AF173619

Oxford University
Roll of Service

E. S. Craig

Alpha Editions

This edition published in 2020

ISBN : 9789354045943

Design and Setting By
Alpha Editions
www.alphaedis.com
email - alphaedis@gmail.com

As per information held with us this book is in Public Domain.
This book is a reproduction of an important historical work. Alpha Editions uses the best technology to reproduce historical work in the same manner it was first published to preserve its original nature. Any marks or number seen are left intentionally to preserve its true form.

EDITOR'S NOTE

THE chief object of this Note is to put in its true perspective the part played by the Editor in the production of this work.

Since the summer of 1916, he has always been fortunate enough to find helpers who have taken such interest in the work and displayed so much ability over it, as to leave him increasingly little to do beyond making suggestions and taking decisions. The name of the first of these helpers, J. F. Willoughby, is on the Roll which he helped to compile. He died in 1918 in the Oxford Base Hospital, when on the point of receiving his Commission after a most promising career in one of the Officer Cadet Battalions.

From the summer of 1918 the Editor has had the assistance of Miss W. M. Gibson. Since the Armistice she has practically taken over the editorial duties, and to her unremitting labour the production of this final edition is chiefly due.

Besides these two, many friends have helped at one time or another; conspicuous among them being Miss Evelyn Davenport, who after five years of strenuous war service found relaxation in helping to compile these lists.

In every successive edition the Editor has borne testimony to the excellence of the work done by the College compilers. It would be impertinent for him to praise them for what they have done out of the fullness of their collegiate pride and love, but he may be permitted to thank them heartily for the ready help and consideration which they have always given him.

E. S. C.

ADDENDA ET CORRIGENDA

Page 53. Kerry, Earl of. *Add* Croix de Chevalier de la Légion d'Honneur.

„ 57. **Mann, J. S.** Assistant Political Officer, Umm Al Ba'rur. Killed in action, Mesopotamia, July 22, 1920.

„ 58. 1919 Maxwell-Hyslop, J. E. (Jan. 4, 1918). 2nd Lt. R.F.A. France 1918.

„ 101. *For* Colyer-Ferguson *read* Colyer-Fergusson.

„ 115. *Delete* Oliver, R. G. from the Exeter College Roll.

„ 335. *For* Andrewes, F. W. *read* [Andrewes, Sir F. W., D.M.] and *add O.B.E.* (Mil.).

„ 341. *Delete* Burrowes, A. D. from the Christ Church Roll.

„ 491. Woodward, Rev. C. S. *For* Dec. 27 *read* May 16, and *for* Sept. 25, 1918, *read* Nov. 14, 1916.

„ 511. *For* de Rougemont, G. *read* de Rougemont, G. L. A.

„ 519. Priestley, L. S. *Add D.* March 16, 1919.

„ „ **Rankin, T. W.** Died Jan. 21, 1919.

CONTENTS

INTRODUCTION

The Oxford University Roll of Service contains the names, fourteen thousand five hundred and sixty-one in number, of those members of the University who served in the Military and Naval forces of the Crown during the War. When the War broke out the country was unprepared for it. We had almost completely neglected to produce many of the materials necessary for war. In one thing only we were magnificently provided. We had produced the men. They were so many and so good that they achieved the immense task of forging, during the War itself, the weapon that was to give us victory.

During the eight or nine years before the War there had been a great quickening of military activity in the Universities. Partly, no doubt, this quickening was due to the tension of the political atmosphere and the imminence of the German threat. But it was wisely encouraged by the authorities, and especially by Lord Haldane, who deserves not a little credit for his patient and persevering efforts to enlist the Universities in the cause of national defence. Commissions in the Army were brought within the reach of graduates. Military History was given a recognized position among University studies. A Delegacy was appointed to superintend the instruction of Army candidates, and the University contingent of the Officers' Training Corps grew and flourished. In place of the handful of volunteers who in the mid-Victorian era were regarded by their undergraduate fellows as a body of eccentrics, addicted to an unusual form of sport, the University, a year before the War, turned out, for review by Lord French, some twelve hundred Officer Cadets, very much in earnest, and representative of all the best sides of University life.

Then the War came, and trained, or half-trained, or untrained, the University sprang to arms. An American Rhodes scholar who had come to Oxford a year or two before the War once said that he was sorry for those of his countrymen who left Oxford before the outbreak of war, and equally sorry for those of them who made their first acquaintance with Oxford after the War had begun. None of them, he said, could know Oxford. What he had seen, and could never forget, was that quiet life of sport and leisure leaping and passing like a flame. The War began during the Long Vacation, when very few of the undergraduates were in residence. A Committee of the Military Delegacy sat in a dingy little room in Alfred Street to interview all Oxford men who applied for commissions. A torrent of young life surged through that little room, eager, and even gay, light-hearted but not light-minded, fully conscious of all that was involved in the test that was now at hand. More than two thousand candidates were interviewed in August and September 1914. Of these the great majority received commissions. When the University met again in October the number of undergraduates in residence was reduced to about fourteen hundred, of whom about eight hundred were undergoing an intensive course in the Officers' Training Corps. By the end of the year 1917 there were only three hundred and fifteen students in residence. Of these some fifty were Oriental students, twenty-five were refugees, chiefly Serbians, some thirty were medical students, and about a hundred and twenty were members of the Officers' Training Corps, waiting till their age should qualify them for admission to a Cadet Battalion. The military history of Oxford, during the later years of the War, is to be read among the records of the battle fronts, from Flanders to Mesopotamia.

The services of Oxford to the nation and to the national cause cannot be fully stated in this Roll of Service. Many names deserve remembrance which do not appear in this list. Foremost among these come the names of those young officers who were trained, during the progress of the War, in the Cadet Battalions formed at Oxford and quartered in certain of the Colleges. As early as December 1914 it was decided to found here a School of Instruction for young officers. The School got to work in January 1915, and by March of the following year about three thousand young officers had passed through it. Then it was superseded by the two Officer Cadet Battalions, in which candidates for commissions, many of whom had served in the ranks, underwent a very complete course of training, lasting at first for four months and, later on, as the system developed, for seven months. The strength of each battalion was about seven hundred and fifty, and they were quartered by Companies in Keble, Wadham, Hertford, New College, Magdalen, Trinity, Balliol, St. John's, and Worcester. In 1915 there was also formed at Oxford a School of Military Aeronautics, which began by training young officers, but after a little time was changed into a Cadet School, for the training of about a thousand cadets. The cadets and mechanics were housed in Christ Church, Queen's, Brasenose, Exeter, Lincoln, Jesus, Corpus Christi, and Pembroke; they had their aerodrome at Port Meadow and a camp in the University Parks. Certain of the scientific departments of the University were almost wholly devoted to their needs.

The cadets who passed through Oxford under this scheme were invited to consider themselves Oxford men, and accepted the invitation. The work was hard and the discipline strict, but they lived the collegiate life, and enjoyed it. There were competitive sports—boat-races, football, and cricket—among the several Colleges, and a fervent spirit of College loyalty grew up with amazing rapidity. The consequences of this are not easy to forecast. The cadets who passed through Oxford during the War, who lived in the Colleges, and belonged to them, and paid allegiance to them, are about equal in number to the other living members of the University. They have left Oxford, but they have not forgotten her, and she has now a host of enthusiastic champions and friends in every one of the Dominions. They would not wish to deny to their foster mother the right to feel pride in their doings.

Another group of men, most of whom wore no uniform, rendered good service to the cause. The scientific laboratories of the University were put at the disposal of the Government, and worked hard at the problems referred to them. To enumerate their achievements, in Physics, Chemistry, Physiology, and Pathology, would demand a whole volume. All military operations depend for their success on efficiency at the base, and this War more than any earlier war was based on science. The science of wasting and killing has made enormous progress during the War, but it is sometimes forgotten that the science of saving and healing has kept pace with it. To succeed in war a nation must excel in both sciences, and if ever a complete history of the War shall be written the work of Oxford men of science will have an honourable place in it.

Very early in the War the Examination Schools were converted into the Third Southern General Hospital, and Somerville College was given up by its staff and students to become a branch hospital. Oriel

College lent one of its quadrangles for the housing of the dispossessed Somerville students ; University College provided additional accommodation for hospital patients ; Merton College gave quarters for the nurses.

Destroying and preserving make up the whole art of war. If any one, suffering from mental fatigue or sensual disgust, is tempted to believe that these processes annul each other, and inevitably make of war a wanton and foolish business, Oxford has supplied him with the remedy for that sickness. The Clarendon Press, during the whole progress of the War, though deprived of the services of virtually all its men of military age, was active in the production of books and pamphlets, most of them written by Oxford men, setting forth the causes and issues of the War—a mine of information, and an armoury of apologetics. This War library, being written to vindicate the British cause, may be called special pleading ; but let it be compared and contrasted with the whole body of apologetics produced by the German Universities. The comparison will prove what cannot be proved by the ordeal of battle, that the failure of Germany, on which the War has now set its seal, was a failure in intelligence and sympathy.

Here then is matter for three more volumes of Oxford War Records. But this Roll of Service comes before and above them all. It prints the names of those who through a long series of academic generations were nourished at Oxford, and who, when the call came, because the call came in the name of charity, gave their bodies to be burned. The gift of those who gave their lives is here specially recorded, and indeed, among the early volunteers, these are in a majority. They were the makers of the new army. They had put away all thoughts of safety. They cared only to maintain their cause, to assert their allegiance, and to make a rule and habit of devotion. The wounds and maims of these and others are not here recorded—it would make too long a tale. Nor are the deeds described by which decorations were won, except the deeds of those, sixteen in number, who were given the Victoria Cross. Soldiers themselves honour the Victoria Cross, because they know that it is one of those rare distinctions which are given to none but the deserving. But they know also, better than civilians, that only a fortunate remnant of those who have deserved the Victoria Cross receive the award. The bravest deeds in war are seldom done in the sight of witnesses; no reporters are present when a post is held to the last man. Too much stress must not be laid on decorations. The honour due to the men on this Roll is due to their likenesses rather than to their differences. They lived and fought together. The bravest of those who wear crosses and ribbons could find his fellow, if all were known, in that obscure company who wear no decoration but the single word *Missing* inscribed after their names.

Much thought has been expended, during the War and since, on the fittest way of honouring the dead. They will not come back, and we, who remember them and think of them, like to believe that they will always be remembered. But let us be just to them. They did not ask, when they gave their lives, that their memories should be preserved. There have been nations (there are some to-day) who make divinities of fame and glory. That has never been the habit of thought of the English people. Our dead were content to save England. If they could see Oxford, as Oxford is to-day, with the War won, they would be pleased with that living memorial. Even if they had failed to save England, they well knew (though no one can explain it) that their sacrifice had an absolute value, and was not made in vain. We grope for some sign or token from them, and here and there, far away from the graves where they lie, we find it. Their virtue, which was a live thing, cannot be engraved on stone or printed in a book, but it still is here, to be sought for among other live things. The words Courage and Duty—or rather, the ideas of courage and duty, for Englishmen use the words very sparingly—are enriched by a great bequest. Fellowship and friendship mean more to-day than they meant before the War. The air that children breathe, even when they are at play, now comes to them tonic, from the heights. These things are the touch of live spirits, present or absent. The names here printed in thick type have appeared in many Oxford lists before this. We print them now, with reverence and affection, for the last time, in this final Roll, as a tribute from the University to the dearest of her sons.

W. A. R.

EXPLANATORY NOTE

The details which have been collected about members of the University in this Roll are given, so far as possible, in the following order:

Date of Matriculation.
Name, Degree, and Distinctions gained before the War.
Date of commencement of Service (in brackets).
Rank, Unit, and, in brackets, highest acting rank.
Fields of Foreign Service.
Distinctions gained during the War. (The dates given are those of the Gazettes.)
Mentions in Dispatches.

The following symbols have been employed:

* to denote membership of the University Contingent of the Officers' Training Corps prior to 1915.
‡ to denote Service in the ranks before Commission.
D. to denote mentions in Dispatches.
D. § to denote mentions by the Secretary of State for valuable service in connexion with the War.

The names of those who have lost their lives on Service are printed in heavy type.

The names of some who, after having been accepted for admission to a College, lost their lives in the War before being actually matriculated, have been included in the Roll.

UNIVERSITY COLLEGE

1919 Adams, C. H. N. (Aug. 15, 1918). Gnr. 211th Batt., R.F.A. 2nd Lt. (on demobilization).

1898 Adams, H. W., B.A. (Nov. 13, 1915). Lt. R.A.S.C. *M.B.E.* (Mil.), *D.* § Mar. 1919.

1919 Addleshaw, H. L. (Dec. 10, 1915). Pte. 28th London Regt. (Artists Rifles).

1910 Aitchison,* W. de L., B.A. (Aug. 19, 1917). 2nd Lt. 13th (Garr.) Bn., N. Staffordshire Regt.

1896 **Aldous, S. J.,** B.A. (Mobilized Aug. 1914). Capt. 5th Sherwood Foresters. France. Killed in action on Mar. 25, 1916.

1919 Alford, V. (Jan. 25, 1918). 2nd Lt. 328th Siege Batt., R.G.A. France, 1918–19.

1912 Allan,* J. L., M.A. (July 21, 1915). Lt. 2/3rd W. Lancashire Bde., R.F.A. (T.F.). Empld. at War Office. France, Belgium. *M.B.E.* (Mil.). *D.* § Mar. 1919.

1910 Allen, C. K., M.A. (Jan. 7, 1915). Capt. and Adjt. 13th Middlesex Regt. France. *M.C.*, Sept. 16, 1918.

1882 Allen, Rt. Hon. C. P., M.A. (Sept. 1914). Maj. 5th Gloucestershire Regt. (T.F. Res.). France, 1917, 1918.

1919 Allen, M. (Apr. 1917). 2nd Lt. 353rd Siege Batt., R.G.A. France, 1917–19.

1919 Allen, R. E. T. (Jan. 18, 1916). Lt. D Batt., 181st Bde., R.F.A. France, 1916–19. *M.C.*, June 3, 1919. *D.* France, 1918.

1886 Ambrose, W. G., B.A. (Serving Aug. 4, 1914). Capt. 3rd Cheshire Regt., Res. of Officers, Nigerian Pol. Service. W. Africa. *M.C.*, Jan. 1, 1918. *D.* W. Africa, 1916.

1911 **Anderson,* A. J. R.** (Aug. 15, 1914). 2nd Lt. 2nd R. Irish Regt. France. Killed in action, Nov. 1914.

1893 Armstrong, H. C., M.A. (Sept. 18, 1914). Capt. R.A. (Civil Employment).

1914 Arnold, W. H., B.A. (Aug. 1917). 2nd Lt. 62nd Coast Artillery, U.S. Army. France, 1918–19.

1913 Atkinson, L. O. (Sept. 1, 1914). Lt. 11th King's (Liverpool Regt.) (Capt.). Lt. 854th (K.L.) Area Employment Coy. France.

1895 Attenborough, G., M.A. (Jan. 13, 1915). Maj. R.A.S.C. *D.* § Mar. 1918.

1901 Attlee, C. R., M.A. (Sept. 30, 1914). Maj. 5th S. Lancashire Regt. Gallipoli, 1915; Mesopotamia, 1916; France, 1917, 1918.

1908 **Avery, Sir W. E. T.,** Bt., B.A. (Aug. 29, 1914). Capt., temp. Maj., R.A.S.C. (M. T). (S.R.). France. *M.C.*, Jan. 1, 1917. *D.* France, 1916. Died at Rouen on Nov. 20, 1918.

1900 Avery Wright, F. C., B.A. (Aug. 25, 1915). Lt., temp. Capt., Flying Officer, R.A.F.

1901 Bailey, Rev. C. H., B.A. (Dec. 7, 1914). Chaplain to the Forces (3rd Class). France. *M.C.*, Jan. 1, 1917. *D.* France, 1918, 1919.

1913 Bailward,* A. N. (Aug. 29, 1914). 2nd Lt. N. Somersetshire Yeomanry. (Invalided.)

1903 Baines, J. H., M.A. (Mobilized Aug. 4, 1914). Capt., Acting Maj., C Batt., 58th Bde., R.F.A., 11th Div. France, 1915, 1916–19. *M.C.*, Jan. 1, 1918.

1899 **Baker, B. W.,** B.A. Pte. 5th London Regt. (London Rifle Brigade). France. Died on Apr. 16, 1917, of wounds received in action.

1902 Baker, W. H. B., M.A. (Feb. 14, 1915). Maj. attd. 298th Siege Batt., R.G.A. France, 1917–19. *D.* France, 1917, 1919.

1901 Balfour, A. R., B.A. (Aug. 29, 1914). Capt. Lothians and Border Horse. A.P.M. Salonika. *M.C.*, June 3, 1916. *D.* Salonika, 1916.

1918 Ballinger, O. D. (Apr. 7, 1917). Lt. 1st, attd. 1/6th R. Warwickshire Regt. Belgium, France, 1917 ; Italy, 1917–18.

1895 **Banbury, C. W.** (Serving Aug. 4, 1914). Capt. Coldstream Guards. France. Killed in action on Sept. 26, 1914.

1906 Bankes, R. W., B.A. (Mobilized Aug. 4, 1914). Capt. Montgomeryshire Yeomanry. A.D.C. to Gen. Allenby, E.E.F. Egypt, Palestine. *D.* Palestine, 1919.

1910 Barnard, E., B.A. (Aug. 21, 1914). Maj. 7th Gloucestershire Regt. Gallipoli, 1915 ; Mesopotamia, 1916–18 ; Persia, 1918 ; Caucasus, 1918–19. *D.S.O.*, Sept. 12, 1917. *D.* Mesopotamia, 1917, 1918.

1919 Barnes, L. J. (Sept. 10, 1914). ‡Capt. 2nd K.R.R.C. France. *M.C.*, Aug. 19, 1916 ; *Bar*, Sept. 18, 1918.

1906 Barnes,* W. G., M.A. (Aug. 4, 1914). Pte. H.A.C. (Discharged as medically unfit, May 1915.)

1909 **Barrett, G.,** B.A. (Oct. 5, 1914). Lt. 12th R. Warwickshire Regt., attd. 2nd Hampshire Regt. Gallipoli. Missing, presumed killed in action at Achi Baba on Aug. 6, 1915.

1909 **Barrington-Kennett,* A. H.** (Aug. 1914). 2nd Lt. 3rd Oxf. & Bucks Lt. Infty. France, 1914. Died on Sept. 20, 1914, of wounds received in action in the Battle of the Aisne.

1919 Barwell, C. L. (July 11, 1917). ‡2nd Lt. 3rd Oxf. & Bucks Lt. Infty.

1903 Batchelor, T. B., M.A. (Oct. 12, 1914). Capt., Acting Maj., 5th Cavalry Field Ambulance, R.A.M.C. France, 1915–19. *D.* France, 1918.

1886 Bathurst, Sir C., M.A., *M.P.* (Sept. 10, 1914.) Capt. R.E. Empld. under Board of Agriculture and Fisheries. *K.B.E.* *D.* § Feb. 1917.

1914 **Batty, C. F.** (Nov. 28, 1914). 2nd Lt. 10th Durham L.I. France. Killed in action on Jan. 20, 1916.

1896 Bayly, E. A. J. (Serving Aug. 4, 1914). Maj. 1st R. Welch Fusiliers, attd. 2/4th The Buffs (E. Kent Regt.), attd. Egyptian Army. Egypt. *D.S.O.*, Jan. 1, 1917. Order of the Nile (3rd Class).

1910 Beaufoy, L. S., M.A. (Sept. 15, 1914). ‡2nd Lt. 10th E. Surrey Regt., afterwards Lt., Acting Capt., 4th Field Survey Bn., R.E. France, Belgium, Germany, 1916–19.

1906 Beaumont,* G. E., B.M., M.A. (Sept. 16, 1914). Capt. R.A.M.C., attd. 57th General Hospital, B.E.F. France, Belgium.

1919 Beck, H. H. (Jan. 5, 1917). ‡Lt. 9th Inf. Regt., C.P.R. S. Africa.

1911 Beechman,* F. J., M.A. (July 8, 1915). Lt., Acting Maj., 37th Bn. M.G.C., France. *M.C.*, Jan. 1, 1919. *D.* France, 1918.

1903 Bell, E., B.A. (Mobilized Aug. 4, 1914). Capt. Surrey Yeomanry. France, 1914–16 ; Macedonia, 1916–19. *M.C.*, Jan. 1, 1917. Greek Military Cross, 3rd Class. *D.* France, 1916.

1898 **Bell, E. N.,** B.A. Lt. I.A.R.O., attd. Indian Inf. Mesopotamia. Died at Trimulgherry on Feb. 10, 1918, of illness contracted on active service.

1919 Bell, E. O. L. (July 8, 1916). Lt. R.A.F. France, 1918–19. *D.* France, 1918.

1913 Bessemer, H. D., B.A. (Apr. 2, 1915). Lt. 5th Queen's (R. W. Surrey Regt.) (T.F. Res.).

1905 Bingham,* H. B., B.C.L., M.A. (Sept. 2, 1914). ‡2nd Lt. 14th R. Sussex Regt., afterwards Lt. R.F.A. France, Belgium.

1900 Birch, W. R. (Sept. 30, 1914). Lt. 1st Dragoon Guards (S.R.). France. *M.C.*, June 3, 1919.

1912 Birley,* G. H., B.A. (Mobilized Aug. 4, 1914). Capt. 4th Queen's (R. W. Surrey Regt.). Capt., Flight Commander, R.A.F. *D.* § Jan. 1917. (Invalided.)

1904 Birley, J. L., B.M., M.A. (Aug. 7, 1916). Lt., Temp. Lt.-Col., R.A.M.C. France. *D.* France, 1917.

1906 **Birrell-Anthony, H. A.,** B.A. (Sept. 9, 1914). 2nd Lt. 1st Monmouthshire Regt. France, Belgium. Killed in action at 2nd Battle of Ypres on May 8, 1915.

1919 Black, H. (May 18, 1917). ‡2nd Lt. R.A.F. France, 1918.

1903 Blaikie, T. H. C., M.A. (Aug. 31, 1914). Capt. and Adjt. 11th London Regt. (Finsbury Rifles). Lt. R.F.A. *M.B.E.* (Mil.)

1893 Blake, A. E., B.C.L. (Feb. 6, 1915). 2nd Lt., Acting Capt., 4th Somerset L.I.

1915 **Blyth, J. C.** (July 7, 1916). 2nd Lt. 5th, attd. 1st, K.R.R.C. France. Killed in action near Arras on Apr. 13, 1917.

1910 **Boddington,* M.,** B.A. (Sept. 22, 1914). Capt. 6th Shropshire L.I. France. *M.C.*, June 3, 1916. Killed in action on the Somme on July 1, 1916.

1912 Bolton, G., M.A. (July 30, 1914). Capt. 5th R. Sussex Regt. France, Belgium, 1915, 1916, 1917 ; Italy, 1917–19.

1906 Bonsey,* Rev. H. R., M.A. (Oct. 2, 1914). Chaplain to the Forces (4th Class).

1908 Bourdillon,* R. B., M.A. (Aug. 5, 1914). ‡2nd Lt. Intelligence Corps. Capt., Acting Lt.-Col., R.A.F. France, Italy, 1914–18. *M.C.* Sept. 26, 1917. *A.F.C.*, June 3, 1918.

1911 **Boustead, H. A. R.,** B.A. (Sept. 14, 1914). 2nd Lt. 2/8th Middlesex Regt. Flying Officer, R.F.C. Egypt, France, 1917. *D.* France, 1917. Died on Apr. 5, 1917, of wounds received in action.

1919 Bowyer, R. W. (Nov. 12, 1914). Lt. 9th Sherwood Foresters (Capt.). France.

1901 Boxall, A. P., M.A. (Mobilized Aug. 4, 1914). Lt.-Col. Comdg. 330th Bde., R.F.A. India, 1914–15 ; France, Belgium, 1916–19. T.D. *D.* France, 1917, 1919.

1903 Boyd, A. W., M.A. (Aug. 7, 1914). Capt. 1/7th Lancashire Fusiliers. Egypt, 1914 ; Gallipoli, 1915–16 ; Palestine, 1916 ; France, 1916–18. *M.C.*, Mar. 15, 1916. *D.* Gallipoli, 1916.

1909 **Boyd,* E. F.,** B.A. (Serving Aug. 4, 1914). Lt. Northumberland Fusiliers. France. *D.* France, 1914 ; French Dispatches, 1914. Killed in action on Sept. 19, 1914.

1919 Bradley, G. R. (Mar. 2, 1917). ‡Lt. R.A.F.

1919 Bradley, J. B. G. (Sept. 5, 1917). 2nd Lt., Flying Officer, R.A.F. France, 1918.

1904 **Bradshaw, B.,** M.A. (Mar. 6, 1915). 2nd Lt. 3rd Border Regt. Gallipoli. Killed in action in Gallipoli on June 11, 1915.

1919 Brashaw, A. C. (May 13, 1917). ‡2nd Lt. 3rd Shropshire L.I. France, 1918.

1912 **Brandon-Thomas, J. G.** (Serving Aug. 4, 1914). Lt. R. Inniskilling Fusiliers. France. *D.* France, 1914. Died on Nov. 17, 1914, of wounds received in action.

1896 Bray, Rev. W. H., M.A. (Feb. 15, 1916). Chaplain to the Forces (4th Class).

1905 Brehaut, L., B.Sc., M.A. (1914). Pte. 28th Bn., 2nd Div., C.E.F. France, 1915. (Invalided, Aug. 1915.)

1902 Bridges, R. F., B.M. (Serving Aug. 4, 1914). Capt. R.A.M.C.

1919 Bridgett, H. E. (Sept. 8, 1914). ‡Lt., Acting Capt., D Batt., 330th Bde., R.F.A. Salonika, 1915–16; Belgium, France, 1915, 1917–19. *M.C.*, Oct. 5, 1918. Croix de Guerre.

1896 Bridson, T. R., M.A. (Apr. 6, 1916). Pte. Scots Guards. ‡2nd Lt., R.A. Pioneer R.E. (Signals).

1907 Bristowe,* L. G. (Mar. 10, 1915). 2nd Lt. R.F.A. Lt. R.A.F.

1907 **Broad, A. E.,** M.A. (Feb. 8, 1915). Lt. 6th Dorsetshire Regt. France. *M.C.*, Jan. 14, 1916. *D.* France, 1915. Died at Le Touquet on Mar. 2, 1916, of wounds received in action.

1919 Brocklehurst, R. J. (Mar. 22, 1918). 2nd Lt. Tank Corps.

1906 Brooke, W. H., M.A. (Mobilized Aug. 5, 1914). Maj. 8th W. Yorkshire Regt. (T.F.). France, Belgium, 1915–19. *M.C.*, Jan. 14, 1916. *D.* France, 1915, 1918.

1919 Brown, E. T. (Serving Aug. 4, 1914). Capt. Heavy Artillery, U.S. Army (Maj.). France.

1919 Bruxner, G. M. (Jan. 6, 1918). 2nd Lt. 2nd Scots Guards. France and Germany, 1918–19.

1913 Buller,* E. T. (May 12, 1915). Lt. and Adjt. 1st D.C.L.I. France. *M.C.*, Jan. 1, 1917. *D.* France, 1916.

1911 **Burdon,* R.** (Sept. 24, 1914). Capt. 18th Durham L.I. Flight-Comdr. R.F.C. Killed in aeroplane accident on Jan. 10, 1917.

1898 Burra, L. T., D.M. (Nov. 9, 1915). Capt. R.A.M.C. Malta, 1915–16; Egypt, 1916–17.

1906 Burra,* S. H., B.A. (Apr. 12, 1915). ‡Lt. 4th N. Midland (Howitzer) Bde., R.F.A. (T.F.) (Capt.). France, Belgium, 1915–18.

1907 Burrell, C. M., B.M., M.A. (June 5, 1915). Surgeon Lt. R.N. *D.* Admiralty, 1919.

1904 Butler, R. B., B.A. (Oct. 1915). 2nd Lt. R.G.A.

1919 Butterfield, H. (Apr. 1916). ‡Lt. Sig. Coy., R.E., 2nd Canadian Div. France, Belgium, Germany, 1917–19. *M.S.M.*, Nov. 1917.

1904 **Butterworth, H. M.** (Mar. 11, 1915). 2nd Lt. 9th Rifle Brigade. France, Belgium. Killed in action in the Battle of Loos on Sept. 25, 1915.

1897 Buxton, J. L. (Serving Aug. 4, 1914). Maj., Bt.-Lt.-Col., Rifle Brigade. France. *C.M.G. D.S.O.*, June 3, 1916. *D.* France, 1916 twice, 1917 twice, 1919.

1895 Byles, C. M. Barnard, B.A. (Feb. 19, 1915). Lt. 13th London Regt. Acting Capt. Labour Corps.

1911 Bywater,* J. S., B.A. (Nov. 8, 1915). Lt. R.G.A.

Callard, W. K. (Nov. 21, 1915). Lt. 5th Leicestershire Regt. France. Killed in action on the Somme on July 1, 1916.

1909 Campbell,* E. F., B.A. (Serving Aug. 4, 1914). Capt. 4th, attd. 18th, K.R.R.C. (Maj.). France. *D.S.O.*, Nov. 6, 1918. *D.* France, 1918.

Carnegie, T. A. (Sept. 26, 1916). Lt. 6th, attd. 12th, K.R.R.C. (Capt.). France. Killed in action on Jan. 16, 1917.

1905 **Carpenter, E. B.,** B.A. (Sept. 29, 1914). Capt. Plymouth Bn. R. Marine Bde., R.N. Div. Gallipoli. Died on Aug. 18, 1915, of wounds received in action in Gallipoli.

1913 Carter, A. N., B.A. (Serving Aug. 4, 1914). ‡Lt. 8th York & Lancaster Regt. Lt., Acting Capt., M.G.C. France, 1915–18. *M.C.*, Mar. 6, 1918.

1914 **Cary,* L. S. R.** (Dec. 22, 1914). 2nd Lt. 9th Devonshire Regt. France. Killed in action on July 20, 1916.

1913 **Causton,* J. P.** (Sept. 2, 1914). Lt., Acting Capt., 6th, attd. 1st, Hampshire Regt. France. Killed in action on Apr. 22, 1918.

1901 Cave, P. N., D.M. (Mobilized Aug. 4, 1914). Capt. 2nd London Sanitary Coy., R.A.M.C. (Invalided on account of ill health, Sept. 1918.)

1919 Chalk, L. (Sept. 16, 1914). ‡Lt. 3rd R. Berkshire Regt. (Capt.). France.

1913 Chamberlain, N. J., B.A. (May 3, 1915). Lt. R.F.A. (T.F.). Egypt, Palestine. *D.* Palestine, 1918.

1919 Chapman, R. V. (Aug. 3, 1914). ‡Sub-Lt. R.N.V.R., afterwards Capt. Corps of Guides, Indian Army. Antwerp, 1914; Gallipoli, 1915; France, 1916; India, 1917; Palestine, 1918.

1901 **Cheyne, H.,** B.A. (Mobilized Aug. 4, 1914). Maj. R.F.A. France, Belgium. Killed in action on July 10, 1917.

1907 **Chichester, Hon. R. C. F.,** B.A. Hon. Capt. Serbian Army. Serbia. Died of typhoid fever on July 31, 1915.

1919 Child, P. G. (Oct. 10, 1917). 2nd Lt. R.A.F.

1919 Chilton, G., B.A. (Dec. 30, 1915). Lt. 16th London Regt. (Queen's Westminster Rifles). Intelligence Officer 169th Inf. Bde. France, Belgium, 1916–18. (Invalided on account of ill health contracted on active service, Nov. 1918.)

1910 Chitty,* T. H. W., B.A. (Mobilized Aug. 4, 1914). Capt. R.F.A. (T.F. Res.), attd. Min. of Nat. Service.

1896 Chorley, Rev. E. A., M.A. (Feb. 14, 1917). Chaplain to the Forces (4th Class). *D.* § Aug. 1919.

1912 Christison,* A. F. P., B.A. (Mar. 14, 1914). Maj. 1st, attd. 6th Q.O. Cameron Highlanders. France, 1915, 1916–19. *M.C.* Jan. 14, 1916; *Bar*, July 18, 1917. *D.* France, 1915 twice.

1913 **Christison,* F. J.** (Aug. 26, 1914). Lt. and Adjt. 10th Arg. & Suth'd. Highlanders. Belgium and France. Died on Dec. 4, 1915, of wounds received in action in Belgium.

1894 Christopherson, Rev. D., M.A. (Mobilized Aug. 4, 1914). Chaplain (4th Class) 8th London Bde., R.F.A. (T.F.).

1912 Christopherson,* D., M.A. (Oct. 24, 1915). ‡Lt. 9th K.O.Y.L.I.

1912 Christopherson, N. (Sept. 18, 1914). Capt. R.F.A. (T.F.). *M.C.*, June 3, 1918. *D.* France, 1916.

1905 Church,* G. S., B.A. (Sept. 1914). ‡Maj. R.F.A. France and Belgium. *M.C.*, Dec. 17, 1917.

1896 **Church, J. W.,** M.A. (Mar. 1, 1915). Lt. 1st Hertfordshire Regt., attd. 1st Cambridgeshire Regt. France. Died on Mar. 30, 1918, of wounds received in action.

1913 Clapperton,* J. F. (Sept. 23, 1914). Capt. City of London Yeomanry. Lt. 5th Devonshire Regt.

1912 Clapperton,* R. H., B.A. (Serving Aug. 4, 1914). Capt. 5th Devonshire Regt. Egypt and Palestine. *M.C.*, Apr. 22, 1918. *D.* Palestine, 1918.

1905 Clark,* T. (Mobilized Aug. 5, 1914). Maj. 7th R. Scots. France.

1904 **Clarke, M. E. L. H.** (Serving Aug. 4, 1914). Lt. Worcestershire Regt. France, Aug. 1914. Killed in action on Aug. 26, 1914.

1909 **Clutterbuck,* D.,** B.A. (Feb. 12, 1915). Lt. R.F.A. France, 1915–17. *D.* France, 1917. Died on May 6, 1917, of wounds received in action.

1909 **Coghlan, W. H.** (Serving Aug. 4, 1914). Lt. R.F.A. France and Belgium, Aug. 1914. Killed in action in Aug. 1914.

1899 Coke, D. F. T., B.A. (Nov. 27, 1914), Capt. (Adjt.) 10th Loyal N. Lancashire Regt. France. *D.* France, 1916.

1912 Coleridge, G. C. R. (Oct. 3, 1914). Capt. S. Staffordshire Regt., empld. M.I. Directorate, War Office. France. *M.C.*, Jan. 1, 1917. *D.* France, 1916.

1913 Coles,* G. R. (Aug. 29, 1914). Capt. 7th Hampshire Regt., attd. Indian Cavalry. India.

1913 **Coller, B. T.** (Oct. 5, 1914). 2nd Lt. 10th Norfolk Regt. Lt. General List. Flying Officer, R.F.C. France, 1916. Killed in action on Sept. 26, 1916.

1897 **Collinge, W. R.** (June 21, 1915). 2nd Lt. 6th King's (Liverpool Regt.). France and Belgium. Died on Aug. 7, 1917, of wounds received in action.

1888 Collins, A. E., B.A. (Mobilized Aug. 4, 1914). Maj. Yorkshire Hussars, empld. Ministry of National Service.

1911 Collins, J. L., B.A. (Sept. 20, 1914). Capt. (Adjt.) 6th Lancashire Fusiliers. Gallipoli, Egypt, Sinai Peninsula 1915–16. (Invalided, Jan. 3, 1918, on account of ill health contracted on active service.)

1884 Collins, W. F., B.A. (Serving Aug. 4, 1914). Lt.-Col. 2nd Dragoons, and 6th Res. Regt. of Cavalry. France. *D.S.O.*, June 3, 1918. Order of St. Stanislas (2nd Class). *D.* France, 1916; § Aug. 1919.

1912 Colyer-Fergusson, W. P. (Apr. 26, 1917). 2nd Lt. 3rd, attd. 2nd, Northamptonshire Regt.

1907 Cook, A. H., B.A. (Sept. 1914). Capt. 1/8th Arg. & Suth'd. Highlanders. France, 1915–16, 1918–19. *D.* France, 1916, 1919.

1910 Cope,* A. L. S., M.A. (Mobilized Aug. 4, 1914). Capt. 3rd The Buffs (E. Kent Regt.); Bde. Maj., Dover Inf. Bde., empld. Ministry of National Service. France, 1914. *M.B.E.* (Mil.).

1900 **Corbett, C. D. H.,** D.M. (Dec. 11, 1916). Capt., Acting Lt.-Col., Medical Officer, R.A.F. Died, Nov. 1918, of illness contracted on active service.

1902 Cornwallis, K., B.A. Maj. Special Lists. Temp. Lt.-Col. specially empld. Egypt and Palestine. *C.B.E.* (Mil.). *D.S.O.*, June 4, 1917. Order of El Nahda (2nd Class). Order of the Nile (4th Class). Commander, Order of George I (Greece). *D.* Egypt, 1917; Hedjaz, 1918; Palestine, 1919.

1910 Cory-Wright,* G. (Aug. 15, 1914). Lt. 3rd The Buffs (E. Kent Regt.). Temp. Capt. R.A.F. Mesopotamia. *D.* Mesopotamia, 1919.

1902 **Cowan, G. D.,** B.A. (Mobilized Aug. 4, 1914). Maj. 9th R. Scots. France. *D.* France, 1917. Died on Apr. 23, 1918, of wounds received in action.

1914 Cowan, J. M. 2nd Lt. I.A.R.O. India.

1909 **Cowie, G. R.,** B.M., M.A. (Oct. 13, 1917). 2nd Lt. S. African Medical Corps (Capt.), attd. S. African Bde., R.F.A. France. *D.* France, 1915. Died on Sept. 3, 1918, of wounds received in action.

1912 Cowie, W. N. (Feb. 3, 1915). Capt. C/48th Army Bde., R.F.A., (Maj.). France. *D.S.O.*, June 22, 1918. *M.C.*, June 18, 1917; *Bar*, Feb. 1, 1919. *D.* France, 1916, 1917, 1918.

1907 Cowland, W. S., M.A. (Aug. 1914). Maj. 12th Hampshire Regt. Gallipoli, 1915; Salonika, 1916–18. *D.S.O.*, Jan. 1, 1918. Croix de Guerre. *D.* Salonika, 1918 twice.

1912 Cox, A. B., B.A. (Sept. 19, 1914). Lt. 7th Northamptonshire Regt.

1910 Cox,* G. W., B.A. (Sept. 2, 1914). 2nd Lt. 4th The Black Watch. (Resigned on account of ill health.)

1898 Crabbie, J. E., B.A. (Oct. 5, 1914). Capt. 6th The Black Watch. *O.B.E.* (Mil.).

1908 Craddock,* H. E. F., B.A. (Apr. 5, 1917). 2nd Lt. I.A.R.O. (Cavalry).

1919 Craig, A. B. (Sept. 24, 1914). Capt. 9th Worcestershire Regt. Gallipoli, 1915; Mesopotamia, 1917–18; Persia, Russia, 1918.

1913 **Crebbin,* W. A.** (Oct. 22, 1914). Capt. 8th Rifle Brigade. France and Belgium. *M.C.*, June 4, 1917. Killed in action on Apr. 4, 1918.

1897 Cree, D. C. L., M.A. (Feb. 11, 1916). Lt. R.N.V.R.

1896 Crichton, R. (Jan. 3, 1915). Capt. 7th Highland L.I.

1912 Crole,* G. B., B.A. (Aug. 15, 1914). 2nd Lt. 2nd Dragoon Guards. 2nd Lt. R.F.A. Capt., Flying Officer, R.A.F. France. *M.C.*, Sept. 26, 1917. (Prisoner of War.)

1909 **Croome, W. H.** (Aug. 26, 1914). Capt. 8th Essex Regt. G.S.O. 3. France. Missing, believed killed in action at Gouzeaucourt on Nov. 30, 1917.

1909 Cruickshank, G. G. L., B.A. (Jan. 16, 1915). 2nd Lt. 21st Manchester Regt. Lt. 70th Training Bn.

1907 **Cunliffe,* J. L.,** B.C.L., M.A. (Dec. 4, 1914). Capt. 21st Manchester Regt. France. Killed in action on Sept. 4, 1916.

1919 Curlewis, I., B.A. (Oct. 1914). Galloper to O.C., 13th S. African Mounted Rifles. ‡Lt. R.A.F. S. Africa, 1914–15; France, 1916. *M.C.*, Nov. 14, 1916. (Wounded prisoner of War, 1916–18, released as permanently unfit, Jan. 1918.)

1919 Curran, H. G. (Sept. 6, 1917). Midshipman R.N., H.M.S. *Waterhen*. Grand Fleet.

1919 Currie, J. A. (Jan. 8, 1918). 2nd Lt., Technical Officer, R.A.F.

1908 Dalby, Rev. E. L., M.A. (Jan. 18, 1918). Chaplain to the Forces (4th Class).

1897 Dalhousie, Earl of (Serving Aug. 4, 1914). Capt. Scots Guards, Res. of Officers.

1910 Daly,* T. D., B.A. (Sept. 9, 1914). Capt. R. Welch Fusiliers. G.S.O. 3. Mesopotamia. *M.C.*, Aug. 25, 1917.

1912 **Danckwerts,* R. W.** (Aug. 28, 1914). Lt. Gloucestershire Regt. France. Died on Dec. 22, 1914, of wounds received in action.

1891 Daniell, R. A., B.A. (July 17, 1917). Lt. 15th Worcestershire Regt.

1895 Daniell, R. H. A. (Serving Aug. 4, 1914). Lt.-Col. 3rd Hampshire Regt. *D.* § Feb. 1917.

1895 Dashwood, T. H. K. (Sept. 6, 1915). Capt. R.A.S.C.

1897 Davenport, J. A., B.A. (Serving Aug. 4, 1914). Capt. Lancashire Fusiliers. France, 1914. (Wounded Prisoner of War 1914–17. Interned in Holland 1917–18.)

1908 **Davidson,* F. C.,** B.A. Capt. I.A.R.O., attd. S. Waziristan Militia. India. Killed in action on the frontier on May 10, 1917.

1919 Davie, K. M. (Sept. 6, 1919). Cadet Household Bde. O.C.B.

1906 Davies,* A. A. M. (Serving Aug. 4, 1914). Capt. R.A.M.C. India, 1914–19.

1888 Davies, Rev. T. H., D.D. (Oct. 27, 1915). Chaplain to the Forces (4th Class), attd. 190th Bde., 63rd (R.N.) Div. France, 1916–17. *D.* France, 1917.

1919 Davies, T. L. (Dec. 11, 1915). ‡Lt. 26th Batt., 17th Bde., R.F.A. France, 1917.

1885 Dawes, J. A., B.C.L., M.A,. *M.P.* (Dec. 2, 1914.) Lt.-Commdr. R.N.V.R. (Commdr.). North Sea patrol; Gibraltar (Intelligence Dept.). Croix de Chevalier de la Légion d'Honneur.

1894 Day, G. H. (Jan. 4, 1915). Staff-Sergt.-Maj. R.A.S.C.

1919 Dealtry, L. P. (Oct. 1914). ‡Lt. R.E. (Signals). France and Belgium, 1916, 1917–18. *D.* France, 1917.

1912 de Jongh, L. A. (Nov. 26, 1915). Lt. R.F.A. (S.R.). France. *M.C.*, Feb. 4, 1918.

1906 de la Penha,* A. E. (Sept. 19, 1914). Capt. Labour Corps.

1905 Dendy, N. H. (Apr. 15, 1915). Lt., Acting Capt. and Adjt., 42nd Bde. R.F.A. France. *M.C.*, Jan. 1, 1919.

1896 Denniston, Rev. J. G., M.A. (Aug. 1, 1917). Chaplain, R.N., H.M.S. *Superb.* Grand Fleet.

1905 de Putron, P. Nigerian Land Contingent. W. Africa.

1913 de Selincourt, A., B.A. (Aug. 29, 1914). 2nd Lt. 7th N. Staffordshire Regt. Lt. (Hon. Capt.) R.A.F. Gallipoli, 1915; France, 1917. (Prisoner of War, May 1917–Dec. 1918.)

1914 de Villiers, J. E. (Jan. 14, 1915). Pte. 9th S. African Inf. German SW. Africa, 1915; German E. Africa, 1916–17.

1914 Dickson, A. W. (Jan. 25, 1916). Sub-Lt. R.N.V.R. Greece, 1915–16; Egypt, 1916–18; Palestine, 1918; Salonika, 1918; Constantinople, 1918–19.

1902 Dickson, J. R., B.A. (Apr. 30, 1915). Lt., Acting Capt., 3rd Q.O. Cameron Highlanders, attd. 10th R. Scots.

1912 **Dickson, W. M.** (Jan. 22, 1915). 2nd Lt. 11th Arg. & Suth'd. Highlanders. Gallipoli. Killed in action in Gallipoli on Sept. 26, 1915.

1907 Diggle,* P. R., B.A. Nigerian Land Contingent. W. Africa.

1900 Dillon, E. W. (Oct. 14, 1914). Capt. 4th R. W. Kent Regt. Staff-Capt. Egypt. *D.* Egypt, 1917.

1919 Dodds, W. E. (May 1917). 2nd Lt. K.O.Y.L.I.

1910 Donald,* G., M.A. (Feb. 7, 1916). Capt. R.A.F. (Sea Patrol). *D.F.C.*, Sept. 22, 1918. Greek Military Cross, Class II (' War Cross ').

1909 Donald,* W. A., B.A. (Nov. 22, 1914). Lt. 6th Dragoons (S.R.).

1919 Donaldson, R. H. (Nov. 14, 1914). Lt. 20th Divl. Signal Coy. R.E. (Capt.). France.

1912 Donne, A. C., B.A. (June 20, 1915). Capt. R. Marines.

1908 Downie,* H. F., M.A. (Mobilized Aug. 4, 1914). ‡Lt., Acting Capt., 1st (Garr.) Bn. Norfolk Regt., attd. 9th Worcestershire Regt. Mesopotamia, India. *D.* India, 1917.

1906 Dracopoli, I. N. (May 15, 1916). Capt., Technical Officer, R.A.F. Egypt and Palestine. *D.* Palestine, 1919.

1911 Druce,* J. C., M.A. (Aug. 15, 1914). Lt. and Adjt. 4th, attd. 1st, E. Surrey Regt. France. *M.C.*, Jan. 1, 1918. *D.* France, 1916.

1914 **Drysdale, I. S.** (Dec. 22, 1914). 2nd Lt. 11th Rifle Brigade. France. *D.* France, 1915. Killed in action on Sept. 18, 1915.

1902 Drysdale, R. C., B.A. (Apr. 1, 1915). Lt. General List, empld. with Army Signal Service.

1905 Duigan, W., M.A. (Mobilized Aug. 4, 1914). Capt. R.A.M.C. (T.F.).

1919 Duncan, D. D. (Aug. 17, 1914). ‡Lt. 404th Batt., R.F.A. German SW. Africa, 1914–15; India, 1917; Mesopotamia, 1917–19.

1911 Durno, L. G., B.A. (Oct. 7, 1915). Lt. 3rd Seaforth Highlanders., empld. O.C.B. France, 1916.

1919 Dyde, H. A. (Jan. 1, 1916). Capt. 50th Canadian Inf. France, Belgium, 1917–18. *M.C.*, Sept. 16, 1918; *Bar*, Feb. 15, 1919.

1913 Dyde, W. F., B.A. (Dec. 17, 1914). Lt., Acting Maj., R.A. France. *M.C.*, Sept. 16, 1918.

1907 Earl,* A., B.A. (Dec. 17, 1915). Maj. R.G.A., empld. Ministry of Munitions. *C.B.E.* (Mil.).

1912 Earle, M., Hon. M.A., *D.S.O.* (Serving Aug. 4, 1914). Lt.-Col. Grenadier Guards. G.S.O. 1. Dept. of C.I.G.S., War Office. (Col.). France, Belgium. *C.B.* *C.M.G.* *D.* France, 1915. (Wounded Prisoner in Germany and Switzerland, 1914–17.)

1906 Eddis, A. McD. (Jan. 3, 1916). Lt. R.F.A. (S.R.), attd. H.Q. *D.* § Mar. 1919.

1908 Eddison, C. R., B.A. (Nov. 11, 1914). Capt. R.A.S.C.

1917 Edgell, L. F. A. (June 26, 1918). 2nd Lt. 3rd K.O. Scottish Borderers.

Elliott, G. K. (Mar. 1, 1917). 2nd Lt. 3rd, attd. 25th, R. Welch Fusiliers. France. Killed in action near St. Emilie on Sept. 8, 1918.

1893 Etherington Smith, H. L., M.A. Hon. Capt. R.A.M.C. Temp. Qr.-Master serving with No. 1 British Red Cross Hospital. France. *O.B.E.* (Mil.). *D.* France, 1918.

1913 Faber, E. W., M.A. (Sept. 15, 1914). 2nd Lt. 5th Durham L.I.

1890 Farquharson,* A. S. L., M.A. (Mobilized Aug. 4, 1914). Maj. Unattached List, T.F. Bt.-Lt.-Col. G.S.O. 1. Dept. of C.I.G.S., War Office. (Lt.-Col.). Missions to Belgium, France, 1915, 1917, 1919, and to Italy, 1917. *C.B.E.* (Mil.). Croix d'Officier de la Légion d'Honneur. *D.* § Feb. 1917, § Aug. 1917, § Oct. 1919.

1900 **Farquharson, J. C. L.** (Mobilized Aug. 4, 1914). Lt. 14th London Regt. (London Scottish). France and Belgium. Killed in action at Messines on Oct. 31, 1914.

1906 Farrar, T. C. L. (Oct. 5, 1914). Capt. 12th Loyal N. Lancashire Regt. D.A.P.M.

1899 **Farrer, R. B.** (Mar. 11, 1915). Lt. 15th Leicestershire Regt. France and Belgium. Killed in action on June 8, 1917.
1912 Fay,* R. W., B.A. (Oct. 8, 1914). Lt. 4th Northamptonshire Regt. Egypt and Palestine. *D.* Palestine, 1918.
1909 Featherstone, E., B.A. (Sept. 1914). ‡Capt. 13th Middlesex Regt. (Maj.) France and Belgium. *M.C.*, Feb. 1, 1919.
1903 Fell, M. A. H., B.A. (May 27, 1916). Capt. New Zealand Rifle Brigade. Lt., Technical Officer, R.A.F.
1873 Fell, W., D.M. (June 22, 1915). Capt., Bt.-Maj., R.A.M.C.
1913 Ferard, C. L., B.A. (Sept. 8, 1914). Lt. Divl. Ammunition Column, R.A. Salonika. *M.C.*, June 4, 1917. *D.* Salonika, 1916, 1917.
Ferard, G. D. (Apr. 14, 1915). Lt. 5th, attd. 7th, Devonshire Regt. France. Killed in action on Feb. 21, 1918.
1899 Ferguson, J. A., B.A. (Apr. 1, 1917). Capt. 5th Punjab Light Horse, I.D.F. *O.B.E.* (Civil).
1909 Fishbourne,* W. J. C., B.A. (Oct. 8, 1914). 2nd Lt. Denbighshire Hussars. Capt. 24th R. Welch Fusiliers. Egypt and Palestine.
1915 Fitz-Randolph, A. M. (Sept. 1, 1915). Capt., Aeroplane and Seaplane Officer, R.A.F. North Sea Patrol.
1919 Flack, H. (Nov. 16, 1917). 2nd Lt. 660th Aero Sqdn., U.S. Air Service (Capt.). France.
1901 Flack, M. W., B.M., M.A. (Oct. 21, 1915). Hon. Maj. R.A.M.C. Hon. Wing Commdr. (Lt.-Col.), Director of Medical Research, R.A.F. *C.B.E.* (Mil.). *D.* § Aug. 1917.
1901 Fletcher, P. C., M.A. (Sept. 12, 1914). Lt. 42nd Div. Signal Coy, R.E. (T.F.). Egypt, Gallipoli, Sinai, France, 1914–18. *M.C.*, Jan. 1, 1919.
1897 Follett, W. H. (Oct. 25, 1916). Lt. 8th S. African Inf. E. Africa. *M.C.*, July 27, 1918.
1908 Forbes, T. L. (Nov. 6, 1914). Capt. 5th London Regt. (London Rifle Brigade), attd. R.A.F. (Administrative Officer).
1909 Forrester, G. D., B.A. Rangoon Volunteer Force.
1911 **Foster,* A. D.** (Sept. 12, 1914). Capt. 8th R. Sussex Regt. France. *M.C.*, Oct. 20, 1916. Killed in action on May 5, 1917.
1902 Fox, Rev. A., M.A. (Serving Aug. 4, 1914). Capt. Unattached List, T.F., Lancing College O.T.C.
1919 Fox, T. R. (Feb. 27, 1918). Flight-Cadet, R.A.F.
Francis, B. H. (Aug. 15, 1914). 2nd Lt. 3rd R. Scots. France. Killed in action, Mar. 1915.
1881 Franks, W. Temple. B.C.L., *C.B.* (Oct. 1914). ‡Sub-Lt. R.N.V.R. (Anti-Aircraft Corps).
1893 Freeborn, E. W., M.A. (Mobilized Aug. 4, 1914). Maj. Unattached List, T.F., O.C. Harrow School O.T.C. *D.* § Mar. 1918.
1895 Freeman, J., D.M. (Mobilized Aug. 4, 1914). Capt. R.A.M.C. (T.F.).
1902 **Freeman, N. W.,** B.A. (Sept. 23, 1914). Capt., Acting Maj., 106th Batt., 9th Div. Artillery, R.F.A. France, Gallipoli. *M.C.*, June 3, 1918. *D.* France, 1915, 1916. Killed in action at Ettreillers on Mar. 21, 1918.
1910 Freeman, P. A. M. (Aug. 31, 1915). Lt. R.F.A. (S.R.) Asst. Inspector, Royal Arsenal, Woolwich.

1903 Fremantle, A. E. A., B.A. (1914). Lt. R.N.V.R. Lt. Special Lists (Interpreter). Chevalier, Order of the Redeemer, 5th Class.

1919 Futch, T. L. (Serving Aug. 4, 1914). 1st Lt. 3rd F.A., Bde. Headquarters, U. S. Army. France and Germany.

1903 Fyffe, A. H., B.A. (July 24, 1915). Lt. R.G.A.

1919 Gairdner, A. C. (Aug. 20, 1918). Cadet R.A.F.

1908 **Galletly, I.,** B.A. (Mobilized Aug. 4, 1914). Lt. 1st Lowland Bde. R.F.A. (T.F.). France. Killed in action in France on Aug. 3, 1916.

1919 Gammell, J. L. (Aug. 9, 1917). Capt. 3rd Field Artillery, U.S. Army. France, 1918.

1900 Gardiner, H., B.A. (May 17, 1915). 2nd Lt. R.F.A. (Resigned on account of ill health.)

1900 Gardner, J. S., M.A. (Sept. 5, 1914). Maj. Midland Div. R.E. (T.F.). France. *D.* France, 1915.

1909 **Garnier,* D. K.,** B.A. (Serving Aug. 4, 1914). Capt. Gloucestershire Regt. France. Died on Dec. 7, 1916, of wounds received in action.

1910 Garrod,* A. G. R., M.A. (Aug. 14, 1914). Capt. 3rd Leicestershire Regt. Maj., Acting Lt.-Col., Headquarters Staff, R.A.F., Cologne. Belgium and France, 1914–18; Germany, 1918–19. *M.C.*, Feb. 18, 1915. *D.F.C.*, July 1919. *D.* France, 1915, 1916, 1917.

1908 **Gascoyne-Cecil,* R. W.** (Aug. 1914). ‡Lt. R.H.A. (T.F.), attd. T.M.B. France and Belgium. Killed in action at Mesnières on Dec. 1, 1917.

1896 Gaskell, J. C., M.A. (Mobilized Aug. 4, 1914). Lt.-Col. 2nd Welsh Bde. R.F.A. (T.F.). T.D.

1919 Gaussen, A. R. L. (May 16, 1917). Midshipman R.N.V.R., H.M.S. *Satyr*. Grand Fleet, Harwich Force.

1919 Gawler, D. R. (Sept. 1, 1914). Capt. 11th R. Scots (Maj.), attd. R.A.F. Belgium and France, 1915–16. *M.C.*, May 11, 1917. *D.* France, 1915.

1910 **Geen, W. P.** (Aug. 6, 1914). ‡2nd Lt. 9th K.R.R.C. France and Belgium. Killed in action nr. Hooge on July 30, 1915.

Geoghegan, W. G. R. (Oct. 8, 1915). 2nd Lt. 3rd, attd. 2nd, R. Inniskilling Fusiliers. France. Died on Apr. 13, 1917, of wounds received in action.

1914 **Gerard, T. O.** (Mar. 10, 1915). 2nd Lt. 4th Manchester Regt., attd. M.G.C. France. Killed in action near Contalmaison on July 10, 1916.

1898 Gething, R. E., B.C.L., M.A. (Dec. 4, 1915). Lt., Acting Capt., R.G.A. Courts-Martial Officer.

1905 Gibbs, H. G., M.A. (May 22, 1916). Lt., Acting Maj., Technical Officer, R.A.F.

1892 Gibson, A. G., B.A. (Jan. 6, 1915). Maj. R.A.S.C. Egypt.

1894 Gibson, E. H. (July 7, 1916). Lt. R.G.A.

1919 Gie, A. H. (Aug. 9, 1914). Burgher, 6th S. African Horse. German SW. Africa, German E. Africa. (Invalided, June 1917.)

1919 Gilbert, A. B. (May 26, 1917). Gnr. 12th Canadian Siege Batt. France and Belgium, 1918–19.

1901 Gilliat, J. F. G. (Oct. 6, 1914). Lt. Res. Regt. of 1st Life Guards. Staff-Capt. Dept. of the Adjt.-Gen., War Office. *D.* § Mar. 1919.

1907 Gilray, C. M., B.A. (July 7, 1916). Lt. 6th Rifle Brigade. Temp. Capt., empld. O.C.B. France. *M.C.*, Jan. 1, 1918.

1900 **Goldberg, F. W.,** B.A. (Nov. 20, 1915). 2nd Lt. 3rd Queen's (R. W. Surrey Regt.), attd. 7th R. Dublin Fusiliers. Egypt. Killed in action on Oct. 3, 1916.

1898 **Goldberg, H. W.,** B.A. (Mar. 31, 1915). 2nd Lt. 3rd, attd. 1st, Queen's (R. W. Surrey Regt.) France. Died at Rouen on July 31, 1915, of wounds received in action in France.

1915 Gordon, E. V., B.A. (Aug. 1916). Gnr. Canadian Artillery. (Invalided, Nov. 1916.)

1887 Gordon, Rev. W., M.A. (Mobilized Aug. 4, 1914). Chaplain (4th Class), attd. R.F.A.

1899 Grainger, A. C. (Feb. 2, 1917). Lt. R.A.S.C.

1917 Grantham, H. T. (Oct. 15, 1918). Gnr. 212th Batt., R.F.A.

1891 Gray, D. P. A. (Oct. 26, 1914). Lt. Protection Coy., R. Defence Corps.

1901 Gray, F. H. T. (Sept. 6, 1915). Lt. Special Lists. Order of the White Eagle (5th Class).

1904 Gray, J. N., B.A. (Mobilized Aug. 4, 1914). Capt., temp. Maj., Inns of Court O.T.C. G.S.O. 3, G.H.Q. France, 1914–19. *D.S.O.*, Jan. 1, 1917. *D.* France, 1915.

1914 **Greenlees, C. F.** (Nov. 27, 1914). 2nd Lt. 9th Queen's (R. W. Surrey Regt.), attd. R. Dublin Fusiliers. Gallipoli, Egypt, France. Killed in action in the Battle of the Somme on July 1, 1916.

1903 Grensted, Rev. L. W., M.A. (Nov. 18, 1915). Chaplain to the Forces (4th Class), attd. 2nd Western General Hospital, 1917–19.

1902 Grice-Hutchinson, C. G. (Oct. 15, 1914). Capt. 8th, attd. 9th, S. Staffordshire Regt. France. *M.C.*, June 3, 1916. *D.* France, 1917.

1910 Grimthorpe, Lord (Aug. 4, 1914). Capt. Yorkshire Hussars. 2nd Lt. (Hon. Capt.) Administrative Officer, R.A.F. France, Belgium, 1915–17. *D.* France, 1917.

1918 Groves, S. J. S., B.A. (Sept. 19, 1914). Lt. 10th, attd. 1st and 2nd, York & Lancaster Regt. (Capt.). France, 1915–16. (Invalided on account of wounds, May 1918.)

Gunther, N. O. F. (Sept. 22, 1915). 2nd Lt. R. E. Kent Yeomanry, attd. 6th The Buffs (E. Kent Regt.). France. *M.C.*, July 18, 1917. Killed in action on July 11, 1917.

1919 Gurney, H. L. G. (May 5, 1917). Lt. 1st K.R.R.C. France, 1918.

1911 Hadden,* F. L., B.A. (Sept. 24, 1914). Capt. 4th R. Berkshire Regt. Capt. Special Lists.

1919 Haig, E. F. G. (Aug. 4, 1915). Lt. 3rd Queen's (R. W. Surrey Regt.). (Capt.). France, Italy, Austria, Egypt. *D.* Italy, 1919.

1907 Hallett,* D. B. I., B.M., M.A. (June 10, 1915). Capt. R.A.M.C.

1892 Hallowes, Rev. W. H., B.A. (Nov. 17, 1916). Chaplain (Hon. Capt.) S.A. Labour Corps.

1905 Hamilton, Rev. C. C., M.A. (Sept. 10, 1917). Chaplain to the Forces (4th Class), attd. 183rd Inf. Bde. France, 1917–19.

1906 Hamilton,* P. S., M.A. (Sept. 1914). ‡Lt. 4th Border Regt. Capt. G.S.O. 3, Headquarters Staff, Indian Army. India, NW. Frontier.

1908 Hands, P. A. M., B.A. (Aug. 27, 1915). Maj. S.A. Heavy Artillery, attd. 162nd Siege Batt., R.G.A. France. *D.S.O.*, Jan. 1, 1919. *M.C.*, July 18, 1917. *D.* France, 1918.

1910 Hands, K. C. M., B.A. (Nov. 14, 1915). Lt. 366th Forestry Coy. R.E. France.

1907 **Hands, R. H. M.,** B.A. (Nov. 1914). ‡Capt., Acting Maj., S. A. Heavy Artillery, attd. 73rd Siege Batt., R.G.A. German S.W. Africa. France. Died on Apr. 20, 1918, of wounds received in action.

1912 **Harold, J. P. B.,** B.A. (Aug. 15, 1914). Lt. R.F.A. Flying Officer R.F.C. France. *D.* France, 1916. Died on Feb. 16, 1918, of wounds received in action.

1907 Harper, C. S., M.A. (Nov. 10, 1916). Lt., Acting Capt., I.A.R.O., attd. 104th Wellesley's Rifles. Mesopotamia, 1917–19.

1909 Harris, T. N. C., B.A. (Jan. 12, 1915). Lt. 6th Oxf. & Bucks Lt. Infty. Lt., Acting Capt., 36th Training Res. Bn. France. *M.C.*, Nov. 25, 1916.

Harrison, E. B. (Sept. 21, 1915). 2nd Lt. 7th W. Yorkshire Regt. France. Died on Sept. 29, 1916, of wounds received in action.

1907 Harrison,* E. C., B.A. (Mobilized Aug. 4, 1914). Capt., Acting Maj., R.G.A. (T.F.). France. *M.C.*, Jan. 1, 1919. *D.* France, 1916, 1917.

Harrison, G. (Dec. 22, 1914). 2nd Lt. 12th Hampshire Regt. 2nd Lt. M.G.C. France. Killed in action near Fricourt on July 1, 1916.

1909 **Hart, C. H.** (Sept. 1914). ‡Lt. 5th, attd. 2nd, Bedfordshire Regt. (Capt.). France. Killed in action on Oct. 23, 1918.

1901 **Hartnoll, J.,** M.A. (Mobilized Aug. 4, 1914). Capt., Berks. Batt. R.H.A. Died on May 20, 1917, of enteric contracted on active service.

1909 Harvey-Samuel, F. K. (Mar. 25, 1915). 2nd Lt. 1st Hertfordshire Regt. (Resigned.)

1919 Hastings, J. M. (Sept. 28, 1914). Lt. 2/7th London Regt. (Rifles). Lt. 31st D.C.O. Lancers, Indian Army. Gallipoli, Egypt, France, India, Palestine.

1884 Hawker, H. G., M.A. (Nov. 10, 1914). Capt. 11th Devonshire Regt. (and Depot).

1908 Hawker, M. L. (Apr. 25, 1916). Capt. Paymaster A.P.D.

1913 Hay,* W. R. (Oct. 3, 1914). Lt. 4th Dorsetshire Regt., attd. Indian Army. Mesopotamia. *D.* Mesopotamia, 1919.

1911 **Heath, J. L.** (Mar. 17, 1915). Lt. 1st and 2nd K.O.Y.L.I. France. Killed in action on Oct. 2, 1915.

1909 Hebert,* B. T. M., B.A. (Sept. 1, 1914). Lt., Acting Capt., 2nd Welsh Guards. France, 1916–17; Germany, 1918–19. *M.C.*, Dec. 17, 1917.

1909 Henriques,* B. L. Q., B.A. (Oct. 1915). Lt. 3rd The Buffs (E. Kent Regt.). Capt. Tank Corps. Belgium and France, 1917–18. Italian Silver Medal for Military Valour. *D.* France, 1917, 1918.

1919 Hewart, H. V. (Jan. 1916). Sub-Lt. R.N.V.R.

1905 **Hibbert,* S.,** B.M., M.A. (1914). Asst. Surgeon R.N. Lost in H.M.S. *Formidable* on Jan. 1, 1915.

1902 **Hill, R. H.,** B.A. (Aug. 1914). Sergt. 1/14th London Regt. (London Scottish). France and Belgium. Killed in action on Oct. 13, 1915.

1905 Hill, T. W., B.A. (Feb. 22, 1917). Lt. R.F.A. France. *M.C.*, Dec. 17, 1917.

1893 Hilton, H. A. (Apr. 7, 1915). Maj. R.A.S.C.

1909 Hirst, F. E. (June 17, 1917). Lt. Labour Corps.

1898 **Hodgson, R. D.,** B.A. (Dec. 19, 1914). Capt. R.F.A. France. Killed in action on Mar. 21, 1918.

1909 Hoffnung-Goldsmid,* C. J., B.A. (Serving Aug. 4, 1914). Capt. 9th Lancers. G.S.O. 3. France, 1914–17; Italy, 1917–18. *O.B.E.* (Mil.). Croce di Guerra. Order of the Crown of Italy (Cavalier). *D.* Italy, 1918, 1919.

1901 Holland, Rev. H. St. B., M.A. (May 28, 1918). Chaplain to the Forces (4th Class).

1902 Holland, Rev. J. B., M.A. (Dec. 11, 1916). Chaplain to the Forces (4th Class).

1904 Holland, K. G., B.A. (July. 26, 1915). Capt. R.A.S.C. Gallipoli, Egypt and Palestine. *O.B.E.* (Mil.). Order of El Nahda (4th Class). *D.* Palestine, 1918, 1919.

1909 **Holland,* V. E.,** B.A. (Serving Aug. 4, 1914). Lt., Acting Capt., 7th Hussars. Mesopotamia. *D.* Mesopotamia, 1919. Died on Nov. 8, 1918, of wounds received in action on Nov. 28, 1917, in Mesopotamia.

1918 Hollett, M. M. (Jan. 1916). Sergt. 1st Newfoundland Regt. France, 1916. (Invalided on account of wounds, Aug. 1917.)

1919 Hopkin, S. (Sept. 8, 1914). Cpl. 53rd Div. Cyclist Coy. (Sergt.). Egypt, Palestine, 1916–19.

1919 Hopper, H. L. (Aug. 23, 1915). Lt. 7th W. Riding Regt. France, 1916, 1917–18. *M.C.*, May 13, 1918.

1909 Horne, A. E. (Mobilized Aug. 4, 1914). Capt. Surrey Yeomanry. G.S.O. 3. Salonika. *M.C.*, Jan. 1, 1918. Croix de Guerre. *D.* Salonika, 1917.

1912 **Horne, L. J.** (Mar. 2, 1915). Lt. 4th K.O.Y.L.I. France. Killed in action on June 15, 1918.

1912 **Houghton,* P. S.,** B.A. (Aug. 26, 1914). Capt. 9th London Regt. (Queen Victoria's Rifles). France. Killed in action on the Somme on July 1, 1916.

1919 Howe, L. A. (July 31, 1915). Lt. 3rd Lincolnshire Regt. (Capt.). France, 1916–18; Germany, 1919.

1908 Howell, G. F. (Sept. 26, 1916). Lt., Acting Capt., 5th K.R.R.C. G.S.O. 3. France. Croix de Chevalier de la Légion d'Honneur.

1919 Hunt, J. R. (Mar. 18, 1917). Cadet R.F.A., O.C.B.

1911 **Hunter,* H. M.** (Aug. 15, 1914). Lt. 3rd, attd. 2nd, Wiltshire Regt. France. *D.* France, 1915. Died on Apr. 6, 1915, of wounds received in action.

1897 Hunter, R. C., B.A. (Mobilized Aug. 4, 1914). Lt. Royal 1st Devon Yeomanry (T.F. Res.).

1897 Huntley, F. O. J., B.A. (June 26, 1915). Lt. 6th King's (Liverpool Regt.).

1919 Huskinson, G. N. B. (Feb. 1, 1918). ‡2nd Lt. Grenadier Guards.

1919 Hustler, W. M. C. (Mar. 1918). 2nd Lt. 3rd (Garr.) Bn. R. Irish Fusiliers. Salonika, 1918.

1897 Hutton, R. W. Army Pay Dept.

1899 Huxtable, Rev. A. H., M.A. (Nov. 15, 1916). Chaplain to the Forces (4th Class), attd. Tank Corps. France and Belgium. *M.C.*, Oct. 28, 1917.

1919 Inglis, G. J. (Sept. 10, 1918). ‡2nd Lt. R.F.A.

1882 **Inglis, Rev. R. E.,** M.A. (July 5, 1915). Chaplain to the Forces (4th Class). France, 1915. Killed in action near Ginchy on Sept. 18, 1916.

1908 Inman, R. J., B.M. (July 15, 1915). Temp. Surgeon R.N.

1907 Isaacs-Innes, D. E., M.A. (May 8, 1915). Lt. R.E. Salonika. *M.C.*, June 3, 1918. *D.* Salonika, 1917.
1909 Isherwood,* A. A. M., M.A. Nigerian Land Contingent. W. Africa.
1912 Jameson,* A. St. C. (Oct. 1914). ‡Lt. 3rd, attd. 2nd, Seaforth Highlanders. Belgium, France. (Invalided on account of wounds, May 5, 1917.)
1912 **Jardine,* G. B. T.,** B.A. (July 12, 1915). 2nd Lt. 13th Arg. & Suth'd. Highlanders, attd. 5th Q. O. Cameron Highlanders. France. Missing, believed killed in action on Oct. 18, 1916.
1913 **Jeune, H. St. H.** (Sept. 16, 1914). Capt. 9th Gloucestershire Regt. France. Died on May 12, 1917, of wounds received in action.
1911 Jobson, R. H., B.A. (Sept. 5, 1914). Lt., Acting Capt., and Adjt., 1st E. Anglian Bde. R.F.A. (T.F.). France. *M.C.*, Jan. 1, 1918.
1916 **Johns, L.** (1917). Cadet School, France. Lt. Artillery, U.S. Army. France. Killed in action on Nov. 30, 1918.
1894 Johnson, G. W., M.A. (Oct. 30, 1915). 2nd Lt. 9th Hampshire Regt.
1892 **Jones, A. M.** (Mar. 30, 1915). Lt. 1st Scots Guards. France, 1915-16. Died on Nov. 21, 1916, of wounds received in action.
1906 Jones, Rev. B. E., M.A. (Aug. 31, 1914). ‡Capt. 4th, attd. 7th, R. Welch Fusiliers.
1911 **Jones,* E. K.** (Aug. 22, 1914). Capt. 8th R. Welch Fusiliers. France. Killed in action in the Battle of the Somme on July 3, 1916.
1904 Joseph, A. F., M.A. Lt., temp. Capt., I.A.R.O. Staff-Captain India Northern Command, Bareilly Bde., Meerut Div.
1908 Julius, A. D., B.A. (Jan. 27, 1915). Lt. General List. R.T.O. (1st Class).
1914 **Julius, C. H.** (Apr. 17, 1915). Lt. 1st & 2nd, attd. 3rd, E. Lancashire Regt. France. Killed in action on Apr. 9, 1916.
1905 Keeling, E. H., M.A. (Dec. 2, 1914). Capt. I.A.R.O., attd. 1/119th Inf. Acting Lt.-Col., Asst. Director of Port Traffic (Class X), R.E. (Prisoner of War in Turkey, escaped from Prisoners' camp.) Mesopotamia, Russia, Palestine. *M.C.*, Oct. 16, 1918. *D.* Mesopotamia, 1916.
1899 Kelly, A. L., B.C.L., M.A. (Nov. 22, 1916). Lt. 6th K.R.R.C. Staff-Captain (Courts-martial Officer). France. *O.B.E.* (Mil.). *D.* France, 1919.
1904 Kelly, N. L., B.A. (Jan. 25, 1917). Lt. 1st Monmouthshire Regt.
1901 Kemp,* J. C., B.A. (Nov. 6, 1915). Maj. Quebec Regt., Canadian Contingent. Bde. Maj. France. *D.S.O.*, June 3, 1919. *M.C.*, June 4, 1917. *D.* France, 1919.
1905 Kemp, R. B. H., B.A. (Aug. 15, 1914). Capt., attd. 3rd Irish Guards (S.R.).
1905 **Kennedy, C. G.,** B.A. Capt., Political Officer at Mbozi, German E. Africa. German E. Africa. Died at Durban on Oct. 21, 1918.
1899 Kennedy, N., B.A. (Mobilized Aug. 4, 1914). Maj., temp. Lt.-Col., Ayrshire Yeomanry. A.A.G. Egypt and Palestine. *D.S.O.*, June 4, 1917. *D.* Egypt, 1917.
1919 Kennedy, P. G. (Sept. 26, 1917). ‡2nd Lt. M.G.C. (Armoured Car Unit). Mesopotamia, Persia, Russia, Baku. *M.C.*, Mar. 8, 1919.
1901 Kennedy, W. D., B.M., M.A. (Jan. 7, 1916). Capt. R.A.M.C. France. *D.* France, 1918.

1902 Kerans, P. M. A. (Serving Aug. 4, 1914). Capt., Temp. Maj., 6th Dragoon Guards. G.S.O. 2. France. *M.C.*, June 3, 1918. *D.* France, 1917.

1914 Kerr, F. R. (Sept. 30, 1914). Capt. R.A.M.C. (S.R.). France. *D.S.O.*, Nov. 4, 1915. *D.* France, 1915.

1919 Kidd, H. J. (Jan. 13, 1916). Lt. R.F.A. France, 1916, 1918–19.

1913 **Kimber,* H. C. D.** (Aug. 26, 1914). Lt. 7th London Bde., 1st London Divl. Ammn. Col., R.F.A. (T.F.). France. Died on June 22, 1916, of wounds received in action,

1916 King, E. R. (Feb. 17, 1917). Lt. Warwickshire Yeomanry, attd. Indian Army.

1874 Kinloch, Sir D. A., Bt., B.A., *C.B.*, *M.V.O.*, (Sept. 17, 1914). Brig.-Gen. comdg. 16th Res. Bde. France, 1915–16. *D.* France, 1915, 1916; § Feb. 1917.

1919 Kirwan, G. D. (July 28, 1915). Lt., temp. Capt. R.G.A. (S.R.). Staff-Captain. France, 1915–18. *M.C.*, June 3, 1918. Croix de Guerre.

1912 **Knapp-Fisher, C. E. H.** (Aug. 26, 1914). 2nd Lt. 6th K.O.Y.L.I., Belgium and France. Died on July 31, 1915, of wounds received in action in Belgium.

1919 Knight, H. S. (June 17, 1916). ‡Lt. R. Newfoundland Regt. France and Belgium, 1917–18.

1920 Laming, R. C. (Apr. 22, 1918). Lt. 18th Hussars. Germany, 1918–19.

1898 Lane, C. C. P., B.A. Pte. Wiltshire Regt.

1919 Laver, C. H. (Aug. 4, 1914). ‡Lt. R.F.A. Surgeon-Lt. R.N. (from 1917). Belgium, France, 1914–16.

Laws, P. U. (Sept. 16, 1914). Capt. 16th Sherwood Foresters. France and Belgium. *M.C.*, Oct. 18, 1917. *D.* France, 1916. Killed in action on Sept. 20, 1917.

1902 Le Blanc Smith, G., B.A. ‡Capt. 4th E. Surrey Regt. E. Africa. *M.C.*, Feb. 1, 1917; *Bar*, May 4, 1917. *D.C.M.*

1907 **Leckie,* J. H.**, B.A. (Serving Aug. 4, 1914). Lt. 1st R. Dragoons. France. Killed in action on May 13, 1915.

1904 Ledward, J. C., B.A. (Sept. 1914). Capt. Inns of Court O.T.C., attd. as Adjt. 1/4th Leicestershire Regt. France, 1918.

1908 Ledward, K. H., B.A. (Sept. 16, 1915). Lt. R.G.A. Empld. Dept. of C.I.G.S., War Office.

1896 Lee, E. C., B.A. (Aug. 22, 1916). Lt. R.G.A. (S.R.).

1919 Lee, H. W. (May 22, 1916). ‡Lt., Acting Capt. R.A.F. (Kite Balloons), attd. Grand Fleet.

1913 Lees, G. H. (Nov. 11, 1914). Capt. R. Welch Fusiliers. Maj. General List. France. *M.C.*, Nov. 25, 1916.

1897 Lee-Warner, Rev. A., M.A. (Oct. 31, 1916). Chaplain to the Forces (3rd Class). Egypt, 1915; France, 1916–18. *D.* France, 1919.

1899 Lee-Warner, W. H., B.A. (Sept. 3, 1917). Pte. E. Surrey Regt., attd. Mil. Intelligence Dept., War Office. Hon. Capt. Special Lists (whilst on special service). Egypt (Arab Bureau, Cairo), 1918, 1919; E. Indies, 1918; Aden and Hadhramant Hinterland, 1918–19.

1913 **Le Mesurier,* H.** (Nov. 27, 1914). 2nd Lt. 9th K.R.R.C. France, 1915–16. Killed in action at Delville Wood on Aug. 24, 1916.

1919 Leney, A. M. (Sept. 24, 1917). 2nd Lt. 3rd Hussars. Belgium, Germany, 1919.

1919 Leslie-Smith, A. (Feb. 1, 1918). Gentleman Cadet R.M.A.

1908 Lessing, E. A. (Apr. 1915). Capt. Grenadier Guards. Russia, 1918-19. *O.B.E.* (Mil.). Order of St. Stanislas (Russia). *D.* Russia, 1918.

1897 Lester, Rev. B., M.A. (Oct. 7, 1914). Chaplain to the Forces (4th Class). France. *D.* France, 1919.

1906 **Lester,* E. G.,** B.A. (Dec. 8, 1915). Lt. 1st Central Ontario Regt., Canadian Inf. France. Died on June 25, 1917, of wounds received in action.

1919 Levy, B. W. (Aug. 26, 1918). Cadet 1st Cadet Bn., R.A.F.

1917 Lewis, C. S. (June 1917). 2nd Lt., attd. 2nd Middlesex Regt. France, 1918.

1906 Lewis,* E. J. P., M.A. (June 22, 1915). Lt. 4th (attd. Res. Bn.) R. Berkshire Regt.

1892 **Lewis, R. P.,** M.A. (Serving Aug. 4, 1914). Maj. 1st Devonshire Regt. Lt.-Col. 9th, attd. 1/10th, Manchester Regt. France and Belgium. Died on Sept. 7, 1917, of wounds received in action.

1900 Lewis, W. H. P., M.A. (Sept. 24, 1914). Capt. Glamorganshire Yeomanry. A.D.C. France and Germany, 1916–19. *O.B.E.* (Mil.). *D.* France, 1917, 1918.

1900 Leys,* K. K. M., M.A. (Mar. 1917). Lt., Acting Capt., R.G.A., attd. H.Q. 52nd Div. France, 1918–19.

1919 Lindop, T. E. (Apr. 1918). Flight Cadet R.A.F.

1898 [Lindsay, A. D., M.A.] (Oct. 1914). Lt.-Col. General List. Deputy Controller of Labour. France, 1917–19. *C.B.E.* (Mil.). *D.* France, 1919.

1901 Linton, Rev. H., M.A. (Sept. 11, 1916). Chaplain to the Forces (4th Class).

1912 Llewellin, J. J., M.A. (Sept. 17, 1914). Lt., Acting Maj., R.G.A. France, 1915–19. *M.C.*, Jan. 1, 1918.

1908 Llewellin,* W. W., M.A. (Oct. 22, 1914). Capt. 4th, attd. 1st, Dorsetshire Regt.

1902 Lloyd-Greame, Sir P., B.A. *M.P.* (Aug. 1914). Capt. 5th Yorkshire Regt. Maj. K.R.R.C. Maj. General List, empld. Ministry of National Service. France and Belgium. *K.B.E.* *M.C.*, Jan. 1, 1917.

1914 Long, J. E. S. (Feb. 23, 1915). 2nd Lt. 9th R. W. Kent Regt. Lt. (Wireless Equipment Officer) R.A.F.

1910 Lorenz, R. E., B.A. (Aug. 31, 1914). Sergt. Instr. 15th London Regt. (Civil Service Rifles). France.

1912 Loudoun-Shand, E. G., M.A. (Aug. 1914). 2nd Lt. 8th K.R.R.C., afterwards Capt. General List. A.D.C. France and Belgium, 1915, 1916, 1918. *M.C.*, June 3, 1919. *D.* France, 1916.

1911 **Loxton,* C. E. H.** (Aug. 26, 1914). 2nd Lt. 5th N. Staffordshire Regt. France. Died on May 25, 1915, of wounds received in action.

1912 Lucas,* C. A. (Sept. 2, 1914). Lt., Acting Capt., 5th Hampshire Regt.

1896 Lucas, St. J. W. L., M.A. (Dec. 1915). Pte. Queen's (R. W. Surrey Regt.). ‡2nd Lt. General List. Staff-Lt. (1st Class). Italy, 1916–18.

1898 Lunt, T. R. W. (Oct. 29, 1915). Lt. R.F.A. (S.R.).

1897 Lyon, C. D. G. (Serving Aug. 4, 1914). Maj., Acting Lt.-Col., 187th Bde., R.F.A. France. *D.S.O.*, June 3, 1916. Croix de Guerre. *D.* France, 1915, 1916 twice, 1917, 1918.

1889 Macaulay, D. I. M. (Serving Aug. 4, 1914). Maj. Indian Army (Cavalry). D.A.A.G.

1914 McCracken, A. (Aug. 10, 1916). Capt. I.A.R.O.

1906 McCulloch, A. (Feb. 9, 1917). 2nd Lt. Technical Officer, R.A.F.

1879 **McDonnell, Hon. Sir Schomberg,** *K.C.B., G.C.V.O.* (July 16, 1915). Maj. T.F. Res., Capt. 5th Q. O. Cameron Highlanders. G.S.O. 3. France. Died on Nov. 23, 1915, of wounds received in action.

1919 McEwen, P. A. (Aug. 10, 1914). Pte. E. Surrey Regt. ‡Lt. R.F.A. India, 1914–16; Egypt, 1916; France and Belgium, 1917–18.

1901 Macfarlane, W. N., M.A. (May 29, 1916). Lt. R.A.S.C.

1906 Macfarlane-Grieve,* R. W., M.A. (Feb. 17, 1915). Capt. 3rd, attd. 1/7th, The Black Watch. France, 1915; Mesopotamia, 1916–17; France, 1918. *M.C.*, Oct. 24, 1918.

1919 Machin, B. W. (May 6, 1915). Lt. 1st The Black Watch. France, 1916, 1917.

1904 **McJannet, W. R. B.,** B.A. (Dec. 20, 1914). Capt. 10th, attd. 7th, Seaforth Highlanders. France. Killed in action in the Battle of the Somme on July 14, 1916.

1907 **Mackintosh, E. H.** (Sept. 9, 1914). Lt. 8th The Black Watch. France. Killed in action at the Battle of Loos on Sept. 25, 1915.

McKenna, J. M. (Sept. 9, 1914). Lt. 9th K.R.R.C., and R.F.C. France. Killed in action on Oct. 2, 1917.

1912 McKenna,* T. M., B.A. (Aug. 15, 1914). 2nd Lt. 8th Hussars (S.R.).

1919 Mackenzie, C. W. (Apr. 17, 1918). 2nd Lt. 4th Northumberland Fusiliers. France, 1918–19.

1901 Mackenzie, D., B.A. (Oct. 5, 1914). Capt. and Adjt. 6th The Black Watch, attd. 1/4th Hampshire Regt. India.

1911 McNair, J. B., B.C.L. Lt. Canadian Heavy Artillery.

1917 McNicoll, J. M. (Sept. 20, 1918). 2nd Lt. R.H.A. Palestine.

1919 Macphail, J. G. S. (July 3, 1918). ‡2nd Lt. R. Scots.

1903 **Macrae, A. W. U.,** B.A. (Serving Aug. 4, 1914). Capt. 5th R. Scots. France. Killed in action on Aug. 11, 1918.

1899 **Macrae, F. L.** (Mar. 1, 1915). 2nd Lt. 8th Seaforth Highlanders. France. Killed in action at the Battle of Loos on Sept. 25, 1915.

1902 Macrae, Rev. J. A., M.A. (Oct. 23, 1917). Chaplain to the Forces (4th Class).

1911 McWilliam,* O. G. E., M.A. (Aug. 26, 1914). Capt. 5th R. Inniskilling Fusiliers. Gallipoli, Salonika.

1913 **Maggs,* E. W. B.** (Jan. 30, 1918). 2nd Lt. 8th, attd. 11th, K.R.R.C. France. Killed in action at Lens on Aug. 21, 1918.

1895 Maples, F. C., B.A. (Aug. 27, 1916). Lt. R.F.A. (S.R.).

1912 **Marler,* W. E.** (Apr. 8, 1915). 2nd Lt. 3rd Somerset L.I. France. Died on May 4, 1917, of wounds received in action.

1882 Marrable, A. G. (Serving Aug. 4, 1914). Maj., Bt.-Col. K.O.Y.L.I., Temp. Brig.-Gen., attd. Staff. France. *C.B.*, June 3, 1916. Croix d'Officier de la Légion d'Honneur. Croix de Commandeur de l'Ordre de la Couronne. *D.* France, 1916.

1893 Marsden, W. J. M., M.A. (Oct., 1914). ‡Capt. (Adjt.) 21st Manchester Regt., empld. Dept. of C.I.G.S., War Office (Maj.). *O.B.E.* (Mil.).

1898 Mathews, W. C., B.A. (Mar. 10, 1915). Lt. R.E. (T.F.).

1893 Matterson, W. A. K., B.A. (Nov. 1, 1916). Lt. T.F. Res.

1911 **Matthews, M. L. W.,** B.A. (Aug. 29, 1914). Capt. 6th R. W. Kent Regt. France. *D.* France, 1916. Killed in action on the Somme on July 3, 1916.
1899 **Maughan, A. W.,** B.A. (Nov. 4, 1916). 2nd Lt. 385th Siege Batt., R.G.A. France and Belgium. Killed in action near Messines on June 24, 1917.
1900 Maxwell, G. A., B.A. (Serving Aug. 4, 1914). Capt. 5th Yorkshire Regt. France. *D.* France, 1916 twice, 1917, 1918. (Prisoner of War, 1918.)
1920 Meats, G. W. (Mar. 15, 1915). Capt. 3rd W. Yorkshire Regt., attd. 7th York & Lancaster Regt. France, Belgium, 1916, 1917, 1918, 1919. *M.C.*, Feb. 4, 1918; *Bar*, Feb. 18, 1918.
1876 Meautys, T. A. (Apr. 1916). Lt., Acting Capt., Special Lists. Courts Martial Officer, D.A.A.G.
1901 Medcalf, E. F., M.A. (Dec. 2, 1914). Maj. 8th Oxf. & Bucks Lt. Infty. Salonika. Greek Military Cross (2nd Class).
1893 Mellor, G. R. L., M.A. (Sept. 19, 1914). Capt. 1st (Garr.) Bn. King's (Liverpool Regt.). France. *M.C.*, Sept. 26, 1917.
1919 Melly, A. J. M. (June 29, 1917). Lt. R.F.A. France, 1918–19. *M.C.*, Sept. 18, 1919.
1907 Mendl,* C. T. S. (Feb. 27, 1915). Lt. 3rd Devonshire Regt. Lt., Staff Officer, R.A.F.
1897 Mendl, L. E., B.A. (Nov. 25, 1914). Capt. R.A.S.C.
1911 Mendl,* R. W. S., M.A. (Jan. 1, 1916). Lt., Acting Adjt., 406th Batt., 172nd Bde., R.F.A. (T.F.). Egypt, Palestine, 1917–19.
1904 Mercer, C. W., M.A. (Oct. 5, 1914). Capt. 3rd County of London Yeomanry. Empld. Ministry of National Service. Egypt, Sinai, Salonika.
1904 Meredith, A. E., B.A. (Serving Aug. 4, 1914). Capt. R.E., attd. for Army Signals. Acting Maj. 114th Mahrattas, Indian Army. Mesopotamia. *M.C.*, June 3, 1918. *D.* Mesopotamia, 1917, 1919.
1912 Merriam,* L. P. B., M.A. (Sept. 1, 1914). Lt. 7th Rifle Brigade, afterwards Maj. 7th Tank Corps. France and Belgium. *M.C.*, Nov. 16, 1916.
1911 Middleton, A. L., B.A. (Mobilized Aug. 4, 1914). Capt. 1st W. Riding Bde., R.F.A. (T.F.).
1899 Middleton, H. D., M.A. (Oct. 20, 1915). Lt., Acting Capt., 3/1st W. Riding Ammn. Column, R.F.A. (T.F.). France, Belgium, Germany.
1887 Millar, Rev. F. G., M.A. (Sept. 16, 1915). Chaplain to the Forces (4th Class).
1919 Millican, N. S., B.A. (Sept. 23, 1914). ‡Capt. 4th King's (Liverpool Regt.). France, 1915–18. *M.C.*, Jan. 1, 1917. *D.* France, 1917.
1919 Milligan, W. R. (June 6, 1917). 2nd Lt. 1st (Res. Garr.) Bn. Highland L.I., attd. 2/9th Durham L.I. Lt. and Asst. R.T.O. Salonika, 1918–19.
1901 Mills, G. H., B.A. (Feb. 15, 1915). Lt. R.A.O.C.
1903 **Milne, A. N.,** B.A. (Apr. 25, 1915). 2nd Lt. 6th Manchester Regt. Gallipoli. *D.* Gallipoli, 1915. Killed in action at Suvla Bay on Aug. 7, 1915.
1910 **Miskin,* M. J.,** M.A. (Dec. 7, 1914). 2nd Lt. 9th N. Staffordshire Regt. Lt., Acting Maj., 1st Bn. Tank Corps. France and Belgium. *M.C.*, Feb. 18, 1918; *Bar*, Mar. 8, 1919. Killed in action on Oct. 17, 1918.
1919 Mitchell, H. P. (Aug. 27, 1918). Gentleman Cadet R.M.C., Sandhurst.
1907 **Mitchell,* J. T. R.,** B.A. (Aug. 1914). Maj. 13th R. Scots. Acting Lt.-Col. attd. 11th Arg. & Suth'd. Highlanders. France. *D.S.O.*, Jan. 1, 1917. Croix de Guerre. *D.* France, 1916, 1917, 1918. Died on Apr. 1, 1918, of wounds received in action.

1900 Mocatta, O. E., B.A. (July 17, 1916). Lt. R.A.S.C.

1905 Modera, F. S., M.A. (Oct. 15, 1914). ‡Capt., Bt.-Maj., 20th R. Fusiliers; Acting Lt.-Col. 1st Lancashire Fusiliers. D.A.A.G., G.H.Q., France. France and Belgium. *D.S.O.*, Sept. 16, 1918; *Bar*, Feb. 15, 1919. *M.C.*, Jan. 1, 1917. *D.* France, 1917, 1918, 1919.

1899 Monier-Williams, G. W., M.A. (Sept. 16, 1914). Capt. 12th London Regt. (The Rangers). Maj. Special Lists whilst spec. empld. with R.E. France, 1915–19. *O.B.E.* (Mil.). *M.C.*, Jan. 1, 1917. *D.* France, 1918.

1904 Monier-Williams, R. T., M.A. (Sept. 9, 1914). Capt. 7th The Buffs (E. Kent Regt.). Maj. General List. D.A.A.G., G.H.Q. France. *O.B.E.* (Mil.). *D.* France, 1918 twice.

1900 Monkhouse, C. C., B.A. (July 19, 1916). Lt., Acting Capt., R.G.A. (S.R.). Italy. *M.C.*, June 3, 1918.

1919 Montagu, J. E. (Jan. 25, 1918). 2nd Lt. R.F.A. France, Belgium, Germany.

1896 Moore, A. M., M.A. (Sept. 1, 1918). 2nd Lt. Norfolk Regt. (on demobilization).

1902 **Morgan, R. C.,** M.A. (Dec. 15, 1916). Lt. R. Welch Fusiliers. Temp. Capt., Labour Corps. Asst. Labour Commandant, No. 1 Sub-Area, B.E.F. France. Died on Feb. 18, 1919, of illness contracted on active service.

1904 **Morris,* H. G.,** B.M. (Feb. 8, 1915). Capt. R.A.M.C. France. Killed in action on the Somme on July 14, 1916.

1903 **Morrison, E. W.,** M.A. (Aug. 1914). ‡Lt. 2nd D.C.L.I. France, 1916–17; Salonika, 1917–18. *M.C.*, July 19, 1917. Died at Salonika on Dec. 10, 1918, of illness contracted on active service.

1910 Mort,* E. L., B.A. (Feb. 17, 1915). Lt. 3rd Nigeria Regt. Cameroons, 1915–16; German E. Africa, 1917–18.

1919 Morton, G. M., B.A. (Nov. 2, 1915). Lt. R.G.A. (S.R.) (Maj.). France, 1916–18. *D.* France, 1918.

1891 Mundy, G. B. Massingberd, B.A. (Apr. 27, 1915). Capt. and Adjt. Depot, Lincolnshire Regt.

1894 Muntz, G. D. E. (July 28, 1916). Capt. Special Lists. (Empld. recruiting duties.)

1899 **Mure, G. A. S.** (Jan. 11, 1915). Lt., Officer Comdg. Depot Essex Regt. Capt. Arab Rifles. Egypt. Killed in action on Jan. 3, 1917.

1899 **Murray, G. R.,** B.A. Lt. Lancers, I.A.R.O. Mesopotamia. Died on Dec. 21, 1916, of wounds received in action.

1908 Myles, J. F., B.A. (Sept. 19, 1914). Capt. 8th Seaforth Highlanders.

1905 **Mylne, J. G.,** B.A. (June 14, 1915). Lt. 8th, attd. 1/4th, R. Scots. France. Killed in action on Sept. 2, 1918.

1910 Nason,* C. S., M.A. (Sept. 5, 1914). Capt. 5th Gloucestershire Regt., attd. King's African Rifles. Belgium, France, German E. Africa.

1895 Neilson, J. B. (Mobilized Aug. 4, 1914). Capt. Ayrshire Yeomanry.

1920 Neilson, J. B. (Nov. 11, 1915). Lt. Gordon Highlanders. Maj. M.G.C. France, Belgium, 1916–19. *M.C.*, Jan. 1, 1918; *Bar*, Feb. 1, 1919; *2nd Bar*, Apr. 2, 1919.

1895 **Nelson, T. A.,** B.A. (Mobilized Aug. 4, 1914). Capt. Lothians & Border Horse, attd. Staff. France, 1915–17. *D.* France, 1916 twice, 1917. Killed in action on Apr. 9, 1917.

1908 Nelson,* T. S., B.A. (Mobilized Aug. 4, 1914). Capt. R.A.M.C. (S.R.). France. *D.* France, 1917.

1902 Newton, C. N. (Mobilized Aug. 4, 1914). Capt. 2nd Grenadier Guards (S.R.). France. *M.C.*, Nov. 25, 1916.

1912 Newsum, H. N., B.A. (Feb. 1, 1915). Capt. 9th, attd. 2/5th, Lincolnshire Regt. France. *M.C.*, Nov. 14, 1916.

1912 Nicholson, C. J. H. (Sept. 30, 1914). Lt. 2nd Suffolk Regt. Lt. General List, empld. War Office.

1919 Nisbet, F. C. (Feb. 6, 1918). Pte. 1st The Buffs (E. Kent Regt.). France and Germany.

1915 Nolan, H. G. (Sept. 12, 1916). Capt. 49th Canadian Inf. France and Belgium. *M.C.*, Jan. 1, 1919. *D.* France, 1918.

1915 Northcroft, E. G. D. (Mar. 1, 1917). Lt. 5th Bedfordshire Regt., attd. M.G.C. France. *D.* France, 1918.

1901 **Ogilvie, A. W.,** M.A. (Oct. 4, 1915). Lt. A.S.C. (M.T.). France. Died of pneumonia after gas-poisoning on Oct. 30, 1918.

1903 Ogilvie, S. S., B.A. (Feb. 10, 1915). ‡Lt., Acting Maj., 1st & 2nd Wiltshire Regt. (Lt.-Col.). France. *D.S.O.*, Aug. 25, 1916; *Bar*, Jan. 1, 1918; *2nd Bar*, July 26, 1918. Given Commission for bravery in the field. *D.* France, 1915, 1916, 1917, 1918. (Prisoner of War in Germany, 1918.)

1910 Ormrod,* M. S., B.A. (Aug. 5, 1914). Capt. 2nd, attd. 11th. K.R.R.C. (Maj.). France. *D.S.O.*, Jan. 1, 1919. *D.* France, 1918.

1910 Osborne, E. T. (Dec. 22, 1914). 2nd Lt. 10th Bedfordshire Regt., afterwards Observer Officer R.A.F.

1909 Osmond,* W. R. F., M.A. (Aug. 5, 1914). Lt. R.F.A. Mesopotamia and India, 1915–19.

1905 Otter, F. L., B.A. (Sept. 1914). ‡Capt. 5th London Regt. (London Rifle Brigade). Lt., Acting Capt., R.E. France, 1917–18. *M.C.*, Oct. 28, 1917.

1900 Otter, R. E., B.A. (Mobilized Aug. 5, 1914). Capt., Bt.-Maj., 5th London Regt. (London Rifle Brigade). (Maj. D.A.Q.M.G.) France, 1914–19. *M.C.*, Jan. 1, 1917. Croix de Guerre with palm. *D.* France, 1918, 1919.

1911 Owen, G. S., B.A. (June 16, 1916). Lt. R.E. Salonika. *D.* Salonika, 1918.

1919 Owen, R. E. (Mar. 12, 1918). 2nd Lt. R.M.A. France.

1911 Page, L. F., B.A. (Jan. 11, 1915). Lt. R.F.C. (Invalided.)

1898 Paige, G. P., B.A. (Mobilized Aug. 4, 1914). Capt., Acting Lt.-Col., 1/4th D.C.L.I. Egypt and Palestine. *D.* Palestine, 1918, 1919.

1914 Pain, J. C. (Dec. 2, 1914). Lt., temp. Capt., 9th Devonshire Regt. France; N. Russia. *M.C.*, June 4, 1917. *D.* N. Russia, 1919.

1920 Pakenham-Walsh, W. P. (Jan. 18, 1916). Lt. R.F.A., attd. Hdqrs. Lancashire Divl. Artillery. Lt. R.A.F. France. *D.* France, 1917.

1905 Palmer, A. N., B.A. (Sept. 30, 1914). Capt. 4th R. Berkshire Regt., empld. Commd. School.

1912 Palmer,* H. A., B.A. (Sept. 14, 1914). Lt. 8th Middlesex Regt. Capt. I.A.R.O., attd. 1/91st Punjabis. India.

1907 **Palmer, Hon. R. S. A.,** M.A. (Sept. 2, 1914). Capt. 6th, attd. 4th, Hampshire Regt. Mesopotamia. Died on Jan. 21, 1916, of wounds received in action at the Battle of Um El Hannah.

1883 Papillon, P. R. (Serving Aug. 4, 1914). Lt.-Col. 13th Essex Regt. France. *D.S.O.*, Oct. 20, 1916. *D.* France, 1916.

1901 **Pardoe, Rev. G. S.,** B.A. (Apr. 10, 1917). Chaplain to the Forces (4th Class). Died on Oct. 15, 1918.

1906 Parker,* Rev. C. L., M.A. (Jan. 1, 1915). Chaplain to the Forces (4th Class). (Resigned on account of ill health.)

1910 Parry, J. H. (Oct. 12, 1915). 2nd Lt. 3rd The Buffs (E. Kent Regt.) empld. under Ministry of Munitions.

1901 Parsons, Rev. R. G., M.A. (Aug. 15, 1916). Chaplain to the Forces (4th Class).

1919 Pasley, R. M. S. (Nov. 2, 1917). 2nd Lt. D Batt., 160th Bde., R.F.A. France, 1918.

1902 Paterson, A. H., M.A. (Aug. 12, 1914). ‡Capt. 1/22nd London Regt. (The Queen's). France, 1915–19. *M.C.*, June 3, 1918. *D.* France.

1919 Paterson, I. H. B. (Sept. 1917). 2nd Lt. 10th R. Fusiliers. France, 1918.

1919 Paton, V. A. L. (May 1917). Lt. Grenadier Guards. France, Belgium.

1902 Payne, J. B., B.A. (May 12, 1915). Lt. 7th, attd. 10th, York & Lancaster Regt., empld. O.C.B. France.

1880 Payne, P. G. S., B.A. (Sept. 23, 1914). Lt. Bedfordshire Yeomanry.

1905 Peacock, G. S. (Apr. 19, 1915). Maj., Acting Lt.-Col., Staff Officer, R.A.F. *O.B.E.* (Mil.).

1896 Pearson, H. F., B.A. (Aug. 2, 1916). Capt. 21st Middlesex Regt. France. *M.C.*, June 3, 1918. (Prisoner of War in Germany, 1918.)

1907 Pearson,* H. W., B.A. (Mobilized Aug. 4, 1914). Capt. E. Riding of Yorkshire Yeomanry, attd. M.G.C.

1903 Pearson,* W. J., D.M. (Mar. 12, 1915). Capt., Acting Maj., R.A.M.C. D.A.D.M.S. France, 1916–17; Italy, 1917–19. *D.S.O.*, June 3, 1918. *M.C.*, Oct. 28, 1917. *D.* Italy, 1918.

1897 Pearson, W. O., M.A. (1916). ‡2nd Lt. 2nd Middlesex Regt. France. *M.M.* (Prisoner of War.)

1906 Pease, G. B. R. (Serving Aug. 4, 1914). Capt. R.F.A. (S.R.). Acting Maj. R.H. and R.F.A.

1901 Pegg, Rev. W. H. F., B.A. (Serving Aug. 4, 1914). Chaplain to the Forces (4th Class), attd. Cavalry Field Ambulance. France, 1914. *D.* France, 1914. (Invalided.)

1908 Pellatt, H. F. M. (Sept. 25, 1915). Lt., Acting Maj., 3rd R. Irish Regt. Staff-Captain, Dept. of Asst. Director-Gen. of Movements and Railways, afterwards Q.M.G's Dept., War Office. France. *M.B.E.* (Mil.). *M.C.*, Sept. 22, 1916. *D.* § Mar. 1919.

1908 Pereira, A., B.A. (Apr. 21, 1918). Capt., Paymaster A.P.D. *D.* § Aug. 1919.

1908 Perry, G. B., M.A. (Aug. 31, 1914). Lt. 11th London Regt. (Finsbury Rifles) (Capt.). Lt. T.F. Res.

1912 **Phillips, E. E. L.** (Oct. 24, 1914). 2nd Lt. 6th R. Berkshire Regt. France. Killed in action on Oct. 30, 1915.

1913 Pigeon, A. L. (Oct. 13, 1914). Lt. R.A.

1910 Piggott,* C. F. L., M.A. (Oct. 6, 1914). Capt. S. Wales Borderers. Staff-Captain. France. *D.* France, 1916.

1909 Pilcher,* K. R., M.A. Gnr. R.G.A.

1919 Pilling, J. L. (June 9, 1917). 2nd Lt. R.F.A. France and Germany, 1917–19. *M.C.*, Sept. 28, 1918.

1913 **Pim,* E. W. B.,** B.A. (Aug. 3, 1914). Lt. R.F.A. Died on July 5, 1918.

1902 Pinsent, R., B.A. (Jan. 4, 1916). Lt. R.E. (Signals). Egypt, Palestine, Syria.

1894 **Pirie, G. L.** (Sept. 12, 1914). 2nd Lt. Northamptonshire Yeomanry. Gallipoli. Died on June 16, 1915, of wounds received in action.

1910 **Pollock-Hodsoll, G. B.** (Serving Aug. 4, 1914). Capt. 3rd Suffolk Regt. France. Killed in action on Nov. 9, 1914.

1900 Pope, P. F. (Serving Aug. 4, 1914). Capt. Indian Army.

1898 Pope, S. F., B.A. (Oct. 1, 1914). Capt., temp. Maj., 6th Devonshire Regt. D.A.Q.M.G. Mesopotamia. *O.B.E.* (Mil.). *D.* Mesopotamia, 1918.

1890 Portman, Rev. A. B., M.A. (July 4, 1916). Chaplain to the Forces (4th Class).

1903 Pott, W. T., B.A. (Aug. 15, 1914). Lt., Acting Capt. and Adjt., 9th Lancers. France. *M.C.*, July 26, 1918.

1913 **Potts, H.** (Dec. 22, 1914). 2nd Lt. 7th Bedfordshire Regt., attd. 1st Essex Regt. France. Died on Oct. 1, 1916, of wounds received in action.

1889 Powell, E. A. L. (Sept. 1, 1914). Capt. 3rd Leicestershire Regt.

1906 Powell,* J. J., B.A. (Serving Aug. 4, 1914). Capt., temp. Maj., 1st Oxf. & Bucks Lt. Infty. G.S.O. 3. Mesopotamia, 1915–16; France, 1918. *D.* Mesopotamia, 1915.

1909 **Power, W.** Lt. Cape Coloured Regt., S. African Inf. German E. Africa. Killed in action at Hattias on Nov. 6, 1917.

1905 Prendergast-Arnold,* G. A., B.A. (Dec. 22, 1914). Lt. 13th K.R.R.C.

1902 Preston, Rev. A. L., M.A. (May 14, 1915). Chaplain to the Forces (4th Class).

1907 **Prior, E. F.,** M.A. (Mobilized Aug. 4, 1914). Capt. 8th Rifle Brigade. France and Belgium. Killed in action on Sept. 16, 1916.

1898 Prior, P. N., B.A. Pte. Somerset L.I., attd R. Warwickshire Regt.

1914 **Quinn, J. P. C.** (Mar. 25, 1915). 2nd Lt. 7th R. Dublin Fusiliers (resigned), afterwards Pte. 1st H.A.C. France, 1916. Killed in action at Beaucourt on Nov. 14, 1916.

1919 Raiment, P. C. (Oct. 21, 1914). Capt. R.A.M.C. Gallipoli, 1915; France, 1916.

1906 Ramsbotham,* H., B.A. (Sept. 12, 1914). Maj. General List. D.A.A.G. France. *O.B.E.* (Mil.). *M.C.*, Jan. 1, 1917. *D.* France, 1917 twice, 1918.

1899 Rankin, J. S., M.A., *M.P.* (Mar. 16, 1915). Capt. R.A. Staff Appointment, Class FF.

1914 Rathbone,* R. B., B.A. (Nov. 27, 1914). Capt. 6th Loyal N. Lancashire Regt. Gallipoli, Egypt, India, Mesopotamia. *D.* Mesopotamia, 1918, 1919.

1905 Rawle, J., B.A. (Aug. 15, 1914). Lt. Dragoon Guards (S.R.), attd. 4th Dragoon Guards. France.

1892 Ray, R. A. (Serving Aug. 4, 1914). Maj. 1st King's Own (R. Lancaster Regt.). Lt.-Col. whilst Chief Instr., School of Instruction. France. *D.S.O.*, June 3, 1918. Belgian Croix de Guerre. *D.* France, 1918.

Rayner, J. (July 24, 1915). 2nd Lt. 10th Middlesex Regt., attd. 5th The Buffs (E. Kent Regt.). Mesopotamia. Died at Amara on July 6, 1916, whilst on active service.

1910 Read, J. E., B.C.L. (Nov. 5, 1914). Capt. Canadian Field Artillery (Maj.). France. *D.* France, 1917.

1908 Rees-Mogg, E. F., B.A. (Oct. 18, 1915). Lt. R.A.S.C.

1893 **Reid, C. J.,** B.A. (Mobilized Aug. 4, 1914). Capt. 9th Warwickshire Regt. Gallipoli. Presumed killed in action on Aug. 10th, 1915.

1899 Rendel, S. G., B.A. (Aug. 30, 1915). Lt. R.A.S.C.

1919 Rhys, G. (Sept. 13, 1916). ‡2nd Lt. 1/8th W. Yorkshire Regt. France, 1917.

1894 Rigg, W. T., B.A. (Jan. 20, 1916). Maj. 6th R. Irish Rifles. France. Croix de Guerre. *D.* France, 1917.

1897 Riley, O. C. H. (Dec. 28, 1914). Lt. R.F.A. (S.R.). Acting Maj. R.H. and R.F.A.

1913 Ritchie, H. P. (Sept. 29, 1914). Capt. 12th Arg. & Suth'd. Highlanders. France, 1915; Salonika, 1915–16. *D.* § Mar. 1919.

1905 Robertson-Durham, J. A., B.A. (Sept. 19, 1914). Capt. Gordon Highlanders, empld. War Office. *O.B.E.* (Mil.).

1900 **Robertson-Walker, A. M. M.** (Dec. 1, 1914). Capt. 8th R. Fusiliers. France. *D.* France, 1916. Killed in action at Ovillers on July 7, 1916.

1905 **Robin, C. H.** (Mobilized Aug. 4, 1914). Capt. 2nd R. Jersey Militia, attd. as Capt. and Adjt. 13th York & Lancaster Regt. France. Killed in action on May 11, 1917.

1908 Robin, G. J. (Mobilized Aug. 4, 1914). Capt. R. Jersey Militia Artillery. A.D.C. to the Lt.-Governor, Jersey.

1902 Robinson, G. A. H., B.A. (Feb. 3, 1915). Capt. 4th Oxf. & Bucks. Lt. Infty. Asst. Inspector of Qr.-Master-General's Services.

1912 Robinson, G. P., B.A. (Jan. 31, 1915). Lt. 8th Middlesex Regt., attd. R.A.F.

1911 Robinson, R. W. G., M.A. (Oct. 21, 1914). Capt. 5th Durham L.I., attd. 93rd Bde. R.G.A. as Education Officer. France, 1916–18; Germany, 1919. *M.C.*, Sept. 16, 1918. (Prisoner of War, 1918.)

1919 Rogers, N. McL. (Feb. 12, 1915). ‡Lt. 246th Bn. Nova Scotia Highlanders. Belgium, France, 1915–16.

1905 Rolland, J. F., B.A. (Sept. 23, 1914). Lt. E. Riding of Yorkshire Yeomanry, empld. Army Signal Service. Palestine. *D.* Palestine, 1918.

1908 Rolt, J. H. (Dec. 6, 1915). Capt., temp. Maj., R.A.S.C. D.A.D. of Transport. France, 1918, 1919. *D.* France, 1918, 1919.

1887 Rooth, J. A., B.A. (Mobilized Aug. 4, 1914). Capt. R.A.M.C.

1904 Rowe, F. C., B.A. (Jan. 10, 1916). Maj., Technical Officer, R.A.F.

1913 Rowlatt,* C. J., M.A. (Oct. 22, 1914). Capt. 13th Rifle Brigade. Capt. General List. G.S.O. 3, Dept. of C.I.G.S., War Office. France, 1915–16. *M.B.E.* (Mil.). *D.* § Mar. 1919.

1913 Rucker, C. E. S., B.A. (Aug. 1914). ‡Lt. 10th Rifle Brigade. Gallipoli, 1915 (attd. 1st R. Dublin Fusiliers); France, 1915–16. *M.C.*, Jan. 22, 1916.

1919 Rucker, P. W. (Sept. 5, 1918). Cadet Household Bde. O.C.B.

1908 Ruffer, M. E. (Oct. 11, 1915). Lt. R.G.A. (S.R.).

1908 Rushton, W. O., B.A. (Apr. 20, 1915). Capt. General List. Staff-Captain. France. *M.C.*, June 3, 1918.

1894 **Russell, A. C. H.,** M.A. (Dec. 12, 1914). Capt. A.O.D. Died on Oct. 27, 1918, of illness contracted while on active service.

1913 Russell, G. C. (Aug. 15, 1914). Capt. 68th Batt. R.F.A. Acting Lt.-Col. R.H. and R.F.A. France, Salonika, Palestine. *M.C.*, June 4, 1917. Italian Silver Medal for Military Valour. *D.* Salonika, 1917.

Russell, J. W. B. (Dec. 27, 1914). 2nd Lt. 9th W. Riding Regt. (Lt.). Belgium and France. Killed in action south of Mametz Wood on July 7, 1916.

1880 Salisbury, The Marquess of, M.A., *K.G.*, *G.C.V.O.*, *C.B.*, T.D. (Serving Aug. 4, 1914). *A.D.C.* to the King. Hon. Maj.-Gen. Col. 4th E. Anglian Bde., R.F.A. *D.* § Feb. 1917.

1911 **Salvesen, E. M.** (Oct. 27, 1914). 2nd Lt. 4th R. Dublin Fusiliers. France and Belgium. Killed in action near St. Julien on Apr. 25, 1915.

1911 Salvesen,* N. G., B.A. (Aug. 29, 1914). Capt. 7th R. Scots. Staff Officer Class FF. Empld. in Dept. of C.I.G.S., War Office.

1919 Salvesen, T. N. F. (Sept. 16, 1917). Paymaster Cadet, H.M.S. *Renown.* Mediterranean.

1906 **Sandeman,* S. R.,** M.A. (Aug. 31, 1914). Lt. 2nd London Bde. R.G.A. (T.F.). Belgium. Missing, believed killed in action near St. Julien, Ypres, on Apr. 22, 1915,

1890 Sanderson, A. A., B.A. (Feb. 12, 1915). Lt. R.N.V.R.

1919 Sandford, K. S. (Apr. 29, 1918). 2nd Lt. R.F.A.

1912 Sassoon, R. E. (Oct. 15, 1914). Capt. S.R. Bn. attd. 2nd Irish Guards, France. *M.C.*, Sept. 26, 1917.

1902 Sawbridge, B. F., M.A. (May 1915). Lt. 5th London Regt. (London Rifle Brigade). Acting Capt. whilst in charge of Anti-Gas School. France, 1916–18.

1906 Sawbridge, Rev. H. F. F., M.A. (Nov. 13, 1915). Chaplain to the Forces (4th Class). France. *M.C.*, Nov. 25, 1916.

1905 Sayer, A. C., B.A. (Mobilized Aug. 4, 1914). Maj. Sussex Dragoons, attd. 16th R. Sussex Regt. Palestine, France. *D.S.O.*, June 3, 1919. *M.C.*, Feb. 4, 1918. *D.* Palestine, 1917 ; France, 1919.

Scott, B. (Sept. 18, 1914). Lt. 15th London Regt. (Civil Service Rifles). France. Presumed killed in action at Loos on May 21, 1916.

1904 Scott, E. L., B.A. Maj. R.A.S.C. Asst. Director of Labour, German E. Africa. German E. Africa. *O.B.E.* (Mil.). *M.C.*, Feb. 1, 1917.

1900 **Scott, J. Y.,** M.A. (Sept. 12, 1914). Lt. 10th Rifle Brigade. France. Killed in action on the Somme on Sept. 3, 1916.

1904 Scott-Tucker, J. R. L. H., B.A. (Serving Aug. 4, 1914). Capt. & Adjt., Bt.-Maj. Gloucestershire Regt. D.A.A.G., G.H.Q. France. Croix de Guerre. *D.* France, 1917, 1918.

1910 **Scrimgeour, M.** (Aug. 22, 1914). 2nd Lt. 8th Rifle Brigade. Belgium and France. Killed in action at Hooge on July 31, 1915.

1915 **Sears, J. P.** (Jan. 30, 1918). 2nd Lt. attd. 2nd Oxf. & Bucks. Lt. Infty. France. Killed in action on Aug. 20, 1918.

1911 Sebastian, E. G. (Oct. 16, 1914). Lt. 6th, attd. 2nd, The Buffs (E. Kent Regt.). France. *D.S.O.*, Mar. 3, 1917.

1905 **Sebastian, S. R.,** B.A. (Mar. 6, 1915). Lt., Acting Lt.-Col., 3rd Hampshire Regt., attd. 6th Oxf. & Bucks. Lt. Infty. France. *M.C.*, Jan. 1, 1917. *D.* France, 1917 twice. Died on Mar. 27, 1918, of wounds received in action near Ham.

1895 Shakspeare, W., B.A. (Mobilized Aug. 4, 1914). Maj. 3rd N. Staffordshire Regt. France and Belgium, 1917 (attd. 8th Bn.).

1919 Sharp, H. F. B. (Sept. 1914). Lt., temp. Capt., R.F.A. (S.R.). France, 1916–17; Italy, 1917–19. *M.C.*, Oct. 28, 1917; *Bar*, Nov. 26, 1917. Italian Silver Medal for valour. Croix de Guerre. *D.* France, 1916, 1917.

1909 Sharp,* H. S. (Aug. 4, 1914). Capt. 1/1st Fife & Forfar Yeomanry, attd. 14th The Black Watch. Gallipoli, 1915; Egypt and Palestine, 1915–18; France, 1918. *D.* France, 1919.

1911 **Shaw,* P. H.** (Aug. 15, 1914). 2nd Lt. 8th The Black Watch. France. Killed in action in the Battle of Loos on Sept. 25, 1915.

1914 Shaw, R. W., M.A. (Sept. 24, 1915). Lt. 7th Northumberland Fusiliers. R.T.O.

1912 **Shaw-Stewart,* N.,** B.A. (Aug. 16, 1914). Lt. 1st Rifle Brigade. France. Killed in action on Aug. 21, 1916.

1896 **Shepherd-Cross, C. H. S.** (Mobilized Aug. 4, 1914). Capt. D. of Lancaster's Own Yeomanry. Acting Maj. M.G.C. France and Belgium. Died on Oct. 15, 1917, of wounds received in action.

1913 Shone, T. A. (Aug. 25, 1914). Capt. 10th Hampshire Regt., afterwards Capt. Intelligence Corps. Gallipoli, 1915; Belgium, 1917; Italy, 1917–18; France and Belgium, 1918. *D.* France, 1918.

1901 **Sidgwick, A. H.,** M.A. (Jan. 3, 1916). 2nd Lt., Acting Capt. & Adjt., 157th Siege Batt. R.G.A. (S.R.). France and Belgium. Died on Sept. 17, 1917, of wounds received in action.

1919 Simpson, P. O. (Jan. 4, 1918). 2nd Lt. R.F.A. France, Germany, N. Russia.

1905 Sinclair, D., B.A. (Nov. 28, 1917). 2nd Lt. 6th R. Scots.

1919 Sinnett, J. L. M. (Sept. 15, 1916). Lt. R.F.A. (S.R.). France, 1917–18. *M.C.*, Sept. 16, 1918.

1911 **Skinner,* D. H.,** B.A. (Sept. 16, 1914). Lt., temp. Capt., 7th R. W. Kent Regt. France. Died on July 16, 1916, of wounds received in action on the Somme.

1904 Small, E. M., B.A. (Jan. 5, 1917). Lt. R.A.S.C.

1908 **Smeathman,* C.** (Serving Aug. 4, 1914). Lt. 1st Leicestershire Regt. France. Killed in action in Oct. 1914.

1912 Smith, E. E., B.A. (July 15, 1915). Lt. 1/4th Oxf. & Bucks. Lt. Infty. afterwards attd. War Trade Intelligence Dept. France, 1916.

1919 Smith, H. F. (Feb. 7, 1918). Pte. 5th R. Fusiliers.

1890 **Smith, H. G.,** M.A. (Sept. 3, 1914). Capt., Acting Maj., R.A.S.C. France. *M.C.*, June 3, 1916. Croce di Guerra. Died on Feb. 16, 1919, of illness contracted on active service.

1897 Smith, L. A., B.C.L., M.A. (Mar. 22, 1916). ‡2nd Lt. 1st R. Sussex Regt. Mesopotamia, 1917; India, 1917–19.

1905 Smith, L. B., M.A. (Jan. 17, 1916). Lt. R.F.A. (S.R.). France.

1919 Smith, R. W. (Nov. 9, 1917). 2nd Lt. Welsh Guards. France.

1899 Smith, T. C., M.A. ‡2nd Lt. M.G.C. Staff-Lt. (2nd Class). Draft Conducting Officer.

1908 Snow, S. R. E., B.A. (Mobilized Aug. 4, 1914). Capt. Royal 1st Devon Yeomanry, attd. 16th Devonshire Regt. Gallipoli, 1915; Egypt and Palestine. (Prisoner in Turkey.)

Sorley, C. H. (Aug. 26, 1914). Capt. 7th Suffolk Regt. France, 1915. Killed in action near Hulluch on Oct. 13, 1915.

1887 Sowler, H., M.A. (Mobilized Aug. 4, 1914). Lt.-Col. 2nd E. Lancashire Bde., R.F.A. (T.F. Res.), empld Artillery Horse Lines. T.D.

1904 **Spafford, A. D. D.,** B.A. (1914). 2nd Lt., Acting Capt., 3rd, attd. 2nd, R. Scots. France. Killed in action on Nov. 13, 1916.

1013 **Sparks,* J. E.** (Aug. 1914). Lt. 1st R. Fusiliers. France. Killed in action in the Battle of the Somme on July 21, 1916.

1910 Spencer, W., B.A. (Aug. 1914). Capt. 13th R. Fusiliers, empld. O.C.B. France, 1915–16.

1909 Spurrier, Rev. H. S. C., B.A. (June 7, 1918). Chaplain to the Forces (4th Class).

1906 Stanley-Clarke, A. C. L., B.A. (Serving Aug. 4, 1914). Capt., temp. Lt.-Col., 2nd, attd. 10th, Cameronians, comdg. Corps School. France. *D.S.O.*, Jan. 1, 1918; *Bar*, July 26, 1918. Croix de Chevalier de la Légion d'Honneur. Croix de Guerre. *D.* France, 1916, 1917 twice, 1918.

1919 Stern, A. M. (Apr. 5, 1918). 2nd Lt. Grenadier Guards.

1900 Stevenson, G. H., M.A. (May 5, 1915). Lt. 3/4th Oxf. & Bucks. Lt. Infty. Staff-Lt. Intelligence Corps, G.H.Q., France. France, 1918.

1913 Stevenson, R. C. S. (Sept. 25, 1915). Capt. 2nd Rifle Brigade. France. (Prisoner of War.)

Stevenson, R. D. (Oct. 14, 1914). Capt. 11th Arg. & Suth'd. Highlanders. France, Belgium. Killed in action in Belgium on May 17, 1916.

1904 **Steward, H. N.,** B.A. (Serving Aug. 4, 1914). Capt. Indian Cavalry, attd. R.F.C. Accidentally killed on Dec. 3, 1916.

1911 Stewart,* A. C., B.A. (Aug. 6, 1914). Capt. 6th, attd. 5th, Cameronians. France, 1915–17, 1918–19; Egypt, 1918. *M.C.* Feb. 1, 1919; *Bar*, Mar. 8, 1919.

1902 Stewart, Rev. G. W., M.A. (June 26, 1917). Chaplain to the Forces (4th Class).

1908 **Stewart, J. J. E. B.,** B.A. (Sept. 14, 1914). 2nd Lt. 7th, attd. 12th, R. Scots. France. Died on June 12, 1917, of wounds received in action.

1905 Stewart, L. T., B.A. Pte. R. Fusiliers. France. *M.M.*

1913 Stewart-Smith, D. C., B.A. (Oct. 31, 1914). Lt. 3rd The Black Watch. France. (Prisoner of War.)

1909 **Steyn, S. S. L.** (Dec. 8, 1914). Lt. 117th Bde., R.F.A. Salonika, Palestine. Killed in action in Palestine on Dec. 8, 1917.

1893 Stiebel, A., M.A. (Dec. 14, 1914). ‡Lt. 4th R. W. Kent Regt. France, 1917.

1913 Stigant, F. C., B.A. (Sept. 9, 1914). Lt. 5th R. Inniskilling Fusiliers, empld. O.C.B.

1911 Stirling-Stuart,* D. R. (Aug. 26, 1914). Lt. 2nd Dragoons. France, 1915–19.

Stockwood, L. F. (June 17, 1915). 2nd Lt. Res. Household Bn., attd. Household Bn. France and Belgium. Died on Oct. 12, 1917, of wounds received in action.

1901 Stoop, A. D., B.A. (Sept. 3, 1914). Capt. 5th Queen's (R. W. Surrey Regt.). Mesopotamia. *M.C.*, Jan. 11, 1919.

1913 Strachey, J. F. Sub-Lt. R.N.V.R. (invalided). Cadet Inns of Court O.T.C.

1919 Strater, E. La N. (Apr. 1, 1917). 2nd Lt. Field Artillery, U.S. Army. France.

1903 [Streatfeild, Rev. F., B.D.] (Oct. 10, 1914). Chaplain to the Forces (4th Class), attd. 4th Oxf. & Bucks Lt. Infty. France, 1915–16.

1920 Streit, C. K. (June 21, 1917). Sergt. Intelligence Section, U.S. Army. France, 1917–19.

1896 Struben, C. F. W., M.A. (Aug. 4, 1914). Lt., Acting Comdr., R.N.V.R., S. African Div. Cape Station, 1914–15; Ægean, 1916–18. *O.B.E.* (Mil.).

1908 Stuart, A. H. (Apr. 20, 1915). Capt. Special Lists.

1874 Studd, E. F., B.C.L., M.A. (July 9, 1915). Capt. Special Lists. Salonika. *D.* Salonika, 1917.

Summerhayes, J. A. (July 15, 1917). 2nd Lt. Labour Corps. Acting Capt. 13th R. Inniskilling Fusiliers. France. Killed in action on Aug. 27, 1918.

1904 Sutton, B. E., B.A. (Oct. 19, 1914). Capt. Westmorland & Cumberland Yeomanry. Maj., Acting Lt.-Col., Flying Officer, 7th Sqdn., R.A.F. France. *O.B.E.* (Mil.). *D.S.O.*, Sept. 26, 1917. *M.C.*, Jan. 1, 1917. Belgian Croix de Guerre. *D.* France, 1917, 1918 twice.

1890 Swifte, E. G. M., B.A. (Sept. 10, 1914). Maj. R.A. and Tank Corps, attd. Staff. France, Germany.

1898 Swinson, J. H., B.A. (Oct. 24, 1915). Lt. 6th Rifle Brigade, empld. War Office.

Swire, A. G. (Mobilized Aug. 4, 1914). 2nd Lt. Essex Yeomanry. France. Killed in action on May 13, 1915.

1910 Swire,* J. K., B.A. (Aug. 26, 1914). Lt. Essex Yeomanry. France, 1915–16.

1883 Symonds, G. D. (Mobilized Aug. 4, 1914). Maj., Bt.-Lt.-Col., R.F.A. Res. of Officers. G.S.O. 2, Dept. of C.I.G.S., War Office. Croix de Chevalier de la Légion d'Honneur. Order of St. Stanislas (2nd Class). Chevalier de l'Ordre de Leopold. *D.* § Feb. 1917.

1906 **Tarr,* F. N.,** B.A. (Serving Aug. 4, 1914). Lt. 4th Leicestershire Regt. Belgium and France. Killed in action near Ypres on July 18, 1915.

1894 Tasker-Evans, C. T. (Nov. 15, 1914). Lt. R. Defence Corps.

1911 Tatton,* T. A., B.A. (Aug. 26, 1914). Capt. Rifle Brigade. France. *M.C.*, Jan. 8, 1918.

1904 Taylor,* C. J. G., D.M., (Mobilized Aug. 4, 1914). Surgeon Lt. R.N.V.R.

1898 Terry, H. F., B.A. (Oct. 14, 1916). Lt. R.F.A. (T.F.).

1902 **Terry, H. M.,** B.A. (Oct. 1, 1916). 2nd Lt. R.E. France. Killed in action on June 28, 1917.

1911 Thomas,* A. E., B.M. (Dec. 22, 1914). 2nd Lt. 7th S. Wales Borderers.

1919 Thompson, J. de F. (Jan. 1, 1918). Cadet R.F.A.

1895 Thomson, F. C., B.A., *M.P.* (Sept. 22, 1914). Lt. Scottish Horse, attd. 2/1st Lovat's Scouts, empld. Dept. of C.I.G.S., War Office. Egypt, 1916; Salonika, 1916–18. *M.B.E.* (Mil.).

1910 **Thomson,* F. W.** (Aug. 29, 1914). Lt. 7th, attd. 1st, R. Scots. Gallipoli. Killed in action in Gallipoli on June 28, 1915.

1906 **Thomson, K. D.,** B.A. (Aug. 1914). ‡2nd Lt. 10th Arg. & Suth'd. Highlanders. France. Killed in action in the Battle of the Somme on July 18, 1916.

1914 **Thurlow, G. R. Y.** (Dec. 22, 1914). 2nd Lt. 10th Sherwood Foresters. France. Killed in action near Monchy on Apr. 23, 1917.

1898 [**Tiddy,* R. J. E.,** M.A.] (Feb. 16, 1915). Lt. 2/4th Oxf. & Bucks Lt. Infty. France. Killed in action on Aug. 10, 1916.

1910 Tinne,* C. E., M.A. (Aug. 14, 1914). Capt. 19th Bde. Amm. Col., 27th Div., R.F.A. France, 1914; Salonika, 1916; Russia, Caucasus, 1919. *D.* Salonika, 1918, 1919.

1896 Tinne, J. A., M.A. (Jan. 7, 1916). Capt. 281st Bde., R.F.A. France, Belgium, Italy.

1919 Todd-Jones, G. B. (Sept. 1, 1916). Lt. 232nd Bde., R.F.A. France.

1912 **Todd-Naylor, W. B.** (Aug. 26, 1914). 2nd Lt. 8th K.R.R.C. France and Belgium. Killed in action at Delville Wood on Aug. 24, 1916.

1919 Tolley, C. J. H. (Nov. 1915). Lt. Tank Corps (Capt.). France and Belgium, 1917. *M.C.*, July 31, 1917. (Prisoner of War, Nov. 1917–Dec. 1918.)

Tolson, J. M. (1916). ‡2nd Lt. R.F.A. France, 1917, 1918. Died on Oct. 20, 1918, of wounds received in action.

1900 Tomlinson, B. M., B.A. (Sept. 15, 1914). Capt., Temp. Maj., 24th Middlesex Regt. G.S.O. 3, Dept. of C.I.G.S., War Office.

1896 Tomlinson, F. W. (Serving Aug. 4, 1914). Maj. The Buffs (E. Kent Regt.). Class BB Officer in Dept. of C.I.G.S., War Office, afterwards empld. Ministry of Labour. France. (Prisoner of War, 1914–18.)

1898 Tomlinson, G. J. F., M.A. Nigerian Land Contingent. W. Africa.

1914 Touche, G. C. (Feb. 18, 1915). Lt. R.A.S.C. Gallipoli, 1915; Egypt and Palestine, 1915–19.

1906 Touche, N. G., B.A. (Aug. 1915). Lt. R.A.S.C. France, 1915; Salonika, 1915–19.

1905 **Trevor, Rev. E. W.,** M.A. (Dec. 4, 1915). Chaplain to the Forces (4th Class). France, 1916. Killed in action on Nov. 14, 1916.

1911 Tudor-Craig,* A. R., B.A. (Sept. 9, 1914). Capt. 5th R. Irish Fusiliers. Egypt and Palestine. *M.C.*, Nov. 25, 1916. *D.* Palestine, 1918.

1913 Tudor-Craig,* P. C., B.A. (Sept. 9, 1914). Capt. 6th R. Irish Fusiliers, attd. Indian Army. Gallipoli, Salonika. *D.* Gallipoli, 1915; Salonika, 1917.

1910 **Tuke,* A. H. S.** (Aug. 15, 1914). 2nd Lt. 3rd, attd. 2nd, Northumberland Fusiliers. Belgium. Killed in action near Ypres on May 7, 1915.

1897 Turnbull, H. G. D., M.A. Capt. I.D.F. Adjt. Bombay University Inf., empld. Intelligence Dept., Bombay, 1917–18.

1906 Turner, A. B., B.A. Capt. 6th R. Warwickshire Regt., attd. Staff. France. *M.C.*, Jan. 1, 1917.

1903 Turner, H. B. (Nov. 20, 1914). Capt. Lancashire Hussars (Yeomanry).

1919 Turner, H. W., B.A. (Dec. 1915). ‡2nd Lt. 1st Hampshire Regt. France, 1917.

1915 Vaughan, A. G. (Feb. 27, 1918). 2nd Lt. S. Wales Borderers.

1899 **Venables, G. R.,** B.A. (Aug. 1914). 2nd Lt. 3rd, attd. 2nd, Shropshire L.I. France, Belgium. Killed in action on Mar. 7, 1915.

1907 Venn,* E. N. L., B.A. (Serving Aug. 4, 1914). Lt., temp. Capt., 17th Lancers.

1909 Vertue, H. St. H., B.M., M.A. (Feb. 1, 1917). Capt. R.A.M.C. (S.R.). France. *M.C.*, 1918.

1919 Vessey, G. P. D. (Jan. 4, 1918). Corpl. 3rd Oxf. & Bucks. Lt. Infty.

1898 Vickers, H. R., B.A. (Jan. 15, 1915). 2nd Lt., Acting Capt., W. Riding Divl. Ammn. Column, R.F.A. (T.F.).

1906 Vickers, J. H., B.A. Capt., Acting Maj., Airship Officer R.A.F. *D.* § Jan. 1919.

1911 Villiers,* A. E., M.A. (Aug. 14, 1914). Lt. (S.R.), attd. 15th K.R.R.C., then attd. R.E. for Army Signals (Capt.). France, 1917–19.

1911 Wakefield, G. E. (Aug. 1914). Capt. 3rd R. Scots Fusiliers, empld. Dept. of C.I.G.S., War Office. France. *D.* § Mar. 1918.

1907 Wakefield, H. R., B.A. (Aug. 15, 1914). Lt. 3rd R. Scots Fusiliers. Empld. Ministry of Labour.

1913 **Walker, A. T.** (Dec. 2, 1914). 2nd Lt. 8th Rifle Brigade. Belgium and France. Killed in action at Hooge on July 30, 1915.

1889 Walker, C. H. H., M.A. (Nov. 5, 1914). Capt. 5th Border Regt., attd. 27th King's (Liverpool Regt.).

1890 Walker, E. W. A., D.M., D.Sc. (Aug. 1914). Capt. O.U.O.T.C. and R.A.M.C. (T.F.). Special duty, Medical Research Committee.

1905 Wallace,* R. J., M.A. (Oct. 1905). Capt. 9th R. Scots. 2nd Lt. (Hon. Capt.), Acting Capt., Technical Officer, attd. Staff R.A.F.

1910 Waller,* A. J. R., M.A. (Serving Aug. 4, 1914). Capt. 2nd Essex Regt. Capt. Administrative Officer, R.A.F. France and Belgium, 1914, 1916–18. Belgian Croix de Guerre.

1903 **Waller, R. A.,** B.A. (Apr. 26, 1917). 2nd Lt. 5th, attd. 1st, R. Fusiliers. France, 1917. Died in hospital on Nov. 1, 1917.

1904 Waller,* W. E., B.M. (Jan. 1, 1916). Capt. R.A.M.C. Mesopotamia, 1916–19. *D.* Mesopotamia, 1918.

1900 **Wallis, N. V.,** B.A. (Mar. 1, 1915). 2nd Lt. 12th, attd. 9th, Cheshire Regt. Egypt and Salonika. Killed in action on Apr. 10, 1917.

1907 Walters,* F. P., M.A. (Aug. 15, 1914). Capt. 3rd Oxf. & Bucks. Lt. Infty. G.S.O. 3, Dept. of C.I.G.S., War Office. *D.* § Mar. 1918; § Aug. 1918.

1911 **Warburton, H. C.** Lt. Nigerian Police Force. Drowned, Jan. 1918.

1919 Ward, A. O. (June 11, 1917). ‡2nd Lt. 5th Essex Regt. France.

Warlow, T. W. (Aug. 22, 1914). Lt. 6th K.O.Y.L.I. Belgium. Died on July 28, 1915, of wounds received in action.

1896 Warrand, D. G., M.A. (Mobilized Aug. 4, 1914). Capt., temp. Maj., 3rd Seaforth Highlanders. D.A.A.G., empld. Ministry of Labour. France, 1914–18. *O.B.E.* (Mil.). *D.* France, 1916, 1917, 1918.

1919 Webster, A. P. (May 10, 1918). 2nd Lt. Grenadier Guards (S.R.).

1887 Weigall, J. W. W., B.A. (Mar. 26, 1917). Lt. Special Lists, empld. Ministry of National Service.

1919 Wellacott, W. L. B. (Aug. 19, 1917). 2nd Lt. 126th Field Coy. R.E. France and Belgium, 1918–19.

1914 **Wentzel, E. F.** (Apr. 8, 1915). Lt., Acting Capt., 3rd, attd. 8th, E. Surrey Regt. France. Killed in action near La Fère on Mar. 23, 1918.

1919 Westendarp, H. E. A., B.A. (Jan. 24, 1916). ‡Lt. 2/1st W. Kent Yeomanry, attd. 6th R. W. Kent Regt. France, 1918.

1907 Weyman,* A., M.A. (Serving Aug. 4, 1914). Capt. & Adjt., Bt.-Maj. 1st Leicestershire Regt. Bde. Maj. France and Belgium, 1914–18. *M.C.*, Jan. 1, 1917. Croix de Chevalier de la Légion d'Honneur. Croix de Guerre (avec Palme). *D.* France, 1917, 1918.

1902 Whatley, A. P., M.A. Pte. 20th London Regt. (Discharged, medically unfit.)

1893 Whitaker, C. W., M.A. (Serving Aug. 4, 1914). Maj. 3rd King's (Liverpool Regt.), empld. 1st Newfoundland Regt. *D.* § Feb. 1917.

1896 White, E. H., D.M. (Dec. 11, 1916). Capt. R.A.M.C. Egypt.

1903 White, Rev. G., M.A. (Nov. 1, 1917). Chaplain to the Forces (4th Class).

1896 White, I. H. G., M.A. (Sept. 26, 1914). Capt. 3rd R. Warwickshire Regt., attd. Labour Corps. France, 1915.

1905 **White, S. A.,** M.A. (Feb. 17, 1915). Capt. and Adjt. 21st Northumberland Fusiliers. France. Killed in action on the Somme on July 3, 1916.

1919 Whitfeld, L. O'G. (Serving Aug. 4, 1914). 2nd Lt. 3rd Manchester Regt., attd. as Lt. R.A.F. France and Belgium, 1916, 1918.

1907 Whitwill,* M. (Mobilized Aug. 4, 1914). Lt. 2nd S. Midland Field Coy. R.E. (T.F.). Acting Lt.-Col. C.R.E. 38th (Welsh) Div. France and Belgium, 1915, 1916–19. *D.S.O.*, Apr. 19, 1918. *M.C.*, Jan. 1, 1918. *D.* France, 1917, 1918.

1895 Whyte, H., B.A. (Jan. 1918). ‡2nd Lt. R.A.S.C. Temp. Capt. and Education Officer.

1909 Wigan,* C. R., B.A. (Aug. 5, 1914). Capt. 5th Queen's (R. W. Surrey Regt.). A.D.C. to G.O.C. 15th (Indian) Div. India, 1914–15; Mesopotamia, 1915–19. *M.C.*, Nov. 25, 1916.

Wigan, W. L. (Nov. 11, 1914). 2nd Lt. 1st, attd. 8th, R. W. Kent Regt. Died on Feb. 23, 1916, of wounds received in action.

1909 Wigram,* R. F., B.A. (Feb. 21, 1915). Capt. Special Lists. G.S.O. 3, Dept. of C.I.G.S., War Office, afterwards at H.M. Embassy, Washington.

1912 Wilcox,* J. J. (Serving Aug. 4, 1914). Lt. Somerset L.I. Salonika. *M.C.*, June 4, 1917. *D.* Salonika, 1916, 1917.

1914 Wilkinson, D. F. (Nov. 28, 1914). Capt. 13th King's (Liverpool Regt.). France and Belgium, 1915–17. *M.C.*, May 3, 1917.

1894 Wilkinson, E. A. G., B.A. (Serving Aug. 4, 1914). Surgeon Commdr. R.N., H.M.S. *Revenge*. *O.B.E.* (Mil.).

1899 Wilkinson, G. E., M.A. (Sept. 12, 1914). Capt. 6th Northumberland Fusiliers, attd. M.G.C. France. *M.C.*, June 3, 1918. *D.* France.

1910 [Wilkinson,* W. A. C., B.A.] (Nov. 3, 1914). 2nd Lt. A.S.C. Lt. Coldstream Guards. France. *M.C.*, Sept. 26, 1917; *Bar*, Feb. 18, 1918.

1893 Wilkinson, W. H. J., B.A. (Sept. 15, 1914). Capt. Special Lists. G.S.O. 3. G.H.Q., France. India, France. *C.I.E.* Croix de Chevalier de la Légion d'Honneur. Chevalier de l'Ordre de Leopold. *D.* France, 1916 twice, 1919.

1890 Willett, J. A., D.M. (Oct. 1, 1915). Capt., Acting Maj., R.A.M.C. (T.F.). Mesopotamia, 1916; France, 1917–19.

1904 Williams, F. A., B.A. (Mobilized Aug. 5, 1914). Maj. 5th London Bde. R.F.A. (T.F.). France, 1915, 1917, 1918–19. Croix de Guerre. *D.* French Dispatches, 1918.

Williams, V. F. (July 1916). 2nd Lt. R.F.C. France, 1917. Killed in action near Heudicourt on Apr. 2, 1917.

1883 Williams Wynn, F. R., B.A. (Sept. 15, 1914). Capt., Acting Maj., 5th, attd. 19th, Queen's (R. W. Surrey Regt.).

1912 Wilson, C. S., B.A. (Nov. 21, 1914). Capt. 2/7th W. Yorkshire Regt., attd. Depot (Qr.-Master).

1913 Wilson, H. McD., M.A. (Sept. 1915). Lt. B Batt., 246th Bde. R.F.A. (T.F.) (Capt.). France. *M.C.*, Sept. 26, 1916.

1907 Winter, H. A., B.A. (May 10, 1917). 2nd Lt. (Pilot) R.A.F.

1909 Wise,* J. H., B.A. (Apr. 9, 1915). Capt. I.A.R.O., attd. 92nd Punjabis. India, Mesopotamia, Palestine. *D.* Mesopotamia, 1917.

1900 **Wodehouse, A. P.** (Serving Aug. 4, 1914). Capt. Indian Army, attd. 110th Mahratta L.I. Mesopotamia. Killed in action in Mesopotamia on Nov. 22–4, 1915.

1911 **Wollocombe, F.** (Dec. 7, 1914). 2nd Lt. 9th Devonshire Regt. France. Died on Sept. 10, 1916, of wounds received in action.

1905 Wolmer, Viscount, M.A., *M.P.* (Mobilized Aug. 4, 1914). Capt. 3rd Hampshire Regt.

1908 Womersley, A. D. (Sept. 12, 1914). Capt. 10th Essex Regt. Capt. General List, empld. Dept. of C.I.G.S., War Office. A.D.C. to G.O.C. Sierra Leone. France, 1916.

1910 Womersley, L. D., B.A. (Nov. 2, 1914). Capt. 5th Essex Regt.

1905 Wood,* J. A., B.M., M.A. (May 29, 1917). Capt. R.A.M.C., attd. 27th Div. Salonika, Trans-Caucasia.

1902 Woodhouse, Rev. J. W., M.A. (Feb. 19, 1915). Chaplain to the Forces (4th Class).

1909 **Woodhouse,* R. C. H.,** B.A. (Serving Aug. 4, 1914). Lt. 56th Punjabi Rifles, Indian Army. Mesopotamia. *D.* Mesopotamia, 1916. Killed in action, Jan. 13–14, 1916.

1907 Woodley, F. S., B.A. (Sept. 26, 1914). ‡Capt. 1st R. Munster Fusiliers. France, 1915–18. *M.C.*, Nov. 14, 1916.

1904 **Woodroffe, L.,** M.A. (Mobilized Aug. 4, 1914). Capt. Unattached List, T.F. Capt. 14th, attd. 8th, Rifle Brigade. France and Belgium. *M.C.*, Jan. 14, 1916. *D.* France, 1915. Died on June 4, 1916, of wounds received in action at Ypres.

1913 Woolf, H. M., B.A. (Sept. 11, 1914). ‡Lt. 3rd Border Regt., attd. M.G.C. (Capt.). France, 1916–17; Salonika, 1917–18.

1911 Worsley, E. M. (Aug. 22, 1914). Lt. 6th Yorkshire Regt.

1893 Worsley Taylor, F. E., M.A. Singapore Volunteers.

1884 Worthington, F., B.M. (Serving Aug. 4, 1914). Capt., Acting Lt.-Col., 43rd Fd. Amb., R.A.M.C. France. *O.B.E.* (Mil.). *D.S.O.* Jan. 14, 1916; *Bar*, Jan. 1, 1918. *D.* France, 1915, 1917, 1918.

1910 Wright, C. C. de Vire. Lt. 3rd King's African Rifles. E. Africa.

1901 Wright, G. L. (Oct. 13, 1914). Lt., Acting Maj., 2nd N. Midland Bde. R.F.A. (T.F.) France. *M.C.*, June 4, 1917.

1915 Wright, R. B. B. (Dec. 22, 1915). Lt. 3rd, attd. 5th, Grenadier Guards. France. *D.* France.

1890 Wright, R. G., B.A. (Dec. 1, 1914). Lt. R. Defence Corps. (T.F. Res.)

1899 Wurtzburg, W. F., B.A. Sanitary Section R.A.M.C.

1919 Wyllie, B. P. (Apr. 11, 1917). 2nd Lt. R.F.A. (S.R.). France.

1908 Yerburgh, R. D. T. (Feb. 17, 1915). Capt. R.A.S.C.

1910 Young, W. R., M.A. (Dec. 7, 1914). Capt., Acting Maj., 101st Bde., 22nd Divl. Art. R.F.A. France. *M.C.*, Dec. 17, 1917; *Bar*, Sept. 16, 1918.

BALLIOL COLLEGE

1901 Abbott, R. S., B.A. (Serving Aug. 4, 1914). Capt., Bt.-Maj., 38th (K.G.O.) Central India Horse. (G.S.O. 2.) France, 1914–17. *M.C.*, Jan. 1, 1917. *D.* France, 1916, 1917.

1919 Abdul Hamid, M. (Oct. 1, 1917). Lce.-Cpl. 1st Madras Inf., I.D.F.

1918 Abernethy, D. A. (Mar. 29, 1917). Lt. R.F.A. France, 1917–18.

1893 Acland, Rt. Hon. F. D., *M.P.* (July 23, 1915). Lt. University of London O.T.C.

1919 Acton, C. R. (Aug. 5, 1914). ‡2nd Lt. E. Surrey Regt. (Lt.). France and Belgium.

1912 **Adam,* A. I.** (Aug. 1914). Capt. 1/1st Cambridgeshire Regt. France. Presumed killed in action near Hamel on Sept. 16, 1916.

1895 Adams, J. D., B.A. (Jan. 1915). Pte. R.A.S.C. (Motor Transport Service). Died on Nov. 29, 1919.

1900 Albery, B. J., B.A. (Jan. 1, 1917). Lt. R.N.V.R.

1913 **Alexander, P. J.** (Apr. 12, 1915). Capt. 8th The Black Watch. France, Belgium. *M.C.*, July 26, 1917. Killed in action at Passchendaele on Oct. 12, 1917.

1912 Allen, G. W., M.A. (Sept. 1, 1914). Capt. and Adjt. 5th Leicestershire Regt. (Bde. Maj.). France, 1915–19. *D.* France, 1917.

1917 Allott, E. N. (July 1917). Lt. R.A.F. France, 1918.

1919 Althaus, F. R. (Aug. 26, 1914). Capt. 7th Suffolk Regt. France, Belgium, 1915–16; Palestine, 1917–18. *D.* France, 1916.

1892 [Amery, L. C. M. S., M.A.] (Oct. 6, 1914). Hon. Capt. 14th R. Warwickshire Regt. and Intelligence Corps. Temp. Lt.-Col. General List. G.S.O. 1, War Office. Belgium and France, 1914–15; Balkans, 1915; Gallipoli, 1915; Salonika, 1916; Supreme War Council, Versailles, 1917–18. Serbian Order of the White Eagle (4th Class). Greek Order of the Redeemer (Officier).

1904 Anderson, A. J. G., B.A. (Mobilized Aug. 1914). ‡Capt. 14th London Regt. (London Scottish). Maj. R.A.F. Egypt and Palestine. *D.* § Mar. 1918; Palestine, 1918, 1919.

1919 Anderson, R. J. B. (Oct. 5, 1917). 2nd Lt. R.G.A. (S.R.). France, 1918; Salonika, 1918–19.

1911 Angus, H. F., B.C.L., M.A. (Aug. 26, 1914). Capt. 1/4th Wiltshire Regt. India, 1914–16; Mesopotamia, 1916–19. *D.* Mesopotamia, 1918 twice.

1914 Appleby, G. E. (Nov. 5, 1914). Lt., Acting Capt., 12th K.R.R.C. France and Belgium, 1915–19. *M.B.E.* (Mil.).

1898 Argles, H. D., M.A. (Jan. 1916). Lt. 3rd County of London Yeomanry, attd. H.Q. 3rd Cavalry Division. France.

1906 Armitage,* V. L., M.A. (Aug. 26, 1915). Lt. 4th Northamptonshire Regt. Lt. Provost Branch (Capt.). France, Germany.

1911 Armour, J. S. (Oct. 11, 1916). Lt. I.A.R.O., attd. Intelligence Dept., G.H.Q. Mesopotamia.

1919 Armstrong, R. A. (Nov. 1915). ‡Lt. R.A.S.C., attd. R.G.A., VI Corps H.Q. Belgium and France, Germany.

1901 Arundel, A. D. S., B.A. (Mar. 23, 1915). Capt. R.A.S.C. France and Belgium.

1919 Ashton, A. L. B. (July 6, 1917). Lt. R.G.A.

1908 **Ashton,* E. D.,** B.A. (Sept. 1914). 2nd Lt. 9th Lancashire Fusiliers (Lt.). Gallipoli, France. Killed in action at Thiepval on July 1, 1916.

1909 [Asquith, C., M.A.] (Nov. 18, 1914). Capt. 16th London Regt. (Queen's Westminster Rifles), empld. Ministry of Munitions (1916–18).

1900 Asquith, H. (Nov. 27, 1914). Lt. R. Marines. Capt. R.F.A. Belgium, 1915; France and Belgium, from 1917.

1897 [**Asquith, R.,** M.A.] (Dec. 1914). Lt. 3rd Grenadier Guards. France. *D.* France, 1916. Killed in action in the Battle of the Somme, on Sept. 15, 1916.

1893 Aston, E. J. S., M.A. (Dec. 3, 1917). 2nd Lt. Equipment Officer, R.A.F.

1904 Auld, W. J., B.A. (Nov. 13, 1915). Pte. 1st Garrison Bn., Highland L.I. France, 1916–17. (Invalided Jan. 8, 1919.)

1913 Bacon, R. S. (Aug. 21, 1914). Capt. 8th Cheshire Regt. Gallipoli, 1915; Egypt, 1916; Mesopotamia, 1916; France, 1917; Gibraltar, 1918–19.

1920 Baddeley, E. L. O. (Aug. 15, 1914). Capt. 6th Middlesex Regt. France, Belgium, 1915–18, 1918–19; N. Russia, 1919. *D.* France, 1916.

1919 Baer, A. M. (Jan. 5, 1915). Capt. 18th Middlesex Regt. Gallipoli, 1915; France, 1916–18. *D.* France, 1918.

1896 Baillie, G. E., B.A. (Aug. 15, 1916). Pte. 2nd Seaforth Highlanders. France. (Discharged physically unfit, July 1918.)

1911 Baines,* F. J. T., M.A. (Aug. 29, 1914). Capt. 1/4th Somerset L.I. Mesopotamia.

1907 Baker, F. C., B.A. (Aug. 4, 1914). Lt. D.C.L.I. (till Dec. 1915). Maj., Flying Officer, 102nd Sqdn., R.A.F. France, 1915–18. *D.F.C.*, Jan. 1, 1919. *A.F.C.*, Nov. 2, 1918. Croix de Chevalier de la Légion d'Honneur. *D.* France, 1917.

1906 Baker,* H. L. P. (Sept. 2, 1914). ‡Lt. R.G.A. France.

1916 Baldwin, R. M. (Sept. 6, 1916). Lt. R.E. France.

1901 Balfour, Hon. H. R. C., B.A. (Aug. 1914). ‡Capt. 3rd R. Scots. France and Belgium, 1914–15.

1897 Balfour, Hon. J. M., B.A. (Aug. 25, 1914). Lt. (Hon. Capt.) Scottish Horse. Staff Capt. General List. France. *O.B.E.* (Mil.).

1900 Balfour, Hon. J. R. B., B.A. (Jan. 1915). Lt.-Comdr. R.N.V.R. France, Belgium, Russia. Order of St. Stanislas (3rd Class).

1903 Balfour, Rev. The Hon. N. F. W., M.A. (Sept. 3, 1915). Pte. 3/2nd Lowland Field Ambulance, R.A.M.C., afterwards Chaplain to the Forces (4th Class). Gibraltar.

1904 Ballantyne, J. (Aug. 5, 1914). Capt. 1/8th Highland L.I., attd. 1/7th R. Scots. Gallipoli, Egypt, France. *M.C.*, Dec. 2, 1918.

1911 **Balmforth, A.** (Oct. 1914). Lt. 8th Manchester Regt. Acting Capt. 6th King's (Liverpool Regt.). Belgium. Killed in action on July 31, 1917.

1916 Barclay, N. (May 7, 1915). 2nd Lt. 2/8th London Regt. (Post Office Rifles). Empld. F.O.

1900 **Barnes, E. L.,** B.A. (Sept. 12, 1914). Capt. and Adjt. 8th King's Own (R. Lancaster Regt.). France and Belgium. *D.* France, 1916. Killed in action at St. Eloi on Apr. 3, 1916.

Barnett, D. O. (Jan. 1, 1915). Lt. Leinster Regt. France. Died on Aug. 16, 1915, of wounds received in action.

1919 Barr, F. S. (May 28, 1917). Hospital Sergt. Sanitary Corps, U.S. Army.

1917 Barratt, S. (Aug. 1, 1918). Signaller R.G.A.

1906 **Barrington-Kennett, V. A.,** B.A. (Aug. 6, 1914). Maj. and Squadron-Comdr. R.F.C. France. *D.* France, 1915. Killed in action at Serre on Mar. 13, 1916.

1909 Barrington-Ward, R. M., B.A. (Aug. 21, 1914). Capt. D.C.L.I. Maj. G.S.O. 2, General List. Belgium, France, 1915–19. *D.S.O.*, Jan. 1, 1918. *M.C.*, Jan. 1, 1917. *D.* France, 1915, 1916, 1917.

1919 Barry, P. R. (Jan. 1917). Lt. 1st Irish Guards (Adjt.). France, 1918; Germany, 1918–19. *M.C.*, Feb. 1, 1919.

1878 Basing, Lord, B.A. (Mobilized 1914). Hon. Brig.-Gen. T.F. Reserve *C.B.* *D.* § Feb. 1917; § Feb. 1918. Died on Apr. 8, 1919.

1911 Batchelor, F. (July 1, 1915). Lt. 7th The Black Watch. France.

1904 Bate, Rev. F., B.Litt. (Apr. 27, 1917). Chaplain to the Forces (4th Class).

1875 Baynes, Rt. Rev. A. H., M.A., Hon. D.D., T.D. (Mobilized Aug. 20, 1914). Chaplain (1st Class), attd. S. Nottinghamshire Hussars.

1920 Baynes, C. H. (May 17, 1918). 2nd Lt. R.E. (Signal Service).

1901 Beal, H. E. (Aug. 26, 1916). Lt., temp. Capt., I.A.R.O., attd. Rajput Garrison Coy. India.

1886 Beatson-Bell, N. D., B.A. (Aug. 1914). Maj. Calcutta Scottish Volunteers, I.D.F. India. *C.I.E.* *C.S.I.* *D.* India.

1903 [Beazley, J. D., M.A.] (July 8, 1917). Lt. R.N.V.R.

1911 Beddington, J. L., B.A. (Aug. 4, 1914). Capt. K.O.Y.L.I. (attd. War Office) (Staff Capt.). France until 1916.

1877 Bedford, Duke of, *K.G.* (Mobilized Oct. 1914). *A.D.C.* to the King. Col. comdg. Command Depot, late 3rd Bedfordshire Regt. *K.B.E.* *D.* § Feb. 1917.

1919 Beechman, N. A. (May 25, 1915). Lt., Acting Capt., 5th E. Surrey Regt., attd. No. 6 O.C.B. France. *M.C.*, Sept. 26, 1917.

1919 Bell, G. F. (July 30, 1915). Capt. R.F.A. (S.R.), attd. 106th Bde. France, 1916–17, 1917–19. *M.C.*, June 3, 1919. *D.* France, 1916.

1909 [Bell, J., B.A.] (Dec. 11, 1914). Lt. 2/5th Somerset L.I. (Capt.). India.

1901 Bell, J. J., M.A. (Mobilized Aug. 4, 1914). Capt. 20th London Regt., (T.F. Res.), attd. War Office. France, 1915–16. *D.* France, 1916.

1903 Bell, K. N., M.A. (Aug. 2, 1914). Lt. R.G.A. (Maj.). Belgium, France. *M.C.*, Dec. 17, 1917.

1919 Bell, W. (June 1916). ‡2nd Lt. R.G.A. France.

1917 **Bellord, C. E.** (Jan. 1918). 2nd Lt. Observer, R.A.F. France. Killed in action at Metz on Sept. 15, 1918.

1913 Benson, C. E. (Aug. 4, 1914). Lt., Acting Capt., 5th Grenadier Guards. France. *D.S.O.*, Oct. 18, 1917. *D.* France, 1917.

1907 Benson, G. H. (Mobilized Aug. 1914). Capt. W. Kent Yeomanry, attd. 9th Lancers. Gallipoli, 1915–16; France, 1916–19.

1908 Benson, R. L. (Serving Aug. 4, 1914). Capt., temp. Maj., 9th Lancers. G.S.O. 2. France, 1914–15 and 1917–18. *D.S.O.*, June 3, 1918.

M.C., Feb. 18, 1915. Croix de Chevalier de la Légion d'Honneur. Croix de Guerre with palm. *D.* France, 1914, 1915, 1917, 1918.

1900 Beresford, S. de la P., B.A. (July 7, 1916). Lt. R.G.A. (S.R.). Acting Capt. Education Officer, Rhine Army. Germany, 1919.

1895 Berman, L. E., B.A. (April 8, 1916). Pte. Middlesex Regt. France.

1913 **Berrill,* B. F. G.** (Aug. 14, 1914). Lt. 4th R. Fusiliers. Belgium. Killed in action at Hill 60 on Mar. 17, 1915.

1904 Bertie, Hon. A. M. C. (Nov. 9, 1914). Maj. 11th Rifle Brigade (Lt.-Col.). France and Belgium, 1915–18. *D.S.O.*, June 18, 1917. *M.C.*, Feb. 18, 1918. *D.* France, 1917 twice.

1909 Bertie, A. W. (Serving Aug. 4, 1914). Capt. R.F.A. France. *M.C.*, June 3, 1918. *D.* France, 1917.

1910 Besly, E. F. W., B.A. (Sept. 1, 1914). ‡Lt., Acting Capt., Seaforth Highlanders. Staff Capt. G.H.Q., France. France.

1877 Bevan, Rev. J., M.A. (May 14, 1915). Chaplain to the Forces (4th Class).

1919 Bickersteth, J. R. (June 1915). Capt. Yorkshire Hussars. Capt. C.M.O. and Intelligence Officer. France.

1913 Bicknell, A. (Sept. 1914). Capt., Bt.-Maj., 2/5th Gloucestershire Regt. Staff Capt. 184th Inf. Bde. France. *M.C.*, Jan. 1, 1918. *D.* France, 1919.

1911 Biddle, A. A. (May 8, 1917). Capt. Field Artillery, A.D.C. U. S. Army. Asst. G. 1, 88th Div. (Maj.). France.

1916 Bigelow, H. R. (Oct. 16, 1917). Interpreter, Intelligence Section, U.S. Army. France, Italy.

1919 Binney, R. C. C. J. (July 17, 1916). Lt. 8th R. W. Kent Regt. France, 1918; Germany, 1919.

1918 Birch, H. R. (Mar. 9, 1916). Pte. 5th Field Ambulance, A.I.F. France, Belgium.

1902 Birchenough, C., M.A. (Apr. 1916). Lt. 105th Siege Batt., R.G.A. France, 1917; Italy, 1917–19. *D.* Italy, 1918.

1914 Birnie, A. (Aug. 6, 1915). Sergt. 102nd Field Amb., R.A.M.C. France, 1916–19.

1908 Black, J. B., M.A. (Mar. 16, 1915). Lt. 10th Highland L.I. France. (Prisoner of War, Mar.–Nov. 1918.)

1914 Blacker, C. P. (July 15, 1915). Capt. 2nd Coldstream Guards. France, 1915–19. *M.C.*, Nov. 14, 1916. *D.* France, 1918 twice.

1891 **Blackwood, Lord B.** (Aug. 6, 1914). 2nd Lt. Grenadier Guards. France. Killed in action on July 3, 1917.

1910 Blair,* P. J., M.A. (Mobilized Aug. 4, 1914). Lt.-Col. 13th (Scottish Horse) Bn. The Black Watch. France, Belgium. *D.S.O.*, June 3, 1919. Croix de Guerre with gold star. *D.* France, 1917, 1919.

Blake, J. M. (May 1, 1917). 2nd Lt. Devonshire Regt. France and Belgium. Killed in action on Oct. 4, 1917.

1906 Blight, E. C., B.A. (Mobilized Aug. 4, 1914). Capt. 8th London Regt. (Post Office Rifles) (T.F. Res.). Capt. Administrative Officer, R.A.F. France, 1915. *D.* § Aug. 1919.

1900 Bliss, H. J. W., B.A. (Sept. 15, 1914). Capt., Acting Maj., R.A.S.C. (M.T.). France.

1917 Bloomfield, P. (June 1917). Cadet R.F.A. Cadet School. (Discharged medically unfit, Apr. 1918).

1900 Bomford, H., B.A. (Serving Aug. 4, 1914). Cpl. 7th United Provinces Light Horse, I.D.F. India.

1886 **Bonham-Carter, N.** (May 1915). 2nd Lt. Household Bn. (Lt.). Belgium, France, 1916–17. Killed in action at Rœux on the Scarpe on May 3, 1917.

1910 Borley, G. C. H., B.A. R.G.A., attd. Intelligence Dept.

1914 Bosanquet, C. H. (Dec. 22, 1914). Capt. 3rd Field Survey Bn. R.E. France, Belgium. *D.* France, 1917, 1919.

1913 Boswell, R. H., B.A. (Oct. 30, 1915). Pte. R.A.M.C. France, 1916–19.

Boulton, C. H. E. (Sept. 5, 1914). Lt. Gen. List, attd. 5th Q. O. Cameron Highlanders. France and Belgium. Killed in action in Belgium on Oct. 12, 1917.

1878 Boulton, Sir H. E., Bt., M.A., *C.V.O.* (Mobilized 1914). Capt. City of London Yeomanry (T.F. Res.). Capt. Labour Corps. *C.B.E.* (Civil).

1884 Boulton, O. E., M.A., T.D. (Mobilized 1914). Lt.-Col. 2/3rd County of London Yeomanry. *D.* § Feb. 1917.

1908 [Bourdillon,* R. B., M.A.] (Aug. 5, 1914). ‡2nd Lt. Intelligence Corps. Lt.-Col. R.A.F. France. *M.C.*, Sept. 26, 1917. *A.F.C.*, June 3, 1918.

1915 Bowen, E. J., B.A. (Feb. 16, 1917). Lt. R.G.A. France, 1917–19.

1909 Bowlby,* H. R. (Serving Aug. 4, 1914). Capt. Rifle Brigade. Lt. R.N.V.R.

1911 Bowlby,* H. S., B.A. (Aug. 22, 1914). Maj. 7th R. Sussex Regt. France, 1915–19. *M.C.*, June 26, 1916.

1919 Boyce, H. L. (Aug. 1914). Lt. 10th Bn. A.I.F. (Staff Lt.). Egypt, Gallipoli, 1915 (with 27th Bn.); France and Belgium, 1916, 1917, 1918.

1892 Boyd Carpenter, A., B.A. (Mobilized Aug. 1914). Hon. Capt. Res. of Officers. Bt.-Maj. D.A.D., Dept. of Under-Secretary of State for War. France. *D.* § Feb. 1917.

1917 Boyle, A. R. (July 5, 1917). Lt. 1st Irish Guards. France.

1911 Brabant,* Rev. F. H., M.A. (Mar. 1916). Lce.-Cpl. 10th R. Fusiliers (attd. Intelligence Corps). France, 1916–19.

1903 Brander, W. B. (Aug. 1914). Capt. 14th Tenasserim Bn., I.D.F. Burma. *C.B.E.* (Civil).

1906 [**Brandt,* D. R.,** B.A.] (Aug. 4, 1914). Lt. 6th, attd. 1st, Rifle Brigade. France and Belgium. Killed in action in Belgium on July 6, 1915.

1882 Brassey, Earl, M.A., Hon. D.C.L. (Mobilized 1914). Lt.-Col. 2nd W. Kent Yeomanry (T.F. Res.). Italy. T.D. Commander of the Order of the Crown of Italy. *D.* § Feb. 1917. Died as the result of an accident on Nov. 12, 1919.

1897 Bremer, J. L. (Dec. 9, 1915). Surgeon U.S. Medical Reserve (Acting Maj. R.A.M.C., 1915–16). France, 1915–16.

Brewerton, W. L. Pte. R. Fusiliers. Died on Aug. 23, 1918.

1891 Brinton, Rev. P. R., M.A. (Sept. 30, 1918). Pte. R.A.M.C.

1916 Brodie, Rev. I. (Jan. 1918). Chaplain to the Forces (4th Class). France and Belgium, 1918–19.

1907 Brodrick, Hon. G. S. J. (Mobilized Aug. 29, 1914). Lt.-Col. Surrey Yeomanry. Maj. R.A.F. Gallipoli, France. *M.C.*, Feb. 2, 1917. Croix de Chevalier de la Légion d'Honneur. *D.* Gallipoli, 1915; § Jan. 1919. (Relinquished Commission on account of ill health contracted on active service.)

1881 Bromley-Davenport, W., *D.S.O.*, T.D. (Mobilized Aug. 1914). Lt.-Col. Staffordshire Yeomanry. Col. Labour Commandant (Brig.-Gen.). Egypt, France, Italy, Belgium, Germany. *C.M.G.* *C.B.E.* (Mil.). Croix d'Officier de la Légion d'Honneur. Order of the Crown of Italy. Belgian Croix de Guerre. *D.* Italy, 1919.

1914 Bronner, R. (Apr. 26, 1917). Lt. 5th London Regt. (London Rifle Brigade).

1911 Brooke, J. R. I. (Sept. 11, 1914). Lt., temp. Capt., R.G.A. Staff-Captain. France, Salonika. *M.B.E.* (Mil.). Greek medal for Military Merit (4th Class). *D.* France, 1915; Salonika, 1918, 1919.

1912 **Brown, D. W.,** B.A. (Aug. 1914). Capt. 6th Leicestershire Regt. France. Killed in action at Bazentin-le-Petit on July 14, 1916.

1910 **Brown,* J.,** B.A. (Sept. 1914). ‡Lt. 6th Seaforth Highlanders. France and Belgium. *M.C.*, July 18, 1917. Killed in action at Wytschaete on Apr. 11, 1918.

1905 [**Brown, J. R.,** M.A.] (Apr. 13, 1914). Capt. 7th Highland L.I. Gallipoli, 1915; Egypt, Palestine, 1916–17. Died on Apr. 23, 1917, of wounds received in action at Gaza.

1909 Brown, L. G., D.M. (Feb. 22, 1915). Capt. R.A.M.C. Lt.-Col. No. 15 Convalescent Depot. France, Belgium. *M.C.*, June 4, 1917. *D.* France, 1918.

1883 Brown, W. B., B.A. (Sept. 29, 1917). 2nd Lt. Labour Corps, attd. Indian Labour Corps. Capt. Summary Court Officer. France, Belgium, Germany.

1918 Browne, G. S. (Dec. 1915). Lt. 10th T.M.B., A.I.F. France. *M.C.*, Aug. 25, 1917.

1912 Browning, A. (1917). 2nd Lt. R.G.A.

1917 Bruce, R. E. Motor Transport, A.I.F.

1913 Bruce, R. F. D. (Mobilized Aug. 1914). Capt. 5th The Black Watch. D.A.P.M. France, Belgium, and Germany, 1914–19.

1913 Bruce-Gardyne, I. M., B.A. (Mobilized Aug. 4, 1914). Lt. 5th The Black Watch (Capt.). France. *M.C.*, June 23, 1915. *D.* France, 1915.

1918 Bryan-Brown, A. N. (Aug. 8, 1918). Cadet No. 13 O.C.B.

1900 **Buch, C. J.,** B.A. (Aug. 14, 1915). 2nd Lt. 10th Bedfordshire Regt. France. Killed in action in France on Sept. 13, 1916.

1919 Buchanan, S. M. (June 4, 1918). ‡Ensign U.S. Naval Reserve Force.

1909 Bulkeley-Johnson,* V. F. (Serving Aug. 4, 1914). Capt. Rifle Brigade (Maj.). A.D.C. to Governor-General of Canada. France, 1914–15.

1891 Burkitt, W. J. D. Maj. I.D.F. India.

1881 Burnham, Lord, M.A., *K.C.V.O.* (Mobilized 1915). Hon. Col. R. Bucks Hussars. Lt.-Col. T.F. Reserve. T.D. Companion of Honour. Légion d'Honneur. Commander of the Order of Leopold of Belgium. *D.* § Feb. 1917.

Burnside, E. B. C. (Aug. 14, 1914). Capt. 7th The Buffs (E. Kent Regt.) (Capt. and Adjt.). France and Belgium, 1915, 1916, 1917. *D.* France, 1916. Killed in action at Poelcappelle on Oct. 12, 1917.

1911 Burrows, J. H., B.A. (Sept. 1, 1915). Instructor Lt. R.N. Grand Fleet, 1915–19.

1913 Burrows,* M. B., B.A. (Aug. 4, 1914). Lt. 5th Dragoon Guards. Temp. Capt. and Liaison Officer, N. Russia (Maj.). Belgium, France, 1914;

North Russia, 1919. *D.S.O.*, Sept. 13–14, 1919. *M.C.*, May, 1919. Order of St. George (4th Class). Order of St. Vladimir (4th Class). Order of St. Anne (3rd Class). (Prisoner of War from Sept. 1914 to Feb. 1918.)

1919 Burt, H. T. (May 1916). ‡Lt. R.F.A. 2nd Lt. Flying Officer, R.A.F. France, 1916–17 and 1918–19.

1902 [Butler, H. B., M.A.] (Mobilized Aug. 4, 1914). Capt. Inns of Court O.T.C. Seconded for work at Home Office. *C.B.*

1919 Buxton, D. A. J. (Sept. 8, 1914). ‡Lt. 6th W. Riding Regt., attd. R.A.F. Gallipoli, 1915; Egypt, 1915–16.

1914 Byers, J. A. (Nov. 28, 1914). Lt. Cheshire Regt. Lt. R.E., attd. for Army Signal Service. Mediterranean, 1915–16; Mesopotamia, 1916 and 1917–18; India, 1916–17 and 1918–19.

1919 Byth, H. V. (May 8, 1918). ‡2nd Lt. Education Service, A.I.F. Egypt.

1917 Cade, J. F. (Apr. 5, 1918). 2nd Lt. King's (Liverpool Regt.). France, 1918–19.

1889 Cadell, P. R. (Mobilized Aug. 1914). Lt.-Col. Bombay Bn. I.D.F. (Hon. Col. and A.D.C. to the Viceroy of India.) India, Mesopotamia. *C.S.I.* V.D.

1899 Cadogan, Hon. E. C. G., B.A. (Mobilized Aug. 4, 1914). Capt. Suffolk Yeomanry. Maj. G.H.Q., E.E.F. Gallipoli, Egypt, Palestine. *D.* Palestine, 1919.

1919 Cairns, H. W. B. (May 1915). Capt. Australian A.M.C. Lemnos, 1915; Egypt, 1916; France, 1918.

1919 Caldwell, W. (Aug. 15, 1915). Capt. 48th Bn., A.I.F. Egypt, France.

1906 Cameron, A. G., B.A. (Mobilized Aug. 1914). Capt. King Edward's Horse, attd. 4th R. Berkshire Regt. France.

1896 Cameron, E. C., B.A. (Mobilized Aug. 4, 1914). Maj. 1st Lovat's Scouts. G.S.O. 3. (Relinquished Commission on account of ill health.)

1902 Camoys, Lord (Mobilized Aug. 1914). Lt. Q. O. Oxfordshire Hussars (Capt.). Lt. Technical Officer, R.A.F. (Resigned on account of ill health.)

1903 [Campbell, Rev. J. McL., M.A.] (Aug. 10, 1914). Chaplain to the Forces (3rd Class), attd. 4th Div. France. *M.C.*, Jan. 1, 1919. *D.* France, 1917.

1904 **Campbell, N. P.,** M.A. (Jan. 15, 1915). Capt. R.E. France, 1915–17. Killed in action at Pelves Lane on the Scarpe on May 3, 1917.

1897 Campbell, P. G. C., M.A. (June 1, 1915). Lt.-Col. 253rd Bn., C.E.F. France, 1917–18. *M.C.*, Jan. 10, 1918.

1894 Campbell-Johnston, D. G. (Jan. 1916). Pte. Foreign Legion (French Army). 2nd Lt. Special Lists (Censor Staff) (English Army). France, 1916–17. Croix de Guerre.

1908 Carpenter, R., M.A. (1918). 1st Lt. Mil. Intelligence, U. S. Army, attd. Peace Commission, Paris.

1911 Carré, M. H., B.A. (Nov. 24, 1914). Capt. R. W. Kent Regt. attd. H.Q., R.A.S.C. (M.T.) (Education Officer). France, 1915, 1916. *M.C.*, Jan. 1, 1916. *D.* France, 1915.

1919 Carter, M. O. (Feb. 20, 1917). Lt. R.F.A. (S.R.). Belgium, France. *M.C.*, Sept. 16, 1918.

1899 Carton de Wiart, A. (Serving Aug. 4, 1914). Maj., Bt.-Lt.-Col., 4th Dragoon Guards. Temp. Brig.-Gen., Chief of British Mil. Mission to Poland. Somaliland, 1914; France, 1915–18. *C.B. C.M.G. D.S.O.*, May 15, 1915. Ordre de la Couronne. Ordre de Léopold. Belgian Croix de Guerre. Belgian War Medal. *D.* France, 1916, 1917 twice, 1918, 1919. **V.C.** won at La Boisselle, July 2–3, 1916.

For most conspicuous bravery, coolness, and determination during severe operations of a prolonged nature. It was owing in a great measure to his dauntless courage and inspiring example that a serious reverse was averted.

He displayed the utmost energy and courage in forcing our attack home. After three other Battalion Commanders had become casualties, he controlled their commands, and ensured that the ground won was maintained at all costs.

He frequently exposed himself in the organization of positions and of supplies, passing unflinchingly through the fire barrage of the most intense nature.

His gallantry was inspiring to all.

1916 Carton de Wiart, F. X. Sous-Lt. Infanterie, Belgian Army. Belgium.

1913 Carus-Wilson,* M. M., B.A. (Oct. 4, 1914). Lt. 1/4th Dorsetshire Regt. India, 1915–16; Mesopotamia and India, 1916–19.

1919 Cavanagh, B. A. M. (Aug. 2, 1918). Pte. R.E. (Special Bde.). France, 1918–19.

1917 Cave, J. D. (Apr. 1918). Conducteur, Croix rouge française. France, Belgium.

1919 Chambers, J. C. (June 7, 1918). 2nd Lt. R. W. Kent Regt. (on demobilization).

1908 **Champneys, J. D.,** B.A. (Aug. 26, 1914). Lt. 6th Leicestershire Regt. France. Died as a prisoner on Nov. 23, 1915, of wounds received in action.

1911 **Chaplin,* H. M.** (Aug. 15, 1914). Lt. 3rd Cheshire Regt. France and Belgium. Killed in action near Ypres on May 9, 1915.

1887 Charteris, Hon. E. E. (Sept. 16, 1914). Capt. Special Lists. Capt. Tank Corps. G.S.O. 3. France. *D.* § Feb. 1917.

Charteris, Hon. I. A. (Feb. 27, 1915). 2nd Lt. Grenadier Guards. France and Belgium. Killed in action on Oct. 17, 1915.

1908 Chavasse,* F. B., D.M. (May 1, 1915). Capt. 96th Field Ambulance, R.A.M.C. (Maj.). Egypt, Mediterranean, France, Belgium. *M.C.*, Sept. 26, 1917.

1906 **Cheatle, W. J. N.,** B.A. (Serving Aug. 4, 1914). Lt. 1st K.O. Scottish Borderers. Egypt and India, 1914; Gallipoli, 1915. Killed in action in Gallipoli on Apr. 26, 1915.

1912 Chitty, C., B.A. (Sept. 24, 1914). Lt. 4th Hampshire Regt. Mesopotamia. (Prisoner of War in Turkey.)

1900 Chute, Rev. J. C., M.A. (Serving Aug. 4, 1914). Capt. Unattached List, T.F., Eton College O.T.C.

1919 Clark, A. M. (Apr. 27, 1916). Capt. R.A.M.C. Belgium, France, Germany. *M.C.*, Dec. 2, 1918.

1898 Clark, E. G. U., M.A. (June 1916). ‡2nd Lt. 7th Norfolk Regt. France. (Prisoner of War from Mar. 1918.)

1911 Clark, F. L. G., B.A. (Sept. 15, 1914). ‡Lt. 1st Hampshire Regt. France, 1915–16, 1916–18.

1908 [Clark, G. N., M.A.] (Mobilized Aug. 1914). Lt., temp. Capt., 8th London Regt. (Post Office Rifles). France. (Prisoner of War, May 1916.)

1919 Clark, J. B. (June 1, 1917). 2nd Lt. R.A.S.C. France.

1910 Clark, R. T., B.A. (Nov. 1915). Lt. 9th The Black Watch. France, 1916–18.

1884 Clarke, Sir R. T. H., Bt. (Apr. 12, 1915). Lt. A.S.C. Salonika, 1915–16. (Invalided Jan. 1916.)

1919 Clarke, S. S. (Sept. 7, 1916). 2nd Lt. R.G.A. Belgium, France, Germany.

1904 Clay, C. T., M.A. (June 1915). Lt., temp. Maj., Royal 1st Devon Yeomanry. D.A.Q.M.G., G.H.Q., France. France. Chevalier de l'Ordre de Léopold. Belgian Croix de Guerre. Chevalier de l'Ordre du Mérite Agricole. *D.* France, 1917, 1918.

1899 **Clay, L. P.,** M.A. (Mobilized Aug. 4, 1914). Capt. Yorkshire Dragoons (Maj.). France. Killed in action at Templeux la Fosse on Feb. 18, 1918.

1904 Clear, T., M.A. (Nov. 3, 1917). Lt. Indian Cavalry, I.A.R.O. India.

1919 Cleare, C. R. (Sept. 9, 1916). Lt. R.G.A. France.

1906 Clifton, E. W. V., M.A. (June 22, 1916). ‡Capt. I.A.R.O. India.

1909 Cluer, R. M., B.A. (1914). Pte. R.A.S.C. (M.T.). France.

1909 **Clutterbuck, B. V.,** B.A. (Apr.. 1915). ‡2nd Lt. R.F.A. France and Belgium. Killed in action at Bœsinghe on July 14, 1917.

1912 Coats, J. D. O., B.A. (Sept. 14, 1914). Lt. 5th The Black Watch. Capt. M.G.C. France, Mesopotamia.

1893 **Cobb, K. R.,** B.A. (Sept. 1914). Capt. 15th K.R.R.C., attd. 1st R. Inniskilling Fusiliers. Gallipoli. Killed in action in Gallipoli on July 1, 1915.

1899 Cockayne, E. A., D.M. (July 17, 1915). Surgeon-Lt. R.N. White Sea Fleet, 1917. *D.* Admiralty, 1919.

1911 **Coleridge, L. F. R.** (1914). 2nd Lt. 1st Coldstream Guards. France; Belgium. Killed in action at Givenchy-lez-la-Bassée on Dec. 22, 1914.

1908 Collier,* W. T., B.M., M.A. (Feb. 10, 1915). Capt. R.A.M.C. Egypt, Palestine, and Hedjaz. *M.C.*, Jan. 1, 1918. *D.* Palestine, 1918.

1897 Collins, L. C. (Nov. 6, 1915). Lt. 5th Durham L.I. France.

1919 Collis, J. S. (June 12, 1918). 2nd Lt. Irish Guards.

1911 **Compton, Lord S. D.** (Mobilized Aug. 4, 1914). Lt. Household Cavalry. France, Belgium. Killed in action on May 13/14, 1915.

1902 Compton-Bracebridge, C., B.A. (June 5, 1915). Lt. R.A.S.C. (M.T.) (till Sept. 1916). Capt. R.A.F. France.

1919 Considine, A. E. (Sept. 21, 1914). Capt. 13th R. Scots. France, 1915, 1917–19. *M.C.*, July 26, 1918; *Bar*, Oct. 16, 1918.

1907 Conway, F. J., B.A. (Sept. 1914). ‡Lt. R.F.A. France, India, Mesopotamia.

1886 Cookson, G. M., B.A. (Oct. 3, 1914). Capt. 2/4th Dorsetshire Regt., attd. Gen. Staff. India, 1914–16.

1895 Coolidge, J. L., B.Sc. (Jan. 1, 1918). Maj. Ordnance Dept., U.S. Army. Commdt. American E.F. School Detachment, Paris. France, 1918–19. Croix de Chevalier de la Légion d'Honneur.

1908 Cooper, G. J. R. (Serving Aug. 4, 1914). Lt., Acting Capt. and Adjt., 2nd Dragoons (R. Scots Greys). France, Belgium. Order of St. Stanislas (3rd Class). Chevalier, Ordre de Léopold (avec Palme). Belgian Croix de Guerre. *D.* France, 1914.

1912 Coote, C. R., *M.P.* (Mobilized Aug. 4, 1914). ‡Capt. 5th Gloucestershire Regt. France, Italy. *D.S.O.*, Sept. 24, 1918. *D.* Italy, 1918.

1919 Corbett, P. E. (June 1915). Lt. 13th R. Highlanders of Canada (Capt.). France and Belgium. *M.C.*, July 26, 1917.

1897 Costley-White, Rev. H., M.A. (Feb. 1915). Capt. Unattached List, T.F., Rugby School O.T.C.

1881 Cottesloe, Lord, V.D. (Mobilized Oct. 1914). Lt.-Col. (Hon. Col.) 4th Oxf. & Bucks. Lt. Infty. (T.F. Res.). *D.* § Feb. 1917.

1904 **Cowie, A. W. S.,** B.A. (Jan. 28, 1915). 2nd Lt. 7th Lincolnshire Regt. France. Killed in action on the Somme on July 8, 1916.

1919 Cox, C. W. M. (May 17, 1918). 2nd Lt. R.E. (Signals).

1915 **Coxe, C. H.** (Dec. 13, 1915). 2nd Lt. R.F.C. France. Died as a prisoner on July 2, 1916, of wounds received on the previous day.

1898 [Craster, H. H. E., M.A., D.Litt.] (Mar. 28, 1917). ‡Lt. Special Lists, empld. War Office (Intelligence Directorate).

Cresswell, F. (Aug. 10, 1914). ‡2nd Lt. 9th Leicestershire Regt. (Adjt.). France, Belgium. Killed in action near Arras on May 18, 1916.

1898 Cross, A. (Mobilized Aug. 1914). Lt. Q.O.R. Glasgow Yeomanry. Egypt, 1917–19.

1913 Cross,* A. R. (Aug. 15, 1914). Capt. 3rd Gordon Highlanders. D.A.P.M. France, 1915, 1916, 1917–19. *M.C.*, July 18, 1917. *D.* France, 1918.

1918 Cross, F. L. (Sept. 5, 1918). Pte. 28th London Regt. (Artists Rifles O.T.C.).

1906 Crosse, Rev. E. C., M.A. (Jan. 15, 1915). Chaplain to the Forces (3rd Class), attd. 7th Division. France, Italy. *D.S.O.*, Jan. 1, 1917. *M.C.*, Dec. 17, 1917. Croce di Guerra. *D.* France, 1916, 1917; Italy, 1919.

1912 Crossley,* Hon. J. de B. (Aug. 4, 1914). Capt. Suffolk Yeomanry, attd. R.A.F. Mudros, Salonika, Egypt, Palestine, France.

1905 Crosthwaite,* Rev. G. B., B.A. (Feb. 1917). Chaplain to the Forces (4th Class) (1917–18). Pte. R.A. (1918). ‡2nd Lt. R.H.A. (1918). France, Belgium.

1919 Cunliffe, T. (Dec. 1914). Lt. R.F.A. (S.R.) (Capt.). Belgium and France, 1915; Salonika, 1915–18.

1906 **Cunningham, J. C.** (Feb. 2, 1915). Pte. Princess Patricia's Canadian L.I., C.E.F. (Sergt. Instructor). France. Killed in action at Monchy le Preux on Aug. 26, 1918.

1902 Dakyns, A. L., M.A. (Sept. 11, 1914). 2nd Lt. A.S.C. France, Belgium. (Invalided, Dec. 27, 1915.)

1899 Daman, G. W., M.A. (Aug. 26, 1914). Capt. R. Fusiliers.

1906 Danckwerts, H. O., M.A. (Mobilized Aug. 2, 1914). ‡Lt. E. Riding of Yorkshire Yeomanry (Capt.). *D.* § Aug. 1918.

1897 **Darbishire, A. D.,** B.Sc., M.A. (July 1915). ‡2nd Lt. R.G.A. (S.R.). Died on Dec. 26, 1915, of illness contracted on active service.

1888 Darbishire, O. V., B.A. (Aug. 1914). Lt. Unattached List, T.F., Bristol University O.T.C. *D.* § Mar. 1919.

1905 Davey, A. F. C. Pte. R.A.M.C.

1919 Davidson, H. H. (Nov. 5, 1916). Lt. R.G.A. (S.R.). Belgium, France.

1911 Davidson, L. H., B.A. (1914). Pte. 14th London Regt. (London Scottish) (empld. Permit Office).

1888 Davies, E. R., M.A. (Mobilized Aug. 1914). Maj. R.A.S.C., 1st London Divisional Train (T.F. Res.). *D.* § Feb. 1917.
1919 Davies, I. M. (Aug. 1914). 2nd Lt. Welsh Regt., afterwards Capt. Flight Commander, R.A.F. France. *D.* § Jan. 1919.
1920 Davies, J. A. V. (July 23, 1918). Flying Cadet, U.S. Air Service.
1906 Davies, R. L. (Nov. 9, 1914). ‡Lt. 1/8th King's (Liverpool Regt.) (Capt.). Staff-Lt. Intelligence Dept., War Office. Belgium and France.
1899 Davis, H. D., B.M. (Mobilized Aug. 1914). Capt. R.A.M.C. (T.F.). Egypt.
1909 Davy, M. B. (Aug. 5, 1914). ‡Lt. R.G.A. (S.R.) (Capt.). Burma, France, 1916–17.
1886 Dawkins, T. F., B.A. (Mobilized Aug. 4, 1914). Maj. T.F. Res., empld. War Office. Croix de Guerre.
de Bless, G. A., (Sept. 1915). Midshipman R.N. Died at sea on Mar. 23, 1916.
1905 de Gramont, Duc (1914). Lt. État-Maj. French Army. France.
1902 **Dehn, T. G. R.,** B.A. (Aug. 1916). 2nd Lt. 3rd Wiltshire Regt. France. Died on Apr. 19, 1917, of wounds received in action at Mitry-en-Foutare.
1902 de Liedekerke, Count R. (Aug. 4, 1914). Lt. d'Infanterie, Belgian Army. Belgium. *D.* Belgian Dispatches, 1917.
1912 **Dendy, R.,** B.A. (Aug. 31, 1914). Capt. R.A.S.C., attd. 2nd S. Wales Borderers. France, Belgium. *M.C.*, Mar. 8, 1919. Killed in action near Rolligham-Capelle on Oct. 15, 1918.
1912 Denham, H. J., M.A. (Aug. 1914). ‡Lt. R.G.A. (Capt.). France, 1915–18. *D.* France, 1917.
1911 Denham, H. K., M.A. (Apr. 1915). Surgeon Sub-Lt. R.N.V.R. H.M.S. *Lark*, H.M.S. *Heather*, H.M.S. *Marshfort*. North Sea, 1915–16; Atlantic, 1916–18; Mediterranean, 1918. *D.* Nov. 1917.
1896 Denman, Hon. R. D., B.A., *M.P.* (Nov. 1915). Lt. and Adjt. R.F.A. France, 1916–17.
1915 de Salis, Count A. D. R. (Apr. 20, 1916). Lt. Irish Guards (S.R.), empld. Guards M.G.R.
1910 de Salis,* Count J. E., M.A. (Sept. 24, 1914). Lt. Irish Guards. Capt. whilst holding Special Appt. Balkans. Croix de Chevalier de la Légion d'Honneur. Montenegrin Military Medal. Montenegrin Silver Medal for Bravery.
1898 **de Trafford, H. J.,** B.A. (Serving Aug. 4, 1914). Capt. 3rd S. Staffordshire Regt. Belgium, France. Killed in action in France on Sept. 25, 1915.
1905 Dewar, R. (Aug. 4, 1914). Lt. University College, Reading, O.T.C. Capt. 4th Hampshire Regt. Acting Capt. Administrative Officer R.A.F.
1919 Dickinson, A. E. F. (Jan. 25, 1918). 2nd Lt. R.G.A.
1900 **Dickinson, H. N.,** B.A. (Jan. 6, 1915). 2nd Lt. 3rd R. W. Kent Regt. France. Died on Oct. 13, 1916, of wounds received in action on the Somme.
1905 Dixon, G. C., B.A. (Sept. 1914). Capt. R.A.M.C. France, Quetta, 1915–16; Mesopotamia, 1916–19; Punjab, 1919.
1910 Dixon, Ll. (Dec. 1914). 2nd Lt. Unattached List, T.F., Weymouth College O.T.C.
1910 Dodd,* C. E. S. (Sept. 1914). Capt. Welsh Guards. Staff Lt. (2nd Class). France, Belgium, Germany.

1913 Dodd, R. J. S., B.A. (Apr. 10, 1915). Lt. 3rd R. Berkshire Regt., attd. M.G.C. (Capt.). France, 1915–16, 1918–19.

1909 Dodgson, R. C. F. (Sept. 28, 1914). 2nd Lt. R. Marines. Belgium, France.

1904 Dodson, J. E. (1915). Lt. Unattached List, T.F., Liverpool College O.T.C.

1916 Dodwell, D. W. (Sept. 15, 1916). 2nd Lt. 1st R. Warwickshire Regt. Egypt, 1918–19.

1913 Doe, A. B. (1917). Pte. U.S. Army. France, 1914–15 (with British Red Cross).

1902 Downes, O. C. (Jan. 4, 1904). Maj. Rifle Brigade. G.S.O. 2. France. *D.S.O.*, Aug. 25, 1915. *M.C.*, Jan. 1, 1919. *D.* France, 1915, 1916.

1903 Dowson, S. H., B.A. (Sept. 1914). ‡Lt. 1st R. Warwickshire Regt. (Capt.). France. *M.C.*, Jan. 1, 1919.

1902 Drake, J. C. B. (Sept. 1, 1918). 2nd Lt. I.A.R.O., attd. 16th Cavalry (Maj.). India. *O.B.E.* (Civil).

1887 du Boulay, Sir J. H., *K.C.I.E.* (Serving Aug. 4, 1914.) Lt.-Col. Simla Rifles, I.D.F. India.

1907 Duff, C. P., B.A. (Serving Aug. 1914). ‡Capt. R.A., H.Q. 14th Indian Division. Gallipoli, 1915–16; Egypt, 1916; France, Belgium, 1916–17; Mesopotamia, 1917–19. *D.* France, 1916, 1917.

1895 Dugdale, E. T. S. (Mobilized Aug. 1914). Capt. Leicestershire Yeomanry, empld. Postal Censorship, War Office. France.

1920 du Luart, L. C. L. (Aug. 20, 1918). Interpreter, French Liaison Service, attd. U.S. Army. Germany.

1904 Duncan, H. H., M.A. (Mobilized Aug. 5, 1914). Capt. Norfolk Yeomanry. Staff Lt. (3rd Class). France, Belgium, Italy, 1917–18.

1903 Duncan, Rev. J. M., M.A. (May 1915). Chaplain to the Forces (4th Class). Gallipoli, 1915; Egypt, 1916; France, 1918–19.

1897 **Dyer,* C. N.,** B.A. (Mobilized Aug. 1914). Capt. H.A.C. Suez Canal, 1915–16; Egypt (NW. Frontier), 1916. Died at Suez on July 14, 1916, of illness contracted on active service.

1901 **Dyer, S. B. B.** (Serving Aug. 4, 1914). Maj. 2nd Life Guards, and General Staff. Attaché, British Embassy, Madrid. Died on Jan. 27, 1917.

1919 Dyson, W. E. (Sept. 11, 1914). ‡2nd Lt. Devonshire Regt. France. (Prisoner of War.)

1919 Edinger, G. A. (May 3, 1917). 1st B.R.C. Field Ambulance Convoy, Italy. 2nd Lt. American Red Cross. Italy, 1917–18.

1912 **Edinger,* W. M. V.** (Sept. 2, 1914). ‡Lt. 14th R. Warwickshire Regt. France. Killed in action at Bapaume on Aug. 23, 1918.

1912 Egerton,* A. E., M.A. (Aug. 15, 1914). Lt. 3rd W. Yorkshire Regt. Lt. General Staff (Intelligence). Egypt, France, Palestine, Syria. *M.C.*, Mar. 30, 1916.

1901 Elgin and Kincardine, Earl of. (Mobilized Aug. 5, 1914). Maj. R.G.A. Col. Labour Commdt., IV Corps. France. *C.M.G.* *D.* 1918 twice.

1911 Elgood,* C. L., M.A. (Aug. 26, 1914). Capt. 10th Middlesex Regt. Lt. Indian Army. India.

1911 Elton, G., B.A. (Sept. 1914). Capt. 4th Hampshire Regt. India and Mesopotamia, 1915. (Prisoner in Turkey, 1916–18.)

1913 Emery, A. (1917). 2nd Lt. 1st (Garr.) Bn. K.O.Y.L.I.

1916 Entwistle, H. (Mar. 21, 1917). Lt. R.A.F. France, Belgium. Belgian Croix de Guerre.

1907 Erleigh, Viscount G. R. (Aug. 7, 1914). Capt. R. Fusiliers. Staff Capt. and D.A.A.G. France. *M.C.*, June 3, 1918. Croix de Guerre.

1898 [**Everett, A. F.**] Rfln. 16th London Regt. (Queen's Westminster Rifles). France. Killed in action on Apr. 14, 1917.

1919 Evershed, F. R. (Feb. 4, 1918). ‡2nd Lt. 2nd Field Squadron, R.E. France.

1912 **Falcon, G. W. L.** (Oct. 1914). Lt. 11th E. Surrey Regt., attd. 2nd Hampshire Regt. Gallipoli. Killed in action at Krithia on Aug. 6, 1915.

1885 Farmer, G. W. S., B.M., M.A., M.Ch. Capt. R.A.M.C. (Brisbane).

1901 Farrer, H. M., M.A. (Oct. 1, 1914). Lt. R.N.V.R. Maj. General List; D.A.Q.M.G. Egypt, Gallipoli, France. *D.* France, 1918.

1907 Farrer,* S. J. (Oct. 1914). Lt. 12th R. Sussex Regt. (Capt.). France, 1916–19. *D.* France, 1916.

1890 Faunthorpe, J. C. (Sept. 1914). Lt.-Col., Special Lists. G.S.O. 2. Intelligence G.H.Q., France. France, Belgium. *C.B.E.* (Civil). *M.C.*, Jan. 1, 1917. V.D. *D.* France, 1915.

1903 [Feiling, K. G., M.A.] (Dec. 30, 1914). Capt. 3rd The Black Watch. Capt. A.H.Q., India. India, 1916–19. *O.B.E.* (Mil.).

1913 **Fellowes, R. C. B.** (Aug. 1914). Lt. Somerset L.I. Capt. General List. Capt. Coldstream Guards. France. Killed in action near Moyenville on Aug. 21, 1918.

1905 Field, G. C., B.Sc., M.A. (Sept. 10, 1914). Lt. 8th R. Warwickshire Regt. attd. War Office (Capt.). France. (Prisoner of War in Germany.)

1902 Field, H. St. J. (Oct. 8, 1914). ‡Lt. R.G.A. (S.R.). France, 1918–19.

1874 Findlay, R. E., M.A. (Mobilized July 25, 1915). Maj. Q.O.R. Glasgow Yeomanry. T.D. *D.* § Feb. 1917.

1905 **Findlay,* R. S.**, B.A. (Mobilized Aug. 1914). Capt. 9th Arg. & Suth'd Highlanders. France, 1915. Killed in railway accident at Gretna on May 22, 1915.

1908 **Finlay, E. N. A.**, M.A. (Apr. 1915). 2nd Lt. 16th Rifle Brigade. France, Belgium, 1916. Killed in action near Festubert on July 4, 1916.

1907 Fisher, E. A., B.Sc. (Jan. 4, 1915). Lt. R.G.A. (empld. on Anti-Aircraft duties).

1891 Flemmich, A. H., B.A. (June 15, 1915). Capt. R.A.S.C. France, 1915–18.

1899 Flemmich, M. D., M.A. (May 31, 1915). Capt. R.A.S.C. East Africa, 1917–19.

1910 **Fletcher,* R. W.**, B.A. (Aug. 4, 1914). 2nd Lt. R.F.A. France, Belgium. Killed in action at Veldhoek on Oct. 31, 1914.

1906 **Fletcher,* W. G.**, M.A. (Aug. 6, 1914). 2nd Lt. 2nd R. Welsh Fusiliers. France, Belgium. *D.* France, 1914, 1915. Killed in action near Bois Grenier on Mar. 20, 1915.

1914 Flint, W. W. (Mar. 1918). 1st Lt. Q.M. Corps, U.S. Army. France.

1903 Forbes, N., M.A. (Oct. 1, 1917). Lt. R.N.V.R. Salonika, 1918.

1877 Fowler, H. W., M.A. (Apr. 1915). Pte. 30th R. Fusiliers. France, 1915–16.

1898 Fox, A. D. (Nov. 29, 1915). ‡Lt. Labour Corps. France, Belgium, 1917–19.

1917 Franklin, A. V. (May 1, 1918). ‡2nd Lt. R.G.A. (on demobilization).

1883 Fraser, C. J. R., B.A. (Sept. 24, 1914). Capt. Manchester Regt. Capt. Labour Corps.

1919 Freeman, R. E. (June 7, 1916). Lt. 180th Bde. R.F.A. France.

1891 Fremantle, F. E., B.M., M.Ch., M.A. (Mobilized Aug. 6, 1914). Lt.-Col. R.A.M.C., D.A.D. of Medical Services. Gallipoli, Egypt, Mesopotamia. *O.B.E.* (Mil.). *D.* Mesopotamia, 1918, 1919.

1909 Fry, H. K., B.Sc. (Aug. 20, 1914). Lt.-Col. Australian A.M.C. (Col.). Egypt, 1914–15, 1916; Gallipoli, 1915; France, 1916–18, 1919. *D.S.O.*, Jan. 1, 1917. *D.* France, 1916, 1917.

1900 Fulford, H. E., M.A. (Nov. 3, 1914). Maj. R.A.S.C. France, Italy. *O.B.E.* (Mil.). Croce di Guerra. *D.* France, 1917; Italy, 1918, 1919.

1913 Fullerton-Carnegie, G. D. H. (Jan. 29, 1915). Lt., Acting Capt., 7th The Black Watch. 2nd Class Agent, Intelligence Corps (graded as Staff-Lt., 1st Class). France. *M.C.*, Jan. 14, 1916. *D.* France, 1915, 1916.

1906 Furse, R. D., B.A. (Mobilized Aug. 4, 1914). Maj. 1st Regt. King Edward's Horse. France, 1915–17; Italy, 1917; France, 1918. *D.S.O.*, July 26, 1918; *Bar*, Mar. 8, 1919. *D.* France, 1918, 1919.

1917 Fyfe, D. P. M. (July 4, 1918). 2nd Lt. Scots Guards.

1909 Fyson, C., M.A. (Mobilized Aug. 1914). Lt. 3rd Worcestershire Regt. France, 1914–15.

1910 Galbraith, V. H., M.A. (Jan. 19, 1915). Lt. 5th Queen's (R. W. Surrey Regt.) (Capt.). Palestine, France. Croix de Guerre.

1918 Gallop, C., B.C.L. (May 11, 1916). Pte. A.V.C.

1913 Galpin, P. C. (May 10, 1917). Capt. Field Artillery, U.S. Army. France, 1917–19. Chevalier de l'Ordre de la Couronne.

1903 Gamlen, J. C. B., M.A. (Oct. 1914). Lt. 1/4th Oxf. & Bucks. Lt. Infty. (Staff Capt.). France, Belgium, 1916–17; Italy, 1917–19. *M.C.*, June 3, 1919.

1906 **Gardiner, E. H.,** M.A. (July 1915). Lt. 1/7th Cheshire Regt. Egypt and Palestine, 1916–18; France, Belgium, 1918. Died on Oct. 7, 1918, of wounds received in action at Menin.

1898 **Gathorne-Hardy, A. C.,** B.A. (Sept. 5, 1914). Capt. 9th Cameronians. France. Killed in action at the Battle of Loos on Sept. 25, 1915.

1919 Gatliff, H. E. C. (Jan. 15, 1917). 2nd Lt. 5th Coldstream Guards.

1899 Gere, R. H., B.A. (Nov. 4, 1914). ‡Lt. K.O. Scottish Borderers (Capt.). France, Egypt.

1903 Gibbon, Rev. H. H., M.A. (Nov. 30, 1914). Chaplain to the Forces (2nd Class). France. *O.B.E.* (Mil.). *D.* France, 1918.

1907 **Gibson,* R.,** M.A. (Mobilized Aug. 4, 1914). Capt. 3rd, attd. 2nd, K.O. Scottish Borderers. France and Belgium. *D.* France, 1915. Killed in action at Hill 60 on May 5, 1915.

1911 **Gilmour, A. K.** (Aug. 1914). ‡Capt. 7th K.O. Scottish Borderers. France. Killed in action on the Somme on Aug. 15, 1916.

1911 Glover, C. H., M.A. (Oct. 1914). Lt. 10th Middlesex Regt. Lt. Intelligence Corps. France, Belgium. *D.* France, 1918.

1915 **Glover, R. H.** (Apr. 1916). 2nd Lt. R.F.A. France, Belgium. Died on Sept. 25, 1917, of wounds received in action.

1874 [Godley, A. D., M.A., Hon. D.Litt.] (Aug. 1914). Lt.-Col. 2nd Vol. Bn. Oxf. & Bucks. Lt. Infty. *O.B.E.* (Mil.). *D.* § Mar. 1919.

1892 Godwin, G. H. (1917). Sergt. R.A.F. ‡2nd Lt. Special Lists, attd. Army General and Commercial College, Cologne. Italy, 1917–19; Germany, 1919.

1896 Goldsmith, E. T., B.Sc. (Serving Aug. 4, 1914). Instructor Commdr. R.N.

1899 Goodwin, F. S., M.A. (Serving Aug. 4, 1914). Major Emanuel School, Wandsworth, O.T.C., empld. War Office.

1901 Gordon-Walker, A. L., B.A. (Nov. 1916). Capt. General List (Lt.-Col.). (Military Governor and Political Officer, Basrah.) Mesopotamia. *D.* Mesopotamia.

1903 Gorell, Lord, M.A. (May 29, 1915). Capt. General List. Col. Deputy Director of Staff Duties, War Office. France and Belgium. *C.B.E.* (Mil.) *M.C.*, Jan. 1, 1917. *D.* France, 1918.

1899 **Goschen, C. G.** (Sept. 1914). Capt. Grenadier Guards (S.R.), attd. 4th Bn. France, Belgium. Killed in action at Lesbœufs on Sept. 25, 1916.

1885 Goschen, Viscount G. J., v.d. (Sept. 1914). Lt.-Col. 2/5th The Buffs (E. Kent Regt.) (Hon. Col.). (Served under Board of Agriculture since June 1917.) *C.B.E* (Civil)..

1913 **Gough, H. S.** (Nov. 24, 1914). 2nd Lt. 11th K.R.R.C. France and Belgium. Killed in action near Ypres on June 16, 1916.

1909 Govare, J. P. (Aug. 4, 1914). ‡2nd Lt. Infantry Corps, French Army. France. Croix de Guerre. Médaille du Mérite Militaire. *D.* French Despatches.

1913 Gover, W., B.M. (Dec. 18, 1917). Surgeon Lt. R.N. H.M.S. *Fearless.*

1919 Gradwell, J. L. A. (Sept. 24, 1917). Midshipman R.N.V.R. H.M.S. *Lochinvar.*

1901 Graham, A. K. (Apr. 5, 1915). Lt. Lothians & Border Horse. Lt. M.G.C. (Cavalry). France, 1915; Salonika, 1915–17; France, 1918.

1900 Grant, C. F. (May 7, 1915). Capt. I.A.R.O., attd. 170th Burma Rifles. Persia, 1915–17; Mesopotamia, 1918; Palestine, 1918–19.

1894 Grant, W. L., M.A. (June 26, 1915). Maj. 5th Canadian Reserve Bn., C.E.F. France until 1917.

1914 **Graves, A. H.** (Dec. 24, 1914). Capt. 8th Norfolk Regt. Capt. M.G.C. France, Belgium, 1916–18. *M.C.*, Aug. 25, 1916; *Bar*, Aug. 25, 1917. Killed in action on Mar. 22, 1918.

1889 Graves, H., B.A. (Nov. 1914). Capt. 6th Suffolk Regt. France.

1899 Green, C. J. S., B.A. (Mobilized Aug. 4, 1914). Lt.-Col. 7th London Regt. France, 1915–18, 1919. *D.S.O.*, June 4, 1917. *M.C.*, June 3, 1916. Belgian Croix de Guerre. *D.* France, 1915, 1917 twice, 1918.

1909 **Grenfell,* Hon. G. W.** (Sept. 14, 1914). 2nd Lt. 8th Rifle Brigade. France and Belgium. Killed in action near Hooge on July 30, 1915.

1906 **Grenfell, Hon. J. H. F.** (Serving Aug. 4, 1914). Capt. 1st R. Dragoons. France and Belgium, 1914–15. *D.S.O.*, Jan. 1, 1915. *D.* France, 1914, 1915. Died at Boulogne on May 26, 1915, of wounds received in action near Ypres.

1913 Grey-Edwards, H. B. R., B.A. (Nov. 9, 1914). Lt. R.A. Maj. R.A.F. France. *M.C.*, Oct. 29, 1915. *D.* France, 1915.

1908 Griffith, F. K., M.A. (Aug. 15, 1914). Capt. 3rd Lincolnshire Regt. 1st Class Asst. Instructor. France, 1914–18. *M.C.*, Oct. 18, 1917.

1898 [Griffith, I. O., M.A.] (Sept. 5, 1915). Maj. Technical Officer, R.A.F. *A.F.C.*, Nov. 2, 1918.

1858 Grove, Sir C., B.A., *K.C.B.* Col. E. Yorkshire Regt. Maj.-Gen. Ret. Pay. *D.*

1910 Grove, E. T. N., B.A. (Sept. 14, 1914). Capt. R. Bucks. Hussars, attd. Egyptian Army. Gallipoli, Egypt, Central Africa.

1919 Guerrier, K. J. (Apr. 7, 1917). 2nd Lt. 2nd Rifle Brigade. France, 1918.

1919 Gundry, R. E. (May 8, 1916). Lt. 8th Middlesex Regt. Belgium, France, 1917.

Guthrie, C. W. (Mar. 28, 1917). 2nd Lt. R. Scots. France. Missing, believed killed in action in France on Aug. 1, 1917.

1911 **Haldane,* R. P.** (Aug. 12, 1914). Lt. 6th The Black Watch. France. Died on June 14, 1915, of wounds received in action in France.

1911 **Hall,* R. H.** (Sept. 1914). ‡Capt. and Adjt. R.F.A. France, Belgium. Died on July 11, 1917, of wounds received in action in Belgium.

1891 Hallifax, H. F. (Feb. 18, 1915). Capt. Special Lists. Capt. and Adjt. 20th Deccan Horse. France, Egypt, India.

1894 Hallifax, H. W., B.A. (Sept. 15, 1914). ‡Lt. 147th Army Troops Coy., R.E. B.E. Africa, Egypt, France. *D.* France, 1919.

1901 Hallward, B. M., B.A. (Sept. 14, 1914). Lt. 6th Rifle Brigade. (Maj. Special Service in Russia.) Russia. *D.S.O.*, June 4, 1917. *D.* § July, 1917; Russia, 1919.

1905 Hamilton, G. M., M.A. (Mar. 23, 1915). Maj. Special Lists. Graves Registration Commission. France. *D.* France, 1917.

1919 Hamilton, P. M. (Mar. 29, 1915). Sergt. 4th Australian Light Horse Field Ambulance. Egypt, 1915; Sinai, 1916; Palestine, 1917–18; Syria, 1918. *D.* Egypt, 1917.

1913 **Hamilton-Fletcher, G.** (Sept. 19, 1914). 2nd Lt. 3rd Grenadier Guards, attd. 1st Scots Guards. France. Killed in action at Givenchy-lez-la-Bassée on Jan. 25, 1915.

1919 Handford, S. A. (Oct. 10, 1917). 2nd Lt. Labour Corps. France, 1918–19.

1903 **Handyside, J.,** M.A. (July 8, 1915). 2nd Lt. 18th King's (Liverpool Regt.). France. Died on Oct. 18, 1916, of wounds received in action on the Somme.

1894 Hankey, C. T. A., B.A. (Mobilized Aug. 4, 1914). Capt. 4th R. Sussex Regt. Staff Capt., Camp Commdt.

1919 Harford, J. D. (Aug. 10, 1917). Lt. 2nd Essex Regt., attd. 277 P.O.W. Camp. France.

1917 Harris, A. M. (July 25, 1918). 2nd Lt. R.G.A.

1889 Harrison, B. O. (Feb. 7, 1917). ‡2nd Lt. Special Lists. Staff Lt. (2nd Class). France.

1892 Harrison, C. W. (Serving Aug. 4, 1914). ‡2nd Lt. Malay Vol. Regt. British Malaya.

1887 Harrison, H. (Mar. 20, 1915). Lt. R. Irish Regt. France, Belgium, 1916–17. *O.B.E.* (Mil.). *M.C.*, Dec. 11, 1916; Bar, Feb. 18, 1918.

1897 Hartley, H. B., M.A. (Oct. 12, 1914). Capt. 7th Leicestershire Regt. Maj., Acting Lt.-Col., R.E. Temp. Brig.-Gen. Controller, Chemical Warfare Dept., Ministry of Munitions. France. *C.B.E.* (Mil.). *M.C.*, Jan. 1, 1916. *D.* France, 1915, 1918, 1919.

1915 Hartley, L. P. (Apr. 12, 1916). ‡2nd Lt. Norfolk Regt. (T.F.). (Invalided Sept. 1918.)

1910 Hartog,* D. H., B.A. (Sept. 2, 1914). Capt. 1/6th Gloucestershire Regt. D.A.P.M. France, Belgium, Italy. *M.C.*, Jan. 14, 1916. Croce di Guerra. *D.* France, 1915.

1903 Harvey, W. F., B.M., M.A. (Sept. 1914). Surgeon-Lt. R.N. France, Belgium, North Sea. Albert Medal, June 1918.

1912 Harwood, H. C. (Feb. 27, 1917). Lt. 1st (Res. Garr.) Bn. Suffolk Regt.

1914 **Hawkins, C. F.**, B.Sc. (1917). Lt. Chemical Warfare Dept., U.S. Army. Killed whilst doing experimental work on July 27, 1918.

1912 Hayhurst-France,* A. H., B.A. (Aug. 26, 1914). Lt. 4th Hussars. France. *M.C.*, Nov. 6, 1918.

1882 Head, H. F. (Serving Aug. 4, 1914). Lt.-Col. R.G.A. *D.* § Feb. 1917.

1898 Headlam, G. W., B.A. (Aug. 1914). 2nd Lt. 1st Coldstream Guards. France, 1917–18.

1894 Heathcote, W. J. (Jan. 1, 1915). 2nd Lt. Interpreter (1915–16.)

1908 **Heinemann, J. W.**, B.A. (Oct. 1914). Capt. 20th R. Fusiliers. France. Died on Mar. 6, 1916, of wounds received in action.

1905 Hely-Hutchinson, M. R., B.A. (Oct. 3, 1915). Lt. Irish Guards (Capt.). G.S.O. 3. France, 1916–18. *M.C.*, June 4, 1917. *D.* France, 1916.

1913 **Henderson, A. W.** (Aug. 26, 1914). Capt. Rifle Brigade. France. Killed in action in the battle of the Somme on July 2, 1916.

1893 Henderson, J. H., B.A. (May 17, 1917). Hon. Lt. Special Lists.

Henderson, T. H. (Jan. 20, 1915). Capt. and Adjt. 10th Rifle Brigade. France, Belgium. *M.C.*, Mar. 30, 1916; *Bar*, Sept. 26, 1917. *D.* France, 1917. Killed in action near Cambrai on Nov. 30, 1917.

1891 Henley, Hon. A. M., B.A. (Serving Aug. 4, 1914). Lt.-Col., Bt.-Col., 5th Lancers. Temp. Brig.-Gen. 127th Infantry Bde. France and Belgium, 1914–19. *C.M.G.*, Jan. 1, 1919. *D.S.O.*, June 3, 1916. *D.* France, 1915, 1916 twice, 1917 twice, 1918 twice, 1919.

1896 Henley, Hon. F. R., M.A. (Sept. 1914). Lt. R.N.D., R.N.V.R. Gallipoli. *D.* Gallipoli, 1916.

1885 Henniker, F. C. (Mar. 18, 1915). Capt. 1st Cambridgeshire Regt.

1898 Herbert, Hon. A. N. H. M., B.A., *M.P.* (Aug. 12, 1917). Capt. Irish Guards (S.R.). Temp. Lt.-Col. Chief of Military Mission to Albania. France, Salonika, Gallipoli, Mesopotamia, Albania. Order of the White Eagle (5th Class) (with swords).

1911 Herbert,* M. G. (Sept. 9, 1914). 2nd Lt. R. Wiltshire Yeomanry. Lt. Household Cavalry, empld. Guards M.G. Regt. France.

1897 **Herbert, R. Y.**, M.A. (July 8, 1915). Lt. R.F.A. France, Belgium. *D.* France, 1916. Killed in action at Wytschaete Wood on Sept. 23, 1917.

1908 Herbert, S. (Mobilized Aug. 4, 1914). Lt. R. Horse Guards. Capt. and Adjt. Guards M.G. Regt. France. *D.* France, 1918.

1912 **Herbertson, A. H.**, B.A. (Oct. 1914). Lt. K.R.R.C. (Capt.). France and Belgium. Killed in action at Chérisy on May 16, 1917.

1912 **Hewart,* G. M.** (Nov. 14, 1914). 2nd Lt. 6th Lincolnshire Regt. Gallipoli. Killed in action in Gallipoli on Aug. 9, 1915.

1911 **Hewett, S. H. P.** (Jan. 15, 1915). Lt. 13th R. Warwickshire Regt. France. Killed in action near Pozières on July 22, 1916.

1909 Hibbert, J. G., B.A. (Aug. 6, 1914). ‡Capt. R.A.O.C. (Maj.). D.A.D. of Ordnance Services. France, Belgium. *M.C.*, Jan. 1, 1917. *D.* France, 1917.

1914 Hickey, J. S. (Oct. 8, 1915). Lt. R.N.V.R. North Sea, Atlantic.

1893 Hide, P., M.A. Sergt. I.D.F., empld. Training School for Indian Cadets. India.

1919 Higgins, E. M. (Dec. 19, 1917). Gunner 6th F.A. Bde., A.I.F. (Cpl.). France.

1897 Higgins, G. H., B.C.L., M.A. (Nov. 2, 1914). Capt. Queen's (R.W. Surrey Regt.) (Lt.-Col.). Capt. General List. France. *D.* France, 1919.

1906 **Higgins, M. B.,** B.A. (Nov. 4, 1914). ‡Capt. and Adjt. 8th Australian Light Horse. Gallipoli, Egypt, Sinai, 1915–16. *D.* Egypt, 1917. Killed in action at El Magdhaba on Dec. 23, 1916.

1907 **Higginson,* T. A.,** B.A. (Aug. 1914). Capt. 6th Shropshire L.I. France. Accidentally killed in France on Sept. 19, 1915.

1896 **Hill, C. P.,** B.A. (Sept. 1914). Capt. 4th, attd. 1st, N. Staffordshire Regt. Belgium and France, 1915–16. Killed in action at Guillemont on Aug. 19, 1916.

1891 Hill, G. R., M.A. (Mar. 1916). Capt. Administrative Branch, R.A.F.

1920 Hill, J. C. (Jan. 28, 1918). Flight Cadet, 52nd Sqdn., R.A.F.

1885 Hills, J. W., B.A., *M.P.* (Oct. 5, 1914). Maj. 4th Durham L.I. (Lt.-Col.). France, Belgium. *D.* France, 1916.

1913 **Hitchcock, H. W.** (Mar. 27, 1915). Lt. M.G.C. France. Killed in action on Nov. 13, 1916.

1873 Hoare, A. F., M.A., *C.B.*, V.D. (Mobilized Aug. 4, 1914). Hon. Col. Haileybury O.T.C. Maj. Hertfordshire Regt. (T.F. Res.).

1900 Hodges, T. O. (Apr. 1, 1917). 2nd Lt. Madras Volunteer Guards, I.D.F.

1895 [Hodgkin, R. H., M.A.] (Dec. 11, 1914). Capt. 7th Northumberland Fusiliers, empld. War Office.

1919 Hoggan, R. (June 1916). Lt. R.G.A. (S.R.). France and Belgium, 1917–19.

1883 Hole, H. Marshall, B.A. (Jan. 20, 1915). Lt.-Col. 4th Norfolk Regt., attd. Administrative Staff Northern Command. France. *D.* § Aug. 1919.

1920 Holliday, G. C. (Jan. 31, 1918). 2nd Lt. 2/5th Lancashire Fusiliers. France 1918–19.

Hollins, W. H. (Sept. 2, 1914). 2nd Lt. 8th Sherwood Foresters. France. Killed in action on June 15, 1916.

1913 Hollway, C. R. (Nov. 27, 1914). 2nd Lt. K.R.R.C. Staff Lt. (2nd Class) R.T.O. France, 1915–16; Italy, 1917–19.

1898 **Holmes, A.,** M.A. (Aug. 31, 1914). ‡Lt. 2nd Essex Regt. France. Killed in action at Beaumont Hamel on July 1, 1916.

1888 Holmes, Rev. F. W. R., M.A. (Jan. 1916). Chaplain to the Forces (4th Class). Gibraltar.

1909 Holmes,* H. C., M.A. (Sept. 8, 1914). Lt. Irish Guards. Staff Capt. Camp Commdt. (Maj.). France.

1909 Holmes, H. W., M.A. (Aug. 30, 1914). ‡Lt. R.A.F. France.

1904 Holmes, M. G., B.A. (Sept. 15, 1914). Maj. R.A.S.C. (Lt.-Col.). France, Belgium, Egypt, and Palestine. *O.B.E.* (Mil.). Order of the Nile (4th Class). *D.* Egypt, 1916; Palestine, 1919.

1913 Hope, T., B.A. (Apr. 26, 1915). Pte. R.A.M.C. (Lce.-Cpl.). France, 1917–19.

1919 Hopkins, C. (Aug. 27, 1917). 2nd Lt. 302nd Machine Gun Bn., U.S. Army. France.

1910 Hopkins,* G. W. S., B.A. (Oct. 14, 1914). Capt. 5th R. Warwickshire Regt., attd. T. M. B. France, Belgium, 1916–18. *M.C.*, Jan. 1, 1917. (Prisoner of War, Mar.–Nov. 1918.)

1907 Hornby, Rev. H. L., M.A. (Oct. 2, 1914). Chaplain to the Forces (3rd Class), attd. 2nd Div. France. *M.C.*, July 27, 1916. *D.* France, 1916.

1912 **Hornby, W.** (Sept. 1914). ‡2nd Lt. 17th King's (Liverpool Regt.). France, 1915–16. Killed in action near Flers on Oct. 12, 1916.

1906 **Horner, E. W.** (Aug. 1914). Lt. 18th Hussars. France, Egypt. Died on Nov. 21, 1917, of wounds received in action at Noyelles, near Cambrai.

1919 Horsley, H. M. (Sept. 14, 1916). Lt. R.G.A. (S.R.). France, 1917–18.

1918 Howard, S. G. (Apr. 22, 1916). Lt. R.A.F.

1914 Howell, C. H. (Dec. 13, 1915). Lt. R.A.F. France.

1912 **Hoyle, B. W. E.** (Sept. 1914). Capt. 9th R. Welch Fusiliers. France. Killed in action at Festubert on Sept. 25, 1915.

1919 Hudson, B. M. M. (Aug. 9, 1914). ‡Capt. 1st County of London Yeomanry. Lemnos and Egypt, 1915; Salonika, 1917; Egypt, 1917; Palestine, 1918–19.

1919 Hughes, H. B. L. (Sept. 1917). 2nd Lt. R.G.A. (S.R.).

1919 Hughes-Hughes, E. P. A. de B. (Feb. 12, 1916). Lt. Welsh Guards, attd. Guards M.G. Regt. (Capt.). France, Belgium, Germany, 1917–18.

1907 **Hulse, Sir E. H. W.,** B.A. (Serving Aug. 4, 1914). Lt., Acting Capt., 2nd Scots Guards. Belgium, France, 1914–15. *D.* France, 1915. Killed in action at Neuve Chapelle on Mar. 14, 1915.

1897 Hunt, A. P., B.A. (Dec. 12, 1917). 2nd Lt. Unattached List, T.F., Sheffield Univ. O.T.C. (O.C.).

1899 Hunt, C. B., M.A. (Oct. 25, 1915). Lt. 2/4th Oxf. & Bucks. Lt. Infty. France, 1916–17. (Wounded and Prisoner of War, 1917–18.)

1893 Hunt, E. H., B.M., M.A., M.Ch. (Serving Aug. 4, 1914). Surgeon-Maj. 26th Hyderabad Volunteer Rifles, I.D.F. India.

1903 Hunt, J. W. B., B.A. (Jan. 19, 1915). Capt. M.G.C. and Lincolnshire Yeomanry. France. *D.* France, 1915.

1892 Hunter, J. L., B.A. (Sept. 12, 1914). 2nd Lt. 12th K.R.R.C., empld. in Food Production Dept. (Capt.). France.

1904 **Hunter, J. M.**, B.A. (Dec. 1914). 2nd Lt. 6th Wiltshire Regt. France. Killed in action at La Boisselle on July 3, 1916.

1888 Hunter, W. C. (Mobilized Aug. 2, 1914). Capt. Oxf. & Bucks. Lt. Infty. (Res. of Officers), temp. Lt.-Col. Prisoners of War Camp. France. *D.* France, 1916.

1907 Hunter-Blair, J., B.A. (Mar. 13, 1915). Lt. 3rd Seaforth Highlanders, attd. R.E. (Army Signals).

1913 Huxley, G. (Aug. 15, 1914). Capt. 3rd E. Yorkshire Regt., attd. Intelligence Corps. France, Belgium, 1914–18. *M.C.*, June 3, 1919. *D.* France, 1917.

1906 [Huxley, J. S., M.A.] (Apr. 1917). 2nd Lt. A.S.C. 2nd Lt. Intelligence Corps (Staff Lt.). Italy.

1919 Impey, M. E. (Sept. 16, 1914). Sub-Lt. R.N.D. Antwerp, 1914. (Interned in Holland, 1914–18.)

1909 Irby, G. N. (Apr. 15, 1915). Capt. Bucks. Bn. Oxf. & Bucks. Lt. Infty. (Invalided Jan. 8, 1918.)

1894 Irving, M., B.A. (Feb. 20, 1917). Capt., temp. Lt.-Col., I.A.R.O.; A.A.G. India. *O.B.E.* (Mil.). *D.* India, 1918.

1919 Isaac, W. R. M. (Apr. 28, 1915). Lt. R.F.A. France, 1915–16, 1917.

1912 [Jacks, M. L., M.A.] (Nov. 24, 1914). Lt. K.R.R.C. Acting Capt. No. 4 O.C.B. France, 1915–16.

1919 Jacks, S. B. L. (July 1915). Maj. 'D' Batt., 165th Bde., R.F.A. Egypt, France. *M.C.*, Dec. 11, 1916.

1905 Jackson, B. H. (Sept. 15, 1914). Maj. Leicester R.H.A. Egypt, Palestine, Syria. *M.C.*, Jan. 1, 1918. *D.* Palestine, 1917.

1919 Jackson, F. H. (Aug. 15, 1914). Lt. 3rd R. Sussex Regt. Lt. R.A.F. France. (Interned in Holland, July 1918 to Jan. 1919.)

1913 **Jackson,* G. L.** (Aug. 4, 1914). Capt. 1st Rifle Brigade. France, Belgium. *D.* France, 1915. Killed in action near Fampoux on Apr. 9, 1917.

1919 Jackson, L. N. (Feb. 1, 1917). Lt. 46th Bde., R.F.A. France, 1917–19. *M.C.*, Jan. 1, 1919. *D.* France, 1919.

1913 **James,* B. A.** (Aug. 1914). Capt. 13th Middlesex Regt. France, Belgium. Killed in action near Guillemont on Aug. 18, 1916.

1919 James, B. C. L. (Oct. 9, 1918). Cadet R.A.F.

1896 Jameson, J. G., B.A. (Sept. 20, 1914). Capt., temp. Maj., 2nd Scottish Horse. Capt. Labour Corps. France.

1890 Jeffrey, R., B.A. (Feb. 4, 1915). Lt. 2/1st Lothians and Border Horse. Capt. M.G.C. France, Belgium, 1916–17, 1918.

1911 **Jenkins, A. L.** (Aug. 1914). ‡Lt. D.C.L.I., attd. R.F.C. India, 1914–15; Aden, 1916; Palestine and Egypt, 1917. Killed on duty, whilst flying in Yorkshire on Dec. 31, 1917.

1907 Jenkins, Rev. C., M.A. (Jan. 28, 1916). Chaplain to the Forces (4th Class), attd. 60th (London) Div. France, Salonika, Palestine, Egypt.

1919 Jenkins, D. Ll. (Feb. 7, 1918). 2nd Lt. 12th Rifle Brigade. France, 1918–19.

1914 Jenkins, E. M. (Dec. 16, 1914). ‡Lt. I.A.R.O., attd. 1/91st Punjabi L.I. (Capt.). France, 1915; Salonika, 1915–17; India and Burma, 1917–18; Palestine, 1918–19.

1901 Jenkyns, S. S., M.A. (Dec. 11, 1914). Capt. 6th Rifle Brigade. Acting Lt.-Col. 9th N. Staffordshire Regt. France, 1915, 1916, 1917–18. *M.C.*, June 3, 1918.

1908 Jenness, D., B.A. (Apr. 1917). Pte. Canadian Corps Survey Section (Cpl.). France, Belgium, and Germany, 1917–19.

1895 Jervis-Smith, E. J. (Serving Aug. 4, 1914). Maj. 3 C Res. Bde., R.F.A. (Aldershot Command). India. *D.* § Aug. 1919.

1910 Jessel, G., M.A. (Aug. 22, 1914). Capt. 5th The Buffs (E. Kent Regt.). India, Mesopotamia. *M.C.*, Dec. 22, 1916. *D.* Mesopotamia, 1916.

1920 Jessel, R. W. A. (Nov. 1917). †Lt. 4th R. Sussex Regt. Belgium, Germany, 1918–19.

1912 **John, I. G.** (Apr. 12, 1915). 2nd Lt. 1st S. Wales Borderers. France. Killed in action at Loos on Feb. 25, 1916.

1897 Johnston, C. E. L., B.A. (Serving Aug. 4, 1914). Maj. R.A., temp. Lt.-Col. Indian Ordnance Dept. Asst. Director of Ordnance Stores Section. India.

1913 Johnstone, H., B.A. (June 16, 1915). Lt. Rifle Brigade (Capt.).

1882 **Jones, Rev. A. W.** (Feb. 1, 1916). Lt. R.A.M.C. (Invalided 1916.) Died on Dec. 4, 1917.

1901 Jones, B. M., M.A. (Sept. 2, 1914). ‡Lt.-Col. Special Lists. Director, Central Laboratory, G.H.Q. France. *D.S.O.*, June 3, 1917. *D.* France, 1916 twice, 1917.

1905 Jones, E. H. (July 7, 1915). ‡2nd Lt. I.A.R.O. Mesopotamia, 1915–16. (Taken prisoner by the Turks at the fall of Kut.)

Jones, H. P. M. (Apr. 15, 1915). 2nd Lt. A.S.C. Lt. M.G.C. France and Belgium. Killed in action in France on July 31, 1917.

1904 Jones, L. E., B.A. (Mobilized Aug. 1914). Capt. Bedfordshire Yeomanry. Temp. Maj. 19th Bn. M.G.C. France, Belgium, 1915–18. *M.C.*, Dec. 2, 1918. *D.* France, 1916, 1917. (Wounded and Prisoner of War, Mar.–Nov. 1918.)

1919 Jones, W. M. (Sept. 24, 1914). ‡2nd Lt. R.F.A. Egypt, 1914–15 ; Gallipoli, 1915 ; France, 1916–17.

1913 **Joseph, C. G. J.** (Aug. 1914). 2nd Lt. London Regt. Died Oct. 1914.

1908 **Kay-Shuttleworth,* Hon. E. J.**, B.A. (Aug. 20, 1914). Capt. Rifle Brigade. Staff Capt. 218th Inf. Bde. France, Belgium, 10 months. *D.* § Feb. 1917. Accidentally killed at Witham on July 10, 1917.

1906 **Kay-Shuttleworth,* Hon. L. U.**, B.A. (Feb. 1, 1915). Capt. and Adjt. 11th Bde., R.F.A. France, Belgium. *D.* France, 1915. Killed in action at Vimy Ridge on Mar. 30, 1917.

1883 Keeling, J. H., M.A. (Dec. 27, 1914). Capt. 5th London Regt. (London Rifle Brigade), attd. R.E.

1908 **Keen, W. A.**, B.A. (Jan. 31, 1915). Capt. 7th Middlesex Regt., attd. 12th Somerset L.I. Egypt, Palestine, France. Died on Sept. 6, 1918, of wounds received in action at Moislains on Sept. 2.

1900 **Kelly, F. S.**, M.A. (Aug. 1914). ‡Lt.-Commdr. R.N.V.R., Hood Bn. R.N.D. Gallipoli, France. *D.S.C.*, 1916. *D.* Gallipoli, 1915. Killed in action at Beaucourt-sur-Ancre on Nov. 13, 1916.

1897 Kennaway, Sir J., Bt., M.A. (Aug. 4, 1914). Capt. 1/4th Devonshire Regt. India, Mesopotamia.

1901 Kennedy, G. L. (May 26, 1916). Lt., Acting Capt., R.G.A. France. *D.* France, 1917.

1909 Ker, E., M.A. (Sept. 1, 1914). Lt. 5th Highland L.I., attd. R.E. for Army Signal Service. North Russia.

1911 **Ker,* W.** (Aug. 1914). Lt. R.N.V.R., Hawke Bn. R.N.D. Gallipoli, France. Killed in action at Beaucourt-sur-Ancre on Nov. 13, 1916.

1905 Kermack, W. R., B.A. (Mobilized Aug. 1914). Capt. 1/7th R. Scots. Gallipoli, Egypt and Palestine, France and Belgium. *M.C.*, Mar. 26, 1918. *D.* Palestine, 1917 ; France, 1919.

1890 Kerry, Earl of, M.A., *D.S.O.*, *M.V.O.* (Serving Aug. 4, 1914). Maj. Irish Guards, Res. of Officers (Lt.-Col.). G.S.O. 2, Dept. of C.I.G.S., War Office. *D.* § Feb. 1917.

1895 Kershaw, P. S. (Sept. 20, 1914). Lt. R.N.D. Capt. R.A.F. Gallipoli, France.

1912 King, W. A. H., B.A. (Dec. 1914). Lt. 3rd R. Sussex Regt., attd. War Office.

1898 Kingan, T. D., M.A. (Nov. 13, 1914). Lt., Acting Capt., 13th R. Irish Rifles. France, Belgium.

1919 Kingdon, H. E. (May 15, 1916). Cpl. 11th R. Scots Fusiliers, attd. Army Pay Corps. France, 1918–19.

1889 Kinross, Lord, B.A. (Mar. 1915). Maj. Special Lists (Claims Commission). France. Chevalier de l'Ordre du Mérite Agricole. *D.* France, 1918.

1895 Kitto, J. V., B.A. (June 3, 1915). Capt. and Adjt. R.G.A. (S.R.). *D.* § Feb. 1919.

1918 Knapp, C. P. C. (Sept. 7, 1914). ‡2nd Lt. 7th King's (Liverpool Regt.). France, 1915–16.

1907 **Knatchbull-Hugessen, M. A.** (Oct. 1914). ‡Lt. Grenadier Guards (S.R.), attd. 2nd Bn. France. *M.C.*, Nov. 18, 1915. *D.* France, 1915. Killed in action in the Battle of Loos on Sept. 25, 1916.

1910 Knight,* G. N., M.A. (Aug. 14, 1914). Capt. 7th E. Surrey Regt., attd. War Office. France, 1915.

1901 **Kylie, E. J.**, M.A. (Aug. 6, 1914). Capt. and Adjt. C.E.F. France. Died on May 14, 1916, of illness contracted while on active service.

1907 **Lacaita,* F. C.**, B.A. (Serving Aug. 4, 1914). Lt. 17th Lancers. Capt. M.G.C. France. *M.C.*, Mar. 3, 1917. Killed in action near Hamel-sur-Somme on Apr. 4, 1918.

1913 Lacey, W. G. (Oct. 8, 1914). Lt. Bedfordshire Regt. Lt. M.G.C. France, 1916, 1918.

1906 Laffan,* Rev. R. G. D., M.A. (Sept. 26, 1914). Chaplain to the Forces (4th Class), attd. A.S.C., with Serbian Army. Salonika, 1916–18. Serbian Order of St. Sava, 4th Class (1918); 3rd Class (1919).

1919 Lance, A. E. (Jan. 1916). Maj. Maltese Mining Coy., R.E. France and Italy. *D.* France, 1918.

1917 Landreth, S. (June 29, 1917). ‡2nd Lt. Northumberland Fusiliers.

1912 Lane, K. W., B.A. (July 12, 1915). Lt. 3/2nd S. Midland Bde., R.F.A., empld. Ministry of Munitions. France, 1915–16.

1887 Latham, A. C., D.M. (Serving Aug. 4, 1914). Capt. R.A.M.C.

1913 Latham, P. M. S., M.A. (Oct. 27, 1914). Lt. 2/5th Hampshire Regt. India, 1915; Egypt, 1917, 1918; Palestine, 1917–18.

1919 Lavin, G. E. (Jan. 5, 1918). 2nd Lt. R.A.F.

1874 Lawrence, E., B.A. (Nov. 13, 1914). Capt. 2/6th King's (Liverpool Regt.) (T.F. Res.).

1910 Lawrence, H. W. N. (Sept. 2, 1914). Lt. Coldstream Guards. France.

1877 Lawrence, Sir W. R., *G.C.I.E.* (Nov. 12, 1914). Col. Special Lists (Commissioner of Indian Hospitals). Hon. Col. R.A.F. (Maj.-Gen.). France. *G.C.V.O.*, *C.B.* *D.* § Jan. 1917. *D.* France, 1919.

1909 Lawson, E. F., B.A. (Mobilized Aug. 1914). Capt. R. Bucks. Hussars. Temp. Lt.-Col. 1st County of London Yeomanry. Gallipoli, Egypt, Syria. *D.S.O.*, Mar. 8, 1919. *M.C.*, Feb. 18, 1918. *D.* Gallipoli, 1916; Palestine, 1918.

1911 Layng,* T. M., B.A. (Serving Aug. 4, 1914). Capt. Indian Army, attd. 10th Jhats. France, 1914–15; Mesopotamia, 1916; India, 1919. *M.C.*, Jan. 14, 1916. *D.* France, 1915.

1913 **Leather,* J. F.** (Serving Aug. 4, 1914). Capt., Acting Maj., A.S.C., attd. 1/4th Shropshire L.I. Gallipoli, 1915; Belgium, France, 1916–18. *D.* France, 1917. Died on Oct. 16, 1918, of illness contracted while on active service,

1904 Le Breton, J. G. B., B.A. (Aug. 8, 1914). ‡Capt. 3rd King's African Rifles. German East Africa. *D.* East Africa, 1917.

1900 Lee, A. E. J. (May 26, 1915). Sub-Lt. R.N.V.R. (Relinquished Commission on grounds of ill health, June 15, 1916.)

1905 Lefroy, L. M., B.A. (Oct. 15, 1914). Lt. 5th R. Irish Regt. Capt. General

List. G.S.O. 3. Gallipoli, 1915; Italy, 1915; Salonika, 1915–18; Constantinople, 1918–19. *O.B.E.* (Mil.). *D.* Salonika, 1917, 1918.

1913 Legros, R. P. (Aug. 23, 1914). Mal. des Logis, Aviateur, Instructor on Aerial Gunnery, French Army. France.

1911 Leigh-Smith, P., M.A. (Sept. 15, 1914). Lt. Special Lists. Staff Lt. (2), Intelligence Corps. France. *D.* France, 1915.

1897 Leiper, R. J., B.A. (Oct. 20, 1915). Lt. (Interpreter) Q.O.R. Glasgow Yeomanry. North Russia, 1918–19. *D.* Murmansk, 1919.

1886 **Le Patourel, Rev. W. M.,** M.A. Chaplain, R.N., H.M.S. *Defence*. Grand Fleet. Killed in action at the Battle of Jutland on May 31, 1916.

1919 Leslie, A. A. (Aug. 11, 1915). Lt. R.F.A. France, 1916–17; Italy, 1918. *M.C.*, Jan. 1, 1918.

1912 Leslie-Melville, Hon. I., B.A. (Mobilized Aug. 1914). Capt. 2nd Lovat's Scouts. A.D.C. Gallipoli, 1915; Egypt, 1916; France, 1917–18.

1915 **Lester-Smith, H.** (Oct. 1915). ‡2nd Lt. 4th Cheshire Regt. Belgium. Killed in action at Wytschaete on July 14, 1917.

1885 Leveson-Gower, G. C. G., M.A. (Nov. 1914). Capt. (Hon. Maj.) W. Kent Yeomanry (T.F. Res.). *D.* § Feb. 1917.

1895 Lewis, N. Somers, B.A. (Oct. 13, 1915). ‡2nd Lt. 13th London Regt. (T.F. Res.). France.

1904 Lewis, P. T., B.A. ‡Lt., Acting Capt., R.F.A. (S.R.). Gallipoli, 1915; Egypt, 1916; France, 1916, 1917. *M.C.*, Oct. 20, 1916. *D.* France, 1916, 1917.

1885 Leycester-Penrhyn, A. L., M.A. (Oct. 14, 1914). Maj. 6th E. Surrey Regt., attd. R.A.F.

1918 Leys, D. G. (Oct. 8, 1914). Lt. 7th Bedfordshire Regt. Belgium, France.

1918 Leys, J. A. (Aug. 25, 1915). Lt. R.G.A. France, 1916.

1908 **Liddell, J. A.** (Serving Aug. 4, 1914). Capt. 3rd Arg. & Suth'd. Highlanders, attd. R.F.C. France and Belgium, 1914–15. *M.C.*, Feb. 18, 1915. *D.* France, 1914. Died on Aug. 31, 1915, of wounds received in action at La Panne, Belgium. **V.C.**

For most conspicuous bravery and devotion to duty on July 31, 1915.

When on a flying reconnaissance over Ostend–Bruges–Ghent he was severely wounded (his right thigh being broken), which caused momentary unconsciousness, but by a great effort he recovered partial control after his machine had dropped nearly 3,000 feet, and notwithstanding his collapsed state succeeded, although continually fired at, in completing his course, and brought the aeroplane into our lines—half an hour after he had been wounded.

The difficulties experienced by this officer in saving his machine, and the life of his observer, cannot be readily expressed, but as the control wheel and throttle control were smashed, and also one of the under-carriage struts, it would seem incredible that he could have accomplished his task.

1920 Lindon, L. C. E. (Feb. 8, 1915). Pte. Australian A.M.C., No. 1 Stationary Hospital (Cpl.). Egypt, Lemnos, Gallipoli, 1915–16.

1898 Lindsay,* A. D., M.A. (Oct. 1914). Lt.-Col. General List. Deputy Controller of Labour. France, 1917–19. *C.B.E.* (Mil.). *D.* France, 1919.

1907 Lindsay, T., B.A. (Oct. 2, 1918). Pte. 28th London Regt. (Artists Rifles O.T.C.).

1906 **Lister, Hon. C. A.** (Dec. 8, 1914). 2nd Lt. 1st County of London

Yeomanry. Lt. R. Marines (from Feb. 1915). Egypt, Gallipoli. *D.* Egypt, 1915. Died on Aug. 28, 1915, of wounds received in Gallipoli.

1898 Littlehailes, R., M.A. (Mobilized 1914). 2nd Lt. 1st Madras Guards, I.D.F. India.

1893 Lloyd-Goring, L. H., M.A. (Sept. 19, 1914). Capt. Special Lists, empld. as Draft-Conducting Officer. France, 1916–19.

1910 Lodge, W. J., B.A. (Oct. 9, 1914). Maj. R. Scots (Lt.-Col.).

1910 **Lowden, J. H.,** B.A. (June 1915). Lt. 7th S. African Infantry. German S.W. Africa, German E. Africa. *D.* E. Africa. Killed in action on Mar. 11, 1916.

1907 Lowther, A. J. B. (Aug. 6, 1914). Capt. 3rd Suffolk Regt. France. (Invalided, July 1917, on account of wounds.)

1911 **Lowy, W. A.** (Oct. 1914). Capt. 10th Hampshire Regt. Salonika, 1915–18. Died on Sept. 3, 1918, of wounds received in the Struma Valley.

1912 **Lubbock, Hon. E. F. P.,** B.A. (Sept. 1914). ‡Capt. A.S.C., attd. R.F.C. (Flight Comdr.). France, Belgium. *M.C.*, Nov. 18, 1915. *D.* France, 1915 twice. Killed in action near Ypres on Mar. 11, 1917.

1895 **Lucas and Dingwall, Rt. Hon. Lord,** B.A. (Mobilized 1915). Capt. Hampshire Yeomanry. Flight Comdr., R.F.C. Egypt, 1915–16; France, 1916. Order of Karageorge (4th Class) (with swords). *D.* Egypt, 1916. Killed in action in France on Nov. 3, 1916.

1885 Ludlow, Rt. Hon. Lord, M.A. (1917). Capt. Special Lists. Staff Lt. (3rd Class). France, Belgium.

1917 Ludlow, R. R. (Oct. 1, 1915). 2nd Lt. 7th D.C.L.I. France.

1893 Lushington, Rev. P. A., M.A. (Serving Aug. 4, 1914). Chaplain (4th Class), attd. A.S.C.

1901 Lusk, Rev. D. C., M.A. (Aug. 29, 1916). Chaplain to the Forces (4th Class), attd. 1/14th London Regt. (London Scottish). France, Belgium, Germany. *M.C.*, Jan. 1, 1918; *Bar*, Dec. 2, 1918. *D.* France, 1917.

1907 **Lyell, D.,** B.A. (Sept. 1914). 2nd Lt. 7th R. Scots. Egypt, Gallipoli. Killed in action in Gallipoli on July 12, 1915.

1905 **Lyon,* W. S. S.,** B.A. (Mobilized Aug. 4, 1914). Lt. 9th R. Scots. France and Belgium. Killed in action near Ypres on May 8, 1915.

1915 **Lyons, V. A.** (Jan. 2, 1916). 2nd Lt. 18th Highland L.I. Belgium, France. Died on Aug. 23, 1917, of wounds received in action in Belgium.

1887 McAlester, C. G., B.A. (Aug. 8, 1915). Lt.-Col. 3/5th R. Scots Fusiliers.

1894 Macaulay, T. C. (Mar. 10, 1915). Lt. R.A. Capt., Staff Officer, R.A.F. Gallipoli, Palestine. *M.C.*, May 31, 1916. *D.* Gallipoli, 1915; Palestine, 1918.

McCleave, H. A. Lt. 13th Canadian Infantry. France and Belgium. Died on Oct. 10, 1916, of wounds received in action.

1919 McDonald, J. R. (Aug. 8, 1917). Cadet R.G.A.

1912 **Macdonell, A. S.** (Sept. 14, 1914). 2nd Lt. 1st Q. O. Cameron Highlanders. France. Killed in action at Hulluch on Oct. 13, 1915.

1909 Macdonnell, H. W., B.A. (June 28, 1915). Capt. P.P.C.L.I., Canadian E.F. France. (Prisoner of War.)

1905 Macdonnell, J. M., B.A. (Aug. 8, 1914). Maj. Canadian Field Artillery. Bde. Maj. 3rd Canadian Divl. Artillery. France, Belgium. *M.C.*, June 4, 1917. Croix de Guerre. *D.* France, 1917.

1907 Macdonnell, N. S., B.A. (Aug. 13, 1914). Capt. 302nd Bde., R.F.A. (Maj.). France, 1915–16; Egypt, Palestine, 1917–18. *D.* France, 1916.
1919 McEwen, R. B. (Apr. 20, 1917). 2nd Lt. R.G.A. (T.F.), attd. R.A.F.
1912 **Macfarlane, A. H.** (Oct. 4, 1914). 2nd Lt. 9th R. Scots. France and Belgium. Killed in action near Ypres on May 12, 1915.
1919 McIntyre, J. G. (Oct. 1914). Capt. Ayrshire Yeomanry, attd. 12th R. Scots Fusiliers. Gallipoli, Egypt, Palestine, France. *M.C.*, Feb. 4, 1918; *Bar*, Nov. 6, 1918. Croix de Guerre.
1898 **Mackay, S. F. H.**, B.A. (Feb. 7, 1915). Capt. 5th E. Lancashire Regt. France. Died of wounds in a German Hospital, June 1917.
1912 **Mackenzie, I.** (Dec. 1914). Capt. and Adjt. 5th Seaforth Highlanders. France. *M.C.*, Feb. 4, 1918. Killed in action at Louverval on Mar. 21, 1918.
1901 **Mackenzie, K.**, M.A. (Oct. 4, 1914). Capt. 9th R. Scots (Maj.). France. Killed in action at Heuinel on Aug. 27, 1918.
1893 McKerron, R. G. (1916). Lt. Graves Registration Committee.
1905 **McLaren, Hon. F. W. S.**, B.A., *M.P.* (Sept. 1914). Lt. R.N.V.R. (Lt.-Comdr.). 2nd Lt. R.F.C. France, Belgium, Gallipoli, Egypt. Accidentally killed at Montrose on Aug. 30, 1917.
1905 MacLehose, H. A., B.A. (Mobilized Aug. 1914). Maj. 8th Cameronians. Gallipoli, 1915.
1908 **MacLehose,* N. C.**, B.A. (Mobilized Aug. 1914). Lt. 8th London Regt. (Post Office Rifles). Belgium, France. Killed in action at Festubert, May 26, 1915.
1906 MacLeod, A. R. (1917). Lt. R.G.A. France.
1904 Macmillan, D. de M., M.A. (Sept. 26, 1914). 2nd Lt. 14th K.R.R.C.
1912 Macmillan, M. H., B.A. (Nov. 19, 1914). Lt. Grenadier Guards.
1913 Macmurray, J. (Sept. 23, 1914). ‡2nd Lt. 7th Q.O. Cameron Highlanders. France, 1915–18. *M.C.*, Mar. 28, 1918.
1919 MacNeil, N. H. (Sept. 11, 1914). Lt. 16th Highland L.I. (Capt.). Lt. R.A.F. France. *M.C.*, Nov. 4, 1915. *D.* France, 1915.
1895 [McNeile, Rev. R. F., M.A.] (Oct. 1915). Chaplain to the Forces (4th Class). Egypt and Palestine, 1915–18.
1913 Madan, G. S. (Aug. 1914). ‡Capt. King's Own (R. Lancaster Regt.). Instructor, School of Trench Mortars. France, Germany, Italy, Egypt, Gallipoli, Salonika, Constantinople, Mesopotamia, India.
1899 Main, Rev. A., B.A. (July 8, 1918). Chaplain to the Forces (4th Class). France, Belgium, Germany.
1912 Malik, H. S., B.A. (Apr. 6, 1917). Lt. R.A.F. France, Italy.
1919 Mallet, R. E. A. (June 8, 1915). Lt. Technical Officer, R.A.F. France, 1916–17, 1918. *M.C.*, Oct. 18, 1917.
1911 Mallet, V. A. L., B.A. (Sept. 1914). Capt. Cambridgeshire Regt. (Staff Capt.) France, 1915–16; Persia.
1919 Mallet, W. I. (Oct. 7, 1918). Cadet R.E.
1912 Mann,* J. S., M.A. (Aug. 26, 1914). Lt. 6th R.W. Kent Regt. Capt. General List (Intelligence Corps). France, 1915, 1917–19. Croix de Guerre with Gold Star. *D.* France, 1918.
1910 **Manners,* Hon. J. N.** (Serving Aug. 4, 1914). Lt. Grenadier Guards. France, Belgium. Killed in action near Villers Cotterets on Sept. 1, 1914.

1903 [Marsden, G., M.A.] (Nov. 1915). Sub-Lt. R.N.V.R. H.M.S. *President.* North Sea. Order of the Sacred Treasure (5th Class).

1911 Marshall, A. G., B.A. (Aug. 7, 1914). ‡Capt. R.E. France, 1914–15; Gallipoli, 1915–16; Egypt, 1916; Mesopotamia, 1916–19.

1907 Martin, H. (Dec. 2, 1914). Maj. R.F.A. France, 1915–18. *D.S.O.*, June 4, 1917. *D.* France, 1917, 1919.

1909 Martin, H. F., B.A. (Oct. 1914). Lt. 16th Highland L.I. (Capt.). France.

1910 Martin, W., B.C.L. (1916). Capt. Canadian M.G.C., 'Section D' (Tank Branch).

1911 Massey,* C. V., M.A. (July 19, 1915). Maj. Canadian Officers Training Corps (Lt.-Col.). *D.* § Feb. 1919.

1919 Massey, R. H. (Aug. 30, 1915). Lt. 85th Batt., Canadian F.A. (Capt.). France, 1916; Siberia, 1918.

1919 Masterman, C. A. (Mar. 31, 1915). Lt. 3rd Hampshire Regt. (empld. R.E.) (Capt.). France, 1916, 1918–19.

1891 Matheson, A., B.A. (Nov. 2, 1914). Capt., Acting Lt.-Col., R.E. (Postal Section). France. *D.S.O.*, June 4, 1917. *D.* France, 1917.

1914 Matheson, D. M. (Mar. 1915). Lt. R.G.A. (Capt.). France. (Invalided, May 1918.)

1919 Mathew, T. (Jan. 1917). Lt. Welsh Guards. France.

1903 **Maude, J. W. A.** (Dec. 1914). 2nd Lt. 10th K.R.R.C. France. Killed in action at Laventie on Aug. 23, 1915.

1896 Maughan, J. M., B.A. (Aug. 12, 1914). Maj. 20th Bn., A.I.F. (Lt.-Col.). German New Guinea, 1914–15; Gallipoli, 1915; Egypt, 1916; France, 1916–17. *D.S.O.*, Sept. 26, 1916.

1892 Maxwell, T. D., B.A. (Nov. 22, 1914). Lt. Intelligence Officer, Cross River Column, Cameroons E.F. W. Africa, 1914–15.

1905 May, C. H., B.A. (Aug. 4, 1914). ‡Capt. M.G.C. Acting Maj. Tank Corps. France, 1915–18. *M.C.*, June 18, 1917.

1909 **May, R. T.,** B.A. (Aug. 4, 1914). Capt. 7th R. Sussex Regt. France, 1915–16. *D.* France, 1916. Killed in action at Ovillers on July 6, 1916.

1919 Mayhew, A. G. H. (Oct. 5, 1914). Capt. R. E. France, 1915–19. *M.C.*, June 3, 1919.

1910 Mayne, A. B., M.A. (Sept. 1917). 2nd Lt. Unattached List, T.F., Taunton School O.T.C.

1903 Mead, L., B.A. (Aug. 4, 1914). Maj. City of London Yeomanry. A.P.M. (graded as Staff-Captain). Egypt, 1915–16; France, 1918. *D.* Egypt, 1916. *D.* § Aug. 1919.

Mead, R. J. (Aug. 23, 1914). 2nd Lt. 8th R. Fusiliers. France and Belgium. Died on Aug. 2, 1915, at Armentières Hospital, of wounds received in action.

1899 Meade, C. F. (Oct. 1914). Lt. 1/1st Surrey Yeomanry. Salonika.

Medley, B. A. (Oct. 1914). 2nd Lt. 2nd Highland L.I. France. *D.* France, 1915. Died on Sept. 26, 1915, of wounds received in action.

1912 Mellor, R. W. H., M.A. (Aug. 7, 1914). ‡Capt. 130th Field Coy., R.E. France, 1914–15, 1915–18. *M.C.*, June 3, 1918. *D.* France, 1916, 1917, 1918.

1906 Meredith, L. A. de L., B.A. (Nov. 7, 1914). 2nd Lt. 3rd Gloucestershire Regt.

1913 Merrill, R. V., B.A. (Apr. 1, 1917). Capt. U.S. Infantry. A.D.C.

1897 Merriman, R. B. (May 1, 1918). Capt. A.D.C., U.S. Army. Siberia.
1906 Merton, T. R., M.A., D.Sc. (June 1916). Lt. R.N.V.R. *D.* § Aug. 1917.
1913 Miles, F. F., M.A. (Sept. 12, 1914). ‡Capt. 9th Gloucestershire Regt. Salonika, 1915, 1916, 1917, 1918; France, 1915, 1918–19.
1913 Miles, J. E., B.A. (July 10, 1915). Friends Ambulance Unit, B.R.C.S. France, Belgium, 1915–19.
Milholland, F. R. (Dec. 18, 1914). Capt. 6th Yorkshire Regt. France, Belgium. Died on Feb. 27, 1918, of wounds received in action near Bethune.
1900 Mirrielees, F. D., B.A. (Mobilized Aug. 1914). Maj. Surrey Yeomanry. France, Egypt, Salonika, Caucasus.
1889 Mitchell, A., B.A. (Mobilized Aug. 1914). Lt.-Col. Fife and Forfar Yeomanry (T.F. Res.). Staff Lt. (2nd Class). Gallipoli, Egypt, Belgium, France, Germany. T.D. *D.* § Feb. 1917.
1896 Mitchell Thomson, Sir W., Bt., B.A., *M.P.* (Nov. 1914). Hon. Lt. R.N.V.R. (British Representative, Supreme Economic Council, 1919.) North Sea, Mediterranean. *K.B.E.* Croix de Chevalier de la Légion d'Honneur. Officer of the Order of the Crown of Italy.
1919 Moir, J. W. (May 1917). 2nd Lt. 2nd Scots Guards. France, 1917–18.
1919 Monckton, R. (Jan. 7, 1918). Pte. 12th E. Surrey Regt. (Cadet). France and Belgium, 1918.
1910 Monckton,* W. T., M.A. (June 7, 1915). Lt. 4th R. W. Kent Regt. attd. H.Q. 17th Div. (Maj.). France. *M.C.*, June 3, 1919. *D.* France, 1917.
1909 Monins, J. E., B.A. (Aug. 29, 1914). Capt. 4th The Buffs (E. Kent Regt.) (Maj.). Aden, India, Afghanistan.
1900 Munro, H. R. (Dec. 27, 1917). 2nd Lt. 3rd The Black Watch.
1901 **Montagu, R. H.** (Jan. 1915). Lt. 8th Hampshire Regt. France and Belgium. Killed in action at Menin Road on Sept. 21, 1917.
1885 Montague, C. E. (Dec. 23, 1914). ‡Capt. General List. Staff Lt. (1st Class). France, Belgium, Germany, 1915–19. *O.B.E.* (Mil.). Order of Crown of Rumania (with swords). *D.* France, 1917, 1918, 1919.
1908 Montefiore,* L. N. G., B.A. (Mobilized 1914). Capt. 1/9th Hampshire Regt. India, Siberia. *O.B.E.* (Mil.). *D.* Siberia, 1919.
1904 Monteith, J. H. I. (Sept. 4, 1914). ‡Maj. 10th S. Wales Borderers. France, 1915–19. *D.* France, 1917, 1919.
1895 Moorhead, G. H., B.A. (Nov. 6, 1914). Capt. 6th Dragoons.
1897 Morgan, J. H., B.A. (Aug. 7, 1916). Lt.-Col. General List. Temp. Brig.-Gen. (D.A.G.), A.G.'s Staff, Inter-Allied Commission of Control for Germany. France, 1914–15, 1916. *D.* § Aug. 1917.
1893 Morgan, P. V. (Aug. 4, 1915). Capt. R.A.O.C. France, Belgium.
1909 Morison, B. H. (Aug. 5, 1914). Capt. 2nd Wellington Regt., N.Z.E.F. Egypt, 1914–15; Gallipoli, 1915; France, 1916–18. *M.C.*, Jan. 1, 1918. *D.* France, 1917.
1899 Morison, C. G. T., M.A. (Oct. 1915). 2nd Lt. O.U.O.T.C. Capt. Unattached, H. Q. Third Army. France, 1916. Co. Officer, R.M.C., Camberley.
1907 Morison, R. W. (Oct. 10, 1914). Lt. 3rd County of London Yeomanry. Lt. Technical Officer, R.A.F.
1879 Morison, Sir W. T., *K.C.S.I.* (July 24, 1915). Lt.-Col. R.A.O.C. France. *C.M.G.* *D.* France, 1916, 1919.

1919 Morris, J. F. (Sept. 1918). 2nd Lt. R.F.A.
1887 Mortimer, M. W., M.A. (Nov. 18, 1914). Maj. Suffolk Yeomanry (T.F. Res.).
1916 Mostyn, G. A. (Feb. 5, 1917). 2nd Lt. 6th K.R.R.C. France.
1904 Moyse, C. S., M.A. (Feb. 18, 1916). ‡Lt. General List, Canadian E.F.
1914 **Muir, A. B.** (Feb. 1, 1916). 2nd Lt. Arg. & Suth'd. Highlanders. France, Belgium. *D.* France, 1917. Killed in action near Ypres on Sept. 20, 1917.
1916 **Muirhead, L.** (Mar. 1917). 2nd Lt. B/59th Bde., R.F.A. France. Killed in action near Cambrai on Sept. 29, 1918.
1912 **Munster,* J. F.** (Aug. 1914). Lt. 13th Hussars. France, Mesopotamia. Killed in action at Kut on Feb. 4, 1917.
1917 Murphy, J., B.A. Field Ambulance, A.I.F. France.
1906 **Myers,* K.,** M.A. (May 1916). Pte. 72nd Canadian Inf. (Sergt.). France. Died on July 22, 1918, of wounds received in action.
1908 Namier, L. B., M.A. (Sept. 5, 1914). Pte. 20th R. Fusiliers. (Discharged Feb. 1915 to take up work under the Foreign Office.)
1872 Neave, S. H. M., B.A. (Mar. 1915). Capt. R.A.M.C.
1919 Nettlefold, J. K. (Aug. 1916). Lt. R.G.A. (T.F.). Salonika.
1910 Neumann,* Sir C. J. G., Bt., M.A. (Mobilized Aug. 1914). Capt. Norfolk Yeomanry. Staff-Captain. Mudros, Egypt, 1916. *D.* § Aug. 1919.
1919 Newboult, H. O. (Aug. 1, 1916). ‡Lt. R.G.A. (S.R.). Italy, 1917; Mesopotamia, 1917–18; Egypt, 1918; Salonika, 1918–19.
1888 Newman, A. P. S., M.A. (Serving Aug. 4, 1914). Maj. Unattached List, T.F., Cheltenham College O.T.C. *D.* § Mar. 1919.
1919 Newnham, H. A. (Apr. 1, 1917). Capt. and Staff Lt. R.A.S.C. (Administrative Staff). France.
1903 Newsholme, H. P., D.M. (Sept. 3, 1915). Capt. R.A.M.C. France, Italy.
1914 **Nicholls, D. W. A.** (Dec. 1914). Capt. 7th Suffolk Regt. France. *M.C.*, Aug. 25, 1916. Killed in action at Arras on Apr. 10, 1917.
1917 Nichols, J. B. (Apr. 19, 1917). 2nd Lt. Labour Corps.
1913 Nichols, P. B. B., B.A. (Aug. 27, 1914). Capt. 7th Suffolk Regt. Capt. General List. Bde. Maj. 125th Inf. Bde. France, Belgium, 1915–16, 1916–19. *M.C.*, June 3, 1916. *D.* France, 1918.
1916 Niven, C. R. (June 29, 1917). 2nd Lt. R.F.A. (S.R.). Italy, France, Belgium, Germany. *M.C.*, Apr. 2, 1919.
1904 Nixon, P. (Apr. 1918). 2nd Lt. Inf. U.S. Army.
1919 Norman, R. T. (Oct. 16, 1914). Lt. 1/7th Cheshire Regt., attd. 102nd T.M.B. Egypt, Palestine, France, 1916–19. Belgian Croix de Guerre.
1903 Northampton, Marquis of, B.A. (Serving Aug. 4, 1914). Capt. R. Horse Guards. Acting Maj., attd. R.E. (for Army Signals). France, 1914–17; Palestine, 1917–19. *D.S.O.*, June 3, 1919. *D.* Palestine, 1918, 1919.
1912 Norton, J. E., B.A. (Serving Aug. 4, 1914). ‡Lt. R.F.A. (Capt.). Gallipoli, Egypt, France. *M.C.*, Jan. 26, 1917; *Bar*, Apr. 2, 1919.
1919 Norway, N. S. (Oct. 7, 1918). Pte. 1st (Res.) Suffolk Regt.
1884 **O'Beirne, H. J.,** *C.B.*, *C.V.O.* Diplomatic Service, attd. Lord Kitchener's Mission to Russia. Drowned in the sinking of H.M.S. *Hampshire* on June 6, 1916.
1900 Odgers, W. B., M.A. (Nov. 24, 1915). Lt. A.S.C. Capt. Special Lists (Courts Martial Officer). France, 1916–19.

1920 O'Dwyer, J. C. (Dec. 11, 1918). Lt. 31st Lancers, Indian Army. Staff Lt. Indian Frontier, 1919.

1910 Ogilvie, E. D., B.A. (Aug. 14, 1914). Lt. 1st Life Guards (S.R.), attd. Guards M.G. Regt. France, Belgium.

1911 Ogilvie,* F. W., M.A. (Aug. 15, 1914). Capt. 4th Bedfordshire Regt. Belgium, France.

1893 Okell, G., B.A. (Feb. 2, 1915). Lt. 15th Welsh Regt. France, Belgium.

1905 Orr, J., B.Litt., M.A. (Aug. 1914). 2nd Lt. Unattached List, T.F., attd. Intelligence Corps. France, 1918.

1900 Ottley, R. B. H. (Sept. 1914). Capt. and Adjt. R.A.S.C. Staff-Captain War Office. France, Egypt. *M.B.E.* (Mil.). *D.* § Mar. 1918; § Mar. 1919.

1912 **Paddison, G. M.** (Aug. 1914). Lt. 6th D.C.L.I. France and Belgium. Killed in action at Hooge on July 30, 1915.

1919 Paddison, R. M. (Aug. 1, 1916). Lt. 3rd D.C.L.I. France. (Prisoner of War, Apr. 1917–Nov. 1918.)

1902 Pallis, A. A. (Sept. 1916). 2nd Lt. Archipelago Division, Greek Army. Lt. Special Lists. Deputy Governor-General of Salonika Province. Salonika. *M.B.E.* (Mil.). Chevalier of the Order of the Redeemer. *D.* Salonika, 1917.

1908 **Palmer,* R. W. Poulton,** B.A. (Mobilized Aug. 1914). Lt. 4th R. Berkshire Regt. France and Belgium. Killed in action at Ploegsteert Wood on May 5, 1915.

1914 Paradise, S. H., B.A. (Dec. 24, 1917). 2nd Lt. Field Artillery, U.S. Army. France.

1919 Parkin, G. R. (Sept. 5, 1914). Lt. R.E. Gallipoli, 1915; France, 1916, 1918–19.

1913 Parry, J., M.A. (Apr. 1915). Lt. A.S.C. Capt. (Flight Comdr.) R.A.F. France.

1892 Parsons, Hon. G. L., M.A. (Dec. 29, 1916). Lt. General Lists, empld. Ministry of Munitions.

Pasley, T. E. S. (Aug. 27, 1917). 2nd Lt. 1st K.O. Scottish Borderers. France. Believed killed in action on Apr. 11, 1918.

1890 **Paton, M. B.,** B.A. (Nov. 1914). Capt. 10th S. Lancashire Regt., attd. Lancashire Fusiliers. Gallipoli. Killed in action in the attack on Achi Baba on Aug. 7, 1915.

1907 Payne, C. E., B.A. (Jan. 1914). Capt. Unattached List, T.F., Clifton College O.T.C.

1911 Pearce, C. F. B., B.A. (Dec. 1, 1914). Lt. 2/5th Somerset L.I. Lt., Acting Capt., 2/17th Infantry, Indian Army. India, 1915–19.

1919 Pearson, C. H. (Feb. 8, 1918). 2nd Lt. 5th Guards M.G. Regt.

1914 Pearson, H. C. (Feb. 23, 1915). Lt. 1st K.R.R.C. (till 1918). Capt., Staff-Captain, Indian Army, attd. 2nd Gurkha Rifles. France, India. *M.C.*, Dec. 11, 1916.

1899 **Peckham, A. N.** (Mar. 1915). Lt., Acting Capt., I.A.R.O., attd. 112th Infantry, Indian Army. India, Mesopotamia, 1915–18. Accidentally killed at Akab on Feb. 14, 1918.

1904 **Peebles, W. F.** (Sept. 2, 1914). 2nd Lt. 10th Border Regt. 2nd Lt. M.G.C. Gallipoli, Egypt, Mesopotamia, France, Belgium. Killed in action, at Ypres on Apr. 30, 1917.

1905 Peel, D. H., M.A. (Sept. 1914). 2nd Lt. Unattached List, T.F., Rossall School O.T.C.

1885 Peel, Viscount, B.A. (Mobilized Aug. 4, 1914). Lt.-Col. Bedfordshire Yeomanry (T.F. Res.). *G.B.E.* (Civil Div.). American Distinguished Service Medal. *D.* § Feb. 1917.

1920 Peel, W. R., M.A. (Sept. 19, 1914). Lt.-Col. 6th Yorkshire Regt., attd. 1/10th Manchester Regt. Gallipoli, 1915; Egypt, 1916; France, Belgium, 1916–19. *D.S.O.*, June 4, 1917; *1st Bar*, Sept. 16, 1918; *2nd Bar*, Apr. 2, 1919. *D.* France, 1916, 1917, 1918, 1919.

Pember, E. H. (July 1, 1915). Lt. R.F.A., attd. R.F.C. France and Belgium. Killed in action in Belgium on Sept. 30, 1917.

1894 Pember, G. R., M.A. (June 11, 1915). Lt. R.F.A. (S.R.).

1904 Pemberton, R. O. W., B.A. (Mobilized Aug. 4, 1914). Capt. Suffolk Yeomanry, attd. 15th Suffolk Regt. Salonika, Egypt, Palestine.

1901 Perceval, F. W., B.A. (Nov. 24, 1915). Capt., Bt.-Maj., R.A.O.C. *O.B.E.* (Mil.). *D.* § Aug. 1917, § Mar. 1918, § Aug. 1918, § Mar. 1919.

1913 Peto,* J. M. (Dec. 29, 1914). Capt. Coldstream Guards. France, 1915–17, 1918. *D.* France, 1916.

1901 [Phelps, W., M.A.] (Oct. 10, 1914). Maj. Lancashire Fusiliers. France, 1916–17.

1897 Phillips, E. R., B.A. (Aug. 1917). Lt., M.G.O., 12th W. Riding Vol. Regt.

1871 Phillips, F. B. W., D.M. (Mobilized Aug. 1914). Capt. R.A.M.C., Sanitary Officer.

1908 Phillips,* F. R., B.A. (Aug. 1914). Capt. Surrey Yeomanry. Staff-Captain. Belgium, France, Macedonia, Bulgaria, Turkey. *M.C.*, June 3, 1918. *D.* Salonika, 1917.

1915 Phillips, J. N. (Jan. 17, 1916). Lt. R.A.S.C. (M.T.) (Capt.). Salonika, 1917–19.

1890 Phillpotts, R. B., B.A. (Aug. 5, 1914). Lt. Royal 1st Devon Yeomanry, (T.F. Res.). Staff-Captain. Gallipoli, Egypt, 1915.

1898 Phipps, P., B.A. (Oct. 1914). Capt., temp. Maj., 3rd Sherwood Foresters. Deputy Asst. Director of Movements and Railways. France. *D.* § Mar. 1918.

1919 Pinnell, L. G. (Aug. 26, 1915). Lt. 10th Bedfordshire Regt. Lt. M.G.C. (Capt.). Salonika, 1916; France, 1918–19.

1913 **Pinsent, R. P.** (Sept. 1914). 2nd Lt. 10th R. Warwickshire Regt. France. Killed in action at Richebourg St. Vaast on Oct. 8, 1915.

1918 Plane, A. A. (Aug. 18, 1914). ‡Capt. 15th Bn. A.I.F. Egypt, France.

1919 Platt, W. J. (Jan. 6, 1917). ‡2nd Lt. N.Z. Rifle Brigade. France.

1906 Plimsoll,* S. R. C. (Aug. 5, 1914). Capt. R.F.A., attd. T.M.B. France and Belgium, 1915–18. *M.C.*, Jan. 1, 1917; *Bar*, Oct. 28, 1917. *D.* France, 1916. (Prisoner of War, 1918.)

1907 Plowden, P. P. M. C., M.A. (Mobilized 1914). Lt. 19th Agra Coy. I.D.F.

1898 Pocklington, G. R., B.A. (Mar. 13, 1916). ‡Lt. 12th Suffolk Regt. France, Belgium.

1902 **Pollexfen, G. B.** (Aug. 1914). Pte. 10th King's (Liverpool Regt.) (Liverpool Scottish). France and Belgium. Killed in action at Ypres on Jan. 26, 1915.

1888 Pomeroy, Hon. R. L., B.A. (Aug. 16, 1914). Capt. 5th Dragoon Guards (Res. of Officers). Temp. Maj. 4th Res. Regt. of Cavalry. *O.B.E.* (Mil.).

1919 Ponder, A. O. (May 28, 1915). ‡Lt. 1st Canterbury Regt., N.Z.E.F. Egypt, 1915–16; France, Belgium, and Germany, 1916–18. *M.C.*, Feb. 15, 1919. *D.* France, 1917.

1898 Ponsonby, C. E., B.A. (Aug. 4, 1914). Capt., Acting Maj., 10th (W. Kent Yeomanry Bn.) The Buffs (E. Kent Regt.) (Lt.-Col.). Gallipoli, 1915; Egypt, 1916–17; Palestine, 1917–18; France, 1918–19. Croix de Guerre.

1913 Potocki, Count J. (1914). Lt. Russian Cavalry. Russia.

1912 Potter,* K. R., M.A. (Dec. 10, 1914). Lt. 7th Norfolk Regt. (Capt.). France, 1915–16, 1917. *M.C.*, Sept. 26, 1916. (Wounded and Prisoner of War, Nov. 1917.)

1892 Poynting, J. W. E., B.A. (Oct. 30, 1915). Capt. 9th K.O. Scottish Borderers. Staff-Captain G.H.Q., Ireland.

1919 Prickett, Rev. G. (July 30, 1915). ‡Chaplain (4th Class), A.I.F. Egypt, France.

1907 Primrose, A. H. R. (June 16, 1915). Lt., temp. Capt., 3rd Scots Guards (S.R.). France.

1912 Prince, A. E. (July 1, 1915). Lt. 1/5th Manchester Regt. (Adjt.). Staff Lt. O.E.T. Administration, Haifa, Palestine. Gallipoli, Egypt, Palestine. *D.* Palestine, 1918.

1910 **Purcell,* C. F.,** B.A. (Oct. 1914). Lt. Irish Guards. France, Belgium. Killed in action at Cuinchy on Sept. 15, 1916.

1904 [**Radcliffe, J. D. H.,** B.C.L., M.A.] (Aug. 6, 1914). Capt. 7th K.R.R.C. France and Belgium. Killed in action near Hooge on July 30, 1915.

1915 Radcliffe, J. N. (Dec. 10, 1915). Capt. R.G.A. (S.R.). Staff Captain 5th Corps R.A. France. *M.C.*, Jan. 1, 1918.

1902 Rae, C. E. L., B.C.L., M.A. (Aug. 3, 1914). Lt. R.N.V.R. Antwerp, 1914. H.M.S. *Emperor of India*, 1917–19.

1907 **Rae,* T. K. H.,** M.A. (Dec. 1914). 2nd Lt. 8th Rifle Brigade. France and Belgium. Killed in action at Hooge on July 30, 1915.

1910 [Raikes,* H. R., M.A.] (Mobilized Aug. 4, 1914). Capt. The Buffs (E. Kent Regt.) (S.R.). Maj. R.A.F. France. *A.F.C.*, June 3, 1918.

1903 Ramsay, Hon. C. F. M. (Sept. 30, 1914). Interpreter, attd. 1st Life Guards. Lt. Northumberland Yeomanry. Belgium and France, 1914, 1915–18; Germany, 1918–19. *M.C.*, Nov. 26, 1917; *Bar*, Apr. 2, 1919. *D.* France, 1917.

1901 Ramsbotham, Rev. E. F. S., M.A. (Sept. 6, 1918). Chaplain to the Forces (4th Class).

1908 Randolph, G. A., B.A. (Dec. 2, 1915). Lt. N. Somerset Yeomanry, attd. R.A.F. France.

1894 Ranken, T., B.A. (Aug. 5, 1914). Capt. (Hon. Maj.) 8th R. Scots. Maj., attd. General Staff, Northern Command.

1905 Ranking, G. S. A., M.A. (Mobilized Aug. 1914). Lt.-Col. R.A.M.C., 3rd Southern General Hospital. *C.M.G.* *D.* § Feb. 1917, § July 1917.

1891 Rattigan, A. M. (Sept. 24, 1914). Capt. K.O. Scottish Borderers. Belgium, 1914; France, 1918–19. *D.* France, 1919.

1870 Rawnsley, Rev. Canon H. D., M.A., T.D. (Serving Aug. 4, 1914). Chaplain (1st Class), attd. Border Regt. Died on May 28, 1920.

1911 **Rawsthorn,* A. E.** (Sept. 1914). 2nd Lt. 4th Loyal N. Lancashire Regt. France. Killed in action at Festubert on June 15, 1915.

1913 Rayner,* C. S. W. (Nov. 27, 1914). Capt. 8th Oxf. & Bucks. Lt. Infty. Lt., Acting Capt., 1/48th Pioneers, Indian Army. France, 1915; Salonika, 1915–17; India, 1917–19. *D.* Salonika, 1917.

1916 Rayner, H. L. (July 27, 1918). Surgeon Sub-Lt. R.N.V.R.

1875 [Reichel, Sir H. R., M.A.] (Serving Aug, 4, 1914). Capt. Unattached List, T.F., Bangor University College O.T.C.

1902 Reiss, R. L., B.A. (Feb. 13, 1915). Capt. 6th Loyal N. Lancashire Regt., empld. Min. of Reconstruction. Gallipoli, Egypt, Mesopotamia, India, until 1917.

1907 **Reiss, S. L.**, M.A. (Aug. 1914). Lt. 5th R. Berkshire Regt. France, Belgium. Killed in action at Loos on Oct. 13, 1915.

1906 Reynell, W. R., D.M. (Aug. 15, 1914). Capt. R.A.M.C., Australian Medical Unit. France.

1901 Reynolds, L. G. S. (Mobilized Aug. 1914). Maj. 8th London Regt. (Post Office Rifles). Capt. R.A.F. (Maj.). France. *O.B.E.* (Mil.). Croix de Chevalier de la Légion d'Honneur. *D.* § Jan. 1919. (Prisoner of War, 1918).

Rhys-Davids, A. P. F. (Jan. 28, 1916). Lt. R.F.C. France. *D.S.O.*, Oct. 28, 1917. *M.C.*, July 18, 1917; *Bar*, July 18, 1917. *D.* France, 1917. Killed in action on Oct. 27, 1917.

Rice, B. N. (Aug. 29, 1914). Capt. E. Yorkshire Regt. France. Died on July 10, 1917, of wounds received in action in France.

Richards, H. S. (Nov. 1, 1915). 2nd Lt. 10th Essex Regt., attd. R.A.F. Accidentally killed, Aug. 1918.

1899 **Richmond, H. C.** (Serving Aug. 4, 1914). Capt. 1st Gloucestershire Regt. Staff-Captain. France, Belgium. Killed in action near La Bassée on Jan. 25, 1915.

1900 Richter, A. J. P., B.A. (Aug. 1914). Lt. 1st Imperial Light Horse. Capt. Headquarters Staff, S. African Army. German S.W. Africa, German E. Africa. *D.* S.W. Africa.

1905 Ridley, Hon. J. N., B.A. (Mobilized Aug. 1914). Maj. Northumberland Yeomanry. D.A.A.G., XIX Corps. France, Belgium. *O.B.E.* (Mil.). Croix de Chevalier de la Légion d'Honneur. *D.* France, 1918, 1919.

1909 Ridley,* M. R., M.A. (Serving Aug. 4, 1914). Capt. Unattached List, T.F., Clifton College O.T.C.

1893 **Ridley, Viscount,** B.A. (Mobilized Aug. 4, 1914). Lt.-Col. Northumberland Yeomanry (T.F. Res.). Died on Feb. 15, 1916.

1906 Rieu, E. V. (Aug. 1918). 2nd Lt. I.A.R.O., attd. 105th Mahratta L.I. India.

1895 Rivière, E., B.A. (1914). Anti-Aircraft Corps, R.N.V.R.

1913 Roberts, R. T. F. D., B.M. (Dec. 29, 1917). Surgeon Lt. R.N. H.M.S. *Sydney*.

1911 Robertson, H. A., M.A. (Aug. 26, 1914). Capt. 8th Devonshire Regt. France, 1915–16, 1917; Italy, 1917–19.

1887 Robertson, J. H. (May 25, 1915). ‡2nd Lt. 23rd R. Fusiliers, attd. General Staff, G.H.Q., France. France and Belgium, 1915–17. Died on Oct. 9, 1919.

1919 Robertson, J. W. (May 23, 1917). 2nd Lt. The Black Watch.
1913 Robinson, H. W., B.A. (Feb. 19, 1915). Lt. R.G.A. (Capt.). Mesopotamia, 1916–18. *D.* Mesopotamia, 1919.
1883 Robinson, Rev. T. W., B.A. (Serving Aug. 4, 1914). Chaplain R.N. Naval Instructor.
1912 Robson, A. J. (Apr. 12, 1915). Capt. R.A.S.C.
1883 Rochdale, Lord (Mobilized Aug. 1914). Col. 1/6th Lancashire Fusiliers (T.F. Res.), (Brig.-Gen.). Egypt, Gallipoli, 1914–15.
1913 Rodd,* F. J. R. (Sept. 19, 1914). Lt. R.F.A. Staff-Captain (Intelligence Corps). France, Italy, Egypt, Palestine, Syria, N. Africa. Cavalier of the Order of St. Maurice and St. Lazarus. *D.* Palestine, 1917, 1918.
1919 Rodger, A. B. (Sept. 1914). Lt. 11th Highland L.I. (Capt.), attd. R.A.F. France. *D.* France, 1917.
1904 Roe, A. S., B.M. (1917). Capt. Australian A.M.C.
1900 Roe, R. C., M.A. (Aug. 4, 1914). Lt. 1/6th Lancashire Fusiliers (T.F. Res.) (Capt.). Egypt, Gallipoli, 1914–16.
1889 Rogers, T. P. (July 6, 1918). Lt. R.N.V.R. H.M.S. *Ganges.*
1904 Romilly, F. C., B.A. (Oct. 1914). Lt. R.G.A. France.
1917 Rooke, Rev. G. L. W. (Oct. 1914). Pte. Field Ambulance, A.I.F. ‡Chaplain (4th Class), A.I.F. Egypt, Gallipoli, France, Belgium.
1906 Rooker, J. K., B.A. (Sept. 8, 1914). Lt., Acting Capt., M.G.C. (Staff Captain). France, 1914–18; Salonika, 1918–19. *M.C.*, Sept. 16, 1918.
1887 **Roos, G. O.,** B.C.L., M.A. (Oct. 3, 1915). Capt. York & Lancaster Regt. France. Killed in action on the Somme on July 1, 1916.
1904 [Rose, H. J., M.A.] (1914). ‡Lt. Princess Patricia's Canadian L.I. Lt. Canadian Khaki University. France.
1885 Ross, A. Gordon (July 18, 1917). Capt. General List, R.T.O. Russian Order of St. Stanislas (3rd Class).
1896 [Ross, W. D., M.A.] (Apr. 22, 1915). Maj. Special Lists. Inspector Min. of Munitions. *O.B.E.* (Mil.). *D.* § Jan. 1917.
1917 Rothstein, A. (July 6, 1917). Lce-Cpl. R.E.
1882 Ruggles-Brise, Sir H. G., *M.V.O.* (Serving Aug. 4, 1914). Maj.-Gen. Military Secretary, G.H.Q. France. *K.C.M.G. C.B.* Commandeur de l'Ordre de Leopold. Belgian Croix de Guerre. *D.* France, 1914, 1917 twice, 1918, 1919.
1904 Russell, A. J. G., B.A. (Oct. 12, 1916). ‡2nd Lt. Labour Corps.
1891 Russell, C. F. W., M.A. (Mobilized Aug. 5, 1914). Capt. Bedfordshire Yeomanry (T.F. Res.). France.
1897 Russell, C. G. E. (Mobilized Aug. 5, 1914). Capt. 1st Bedfordshire Yeomanry. France and Belgium, 1915–18.
1909 **Russell,* D. A. C.** (Dec. 1914). Pte. Rhodesian Rifles. Central German Africa, N. Rhodesia. Died on Oct. 31, 1915, of fever contracted on active service.
1893 Russell, G. B. A. (Mobilized Aug. 5, 1914). Maj. Grenadier Guards (Staff-Captain, War Office). France. *D.* § Aug. 1918.
1919 Ryan, A. (Sept. 9, 1918). ‡2nd Lt. R.F.A.
1892 Salt, A. E. W., B.A. (May 24, 1916). Lt. General List. Staff Lt. Capt. Educational Officer. Salonika. *D.* Salonika, 1917.

1919 Samuel, E. H. (Apr. 1917). 2nd Lt. R.G.A. 3rd Class Agent, Intelligence Corps. Palestine.

1909 **Samuel, W. G.** (Sept. 1, 1914). ‡Lt., Acting Capt. and Adjt., 6th Suffolk Regt., attd. 2nd Bedfordshire Regt. France. Killed in action at Ronssoy on Sept. 21, 1918.

1907 Sanders, J. H., M.A. (July 11, 1916). Lt., Acting Capt., I.A.R.O., attd. 5th Cavalry, afterwards attd. Recruiting Staff. India.

1886 Sanders, Sir R. A., Bt., M.A., *M.P.* (Aug. 1914). Lt.-Col. 16th Devonshire Regt. Gallipoli, Egypt, Palestine. T.D. *D.* Egypt, 1916.

1919 Sandford, F. H. (Serving Aug. 4, 1914). Commdr. R.N. Dardanelles, Belgium. *D.S.O.*, Aug. 16, 1915. Croix de Guerre avec palme. (Promoted for service at Zeebrugge, 1918.)

1919 Sandral, D. M. (July 8, 1915). ‡Lt. 46th Bn., A.I.F. Egypt, Belgium.

1917 Sandwith, C. F. C. (May 22, 1918). Pte. 3rd Queen's (R. W. Surrey Regt.).

1909 Sandys,* M. K. T., M.A. (Oct. 21, 1914). Capt. 2/4th D.C.L.I. India, 1915–19.

1919 Saunders, H. A. St. G. (Jan. 18, 1916). Lt. Welsh Guards (S.R.), attd. 1st Bn. France, 1917–18; Germany, 1918–19. *M.C.*, Apr. 2, 1919.

1912 Scanlan,* J. F. (Mar. 1917). Lt. R.A.S.C. Italy, 1918–19.

1892 Scargill, L. W. K. (Mar. 15, 1915). Lt. R.A.M.C. Malta.

1909 Scholfield,* W. S. (Oct. 10, 1914). Capt. 1/7th W. Yorkshire Regt. G.S.O. 3. France, Belgium. *D.* France, 1918.

1911 **Scott, A. N. H.** (Aug. 6, 1914). Lt. 2nd Scots Guards. France. Killed in action at Festubert on May 16, 1915.

1919 Scott, D. H. (Apr. 14, 1918). 2nd Lt. R.E.

1919 Scott, F. P. D. (Sept. 1, 1916). 2nd Lt. R.A.F. Mesopotamia.

1893 Scriven, J. T., M.A. (Sept. 1914). Bde. Maj. 36th Ulster Div. Capt. Motor M.G.C.

1919 Scrutton, G. M. (Sept. 6, 1916). Lt., Acting Capt. and Adjt,. D/112th Bde. R.F.A. France. *M.C.*, Jan. 30, 1919.

1901 **Sebag-Montefiore, R. M.**, M.A. (Mobilized Aug. 4, 1914). Capt. R. E. Kent Yeomanry. Gallipoli, 1915. Died at Alexandria on Nov. 9, 1915, of wounds received in Gallipoli.

1919 Segnit, R. W. (May 15, 1915). ‡Lt. 10th Inf. Bn., A.I.F. Lemnos, 1915–16; Egypt, 1916; France, 1916–19.

Seward, R. (Sept. 20, 1915). Sergt. 21st K.R.R.C. Belgium, France, 1916. Killed in action at Ploegsteert on June 1, 1916.

1912 **Sewart, G. E. S.** (Aug. 1914). 2nd Lt. 10th Durham L.I. France. Killed in action at Arras on May 8, 1916.

1905 Sharpe,* R. L., B.A. (Mobilized Aug. 5, 1914). Capt. 1st London Regt., attd. O.C.B. Egypt, Gallipoli, France.

1897 Sharpe, W. S., M.A. (Dec. 10, 1914). Capt. 1st London Regt. Gallipoli, 1915; France, 1917.

1919 Shavaksha, K. S. (Oct. 16, 1918). Rifleman 5th London Regt. (London Rifle Brigade).

1907 Shaw, D. P., M.A. (Sept. 1914). Maj. 6th Dorsetshire Regt. (Lt.-Col.). Belgium, France. *D.S.O.*, Dec. 2, 1918. *D.* France, 1918.

1914 Shaw,* J. P. (Dec. 4, 1914). Lt. 6th Shropshire L.I. France, Belgium. *M.C.*, Aug. 19, 1919. (Prisoner of War.)

1907 **Shaw-Stewart, P. H.,** M.A. (Sept. 25, 1914). Lt.-Commdr. R.N.V.R. G.S.O. 3. Gallipoli, Salonika, France. Croix de Chevalier de la Légion d'Honneur. Croix de Guerre. Killed in action in France on Dec. 30, 1917.

1910 Shepardson, W. H., B.A. (1917). 2nd Lt. F.A., U.S. Army, attd. Peace Commission, Paris.

1919 Sherborne, H. F. (Jan. 1, 1918). Lt. R.E. France, Germany. *M.C.*, Mar. 8, 1919.

1901 [**Sidgwick, A. H.,** M.A.] (Jan. 3, 1916). 2nd Lt., Acting Capt., and Adjt. 157th Siege Batt. R.G.A. France and Belgium. Died on Sept. 17, 1917, of wounds received in action.

1919 Simpson, C. W. (Sept. 7, 1916). Lt. R.G.A. France.

1901 Simpson, Sir James W. M., Bt. R.A.F.

1904 **Siordet, G. C.** (Sept. 1914). ‡2nd Lt. 13th Rifle Brigade, attd. 6th King's Own (R. Lancaster Regt.). France, Mesopotamia. *M.C.*, Sept. 22, 1916. Killed in action near Kut on Feb. 9, 1917.

1895 Skinner, E. J., B.A. (Serving Aug. 4, 1914). Maj., Acting Lt.-Col., R.H.A. (in Command of Cadet School). France. *D.S.O.*, June 3, 1916. *D.* France, 1915, 1916, 1917 twice.

1899 **Skrine, H. L.,** B.A. (Mobilized Aug. 1914). Capt. 6th Somerset L.I. Belgium and France. Killed in action at the Battle of Loos on Sept. 25, 1915.

1904 Sloman, H. N. P., M.A. (Sept. 1916). Lt. 11th Rifle Brigade, attd. No. 23 O.C.B. France and Belgium, 1917. *M.C.*, Sept. 26, 1917.

1899 [Smith, A. L. F., M.A., *M.V.O.*] (Sept. 1914). Capt. 2/7th Hampshire Regt. (spec. empld.). India, Mesopotamia.

1876 Smith, F. J., D.M. (Mobilized Aug. 4, 1914). Maj. R.A.M.C. Died on Apr. 30, 1919.

1909 Smith, G. M., M.A. (1916). Capt. E. Ontario Regt., Canadian Contingent, attd. H.Q. 1st Corps Heavy Artillery. France, 1916–17. *M.C.*, Nov. 14, 1916.

1917 Smith, H. J. F. (Jan. 1918). 2nd Lt. 5th Coldstream Guards.

1913 Smith, H. P. Pte. Gloucestershire Regt.

1913 Smith, N. F., B.M., M.A. (Oct. 1914). Surgeon Lt. R.N. H.M.S. *Benbow*, Grand Fleet.

1900 Smith, W. E., M.A. (Sept. 18, 1915). Capt. R.A.M.C. (T.F.). Senior Chemist, No. 3 Water Tank Coy. France, 1916–18.

1919 Snow, T. W. (Mar. 17, 1915). Lt. 16th London Regt. (Queen's West minster Rifles). Lt. 286th Bde., R.F.A. (Capt.). France, 1916, 1917–19. *M.C.*, Jan. 1, 1919.

1876 Somerleyton, Lord, B.A., *K.C.V.O.* (Aug. 1914). Capt. Suffolk Regt. (T.F. Res.). Hon. Lt.-Col. (in Army). Hon. Col. (S.R.). Empld. Recruiting Duties. France and Belgium.

1894 Somerset, H. C. S. A. (Sept. 22, 1914). Capt. Gen. Staff. King's Messenger, War Office. France, Belgium, Russia, Italy, Serbia, Gallipoli, Egypt, Germany. *D.* France, 1917 twice.

1911 Sproule, G. M., B.A. (Aug. 21, 1914). Capt. R.A.S.C., attd. R. Dublin Fusiliers. Salonika, 1916–17; France, 1918. *M.C.*, Jan. 1, 1918. *D.* Salonika, 1916, 1917.

1894 Stanley, Hon. Sir A. L., M.A., *K.C.M.G.* Capt. Cheshire Yeomanry. Governor of Victoria.

1909 Stanton, R., M.A. (Mar. 8, 1916). ‡Lt. R.A.S.C. (M.T.). France, 1916–18.

1901 **Starkey, V. G.,** B.A. (Feb. 1, 1915). Lt. 7th K.O.Y.L.I. France. Killed in action in France on Oct. 14, 1915.

1910 Stein, H. K., B.C.L., M.A. (Feb. 1, 1916). ‡Lt. R.E. (Wireless Section). France, Belgium, Germany.

1906 Stein,* L. J., B.A. (Mobilized Aug. 4, 1914). Capt. 12th London Regt. (The Rangers). D.A.A. (Staff Capt.), attd. Political Branch, G.H.Q., E.E.F. France, 1914–15, 1917–18; Palestine, 1918–19.

1916 Stephenson, R. M., B.A. (July 4, 1917). 2nd Lt. R.F.A. France. (Placed on retired list on account of ill health caused by wounds.)

1905 Stevens, A. M. (Mar. 24, 1917). Lt. Medical Corps, U.S. Naval Reserve, attd. U.S. Naval Aviation. France, Belgium. (Prisoner of War, July–Nov. 1918.)

1913 **Stevens, L. B.** (Sept. 4, 1914). ‡2nd Lt. 3rd S. Staffordshire Regt. France, 1915. Killed in action at Fromelles on May 9, 1915.

1900 [Stevenson, G. H., M.A.] (May 5, 1915). Lt. 4th Oxf. & Bucks. Lt. Infty. Staff Lt., Intelligence Corps. France, 1918.

1904 Stevenson-Reece, G. M., M.A. (Mobilized Aug. 1914). ‡Lt. 2nd Dragoons (Staff Capt.). France, 1914–18. *D.* France, 1915, 1917.

Stitt, I. d'A. S. (Dec. 1916). 2nd Lt. 1/16th London Regt. (Queen's Westminster Rifles). France. Killed in action at Towey Post, near Arras, on Mar. 18, 1918.

1912 Stokes, H. B., B.A. (Sept. 29, 1914). Capt. General List. Staff Capt. R.T.O. France.

1919 Struve, G. P. (July 19, 1917). Pte. Gen. Kornilov's Volunteer Army, Russia.

1905 Stuart, A. N., M.A. (Nov. 11, 1914). Maj. 8th S. Lancashire Regt. Maj., Administrative Officer, R.A.F. France.

1911 Stuart, J. McA., M.A. (June 15, 1916). Sub-Lt. R.N.V.R., attd. R.N.A.S. 2nd Lt. R.E. France. (Invalided, Apr. 1918.)

1889 Stuart, L. (Mobilized 1914). Lt.-Col. 5th Lucknow Group Garr. Art. India. *C.I.E.*, Sept. 13, 1919. *D.* India, 1918.

1910 Stuart, W. A. (May 14, 1917). Maj. 44th Art. Bde., U.S. Army.

1909 Stuart-Wortley,* N. R. M. (Mobilized Aug. 1914). Lt. Hampshire Yeomanry. Capt. R.A.F. France. *M.C.*, Apr. 22, 1918. *D.* France, 1916 twice.

1899 Sturgis, J. B., B.A. (Apr. 1915). Lt. Surrey Yeomanry, attd. 8th Queen's (R. W. Surrey Regt.) (Capt.). France, 1918.

1912 [Sumner, B. H., M.A.] (Aug. 15, 1914). Capt. 6th K.R.R.C., empld. War Office. France, 1914–17; Paris, Peace Conference, 1919. *D.* § Mar. 1919.

1908 Sutherland-Leveson-Gower, Lord A. St. C. (Serving Aug. 4, 1914). Capt. R. Horse Guards. A.D.C. France. *M.C.*, July 24, 1915. *D.* France, 1915 twice.

Sutton, E. M. (Feb. 16, 1915). Lt. R.E., attd. Signal Service, 35th Div. France. *D.* France, 1918. Killed in action on Mar. 24, 1918.

1896 Swan, K. R., B.A. (Aug. 28, 1914). Lt.-Commdr. R.N.V.R. Scapa Flow, 1914–18. *O.B.E.* (Mil.).

1897 Swann, C. D., M.A. Acting Paymaster, A.P.D.

1897 **Talbot, J. A. W.** (Mobilized Aug. 4, 1914). Maj. R. Gloucestershire Hussars. Died on Nov. 1, 1918, of illness contracted on active service.

1903 Talbot, Rt. Rev. N. S., D.D., Bishop of Pretoria (Aug. 21, 1914). Chaplain to the Forces (1st Class) (Asst. Chaplain-General). France. *M.C.*, Jan. 14, 1916. *D.* France, 1915 twice, 1916.

1903 Tallents, S. G., B.A. (Sept. 1914). Capt. Irish Guards, temp. Lt.-Col. whilst on Continental Supreme Council of Supply and Relief. France, 1915; Finland & Baltic States. *C.B.* *C.B.E.* (Mil). *D.* § Feb. 1917; *D.* Finland, 1919.

1919 Tallents, T. F. (Sept. 1914). Capt. Irish Guards (S.R.), attd. 4th Guards M.G. Regt. (Maj.). France. *M.C.*, June 3, 1916; *Bar*, Dec. 2, 1918. *D.* France, 1916.

1905 Tatham, M., M.A. (Mar. 25, 1915). Capt. Special Lists (whilst with Amb. Unit). France, Belgium, 1915–19. Chevalier de l'Ordre de la Couronne.

1899 Tawney, R. H., B.A. (Nov. 26, 1914). Sergt. 22nd Manchester Regt. France, 1915–16.

1899 **Taylor, H.,** B.A. (Serving Aug. 4, 1914). Capt. 2nd Scots Guards. France. *D.* France, 1914. Killed in action at Rouge Bancs on Dec. 18, 1914.

1919 Tenen, I. (Sept. 22, 1916). Pte. 6th I. L. Coy., Middlesex Regt. France.

1911 Terry, C. H. (Nov. 1914). Surgeon Lt. R.N. North Sea.

1917 Terry, F. E. (Aug. 24, 1917). Gunner 120th Siege Batt., R.G.A. (Lce.-Cpl.). France.

1911 Thompson, D. C., B.A. (Aug. 29, 1914). Capt. 4th Devonshire Regt. Capt. Labour Corps. India, 1914–16; Mesopotamia, 1916–19.

1910 Thomson, H., M.A. Maj. 50th S. Australian Force, A.I.F. France. *M.C.*, June 3, 1918.

1894 **Thomson, H. T.,** B.C.L., M.A. (Oct. 1914). Lt. 7th S. Staffordshire Regt. Gallipoli. Died on Sept. 26, 1915, of wounds received on Aug. 7 in Gallipoli.

1911 Thornton, R. H., M.A. (Sept. 20, 1914). Maj. General List. G.S.O. 2. France, 1915–18. *M.C.*, June 3, 1918. *D.* France, 1917, 1918.

1891 **Thynne, Lord A.** (Mobilized Aug. 4, 1914). Lt.-Col. R. Wiltshire Yeomanry, attd. Wiltshire Regt. France. *D.S.O.*, Jan. 1, 1917. Croix de Guerre. *D.* France, 1916, 1917. Killed in action near Bethune on Sept. 15, 1918.

1894 Timmis, W. U., B.A. (Nov. 20, 1916). Lt. 5th Grenadier Guards. France, 1917–18.

1917 Titchmarsh,* E. C. (Dec. 1, 1917). ‡2nd Lt. R.E. (Signals). France, Belgium, 1918–19.

1908 Todd, J. E., M.A. (May 12, 1916). Lt. Cameronians. Mesopotamia, India.

1896 Tomkinson, C. W., B.A. (Mobilized Aug. 1914). Maj. Cheshire Yeomanry. A.D.C. to G.O.C. 3rd Cavalry Div. Egypt, Palestine, France.

1898 Tomkinson, J. E. (Sept. 15, 1914). Capt. Cheshire Yeomanry. Staff-Capt. Egypt, Palestine.

1905 Trevor, S. L., M.A. (Mobilized Aug. 1914). Capt. Bedfordshire Yeomanry, attd. Labour Corps. France, 1915.

1900 **Tristram, L. B. C.** (Serving Aug. 4, 1914). Capt. 2nd Leicestershire Regt. India, France. Killed in action near Bethune on Oct. 31, 1914.

1904 Troup, Rev. G. E., M.A. (July 23, 1915). Chaplain, R.N. Division. France.

Turner, G. A. (Jan. 1916). 2nd Lt. R. W. Kent Regt., attd. 7th Loyal N. Lancashire Regt. France. Killed in action near Grandcourt on Nov. 17, 1916.

1908 **Turton, E. S.,** B.A. (Mobilized Aug. 4, 1914). Lt. Yorkshire Hussars, attd. 8th Sherwood Foresters. Belgium. Killed in action near Ypres on Aug. 31, 1915.

1879 Turton, R. B., M.A. (Sept. 19, 1914). Maj. General List. Temp. Maj., Staff. France.

Twist, F. C. O. (Aug. 1914). 2nd Lt. 18th Manchester Regt. France. *D.* France, 1916. Killed in action near Guillemont on July 30, 1916.

1911 **Tyrrell,* F. C.** (Sept. 1914). 2nd Lt. Coldstream Guards (S.R.). France. Died on Feb. 16, 1915, of wounds received in action.

1911 Underhill, F. H., M.A. (Sept. 26, 1915). ‡Lt. 1st Hertfordshire Regt. France.

1876 Upcott, E. A., M.A. (Sept. 1914). Maj. Wellington College O.T.C.

1914 **Ursell, V. G.** (Sept. 5, 1914). ‡2nd Lt. 8th, attd. 7th, Shropshire L.I. France, 1915; Salonika, 1915–16; France, 1917. Killed in action near Arras on May 3, 1917.

1911 Vallance, G. A. (Dec. 1, 1914). Capt. 2/5th Somerset L.I. Capt., Bde. Maj., Sialkot Bde., India. India, 1914–19.

1909 **Van den Bergh, S. J. H.,** B.A. (Mobilized Aug. 1914). Capt. 1st County of London Yeomanry. France, Egypt, Palestine, Salonika. Killed in action at Beersheba on Oct. 27, 1917.

1881 Vane-Tempest, F. F. A. (Nov. 1914). Capt. Durham L.I. (spec. empld.). Staff-Capt.

1888 Vanneck, A. P., M.A. (Oct. 28, 1914). ‡Lt. R.G.A. (spec. empld.). Staff-Lt. *M.B.E.* (Mil.).

1898 Varley, R. S., M.A. (Oct. 1914). Lt. N. Staffordshire Regt. (Capt.). France, 1917.

1870 Vaughan, E. L., M.A. (Serving Aug. 4, 1914). Qr.-Master and Hon. Capt. Unattached List, T.F.

1919 Vaughan-Morgan, G. C. (Sept. 5, 1916). Lt. 3rd Irish Guards. France, 1917.

1900 Verney, Sir H. C. W., M.A. (Jan. 1916). Lt.-Col. General List. Asst. Director of Labour. A.Q.M.G. France, Mesopotamia. *D.S.O.*, Jan. 1, 1918. *D.* France, 1916, 1917.

1897 Waddy, Rev. P. S., M.A. (Aug. 1914). Chaplain to Australian Forces (3rd Class). France, 1916–17; Egypt, 1917; Palestine, 1917–18.

1909 Waddy, R. G., B.Sc., B.M., M.Ch. (Aug. 5, 1914). Capt. R.A.M.C. Salonika, Egypt.

1897 **Wahl, B. W.,** M.A. (1916). 2nd Lt. I.A.R.O., Cavalry Branch. Mesopotamia. Killed in action, Oct. 1916.

1906 Waley, S. D., B.A. (Nov. 22, 1916). ‡Lt. 22nd London Regt. (The Queen's). France, 1917–18. *M.C.*, Oct. 16, 1918.

1897 Waley-Cohen, C., M.A. (Feb. 1915). Lt.-Col. Special Lists. A.Q.M.G.. Asst. Director of Requisition Service. Salonika, France. *C.M.G.* Croix de Chevalier de la Légion d'Honneur. *D.* Salonika, 1916, 1917; France, 1919.

1900 **Walford, G. N.** (Serving Aug. 4, 1914). Capt., Bt.-Maj., R.H.A. Gallipoli. Killed in action in Gallipoli on Apr. 30, 1915. **V.C.** won on Apr. 26, 1915.

Subsequent to a landing having been effected on the beach at a point on the Gallipoli Peninsula, during which both Brigadier-General and Brigade Major had been killed, Lt.-Col. Doughty-Wylie and Capt. Walford organized and led an attack through and on both sides of the village of Sedd-el-Bahr on the Old Castle at the top of the hill inland. The enemy's position was very strongly held and entrenched, and defended with concealed machine-guns and poms-poms.

It was mainly due to the initiative, skill, and great gallantry of these two officers that the attack was a complete success.

Both were killed in the moment of victory.

1894 **Walker, E. W.,** B.A. (Serving Aug. 4, 1914). Capt. 1st E. Yorkshire Regt. France and Belgium. Killed in action near Armentières on Oct. 28, 1914.

1908 Walker, N. M. L., B.A. (Sept. 12, 1914). ‡Lt. R. Scots (Capt.). France, 1916; Russia, 1918–19.

1887 Walker, R. J., B.A. Lt. R.N.V.R.

1912 **Wallace, A.** (Oct. 11, 1914). Sergt. New Zealand Engineers, N.Z.E.F. Gallipoli. *D.* Gallipoli, 1915. Died on May 10, 1915, of wounds received in Gallipoli.

1896 Wallace, W. J. L., M.A. (June 1915). Capt. 1/4th Oxf. & Bucks Lt. Infty. France, 1917.

1907 Wallace, W. S., M.A. (Dec. 7, 1915). Maj. 3rd Canadian Res. Bn. France.

1902 Wallis, H. B., B.A. (Sept. 24, 1914). Capt. R. Marines, Reserve of Officers. France, 1914; Gallipoli, 1915. *D.* Gallipoli, 1915.

1919 Wallop, G. V. (Jan. 1917). Lt. 2nd Life Guards. France, 1918–19.

1885 Warburton, H. G. (Dec. 29, 1915). Maj. I.A.R.O., attd. Intelligence Branch. (Lt.-Col., A.Q.M.G., 8th Lucknow Div.) Mesopotamia, 1917–18; Persia, 1918; Trans-Caucasia, 1919.

1895 Ward, A. S., M.A. (Mobilized 1914.). Lt. Hertfordshire Yeomanry (T.F. Res.).

1887 Ward, B. R. (Serving Aug. 4, 1914). Col. R.E. *C.M.G.* *D.* § Jan. 1917.

1905 **Ward, F. W.,** B.A. (Mobilized Aug. 4, 1914). Capt. 1/4th Gloucestershire Regt. France, Belgium. Killed in action near Poelcappelle on Oct. 9, 1917.

1912 Ward,* H. J., M.A. (Aug. 29, 1914). Capt. 4th Devonshire Regt. India, 1914–16; Mesopotamia, 1916–19.

1911 Warde-Aldam,* J. R. P., M.A. (Mobilized Aug. 4, 1914). Capt. 1st Yorkshire Dragoons. France, 1916–18.

1896 Warre, E. L. (Nov. 2, 1914). Capt. K.R.R.C., attd. R.A.F. Staff-Capt. Belgium.

1897 Warre, F. W. (Nov. 1914). Lt. 11th K.R.R.C. Maj. General List. G.S.O. 3. France. *O.B.E.* (Mil.). *M.C.*, Jan. 22, 1916. *D.* France, 1917, 1918.

1891 Waterhouse,* A. T., D.M. (Mobilized Aug. 4, 1914). Maj. R.A.M.C., empld. 2/2nd S. Midland Field Ambulance. France and Belgium, 1916–19.

1907 Waterhouse, M. T., B.A. (Mobil'zed Aug. 8, 1914). Maj. 1st Nottinghamshire Yeomanry. Egypt, Gallipoli, Salonika, Palestine, Syria. *M.C.*, Jan. 1, 1917. *D.* Salonika, 1916.

1910 Watson, W. H. L., B.A. (Aug. 5, 1914). Pte. R.E. (Motor Cyclist). ‡Maj. 4th Bn. Tank Corps. France and Belgium, 1914–15, 1915–18. *D.S.O.*, June 3, 1919. *D.C.M.*, Apr. 1, 1915. *D.* France, 1919.

1899 Watt, J. Crabb, B.A. Penang Volunteers.

1919 Watt, R. P. (Apr. 28, 1916). Lt. 5th Lancers. France, Belgium.

1911 Wedderburn, A. H. M., B.A. (Aug. 5, 1914). Capt. 5th The Black Watch. Staff-Capt. 9th Inf. Bde. France and Germany, 1914–19. *D.* France, 1917.

1919 Wendell, R. L. (Oct. 1918). Cadet Household Bde., O.C.B. France, 1917 (with American Red Cross, attd. French Army).

1907 Wernher, Sir D. J. (Mar. 28, 1915). Capt. R.A.S.C. (Maj.) (attd. R.A.F., 1917). France, Salonika. Croix de Guerre. *D.* France, 1917.

1910 **West, A. G.,** B.A. (Feb. 1915). ‡2nd Lt. 6th Oxf. & Bucks. Lt. Infty. (Capt.). France. Killed in action near Bapaume on Apr. 3, 1917.

1891 West, C. E., B.A. (Jan. 1915). Capt. R.A.M.C., attd. 1st London Gen. Hospital.

1900 **West, H. C.** (Serving Aug. 4, 1914). Capt. R.H.A. Mesopotamia. *M.C.*, Oct. 29, 1915. *D.* Mesopotamia, 1915. Killed in action near the Persian Gulf on Nov. 23, 1915.

1912 Wheeler, A. R., M.A. (May 15, 1917). Capt. 312th Inf., attd. Intelligence, 78th Div. H.Q., U.S. Army. France, 1918; Austria, 1919.

1917 White, A. (Feb. 1918). 2nd Lt. Labour Corps.

Whitehead, E. A. (May 24, 1917). 2nd Lt. R.A.F. France. Killed in action over the Farêb de Gobain on Mar. 13, 1918.

1914 Whitehead, G. R. B. (Apr. 26, 1915). Lt. R.A.S.C. France, 1915–16, 1917.

1916 Whitehead, G. S., M.A. (Sept. 1, 1917). 2nd Lt. 313th M.G. Bn., U.S. Army. France, 1918.

1897 Whitlaw, C. F. (Feb. 4, 1915). 2nd Lt. 4th Devonshire Regt., empld. 6th Wiltshire Regt. France.

1906 **Whitley, C.,** B.A. (Aug. 1914). ‡Capt. 7th K.R.R.C. France. *M.C.*, Oct. 20, 1916. *D.* France, 1917. Killed in action at Wancourt, near Arras on Apr. 11, 1917.

1913 Whitridge, A. (Mar. 20, 1915). Lt. R.F.A. Capt. U.S. Field Artillery. Maj., General Staff, U.S. Army. France and Belgium. *M.C.*, May 16, 1916. *D.* France, 1916.

1910 Whittle, F., B.A. (July 30, 1917). 2nd Lt. Labour Corps. France.

1911 **Whyte, R. B.,** B.A. (Aug. 5, 1914). 2nd Lt. 3rd, attd. 1st, The Black Watch. France. Killed in action at Hulluch on Sept. 25, 1915.

1887 Wild, C. E. (Apr. 1, 1917). Lt. 7th United Provinces Horse, I.D.F.

1919 Wilkinson, T. C. S. (July 6, 1915). Sub-Lt. R.N., H.M.S. *Wakeful.* The Baltic, 1918–19.

1909 Williams, A. de C., B.A. (Nov. 25, 1916). 2nd Lt. Cavalry Branch, I.A.R.O., attd. No. 5 M.T. Coy. India.

1919 Williams, F. E. (June 8, 1915). Lt. 32nd Inf. Bn., A.I.F. Temp. Capt. Special Service List (Dunster Force). Egypt, France, 1916–18. N.W. Persia, 1918.

1902 Williams, O. C. (Mar. 13, 1915). Major Special Lists. G.S.O. 2, War Office. Gallipoli, 1915; Egypt, 1916–17; Palestine, 1917–18. *M.C.* June 3, 1916. Croix de Chevalier de la Légion d'Honneur. Italian Silver Medal for Military Valour. *D.* Gallipoli, 1916; Egypt, 1916, 1917.

1895 Williamson, F. H. (May 5, 1915). Brig.-Gen. Postal Section R.E. (S.R.). Egypt, Gallipoli, 1915. *C.B.E.* (Mil.).
1914 Willis, J. R., B.A. (Jan. 11, 1916). Lt. Worcestershire Regt., attd. R.A.F. France, 1917; Italy, 1917–18. *M.C.*, Mar. 7, 1918.
1910 **Wilson, J. N.** (Aug. 1914). Capt. 6th The Black Watch. France and Belgium. Died on July 4, 1917, of wounds received near Ypres.
1902 Wilson, Sir J. R., B.A. (Mobilized Aug. 4, 1914). Capt. Lanarkshire Yeomanry (Maj.). Gallipoli, Palestine, Egypt.
1898 Wilson, R. W., B.A. Lt. Army Political Officer, German E. Africa. E. Africa.
1908 Wingate, R. E. L., B.A. (Sept. 1917). Asst. Political Officer, M.E.F. Mesopotamia. *D.* Mesopotamia, 1919.
1919 Winkworth, W. W. (May 28, 1916). ‡Lt. 38th Bde. R.F.A. Belgium and France, 1916–18. *M.C.*, Jan. 1, 1918.
1919 Wintringham, T. H. (June 5, 1916). Air Mechanic, R.A.F. France, 1916–18.
1901 Withers, Rev. G. M., M.A. (Aug. 7, 1917). Chaplain to the Forces (4th Class). France.
1906 Wood, A. L. S., B.A. (Mobilized Aug. 4, 1914). Maj. R.A.S.C. (T.F.), attd. 8th Divl. Train. France and Belgium, 1915–19. *O.B.E.* (Mil.). *D.* France, 1917 twice, 1918.
1917 Wood, N. (May 9, 1918). 2nd Lt. Northumberland Fusiliers.
1914 Wood, Rev. W. L. (1917). Chaplain U.S. Army.
1899 [Woodd, G. N., M.A.] (Jan. 28, 1916). Lt. Unattached List, T.F., Bury Grammar School O.T.C.
1918 Woods, J. H. E. (Sept. 28, 1914). Lt. 22nd R. Fusiliers. France, 1915–16. (Invalided on account of wounds, Mar. 1918.)
1883 Wootten, H. E. (Oct. 9, 1914). Maj. (Hon. Lt.-Col.) 9th Border Regt. Temp. Lt.-Col. President, Area Quartering Committee. France. *D.S.O.*, June 3, 1917.
1917 Wordsworth, J. T. (Feb. 15, 1917). Lt. 4th R. Welch Fusiliers. France, 1918; Gibraltar, 1918–19.
1905 Worsley, R. M. M., B.A. (Aug. 4, 1914). Capt., Acting Maj., R.G.A., attd. 1/2nd Lancs. Heavy Batt., R.G.A. (T.F.). Ceylon, France. *M.C.*, Jan. 1, 1919. Italian Silver Medal for Military Valour. *D.* France, 1916.
1918 Wrench, J. C., B.A. (Sept. 1914). 2nd Lt. Northumberland Fusiliers. France.
1897 Wright, E., B.A. (June 1915). Lt. R.N.A.S., Armoured Car Section. Capt. M.G.C. (Asst. Sec. Supreme War Council). Belgium, France.
1912 **Wright, E. G. E.** (Sept. 18, 1914). 2nd Lt. 7th Somerset L.I. France and Belgium. *M.C.*, Mar. 15, 1916. Killed in action at Ypres on June 16, 1916.
1919 Wrong, H. H. (July 20, 1915). Lt. 1/4th Oxf. & Bucks. Lt. Infty. Capt. Administrative Officer, R.A.F. France and Belgium, 1915–16. *D.* § Jan. 1919.
1889 Wyatt, J. A.I.F.
1899 Wykes, P. H., M.A. (Nov. 1914). Lt. Unattached List, T.F., Bradford Grammar School O.T.C.
1910 **Wyley, W. R. F.** (Mobilized Aug. 1914). Lt. and Adjt. 240th Bde., R.F.A. France, 1915–16. Killed in action at Ovillers on Sept. 19, 1916.

1884 [Wylie, F. J., M.A.] (June 5, 1915). Capt. T.F. Res., empld. No. 4 O.C.B.

1882 Wynch, L. M., B.A. (Apr. 1916). Hon. Maj. Special Lists (whilst empld. with British Red Cross Society). Serbia, 1915; France. *C.B.E.* (Civil). *C.I.E.* Order of St. Sava (4th Class). *D.* France, 1916, 1919.

1913 **Wynne, C. W.** (Feb. 1915). Capt. R.G.A. France, 1916–17. Died at St. Omer on June 24, 1917, of wounds received in action at Armentières.

1885 Young, D. J., M.A. (Sept. 22, 1914). Capt. Central London Vol. Regt. Qr.-Master 2nd British Farmers' Serbian Relief Hospital. Serbia. Croix d'Officier de l'Instruction Publique.

1901 Young, H. S., M.A. (Aug. 19, 1914). Capt. Army Pay Dept. France. *D.* France, 1916.

Young, J. H. (Dec. 31, 1914). 2nd Lt. Northumberland Fusiliers, attd. 5th Bn. France. Died on June 9, 1918, of wounds received in action.

1910 Younger,* J. P. (Aug. 1914). Capt. 3rd, attd. 2nd, Arg. & Suth'd. Highlanders. France, 1915–17.

1876 Younghusband, R. E., B.A. (Dec. 11, 1914). Maj. R.A.S.C. *C.S.I.* *D.* § Aug. 1919.

1919 Yoxall, H. W. (July 1915). Capt. 8th K.R.R.C. Capt. General List. France and Belgium, 1916–17. *M.C.*, Jan. 1, 1917; *Bar*, Oct. 28, 1917.

1908 Ziman, S. N., B.A. (July 22, 1916). Lt. 35th Scinde Horse, I.A.R.O. Temp. Capt., Staff-Capt., Bannu Bde. India, N.W. Frontier.

MERTON COLLEGE

1919 Abbott, W. S. (Aug. 20, 1917). 2nd Lt. 10th Devonshire Regt.
1910 **Ackerley,* R. H.** (Aug. 8, 1914). Lt. 1st R. Welch Fusiliers. France, Belgium. Killed in action at Festubert on May 16, 1915.
1913 Adams, W. C. (May 26, 1915). Lt. 2nd, attd. 5th, R. Berkshire Regt. France. *M.C.*, May 26, 1917. *D.* France, 1917.
1914 **Adamson, G. E.** (Mar. 5, 1915). Lt. 7th Middlesex Regt. France, Belgium. *M.C.*, Sept. 16, 1918. Killed in action in the attack on Summit Trench, Croisilles, on Aug. 24, 1918.
1919 Adamson, F. J. (Aug. 11, 1914). Capt. Highland L.I.; Instructor, O.C.B. France, 1915–16.
1910 Aitken, Rev. W. H. M., B.A. (Feb. 21, 1917). Chaplain to the Forces (4th Class).
1906 Allen, W. A. C., M.A. (Dec. 1916). 2nd Lt. R.A.F.
1894 Allfrey, H. C. (Dec. 7, 1914). Capt. Leicestershire Yeomanry, afterwards Capt. R.A.
1916 Armstrong, J. B. (1917). 2nd Lt. 23rd Inf. U.S. Army. France, 1918–19.
1899 Aronson, V. R., B.C.L., M.A. (Mar. 27, 1916). Lt. R.A.S.C.
1896 Ascherson, C. S., B.A. (June 15, 1916). Lt. Special Lists, empld. at War Office. *D.* § Mar. 1918.
1892 Attlee, Rev. B. H. B., B.D. (Sept. 1, 1915). Chaplain, R.N.D. Gallipoli, Egypt, Mudros, France. (Invalided, Sept. 16, 1916.)
1903 Bailey, E. A. H., M.A. (Mobilized Aug. 1914). Lt.-Col. R.F.A. (T.F.). Egypt, Palestine. *D.S.O.*, Jan. 1, 1918. *D.* Palestine, 1918.
1890 **Baker, C. D.,** M.A. (Sept. 21, 1915). Capt. Grenadier Guards. France, Belgium. Killed in action on July 29, 1917.
1909 Baldock, Rev. F. R., M.A. (July 1918). Pte. 28th London Regt. (Artists Rifles).
1899 Balfour, A. E. (Oct. 18, 1914). Capt. 8th Gordon Highlanders, afterwards Capt. General List.
1908 Ball, A. K. M., M.A. (Mobilized Aug. 1914). Capt. R.A.S.C.
1906 [Barber, E. A., M.A.] (Aug. 26, 1915). Lt. 4th Shropshire L.I.; Lt. Special Lists; Staff Lt. (1st Class). Salonika, 1918–19. *D.* Salonika, 1919.
1919 Barker, E. J. (Dec. 11, 1915). Lt. King's (Liverpool Regt.).
1909 Barnard, H. W., M.A. (Nov. 6, 1914). Capt. 5th R. W. Kent Regt. (T.F.).
1877 Barnardiston, N. W., *M.V.O.* (Serving Aug. 4, 1914). Maj.-General. Staff. *C.B.* *C.M.G.* Order of the Rising Sun (2nd Class). Tsing-Tau. *D.* §Aug. 1917. Died on Aug. 18, 1919.
1894 Bartleet, L., M.A. R.G.A.
1887 Bartrum, Rev. E. S., M.A. (Oct. 23, 1917). Chaplain to the Forces (4th Class).
1897 Baskervyle-Glegg, J. (June 23, 1916). Lt. Montgomeryshire Yeomanry.

1918 Bates, R. B. (Aug. 19, 1914). Lce.-Sgt. 7th Bn. A.I.F. Suez Canal, 1915, 1916; Gallipoli, 1915; France, from 1916. *M.M.*, Oct. 27, 1915; *Bar*, Dec. 16, 1916.

1898 Baxendale, J. F. N. (Mobilized Aug. 1914). Lt.-Col. Hampshire Yeomanry. France. *D.* France, 1917.

1919 Baynes, T. A. H. (Jan. 29, 1916). Lt. 7th Divl. Signal Coy., R.E. France, 1916–17. Italy, 1917–19.

1906 Baynham, A. G., B.A. (1915). ‡Lt. M.G.C., afterwards Lt. Tank Corps. France. *M.C.*, Jan. 1, 1918.

1914 Bean, E. L. (Aug. 4, 1915). Sergeant X/47th T.M.B., 7th London Bde., R.F.A. France, 1916–19.

1905 Beech, Rev. G., M.A. (Jan. 1, 1916). Chaplain to the Forces (4th Class).

1919 Beighton, H. (Oct. 1916). 2nd Lt. 3rd Queen's (R. W. Surrey Regt.) France, 1917.

1911 Beirne, F. F., B.A. (May 4, 1917). 1st Lt. U.S. Infantry. France.

1913 **Bellasis,* P. J.** (Aug. 22, 1914). Capt. 5th Shropshire L.I. France, 1915–16, Belgium. Killed in action at Delville Wood on Aug. 24, 1916.

1910 **Benson, J. M.** (Sept. 1914). 2nd Lt., Acting Capt., 4th Northumberland Fusiliers, comdg. 149th T.M.B. France. Killed in action between Craonne and Pontavert on the Aisne on May 27, 1918.

1905 Bewsher, F. W., B.A. (Mobilized Aug. 4, 1914). Capt. 5th London Regt. (London Rifle Brigade.). G.S.O. 2, IV Corps (Lt.-Col.). France. *D.S.O.*, June 3, 1919; *M.C.*, June 4, 1917. *D.* France, 1917, 1919.

1894 Bickerton, J. M. N. S., B.M., M.A. (Jan. 26, 1917). Capt. R.A.M.C.

1886 Bingley, A. G. E. (1914). Maj., Special Lists (late R. Berkshire Regt.). E. Africa.

1912 Birch, A. E., M.A. (Sept. 9, 1914). ‡Capt. 8th R. Welch Fusiliers. Egypt, Mesopotamia, India. *D.* Mesopotamia, 1918.

1915 Bird,* O. S. (July 1916). ‡Lt. 3rd E. Lancashire Regt. France.

1912 Bird, R., B.A. (Sept. 11, 1914). ‡Lt. 6th York and Lancaster Regt. (Adjt.). Egypt, 1915–16; France, 1916–17 and 1917–19.

1891 Birkenhead, Lord, B.C.L., M.A. (Aug. 1914). Hon. Capt. Q.O. Oxfordshire Hussars. Lt.-Col. H.Q. Staff, Indian Army Corps. France, Belgium. *D.* France, 1915.

1903 Birks, A. H., B.A. (Nov. 19, 1914). C.S.M. Inns of Court O.T.C.

1901 Birts, W. T. W., M.A. (Apr. 2, 1916). Lt. 16th London Regt. (Queen's Westminster Rifles), empld. Min. of Mun.

1913 Blanshard, P. V., B.Sc. (1918). Sergt. U.S. Base Hospital No. 123. France, 1918–19; Mesopotamia, India, 1915–17 (with Y.M.C.A.).

1900 Blundell, F. N., B.A. (Aug. 19, 1914). Capt. Lancashire Hussars. France, Belgium, 1915–19. *D.* France, 1919.

1902 **Boddington, R. T.,** M.A. (Feb. 1916). 2nd Lt. 1/10th London Regt. Egypt, Palestine. Killed in action at 'Rafa Belah ridge', Gaza, on Nov. 2, 1917.

1919 Bolton, E. J. (Dec. 1915). Lt. 3rd Dorsetshire Regt., Lt. Special Lists, attd. Naval Intelligence Dept. France. *M.C.*, Oct. 18, 1917.

1905 Bond, E. Fitz-G., M.A. (Apr. 15, 1916). Lt. 27th Bde., R.G.A. France. *M.C.*, Feb. 4, 1918.

1909 **Booth,* F. H. F.,** B.A. (Aug. 1914). ‡Capt. 2nd Worcestershire Regt. France, Belgium. Missing, believed killed in action near Gheluvelt, on Sept. 25, 1917.

1903 Boraston, J. H., B.C.L., M.A. (Aug. 1914). Lt.-Col. R.F.A. (T.F.). France. *C.B.* *O.B.E.* (Mil.). Croix de Chevalier de la Légion d'Honneur. *D.* France, 1917, 1918, 1919.

1919 Boswell, K. C. (Aug. 29, 1916). ‡Lt. R.G.A. France. (Prisoner of War, Mar.–Nov. 1918.)

1881 Bourne, G. C., M.A., D.Sc. (Nov. 31, 1914). Supervising Officer, Y.O. Coy., Res. Inf. Bde. Late Maj. 12th Worcestershire Regt. (Hon. Colonel).

1903 **Bowen, A. J. H.,** M.A. (Mobilized Aug. 4, 1914). Maj. 2nd Monmouthshire Regt. (Lt.-Col.). France, Belgium. *D.S.O.*, July 3, 1915; *Bar*, Mar. 12, 1917. *D.* France, 1915, 1916, 1917. Killed in action on Mar. 2, 1917.

1913 Bowen, E. I. P., B.A. (Nov. 1914). Lt. R.E. (Capt.). France.

1919 Bradshaw, N. R. J. (Dec. 8, 1915). ‡Lt. 1st (Garr.) Bn. Worcestershire Regt.; Acting Capt. and Adjt. 74th Labour Group, Labour Corps. France.

1904 **Brandon, A. C.,** B.A. (Mobilized Aug. 1914). Capt. 4th Hampshire Regt. Mesopotamia. Killed in action on Jan. 21, 1916.

1899 Brook, Rev. R., M.A. (Aug. 3, 1916). Chaplain to the Forces (4th Class) (S.C.F.). France, 1915–16 (as Acting Chaplain). *D.* § Mar. 1918.

1919 Brown, C. R. (Apr. 27, 1917). Lce.-Cpl. 8th R. W Kent Regt. France. *M.M.*

1919 Brown, H., B.A. (Sept. 4, 1914). ‡Capt. 2/5th King's Own (R. Lancaster Regt.). France, 1915–16, 1917–19.

1909 Browne, T. L. (Mar. 19, 1915). Capt. 10th Northumberland Fusiliers. France, Italy. *M.C.*, Nov. 19, 1917. Italian Silver Medal for Valour.

1910 Bryan, W. S., M.A. (1917). Lt. Intelligence Service, U.S. Army, attd. G.H.Q. France.

1912 Bryans,* W. B. (Aug. 14, 1914). Capt. 3rd Norfolk Regt. Adjt. R.A.F. France, Belgium, 1915.

1912 Buckland, C. S. B. (Oct. 1915). Capt. and Adjt. R.G.A. France, Belgium, 1916–19.

1913 Bullen, J. G., B.A. (Aug. 21, 1914). Maj. 9th, attd. 3rd, Essex Regt. France. *D.* France, 1916.

1911 Bullivant, W. (Jan. 9, 1916). Lt. 7th Sherwood Foresters.

1913 **Bulmer, J. L.** (Oct. 1915). 2nd Lt. 5th Oxf. & Bucks. Lt. Infty. France. Reported missing, presumed killed in action on May 3, 1917.

1904 Burchardt-Ashton, J. F. (Oct. 15, 1914). Lt. R.F.A. Lt. R.A.S.C.

1904 **Burdekin, S.** (Feb. 20, 1915). 2nd Lt. R.F.A. France. Killed in action on Sept. 28, 1915.

1913 Burge, B. E. J. (Sept. 7, 1914). Lt. 23rd Rifle Brigade. (T.F.) (Capt.). Malta, Egypt, Sudan, Gallipoli, 1914–15. India, 1916–19.

1881 Burges, G. H., B.A. (Serving Aug. 4, 1914). Lt.-Col., Bt.-Col., 8th Gloucestershire Regt. *D.* § Feb. 1917.

1905 Burney, E., B.A. (Sept. 2, 1914). 2nd Lt. Intelligence Corps, afterwards Capt. Staff Officer, R.A.F. France, S. Russia. *M.C.*, June 3, 1916.

1905 Burt, M. S. (Jan. 1918). Pte. Air Service, U.S. Army.

1911 Burton, C. E., M.A. (Sept. 7, 1914). ‡Lt. Army Cyclist Corps. France.

1912 Burton, T. K., B.A. (Aug. 15, 1914). Lt. Cameronians and R.A.F. Salonika, 2 years. Egypt, 11 months.

1911 Buxton, A., M.A. (Aug. 13, 1915). Lt. R.G.A. (T.F.). France, for 2 years.

1920 Cairns Smith, A. F. (June 1, 1917). Lt. 'C.' Batt., 310th Bde., R.F.A. France 1917–18; Germany 1918–19.

1908 Campbell, W. S. (May 11, 1917). Capt. 335th Field Artillery, U.S. Army (Maj.). France, 1918.

1908 Cartmel-Robinson, H. F. (1914). ‡2nd Lt., Acting Capt. and Adjt., R.F.A. W. Africa.

1903 **Caton, F. W.,** M.A. (1915). 2nd Lt. R.E. France. Killed in action on June 28, 1916.

1910 **Cattley, H. P.** (1914). Pte. Manchester Regt. France. Killed in action on Mar. 14, 1917.

1913 **Chamberlayne, T. E. O.** (Oct. 6, 1914). Lt. 73rd Bde., R.F.A. France, 1915–16. Killed in action on the Somme on Aug. 18, 1916.

1905 [Cheshire, G. C., B.C.L., M.A.] (Jan. 7, 1915). Capt. 6th Cheshire Regt. Capt. R.A.F. (since Nov. 1916). France, Belgium.

1920 Clark, C. B. (Dec. 1915). †Lt. 38th Bn. C.E.F. Flying Officer, Airship Section, R.A.F. France, Belgium, 1917–18.

1908 Clark,* J. E., B.A. (Aug. 4, 1914). Capt. 5th R. Inniskilling Fusiliers. Belgium, France, Italy. *M.C.*, Sept. 24, 1918. *D.* France, 1917.

1903 Clarke, N. O., M.A. (Aug. 15, 1914). Capt. 3rd N. Staffordshire Regt. France, Belgium, 1915–16.

1904 **Clerk, R. M.,** B.A. (Oct. 29, 1914). Capt. King's Own (R. Lancaster Regt.), attd. 6th Queen's (R. W. Surrey Regt.). France. Killed in action at Arras on Apr. 9, 1917.

1903 **Coburn, C.,** B.A. (Apr. 26, 1917). 2nd Lt. K.R.R.C. France, Belgium. Killed in action on July 31, 1917.

1907 [Cocker,* N.] (1917). ‡2nd Lt. Lincolnshire Regt.

1919 Cockman, H. J. (Feb. 13, 1917). Lt. R.A.F. France. *D.F.C.*, Dec. 3, 1918.

1892 Cohen, J. W., B.A., T.D. (Mobilized Aug. 1914). Lt.-Col. 16th London Regt. (Queen's Westminster Rifles), attd. Independent Force, R.A.F. France. *D.S.O.*, June 3, 1916. *D.* France, 1916 twice, 1917, 1918.

1887 Collison, H., M.A. (July 29, 1915). Capt. Army Cyclist Corps. Lt. General List, attd. Indian Army. India.

1911 Collymore, E. A., M.A. (Sept. 29, 1914). Capt. 8th E. Lancashire Regt. General List.

1911 **Conn,* J. F. C.,** B.A. (Oct. 5, 1914). Capt. 7th Arg. & Suth'd. Highlanders. France, 1915, 1917. Died at Wimereux on May 1, 1917, of wounds received in action on Apr. 23, 1917.

1919 Conner, C. (Aug. 15, 1918). 2nd Lt. R.G.A.

1919 Cooke, D. E. (Sept. 1915). Lt. Durham L.I., attd. R.E. France. *M.C.*, Sept. 16, 1918.

1902 Cooke, O. H., B.C.L., M.A. (Aug. 12, 1914). Lt. 3rd K.O.Y.L.I. (Capt.). France. *M.C.*, Nov. 25, 1916; *Bar*, Nov. 17, 1917.

1919 Cooke, R. A. (Sept. 8, 1914). ‡Lt. 7th Cheshire Regt., attd. M.G.C. (Capt.). Palestine, 1916–19.

Coupland-Smith, F. V. (Sept. 10, 1914). ‡2nd Lt. 173rd Bde., R.F.A. Egypt, Serbia, France, Belgium. Killed in action at Wytschaete on July 2, 1917.

1908 Cowan, J. R. C. (Mobilized Aug. 4, 1914). Capt. 2nd Scottish Horse. Gallipoli, Egypt. (Discharged on account of ill health, Jan. 1918).
1899 Cowderoy, T. A., M.A. No. 2 Cadet School, R.G.A.
1911 Coxon, R. E., B.A. (June 16, 1915). Lt. 1st Irish Guards, attd. O.C.B.
1919 Crawford, H. L. (June 26, 1918). Pte. 2nd Artists Rifles, O.T.C.
1912 Crawford,* J. G. (Aug. 29, 1914). Capt. 5th Cheshire Regt. France.
Crawhall, F. P. (Aug. 15, 1914) 2nd Lt. 6th K.R.R.C. France. Killed in action at Givenchy-lez-la Bassée on Mar. 10, 1915.
1905 Croysdale, T. P., B.A. (Mobilized Aug. 4, 1914). Capt. 10th London Regt. (Maj.). France, Egypt. *D.* § Mar. 1919, § Aug. 1919.
1894 Cruickshank, R. B., B.A. (Aug. 11, 1916). Lt. R.G.A.
1912 **Culpin, K. H.** (Apr. 1916). 2nd Lt. 2nd Gloucestershire Regt. France. Died on May 15, 1917, of wounds received in action near Fresnois.
1890 Curtis, H., M.A. Pte. Q. O. Cameron Highlanders.
1919 Davis, G. I. (Oct. 27, 1917). 2nd Lt. R.E. (Signal Service). France.
1913 Davison, W. C., B.A., B.Sc. (June 21, 1917). Capt. Medical Corps, U.S. Army. France, 1917–19. (Served with B.R.C.S. in France and Serbia, 1914–16).
1899 Deed, S. C., B.A. (Nov. 21, 1914). Lt. Reserve of Cavalry, attd. 10th Hussars, afterwards Maj., Special Lists ; D.A.A.G. France, Palestine. *M.C.*, Mar. 30, 1916. Order of the Nile (4th Class). *D.* Palestine, 1919.
1898 de Labillière, Rev. P. F. D., M.A. (Mar. 21, 1916). Chaplain to the Forces (4th Class). Egypt, 1917–19. *D.* § Mar. 1918.
1879 De Winton, A. J., M.A. (Oct. 29, 1914). Hon. Maj. Labour Corps. France, Belgium.
1897 [de Zulueta,* F., M.A., D.C.L.] (Dec. 30, 1914). Capt. 2nd Worcestershire Regt. France, 1918–19.
1911 **Dickson,* A. J.,** B.A. (Serving Aug. 4, 1914). Lt. 2nd Highland L.I. France, Belgium. Killed in action near Zonnebeke on Nov. 14, 1914.
1900 Dickson, M. R., B.A. (Aug. 1914). Lt.-Col. 12th Arg. & Suth'd. Highlanders. Salonika. *D.S.O.*, June 3, 1918. Croix d'Officier de la Légion d'Honneur. *D.* Salonika, 1917–18.
1908 Diggle,* Rev. R. F., M.A. (Jan. 1, 1918). Chaplain to the Forces (4th Class), attd. 2nd London Regt. France. *M.C.*, Dec. 2, 1918.
1908 Distin, C. W., B.A. (Oct. 28, 1917). 2nd Lt. R.F.A. France. *M.C.*, Feb. 15, 1919; *Bar*, Jan. 1, 1919.
1910 Doake,* R. L. V., B.A. (Sept. 12, 1914). Capt. 7th, attd. 2nd, Bedfordshire Regt. France. *D.S.O.*, Mar. 8, 1919. *M.C.*, Sept. 16, 1918. *D.* France, 1919.
1911 Domville, C. L., B.A. (Nov. 1914). Capt. 5th K.R.R.C. France, Belgium, 1915–18. (Prisoner of War, 1918.) *M.C.*, Oct. 18, 1917. *D.* France, 1916 twice.
1883 Douglas, J. A., M.A. (Sept. 21, 1914). Maj. Special Lists ; D.A.Q.M.G., British Mission to Serbian Army. Serbia. Order of St. Sava (4th Class).
1895 **Douglas, J. C. E.,** B.A. (1914). Capt. 10th Yorkshire Regt. France. Died on Dec. 18, 1915, of wounds received in action.
1915 Dove, F. S. (Nov. 6, 1916). Pte. Tank Corps. Cadet R.A.F. France. *M.M.*, Mar. 13, 1918.

Drummond, J. C. G. (Jan. 5, 1918). 2nd Lt. R.A.F. France. Killed in action on Oct. 8, 1918.

1919 Dunbar, G. A. (July 1915). ‡Capt. 42nd Bn. A.I.F. Egypt, France 1916–18. *M.C.*, June 3, 1919. Belgian Croix de Guerre. *D.* France, 1917, 1918.

1914 **Dunlop, L. L. B.** (1914). 2nd Lt. 11th Cheshire Regt. France. Killed in action in Battle of the Somme on July 4, 1916.

1909 **Dunnage,* A.** (Sept. 1, 1914). ‡2nd Lt. 5th Rifle Brigade. France. Killed in action at Delville Wood on Sept. 1, 1916.

1910 Dunthorne,* R. G., B.A. (Aug. 7, 1914). ‡Capt. 11th S. Lancashire Regt. Instructor No. 14 O.C.B. (since May 1918). France, 1915; Salonika, 1915–16; France, 1917–18.

1902 Duveen, G. E., M.A. (Sept. 28, 1914). Lt. R.N.V.R. Antwerp, Mediterranean, North Sea.

1911 **Eddison,* T. D.** (Sept. 1, 1914). ‡2nd Lt. 19th King's (Liverpool Regt.). France. Killed in action in Trônes Wood on July 30, 1916.

1899 Edmonds-Smith, Rev. E., M.A. (Serving Aug. 4, 1914). Chaplain to the Forces (3rd Class). Malta. *D.* § Mar. 1918.

Edsall, T. H. (1917). Base Hospital Unit, California. Died Jan. 1918.

1908 Edwards,* E. M., M.A. (Sept. 15, 1914). Capt. 48th Divl. Train, R.A.S.C. France, Italy. *M.C.*, Apr. 2, 1919. *D.* Italy, 1918.

1909 Edwards, F. B., B.A. R.G.A., Tasmania.

1905 Farren, Rev. W. M. A., M.A. (Serving Aug. 4, 1914). Chaplain to the Forces (4th Class). Malta. *D.* § Mar. 1918, § Aug. 1919.

1895 Fennell, W. W., M.A. (June 4, 1915). Lt. R. Defence Corps.

1911 [Fielding, M. G., M.A.] (1914). ‡Lt. 2nd Oxf. & Bucks. Lt. Infty. (Capt.). France. *M.C.*, Feb. 13, 1917.

1919 Finch, J. P. G. (Mar. 16, 1917). 2nd Lt. 24th Heavy Batt., R.G.A. France, Belgium.

1903 Firth, J. C. B., B.A. (Aug. 28, 1914). Lt. Shropshire L.I. (till Dec. 1916). Major R.A.F. France, Italy. *M.C.*, Feb. 18, 1918. Italian Bronze Medal for Military Valour.

1911 Fletcher, G. D. A., B.A. (Aug. 10, 1914). ‡Maj. 5/6th R. Scots (Lt.-Col.). France, 1915–16; Belgium, 1916–18. *M.C.*, June 3, 1916. *D.* France, 1918.

1908 **Fletcher, H. W.,** B.A. (Sept. 6, 1914). ‡Lt. 9th R. Welch Fusiliers. Gallipoli, 1915; Egypt and Palestine, 1916–17. Died on Mar. 26, 1917, of wounds received in action at the 1st battle of Gaza.

1915 Fossick, W. G. (Feb. 28, 1916). Pte. H.A.C., attd. Censor Section, Havre. France, Belgium.

1895 Foster, T. S., M.A. (Feb. 1917). Lt. R.A.O.C.

1899 Fox, L. D'A. (Serving Aug. 4, 1914). Maj. 1st R. Welch Fusiliers, attd. Gold Coast Regt. West Africa.

1901 **Fry, C. E.,** B.A. (1914). Lt. R.A. France. Killed in action on Apr. 17, 1917.

1914 Fuller, E. A. (Dec. 22, 1914). Lt. 3rd Middlesex Regt. France, 1916–18.

1897 Fyfe, W. H., M.A. (Jan. 1915). Lt. O.U.O.T.C., afterwards Maj. H.Q. General Staff. *D.* § Mar. 1918.

1902 **Gair, H. B.** (Nov. 1916). 2nd Lt. 4th Dorsetshire Regt., attd. 206th Field Coy., R.E. France. Died on May 15, 1918, of wounds received in action at Bretencourt.

1909 Gardner,* H. M., B.A. (Sept. 1915). ‡Lt. King's African Rifles. German East Africa.

1900 Garrett-Pegge, R. O., M.A. (June 7, 1916). 2nd Lt. R.A.S.C. France, Belgium.

1900 Garrett-Pegge, W. G., M.A. (Feb. 15, 1916). Lt. R.A.S.C. France, Belgium, 1916–19.

1909 Garsia,* M. de la P., B.A. (Oct. 10, 1914). Lt. 3rd Somerset L.I. France.

1905 Gartside, L., B.A. (Mobilized Aug. 1914). Capt. 1/7th Arg. & Suth'd. Highlanders. France. *D.S.O.*, Oct. 15, 1918. Croix de Chevalier de la Légion d'Honneur. *D.* France, 1916, 1918, 1919.

1918 Gatenby, E. J. B., B.A. (July 5, 1915). ‡Lt. 12th King's (Liverpool Regt.) France, 1915–17.

1902 Gay, C. H. (Serving Aug. 4, 1914). Capt., Bt.-Maj., temp. Lt.-Col., R.G.A. A.Q.M.G. France. *D.S.O.*, Jan. 1, 1918. Chevalier de l'Ordre de Léopold. Belgian Croix de Guerre. *D.* France, 1917, 1918.

1889 Gee, W. H., M.A. Canadian E.F. France, Belgium. (Prisoner of War.)

1914 George, H. E. (July 1915). ‡2nd Lt. R.G.A. (S.R.). Egypt, France, Salonika.

1898 Gethin, F. D. S. (Serving Aug. 4, 1914). Maj., Bt.-Lt.-Col., R.F.A., attd. Ministry of Munitions, 1916–19. *D.* § Mar. 1918.

1907 Giffey,* C. K. O. B., B.A. (Serving Aug. 4, 1914). Capt. 2nd Worcestershire Regt. France, 1914–15; Mesopotamia, 1917–18; Persia, 1918; S. Russia, 1918–19.

1902 Gill,* W. B., B.Sc., M.A. (Sept. 1914). Sergt. 9th Hampshire Regt., afterwards ‡Maj. R.E. (Wireless). Egypt, Salonika, 1916–17. *O.B.E.* (Mil.). *D.* Palestine, 1918 twice.

Gillies, H. G. (July 18, 1916). 2nd Lt. 1st R. Scots Fusiliers. France. Missing, presumed killed in action at Serre on Nov. 13, 1916.

1892 Glynn, E. F., B.A. (Mobilized Aug. 4, 1914). Capt., Acting Maj., R.F.A. (T.F.). India, France.

1905 Goddard, E., M.A. (Oct. 1916). Staff Lt. H.Q. Eastern Command (Intelligence Officer). *M.B.E.* (Mil.).

1896 Gosling, Rev. W. C., M.A. (May 1, 1917). Chaplain to the Forces (4th Class).

1890 Goudge, Rev. T. S., M.A. (Serving Aug. 4, 1914). Chaplain to the Forces (1st Class). France. *D.S.O.*, Jan. 1, 1918. *D.* France, 1917.

1919 Gough, J. W. (Aug. 15, 1918). 2nd Lt. R.G.A. (on demobilization).

1909 Gould,* E. R. (Sept. 4, 1914). ‡Capt. 2nd E. Surrey Regt., attd. 11th R. Welch Fusiliers. France, 1915; Salonika, 1915–18; Constantinople, 1918–19. Chevalier, Order of the Redeemer.

1908 Graham,* H., M.A. (May 15, 1915). Lt. I.A.R.O., attd. 9th Gurkhas and later to Nepalese Contingent (Capt.). Mesopotamia, 1916.

1912 Gray, D. (Oct. 31, 1914). Lt. R.N.V.R. (Naval Intelligence Division). Belgium, France, Italy, Mediterranean.

1919 Green, J. B. (July 23, 1917). Telegraphist, R.N.V.R. North Sea, Mediterranean.

1919 Griffith, E. S. (May 7, 1918). Student Flight Officer, U.S. Naval Aviation.

1902 Gullick, T. E., B.A. (Sept. 3, 1914). ‡Maj. R.A.S.C. France, Belgium. *M.C.*, June 3, 1916. *D.* France, 1917.

1903 Guy, P. L. O. (Mar. 11, 1915). 2nd Lt. 11th Cameronians, afterwards Capt. M.G.C. (Education Officer).

1905 **Hales, C. E. H.** (Dec. 4, 1914). 2nd Lt. 3rd Wiltshire Regt. Died on Nov. 22, 1917, of illness contracted on active service.

1919 Hall, R. R. P. (Sept. 6, 1915). Pte. 53rd Field Ambulance, R.A.M.C. (Lce.-Cpl.). France.

1893 Hamilton, H. C. H., B.A. (Apr. 6, 1915). 2nd Lt. 18th R. Fusiliers.

1919 Hamilton-Gay, G. B. W. (Mar. 31, 1915). ‡Lt. R.G.A.

1904 Hancock, C. G., B.A. (1914). Capt. 9th Middlesex Regt. (T.F.).

1894 Hands, Rev. L., B.D. (Apr. 17, 1917). Chaplain to the Forces (4th Class).

1885 Hardman, H. FitzW., B.A. (Serving Aug. 4, 1914). Lt.-Col. 2nd Somerset L.I. *D.* § Aug. 1918.

1901 **Hardy, G. J. M.** (Apr. 13, 1915). Lt. 4th, attd. 3rd, Coldstream Guards (Capt.). France. Killed in action on Aug. 1, 1917.

1891 **Harford, E. B.** (Sept. 1914). Capt. 2/4th Somerset L.I. (Col.). India, Palestine. *D.* Palestine, 1918. Wounded at Gaza (Nov. 1917), invalided home, and died at Eastbourne on July 15, 1918.

1906 Harland, C. C., M.A. (Aug. 15, 1914). Lt. S. Staffordshire Regt. (Capt.). France. *M.C.*, Jan. 1, 1918. Croix de Guerre. *D.* France, 1918, 1919.

1909 Harrington,* H. N., B.A. (Serving Aug. 4, 1914). Capt. 3rd, attd. 1st, Cheshire Regt. France. *D.* May 5, 1920. (Prisoner of War.)

1895 **Harrison, C. R.,** B.A. (Sept. 1914). Lt. 3rd, attd. 2nd, Leicestershire Regt. France. Died on May 23, 1915, of wounds received at Festubert.

1914 **Harrison,* W. B.** (July 1915). Pte. 20th R. Fusiliers. France. Killed in action at High Wood on July 20, 1916.

1901 Harrop, H. R., M.A. (June 18, 1915). Lt. I.A.R.O. India.

1913 **Hart, R. G.** (Sept. 1914). 2nd Lt. 3rd R. Warwickshire Regt. France. Presumed killed in action, June 1916.

1905 **Hartley, C.,** B.A. (Aug. 26, 1914). Lt. C Batt., 210th Bde., R.F.A. Egypt, France, Belgium. Killed in action at Ypres on Sept. 1, 1917.

1910 **Hartley,* D'A. J. J.** (Sept. 1914). Lt. 7th Dragoon Guards, attd. M.G.C. France, 1915–16. Killed in action in Battle of the Somme on July 14, 1916.

1906 Harvey-Samuel, G. D., M.A. (1915). Lt. 10th, attd. 2nd, Middlesex Regt. France. (Prisoner of War, Mar. 1918.) *D.* France, 1918.

1904 Haslam, P. L. C. (Serving Aug. 4, 1914). Capt. 18th Hussars, Lt.-Col. 4th Bn. Tank Corps, France, Belgium. *D.S.O.*, Jan. 1, 1918. *D.* France, 1917.

1903 Hastings, C. E. P., B.A. (Sept. 1, 1914). Capt. Army Cyclist Corps. France.

1900 Hastings, W. G. W., B.A. (Mar. 26, 1915). Capt. Special Lists. Maj. D.A.D. of Transport.

1881 Hatchard, F. S. U., M.A. (May 1915). Lt. General List (T.F. Reserve), empld. Recruiting duties.

1911 Hawkes,* F. C., B.A. (Sept. 15, 1915). Lt. A.S.C. (until Jan. 1918). Lt., Acting Capt., R.G.A. France.

1919 Hawking, J. L. (Aug. 9, 1918). Pte. 28th London Regt. (2nd Artists Rifles O.T.C.).

1908 Heath,* R., B.A. (Nov. 15, 1914). Lt. 8th E. Surrey Regt., afterwards Capt. 252nd Tunnelling Coy., R.E. France. *D.* France, 1917.

1914 Henderson, H. Y. G. (Dec. 2, 1914). Lt., Acting Capt., 14th Highland L.I. France, 1916–17, 1917–18. (Prisoner of War, Apr.–Nov. 1918.)

1907 Herring, D. G., M.A. (1917). Lt. U.S. Ordnance Corps. France.
1909 Higgins, J. G., B.A. Pte. Ambulance Corps, Canadian E.F.
1910 Higham,* E. E. (Sept. 4, 1914). ‡Lt. 5th London Regt. (London Rifle Brigade). France, 1917.
1905 Hill, J. E., M.A. (Mobilized Aug. 4, 1914). Major 5th Bedfordshire Regt. (D.A.A.G., 1917). Gallipoli, Egypt, Palestine. *O.B.E.* (Mil.). *D.* Palestine, 1918 twice.
1902 **Hill, R. W.,** M.A. (Aug. 11, 1915). Lt. 1st Cambridgeshire Regt. (Capt.). France, Belgium. Died on July 31, 1917, of wounds received in action at St. Julien.
1915 Hill-Wilson, A. C. R.A.S.C. (M.T.).
1907 **Hobbs, O. J.,** M.A. (1914). ‡Sub-Lt. R.N.V.R., Anson Bn., R.N.D. Gallipoli, France. Killed in action at Beaumont Hamel on Nov. 13, 1916.
1908 Hodges,* J. F., B.A. (Serving Aug. 4, 1914). Capt. 2nd R. Irish Fusiliers. Belgium, 1914 ; France, 1915 ; Salonika, 1915–17 ; Palestine, 1917–18 ; Egypt. *M.C.*, June 23, 1915 ; *Bar*, Feb. 4, 1919. *D.* France, 1915.
1904 Hodgkinson, J., M.A. (Mobilized Aug. 4, 1914). Capt. 5th N. Staffordshire Regt. Temp. Maj. Tank Corps. France, 1917, 1918–19.
1904 Hodson, H. S., M.A. (Sept. 14, 1914). Capt. Staffordshire Yeomanry and Adjt. 1st Vol. Bn. Northamptonshire Regt.
1900 Hole, W. G., B.A. (Mobilized Aug. 1914). Maj Royal 1st. Devon Yeomanry. Palestine. *D.* Palestine, 1918, 1919.
1906 **Holland, A. C.,** B.A. (Aug. 1914). ‡2nd Lt. 4th Bedfordshire Regt. France. Killed in action at Delville Wood on July 27, 1916.
1902 Holland, W. A., B.A. (Sept. 3, 1914). ‡Lt. R.F.C., afterwards Lt. 3rd Dorsetshire Regt. (Capt.). Gallipoli, 1915.
1898 **Horlock, A. I. W.,** M.A. Pte. R. Fusiliers. France, Belgium. Killed in action on July 3, 1917.
1908 Horsley,* S. S., M.A. (Aug. 15, 1914). Capt. 3rd E. Surrey Regt., and Unattached List, T.F.
1909 Horton,* L. E. L., B.A. (Serving Aug. 4, 1914). Capt. 1st King's (Liverpool Regt.), empld. Min. of National Service. France, Aug.–Sept. 1914.
1895 Horton, W., B.A. (Nov. 10, 1915). Lt. 6th S. Staffordshire Regt. (T.F.).
1909 Howe, H. W., M.A. Middlesex Regt.
1900 Howell, O. B., M.A. (July 1916). Lt. R.A.F. (Flight Comdr.). France.
1908 **Huggard,* H.** (Aug. 1914). Lt. 6th E. Yorkshire Regt. Egypt, Gallipoli. Presumed killed in action at Suvla Bay on Aug. 9, 1915.
1898 Hughes, J. J., B.A. 2nd Lt. Welsh Regt.
1911 **Hunt,* A. N. C.** (Aug. 17, 1914). Capt. 2nd Oxf. & Bucks. Lt. Infty. France. Killed in action on June 6, 1916.
1911 Hunt, R. N. C. (May 19, 1915). Lt. 1/4th Oxf. & Bucks. Lt. Infty., attd. War Office. France, 1916.
1898 Hunter, F. J. W. (Apr. 28, 1915). Lt. 7th The Black Watch (T.F.).
1907 Husband, R. O. F., B.A. (Sept. 15, 1915). Lt. 5th Rifle Brigade ; Staff Lt. (2nd Class).
1907 Hutton,* T. W., B.A. (Jan. 13, 1916). Lt. Warwickshire Regt.
1910 **Hutton,* R.** (Sept. 1914). 2nd Lt. 3rd Leicestershire Regt., attd. 2nd R. Warwickshire Regt. France, Belgium. Reported missing, presumed killed in action near Ypres on Nov. 9, 1914.

1903 Innes, A. G., M.A. (1914). Lt. R.N.V.R.

1912 Jack, A. L., M.A. (Jan. 25, 1915). Lt. K.O.Y.L.I.

1898 Jackson, F. W. J., M.A. (Aug. 4, 1914). Lt. R.A.S.C. (Capt.). France, 1916–18.

1913 Jagger,* A. H. (Aug. 29, 1914). Capt. 7th R. Warwickshire Regt. Belgium, France, 1915–16, 1917, 1918.

1892 James, A. H. C., B.A. (Serving Aug. 4, 1914). Maj., temp. Lt.-Col., S. Staffordshire Regt.; Provost Marshall. France. *M.V.O.* *D.S.O.*, Feb. 18, 1915. *D.* France, 1918.

1900 Jameson, H. P., *M.P.* (Aug. 4, 1914). Capt. R.M.C., Sandhurst. France.

1909 **Jarintzoff, D.** (1914). ‡Capt. E. Lancashire Regt., attd. 8th Bn. Gallipoli, France, Belgium. *M.C.*, June 3, 1916. *D.* Gallipoli, 1916. Killed in action on Oct. 8, 1917.

1906 **Jesson, R. W. F.,** B.A. (Aug. 5, 1914). Maj. 5th Wiltshire Regt. Gallipoli, Mesopotamia. *D.* Mesopotamia, 1917. Killed in action at Kut on Feb. 22, 1917.

1904 Jessop, J. W., M.A. (Jan. 31, 1916). Lt. 2nd Bn. M.G.C. France, Belgium, Germany.

1913 Johnson, C. W., B.A. (Jan. 25, 1915). Pte. R.A.M.C. France, Belgium.

1918 Johnston, C. E., B.Litt. (1915). Canadian Engineers.

1913 Johnston, P. R., B.A. (Apr. 10, 1915). Lt. E. Surrey Regt. France.

1919 Johnstone, G. H. (Nov. 10, 1917). Signaller 14th London Regt. (London Scottish).

1915 Joll, A. E. (June 15, 1916). ‡Lt. 2nd (Garr.) Bn. Bedfordshire Regt., attd. 1/6th Hampshire Regt. India, 1917–18; Mesopotamia, 1918–19.

1897 **Jones, C. E. C.** (Dec. 26, 1914). Capt. 10th R. Warwickshire Regt. France. Killed in action near La Boisselle on July 4, 1916.

1897 Joyce, L. W. (Mobilized Aug. 4, 1914). Maj. R.H.A. (T.F.).

1908 Judd,* Rev. A. F., M.A. (Oct. 5, 1917). Chaplain to the Forces (4th Class), attd. 61st Inf. Bde. France, 1917–19.

1902 **Kay-Mouat, E. W.** (Sept. 1914). Bowker's Horse (British E. Africa). E. Africa. Killed at Longido on Nov. 4, 1914.

Kelly, E. R. (Jan. 27, 1915). 2nd Lt. 3rd Border Regt., attd. Lancashire Fusiliers. France, Belgium. Killed in action at Pilkem, near Ypres, on July 8, 1915.

1910 Kemm, A. H., B.A. (Aug. 14, 1916). 2nd Lt. I.A.R.O., attd. 2nd Queen Victoria's Own Corps of Guides (Frontier Force). India.

1883 Kewley, A. G., M.A. (Mobilized Aug. 1914). Capt., Acting Maj., R.A.M.C.

1905 Kewley, T. C. (Sept. 5, 1914). Lt. 4th Yorkshire Regt. (T.F.). Lt. R.F.A. (Capt.). France. *D.* France, 1919.

1894 **King-Pierce, W. G.,** B.A. (Serving Aug. 4, 1914). Capt. Manchester Regt. France, 1914. Killed in action, Oct. 1914.

1902 Kirby, S. H., B.A. (Nov. 19, 1914). Lt. 7th Warwickshire Regt., and Lt. R.G.A. (T.F.).

1894 Kirk, A. H. (Mobilized Aug. 1914). Maj. R.H.A. (T.F.).

1888 Kyle, H. G., D.M. (May 24, 1915). Capt. R.A.M.C.

1874 Laffan, Rev. R. S. de C., M.A. (Feb. 4, 1916). Chaplain to the Forces (4th Class). *D.* § Feb. 1917, § Aug. 1919.

1900 Lambert, B., M.A. (Feb. 1, 1916). Maj. R.E. (O.C. Respirator Design. Min. of Mun.) France. *O.B.E.* (Mil.). *D.* France, 1916, 1917.

1913 Lambert, C. J. (Aug. 29, 1914). Capt. 16th R. Scots. France, Belgium. (Prisoner of War in Germany, Mar.–Nov. 1918.)

1910 **Lambert, J. F.** (Apr. 1915). Lt. 9th K.R.R.C. France, Belgium. Killed in action at Hooge on July 30, 1915.

1901 Lamport, A. J., B.A. (1914). ‡Lt. Welsh Regt. Lt. M.G.C. France. (Prisoner of War.)

1898 Lamport, H. C., B.A. (Mobilized Aug. 1914). Lt.-Col. R.A.M.C. (T.F.).

1902 **Langdale, E. G.,** M.A. (Mobilized Aug. 5, 1914). Capt. 5th Leicestershire Regt. France. *D.* France, 1915. Killed in action at the Hohenzollern Redoubt on Oct. 13, 1915.

1901 Laurie, R. D., M.A. (1916). Capt. R.A.M.C. France. *O.B.E.* (Mil.). *D.* France, 1917, 1918.

1912 Lawrence, A., B.A. (Aug. 26, 1914). Lt. 7th S. Staffordshire Regt.

1912 Lawson, J., M.A. (June 7, 1915). Lt. 4th Sherwood Foresters. Asst. to Officer in charge of Records, Labour Corps. France. *D.* § Aug. 1918.

1894 Leach, R. E. H., D.M. (1916). Capt., Acting Maj., R.A.M.C. Egypt, Palestine. *O.B.E.* (Mil.).

1905 Lee, E. M., B.A. (1914). Lt. R.N.V.R. Transport Officer, 2nd Grade, *O.B.E.* (Mil.). *D.* Naval Dispatches. *D.* Palestine, 1918.

1901 Lee, G. B. (Sept. 16, 1914). Capt. R. Irish Rifles. Staff Capt. Mesopotamia. *D.* Mesopotamia, 1917 twice.

1910 **Lee,* L. S.,** B.A. (Aug. 26, 1914). 2nd Lt. 5th Oxf. & Bucks. Lt. Infty. France. *D.* France, 1915. Missing, presumed killed in action in the Battle of Loos in Oct. 1915.

1902 Lee, Rev. T. E., M.A. (Sept. 6, 1918). Chaplain to the Forces (4th Class).

1897 Leicester-Warren, C. (Dec. 11, 1914). Capt. 16th London Regt. (Queen's Westminster Rifles).

Leighton, R. A. (Oct. 21, 1914). Lt. 7th Worcestershire Regt. France, Died on Dec. 23, 1915, of wounds received in action.

1913 Leonard, S. B., B.A. (Jan. 1916). Lt. 4th The Buffs (E. Kent Regt.). France, 1917.

1899 **Levin, W. Fitz G.** (Nov. 21, 1914). Maj. Wellington Mounted Rifles, N.Z.E.F. Gallipoli. Died on Dec. 25, 1915, of wounds received in Gallipoli.

1896 **Lewin, F. H.,** B.A. (Mobilized Aug. 4, 1914). Capt. 3rd Connaught Rangers. Died on Dec. 8, 1915, of wounds caused by grenade accident.

1914 Lewis, R. P. A. (1916). ‡2nd Lt. Hertfordshire Regt.

1900 [Leys, K. K. M., M.A.] (Mar. 1917). Lt., Acting Capt., R.G.A., attd. H.Q. 42nd Div. France, 1918–19.

1902 Limbert, N. A., M.A. (Nov. 22, 1916). 2nd Lt. Bedfordshire Regt. Lt., Acting Capt., Labour Corps.

1919 Lindsey, A. (Dec. 12, 1915). Lt. R.F.A. Salonika, 1917; Palestine, 1917; Egypt, 1917–18; France, 1918.

1907 Lloyd, F. N. (Sept. 16, 1914). Lt. 3rd Guards Machine Gun Regt. France, Belgium.

1909 Lloyd,* J. R. (Oct. 8, 1914). Lt. E. Riding of Yorkshire Yeomanry, attd. M.G.C.

1907 Longland, A. C., M.A. (Nov. 28, 1914). Capt. 7th Wiltshire Regt. France, 1915; Salonika, 1915–18; France, 1918. *D.* Salonika, 1918.

1894 Longworth, T. J. (Mobilized Aug. 1914). Maj. R. Gloucestershire Hussars. Egypt, 1915; Gallipoli, 1915; France, 1916; Syria and Palestine, from 1916.

1910 **Low, J. M.** (Aug. 4, 1914). Lt. 2nd Seaforth Highlanders, attd. M.G.C. France. Reported missing, presumed killed in action in the Battle of the Somme on July 1, 1916.

1913 Lowe,* W. G., B.A. (1916). ‡2nd Lt. Middlesex Regt.

1912 Lowengard, A. C. G. (July 30, 1914). ‡Lt. 35th Regt. Infanterie de Ligne, French Army. France, 1914–18. Croix de Guerre. *D.* France, 1915, 1916.

1903 Lydall, H. H. W., B.A. (Oct. 8, 1914). Capt. R.A.S.C. France. *D.* France, 1918 twice.

1914 **Lynch-Staunton, G.** (Feb. 13, 1916). 2nd Lt. 13th Hussars (Lt.). France, Mesopotamia. Killed in action at Lajj on Mar. 5, 1917.

1911 Lyne,* H. W. (July 24, 1915). Lt. Acting Capt. 1st K.O.Y.L.I. France. *M.C.*, Mar. 8, 1919.

1904 Lyon, K., B.A. (Jan. 3, 1917). Capt. R.G.A. Staff Capt. France, 1916–18. *O.B.E.* (Mil.). *D.* § Feb. 1917; France, 1917.

1914 Lytle, R. R. (1915). American Amb. 1915–16. Lt. F.A., U.S. Army, afterwards Capt. 11th U.S. Cavalry. France, 1915–16.

1897 MacAlister, G. I., B.A. (Sept. 15, 1916). Lt. R. Defence Corps.

1896 Macbeth, P. (Feb. 1915). 2nd Lt. 11th (Res.) S. Staffordshire Regt.

1919 McDougall, J. (Aug. 8, 1917). Lt. 2/33rd Punjabis, Indian Army. N.W. Frontier, India.

1895 McEwen, G. L. (Mobilized Aug. 1914). Capt. 6th The Black Watch.

1898 Macfie, C. (Serving Aug. 4, 1914). Maj. Seaforth Highlanders; D.A.A.G. France. *D.S.O.*, June 3, 1918. *D.* France, 1918.

1908 Mackintosh,* A. B., B.A. 2nd Lt. I.A.R.O. India.

1897 Mackintosh, C. A. G., B.A. (1914). Lt. R.F.C., I.E.F. Maj. Special Lists. France.

1911 MacLachlan,* A. M. R.A.M.C.

1920 McLaughlin, T. O. (Feb. 1918). Pte. R.E. (Signal Corps), attd. Infantry. France.

1894 McMullen, A. P., M.A. (Aug. 20, 1914). Lt. R.N.V.R., H.M.S. *Agincourt.* Grand Fleet. *D.* Naval Dispatches.

1901 Macpherson, A. G., M.A. (1915). Lt. Unattached List, T.F., Radley College O.T.C.

1913 Mahony, M. R. (Nov. 11, 1914). Lt. R. Irish Fusiliers. Lt. R.A.F. (since June, 1917). France, 1915; Salonika, 1916; Egypt, 1917; France, 1918.

1919 Malcolm, J. W. K. (Nov. 1, 1917). Pte. 14th London Regt. (London Scottish).

1906 Marsden, H. K., M.A. (Serving Aug. 4, 1914). Qr.-Master and Hon. Capt. Eton College O.T.C. *D.* § Mar. 1919.

1902 Marshall, W. T., M.A. (Mobilized Aug. 1914). Lt. 6th Sherwood Foresters (empld. with Timber Supply Dept.).

1891 Marsham, C. G. B., M.A. (Mobilized Aug. 1914). Maj. W. Kent Yeomanry.

1919 Masson, J. R. (June 6, 1917). Lt. 3rd, attd. 6th, K.O. Scottish Borderers. France, 1917–18. (Prisoner of War, Mar.–Dec. 1918.)

1895 Master, E. T., M.A. (Aug. 25, 1915). Capt. 2/7th W. Yorkshire Regt. France.

1893 Masters, G. (Serving Aug. 4, 1914). Maj., Acting Lt.-Col., R.F.A. France. *D.S.O.*, Sept. 16, 1918. Croix de Chevalier de la Légion d'Honneur, Croix de Guerre. *D.* France, 1914, 1918 twice.

1919 Mathias, T. W. (July 1916). ‡Lt. 121st Hy. Batt., R.G.A. France 1917–18; Germany, 1918–19.

1895 Maxwell-Lyte, J. (Mobilized Aug. 5, 1914). Capt., temp. Maj., 3rd Northumberland Fusiliers; Asst. Embarkation Staff Officer.

1911 Means, T. (1917). 2nd Lt. Motor Transport, U.S. Army. France.

1903 Meiklejohn, G. S. (Aug. 29, 1914). 2nd Lt. 12th R. Scots. (Resigned on account of ill health.)

1905 **Mellers, G. H. R.,** B.A. (Mobilized Aug. 1914). Capt. 1/7th Sherwood Foresters (Adjt.). France, Belgium. Killed in action in an attack upon the Hohenzollern Redoubt on Oct. 13, 1915.

1882 Menzies, A. I., M.A. (Sept. 1, 1914). Maj. 1st Gloucestershire Regt. France, Belgium.

1894 Messel, H. G. (Oct. 1914). Lt. 4th R. Sussex Regt.

1890 Messel, L. C. R., M.A., T.D. (Rejoined T.F. Oct. 1914). Lt.-Col. 4th The Buffs (E. Kent Regt.). *O.B.E.* (Mil.). *D.* § Feb. 1917.

1909 **Meugens,* G. E.,** B.A. (Aug. 29, 1914). Capt. 11th Manchester Regt. Maj. Tank Corps. France. *D.* France, 1918. Died on Oct. 30, 1918, of illness contracted while on active service.

1900 Micklewright, H. G. F., M.A. (Serving Aug. 4, 1914). Capt. Unattached List, T.F., Whitgift Grammar School O.T.C. *D.* § Mar. 1918.

1897 Middleton, W. H. (Serving Aug. 4, 1914). Lt.-Col. 1st Hampshire Regt. France, Belgium, 1915–17; Italy, 1917–19. *D.S.O.*, June 4, 1917. Italian Silver Medal for Military Valour. *D.* France, 1916, 1917; Italy, 1918.

1919 Millard, L. MacV. (July 16, 1918). Cadet No. 3 R.F.A. Cadet School.

1907 Miller, A. H., M.A. (Dec. 1915). Lt. 1st Bde. Canadian G.A. France, 1917–19.

1913 Millis,* C. H. G. (Aug. 14, 1914). Maj. Sherwood Foresters. Bde. Maj. 89th Inf. Bde. France. *D.S.O.*, Sept. 24, 1918. *M.C.*, Jan. 1, 1917 *Bar*, Sept. 26, 1917. Croix de Guerre. *D.* France, 1918.

1909 Mills,* A. L. S., B.A. (Oct. 26, 1914). Maj. 24th Bn. Victoria Rifles, C.E.F. D.A.A.G. H.Q. Staff, Ottawa. France, 1915–17. *D.S.O.*, July 18, 1917. *D.* France, 1917.

1911 **Milner,* L. F.** (Aug. 1914). Lt. 1/9th King's (Liverpool Regt.). France. Killed in action at Loos on Sept. 25, 1915.

1911 Mitchell,* C. A. D., M.A. (Aug. 9, 1914). Capt. 4th Devonshire Regt., attd. M.G.C.

1900 [Moberly, W. H., M.A.] (July 12, 1915). Lt. 2/4th Oxf. & Bucks. Lt. Infty. (Capt.). France, 1915–16, 1917. *D.S.O.*, Oct. 18, 1917. *D.* France, 1916, 1917.

1912 Mold,* G. L. (Oct. 8, 1914). Lt. 4th Devonshire Regt. Capt. 27th Punjabis, Indian Army. India, N.W. Frontier, Mesopotamia, Palestine.

1903 Monteath, H. H., B.A. (Dec. 30, 1914). Capt. R.A.S.C. Mesopotamia. *D.* Mesopotamia, 1919.

1898 Montgomery, R. H. (Aug. 15, 1914). Lt. 4th E. Surrey Regt. (Staff Lt.). *D.* § Feb. 1917.

1905 Moon, J., B.A. (May 4, 1915). Lt. R.F.A. Egypt, Palestine, 1915–16; France, 1916–17. (Relinquished Commission on account of wounds, 1917.)

1911 Moorat, S. A. J., B.A. (May 3, 1917). Lt. 1/13th London Regt. France, Belgium.

1884 Moran, Rev. W. I., M.A. (Sept. 18, 1917). Chaplain to the Forces (4th Class).

1907 Morgan,* F. A., M.A. (Mobilized Aug. 1914). Lt. 5th, attd. 1/6th, S. Staffordshire Regt. France. *M.C.*, Mar. 8, 1919.

1915 Morton,* V. C. (Apr. 17, 1916). Sapper R.E. (Lce.-Cpl.). France.

1919 Moseley, J. O. (May 10, 1917). 1st Lt. 32nd Div. U.S. Army (Capt.). France, Germany, 1917–19.

1909 Mott,* A. S., B.A. (Oct. 1915). Capt. R.F.A. France, 1916–17; Italy, 1917–18; France, 1918.

1912 Muller, J. E., M.A. (Mobilized Aug. 1914). ‡Capt. R.F.A. France, 1915–16, 1917–18. *M.C.*, Nov. 25, 1916.

1912 Mure,* G. R. G., M.A. (Aug. 25, 1914). Capt. Warwick R.H.A. (Maj.). France, Germany, 1915–19. *M.C.*, June 3, 1919. Chevalier de l'Ordre de la Couronne. Belgian Croix de Guerre. *D.* France, 1917, 1918.

1890 Nelson, A. L., B.A. (Feb. 7, 1916). Capt. R.A.S.C., attd. R.A.F.

1896 Nelson, C. (Serving Aug. 4, 1914). Capt. 15th Hussars. Bde. Maj. 10th Cav. Bde., Northern Command. France, Aug. 1914–16; Mesopotamia, 1916; India, 1916–19; Afghanistan, 1919. *D.S.O.*, Mar. 24, 1915. *D.* France, 1914.

1911 **Newall,* L.** (Aug. 1914). 2nd Lt. 1st R. Fusiliers (Lt.). Malta, 1914–15; France, 1915. Killed in action on Sept. 2, 1915.

1890 Newsom, Rev. G. E., M.A. (1915). Chaplain to the Forces (4th Class).

1910 **Nield,* W. H. E.,** B.A. (Sept. 1914). Lt. 11th R. Fusiliers (Capt.). France, 1915–16. Killed in action at Mametz on July 1, 1916.

1903 **Nimmo, K. P.** (Sept. 1914). Pte. 17th King's (Liverpool Regt.) France. Killed in action at Maricourt on June 28, 1916.

1896 **Niven, W. E. G.** (Mobilized Aug. 1914). Lt. Berkshire Yeomanry. Gallipoli. Missing, presumed killed in Gallipoli on Aug. 21, 1915.

1919 Nuttall, R. H. (Oct. 1917). 2nd Lt. R.F.A. France.

1901 Oldham, N. H. (Aug. 13, 1915). Lt. R.A.S.C.

1913 O'May, J., B.A. Malay States Volunteer Rifles.

1918 Orton, H. (June 7, 1917). Lt. 5th Durham L.I. France. (Invalided on account of wounds, Aug. 1918.)

1899 Overbury, J. G., B.A. (Mobilized Aug. 1914). Maj. 10th Middlesex Regt. (T.F.) Bde. Maj. Mesopotamia. *D.* Mesopotamia, 1917.

1889 Parker, F. M. S., B.A. (Nov. 13, 1914). Capt. 2/5th Queen's (R. W. Surrey Regt.). Capt. Intelligence Dept., War Office. *D.* § Aug. 1918.

1920 Parkes, N. (Apr. 16, 1915). ‡Lt. Middlesex Regt., and M.G.C. (Maj.). France, Germany.

1920 Paterson, F. W. (Jan. 7, 1918). Pte. 15th Bn., A.I.F. (Sergt.). France, Belgium, 1918–19.

1903 Paterson, J., M.A. (Mobilized Aug. 4, 1914). Capt. 14th London Regt. (London Scottish) (Lt.-Col.). France, 1914; Italy, 1917. *M.C.*, June 23, 1915. *D.* France, 1915, 1916 twice.

1906 Paterson, W. A., B.A. (1916). Lt. R.A.S.C.
1919 Paul, T. G. (Aug. 17, 1914). ‡Capt. 6th Inf. Bn., A.I.F. Egypt, 1914; Gallipoli, 1915; France, 1916–19. *M.C.*, Jan. 1, 1919.
1901 Pawle, F., B.A. (Sept. 4, 1914). Capt. 1st Hertfordshire Regt. (Maj.). France.
1887 Payne, C. H., M.A. (June 1, 1916). Capt. 18th Rifle Brigade (T.F.).
1910 Peach, T. H., B.A. (Aug. 13, 1915). Lt. 3rd N. Staffordshire Regt. France. *D.* § Aug. 1919.
1910 Pearce-Gould, H., M.A. (May 9, 1916). Lt. Welsh Guards.
1882 **Pell, A. J.,** B.A. (Serving Aug. 1914). Bde. Maj. General Staff; Divisional Musketry Officer, Western Command. Died on Aug. 28, 1916, of illness contracted on active service.
1911 Pelly,* H. A. (Aug. 1914). Lt. 7th Hussars (Capt.). France, Belgium, 1915–17; Mesopotamia, 1918–19. *M.C.*, Apr. 2, 1919.
1914 Penfield, W. G., M.A. (1917). U.S. Medical Reserve Corps. France, 1916–18 (with Red Cross).
1913 **Perks,* R. C.** (Jan. 19, 1915). Capt. 10th W. Riding Regt. France, Belgium, Italy. *D.S.O.*, Sept. 26, 1916. *D.* France, 1916. Killed in action on the Piave on Oct. 27, 1918.
1899 Phillimore, J. G., M.A. R.A.M.C. (Discharged.)
1910 Phillips, H., B.A. (Nov. 1914). Capt. 9th Essex Regt. France.
1911 Pippet, G. K. (Nov. 13, 1914). 2nd Lt. 12th K.R.R.C. (Resigned on account of ill health.)
1907 **Pixley, J. N. F.** (Apr. 13, 1916). Capt. Grenadier Guards. Belgium. Killed in action on Oct. 12, 1917, near Houlthurst Forest.
1910 **Pollard,* R. T.** (Aug. 1914). Lt. 5th R. Berkshire Regt. France. *D.* France, 1915. Killed in action near Hulluch on Oct. 13, 1915.
1897 Pope, M. E. W. (Mobilized Aug. 1914). Maj. Yorkshire Hussars.
1907 Powell, Rev. E., M.A. (Sept. 12, 1917). Chaplain to the Forces (4th Class).
1896 Powell, Rev. G. H., M.A. (July 31, 1915). Chaplain to the Forces (4th Class). *D.* § Mar. 1918.
1901 Poyser, K. E. (Aug. 4, 1914). Lt.-Col. 9th Loyal N. Lancashire Regt. Maj., attd. Headquarters Staff. France, Belgium, Italy. *D.S.O.*, Jan. 1, 1917. *D.* France, 1916 twice.
1888 Prance, C. H. G. (Feb. 4, 1916). Capt. R.A.M.C. Malta, Italy. *D.* § Mar. 1918; Italy, 1919.
1888 Previté, H. F., M.A. (Sept. 12, 1914). Maj. 22nd London Regt. (The Queen's).
1912 **Pringle, R. W. H.** (Sept. 1914). Capt. W. Yorkshire Regt. Egypt, France. Killed in action on the Somme on July 1, 1916.
1901 Pritchard, G., B.C.L., M.A. (Dec. 21, 1915). Lt. 8th Worcestershire Regt. France. *M.C.*, June 18, 1917.
1919 Raikes, D. T. (Apr. 30, 1915). Lt. 3rd S. Wales Borderers. Maj. 14th Bn. Tank Corps. France. *D.S.O.*, Feb. 18, 1918. *M.C.*, Feb. 4, 1918; *Bar*, Sept. 16, 1918. *D.* France, 1916, 1917, 1918.
1911 Raikes,* W. T. (Aug. 14, 1914). Capt. 3rd S. Wales Borderers. Lt.-Col. 25th Bn. M.G.C. France, 1915–16, 1917–19. *D.S.O.*, June 3, 1919. *M.C.*, Feb. 4, 1918; *Bar*, Sept. 16, 1918. *D.* France, 1916 twice.
1902 Ratto, F. L., B.A. (1915). Capt. R. Welch Fusiliers. France, Belgium. *M.C.*, Jan. 1, 1918.

1908 **Rawlins, G. E. A.**, B.A. (Sept. 12, 1914). Capt. 8th R. Fusiliers. France, 1915–16. Killed in action near Albert on July 7, 1916.

1876 Rawnsley, W. H., M.A. (Sept. 2, 1914). Maj. 10th Cheshire Regt.

1879 Redmayne, J. F. de C. S., M.A. (Oct. 1914). Capt. C.R.O., Canadian Forces. *D.* § Aug. 1918.

1909 Redwood, E., M.A. (June 15, 1915). Lt. R.A.S.C. (Capt.). France, Salonika, Palestine, Egypt.

1911 **Reid, J. B.**, B.A. (July, 1915). Friends Ambulance Unit, B.R.C.S. France, 1915. Died on July 6, 1916.

1919 Renwick, W. L. (1914). Capt. 10th Cameronians. Capt. Labour Corps. France. *M.C.*, Jan. 1, 1918.

1909 **Reynolds, W. K.** (Sept. 3, 1914). Lt. 3rd Leicestershire Regt. France, Belgium. Killed in action near Ypres on Sept. 10, 1915.

1919 Reynolds, H. E. (Jan. 12, 1917). Sergt. (temp. W.O. 1st Class) 1st Auckland Inf. Bn., N.Z.E.F. France.

1889 Riccardi-Cubitt, Count H. (Sept. 14, 1917). Lt. Special Lists, R.T.O.

1912 Rishbeth, O. H. T., M.A. (Oct. 1916). Lt. R.N.V.R., Admiralty Intelligence Dept. Greece and the Aegean, 1916–17. Chevalier of the Order of the Redeemer. *D.* Admiralty Dispatch, 1918.

1919 Ritchie, K. J. (May 1915). Lt. 1st Hertfordshire Regt., attd. No. 13 O.C.B. (Capt.). France, 1916–17, 1918. *D.* France, 1917.

1888 Robeson, F. E., M.A. (Serving Aug. 4, 1914). Lt.-Col., Unattached List, T.F., Eton College O.T.C. *D.* § Mar. 1918. (Resigned Aug. 1917.)

1912 Robinson, A. J. (Apr. 20, 1915). Lt. 6th Middlesex Regt. Acting Capt. 4th Oxf. & Bucks. Lt. Infty. France. *D.* France, 1917.

1905 **Robinson, J. Y.**, M.A. (Sept. 1, 1914). Capt. and Adjt. 7th N. Staffordshire Regt. Gallipoli, Mesopotamia. *M.C.*, Feb. 2, 1916. *D.* Gallipoli, 1915. Died on Aug. 23, 1916, of wounds received in action at Umm El Hannah.

1919 Roe, W. N. (Apr. 10, 1917). Lt. 2nd Coldstream Guards. France, 1918. *M.C.*, Dec. 2, 1918; *Bar*, Feb. 1, 1919.

1919 Rogers, T. F. (Apr. 19, 1917). Pte. 17th R. Sussex Regt. France, 1918–19.

1909 **Rogers,* W. F.**, B.A. (Serving Aug. 4, 1914). Maj. 45th Batt., R.F.A. France, Aug. 1914–17. *D.S.O.*, June 4, 1917. *D.* France, 1917. Killed in action near Arras on May 19, 1917.

1919 Roney, E. J. (Oct. 25, 1918). Cadet R.N.

1896 [Ross, W. D., M.A.] (Apr. 22, 1915). Maj. General List, attd. to Ministry of Munitions (1915–19). *O.B.E.* (Mil.). *D.* § Jan. 1917.

1912 Rossdale,* G. H., B.M. (Serving Aug. 4, 1914). Capt. R.A.M.C. Mesopotamia.

1919 Roth, C. (Feb. 14, 1917). Pte. 11th Somerset L.I. France, Belgium.

1894 Rothfeld, O., B.A. Poona Volunteer Rifles.

1915 Rushworth, T. A. (Sept. 1914). Sen. Wireless Operator, R.N.V.R.

1888 St. Aubyn, G. S. (Mobilized Aug. 1914). Lt.-Col. K.R.R.C. (T.F. Res.). *D.* § Feb. 1917.

1913 St. George, C. F. L., M.A. (Oct. 5, 1914). 2nd Lt. 4th R. Sussex Regt. Gallipoli, 1915. (Resigned Commission on account of ill health Dec. 1917.)

1914 Sackett, A. B. (Jan. 25, 1915). Lt., Acting Capt., 15th Northumberland Fusiliers, attd. 1/5th Lancashire Fusiliers. Gallipoli, 1915; Egypt and Sinai, 1916–17; France, 1917–18. *M.C.*, Oct. 28, 1917.

1901 **Samson, A. L.** (Serving Aug. 4, 1914). Capt. 2nd R. Welch Fusiliers. India, France. *M.C.*, June 23, 1915. *D.* France, 1915. Killed in action at Loos on Sept. 25, 1915.

1919 Samuel, G. H. (Apr. 29, 1915). Lt. 2nd Middlesex Regt. (Capt.). France. *D.* France.

1903 Savill, G. L. (Oct. 14, 1916). Lt. R.F.A. (S.R.).

1919 Schaffer, R. J. (Aug. 2, 1918). Pte. 19th London Regt.

1905 Schmitt, B. E. (Aug. 1918). 2nd Lt. F.A., U.S. Army.

1907 Scoon, R. M., B.A. (1917). Lt. U.S. Infantry.

1903 Scott, A. J. L., B.A. (Mobilized Aug. 1914). Capt. Sussex Yeomanry. Lt.-Col. R.A.F. France. *C.B.*, Oct. 11, 1919. *M.C.*, July 26, 1917. *A.F.C.*, Jan. 1, 1919.

1919 Scott, D. G. (Aug. 1, 1916). ‡Lt. 2/6th Sherwood Foresters, attd. General Staff. France, Belgium, Germany.

1908 Scott,* Rev. D. W., M.A. (1918). Chaplain to the Forces (4th Class), attd. 36th Northumberland Fusiliers. France, 1918.

1906 Scott, F. G. L., B.A. (1914). Surgeon-Lt. R.N.

1916 Scott, N. D., M.A. (Dec. 7, 1917). Pte. 1st Class, C. Coy., 1st Gas Regt., U.S. Army. France, 1918–19.

1885 Scott-Crickett, P. S. H., M.A. Hon. Lt. Recruiting Officer.

1919 Scroggs, A. F. (Aug. 18, 1916). Flying Officer 113th Sqdn. R.A.F. France, Egypt.

1919 Scudder, E. S. (May 15, 1917). American Ambulance, attd. 10th French Army; 1st Lt. Automobile Services, 3rd Italian Army. France, 1917; Italy, 1917–19. Medaglia di Valore. *D.* Italian Dispatches, 1918.

1908 Sells,* C. P. (1914). Capt. R.A.M.C. France. *M.C.*, June 3, 1918.

1919 Sergeant, T. W. (Apr. 5, 1918). 2nd Lt. K.R.R.C. (on demobilization).

1913 Sheldon, O., B.A. (Oct. 1914). Lt. 10th Signal Coy., R.E. (Capt. and Adjt.). Salonika, Egypt, Palestine. *D.* Salonika, 1917.

1913 Shelswell,* O. H. C., B.A. (Aug. 22, 1914). Lt. 6th K.O.Y.L.I. and M.G.C. Capt. 40th Pathans, Indian Army. France, South Africa, India, Afghanistan.

1908 Sherlock,* C. C., B.A. (May 21, 1915). Lt. 19th Middlesex Regt. France. *M.C.*, Oct. 28, 1917. *D.* France, 1918.

Simpson, G. R. (Aug. 15, 1914). Lt. 3rd, attd. 1st, Cheshire Regt. France. Died on Aug. 30, 1918, of wounds received in action.

1919 Skeet, C. H. L. (Sept. 1914). Lt. 12th R. Fusiliers. France. (Prisoner of War, 1915–18.)

1895 Skrimshire, C. R., M.A. 2nd Lt. Unattached List, T.F., Wellington College O.T.C.

1903 Sleeman, S. B., B.A. (Mar. 27, 1915). Lt. 6th Devonshire Regt.

1900 Sloane, A. D. (Serving Aug. 4, 1914). Capt. Dragoon Guards (S.R.) (Ret. pay), late 2nd Dragoon Guards. France. *D.* France, 1915.

1892 Slocock, E., M.A. (Oct. 1914). A.B. R.N. Division. Gallipoli, 1915–16; France, 1916–17.

1909 Smith, A. R. (Aug. 31, 1914). Capt. R.A.S.C., attd. 19th Bde., R.G.A. France, Belgium, 1915–18. *M.C.*, June 4, 1917.

1903 Smith, G., M.A. (Aug. 24, 1915). Maj. R.A.O.C. Maj. D.A.D.O.S. France, 1915–19.

1907 Smith, H. F. E. (Aug. 14, 1914). Capt., temp. Lt.-Col., 2nd K.R.R.C. France. *D.S.O.*, Sept. 17, 1917. Croix de Chevalier de la Légion d'Honneur. *D.* France, 1917 twice.

1904 Smith, L. C., M.A. (Sept. 1914). Lt. Unattached List, T.F., St. Paul's School O.T.C.

1907 Smith,* W. O., B.A. (Jan. 18, 1915). Maj. 16th Lancashire Fusiliers. *D.* § Aug. 1919.

1900 Soames, J. G. L., B.A. (1914). Maj. R.A.S.C. France. *D.* France, 1916, 1917.

1913 Solomon, P. H. (Aug. 1914). ‡Maj. A Batt., 52nd Bde., R.F.A. France, Belgium. *M.C.*, June 3, 1919. *D.* France, 1918.

1903 **Somers-Smith, R. W.** (Jan. 1915). 2nd Lt. K.R.R.C. France, Belgium. Killed in action at Hooge on June 30, 1915.

1919 Speller, C. A. (Aug. 5, 1914). ‡Lt. King's African Rifles. East Africa.

1908 Spicer, A. C. N., M.A. (Nov. 18, 1914). 2nd Lt. 7th S. Staffordshire Regt. Lt., Acting Capt., General List, attd. O.C.B.

1895 **Spurrell, H. G. F.,** B.M., M.A. (June 1, 1917). Capt. R.A.M.C. Egypt. Died at Alexandria on Nov. 8, 1918, of illness contracted while on active service.

1919 Stanford, L. J. (Aug. 1916). ‡Lt. 8th London Regt. (Post Office Rifles). France, Belgium. (Invalided on account of wounds.)

1878 Stather-Hunt, Rev. Canon D. J., M.A. (Aug. 4, 1914). Chaplain to the Forces (1st Class). Belgium, France, Holland, Germany. T.D. *D.* France, 1915.

1903 Stedall, L. P. (Aug. 19, 1914). Capt. 1st City of London Yeomanry. Egypt, Palestine. *D.S.O.*, Jan. 18, 1918. *D.* Egypt, 1916.

1884 Steele, W. K. (Aug. 9, 1914). Lt.-Col. R.A.M.C. (S.R.).

1900 Steer, E. P. (Oct. 1, 1914). Lt. 1st Monmouthshire Regt. Staff Capt. Welsh Res. Bde.

1910 Stephenson, E. K., M.A. (Aug. 15, 1914). Capt. Coldstream Guards. France, India.

1902 Stevenson, J. A., B.A. Lt. Cameron Highlanders, C.E.F.

1919 Story, G. F. E. (Sept. 6, 1918). Cadet Household Bde., O.C.B.

Stott, P. H. (Nov. 1916). 2nd Lt. 1/5th W. Yorkshire Regt. France, Belgium. Killed in action at Wytschaete Ridge on April 25, 1918.

1907 Sturgeon,* G. V., B.A. (Aug. 1914). Lt. R. Sussex Regt. France.

1912 **Sugden,* C. B.** (Sept. 1, 1914). 2nd Lt. 1/4th K.O.Y.L.I. France, 1915. Killed in action at Armentières on May 25, 1915.

1908 Sutch,* Rev. R. H., M.A. (Dec. 11, 1918). Chaplain to the Forces (4th Class). France.

1904 Sweet-Escott, H. H. (June 23, 1917). Lt. R.A.S.C.

1912 Swift,* C. B. (Serving Aug. 4, 1914). Capt. 1st Norfolk Regt. France, Belgium, Egypt.

1919 Symonds, E. N. C. (Nov. 3, 1915). Lt. C Batt., 270th Bde., R.F.A. (Capt.). Egypt, Palestine. *M.C.*, Jan. 1, 1918. *D.* Egypt, 1917.

1919 Taylor, A. B. (Sept. 23, 1915). Pte. N.Z.E.F. Egypt, 1915–16; France, Belgium, 1916–17.

1896 Taylor, H. I., M.A. London Regt.

1886 Thomas, A. E., D.M. (Mobilized Aug. 1914). Capt., Sanitary Officer, R.A.M.C.

1907 Thomas,* A. R. (Sept. 24, 1915). Lt. I.A.R.O., attd. Supply and Transport Corps. India.

1911 Thompson, E. G., B.A. (May 1917). ‡Lt. R.N.V.R. Lt. R.A.F.

1909 Thompson,* M. R. (Serving Aug. 4, 1914). Capt. 20th Hussars. France. *D.* France, 1915, 1917.

1919 Thompson, V. U. M. (Sept. 3, 1914). Pte. 2/4th Wiltshire Regt. (Sergt.). India, 1914–17; Mesopotamia, 1917–19.

1906 Thomson,* I. K., B.A. (Aug. 4, 1914). ‡Lt. 3rd Yorkshire Regt. France, 1916; Salonika, 1917–19. *D.* Salonika, 1918 twice.

1903 Tilden-Smith, L., M.A. (Feb. 5, 1915). 2nd Lt. 14th Middlesex Regt. Lt. R.A.F.

1902 Tippetts, C. M. (Serving Aug. 4, 1914). Capt., Bt-Major, 2nd S. Wales Borderers & M.G.C. Maj. Tank Corps. France, N. Russia. *D.* France, 1917; Russia, 1919.

1897 Tippetts, S. A., B.A. Governor of Sudan Province. Egypt. *D.* Egypt.

1897 Tompson, R. H. D., M.A., *D.S.O.* (Serving Aug. 4, 1914). Maj., Bt.-Lt.-Col., R.A. Temp. Lt.-Col., Special Lists; A.Q.M.G. France. *D.* France, 1915 twice, 1916 twice, 1918, 1919.

1907 **Tooke, B.** (Sept. 1914). ‡Capt. 18th W. Yorkshire Regt. France. *D.* France, 1917. Killed in action at Bullecourt on May 3, 1917.

1899 Topham, E. A. C. (July 29, 1917). 2nd Lt. R.A.S.C.

1913 Towson, H. D., B.A. (Apr. 1918). Cpl. 328th Inf., U.S. Army (Sergt.). France 1918. Died in America, 1919.

1905 Trelawney-Ross,* A. H., M.A. (Serving Aug. 4, 1914). Lt. Unattached List, T.F., Sherborne School O.T.C.

1903 Trelawney-Ross, Rev. W. E. T., M.A. (May 8, 1917). Chaplain to the Forces (4th Class). France. *M.C.*, Oct. 15, 1918.

1906 **Trench, C. R. Chenevix,** B.A. (Mobilized Aug. 1914). Capt., Acting Maj., 5th Sherwood Foresters. France. *D.* France, 1918. Killed in action on Mar. 21, 1918.

1911 **Troup,* S. H.** (Sept. 1914). Lt. 2nd R. Berkshire Regt. (Capt.). France, 1915; Salonika, 1915–17; France, Belgium, 1917. Killed in action at Passchendaele on Dec. 2, 1917.

1899 Trumpler, S. A. H., M.A. (Dec. 4, 1915). Lt. R.A.S.C.

1919 Tudor, O. M. (Mar. 1, 1918). Gunner, R.F.A.

1907 **Turnbull, A. P.,** B.A. (Oct. 6, 1914). ‡2nd Lt. Australian Light Horse. Gallipoli. Killed in action at Walker's Ridge, Gallipoli on Aug. 7, 1915.

1898 Turner, A. M. (Serving Aug. 4, 1914). Maj. 1st Dragoon Guards. G.S.O. 2. France. *D.S.O.*, Jan. 14, 1916. *D.* France, 1915.

1913 **Turner,* H.** (July 16, 1915). 2nd Lt. 13th Sherwood Foresters (until Sept. 1916). Capt. R.A.F. (Flight Commander). France. Croix de Guerre. Presumed killed in action south of Curvilly on June 5, 1918.

1908 Turton,* N. H., M.A. R.G.A., Sierra Leone.

1909 Verschoyle,* Rev. G. J. F., M.A. (Jan. 4, 1917). Chaplain to the Forces (4th Class).

1914 Vagliano, A. Cuirassiers, French Army. France.

1913 Vickers,* C. G., B.A. (Sept. 2, 1914). Capt., Acting Maj., 7th Sherwood Foresters. France, Belgium. Croix de Guerre. *D.* France, 1918. **V.C.**

For most conspicuous bravery on October 14, 1915, in the Hohenzollern redoubt. When nearly all his men had been killed or wounded, and with only two men available to hand him bombs, Captain Vickers held a barrier for some hours against heavy German bomb attacks from front and flank. Regardless of the fact that his own retreat would be cut off, he had ordered a second barrier to be built behind him in order to ensure the safety of the trench. Finally he was severely wounded, but not before his magnificent courage and determination had enabled the second barrier to be completed. A critical situation was thus saved.

1904 **Vint, W. G.,** M.A. (Mar. 27, 1916). Pte. 8th W. Riding Regt. France. Killed in action at Beaucourt on Dec. 8, 1916.

1899 Vizard, J. T., B.A. (Feb. 22, 1915). Lt. R.G.A. (Capt.). Italy, 1917–18. Italian Bronze Medal for valour.

1910 Wagner, D. P., B.A. (Jan. 25, 1917). Lt. 11th, attd. 1st, Dublin Fusiliers. France. *M.C.*, Sept. 26, 1917; *Bar*, Mar. 8, 1919.

1903 Waldy, J. N. (Dec. 28, 1915). Capt. 18th K.R.R.C. France, Italy. *D.* Italy, 1918.

1905 Walker, E. A., M.A. Lt. Cape of Good Hope Garrison Artillery. Africa.

1901 Walker, P. L. E. (Serving Aug. 4, 1914). Capt., Acting Lt.-Col., 7th Hussars, attd. 1st E. Lancashire Regt. France. *D.S.O.*, Oct. 27, 1918.

1895 Walker, T. H., B.A. (Serving Aug. 4, 1914). Maj. R.F.A. (Lt.-Col.). France, 1915–16; Egypt, Palestine, 1916–19. *D.S.O.*, Jan. 1, 1919. *D.* Palestine, 1918.

1912 **Wallace,* H. S. H.** (Oct. 1914). Capt. 10th Worcestershire Regt. France. Killed in action at Bazentin-le-Petit on July 22, 1916.

1919 Walmsley, A. A. (June 9, 1916). Lt. 17th London Regt. France, Belgium.

1913 Wanless,* R. P. (Feb. 12, 1917). Surgeon Probationer, R.N.V.R.

1911 Warner, J. E., B.A. (Aug. 22, 1914). Capt. 5th R. Berkshire Regt., empld. Ministry of Labour. France.

1908 Waters,* J. D., B.A. (Sept. 12, 1914). Lt.-Col. 10th R. Fusiliers. France. *D.S.O.*, May 13, 1918. *D.* France, 1916, 1917, 1918, 1919.

1920 Watmough, H. G. (Apr. 2, 1917). Sergt. VI Corps, I.C.S., R.A.O.C. France, Germany, 1917–19.

1899 Watson, J., B.A. (Mobilized Aug. 1914). Maj. R.F.A. (T.F.).

1905 Watson, W. T., B.A. 2nd Lt. R.A.F.

1911 Webster,* P. L. C., B.A. (Aug. 15, 1914). Capt. 3rd Oxf. & Bucks. Lt. Infty. France, 1915–16.

1919 Weir, J. A. (Nov. 1915). Pte. C.A.M.C. Lt. R.A.F. France.

1890 Welch-Thornton, H. (Oct. 1, 1917). Capt., Acting Lt. Col., R.A.O.C. *D.* § Aug. 1919.

1899 Wells, W. W., B.M., M.A. (Oct. 1, 1915). Capt. R.A.M.C.

1914 Westgarth, F. C. (May 26, 1917). Pte. R.A.V.C. France, 1917–18.

1903 Wheatcroft, C. J., M.A. (Aug. 5, 1914). Capt. 1/6th Sherwood Foresters. Capt., Bde. Maj., General Staff. France, 1915–17. *D.* France, 1917.

1896 Wheatcroft, H. A., M.A. (Mar. 1915). Capt. R.A.S.C. (T.F.). *D.* § Aug. 1919.

1908 **Whitefoord, Rev. C.** (Nov. 29, 1916). Chaplain to the Forces (4th Class). France, 1916–18. Died on May 30, 1918, of wounds received in action.

1901 Whitfield, A. B., M.A. (Oct. 9, 1914). Capt. 6th R. Warwickshire Regt., Courts Martial Officer.

1919 Whitley, J. (Oct. 1, 1916). ‡Lt. R.F.A. France, Belgium. (Discharged on account of wounds.)

1889 Whittington, R., D.M. (Aug. 5, 1914). Capt., Acting Maj., R.A.M.C. (T.F.).

1892 Wigram, R. (Dec. 21, 1914). Lt. 12th K.R.R.C.
1904 Wilkie, D., B.A. (Mobilized Aug. 1914). Capt. 3rd Yorkshire Regt., empld. Recruiting Duties.
1913 **Williams, P. C.** (Sept. 1, 1914). Lt. 10th Hampshire Regt. Gallipoli. Killed in action at Suvla Bay on Aug. 10, 1915.
1919 Willis, J. D. (Mar. 2, 1917). 2nd Lt. R.E.
1897 Winch, I. G., B.A. (Mobilized Aug. 5, 1914). Maj. R. E. Kent Yeomanry, attd.Tank Corps (1918). Gallipoli, 1915. *D.* § Feb. 1917.
1891 Winch, T. M., B.A. (Oct. 1914). Lt. Lincolnshire Yeomanry. Lt. R.A.F.
1899 Witts, E. F. B. (Apr. 1915). Maj. 9th Gloucestershire Regt. France, 1915; Salonika, 1916, 1917, 1918; France, 1918. *D.S.O.*, June 3, 1918. *D.* Salonika, 1917, 1918.
1910 **Wood,* A. W.,** B.A. (Aug. 15, 1914). 2nd Lt. 3rd, attd. 2nd, Oxf. & Bucks. Lt. Infty. France. Died on Sept. 29, 1915, of wounds received in action.
1888 Wood, G. R., M.A. (Mobilized Aug. 1914). Capt. 4th Oxf. & Bucks. Lt. Infty.
1919 Wood, H. G. W. (Feb. 28, 1917). Pte., Acting Cpl., 336th Coy. R.E. France, 1917–19.
1906 Wood, W. de B., M.A. (Sept. 1914). Maj. 7th Shropshire L.I. Maj. G.S.O. 3, War Office. France.
1898 **Wood, W. J.** (Oct. 8, 1914). 2nd Lt. 15th Middlesex Regt., attd. 16th London Regt. (Queen's Westminster Rifles). France. Killed in action on Nov. 7, 1915.
1912 Woodbury, E. B. C. (Sept. 18, 1916). Lt. 1st Coldstream Guards (Capt.). India, France.
1903 Woodgate, H. G., B.A. (Jan. 26, 1915). 2nd Lt. Unattached List, T.F., Whitgift Grammar School O.T.C.
1897 Wood Hill, B., M.A. (Jan. 12, 1916). Lt. K.R.R.C. France, Belgium, 1917.
1902 Wood Hill, C., B.A. (Mobilized Aug. 1914). Capt. Northamptonshire Yeomanry. G.S.O. 3. France, 1915–19.
1909 Woodhouse,* R. M., B.A. (Oct. 18, 1914). Lt. 4th Dorsetshire Regt. (Capt.). India, Mesopotamia, Palestine.
1914 **Woolnough, C. W. F.** (Jan. 26, 1915). 2nd Lt. 10th Bedfordshire Regt. 2nd Lt. 69th Coy. M.G.C. France, 1916. Killed in action near Loos on Mar. 21, 1916.
1912 Worthington, P. (Sept. 1, 1914). ‡2nd Lt. 16th Middlesex Regt. (till May 1916). Capt. R.A.F. France. *M.C.*, June 3, 1916. *D.* France, 1918.
1919 Wotherspoon, G. R. H. (July 7, 1916). Gunner No. 2 Siege Art. Res. Bde. (Cpl.).
1919 Wright, H. H. S. (May 25, 1917). Lt. R.G.A. (S.R.). France, 1917–18.
1888 Wyld, C. E. (Sept. 1914). Lt.-Col. 16th K.R.R.C. France, 1915–17.
1913 Wylie, H. (July 3, 1915). Lt. 9th S. Wales Borderers, attd. 1/4th Welsh Regt. France, 1916–17; Palestine, 1917–18; Egypt, 1918–19.
1897 **Yates, C. C.,** B.A. (Nov. 1914). Lt. 9th Loyal N. Lancashire Regt. France, Belgium. Killed in action at Vimy Ridge on May 15, 1916.
1907 Youle,* J. S., B.A. (Dec. 14, 1914). Capt., Acting Maj., R.G.A. France, 1915–18.
1910 Young,* D. F. (Aug. 1914). Maj. 9th K.R.R.C., attd. 1/15th London Regt. (Civil Service Rifles) (Lt.-Col.). Belgium, France. *M.C.*, July 26, 1918.

EXETER COLLEGE

1907 **Abbott,* L. P.,** B.A. (Dec. 16, 1914). Lt. 7th Leicestershire Regt. France. *D.* France, 1916. Killed in action at Mametz Wood on July 14, 1916.

1919 Adams, J. H. (Nov. 1916). Pte. R. W. Kent Regt. France.

1897 Adams, P. E. H., B.M., M.A. (Feb. 1915). Capt. R.A.M.C.

1909 Adams,* W. B., B.A. (Sept. 3, 1914). Capt. S. Staffordshire Regt. (till Aug. 1916). Lt.-Col., Staff Officer, 1st Class, R.A.F. France, 1915; Egypt, 1917, 1918. *D.* Egypt, 1918; § Aug. 1919.

1914 Addis, T. (Aug. 1914). ‡Lt. R.F.A. France, Italy.

1896 Adlard, M., M.A. (July 1915). Capt. Unattached List, T.F., N. E. County School O.T.C.

1905 Agius, A. V. L. B., B.A. (Mobilized Aug. 4, 1914). Maj. 3rd London Regt. Malta, France. *M.C.*, Jan. 14, 1916. *D.* France, 1915.

1886 Allen, Ven. W. C., M.A. (Nov. 22, 1915). Chaplain to the Forces (4th Class) 2nd W. Command, Manchester Hospitals. *D.* § Feb. 1917.

1911 **Allpass, H. B. K.,** B.A. (Jan. 7, 1915). 2nd Lt. Essex Regt. France. Killed in action, Sept. 1916.

1919 Anderson, C. I. (Jan. 1916). Lt. 498th Siege Batt. R.G.A. France, 1918–19.

1912 Anderson, E. J. (1914). R.N.V.R.

1905 Anne, G. C. (Aug. 29, 1914). Capt. K.O.Y.L.I. Capt., Acting Maj., Staff Officer, R.A.F. Palestine. *O.B.E.* (Mil.). *D.* Palestine, 1918.

1919 Ansdell, G. A. R. W. (Aug. 4, 1914). ‡Lt. R. Bucks. Hussars. Egypt, Turkey in Asia.

1898 Arbuthnot-Brisco, R. J. W. (Dec. 1, 1914). Maj. 7th R. Welch Fusiliers, attd. Labour Corps.

1903 Archer, P. A. E., B.A. (Sept. 27, 1914). Capt. Royal 1st Devon Yeomanry, attd. Staffordshire Yeomanry.

1912 **Arnell,* R. B.** (Aug. 28, 1914). 2nd Lt. 7th K.R.R.C. France, Belgium. Killed in action at Hooge on July 30, 1915.

1908 Ashpitel, G. F. (Feb. 9, 1916). Lt., Acting Capt., 5th, attd. 1st Queen's (R. W. Surrey Regt.). France. *M.C.*, Sept. 16, 1918; *Bar*, March 8, 1919. *D.* France, 1917.

1912 **Ashworth,* B. W.** (Sept. 1914). 2nd Lt. 11th R. W. Kent Regt. France, Belgium. Died on Aug. 4, 1917, of wounds received at Hollebeke.

1919 Ashworth, R. (1918). U.S. Marine Corps.

1912 Aston,* C. C., B.A. (Aug. 15, 1914). Capt. 4th Bedfordshire Regt., attd. 8th Welsh Regt. France, 1915; Gallipoli, 1915–16; Egypt, 1916; Mesopotamia, 1916–18.

1893 Atkinson,* C. T., M.A. (Serving Aug. 4, 1914). Capt. O.U.O.T.C., attd. Gen. Staff, War Office (1914–15), attd. Committee of Imperial Defence (1915–19).

1919 Atherly, S. E. P. (July 1917). ‡2nd Lt. 10th Hussars.

1919 Bacon, C. E. (Dec. 28, 1916). Lt. R.A.F. France and Belgium, 1917–18.

1905 *Baggallay, Rev. F. W., M.A. (Oct. 25, 1915). Chaplain to the Forces (4th Class). France. *D.* France, 1918, 1919.
1901 **Bailey, J. W.,** M.A. (Nov. 1915). 2nd Lt. and Instructor, R.F.C. Killed in action during a Zeppelin raid on March 31, 1916.
1899 Baines, M. B., D.M. (Aug. 22, 1914). Capt. R.A.M.C. France. *M.C.*, Dec. 4, 1916.
1905 Baines, N. A., B.A. (Sept. 18, 1914). ‡Lt. 3rd R. Scots, attd. 2nd Gloucestershire Regt. (Capt.). Gallipoli, Egypt, France, Macedonia. Chevalier of the Crown of Rumania.
1894 Baines, S. H., M.A. (Sept. 15, 1914). ‡Lt. Sherwood Foresters; Lt. Labour Corps. France, Belgium.
1881 Ball, Rev. F., M.A. (Serving Aug. 4, 1914). Chaplain R.N.
1903 Balleine, Rev. A. H., M.A. (Sept. 22, 1914). Chaplain to the Forces (3rd Class). France. *O.B.E.* (Mil.). *D.* France, 1916, 1917, 1918, 1919.
1902 **Balleine,* C. F.,** M.A. (Serving Aug. 4, 1914). Capt. 8th Rifle Brigade. France, Belgium. Killed in action on July 2, 1915.
1911 Bamford, H. J., B.A. (Mobilized Aug. 4, 1914). Capt. R.F.A. (T.F.). France, Belgium, 1915–18.
1896 **Bannatyne, D. A.,** B.A. (Jan. 1915). Lt. 9th R. Scots. France. Killed in action near Soissons on Aug. 1, 1918.
1911 Barber, B. H., B.A. (Mobilized Aug. 4, 1914). Capt., Temp. Maj., 2nd King Edward's Horse; G.S.O. 2. France. *M.C.*, Jan. 1, 1919.
1906 Barber, E. A., M.A. (Aug. 26, 1915). Lt. 4th Shropshire L.I.; Lt. Special Lists; Staff Lt. (1st Class). Salonika, 1918–19. *D.* Salonika, 1919.
1910 Barker, F. D., B.A. (Nov. 1915). ‡2nd Lt. 3rd Essex Regt. France. (Invalided on account of wounds, Mar. 9, 1918.)
1908 Barnes, E. F. (May 20, 1915). Lt. 3rd Monmouthshire Regt.
1911 Barnett, A. (1917). U.S. Army.
1903 **Barr, W. A.** (Sept. 1914). ‡Lt. 328th Siege Batt., R.G.A. Belgium, France, 1914–18. Killed in action near Croisilles on Aug. 27, 1918.
1912 Barrow, R. H., B.A. (Dec. 30, 1915). Lt. 6th Manchester Regt. France. (Invalided Aug. 1918.)
1919 Barton, H. R. (Aug. 8, 1914), Pte. 13th London Regt. (Cpl.). Salonika, Egypt, Palestine.
1914 Barstow, H. L. (Nov. 1, 1915). Lt. M.G.C., attd. 2/4 Gurkha Rifles, Indian Army. India.
1910 **Bastard,* W.,** B.A. (Serving Aug. 4, 1914). Lt. 2nd Bedfordshire Regt. Belgium. *D.* France, 1915. Killed in action at Ypres on Oct. 26, 1914.
1888 Bates, Rev. G. L. (April 4, 1916). Chaplain to the Forces (4th Class).
1896 Battersby, C. W. (Aug. 24, 1916). Lt., Acting Captain, R.A.O.C.; D.A.D. Ordnance Services. Palestine. *D.* Palestine, 1919.
1919 Baxter, H. J. (March 25, 1918). 2nd Lt. Rifle Brigade (on demobilization).
1908 **Bayfield,* H. L.,** B.A. (Serving Aug. 4, 1914). Lt. 1st Leicestershire Regt. France and Belgium. *D.* France, 1915. Died on March 12, 1915, of wounds received in action.
1898 Beardmore, Rev. C. L. H., M.A. (Serving Aug. 4, 1914). Chaplain to the Forces (3rd Class). Gallipoli, Salonika. Order of the White Eagle (5th Class). *D.* Gallipoli, 1915.

1907 Bedale,* Rev. F. B., B.A. (Aug. 21, 1917). Chaplain, R.N., H.M.S. *Erin*. Grand Fleet.

1913 **Bedwell, V. L. S.** (Oct. 1914). 2nd Lt. 4th Suffolk Regt. France. Killed in action in High Wood on Aug. 18, 1916.

1885 **Bell, F. de B.,** B.A. (Serving Aug. 4, 1914). Maj. 2nd Norfolk Regt. Mesopotamia. *D.* Mesopotamia, 1915. Died on April 24, 1915, of wounds received in action.

1911 **Bellamy, G. G.,** B.A. (Sept. 12, 1914). Maj. 7th Devonshire Regt., attd. M.G.C. France. Died on Sept. 1, 1918, of wounds received in action at Bus en Artois.

1919 Benson, T. N. (Aug. 4, 1915). ‡Capt. 1/4th Gloucestershire Regt. France, 1916–17; Italy, 1917–19. *M.C.*, June 18, 1917.

1896 Bentinck, B. W., M.A. (Sept. 4, 1914). ‡Capt. R.A.F. (Maj.). France, Belgium, Italy. *D.* France, 1917.

1912 **Bernheim, G. E.** (Sept. 1914). Artillerie Lourde, French Army. France. Croix de Guerre. Médaille Militaire. *D.* French Dispatches. Killed in action at Tahure, Champagne, on Oct. 5, 1915.

1911 **Berry,* T. C. H.,** B.A. (Sept. 1914). Capt. 14th Welsh Regt. France, 1916, 1917, 1918. Killed in action at Morval on Aug. 30, 1918.

1914 Bicknell, R. L. (June 22, 1915). Lt. R.G.A.

1911 **Biddulph,* R. A.** (Oct. 21, 1914). 2nd Lt. 2nd Dragoon Guards. France. Died on Nov. 19, 1916, of illness contracted on active service.

1884 Bidlake, Rev. W., M.A. (Serving Aug. 4, 1914). Chaplain to the Forces (4th Class), attd. R.F.A.

1907 **Blackburn, R. H.** (Feb. 10, 1915). Lt. 8th Bedfordshire Regt. Died on Nov. 5, 1918, of illness contracted while on active service.

1888 Blake, C. F. S. (Nov. 16, 1915). Capt. R.A.S.C. *O.B.E.* (Mil.).

1906 Blandy,* W. E. M., M.A. (Mobilized Aug. 4, 1914). Capt. 4th R. Berkshire Regt. France, 1915–16.

1910 Blomfield,* A., B.A. (Aug. 31, 1914). Lt. 5th R. Sussex Regt.; Lt. R.A.F. France, 1915, 1916, 1917, 1918.

1893 Bloxam, Rev. J. F., M.A. (July 3, 1917). Chaplain to the Forces (4th Class). France. *M.C.*, Nov. 26, 1917; *Bar*, Feb. 15, 1919.

1908 Bodkin, P. R. (Apr. 15, 1915). Lce.-Cpl. 19th London Regt. France, 1915–18. (Prisoner of War, Mar.–Dec. 1918.)

1900 Bond, Rev. W. F., M.A. (Serving Aug. 4, 1914). Maj., Unattd. List, T.F., Lancing College O.T.C.

1884 Booker, G. E. N. (Aug. 11, 1914). Lt.-Col. 4th Reserve Regt. of Cavalry. *C.B.E.* (Mil.). *D.* § Feb. 1917.

1917 Boulton, C. D. C., B.A. (Oct. 2, 1916). Paymaster Sub-Lt. R.N.V.R. H.M.S. *Niobe*, 1916–17; H.M.S. *Thalia*, 1917–19.

1911 **Bowen, R. G. B.** (Mobilized Aug. 4, 1914). Lt. 1st London Regt. France and Belgium. Killed in action at Aubers Ridge on May 9, 1915.

Bowman, C. H. (Dec. 19, 1916). 2nd Lt. Oxf. & Bucks. Lt. Infty. Belgium. Killed in action in Belgium on Aug. 16, 1917.

1919 Boyce, E. K. A., B.A. (Aug. 1914). ‡Lt. 6th Dorsetshire Regt. France, 1916. (Invalided on account of wounds.)

1901 Boyd, A. K., B.A. (Sept. 1914). Capt. 2/4th Queen's (R. West Surrey Regt.). Gallipoli. (Invalided May 1918.)

1912 **Boyd,* W. N. L.** (Aug. 1914). Lt. 2nd Seaforth Highlanders. France, Belgium. Presumed killed in action at St. Julien on Apr. 25, 1915.

1908 Boyle, Rev. N. S. S., B.A. (Aug. 2, 1914). Chaplain to the Forces (4th Class), attd. 16th K.R.R.C.

1898 Brabazon, C. P., M.A. (Nov. 27, 1914). Capt. 3rd K.O. Scottish Borderers.

1913 Brée, P. G. (Dec. 28, 1917). Lt. 3rd Suffolk Regt., attd. 66th Punjabis. I.A. India.

1905 Brendon, J. A., B.A. (June 1916). ‡Lt. R.G.A. France, 1916–18.

1919 Briggs, A. H. P. (May 1, 1918). Cadet, No. 8 School of Aeronautics, R.A.F.

1899 Briggs, Rev. H. S., M.A. Chaplain to the Forces (4th Class).

1910 Brindley,* W. H., M.A. (Sept. 1914). Maj. 10th R. Warwickshire Regt. (Lt.-Col.). France, Belgium. *M.C.*, June 4, 1917. *D.* France, 1918.

1905 **Bromfield-Williams, J.** (Aug. 1914). ‡Lt. 5th Q. O. Cameron Highlanders. France, Malta, 1914; France, 1915. Killed in action at Loos on Sept. 25, 1915.

1903 **Brook, A. C.,** B.A. (Sept. 12, 1914). 2nd Lt. 5th Manchester Regt. Gallipoli. Killed in action on June 14, 1915.

1880 Brooke, Rev. W. I., M.A. (Oct. 9, 1917). Chaplain to the Forces (4th Class).

1919 Brookfield, G. P. (Dec. 2, 1914). ‡Lt. Royal Canadian G.A.

1914 Brough, P. H. L. (June 16, 1915). Lt. 1st Northumberland Fusiliers, attd. 4th King's (Liverpool Regt.). France and Belgium. *M.C.*, Oct. 26, 1919. *D.* France, 1917.

1910 **Broughton-Adderley, P. H.** (Sept. 11, 1914). 2nd Lt., Acting Capt., Scots Guards. France. *M.C.*, Feb. 1, 1919. Died on Oct. 16, 1918, of wounds received in action at the Selle River.

1884 Brown, C. H., M.A. (Oct. 4, 1914). Lt., Acting Maj., R.A.S.C. Egypt and Palestine. *D.* Palestine, 1918 twice.

1905 **Brown, *D. H.** (Oct. 1914). Capt. 6th K.O. Scottish Borderers. France. Killed in action at the Battle of Loos on Sept. 25, 1915.

1911 **Brown, W. R.,** B.A. Pte. 28th London Regt. (Artists' Rifles). France, Belgium. Killed in action on Oct. 30, 1917.

1892 Brunskill, H. F. (July 18, 1915). Lt. R. Wiltshire Yeomanry. A.P.M.

1919 Bucknall, G. A. F. (May 2, 1918). 2nd Lt. R.A.F.

1919 Bunn, R. F. I. (Jan. 10, 1918). 2nd Lt. 4th The Buffs (E. Kent Regt.).

1887 Burbey, J. L., M.A. (Serving Aug. 4, 1914). Maj. 11th Loyal N. Lancashire Regt. *D.* § Feb. 1917; § Aug. 1919.

1911 Burdon,* C. C. (Nov. 13, 1914). Lt. K.R.R.C.; Staff Lt. (2nd Class). France, Macedonia.

1909 Burke,* E. H. R., M.A. (Mar. 2, 1916). Lt. Irish Guards. France, Belgium.

1902 Burlton, F. A. (Mar. 15, 1915). Lt. Hertfordshire Yeomanry, attd. M.G.C.

1903 **Burrell, J. S. G.,** M.A. (Sept. 1914). ‡2nd Lt. 1/4th Cheshire Regt. Gallipoli. Killed in action at Suvla Bay on Aug. 9, 1915.

1903 Burrows, E. A. (Jan. 5, 1915). Lt. 3rd Res. Regt. of Cavalry, attd. 19th Hussars.

1903 **Burton, J. S.,** M.A. (Oct. 27, 1914). 2nd Lt. Grenadier Guards. Belgium. Killed in action near Ypres on May 16, 1916.

1910 Butcher,* P. G. (Aug. 21, 1915). Lt. 8th Devonshire Regt. France.

1908 Buxton, L. H. D., M.A. (Oct. 1914). Capt. R.F.A.; Staff Lt. (2nd Class), Intelligence Corps. France.

1911 **Byng, P. H.** (Apr. 1915). 2nd Lt. R.F.A. India and Mesopotamia, 1916. Died on Sept. 25, 1916, of illness contracted on active service.

1901 Byrne, E. le C., M.A. (1914). R.N.V.R.

1915 Cameron, C. W., B.A. (Jan. 14, 1916). Gunner 232nd Bde., R.F.A. France.

1906 **Campbell, I. S.** Orderly, Lady Paget's Serbian Hospital Unit. Serbia, Roumania. Died on June 27, 1917, of illness contracted while on active service.

1905 Campden, Viscount (Mobilized Aug. 1914). Maj. 5th Gloucestershire Regt. Dep. Asst. Military Secretary. France, Belgium. *O.B.E.* (Mil.). T.D. *D.* § Aug. 1918.

1906 Carey, A. de J. (Oct. 9, 1915). Lt. R.N.V.R.

1891 Carey, G. M., M.A. (Dec. 21, 1915). 2nd Lt., Unattd. List, T.F., Sherborne School O.T.C.

1893 Carleton, P. R. N., B.A. (Oct. 1914). Lt., Acting Captain, 7th Training Reserve Bn.

1905 Carnelley, S. H. (1915). Capt. E. African Protectorate Forces. E. Africa, 1915–18.

1903 Carrington, S. (1914). ‡2nd Lt. W. Riding Regt.

1910 Cartwright, *C., B.A. (Aug. 21, 1914). Maj. 6th York & Lancaster Regt. (Lt.-Col.). Gallipoli, Egypt, France. *D.S.O.*, Feb. 15, 1919. *M.C.*, Mar. 3, 1917. *D.* France, 1917.

1913 Cassidy, J. R., B.A. (Nov. 25, 1914). Capt. R.A.S.C. Capt. R.A.F. Gallipoli, 1915; Egypt, 1916; Grand Fleet, 1918–19. *D.* Gallipoli, 1915.

1902 Castle, E. R. M., B.A. (Mar. 1, 1915). Capt. R.A.S.C.

1890 Cattell, Rev. R. H. B., M.A. (Aug. 9, 1915). Chaplain to the Forces (4th Class).

1913 Challacombe, C. N. (Dec. 11, 1914). Lt. 1st E. Surrey Regt., attd. 10th Lincolnshire Regt. France.

1905 Challinor, J. M., B.A. (Aug. 15, 1914). Capt. 3rd K.O. Scottish Borderers, attd. War Office. France. *M.C.*, Jan. 14, 1916. *D.* France, 1915.

1913 **Chambers,* W. J.** (Dec. 11, 1914). Lt. 11th E. Surrey Regt. France. Killed in action on Aug. 18, 1916.

1900 Chapman, H. R., M.A. (Sept. 2 1914). ‡Capt. 5th Yorkshire Regt. France and Belgium. *D.* France, 1917.

1886 Chapman, Rev. T. A., B.D. (Serving Aug. 4, 1914). Chaplain to the Forces (4th Class) (T.F.), attd. R.F.A.

1919 Chavasse, C. (Jan. 6, 1916). Lt. D/48th Bde., R.F.A. France.

1905 Cheshire, G. C., B.C.L., M.A. (Jan. 7, 1915). Capt. 6th Cheshire Regt., Capt. Balloon Officer, R.A.F. France, Belgium.

1908 Chichester Constable,* R. C. (Serving Aug. 4, 1914). Capt., Bt.-Maj., Rifle Brigade; G.S.O. 3. France. *D.S.O.*, Jan. 14, 1916. *D.* France, 1915, 1917, 1918.

1914 Christie-Crawfurd, G. N. O.T.C., Ayrshire. Died on Oct. 22, 1918.

1919 Christopoulos, C. (June 15, 1918). Lt. 9th Inf. Regt., Greek Army. Salonika.

1901 Clarence, A. A., M.A. (Mar. 18, 1915). Capt. Hampshire Yeomanry. R.T.O. Mediterranean, Italy. *O.B.E.* (Mil.). *D.* Mediterranean, 1916; Italy, 1918.

1919 Clarke, M. N. (Feb. 3, 1916). Lce.-Cpl. Inns of Court O.T.C.

1905 Clayton, Rev. P. T. B., M.A. (May 26, 1915). Chaplain to the Forces (4th Class); Garrison Chaplain, Poperinghe. France, Belgium, 1915–18. *M.C.*, Jan. 1, 1918.

1902 Cleave, A. (Aug. 12, 1914). Capt. 2nd Suffolk Regt. (1914–15); Capt. R.A.F. (1918). France, 1914. (Invalided, 1915; rejoined, 1918.)

1901 **Clemson, J. O.** (Mobilized Aug. 1914). Lt. R.N. Devon Yeomanry. Gallipoli. Died on Dec. 9, 1915, of wounds received in action.

1898 Coates, E. C. (Mobilized Aug. 6, 1914). Capt. 15th Hussars, Res. of Officers. A.P.M. France. *O.B.E.* (Mil.). *D.* France, 1919.

1905 Cockburn, A. S. (1914). Pte. 16th Middlesex Regt. (Public Schools Bn.).

1919 Coghill, G. H. (Feb. 18, 1918). Pte. 2/28th London Regt. (Artists Rifles).

1919 Coghill, N. H. K. A. (Nov. 16, 1917). 2nd Lt. B./116th Bde., R.F.A. Salonika, Rumania, 1918–19.

1903 Coleman, H. O., B.A. (Aug. 5, 1916). Lt. 4th King's Own (R. Lancaster Regt.). Staff-Lt. (2nd Class). France.

1910 Coles,* J. L. (Serving Aug. 4, 1914). Lt. 2nd York & Lancaster Regt. (Capt.). France, 1915; Salonika, 1915–18.

1887 Collier, W., M.A. (Mobilized Aug. 1914). Lt.-Col. R.A.M.C. (T.F.). Consulting Physician to the Southern Command. *D.* § Aug. 1919.

1903 Coltart, A. H., M.A. (Serving Aug. 4, 1914). Capt. 4th King's (Liverpool Regt.). France, Belgium.

1887 **Colthurst, A. B.,** B.A. (Dec. 22, 1914). Capt. 14th Gloucestershire Regt. France. Killed in action on Oct. 25, 1916.

1910 Colyer-Ferguson, M. C. H. (Oct. 28, 1914). Capt. R.A.S.C.

1907 Constable, L. G. A. (Sept. 12, 1914). Capt. 8th R. Inniskilling Fusiliers. France. *M.C.*, June 24, 1916.

1913 **Cooke, T.** (Jan. 1915). Lt. R.G.A. (Adjt. 1st Heavy Artillery Group). France. *D.* France, 1916. Died on June 30, 1917, whilst on active service.

1889 Coop, Rev. J. O., M.A. (Mobilized 1914). Chaplain to the Forces (1st Class), attd. R.A. (T.F.). France. *D.S.O.*, Jan. 1, 1918. T.D. *D.* France, 1916, 1917.

1914 Cooper, R. S. F. (Dec. 19, 1914). Capt. Cheshire Regt. Salonika. *M.C.*, March 5, 1918. Order of the White Eagle (5th Class) (with swords).

1915 Cooper, J. V. (Feb. 15, 1916). Lt. 3rd, attd. 6th, Somerset L.I. France, 1916–18.

1891 Coote, A. B., M.A. Inns of Court O.T.C.

1904 Coote, D. V. (Oct. 1914). Lt. The Buffs (E. Kent Regt.).

1910 Copner,* C. J. P., B.A. (Serving Aug. 4, 1914). Capt. 1st S. Wales Borderers. Hon. Capt. R.A.F. France. *D.* France, 1917.

1907 **Cousins, D. T.,** B.A. (Sept. 20, 1915). Lt. 4th, attd. 6th, The Buffs (E. Kent Regt.). France. Killed in action on Apr. 10, 1917.

1895 Cowlard, J. F. (Serving Aug. 4, 1914). Capt. 20th Hussars.

1913 **Cox,* C. R.,** (Nov. 1914). Capt. 12th R. Sussex Regt., attd. R.F.C. France. Died on Apr. 13, 1917, of wounds received in action.

1905 **[Cozens-Hardy, R.]** (Sept. 1914). Lt. 1st Norfolk Regt. (Captain). France, Belgium. Killed in action at Poldershoek on Oct. 9, 1917.

1911 Craddock,* A. B., B.A. (Serving Aug. 4, 1914). Capt. R. Warwickshire Regt. Capt. Indian Army, attd. 2nd Rajputs. India.

1914 Craig, E. D., B.A. (Oct. 22, 1916). Lt. R.A.S.C.

1875 Crane, C. P., M.A., *D.S.O.* (Mobilized 1914). Lt.-Col. York & Lancaster Regt. (T.F. Res.). *O.B.E.* (Mil.). *D.* § Feb. 1917.
1907 Crane,* M. E., B.A. (Serving Aug. 4, 1914). Capt. 1st W. Riding Regt. India.
1905 Cranswick, C. F. (1916). ‡2nd Lt. 1st S. African Inf. France, 1917–18.
1919 Crawshaw, C. F. H. (July 15, 1915). Lt. 9th King's Own (R. Lancaster Regt.). France, Salonika.
1919 Crawshaw, E. J. (March 13, 1917). 2nd Lt. 51st K.R.R.C.
1912 **Crichton, C. A. W.** (Mobilized Aug. 1914). 2nd Lt. 3rd London Regt. France. Killed in action at Neuve Chapelle on Mar. 10, 1915.
1903 Crocker, J. P. (1914). ‡2nd Lt. R. Fusiliers.
1914 Crompton, F. C. B. (July 26, 1915). Lt. R.A.S.C. France.
1913 **Cruddas,* S. G. P.** (Nov. 28, 1914). 2nd Lt. 6th D.C.L.I. France and Belgium. Killed in action at Ypres on Sept. 21, 1915.
1900 Cruwys, L. G., B.A. (Sept. 21, 1915). Capt. Special Lists, empld. Ministry of National Service.
1889 Currie, L. C., M.A. (April 10, 1915). Capt. R.A.S.C.
1887 Cuthbertson, J. O., B.M. (Dec. 20, 1915). Capt. R.A.M.C. (T.F.).
1912 **Daffen,* H. C.** (Sept. 1914). Lt. 2/8th Sherwood Foresters. *D.* §. Killed in Dublin Rebellion on April 29, 1916.
1908 Daniell, T. E. St. C., B.A. (June 7, 1916). Lt.-Col. Special Lists. Dep.-Director of Aircraft Equipment. *O.B.E.* (Mil.). *M.C.*, Jan. 1, 1917. *D.* § March, 1918.
1900 **Darley-Waddilove, C. J.** Pte. R.A.M.C. France. Killed in action, May 1–5, 1917.
1898 Davidson, Rev. H. F., M.A. (Oct. 4, 1915). Chaplain R.N., H.M.S. *Leviathan*. North Atlantic, Red Sea, Indian Ocean, North Sea.
1914 Davies, C. G. (Mobilized Aug. 1914). Lt. 24th London Regt. (The Queen's). Maj. 24th Bn. M.G.C. France, 1915–18, 1918–19. *M.C.*, July 24, 1915. *D.* France, 1915, 1918.
1919 Davies, E. H. (Aug. 30, 1914). Capt. 9th Lancashire Fusiliers. Gallipoli, 1915; Egypt, 1916; France, 1916. (Prisoner of War in Germany, Sept. 1916–Dec. 1918.) *D.* Gallipoli, 1916.
1919 Davies, E. R. (Dec. 10, 1915). ‡2nd Lt. 5th Res. Regt. Hussars. France.
1912 **Davies,* G.** (Sept. 26, 1914). 2nd Lt. 24th London Regt. (The Queen's). France. Died on May 1, 1915, of wounds received in action.
1906 Davies,* I., B.A. (Mobilized Aug. 4, 1914). Capt. 6th Sherwood Foresters (attd. R.A.F., 1917–18.) France and Belgium. *D.* § Aug. 1919.
1920 Davies, L. L. (Aug. 2, 1916). Lt. 4th Lancashire Fusiliers. France, Belgium, 1917–19.
1909 Davy, T. A. L., B.A. (Dec. 8, 1915). Lt. 217th Bde., R.F.A. (T.F.). (Capt.). India.
1899 Dawson, J. K. B., B.A. (Sept. 26, 1916). Lt. Army Cyclist Corps.
1919 Dawson, W. T. (Aug. 18, 1916). ‡Lt. Canadian Res. Artillery. France, 1917–18.
1895 Day, W. L. M., D.M. (Mar. 16, 1917). Capt. R.A.M.C. *O.B.E.* (Mil.).
1919 Day, W. R. (Mar. 13, 1916). Sapper R.E.
1915 de Brisay, A. C. D. (Sept. 5, 1915). Lt. 5th Lincolnshire Regt.
1910 de Jongh, K. G. (April 10, 1915). Lt. 3rd Hampshire Regt. Lt. R.A.F.
1910 Dennis, G. P., M.A. (Sept. 18, 1915). Paymaster, Army Pay Dept.

1914 de Souza, L. L. (May 22, 1915). Lt. M.G.C.
1903 D'Esterre, S. B. W., M.A. (1914). ‡Hon. Capt. and Q.M., British Columbia Regt., Canadian E. F. France.
1919 de Vall, T. G. C. (Feb. 8, 1917). ‡Lt. R.A.F.
1919 Dickinson, E. C. (June 11, 1917). Lce.-Cpl. R.E.
1903 Dickson, T. W., B.A. (Aug. 5, 1914). ‡Capt. R.E. France and Belgium. *M.C.*, June 3, 1918.
1904 Dixon, Rev. F. R., B.A. Chaplain to the Forces (4th Class).
1919 Dixon, T. D. (Feb. 2, 1915). Lt. 14th R. Warwickshire Regt. (Capt.). France, 1915–16, 1917, 1918; Italy, 1917–18.
1899 **Dobson, H. P.** (Serving Aug. 4, 1914). Capt. Worcestershire Regt., attd. 9th Bn. Mesopotamia. *D.* Mesopotamia, 1916. Killed in action, on Apr. 4–5, 1916.
1898 **Dobson, W. J.,** B.A. (Aug. 12, 1914). ‡Capt. 1st Canadian Infantry (Maj.). France, Belgium. Killed in action at Zillebeke on July 9, 1916.
1910 Dodd,* B. F., B.A. (May 14, 1916). Lt. E. Surrey Regt., attd. 2/107th Pioneers, Indian Army. India.
1881 Donovan, Rev. P. J., M.A. (April 1, 1916). Chaplain (4th Class), A.I.F.
1908 Dover,* G. C., B.A. (Serving Aug. 4, 1914). Lt. Unattached List, T.F., King's School, Bruton, O.T.C.
1910 Drake-Brockman, K. E., B.A. (Apr. 8, 1915). Lt., Acting Capt., 5th R. Fusiliers.
1904 Drought, J. V., B.A. (Serving Aug. 4, 1914). Capt. 1/124th Duchess of Connaught's Own Baluchistan Infantry, attd. 2/130th King George's Own Baluchis (Maj.). India.
1905 Drury, Rev. W. E., M.A. (July 27, 1915). Chaplain to the Forces (4th Class), attd. 101st Bde., R.G.A. Egypt, France, Mesopotamia.
Duff-Gordon, C. L. (Sept. 22, 1914). Lt. Hertfordshire Regt., attd. M.G.C. France. Killed in action on Sept. 3, 1916.
1912 Duff-Gordon,* D. F. (Aug. 30, 1914). Lt. Montgomeryshire Yeomanry. Lt. Scots Guards (S.R.).
1898 Duke, N. O., B.A. (1915). Lt. R.N.V.R.
1919 Dunkle, D. F. (Aug. 5, 1917). Capt. 64th Inf., U.S. Army. France.
1914 Dunstan, A. E. A. (Sept. 3, 1914). Capt. 1st King's Own (R. Lancaster Regt.), attd. Political Dept., Mesopotamia. India, Mesopotamia, Persia, 1914–19.
1910 Dyke, S. C., B.M. (April 1, 1915). Capt. R.A.M.C. France.
1919 Dyson, H. V. D. (Aug. 18, 1915). Lt. 1st R.W. Kent Regt. France and Belgium, 1916–18.
1903 Eagar, W. McG., B.A. 2nd Lt. R.F.A.
1919 Eales, C. (Oct. 1, 1915). 2nd Lt. 3/4th Devonshire Regt. Capt. R.A.F. France, 1916–18.
1907 **Eames,* W. S.,** B.A. (Feb. 1915). Lt. 7th, attd. 12th, R. Fusiliers. France, Belgium. Killed in action at Ypres on Feb. 16, 1916.
1919 East, R. M. (May 11, 1917). Lt. 109th Siege Batt., R.G.A. France, Belgium.
1905 Ebdon, R. A., B.Mus. (Feb. 4, 1918). 2nd Lt. R.G.A. (S.R.).
1905 Edmunds, M. W. (Aug. 1914). Capt. 1/4th Oxf. & Bucks. Lt. Infty. France, 1915–16, 1917; Italy, 1918–19. *D.* § Aug. 1919.

1919 Edwards, D. A. (Aug. 4, 1915). Pte. 20th R. Fusiliers. 2nd Clerk, R.A.F. (Schoolmaster Sergt.). France.

1913 Elliot,* G. G., B.A. (Dec. 8, 1914). Lt. 8th Sherwood Foresters (Capt.). France, 1915–16, 1917–18. *M.C.*, Dec. 17, 1917.

1907 Ellis-Danvers, G. R. (Mar. 10, 1917). Lt., Acting Capt., and Adjt., Labour Corps.

1908 Ely,* D. M., B.A. (May 19, 1915). Lt. R.F.A. (S.R.).

1908 Evans, H. W. D., B.A. (Dec. 1915). Lt. 1st Shropshire L.I. France, Belgium. (Prisoner of War, Mar.–Nov. 1918.)

1899 **Eve, W. H.** (Serving Aug. 4, 1914). Capt. 13th Hussars. France, Mesopotamia. Killed in action at Lajj on Mar. 5, 1917.

1919 Ewing, J. H. (Nov. 29, 1917). ‡2nd Lt. 13th Middlesex Regt. France and Belgium, 1918–19.

1911 Fairbank,* C. A. H. (Dec. 10, 1915). Lt. attd. 49th Batt., R.F.A. (Capt.). France, 1916–19. *M.C.*, Jan. 30, 1919. *D.* § Mar. 1919.

1919 Fairweather, I. (Serving Aug. 4, 1914). Lt. 2nd Cheshire Regt. (Capt.). Belgium.

1896 Fallaize, E. N., B.A. (Mar. 28, 1917). Lt. 5th Worcestershire Regt., attd. 13th Cheshire Regt. France.

1899 Falle, E. H., M.A. (Serving Aug. 4, 1914). Lt. Unattached List, T.F., University College O.T.C.

1908 Fannin, C. G., B.A. (Feb. 7, 1915). Lt. R.G.A. (T.F.), empld. Ministry of Munitions. France. *M.C.*, Jan. 1, 1918. *D.* France, 1916.

1902 Fendick, Rev. G. H., M.A. (Feb. 1916). Chaplain to the Forces (4th Class). France, 1916.

1919 Fenton, F. C. (Aug. 27, 1917). Lt. 72nd Coast Artillery Corps., U.S. Army. France.

1903 Fenwick-Owen, G. (Oct. 1, 1914). Capt. Norfolk Yeomanry, attd. 12th Norfolk Regt. Egypt and Palestine. *M.C.*, Feb. 4, 1918.

1905 Ferrers, C. R., M.A. Malay States Volunteer Rifles.

1900 Ferrers, E. A. J. (Mar. 7, 1915). Capt. 4th E. Surrey Regt. Staff-Captain.

1905 Fetherstonhaugh, C. F. C., B.A. (Sept. 1914). ‡Capt. 3rd, attd. 11th, Essex Regt. Belgium and France. *M.C.*, Jan. 1, 1919. *D.* France, 1917.

1896 Field, Rev. G. H., B.A. (Nov. 27, 1915). Chaplain to the Forces (4th Class). Egypt, 1916; France, 1918.

1911 Field,* G. S., B.A. (Aug. 26, 1914). Capt. 4th R. Berkshire Regt.

1906 Fish, C. B., B.A. (Dec. 20, 1916). Lt. Q.O. Oxfordshire Hussars.

1884 Fitzgerald, Rev. J. C., M.A. (Dec. 5, 1914). Chaplain to the Forces (3rd Class). Palestine. *O.B.E.* (Mil.). *D.* Palestine, 1918 twice 1919.

1899 Fleming-Struthers,* R. de J., B.Sc., M.A. (1914). 2nd Lt. Res. of Cavalry.

1909 Fletcher, J. M. (Mar. 1, 1917). Lt. Special Lists, whilst R.T.O.

1899 Flower, N., B.M., M.A. (Jan. 1917). Capt. R.A.M.C. Surgeon Specialist, Malta Command. Malta.

1906 Floyd,* B. E., B.A. (Serving Aug. 4, 1914). Capt., Acting Maj., R.G.A. France, E. Africa. *M.C.*, Jan. 1, 1918. Croix de Guerre. *D.* E. Africa, 1916, 1918.

1919 Follett, F. V. (Mar. 1917). Lt. 12th (Norfolk Yeomanry) Bn., Norfolk Regt. France.

1919 Forsyth, I. M. (Feb. 9, 1917). Lt. 3/8th Gurkhas, Indian Army (Capt.). India, 1918–19 ; N.W. Frontier, 1919.

1910 Fortescue, L. S. (Dec. 17, 1914). Capt. I.A.R.O., attd. Supply and Transport Corps. India.

1914 Forty, G. H. (Sept. 1, 1914). Maj. 10th D.C.L.I. France. *M.C.*, Nov. 14, 1916. *D.* France, 1916, 1918.

1911 **Foster, A. C.** (Sept. 18, 1914). ‡2nd Lt. 1st Grenadier Guards. France. Died on Mar. 12, 1915 at Merville of wounds received in action at Neuve Chapelle.

1919 Fraser, P. A. (Nov. 6, 1918). 2nd Lt. 3rd Cavalry Reserve.

1872 Freeborn, J. C. R., M.A. (Mobilized Aug. 1914). Maj. R.A.M.C. (T.F.). 3rd S. Gen. Hospital.

1912 **Freston, H. R.** (April 10, 1915). 2nd Lt. 6th R. Berkshire Regt. France. Killed in action on Jan. 24, 1916.

1919 Frost, Rev. F. G. (Oct. 21, 1914). Pte. 28th Bn. C.E.F. ‡Hon. Capt. and Chaplain, attd. 10th Canadian Inf. Bn. France, 1915–16, 1918. *D.C.M.*, Sept. 15, 1916.

1905 Fry, Rev. H. E. K., M.A. (Sept. 4, 1917). Chaplain to the Forces (4th Class).

1906 Fry, J. G., B.A. (Dec. 29, 1916). 2nd Lt. 21st Siege Batt., R.G.A. France.

1889 Fulford, Rev. J. L. L., D.D. (Sept. 15, 1916). Chaplain to the Forces (4th Class).

1908 **Galton,* T. H.** (Aug. 15, 1914). 2nd Lt. 6th, attd. 3rd, Worcestershire Regt. France. Killed in action at Aubers Ridge on Oct. 21, 1914.

1906 Gamage, L. C., M.A. (Sept. 10, 1914). Capt. 24th London Regt. (The Queen's). France, 1915–16, 1917–18. *M.C.*, Jan. 1, 1917.

1895 Gamlen, R. B., M.A. N.Z.A.M.C.

1905 Gandy, C., B.A. (Oct. 30, 1914). Lt. R.F.A. France, Belgium.

1919 Garrad, B. L. (Dec. 2, 1914). Lt. R.G.A. (Capt. and Adjt.). France.

1914 **Garrard, R. H.** (Jan. 21, 1916). 2nd Lt. 16th K.R.R.C. France. Killed in action on April 23, 1917.

1907 George,* G. E., B.A. (Aug. 8, 1914). Capt. 3rd Wiltshire Regt. Lt. R.N.V.R. France, Belgium, 1914–15 ; Patrol Boats, 1915–17. *D.* France, 1914, 1915.

1912 **Gibson,* M. R.** (Aug. 22, 1914). Lt. 7th E. Surrey Regt. France. Killed in action at Loos on Oct. 8, 1915.

1907 **Gibson, S. A. C.,** B.A. (July 24, 1915). 2nd Lt. 3rd Wiltshire Regt., attd. Bucks. Bn. Oxf. & Bucks. Lt. Infty. France, Belgium. *M.C.*, Sept. 26, 1917. Died on Aug. 26, 1917, of wounds received in action.

1909 Gilbert, Rev. J., B.A. (May 8, 1915). Chaplain to the Forces (4th Class).

1919 Gilbert, P. D. (Nov. 10, 1914). Sergt. 2/4th Wiltshire Regt. India, 1915–19.

1908 **Gill, C. T.,** B.A. (Sept. 1914). ‡2nd Lt. 22nd Manchester Regt. France, 1916. Killed in action at Mametz on July 1, 1916.

1897 Gillson, F. W. C., B.A. (May 12, 1915). Lt. 1st W. Yorkshire Regt.

1914 Glenn, J. L., B.A. (May, 1917). Capt. 26th Inf., U. S. Army. France, 1917–18. Croix de Guerre with Palm. L'Ordre de la Couronne.

1896 Goddard, Rev. F. G., B.D. (Feb. 6, 1918). Chaplain to the Forces (4th Class).

1919 Godfrey-Isaacs, D. (Aug. 9, 1914). ‡Lt. 2nd R. Welch Fusiliers (Capt.). France, Italy.

1919 Gold, D. G. (Mar. 1917). Lt. R.F.C. France. (Prisoner of War.)

1898 Goldring, C., M.A. (Nov. 22, 1916). Lt. General List.

1911 **Goodman, H. H.** (Sept. 22, 1914). ‡2nd Lt. 3rd, attd. 2nd, Devonshire Regt. (Capt.). France, Belgium, 1915. Killed in action at Ypres on Aug. 16, 1917.

1911 **Gordon, A. McD.** (Serving Aug. 4, 1914). Capt. B/246th Bde., R.F.A. (Bde.-Maj. 49th Div. Artillery). Belgium, France. *M.C.*, Jan. 14, 1916. Killed in action at Passchendaele on Nov. 6, 1917. *D.* France, 1915.

1906 Gordon,* E. G. S. (Sept. 13, 1914). Lt. Highland L.I. Lt. R.A.F. France. (Prisoner of War.) *D.* France, 1916.

1911 **Gordon,* R. H.** (Sept. 10, 1914). 2nd Lt. 8th King's (Liverpool Regt.). France. Killed in action, Aug. 1916.

1908 Gordon, S. P., B.A. (Oct. 1914). Lt. R.N.V.R. (Intelligence Officer).

1902 Goulding, W. L. A. (Mobilized Aug. 1914). Capt. R. Irish Fusiliers. A.D.C.

1909 **Gramshaw,* R. W. R.,** B.A. (Aug. 15, 1914). 2nd Lt. 3rd, attd. 2nd, R. Sussex Regt. Belgium, France. Died on Jan. 27, 1915, of wounds received in action at Cuinchy.

1912 **Grant,* J. Cardross** (Sept. 1914). Capt. 10th Cameronians (Capt. and Adjt.). France. *M.C.*, Jan. 14, 1916. *D.* France, 1915. Killed in action near Bethune on Jan. 27, 1916.

1907 Grant-Dalton, L. (Serving Aug. 4, 1914). Capt. Dorsetshire Regt. France. (Prisoner of War.)

1919 Green, G. H. (July 14, 1915). Acting Sergt. R.A.M.C. East Mudros, 1915–16; Egypt and Palestine, 1916–19.

1896 **Green, H. W.,** B.A. (Serving Aug. 4, 1914). Maj., Bt. Lt.-Col., The Buffs (E. Kent Regt.), attd. 1st Queen's (R. W. Surrey Regt.) (Brig.-Gen. 10th Inf. Bde.). Cameroons, 1914; France, 1916, 1917. *D.S.O.*, Jan. 1, 1917. *D.* France, 1916, 1917. Died on Dec. 31, 1918, of wounds received in action near Landrecies on Nov. 7, 1918.

1904 **Green, R. C.,** B.A. (Oct. 6, 1914). Lt. 1st Bedfordshire Regt. France. Killed in action near Arras on May 18, 1916.

1914 Greenhill, F. A., B.A. (Jan. 1916). Lt. R.F.A. France and Belgium.

1895 Grigg, E. W., B.A. (Sept. 29, 1914). Maj. General List (specially empld.).

1903 Griggs, Rev. D. B., M.A. (Sept. 30, 1914). Chaplain to the Forces (4th Class), attd. R.A. (T.F.).

1881 Grimshawe, E. S. V. (Mobilized 1914). Lt.-Col. 4th Durham L.I. Maj. Special Lists. President, Area Quartering Committee. *D.* § Mar. 1919.

1919 Gripper, H. E. (Jan. 30, 1916). 2nd Lt. 1/5th R. W. Kent Regt. India.

1913 Grizelle,* H. F., B.A. (Oct. 1914). Maj. 16th London Regt. (Queen's Westminster Rifles). France, 1915–19. *M.C.*, Jan. 1, 1917. *D.* France, 1916.

1907 Groom, R. G., B.A. (Oct. 27, 1914). Capt. General List. Staff-Lt. *D.* § Aug. 1918.

1892 Gwyther, E. N., M.A. (Dec. 6, 1914). Lt. 1st (Garr.) Bn. Bedfordshire Regt. India, 1916.

1897 Haig, K. G. (July 27, 1916). Capt. R.A.M.C.

1902 Halford-Adcock, H. (July 1915). 2nd Lt. 3rd Durham L.I. (Capt.) (attd. Headquarters, 93rd Bde.). France.

1904 Hall, P. J., M.A. (June 3, 1915). Lt. Hampshire Regt., attd. 34th Training Reserve Bn.

1911 **Hall,* W. E.** (Aug. 15, 1914). Lt. 5th, attd. 2nd, R. Fusiliers. Gallipoli. Killed in action near Krithia on May 23, 1915.

1919 Hampden, J. A. C. (June 17, 1915). Sergt. R.A.M.C. Salonika, 1915–19. *D.* Salonika, 1919.

1914 Hancock, H. D. (Mar. 23, 1915). Lt. 2/5th Sherwood Foresters, attd. Intelligence Corps. France, Germany. *D.* France, 1919.

1919 Hancock, K. M. (Nov. 1917). 2nd Lt. Somerset L.I. France, 1918.

1913 Hancock, O. L. (Aug. 22, 1914). Capt. 7th D.C.L.I. Staff Officer, Barbados Local Forces. France, 1915.

1902 Handley, G. L., M.A. (Sept. 1, 1914). Capt. R.A. Mesopotamia. *M.C.*, Jan. 11, 1919. *D.* Mesopotamia, 1917.

1914 Hardy, A. C. (Jan. 27, 1915). Lt. 2/1st Northern Cyclist Bn., attd. R.E. (Capt.). France, 1918–19.

1908 Hardy,* W. H. C., B.A. (Aug. 1914). Capt. 3rd R. Sussex Regt. G.S.O. 3, G.H.Q., B.E.F. France, 1914, 1915, 1917–19. *M.C.*, Feb. 18, 1918.

1895 Harington, H., B. A. (Serving Aug. 4, 1914). Capt. 1st W. Yorkshire Regt. France.

1919 Harland, M. H. (Dec. 5, 1914). Lt. 13th W. Yorkshire Regt. Lt. R.F.A. Lt. R.A.F. France, 1915–17, 1918.

1912 **Harries-Jones,* L. A.,** (Dec. 10, 1914). 2nd Lt. 18th Manchester Regt. Missing, believed killed in action.

1902 Harrild, F., M.A. (June 26, 1916). Lt. R.A.S.C.

1904 Harris, Rev. A. G., M. A. (July 7, 1916). Chaplain to the Forces (4th Class). France. *D.* France, 1919.

1907 Harris, P. G. K. (Oct. 16, 1914). Lt. Somerset L.I. France. *M.C.*, Mar. 8, 1919. *D.* France, 1918.

1919 Harrison, G. J. C. (Aug. 29, 1914). Capt. and Adjt. 7th Indian D.A.C., R.F.A. Egypt, Palestine, Syria.

1882 Harrison, M. C. C., M.A. (Mobilized Aug. 4, 1914). Maj. 3rd Loyal N. Lancashire Regt., attd. Labour Corps.

1903 Harrison, T. St. C., B.A. (July 3, 1918). Lt. 3rd Nigeria Regt., W.A.F.F. German E. Africa.

1919 Hart, F. A. A. (Mar. 13, 1915). Lt. R.F.A. (Capt.). India, 1915–16, 1917–19; Mesopotamia, 1916–17; Afghanistan, 1919. *D.* Mesopotamia, 1917.

1904 Harvey, Rev. L. F., B.A. (May 5, 1915). Chaplain to the Forces (4th Class) (T.F.), attd. Yorkshire Dragoons.

1910 **Harvey,* R. E.** (Oct. 3, 1914). Capt. and Adjt. 9th The Black Watch. France. Died on Sept. 25, 1915, of wounds received in action at Loos.

1897 Harvie, Rev. H. M., M.A. (July 27, 1916). Chaplain to the Forces (4th Class).

1919 Harwood, E.H. (Dec. 1916). ‡2nd Lt. 2nd R. Warwickshire Regt. France, Italy, 1917–19.

1919 Hawkins, H. A. (Aug. 20, 1916). Lt. 4th S. Staffordshire Regt. France, Belgium. *M.C.*, Sept. 24, 1918.

1905 Hayes, B. H. (April 8, 1915). Lt. 3rd (Garr.) Bn. Bedfordshire Regt. India, 1917.

1909 Hayley,* G. W., B.A. (Jan. 26, 1915). Lt. R.F.A. Italy. *D.* Italy, 1918.

1919 Heelis, H. L. (June 1, 1916). ‡2nd Lt. 10th Lancashire Fusiliers. France, Belgium. (Prisoner of War, June–Dec. 1918.)

1901 Helm, Rev. G. F., M.A. (Mar. 4, 1911). Chaplain to the Forces (4th Class) (T.F.), attd. 5th Gloucestershire Regt. France. *M.C.*, Jan. 1, 1918.

1890 Henderson, B. W., M.A., D.Litt. (July 4, 1918). Cadet, Garr. O.C.B., Cambridge.

1899 Henderson-Scott, A. M., B.C.L., M.A. (Serving Aug. 4, 1914). Capt., Bt.-Maj., 1st R. Inniskilling Fusiliers. Lt.-Col. Special Lists, whilst A.A.G. (War Office). France. *C.B.E.* (Mil.). *D.* France, 1915; § Aug. 1917.

1900 **Henry, C.** (Serving Aug. 4, 1914). Lt. 3rd, attd. 1st, Worcestershire Regt. France. Killed in action at Vailly sur Aisne on Sept. 20, 1914.

1887 Herbert, H. B., M.A. (Serving Aug. 4, 1914). Capt. Unattached List, T.F. Berkhamsted School O.T.C.

1919 Heslop, W. R. C. (Aug. 21, 1915). Lt. R.G.A. Belgium, France.

1909 Hewat,* J. S. (Jan. 25, 1915). Lt., Acting Capt., E. Surrey Regt. France. *M.C.*, Jan. 14, 1916. *D.* France, 1915.

1913 **Hibbs, L. B.** (Aug. 1914). Lt. R. Jersey Militia, attd. 7th R. Irish Rifles. France. Died at Lapuquoy on Mar. 21, 1916, of illness contracted on active service.

1910 **Hill,* G. C. D.,** B.A. (Aug. 25, 1914). Lt. 2nd Shropshire L.I. (Capt.) France, 1915; Macedonia, 1915–17. Drowned near Genoa on May 4, 1917, in sinking of s.s. *Transylvania* by a German submarine.

1911 Hill, H. B., B.A. (Aug. 28, 1914). Capt. 5th Dorsetshire Regt. Staff-Captain 32nd Inf. Bde. Egypt, 1916; France, 1916–19. *M.C.*, June 3, 1918. *D.* France, 1917.

1903 Hillyard, T. G., M.A. (Nov. 1914). Capt. 3rd Devonshire Regt. France, 1915–16, 1917–19.

1900 Hilton-Simpson, M. W. (Sept. 29, 1914). Capt. R.A.S.C. France, 1915–18. *D.* France, 1916.

1918 Hindle, C. J. Pte. 6th R. Fusiliers. France.

1906 Hirst, C. J., B.A. (Mobilized Aug. 1914). Capt. 1/1st Q. O. Yorkshire Dragoons. France, 1915–18. *M.C.*, June 3, 1918. Belgian Croix de Guerre.

1912 Hobbs, F. F. B., B.A. (Nov. 26, 1914). Lt. 149th Siege Batt., R.G.A. (Capt.). France, Belgium.

1902 Hocart, A. M., M.A. (Sept. 6, 1914). Capt. General List. Staff-Lt. France. *D.* France, 1917.

1911 **Hodge, A. B.** (Jan. 30, 1915). Lt. 3rd, attd. 2nd, Leinster Regt. (Capt.). France and Belgium. Killed in action near Zillebeke on July 31, 1917.

1919 Hodge, W. E. (Dec. 11, 1915). ‡Lt. 2/4th D.C.L.I. India.

1919 Holborow, G. (Sept. 23, 1914). Capt. 5th Connaught Rangers. France and Germany, 1915–19.

1893 **Holden, Rev. O. A.,** M.A. (Dec. 27, 1916). Chaplain to the Forces (4th Class). France. Killed in action on Dec. 1, 1917.

1898 Hole, G. B. (Nov. 5, 1914). Capt. 8th Res. Bn. Indian Inf., attd. 4th Devonshire Regt. India.

1895 [Holland, Hon. S. L.] (Mobilized 1914). Capt. 6th Dragoons, Res. of Officers. A.P.M. France. *D.* France, 1919.

1902 Holt, E. (July 4, 1916). Lt. Oxf. & Bucks. Lt. Infty. France, Belgium. *M.C.*, Nov. 26, 1917.
1885 Holt, Rev. V., M.A. (Mobilized 1914). Chaplain to the Forces (4th Class) (T.F.), attd. 4th Gloucestershire Regt. France.
1919 Holtham, R. (Jan. 26, 1916). Lt. 4th Australian M.G. Bn. (Education Officer). France, Belgium.
1902 Hony, H. C., B.A. (July, 1917). Lt. Special List, Indian Army. (Capt.). India, Mesopotamia. *M.B.E.* (Mil.). *D.* Mesopotamia, 1918.
1897 Hook, Rev. A. J., M.A. (June 15, 1917). Chaplain to the Forces (4th Class).
1913 Hopkinson,* A. J. (Aug. 15, 1914). Capt. 4th Durham L.I., attd. Intelligence Corps. France.
1919 Hopper, B. C. (April 19, 1917). ‡Capt. 96th Aero Squadron, American Air Service (Flight Commander). France. Croix de Guerre. Aero Medal of Valor.
1913 Horn, T. (Jan. 1, 1916). Lt. 15th W. Yorkshire Regt. France, 1916–18, 1918–19.
1911 Horniman, L. I., B.A. (Sept. 13, 1914). ‡Capt. 13th Middlesex Regt. France.
1904 Howard, K. N. Lt. R.A.S.C.
1913 Howard-Flanders, W. E., B.A. (1914). ‡2nd Lt. R.E.
1911 **Hudson, E. S.,** B.A. (Sept. 7, 1914) 2nd Lt. 10th Devonshire Regt. Egypt, Salonika. Died on Feb. 13, 1917, of wounds received near Lake Doiran.
1910 Hughes,* C. V. (1914). Pte. 16th Middlesex Regt. (Public Schools Bn.).
1901 Hughes, G. R., M.A. (Aug. 28, 1916). Lt. R.A.M.C.
1909 Hughes,* L. D. C., B.A. (1917). Lt. 7th R. Warwickshire Regt. France, 1917; Italy, 1917–18; France, 1918. *M.C.*, Apr. 2, 1919. Italian Silver Medal for Military Valour. *D.* Italy, 1918.
1886 Hughes, Rev. O. R. F., M.A. (Serving Aug. 4, 1914). Chaplain, R.N.
1894 Hunt, Rev. A. A., M.A. (June 15, 1917). Chaplain to the Forces (4th Class).
1899 Hunt, E. G., B.A. (Jan. 1915). Lt. N. Staffordshire Regt. Lt., Acting Capt., Unattd. List.
1912 Huntingdon, J. F., B.A. (Sept. 4, 1914). Lt. 2/22nd London Regt. (The Queen's). France, Salonika, Egypt.
1919 Hyde, E. L. (Sept. 7, 1914). ‡2nd Lt. R. Berkshire Regt. Staff-Capt. R.A.F. France. *D.* France, 1915.
1894 Hyde, G. F. (Aug. 27, 1914). 2nd Lt. 6th R. Sussex Regt.
1882 Hyde, J. G. (Dec. 4, 1914). Sergt. 24th R. Fusiliers. France, 1915–18.
1919 Imrie, W. T. M. (Oct. 19, 1914). ‡Capt. 55th Coke's Rifles (Frontier Force), Indian Army. France, Persia, India.
1894 Ingram, H., B.A. (1915). Lt. R.N.V.R.
1907 Irvine, Q. H. I., B.A. (Apr. 21, 1915). Lt. 3rd Arg. & Suth'd. Highlanders, empld. Ministry of Labour.
1914 Irving, W. H., B.A. Cadet, R.A.F. (Canada).
1919 Isaacs, J. (May 19, 1917). Lt. R.G.A. (T.F.).
1911 **Isaacs, V. H.,** B.A. (Feb. 27, 1918). 2nd Lt. 9th R. Fusiliers. France. Killed in action at Epéhy on Sept. 21, 1918.
1885 Ismay, J. H., M.A. (Oct. 1, 1914). 2nd Lieut. Dorset. Yeomanry (Staff-Captain).

1912 Jackson, A. B. (Apr. 1, 1917). Maj. 10th S. Provinces Mounted Rifles. India.

1909 **Jackson, G. C.,** (Oct. 1914). Lt. 6th K. O. Scottish Borderers. France. Killed in action at Loos on Sept. 25, 1915.

1919 Jackson, W. D. (June 4, 1916). Capt. R.A.F. Grand Fleet, 1917–19. *D.F.C.*, Sept. 21, 1918.

1911 James, W. F. T., B.A. (Aug. 10, 1914). Capt. Glamorganshire Yeomanry, attd. R.A.F. France.

1910 Jeffreys, M. D. W. (Oct. 11, 1916). Lt. Special Lists. German E. Africa, 1916–17. (Prisoner of War, 1917.) *D.* E. Africa, 1917.

1895 Jelf, A. S., M.A. (Sept. 1914). Capt. G.S.O. 3, Straits Settlements Command. Capt. General List, attd. War Office. Malay, 1914–16.

1905 **Jelf, C. G.,** B.A. (Oct. 27, 1914). 2nd Lt. 6th The Buffs (E. Kent Regt.). France. *D.* France, 1915. Killed in action near Loos on Oct. 13, 1915.

1919 Jenkins, P. W. (Nov. 24, 1914). Lt. 9th Welsh Regt. France, Belgium.

1904 Jenkins, R. H. (July 24, 1915). Lt. Gloucestershire Regt.

1890 **Jenkinson, J. W.,** B.Sc., M.A., (Jan. 10, 1915). Capt. 12th Worcestershire Regt., attd. R. Dublin Fusiliers. Gallipoli. Killed in action on June 4, 1915.

1890 Jobling, G. C., B.A. (Nov. 21, 1915). Lt. Special Lists, empld. under Directorate of Requisitions and Hiring.

1913 Johnes,* R. P. (Dec. 15, 1914). Lt. 1st Somerset L.I. France.

1919 Johns, W. C. S. (Mar. 5, 1915). 2nd Lt. Unattached List., T.F., Monkton Combe School O.T.C.

1874 Johnson, Rev. G. H., M.A. (Dec. 26, 1915). Chaplain to the Forces (4th Class).

1908 **Johnston, A. L.,** B.A. (Serving Aug. 4, 1914). Lt. Shropshire L.I. France and Belgium. Killed in action near Ypres on Apr. 22, 1916.

1903 Jones, A. M., M.A. (Sept. 21, 1914). Lt. Unattached List, T.F., St. Paul's School O.T.C.

1909 Jones, F. E. A., B.A. (Aug. 30, 1917). Lt. R.N.V.R.

1902 Jones, G. O., B.A. (Feb. 6, 1916). Lt. Welsh Regt.

1913 Jones, T. H. (1917). U.S. Field Artillery.

1905 **Judd, Rev. A. C.,** M.A. (Jan. 31, 1916). Chaplain to the Forces (4th Class), attd. 2/5th Sherwood Foresters. France. *M.C.*, Dec. 17, 1917. Killed in action on March 21, 1918.

1919 Jupe, A. C. (Aug. 1, 1916). ‡2nd Lt. R.F.A. Belgium, France.

1909 Kearley,* Hon. G. C. (Jan. 11, 1916). Sub-Lt. R.N.D. Lt. 1st Scots Guards, attd. Remount Dept. France.

1896 Kember, Rev. T. L., B.A. (Oct. 26, 1916). Chaplain to the Forces (4th Class).

1911 Kemp, J. T. (Feb. 1, 1917). Lt. W. African Carrier Corps. E. Africa.

1899 Kennedy, C. C. M., B.A. (Mobilized Aug. 1914). Maj. Hertfordshire Regt. G.S.O. 2. France. *M.C.*, Jan. 1, 1917. *D.* France, 1918.

1911 Kennedy, J. D. (Oct. 13, 1914). Capt. R. W. Kent Regt., attd. General Staff, War Office (Maj.). France.

1913 **Kenyon,* C. W.** (Nov. 13, 1914). 2nd Lt. 10th R. Sussex Regt. France. Killed in action on Mar. 16, 1916.

1913 Killick, A. H., B.A. (Sept. 1, 1914). Lt. 10th E. Surrey Regt. Capt. S. Lancashire Regt., attd. M.G.C. (Lt.-Col. 10th M.G. Bn.). France,

Salonika, Egypt, Palestine. *D.S.O.*, June 3, 1919. *M.C.*, June 3, 1918. Order of the Nile (4th Class). *D.* Palestine, 1919.

1912 Kindersley,* J. B., B.A. (Aug. 30, 1914). Maj. 63rd Bde., R.F.A. France, Belgium. *D.S.O.*, Jan. 1, 1919. *M.C.*, Jan. 1, 1917; *Bar to M.C.*, Feb. 18, 1918. *D.* France, 1918.

1877 Kindersley, R. S., M.A. (Serving Aug. 4, 1914). Capt. Unattached List, T.F., Eton College O.T.C.

1900 **King, T. S.** (Mar. 1915). Capt. 4th, attd. 7th, E. Surrey Regt. France. Killed in action on May 3, 1917.

1912 Kitchin, C. H. B., B.A. (Sept. 9, 1915). Lt. 8th R. Warwickshire Regt., attd. M.G.C. France, 1916–17, 1917–18.

1902 Knight, Rev. C. B. H., M.A. (Aug 1, 1915). Chaplain to the Forces (4th Class), attd. 7th Lincolnshire Regt. France. *M.C.*, Jan. 11, 1919.

1909 Knighton, G. F., B.A. (Dec. 19, 1916). Lt. 5th Sherwood Foresters, attd. Labour Corps.

1910 Knowles, R. S. (May 9, 1916). Lt. 13th Essex Regt. France. (Invalided.)

1886 Knox, H. V., M.A. (Sept. 3, 1914). Capt. 5th Oxf. & Bucks. Lt. Infy. Capt. R.A.F. France, 1916–17.

1910 Knox, R. S., B.A. (Nov. 22, 1916). Lt. 3rd Gordon Highlanders.

1919 Kress, W. J. (May 11, 1917). Lt. Quartermaster Corps, U.S. Army. France.

1913 Lafitte, L. S. (1917). 2nd Lt. Field Artillery, U.S. Army.

1907 Lailey, G. P. B., B.A. (Oct. 18, 1914). Lt. D.C.L.I. Capt. Special Lists. Courts Martial Officer.

1897 **Lamb, Cameron** (Serving Aug. 4, 1914). Capt. 2nd Border Regt. Belgium, France. *D.S.O.*, Dec. 1, 1914. Killed in action near Fleurbaix on Dec. 29, 1914.

1894 Landman, Rev. L. H., M.A. (Serving Aug. 4, 1914). Chaplain, R.N. North Sea, Mediterranean.

1907 Larsen, T., B.A. Sergt. Canadian Infantry. Cadet. No. 7 O.C.B.

1919 Leadbetter, T. H. (Apr. 1916). H.A.C. (Invalided, July 1917.)

1906 **Leechman,* C. B.**, B.A. (Serving Aug. 4, 1914). Lt. 3rd Hussars. Belgium, France. Killed in action near Vailly sur Aisne on Sept. 24, 1914.

1919 Leeman, F. W. (June 21, 1915). ‡Lt. Suffolk Regt. (Capt.). France.

1897 **Lees, E. B.**, M.A. (Mobilized Aug. 1914). Maj. Westmorland and Cumberland Yeomanry, attd. Sherwood Foresters. France, 1915, 1918. Killed in action near Albert on July 31, 1918.

1912 Le Feuvre, R. (Mobilized Aug. 4, 1914). Capt. 6th Loyal N. Lancashire Regt. Gallipoli, 1915.

1900 Lefroy, G. F., B.A. (June 9, 1915). Lt. R.F.A. France. *D.* France, 1917.

1906 Legge,* A. M., B.A. (Oct. 4, 1914). Lt. 16th (Sussex Yeomanry) Bn. R. Sussex Regt. France.

1892 Le Marchant, W. G., B.A. (Jan. 9, 1915). ‡Lt. 6th. K.R.R.C. (Capt.). France.

1919 Le Quesne, A. R., B.A. (Feb. 4, 1918). 2nd Lt. 1st King's (Liverpool Regt.). France, 1918–19.

1886 Lethbridge, F. W. (Sept. 1914). Lt.-Col. 10th W. Riding Regt. France, Italy. *D.S.O.*, Oct. 28, 1917. Italian Silver Medal for Military Valour. Croce di Guerra. *D.* France, 1917; Italy, 1918, 1919.

1899 Lethbridge, Rev. H. C. B., M.A. (Sept. 1, 1916). Chaplain to the Forces (4th Class).

1901 Leuchars, R., M.A. (1914). ‡2nd Lt. R.A.S.C.

1919 Levy, E. M. (June 1917). Chaplain to the Forces (4th Class). France, 1917–18.

1904 Lewis, A. C. W., B.A. (Nov. 21, 1914). Maj., Asst. Director, Army Printing and Stationery Services. France, Egypt.

1903 Lewis, C. E. T. (June 17, 1915). Lt. M.G.C.

1914 **Littlewood, F. W.** (Feb. 23, 1915). Lt. 8th York and Lancaster Regt. France. Killed in action on March 5, 1916.

1898 Little, D. S. (1914). Lt. Nyasaland Field Force. East Africa.

1914 Llewellyn-Davies, A. H. P. (Feb. 8, 1916). Lt. Tank Corps. France, 1917, 1918.

1919 Lloyd, A. H. (Apr. 28, 1915). ‡Lt. R.E. France, Belgium, 1916–18; Germany, 1918–19. *M.C.*, Sept. 17, 1917; *Bar*, Feb. 15, 1919.

1893 Lloyd, Rev. H. T., M.A. (June 23, 1915). Chaplain to the Forces (4th Class). Gallipoli, Egypt, Palestine. *M.C.*, Jan. 1, 1918. *D.* Gallipoli, 1916; Palestine, 1917.

1901 **Lockhart, H. K.**, M.A. (1914). Motor Cyclist Section, R.E. Accidentally killed at Bearden Camp, Hitchin, on June 19, 1915.

1903 Lockhart, L. A. (May 20, 1916). Lt. 8th King's (Liverpool Regt.), attd. Labour Corps.

1913 Lockwood, T. P., B.A. (1917). Lt. F.A. & 88th Aero Squadron, U.S. Army. France.

1914 Loewe, H. M. J., M.A. (July 24, 1915). Lt. 1st (Garr.) Bn. Lincolnshire Regt. India.

1903 Longmore, P. E., M.A. (Mobilized Aug. 4, 1914). Maj. Hertfordshire Regt. France, 1914–17; Italy, 1917–18; France, 1918–19. Cavalier of the Order of St. Maurice and St. Lazarus. *D.* France, 1915, 1916.

1894 Lory, F. B. P., M.A. (July 17, 1916). Lt. I.A.R.O., attd. 35th Poona Bn. I.D.F. (Capt.). India.

1907 Lund, H. H., B.A. (Sept. 1915). Capt. 6th K.R.R.C., empld. Ministry of Munitions. German S.W. Africa, France. *D.* § Mar. 1919.

1905 Lunt, Rev. G. C. L., M.A. (Feb. 6, 1917). Chaplain to the Forces (4th Class). France. *M.C.*, June 3, 1918.

1904 Lyall, J. H., B.A. (Oct. 6, 1916). Lt. I.A.R.O. India.

1907 Lyne-Stephens, S. E. V. (Oct. 22, 1914). Lt. W. Yorkshire Regt. France. *D.* France, 1915, 1917.

1896 McComas, A. (Mobilized Aug. 1914). Capt. 22nd London Regt. (The Queen's).

1910 Macdonald, I. P., B.A. (Jan. 1915). ‡Lt. I.A.R.O., attd. 28th Punjabis, Indian Army. Mesopotamia.

1903 McDougal, T. W. H. (Jan. 27, 1917). Lt. Special Lists (empld. Recruiting Duties).

1911 McEvoy, T. L. (Serving Aug. 4, 1914). ‡Maj. 'F' Batt., A.A.R.A. France, Belgium, 1915–19. *D.* France, 1916, 1918, 1919.

1913 McFarland,* W. C. D. (Aug. 15, 1914). Capt. 1st Highland L.I. France, 1915; Mesopotamia, 1916–19; N. Russia, 1919. *M.C.*, May 26, 1919.

1896 MacGregor, R. D., B.M. (Dec. 16, 1914). Capt. R.A.M.C.

1911 Mackarness, G. C. N., B.A. (Sept. 15, 1914). ‡Capt. General List, attd. Headquarters V Corps. France.

1904 Mackarness, H. J. C., B.A. (Aug. 26, 1914). Capt. E. Lancashire Regt. Mesopotamia, India.

1886 McKee, Rev. J. R., M.A. (June 24, 1915). Chaplain to the Forces (4th Class), attd. Headquarters Staff, Shorncliffe. *D.* § Mar. 1918.

1901 McKelvie, Rev. R. F. S., D.D. (Jan. 30, 1918). Chaplain to the Forces (4th Class).

1919 Mackereth, J. (Mar. 8, 1917). Capt. R.A.F. France, Italy.

1913 **Mackirdy,* C. D. S.** (Nov. 11, 1914). Lt. 11th Hussars. France, 1915–18. Killed in action on Mar. 22, 1918.

1911 **Mackreth,* J.** (Sept. 8, 1914). Lt. R.E. France. Killed in action on Sept. 15, 1916.

1897 **Magor, A. C.** (Mobilized Aug. 4, 1914). Capt. 2nd Wiltshire Regt. Belgium. Killed in action at Ypres on Oct. 14, 1914.

1891 Maling, A. F., M.A. (Aug. 21, 1916). Lt. General List (T.F. Res.), empld. Ministry of National Service.

1907 Maling, G. A., B.M., M.A. (Jan. 1915). Capt. 34th Field Amb. R.A.M.C. France, Belgium. *D.* France, 1915. **V.C.**

For most conspicuous bravery and devotion to duty during the heavy fighting near Fauquissart on September 25, 1915.

Lt. Maling worked incessantly with untiring energy from 6.15 a.m. on the 25th till 8 a.m. on the 26th, collecting and treating in the open under heavy shell fire more than 300 men. At about 11 a.m. on the 25th he was flung down and temporarily stunned by the bursting of a large high-explosive shell, which wounded his only assistant and killed several of his patients. A second shell soon after covered him and his instruments with débris, but his high courage and zeal never failed him, and he continued his gallant work single-handed.

1906 **Manlove, L. C. T.,** B.A. (Sept. 1914). ‡2nd Lt. 3rd, attd. 2nd, Hampshire Regt. France and Belgium. Killed in action near Ypres on Aug. 3, 1916.

1913 Margary, I. D., B.A. (Apr. 8, 1915). Lt. 3rd R. Sussex Regt. (attd. 7th Bn.). France, 1916–17, 1917.

1919 Mark, J. (Nov. 1916). ‡2nd Lt. R.F.A. France.

1900 Marsden, H. R. (Sept. 10, 1914). ‡Lt. 8th London Regt. (Post Office Rifles). France and Belgium, 1916, 1917.

1912 **Marshall,* E. W.** (Aug. 15, 1914). Lt., Acting Captain, 1st Somerset L.I. France and Belgium, 1914–15, 1916–18. *M.C.*, June 3, 1917. Killed in action at Pacaut Wood on Apr. 22, 1918.

1914 **Marston, F. W.** (Nov. 18, 1914). 2nd Lt. 10th R. Warwickshire Regt. France. Died on July 24, 1916, of wounds received in action in the Battle of the Somme.

1919 Martin, J. B. (Jan. 7, 1917). ‡2nd Lt. 1st R. Warwickshire Regt. France, 1918–19.

1896 Martyn, H. (Oct. 14, 1914). Lt. Rifle Brigade (T.F. Res.).

1912 **Mason,* A. E. K.** (Aug. 15, 1914). Capt. 9th R. Fusiliers. France. Killed in action near Vermelles on Mar. 2, 1916.

1911 **Massiah-Palmer,* W. W. T.,** B.A. (Sept. 1914). Lt.-Col. 13th Northumberland Fusiliers. Lt.-Col. General List. Assist. Director of Graves

Registration and Inquiries. France, Egypt, Palestine, Salonika, Gallipoli. *O.B.E.* (Mil.). *D.* Palestine, 1919. Died on Feb. 17, 1919, of illness contracted at Salonika.

1906 Mather, E. E., B.M., M.A. (Dec. 2, 1914). Capt. R.A.M.C. France. (Prisoner of War.)

1905 Mathew, M. A., B.A. R.G.A.

1906 Matthew, Rev. H. E. J., M.A. (June 24, 1915). Chaplain, R.N., H.M.S. *Royal Sovereign.*

1905 **Maxwell, R. E. W.,** B.A. (Serving Aug. 4, 1914). Maj. 6th K. O. Scottish Borderers. France. Killed in action at Loos on Sept. 25, 1915.

1886 Master, A. G., M.A. (Serving Aug. 4, 1914). Lt.-Col. R.A.S.C. France. *D.S.O.*, Mar. 24, 1915. *D.* France, 1917.

1895 Maurice, R. FitzG., B.A. (Apr. 1916). Capt. 11th D.C.L.I. Maj. Tank Corps. France, 1917–18. *M.C.*, June 3, 1919. *D.* France, 1918.

1905 Mead, J. P. (Jan. 25, 1917). Lt. 4th E. Surrey Regt., attd. Egyptian Army. Egypt.

1919 Mears, R. A. F. (July 27. 1915). Lt. 17th Sherwood Foresters. France and Belgium.

1882 Merry, Rev. W. M., M.A. (Aug. 10, 1917). Chaplain to the Forces (4th Class).

1902 Miller, E. C. (Dec. 27, 1916). Lt. R. G. A., attd. Indian Army. India.

1919 Milne, A. (July 31, 1916). Signaller, Div. Signal Coy., S. African Force. German E. Africa, 1916–17.

1906 Milner, C. E. (May 14, 1915). Lt. I.A.R.O. (Cavalry). India.

1893 Mitchell, F. C. (Aug. 8, 1914). Maj. 3rd R. Berkshire Regt., attd. 19th (Garr.) Bn. Hampshire Regt. Belgium and France, 1916–19. *D.* France, 1919.

1910 Moberly, G. H., B.A. (Oct. 23, 1914). 2nd Lt. 9th King's Own (R. Lancaster Regt.). Lt., Acting Captain, M.G.C. Gallipoli, 1915–16; Egypt, 1916; France, 1916–18. *M.C.*, Jan. 1, 1918. *D.* France, 1918.

1912 Molony, J. T., B.A. (Apr. 3, 1915). Lt. 4th Dorsetshire Regt., attd. 1st Oxf. & Bucks. Lt. Infty. India, 1915–18; Mesopotamia, 1918.

1896 Moore, Rev. C. W. G., M.A. (Sept. 15, 1914). Chaplain R.N., attd. R.N.D. France. *D.S.O.*, June 4, 1917. *D.* France, 1917.

1908 **Moore, Rev. E. N.,** B.A. (Sept. 12, 1916). Chaplain to the Forces (4th Class), attd. 20th King's (Liverpool Regt.). France and Belgium. *M.C.*, July 31, 1917. Killed in action near Ypres on Jan. 5, 1918.

1901 Moore, T. (Sept. 16, 1914). Capt. 1/5th Somerset L.I. India, 1914–17; Egypt, Palestine, 1917–18. *D.* Palestine, 1919.

1909 Moore,* W. C., B.A. Nigerian Land Contingent. W. Africa.

1895 Mordaunt, O. C. (Serving Aug. 4, 1914). Lt.-Col. Somerset L.I., Commandant, Army Signal School, Dunstable (Col.). Gallipoli, 1915; France and Belgium, 1916–17; Italy, 1917–18. *D.S.O.*, June 3, 1917. Croix de Guerre (avec palme). Croix de Guerre (avec étoile). Croce di Guerra. *D.* France, 1917 twice; Italy, 1918, 1919.

1905 Morgan, N. A., M.A. (Serving Aug. 4, 1914). Capt. 2nd Leicestershire Regt. France. *M.C.*, March 27, 1915. *D.* § March and June, 1918.

1919 Morley, A. K. C. (Nov. 26, 1916). Pte. R.A.S.C. France.

1912 Morris, H. M., B.A. (Nov. 1914). Capt. R.A.S.C. Supply Officer, 122nd Inf. Bde. France, 1916–17, 1918; Italy, 1917–18. *D.* France, 1918.

1919 Morris, W. E. (Nov. 10, 1915). Sapper-Surveyor, R.E.
1903 Morrison, B. C. (Dec. 21, 1916). Lt. R.A.S.C.
1912 Morton, R. (Sept. 4, 1914). Lt., Acting Captain, 2nd Cheshire Regt. France, Salonika. *M.C.*, Jan. 1, 1918. Greek Military Cross. *D.* France, 1917, 1918; Salonika, 1919.
1898 Murdoch, C. H. C., B.A. (Dec. 27, 1915). Lt. 6th, attd. 11th, Rifle Brigade. France. *M.C.*, Jan. 1, 1917.
1908 Murphy, F. (Feb. 2, 1916). Lt., Acting Capt., Technical Officer, R.A.F. *D.* § Mar. 1918.
1909 Murray, A. M., B.A. (Jan. 4, 1915). Lt. Middlesex Regt. France. (Prisoner of War.)
1901 Myles, C. D., B.A. (Nov. 8, 1915). Lt. R.G.A. (S.R.), (specially empld.).
1900 **Nash, M. V. J.,** M.A. (Mar. 28, 1917). 2nd Lt. 25th, attd. 10th, London Regt. Egypt and Palestine. Killed in action at Gaza on Nov. 2, 1917.
1903 Neligan, G. E., B.M., M.A. (Sept. 15, 1914). Maj. 7th C.C.S., R.A.M.C. France and Belgium. *M.C.*, Jan. 14, 1916. *D.* France, 1915.
1919 Nethercot, A. H. (May 15, 1917). ‡2nd Lt., 146th F.A., U.S. Army. France and Germany.
1919 Newboult, A. T. (Dec. 9, 1914). ‡Lt. D.C.L.I. Gallipoli, France, Belgium. *M.C.*, Nov. 7, 1918.
1905 Newton, L. A., B.A. (Aug. 5, 1914). Capt. Border Regt. France and Belgium, 1915–16.
1907 Nicol, C. G. (Nov. 20, 1916). Lt. R.G.A. (S.R.).
1900 Nixon, Rev. F. J., M.A. (May 3, 1918). Chaplain to the Forces (4th Class).
1902 Norris, R., M.A. (Oct. 10, 1914). 2nd Lt. 4th Cheshire Regt. (T.F. Res.).
1912 Norton, Hon. R. H. B. (Aug. 15, 1914). Capt. Scots Guards (S.R.). Staff-Captain, War Office. *D.* § Feb. 1917.
1894 **Norwood, J., V.C.** (Mobilized Aug. 1914). Capt. 2nd County of London Yeomanry (Res. of Officers), attd. 5th Dragoon Guards. France. Killed in action at Petit Morin on Sept. 8, 1914.
1919 Oakley, R. (Sept. 26, 1917). Midshipman, R.N., H.M.S. *Emperor of India*. North Sea. (Invalided, Feb. 21, 1918.)
1907 **O'Beirne, A. J. L.** (Aug. 1914). Lt. Q.O. Oxfordshire Hussars, attd. R.A.F. E. Africa, 1914–15; Belgium, 1917. Died on July 28, 1917, of wounds received in air fighting over Houthulst Forest.
1888 Occleston, S. V. (Sept. 2, 1914). Capt. 11th Hussars (Res. of Officers). Maj. Special Lists, whilst Commdt., Reception Camp. France. *D.* France, 1916.
1913 **O'Daly,* D. R. D.** (Aug. 14, 1915). 2nd Lt. 7th Northumberland Fusiliers. France and Belgium. Killed in action at Warlencourt on Nov. 14, 1916.
1905 Ogilvie, D. D., B.A. (Mobilized Aug. 4, 1914). Maj. 14th (Fife and Forfar Yeomanry) Bn. The Black Watch (Lt.-Col.). Gallipoli, Egypt, Palestine, France, Belgium. *D.* Egypt, 1917.
1910 Oliphant,* D. A., B.A. (Mar. 24, 1916) Lt., Acting Capt., I.A.R.O., attd. 9th Gurkha Rifles. India, Mesopotamia.
1911 Oliphant,* T. (Mobilized Aug. 4, 1914). Capt. 5th Norfolk Regt. Staff Captain. Gallipoli, 1915.
1903 Oliver, R. G., B.A. (May 6, 1917). 2nd Lt. R.F.A. (S.R.). France. *M.C.* Nov. 19, 1917.

1897 Onslow, F. R. D., B.A. (Mar. 6, 1916). Lt. Special Lists (whilst on Special Service). *D.* § Feb. 1917.

1894 **O'Rorke, Rev. B. G.,** M.A. (Serving Aug. 4, 1914). Chaplain to the Forces (2nd Class). France. (Prisoner of War in Germany for ten months, 1914–15.) *D.S.O.*, Jan. 1, 1917. *D.* France, 1916. Died on Dec. 25, 1918, of illness contracted while on active service.

1919 O'Shea, D. G. (Jan. 1918). 2nd Lt. R. Wiltshire Yeomanry.

1895 Oxland, W. C., M.A. (1914). ‡Capt. 2nd King's African Rifles. E. Africa. *M.C.*, Jan. 1, 1919. *D.* E. Africa, 1918.

1913 Packe,* E. A. (Aug. 4, 1914). ‡Lt. Oxf. & Bucks. Lt. Infty. Flight Lt. R.A.F. France and Belgium. *D.F.C.*, Oct. 11, 1919. *D.* France, 1918.

1919 Page, E. A. (July 24, 1915). Pte. R.A.M.C. France, 1916; Salonika, 1917–18.

1913 Pagett,* R. K., B.A. (Nov. 22, 1915). A.B., R.N.V.R., A.A. Corps. ‡2nd Lt. R.G.A. France.

1900 Paige, C. P. (Serving Aug. 4, 1914). Maj. 1/109th Inf., Indian Army. G.S.O. 2. *C.I.E.* India, N.W. Frontier, Waziristan.

1903 Palmer, C. E. (May 1, 1915). Lt. Guards M.G. Regt.

1911 [Paramore, J. R. P.] (Jan. 27, 1915). Lt. 3rd D.C.L.I. (Capt.). attd. R.A.F. (1917–19). France, 1915, 1916–17.

1902 [Parham, Rev. A. G., M.A.] (Oct. 28, 1914). Chaplain to the Forces (2nd Class), D.A.C.G. XVII Corps. Egypt, 1915–16; Gallipoli, 1915; France, 1917–19. *M.C.*, June 3, 1916. *D.* Gallipoli, 1916; France, 1918.

1919 Parham, F. D. (Aug. 1917). Capt. 11th F.A., U.S. Army. France.

1906 Park, Rev. W. R., M.A. (Serving Aug. 4, 1914). Chaplain to the Forces (2nd Class). India, Mesopotamia. *C.I.E.*, *O.B.E.* (Mil.). *D.* Mesopotamia, 1917, 1919.

1915 **Parry, H.** (Jan. 1916). 2nd Lt. K.R.R.C. (Capt.). France, Belgium. Killed in action at Ypres on May 6, 1917.

1902 Parry, Rev. L. W., M.A. (1914). Chaplain (4th Class) A.I.F.

1909 **Parry-Crooke,* L. W.,** B.A. (1914). Pte. 21st R. Fusiliers. France. Killed in action on July 27, 1916.

1903 Parsons, A. E. B. (Serving Aug. 4, 1914). Capt. 52nd Sikhs (Frontier Force), Indian Army, attd. N.W. Frontier Province Political Dept. India. *D.* India, N.W. Frontier, 1916.

1898 Pauling, G. H. R. (Sept. 21, 1915). Lt. R.N.V.R.

1914 **Payne, E. O.** (Dec. 7, 1914). Lt. 2nd R. Berkshire Regt. France. Killed in action at Ovillers, July, 1916.

1903 Pearce, R. E. S. (Oct. 12, 1914). Lt. 2/7th Hampshire Regt. (Capt.). India. Mesopotamia.

1911 Peel, Rev. D. K. M., M.A. (June 24, 1915). Lt. 3rd Oxf. & Bucks. Lt. Infty.

1897 Pemberton, E. G., M.A. (Mobilized Aug. 4, 1914). Capt. Warwickshire Yeomanry. G.S.O. 3. Egypt and Palestine. *O.B.E.* (Mil.). *M.C.*, Mar. 3, 1917. *D.* Egypt and Palestine, 1917, 1919.

1919 Pengilley, E. E. (Oct. 3, 1916). Lt. 23rd R. Fusiliers. France. (Wounded and Prisoner of War, May, 1917–Dec. 1918.)

1909 Philippi, G. (Oct. 14, 1914). Lt.-Col. R.A.F. France. *M.C.*, Nov. 14, 1916. *D.* § Mar. 1918.

1902 Phillips, W. T., M.A. (May 20, 1915). Lt. 5th R. Munster Fusiliers.

1911 **Pickop,* J. T. G.,** B.A. (Aug. 1914). Lt. 1st R. Fusiliers (Capt.). France. Died on June 21, 1917, of wounds received in action at Vimy Ridge.

1903 [Pidduck, F. B., M.A.] (Jan. 1, 1916). Capt. Special Lists (whilst Asst. Proof Examining Officer). *D.* § Mar. 1918.

1919 Pilley, J. G. (Feb. 23, 1918). 2nd Lt. R.E.

1910 Pirie, J. W. (Dec. 20, 1914). Lt. 4th Hampshire Regt., attd. M.G.C. India.

1888 Pott, C. S., B.A. (Sept. 28, 1914). Capt. W. Kent Yeomanry. Staff-Captain.

1888 Powell, A. T. (Mobilized Aug. 1914). Lt.-Col. R.A. (T.F.), empld. R.G.A. Palestine. T.D. Order of the Nile (3rd Class). *D.* Palestine, 1918.

1874 Power, Sir D'Arcy, B.M., M.A. (Mobilized Aug. 1914). Lt.-Col. R.A.M.C. (T.F.), attd. 1st London General Hospital. *K.B.E.*. *D.* § Apr. 1917.

1891 Poynton, Rev. E. W., M.A. (Apr. 26, 1916). Chaplain to the Forces (4th Class).

1912 **Pratt,* G. C. S.** (Sept. 1914). Lt. R.H. and R.F.A., attd. No. 14 Anti-Aircraft Section. France, 1915. *D.* France, 1916. Died on Nov. 27, 1915, of wounds received in action at Houplines.

1919 Prescot, H. K. (Apr. 24, 1917). 2nd Lt. 206th Siege Batt., R.G.A. France.

1913 Price,* G. C., B.A. (Dec. 5, 1914). 2nd Lt. 8th S. Staffordshire Regt. Rifleman 5th London Regt. (London Rifle Brigade). (Resigned Commission, 1915, on medical grounds, and re-enlisted.) Belgium and France, 1916–17, 1918–19.

1911 Price,* H. S. (Nov. 1914). Capt. and Adjt. 16th London Regt. (Queen's Westminster Rifles). France, 1915–19. *M.C.*, Jan. 1, 1918. *D.* France, 1916, 1917.

1878 Pring, Rev. D. J., M.A. (Aug. 23, 1917). Chaplain to the Forces (4th Class).

1904 Pring, F. J. H., B.A. (Serving Aug. 4, 1914). Capt. Cheshire Regt., attd. W.A.F.F. (Maj.). Cameroons, 1914–16; E. Africa, 1916–17. *M.C.*, June 26, 1916; *Bar*, July 19, 1917. *D.* E. Africa, 1916, 1918.

1891 Pringle, J. C., M.A. (May 9, 1918). 2nd Lt. R.F.A.

1905 **Prior, H. G. R.** (July 14, 1915). Lt. 11th R. W. Kent Regt. France. Killed in action on Oct. 7, 1916.

1901 Pritchard, T. M., B.A. (Sept. 1914). ‡Lt. M.G.C. (Capt. and Adjt.). France. *D.* France, 1918.

1894 Pullen-Baker, R. C. W., M.A. (July 1918). ‡2nd Lt. General List.

1909 Pyemont, W., B.A. (Nov. 3, 1914). Lt., Acting Capt., R.E. France. *M.C.*, June 4, 1917; *Bar*, Jan. 18, 1918. *D.* France, 1917.

1899 Rabbits, C. W. (Dec. 16, 1914). Lt. R.A.

1896 Radcliffe, J. C., B.A. (Nov. 10, 1914). Lt. R.N.V.R., attd. Staff of Rear Admiral, Stornoway. Dunkerque.

1904 Ram, L. A. J. G., B.A. (Mobilized Aug. 4, 1914). Capt. Hertfordshire Yeomanry. Egypt, Gallipoli, France. *D.* § Aug. 1919.

1913 Randall, D. E., B.A. (Nov. 18, 1914). Maj. R.F.A. France, 1915–18. *M.C.*, Jan. 1, 1917.

1902 Rashleigh, H. P., M.A. (Aug. 4, 1914). ‡Capt. 9th London Regt. (Queen Victoria's Rifles), attd. R.A.F. France, 1915.

1919 Rawlinson, J. C. (Jan. 8, 1917). Lt. Tank Corps (Adjt.). France, 1917.

1919 Rees, D. I. (Oct. 18, 1915). Lt. 18th R. Welch Fusiliers. France.

1911 Rees, H. J. V. (Aug. 15, 1914). Capt. 4th S. Wales Borderers, attd. M.G.C. Aden, India.

1919 Rees, J. W. (Apr. 14, 1915). Lt. 331st Batt. R.F.A. France and Belgium, 1916–19.

1919 Reeves, E. F. (Apr. 1917). Lt. 6th Queen's (R. W. Surrey Regt.). France, Belgium, Germany. *M.C.*, Oct. 15, 1918.

1892 Reynolds, L. W., B.A. (Oct. 29, 1914). Capt. Special Lists. France. *C.I.E.* *M.C.*, Jan. 14, 1916. *D.* France, 1915.

1909 Rhymes, W. C., B.A. (Dec. 10, 1915). ‡Lt. 162nd Siege Batt., R.G.A. France, 1917–18.

1911 **Richardson,* A. T. L.** (Aug. 29, 1914). Capt. W. Somerset Yeomanry. Gallipoli, Egypt, Palestine. Killed in action in Palestine on Nov. 6, 1917.

1912 Richardson,* M. C. (Sept. 14, 1914). Lt. 2/4th Oxf. & Bucks. Lt. Infty. Captain R.E. France, 1915–16.

1919 Riddoch, I. P. (June 1, 1916). ‡2nd Lt. Tank Corps. France.

1912 Roberts, F. N., B.A. (Dec. 5, 1914). Lt., Acting Capt., R.G.A. Gallipoli.

1908 Roberts, Rev. H. C., M.A. (April 24, 1917). Chaplain to the Forces (4th Class).

1919 Roberts, J. G. (May 11, 1917). Capt. 328th Inf., U.S. Army. France. *D.* American Div. Orders.

1919 Roberts, G. W. P., B.A. (Jan. 1916). Pte. 28th R. Fusiliers.

1911 **Roberts, N. H.** (1914). ‡2nd Lt. 3rd, attd. 1st, K.O. Scottish Borderers. France. Killed in action near Arras on Apr. 23, 1917.

1907 Roberts, O. D., B.A. (March 10, 1917). 2nd Lt. Labour Corps.

1910 **Robertson,* G. S.** (Nov. 11, 1914). Capt. 13th R. Scots. France. Killed in action at Loos, Sept. 25–7, 1915.

1908 Robertson, S. R. (Feb. 3, 1915). Lt. 3rd R. Scots. E. Africa. *D.* E. Africa, 1916.

1907 Robinson, G. S., B.M., M.A. (Feb. 7, 1916). Capt. R.A.M.C., attd. 2nd Middlesex Regt. (Invalided, Sept. 24, 1918.)

1911 **Robinson, P. D.** (Sept. 1914). Capt. 9th Northumberland Fusiliers. France. Killed in action at Contalmaison on July 7, 1916.

1906 Rochford,* B., B.A. (Jan. 1917). Lt. Grenadier Guards. France.

1911 Rodda, F. S. T., B.A. (March 3, 1915). Sergt. 2/2nd London Regt. France.

1912 **Rodney-Ricketts, S. A.** (Jan. 9, 1915). Lt., Acting Capt. R.F.A. France and Belgium. *M.C.*, Jan. 10, 1917. Killed in action on Oct. 31, 1917.

1912 Rodoconachi, P. H. (Aug. 27, 1914). ‡Lieut. R.F.A. (T.F.) (Capt.). France, 1915; Salonika, 1915–16.

1880 Rogers, B. M. H., D.M. (Mobilized Aug. 4, 1914). Maj., Bt. Lt.-Col., R.A.M.C. (T.F.).

1909 Rogers, T. M. (Aug. 6, 1914). Maj. R.A.F. *O.B.E.* (Mil.). *D.* § 1916.

1919 Rolph, J. (Sept. 11, 1914). ‡2nd Lt. 12th R. Warwickshire Regt. Lt. M.G.C. Gallipoli, France, Belgium.

1919 Roots, H. S. (July, 1915). 2nd Lt. 1st London Regt. France, 1915, 1918.

1896 Rose, G. A., B.A. (Oct. 26, 1916). Lt. R.A.S.C.

1904 Rose, H. J., M.A. (1914). ‡Hon. Lt. General List, C.E.F.

1919 Roskin, H. H. (May 5, 1915). Capt. and Adjt., 1st (Garr.) Bn. Yorkshire Regt. India, 1916–19.

1915 Roth, L. (June 1916). ‡Lt. 40th R. Fusiliers. France.

1905 Round, C. J. (Sept. 16, 1914). Lt. Essex Yeomanry (Capt.). France, 1915.

1898 **Rowley-Conway, G. S.** (Serving Aug. 4, 1914). Maj. 6th Loyal N. Lancashire Regt. Gallipoli. Killed in action at Sari Bair on Aug. 10, 1915.

1893 Russell, W. P. M., M.A. (Mobilized Aug. 4, 1914). Capt. 10th London Regt. Gallipoli. *M.C.*, Jan. 22, 1916. *D.* Gallipoli, 1915.
1903 Ryder-Mitchell, Rev. A. S., M.A. (Dec. 1, 1916). Chaplain to the Forces (4th Class).
1904 Rylands, G. G. (Sept. 1, 1914). Capt. 17th King's (Liverpool Regt.). France.
1887 **Ryley, H. B.,** B.A. (1916). Lt. Suffolk Regt. Killed in action on Dec. 15, 1917.
1910 **Sanders,* A. E.,** B.A. (Sept. 1914). Capt. 2nd York & Lancaster Regt. France. *D.* France, 1916. Died on May 19, 1916, of wounds received in action.
1910 Sanders,* E., B.A. (Aug. 26, 1914). Capt. 5th Dorsetshire Regt. Gallipoli. (Resigned.)
1912 Saunders, V. T., M.A. (June 3, 1915). Lt., Acting Capt., R.G.A. (S.R.).
1910 **Schofield,* A. T.** (Nov. 18, 1914). Capt. Kent Cyclist Bn., attd. R. W. Kent Regt. France. Died on Nov. 10, 1918, of wounds received in action.
1907 Scobell, W. B. (Sept. 1914). ‡Capt. R. Berkshire Regt. France.
1917 Scott, H. R. (Jan. 4, 1918). ‡2nd Lt. Lincolnshire Regt.
1908 Scott, H. S., B.A. (Oct. 13, 1914). Capt. 15th Bde., R.F.A. France, 1916 and 1918; Salonika, 1916–17; Palestine, 1917–18.
1898 **Scott, W. McD. W.,** M.A. 2nd Lt. R.A.S.C. Died on Sept. 2, 1918.
1892 Selby-Lowndes, E. A., M.A. (Feb. 20, 1918). 2nd Lt. Special Lists. Staff-Lieutenant.
1912 Shairp,* J. W., B.A. (Nov. 20, 1914). Lt. 12th (Ayrshire & Lanarkshire Yeomanry) Bn. R. Scots Fusiliers. Gallipoli, 1915–16; Egypt and Palestine, 1916–18; France, 1918.
1914 Sharp, S. S., B.A. (May, 1917). ‡Lt. 148th F.A., U.S. Army. France, 1918.
1919 Shaw, E. F. (June 4, 1918). 2nd Lt. R.A.F.
1897 Shelmerdine, N., M.A. (Jan. 31, 1915). ‡Lt. 7th Worcestershire Regt.
1919 Shepherd, R. O. (Feb. 27, 1918). 2nd Lt. R.G.A.
1906 **Shirley, A. V.** (Jan. 22, 1915). 2nd Lt. Welsh Horse, attd. R.F.C. Killed on June 8, 1917.
1900 **Shirreff, F. G.,** M.A. (June 2, 1915). 2nd Lt. R. Berkshire Regt. France. Killed in action on the Somme on July 1, 1916.
1912 Shuttleworth,* F. J., B.A. (Oct. 3, 1915). Lt., Acting Capt., C/150th Bde. R.F.A. (T.F.) France, 1916–18. *M.C.*, Feb. 15, 1919; *Bar*, March 8, 1919. *D.* France, 1918.
1912 Sim,* C. A. G. S. (Aug. 15, 1914). Lt. 1st D.C.L.I. (Maj. M.G. Bn.). France, 1915–16; Palestine, 1917–19. *D.* Palestine, 1919.
1907 **Sim,* H. A. C.,** B.A. (Serving Aug. 4, 1914). Lt. 2nd Cameronians. France and Belgium. Killed in action at Fromelles on May 9, 1915.
1897 Simner, P. R., M.A. (Aug. 1914). ‡Lt.-Col. 10th W. Riding Regt. France. (Prisoner.) *D.S.O.*, Jan. 1, 1917. *D.* France, 1916 twice, 1917, 1918.
1906 **Single,* F. A.,** B.A. (Serving Aug. 4, 1914). Capt. 2nd Dragoon Guards (Maj.). France, 1914–18. *M.C.*, Jan. 1, 1917. Died on March 30, 1918, of wounds received in action.
1919 Skinner, T. G. (Jan. 10, 1918). 2nd Lt. R.A.F. France, 1918.
1911 Slater,* P. J., B.A. (Serving Aug. 4, 1914). Capt. 6th S. Staffordshire Regt., attd. R.A.F. France. *D.F.C.*, Dec. 2, 1918. *D.* France, 1916.

1908 **Slingsby,* A. E. K.** (Serving Aug. 4, 1914). Lt., Acting Capt., 6th W. Riding Regt. France and Belgium. Killed in action at Ypres on July 14, 1915.

1911 Smith,* A. H., B.A. (Sept. 15, 1914). R.N.V.R. H.M.S. *Shannon*, H.M.S. *Brilliant.*

1919 Smith, C. C. B. (Apr. 7, 1917). 2nd Lt. Wiltshire Regt., attd. 4th R. Berkshire Regt. France, Italy.

1919 Smith, E. C. (June 1917). 2nd Lt. Labour Corps. France.

1912 Smith, F. M., B.A. (Serving Aug. 4, 1914). ‡Lt. York & Lancaster Regt. Lt. R.A.F. France, 1915–17.

1906 Smith, P. de S. (Apr. 16, 1917). Capt. R.A.M.C.

1907 Smith, S., B.Sc., M.A. (1916). Lt. R.N.V.R.

1896 Smith, T. C., M.A. (Mobilized Aug. 1914). Capt. R. Bucks. Hussars.

1908 Smith-Carington, H. F., B.A. (Sept. 6, 1914). ‡Capt. Manchester Regt. Gallipoli, 1915; Egypt, 1916; France, 1916–17.

1907 **Smith-Sligo, A. G. R. J.,** B.A. (Serving Aug. 4, 1914). 2nd Lt. 1st Q. O. Cameron Highlanders. France. Killed in action at Troyon sur Aisne on Sept. 14, 1914.

1912 **Solomon, E. J.** (Dec. 26, 1914). ‡2nd Lt. 8th S. Lancashire Regt. France, Belgium. Killed in action at Ypres on Aug. 3, 1917.

1899 Somerset,* W. H. B., M.A. (Oct. 1, 1914). Lt. 3rd Monmouthshire Regt. France, Belgium.

1898 Sopper, F. W. (Serving Aug. 4, 1914). Capt. 18th Hussars (Lt.-Col.). France, Belgium. *D.* France, 1915.

1913 Souchon, G. H. (Dec. 14, 1914). Lt. 17th Lancers. India.

1908 Spread,* Rev. R. A. R. (Apr. 2, 1917). Chaplain to the Forces (4th Class). France. *D.* France, 1918.

1897 Sprules, R. G. W., M.A. (Nov. 12, 1914). Maj. R.A.O.C. France, 1915–19. *D.* France, 1918.

1912 Stafford,* H. W. (Sept. 28, 1914). Lt. R.E. (attd. R.F.C., 1916). Staff-Lieutenant. France and Belgium.

1902 **Stanfield, C. C.** (Mobilized Aug. 4, 1914). Capt. 3rd The Buffs (E. Kent Regt.). Died on May 31, 1917.

1911 **Staples, O. O.** (Serving Aug. 4, 1914). 2nd Lt. 6th R. Scots Fusiliers. France. Killed in action near Loos on Sept. 25, 1915.

1909 Stenner,* C. L. R., B.A. (1914). Capt. R.A.S.C. France.

1914 Stevens, D. B. (Apr. 1, 1915). Sub-Lt. R.N.V.R., attd. R.N.D. Lt. R. Marines, R.M.A. Howitzer Bde. France and Belgium, 1916. (Invalided, July 1917.)

1901 Stevens, G. B., M.A. (Oct. 23, 1917). 2nd Lt. Hampshire Regt. France, 1915.

1919 Stileman, D. F. (Aug. 21, 1914). ‡Capt. 8th R. Berkshire Regt. France, 1916.

1912 **Stirling,* R. K.** (Aug. 1914). Lt. 5th, attd. 1st, R. Fusiliers. France, Belgium. Killed in action at Hooge on Aug. 21, 1915.

1900 Stone, K. W. (Nov. 16, 1915). Lt. R.A.O.C.

1898 Stow, J. L., M.A. (Nov. 1914). Capt. General List. A.D.C. to G.O.C. 8th Div. France, 1915, 1918.

1902 Stow, V. A. S. (Apr. 1, 1917). Lt. I.A.R.O., attd. Sappers and Miners. Mesopotamia.

1915 Struth, M. le V., B.A. (Jan. 1916). Cpl. 1/28th London Regt. (Artists' Rifles). France, 1916–18.

1908 Styles, H. W. (Mobilized Aug. 4, 1914). Capt. 1/4th R. W. Kent Regt. India.
1919 Sutherland, I. H. (Mar. 20, 1918). Pte. 13th Reinforcements, A.I.F.
1919 Sweet, J. McC. (Jan. 19, 1915). Lt. 11th Cheshire Regt. France.
1907 Sweet-Escott, T., B.A. (Aug. 15, 1914). Lt., Acting Capt., 2nd S. Lancashire Regt. France and Belgium.
Sydenham, H. St. B. (Oct. 1914). Lt. Devonshire Regt. India. Died on Oct. 8, 1916, of illness contracted on active service.
1908 Sylvester, Rev. D. K., M.A. (Nov. 11, 1915). Chaplain to the Forces (4th Class). France and Belgium, 1915–19; Germany, 1919.
1912 Taglis,* E. C. A., B.A. (Nov. 3, 1914). Capt. 5th W. Riding Regt. France, 1915. (Invalided, Sept. 1915.)
1914 Tatham, W., B.A. (Aug. 9, 1914). Cpl. 1st Bn. H.A.C. Inf. 2nd Lt. O.U.O.T.C. (1917). France and Belgium, 1914–15. (Invalided, Aug. 1915.)
1918 Taylor, F. A. (May 9, 1915). Capt. 2nd Auckland Regt., N.Z.E.F. Egypt, 1915–16; France and Belgium, 1916–17. (Discharged on account of ill health caused by wounds.)
1908 Taylor, H. L. J. (Feb. 8, 1915). Lt. 23rd London Regt.
1896 Taylour, A. R., B.A. (Sept. 28, 1914). Capt. 1st London Regt., attd. H.Q., L. of C. Area, France. France, 1916–19. *D.* France, 1918.
1900 Terrell, A. à B. K., B.A. (Nov. 20, 1914). Lt., Acting Capt., R.F.A. (T.F.).
1911 Teviot-Kerr,* A. E. K. (July 20, 1915). Lt. I.A.R.O., attd. 9th Gurkha Rifles. India.
1919 Therrel, C. (June 16, 1916). ‡Maj. 328th Inf., U.S. Army. France. *D.* American Div. Orders.
1894 Thomas, Rev. C. S., M.A. (Oct. 3, 1914). Chaplain to the Forces (4th Class).
1919 Thomas, D. E. (Dec. 17, 1917). Ord. Seaman R.N.V.R.
1919 Thomas, E. M. (Mar. 9, 1917). 2nd Lt. C/103rd Bde., R.F.A. France, Italy. *M.C.*, Apr. 2, 1919.
1902 Thomas, W. G., B.A. (Feb. 1915). Lt. 9th R. Welch Fusiliers. Capt. M.G.C. France. *M.C.*, Jan. 14, 1916.
1904 Thompson, H. (July 15, 1915). Lt. R.F.A.
1911 Thompson,* L. L. H., B.A. (Sept. 5, 1914). Capt. 1/7th Cheshire Regt. (Maj.). France, Belgium, 1917–18.
1893 Thomson, C. L. C. (Dec. 15, 1915). Lt. R.N.V.R.
1900 Thursby-Pelham, Rev. H. C., B.A. (May 28, 1918). Chaplain to the Forces (4th Class).
1892 Tibbits, Rev. J. K., B.A. (Apr. 16, 1917). Chaplain, Canadian Forces.
1910 **Tolhurst, B. J.** (Oct. 17, 1914). Lt. 9th W. Riding Regt., attd. R.F.C. France. Died on Apr. 22, 1917, of wounds received in action near Arras.
1911 Tolkien, J. R. R., M.A. (July 15, 1915). Lt. Lancashire Fusiliers.
1919 Tonks, O. J. (Nov. 29, 1916). ‡2nd Lt. 17th R. Welch Fusiliers. France, 1918–19.
1906 Trefusis, Rev. F. M., B.A. (Dec. 17, 1915). Chaplain to the Forces (4th Class).
1911 Trimingham,* H. G. L., M.A. (Mar. 25, 1915). Capt. 16th London Regt. (Queen's Westminster Rifles), attd. Tank Corps. France.

1907 Trower, H. M. (Apr. 11, 1915). Lt. 6th, attd. 16th, Middlesex Regt. France, 1916–17. *M.C.*, Feb. 4, 1918.

1914 **Tulloch, E. St. C.** (Dec. 22, 1914). Lt. Northumberland Fusiliers. France. Killed in action on the Somme on July 7, 1916.

1914 Tunnicliffe, O. A. (Dec. 28, 1914). Capt. 10th N. Staffordshire Regt., attd. 1st S. Staffordshire Regt. Staff-Captain 152nd Inf. Bde., 51st Div. France, 1915–19. *M.C.*, July 27, 1916.

1907 **Turnbull, J. O.,** M.A. (Oct. 21, 1914). Capt. Welsh Regt. Belgium, France. Killed in action at High Wood on Sept. 8, 1916.

1882 Turrell, W. J., D.M. (Mobilized Aug. 4, 1914). Maj. R.A.M.C. (T.F.). 3rd S. General Hospital.

1900 Tyler, H. G., B.A. (Mobilized Aug. 1914). Capt. 3rd Monmouthshire Regt. France and Belgium.

1919 Tyringham, H. D. (Jan. 1918). 2nd Lt. 1st Scots Guards. France.

1911 Vanneck, R. G. (Nov. 1914). Capt. 13th R. Fusiliers. France, 1915–18. *M.C.*, July 18, 1917.

1907 Vardon, H. G. E. (Dec. 19, 1916). Lt. R. Wiltshire Yeomanry.

1912 Vibart,* H. H. R., B.A. (Jan. 24, 1916). Lt. R.A.S.C. (Adjt.). Malta, 1916–17; Salonika, 1917–18.

1908 Waddington,* T. T. (Oct. 1914). Capt. R. W. Kent Regt. France. *M.C.*, Mar. 30, 1916.

1890 Wade, R. R., D.M. (July 16, 1917). Capt. R.A.M.C.

1904 Wale, Rev. L. W., M.A. (Serving Aug. 4, 1914). Chaplain R.N. H.M.S. *Cochrane*, 2nd Cruiser Squadron, 1913–16; H.M.S. *Diligence*, 12th Destroyer Flotilla, from 1916.

1909 Walker, P. H., B.A. (Sept. 13, 1914). Lt. R.F.A. (Maj.). France. *M.C.*, June 3, 1918; *Bar*, Apr. 2, 1919; *2nd Bar*, Apr. 2, 1919. *D.* France.

1914 Walker, T. C. Manchester Regt.

1896 Wallace, J., B.M., M.A. (Mobilized Aug. 4, 1914). Capt. R.A.M.C. Commdt. Auxiliary Hospital, Weston-super-Mare. *M.B.E.* (Civil).

1909 Walsh, L. P. (1914). ‡Lt., Acting Capt., K.R.R.C. France. *M.C.*, Dec. 11, 1916; *Bar*, Feb. 15, 1919.

1909 Walton, F. W., B.A. (Apr. 9, 1915). Capt. R.H.A. (T.F.). France, 1916.

1915 **Warburton, F. E.** (Jan. 19, 1916). Lt. R.F.A. France and Belgium. Killed in action at Zonnebeke on Oct. 14, 1917.

1880 Ward, Rev. W. J., B.A. (Serving Aug. 4, 1914). Chaplain to the Forces (1st Class).

1919 Wardle, C. R. (May 6, 1915). Lt. S. Wales Borderers. France, 1916–17.

1915 Waring, H. E. A. (Mar. 1916). ‡Lt. R.A.F. France. (Prisoner of War.)

1909 Warner, H. H. M., B.A. (Aug. 28, 1914). Capt. R.G.A. France and Belgium.

1914 **Warnington, C.** (Dec. 28, 1914). 2nd Lt. 6th The Buffs (E. Kent Regt.). France. Missing, later presumed killed in action at Monchy-le-Preux on May 3, 1917.

1912 Waterfield, A. C., B.A. (Jan. 11, 1915). Lt. Shropshire L.I. Capt. Special Lists, whilst comdg. T.M.B. France. *M.C.*, Jan. 1, 1919.

1919 Watkin, W. R. (Jan. 1917). Pte. M.G.C. France.

1907 Watson,* Rev. A. R. A., M.A. (Jan. 9, 1917). Chaplain, R.N., H.M.S. *Brenda*.

1908 Watson, B. W., B.A. (Mar. 6, 1915). Lt. Q.O. Oxfordshire Hussars.

1919 Watterson, J. S. Q. (Oct. 9, 1915). Lt. 4th Somerset L.I. India, 1916–18.
1919 Watts, C. (Nov. 17, 1915). 2nd Writer R.N. (Naval Schoolmaster). Belgian Coast.
1905 Webster, Rev. F. G. D., M.A. (Serving Aug. 4, 1914). Chaplain to the Forces (3rd Class). France. *D.* France, 1917 ; § Aug. 1919.
1913 **Wells, H. T.** (Oct. 11, 1915). 2nd Lt. A.S.C. Died on Apr. 2, 1916.
1908 West, H. W., B.A. (June 15, 1915). Lt. Special Lists. Staff-Lieutenant, attd. General Staff.
1886 Wheeler, D. W., M.A. (Feb. 20, 1915). Lt. R.A.S.C. R.T.O. (1918). France, 1918.
1919 Wheway, C. G. (Nov. 25, 1916). Lt. D/104th Bde., R.F.A. France.
1912 Wheway,* G. D., B.A. (Aug. 1914). Lt. 7th N. Staffordshire Regt. Maj. 185th Coy. M.G.C. Gallipoli, Mesopotamia. Cavalier, Order of the Crown of Italy. *D.* Mesopotamia.
1913 Whiffen,* N. H. (Aug. 29, 1914). Lt. 1/5th E. Surrey Regt. Lt. M.G.C. India, 1914–18 ; Egypt, 1918 ; France, 1918.
1892 Whitaker, B., B.A. (Sept. 1914). Lt. 2/1st Q.O. Oxfordshire Hussars (Capt.). France and Belgium. *D.* § Feb. 1917.
1909 Whitaker,* C. H., M.A. (Apr. 6, 1915). Capt. R.A.S.C. E. Africa. *D.* E. Africa, 1917.
1919 White, G. (Nov. 8, 1915). Pte. H.A.C. France.
White, W. A. (Mar. 25, 1918). 2nd Lt. K.R.R.C. France. Killed in action on Oct. 3, 1918.
1907 Whitehead, A. P., B.A. (Sept. 10, 1914). ‡Lt. 3rd S. Staffordshire Regt. (Capt.). France, 1915–17, 1918–19. *M.C.*, Mar. 8, 1919. *D.* France, 1916.
1902 Whitehead, C. d'O. J., B.A. (June 20, 1915). Lt. 4th Dorsetshire Regt India.
1908 Whitehead, T. C., B.A. (May 1916). ‡Lt. 2nd H.A.C. Italy, 1917–18.
Whiteman, H. E. R.F.C. Killed whilst flying, Oct. 1916.
1919 Whitfield, A. S. Labour Corps.
1919 Whitmore, W. E. (Sept. 10, 1915). Pte. R.A.M.C. France, 1916–17.
1889 Whitworth, R. H., B.A. (Feb. 20, 1915). Capt. R.A.S.C. *D.* § Aug. 1919.
1894 Wilder, G. M. (Mobilized Aug. 4, 1914). Maj. Berkshire Yeomanry. Egypt and Palestine.
1900 Wildy, H. A., B.A. (Aug. 22, 1914). Capt. 1/25th London Regt., attd. M.M.G.C. India. *O.B.E.* (Mil.).
1910 Williams,* A., B.A. (Sept. 4, 1914). Capt. 17th London Regt. France, 1917–18.
1913 Williams, B. W. (Sept. 26, 1914). ‡Capt. R.F.A. France, 1915 ; Macedonia, 1915–18. *D.* France, 1916 ; Salonika, 1917.
1910 **Williams,* C. M.** (Oct. 18, 1915). 2nd Lt. 16th Manchester Regt. France. Died on July 29, 1916, of wounds received in action.
1912 Williams, F. C. (July 14, 1915). Lt. S. Wales Borderers (specially empld.).
1914 **Williams, H. M.** (Mar. 1916). 2nd Lt. 10th Welsh Regt. France and Belgium. Killed in action at Ypres on June 24, 1917.
1902 Williams, Rev. N. P., M.A. (Jan. 16, 1918). Asst. Chaplain, R.N. College, Dartmouth.
1914 Willis, A. J. (Sept. 22, 1914). Maj. 10th York & Lancaster Regt. France, 1915, 1916.

1898 Willis, Rev. E., M.A. (July 12, 1916). Chaplain to the Forces (4th Class).

1906 **Willis, R.,** M.A. (Aug. 5, 1914). ‡Lt. Loyal N. Lancashire Regt. France. Killed in action at Vimy Ridge on May 15, 1916.

1919 Wilson, C. S. (Nov. 2, 1917). Cadet R.F.A.

1911 **Wilson,* R. M.** (Aug. 26, 1914). Lt. 6th Loyal N. Lancashire Regt. Gallipoli. Killed in action at Sari Bair on Aug. 11, 1915.

1905 Winans, P. (May 1, 1916). 2nd Lt. R.A.S.C.

1911 **Windle,* M. W. M.** (Aug. 22, 1914). Lt. 8th Devonshire Regt. France. Killed in action at the Battle of Loos on Sept. 25, 1915.

1914 Wintersgill, D. S. (Feb. 23, 1915). Capt. 6th York & Lancaster Regt. Gallipoli, 1915; Egypt, 1916; France, 1916–17.

1906 Wippell, D. H., B.A. (Aug. 1914). Capt. Yorkshire Regt. France.

1902 Wippell, Rev. J. C., M.A. (Aug. 11, 1917). Chaplain to the Forces (4th Class).

1910 **Wood,* G. D.** (Aug. 27, 1914). Lt. 7th Suffolk Regt. France. Killed in action at the Quarries near Hulloch on Oct. 13, 1915.

1906 **Woodhead, H.,** B.A. Maj. 1st (Res.) Bn. S. African Forces. Missing, believed killed in action.

1903 Woods, G. S., M.A. (1917). Lt. R.N.V.R., attd. Admiralty (Intelligence Branch).

1919 Woollcombe, L. A. W. (Jan. 1917). 2nd Lt. 1st S. Staffordshire Regt., attd. 10th R. Warwickshire Regt. France, 1918.

1912 Worth, J. G. (Oct. 11, 1915). Lt. R.A.S.C., Supply Officer, 11th Cav. Bde., 4th Cav. Div. Egypt, Palestine, 1918–19.

1906 Wortley, H. E., B.A. (Oct. 1914). ‡Lt. 3rd Suffolk Regt., attd. R.A.F. Salonika, Mesopotamia.

1919 Wreford, J. M. R. (Feb. 8, 1917). Lt. Irish Guards. France.

1915 Wright, G. P. (May 1916). Lt. 21st Siege Batt., R.G.A. France and Belgium, 1917–19.

1919 Wrigley, E. J. (Sept. 21, 1914). ‡Lt. 6th R. Welch Fusiliers. Egypt, Hedjaz, Salonika, Bulgaria, Turkey, 1917–18.

1902 **Wyatt, A. T. E.** (Mobilized Aug. 4, 1914). Capt. 3rd, attd. 1st, Lincolnshire Regt. France, 1914. (Prisoner of War, Feb.–July 1915.) Died on Feb. 19, 1917, as the result of wounds received in action.

1906 **Wyatt, W. H.,** B.A. (April 23, 1915). Lt. E. Yorkshire Regt. France. Killed in action on May 4, 1916.

1905 Yates, H. G. N. (July 20, 1915). Lt. Tank Corps. France.

1895 Yates, R. E. (Oct. 9, 1918). Lt. R.G.A. (after demobilization).

1904 Yeoman, W. F., M.A. (Sept. 24, 1915). Lt. 6th K.R.R.C. France.

1897 Yonge, A., B.M. (Apr. 6, 1915). Capt. R.A.M.C.

1919 Yorke, A. F. (Nov. 8, 1915). ‡Lt., Acting Capt., 1st W. Yorkshire Regt. France, Belgium.

1898 Young, B. W. D., B.A. (Mar. 13, 1916). Lt. General List, T.F. Res.

1919 Young, C. E. (Jan. 28, 1915). Lt. 27th Div. Train, R.A.S.C. Lt. R.A.F. (Capt.). France, 1915–17, 1917–18.

1897 Yule, C. B. B. (Jan. 21, 1915). Lt. R.G.A. Capt. Special Lists (Special Appointment, Ministry of Munitions). *O.B.E.* (Mil.). *D.* § Mar. 1918.

ORIEL COLLEGE

1896 Adair, H. S. (Serving Aug. 4, 1914). Maj. Cheshire Regt. (Lt.-Col.). G.S.O. 2 (G.S.O. 1). France and Belgium. *D.S.O.*, Jan. 1, 1918. *D.* France, 1916 twice, 1917 twice.

1878 Adams, Rev. W. J. (Serving Aug. 4, 1914). Chaplain to the Forces (4th Class), attd. R.A. V.D. *D.* § Mar. 1918.

1907 Agar, W., B.A. (Oct. 1916). Capt. R.A.M.C., attd. 27th C.C.S. Mesopotamia, India, Salonika.

1894 Aitchison, Rev. W., M.A. (Apr. 2, 1917). Chaplain to the Forces (4th Class).

Aitken, J. M. (Apr. 1917). 2nd Lt. R.F.A. France, 1918. Died on Oct. 12, 1918, of wounds received in action near Le Cateau.

1881 Allan, J. B., B.C.L., M.A. (Sept. 17, 1915). Lt. R.N.V.R. Egypt.

1897 Allen, H. I., B.A. (Mar. 1, 1915). Lt., Technical Officer, R.A.F.

1892 Allen, R. W., M.A. (Sept. 2, 1914). Capt. 8th Hussars, Res. of Officers.

1919 Amacker, D. M. (June, 1917). Sergt. Interpreters' Corps, Divl. H. Q. 42nd Div., afterwards 1st Lt. H. Q. 1st Army, U.S. Army. France, 1918.

1898 **Amphlett, R. F.,** B.A. (July 21, 1916). 2nd Lt. 8th Worcestershire Regt. France, 1916–17. Killed in action at Hardecourt on Apr. 6, 1917.

1911 **Anderson, J. M.** (Dec. 18, 1914). Lt. 3rd, attd. 2nd, R. Scots. France and Belgium. Killed in action in Belgium on June 19, 1915.

1899 Anderson, N., B.A. (June 1, 1916). Capt. 5th London Regt. (London Rifle Brigade). D.A.A.G. France. *O.B.E.* (Mil.). *D.* France, 1918 twice.

1913 Andrew, W. M., M.A. (Apr. 18, 1915). Lt. 9th Highland L.I. France. (Prisoner of War.)

1914 Andrewes, G. L. (Nov. 1, 1915). 2nd Lt. 10th Suffolk Regt. Lt. Labour Corps (Capt. and Adjt.).

1889 **Andrews, M. P.,** M.A. (Serving Aug. 4, 1914). Capt. 4th W. Riding Regt. France. *D.* France, 1915. Killed in action on Aug. 14, 1915.

1920 Ardagh-Walter, P. F. (Jan. 24, 1918). 2nd Lt. 62nd Batt., R.G.A. France, Germany, 1918–19.

1898 Arkwright, B. H. G. (Mobilized Oct. 1914). Capt. 1/1st Derbyshire Yeomanry. Bde. Maj. Cavalry Bde., B.S.F. Egypt, The Balkans. *D.* Egypt, 1915.

1909 Arkwright,* C. G., B.A. (Dec. 1914). Capt. 4th Northumberland Fusiliers (Maj.). France. *M.C.*, Jan. 1, 1917. *D.* France, 1916.

1909 Arkwright,* C. H. (May 7, 1915). Capt. R.F.A. (T.F.).

1910 Armitage,* K. L. F., B.A. (Aug. 12, 1914). 2nd Lt. 9th R. Warwickshire Regt., afterwards Capt. 2/21st Punjabis (Lt.-Col. i/c 30th Punjabis). India, 1914–16 and from 1917; E. Africa, 1916–17. *D.* E. Africa, 1917.

1905 Armstrong, E. M., B.Sc. (1917). U.S. Medical Res. Corps.

1901 Armstrong, G. G., M.A. (Nov. 27, 1914). Cpl. Madras Motor Cyclists Detachment, afterwards Lt.-Col. General List. France. *O.B.E.* (Mil.); *M.C.*, Jan. 14, 1916. *D.* France, 1915, 1919.

1913 Arthur,* J. S. (Aug. 15, 1914). Lt. R.A., afterwards Lt., Flying Officer, R.A.F. France. *M.C.*, Jan. 1, 1917. *D.* France, 1915.

Astley, E. D. D'O. (July 24, 1915). Capt. 3rd R. Berkshire Regt. France. *D.* France, 1917. Killed in action on June 1, 1918.

1905 Atkins, H., B.A. (1916). Lt. R.A.F. (Maj.) (Staff Officer, 2nd Class).

1913 **Atkinson,* G. J. B.** (Aug. 15, 1914). Lt. 5th Worcestershire Regt. Gallipoli. Killed in action in Gallipoli on June 22, 1915.

1919 Attlee, C. M. (Nov. 19, 1916). Lt. R.A.F. France.

1900 **Auret, Ben.**, B.A. (Aug. 1914). Capt. R.F.A. France, 1915–16. Killed in action on Sept. 21, 1916.

1911 **Austin,* T. C. McD.**, B.A. (Aug. 22, 1914). Capt. 4th S. Wales Borderers. Gallipoli, Mesopotamia. *D.* Gallipoli, 1915. Killed in action at Sanna-i-yat on Apr. 9, 1916.

1896 Bacon, A. F. L., M.A. (Dec. 12, 1914). Lt. 4th Hampshire Regt. (Capt.).

1905 Baker, E. C. A., B.A. (Mar. 27, 1915). 2nd Lt. Rifle Brigade. Lt. General List, attd. Rifle Record Office (Staff-Lt., 2nd Class). *D.* § Mar. 1919.

1903 Baker, F. S. A., M.A. (Aug. 15, 1914). Capt. 3rd Seaforth Highlanders. Capt., Acting Maj., R.A.F. (Staff). France. *D.* France, 1917.

1915 **Baker, G. L. J.** (Oct. 28, 1916). 2nd Lt. 1st, attd. 6th, Middlesex Regt. France, 1916–17. Killed in action at the 2nd Battle of Arras on Apr. 23, 1917.

1913 **Balcombe-Browne,* R.** (Dec. 12, 1915). Capt. R.F.A. Maj. R.A.F. France. *M.C.*, July 27, 1916. *D.* § Mar. 1918. Accidentally killed, 1918.

1912 **Balcombe-Brown,* W. E.** (Serving Aug. 4, 1914). Lt. R.F.A. France and Belgium. Killed in action in Belgium on June 29, 1915.

1901 **Balfour-Melville, J. E.**, B.A. (Nov. 4, 1914). 2nd Lt. 3rd The Black Watch. France, 1915. Killed in action at Loos on Sept. 25, 1915.

1894 Bannon, B. D., B.A. (Aug. 3, 1915). S. Soldat, Section Sanitaire Anglaise, 1ère Armée française. France, 1915–16. (Verdun, July 12, 1916.)

1917 Bardsley,* W. L. F. (Aug. 21, 1918). 2nd Lt. 5th Grenadier Guards.

1917 **Barnes, E.** (June 20, 1917). 2nd Lt. R.F.C. Killed while flying on Jan. 27, 1918.

1895 **Barrett, P. G.**, B.A. (Serving Aug. 4, 1914). Capt. R. Munster Fusiliers. France and Belgium, Aug. 1914. Killed in action on Aug. 27, 1914.

1913 Barry, A. G. (Aug. 1914). Lt. 9th Lancashire Fusiliers. Capt. Manchester Regt. Lt.-Col. M.G.C. Gallipoli and Egypt, 1915–16. France, from 1916. *D.S.O.*, June 3, 1919. *M.C.*, June 3, 1916. *D.* Gallipoli, 1916; France, 1917.

1908 Barry,* Rev. F. R., M.A. (Nov. 11, 1915). Chaplain to the Forces (2nd Class) (D.A.C.G.). Egypt, 1915–16. France, 1916–19. *D.S.O.*, Nov. 25, 1916. Montenegrin Silver Medal for Bravery. *D.* France, 1916.

1897 Barton, C. T., B.A. (Apr. 1, 1914). 2nd Lt. 1/4th Oxf. & Bucks. Lt. Infty. (Capt.).

1890 Bathurst, A. H. (Rejoined Aug. 1914). Capt. Res. of Officers (Maj.). D.A.A. and Q.M.G. 40th Div.; D.A.A.G. 8th Corps. France and Belgium, 1915–17. *D.* France, 1916.

1895 Batley, Rev. W. Y., M.A. (Aug. 29, 1916). Chaplain to the Forces (4th Class). France and Belgium, 1916–17. *M.C.*, Oct. 18, 1917.
1905 Bax, C. E. O., M.A. (Mar. 9, 1915). Lt. 9th Middlesex Regt. Capt. Stationery Service.
1902 Baxter, W. E. E. (Aug. 15, 1914). 4th Lt. Section Sanitaire Anglaise, No. 10, French Army. France, Verdun.
1875 Baynes, Rt. Rev. A. H., D.D. (Serving Aug. 4, 1914). Chaplain to the Forces (1st Class), attd. Nottinghamshire Hussars. T.D.
1899 Beazley, H. L., B.A. (July 1916). 2nd Lt. King's (Liverpool Regt.). Staff-Captain H.Q. 1st Army. France, 1917–19. *D.* France, 1919.
1903 Beazley, J. G. B., M.A. (Mobilized Aug. 5, 1914). Maj. 6th King's (Liverpool Regt.). (D.A.A.G., Western Command, 1918.) France, 1917–19. *M.C.*, Jan. 1, 1918.
1882 Bedford, Rev. A. W., M.A. (Nov. 22, 1915). Chaplain to the Forces (4th Class). *D.* § Aug. 1919.
1883 Beeching, H. A., M.A. (Dec. 1914). Capt. 4th R.W. Kent Regt. (Retired owing to ill health, Jan. 1917.)
1913 Beeton,* W. G. R. (Aug. 16, 1914). ‡Lt. Queen's (R. W. Surrey Regt.). Lt. M.G.C. (Capt.). France and Belgium. *D.* France, 1917.
1882 Behrens, O. P. 2nd Lt. Cheshire Regt. Vol. Bn.
1899 **Benedict, A. E. J. W. S.,** B.A. (Dec. 29, 1914). Lt. R. Bucks. Hussars (Adjt.). Died at King's Lynn, Norfolk, on Dec. 16, 1915.
1909 **Benn, J. R. T.** (Mobilized Aug. 4, 1914). Capt. 4th W. Riding (Howitzer) Bde., R.F.A. (T.F.). France and Belgium. Killed in action near Ypres on Sept. 1, 1915.
1919 Bennett, J. D. (Feb. 5, 1918). 2nd Lt. Grenadier Guards.
1888 Bent, Rev. G. T., M.A. (Nov. 29, 1915). Chaplain to the Forces (4th Class). France.
1914 Berry,* T. T., B.A. (May 3, 1915). Lt. 3rd Somerset L.I. France.
1910 Best,* H. M., M.A. (June 21, 1917). ‡2nd Lt. 10th D.C.L.I. France.
1879 Bienemann, Rev. G. A., B.A. (Aug. 5, 1915). Chaplain to the Forces (4th Class).
1913 **Billman, W. M.** (Aug. 10, 1914). ‡2nd Lt. 6th, attd. 1st, Middlesex Regt. France. Died on Nov. 6, 1916, of wounds received in action on the Somme.
1894 Birch, A. L., M.A. (Nov. 27, 1915). Lt. 5th Cheshire Regt.
1898 Birch, Rev. J. G., M.A. (Nov. 5, 1917). Chaplain to the Forces (4th Class).
1910 **Birch, W. R.,** B.A. (Aug. 7, 1914). Capt. ‡5th Oxf. & Bucks. Lt. Infty. France and Belgium. *D.* France, 1915. Killed in action at Le Sars on Oct. 7, 1916.
1900 **Birt, W. B.,** B.A. (Sept. 1914). Capt. 9th E. Surrey Regt. France. Wounded and taken prisoner at Loos, Sept. 1915. Died in hospital at Cologne on Apr. 18, 1916.
1894 Bishop, D. W. Capt. S. African Medical Corps.
Blackie, J. S. (Aug. 14, 1915). 2nd Lt. 5th Rifle Brigade. France. Killed in action, Oct. 1916.
1902 Blackiston, H., B.A. (Mobilized Aug. 4, 1914). Capt. R.F.A. (S.R.). *D.* § Aug. 1919.
1909 **Blackwell, A. F.** (Mar. 1915). Lt. R.F.A. France. *M.C.*, Sept. 26, 1916. Killed in action on June 2, 1917.

1919 Blaxland, L. B. (Aug. 28, 1916). Capt. 61st Squadron, R.A.F. France, 1917.

1905 Blencowe, Rev. J. W., M.A. (Sept. 17, 1915). Chaplain to the Forces (4th Class).

1915 Bles, J. L. W. (Apr. 18, 1915). Lt. 2/5th Cheshire Regt., attd. 4th (Res.) Bn. (Lt. R.F.C., 1916.) France, 1917.

1891 Bliss, E. C., M.A. (Dec. 19, 1915). 2nd Lt. R.G.A. (S.R.). Staff-Captain Southern Command. *D.* § Aug. 1919.

1900 Blomfield, H. M., B.A. (Mobilized Aug. 22, 1914). Capt. 1/5th The Buffs (E. Kent Regt.). Staff-Captain. India, 1914–15, 1917–18; Mesopotamia, 1915–16, 1916–17; Palestine, 1918; Egypt, 1919.

1912 Blyth (Bleistein), G. J., B.A. Sergt.-Maj. Middlesex Regt.

1920 Bocree, A. R. (Aug. 4, 1914). ‡Lt. Suffolk Regt. Capt. R.A.F. (Flight Commdr.). France. *D.* Jan. 1919.

1889 **Boone, C. F. de B.** (Serving Aug. 4, 1914). Capt. Essex Regt. France. Died on Sept. 23, 1914, of wounds received in action.

1913 Boothroyd, R. H. (Nov. 28, 1914). Lt. 5th K.R.R.C. France and Belgium.

1897 Bosanquet, B. J. T. (Apr. 1, 1918). Lt., Kite Balloon Officer, R.A.F.

1911 **Bourne,* S. M.** (Sept. 1914). Lt. 8th R. Fusiliers. France, Egypt, Mesopotamia. Killed in action near Sanna-i-yat on Apr. 5, 1916.

1910 Bowen, R. L. (Aug. 29, 1914). Maj. 8th K.R.R.C. (Lt.-Col.). France and Belgium, 1915–18. *M.C.*, Jan. 1, 1918. (Prisoner of War, Mar.–Dec. 1918.)

1919 Bower, P. S. S. (May 15, 1917). 2nd Lt. R.G.A. France.

1894 [Boycott, A. E., B.Sc., D.M.] (June 25, 1917). Capt., Bt.-Maj., R.A.M.C. *D.* § Aug. 1918.

1898 Bracken, G. T. H., B.A. (June 6, 1916). 2nd Lt. R.G.A. Mesopotamia, 1916–18. *D.* Mesopotamia, 1917.

1907 Braddell, R. L. L., B.A. (July 22, 1917). ‡2nd Lt. R.G.A.

1913 Bradley,* R. L., B.A. (Sept. 1914). Capt. 22nd London Regt. (The Queen's). Instructor, O.C.B. France, 1915–16. *M.C.*, Nov. 14, 1916. *D.* § Mar. 1919.

1919 Brain, J. H. P. (Aug. 15, 1914). Capt. 3rd Welsh Regt. Capt. Airship Pilot, R.A.F. France, 1915–17.

1919 Bredin, G. R. F. (Dec. 16, 1917). 2nd Lt. 64th Field Coy., R.E. France and Belgium. *D.* France, 1919.

1911 **Bren, H. A. H.** (Aug. 1914). ‡Lt. 4th Leinster Regt. France. Killed in action at Guillemont on Sept. 9, 1916.

1911 Bridges, G. H., M.A. (Sept. 5, 1914). ‡Lt. 9th E. Surrey Regt. France and Belgium, 1916, 1917, 1918.

1918 Brigden, J. B., B.A. Pte. Inf., A.I.F.

1895 Broadbent, H. P. O. (Mar. 9, 1915). Lt. Bedfordshire Yeomanry.

1920 Brodie, W. J. W. (Jan. 1918). ‡2nd Lt. R.A.F. France.

1909 Brodrick-Dale,* E. C., M.A. (Serving Aug. 4, 1914). Capt. 112th Batt., 24th Bde., R.F.A. (Maj.). Belgium and France, 1914–18 *M.C.*, June 4, 1917. *D.* France, 1916 twice, 1917 twice.

1910 Brooke,* R. St. C., M.A. (Sept. 16, 1914). Capt. 7th K.O.Y.L.I. France. *M.C.*, June 3, 1916.

1909 Broome, F. N., B.A. (Aug. 31,1914). ‡Capt. 173rd Bde., R.F.A. German S.W. Africa, France, Belgium, 1914–18. *M.C.*, June 3, 1918.

1907 Brown, A. M., B.A. (May 1915). 2nd Lt. Duke of Lancaster's Yeomanry, afterwards Lt. Grenadier Guards (S.R.), attd. 1st Bn. France, 1916–18. *M.C.*, Sept. 27, 1918.

1899 Brown, E., B.A. (Dec. 31, 1915). Lt. 5th Queen's (R. W. Surrey Regt.).

1919 Brown, J. D. (May 8, 1918). 2nd Lt. 5th K.O. Scottish Borderers.

1920 Brown, J. M. (May 15, 1917). Pte. 2/10th R. Scots (Lce.-Cpl.). N. Russia.

1913 **Bryson,* G. L. U.** (1914). Capt. and Adjt. 14th R. Warwickshire Regt. France. Killed in action on July 30, 1916.

1904 Budd, C. H., B.M., M.A. (Aug. 1914). Capt. R.A.M.C. (T.F.). Egypt and Palestine. *M.C.*, July 26, 1918. *D.* Palestine, 1918.

1885 Bullock, E. C., M.A., T.D. (Mobilized Aug. 4, 1914). Lt.-Col. R.F.A. (T.F.). Belgium, 1915; France, 1915–16, 1917–18. *D.* France, 1915; § Feb. 1917.

1889 Bunbury, Rev. G. A., M.A. (Oct. 9, 1916). Chaplain to the Forces (4th Class).

1919 Burch, J. C. (July 1915). ‡Lt. R. Sussex Regt.

1910 Burden-Muller, R. (Mar. 25, 1918). 2nd Lt. Special Lists. Staff-Lt. (3rd Class).

1901 Burn, R. C. W., B.A. (Mobilized Aug. 1914). Capt. Sussex Yeomanry. Maj. M.G.C. (Cavalry).

Burne, T. O. (June 27, 1917). 2nd Lt. 2nd R. Berkshire Regt. France. Missing, believed killed in action near Morchain on Mar. 25, 1918.

1919 Burney, O. R. (June 1, 1917). Pte. 15th London Regt. (Civil Service Rifles).

1913 Burnie,* A. I., B.A. (Oct. 29, 1914). 2nd Lt. The Buffs (E. Kent Regt.). Lt., Flying Officer, R.A.F. France. (Prisoner of War.)

1919 Burrell, E. B. (Jan. 16, 1916). Lt. R.M.A., Siege Guns. Grand Fleet, Belgian Coast.

1894 Burroughes, C. FitzP. (Dec. 21, 1914). Capt. 2/1st Leicestershire Yeomanry.

1907 **Burrows,* L. R.**, B.A. (Oct. 23, 1914). 2nd Lt. 9th Northumberland Fusiliers. France and Belgium. Killed in action at Hill 60 on Oct. 2, 1915.

1901 **Burton, R. C.** (Serving Aug. 4, 1914). Capt. Rifle Brigade. France. Died on Mar. 16, 1915, of wounds received in action.

1912 Byng, F. G., B.A. (Aug. 4, 1914). Pte. 28th London Regt. (Artists' Rifles) (discharged through ill health, Oct. 1914; rejoined 1916). ‡2nd Lt. R.F.A. France, 1917–18.

1919 Byworth, H. A. (Apr. 23, 1917). Capt. 13th Bedfordshire Regt. (Adjt.). *D.* § Aug. 1919.

1893 Caldecott, E. L., B.A. (Serving Aug. 4, 1914). Lt.-Col. R.A. France, 1914–19. *D.S.O.*, June 3, 1916. *D.* France, 1916 twice, 1917, 1918.

1919 Campbell, E. (Dec. 29, 1915). Lt. R.F.A. France and Belgium, 1917; N. Russia, 1919. *M.C.*, Sept. 18, 1917.

1894 Campbell, H. (1914). Capt. General List (Staff-Captain). D.A.A.G. Salonika. *M.C.*, Jan. 1, 1918. Greek Order of the Redeemer. *D.* Salonika, 1917.

1904 Campbell, L. H. (1916). Lt. R.N.V.R.

1901 Canning, C. B., M.A. (Dec. 31, 1916). 2nd Lt. Unattached List, T.F., attd. Marlborough College O.T.C.

1907 Carew,* Rev. W. H., B.A. (Oct. 1, 1914). Chaplain to the Forces (4th Class). France and Belgium, 1917–19. *M.C.*, Sept. 16, 1918.

1899 Carpenter-Garnier, Rev. M. R., M.A. (June 13, 1918). Chaplain to the Forces (4th Class), attd. 83rd (Dublin) General Hospital. France.

1896 Carr-Gomm, H. W. C., M.A. (Oct. 14, 1914). Capt. 22nd London Regt. (The Queen's), (T.F. Res.).

1899 Carrington, C. W., M.A. (Aug. 24, 1916). Lt. 5th Grenadier Guards. France. *D.S.O.*, Feb. 18, 1918. *D.* France, 1918.

1900 Carter, G. F., B.A. (Aug. 10, 1914). Lt. (Q.M.) R.A.M.C. Capt. Special Lists. Courts Martial Officer.

1890 Carwithen, Rev. R. M., B.A. (July 10, 1917). Chaplain to the Forces (4th Class).

1919 Caudwell, F. W. H. (May 30, 1917). 2nd Lt. 1/4th Oxf. & Bucks. Lt. Infty. France, Italy, 1918–19.

1914 Cayzer, Sir C. W., Bt. (Oct. 20, 1915). Lt. 19th Hussars. France. (Prisoner of War.)

1908 **Chalmers, R.,** M.A. (Serving Aug. 4, 1914). Capt. Suffolk Regt. A.D.C. France. Killed in action on May 10, 1915.

1909 Chalmers, W. K., M.A. (Oct. 5, 1914). Lt., Acting Capt., C Batt., 275th Bde., R.F.A. (Maj.). France and Belgium.

1897 Chamberlayne, W. F. T. (Mobilized Aug. 1914). Capt. 4th R. Warwickshire Regt.

1900 Champion, Rev. G., M.A. (Jan. 1, 1918). Chaplain to the Forces (4th Class), attd. 66th Labour Corps. Belgium, France.

1910 Champneys,* W. (Jan. 25, 1915). Lt. Grenadier Guards, attd. T.M.B.

1895 Chancellor, W. G. (Jan. 31, 1915). ‡Lt. R.N.V.R., Wireless Telegraph School. King's Messenger. Malta, Rome, Paris.

1902 Chapman, R. W., M.A. (Mar. 26, 1915). Capt. 43rd Siege Batt., R.G.A. Salonika, 1915–18.

1902 Cheale, A. R., B.A. (Serving Aug. 4, 1914). Maj. 4th R. W. Kent Regt.

1911 Clapton,* E. V., M.A. (Sept. 5, 1914). ‡Lt. 1/6th Essex Regt. (Capt.). Egypt, 1915–17; Palestine, 1917–18.

1908 Clark, G. N., M.A. (Mobilized Aug. 1914). Lt., temp. Capt., 8th London Regt. (Post Office Rifles). France. (Prisoner of War, May, 1916.)

1892 Clark, J. N. D'A., B.A. (Serving Aug. 4, 1914). Maj. Derbyshire Yeomanry. Egypt and Salonika. *D.* Salonika, 1917.

1919 Clarke, G. R. (Sept. 1, 1914). Sergt. 1/4th Oxf. & Bucks. Lt. Infty. France and Belgium, 1915–17; Italy, 1917–18. (Prisoner of War in Austria, June–Dec. 1918.)

1902 Clarke, H. E., M.A. (Dec. 10, 1916). Lt. R.G.A., attd. 291st Siege Batt. France. *D.* France, 1918.

1904 Clarke, L. J., B.A. (Mobilized Aug. 4, 1914). Capt. 22nd London Regt. (The Queen's). Commdr. Inf. Bde., R.E., Signal Section. France and Belgium. *M.C.*, Sept. 17, 1917. *D.* France, 1916.

1919 Clarke, R. T. V. (Mar. 1916). 2nd Lt. R.M.A., afterwards Sub-Lt. R.N.V.R. East Coast Patrol and 4th Destroyer Flotilla.

1879 Clarke, Rev. T. G., M.A. (Jan. 21, 1917). Chaplain to the Forces (3rd Class), attd. Northamptonshire Regt.

1887 Clifford, A. N. (May, 1916). Lt. Special Lists.

1911 **Coker,* C. J.** (Sept. 15, 1914). Lt. 1st Welsh Regt. France and Belgium, 1915. Killed in action at St. Eloi on June 22, 1915.

1913 Colbourne,* M. D. (Aug. 15, 1914). Capt. 3rd, attd. 2nd, R. Berkshire Regt., afterwards attd. R.A.F. France, 1915.

1913 **Coller, C. M.** (Oct. 1914). Capt. 9th Norfolk Regt. France, 1917–18. Killed in action at Lagnicourt on Mar. 21, 1918.

1919 Coller, R. G. (Jan. 24, 1917). Lt. R.F.A. (S.R.). France, 1917–19.

1896 Collett, A. K., M.A. (Apr. 3, 1916). ‡Lt. 8th London Regt. (Post Office Rifles). France, 1917–18.

1895 Collett, C. M. (Apr. 23, 1915). Lt. I.A.R.O. India.

1912 Collier, A. L. (Sept. 8, 1914). ‡Capt. Q.O. Cameron Highlanders (Maj.). France and Belgium, 1915; Salonika, 1915–18; Trans-Caucasia, 1919. *M.C.*, Jan. 1, 1918. Order of the White Eagle (5th Class) (with swords). *D.* Salonika, 1917, 1919.

1892 Collingwood, J. C. (Serving Aug. 4, 1914). Capt. K.O. Scottish Borderers (Adjt.). Capt. Special Lists.

1906 **Collinson, J. L. W.,** B.C.L., M.A. (Feb. 13, 1915). 2nd Lt. 3rd, attd. 2nd, S. Lancashire Regt. (Capt.). France, 1915–16. Killed in action at Ovillers on July 15, 1916.

Colyer-Fergusson, T. R. (Sept. 1914). ‡2nd Lt., Acting Capt., 2nd Northamptonshire Regt. France and Belgium, 1915–17. Killed in action at Bellewaarde on July 31, 1917. **V.C.** won at Bellewaarde, on July 31, 1917.

For most conspicuous bravery, skilful leading, and determination in attack. The tactical situation having developed contrary to expectation, it was not possible for his company to adhere to the original plan of deployment, and, owing to the difficulties of the ground and to enemy wire, Capt. Colyer-Fergusson found himself with a sergeant and five men only. He carried out the attack nevertheless, and succeeded in capturing the enemy trench and disposing of the garrison. His party was then threatened by a heavy counter-attack from the left front, but this attack he successfully resisted.

During this operation, assisted by his orderly only, he attacked and captured an enemy machine gun and turned it on the assailants, many of whom were killed and a large number were driven into the hands of an adjoining British unit. Later, assisted only by his sergeant, he again attacked and captured a second enemy machine gun, by which time he had been joined by other portions of his company, and was enabled to consolidate his position. The conduct of this officer throughout forms an amazing record of dash, gallantry, and skill, for which no reward can be too great having regard to the importance of the position won. This gallant officer was shortly afterwards killed by a sniper.

1919 Comstock, H. (Mar. 26, 1917). Maj. 120th Inf., U.S. Army. France, 1918–19.

1915 Cooke, A. T. S. (Jan. 25, 1916). ‡2nd Lt. 1st S. Wales Borderers. France, Germany.

1884 Cooke, F. J. (Dec. 1, 1915). Lt. R.A.S.C. Lt. Labour Corps (Capt.).

1913 Cooper, O., B.A. (Aug. 29, 1914). Capt. 6th Lancashire Fusiliers. Gallipoli and Egypt, 1915.

1896 Cooper, R. T., M.A. (Mobilized Aug. 4, 1914). Capt. R.A.S.C. France, 1916–19.

1893 Corbett, B. O., B.A. (Sept. 1916). ‡Lt., Acting Capt., R.G.A. (S.R.) (Adjt.).

1920 Cornwall, A. E. C. (Apr. 1917). Lt. R. Gloucestershire Hussars. Egypt.
1899 Cossar, G. C. (Oct. 1914). Capt. R.A.M.C. France and Belgium. *M.C.*, Sept. 16, 1918.
1897 Cossins, H. (Mar. 15, 1917). Pte. Queen's (R. W. Surrey Regt.). Cpl. R.A.S.C., attd. G.H.Q. Belgium and France.
1912 Cotterill,* L. D., B.A. (Aug. 26, 1914). Capt., Bt.-Maj., General List. D.A.A.G., War Office Staff (Maj.). France and Belgium, 1915–16. *M.C.*, Mar. 30, 1916. Chevalier de l'Ordre de la Couronne.
1903 Craggs, G. S., M.A. (Aug. 14, 1914). Maj. Alberta Regt., Canadian Inf. France, 1915–16. *D.* France, 1916.
1905 Cranstoun, G., B.A. (Nov. 13, 1915). Capt. R.A.M.C.
1892 **Crawley, G. R. E.** (Nov. 1, 1914). Lt. 10th R. Inniskilling Fusiliers. France. Killed in action on Feb. 26, 1917.
1904 Cripps, E. S., B.A. (Apr. 29, 1915). Capt. R.A.F. (Maj.). *D.*
1901 Cripps, F. E. (Oct. 15, 1914). Lt. R.A.S.C., attd. H.Q. 1st Cavalry Bde. Salonika, 1915–16; France, 1918–19. *D.* France, 1919.
1889 Crossman, D., M.A. Capt. Huntingdonshire Vol. Regt.
1919 Dalmahoy, P. J. E. (Aug. 28, 1914). Capt. R.F.A. (T.F.). France, 1915–18.
1919 Dance, B. M. (June 7, 1918). Pte. 5th R. Fusiliers.
1906 Dandridge, Rev. E. P. Chaplain U.S. Army.
1876 Darling, A. M. (Sept. 1914). Lt. 18th Vol. Bn. R. W. Kent Regt.
1920 Darling, J. M. (Jan. 18, 1918). 2nd Lt. R.F.A. France.
1918 Dashwood, F. A. Lt. S. Lancashire Regt., attd. R.A.F.
1910 Davenport,* C. T., B.A. (Sept. 7, 1914). A.B. R.N. Div. ‡Lt. 3rd, attd. 1/4th, Oxf. & Bucks. Lt. Infty. (Capt.). Mesopotamia, 1916; Italy, 1918–19.
1904 **Davenport, H. N.**, M.A. (Sept. 14, 1914). Capt. 2/4th Oxf. & Bucks. Lt. Infty. Maj. 2/6th R. Warwickshire Regt. France, 1915–18. *M.C.*, June 4, 1917. *D.* France, 1918. Missing, believed killed in action near Ham on Mar. 26, 1918.
1895 Davey, Rev. G. L., M.A. (Apr. 1916). Pte. R.A.M.C., afterwards Chaplain to the Forces (4th Class).
1883 Davey, Hon. H. S. (Serving Aug. 4, 1914). Lt.-Col. 18th Hussars, Res. of Officers, attd. Staff, Class BB., *C.M.G.* *D.* § Feb. 1917.
1899 David, C. J. E., B.A. (May 28, 1916). Lt. R.E. (Maj.). France, 1916–19.
1900 Davies, C. E. (Serving Aug. 4, 1914). Maj. R. Warwickshire Regt., attd. 16th R. Welch Fusiliers. Salonika, France. *D.S.O.*, Dec. 2, 1918. *D.* Salonika, 1917; France, 1918.
1919 Davies, C. E. P. (May 28, 1918). ‡2nd Lt. R.A.S.C. (M.T.). France, Germany.
1910 **Dawson,* W. R. A.** (Serving Aug. 4, 1914). Capt., Bt.-Maj., temp. Lt.-Col., 6th R. W. Kent Regt. France and Belgium. *D.S.O.*, Apr. 15, 1916; *Bar*, July 18, 1917; *2nd Bar*, June 22, 1918; *3rd Bar*, Mar. 8, 1919. *D.* France, 1916, 1917, 1918 twice, 1919. Died on Dec. 3, 1918, of wounds received on Oct. 22, at St. Amande.
1901 **Dean, R. F. M.** (Aug. 1914). 2nd Lt. 4th R. Warwickshire Regt., attd. M.G.C. E. Africa, France. Killed in action on the Somme on July 1, 1916.
1919 de Bruyne, H. B. A. (June 17, 1917). 2nd Lt. R.F.A. France, 1918–19.

1880 Deedes, Rev. Canon A. G., M.A. (Oct. 1, 1914). Chaplain to the Forces (4th Class). Died Dec. 1916.

1905 Dehn, R. M. R., B.A. Pte. Middlesex Regt.

1906 Deneke, R. H., B.A. (Nov. 22, 1916). 2nd Lt. R. Fusiliers. France.

1895 **Denman-Jubb, C. O.,** B.A. (Serving Aug. 4, 1914). Capt. and Adjt. W. Riding Regt. Belgium. *D.* France, 1914. Killed in action at Wasmes, near Mons, on Aug. 24, 1914.

1913 de Selincourt, M. J. (Sept. 2, 1914). ‡2nd Lt. 14th Middlesex Regt.

1913 **Dickie,* W.** (Oct. 1914). 2nd Lt. 1st K.O. Scottish Borderers. Gallipoli, 1915; Egypt, 1916; France, 1916. Killed in action in the attack on Beaumont-sur-Ancre on July 1, 1916.

1873 Ditchfield, Rev. P. H., M.A. Acting Army Chaplain.

1896 **Dobie, J. J.,** B.A. (Serving Aug. 4, 1914). Capt. 3rd Hussars (Maj.). France. *D.S.O.*, June 3, 1918. *M.C.*, July 26, 1918. *D.* France, 1914, 1918. Killed in action near Crevecœur on Sept. 30, 1918.

1896 **Docker, G. A. M.** (Serving Aug. 4, 1914). Capt. and Adjt. R. Fusiliers. France. Killed in action on Nov. 19, 1914.

1900 Dodsworth, B., B.A. (Apr. 1915). Lt. T.F. Res. Temp. Capt. in the Army, Staff-Captain. France, 1916–18. *O.B.E.* (Mil.). *D.* France, 1917, 1919.

1919 Donaldson, E. P. (Jan. 12, 1915). Lt. Rifle Brigade. Maj. 12th Bn. M.G.C. France, 1916–19.

1889 Dott, Rev. W. P., M.A. (June 19, 1917). Chaplain to the Forces (4th Class).

1913 Douglas, R. (Aug. 14, 1916). 2nd Lt. I.A.R.O. India.

1910 Dowding, Rev. A. T. W., B.A. (Jan. 11, 1916). Chaplain to the Forces (4th Class). France.

1907 [Dreyer, G., M.A.] (July 1915). Hon. Lt.-Col. R.A.M.C. Colonel R.A.F. France, 1915–19. *C.B.E.* (Mil.). *D.* France, 1918.

1907 Du Buisson, J. M., B.A. (Aug. 7, 1914). Capt. 7th Queen's (R. W. Surrey Regt.). France.

1913 Duckworth,* G. S. (Dec. 14, 1914). Lt. 10th King's (Liverpool Regt.), attd. M.G.C.

1908 Duncan, H. S., B.A. (Mobilized Aug. 4, 1914). Capt. D/236th Batt., R.F.A. (T.F.) (Maj.). France and Belgium, 1915–19. *M.C.*, Jan. 1, 1918. *D.* France, 1916.

1919 Dunlap, R. W. (June,1917). American Ambulance, afterwards Ensign, U.S. Naval Aviation Forces. France, 1917–19.

1910 Dunn, A. I., B.A. (Nov. 11, 1915). ‡Lt. R. Monmouthshire R.E. (Capt.). Belgium and France. *D.* France, 1919.

1913 **Dymock,* R. T. V.** (Dec. 1914). 2nd Lt. Shropshire L.I. France and Belgium. Died on Oct. 27, 1915, of wounds received in action near Ypres.

1895 Eardley-Wilmot, E. G., M.A. (Jan. 26, 1915). Capt. 7th R. Welch Fusiliers. R.T.O. *D.* § Mar. 1918; § Aug. 1918; § Aug. 1919.

1919 Easton, J. (Aug. 31, 1914). ‡Lt. 12th R. Fusiliers. France, 1915. (Prisoner of War, 1915–18.)

Eccles, J. D. (Sept. 1914). Capt. 9th London Regt. (Queen Victoria's Rifles). France, 1915, 1916. *M.C.*, June 3, 1916. Died on Sept. 27, 1916, of wounds received in action at Combles.

1900 Eccles, P., B.A. (Apr. 1, 1917). Capt. 2nd Madras Garrison Artillery, I.D.F. India.

1904 **Edgar, R. G.,** B.A. (Serving Aug. 4, 1914). Capt. 6th Manchester Regt. Egypt and Gallipoli. Killed in the assault on Achi Baba on June 4, 1915.

Edwardes, O. (Oct. 20, 1915). 2nd Lt. K.R.R.C. France. Killed in action on the Somme on July 1, 1916.

1902 Edwards, H. I. P., B.A. (Serving Aug. 4, 1914). Maj. 16th R. Sussex Regt. (Lt.-Col.). France. *D.S.O.*, June 3, 1919. *D.* France, 1919.

1906 Edwards, W. G. (Mobilized Aug. 5, 1914). ‡Maj. 3rd King's African Rifles. British, German, and Portuguese E. Africa. *M.C.*, July 27, 1918. *D.* E. Africa, 1917.

1894 Elgee, E. A., B.A. (Apr. 1915). Capt. Special Lists, empld. Remount Duties. *O.B.E.*

1910 **Elgey,* E.** (Dec. 1, 1915). 2nd Lt. R.F.A., afterwards 2nd Lt. 49th Squadron, R.F.C. France. Killed flying near Croisilles on Mar. 19, 1917.

1910 Elliott, W. S., M.A. (June 26, 1915). 2nd Lt. 4th Highland L.I. (invalided), afterwards Asst. Recruiting Officer.

1905 Empson, A. H. A. (Serving Aug. 4, 1914). Lt. 8th Indian Cavalry (Capt.). India, France. *D.* France, 1916.

1908 Evans,* A. J., B.A. (Apr. 15, 1915). 2nd Lt., Staff-Lt., Intelligence Dept. Capt., Flight Commdr., R.A.F. France, Mesopotamia, *M.C.*, Jan. 14, 1916; *Bar* (for escaping from Germany), Dec. 16, 1919. *D.* France, 1915 (Prisoner of War, escaped from Germany. Prisoner of War in Turkey, Mar.–Dec. 1918.)

1892 Evans, E. F. H. (Oct. 13, 1914). Capt. 10th Worcestershire Regt., attd. 51st Bedfordshire Regt. France, 1915–16.

1887 Farran, Rev. G. E., D.D. Secretary and Registrar, Baltic and Corn Exchange (No. 8 Red Cross) Hospital. France, 1914–19. ***M.B.E.***

1904 Fawcus, R. A., B.M. (Sept. 20, 1915). Capt. R.A.M.C.

Fawdrey, A. G. (Aug. 1915). 2nd Lt. 2nd R. Warwickshire Regt. France. Killed in action near Bullecourt on May 4, 1917.

1919 Fergusson, A. M. (Jan. 5, 1916). Lt. 5th King's (Liverpool Regt.) (Capt.). France.

1915 Ffooks, E. C. (Sept. 1918). 2nd Lt. R.A.S.C. (M.T.).

1911 Ffooks, W. A., B.A. (Sept. 26, 1914). Capt. 8th D.C.L.I. Capt. General List, Staff-Captain. France, 1915; Salonika and Egypt, 1915–19. *O.B.E.* (Mil.).

1899 Findlay, W., B.A. (July, 1915). Capt., Acting Maj., R.A.O.C. *D.* § Aug. 1918.

1913 **Fitzroy, M. A.** (Aug. 27, 1914). Capt. 4th Seaforth Highlanders. France, 1914–15. Killed in action near Neuve Chapelle on Apr. 17, 1915.

1883 Flynn, Rev. H. F. (June 19, 1916). Chaplain to the Forces (4th Class).

1914 Fookes, T. G. (Aug. 3, 1915). ‡Lt. I.A.R.O., attd. 49th Bengalis. Gallipoli, Egypt, India, Mesopotamia.

1919 Forbes, A. H. d'E. (Oct. 31, 1917). 2nd Lt. 6th Queen's (R. W. Surrey Regt.), attd. E. Surrey Regt. France. *M.C.*, Oct. 16, 1918.

1912 Forbes,* W. R. T., B.A. (Sept. 7, 1914). Capt. 8th The Black Watch. France.

1903 Ford, J. C., B.A. (Oct. 11, 1915). Maj. R.A.S.C., comdg. R.A.S.C., W. Africa. W. Africa.
1900 Forman, A. T., B.A. (Nov. 25, 1915). Capt. R.A.O.C. Mesopotamia, 1916–18. *D.* Mesopotamia, 1918.
1898 Forman, R. S., B.A. (Jan. 30, 1916). ‡Lt. R.A.S.C. Salonika, 1917–18.
1898 Forster, E. S., M.A. (Nov. 22, 1915). Lt. Special Lists. Temp. Maj. Intelligence Corps, B.S.F. Salonika, 1915–18; Constantinople, 1918–19. *M.B.E.* (Mil.). Order of St. Sava (5th Class). *D.* Salonika, 1918, 1919.
1885 Foster, Rev. F. E., M.A. (Oct. 9, 1917). Chaplain to the Forces (4th Class).
1898 **Fox, G. H.,** B.C.L., M.A. (July 15, 1915). 2nd Lt. R.F.A. (S.R.). Mesopotamia. Killed in action at Katia on Apr. 23, 1916.
1914 Fox, Rev. H. W., M.A. (Aug. 28, 1914). Chaplain to the Forces (3rd Class). France and Belgium. *D.S.O.*, Jan. 1, 1919. *D.* France, 1914, 1917.
1910 Fox, J. E. J., B.A. (Aug. 28, 1914). ‡Capt. R. Newfoundland Regt. Staff-Captain. Gallipoli, 1915; Egypt, 1916; France, 1916.
1919 Francis, E. L. (Aug. 15, 1914). Capt. (Adjt.) 3rd Wiltshire Regt. France, 1914–15. *D.* France, 1915.
1909 Fraser, A. C., B.A. (Oct. 5, 1914). Lt. C Batt., 264th Bde., R.F.A. (Capt.). Gallipoli, Egypt, Palestine, Syria.
1894 **Freeman, E.** (Serving Aug. 4, 1914). Maj. 10th R. Welch Fusiliers. France. Killed in action on Mar. 3, 1916.
1908 Freeman, R. C. (Dec. 5, 1912). Capt. R.E. (G.S.O. 3). France. *M.C.*, June 3, 1919.
1919 Freudenthal, N. F. H. (May 16, 1916). ‡Lt. Grenadier Guards. France.
1916 Frost, H. C. (July 15, 1916). Lt. 13th Somerset L.I. France, 1916–17.
1881 Froude, A. A., B.A. (June 13, 1916). Lt.-Comdr. R.N.V.R. (Comdr.). *C.M.G.* *O.B.E.* (Mil.).
1905 Fuller-Maitland, G. A., B.A. (June 14, 1915). Lt. Military Labour Corps, S. African F.F. Capt. Political Service. B.E. Africa, 1915–17. German E. Africa, 1917–18.
Furley, W. H. (July 12, 1915). Lt. 3rd, attd. 12th, R. Scots (Capt. and Adjt.). France and Belgium, 1916, 1917, 1918. *D.* France, 1917. Killed in action near Kemmel on Apr. 25, 1918.
1919 Gamble, A. M. (Aug. 19, 1917). Lt. R.E. France and Belgium.
1919 Gardner, F. D., B.A. (July 4, 1915). Lt. 8th Sherwood Foresters, attd. R.E. (Staff-Lt., 2nd Class). France and Belgium.
1894 Garnier, E. T., M.A. (Feb. 6, 1915). Lt. A.S.C., afterwards Capt. R.G.A. Mesopotamia, 1916–18; France, 1918.
1899 Garnier, Rev. G. R., M.A. (1916). Lce.-Cpl. M.T., R.A.S.C. France.
1899 George, E. B. (July 5, 1915). Capt. R.A.S.C.
1913 Gibson-Taylor, Rev. A. W. H. (Oct. 7, 1914). Chaplain to the Forces (4th Class).
1912 Gilkes,* M. H., M.A. (Sept. 23, 1914). Capt. 21st London Regt., attd. Ministry of Munitions. France. *M.C.*, Oct. 29, 1915.
1919 Gillmor, E. R. W. (June 7, 1918). 2nd Lt. R. Berkshire Regt.
1919 Glennie, H. D. (Sept. 20, 1918). Midshipman R.N.V.R.
1902 [Gordon, G. S., M.A.] (Serving Aug. 1914). Capt. 6th W. Yorkshire Regt. Special Staff appointment. *D.* § Mar. 1919.

1905 Gordon, J. E., B.A. (Nov. 28, 1917). Lt. 7th Arg. & Suth'd. Highlanders.
1919 Gott, J. B. (Sept. 1918). Cadet 21st O.C.B.
1905 Gotto, G. W., B.A. (Aug. 16, 1915). Capt. R.A.S.C.
1912 **Graham,* J. H. T.** (Oct. 17, 1914). Lt. 6th K.O. Scottish Borderers. France. Killed in action at Bernafoy Wood on the Somme on July 6, 1916.
1909 Grant,* F., M.A. (Sept. 1914). Capt. R.G.A. France and Belgium, 1916–17. *M.C.*, Jan. 1, 1918. (Invalided on account of wounds, Aug. 1917.)
1920 Gravem, A. B. (Nov. 6, 1917). ‡2nd Lt., Acting Lt., F.A., U.S. Army.
1895 Graves, P. P., B.A. (Dec. 1915). Capt. Special Lists. Staff-Captain. Egypt and Palestine. Croix de Chevalier de la Légion d'Honneur. *D.* Egypt.
1895 Gray, G. H. E., B.A. (Nov. 1, 1917). 2nd Lt. R.F.A. (S.R.).
1901 Greene, E. A. (Mobilized Aug. 4, 1914). Capt. Suffolk Yeomanry. Staff-Captain. France. *M.C.*, June 3, 1918.
1888 Greene, Sir W. R., Bt., B.A. (Aug. 21, 1914). Lt.-Col. County of London Yeomanry, T.F. Res. G.S.O. 2. France. *D.S.O.*, Jan. 14, 1916. T.D. *D.* France, 1915 ; § Feb. 1917.
1898 Greenshields, J. D. (Oct. 24, 1914). Capt. 20th King's (Liverpool Regt.) (Maj.). France. *D.* France, 1916.
1907 Grieve, A. McL., M.A. (Mobilized Aug. 4, 1914). Capt. 3rd, attd. 2nd, The Black Watch. France, 1914 ; Mesopotamia and India, 1916, 1917 ; Egypt, Palestine, Hedjaz, 1918. *D.* Palestine, 1919.
1898 Grieveson, E. R., M.A. Capt. R.A.M.C.
1909 Guillebaud, H. L., B.A. (Oct. 15, 1914). ‡Capt. 43rd (Garr.) Bn. R. Fusiliers. France.
1919 Gunn, J. L. (Jan. 16, 1914). Lt. 5th R. Scots. Capt. 74th Bn. M.G.C. Gallipoli, 1915 ; France, 1916, 1918 ; Egypt and Palestine, 1917–18.
1906 **Gurney, K. G.,** M.A. (May 1916). 2nd Lt. 2/6th Gloucestershire Regt. France, 1917. Died on Dec. 17, 1917, at German Military Hospital at Walincourt, of wounds received in action near Cambrai.
1903 Guy, Rev. C. A., M.A. (Jan. 20, 1915). Chaplain, R.N., H.M.S. *Diana.*
1902 Guy, E. M., B.A. (Nov. 28, 1914). Capt. 2/1st Northumberland Hussars. G.S.O. 3. France, 1917–18. *O.B.E.* (Mil.).
1900 **Gye, D. A.,** B.A. (Aug. 1914). ‡Lt., Acting Capt., R.H.A. Egypt, Gallipoli. Killed in action on Feb. 28, 1917.
1919 Habershon, A. W. (Oct. 8, 1915). Lt. R.A.S.C., attd. 75th Bn. Labour Corps. France and Belgium. R. Humane Society Bronze Medal. *D.* France, 1919.
1896 Hadow, A. L. (Serving Aug. 1914). Maj. Norfolk Regt., attd. Labour Corps. Gallipoli, France. *C.M.G.* Order of the Nile (4th Class). *D.* Gallipoli, 1916 ; France, 1917 ; § Aug. 1919.
1890 Hainsselin, Rev. S., M.A. (Aug. 5, 1914). Chaplain R.N. Lt. D.C.L.I. France and Belgium, 1917–18.
1884 Hall, A. N. (Aug. 1914). Lt.-Col. Q.O. Oxfordshire Hussars, T.F. Res. *O.B.E.* (Mil.).
1913 Hall, P. M. (Sept. 7, 1914). Lt. 1st Wessex Bde., R.F.A. (Maj.). India, 1914–16 ; Mesopotamia, 1916–18. *M.C.*, Feb. 7, 1918. *D.* Mesopotamia, 1917, 1918.

1912 **Hall, T. N.** (Jan. 1915). Lt. Bucks. Bn., Oxf. & Bucks. Lt. Infty. France, 1916. Died on Aug. 15, 1916, of wounds received in action.

1883 Hallett, Ven. C., M.A. (Nov. 1, 1917). Chaplain to the Forces (4th Class). E. Africa, 1917–19. (Interned in German E. Africa, 1914–16.)

Hanbury-Sparrow, B. H. (Jan. 7, 1915). Capt. 3rd Shropshire L.I., attd. 7th N. Staffordshire Regt. Gallipoli, Mesopotamia, Russia. *M.C.*, 1918. *D.* Mesopotamia. Killed in action at Baku on Aug. 26, 1918.

1909 **Hancocks, W.** (Jan. 7, 1914). Capt. 7th Worcestershire Regt. France. Killed in action on Oct. 9, 1917.

1905 **Hanington, G. J.,** B.A. (Aug. 5, 1914). Capt. A.S.C. Accidentally killed, Oct. 1915.

1912 Hansell, H. M., M.A. (Oct. 4, 1914). Capt. 5th Durham L.I.

1919 Harding, H. E. (July 24, 1918). Pioneer R.E., Anti-Gas Establishment.

1905 Harper, P. H., B.A. (Oct. 18, 1917). Lt. Australian Engineers. Egypt, Palestine.

1916 Harrild,* H. V. (May 1, 1916). Lt. King's (Liverpool Regt.). France, Salonika.

1911 Harrild, W. L., M.A. (Sept. 29, 1914). Lt., Acting Capt., 12th London Regt. (The Rangers) (Adjt.). France, 1915–16, 1917–18.

1906 Harris,* G. S., M.A. (Dec. 19, 1916). 2nd Lt. Loyal N. Lancashire Regt. France. *D.* France, 1918.

1894 Harrison, W. E. (Mobilized Aug. 4, 1914). Lt.-Col. comdg. Special Bde. Depot, R.E. *O.B.E.* (Mil.). *D.* § Feb. 1917.

1901 Hartley, A. G., B.A. (Oct. 9, 1914). Lt. 5th Bedfordshire Regt. Gallipoli, 1915. (Relinquished Commission on account of ill health, 1917.)

1906 Harvey, H. L., B.A. (1916). ‡Lt. 9th Bn., A.I.F. France, 1916–19.

1919 Hay, A. (Feb. 1916). ‡Lt. 14th Siege Batt., R.G.A. France and Germany.

1911 **Hay, D. Y.** (Sept. 1914). Lt. 2/5th R. W. Kent Regt. Pilot 20th Squadron, R.F.C. France, 1917. Killed in action on Aug. 11, 1917.

1907 Hay,* J. H., B.A. (Mobilized Aug. 1914). Capt. 1/5th R. W. Kent Regt. (Maj.). India, 1914–17; Mesopotamia, 1917–19. *D.* Mesopotamia, 1919.

1908 **Heath,* R. M.,** B.A. (Sept. 1915). ‡2nd Lt. 9th, attd. 3rd, Somerset L.I. (Adjt.). France, 1916. Killed in action near Delville Wood on Sept. 16, 1916.

1908 Henderson,* J. G., B.A. (Aug. 4, 1914). Maj., Acting Lt.-Col., Postal Section, R.E. D.D. Army Postal Services, B.S.F. France, 1914–15; Gallipoli, 1915; Macedonia, 1916–18; Turkey, 1919. *O.B.E.* (Mil.). *M.C.*, June 6, 1916. Order of the White Eagle. *D.* France, 1915; Salonika, 1916, 1917, 1918, 1919.

1909 Henderson, S., B.A. (Sept. 25, 1914). Lt. 9th Essex Regt. Capt. R.A.F., attd. Staff, Air Ministry. Belgium, 1915–16; Italy, 1918.

1895 **Henderson, W. A.,** B.A. (Serving Aug. 4, 1914). Capt. 1st Arg. & Suth'd. Highlanders. France. Killed in action on Dec. 10, 1914.

1902 Henley, F. A. H., B.A. (Mar. 4, 1916). Lt. R.A.S.C. Egypt and Palestine. *M.B.E.* (Mil.). *D.* Palestine, 1918.

1915 Hepburn, S. F. (Jan. 27, 1916). Lt. R.A.S.C., attd. 193rd Siege Batt., R.G.A. France, 1916–19.

1903 **Hepton, W.,** M.A. (Jan. 9, 1917). ‡2nd Lt. 5th Dragoon Guards. Died on Nov. 9, 1918, of illness contracted while on active service.

1911 Hering, H. B. (1917). Capt. 308th Inf., U.S. Army. (Discharged on account of ill health, Nov. 1917.)
1898 Hetherington, E. C., M.A. (June 12, 1916). Lt. R.A.S.C.
1919 Hett, A. S. (May 27, 1916). Lt. R.A.F.
1912 **Hewetson, R. J. P.** (Aug. 15, 1914). Capt. 3rd Loyal N. Lancashire Regt. Qr.-Master and Adjt. 2nd Corps A.R.C. France, 1915, 1917, 1918. (Prisoner of War, May 27, 1918.) Died in a German hospital on July 3, 1918, of wounds received in action at Beaurieux.
1907 Heywood, N., M.A. (Nov. 1916). Capt. R.A.S.C., attd. War Office. *O.B.E.* (Mil.). *D.* § Mar. 1918.
1915 Heywood-Waddington, A., B.A. (Jan. 25, 1917). 2nd Lt. 3rd Somerset L.I.
1912 Higham, R. L., M.A. (June 7, 1916). Lt. R.G.A. France, 1917, 1918.
1897 Hill, P. M. T., B.A. (May 30, 1916). Capt. Technical Officer R.A.F.
1889 Hill, V. T., M.A. (Dec. 7, 1914). Maj. 5th K.R.R.C. France, 1915–16.
1911 **Hind,* J. F. M.** (Aug. 1914). Lt. 9th Sherwood Foresters. Gallipoli, 1915; Egypt, 1916; France, 1916. Killed in action at Thiepval on Sept. 27, 1916.
1910 **Hinde,* W. H. R.**, M.A. (Sept. 26, 1914). Capt. R.A.S.C. T.D. *D.* § Mar. 1918. Died on Oct. 22, 1918, of illness contracted on active service.
1906 **Hislop, J. A.**, B.A. Capt. 19th Manchester Regt. France. Died at Somerville Hospital on July 9, 1916, of illness contracted on active service.
1904 Hoare, J. E., M.A. (Sept. 1914). Lt. 4th Canadian Engineers (Signal Coy.). France.
1920 Hogben, S. J. (Apr. 7, 1917). Lt. 3rd Arg. & Suth'd. Highlanders. France.
1901 Holding, H. E., M.A. (Sept. 1914). 2nd Lt. R.A.S.C. (Resigned on account of ill health.)
1892 Holland, R. E. (Serving Aug. 4, 1914). Maj. 4th Simla Rifles, Indian Army (Lt.-Col.). India.
1919 Holms, J. F. (May 14, 1915). Lt. 1st Highland L.I. France. *M.C.*, Mar. 26, 1917.
1901 Holt, W. V. (Dec. 28, 1914). Lt. R.E., Signal Service.
1909 **Hooton, E. C.**, B.A. (Sept. 1914). Lt. 2/8th R. Warwickshire Regt. France. Killed in action near Neuve Chapelle on June 27, 1916.
1903 **Horsfall, A. M.**, M.A. (Aug. 1914). Lt. Munster Fusiliers. France. *D.* France, 1915. Killed in action on May 19, 1915.
1897 Hoskins-Master, C. E., B.A. (Serving Aug. 4, 1914). Capt. 5th Queen's (R. W. Surrey Regt.). (Invalided.)
1913 Houghton,* R. A. (Aug. 15, 1914). Lt. K.O.Y.L.I., attd. R.A.S.C. (M.T.). France, 1915, 1916, 1917. *M.C.*, Jan. 11, 1919. (Placed on half-pay list on account of ill health contracted on active service.)
1904 Howe-Brown, N. F., B.A. (Mar. 14, 1917). Lt. S. African Inf. E. Africa.
Howell, J. (Dec. 11, 1914). 2nd Lt. 9th K.R.R.C. France. Killed in action at the Battle of Loos on Sept. 25, 1915.
1913 Howell, M., B.A. (Aug. 31, 1914). Lt. R.F.A. (Capt.). France. *D.* France, 1917.
1879 Hughes, M. J. (Nov. 1914). Lt.-Col. 7th R. Inniskilling Fusiliers. *D.* § Feb. 1917.
1906 **Humbert, E. G. J.**, B.A. (Oct. 20, 1914). Lt. 9th R. Berkshire Regt. Gallipoli. Died on June 8, 1915, of wounds received in action in Gallipoli.

1910 Hunt,* E. D. C., B.A. (Jan. 19, 1912). Capt. Suffolk Regt. (Bde. Maj.). France and Belgium. *M.C.*, Jan. 1, 1917; *Bar*, July 26, 1918.

1911 Hutton,* P. H. S., B.A. (Aug. 15, 1914). Capt. 5th R. Fusiliers. France and Belgium, 1915, 1917–18.

1900 Huyshe, R. R., M.A. (Dec. 12, 1914). Capt. R.A.S.C. *M.B.E.* (Mil.). *D.* § Feb. 1917; § Mar. 1918.

1919 Iles, H. F. B. (June, 1918). 2nd Lt. R.E. (Tunnelling Section).

1918 Inglis, K. A. M. (Sept. 1914). Lt. 14th London Regt. (London Scottish). France.

1919 Innes, A. L. (Oct. 1916). Lt. R.F.A. (S.R.).

1892 **Isaac, A. W.,** B.A. (Aug. 6, 1915). 2nd Lt. 1st Worcestershire Regt. France, 1916. Killed in action at Contalmaison on July 7, 1916.

1890 Isaac, E. S. W., B.A. (Sept. 28, 1914). ‡Lt. R.A.S.C. France, 1914–19.

1900 Isaac, F. S. (Aug. 17, 1914). Capt. 5th Worcestershire Regt. Lt.-Col. R.A.F. France.

1908 Isham, V. A. R., B.A. (Jan. 22, 1913). Capt. 2nd Suffolk Regt. Maj. D.A.A.G. France, Belgium, N. Russia. *M.C.*, Aug. 8, 1916. Russian Order. *D.* France, 1916; Archangel, 1919.

1912 **James,* E. G.** (Aug. 1914). Capt. and Adjt. 1st Shropshire L.I. France, 1915–16. *D.S.O.*, Nov. 14, 1916. *D.* France, 1916. Died on Oct. 15, 1916, of wounds received in action.

1898 Jameson, H., M.A. (Apr. 1915). Lt. R.A.S.C.

1898 Jelf-Reveley, A. E. R., B.A. (Serving Aug. 4, 1914). Lt.-Col. 7th R. Welch Fusiliers. Gallipoli. *D.* Gallipoli, 1916; § Feb. 1917.

1918 Jennings, R. W. (Aug. 16, 1916). Lt. 1st R. Fusiliers. France.

1914 Jessop, H. W. (Dec. 22, 1914). Capt., Acting Adjt., 1st (Garr.) Bn. W. Yorkshire Regt. Malta, 1915–19.

1919 Jessop, L. A. (Dec. 31, 1916). Lt. R.A.F., attd. E. Mediterranean Squadron, R.N. Salonika. *D.F.C.*, Dec. 3, 1918.

1913 **Johns, B. D.** (Sept. 14, 1914). Capt. 10th R. Welch Fusiliers. France and Belgium. Killed in action near Wytschaete on Feb. 17, 1916.

1910 Johnson, A. J. (Nov. 25, 1914). Lt. A.S.C., afterwards Capt. and Adjt. H.Q. 62nd Bde., R.F.A. France, 1915–19. Croix de Guerre.

1919 Johnson, H. T. (1918). Cadet R.G.A.

1904 Joynson, W., B.A. (Serving Aug. 4, 1914). Capt. 18th Hussars. France. *M.C.*, Jan. 18, 1918.

1886 **Karslake, W. R.,** M.A. (Aug. 1914). Lt. Pembrokeshire Yeomanry (Capt.). France, Belgium, Serbia. Died on Dec. 29, 1917, of illness contracted while on active service.

1907 Kaye, H. G., M.A. (Aug. 17, 1914). Capt. 6th K.O.Y.L.I. Capt., Flight Commdr., R.A.F. France, 1915; Egypt, 1916–17; Salonika, 1917. (Invalided 1918 owing to injuries received in Salonika.)

1919 Kemble, A. E. (Nov. 11, 1914). Capt. 2nd K.O.Y.L.I. France. *D.S.O.*, Apr. 2, 1919. *D.* France, 1918 twice.

1899 Kendal, N., B.A. (Mar. 1, 1915). Lt. 5th Cheshire Regt.

1903 Kendle, W. E. C. (Jan. 16, 1915). Lt. Indian Army, attd. Supply and Transport Corps. India.

1913 Kendrick, T. D. (Aug. 29, 1914). Lt. 2nd R. Warwickshire Regt. attd. Lancashire Fusiliers (Capt.). France, 1915.

1900 **Kennaway, A. L.,** B.A. (Aug. 1914). Lt. Dorset. Yeomanry. Gallipoli, 1915. Killed in action at Suvla Bay on Aug. 21, 1915.

1897 **Kennedy, A. E.** (Serving Aug. 4, 1914). Capt. Arg. & Suth'd. Highlanders. France and Belgium. Killed in action on Aug. 26, 1914.

1919 Kenrick, J. T. (Apr. 26, 1917). Lt. Worcestershire Yeomanry.

1895 Kettlewell, H. W. (Serving Aug. 4, 1914). Maj., Bt.-Lt.-Col., Shropshire L.I. D.A.Q.M.G. France, 1915–19. *D.* France, 1917, 1918, 1919.

1909 **King, J. P.,** B.A. (1917). No. 6 Coy., New York Divn., U.S. Army. France. Croix de Guerre. Died on May 29, 1919.

1897 **King-Church, C. E.,** B.A. (Mobilized Aug. 1914). Capt. 7th London Regt. France. Killed in action at the Battle of Loos, Sept. 25–6, 1915.

1910 Kinnison, C. H., B.A. (Sept. 1914). Lt. 9th London Regt. (Queen Victoria's Rifles). Maj. 19th Bn. Tank Corps. France, 1915–18. *M.C.*, Sept. 26, 1917 ; *Bar*, Feb. 18, 1918.

1914 Kitchingman, G. D., B.A. (May 25, 1915). Lt. General List, attd. 32nd Divl. Signals, R.E. France and Belgium.

1902 Kneeshaw, W. S., B.A. (Nov. 11, 1914). Lt. 4th R. Welch Fusiliers.

1889 Knipe, C. (Serving Aug. 4, 1914). Capt. 8th Inniskilling Fusiliers.

1892 **Labouchere, A. M.,** B.A. (Dec. 6, 1914). Maj. 5th Oxf. & Bucks. Lt. Infty. France. *D.S.O.*, July 26, 1918. *D.* France, 1918. Died of wounds as a prisoner on Apr. 20, 1918.

1908 **Lagden, R. O.,** B.A. (Aug. 4, 1914). Capt. 4th K.R.R.C. (Maj.). France and Belgium. *D.* France, 1915. Killed in action at St. Eloi on Mar. 6, 1915.

1902 Lake, H. W., B.A. (Jan. 25, 1917). Lt. Coldstream Guards, attd. 2nd Bn. France. *M.C.*, Jan. 11, 1919.

1909 Laskey, F. S., B.C.L., M.A. (Mobilized Aug. 1914). Capt. 4th Manchester Regt. (Lt.-Col.). Maj. Tank Corps. Dep. Asst. Inspector of Training. France. *M.C.*, June 3, 1918.

1890 Law, C. A., B.A. (Serving Aug. 4, 1914). Maj. 2nd Wiltshire Regt. France, Belgium, 1914. (Prisoner of War from 1914.)

1894 Law, W. H. P., B.A. (Serving Aug. 4, 1914). Maj., Bt.-Lt.-Col., R.A.S.C. (Lt.-Col.). France, 1915–19. *D.S.O.*, Jan. 1, 1917. *D.* France, 1915, 1916, 1918.

1905 **Lawford, H. M. B.,** B.A. (Oct. 29, 1914). Capt. 9th R. Fusiliers. France, 1915–16. Killed in action near Flers on Oct. 7, 1916.

1919 Lawrence, G. N. (Nov. 9, 1917). 2nd Lt. 1st Coldstream Guards. France and Germany.

1906 Lawson, E. C. H., M.A. (Feb. 23, 1917). ‡Lt. R.G.A. (S.R.).

1889 Lea, Rev. E. E., M.A. (Apr. 1915). Chaplain to the Forces (4th Class). France.

1906 Le Bas, R. S., B.A. (Aug. 14, 1914). Capt. Queen's (R. W. Surrey Regt.), attd. Somerset L.I. France.

1901 **Lee, R.,** B.A. (Oct. 1914). 2nd Lt. 7th Suffolk Regt. France. Killed in action at the Hohenzollern Redoubt on Oct. 13, 1915.

1897 Lee, R. T., M.A. (Serving Aug. 4, 1914). Maj., Bt.-Lt.-Col., Queen's (R. W. Surrey Regt.) (Lt.-Col.). G.S.O. 1. France. *C.M.G.*, Jan. 1, 1919. *D.S.O.*, Jan. 1, 1917. Officier de l'Ordre de la Couronne. Croix de Guerre. Belgian Croix de Guerre. *D.* France, 1914, 1916 twice, 1917, 1918.

1907 Leese, C. P., B.A. (Feb. 2, 1915). Lt. 7th Lancashire Fusiliers (Resigned.)

1908 Leonard,* Rev. M. P. G., M.A. (Oct. 9, 1914). Chaplain to the Forces (4th Class). Belgium and France, 1915–18; Germany, 1918–19. *D.S.O.*, Nov. 14, 1916. *D.* France, 1916.

1913 Lermit,* H. W. J., B.A. (Sept. 25, 1914). Capt. 15th Lancashire Fusiliers. France, 1916, 1918; Belgium, 1917, 1918. *D.* France, 1917.

1897 L'Estrange Malone, E. G. S. (Serving Aug. 4, 1914). Lt.-Col. 7th R. Fusiliers, empld. F.O. France and Belgium. *D.* France, 1916; § Feb. 1917.

1907 Letchworth,* H. M., M.A. (Apr. 3, 1915). Lt. R. Dublin Fusiliers (Capt.). France. (Prisoner of War.)

1912 **Lewin, E. C.** (Aug. 26, 1914). Lt. 1st R. W. Kent Regt. India, France. Killed in action at Gouzeaucourt on Sept. 27, 1918.

Lewin, F. H. (Nov. 1914). Capt. 7th R. W. Kent Regt. France, Belgium. *M.C.*, Oct. 20, 1916. *D.* France, 1917. Killed in action at Poelcappelle on Oct. 12, 1917.

1913 Leycester, P. W., B.A. (Oct. 24, 1914). Lt. R.A.S.C. Capt. R.A.F. (Observer Officer). France, Belgium, Salonika, Constantinople, S. Russia. *M.B.E.* (Mil.).

1912 **Lipscomb,* E. L.** (Aug. 15, 1914). Lt. 2nd R. Berkshire Regt. France. Killed in action at Fromelles on May 9, 1915.

1912 **Littleboy,* F. G.** (Aug. 5, 1914). Motor Cyclist Dispatch-Rider. ‡Lt. 1st R. W. Kent Regt. France, Belgium, Gallipoli, 1914–15. Died on Dec. 7, 1915, of wounds received in action at Suvla Bay.

1919 Littleboy, R. R. P.F.O., R.N.A.S.

1903 **Littlewood, A. F. B.** H.A.C. France. Killed in action on July 7, 1915.

1907 Lloyd, D. J., M.A. (Aug. 1917). 2nd Class Aircraftsman, R.N.A.S.; Sergt. R.A.F.

1907 **Lloyd, G. L. B.,** B.A. (Aug. 26, 1915). Capt. 5th Dorsetshire Regt. Gallipoli. Killed in action at Suvla Bay on Aug. 7, 1915.

1892 Locker, W. J., B.A. (Mobilized Aug. 4, 1914). Capt. 4th N. Staffordshire Regt. (Lt.-Col. 8th N. Staffordshire Regt., 1914–16). France and Belgium, 1915–16. *D.* France, 1916.

1905 Logan, I. B., B.A. (Mar. 6, 1917). ‡2nd Lt. 2nd Bn. Otago Regt. N.Z.E.F. France.

1911 Longrigg, S. H., B.A. (Sept. 5, 1914). ‡Maj. 9th R. Warwickshire Regt. Maj. Special Lists, whilst empld. as Political Officer. Gallipoli, 1915; Mesopotamia, 1916–19. *D.* Mesopotamia, 1918.

1906 Lowe, J. C. M., B.A. (Nov. 27, 1915). Lt.-Commdr. R.N.V.R.

1905 Loxley, G. H., B.A. (Feb. 1915). Lt. R.N.V.R. Maj. R.A.F. Dept. Aircraft Production, Paris. Croix de Chevalier de la Légion d'Honneur. Officer of the Crown of Italy.

1912 Lyon,* P. H. B., M.A. (Oct. 14, 1914). Capt. 6th Durham L.I. France and Belgium, 1915, 1917–18. *M.C.*, Jan. 18, 1918. (Prisoner of War, May–Dec. 1918.)

1910 Macan, V. T. W. (Nov. 26, 1917). 2nd Lt. General List. Staff-Lt. (3rd Class).

1903 **McDermott, R. K.,** M.A. (Aug. 15, 1914). Capt. 3rd, attd. 1st, Seaforth Highlanders. France. Killed in action on Sept. 20, 1918.

1904 McDonald, D. P., B.M. (June, 1917). Capt. R.A.M.C.

1914 **McGregor, A. W.** (Nov. 27, 1914). 2nd Lt. 9th The Black Watch. France. Killed in action on Feb. 27, 1916.

1911 **McGusty, G. R.** (Nov. 14, 1914). Lt. 8th R. Irish Rifles. France. Died on June 14, 1916, of wounds received in action.

Mackay, J. W. (Dec. 15, 1914). Lt. 7th Q.O. Cameron Highlanders. France and Belgium. Died on Aug. 20, 1917, of wounds received in action.

1892 Mackenzie-Murray, E., B.A. (Serving Aug. 4, 1914). Capt. 14th The Black Watch, attd. Ministry of Labour.

1913 McLeod, G. F., B.A. (Sept. 1914). Capt. and Adjt. 8th Arg. & Suth'd. Highlanders. France, 1915; Salonika, 1915–16; France, 1917–19. *M.C.*, Oct. 18, 1917. Croix de Guerre (avec Palme).

1907 **MacPhail, P. J. S.,** M.A. (Sept. 1915). Lt. 128th Heavy Batt., R.G.A. France. Died at Winchester on Nov. 26, 1918, of illness contracted while on active service.

1900 Magrath, C. J. K., M.A. (1915). Capt. General List (Maj.). France, Belgium, 1915–19. *O.B.E.* (Mil.). Belgian Croix de Guerre.

1899 Maitland-Makgill-Crichton, A. G. (Oct. 1914). Lt.-Col. 5th Q.O. Cameron Highlanders. France, Belgium. *D.S.O.*, Oct. 12, 1917. *M.C.*, Jan. 1, 1917. *D.* France, 1916, 1918.

1900 **Makins, H.,** B.A. (Jan. 24, 1915). Capt. 16th London Regt. (Queen's Westminster Rifles). France and Belgium. Killed in action at Vlamertinghe on Nov. 4, 1915.

Manoukian, Z. S. (Oct. 31, 1917). 2nd Lt. 6th Lancashire Fusiliers. France. Killed in action on Sept. 3, 1918.

1908 Marcon,* C. W. S., B.A. (Sept. 14, 1914). Capt. 2/4th Oxf. & Bucks. Lt. Infty., attd. Staff Divl. H.Q., U.S. Army, 1918. France, 1916–18.

1906 Margoliouth,* H. M., M.A. (Sept. 16, 1914). Capt. 6th Northamptonshire Regt. France, Belgium.

1896 Marsden, M. H., B.A. (Feb. 1916). ‡Lt. R.A.S.C. Belgium, France.

1920 Marshall, H. P. (Aug. 20, 1918). Midshipman, R.N.V.R. Home Fleet.

Marshall, R. B. (Aug. 22, 1914). 2nd Lt. 7th E. Surrey Regt. France, 1916; N. Russia, 1919. *D.* France, 1916. Died on Sept. 14, 1919, of wounds received in action in N. Russia.

1897 Martin, A. W., M.A. (Nov. 26, 1915). Capt. R.A.S.C. Egypt, Palestine, 1916–18.

1891 Massey, A. S., M.A. Anti-Aircraft Corps, R.N.V.R.

1901 **Maton, L. E. L.** (June 1905). Capt. 1st Devonshire Regt. Bde. Maj. France, 1914–15, 1916–17. *M.C.*, Jan. 1, 1916. *D.* France, 1916. Killed in action at Fresnoy on May 9, 1917.

1904 Maude, A. H., M.A. (Mar. 1909). Maj. 47th London Divl. Train, R.A.S.C. (Lt.-Col.). France, Belgium, 1915–19. *C.M.G.*, Jan. 1, 1919. *D.S.O.*, Jan. 1, 1917. *D.* France, 1916, 1918.

1907 Maude, G. W. E. (Serving Aug. 4, 1914). Capt. 1st Yorkshire Regt., attd. M.G.C. India, 1914–16; Afghanistan, 1919.

1912 **Mawdsley, N. H.** (Apr. 30, 1915). Lt. 6th R. Fusiliers. France. Killed in action on June 17, 1918.

1901 **Maxwell, W. J.** (Serving Aug. 4, 1914). Capt. Q.O. Cameron Highlanders, attd. 10th Sudanese Regt., Egyptian Army. Egypt. *D.* Egypt. Died at Abiad-Darfur on Aug. 26, 1916, of illness contracted while on active service.

1884 Mellor, C., B.A. (Jan. 23, 1917). Capt. 15th Vol. Bn. Lancashire Regt.
1909 **Merewether, C. K.** (Aug. 1914). Capt. 1/4th Wiltshire Regt. India, 1914–17; Palestine, 1917. Died in hospital at Port Said on Dec. 20, 1917, of wounds received in action.
1882 Middleton, F. T., B.A. (May 23, 1915). Lt. 12th Lancers. Lt. General List, T.F. Res.
1908 Miles, C. J., B.A. (Sept. 24, 1915). Lt. R.E., Postal Section (Maj.. Egypt and Palestine. *M.B.E.* (Mil.). *D.* Egypt, 1917.
1911 Milling, H. B., M.A. (Nov. 21, 1914). Lt. R.A.F. France. (Prisoner of War.)
1897 Mills, J. D., B.A. (Mobilized Aug. 1914). Maj. Warwickshire Yeomanry, attd. 100th Bn. M.G.C. Egypt, Gallipoli, Palestine, France. *D.* Gallipoli, 1916; Palestine, 1918; France, 1919.
Moller-Gjems, A. O. (Mar. 28, 1917). 2nd Lt. 5th R. Fusiliers. France and Belgium. Killed in action on Aug. 8, 1917.
1903 Monckton, P. M. (Dec. 15, 1915). Lt., Acting Capt., 4th Divl. Train, R.A.S.C. France, Belgium.
1887 Money-Kyrle, Rev. C. L., M.A. (May 30, 1915). Chaplain to the Forces (3rd Class), attd. 1st Div., B.E.F. France, Belgium. *M.C.*, Jan. 1, 1916. *D.* France, 1915.
1904 Monfries, C. B. S., B.A. (Apr. 15, 1915). Capt. 8th R. Scots. Maj. General List. *C.B.E.* (Mil.). Officer of the Order of the Crown of Italy.
1904 **Monro, D. H. C.,** B.A. (Sept. 1914). Lt. 29th, attd. 16th, Canadian Inf. France, 1915–16. Died on May 4, 1916, of wounds received in action.
1919 Morales, C. McL. (Sept. 16, 1916). Gnr. 315th Siege Batt., R.G.A. Italy, 1917–19.
1896 Morgan-Owen, M. M., M.A. (Mobilized Aug. 4, 1914). Lt.-Col. 10th Rifle Brigade. Anzac and Suvla Bay, 1915; France and Belgium, 1916–18. *D.S.O.*, Mar. 5, 1918. *D.* France, 1917, 1918.
1903 **Morland, K. I. T.,** M.A. (1915). ‡2nd Lt. 6th Oxf. & Bucks. Lt. Infty. France and Belgium. Killed in action near Guillemont on Sept. 3, 1916.
1895 Morrell, Rev. G. L., M.A. (June 8, 1915). Chaplain to the Forces (4th Class).
1907 Morris, Rev. A. E., M.A. (April 4, 1918). Chaplain to the Forces (4th Class).
1911 Mortimer,* A. B. (Nov. 4, 1915). Lt., Acting Capt., Canadian Artillery, (Divl. Gas Officer). France.
1898 Moss, W. L. H., B.A. (1915). Capt. R.A.S.C.
1888 Mott, C. E., B.A. (May 26, 1915). Capt. R.A.S.C. Gallipoli, 1915; Egypt, Palestine, Syria, 1915–19.
1913 **Mott, H. F.** (Sept. 1914). Capt. 16th London Regt. (Queen's Westminster Rifles). France. *M.C.*, June 3, 1916. Killed in action at Gommecourt on July 1, 1916.
1908 Muirhead,* J. S., B.A. (Mobilized Aug. 5, 1914). Maj. 51st (Highland) Div. Sig. Coy., R.E. France, 1915–18. *D.S.O.*, June 3, 1918. *M.C.*, June 3, 1916. *D.* France, 1918 twice.
1888 Murray, E. (Aug. 1914). 2nd Lt. General List. France. (Invalided.)
1909 Napier, H., M.A. (Oct. 10, 1915). Lt. 2/16th London Regt. (Queen's Westminster Rifles). France, 1916; Salonika, 1916–17; Palestine, 1917.

1913 Nason, W. (Sept. 16, 1914). ‡Capt. and Adjt. 9th Sherwood Foresters. Gallipoli, 1915–16; Egypt, 1916; France and Belgium, 1916–19. *M.C.*, Sept. 17, 1917. *D.* France, 1917.

1900 **Neate, A. B.,** M.A. (Aug. 7, 1915). Lt. R.F.A. (S.R.). France. Died on Apr. 23, 1917, of wounds received in action.

1895 Nevill, H. R., B.A. (Apr. 1, 1904). Lt.-Col. I.A.R.O., 7th United Provinces Horse. Asst. Adjt.-Gen. India. *O.B.E.* (Mil.).

1913 Newbold, D. (Aug. 1914). ‡Lt. Dorset Yeomanry. Mudros, France, Egypt, Sinai, Palestine, 1915–18.

1906 **Newbold, P.,** B.A. (Aug. 28, 1914). ‡2nd Lt. 7th R. W. Kent Regt. France. Killed in action at Trônes Wood on July 13, 1916.

1904 Newton, W. G., M.A. (Mobilized Aug. 1914). Maj., Acting Lt.-Col., 1/21st London Regt. A.D.C. France, Belgium, 1914–19. *M.C.*, Nov. 14, 1916.

1901 Nicholson, D. H. S., M.A. (Feb. 8, 1917). Capt. R.F.A. (S.R.). Staff-Captain.

Noaks, G. V. (July 14, 1915). 2nd Lt. Northamptonshire Regt. France. Died on Aug. 18, 1916, of wounds received in action.

1898 Norbury, B., B.A. (Dec. 24, 1914). Capt. 7th Manchester Regt.

1894 Norman, H. C., B.A. (Dec. 10, 1915). Capt. 4th The Buffs (E. Kent Regt.). France, 1918.

1902 Normand, W. G., B.A. (June 5, 1915). Lt. 592nd Fortress Coy., R.E.

1902 Norris, O. T. (Oct. 30, 1916). Lt. R.A.S.C.

1906 North, C. F. J., B.A. (Nov. 8, 1915). Lt. Administrative Officer, R.A.F.

1912 Nuttall, R. W., B.A. (Oct. 8, 1914). Lt. 10th E. Surrey Regt. (Capt.). Egypt, Palestine, France, 1916–19. *M.C.*, Feb. 18, 1918.

1920 O'Brien, E. (Sept. 1915). Lt. 8th R. Warwickshire Regt. (Capt.). France.

1904 Oliver, W. J., B.M., M.A. (Feb. 7, 1917). Capt. R.A.M.C.

1906 Osborne, G., B.A. (Serving Aug. 4, 1914). Capt. 19th Hussars. France. *D.* France, 1915.

1909 Ould,* R. F., B.A. (Sept. 1914). Capt. 11th Rifle Brigade. France and Belgium.

1914 Owen, L. (Nov. 1914). Lt. General List, T.F. Res.

1900 Palairet, R. C. N., B.A. (Serving Aug. 4, 1914). Capt., temp. Maj., 2/6th Devonshire Regt. A.D.A.D. Equipment and Ordnance Stores Dept., Indian Army. India.

1919 Palmer, C. R. (Aug. 1916.) Lt. 1/19th London Regt. Lt. R.A.F. France. *M.C.*, Aug. 16, 1917; *Bar*, Feb. 18, 1918.

1904 Panckridge, H. R., B.A. (Dec. 4, 1914). Lt., Acting Capt., I.A.R.O. France, 1915–18; Palestine, 1918. *D.* Palestine, 1918.

1911 **Parke, J. A.** (Sept. 1914). Lt. 10th Durham L.I. France. Missing, believed killed in action, July 1915.

1904 Parker, J. O., B.A. (Mobilized Aug. 4, 1914). Maj. Essex Yeomanry. France. Belgian Croix de Guerre. *D.* France, 1917.

1913 **Parker,* W. L. O.** (Aug. 4, 1914). Lt. 13th Squadron, R.F.C. France. Killed in action on Oct. 31, 1917, when flying over the German Lines.

1894 Parkin, I. U. (Sept. 16, 1917). Lt. Labour Corps.

1898 Parr, E. M. M., M.A. (May 7, 1915). Lt. 14th Sherwood Foresters.

1901 **Parr, H. W. M.**, M.A. (Mobilized Aug. 1914). Lt. 5th S. Staffordshire Regt. France. Killed in action on May 15, 1915.
1919 Patten, A. J. H. (Nov. 11, 1914). Capt. 9th Norfolk Regt., attd. No. 20 O.C.B. France and Belgium. *M.C.*, Sept. 26, 1917; *Bar*, Jan. 18, 1918. *D.* France, 1917.
1892 Pattinson, Rev. R., M.A. (serving Aug. 4, 1914). Chaplain to the Forces (4th Class), attd. R.F.A.
1908 **Peake, H. A. W.**, B.A. (Aug. 4, 1914). Capt. 3rd, attd. 2nd, Essex Regt. France, 1914–16. Killed in action near Ovillers on July 3, 1916.
1912 **Peake, K. J. W.** (Aug. 1914). Lt. 6th Lincolnshire Regt. Gallipoli, 1915. Missing, believed killed in action at Oghratina (Chocolate Hill) on Aug. 9, 1915.
1916 Pearl, W. A. (1917). American Ambulance. France. Croix de Guerre. Médaille Militaire.
1910 **Pearson, M. M.** (Aug. 1914). ‡2nd Lt. Worcestershire Hussars. Egypt. Killed in action at Oghratina, Eastern Egypt, on Apr. 23, 1916.
1899 Pennefather, E. C., B.A. (Aug. 18, 1915). Maj. Special Lists, D.A.A.G. Egypt and Palestine. *M.B.E.* (Mil.).
1912 Penney,* J. C., B.A. (Feb. 8, 1915). Capt. and Adjt. 4th The Black Watch. France. *M.C.*, Sept. 26, 1917.
1893 Pepys, Rev. C. S., B.D. (Jan. 8, 1917). Chaplain to the Forces (4th Class). Salonika. *D.* Salonika, 1917.
1902 Perkins, H. B., B.A. (Aug. 5, 1916). Lt. 3rd Monmouthshire Regt.
1905 **Perks, M. C.**, M.A. (Sept. 19, 1914). 2nd Lt. Loyal N. Lancashire Regt. France. Killed in action on Apr. 23, 1917.
1906 Phillips, S. P. V., B.A. (Mar. 22, 1915). Lt. R.N.V.R. Maj. R.A.F. Gallipoli, 1915; Dunkerque, 1916. *D.* § Jan. 1919.
1914 **Phillips-Jones, L.** (Aug. 1914). ‡Lt. R. Berkshire Regt. Gallipoli. Killed in action at Achi Baba, Gallipoli, on June 7, 1915.
1915 Philpott,* R., B.A. (Nov. 4, 1915). 2nd Lt. 4th E. Yorkshire Regt., attd. 25th Prov. Bn. (Commission relinquished.)
Pilgrim, S. A. F. (Apr. 1917). 2nd Lt. Tank Corps. France. Died on Sept. 24, 1918, of wounds received in action near Peronne.
Pitcairn-Jones, E. (Sept. 15, 1915). 2nd Lt. 5th, attd. 9th, Rifle Brigade. France. Died on May 13, 1916, of wounds received in action in France.
1888 Pitman, H., M.A. (Feb. 1, 1915). Capt., Acting Maj., D.A.D. Inland Water Transport. France.
1888 Pollard, A. E. St. V. (Serving Aug. 4, 1914). Lt.-Col. Border Regt. Gallipoli. *O.B.E.* (Mil.). *D.* Gallipoli, 1916.
1888 Powell, T. P. P., B.A. (Sept. 1914). Lt., Acting Capt., 2/1st Montgomeryshire Yeomanry; A.D.C. Salonika, Palestine, Egypt. *M.B.E.* (Mil.). *D.* Salonika, 1917; Palestine, 1919.
1914 Powell,* V. (Dec. 18, 1914). R.A.M.C. Gnr. R.F.A. (Bomdr.). India, 1916; Mesopotamia, 1916–19.
1909 Powell-Edwards, W. H. G., B.A. (Mobilized Aug. 1914). Maj. Sussex Yeomanry. France. *M.C.*, Feb. 4, 1918.
1912 Powys-Jones, L., B.A. (July 31, 1918). 2nd Lt. 4th K.R.R.C.
1903 Poyntz, R. S. P., B.A. (Jan. 8, 1915). 2nd Lt. 8th R. Berkshire Regt. Lt. General List, attd. School of Instruction (Capt.).

1910 Prentice,* C. H. C., B.A. (Sept. 22, 1914). Lt. D/84th Bde., R.F.A. France, Belgium, 1915–18.

1910 Prestige,* H. H. C., B.A. (Mobilized Aug. 1914). Capt. 1/10th London Regt. Gallipoli, 1915; France, 1917–18.

1887 Prichard, B. C. R. Fusiliers. (Invalided.)

1915 Prichard, E. C. (Nov. 1, 1918). Pioneer, R.E., attd. Bedford 'A' Signal Depot.

1890 Pringle, J. L., M.A. (Mobilized Aug. 4, 1914). Capt. Lothians & Border Horse. France, 1915–19.

1913 **Pullan, C. E. A.** (Sept. 18, 1914). 2nd Lt. 16th Durham L.I. France and Belgium. Killed in action at Houplines, Armentières, on Dec. 30, 1915.

1911 Quick, T. S. Q. P., B.A. (Apr. 9, 1915). Lt. 4th Leinster Regt., attd. King's African Rifles. E. Africa.

1913 Radcliffe, W. H., B.A. (Sept. 20, 1914). ‡Lt. 2nd Devonshire Regt. (Capt.). India, 1915–16; Mesopotamia, 1916–17; France, 1917–18, 1918–19. *D.* France, 1918, 1919.

1908 Rand, O. R., B.A. (1917). U.S. Army.

1902 **Rathbone, G. B.,** B.A. (Feb. 1, 1915). Capt. 7th Gloucestershire Regt. Gallipoli. *D.* Gallipoli, 1916. Killed in action on Apr. 21, 1916.

1893 Rawlence, J. (Serving Aug. 4, 1914). Capt. 1/7th Hampshire Regt. India.

1907 Rayner, O. T., M.A. (Nov. 1915). Capt. General List. Staff-Captain. *M.B.E.* (Mil.).

1913 **Rayson,* W. H. R.** (Oct. 13, 1914). Capt. C/47th Batt., R.F.A. France, Salonika. Died as a prisoner of war on Mar. 27, 1918, of wounds received near Essigny-le-Grand on Mar. 21.

1903 Reader, G. E. H., B.A. (1914). ‡Lt. R.A.O.C.

1892 Reeves, T. S., M.A. (July 20, 1915). Capt. R.A.M.C.

1904 Reid, F., B.A. S. African Inf.

1911 Reid,* G. L. P. (Feb. 26, 1915). Lt. R.G.A. (T.F.).

1897 **Reid, G. W.** (Mobilized Aug. 1914). Capt. and Adjt. 3rd Hampshire Regt. Gallipoli, 1915. Killed in action at Krithia on May 4, 1915.

1911 Reid, N., B.A. (Sept. 1914). ‡Lt. R.F.A. (S.R.) (Capt.). German S.W. Africa, 1914–15; France and Belgium, 1916–19. *D.S.O.*, June 3, 1919. *M.C.*, Jan. 1, 1918. *D.* France, 1919.

1912 **Reid, W. G.** (1915). ‡2nd Lt. Cameronians. France. Died on Feb. 23, 1917, of wounds received in action.

1903 Reiss, P. J., B.A. (1914). ‡Lt. 3rd Bedfordshire Regt. France. *M.C.*, July 26, 1917; *Bar*, Oct. 16, 1918.

1908 Reynolds, C. B., M.A. Pte. Canadian Rifles.

1899 Reynolds, G. N. (Serving Aug. 4, 1914). Capt. 21st Lancers, attd. 9th Lancers, now empld. Remount Service. France, 1914. *M.C.*, Jan. 18, 1919. (Wounded and Prisoner of War, Oct. 1914–18.)

1901 Richards, A. P., B.A. (Oct. 9, 1914). Capt. 4th Durham L.I. India.

1912 Richardson, J. N., B.A. (Sept. 9, 1914). Capt. 6th R. Berkshire Regt. France. *M.C.*, Oct. 20, 1916; *Bar*, Sept. 16, 1918.

1919 Richardson, S. G. (Dec. 29, 1916). Lt. 26th Batt., R.F.A. France.

1919 Rissik, S. A. (July 31, 1915). Lt. 312th Bde., R.F.A. France, 1917–18.

1912 Ritchie, T. R., M.A. (June 6, 1917). 2nd Lt. R.F.A. (S.R.).

1908 **Robb, T. D.,** B.A. (June 25, 1914). Capt. 17th London Regt. France. Killed in action at Loos on Sept. 26, 1915.

Robertson, G. (Feb. 6, 1915). 2nd Lt. 3rd, attd. 1st, Q. O. Cameron Highlanders. France. Killed in action at the Battle of Loos on Sept. 25, 1915.

1901 Robertson, M., M.A. (Oct. 14, 1914). Capt. 9th W. Riding Regt. Maj. General List. France. *O.B.E.* (Mil.). *M.C.*, June 4, 1917. *D.* France, 1916; § Aug. 1918.

1896 **Robinson, F. W.** (Serving Aug. 1914). Maj. R.F.A. France. *D.S.O.*, Jan. 1, 1917. *D.* France, 1916. Killed in action, Apr. 1917.

1891 Robinson, T. C., M.A. (Mobilized Aug. 4, 1914). Lt.-Col. 4th E. Lancashire Regt. A.A. and Q.M.G. Egypt, 1914; Gallipoli, 1915; Palestine and Syria, 1915–19. *D.S.O.*, Jan. 1, 1918. T.D. Order of the Nile (3rd Class). *D.* Palestine, 1917, 1918.

1910 Rodney,* Lord, B.A. (Nov. 15, 1914). Capt. 2nd Dragoon Guards, Res. of Officers.

1895 Rogers, H. S., M.A. (Nov. 1, 1916). ‡Lt. General List. Lt. R.A.F. (Capt. G.S.O. 3.).

1892 Romney, F. W., B.A. Lt. Recruiting Officer.

1917 Roper, E. A. F., B.A. (Oct. 13, 1914). Lt. 9th E. Lancashire Regt. (Invalided.)

Rose, H. P. (Aug. 10, 1916). 2nd Lt. 2nd Seaforth Highlanders. France. Killed in action near Fampoux on Apr. 11, 1917.

1896 Ross, W. D., M.A. (Apr. 22, 1915). Maj. General List, attd. Ministry of Munitions. *O.B.E.* (Mil.). *D.* § Jan. 1917.

1897 Rostron, P. S. (Serving Aug. 1914). Maj. R.H.A. *O.B.E.* (Mil.). *D.* § Feb. 1917.

1895 Russell, C. A. H. (Oct. 20, 1915). Capt. R.A.S.C.

1899 Rutherford, W. (Mar. 24, 1915). Lt. 4th Devonshire Regt.

1907 Rylands,* F., M.A. (Dec. 2, 1914). Capt. 3rd Wiltshire Regt. France. (Prisoner of War.)

1905 Sainsbury,* J., B.M. (Aug. 9, 1914). Capt. R.A.M.C. France, 1914–16.

1883 Salt, Sir T. A., Bt. (Mobilized Aug. 1914). Maj. Res. of Officers; Lt.-Col. 3rd County of London Yeomanry. Lt.-Col. 103rd Bn. M.G.C. France, 1914–16; Balkans, 1916–17; Egypt and Sinai, 1917; Palestine, 1917–18. *D.S.O.*, Jan. 24, 1917. Order of the Nile (4th Class). *D.* § Jan. 1917.

Sampson, R. M. (Jan. 1917). 2nd Lt. 122nd Siege Batt., R.G.A. France, 1918. Killed in action at Croisilles on Aug. 30, 1918.

1906 **Sanderson, T. E.,** B.A. (Oct. 13, 1915). Lt. 4th York & Lancaster Regt. France. *D.* France, 1917. Killed in action on Apr. 13, 1918.

1905 Sandford, T. F. Capt. N. Rhodesia Rifles. Africa. *M.B.E.*

1919 Sands, H. H. A. (Mar. 21, 1915). Lt., Acting Capt., 3rd R. Warwickshire Regt. France, 1915–16.

1911 **Sands,* L. K.** (Aug. 1914). ‡Capt. 10th Lancashire Fusiliers. Belgium, France. Died at Bailleul on Apr. 28, 1916, of wounds received in action at Armentières.

1908 Sargent, J. P., B.A. (Nov. 1914). Capt. 379th Siege Batt., R.G.A. France. *D.* France, 1918.

1897 Sarson, E. V. (Aug. 12, 1914). Maj., Acting Lt.-Col., R.F.A. India,

Mesopotamia, France. *D.S.O.*, Jan. 1, 1918. *D.* Mesopotamia, 1915, 1916; France, 1917, 1918.

1907 Satterthwaite, R. E., B.A. (Serving Aug. 4, 1914). Capt. 1/5th R. W. Kent Regt. Bde. Maj. 11th Bde., I.A. India, Afghanistan.

1911 Saxon,* E. (Aug. 28, 1914). Lt., Acting Maj., 75th Batt., 10th Div., R.F.A. France, 1915–16. Egypt and Palestine, 1916–19.

1906 Schwartze, H. E., B.A. (Feb. 1915). Lt. 4th Durham L.I. Capt. Special Lists. Courts Martial Officer, XIX Corps. France.

1913 Scott,* C. F., B.A. (Sept. 16, 1914). 2nd Lt. 8th Rifle Brigade. France and Belgium, 1915. (Invalided, 1916.)

1913 **Scott, R. W. T. G.** (May 31, 1915). 2nd Lt. 7th Seaforth Highlanders. France. Died on Aug. 15, 1916, of wounds received on July 14, 1916, at Longueval.

1900 **Scrase, R. G.,** M.A. (Jan. 1915). Lt. 4th Gloucestershire Regt. France. Killed in action on July 20, 1916.

1907 Seldon, A. A., B.A. (Apr. 7, 1917). Capt. King's African Rifles. German E. Africa.

1919 Sellar, W. C. (Oct. 31, 1917). 2nd Lt. K.O. Scottish Borderers.

1903 Seth-Smith, D., M.A. (1915). ‡Lt. King's African Rifles. E. Africa. *M.C.*, June 4, 1917.

1878 Seton-Karr, H. W. (Sept. 29, 1914). Capt. 22nd London Regt. (The Queen's), attd. 3rd Echelon, Egypt. Egypt, 1917–19.

1909 **Shairp,* N.,** B.A. (Mobilized Aug. 1914). Capt. Ayrshire Yeomanry. Gallipoli, Egypt, Palestine. *M.C.*, Jan. 1, 1919. *D.* Palestine, 1918. Died on Oct. 13, 1918, of malaria, contracted on active service.

1880 Shaw, Rt. Rev. E. D., Bishop of Buckingham, D.D. (Serving Aug. 4, 1914). Chaplain to the Forces (3rd Class), attd. R. Bucks. Hussars.

1899 Shaw, F., M.A. (Mobilized Aug. 1914). Capt. Duke of Lancaster's Own Yeomanry. Egypt, Constantinople.

1876 Shaw, Sir F. W., Bt., *D.S.O.* (Serving Aug. 4, 1914). Lt.-Col. (Hon. Col.) 8th R. Irish Regt. France, 1915, 1916, 1918.

1898 **Sheffield, L. H.,** B.A. (June 2, 1915). Capt. 3rd, attd. 2nd, Dorsetshire Regt. France. Killed in action on Mar. 25, 1917.

1897 Sherston, C. J. T., M.A. (Apr. 10, 1915). Capt. 2/1st Yorkshire Hussars.

1908 Sherwood-Smith, A. D., B.A. (Sept. 3, 1917). 2nd Lt. Intelligence Corps. France.

1899 Shield, G. E. R., B.A. (Oct. 1, 1914). Lt. 4th Devonshire Regt.

1908 Sidebotham, J., B.A. (May 3, 1918). 2nd Lt. R.A.F.

1906 **Sillem, A. C. H.** (Feb. 21, 1915). 2nd Lt. R.F.A. France. Killed in action at Delville Wood on July 18, 1916.

1908 Sillem, H. N., B.A. (Sept. 15, 1914). Interpreters Corps, Indian Army. ‡Lt. 18th Hussars. France. (Granted Commission for services in the Field, Dec. 15, 1914.)

1907 Simeon, G. N. (Oct. 28, 1915). Lt. 3/3rd Gurkha Rifles, Indian Army (Capt.). Egypt and Palestine, 1917–19.

1919 Simmons, W. M. (May 10, 1917). Capt. 364th Inf., U.S. Army. France and Belgium.

1911 **Simpson, C. W.** (Sept. 1914). 2nd Lt. 7th Leicestershire Regt. France. Killed in action at Bazentin Wood on July 14, 1916.

1911 Sinclair,* R. J. (Aug. 28, 1914). Lt. 5th K.O. Scottish Borderers, attd. Ministry of Munitions. Gallipoli. *M.B.E.* (Mil.). *D.* Gallipoli, 1915.

1913 Sinclair, R. S. B., B.A. (Jan. 15, 1915). Capt. 2/5th Gloucestershire Regt. France. *M.C.*, June 18, 1917 ; *Bar*, Mar. 8, 1919.

1898 **Skinner, F. J.,** M.A. (Aug. 1914). Capt. 12th Hampshire Regt. France. Killed in action on the Somme on Sept. 3, 1916.

1907 Smail, W. M., M.A. (Mar. 15, 1912). Lt.-Commdr. R.N.V.R.

1919 Smith, P. H. (June 1915). Lt .Scottish Horse. Palestine, 1917–18 ; France and Belgium, 1918–19.

1902 Smith, R. B., B.A. (Apr. 1, 1917). 2nd Lt. 19th Lancers. (Staff Lt. 1st Class). France, 1917–18 ; Palestine, 1918–19.

1884 Smith, W. N. E. (Aug. 7, 1914). Capt., Bt.-Maj., R. Marines (Res. of Officers).

1911 Smithers, K. O., M.A. (Sept. 2, 1914). Lt. 1/5th R. W. Kent Regt. (Capt.). India, 1914–19.

1913 **Soames,* R. E.** (Sept. 16, 1914). Lt. 8th E. Surrey Regt. France. Killed in action on the Somme on July 1, 1916.

1914 Sorley, K. W., B.A. (July 1918). Pte. 2/28th London Regt. (Artists' Rifles O.T.C.).

1880 Sorsbie, Rev. W. F., M.A. (Serving Aug. 4, 1914). Chaplain to the Forces (1st Class). *D.* § Feb. 1917.

1911 **Southern, E. B.,** B.A. (Sept. 1914). Pte. 20th R. Fusiliers. France. Died on July 20, 1916, of wounds received in action at High Wood.

1899 Spencer, A., M.A. (Nov. 24, 1915). Lt. 2/11th London Regt. (Finsbury Rifles). France. *M.C.*, Jan. 18, 1919. (Prisoner of War.)

1919 Spicer, F. P. (Jan. 1918). Cadet R.M.C., Sandhurst.

1889 [Stainer, C. L., M.A.] (May 6, 1915). Lt. 4th Oxf. & Bucks. Lt. Infty. (T.F. Res.).

1900 Steel, C. G., B.A. (Dec. 10, 1914). Capt. 10th Loyal N. Lancashire Regt.

1913 Steel, G. (Sept. 1914). Capt. 15th R. Fusiliers. Capt. 3/2nd King's African Rifles (Adjt.). German E. Africa.

1919 Steele, J. D. (Oct. 24, 1915). Flt.-Sub.-Lt. R.N.A.S. Capt. 13th Essex Regt. France, 1916–18.

1915 Stephen-Jones, W. (Sept. 17, 1915). Lt. 7th Sherwood Foresters. France, 1916–17.

1884 Sterling, A. H. B. Lt. T.F. Res., empld. Ministry of National Service.

1912 Stevens, J. L., B.A. (Aug. 1914). ‡Lt. 1/4th D.C.L.I. (Capt.). France, 1914–17 ; Palestine, 1917–18.

1911 Stevens,* T. (Sept. 29, 1914). Lt. R.A. France. *D.* France, 1916.

1912 Stevens, W. T. (Aug. 8, 1914). ‡Lt., Acting Capt., 6th Lancashire Regt. France. *D.* France, 1917.

1905 Stewart, J. C., M.A. (Nov. 9, 1914). Lt. R. Scots.

1908 Stocks, A. H., M.A. (Mar. 10, 1917). Lt. W. African Frontier Force. German E. Africa, 1917–18 ; Portuguese E. Africa, 1918.

1919 Stokoe, G. C. (Feb. 15, 1917). Lt. R.G.A. (S.R.), attd. 244th Siege Batt. France, 1917–19. *D.* France, 1919.

1913 **Stokoe, H. B.** (Sept. 7, 1914). 2nd Lt., temp. Capt., 6th K.O.Y.L.I. France, Belgium, 1915. Accidentally killed near St. Eloi, by the explosion of a rifle grenade, on Oct. 12, 1915.

1920 Stonex, E .A. P. (Sept. 26, 1914). Capt. 5th Cheshire Regt. Staff Capt. (D.A.A.G.). Salonika, Black Sea, 1917–19. *D.* Salonika, 1919.

Stoney, T. S. V. (Sept. 1917). 2nd Lt. 1st Irish Guards. Belgium. Killed in action at Passchendaele on Oct. 9, 1917.

1899 Stormonth-Darling, R., B.A. (Feb. 1915). Lt., Acting Capt., 2/1st Lothians & Border Horse. Maj., A.D.C. to G.O.C. 51st Div. France.

1908 Stotesbury, S. J., B.A. (Oct. 16, 1914). Capt. Gloucestershire Regt. France. *M.C.*, Feb. 4, 1918. *D.* France, 1917.

1909 **Stowell,* T. B.,** B.A. (Nov. 22, 1916). 2nd Lt. 3rd, attd. 8th, S. Lancashire Regt. France. *M.C.*, Aug. 16, 1917. Died on Nov. 19, 1917, of wounds received in action.

1919 Stranack, J. R. S. (Feb. 25, 1916). Lt. 3rd, attd. 9th, Seaforth Highlanders. France, Belgium, Germany, 1916–19. *M.C.*, Jan. 1, 1919. *D.* France, 1918.

1905 **Strathairn, H. W.,** B.A. (Aug. 8, 1915). 2nd Lt. 6th The Black Watch. France. Died on Nov. 16, 1916, of wounds received in action.

1912 Strong, H. W., B.A. (Oct. 7, 1914). Capt. 3rd, attd. 1/4th, Loyal N. Lancashire Regt. France, 1915–16.

1909 Strong,* J. E., M.A. (Nov. 20, 1914). Capt. Cheshire Regt., attd. No. 16 O.C.B. Gallipoli, 1915; France, 1916.

1914 Sullivan, J. (May 3, 1915). 2nd Lt. 11th S. Staffordshire Regt. Lt. R.E.

1917 Summerfield, W., B.A. (Aug. 22, 1916). Pte. Durham L.I. Salonika, Egypt.

1882 Surtees, E. A., M.A. (Serving Aug. 4, 1914). Maj. Unattached List, T.F., Repton School O.T.C.

1919 Sutcliffe, H. (Jan. 18, 1917). Lt. R.F.A. (S.R.). France, 1917–19.

1886 Sykes, Sir A. J., Bt., M.A. Lt.-Col. Cheshire Vol. Regt.

1888 Tarver, M. A. J., M.A. (July 28, 1916). 2nd Lt. Unattached List, T.F., attd. Trent College O.T.C.

1911 Taverner, E. S., B.A. (Dec. 28, 1915). Lt. 4th R. Warwickshire Regt. Lt. R.A.F. (Capt., Administrative Officer).

1914 **Tawney, R. L.** (Mar. 18, 1915). Lt. 7th Somerset L.I. (Capt.). France. *M.C.*, May 16, 1916. Missing, believed killed in action near Cambrai on Nov. 30, 1917.

1905 Teesdale, H., B.A. (Aug. 6, 1916). Lt. Inns of Court O.T.C.

1903 **Tetley, J. C. D.,** M.A. (Nov. 19, 1914). Capt. Grenadier Guards, attd. 3rd Bn. France and Belgium. Killed in action on Oct. 9, 1917.

1914 Tetlow, J. L. (Dec. 1914). Capt. 1/7th W. Riding Regt. Staff-Captain 147th Inf. Bde. France. *M.C.*, Jan. 1, 1919.

1899 Thackeray, F. S. (Serving Aug. 4, 1914). Capt. Highland L.I., attd. 9th R. Dublin Fusiliers (Lt.-Col.). France. *D.S.O.*, Jan. 1, 1917. *M.C.*, June 23, 1916. *D.* France, 1916, 1918 twice.

1912 **Thomas,* A. V.** (Oct. 8, 1914). Capt. 11th E. Surrey Regt., attd. 2nd Hampshire Regt. Gallipoli. Killed in action at Krithia on Aug. 6, 1915.

1919 Thomas, C. A. G. (Sept. 21, 1914). 2nd Lt. 7th Worcestershire Regt. 2nd Lt. R.G.A. (S.R.).

1916 Thomson, A. W., B.A. Pte. R.A.M.C. (Invalided.)

1905 Thomson, Rev. H. A., M.A. (Mar. 4, 1915). Chaplain to the Forces (4th Class).

1907 Thomson,* J. S., M.A. (Nov. 13, 1914). Lt. I.A.R.O. (Cavalry), attd. Staff. Mesopotamia. *D.* Mesopotamia, 1917.

1902 Thornton, G. E., B.M., M.A. (June 7, 1917). Capt. R.A.M.C.

1919 Thorp, G. L. (Sept. 22, 1914). 2nd Lt. 8th The Buffs (E. Kent Regt.). Lt. R.E., Signal Service (Capt.). France, 1915–19. *D.* France, 1919.
1903 Tingey, A. J. C., B.A. (Apr. 1915). Capt. R.A.M.C.
1904 Tizard, H. T., M.A. (Oct. 1914). Lt.-Col., Technical Officer, R.A.F. *A.F.C.*, Nov. 2, 1918. *D.* § Mar. 1918.
1897 Tod, M. N., M.A. (Nov. 15, 1915). Capt. Intelligence Corps (1st Class Agent). Salonika, 1915–19. *O.B.E.* (Mil.). Croix de Guerre. *D.* Salonika, 1916, 1918, 1919.
1902 Toms, E. B. (Nov. 29, 1917). Sub-Lt. R.N.V.R.
Trustram, R. P. (Feb. 1916). Lt. R.F.A. France, Belgium, Italy. *M.C.*, Oct. 10, 1917. Died on Aug. 28, 1918, of wounds received in action.
1919 Tucker, R. F. S. (Aug. 1918). 2nd Lt. R.G.A.
1914 Turner, V. C., B.A. (May 20, 1918). 2nd Lt. R.A.F. (Lt.).
1907 Tyler, G. E., B.A. (July 30, 1915). Lt. Motor M.G.C. Lt., Flight Officer, R.A.F.
1919 Unwin, J. D. (Nov 1914). Capt. 6th Northamptonshire Regt. Capt. 15th Bn. Tank Corps. France. *M.C.*, Dec. 2, 1918. *D.* France, 1918.
1895 **Valpy, O. H.** (Sept. 19, 1914). 2nd Lt. R.A.S.C. Died at Aldershot on Oct. 31, 1914.
1919 Vandeleur, C. R. P. (Oct. 1914). Inns of Court O.T.C.
1913 Van Santwood, G., B.A., B.Litt. (Jan. 1918). ‡2nd Lt. 167th Inf., U.S. Army. France. Croix de Guerre.
1914 **Vaughton,* G. E.** (Oct. 1915). 2nd Lt. 1/8th Essex Cyclist Regt. France. Killed in action near Cambrai on Nov. 20, 1917.
1891 Vincent, R. H. (June 1915). Capt. R.A.M.C.
1911 **Vincent-Jackson, M. J.** (Sept. 1914). Lt. 11th Sherwood Foresters (Capt.). France. Killed in action near Armentières on Feb. 5, 1916.
1898 Waddell-Dudley, A. N. (Serving Aug. 4, 1914). Maj. R.H.A. France. *D.* France, 1918.
1919 Waddington, A. H. (Oct. 8, 1916). Lt. 3rd, attd. 1/5th, Somerset L.I., Egypt.
1884 Waddington, C. W., M.A., *C.I.E.*, *M.V.O.*, (Apr. 1, 1917). Lt.-Col. I.A.R.O., attd. 2/17th Bombay, Baroda, and Central India Railway Bn. India.
1919 Waddington, W. P. (May 29, 1915). ‡Lt. 18th Lancashire Fusiliers. France.
Walford, W. G. (Aug. 15, 1914). Lt., Acting Capt., R.E. (S.R.), attd. R.A.F. France. Killed in action on Nov. 4, 1918.
1893 Walker, A. W. (Oct. 20, 1914). Capt. Staffordshire Yeomanry, attd. 6th S. Staffordshire Regt. (Maj.). France.
1910 Walker, J. P. S., B.M., M.A., (Feb. 1916). Surgeon Lt. R.N. North Sea, 1916; Aegean Sea; Dover and Belgian Coasts.
1902 Wallace, D., B.A. (July 28, 1917). Sub-Lt. R.N.V.R.
1913 **Wallace,* J. R.** (Aug. 6, 1914). 2nd Lt. 1st R. Scots Fusiliers. France, Belgium. Died on Apr. 22, 1915, of wounds received in action near Ypres.
1881 Walters, P. M., M.A. (Aug. 5, 1914). ‡2nd Lt. Inns of Court O.T.C. Acting Capt. attd. No. 14 O.C.B.
1908 **Wand-Tetley,* C. E.,** B.A. (Aug. 22, 1914). Lt. 9th Lancashire Fusiliers. France, 1914–15. *D.* France, 1914. Missing, presumed killed in action, on Aug. 22, 1915.

1892 Warner, P. F., B.A. (Aug. 12, 1914). Capt. Inns of Court O.T.C., attd. R.A.F. *M.B.E.* (Mil.). *D.* § Feb. 1917.

1910 **Waterhouse,* A.,** B.A. (Aug. 17, 1914). 2nd Lt. King's Own (R. Lancaster Regt.). Belgium. Killed in action at Meteren, near Hazebrouck, on Oct. 13, 1914.

1911 Watkins, J. K., B.C.L. (1917). Maj. Field Artillery, U.S. Army.

1919 Watson, H. G. (Sept. 28, 1914). Capt. 16th Manchester Regt. France. *M.C.*, May 5, 1919.

1882 Watson, H. S., B.A. (Mobilized Aug. 1914). Capt. Glamorgan Yeomanry,

1898 Watson, J. M. H., M.A. Lce.-Corpl. R. Sussex Regt.

1913 Watson,* L. H., B.A. (Aug. 19, 1914). Capt. 5th Highland L.I. Gallipoli, 1915; Egypt, 1916; Palestine, 1918; France, 1918. *M.C.*, Aug. 24, 1918.

1919 Watt, R. C. (Apr. 2, 1917). Lt. R.G.A.

1898 **Welch, H. E.** (Serving Aug. 4, 1914). Lt.-Col. 6th Shropshire L.I. France, Belgium. *D.S.O.*, Nov. 19, 1917; *Bar*, Feb. 18, 1918. *D.* France, 1917, 1918. Killed in action south of Amiens on Mar. 29, 1918.

1914 Wharton, L. E., B.A. (Apr. 7, 1915). ‡2nd Lt. H.Q. 19th Bde., R.H.A. Egypt, Palestine, Syria.

1919 Whinney, H. C. D. (Sept. 1918). Cadet R.E.

1884 Whitehouse, A. W., B.A. (1917). Capt. U. S. Army.

1911 Whitfield,* H. F., M.A. (Aug. 29, 1914). Lt. 1/4th The Buffs (E. Kent Regt.) (Capt.). Aden, 1915–16; India, 1914–15, 1916–19.

1909 Whitfield,* J. G., M.A. (Dec. 27, 1914). Lt. 4th The Buffs (E. Kent Regt.). France.

1919 Whitmore, A. (Jan. 1917). ‡Lt. King's Own (R. Lancaster Regt.). France.

1914 **Wiggett, A. J.** (Mar. 1915). 2nd Lt. 13th K.R.R.C. France and Belgium. Died on Mar. 15, 1916, at Ayette, as prisoner of war, of wounds received in action at Bailleul on Mar. 8.

1911 Wiggin,* A. F. H. (Oct. 1914). Capt. 13th Rifle Brigade. Staff-Captain, Arab Bureau, Cairo. France, 1915; Egypt, 1918–19.

1910 Wightwick, H. E. (Aug. 14, 1914). Capt. 4th Cameronians, W. Africa.

1907 Wightwick,* H. W., B.A. (Mobilized Aug. 4, 1914). Capt. 12th London Regt. (The Rangers) (Staff-Captain). France. *M.C.*, Apr. 25, 1918.

1899 Wild, C. H., B.A. (Sept. 11, 1914). Capt., Acting Maj., 8th London Regt. (Post Office Rifles) (Lt.-Col.). France and Belgium, 1915–19; Italy, 1917–18. *D.* France, 1915.

1908 Wiles,* H. H., M.A. (Oct. 3, 1914). 2nd Lt. Indian Army. Capt. Labour Corps (Maj.). India. *D.* § Aug. 1919.

1907 Wilkins,* Rev. B. D., M.A. (June 15, 1916). Chaplain to the Forces (4th Class), attd. 9th Norfolk Regt. France, 1916–19. *M.C.*, Mar. 8, 1919.

1910 Wilkins,* H. G., M.A. (Aug. 24, 1914). Capt. 4th Gloucestershire Regt. Italy.

1910 Wilkinson,* A. M., B.A. (Aug. 1914). Capt. 9th Hampshire Regt. Maj. R.A.F. (Lt.-Col.). France. *D.S.O.*, Oct. 20, 1916; *Bar*, May 26, 1917. *D.* France, 1916, 1917.

1903 Wilkinson, N. R. E., B.A. (Aug. 20, 1914). Capt. 19th Divl. Train, R.A.S.C. France, 1915–19. *O.B.E.* (Mil.). *D.* France, 1918, 1919.

1919 Williams, C. W. (Sept. 1917). Lt. Coldstream Guards. France, 1918.
1908 Williams, E. H., B.A. (Jan. 24, 1915). Capt. 9th Queen's (R. W. Surrey Regt.). (Resigned on account of ill health.)
1908 Williams, Rev. J. L., M.A. (Mar. 1, 1918). Chaplain to the Forces (4th Class).
1919 Williams, J. M. (June 6, 1917). ‡2nd Lt. 43rd Cavalry, U.S. Army.
1884 Williams, Sir Rhys, Bt., B.A., *K.C.* (Mobilized Aug. 5, 1914). Lt.-Col. Welsh Guards, empld. Admiralty. Belgium, France, Russia, Italy. *D.S.O.*, Nov. 4, 1915. Order of Vladimir (4th Class). Persian Order of the Lion and Sun (2nd Class). *D.* France, 1915.
1903 Williams, R. W., B.A. (Apr. 10, 1915). Lt. R.F.A.
1912 **Williams,* T. W.** (Sept. 1914). Lt. 3rd Northamptonshire Regt., attd. Loyal N. Lancashire Regt. Belgium and France, 1914–15. Killed in action at Rue du Bois, near Richebourg St. Vaast, on May 9, 1915.
1912 **Wills,* A. G.** (Sept. 4, 1914). Lt. 9th Sherwood Foresters. Gallipoli. Killed in action at Suvla Bay on Aug. 9, 1915.
1916 Willway, A. C. C. (May 12, 1917). 2nd Lt. R.E. Egypt, 1918–19. (Invalided, Apr. 2, 1919.)
1895 Wilson, Rev. C. H., M.A. (May 14, 1918). Chaplain to the Forces (4th Class).
1893 Wilson, Rev. L. H., M.A. (Jan. 1, 1918). Chaplain to the Forces (4th Class).
1901 Wilson, Rev. P. H., M.A. (July 16, 1915). Chaplain to the Forces (4th Class). France. *O.B.E.* (Mil.). *D.* § Feb. 1917; France, 1915, 1919.
1909 Wilson, R. E. (Serving Aug. 4, 1914). Capt. 3rd Hampshire Regt. Lt., Flying Officer, R.A.F. France. (Prisoner of war.)
1902 Winterbotham, J. P., B.A. (Sept. 18, 1914). ‡Capt. 1/5th Gloucestershire Regt. France and Belgium. *M.C.*, Jan. 1, 1918. *D.* France, 1917 twice.
1910 Wise, H. D. (Aug. 1914). ‡Lt. 18th Hussars (Capt. and Adjt.). France, 1915–18; Germany, 1918–19. *M.C.*, Jan. 1, 1919. *D.* France, 1917.
1912 Wisely,* G. L. K. (Aug. 26, 1914). Capt., Acting Maj., R.F.A. France. *M.C.*, Jan. 1, 1918. *D.* France, 1918.
1899 Wix, E. H. Cadet, O.C.B.
1920 Wood, A. H. (June 6, 1917). Lt. R.A.F.
1884 Woodbridge, C. M., B.A. Capt. Bucks. Vol. Regt.
1903 Woodcock, J. B. H., M.A. (Mobilized Aug. 1914). Maj. Pembrokeshire Yeomanry, attd. 24th Welsh Regt. France. *D.S.O.*, June 3, 1919. *D.* France, 1919.
1912 Woodhouse, A. C., B.A. (Aug. 1914). Capt. Essex Regt., attd. 52nd Bedfordshire Regt. France, 1915. *D.* § Mar. 1919.
1900 Woodhouse, H. M., B.A. (May 28, 1915). Lt. Nottinghamshire Yeomanry, attd. R.A.F.
1902 Woodhouse, R. P., B.A. (May 26, 1915). Capt. Suffolk Yeomanry (Maj.). Capt. M.G.C.
1910 **Woods, B. H.** (Aug. 4, 1914). 2nd Lt. R.E. Egypt. Accidentally killed at the Suez Canal on Dec. 17, 1914.
1883 Woods, Rev. W. M., M.A. (Mobilized 1914). Chaplain to the Forces (4th Class, Hon. 2nd Class). Egypt and Palestine. *O.B.E.* (Mil.). V.D. *D.* Palestine, 1918.

1897 Workman, E. S., M.A. (Sept. 1916). Lt. R.G.A. (S.R.).

1903 **Worthington, S.,** B.A. (Nov. 1914). Lt. 1/1st Leicestershire R.H.A. Egypt, Palestine. Killed in action near Beth Horan on Nov. 28, 1917.

1907 **Worthington,* W. G.,** B.A. (Mobilized Aug. 4, 1914). Maj. 12th London Regt. (The Rangers). France and Belgium, 1914–18. *M.C.*, Jan. 1, 1917. Died on Apr. 27, 1918, of wounds received in action.

1886 Wreford-Brown, C., B.A. (Oct. 14, 1916). Lt. Grenadier Guards, attd. O.C.B.

1893 Wreford-Brown, Rev. G., M.A. (Mar. 9, 1915). Chaplain to the Forces (4th Class).

1909 **Wright, B.,** B.A. Pte. R. Fusiliers. France. Killed in action, May, 1916.

1885 Wyndham, H. J. (June 4, 1915). Lt. R. Defence Corps.

1919 Yeatman, R. J. (Oct. 1914). Lt. R.F.A. France. *M.C.*, Oct. 20, 1916.

1903 **Yorke, J. H. L.,** B.A. (Mobilized Aug. 1914). Capt. Pembrokeshire Yeomanry, attd. 24th Welsh Regt. France. *M.C.*, Feb. 4, 1918. Killed in action on Dec. 27, 1917.

QUEEN'S COLLEGE

1918 Abraham, B. W. (Feb. 5, 1915). Lt. 9th E. Lancashire Regt. and M.G.C. France, 1916–17.

1902 Aglionby, Rev. J. O., M.A. (Apr. 1915). Pte. R.A.M.C. ‡Chaplain to the Forces (4th Class). France, Belgium, 1915–17. *M.C.*, June 4, 1917.

1899 Agnew, H. C., M.A. (Sept. 4, 1914). ‡Lt. 21st King's (Liverpool Regt.). Lt., Acting Capt., 31st Bn. M.G.C. France, 1916–18. *D.* France, 1917, 1919.

1910 Alington, J. M., M.A. Worcestershire Regt.

1919 Allan, S. L. (Aug. 1, 1914). ‡Lt. 10th (Scottish) King's (Liverpool Regt.). France.

1908 Almond,* C. S. (Oct. 8, 1914). Lt. 5th W. Yorkshire Regt., empld. Ministry of Labour.

1891 Alston, C. W. (Oct. 8, 1914). Maj., Acting Lt.-Col., S. African Heavy Artillery. Palestine. Order of the Nile (3rd Class). *D.* Palestine, 1919.

1919 Andrew, T. C. (Jan. 3, 1917). Lt. K.R.R.C. France, 1917–19.

1919 Arkell, A. J. (Aug. 12, 1916). Lt. Flying Officer, R.A.F. France. *M.C.*, May 31, 1918.

1907 **Armitage,* A. W.,** B.A. (Oct. 1914). Capt. 12th, attd. 8th, K.O.Y.L.I. (Adjt.). France. Reported missing, presumed killed in action at Le Sars on Oct. 1, 1916.

1919 Arning, C. W. (Aug. 24, 1917). ‡2nd Lt. R.A.F. France, 1918–19.

1915 Aston, A. V. (July 14, 1916). Lt. R.F.A. France. *M.C.*, July 26, 1917.

1899 Atkinson, C. F. (Sept. 5, 1914). Maj. General List. Intelligence Instructor, American G.H.Q. France. Order of St. Anne (3rd Class). Distinguished Service Medal (America).

1875 Backwell, Rev. H., M.A. (Serving Aug. 4, 1914). Chaplain R.N., R.N. Hospital, Haslar.

1913 Bailey,* V. A., B.A. (June 6, 1918). Pioneer R.E. Signals (Pioneer Instructor).

1903 Baldwin, R. de C., M.A. (June 6, 1917). Capt. W. African Frontier Force. Sierra Leone, German E. Africa, Portuguese E. Africa.

1917 Bannister, W. P. (June 28, 1918). 2nd Lt. Lincolnshire Regt. (on demobilization).

1890 Barber, H. C. (Oct. 1914). Capt. 3rd Vol. Bn. Norfolk Regt.

1919 Barber, S. (June 1, 1918). Lce.-Cpl. 4th Border Regt.

1917 Barford, L. J. (Sept. 5, 1918). 2nd Lt. 5th Bedfordshire Regt.

1911 Barley, L. J. (Aug. 4, 1914). Capt., Bt.-Maj., The Cameronians (S.R.) (Lt.-Col.). Maj., Superintendent Anti-Gas Dept., Ministry of Munitions. France, 1914–17; Italy, 1917–18. *D.S.O.*, Jan. 1, 1917. Croix de Guerre. Cavalier of the Order of St. Maurice and St. Lazarus. Officer of the Order of the Crown of Italy. *D.* France, 1916 twice; Italy, 1918.

1899 **Barr, P. S. St. J.** (Oct. 11, 1914). Cpl. 2nd Canadian Mounted Rifles. France and Belgium. Killed in action at Ypres on July 9, 1916.

1897 Barton, J. H. R., M.A. (Serving Aug. 4, 1914). Lt. Unattached List, T.F., Newcastle-under-Lyne High School O.T.C.

1906 Bass, Rev. W. H., M.A. (Sept. 8, 1916). Chaplain to the Forces (4th Class).

1915 Baxter, J. A. (Apr. 10, 1916). 3rd Writer R.N. H.M.S. *Attentive II*, Dunkerque.

1895 Beattie, Rev. E. H., M.A. (Mar. 21, 1917). Chaplain to the Forces (3rd Class). S.C.F. 57th Div. France, 1917–18; Switzerland, 1918. *M.C.*, Sept. 16, 1918. *D.* France, 1917.

1919 Beckett, T. (Feb. 25, 1918). Pte. 4th K.O.Y.L.I.

1906 Beddard, Rev. F. G., M.A. (May 1916). Chaplain R.N., H.M.S. *Orvieto.* Northern Patrol.

1906 Beech, S. E., B.A. (July 30, 1915). Maj. Canadian Army Medical Corps.

1895 Belcher, Rev. A. H., M.A. (Serving Aug. 4, 1914). Maj. Unattached List, T.F., Brighton College O.T.C.

1909 Bell, J., M.A. (Dec. 11, 1914). Lt. 2/5th Somerset L.I. (Capt. and Adjt.). India.

1911 **Bellamy, J. H.,** B.A. (Sept. 24, 1914). ‡2nd Lt. 11th Sherwood Foresters. Belgium, France, 1915–16. Died on Oct. 4, 1916, of wounds received in action at Le Sars.

1911 **Bender,* A. C.,** B.A. (Sept. 1914). Lt. 15th Hampshire Regt. (Capt. and Adjt.). France and Belgium. Killed in action on Sept. 20, 1917.

1904 **Bentham, T.,** B.Sc. (1916). Lt. R.A.M.C. Malta. *D.* Malta. Died on Mar. 12, 1919, of illness contracted while on active service.

1888 Berridge, R. (Dec. 1914). Lt. R.N.V.R. France, 1914–15.

1910 Berrisford,* E. A., M.A. (Sept. 1, 1914). Maj. Acting Lt.-Col. Special Bde., R.E. France and Belgium, 1915–19. *M.C.*, Jan. 1, 1917.

1917 Berry, E. A. (Sept. 5, 1918). ‡2nd Lt. Grenadier Guards.

1896 Best, J. S., B.A. 2nd Lt. Unattached List, T.F., Brighton College O.T.C.

1919 Beven, F. R. H. (June 7, 1918). 2nd Lt. K.O.Y.L.I. (on demobilization).

1909 Bingemann, L. S., B.A. (Sept. 21, 1918). Lt. Calcutta Light Horse. India.

1919 Bion, W. R. (Dec. 28, 1915). Capt. Tank Corps. France. *D.S.O.*, Feb. 18, 1918. Croix de Chevalier de la Légion d'Honneur.

1906 Birchall,* J. R., M.A. (Oct. 1, 1914). Capt., Acting Maj., 2/4th Devonshire Regt., attd. 1/123rd Outram's Rifles, Indian Army. Egypt and Palestine. *D.* Palestine 1919.

1911 Birch-Jones,* A. F., M.A. (Aug. 22, 1914). Capt. 5th Worcestershire Regt. France, N. Russia. *M.C.*, Aug. 18, 1917.

1907 Blackman, B., B.A. (Nov. 29, 1917). 2nd Lt. Air Service (Aeronautics), U.S. Army.

1911 Blaker,* R. S., M.A. (Sept. 1915). Lt. R.F.A. (S.R.). France, Palestine.

1900 **Bland, A. E.,** B.A. (Aug. 1914). Capt. 22nd Manchester Regt. France. Killed in action in the Battle of the Somme on July 1, 1916.

1906 **Blencowe, L. C.** (Aug. 26, 1916). 2nd Lt. 10th King's (Liverpool Regt.). France and Belgium, 1917. Killed in action in Belgium on June 29, 1917.

Bloomer, A. K. (Aug. 1914). Pte. 6th W. Yorkshire Regt. Belgium, France. Killed in action near Thiepval on July 1, 1916.

1911 Bloomfield,* C. W., B.A. (June 26, 1915). Lt. 3rd S. Staffordshire Regt., attd. 53rd Sherwood Foresters (Capt.). France, Germany. (Prisoner of war, 1917–18.)

1919 Blunden, E. C. (Sept. 2, 1915). Lt. 7th R. Sussex Regt. France. *M.C.*, Jan. 26, 1917.

1896 Bolster, R. C., M.A. (Aug. 4, 1914). ‡Maj. Punjab Light Horse. India.

1898 Bolus, E. J., B.A. (Mobilized 1914). Capt. 26th (Sind) Bn. I.D.F. India.

1907 Bond, C. B. (Oct. 7, 1915). Capt. 5th Middlesex Regt. Capt., Flying Officer, R.A.F. (Maj.). France.

1891 Bousfield, H. D., B.A. (Mobilized Aug. 1914). Lt.-Col. 7th W. Yorkshire Regt. France. *C.M.G.* *D.S.O.*, Jan. 14, 1916. T.D. French Croix de Guerre. Belgian Croix de Guerre. *D.* France, 1915, 1917. (Prisoner of war.)

Bowyer, J. W. (Sept. 1914). Capt. 13th Rifle Brigade. France, 1915–17. Killed in action at Monchy le Preux on Apr. 10, 1917.

1909 Brayshay, K., M.A. (1915). Gnr. Artillery Coy., Hong-Kong Defence Corps.

1912 Briggs,* W. N., B.A. (Aug. 28, 1914). Capt. 1/5th King's Own (R. Lancaster Regt.). Belgium, France, Germany, 1915–19. *D.* France, 1916.

1908 Britton, F. A., M.A. (Oct. 1914). Gnr. R.G.A. Hong-Kong.

1919 Broadbent, C. S. (Feb. 7, 1918). 2nd Lt. Tank Corps.

1899 Brockbank, T., M.A. (Nov. 12, 1915). Pte. 10th Border Regt.

1907 Brooke, Rev. J. M. W. (Nov. 20, 1914). Chaplain to the Forces (4th Class).

1913 **Brown,* A. C.** (Aug. 1914). Lt. 8th S. Staffordshire Regt. France. Killed in action near Fricourt on July 2, 1916.

1891 Brown, A. V., B.A. (Nov. 26, 1914). Pte. Singapore Vol. Corps.

Brown, B. (Sept. 1914). ‡Capt. 16th Rifle Brigade. France. Killed in action in the Battle of the Somme on Sept. 3, 1916.

1896 Brown, W. H., M.A. (Serving Aug. 4, 1914). Lt. Unattached List, T.F., Mill Hill School O.T.C.

1900 Brown, Rev. W. H., M.A. (Sept. 1915). Chaplain to the Forces (4th Class). France, Germany.

1913 Browne, E. S. (Mobilized Aug. 1914.) ‡Lt. R.G.A. Salonika, Palestine, France, N. Russia. *M.C.*, June 26–7, 1919.

1912 Buckley, S. E., B.A. (Aug. 26, 1914). 2nd Lt. General List. Staff-Captain. France. *D.* France, 1919.

1895 Bulkeley, B. W. L., B.A. (Dec. 9, 1915). Capt. 8th Sherwood Foresters (Staff-Captain).

1907 Bunbury, E. J., B.A. (Aug. 4, 1914). ‡Capt. 3rd Grenadier Guards. India, France, Germany. *M.C.*, Feb. 15, 1919.

1899 Burgoyne, A. H. (Sept. 1, 1914). Maj. Middlesex Regt. (Invalided 1916). Maj. attd. Indian Army (1917). Lt.-Col. Special Lists, Controller of Priority Dept., Ministry of Munitions (1918). Belgium, France, Italy, Palestine, Indian Frontier. Croix d'Officier de la Légion d'Honneur. Commander of the Order of the Crown of Italy.

1910 Burridge, E. H., B.A. (Oct. 7, 1914). Lt. 6th Devonshire Regt.

1918 Burton-Baldry, W. B. (Aug. 20, 1914). R.N.V.R. ‡Capt. 3rd Oxf. & Bucks. Lt. Infty., empld. Ministry of National Service. *O.B.E.* (Mil.). *D.* § Aug. 1917, Jan. 1918.

1903 **Butcher, A. J. B.** (Sept. 1915). 2nd Lt. 6th, attd. 17th, K.R.R.C. France. Killed in action at Beaumont Hamel on Sept. 3, 1916.

1919 Butler, G. V. (Sept. 26, 1916). Lt. Tank Corps. France, Belgium, 1917–18.

1919 Butler, H. D. (Jan. 22, 1918). 2nd Lt., Flying Officer, R.A.F.

1912 Butler,* W. E., B.A. (Mobilized Aug. 1914). 2nd Lt. Manchester Regt. (S.R.). France, N. Russia. (Prisoner of war.) *D.* Russia, 1919. *D.* May 5, 1919.

1907 Caiger,* F. E., B.A. (June 1915). ‡Capt. 3rd Manchester Regt. France, Germany.

1891 Cain, Rev. C. S., M.A. (May 11, 1911). Chaplain to the Forces (4th Class), attd. 4th Essex Regt. *D.* § Mar. 1918.

Calvert, R. M. (Apr. 8, 1915). 2nd Lt. 17th Manchester Regt. France. Killed in action in Trônes Wood on July 9, 1916.

1912 **Campbell,* B.** (Aug. 15, 1914). 2nd Lt. 2nd R. Warwickshire Regt. France, 1914. Killed in action near Fleurbaix on Dec. 18, 1914.

1895 Cane, L. A., B.Mus. (Feb. 14, 1915). 2nd Lt. Unattached List, T.F., Mill Hill School O.T.C.

1920 Carpenter, F. E. (Sept. 14, 1914). ‡Capt. 3rd Sherwood Foresters. Egypt, 1915–16 ; France, 1916–18.

1914 Carrie, C. R. Hon. Capt. Canadian Y.M.C.A. France. *D.* France, 1917.

1919 Carruthers, G. I. (Jan. 18, 1918). Pte. R.A.F.

1919 Carter, C. W. (Apr. 13, 1917). 2nd Lt. 45th Bde., R.F.A. (S.R.). France, 1918. (Wounded and prisoner of war, May–Nov. 1918.)

1919 Carter, G. S. H. (Nov. 24, 1916). Lt. R.G.A. Italy, Egypt.

1911 **Carter,* J. A.** (Aug. 1914). Lt. 6th D.C.L.I. (Capt.). France. Died as a prisoner on Apr. 2, 1917, of wounds received in action.

1919 Carter, R. F. A. (Sept. 1918). ‡2nd Lt. R.F.A. (T.F.) (on demobilization).

1913 Carter,* W. N. (Aug. 23, 1914). Capt. 9th London Regt. (Queen Victoria's Rifles). France, 1914–15, 1917–19.

1902 **Caruthers-Little, A. W. P.** (Serving Aug. 4, 1914). Capt. and Adjt. 2nd, attd. 5th, Dorsetshire Regt. Gallipoli. Killed in action at Suvla Bay, Aug. 5–8, 1915.

1909 Chadwick,* A. W. (Aug. 29, 1914). Maj. 11th Hampshire Regt. France, 1915–16, 1917–19. *O.B.E.* (Mil.). *D.* France, 1919.

1900 Charke, Rev. C., M.A. (Feb. 5, 1917). Chaplain to the Forces (4th Class).

1913 Charsley, C. R. (Dec. 4, 1914). Lt. 3rd, attd. 2/5th, Gloucestershire Regt.

1919 Chorley, A. C. (Apr. 8, 1918). Pte. 52nd S. Wales Borderers.

1913 Chorley, R. S. T., B.A. (July 13, 1918). Cadet R.A.S.C., M.T. (Lce.-Cpl.).

1906 Chute,* Rev. C. B., M.A. (Dec. 30, 1916). Chaplain to the Forces (4th Class). Salonika, Asia Minor.

1903 Chute, R. A. J., M.A. (July 1918). Pte. 130th Field Amb., R.A.M.C. France.

1904 Clark, A. J., B.A. (Apr. 11, 1916). Lt. R.A.S.C. Capt. R.A.F. France.

1912 **Clarke, W. H.** (Aug. 5, 1914). 2nd Lt. 3rd Worcestershire Regt. France and Belgium. Killed in action at Spanbroek, Molen, on Mar. 13, 1915.

1914 **Claxton, E. A.** (Nov. 1916). 2nd Lt. 18th K.R.R.C. France and Belgium. Killed in action at Hollebeke on July 31, 1917.

1916 **Clive-Smith, C. M.** (Aug. 29, 1917). 2nd Lt. 12th Rifle Brigade. France. Killed in action on Mar. 24, 1918.
1907 Clough, G. H., B.A. (Dec. 3, 1915). Lt. Unattached List, T.F., Hymers College O.T.C.
1915 Coates, E. T. (Aug. 1916). ‡Lt. R.A.S.C., M.T. France, Mesopotamia.
1896 Cockburn, J. G. H., B.A. (Aug. 5, 1915). Capt. 6th R. Sussex Regt., empld. Military Accts. Dept.
1903 Coe, G. D. (Dec. 24, 1914). Lt., Acting Maj., R.G.A.
1913 **Collett,* A. L.** (1914). 2nd Lt. 8th Gloucestershire Regt. France and Belgium. Died on Sept. 18, 1917, of wounds received in action.
1907 **Collins, H. C.** (Apr. 13, 1915). Lt. 24th Manchester Regt. France. Killed in action on Feb. 11, 1917.
1900 Collins, J. C. (Dec. 2, 1913). Capt. 7th Hampshire Regt., empld. War Office.
1920 Collins, S. E. (Mar. 6, 1916). Sergt. 1st (Garr.) Bn. Gordon Highlanders. India, N.W. Frontier, 1917–19.
1919 Comley, W. J. (Jan. 5, 1917). Pioneer, 20th Corps Signal Coy., R.E. Egypt and Palestine, 1917–19.
1899 Constable, H. L., B.A. (Mar. 22, 1915). Lt. 3rd Yorkshire Regt., attd. 183rd Tunnelling Coy., R.E. France.
1915 **Cook, L. N.** (Dec. 28, 1915). 2nd Lt. 3rd, attd. 11th, King's Own (R. Lancaster Regt.). France, 1916–17. *M.C.*, Oct. 14, 1916. Italian Silver Medal for Military Valour. Killed in action at Villers Plouich on July 7, 1917.
Coombes, J. E. H., (Sept. 24, 1916). Lt. 1/5th Border Regt. France, 1917–18. Died on Apr. 1, 1918, of wounds received in action at Hangard.
1884 Cooper, E. C., M.A. (Sept. 1914). Lt. Victoria College, Jersey, O.T.C.
1919 Cornes, J. (Dec. 1916). 2nd Lt. Northumberland Fusiliers. France. *M.C.*, Dec. 2, 1918; *Bar*, Apr. 2, 1919.
1915 **Coulthwaite, J.** (Jan. 1916). 2nd Lt. 2nd Border Regt. France. Killed in action on Aug. 5, 1917.
1894 Coupland, R. M., B.A. (July 5, 1915). Lt., Acting Capt., 5th K.O.Y.L.I.
1909 **Craven,* Rev. G. E.**, M.A. (1917). Chaplain to the Forces (4th Class). Salonika. Died at Salonika on Dec. 7, 1918.
1913 Cripps, A. C. R.M.C., Sandhurst.
1911 Cripps,* R. T., M.A. (Oct. 23, 1914). Lt. General List, attd. R.E. (Signals). France.
1908 Crisp,* L. L., B.A. (Sept. 3, 1914). ‡Capt. 13th Cheshire Regt. Capt. Labour Corps (since Apr. 1918). France, 1915–16, 1916–19.
Crofts, E. C. L. (July 1916). 2nd Lt. 1st K.O. Scottish Borderers. France. Died on May 1, 1918, of wounds received in action at Estaires on Apr. 11.
1905 Crofts, J. E. V., B.A., B.Litt. R.A.M.C.
1914 **Crompton, A. H.** (Jan. 1, 1915). 2nd Lt. 7th Border Regt. France. Killed in action at Fricourt on July 3, 1916.
1910 Cronshaw,* T. J., M.A. (Mar. 1915). Lt. B/3 Coy., Nigerian Field Force. Cameroons.
1912 Croom-Johnson, H., B.A. (Oct. 1914). Lt., Acting Capt., 4th Worcestershire Regt. Gallipoli, 1915; France, 1916–18. *M.C.*, July 18, 1917; *Bar*, Sept. 16, 1918.
1905 Crowther, W. V. (Feb. 1, 1917). 2nd Lt. R.G.A.

1906 [Cruttwell, C. R. M. F., M.A.] (Aug. 19, 1914). Capt. 4th R. Berkshire Regt. Capt. General Staff, Military Intelligence, War Office. France and Belgium, 1915.

1909 Cuningham, R. M., B.A. (Aug. 1, 1916). 2nd Lt. Special Lists. Staff-Lt. (2nd Class). *D.*

1912 Curtis, P. V. (Sept. 15, 1914). ‡Lt. 2/4th Border Regt. Burma, India.

1898 **Curwen, E. S.,** M.A. (1914). Pte. York & Lancaster Regt. France. Killed in action in the Battle of the Somme on July 1, 1916.

1919 Daldy, A. C. (May 1, 1918). ‡2nd Lt. R.G.A. (on demobilization).

1911 Dalton,* A. H. (Apr. 3, 1914). Lt. 1st County of London Yeomanry. Lt., Flying Officer, R.A.F. (since Apr. 1918).

1904 Daniel, R. E. H. (Dec. 1915). Capt. Administrative Officer, R.A.F. France. *D.* § June, 1919.

1889 Danks, E., B.A. (Apr. 1, 1917). Maj. Volunteer Defence Corps, India. India.

1911 Darke, H. E., D.Mus. (June 19, 1918). Sergt.-Maj. R.A.F.

1892 David, H. L., B.A. (Aug. 21, 1917). Lt. 3rd (Garr.) Bn. R. Welch Fusiliers. India.

1919 Davies, J. A. B. (Feb. 21, 1917). 2nd Lt. R.F.A. (Capt.). France.

1907 **Davies, L.,** M.A. (Oct. 1915). Lt. 9th Rifle Brigade (Capt.). France. Killed in action at Wancourt, near Arras, on June 3, 1917.

1912 Davies,* P. H., B.A. (Nov. 1914). Capt., Acting Maj., 203rd Siege Batt., R.G.A. France, Belgium. *M.C.*, June 3, 1919.

1906 Davis, E. G., M.A. (Sept. 23, 1914). Capt. 8th Essex Regt.

1899 Davis, H. J. (Mar. 3, 1917). Lt. R.N.V.R. (Motor Boat Service).

1909 Davis, L. M. (June 27, 1917). ‡2nd Lt. 3rd County of London Yeomanry. (Invalided.)

1912 Dawson, W. H. H., B.A. (Sept. 22, 1914). Capt. 17th Manchester Regt. France, India, Mesopotamia, Persia. *M.C.*, Jan. 10, 1917.

1919 Dawson, W. W. (Oct. 1916). ‡2nd Lt. Northumberland Fusiliers. Malta.

1909 de Cologan,* A. T. B., B.A. (Mobilized Aug. 1914). Capt. 1/5th London Regt. (London Rifle Brigade). France.

1913 de Ribes, Comte J. E. (Aug. 2, 1914). Sous-Lt. Infanterie, French Army. Attaché, French Embassy, London. France. Croix de Chevalier de la Légion d'Honneur. Croix de Guerre.

1913 de Sausmarez, H. G. T., B.A. (Nov. 12, 1915). Lt. R.G.A. Salonika, 1916–17; Palestine, 1917–18; France and Belgium, 1918.

1903 di Cesnola, Conte A. P., B.Sc. (1915). Tenente d'Artigliera, Italian Army. Italy.

1903 **Dickinson, L. T.,** B.A. (Aug. 12, 1914). Tpr. N. Somerset Yeomanry. France, Belgium. Killed in action at Ypres on Nov. 17, 1914.

1896 Dickinson, N., B.A. (Sept. 2, 1914). Capt. 5th Loyal N. Lancashire Regt.

1912 Disbrowe,* H. C., B.A. (Aug. 15, 1914). Capt. 3rd Lincolnshire Regt. (Capt. and Adjt.). France, Belgium, 1914–15.

1914 **Dixon, O. D.** (Mar. 13, 1915). Lt. K.O.Y.L.I. France, Belgium. Died on service on Nov. 4, 1918.

1915 Dixon, P. E. (Feb. 27, 1916). C.Q.M.S. 141st Army Troops Coy., R.E. France. *M.M.*, Feb. 22, 1918.

1891 Dobson, J., M.A. (Serving Aug. 4, 1914). Capt. Unattached List, T.F., Wellington College O.T.C.

1919 Dodd, T. A. J. M. (Mar. 4, 1918). 2nd Lt. 5th Grenadier Guards.
1916 Dodds, H. R. (Jan. 18, 1917). 2nd Lt. 6th Sherwood Foresters. Belgium, France, 1917–18.
1913 Dodson, G. H. (Sept. 1914). 2nd Lt. 4th Northamptonshire Regt. (Resigned on account of ill health, 1915.) Died on Nov. 13, 1918.
1914 **Douglas, A. G.** (July 2, 1915). Lt. 1st Leicestershire Regt. France. Killed in action at Beaumont Hamel on Aug. 15, 1916.
1919 Douie, C. O. G. (Jan. 9, 1915). Lt. 1st Dorsetshire Regt. Belgium, France, Italy.
1897 Dowding, S. E. H., M.A. (Mar. 30, 1917). Bomdr. R.G.A.
1914 Drescher, H. A. E. (May 6, 1918). Observer Flight Cadet, R.A.F.
Drew, F. J. (June 1917). 2nd Lt. R.G.A. (T.F.). France, 1917–18. Killed in action near Arras on Mar. 28, 1918.
1911 **Duguid,* C. F.** (Feb. 23, 1915). Capt. 22nd Manchester Regt. France. *D.S.O.*, May 11, 1917. *M.C.*, Mar. 3, 1917. *D.* France, 1917. Killed in action at Bullecourt, May 12–15, 1917.
1892 Edmunds, L. W., M.A. (May 2, 1915). Lt.-Commdr. R.N.V.R *O.B.E.* (Mil.).
1919 Edmunds, N. F. (June 25, 1915). Paymaster Lt. R.N.R., H.M.S. *Resolution.* Atlantic, Grand Fleet.
1909 Edmunds,* P. J., B.A. (Nov. 25, 1914). Capt. R.E., empld. War Office. *D.* § Feb. 1917.
Elliott, G. E. (Feb. 1915). 2nd Lt. 13th R. Sussex Regt. France. Killed in action at Festubert on May 20, 1916.
1908 Elliott,* Rev. J. M., M.A. (Jan. 1916). Chaplain to the Forces (4th Class), attd. R.A.M.C.
1913 Ellison, T. F. (Aug. 12, 1914). ‡Lt., Acting Capt., and Adjt. 1st Northumberland Fusiliers. France. *M.C.*, July 26, 1918. *D.* France, 1918.
1911 Elton, G., M.A. (Sept. 1914). Capt. 4th Hampshire Regt. India, 1914; Mesopotamia, 1915. (Prisoner of war, Siege of Kut-el-Amara, Apr. 1916.)
1894 Etty, J. L., M.A. (Feb. 1, 1915). Capt. 2/4th Oxf. & Bucks. Lt. Infty. (Resigned.)
1908 Evans,* Rev. N., M.A. (Nov. 10, 1915). Chaplain to the Forces (4th Class). France, Palestine.
1895 Evers, C. P., M.A. (Aug. 1914). Capt., Bt.-Maj., Unattached List, T.F., Rugby School O.T.C. *D.* § Feb. 1918.
1903 Ewbank, Rev. H., M.A. (Dec. 14, 1915). Chaplain to the Forces (4th Class), 29th Div. France, Belgium, Germany.
1912 **Ewbank, L.** (Mar. 12, 1915). Lt. 5th Border Regt. France. Killed in action on Feb. 23, 1916.
1902 Ewbank, R. B. (1916). Lt. 35th Poona Bn., I.D.F. India.
1909 Eyton,* J. S., B.A. (Apr. 20, 1915). 2nd Lt. 4th D.C.L.I. Lt. 6th K.E.O. Cavalry, Indian Army. India, France, Egypt.
1911 Fagan, B. W., B.A. (Nov. 11, 1914). Capt. 6th Oxf. & Bucks. Lt. Infty. Capt. General List. G.S.O. 3, 3rd Army H.Q. France, Belgium. *M.C.*, Jan. 1, 1918. *D.* France, 1917 twice.
1903 Fanshawe, W., M.A. (July 1915). 2nd Lt. I.A.R.O., attd. 34th P.A.V.O. Poona Horse. India.

1900 Fearenside, E., M.A. (Sept. 19, 1914). Maj., Acting Lt.-Col., 17th Manchester Regt. France, 1915–18. *O.B.E.* (Mil.). *D.S.O.*, Sept. 26, 1916. *D.* France, 1916 ; § Aug. 1919.

1915 Featherstone, E. K. (Jan. 20, 1916). Lce.-Cpl. M.G.C. (Schoolmaster Sergt.).

1886 Fell, B. H., B.A. Chief Petty Officer, R.N.R.

1887 Fenton, C. O'C., M.A. Lt. Canadian Artillery.

1912 Ferrar, W. L., M.A. (Sept. 3, 1914). Sergt. R.F.A. Sergt. Intelligence Corps. France.

1900 Fletcher, Rev. D., M.A. (Sept. 8, 1914). Chaplain to the Forces (3rd Class). S.C.F. 42nd Div. Egypt, 1914–15 ; Gallipoli, 1915 ; Sinai Peninsula, 1916–17 ; France, 1917–19. *D.* France, 1917.

1909 Fletcher,* L. E. (Aug. 28, 1914). ‡Lt. M.G.C., attd. War Office. France.

1907 Floyd, J. F. M., M.A. (Sept. 25, 1915). Lt. 18th Durham L.I. Lt., Acting Capt., M.G.C. France, 1916, 1917–18.

1911 Foligno, C., M.A. (May 20, 1915). Capitano, Comando Generale dell' Arma di Cavalleria, Italian Army. Italy, 1915–19. Croce di Guerra.

1906 **Ford, R. J.,** B.A. (Dec. 1914). Capt. 17th Manchester Regt. France. Killed in action at Glatz Redoubt, Montauban, on July 1, 1916.

1905 **Forsyth, D.,** B.A. (Sept. 1914). ‡2nd Lt. 7th Highland L.I. Died on June 17, 1915, of illness contracted while on active service.

1911 Foster,* R. C. G. (Oct. 29, 1914). Capt. 2nd Queen's (R. W. Surrey Regt.). France. *M.C.*, July 27, 1916. (Prisoner of war.)

1919 Foulston, S. (Nov. 1915). Lt. R.G.A. (S.R.). France, 1916–17. (Invalided, Aug. 30, 1918.)

1893 Fox, P. H., M.A. (Mar. 1, 1915). ‡Paymaster Lt. R.N.R. Murman Coast.

1917 Fuller, C. J. (Sept. 22, 1917). 2nd Lt. R.F.A. France.

1912 Furness, P., M.A. (Dec. 9, 1915). Q.M.S., R.A.S.C. (M.T.). France.

1911 Gabell, I. H. (Aug. 7, 1914). Lt. M.G.C. Bulgaria, Serbia, Macedonia, France.

1908 Gameson,* L., B.M., M.A. (Jan. 28, 1916). Capt. R.A.M.C., attd. 10th Cameronians. France, Belgium. Croix de Guerre.

1919 Gandar-Dower, A. V. (July 1915). Lt. 2nd Dragoon Guards. France.

1901 **Gardner, G. D.** (Sept. 1914). ‡2nd Lt. 9th Suffolk Regt. France. Killed in action in the Battle of the Somme on Sept. 13, 1916.

1911 **Garrard,* W. G. B.** (1914). Lt. 2nd Northumberland Fusiliers. Belgium, 1915 ; Salonika, 1916–17. Accidentally killed at Salonika on Oct. 19, 1917.

1905 **Garside, T. O.,** M.A. (May 1915). 2nd Lt. 4th R. Berkshire Regt. France, 1916–17. Killed in action on Apr. 5, 1917.

1904 Gaunt, R. F., M.A. Pte. Mombasa Defence Force.

1908 Gee,* F., B.A. (Feb. 15, 1915). Capt. and Adjt. R.A.S.C. Salonika.

1917 **Gell, J. B. S.** (Dec. 17, 1917). 2nd Lt. R.F.A. France. Killed in action near Cambrai on Oct. 9, 1918.

1917 Gibbons, A. B. B. (Mar. 18, 1918). 2nd Lt. Labour Corps.

1908 Gibbons, J. F., M.A. London Regt.

1900 Gibson, H. E., D.M. (Sept. 1914). Capt. R.A.M.C. (Invalided, Oct. 1918.)

1919 Giles, E. N. (Feb. 28, 1915). Lt. R.F.A. (T.F.). France, Belgium. *M.C.*, Sept. 26, 1917.

1919 Glover, J. L. (May 10, 1918). 2nd Lt. R. W. Kent Regt. (on demobilization).

1906 Goldspink,* Rev. F. W., M.A. (May 23, 1917). Chaplain to the Forces (4th Class).

1889 Goodwin, H. S., B.A. (Sept. 1914). ‡Capt. 22nd R. Fusiliers. Maj. Staff, 4th Army. France.

1910 Goolden,* R. O. (May 8, 1915). Lt. 3rd Worcestershire Regt. France. *D.* France, 1918. (Prisoner of war.)

1912 **Gordon,* A. M.** (Aug. 15, 1914). Lt. 1st R. Fusiliers. France and Belgium. Missing, believed killed in action near Ypres on Jan. 20, 1916.

1891 Gordon, Rev. E., M.A. Chaplain, Troopship.

1919 Gordon, T. G. (May 1, 1918). 2nd Lt. R.F.A.

1919 Grace, W. A. (Sept. 22, 1914). Capt. 9th Border Regt. France, 1915; Macedonia and Serbia, 1915–19.

1911 Graham, F., B.A. (1914). Lt. Special Lists. Staff-Captain.

1919 Gray, H. M. (Mar. 1917). Lt. 5th Oxf. & Bucks. Lt. Infty. France. (Wounded and prisoner of war in Germany.)

1912 Gray, P. H. H. (Jan. 15, 1915). Lt. 2nd R. Berkshire Regt. France, 1916.

1911 **Greany, J. W.** (Aug. 1914). Capt. and Adjt. 5th Wiltshire Regt. Gallipoli, Mesopotamia. *D.S.O.*, Oct. 20, 1915. *D.* Gallipoli, 1915; Mesopotamia, 1916. Missing, believed killed at Sanna-i-yat on Apr. 9, 1916.

1887 Greenlees, D. C. (Sept. 1914). Maj. 4th Dorsetshire Regt., T.F. Res. India, 1914–17.

1904 Greenstreet, Rev. J. W., M.A. (Aug. 23, 1915). 2nd Lt. Unattached List, T.F., Denstone College O.T.C.

1915 Greenwood, C. C. (Feb. 15, 1916). ‡2nd Lt. 13th King's (Liverpool Regt.). France.

1900 Grenfell, C. H., M.A. (1914). Lt. R.N.V.R.

1888 Grenfell, W. T., Hon. D.M., *C.M.G.* R.A.M.C.

1884 Griffith-Boscawen, Sir A. S. T., M.A., *M.P.* (Serving Aug. 4, 1914). Lt.-Col. 19th Hampshire Regt. France and Belgium, 1916. *D.* France, 1916; § Feb. 1917.

1903 Grinsted, W. F. H. (Serving Aug. 4, 1914). Capt., Acting Maj., R.G.A. France. *M.C.*, Sept. 16, 1918. *D.* France, 1917.

Guillebaud, G. P. (Sept. 14, 1914). Lt. 6th Loyal N. Lancashire Regt. Gallipoli. Killed in action at Chunuk Bair on Aug. 10, 1915.

1912 Gunn, J. A., M.A. (Feb. 1, 1915). Capt. R.A.M.C., 3rd S. Gen. Hospital, empld. Ministry of Munitions.

1910 Gutch, W. L., B.A. R.G.A.

1900 Hadley, F. C. T. (Mobilized Aug. 1914). Capt. 3rd R. Welch Fusiliers. R.T.O., 1917–19. Gallipoli, 1915; France, 1917.

1913 Haggen, G. L., B.C.L. (Dec. 7, 1914). Capt. 8th Oxf. & Bucks. Lt. Infty. Salonika. *D.* Salonika, 1918.

1913 Hall, B. K. B. (Sept. 13, 1914). ‡Lt. 1/4th Wiltshire Regt. (Capt.). India, 1916–17; Palestine, 1917–18. *D.* Palestine, 1918.

Hall, J. G. (Feb. 1916). 2nd Lt. 2/6th W. Yorkshire Regt. France. Killed in action at Bullecourt on May 3, 1917.

1908 Hall,* Rev. T. W., M.A. (July 5, 1918). Chaplain to the Forces (4th Class). France, Belgium.

1919 Halley, E. H. (Aug. 8, 1914). ‡2nd Lt. R.A.F. German S.W. Africa, 1915; German E. Africa, 1916–17.

1919 Handford, C. W. (Apr. 1917). Lt. 6th Queen's (R. W. Surrey Regt.). France, Germany.

1911 **Hanna, W.** (Aug. 1914). Spr. R.E. (Motor Air Line Section). France, Belgium. Killed in action at Poperinghe on Feb. 28, 1916.

1899 Hanson, Rev. R., M.A. (Feb. 1, 1917). Chaplain to the Forces (4th Class). *D.* § Mar. 1918.

1919 Harding, K. G. M. (May 8, 1918). 2nd Lt. 6th K.R.R.C.

1919 Hardy, R. K. (Feb. 17, 1917). Spr. 4th Field Survey Bn., R.E. Belgium, Germany.

1909 **Hardy,* R. L.,** B.A. (Oct. 1914). ‡Capt. and Adjt. 8th K.R.R.C. France and Belgium. *D.* France. Killed in action at Inverness Copse on Aug. 24, 1917.

1895 Harper, W. H. (Dec. 9, 1914). Capt. Special Lists. Temp. Maj., D.A.D. Railway Transport.

1912 Harris,* H. J., M.A. (Sept. 2, 1914). Capt. and Adjt. 1/5th Hampshire Regt. India, Burma.

1908 Harris,* T. A. (Aug. 18, 1914). ‡Maj. Special Bde., R.E. France, 1915–18.

1912 Harrison, A. F., B.A. (Jan. 1, 1916). Lt. 4th Border Regt., attd. R.E. India, N.W. Frontier, 1916–19.

1915 Harrison, J. M. (Feb. 7, 1916). ‡2nd Lt. Labour Corps (Capt.). France, 1916–17, 1918–19.

1910 **Hartley,* W. I. S.,** B.A. (Jan. 28, 1916). Lt. 8th K.O.Y.L.I. France. Killed in action at Ovillers-la-Boisselle on July 1, 1916.

1902 Harvey, J. J. L., B.A. Straits Settlements Vol. Corps, Penang.

1906 Hasell,* E. W., M.A. (Mobilized Aug. 4, 1914). Maj. Westmorland & Cumberland Yeomanry. France.

1865 Hasell, Rev. G. E., M.A. (Serving Aug. 4, 1914). Chaplain (1st Class), attd. Westmorland & Cumberland Yeomanry.

1913 **Hasslacher,* J. C.** (Feb. 19, 1915). Lt. 20th London Regt. France. Killed in action on Dec. 29, 1917.

1914 **Hastwell, W. M.** (Feb. 1915). 2nd Lt. 7th Bedfordshire Regt., attd. M.G.C. France. Killed in action at Arras on Apr. 8, 1917.

1919 Hawkesworth, E. G. (July 11, 1916). Lt. 1st Grenadier Guards. France, Belgium. *M.C.*, Nov. 6, 1918.

1913 **Hawkesworth,* F. H. S.** (Sept. 1914). 2nd Lt. 3rd Border Regt., attd. 2nd Welsh Regt. France. Killed in action at Givenchy on Jan. 25, 1915.

1912 Hawkesworth,* J. L. I. (Apr. 1914). Capt. 1st E. Yorkshire Regt., empld. War Office. France, Belgium.

Hay, R. B. (Sept. 1914). Lt. 3rd W. Yorkshire Regt., attd. R.F.C. France, 1916–17. *M.C.*, July 26, 1917. Died as a prisoner on July 17, 1917, of wounds received in action.

1891 Hazeldine, Rev. F. J., M.A. (June 10, 1915). Chaplain to the Forces (4th Class). France. *M.C.*, Jan. 1, 1918.

1908 Hazeldine, Rev. W. S., M.A. (Aug. 25, 1915). Chaplain to the Forces (4th Class).

1893 Heald, B. H., M.A. (Mobilized 1914). Maj. 34th Bn. I.D.F. Burma, India.

1898 Heanley, R. E. M. (Jan. 8, 1915). Capt. 9th Northumberland Fusiliers, empld. 84th Training Res. Bn. France. (Prisoner of war.)
1919 Hedley, G. W. St. G. (Sept. 1915). ‡2nd Lt. 1st Res. Cavalry (Lancers) (Lt.).
1919 Heffer, A. B. (May 23, 1917). 2nd Lt. Queen's (R. W. Surrey Regt.). France.
1902 Hek, F. W. (May 19, 1911). Maj. 6th Gloucestershire Regt. Acting Maj. 20th Rifle Brigade. Palestine. *D.* Palestine, 1918, 1919.
1919 Hicks, A. N. (Feb. 1917). 2nd Lt. 337th Bde., 18th (Ind.) Div., R.F.A. India, Mesopotamia.
1908 Higham,* Rev. P., M.A. (Sept. 10, 1918). Chaplain to the Forces (4th Class).
1899 Hiley, F. C. W., M.A. (Mobilized Aug. 1914). ‡Lt. 15th Middlesex Regt. (Invalided, July 1915.)
1904 Hiley, W. E., M.A. (Jan 10, 1916). Capt. Special Lists. Asst. Proof and Experimental Officer, Research Dept., Woolwich Arsenal. *O.B.E.* (Mil.). *D.* § Mar. 1918.
1911 Hill,* C. H., M.A. (July 25, 1914). Capt. 3rd S. Staffordshire Regt. France.
1899 Hill, E. E. (Dec. 21, 1916). Lt. R.A.S.C.
1912 Hill,* T. A., B.A. (Aug. 22, 1914). 2nd Lt. 7th R. Sussex Regt. Lt. M.G.C. (Capt.). France, 1915–17.
1908 Hill, T. St. Q., B.A. (Aug. 10, 1917). Pte. 28th London Regt. (Artists' Rifles).
1907 Hippisley, H. H. S. (Nov. 5, 1914). Pte. 14th London Regt. (London Scottish). 2nd A.M., R.A.F. France, Salonika, Egypt, Palestine, Mesopotamia, N.W. Frontier.
1903 Hird, J. S., M.A. (Jan. 1917). Lt. R.G.A. Belgium, France.
1895 Hodgkin, R. H., M.A. (Dec. 11, 1914). Capt. 7th Northumberland Fusiliers, empld. War Office. *D.* § 1920.
1913 Hodgson, G. D. (July 1916). Lt. 13th R. Fusiliers. France.
1905 Hodgson, N., M.A. (1914). Capt. R.A.S.C. France. *D.* France, 1918.
1914 Hodgson, T. B. (Apr. 1, 1918). Surgeon Probationer, R.N.V.R.
1890 Hodson, T. C. (Feb. 1, 1915). Capt. Special Lists. Maj. D.A.D. of Forestry. France. *D.* France, 1917.
Hollowell, F. J. (May 1915). 2nd Lt. 3rd Worcestershire Regt. France. Killed in action in the Leipzig Salient on Aug. 7, 1916.
1903 Holmes, E. B., B.A. (Apr. 1915). Lt. 5th Loyal N. Lancashire Regt.
Holmes, W. B. (Oct. 2, 1916). 2nd Lt. 4th, attd. 6th, Cheshire Regt. (Lt.). France, Belgium. Killed in action at Shrewsbury Forest, near Ypres on Sept. 20, 1917.
1914 Holtzclaw, B. C., M.A. (Aug. 27, 1917). 2nd Lt. 317th Field Artillery, U.S. Army. France, 1918–19.
1919 Honoré, F. M. (June 6, 1917). Lt. R.A.F.
1900 Hope, N. E., M.A. (Oct. 1916). Pte. 1/28th London Regt. (Artists' Rifles). France, Belgium.
1913 **Horser, S. C. S.** (Dec. 30, 1914). Capt. 17th King's (Liverpool Regt.). France. Killed in action in the Battle of the Somme on Oct. 12. 1916.
1919 Hoyle, G. 2nd Lt. R.E.
1910 Hubble, E. P., B.A. (Apr. 1917). Maj. 343rd Inf., U.S. Army. France.

1912 Hughes, C. K., M.A. (Jan. 1, 1917). Pte. 6th Wiltshire Regt. France.

1878 Hughes, Rev. L. R., M.A. (Oct. 1, 1914). Chaplain to the Forces (4th Class), attd. R.E. (S.C.F. to Welsh Army Corps). *D.* § Feb. 1917.

1890 Hughes-Morgan, D. (Rejoined 1914). Maj. 3rd S. Wales Borderers (S.R.).

1889 Hunt, A. S., M.A., D.Litt. (May 1, 1915). Lt. 4th Oxf. & Bucks. Lt. Infty., empld. at War Office (Capt.). France.

1904 Hunt, Rev. K. R. G., B.A. Lt. Unattached List, T.F., Highgate School O.T.C.

1919 Hurd, W. B. (Nov. 14, 1915). Capt. Canadian Education Services. France, Belgium, Germany. *O.B.E.* (Mil.). *D.* France, 1919.

1874 Hurford, A. E., M.A. Capt. (Retired List) Recruiting Officer, Cornwall.

1917 Hutchings, G. A. (Jan. 4, 1918). 2nd Lt. 3rd Lincolnshire Regt.

1919 Hutchins, E. J. (Feb. 14, 1917). 2nd Lt. R.F.A. (S.R.). Palestine.

1913 Ingledow, C. F. E. (Mar. 17, 1915). Lt. 16th Queen's (R. W. Surrey Regt.).

1917 Irvine, I. R. T. (Nov. 30, 1917). 2nd Lt. 2nd King's (Liverpool Regt.). Salonika.

1908 Iselin, A. (1917). Lt. U. S. Army.

1906 Jackson,* A., B.A. (Jan. 27, 1913). Capt., Acting Maj., R.A.M.C. France, Belgium. *D.* § Mar. 1918.

1899 Jackson, C. E., M.A. (Sept. 6, 1918). 2nd Lt. R. Warwickshire Regt.

Jackson, R. W. (Mar. 1, 1917). 2nd Lt. 4th York & Lancaster Regt. France and Belgium. Killed in action on Oct. 9, 1917.

1919 Jacot, E. W. (Aug. 29, 1914). Lt., Acting Capt., 14th R. Warwickshire Regt. France, 1915–16, 1918–19.

1920 Jacques, R. (Feb. 3, 1916). ‡2nd Lt. 2nd W. Yorkshire Regt. France, Belgium.

1902 James, Rev. P. E., M.A. (Sept. 28, 1917). Chaplain to the Forces (4th Class).

1909 Jeffries,* H. S., B.A. (Aug. 24, 1915). Surgeon Lt. R.N. Ascension Island, 1916–19.

1919 Jenkins, E. H. (Aug. 11, 1916). ‡Sub-Lt. R.N.V.R. H.M.S. *Saumarez*, Grand Fleet.

1912 Jenkins, I. S., M.A. (Aug. 1914). Capt. 8th Welsh Regt. Gallipoli, 1915; Mesopotamia, 1916; India, Egypt.

1907 Jessel, A. R. F. Z., B.C.L., M.A. (Feb. 4, 1915). 2nd Lt. 8th Northamptonshire Regt. (Invalided.)

Johnson, L. B. (Apr. 26, 1917). 2nd Lt. 3rd, attd. 1st, Somerset L.I. France. Died on Apr. 15, 1918, of wounds received in action.

1904 **Jones, A. E.,** B.A. Leicestershire Regt. Died on June 5, 1917.

1882 Jones, A. Wentworth, M.A. (Feb. 1, 1916). Lt. R.A.M.C. (Invalided.) Died on Dec. 4, 1917.

1880 Kelly, Rev. H. H., M.A. Chaplain to the Forces (4th Class).

1896 **Kemble, H. H.,** M.A. (Mobilized Aug. 1914). Lt.-Col. 23rd London Regt. France and Belgium. *D.S.O.*, Jan. 1, 1917. *M.C.*, Jan. 14, 1916. *D.* France, 1916, 1917. Died on June 7, 1917, of wounds received in action at Messines Ridge.

1903 **Kenworthy, S.,** M.A. (Dec. 9, 1914). Capt. 17th Manchester Regt. France. *D.* France, 1916. Killed in action in the Battle of the Somme on July 1, 1916.

1919 Kerr, T. S. (Aug. 8, 1915). Lt. 8th R. Sussex Regt. (Capt.). France, 1917–19.
1908 Kerwood,* C. R. 28th London Regt. (Artists' Rifles).
1909 Kidd,* Rev. J. H., M.A. (Feb. 3, 1916). Chaplain R.N., H.M.S. *Resolution*. Mediterranean, 1916–18; North Sea, 1918–19.
1919 Kingham, M. J. (Sept. 10, 1918). Cadet R.M.C., Sandhurst.
1909 Kinross,* K. S., B.A. (Sept. 12, 1916). Lt., Acting Capt., R.G.A. France, 1917–19. *M.C.*, Nov. 26, 1917.
1898 Kinsman, J. C. P., B.A. (Mobilized Aug. 1914). Capt. 15th London Regt. (Civil Service Rifles).
1898 Kirby, W. L. C. (Serving Aug. 4, 1914). Capt., Bt.-Maj., 12th Lancers. Temp. Lt.-Col. A.Q.M.G. France. *D.S.O.*, June 4, 1917. *D.* France, 1917.
1898 Kitchin, C. (May 9, 1918). Pte. 1st S. African Inf. (Sergt.). France, Belgium, 1918–19.
1902 Knight, J. H. (Serving Aug. 4, 1914). Maj. R.G.A., Indian Army (Lt.-Col.). France, 1914–15; Mesopotamia, 1916–18. Order of Karageorge (4th Class) (with swords). *D.* France, 1915; Mesopotamia, 1917.
1919 Lampen, G. D. (Dec. 7, 1917). 2nd Lt. R.F.A. Salonika, 1918; Caucasus, 1918–19.
1914 Larsen, J. A. O., M.A. (July 22, 1918). ‡Lt. Military Intelligence Dept., U.S. Army, attd. American Legation, Copenhagen.
1907 Law,* J. C. S., B.A. (Aug. 20, 1914). Capt. 19th Hampshire Regt. France, Belgium, Italy, Germany, 1916–19.
1908 Lawson,* Rev. E. J. (Aug. 13, 1918). Chaplain to the Forces (4th Class), attd. 69th Labour Group. France, Belgium.
1915 Lawson, F. H. (Dec. 8, 1916). 2nd Lt. R.G.A.
1919 Leach, F. (June 6, 1917). 2nd Lt. R.G.A. France, 1918. *M.C.*, July 26, 1918.
1908 Leather, C. H., B.A. R. Fusiliers.
1899 Lee, Rev. P. E., M.A. (July 30, 1915). Chaplain to the Forces (3rd Class). D.A.C.G. IV Corps. France, Belgium, Germany. *D.* France, 1919.
1895 Lees-Smith, H. B., M.A., *M.P.* (Sept. 1915). Cpl. R.A.M.C. France.
1919 Lefroy, C. B. H. (June 10, 1916). ‡Lt. 43rd Squadron, R.A.F. France, 1917–18. (Prisoner of war, Aug. 1918–Jan. 1919.)
1890 L'Estrange, P. H., B.A. (Sept. 1915). Capt. 7th W. Yorkshire Regt. (Invalided, Apr. 1916.)
1919 Lett, H. N. (Nov. 18, 1917). 2nd Lt. R. Berkshire Regt. Capt. R.A.F. Salonika, 1916–17; Egypt, 1917; France, 1918–19. *D.F.C.*, Feb. 7, 1919.
1881 **Lewis, F. B.** B.E.F. France. Killed in action on Mar. 30, 1917.
Lindsay, B. W. (Aug. 5, 1914). Capt. R.F.A. India, Mesopotamia, France, Belgium. Died on Nov. 22, 1918, of wounds received on Nov. 8 at Kerkhove, near Ingoghem.
1902 Lishman, G. (Oct. 1, 1915). Staff-Sergt. R.A.S.C. Salonika, 1915–17.
1902 Lloyd, A. W. (Sept. 1914). ‡Lt., Acting Capt., 25th R. Fusiliers. German E. Africa. *M.C.*, Jan. 1, 1919. *D.* E. Africa, 1919.
1900 Lloyd, Rev. J. H., M.A. (Oct. 3, 1916). Chaplain R.N., H.M.H.S. *Soudan* North Sea.

1892 Loftus-Tottenham, A. R., M.A. (Apr. 18, 1916). Lt. 2nd King Edward's Own Gurkha Rifles. India.

1893 Lonsdale, J. F. (June 1918). 2nd Lt. Middlesex Regt.

1911 Lowe,* T. G., M.A. (Aug. 28, 1914). Capt. 1/1st Monmouthshire Regt. France. (Prisoner of war.)

1908 McCalman,* Rev. H., M.A. (Jan. 15, 1915). Chaplain to the Forces (4th Class). France. *M.C.*, Jan. 18, 1918. *D.* France, 1917.

1910 **McCance, F.,** B.A. (Nov. 11, 1914). 2nd Lt. 3rd, attd. 2nd, Border Regt. France, Belgium. Died on May 22, 1915, at Base Hospital, Boulogne, of wounds received in action.

1911 McCance, H. B., B.A. (Jan. 5, 1916). Maj. R.E. France, 1916–18; Egypt and Palestine, 1918–19. *D.* France, 1917.

1919 McConkey, O. (Feb. 20, 1916). Gnr. 64th Bn. Canadian Field Artillery (Sergt.). France, 1916.

1907 **McCunn,* F. J.,** B.A., B.Litt. (Sept. 1914). Capt. 6th Q.O. Cameron Highlanders. France. Killed in action at Loos on Sept. 26, 1915.

1905 MacDermot, F. C. J., B.A. (Oct. 7, 1914). Maj. R.A.S.C.; D.A.Q.M.G. France and Belgium. La Medaille de la Reconnaissance française, (3rd class) (in bronze). *D.* France, 1915, 1916, 1917, 1919.

1904 **Mace, Rev. A. B.,** M.A. (May 15, 1915). Chaplain to the Forces (4th Class). France. Killed in action on Oct. 3, 1916.

1906 McEwen, W. L. (Aug. 6, 1914). Capt. Special Lists. G.S.O. 3. France, 1914–17; Italy, 1917–18; Central Europe, 1918–19. *M.C.*, Jan. 14, 1916. *D.* France, 1915 twice; Italy, 1918.

1919 McGreer, Rev. A. H. (Sept. 1914). Hon. Lt.-Col. Canadian Chaplain Service. France, Belgium, Germany. *O.B.E.* (Mil.). *M.C.*, Nov. 14, 1916. *D.* France, 1916.

1896 Machell, L., B.A. (Jan. 12, 1916). Lt. 1st Border Regt. France. *D.* France, 1916.

1912 MacKeith, M. H., B.A. (Sept. 4, 1914). ‡2nd Lt. 3rd (Res.) Yorkshire Regt. France and Belgium, 1915–17.

1910 McLean,* A. E. J., M.A. (1914). ‡2nd Lt. 9th K.R.R.C. Capt. I.A.R.O. France, 1915–16; India, 1918; Palestine, 1918–19.

1912 McLeod,* T. M. (Aug. 15, 1914). Capt. 3rd, attd. 16th, Highland L.I.

1913 Maddox,* A. M., M.A. (July 21, 1915). Lt., Acting Capt., R.E., attd. H.Q., R.A.F. France, 1915–16, 1918; Germany, 1919.

1895 Maidment, W. J. (1915). ‡Lt., Acting Capt., 1st Welsh Regt. Salonika. *M.C.*, Jan. 1, 1918. Given commission for service in the field. *D.* Salonika, 1917.

1919 Maitland, V. K. (Apr. 15, 1916). ‡Lt. 13th Bn. Tank Corps (Capt.). France, Belgium, Germany, 1917–19. *M.C.*, Feb. 15, 1919.

1914 Maldram, F. C. B., B.A. (Sept. 16, 1914). ‡Lt. 75th Bn. M.G.C. France, 1915–16; Mesopotamia, 1917–18; Egypt and Palestine, 1918.

1917 Mallam, P. C. Cadet O.C.B.

1914 Manning, T. W. (Nov. 28, 1914). 2nd Lt. 10th Norfolk Regt., attd. 1/4th Northamptonshire Regt. 2nd Lt. 74th Punjabis, I.A.R.O. Capt. Supply & Transport Corps, I.A.R.O. Egypt and Palestine, 1916–17; India and NW. Frontier, 1917–19.

1907 Maples,* R. C., B.A. (Sept. 22, 1915). Capt. Manitoba Regt., Canadian E.F. France, 1916–19. *M.C.*, Apr. 2, 1919. *D.* France, 1917.

1911 Mappin,* W. H., B.A. (1914). Pte. 12th Gloucestershire Regt.
1907 Marks, L. H., B.A. (Nov. 5, 1915). ‡Lt. R. Sussex Regt. France, 1916–17, 1918.
1895 Marks, W. O., B.A. (Serving Aug. 4, 1914). Maj., Acting Lt.-Col., R.A.S.C. A.D. of Supplies and Transport. France and Belgium. *D.S.O.*, Jan. 14, 1917. *D.* France, 1916 twice, 1917, 1918.
1911 Marshall,* R. C., M.A. (Aug. 22, 1914). Capt. 1st Worcestershire Regt. Gallipoli, 1915; Egypt, 1916; Mesopotamia, 1916; France, 1917–18. (Prisoner of war, 1918.)
1915 Martin, W. T. C., B.A. R.A.F.
1906 Martyr, H. (Dec. 30, 1914). Lt. 6th R. Irish Rifles, empld. Dept. of Information.
1901 Mason, P., B.A. United Provinces Horse, India. India.
1919 Mason, S. P. (June 29, 1917). 2nd Lt. R.F.A. France, 1918–19.
1913 Maurice, M. W. (Dec. 22, 1914). Lt. 8th Somerset L.I. France.
1896 Meadows, E. B. (Mar. 31, 1916). Pte. 2/5th King's Own (R. Lancaster Regt.). Pte. 220th (Divl.) Employment Coy. France.
1909 **Meakin, H. P.** (Oct. 1914). Capt. 3rd Coldstream Guards, attd. 1st Guards T.M.B. France. Killed in action at Lesboeufs on Sept. 25, 1916.
1906 **Merivale,* J. W.,** B.A. (Rejoined Aug. 1914). Capt. 7th Northumberland Fusiliers. France. Killed in action in the Battle of the Somme on Sept. 15, 1916.
1919 Miles, G. C. (Mar. 19, 1917). Sergt. 4th N. Staffordshire Regt. France, Belgium.
1907 Miller, C. F. H. (Feb. 9, 1918). ‡2nd Lt. Aviation Section, Signal Corps, U.S. Army.
1920 Miller, E. S. McG. (Aug. 1914). Capt. Worcestershire Regt. France.
1919 Millward, G. T. (July 3, 1918). Pte. Inns of Court O.T.C.
1919 Milner, H. (Sept. 1, 1917). Cpl. Army Pay Corps.
1898 Mitchell, J. M., B.A. (Dec. 12, 1914). Capt. 8th E. Surrey Regt. Lt.-Col. General List, D.A.A.G. France and Belgium, 1915–19. *O.B.E.* (Mil.). *M.C.*, Jan. 1, 1918. *D.* France, 1917, 1918, 1919.
1919 Moffet, S. (Aug. 8, 1914). Capt. 5th Northumberland Fusiliers. Maj. 3rd Bn. M.G.C. France, 1916–18; Germany, 1919. *M.C.*, Jan. 1, 1918. *D.* France.
1897 Moore, A. Pte. 19th R. Fusiliers.
1919 Moore, G. J. (Nov. 1915). ‡2nd Lt. R.E. (Lt.). France.
1897 Moore, H. (Sept. 9, 1914). Lce.-Cpl. 28th R. Fusiliers. France, 1915–16.
1911 Morgan, W. G. C., B.A. (Feb. 23, 1915). Lt. 6th S. Wales Borderers. Lt. 2/81st Pioneers, Indian Army, afterwards Supply & Transport Corps. France, 1916; India.
1900 Morrice, K. D. R., B.A. (Sept. 1914). ‡Maj. 10th King's (Liverpool Regt.), attd. M.G.C. Mesopotamia.
1906 Morris, R. J. (June 20, 1914). Capt., Bt.-Maj., 4th S. Staffordshire Regt. Acting Lt.-Col. 9th Devonshire Regt. France. *D.S.O.*, Dec. 11, 1916. *D.* France, 1916, 1917.
1909 Mort, S. F., M.A. (June 2, 1915). ‡Capt., 1st Signal Coy., R.E. Gallipoli, 1915; France and Belgium, 1916–18; Germany, 1919. *M.C.*, June 3, 1919. *D.* France, 1918.

1914 **Mortimer, W. L. G.** (1914). 2nd Lt. 6th R. Dublin Fusiliers. Gallipoli. Died on Aug. 10, 1915, of wounds received at Suvla Bay.

1911 Morton,* E. R. M., M.A. (Aug. 3, 1914). Capt. and Adjt. 18th Divl. Train, R.A.S.C. France, Belgium. *O.B.E.* (Mil.). *D.* France, 1919.

1889 Murray, Rev. M. W. (Jan. 16, 1917). Chaplain to the Forces (4th Class).

1902 **Nash, F. H.**, M.A. (Sept. 1914). ‡Capt. 9th N. Staffordshire Regt. France and Belgium. *M.C.*, July 26, 1917. *D.* France, 1917. Killed in action on July 17, 1917.

1914 Neat, C. E. W. (Sept. 13, 1915). Lt. 3rd R. Irish Fusiliers. France, 1916–18.

1902 Newton, J. C., B.A. Nigerian Land Contingent. Africa.

1919 Nicholas, J. O. (Feb. 9, 1917). Cadet 7th O.S.A., Bath. France.

1912 Noake, Rev. A. R., M.A. (Aug. 6, 1916). Chaplain to the Forces (4th Class). Mesopotamia.

1900 Noble, J. A., B.M., M.A. (June 5, 1916). Capt. R.A.M.C. Mesopotamia. *M.C.*, Oct. 26, 1918.

1919 Norrish, G. (Sept. 7, 1917). Midshipman R.N., H.M.S. *Erin.*

1912 Northcote, B., M.A. (Dec. 19, 1915). Lt. 5th W. Yorkshire Regt. France.

1910 Norton, C. J., M.A. (Nov. 13, 1914). Lt. 1/5th Suffolk Regt. Capt. Special Lists, whilst empld. as Acting G.S.O. 3.

1908 Olmsted, J. M. D. Laboratory Asst., Base Hospital No. 7, U.S. Army. France.

1889 Ormerod, Rev. E. W., M.A. (Apr. 1, 1914). Pte. 7th United Provinces Horse.

1897 Ormerod, G. M. (Feb. 4, 1915). Lt.-Col. R.F.A., empld. War Office. G.S.O. 3. France. *D.S.O.*, Jan. 1, 1917. *D.* France, 1916 twice.

1905 Ormerod, H. A., M.A. (June 1, 1915). Lt. R.F.A. (Capt.). France, Greece. *M.C.*, Sept. 26, 1916. Chevalier, Order of King George I (Greece). *D.* France, 1917.

1910 Ormerod,* T. L., M.A. (Aug. 4, 1914). ‡2nd Lt. 6th Queen's (R. W. Surrey Regt.). France, 1916. (Invalided, June 1917.)

1907 **Oughtred, H.**, M.A. (Sept. 15, 1914). ‡2nd Lt. 4th E. Yorkshire Regt. France. Killed in action at Wancourt, Arras, on Apr. 23, 1917.

1919 Palmer, T. L. (July 15, 1917). Lt. R.A.F. Salonika, 1918–19; S. Russia, 1919. Greek Military Cross.

1919 Palmer, W. N. Cadet O.C.B.

1895 Pape, S. W., M.A. Lt. Cape Colony Defence Force. Africa.

1885 **Parker, G. B.** (Aug. 1914). Sergt.-Maj. New Zealand A.S.C. Died at Military Hospital, Wellington, N.Z., on Apr. 5, 1917.

1919 Parkes, G. D. (July 2, 1918). Pioneer R.E. (Anti-Gas Estabt.).

1909 Parlee, M. K., M.A. (1915). ‡Lt. 28th Canadian Inf., attd. R.A.F. Belgium, France.

1906 Patterson,* A. A., B.A. N. Bengal Mounted Rifles. India.

1910 Pauer,* G. O., B.A. Nigerian Land Contingent. W. Africa.

1912 Pavey,* G. P. (Aug. 22, 1914). Lt. 2nd Somerset L.I., attd. Signal Service. India, 1914–19.

1902 **Pearson, A. H.**, M.A. (Apr. 20, 1916). Spr. R.E. Died on June 7, 1918, of illness contracted on active service.

1911 Pearson,* B. L., M.A. (Oct. 27, 1914). Capt. 8th Yorkshire Regt., empld. No. 23 O.C.B. France, Belgium. *D.S.O.*, Jan. 1, 1918. *M.C.*, Nov. 25, 1916. *D.* France, 1916, 1917.

1913 Peele, R. (July 19, 1915). Lt. R.G.A. (S.R.) (Capt.). France, 1916–17.
1901 Peet, T. E., M.A. (Oct. 21, 1915). ‡Lt. 3rd King's (Liverpool Regt.). Salonika, France.
1912 **Pennington, W. H.** (Dec. 22, 1914). 2nd Lt. W. Yorkshire Regt. Died at Penzance of pneumonia on Mar. 2, 1915.
1881 Perceval, A. W. B., B.A. Capt. and O.C. Ixopo Commands, Natal.
1911 **Perham, E.** (June 12, 1915). Capt. 12th W. Yorkshire Regt. France. Killed in action on July 24, 1916.
1919 Perry, H. G. (Feb. 25, 1916). Pte. 9th R. Fusiliers. France.
1914 Petrie, J. A., B.A. (Oct. 22, 1917). Lt. General List.
1891 Phelps, J. H. D., B.M. (May 10, 1918). Capt. R.A.M.C. Malta.
1908 Phillips,* A. A., B.A. Lt. I.A.R.O., 1st Defence Force. India.
1903 Pidduck, F. B., M.A. (Jan. 1, 1916). Capt. Special Lists. Ballistic Research Officer, Woolwich Arsenal. *D.* § Mar. 1918.
1881 Pigot, Rev. E. C., M.A. (1916). Chaplain to the Forces (4th Class).
1911 Pigot,* E. W. (Feb. 26, 1915). Lt. 3rd Shropshire L.I., attd. M.G.C.
1911 Pigott, A. J. K. P. (June 5, 1915). Lt. and Adjt. 1st R. Irish Regt. France, Egypt, Sudan, Palestine.
1907 Pilcher, E. E. I., B.A. (Feb. 27, 1915). Capt. R.E. Egypt, Belgium, France, Italy.
1910 **Pitman,* T. S.,** B.A. (Oct. 1, 1914). ‡Lt. 6th York & Lancaster Regt. France, Belgium. Killed in action at Poelcappelle on Sept. 26, 1917.
1919 Pittar, C. A. (Jan. 15, 1917). Lt. 1st Coldstream Guards. France. *M.C.*, Nov. 6, 1918.
1910 Poole, E. G. C., M.A. (Apr. 1917). Lt. Intelligence Corps. Staff-Lt. France.
1913 Porter, E. F., B.A. (1917). Lt. U.S. Army. France.
1919 Porter, F. A. (Dec. 21, 1917). ‡2nd Lt. Tank Corps.
1902 Potter, G. M., B.A. (Sept. 2, 1914). Pte. 16th London Regt. (Queen's Westminster Rifles). France, Belgium.
1903 Powell, D. H. J., B.A. (Nov. 12, 1914). Lt. R.G.A.
1899 **Pratt, Rev. A. M.,** M.A. (Serving Aug. 4, 1914). Chaplain to the Forces (4th Class). Accidentally killed on June 29, 1917.
1871 Price, J. A. P., D.M. (Mar. 1915). Maj. R.A.M.C. (T.F.).
1910 Proudfoot, F. G., M.A. (Aug. 12, 1914). Maj. R.A.M.C., attd. Q.O. Oxfordshire Hussars. France, 1915, 1916.
1885 Pryce-Mitchell, P. T., M.A. (Mar. 12, 1916). Lt. R. Defence Corps.
1913 Pugh, J. A., B.A. (July 7, 1915). Lt. Welsh Guards. France, Belgium.
1903 Pullinger, H. R., M.A. (Serving Aug. 4. 1914). Capt. Unattached List, T.F., St. Paul's School O.T.C.
Quayle, R. C. (Oct. 31, 1917). 2nd Lt. Leicestershire Regt. France. Killed in action on Oct. 4, 1918.
1902 Quigley, J. H. (Sept. 17, 1915). Lt. Unattached List, T.F., Victoria College O.T.C.
1910 Ragheb, M. E., B.A. Lt. Recruiting Officer.
1892 Randall-MacIver, D., M.A., D.Sc. (Sept. 8, 1914). Capt. Special Lists, D.A.D. of Labour (Staff-Captain). France, 1914–15; Salonika, 1916–18. *D.* Salonika, 1918.
1901 **Randell, H. A.** R. Fusiliers. France. Killed in action on Sept. 8, 1918
1919 Randolph, J. H. (May 11, 1917). Lt. 'D' Batt., 189th Bde., R.F.A. France, 1917–19.

1908 Rea, D. B. (May 3, 1915). Capt. R.A.S.C. France, 1915–16; Mesopotamia, 1916, 1919; India, 1917. *D.* Mesopotamia, 1919.

1908 Reckitt,* C. E. H., B.A. (Aug. 4, 1914). ‡2nd Lt. 2nd, attd. 1st, E. Yorkshire Regt. Lt., Acting Capt. and Adjt., R.E. France, 1914–15, 1915–19. *O.B.E.* (Mil.). *D.* France, 1917, 1919.

1904 Rees, O. M., B.A. (Apr. 4, 1916). Lt. R.G.A. (Capt.). Mesopotamia, 1916–19.

1904 Reiss, H. B., M.A. (Apr. 5, 1916). 2nd Lt. I.A.R.O. India.

1919 Richards, F. R. (Aug. 1, 1917). 2nd Lt. R.G.A. (S.R.). France.

1901 Richardson, A. H. (Mobilized Aug. 1914). Capt. 4th W. Riding Regt. (T.F. Res.). A.P.M. *D.* § Feb. 1917.

1898 Richardson, N., B.A. (Dec. 12, 1914). Lt. R.F.A. (T.F.). France.

1917 Ripley, R. (Dec. 27, 1917). 2nd Lt. R.F.A. France.

1913 **Roberts, A. D.** (Nov. 4, 1914). Lt. 10th Cameronians. Lt. Observer, R.F.C. France. *M.C.*, Nov. 25, 1916. Killed while flying on Aug. 31, 1917.

Robinson, B. O. (Oct. 1916). 2nd Lt. 4th York & Lancaster Regt. France and Belgium. Killed in action at Passchendaele on Oct. 9, 1917.

1909 Robinson,* G. C., B.A. Tpr. Southern Provinces Mounted Rifles. India.

Robinson, G. W. (Sept. 1914). Lt. 10th Gloucestershire Regt. France and Belgium. Killed in action at Loos on Sept. 25, 1915.

1919 Robinson, H. C. (Nov. 7, 1917). 2nd Lt. 1/7th Cheshire Regt. France, Belgium, 1918–19.

1897 Rogers, H. S. (Serving, Aug. 4, 1914). Maj., Bt.-Lt.-Col., Shropshire L.I. P.M., temp. Brig.-Gen. France. *C.B.E.* (Mil.). *D.S.O.*, Jan. 1, 1917. Chevalier, Ordre du Mérite Agricole. *D.* France, 1915, 1916, 1918.

1895 **Ross, H. D.** (Sept. 1915). Pte. 29th R. Fusiliers (Cpl.). France. Killed in action at High Wood on July 20, 1916.

1919 Ross Townsend, R. G. (Sept. 4, 1916). Lt. R.A.F. France, 1917.

1907 Roulston, F. W. H., M.A. (Oct. 1914). 2nd Lt. 4th R. Berkshire Regt. France.

1903 Rowland, A. N. A., M.A. Canadian E.F. France.

1894 Sanderson, F. R., B.A. (Mar. 13, 1915). Capt. R.F.A. Staff-Captain (Lt.-Col.). Egypt, Gallipoli, Palestine. *O.B.E.* (Mil.). Chevalier of the Royal Order of George I (Greece). *D.* Palestine, 1918, 1919.

1903 Saunders, F. G. (Mobilized Aug. 1914). Maj. 3rd Leinster Regt.

1903 **Sayer, C. O.**, B.A. (June 7, 1913). Lt. 7th Durham L.I. France and Belgium. Died in the German Military Hospital at Courtrai, on June 7, 1915, of wounds received in action at Ypres on May 24.

1906 Sayer,* G. R., B.A. (Aug. 4, 1914). ‡Capt. 1st Chinese Labour Bn. Hong-Kong, 1914–15; France, 1916–19.

1913 Sayer,* H. B. (Oct. 17, 1914). Lt. R.E., attd. Egyptian Army (Capt.). France, 1915–17; Sudan, from 1917. *D.* France, 1916 twice; Sudan, 1919.

1881 Scattergood, B. P., M.A. (Mar. 23, 1915). Col.-Sergt. York & Lancaster Regt. Instructor in Musketry.

1916 Schnadhorst, C. E. (Nov. 22, 1916). Lt. 4th N. Staffordshire Regt. France, Belgium. *M.C.*, July 18, 1917.

1916 Schnadhorst, F. E. A. (Apr. 19, 1915). Lt. 4th N. Staffordshire Regt. France, Belgium.

1920 Scotland, P. J. (Oct. 6, 1916). Lt. 3rd The Black Watch. India, Mesopotamia, Egypt, France.
1912 Scott, Rev. F. O., M.A. (July 3, 1917). Chaplain to the Forces (4th Class).
1910 Scott, R., B.A. (July 31, 1918). Pte. Meteorological Section, R.E.
1904 Scott-Wilson, H. W., B.Sc., B.M. (May 26, 1915). Capt. R.A.M.C. Gallipoli, Egypt, Palestine, France.
1913 Senhouse,* H. P. (Oct. 10, 1914). Capt., Acting Maj., R.F.A. France, Belgium, Germany. *M.C.*, June 17, 1917. *D.* France, 1919.
1919 Sharp, R. (Mar. 20, 1918). 2nd Lt. Border Regt.
1919 Sharwood, A. C. (May 8, 1917). Capt. R.A.F., attd. 2nd Light Cruiser Squadron. Grand Fleet. *D.* 1918.
1911 **Shaw,* R. T.** (Aug. 1914). Lt. 2nd R. Sussex Regt. France. Killed in action at Richebourg L'Avoué on May 9, 1915.
1905 Shepherd, C. H. B., M.A. (Dec. 28, 1914). 2nd Lt. Manchester Regt. Capt., Acting Maj., M.G.C. France, Belgium. *M.C.*, Dec. 2, 1918.
1910 **Shepherd,* D. A. M.** London Regt. France. Killed in action on Sept. 20, 1916.
1919 Shepherd, E. C. (Jan. 25, 1915). Sergt. R.F.A.
1914 Shepperd, C. B. (Oct. 1915). Lt. 4th Border Regt. India.
1905 **Shutt, H. C.,** B.A. (Nov. 6, 1914). Lt. 3rd, attd. 1st, R. Scots Fusiliers. France. Killed in action at Serre on Nov. 13, 1916.
1919 Shuttleworth, W. (Sept. 16, 1916). Pte. 4th Devonshire Regt. Egypt, Palestine, France.
1910 **Simmonds,* P. G.,** B.A. (Aug. 1915). 2nd Lt. 9th London Regt. (Queen Victoria's Rifles). France. Killed in action at Gommecourt on July 1, 1916.
1902 Simpson, Rev. F. A., M.A. (Aug. 15, 1915). Chaplain to the Forces (4th Class).
1919 Simpson, J. C. F. (Mar. 14, 1917). Lt. R.A.F. Macedonia.
1902 Simpson, Rev. W. R., M.A. R.A.M.C.
1914 Sisson, G. R. (Aug. 21, 1915). Lt. R.G.A. (S.R.) (Capt.). W. Africa, 1916–17; France, 1917–19.
1919 Smart, G. F. (Aug. 9, 1918). Cadet No. 23. O.C.B.
1920 Smith, C. R. (Apr. 3, 1916). Sergt. 19th Canadian Res. Bn. ‡2nd Lt. 8th London Regt. (Post Office Rifles). France, 1918.
1909 Smith,* E. R., B.A. (Sept. 19, 1914). Lt., temp. Capt., 5th Rifle Brigade, empld. Ministry of National Service. France, 1915. *O.B.E.* (Civil Div.).
1894 Smith, H. A., M.A. (Nov. 16, 1916). Lt. I.A.R.O., attd. Supply & Transport Corps. India, Persia. *D.* Persia, 1919.
1919 Smith, H. I'B. (Oct. 4, 1917). 2nd Lt. Grenadier Guards. France, 1918.
1919 Smith, H. P. (Aug. 4, 1914). Capt. R.F.A. (T.F.) (Maj.). France.
1906 Smith,* N. L., B.A. (1917). Lt., Acting Capt., 1st Chinese Labour Bn. France. Order of Wen-Hu (5th Class).
1904 Smith, Rev. W. L., M.A. (June 1917). Chaplain to the Forces (4th Class). France, Belgium, Germany.
1906 Somers, W. E. (Aug. 11, 1914). Pte. R.A.S.C. France, 1914–18.
1904 Somerset, N. H. P., M.A. (June 10, 1915). Capt. R.A.S.C. Mudros, 1915–16; Egypt, 1916–17; Palestine, 1917–18.
1894 Souttar, H. S., B.M., M.Ch., M.A. (Sept. 19, 1914). Maj. R.A.M.C. Belgium, 1914. *C.B.E.* (Mil.). Officier de l'Ordre de la Couronne.

1893 Spilsbury, A. J., B.A. (Serving Aug. 4, 1914). Capt. O.T.C.
1912 Spokes,* P. S., B.A. (Jan. 30, 1915). Capt. and Adjt. 19th London Regt. France, 1915.
1904 Spyer, J. (Sept. 1914). Lt. 7th S. Wales Borderers. Gallipoli, Salonika, Constantinople.
1897 Stamp, Rev. A. G. C., M.A. (Sept. 25, 1916). Chaplain to the Forces (4th Class).
1917 Starke, H. G. R.E.
1913 **Stephens,* A. M.** (Sept. 1914). ‡2nd Lt. 11th Lancashire Fusiliers. France. *D.* France, 1916. Died on Dec. 30, 1915, of wounds received in action at Armentières.
1913 **Steward,* C.** (Aug. 1914). 2nd Lt. 3rd, attd. 2nd, Shropshire L.I. Belgium. Killed in action at Ypres on May 25, 1915.
1919 Stifter, G. (Dec. 31, 1916). Cadet, Cavalry School, Russian Army. Russia.
1900 Stocken, C. A., M.A. (Feb. 27, 1918). 2nd Lt. 5th Hampshire Regt.
Stokes, P. D. (Dec. 1916). 2nd Lt. 6th, attd. 11th, Rifle Brigade. France, 1917. Died on Apr. 10, 1917, of wounds received in action at Havrincourt Wood.
1910 Stolz, H. R. (June 1, 1917). Capt. U.S. Army Medical Corps. France, 1918–19.
1907 Stonestreet, A. R. (Oct. 3, 1914). Pte. 29th R. Fusiliers.
1899 Storey, F. B. (Mobilized Aug. 1914). Maj., 3rd Queen's (R. W. Surrey Regt.). *D.* § Aug. 1919.
1909 Stork,* H. C., B.A. (Aug. 4, 1916). Capt. 19th Punjabis. Staff-Captain, G.H.Q., M.E.F. (D.A.Q.M.G.). Mesopotamia, Persia, Caucasus.
1879 Stott, F. W. A., B.M., M.A. (Jan. 1915). Capt. R.A.M.C., attd. 2/5th Manchester Regt. (Invalided, Apr. 1917.)
1908 Stuart, W., B.A. (1917). U.S. Army.
1919 Sturt, O. (Sept. 14, 1918). Midshipman R.N.V.R., H.M.S. *Nicator.*
1911 Sutton, E. G. S., M.A. Spr. R.E. (Signal Service).
1915 Sutton, R. B. (Feb. 5, 1917). 2nd Lt. 9th Sherwood Foresters. France, 1918.
1899 Swann, Rev. C. G., M.A. (Feb. 5, 1917). Chaplain to the Forces (4th Class). France, Belgium. *M.C.*, Sept. 26, 1917.
1880 Sweetapple, Rev. H. D. S., D.D. (1915). Chaplain to the Forces (4th Class).
1904 Swete, E. D., M.A. Gloucestershire Regt.
1904 Sykes, W. H., M.A. Nigerian Land Contingent. Africa.
1910 Tait, H. S. (1918). Capt. Canadian A.M.C.
1920 Tallin, G. P. R. (Mar. 1, 1916). Sergt. 196th Inf. C.E.F. ‡2nd Lt. 8th London Regt. (Post Office Rifles) (Capt.). France, 1918–19.
1911 Tansley,* R. G. F., B.A. (Feb. 8, 1916). Lt. R.A.S.C.
1912 Taylor, F., M.A. R.A.M.C.
1913 **Taylor,* W. P.** (Oct. 1915). 2nd Lt. 6th York & Lancaster Regt. France. Killed in action at Bullecourt on May 3, 1917.
1911 Tesh,* W., M.A. (Sept. 11, 1914). ‡Capt., Flying Officer, R.A.F. Gallipoli, 1915; Imbros, 1915; Aegean, 1916–17. (Invalided.)
1907 Thomas, F. A. S., B.A. (Oct. 6, 1916). Lt. I.A.R.O., attd. 114th Mahrattas. Capt. G.S.O. 3, 1st (Peshawar) Div., 1917; D.A.Q.M.G. 6th (Poona) Div., 1918–19. India and NW. Frontier.

1899 Thompson, A. G. J., B.M. (Apr. 21, 1915). Capt. R.A.M.C. Egypt, France, Italy.

1903 Thompson, J. G., B.A. (Aug. 4, 1914). Maj. 7th King's (Liverpool Regt.). D.A.A.G., H.Q., 1st Corps. France, 1915–19. *D.S.O.*, June 3, 1918. *M.C.*, June 3, 1916. *D.* France, 1917, 1918.

1909 **Thornton,* J. H. B.,** B.A. (Mar. 1917). ‡2nd Lt. Labour Corps, attd. Lancashire Fusiliers (Capt.). France. Killed in action near Armentières on Sept. 28, 1918.

1898 Thorold, Rev. E. H., M.A. (Serving Aug. 4, 1914). Chaplain to the Forces (2nd Class). France, from Aug. 1914. *D.* France, 1915, 1916.

1909 Thorp,* A. F. (Serving Aug. 4, 1914). Lt. S. Lancashire Regt. France. (Prisoner of war.)

1919 Till, W. P. (Feb. 14, 1918). 2nd Lt. R.F.A.

1911 Titherington,* G. W., B.A. (Serving Aug. 4, 1914). Capt. and Adjt., Bt.-Maj., 1st Oxf. & Bucks. Lt. Infty. Mesopotamia. *D.* Mesopotamia. 1917, 1918.

1898 **Trousdell, W. H. C.,** B.A. (1914). Lt. Land Contingent, Nigeria, W. Africa. Lost at sea on Mar. 13, 1915.

1891 Tupper, J. H. E., B.A. Poona Vol. Rifle Corps. India.

1919 Turner, N. (July 1, 1918). Pte. 3rd Yorkshire Regt.

1905 **Turrell, H. G.** (Jan. 25, 1917). 2nd Lt. 4th Oxf. & Bucks. Lt. Infty. France. Died on Nov. 3, 1917, of wounds received in action.

1907 Twynam,* C. D. (Dec. 23, 1914). Lt., Acting Capt., R.E. France. *M.C.*, Jan. 1, 1917. *D.* France, 1918.

1903 Udall,* E. H., B.A. (Aug. 22, 1914). Capt. R.A.M.C. (Maj.). Gallipoli, France, Mesopotamia, Persia. *D.* Mesopotamia, 1918.

1901 Udall, T. C. B., M.A. (Apr. 4, 1915). Capt. M.G.C. France, Belgium. *D.* France, 1917. (Prisoner of war.)

1919 Unmack, R. C. (Feb. 8, 1918). 2nd Lt. Dirigible Officer, R.A.F. Anti-Submarine Patrol.

1909 Vallalley, Rev. J. S., M.A. (Nov. 7, 1916). Chaplain to the Forces (4th Class). France.

1919 Vann, L. E. (Nov. 1, 1916). ‡2nd Lt. R.F.A. France.

1892 Veale, R. A., B.A. (Mobilized Aug. 1914). Maj., Acting Lt.-Col., R.A.M.C.

1895 Vernon, A. F. M., M.A. (Jan. 12, 1915). ‡Lt. R.N.V.R. Gallipoli, Malta.

1917 Wain, D. H. (July 15, 1918). 2nd Lt. R.G.A.

1906 Walker, B. H., M.A. (Jan. 1916). Pte. S. African Service Corps (M.T.). German E. Africa, 1916–17. (Invalided, Apr. 1917.)

1905 Walker, E. G. S., B.A. (Aug. 29, 1914). Hon. Capt., Flying Officer, R.A.F. France. *D.* Air Ministry, Dec. 1919. (Prisoner of war.)

1910 Walker, M., B.A. (Oct. 14, 1914). Lt. R.A.S.C., attd. 29th Div. Egypt, Gallipoli, 1915. (Invalided on account of ill health contracted while on active service.)

1903 Walker, W. A. (Sept. 1914). 2nd Lt. 1st Bn. Madras Guards, India Defence Force. India.

1898 Wallace, A. J., M.A. (Oct. 3, 1914). Lt. Postal Section, R.E. France.

1912 Wallace, C. L'E., B.A. (Dec. 12, 1914). 2nd Lt. 8th London Regt. (Post Office Rifles). France. (Prisoner of war.)

1914 Wallis, N. H., B.A. (Oct. 1914). 2nd Lt. 8th S. Wales Borderers. (Relinquished commission on account of ill health, Oct. 1915.)

1892 Warburton, P. E. B. (Oct. 5, 1914). Gnr. I/a Batt., H.A.C. Egypt, Palestine.
1903 Ward, R. O., B.A. (Mobilized Aug. 1914). Capt. R.F.A. Acting Maj. H.A.C. France. *D.S.O.*, June 3, 1919. *M.C.*, June 3, 1918. *D.* France, 1919.
1913 Waring, N. H., M.A. (Mar. 17, 1915). Lt. 10th Border Regt. Lt. Special Lists, empld. Ministry of Munitions. France.
1897 Warren, Rev. J. W. F., M.A. (Aug. 6, 1918). Chaplain to the Forces (4th Class), attd. 4th B.W.I. Regt. France, 1918; Italy, 1918–19.
1914 **Warren, R. H.** American Ambulance (Neuilly-sur-Seine). France. Médaille d'honneur, silver gilt. Died of illness at Bordeaux on Nov. 28, 1916.
1883 Watson, Rev. A. H., M.A. (1916). Senior Chaplain to the Forces.
1888 Weatherley, C. O., B.A. Lt. Vol. Bn. Surrey Regt.
1914 Weber, C. J., M.A. (May 1, 1917). Capt. and Adjt. 69th F.A., U.S. Army.
1911 **Weeks, H. W. M.** (Feb. 23, 1915). Lt. S. Wales Borderers. France and Belgium. Died on Nov. 23, 1917, of wounds received in action.
1899 Welford, A. A., M.A. R.E.
1910 **Wellings, C. H. C.,** B.A. (July 7, 1917). 2nd Lt. Labour Corps. France and Belgium. Killed in action at Ypres on Aug. 11, 1917.
1914 Werlein, P. P., M.A. (Sept. 18, 1917). ‡2nd Lt. 53rd F.A., U.S. Army.
1892 **West, T.** (Oct. 1914). Lce.-Cpl. 23rd (Sportsman's) R. Fusiliers. France, 1915–17. Killed in action near Bourlon on Nov. 29, 1917.
1919 West, W. (June 23, 1916). Lt. R.G.A. Staff-Lt. VI Corps H.Q. France.
1893 Whincup, Rev. R., M.A. (July 1912). Chaplain to the Forces (4th Class). France, Belgium. *M.C.*, Jan. 1, 1917.
1888 White, J., M.A. (Serving Aug. 4, 1914). Instructor in Navigation, Portsmouth.
1910 Whiteley, F. P., M.A. (May 15, 1916). Warrant Schoolmaster, R.N. H.M.S. *Fisgard.*
1915 Whiteley, S. (Mar. 1916). Spr. R.E. (Signals). France, 1916–18.
1918 Whittle, R. A., B.A. (Sept. 3, 1916). ‡Lt. 16th Manchester Regt. France, Belgium, 1917. *M.C.*, Sept. 26, 1917.
1919 Whitwell, F. R. J. (Mar. 1917). Lt. 2nd Scots Guards. France.
1914 **Wigfall, W. E. C.** (Jan. 1915). Lt. 3rd, attd. 8th, E. Yorkshire Regt. (Capt.). Belgium, France. *M.C.*, Oct. 20, 1916. *D.* France, 1916. Died on Aug. 29, 1916, of wounds received in action.
1907 Wilkinson,* H. R., B.A. Indian Vol. Defence Force. India.
Williams, A. I. M. (Jan. 30, 1915). Capt. 13th R. Welch Fusiliers. France. *D.* France, 1918. Died on Oct. 9, 1918, of wounds received in action.
1902 Williams, H. W., B.A. (1914). Sergt. 1st Bn. Behar Light Horse. India.
1911 Williams,* J. (Oct. 30, 1914). Capt. R.G.A., empld. Ministry of Munitions. Belgium, France. *M.C.*, Mar. 30, 1916. *D.* France, 1915.
1916 **Williams, J. Trevor** (Sept. 1917). 2nd Lt. 30th Punjabis, Indian Army. Died of fever on June 7, 1918.
1912 **Williams,* M. F.** (Aug. 1914). Lt. R.F.A. (S.R.). France. Killed iu action at Thiepval on Aug. 11, 1916.
1919 Williams, S. A. G. (Sept. 28, 1917). 2nd Lt. 33rd Batt., R.F.A. France.
1899 Willis, G. M., B.A. R. W. Kent Regt.
1906 Willis, S. F., B.A. (May 6, 1915). Lt. M.G.C.

1908 Wilson,* A. K., M.A. (Serving Aug. 4, 1914). Capt. Unattached List, T.F., Derby School O.T.C.

1902 Wilson, C. C., B.A. (Oct. 6, 1916). Lt. I.A.R.O., attd. 39th Central India Horse, afterwards attd. 12th Bn. (Bengal) Cavalry (Capt.). Mesopotamia, 1917–19.

1895 Wilson, G. F. (Dec. 1915). Capt. R.G.A. (S.R.). France.

1919 Wilson, G. I. (Oct. 18, 1918). Aircraftsman (2nd Grade), R.A.F.

1919 Wilson, J. L. (Dec. 12, 1915). ‡2nd Lt. 13th Durham L.I. France, 1918–19.

1887 Wilson, Rev. J. P. (Apr. 1917). Chaplain to the Forces (4th Class). Egypt, Palestine, Syria, 1917–19. *O.B.E.* (Mil.). *D.* Palestine, 1918.

1911 Wilson, P., M.A. (Sept. 1, 1915). Instructor Lt. R.N.

1916 Wilson, R. (July 24, 1915). Lt. 4th E. Surrey Regt., attd. M.G.C. France. (Prisoner of war.)

1905 Wise, A. F., B.A. (Mar. 10, 1917). Capt. I.A.R.O. Staff-Captain A.H.O., India. India.

Wolfe, A. F. (Apr. 12, 1915). ‡Sub-Lt. R.N. Div. Gallipoli, France. Killed in action near Beaumont Hamel on Feb. 4, 1917.

1878 Wood, Ven. H. S., M.A. (1914). Archdeacon of the Fleet, Greenwich.

1919 Wood, J. C. Cadet, O.C.B.

1909 Wood,* J. T., B.A. (Feb. 1915). Pte. M.G.C. France.

1908 Woodhead,* A. W., B.A. (Nov. 20, 1914). Capt. I.A.R.O., attd. 9th N. Bengal Mounted Rifles. France, Gallipoli, Egypt, Mesopotamia, India, N.W. Frontier.

1902 Woodhouse, H. A., M.A. (Feb. 13, 1915). Capt. Special Lists. Dental Surgeon, attd. R.A.M.C.

1911 Woolley,* G. H. (Aug. 4, 1914). Capt. 9th London Regt. (Queen Victoria's Rifles). G.S.O. 3. France, Belgium. *M.C.*, June 3, 1919. *D.* France, 1915, 1918. **V.C.**

For most conspicuous bravery on Hill 60 during the night of Apr. 20–1, 1915.

Although the only officer on the hill at the time, and with very few men, he successfully resisted all attacks on his trench, and continued throwing bombs and encouraging his men till relieved. His trench during all this time was being heavily shelled and bombed and was subjected to heavy machine gun fire by the enemy.

1886 Wyndham, P., M.A. (1916). Trooper, United Provinces Light Horse.

1906 **Yardley, F. G.,** B.A. (Jan. 9, 1915). 2nd Lt. 8th N. Staffordshire Regt. France, 1915. Died at Calais on Sept. 17, 1915, of wounds received in action near Laventie on Aug. 22, 1915.

1911 **Young,* G. S.,** B.A. (June 21, 1915). Pte. 6th W. Yorkshire Regt. France. Died on Nov. 29, 1916, of wounds received in action.

1917 Zetchevitch, V. (Apr. 1915). Pte. Artillery Unit, Serbian Army. Serbia.

NEW COLLEGE

1911 [Abel Smith, L. R., M.A.] (Dec. 20, 1915). Lt. 5th Grenadier Guards. France and Belgium, 1916, 1917.

1919 Abraham, P. S. (April 27, 1915). Lt. D/159th Bde. R.F.A. (Capt.). France, 1916–19.

1901 Acland-Troyte, H. W., B.A. (Sept. 20, 1914). Capt. Royal 1st Devon Yeomanry. Staff-Captain (Maj.). France, 1916–19. *M.C.*, Jan. 1, 1919. *D.* France, 1918.

1897 Acton, R., M.A. (Nov. 20, 1916). Lt. and Adjt. R.G.A. (Capt.). Egypt and Palestine. *D.* Palestine, 1919.

1895 Adams, J. E. C., B.A. (Apr. 23, 1917). Lt. 3rd (Garr.) Bn. Northumberland Fusiliers.

1912 **Addison, N. G.** (Mobilized Aug. 4, 1916). ‡Lt. King Edward's Horse. France and Italy. *M.C.*, Dec. 2, 1918. *D.* Italy, 1918. Killed in action near Locon, Apr. 10–11, 1918.

1912 Agnew,* E. S., B.A. (Sept. 5, 1914). Lt. 5th Lancers (S.R.). France, 1915–17, 1918; Egypt, 1917. *D.* France, 1915.

1912 Ainger,* E., B.A. (Aug. 26, 1914). Lt., temp. Capt., 3rd Hussars. France. Croix de Guerre. Chevalier, Order of the Star of Rumania.

1914 Aitken, R. (July 1, 1915). Lt. Bucks. Bn. Oxf. & Bucks. Lt. Infty., attd. War Office. France.

1912 Akenhead, D., B.A. (Sept. 1, 1914). Capt. Lincolnshire Regt., attd. O.C.B. Gallipoli, France. (Commission relinquished on account of ill health.)

1900 Akenhead, F., M.A. (Nov. 1914). Capt. 5th Manchester Regt. Gallipoli, 1915–16; Egypt and Sinai, 1916–17. France, 1917–19.

1908 **Alcock, E.,** B.A. (Aug. 1914). Lt. 296th Bde., R.F.A. (T.F.). France. *M.C.*, Sept. 26, 1917. Killed in action on Aug. 20, 1917.

1888 Aldridge, H. H. (Sept. 12, 1914). Capt. Welsh Guards (Staff-Captain). France. *D.* France, 1917.

1901 Alison, C. H. (Feb. 12, 1918). Capt. Paymaster, A.P.D. *M.B.E.*

Allan, R. G. (Oct. 1915). 2nd Lt. K.O. Scottish Borderers. France, 1916, 1917. Killed in action on Vimy Ridge on Apr. 9, 1917.

1887 Allbutt, H. (Feb. 1915). Lt. 2/8th Middlesex Regt. Lt. T.F. Res., Commdt. P. of W. Camp.

1910 Allen, C. K., M.A. (Jan. 9, 1915). Capt. and Adjt. 13th Middlesex Regt. France. *M.C.*, Sept. 16, 1918.

1902 Allen, G. O., M.A. (July 17, 1918). ‡2nd Lt. I.A.R.O. India.

1913 Allen,* G. W. D., B.A. (Aug. 1914). Capt. 4th King's (Liverpool Regt.). Capt., Flying Officer, R.A.F. France. *M.C.*, June 3, 1916.

1900 Allfrey, A. M. St. C., B.A. (Nov. 19, 1914). Lt. R.A.S.C. (Capt. and Adjt.).

1900 **Allport, T. C.,** B.A. (Mobilized Aug. 1914). Capt. 5th York & Lancaster Regt. (T.F.). France. Killed in action in France on Aug. 1, 1915.

1908 Alston,* W. H. S., B.A. (Nov. 1911). Capt., Bt. Maj., 4th Rifle Brigade. Bde. Maj. G.S.O. 2. France. *M.C.*, June 3, 1917. *D.* France, 1916, 1917, 1918, 1919.

1887 Ames, W. H., B.A. (Mobilized Aug. 1914). Col. 4th Oxf. & Bucks. Lt. Infty. (T.F. Res.). France. *D.* § Feb. 1917.

1888 Ampthill, O. A. V., Lord, M.A., *G.C.S.I.*, *G.C.I.E.* (Serving Aug. 1914). Col. 3rd Bedfordshire Regt. France. *D.* France, 1917, 1918; § Feb. 1917, Mar. 1919.

1920 Anderson, R. W. (Dec. 1916). Sergt. Section Sanitaire étrangère, afterwards 1st Lt. 5th F.A., U.S. Army. France, Germany.

1912 Andrews,* A. J. P., B.A. (Sept. 20, 1914). Cpl. R.E. (Signal Section). France, Belgium, Germany. *D.C.M.*, Sept. 4, 1918.

1907 Anson, G. H., B.A. (Mobilized 1914). Capt. Staffordshire Yeomanry (Maj.). Egypt, Palestine. *M.C.*, Jan. 1, 1918. *D.* Palestine, 1917.

Anstie, E. B. (May 1, 1917). 2nd Lt. 2nd Rifle Brigade. France. Killed in action at Parquy on Mar. 23, 1918.

1910 Appleton,* E. R., B.A. (Mar. 17, 1915). 2nd Lt. 5th London Regt. (London Rifle Brigade). (Commission relinquished on account of ill health.)

1903 **Arbuthnot, A. H.,** B.A. (Mobilized Aug. 1914). Capt. 12th London Regt. (The Rangers). France and Belgium. Died on May 15, 1915, of wounds received in action near St. Julien.

1897 **Arthur, H. B. C.,** B.A. (Serving Aug. 4, 1914). Maj. R.F.A. France 1914–16. *D.* France, 1915, 1916 twice. Killed in action in France on Aug. 10, 1916.

1901 Ashby, A. B., M.A. (Sept. 15, 1914). Capt. 2/5th, attd. 19th, Queen's (R. W. Surrey Regt.), Courts Martial Officer. Belgium, France.

1902 Asquith, A. M. (Sept. 23, 1914). Commdr. R.N.V.R., Temp. Brig.-Gen. R.N.D., 189th Inf. Bde. Antwerp, Egypt, Gallipoli, France, Belgium. *D.S.O.*, Apr. 17, 1917; *Bar*, July 18, 1917; *2nd Bar*, Jan. 18, 1918. Croix de Guerre. *D.* France, 1917 twice, 1918.

1909 **Aston, H. S.,** B.A. (June 6, 1914). Capt. Highland L.I. Maj. M.G.C. France and Belgium. *M.C.*, Sept. 16, 1918. Died on July 13, 1918, of wounds received in action.

1905 Astor, Hon. J. J. (Aug. 15, 1914). Capt. 1st Life Guards, empld. R.G.A. France, Belgium. Croix de Chevalier de la Légion d'Honneur. *D.* France, 1919.

1898 Astor, Lord W., B.A., *M.P.* (Oct. 20, 1914). Maj. Special Lists; D.A.Q.M.G. *D.* § Feb. 1917.

1900 Atkinson, J. F. Tindal, B.A. (Nov. 1914). Lt. Grenadier Guards.

1909 [**Atkinson,* L. E.,** B.A.] (Aug. 15, 1914). Lt. 3rd, attd. 2nd, R. Berkshire Regt. France. Killed in action near Fromelles on May 9, 1915.

1906 Aubrey-Fletcher, H. L., *M.V.O.* (Serving Aug. 4, 1914). Capt., Bt.-Maj., Grenadier Guards (Lt.-Col., A.A. and Q.M.G.). France. *D.S.O.*, Jan. 1, 1918. Croix de Guerre. *D.* France, 1915, 1916, 1917, 1918.

1919 Auld, F. C. (May 24, 1916). Lt. 10th Canadian Garrison Artillery. France, Belgium.

1896 **Awdry, C. S.** (Mobilized Aug. 1914). Maj. R. Wiltshire Yeomanry, attd. 6th Wiltshire Regt. (Lt.-Col. XV Corps Cavalry). France. *D.S.O.*, Dec. 2, 1918. *D.* France, 1917. Missing, believed killed in action near Grevillers on Mar. 25, 1918.

1900 Awdry, R. W., B.A. (Mobilized Aug. 1914). Maj. R. Wiltshire Yeomanry, attd. M.G.C. France and Belgium.

1919 Back, J., B.Sc. (Oct. 25, 1915). ‡Lt. 55th Bn. A.I.F. France.

Bailey, A. Y. (May, 1915). Lt. 1st K.R.R.C. France. Killed in action in Delville Wood on July 27, 1916.

1904 Bailey, F. H. (Sept. 28, 1914). Lt. Shropshire Yeomanry, empld. P. of W. Camp. Egypt.

1895 Baird, A. W. F., *D.S.O.* (Serving Aug. 4, 1914). Maj., Bt.-Col. Gordon Highlanders. Temp. Brig-Gen. France and Belgium. *C.B.* *C.M.G.* Croix de Commandeur de la Légion d'Honneur. Croix de Guerre. Commander of the Order of the Redeemer. *D.* France, 1915 twice, 1916 twice, 1917 twice, 1918, 1919.

1919 Baird, M. McC. (Aug. 4, 1916). Lt. 3rd Canadian Garrison Artillery.

Baker, B. H. (Dec. 20, 1915). Lt. 3rd, attd. 13th, Rifle Brigade (Capt.). France. Killed in action at Morin le Bouche on May 22, 1918.

1896 Baker, Rt. Hon. H. T., M.A. (Jan. 1916). Maj. Special Lists; D.A.Q.M.G., attd. R.A.F. *D.* § Feb. 1917.

1910 Balfour,* D. (Feb. 17, 1915). Lt. Lothians and Border Horse. A.D.C. to Governor of Bengal. India.

1906 Balfour Melville, E. W. M., M.A. (June 22, 1917). Lt. General List (T.F. Res.), empld. Recruiting Duties.

1905 Ballance,* A. C., B.M., M.A. (Aug. 5, 1916). Surgeon Lt., R.N., H.M. Monitor 25.

1894 Balston, C. H., B.A. (Mobilized Aug. 4, 1914). Capt., Acting Lt.-Col., 10th (E. Kent Yeomanry) Bn. The Buffs (E. Kent Regt.). Gallipoli, 1915; Egypt, 1916; Palestine, 1917–18; France, 1918–19.

1902 Balston, T., B.A. (Oct. 17, 1914). Lt. 12th Gloucestershire Regt. Maj. General List. D.A.A.G., III Corps. France 1915–19. *O.B.E.* (Mil.). *M.C.*, Jan. 1, 1917. *D.* France, 1917, 1918.

1907 Bampfylde, Hon. H. de B. W., M.A. (Aug. 4, 1914). ‡Maj. King's African Rifles. British and German E. Africa, 1914–17. (Commission relinquished on account of ill health, Nov. 1917.)

1902 **Bannatyne, J. F.,** B.A. (Serving Aug. 4, 1914). Capt. 11th Hussars. Maj. 23rd Manchester Regt. Belgium and France. Died on May 14, 1916, of wounds received in action at Merville.

1906 [Barber, E. A., M.A.] (Aug. 26, 1915). Lt. 4th Shropshire L.I. Lt. Special Lists. Staff-Lieutenant (1st Class). Salonika, 1918–19. *D.* Salonika, 1919.

1906 Bardac, J. H. (Aug. 2, 1914). Sergt. 306me Reg. d'Infanterie, Armée française, secd. London Embassy (Lt.). Belgium, France. Croix de Guerre. (Discharged on account of wounds received in Oct. 1914.)

1899 **Barker, R. V.** (Serving Aug. 4, 1914). Capt. 1st R. Welch Fusiliers. France, Aug. 1914. *D.* France, 1914. Killed in action in France on Oct. 3, 1914.

1903 **Barlow, P. B.,** M.A. (March, 1916). Pte. 1st Grenadier Guards. France. Died at Rouen on Jan. 18, 1917, of blood poisoning, contracted on active service.

1910 Barnes,* A. C., B.A. (Sept. 28, 1914). Maj. 4th Yorkshire Regt. Lt.-Col. 15th Durham L.I. France. *D.S.O.*, Nov. 14, 1916; *Bar*, June 3, 1918. *D.* France, 1916, 1917.

1902 Barnes, G. S., M.A. (Mobilized Aug. 1914). Capt. Pembrokeshire Yeomanry, attd. 24th (Yeomanry) Bn. Welsh Regt. (Maj.). Egypt and Palestine, 1916–18; France and Belgium, 1918–19.

1881 Barnes, Rev. T., M.A. (Sept. 15, 1915). Lt. 457th Coy. R. Defence Corps.

1906 Barratt, A. W., B.A. (Mobilized 1914). Lt., Temp. Maj., 4th Shropshire L.I. G.S.O. 2, Military Attaché at Jassey. France, Russia, Rumania, Italy. *M.B.E.* (Mil.). Order of St. Anne. Order of St. Stanislas. Officer of the Order of the Crown of Italy. Officer of the Order of the Crown of Rumania. Star of Rumania. *D.* § Aug. 1918.

1902 Barron, W. A., M.A. (Apr. 1917). 2nd Lt. Unattached List, T.F., King Alfred's School O.T.C.

1891 Bartleet, Rev. E. B., D.D. (July 20, 1916). Chaplain to the Forces (2nd Class).

1896 **Bartram, H. B.** (Serving Aug. 4, 1914). Capt. E. Batt., R.H.A. France and Belgium, Aug. 1914. Died on Sept. 16, 1914, of illness contracted while on active service.

1917 Bates, H. H. (Feb. 7, 1918). 2nd Lt. R.E. France.

Baumer, D. E. L. V. (Aug. 18, 1915). Lt. R.F.A. (S.R.). France and Belgium. Died on Oct. 21, 1917, of wounds received in action.

1913 Baxter, G. H., B.A. (Sept. 12, 1914). ‡Lt. Kent R.G.A. (T.F.). France, 1916, 1918.

1897 Beaumont, G., B.C.L., M.A. (Mobilized Aug. 1914). Capt., Acting Maj., 2/4th K.O.Y.L.I. France. *M.C.*, Jan. 1, 1918; *Bar*, Apr. 2, 1919.

1896 Beckwith, W. M. (Mobilized Aug. 1914). Maj. Coldstream Guards (Res. of Officers). Temp. Lt.-Col. G.S.O. 1. France, Italy. *D.S.O.*, June 3, 1916. Cavalier of the Order of St. Maurice and St. Lazarus. *D.* France, 1916, 1917; Italy, 1918.

1912 Beddington,* W. R., B.A. (Sept. 1914). Lt. 2nd Dragoon Guards. Egypt, 1914–15; Gallipoli, 1915; Salonika, 1915; Egypt, 1915; France, 1915–18.

1919 Beevor, M. (Aug. 26, 1918). Cadet, R.E.

1900 Behrens, F. E., M.A. (Sept. 12, 1914). Lt. 16th Manchester Regt., attd. War Office M.R. 3. France, 1915. (Commission relinquished on account of ill health.)

1919 Bell, G. S. (Aug. 22, 1918). Cadet O.C.B. (R.E.).

Bell, R. de H. M. (Aug. 1914). Lt. 10th K.R.R.C. (Capt.). France and Belgium, 1915–16. *D.* France, 1915. Killed in action at Guillemont on Sept. 3, 1916.

1906 Benn, I. B. H., B.A. (Serving Aug. 4, 1914). Capt. 1st D.C.L.I. (Maj.). France, 1914–15, 1916, 1918–19. *D.* France, 1915.

1884 Bennett, E. W., B.A. (Sept. 23, 1914). Capt. 4th R. Sussex Regt. (T.F. Res.).

1897 Bennett, J. H. (Serving Aug. 4, 1914). Maj. 3rd Skinner's Horse, Indian Army. India.

1907 **Berlein, C. M.,** B.A. (Aug. 1914). Lt. 5th Oxf. & Bucks. Lt. Infty. France and Belgium. Killed in action near Hooge on June 16, 1915.

1913 **Berridge, W. E.** (Oct. 1914). 2nd Lt. 6th Somerset L.I. France. Died on Aug. 20, 1916, of wounds received in action at Delville Wood.

1909 Bewley, T. K. (Aug. 5, 1914). Lt. 834th Coy., R.A.S.C. France and Belgium.

1910 **Bickmore,* D. F.,** B.A. (Serving Aug. 4, 1914). Lt. 6th King Edward's Own Cavalry, Indian Army. Lt. Norfolk Regt. Acting Lt.-Col. 4th Gordon Highlanders. France, 1914–18. *D.S.O.*, Sept. 16, 1918. *D.* France, 1918. Missing, believed killed in action near Chaumuzy on July 30, 1918.

1896 Biggar, H. P., B.Litt. Lt., 2nd County of London Vol. Regt.
1891 Bill, C. F., B.A. (Aug. 1914). Capt. 4th N. Staffordshire Regt., empld. Ministry of Labour. France, 1916–17.
1896 **Bill, J. H. H.,** B.A. (Oct. 1919). Lt.-Col. Special Duties. Kurdistan. Killed by Kurds on Nov. 3, 1919.
1912 **Bion,* K. N.** (Sept. 1914). Capt. and Adjt. 1st Sherwood Foresters. France. *M.C.*, Jan. 14, 1916. *D.* France, 1915, 1917. Killed in action at Mericourt Wood, March 21–3, 1918.
1894 Birchall, J. D., B.A. (Mobilized Aug. 4, 1914). Maj. R. Gloucestershire Hussars, attd Labour Corps. France. *D.* § Feb. 1917.
1896 Bircham, B. O., B.A. (Oct. 26, 1914). ‡Lt., Acting Capt., 2nd Hampshire Regt. Gallipoli, France, and Belgium. *M.C.*, Nov. 13, 1916.
1902 **Bird, W. S.,** M.A. (Dec. 29, 1914). Lt. 6th K.R.R.C. France. Killed in action in France on Apr. 9, 1915.
1889 Birley, M., M.A. (June 1, 1916). Lt. W. Yorkshire Regt. (T.F. Res.).
1911 Birley,* N. P., B.A. (Sept. 1914). Capt. 3rd S. Staffordshire Regt. Bde.-Maj. France, 1915–18. *D.S.O.*, Jan. 1, 1918. *M.C.*, Sept. 26, 1917. *D.* France, 1917, 1918.
1905 Birrell, J., B.A. (Dec. 21, 1914). Capt. 3rd, attd. 11th, The Black Watch.
1901 Birt, Rev. R. H. C., M.A. (Serving Aug. 4, 1914). Capt. Unattached List, T.F., Radley College O.T.C. (Commission relinquished.)
1916 Black, F. W. (Feb. 28, 1917). Lt. 7th Siege Batt., R.G.A. France.
1907 Blackett-Ord, M., B.A. (Serving Aug. 4, 1914). Capt. Northumberland Fusiliers. India. (Placed on half-pay list on account of ill health.) *D.* § Aug. 1919.
1917 Blair, G. L. (Serving Aug. 4, 1914). Maj. Indian Army. India. (Commission relinquished on account of ill health.)
1901 **Blake, M. F.** (Serving Aug. 4, 1914). Lt. 2nd K.R.R.C. France, Aug. 1914. Killed in action on Sept. 14, 1914.
1908 Blaksley,* J. H., M.A. (Aug. 1914). Capt. Dorset Yeomanry. Salonika, Egypt. *M.C.*, Apr. 4, 1916. *D.* Egypt, 1915.
1910 Blamey, J. N. L., B.M. (July 1916). Capt. R.A.M.C. W. Africa, 1916–17. France, 1918–19.
1908 Blaxland,* Rev. E. C., M.A. (Dec. 1, 1916). Chaplain to the Forces (4th Class).
1899 Blore, J. L., B.A. (Mobilized Aug. 1914). Maj. Unattached List, T.F. Staff-Captain, Southern Command.
1898 **Bodvel-Roberts, H. O.** (Aug. 1914). 2nd Lt. 7th London Regt. France. *M.C.*, Sept. 25, 1915. Died on Nov. 18, 1915, of wounds received at Loos on Sept. 25.
1900 Bolton, C. A. (Serving Aug. 4, 1914) Maj., Bt. Lt.-Col., Temp. Lt.-Col. Manchester Regt. A.Q.M.G. (G.S.O. 2). France, Palestine, Egypt. *C.B.E.* (Mil.). Commander of the Order of the Redeemer. Order of the Nile (3rd Class). *D.* France, 1916; Palestine, 1919.
1896 Bonham-Carter, F. G., B.A. (July 14, 1915). Lt. Grenadier Guards (S.R.), attd. G.H.Q., Italy (Capt.). France, 1915–17; Italy, 1918–19. Croce di Guerra. *D.* France, 1916.
1903 Bonn, W. B. L., B.A. (Mobilized Aug. 1914). Maj. Leicestershire Yeomanry, Acting Capt. 1st Welsh Guards. France. *D.S.O.*, Dec. 2, 1918. *M.C.*, July 26, 1918. *D.* France, 1918.

1913 Bonnerjee,* K. K. E. (Nov. 30, 1914). Capt. 6th R. Sussex Regt. Lt. R.A.F.

1900 Booth, L. C. G., B.A. (Sept. 25, 1914). Maj. 11th W. Yorkshire Regt. France and Belgium. (Commission relinquished on account of ill health.)

1899 Borwick, G., B.A. (Sept. 22, 1914). Capt. 3rd Bedfordshire Regt.

1885 Bosanquet, W. C., D.M. (Mobilized Aug. 1914). Capt., Bt.-Maj., R.A.M.C. (T.F.). (Maj.)

1904 [Bostock, N. F., B.A.] (Sept. 1914). Lt., Acting Capt., 173rd Siege Batt., R.G.A. France.

1911 **Boswell, W. G. K.** (Sept. 1914). Lt., Acting-Capt. 5th, attd. 2nd, Rifle Brigade. France, 1915–16. *D.* France, 1916. Died on July 28, 1916, of wounds received in action in France.

Boucher, A. G. (Nov. 22, 1916). 2nd Lt. 6th K.R.R.C. France and Belgium. Killed in action on July 10, 1917.

1881 [Bourne, G. C., M.A., D.Sc.] (Nov. 31, 1914). Supervising Officer Y.O. Coy. Res. Inf. Bde. Hon. Col. 12th Gloucestershire Regt.

1908 Bourne,* R. C., M.A. (Sept. 2, 1914). Lt. Herefordshire Regt. Capt. T.F. Res. Staff-Lieutenant (1st Class). Gallipoli, 1915; France, 1917.

1914 Bowden, C. G., B.A. (1917). 2nd Lt. R.G.A. Lt. F.A., U.S. Army. France.

1906 **Bowers,* W. A.,** M.A. (Apr. 2, 1915). 2nd Lt. 5th N. Staffordshire Regt. (Lt.). France. Died on July 2, 1916, of wounds received in action at Gommecourt.

1904 Bowes-Lyon, Hon. J. H., B.A. (Sept. 22, 1914). 2nd Lt. The Black Watch (T.F. Res.), empld. Ministry of Munitions. *D.* § Feb. 1917.

1895 **Bowes-Wilson, G. H.,** B.A. (Mobilized Aug. 1914). Capt. 4th Yorkshire Regt. (T.F.). France and Belgium, 1915. Killed in action near Ypres on June 17, 1915.

1905 **Bowman, A. W.** Pte. 23rd London Regt. France. Died of wounds as a prisoner of war on Apr. 17, 1918.

1902 Bowman, C. F., B.A. (Oct. 28, 1914). Maj. 9th Divl. Train, R.A.S.C. France, 1915–19; Belgium. *M.C.*, June 4, 1917. *D.* France, 1916.

1898 Bowman, H. E., M.A. (Oct. 27, 1914). Capt. 18th R. Fusiliers. Capt. General List.

1916 Bowra, C. M. (Mar. 1, 1917). Lt. 298th Bde., R.F.A. France and Belgium.

1904 Bowyer, G. E. W., B.A., *M.P.* (Mobilized Aug. 1914). Capt. Bucks. Bn. Oxf. & Bucks. Lt. Infty., empld. Admiralty (Staff-Captain). France. *M.C.*, Jan. 1, 1917. *D.* France, 1917.

1910 **Boyd,* H. L. F.,** B.A. (Sept. 4, 1914). Capt. 1st The Black Watch (Maj.). France and Belgium, 1914–17. Killed in action near Passchendaele on Nov. 18, 1917.

1912 **Bradshaw,* H. J.** (Aug. 4, 1914). 2nd Lt., Acting Lt., 4th Norfolk Regt. Gallipoli, Egypt, Palestine. *D.* Palestine, 1917. Died on May 19, 1917, as a prisoner of war at Nazareth of wounds received in action at Gaza on Apr. 21.

1899 **Braithwaite, M. L.** (Nov. 15, 1914). Lt. R.A., Flying Officer, R.F.C. Killed on active service on May 17, 1915.

1894 Braithwaite, W. J., B.A. Capt. 6th County of London Vol. Regt.

1911 Branson, D. S., M.A. (Mobilized Aug. 1914). Capt., Acting Lt.-Col. 1/4th York & Lancaster Regt. France, Belgium, Germany. *D.S.O.*,

Jan. 1, 1918; *Bar*, Sept. 16, 1918; *2nd Bar*, Apr. 2, 1919. *M.C.*, Jan. 1, 1917. *D.* France, 1916, 1917, 1918, 1919.

1897 Brassey, E. H., *M.V.O.* (Serving Aug. 4, 1914). Lt.-Col. 1st Life Guards, attd. Guards M.G. Regt. France and Belgium, 1914–19. *D.* France, 1916, 1919.

1912 Bray, J. F. L., M.A. (June 27, 1917). 2nd Lt. Oxf. & Bucks. Lt. Infty. (Lt.).

1919 Braybrooke, P. C. 2nd Lt. Irish Guards (on demobilization).

1909 **Brierley, H. J.**, B.A. (Aug. 29, 1914). Lt. 9th Lancashire Fusiliers. Gallipoli. Killed in action at Suvla Bay on Aug. 7, 1915.

1909 Brierley,* R. W., B.A. (Serving Aug. 4, 1914). Lt. 21st Lancers, attd. M.G.C.

1888 Brinton, R. S. Lt. 1st Vol. Bn. Worcestershire Regt.

Brittain, E. H. (Nov. 19, 1914). Capt. 11th Sherwood Foresters. France, Italy. *M.C.*, Oct. 20, 1916. Killed in action on Asiago Plateau on June 15, 1918.

1885 Bromley-Martin, E. G. (Sept. 14, 1914). Maj. 2nd Worcestershire Hussars. Agricultural Officer, 2nd Army. France and Belgium, 1917–18.

1894 **Brooke, W. J.**, B.A. (Mobilized Aug. 6, 1914). Maj. 3rd Shropshire L.I., attd. 2nd Middlesex Regt. France. Killed in action near Armentières on Apr. 9, 1918.

1913 Brooks, N. B. (Sept. 7, 1915). Lt. Cheshire Yeomanry, attd. 10th Shropshire L.I. (Capt.). Egypt, Palestine, France. *M.C.*, Sept. 21, 1918.

1912 Brooks,* T. M., B.A. (Mobilized Aug. 1914). Capt. Cheshire Yeomanry, attd. 10th Shropshire L.I. Egypt, 1916–17; Palestine, 1917–18; France, 1918. *M.C.*, Feb. 15, 1919. Croix de Guerre.

1898 Brown, Rev. E. K., M.A. (Aug. 6, 1918). Chaplain to the Forces (4th Class).

1910 **Brown,* G. B.**, B.A. (July 29, 1915). Lt. 5th Manchester Regt., attd. Sudan Civil Service. France, Sudan. *M.C.*, Nov. 26, 1917. Died of malaria in the Sudan on Apr. 21, 1918.

1905 **Brown, P. A.**, M.A. (Sept. 1, 1914). ‡Lt. 13th Durham L.I. France. Killed in action near Armentières on Nov. 4, 1915.

1900 Browne, E. C. (June 21, 1915). Capt., Acting Maj., R.A.S.C. *D.* § Mar. 1918.

1904 Bruce, Hon. C. N., B.A. (Sept. 19, 1914). Lt. 2nd Life Guards, attd. Guards M.G. Regt. (Capt.). France.

1899 **Bruce, G. J.** (Sept. 14, 1914). Capt. 13th R. Irish Rifles (Ulster Div.). Bde.-Maj. 109th Inf. Bde. France and Belgium. *D.S.O.*, Mar. 21, 1918; *M.C.*, June 4, 1917; *Bar*, Feb. 18, 1918. *D.* France, 1916, 1918. Killed in action at Dadazelle on Oct. 3, 1918.

1899 **Bruce, Hon. H. L.** (Serving Aug. 4, 1914). Capt. 3rd Scots Guards. France and Belgium, 1914. *D.* France, 1914. Killed in action in Belgium on Dec. 4, 1914.

1908 Bruce, Hon. J. H. (Mobilized Aug. 1914). Lt. Glamorganshire Yeomanry. (Resigned on account of ill health, Apr., 1915.)

1905 Bruce, R. J. (Dec. 1915). Lt. R.A.O.C. *D.* § Aug. 1919.

1910 Bruce,* R. M., B.A. (Serving Aug. 4, 1914). Capt., Bt. Maj., 2/5th Gurkha Rifles, I.A. N.W. Frontier; Mesopotamia. *M.C.*, June 3, 1918.

1907 **Bruce, V. C.**, B.A. (Sept. 1914). ‡Lt. 5th Gordon Highlanders. France. Missing, presumed killed in action on Mar. 26, 1916.

1902 Bruce, W. F., B.A. (Mobilized Aug. 1914). Capt., Acting-Maj. R.E. (Signal Service). France. (Prisoner of war in Germany.) *D.S.O.*, Jan. 1, 1918. *M.C.*, Jan. 14, 1916. *D.* France, 1915, 1916, 1917.

Bryett, L. H. F. (Nov. 3, 1917). 2nd Lt. R.F.A. (S.R.) (61st Div.). France. Died on Oct. 25, 1918, of wounds received in action at Haussy near Cambrai.

1904 Buckmaster, H. S. G., B.A. (Sept. 21, 1914). Capt., Bt.-Maj., Temp. Maj., Bucks. Bn. Oxf. & Bucks. Lt. Infty. G.S.O. 2. *O.B.E.* (Mil.). *D.* § Mar. 1918. (Commission relinquished on account of ill health.)

1919 Buesst, T. N. M. (Jan. 1916). Lt. 18th Middlesex Regt. France and Belgium.

Buist, C. E. (Sept. 29, 1914). Lt. R.G.A. (Capt.). France and Belgium. *M.C.*, Aug. 16, 1917. Died on Oct. 21, 1917, of wounds received in action at Pravenstafel.

1919 Bull, W. H. (Sept. 4, 1918). Cadet, Household Bde., O.C.B.

1910 Burdekin,* B., M.A. (Aug. 15, 1914). Capt. B Batt. 242nd Bde., R.F.A. (Maj.). France, 1914–15, 1917–18.

1913 Burdon-Sanderson, R. L. (Sept. 19, 1914). 2nd Lt. R.F.A. (resigned). 2nd Lt., Acting Capt., Technical Officer, R.A.F.

1913 Burge, M. R. K. (Oct. 3, 1914). Lt., Temp. Capt., The Buffs (E. Kent Regt.). G.S.O. 3, attd. War Office. France. Croix de Guerre (with palm). *D.* § Aug. 1918.

1910 Burger, S. G. H., B.A. (July 31, 1918). 2nd Lt. Lancashire Fusiliers.

Burn, A. S. Pelham (Nov. 5, 1914). Lt. 6th Gordon Highlanders (T.F.). France and Belgium. *D.* France, 1915. Killed in action near Festubert on May 2, 1915.

1884 Burnett, W. F. (June 14, 1915). A.B. Anti-Aircraft Corps, R.N.V.R.

1897 Burr, M., M.A., D.Sc. (Nov. 1915). Capt., Interpreter, Special Lists. Superintendent R.E. Labour Camp. Salonika, 1915–18. Order of the White Eagle (5th Class). Chevalier of the Order of the Redeemer, (5th Class) (Greece). *D.* Salonika, 1918.

1919 Burrell, N. H. F. (1918). 2nd Lt. R.A. (on demobilization).

1906 Burrows, Rev. H. R., M.A. (Sept. 9, 1914). Chaplain to the Forces (4th Class). (Resigned on account of ill health.)

1919 Butcher, A. H. G. (Jan. 18, 1917). Lt. 2nd Coldstream Guards (S.R.). France. *M.C.*, Feb. 18, 1918.

1906 Butler, A. W., B.A. (Oct. 4, 1914). Capt. 4th R. Sussex Regt., attd. M.G.C. Gallipoli, Egypt, Palestine.

1896 Butler, H. E., M.A. (May 30, 1915). Lt., Acting Capt., R.F.A. Staff-Lieutenant (1st Class), attd. British Military Mission, Italy. Italy, 1918.

1907 [**Butler, L. G.,** M.A.] (Aug. 1914). Capt. 3rd Rifle Brigade. France, 1916. Killed in action at Guillemont on Aug. 21, 1916.

1894 Butler, Hon. L. J. P. (Serving Aug. 4, 1914). Lt.-Col. Irish Guards (Brig.-Gen.). France. *C.M.G.* *D.S.O.*, Jan. 14, 1916. *D.* France, 1916, 1917 twice.

1914 Butler-Thwing, F. W. (Dec. 9, 1914). Lt., Acting Capt., Coldstream Guards. France and Belgium, 1916, 1917.

1904 Button, G. T., B.A. (Mobilized Aug. 4, 1914). Capt. 3rd Oxf. & Bucks. Lt. Infty. France, Aug. 1914. (Wounded and prisoner of war from Aug. 1914–18.)

1913 Cade, A. J. M. (Aug. 1914). Pte. 1/5th Gloucestershire Regt. France, 1915. (Invalided.)

1914 Cameron, N. O. M. (Aug. 11, 1915). Lt. 1st Q.O. Cameron Highlanders (Capt. Liaison Officer, attd. R.F.A.). France, 1915–16, 1918–19.

1903 **Campbell, A. W. G.,** M.A. (Serving Aug. 4, 1914). Lt. Coldstream Guards. France, 1914. Died on Sept. 20, 1914, of wounds received on the Aisne.

1906 Campbell,* C. H., B.A. (Jan. 12, 1915). Lt. R.F.A. Salonika, France.

1910 [Campbell,* J. M. H., B.M.] (May 10, 1915). Capt. R.A.M.C. (S.R.). Mesopotamia. *D.* Mesopotamia, 1918.

1891 Campion, Rev. F. H., M.A. (Sept. 1, 1914). Chaplain to the Forces (4th Class), attd. 29th Div. Gallipoli. (Invalided Feb. 1916.)

1889 Campion, W. R., B.A., *M.P.* (Mobilized Aug. 1914). Lt.-Col. 4th R. Sussex Regt. Gallipoli, France, Germany. *D.S.O.*, Jan. 1, 1918. T.D. *D.* Gallipoli, 1915; France, 1919.

Cancellor, D. B. (Apr. 26, 1917). Lt. Hampshire Regt. (S.R.), attd. 1st Bn. France. *M.C.*, Oct. 24, 1918. Killed in action at Présau on Nov. 1, 1918.

1919 Canfield, C. (Feb. 1917). 2nd Lt. 48th F.A., U.S. Army.

1908 Cannon,* P. S., M.A. (Aug. 21, 1914). Capt. 9th Lancashire Fusiliers, attd. T.M.B. and attd. 1st Manchester Regt. Mediterranean, 1915; Mesopotamia, 1916–18; Palestine, 1918–19.

1903 Carpenter, J. A., M.A. (Aug. 22, 1914). Maj. R.E. D.A.D., Engineering Stores. France and Belgium, 1915–19. *D.* France, 1919.

1911 Carritt, R. G. (Feb. 14, 1915). Lt. 1st London Regt. (R. Fusiliers). Lt. Labour Corps (Capt.).

1919 Carroll, D. B. (Aug. 20, 1917). Lt. 364th Inf. Regt., U.S. Army (Capt.). France.

1908 Carson, J. B., B.A. (Jan. 1, 1915). Capt. R.H.A. (Staff-Captain, attd. Intelligence Corps). France and Belgium, 1915–18; Germany, 1918–19. *M.C.*, Jan. 1, 1917. *D.* France, 1916.

1903 Carte, G. W., B.M. (Aug. 6, 1914). Surgeon Lt. R.N.

1888 Carter, Rev. A. A., M.A. (Serving Aug. 4, 1914). Chaplain, R.N. H.M.S. *Marlborough*, Grand Fleet, 1916.

1900 Carter, E. P., B.A. (Sept. 2, 1914). Capt., Temp. Maj., 4th R. Berkshire Regt. D.A.A.G. France. *O.B.E.* (Mil.).

1914 Cartwright, E. C. (Dec. 24, 1914). Capt., Acting Maj., 7th Somerset L.I. France. *M.C.*, Nov. 14, 1916.

1919 Cartwright, G. (Oct. 4, 1918). 2nd Lt. Grenadier Guards (on demobilization).

1908 Cartwright, G. H. G. M., M.A. (Mobilized Aug. 1914). Lt. 5th London Regt. (London Rifle Brigade). Lt. Coldstream Guards (S.R.) (Maj. attd. Guards M.G. Regt.). France and Belgium. *D.* France, 1917.

1908 Casson, S., M.A. (Aug. 15, 1914). Capt. 3rd E. Lancashire Regt. G.S.O. 3, G.H.Q., British Salonika Force. Belgium, 1915; Salonika, 1916–18; Turkey, 1918–19. Greek Order of the Redeemer. *D.* Salonika, 1918.

1919 Catlin, G. E. G. (May 10, 1918). Rfln. 5th London Regt. (London Rifle Brigade). Belgium.

1904 Caton, R. B., M.A. (Sept. 1914). Capt. 1/4th Norfolk Regt. Gallipoli, 1915; Egypt, 1915–17; Palestine, 1917–18; Syria, 1918. *M.C.*, Jan. 1, 1918.

1896 **Cawley, H. T.,** M.A., *M.P.* (Mobilized Aug. 4, 1914). Capt. 6th Manchester Regt.(A.D.C.). Egypt, 1914 ; Gallipoli, 1915. Killed in action in Gallipoli on Sept. 24, 1915.

1901 **Cawley, Hon. O.,** B.A., *M.P.* (Mobilized Aug. 4, 1914). Capt. Shropshire Yeomanry, attd. 10th Shropshire L.I. Egypt, Palestine, France. Killed in action near Merville on Aug. 22, 1918.

1909 Centlivres, A. van de S. (1915). Pte. Duke of Edinburgh's Own Vol. Rifles. German S.W. Africa.

1900 Chambers, G. W., B.A. (Apr. 8, 1917). Lt. R.F.A. (S.R.).

1908 Champenois, J. J., B.Litt. (Aug. 2, 1914). ‡Lt. 13th Infanterie, French Army. France, 1915–17. Croix de Chevalier de la Légion d'Honneur. Croix de Guerre. *D.* France, twice.

1919 Champion, F. W. (Aug. 4, 1914). Capt. Kurram Militia, N.W. Frontier. India, 1914–19 ; Afghanistan, 1919.

1898 Champneys, A. L., B.A. (Nov. 13, 1914). Lt. R.E. (T.F.) (Commission relinquished on account of ill health.)

1919 Chapman, E. G. (Apr. 1917). Capt. 5th M.G. Bn., U.S. Army. France. *American D.S.C.*, Sept. 1917. *D.* France, 1917.

1899 **Chapman, M.** (June 25, 1915). Capt. 4th Grenadier Guards. France. *M.C.*, Feb. 4, 1918. Killed in action at Gars Brugya Farm, near Muris, on Apr. 12, 1918.

1914 Charley, L. W. (Dec. 22, 1914). 2nd Lt. 13th R. Warwickshire Regt. Lt. Intelligence Corps. (Capt.). France. *O.B.E.* (Mil.). *D.* France, 1917, 1919.

1904 Charrington, C. E. W., M.A. (Aug. 15, 1914). Capt. 4th, attd. 7th, S. Staffordshire Regt. (Maj.). Belgium and France, 1915–19. *M.C.*, July 26, 1918.

1897 Chawner, L. C. (Mobilized Aug. 1914). Capt., temp. Maj., 3rd Dorsetshire Regt. D.A.A.G. E. Africa, 1918–19. *D.* § Feb. 1917 ; E. Africa, 1918.

1903 **Cheesman, G. L.,** M.A. (Aug. 26, 1914). Lt. 10th Hampshire Regt. Gallipoli, 1915. Killed in action in the attack on Chunuk Bair on Aug. 10, 1915.

1902 **Cherry, L. A.,** B.A. (1914). Sub-Lt. R.N.V.R., Drake Bn., R.N. Div. Gallipoli, 1915. Killed in action in Gallipoli on May 12, 1915.

1902 Child-Villiers, Hon. A. G. (Mobilized Aug. 1914). Maj. Q.O. Oxfordshire Hussars. France and Belgium. *D.S.O.*, July 18, 1917 ; *Bar*, Sept. 16, 1918. Croix de Guerre. *D.* France, 1917, 1918.

1919 Chitty, J. H. (Aug. 29, 1917). 2nd Lt. 6th, attd. 16th, K.R.R.C. (Lt.).

1919 Cholmondeley, H. (Aug. 1917). 2nd Lt. Coldstream Guards (S.R.). France. *M.C.*, Feb. 15, 1919.

1914 Clark, A. G. (Dec. 10, 1915). ‡Lt. 78th Siege Batt., R.G.A. Malta, 1917–18 ; France, 1918–19.

1900 Clark, H. G. (Oct. 25, 1915). Lt. R.A.S.C. France 1916–19.

1902 **Clarke, A. G.,** B.A. (Dec. 1914). ‡2nd Lt. 5th, attd. 1st, Rifle Brigade. France. Killed in action at Beaumont Hamel, July 1–2, 1916.

1899 Clarke, W. L. R., M.A. (Jan. 5, 1916). ‡Lt. F.A., A.I.F. France.

1907 Clarkson, G. A., B.A. (Feb. 21, 1916). Instructor Lt. R.N.

1889 **Clay, A. J.,** M.A. (Sept. 1914). Maj. 2/6th N. Staffordshire Regt. Died on Feb. 18, 1915, of illness contracted on active service.

1891 Clay, E. C., B.A. (Aug. 12, 1915). Maj. General List. D.A.A.G., War Office. *C.B.E.* (Mil.). *D.* § Feb. 1917.
1893 Clay, S., M.A. (Apr. 7, 1916). Lt. 4th K.O.Y.L.I. Lt. 8th Vol. Bn. W. Riding Regt.
1892 Clay, W. H., B.A. (Sept. 30, 1914). Capt. 6th N. Staffordshire Regt. (Maj.). France, 1917–18, 1918–19. *M.C.*, Dec. 17, 1917.
1903 Clements, E. F. (Sept. 1914). ‡Lt. 3rd Lincolnshire Regt. Acting Capt. Tank Corps. France.
1886 Cobb, C. H., B.A. (1914). ‡2nd Lt. Vol. Bn. 22nd W. Riding Regt.
1907 **Cobb, F. C.,** B.A. (Aug. 22, 1914). Capt. 6th K.O. Scottish Borderers. France. Killed in action in France before Hohenzollern Redoubt on Sept. 25, 1915.
1906 Cockburn,* A. W., B.A. (Dec. 1914). 2nd Lt. R.G.A. Belgium, France.
1895 Cockerell, F. P. (Jan. 2, 1915). Capt. Special Lists (Lt.-Col.). A.P.M. Salonika, Mesopotamia, Dumville Mission. *O.B.E.* (Mil.). *M.C.*, Jan. 1, 1918. Chevalier of the Order of the Redeemer. *D.* Salonika, 1917; Mesopotamia, 1918, 1919.
1897 Codrington, H. W. (Oct. 31, 1918). Lt. R.A.O.C.
1910 Codrington,* W. M. (Serving Aug. 4, 1914). Lt. 16th Lancers, attd. R.E. (Signals) (Capt.). Belgium, France. *M.C.*, June 3, 1919. *D.* France, 1917.
1906 Cohen, L. L., M.A. (Mobilized Aug. 4, 1914). Capt. 13th London Regt. Staff-Captain. France, 1914–15, 1915–16.
1898 Colledge, J. T., B.A. (Mobilized Aug. 1914). 2nd Lt. R. Gloucestershire Hussars. Lt. Guards M.G. Regt. (Capt.).
1904 **Collis-Sandes, M. J.,** B.A. (Aug. 1914). Capt. 11th R. Fusiliers. France. *D.* France, 1917. Killed in action near Miraumont on Feb. 17, 1917.
1912 **Colvill, G. C.** (Aug. 1914). Capt. S. Irish Horse, attd. 7th R. Irish Regt. France. Killed in action near Fontaine-lez-Croiselles on Nov. 30, 1917.
1913 Comins,* C. J., B.A. (Sept. 28, 1914). Capt. R.F.A. (Maj.). Belgium and France, 1915–18. *M.C.*, June 4, 1917; *Bar*, Sept. 16, 1918. (Invalided on account of wounds, 1919.)
1909 **Congleton,* H. F. B., Lord,** B.A. (Serving Aug. 4, 1914). Lt. Grenadier Guards. France and Belgium. *D.* France, 1914. Killed in action near Ypres on Nov. 10, 1914.
1904 Connal-Rowan, G. F. (Serving Aug. 4, 1914). Capt. Arg. & Suth'd. Highlanders. France. (Prisoner of war, Aug. 1914–18.)
1919 Conquest, E. P. (July 24, 1917). Capt. 112th Field Artillery, U.S. Army. France.
1907 Conybeare, J. J., B.M., M.A. (Mobilized Aug. 4, 1914). Maj. 4th Oxf. & Bucks. Lt. Infty., afterwards Capt. R.A.M.C. France, 1915–16; Mesopotamia. *M.C.*, June 3, 1916.
1907 Coode,* B. H., B.A. (Aug. 6, 1914). Lt., Acting Capt., Army Cyclist Corps. France.
1919 Coode-Adams, G. (Feb. 20, 1918). 2nd Lt. 472nd Siege Batt., R.G.A.
1904 **Cook, A. B. K.,** B.A. (Jan. 1915). 2nd Lt. 9th R. Fusiliers. France. Killed in action at Ovillers on July 7, 1916.
1887 Cooke, A., B.M., M.A. (Mobilized Aug. 1914). Maj. R.A.M.C. (T.F.), 1st E. Gen. Hospital.

1898 Cooke, H. H., M.A. (Serving Aug. 4, 1914). Lt. Unattached List, T.F., Fettes College O.T.C.

1887 Cooke, T. P. (Aug. 29, 1914). Maj. 14th R. Warwickshire Regt. France and Belgium, 1915–18.

1908 Cooper, A. D. (Oct. 31, 1917). Lt. Grenadier Guards. France. *D.S.O.*, Dec. 2, 1918.

1898 Cooper, G. A., B.A. (May 19, 1916). Pte. 16th London Regt. (Queen's Westminster Rifles). (Discharged on account of ill health, June 27, 1916.)

1903 Cooper, S. C. P. (Jan. 16, 1915). Lt. 3rd London Regt. (R. Fusiliers). Capt. R.E.

1913 Coote, E. O. (June 12, 1916). ‡Lt. Special Lists (empld. Intelligence Dept.) (Capt.). Italy, 1917–18; Salonika, 1918; Hungary, 1919. *D.* § Aug. 1917. (Civilian prisoner in Germany, Aug. 1914–Mar. 1916.)

1901 Corbett, A. G., M.A. (Oct. 1, 1914). Maj. Sussex Yeomanry, empld. Ministry of Munitions (Lt.-Col.). *D.* § Feb. 1917.

1907 Cork, Rev. W. N., B.A. (Aug. 8, 1918). Chaplain to the Forces (4th Class).

1902 **Cotton, R. C. F.,** M.A. (Oct. 27, 1914). Lt. 1/1st Hampshire Yeomanry and M.G.C. France. Croix de Guerre with star. *D.* French Orders. Died on Mar. 28, 1918, of wounds received at Boix des Essarts.

1903 Counsell, H. E., M.A. (Aug. 1914). Maj. R.A.M.C. (T.F.), 3rd S. Gen. Hospital.

1892 **Courthope, W. G.,** B.A. (Jan. 1915). Capt. 4th Bedfordshire Regt., Staff-Captain R.A.F. France. Died on Oct. 21, 1918, of illness contracted while on active service.

1900 Courtney, H. G., B.A. (Dec. 1915). Lt. 127th Siege Batt., R.G.A. France, 1914–15; Salonika, 1916–18. *D.* Salonika, 1919.

1919 Cousland, K. H. (Aug. 20, 1914). Maj. 17th Bde., R.F.A. France and Belgium, 1916, 1917–19. *M.C.*, Sept. 16, 1918. Croix de Guerre. *D.* France, 1918.

1913 Cox, A. H. G., B.A. (June 21, 1915). Lt. 8th Sherwood Foresters (T.F.), attd. Signal Service. France, 1915–19. *M.C.*, Jan. 1, 1918.

1909 **Cox, R. W. T.,** B.A. (Aug. 5, 1914). ‡2nd Lt. 6th Dorsetshire Regt. France, Belgium. *D.* France, 1916. Died on Feb. 15, 1916, of wounds received in action in Belgium.

1887 Cozens-Hardy, Hon. W. H., M.A. (1914). Hon. Commdr. R.N.V.R. France, Italy, Morocco. Officer of the Order of St. Maurice and St. Lazarus.

1893 Craik, G. L., M.A. (Sept. 1914). Capt. 2nd Lovat's Scouts, empld. Board of Trade. Gallipoli, Egypt, Macedonia, France. *M.C.*, June 3, 1918. *D.* Salonika, 1917.

1919 Crawford, W. F. (June 7, 1915). Capt. 1st Arg. & Suth'd. Highlanders. France, 1915–16; Salonika, 1916–18. *D.* Salonika, 1919.

1884 Crawfurd, R. H. P., D.M. (Aug. 1914). Capt. R.A.M.C., 4th London Gen. Hospital.

1903 Creighton, A. B., B.A. (Sept. 1916). 2nd Lt. 17th London Regt. Staff-Lt. (2nd Class), Intelligence Corps. France.

1905 Crichton, G. H., B.A. (Mobilized Aug. 1914). Capt. 8th Cameronians. (Commission relinquished on account of ill health.)

1901 Cripps, Hon. A. H. S., B.A. (May 5, 1915). Lt. Lincolnshire Yeomanry (Capt.). Courts Martial Officer.
1903 Cripps, Hon. F. H. (Mobilized Aug. 1914). Maj. R. Bucks. Hussars, attd. M.G.C. (Lt.-Col.). Egypt, Palestine, France. *D.S.O.*, Jan. 1, 1918; *Bar*, Mar. 5, 1918. *D.* Egypt, 1917; France, 1919.
1913 Crook, E. A., B.M. (Sept. 1914). Pte. 12th Middlesex Regt. (1914). Surgeon R.N. (1917). H.M.S. *Ceanothus*, Mediterranean, 1917.
1910 **Crook,* P. J.,** B.A. (Mobilized Aug. 1914). Lt. Duke of Lancaster's Own Yeomanry. Egypt and Palestine. Killed in action in Palestine at Wadi Hesi on Nov. 7, 1917.
1919 Cross, P. K. (June 23, 1916). Lt., Acting Capt. and Adjt., 52nd Bde., R.F.A. France and Belgium. *M.C.*, Mar. 8, 1919.
1919 Cross, M. R. (1918). 2nd Lt. R.A.
1919 Crossley, J. S. Midshipman, R.N.
1899 Crosthwaite, A. T., B.A. (Nov. 16, 1914). Lt., temp. Capt., R.A.S.C. Major, D.A.A.G. France. *O.B.E.* (Mil.). *D.* France, 1918, 1919.
1898 Crosthwaite, H. S., B.A. Allahabad Light Horse. India.
1893 Crum, W. E., B.A. (Aug. 4, 1914). Maj. 3rd Calcutta Light Horse, I.D.F. India. *O.B.E.* (Civil).
1909 Crutchley, G. E. V., B.A. (Aug. 15, 1914). Lt. 1st Scots Guards. France. (Prisoner of war.)
1911 Cryan, R. W. W., B.A. (Nov. 4, 1914). Lt. 8th N. Staffordshire Regt. T. M. Officer, attd. 57th Bde. France and Belgium, 1915–18. *D.* France, 1917.
1899 **Cullis, H. T.,** B.A. (June 13, 1915). 2nd Lt. 12th Rifle Brigade. France. Killed in action at Armentières on Dec. 10, 1915.
1906 Culme-Seymour, E. V. (June 1, 1918). 2nd Lt. R. Marines.
1894 [**Cunliffe, Sir F. H. E., Bt.,** M.A.] (Dec. 1914). Maj. 13th Rifle Brigade. France. Killed in action in the Battle of the Somme on July 10, 1916.
1899 Curwen, J. K., M.A. (July 2, 1915). Lt. R.N.V.R. Maj., Staff Officer, Controller-Gen. of Equipment, R.A.F. *D.* § Jan. 1919.
1904 Curwen, J. P. (Mar. 27, 1915). Lt. R.N.V.R., R.N. Armoured Car Div.
1902 Dale, A. B., B.A. (Mobilized Aug. 1914). Capt. 1st County of London Yeomanry. R.T.O. Italy, Macedonia, Egypt, Palestine, Syria.
1913 Daly,* D. W. (Nov. 11, 1914). Lt. 8th Hussars. France.
1886 Darell-Brown, H. F. (Serving Aug. 4, 1914). Maj. 2nd Oxf. & Bucks. Lt. Infty. India, 1914–19. Order of Aviz (Portugal).
1876 David, T. W. E., B.A., Hon. D.Sc. (1915). Lt.-Col. A.I.F. France. *C.M.G. D.S.O.*, Jan. 1, 1918. *D.* France, 1917.
1900 Davies, C. M. (Serving Aug. 4, 1914). Maj., Bt.-Lt.-Col., Rifle Brigade. G.S.O. 1. France, Gallipoli, Egypt. *D.S.O.*, Feb. 18, 1915. Croix de Guerre. *D.* Egypt, 1916; Gallipoli, 1916; France, 1918.
1919 Davies, D. G. (Sept. 25, 1915). Lt. 19th Welsh Regt. France, 1916, 1917–19.
1919 Davies, H. W. (July 5, 1917). Capt. Australian A.M.C. France and Belgium, 1917–19.
1907 Davies,* J. C., D.M. (Aug. 1915). Capt. R.A.M.C. (Maj. Field Amb. 43rd Div.). Belgium, France, Germany, 1915–19.
1908 **Davies,* M. A. M.,** B.A. (Sept. 14, 1914). 2nd Lt. 9th Devonshire Regt. France. Killed in action at Hulluch on Sept. 25, 1915.

1886 Davies, M. F., B.A. Lt. and Adjt. 7th Vol. Bn. Lancashire Regt.
1910 Davies,* W. T., M.A. (Aug. 14, 1914). Capt. 4th Highland L.I., attd. O.C.B. France and Belgium, 1915, 1916–17. *M.C.*, Feb. 14, 1917.
1905 Davis, R. E. J., M.A. (Sept. 24, 1914). 2nd Lt., Acting Capt., Special Lists, attd. R.A.V.C. France and Belgium.
1913 Dawson, H. N., M.A. (Mar. 13, 1915). Lt. 10th Queen's (R. W. Surrey Regt.). France.
1890 Dawson, W. F. Ladybrand Mounted Rifles. S. Africa.
1910 **Dawson-Damer,* Hon. G. S.** (Mobilized Aug. 1914). 2nd Lt. 10th Hussars. France and Belgium. Died on Apr. 12, 1917, of wounds received in action.
1898 Dean, H. R., D.M. (Aug. 19, 1914). Maj. R.A.M.C., attd. 2nd W. Gen. Hospital.
1914 de Beer, E. S. (1916). ‡2nd Lt. 35th Sikhs, Indian Army (Lt.). India.
1886 de Brett, E. A. (Feb. 2, 1915). Lt. R. Defence Corps.
1895 **de Knoop, J. J. J.** (Mobilized Aug. 1914). Capt. Cheshire Yeomanry, attd. Imp. Camel Corps (Maj.). Staff-Captain. France, 1914–15; Egypt, 1916. *D.* Egypt, 1916. Killed in action at Hod-el-Bahein on Aug. 7, 1916.
1920 Demuth, W. H. H. (Mar. 26, 1917). ‡Lt. 13th K.R.R.C. France, Germany. *M.C.*, May 13, 1918.
1905 **de Neufville, E. C.**, B.A. (Aug. 10, 1914). ‡Maj. R.G.A. France, 1916–18. *D.S.O.*, Jan. 1, 1918. Belgian Croix de Guerre. *D.* France, 1917 twice. Missing, believed killed in action at Vaulx Vraucourt on Mar. 21, 1918.
1899 Denison, J. L., M.A. (July 10, 1915). Capt. Courts Martial Officer, Special Lists. France, 1915–18; Italy, 1918.
1897 **Denison, W. F. E.**, M.A. (Sept. 1916). 2nd Lt. 15th Sherwood Foresters. France. Died on Mar. 26, 1918, of wounds received in action near Amiens.
1906 [Denniston, J. D., M.A.] (Sept. 1, 1914). Capt. 7th K.O. Scottish Borderers. Maj. General List. G.S.O. 2, War Office. France, 1915, 1916. *O.B.E.* (Mil.). Croix de Guerre.
1890 Denny, E. W. (Serving Aug. 4, 1914). Maj. 19th Hussars. Bde. Maj., H.Q. 75th Inf. Bde. France. *D.S.O.*, Sept. 16, 1918. *D.* § Feb. 1917; France, 1918.
1912 Denroche-Smith,* L. P., B.A. (Dec. 1915). Lt. 4–5th The Black Watch. France.
1912 Dent,* A. C. (Sept. 1914). Sergt. Essex Yeomanry. ‡Lt. Observer Officer, R.A.F. France, 1914–15; Egypt, 1915; Palestine, 1916; Salonika, 1916; Italy, 1918.
1910 Dewar, A. C., B.Litt. Commdr. R.N. (Ret.), empld. Recruiting Staff.
1911 **Dewar, I. D.** (Aug. 1914). Capt. 5th Q.O. Cameron Highlanders (Adjt.). France and Belgium. Killed in action in Belgium on Mar. 16, 1916.
1903 Dewar, Hon. J., B.A. (Mobilized Aug. 4, 1914). Maj. Scottish Horse, attd. 13th The Black Watch. Gallipoli, Egypt, Salonika, France. *M.C.*, Apr. 2, 1919.
1897 [de Zulueta, F., M.A., D.C.L.] (Dec. 30, 1914). Capt. 2nd Worcestershire Regt. France, 1918–19.
1900 [**Dickens, G.**, M.A.] (Nov. 1914). Capt. 13th K.R.R.C. France, 1915–16. Died on July 17, 1916, of wounds received in action.

1885 [Disraeli, C. R.] (Mobilized Aug. 1914). Maj. R. Bucks. Hussars, attd. R.A.F.

1919 Dixon, R. V. (1918). 2nd Lt. Coldstream Guards.

1911 Dodd, A. H., B.A. (1914). 2nd W. Lancashire Field Amb., R.A.M.C.

1909 Dodsworth, L. L. S., B.A. (Oct. 8, 1914). Lt. 12th W. Yorkshire Regt. (Resigned on account of ill health.)

1912 **Don,* R. M.** (Sept. 1914). Lt. 10th The Black Watch. France, 1915; Salonika, 1915–17. Killed in action on the Doiran front, Macedonia, May 8–9, 1917.

Don, V. G. (Oct. 1914). Lt. 8th R. W. Kent Regt. France. *D.* France, 1915. Killed in action at Loos on Sept. 26, 1915.

1912 **Donald,* A. J. I.** (Aug. 12, 1914). 2nd Lt. 6th Manchester Regt. Egypt, Gallipoli. Killed in action in Gallipoli on June 4, 1915.

1917 Donne-Smith, B. (Apr. 5, 1918). 2nd Lt. K.R.R.C. France, 1918–19.

1893 Donoughmore, R. W. G., Earl of, *K.P.* (Aug. 1917). Col. British Red Cross Society. France, 1915–17. *D.* France, 1916, 1917.

1906 Douglas, Rev. P. S., M.A. (Nov. 1917). Chaplain to the Forces (4th Class), attd. 37th Div. France and Belgium.

1883 Douglas, R. L. (Nov. 12, 1914). Capt. R.A.S.C., Staff-Captain.

1891 Dove, J., M.A. (Nov. 5, 1915). Lt. 3rd Sherwood Foresters (Capt.).

1893 Dowson, A. O. (May 1915). Capt. 12th Rifle Brigade (Maj.). France. *M.C.*, Jan. 1, 1918. *D.* France, 1917.

1899 Dowson, O. F., M.A. (Sept. 29, 1914). Lt., temp. Maj., R.A.S.C. D.A.A.G. France. *O.B.E.* (Mil.). *D.* France, 1918, 1919.

Draper, D. (May 14, 1915). Lt. R.F.A. France. Died on Feb. 21, 1918, of illness contracted while on active service.

1919 Draper, G. N. (Jan. 4, 1918). 2nd Lt. 173rd Bde., R.F.A. France, 1918–19.

1911 [Driver, G. R., M.A.] (Feb. 9, 1915). Capt. Graves Registration Commission. Capt. Intelligence Corps. (Maj. D.A.A.G.). Serbia, France, Belgium, Egypt, Palestine. *M.C.*, Jan. 1, 1918. *D.* France, 1917.

1907 Drury, D. D. (Aug. 6, 1914). Lt. Special Lists, Interpreter. Staff-Lt. (2nd Class). Lt., Hon. Capt., Flying Officer, R.A.F.

1901 Duff, A. C., B.A. (Oct. 31, 1917). Lt. I.A.R.O., attd. 1st Labour Corps; temp. Capt. Political Dept., M.E.F. Mesopotamia. *D.* Mesopotamia, 1918.

1903 Duguid, P., B.A. (Aug. 15, 1914). Capt. 3rd Gordon Highlanders. Belgium, 1914; France, 1915.

1905 Dumville-Lees, A. C. L., B.A. (Serving Aug. 4, 1914). Capt., Acting Maj., Shropshire L.I. W. Africa, France. *D.* French Orders.

1911 Duncan, C. H. S. (Serving Aug. 4, 1914). Capt. R. Scots.

1903 [Dundas, R. H., M.A.] (Jan. 2, 1915). Capt. 2nd The Black Watch. France, 1915; Mesopotamia, 1916–17; India, 1917–19. *D.* Mesopotamia, 1916; India, 1919.

1901 Dundas, R. W., M.A. (July 27, 1915). Lt., temp. Maj., 8th R. Scots. D.A.Q.M.G., H.Q. Tank Corps. France. *M.C.*, June 3, 1918. *D.* France, 1919.

1880 Dunkin, Rev. H., M.A., T.D. (Serving Aug. 4, 1914). Maj. Unattached List, T.F., Sherborne School O.T.C. *D.* § Mar. 1918.

1919 Dunlop, D. C. (Aug. 1915). 2nd Lt. 3rd The Buffs (E. Kent Regt.). Lt., attd. R.E. (Army Signal Service).

1898 **Dunn-Pattison, R. P.,** M.A. (Mobilized Aug. 1914). Capt. and Adjt. 6th Devonshire Regt. (T.F.). Mesopotamia. *D.* Mesopotamia, 1916. Killed in action in Mesopotamia on Mar. 8, 1916.

1912 Dunstan, J. L., B.A. (Dec. 7, 1914). 2nd Lt. R.A., attd. R.F.C. (Died.)

1902 Dutton, H. T., M.A. (May 31, 1916). Gnr. Antrim R.G.A. Sergt. 10th R. Fusiliers, attd. Intelligence Police. France, 1917–19.

1910 Dyer, A. O. (Mobilized Aug. 1914). Capt. R.F.A. (T.F.).

1898 **Dyer, H. A.,** B.Mus. (Dec. 11, 1916). 2nd Lt. R.F.C. France. Killed in action on Dec. 7, 1917.

1912 **Ealand, F. J. A.** (Oct. 1914). 2nd Lt. 8th Somerset L.I. France. Killed in action at Loos on Sept. 26, 1915.

1913 East, C. F. T., B.A. (Feb. 20, 1915). Lt. 3rd, attd. 5th, Northamptonshire Regt. France.

1914 Eastman, G. R. T. (Feb. 9, 1915). Lt. Surrey Yeomanry, attd. 8th E. Surrey Regt. A.P.M.

1880 Eastwood, J. C. B., Hon. M.A. (Serving Aug. 4, 1914). Col. 12th Lancers. Base Commandant at Dieppe, 1918. France, 1914–18. *C.B. C.M.G.* *D.* France, 1916, 1917, 1918.

1908 Eastwood,* J. P. B., B.A. (Aug. 1914). Lt., Acting Capt., R.F.A. (14th Div.). Belgium and France, 1915–19. *D.* France, 1917.

1907 Edelsten, M., B.A. (Nov. 29, 1914). Capt. R.A.S.C. Mesopotamia.

1907 Edge, R. T., M.A. (Apr. 28, 1915). Capt. R.E. France, 1915; Egypt and Palestine, 1916–19. *M.C.*, June 3, 1918.

1895 Edgington, W., B.A. (Aug. 1, 1915). Capt. R.A.S.C., Guards Divl. Train. France. *O.B.E.* (Mil.). *D.* France, 1918.

1890 Edlin, Rev. A. H. C., M.A. (Serving Aug. 4, 1914). Chaplain to the Forces (4th Class).

1891 Edmondson, F., B.A. (Feb. 24, 1915). Lt. 1st Vol. Bn. King's (Liverpool Regt.).

1894 **Edwards, G. O. C.,** B.A. (Sept. 25, 1915). 2nd Lt. 3rd, attd. 9th, W. Riding Regt. France. Killed in action near Contalmaison on July 7, 1916.

1904 **Edwards, H. L. G.,** B.A. (Aug. 1914). Lt. 3rd, attd. 1st, R. Welch Fusiliers. France. Killed in action at Festubert on May 16, 1915.

1914 Ellenberger, G. F., B.A. (Jan. 10, 1915). Capt. 9th K.O.Y.L.I. France, 1915–16, 1917–18. *M.C.*, Jan. 1, 1917; *Bar*, Sept. 16, 1918. (Prisoner of war, May–Dec. 1918.)

1908 **Elliott, G. F.,** B.A. (Sept. 14, 1914). 2nd Lt. 1st S. Staffordshire Regt. (Lt.). France. *D.* France, 1916. Killed in action at Delville Wood on Aug. 31, 1916.

1914 Ellison, R. E. ‡2nd Lt. Labour Corps. France, Germany.

1915 Elphick, H. N. K., B.A. (Dec. 20, 1915). Capt. Howitzer Bde., R. Marine Artillery. France and Belgium. *M.C.*, Nov. 7, 1916.

1913 Emmons, R. V. B., B.A. (May 4, 1916). Pte. American Motor Ambulance Volunteer Corps. France. Croix de Guerre.

1899 Estcourt, T. E. (Serving Aug. 4, 1914). Capt. 2nd Dragoons (R. Scots Greys).

1907 Evans, A. G. (1917). 2nd Lt. Engineers, U.S. Army.

1898 Evans, R. H., B.A. (Sept. 1914). Capt. 2/1st Shropshire Yeomanry (Maj.). France.

1900 Evans, T. K., B.A. (May 1915). Lt. A/104th Bde., R.F.A. (T.F.), attd. Ministry of Munitions. France, 1918–19. *D.* § Aug. 1918.

1909 Evans, W. H. F., B.A. (Oct. 2, 1914). Lt. R.F.A. (T.F.). France, 1916–19.

1898 **Everett, A. F.** Rfln. 16th London Regt. (Queen's Westminster Rifles). France. Killed in action on Apr. 14, 1917.

1891 Everitt, A. F. G., B.A. (Oct. 28, 1914). Capt. General List (Maj.). A.D.C. to G.O.C. 18th Div. France, 1915–19. *D.* France, 1919.

1909 Fagan,* A. W., B.A. (Mar. 22, 1915). 2nd Lt. 10th Middlesex Regt. Capt. I.A.R.O., attd. 92nd Punjabis. I.E.F.

1905 Fairfax,*, J. G., B.A. (Dec. 16, 1914). Capt. 15th Indian Divl. Train, R.A.S.C. Mesopotamia, 1917–19. *D.* Mesopotamia, 1917, 1918 twice, 1919.

1900 **Fairlie, J. O.,** B.A. (Nov. 30, 1914). Capt. 10th Highland L.I. France. Killed in action at Loos on Sept. 26, 1915.

1919 Fancott, E. (Sept. 17, 1914). ‡Lt. Q.O. Oxfordshire Hussars.

1904 **Farmer, C. G. E.** (May 1915). Lt. 15th, attd. 7th, K.R.R.C. France. Killed in action in the Battle of the Somme on Aug. 18, 1916.

1905 **Farmer, H. G.,** B.A. (Aug. 1914). Capt. 7th Seaforth Highlanders. France. Died as a prisoner of war at Jülich, Rheinland, on Nov. 15, 1915, of wounds received in action at Loos on Sept. 25.

1896 Farrer, F. L., B.A. (Feb. 17, 1916). Capt. R.F.A. (Maj.). France. *D.* France, 1918. (Commission relinquished on account of ill health.)

1904 Fawcus, G. E., M.A. (1914). Capt. 39th Chota Nagpur Regt., I.D.F. India.

1908 Fawcus, J. G., M.A. (Sept. 1914). 2nd Lt. Unattached List, T.F., Cranleigh School O.T.C. Lt. 1st R. Berkshire Regt. France, Germany.

1893 Feetham, R., M.A. (Aug. 29, 1916). Lt. Cape Corps, S.A. Inf. East Africa, Egypt.

1919 Fellows, A. E. (Nov. 9, 1917). 2nd Lt. 5th Northamptonshire Regt. France, 1918–19.

1909 Fenwick-Palmer,* R. G., B.A. (Serving Aug. 4, 1914). Capt., Acting Maj., 1st Life Guards, attd. 2nd Guards M.G. Regt. France. *D.* France, 1919.

1912 Finney, A. D., B.A. (Serving Aug. 4, 1914). ‡2nd Lt. R.F.A. Lt., Acting Capt. Staff Officer (3rd Class), R.A.F. Gallipoli, Egypt, Palestine.

1897 Fisher, B. D. (Serving Aug. 4, 1914). Lt.-Col. 17th Lancers. Brig.-Gen. 8th Inf. Bde. France and Belgium. *C.M.G.* *D.S.O.*, Feb. 18, 1915; *Bar*, July 26, 1918. Croix d'Officier de la Légion d'Honneur. *D.* France, 1914, 1915, 1916, 1918, 1919.

1898 **Fisher, G. K. T.,** B.A. (Mobilized Aug. 1914). Capt. 4th Norfolk Regt. Gallipoli, Mesopotamia, Egypt, and Palestine. *D.* Gallipoli, 1915. Died on Sept. 3, 1917, of wounds received in action near Gaza.

1909 Fison,* W. G., B.A. (Sept. 24, 1914). Capt. 60th Divl. Artillery, R.F.A. (T.F.) (Staff-Captain). France, 1916; Salonika, 1916–17; Palestine, 1917–19. *M.C.*, June 3, 1918. *D.* France, 1916; Salonika, 1917.

1919 Fitzherbert-Brockholes, C. (July 5, 1917). 2nd Lt. Coldstream Guards. France, 1918.

1907 Fitzherbert-Brockholes, J. W., B.A. (Mobilized Aug. 1914). Capt. Duke of Lancaster's Own Yeomanry. G.S.O. 3. France, 1915–19. *M.C.*, June 4, 1917.

1905 **Fitzherbert-Brockholes, T. J.** (Serving Aug. 4, 1914). Capt. and Adjt. 2nd Rifle Brigade. France. *D.* France, 1915. Died on Mar. 14, 1915, of wounds received in action near Neuve Chapelle.

1908 Flenley, R., B.Litt. (June 1915). Lt., Acting Capt., R.F.A. (Adjt. 149th Bde.). France, 1915–19. *D.* France, 1917, 1919.

1910 Fletcher, C. E. (formerly Fleischl, C. E.), B.A. (May 5, 1915). Capt. R.A.S.C. France, 1915–19. *M.C.*, Jan. 1, 1918.

1919 Fletcher, H. L. (Aug. 16, 1916). Bomdr. H.A.C. Belgium and France.

1902 Flint, E. C. M., B.A. (June 1, 1916). Capt. Suffolk Yeomanry, attd. 19th Squadron M.G.C. (Maj.). Gallipoli, Egypt, Palestine, Syria. *D.S.O.*, June 3, 1919. *D.* Palestine, 1919.

1902 Fooks, P. E. B., M.A. (Aug. 16, 1915). Lt., temp. Maj., R.G.A. G.S.O. 2. *O.B.E.* (Mil.). *D.* § 1917.

1919 Footman, D. J. (Oct. 13, 1914). Capt. 8th R. Berkshire Regt. France. *M.C.*, June 24, 1916. Belgian Croix de Guerre. (Prisoner of war, Mar.–Nov. 1918.)

1899 Ford, P. J., M.A. (Nov. 20, 1914). Lt., 2/4th Q.O. Cameron Highlanders. Hon. Lt. General Staff, Scottish Command. (Resigned on account of ill health.)

Forrest, R. C. (Aug. 7, 1914). Pte. 14th London Regt. (London Scottish). France and Belgium. Missing, presumed killed in action at Messines on Nov. 1, 1914.

1911 Fortescue,* Hon. D. G. (Mobilized Aug. 1914). Capt. R.N. Devon Yeomanry. Bde.-Maj. 54th Inf. Bde. France. *M.C.* Apr. 2, 1919.

1884 Fothergill, S. R., M.A. (Mobilized Aug. 1914). Lt.-Col. Westmorland & Cumberland Yeomanry. T.D. *D.* § Feb. 1917. (Commission relinquished.)

Fowler, C. G. (Aug. 16, 1914). Lt. 6th Norfolk Regt., attd. 2/8th W. York shire Regt. France, 1917. Killed in action at Ecoust St. Mein on Apr. 6, 1917.

1895 **Fowler, G. H.,** B.A. (Mobilized Aug. 1914). Lt.-Col. 8th Sherwood Foresters (T.F.). France. *D.* France, 1915. Killed in action in France on Oct. 15, 1915.

1919 Fox, J. R. (Aug. 14, 1915). Lt. 7th Seaforth Highlanders (Capt.). France, Belgium, Germany. *M.C.*, Jan. 10, 1917; *Bar*, July 26, 1918.

1913 Franchetti, C. G. F. (1915). Lt. Flying Corps, Italian Army. Italy.

1910 Franchetti, L. (1915). Italian Artillery O.T.C. Italy.

1919 Francis, H. R. (May 15, 1918). Aircraftsman (2nd Class) R.A.F., attd. Airship Dept., Admiralty.

1905 Franklin, S. E., B.A. (Jan. 29, 1915). Paymaster Lt. R.N.R. Dardanelles, 1915–16; Salonika, 1916; Havre Naval Base, 1918–19. *D.* 1916.

1911 Freeston,* L. B., B.A. (Sept. 14, 1914). ‡Lt. 7th London Regt. (attd. British Mission to U.S.A., 1918) (Capt. and Adjt.). France, 1916–18.

1908 **French, Hon. G. P.,** B.A. (Oct. 1914). Lt. 1st, attd. 5th, S. Wales Borderers. Belgium and France. Killed in action at Richebourg l'Avoué on May 9, 1915.

1919 Frick, R. D. (June 1917). 2nd Lt., 115th Field Artillery, U.S. Army.

1910 **Friend, C. P.** (May 26, 1915). Lt. R.F.A. (S.R.), Special Appointment. France and Belgium. Died on Oct. 15, 1918, of illness contracted while on active service.

1906 Fuller, H. J., M.A. (Sept. 25, 1915). Lt. Special Lists (Intelligence Corps). Staff-Lieutenant (1st Class). France. Officier de l'étoile noire de Bénin. *D.* France, 1917.

1913 Furley-Smith, W. A. D., B.A. (Sept. 1914). ‡Lt. R. E. (Signals). France, 1916–18. (Commission relinquished on account of ill health contracted while on active service, Sept. 1918.)

1898 Gadban, V. J., B.A. (Apr. 12, 1915). 2nd Lt. R. West Kent Regt. Capt. Labour Corps. Asst. Labour Commdt. IX Army Corps. France, 1916–19. *O.B.E.* (Mil.). *D.* France, 1919.

1913 **Gaffney,* L. A.** (Aug. 22, 1914). 2nd Lt. 6th R. Munster Fusiliers. Gallipoli. Died on Aug. 12, 1915, of wounds received in action at Suvla Bay.

1913 Gailor, F. H., B.A. 2nd Lt. R.G.A., afterwards F.A., U.S. Army.

1908 **Gair, T.,** B.A. (Aug. 1914). Lt. 276th Bde., R.F.A. France and Belgium. Killed in action near St. Julien on Sept. 9, 1917.

1918 Gammon, S., B.A. (Oct. 5, 1914). Lt. 11th Hampshire Regt. France. (Invalided on account of wounds, Apr. 1918.)

1911 **Garden, C. R. J.,** B.A. (June 27, 1915). 2nd Lt. B/69th Bde., R.F.A. Egypt, 1915–16; Mesopotamia, 1916. Died of cholera at Sanna Post, Mesopotamia, on May 4, 1916.

1896 Gardiner, H. B., B.A. (Feb. 25, 1916). ‡Lt., Interpreter, Special Lists. France.

1905 Garnett, H. H. N. (Sept. 9, 1914). Lt. Duke of Lancaster's Own Yeomanry. (Resigned on account of ill health.)

1897 **Garraway, W. G.** Pte. 28th London Regt. (Artists' Rifles). France and Belgium. Killed in action on Aug. 17, 1917.

1905 Garrod, H. G., B.A. (Dec. 16, 1915). Lt. Unattached List, T.F., City of London O.T.C.

1905 Gater, G. H., M.A. (Aug. 22, 1914). Lt.-Col. 9th Sherwood Foresters. Lt-Col. General List. Temp. Brig.-Gen. 62nd Inf. Bde. Gallipoli, 1915–16; Egypt, 1916; France, 1916–19. *C.M.G.*, 1919. *D.S.O.*, June 3, 1916; *Bar*, Sept. 17, 1917. Croix d'Officier de la Légion d'Honneur. Croix de Guerre. *D.* Egypt, 1916; Gallipoli, 1916; France, 1916, 1917, 1918, 1919.

1896 Gathorne-Hardy, G. M., B.A. (Sept. 1914). Capt. 1/4th R. Berkshire Regt. G.S.O. 2. France and Belgium. *M.C.*, July 24, 1915. Belgian Croix de Guerre. *D.* France, 1915.

1901 **Gay, E.** (Aug. 15, 1914). Capt. 1/5th Norfolk Regt. Gallipoli, 1915. Missing, presumed killed in action at Suvla Bay on Aug. 12, 1915.

1891 George, F. W. B. (Feb. 1915). Maj. 46th Canadian Infantry. (Commission relinquished on account of ill health.)

1895 Gibbons, W. K., B.A. (Aug. 1914). Capt. 9th E. Lancashire Regt. Capt. General List, attd. O.C.B. G.S.O. 3. France, Salonika.

1904 **Gibson, H. O. S.,** B.A. (Aug. 31, 1914). Lt. 1/11th London Regt. (Finsbury Rifles) (Capt.). Gallipoli, 1915; Egypt and Palestine, 1915–17. Killed in action at the second battle of Gaza on Apr. 19, 1917.

1913 **Gibson, R. B.** (Nov. 1914). Lt. 3rd, attd. 2nd, Bedfordshire Regt. (Capt.). France, 1915–16. *D.* France, 1915. Killed in action on July 13, 1916.

1902 Gibson, T. C., B.A. (Oct. 1916). Lt., Acting Capt., 3rd Irish Guards (specially empld.). *O.B.E.* (Mil.).

1888 Gill, J. H., B.A. (Sept. 1, 1914). ‡Maj. 17th W. Yorkshire Regt., attd.

Labour Corps (Lt.-Col.). France and Belgium. *D.S.O.*, Mar. 5, 1918. *D.* France, 1917.

1908 **Gillespie, A. D.,** B.A. (Sept. 1914). ‡2nd Lt. 4th, attd. 2nd, Arg. & Suth'd. Highlanders. France and Belgium, 1915. Killed in action in France at Battle of Loos on Sept. 25, 1915.

1911 **Gillespie,* T. C.,** B.A. (Serving Aug. 4, 1914). Lt. K.O. Scottish Borderers. France and Belgium, Aug.–Oct. 1914. Killed in action near La Bassée on Oct. 18, 1914.

1886 Gilliat, J. B., B.A., *D.S.O.*, T.D. (Oct. 2, 1914). Maj., Hon. Lt.-Col., 2/1st Hertfordshire Yeomanry (T.F. Res.). *D.* § Feb. 1917.

1896 Gillon, S. A., B.A. (Nov. 12, 1914). Capt. 9th K.O. Scottish Borderers. Staff-Lieutenant (1st Class) Intelligence Officer. Gallipoli, 1915–16; Egypt, 1916; France, 1916–17.

1900 Girdlestone, G. R., B.M., M.A. (Nov. 1915). Capt. R.A.M.C., attd. 3rd Southern General Hospital. *D.* § 1920.

1884 Gladstone, R., B.C.L., M.A. (Aug. 4, 1914). ‡Capt. 2nd Vol. Bn. King's (Liverpool Regt.).

1904 **Gladstone, W. G. C.,** B.A., *M.P.* (Sept. 1914). Lt. 1st R. Welch Fusiliers. France and Belgium. Killed in action near Laventie on Apr. 13, 1915.

1899 **Glazebrook, P. K.,** B.A., *M.P.* (Mobilized Aug. 1914). Maj. Cheshire Yeomanry, attd. 10th Shropshire L.I. Egypt, Palestine. *D.S.O.*, Mar. 26, 1918. Killed in action in Palestine on Mar. 7, 1918.

1919 Glossop, G. C. (Jan. 17, 1916). Capt. and Adjt., 91st Bde., R.F.A. France, 1916–19. *M.C.*, Sept. 26, 1917.

1912 Gollancz, V. (Oct. 3, 1915). Lt. 1st (Garr.) Bn. Manchester Regt.

1914 **Gollin, E. B.** (Dec. 22, 1914). Capt. 13th King's (Liverpool Regt.). France and Belgium. Died on May 14, 1917, of wounds received in action between Monchy and Guémappe.

1919 Gompertz, H. C. T. (June 23, 1917). 2nd Lt. R.F.A. 2nd Lt., Observer Officer, R.A.F. France. (Prisoner of war.)

1884 Goodenough, Rev. L. W. V., M.A. (Oct. 9, 1914). Chaplain to the Forces (4th Class). Lt. Special Lists. Staff-Lieutenant (2nd Class). Egypt, 1915–16. Italy, Versailles, Supreme War Council.

1914 Goolden, R. P. H. (Jan. 6, 1915). Lce.-Cpl. R.A.M.C. (T.F.). France.

1919 Gordon, J. B. (Aug. 2, 1917). 2nd Lt. R.F.A. France.

1911 Gore-Browne,* R. F. (Aug. 15, 1914). Capt. R.F.A., empld. under Admiralty. France. (Prisoner of war.)

1907 Gotch, O. H., B.M. (Oct. 1915). Surgeon R.N. Maj., Medical Officer, R.A.F. English Channel, Egypt and Palestine, Belgian Coast, North Sea. *D.* § Jan. 1919.

1908 **Gotch,* R. M.,** B.A. (Aug. 1914). Capt. and Adjt. 7th Sherwood Foresters. France, 1915–16. *D.* France, 1915. Killed in action near Gommecourt on July 1, 1916.

1910 Gough,* Hon. H. W. (Serving Aug. 4, 1914). Capt., Bt.-Maj., Irish Guards. G.S.O. 2. France, 1914–18. *M.C.*, Jan. 1, 1915. *D.* France, 1914, 1918.

1902 Gould, B. J. (Apr. 1, 1917). Lt. I.A.R.O., 4th Simla Rifles. India.

1910 Goulding, A. M. (Apr. 21, 1915). Lt. Canadian F.A. 2nd Lt. R.F.C. (Invalided 1916). Lt. Canadian Army Medical Corps, 1918–19. France, 1916.

1910 Graham, A., B.A. (Aug. 31, 1914). ‡Capt. 4th Highland L.I. (G.S.O. 3). Gallipoli, 1915; France, 1916; Palestine, 1918.

1902 Graham, G. M. A. (Jan. 16, 1915). 2nd Lt. 14th Middlesex Regt. Maj., Asst. to Chief Inspector of Q.M.G. Services, General List. *C.B.E.* (Mil.). *D.* § Aug. 1917.

1909 Graham, J. G. B. P., B.A. (Serving Aug. 4, 1914). Capt. 4th, attd. 2nd, Highland L.I. West Africa, 1915–16; France, 1917–18. *D.* § Aug. 1919.

1895 **Graham, W. L. C.** (Mobilized 1914). Capt. I. A. R. O. (Cavalry) D.A.Q.M.G., Bombay Harbour. Hon. A.D.C. to Viceroy of India. India. Accidentally killed while on duty at Bombay on July 15, 1915.

1910 Grant,* A. E. G., B.A. (Serving Aug. 4, 1914). Capt. 9th Lancers. France. *M.C.*, July 26, 1918; *Bar*, Oct. 16, 1918.

1895 Grant, R. F. S., *M.V.O.*, *D.S.O.* (Serving Aug. 4, 1914). Maj. Rifle Brigade. France and Belgium. *D.* France, 1914. (Placed on Half-Pay List on account of ill health.)

1907 Gray, A., B.A. (Sept. 10, 1914). 2nd Lt. 7th Oxf. and Bucks. Lt. Infty. 2nd Lt. 26th Divl. Cyclist Coy, A.C.C. (Resigned on account of ill health.)

1912 Gray, W. B., B.Litt. (Mobilized Aug. 4, 1914). Capt. 6th R. Scots. G.S.O. 3, Aldershot Command.

1910 Green,* C. E. P. (Oct. 7, 1914). Lt., Acting Capt., Coldstream Guards. Staff Capt., France, 1915–19.

1901 Green, L. H., B.A. (Sept. 20, 1914). Capt. 3rd S. Wales Borderers. France, 1916–19. *M.B.E.* (Mil.).

1919 Greenwood, L. W. (Aug. 15, 1917). 2nd Lt., Flying Officer, R.A.F.

1913 **Greg,* A. T.** (Aug. 1914). Capt. 3rd Cheshire Regt., attd. R.F.C. France, 1914–15, 1915–16, 1917. Killed in aerial action on Apr. 23, 1917.

1911 Greg, R. L., B.A. (Mar. 1, 1915). Capt. Army Pay Dept.

1916 Gregory, T. S. (Nov. 10, 1916). ‡2nd Lt. 13th K.R.R.C. France. *M.C.*, Mar. 8, 1919.

1899 **Gregory, W. R.** (Sept. 24, 1915). 2nd Lt. 4th Connaught Rangers. Maj., Squadron Commander, R.F.C. France, Italy. *M.C.*, July 18, 1917. Croix de Chevalier de la Légion d'Honneur. *D.* France. Killed in action in Italy on Jan. 23, 1918.

1914 Gregson, A. S., B.A. ‡2nd Lt. R.G.A.

1899 Greig, C. A. (Jan. 16, 1916). Lt. Special Lists. G.S.O. 3.

1912 Griffiths,* W. S., M.A. (July 1, 1915). 2nd Lt. R. Welch Fusiliers (relinquished Commission, 1916), afterwards Sapper, No. 3, Airline Section, R.E. France, 1916; Salonika, 1917–19; Bulgaria, 1919; Constantinople, 1919.

1898 Grigg, E. W. M., B.A. (Mar. 13, 1915). Lt. Grenadier Guards (S.R.) (Lt.-Col. G.S.O. 1, Guards Div.) France and Belgium. *C.M.G.* *D.S.O.*, Jan. 1, 1918. *M.C.*, Jan. 1, 1917. *D.* France, 1917, 1918.

Grigson, L. H. S. (Nov. 4, 1916). 2nd Lt. 3rd, attd. 1st, Devonshire Regt. France. Missing, believed killed in action between Fresnoy and Oppy on May 9, 1917.

1890 Groves, H. B. (Aug. 10, 1915). Pte. R.A.S.C. (M.T.). France, 1916.

1911 Grundy,* A. G., M.A. (Nov. 10, 1914). Lt. 6th Welsh Regt. (T.F. Res.). France.

1897 **Grundy, C.,** M.A. (Aug. 1914). Pte. Princess Patricia's Canadian L.I., Canadian Contingent. Belgium and France. Killed in action at Zonnebeke on Apr. 16, 1915.

1910 Gwyther, G. M. (1914). Capt. Suffolk Regt., attd. M.G.C. (Placed on Retired List on account of ill health.)

1909 **Habershon, K. R.,** B.A. (Sept. 19, 1914). Capt. 12th Rifle Brigade. France, Belgium. Killed in action near Ypres on Feb. 13, 1916.

1908 **Haeffner, F. W.,** B.A. (Aug. 1914). ‡2nd Lt. R.F.A. France, 1916. Killed in action in the Battle of the Somme on July 9, 1916.

1900 Haig, H. G., B.A. (May 7, 1915). Capt., Temp. Maj., I.A.R.O. (Cavalry Branch), attd. Railway Troops Bn. India.

1906 Haigh, Rev. M. G., M.A. (Jan. 15, 1917). Chaplain to the Forces (4th Class). E. Africa. *D.* E. Africa, 1919.

1906 **Hain, E.,** B.A. (Mobilized Aug. 4, 1914). Capt. Royal 1st Devon Yeomanry. Gallipoli. Killed in action in Gallipoli on Nov. 11, 1915.

1911 Haldane,* J. B. S., M.A. (Aug. 15, 1914). Capt. 3rd The Black Watch. France, 1915; Mesopotamia, 1916–17; India, 1917–18.

1900 Hall, E. S., M.A. (May 26, 1915). Lt., Acting Capt. and Adjt., 25th, attd. 19th, Queen's (R.W. Surrey Regt.) *D.* § Aug. 1919.

1900 **Hall, G. E.,** B.A. (Aug. 1914). ‡2nd Lt. 1st, attd. 9th, Norfolk Regt. France, 1915–16, 1917. Killed in action at Maroc, Grendy, on Apr. 26, 1917.

1902 Hall, R. E., B.A. Gold Coast Volunteer Force. W. Africa.

1905 Halliday, W. R., B.A., B.Litt. (May 1916). Lt. R.N.V.R. Aegean and Mediterranean. Chevalier of the Order of the Redeemer. *D.* Mediterranean, 1918.

1887 Hambledon, W. F. D., Viscount, B.A. T.D. (Mobilized Aug. 4, 1914). Lt.-Col. Royal 1st Devon Yeomanry (T.F. Res.). Gallipoli, 1915; Egypt, 1916. *D.* Egypt, 1916.

1919 Hamer, P. (June 7, 1917). Pte. 30th Bn. M.G.C. France and Belgium, 1918–19.

1888 Hamilton, A. R., B.A. (Sept. 14, 1914). †Capt. R.A.S.C. France.

1906 Hampton, F. A., B.M. (Aug. 1914). Capt. R.A.M.C. Capt. R.A.F. (Med. Service). France. *M.C.*, Jan. 26, 1917. *D.* France, 1915.

1905 **Hanbury, E. R.** (Mobilized Aug. 1914). Maj. Leicestershire Yeomanry, attd. M.G.C. France and Belgium, 1914–18. *D.* France. Missing, presumed killed in action on Mar. 23, 1918.

1909 **Hankinson,* R. P.,** B.A. (May 1915). 2nd Lt. 4th Queen's (R.W. Surrey Regt.), afterwards 2nd Lt. Corps of Guides, attd. 56th Punjabis, Indian Infantry. Mesopotamia. Died on Feb. 23, 1917, of wounds received in action at Sanna-i-yat.

1909 Hardman, G. W. (Aug. 4, 1914). ‡Capt. General List, R.T.O. France and Belgium, 1915–19.

1908 Hardy, A. C., B.A. (Dec. 1, 1914). Capt., Acting Maj., R.G.A. France and Belgium.

1901 Hardy, H. H., M.A. (Mobilized Aug. 1914). Maj. 8th Rifle Brigade. G.S.O. 3, attd. War Office. France and Belgium, 1917–18. *M.B.E.* (Mil.). *D.* § Feb. 1917, § Feb. 1918.

1900 Hardy, L. H., B.A. (Serving Aug. 4, 1914). Capt., Bt.-Maj., 1st Life Guards (Lt.-Col.). France and Belgium, 1914. *M.C.*, Feb. 18, 1915. *D.* France, 1914.

1889 Hare, P. R. (Mobilized Aug. 1914). Capt. 3rd County of London Yeomanry, empld. Records.

1895 Harmood-Banner, H., M.A. Maj. late S. Wales Borderers, O.C. Administrative Area. (Appointment relinquished on account of ill health.)

1895 Harper, P., B.C.L. (Aug. 11, 1916). Lt. R.G.A. (S.R.).

1887 Harris, G. M., M.A. Major 6th Sussex Vol. Bn. *O.B.E.* (Civil).

1919 Harris, R. L. A. (Aug. 1918). Cadet O.C.B., R.E.

1912 [Harris, W. H.] (Aug. 30, 1917). Pte. 28th London Regt. (Artists' Rifles).

1919 Harrod, H. R. F. (Sept. 10, 1918). 2nd Lt. R.G.A. (on demobilization).

1907 **Hart, L.** Lce-Cpl. R.W. Kent Regt. France and Belgium. Died on Oct. 18, 1917, of wounds received in action 3 days previously.

1893 Hart-Davis, C. H., B.A. (July 15, 1915). Capt. R.E. Kent Yeomanry. G.S.O. 3. Salonika. *D.* Salonika, 1917.

1910 **Hartley,* R.** (Sept. 9, 1914). Lt. 10th Worcestershire Regt. France, 1915. Killed in action at Festubert on Oct. 26, 1915.

1906 [**Hatfeild, C. E.**] (Mobilized Aug. 4, 1914). Capt. R.E. Kent Yeomanry, attd. 10th The Buffs (E. Kent Regt.). Gallipoli, Egypt, Palestine, France. *M.C.*, Feb. 15, 1919. *D.* Palestine, 1917. Killed in action near Cambrai on Sept. 21, 1918.

1919 Haworth, A. G. (Dec. 30, 1914). Lt. 3rd R.W. Kent Regt., attd. M.G.C. (Capt.). Serbia, 1915; Salonika, 1915–17; Palestine, 1917–19. *D.* Salonika, 1917.

Haworth, P. T. (Aug. 1915). 2nd Lt. R.F.A. (Capt.). France, 1915–17. Died on May 3, 1917, of wounds received in action at Gavrelle, near Vimy.

1911 Hayes,* W. E., B.A. (Aug. 6, 1914). ‡Lt. Anzac Signal Coy., R.E. (Capt.). France and Belgium.

1913 Hayes,* W. W. (Aug. 1914). Lt. 16th Lancers. France and Belgium.

1909 Haynes, J. F., B.A. (Oct. 30, 1916). Surgeon Lt., R.N.

1905 **Heath, A. G.**, M.A. (Aug. 1914). Lt. 6th R.W. Kent Regt. France and Belgium. Killed in action at Hulluch on Oct. 8, 1915.

1907 Heathcote, R. St. A., D.M. (Sept. 27, 1917). Surgeon Lt., R.N.

1892 Hele, J. C., B.Mus. (Dec. 1914). Capt. R. Defence Corps.

1899 Henderson, H. L., M.A. (Jan. 14, 1915). Lt. 1st (Garr.) Bn. Devonshire Regt., afterwards Lt. General List (Capt. G.S.O. 2). Egypt, Singapore.

1898 Henderson, R. B., M.A. (Nov. 5, 1915). Lt., Acting Lt.-Col., 117th Siege Batt. R.G.A. France, Belgium, Germany. *D.* France, 1919.

1904 Henderson-Roe, C. G. (Dec. 1914). Capt. 3rd R.W. Kent Regt. France and Belgium. *D.S.O.*, July 26, 1917. *M.C.*, Nov. 7, 1917. *D.* France, 1917.

1899 Henriques, J. Q., B.A. (Mobilized Aug. 1914). Maj. 16th London Regt. (Queen's Westminster Rifles), attd. War Office (Education Dept.) France. T.D.

1913 **Henriques,* P. B. G.** (Aug. 15, 1914). 2nd Lt. 8th K.R.R.C. France and Belgium. Died on July 24, 1915, of wounds received the previous day at Ypres.

1914 Henry, H. A., B.A. (Nov. 24, 1914). Lt. 7th Oxf. & Bucks. Lt. Infty. Lt. (Hon. Capt.), Flying Officer, R.A.F. France, Macedonia, Egypt, Mesopotamia, Persia.

1919 Henty, B. E. A., B.A. (June 4, 1917). 2nd Lt. R.G.A. (S.R.). France, 1917–18.

1910 Herbert, A. P. (Mar. 10, 1915). ‡Lt. R.N.V.R. Gallipoli. *D.* Gallipoli, 1916. (Commission relinquished on account of ill health.)

1912 **Herbert-Smith,* V.,** B.A. (Aug. 15, 1914). 2nd Lt. 5th, attd. 3rd, Rifle Brigade. France, 1915. Killed in action near Neuve Chapelle on Mar. 21, 1915.

1915 Hern, J. R. B. (June 9, 1917). 2nd Lt. R.F.A. France, 1918.

1912 Herring,* E. F., B.C.L., M.A. (Aug. 4, 1914). ‡Lt., Acting Maj., B/99th Batt., R.F.A. France, Salonika, Serbia, Bulgaria. *D.S.O.*, June 3, 1919. *M.C.*, July 26, 1917. *D.* Salonika, 1919.

1912 **Herron,* A. R.** (Aug. 9, 1914). 2nd Lt. 6th, attd. 1st, K.R.R.C. France. Killed in action at Givenchy on Mar. 10, 1915.

1910 **Hess,* A. G.,** B.A. (Serving Aug. 4, 1914). Lt. R.H.A. France. Died on Feb. 24, 1915, of wounds received in action.

1894 Hewett, W. P., B.A. (Mobilized Aug. 1914). Lt.-Col. 9th Middlesex Regt. (T.F.). Mesopotamia. *D.* Mesopotamia, 1918.

1906 Hextall, H. C., B.A. (Oct. 5, 1915). Capt. R.A.S.C.

1889 Heywood-Lonsdale, J. P. H. (Mobilized Aug. 1914). Maj. Shropshire Yeomanry, attd. 10th Shropshire L.I. (Lt.-Col.). Egypt, 1916–17; Palestine, 1917–18; France, 1918–19. *D.S.O.*, Jan. 1, 1919. T.D. *D.* France, 1918.

1902 Hicks, F. M., M.A. (Sept. 17, 1914). Capt. 10th Hampshire Regt. Flight Commander, R.A.F. Gallipoli, Macedonia, Egypt, Palestine. Croix de Guerre. *D.* Gallipoli, 1915.

1904 Hill, Rev. A. P., M.A. (Apr. 1917). Lt. S. African Inf., afterwards Chaplain to the Forces (4th Class). France.

1906 Hill, M. V. B., B.A. (Aug. 15, 1914). Capt. 5th R. Fusiliers. Temp. Lt.-Col. 9th R. Sussex Regt. France and Belgium, 1914–18, 1918–19. *D.S.O.*, Aug. 25, 1917; *Bar*, Sept. 16, 1918. *M.C.*, June 3, 1916. *D.* France, 1916, 1917, 1918, 1919.

Hill, N. W. (Oct. 20, 1915). 2nd Lt., Acting Capt., Oxf. & Bucks. Lt. Infty. France. *M.C.*, Feb. 13, 1917. Killed in action on Jan. 16, 1917.

1877 Hill, R. M., B.A. (Mar. 31, 1917). Lt. R. Defence Corps.

1880 Hine-Haycock, Rev. T. R., M.A. (Jan. 1, 1918). Chaplain to the Forces (4th Class), attd. 8th London Regt. (Post Office Rifles).

1910 Hislop, G. (Sept. 9, 1914). ‡Lt. 2nd Durham L.I. Gallipoli, Egypt, France.

1894 Hoare, C. H. (Mobilized Aug. 1914). Capt. W. Kent Yeomanry. Lt.-Col. M.G.C. France. *D.S.O.* June 4, 1917; *Bar*, Feb. 4, 1918. *D.* France, 1917 twice.

1899 Hoare, G. S., M.A. (Mobilized Aug. 1914). Maj. R.G.A.

1899 Hoare, Sir S. J. G., Bt., M.A., *M.P.* (Sept. 1914). Lt.-Col. Norfolk Yeomanry. G.S.O. 1. Russia, Italy. *C.M.G.* Commander of the Orders of St. Anne and St. Stanislas (2nd Class). Officer of the Order of St. Maurice and St. Lazarus. Czecho-Slovak Croix de Guerre. *D.* § July, 1917; Italy 1918.

1879 Hobhouse, E., D.M. (Mobilized Aug. 1914). Lt.-Col. R.A.M.C. (T.F.). 2nd E. General Hospital.

1919 Hobhouse, E. G. (Feb. 6, 1918). 2nd Lt. R.F.A.

1907 Hobhouse, E. W. N., B.M., M.A. (Feb. 1, 1916). Capt. R.A.M.C.

1911 Hobhouse,* J. R. (Jan. 1917). Capt. R.G.A. (S.R.) (Maj.). France and Belgium. *M.C.*, Sept. 26, 1917.

1912 **Hobhouse, P. E.** (Sept. 1914). Capt. 6th Somerset L.I. (Maj.). France and Belgium. *D.* France, 1917; May 5, 1919. Killed in action at Benay on Mar. 21, 1918.

1899 Hobson, A. J., B.A. (Sept. 27, 1916). Lt. B/83rd Batt., R.F.A. France and Belgium. *M.C.*, Sept. 26, 1917.

1910 Hobson,* F. G., B.A. (Aug. 6, 1914). ‡Capt. W. Yorkshire Regt. Bde. Maj., 21st Inf. Bde. France, from 1914. *D.S.O.*, Aug. 25, 1916. *D.* France, 1914, 1915, 1916, 1917.

1901 Hobson, J. F., M.A. (Sept. 4, 1914). ‡Lt. 8th Durham L.I. (Capt.). France. *M.C.*, Sept. 16, 1918.

1913 **Hodgson,* R. E.** (Aug. 1914). Lt. 4th King's (Liverpool Regt.), attd. R.A.F. France, 1915–17; Belgium, 1918. Killed in action near Dunkirk on Sept. 15, 1918.

1905 Hoernle, E. S., B.A. (June 13, 1917). Capt. I.A.R.O., Indian Labour Corps, attd. 90th Punjabis.

1896 Holliday, R. J. M., M.A. (Serving Aug. 4, 1914). Instructor Lt.-Commdr., R.N., lent to Australian Government.

1914 Holman,* A. (June 29, 1915). Lt. R.F.A. Staff-Lieutenant (1st Class), attd. Headquarters, 21st Div. Artillery. France, 1915–19. *M.C.*, June 3, 1918. *D.* France, 1918.

1895 Holt, P. D., B.A. (Nov. 7, 1914). Maj. King's (Liverpool Regt.). France and Belgium (3 years).

1903 Hood, G. F., M.A. (Feb. 14, 1911). Capt. Nottingham High School O.T.C. Acting Capt. R.E. (Gas Services). France.

1912 Hope, M. B., B.A. (Oct. 24, 1914). Lt. 6th, attd. 4th, K.R.R.C. France. (Prisoner of war.)

1919 Hopper, C. A. (Apr. 10, 1917). ‡Lt. 8th E. Surrey Regt. France, 1917–18, 1918–19.

1919 Hornby, M. C. St. J. (Apr. 24, 1918). 2nd Lt. 3rd Grenadier Guards. France, Germany.

1895 Hornby, R. P. (Sept. 3, 1914). Capt. 6th Lancashire Fusiliers, attd. Headquarter Staff, 42nd Div. Egypt, 1914; Gallipoli, 1915; Palestine. 1916; France, 1917–18. *M.C.*, Nov. 8, 1915. *D.* Gallipoli, 1915.

1914 Horne, H. O., B.A. (Mar. 2, 1916). Sergt. R.A.M.C.

1912 Hossie, D. N., M.A. (Serving Aug. 4, 1914). ‡Maj. D/129th Bde., R.F.A. (Lt.-Col.). France, 1915–16; Salonika, 1916–19. *D.S.O.*, Jan. 1, 1919. Order of the White Eagle (4th Class) (with swords). *D.* Salonika, 1917, 1918 twice.

1895 Houghton, R. J., M.A. (Mobilized Aug. 4, 1914). Capt., temp. Maj., Cheshire Yeomanry, empld. Imp. Camel Corps. Egypt and Palestine, 1916–19. *O.B.E.* (Mil.). *D.* Palestine, 1918.

1911 Houstoun-Boswall,* W. E., B.A. (Aug. 4, 1914). Capt. The Black Watch. Maj. D.A.Q.M.G. France, Belgium, Italy. *M.C.*, Mar. 8, 1919. Croix de Guerre. *D.* France, 1916, 1919; Italy, 1918.

1904 **Howard, L. W. M.** (Oct. 1914). Lt. 7th Queen's (R. W. Surrey Regt.). France. Killed in action near Arras on Sept. 15, 1915.

1919 Howell, C. (May 15, 1917). Maj. 326th Infantry, U.S. Army. France.

1919 Hughes, J. S. (Feb. 19, 1917). Spr. R.E. (Signals). France, 1918–19.

1917 Hughes, R. W. (1917). 2nd Lt. attd. R.E. Recalled for civilian service under Egyptian Government.
1897 Hulbert, T. E. (Serving Aug. 4, 1914). Maj. 3rd Skinner's Horse, Indian Army. France, 1914–16; Mesopotamia, 1916–17. *O.B.E.* (Mil.). *D.* France, 1917, 1919.
1919 Hull, H. K. (June 6, 1917). 2nd Lt. R.G.A.
1904 [**Hulton, A. E. G.,** M.A.] (Sept. 14, 1914). ‡Lt. R.A.S.C. France and Belgium. Died on June 6, 1915, of wounds received in action at St. Jean, near Ypres.
1919 Humphry, J. McN. (Sept. 11, 1915). Lt. 3rd, attd. 2nd, Arg. & Suth'd. Highlanders. France, 1916–18. *M.C.*, Oct. 15, 1918. Croix de Guerre.
1901 Hunter, A. R., M.A. (Aug. 16, 1915). Capt., temp. Maj., R.A.S.C. France, 1917–18.
1900 Hunter, K. O., B.A. (Jan. 30, 1918). 2nd Lt. Coldstream Guards.
1905 **Hunter, L. W.,** M.A. (Apr. 1915). Lt. 1/4th Oxf. & Bucks. Lt. Infty. France, 1916. Killed in action at Pozières on Aug. 13, 1916.
1910 Hunter, N. B., B.A. (Mobilized Aug. 1914). Capt. 4th Highland L.I., attd. Egyptian Army (Maj.). France, 1915; Mesopotamia, 1916.
1913 Hurst, S. R., B.A. American Ambulance Corps, Croix rouge française. France. Croix de Guerre.
1908 Huson, A. C., B.A. (May 4, 1917). Lt. R.G.A. (S.R.). (Capt. and Adj.).
1915 Hutchinson, A. S. (Mar. 3, 1916). Lt. 24th Middlesex Regt. France.
Hutchinson, H. W. (Dec. 19, 1916). 2nd Lt. 3rd, attd. 4th, Leicestershire Regt. France. Killed in action on Mar. 13, 1917.
1909 [**Hutchison, R. H.,** B.A.] (Sept. 1914). Lt. 8th, attd. 1st, The Black Watch. France. Killed in action near Hulluch on Oct. 13, 1915.
1910 **Hutton,* Rev. S. F.,** B.A. (Jan. 16, 1916). Pte. 29th R. Fusiliers. France. Killed in action at Flers on Oct. 7, 1916.
1906 Huxley, J. S., M.A. (Apr. 1917). 2nd Lt. A.S.C. 2nd Lt. Intelligence Corps (Staff Lt.). Italy.
Imroth, L. (Dec. 27, 1915). Lt. 11th Hampshire Regt. E. Africa. Died at Johannesburg on Nov. 7, 1918, of wounds received on Nov. 30, 1917.
1913 **Inchbald, J. C. E.** (Sept. 1914). Capt. 9th Devonshire Regt. France, 1915–17. *D.* France, 1916. Killed in action at Ecoust-St.-Mein, near Bullecourt, on Apr. 2, 1917.
1916 Ireland, E. W. (Nov. 1916). Pte. No. 4 Canadian C.C.S., afterwards Lce.-Cpl. 20th Bn. M.G.C. France, Siberia.
1900 Irvine, A. F., B.A. (Sept. 5, 1914). ‡Lt. 5th Grenadier Guards. France and Belgium. (Invalided on account of wounds.)
1911 Izard, H. (Jan. 12, 1917). Lt. Intelligence Corps. Lt. Flying Officer, R.A.F. E. Africa.
1919 Jackson, T. F. (Dec. 14, 1915). Lt. 21st W. Yorkshire Regt.
1895 **Jackson, T. R.** (May 1915). Capt. 7th D.C.L.I. France. *M.C.*, Jan. 1, 1917. Died on Mar. 25, 1918, of wounds received on previous day.
1913 Jacob, E. F., B.A. (Aug. 24, 1915). Capt. 1st Hampshire Regt., attd. No. 6 O.C.B. France, 1916, 1917. *D.* § Mar. 1919.
1919 James, C. J. B. (1917). 2nd Lt. 12th London Regt. (The Rangers).
1890 James, E. L. H. (Serving Aug. 4, 1914). Lt.-Col. R.A.O.C. Asst. Director of Army Ordnance Services. *O.B.E.* (Mil.).
1916 James, F. E. S., B.A. (June 5, 1917). 2nd Lt. 32nd Siege Batt., R.G.A. France, 1917. (Prisoner of War, Nov. 1917–Dec. 1918.)

1903 Jamieson, A. G. Auldjo, B.A. (Sept. 1914). Lt. 8th R. Scots, attd. War Office (Capt.). France. *M.C.*, Jan. 14, 1916. *D.* France, 1915.
1897 Jamieson, J. H. I. Auldjo, B.A. (Jan. 6, 1915). Lt. 8th R. Scots. Acting Maj. attd. M.G.C.
1893 Jebb, R., M.A. (Mobilized Aug. 1914). Capt. 4th Shropshire L.I. Staff-Captain.
1908 [Jenkin, C. F., M.A.] (Apr. 1915). Lt. R.N.V.R., afterwards Lt.-Col., Section Director, Technical Dept., R.A.F. *C.B.E.* (Mil.).
1919 Jennings, R. A. U. (Oct. 4, 1917). 2nd Lt. 2/4th Queen's (R. W. Surrey Regt.). France, 1918.
1895 **Jerrard-Parsons, K. T.,** B.A. (Nov. 28, 1914). Capt. 6th R. Irish Rifles (Col. D.A.A.G.). Gallipoli, 1915; Serbia, 1915; Macedonia, 1915–17. *D.* Salonika, 1916. Died on Aug. 14, 1917, of illness contracted while on active service.
1912 Jerrold, D. F. (Aug. 6, 1914). ‡Lt. R.N.V.R., i/c Bde. Officers' School, 63rd R.N. Div. Res., Aldershot. Gallipoli, France. *D.* Gallipoli, 1916. (Invalided on account of wounds, June 1918.)
1884 Jessel, Sir H. M., Bt., B.A. (Mobilized Aug. 1914). Hon. Col. 1st London Regt. (R. Fusiliers). Deputy Director of Remounts. *C.B. C.M.G.* T.D. Officier, Ordre de Léopold. *D.* § Feb. 1918.
1905 Johnson, B. H., B.A. (Apr. 8, 1915). Lt. 1st Hertfordshire Regt. (Capt.). France and Belgium. *D.* § Mar. 1919.
1913 Johnson,* H. B. (1915). Capt. R. Marines.
1893 Johnson, R. A., M.A. (Mobilized Aug. 1914). Lt.-Col. 9th (Cyclist Bn.) Hampshire Regt. India, Siberia. *C.B.E.* (Mil.). T.D. *D.* Siberia, 1919.
1891 Johnson, W. L., B.A. (Aug. 1914). Lt.-Col. 2/5th Durham L.I. (T.F. Res.), attd Ministry of Munitions. *D.* § Feb. 1917.
1896 Johnston, C. E., M.A. (Sept. 20, 1914). Lt.-Col. 5th London Regt. (London Rifle Brigade) (T.F. Res.). France. *D.S.O.*, Nov. 6, 1918. *M.C.*, June 3, 1918. *D.* France, 1918.
1908 **Johnston,* G. S.,** B.A. (Mobilized Aug. 4, 1914). Lt. Essex Yeomanry. France and Belgium. Killed in action near Hooge on May 13, 1915.
1904 [**Johnston, J. L.,** M.A.] (Aug. 1914). 2nd Lt. 3rd, attd. 2nd, Oxf. & Bucks. Lt. Infty. (Capt.). France. Missing, presumed killed in action at Festubert on May 12, 1915.
1919 Johnston, J. W. (Jan. 26, 1916). 2nd Lt. R.A.S.C.
1912 **Johnston, R. G.** (Nov. 17, 1914). ‡Lt., temp. Capt., Intelligence Officer, 7th Seaforth Highlanders. France. *M.C.*, June 3, 1916. Killed in action on July 18, 1916.
1885 Jones, E. M., M.A. (Mobilized Aug. 1914). Maj. 1st Hertfordshire Regt.
1919 Jones, I. D. (Sept. 9, 1917). Probationary Flight and Observer Officer, R.A.F. (Commission relinquished on account of ill health.)
1917 Jones, K. M. (June 4, 1917). Pte. Labour Corps (Lce.-Cpl.). (Discharged on account of ill health.)
1890 Jones, R. T., B.A. (Aug. 20, 1914). Capt. 1/1st Shropshire Yeomanry. Egypt and Palestine. (Invalided on account of wounds, July 1918.)
1886 Joseph, H. W. B., M.A. (1916). Lt. 1st Vol. Bn. Oxf. & Bucks. Lt. Infty.
1889 Jowers, H. Hon. Maj. Political Dept., E. African F.F. E. Africa. *D.* E. Africa.
1903 Jowitt, W. A., B.A. (1914). Anti-Aircraft Corps, R.N.V.R.

1899 Joy, F. D. H., M.A. (Oct. 1, 1914). Capt. 3rd, attd. 1st, K.O. Scottish Borderers. G.S.O. 3. France. *D.* France, 1918.

1907 **Kay, G. C.,** B.A. (Mobilized Aug. 1914). Capt., Acting Maj., 1/5th Lancashire Fusiliers, attd. M.G.C. Gallipoli and France. Killed in action at Bucquoy on Mar. 29, 1918.

1914 **Keating, H. F. A.** (Oct. 1, 1914). Lt. R.E. France. Killed in action on June 28, 1918.

1919 Keir, D. L. (Oct. 10, 1914). Lt., Acting Capt., 1st K. O. Scottish Borderers. France, Belgium, Germany.

1919 Keith, C. G. (Feb. 1915). Capt. Grenadier Guards (S.R.). Staff-Captain 3rd Guards Bde. France, Belgium. *M.C.*, Nov. 14, 1916.

1906 Keith-Falconer,* A. W. (Mobilized Aug. 1914). Capt., Acting Maj., Q.O. Oxfordshire Hussars. D.A.Q.M.G., British Armistice Commission. France, Belgium, 1914–19.

1910 Keith-Jopp, W. L. S. (Jan. 23, 1915). Lt. 21st Rifle Brigade (Capt.). Lt., Flying Officer, R.A.F. Egypt, 1916; France, 1917.

1888 Kennard, A. C. H., M.A. (Rejoined Aug. 1914). Capt. Res. of Officers, late Lt.-Col. 1st. London Regt. Lt.-Col. whilst comdg. 69th Labour Group. France. *D.* France, 1918.

1898 Kenworthy-Browne, Rev. E. (Aug. 6, 1918). Chaplain to the Forces (4th Class).

1882 [Kenyon, Sir F. G., M.A., *K.C.B.*] (Aug. 5, 1914). Lt.-Col. Inns of Court O.T.C., attd. Imperial War Graves Commission. France, 1914. T.D. *D.* § Mar. 1918.

1897 **Kenyon, J.,** M.A. (Mobilized Aug. 1914). Maj. 5th Lancashire Fusiliers. Egypt and Gallipoli. Died on Nov. 22, 1918, of illness contracted on active service.

1911 **Kerr,* D. A.** (Aug. 7, 1914). 2nd Lt. 2nd R. Scots. France. Killed in action near Bethune on Oct. 13, 1914.

1920 Kershaw, R. N. (Mar. 1916). ‡Lt. 22nd M.G. Bn., A.I.F. France, 1917, 1918. *M.C.*, Sept. 24, 1918.

1901 Killby, L. G., B.Sc., M.A. (Feb. 1916). Capt. Special Lists. France, 1916. *D.* § Mar. 1918.

1907 **King, Rev. B. W.,** B.A. (May 13, 1918). Rfln. 2nd K.R.R.C. France, 1918. Killed in action near Le Cateau on Oct. 23, 1918.

1897 King, L. R., M.A. (Mobilized Aug. 4, 1914). Maj. 7th Middlesex Regt. Lt.-Col. 14th Welsh Regt. France. *D.* France, 1916. (Invalided, Aug. 13, 1917.)

1900 King, R. B., B.A. (Oct. 28, 1914). 2nd Lt. 7th Arg. & Suth'd. Highlanders. France and Belgium.

1905 King-French, M., B.A. (Sept. 23, 1914). Lt., Acting Maj., R.F.A. France, 1915–19.

1920 Kingsmill, H. Ll. (May 15, 1917). Pte. 2nd M.G. Bn., A.I.F. France, Belgium, 1918–19.

1913 Knollys,* Hon. E. G. W. T. (Sept. 26, 1914). Capt. 16th London Regt. (Queen's Westminster Rifles). Capt., Kite Balloon Officer, R.A.F. France. *M.B.E.* (Mil.). *D.F.C.*, Oct. 11, 1919. Chevalier de l'Ordre de la Couronne. Belgian Croix de Guerre.

Knowles, W. V. (May, 1917). 2nd Lt. 3rd, attd. 2nd, R. Berkshire Regt. Belgium, 1917. Killed in action at Passchendaele on Dec. 31, 1917.

1903 Knowling, A. E. G., M.A. (Feb. 28, 1916). ‡Capt. R.A.S.C. France and Belgium, 1916–18. *O.B.E.* (Mil.). *D.* France, 1919.

1888 Koecher, J. E. (Sept. 21, 1914). Capt., temp. Maj., R.A.S.C., attd. H.Q. 3rd Cavalry Div. France. *D.* France, 1919.

1907 Laidlaw, W., B.A. (Aug. 12, 1914). Lt. 8th R. Scots (T.F.) (Capt.).

1910 Laidlay,* N., B.A. (1914). ‡Lt. R. Fusiliers, empld. Ministry of Munitions.

1914 **Laird, H. B.** (June 26, 1915). 2nd Lt. 3rd, attd. 2nd, Yorkshire Regt. France. Killed in action in the Battle of the Somme on July 8, 1916.

1896 Lake, E. D. C., M.A. (Jan. 1915). 2nd Lt. Unattached List, T.F., Charterhouse O.T.C.

1894 Lakin, H. G., B.A. 2nd Lt. 2nd Vol. Bn. R. Warwickshire Regt.

1901 Lambert, J. B. W. (Nov. 22, 1915). Lt. R.A.S.C.

1892 Lane, R. C., B.A. (Dec. 14, 1914). Maj. R.A.F., Liaison Officer with War Office. France, 1915–17. *D.*

1893 Lane-Fox, E. (Aug. 28, 1914). Capt. Yorkshire Hussars.

1889 Lane-Fox, G. R., B.A., *M.P.* (Mobilized Aug. 4, 1914). Maj. Yorkshire Hussars (T.F. Res.). France. Chevalier de l'Ordre du Mérite Agricole. *D.* France, 1916.

1913 **Lang,* A.** (Oct. 2, 1914). Lt. 6th Arg. & Suth'd. Highlanders. France. Killed in action on Aug. 29, 1916.

1907 **Langdon, W. M.,** B.A. (Sept. 1914). ‡Capt. 10th Cheshire Regt. France. Killed in action on Vimy Ridge on May 21, 1916.

1899 Langton, G. P., B.A. (Oct. 14, 1914). Capt. R.G.A., empld. Ministry of Munitions.

1919 Lanyon, J. A. (July 31, 1918). 2nd Lt. R.G.A.

1905 **Large, E. L.,** B.A. (Mobilized Aug. 1914). Capt. 5th London Regt. (London Rifle Brigade). Belgium. Died on May 21, 1915, of wounds received at St. Jean, near Ypres, on May 1.

1919 Laver, J. (Mar. 9, 1918). 2nd Lt. 2/5th King's Own (R. Lancaster Regt.). France.

1911 Law, G. E. Rhodesian Regt. Africa.

1893 Lawrence, Sir A. W., Bt., M.A. A.B., R.N.A.S. (Anti-Aircraft).

1898 Lawrence, C. T. (Serving Aug. 4, 1914). Maj., Acting Lt.-Col., R.F.A. Salonika, Russia. *D.S.O.*, Jan. 1, 1918. *D.* Salonika, 1917; Russia, 1919 twice.

1899 Lawrence, G. (Sept. 1914). Maj. E. Anglian Bde., R.F.A. (Lt.-Col.). France, Egypt, Palestine. *D.S.O.*, Jan. 1, 1918. *D.* Palestine, 1917.

1905 Lea-Wilson, P., B.A. (1915). Capt. 18th R. Irish Regt. Murdered on June 15, 1920, while on duty in Ireland with R.I.C.

1904 Leach, A. G., B.A. (Oct. 5, 1917). Lt. I.A.R.O., attd. 1/9th Gurkha Rifles. India.

1904 Leach, G. S., M.A. (Oct. 1914). Capt. 12th K.O.Y.L.I. (Pioneers). Egypt, 1915–16; France, 1916–18. *M.C.*, July 26, 1918.

1895 Leathart, A. H., B.A. (Sept. 1914). Lt., Acting Maj., R.F.A. (T.F.). France, 1915–19. *M.C.*, Nov. 6, 1918. Croix de Guerre with Gold Star. *D.* France, 1918.

1886 Leather, P. C. du S. (Sept. 1914). Capt. 4th Yorkshire Regt. France and Belgium, 1915. (Commission relinquished on account of ill health.)

1909 **Lees,* J.,** B.A. (Sept. 1914). 2nd Lt. 4th Highland L.I., attd. Nigeria Regt. Lost at sea in the sinking of s.s. *Falaba* on Mar. 28, 1915.

1919 Lees, L. M. (June 25, 1917). Lt. Labour Corps. France, 1918.
1911 Leeson,* S. S. G., M.A. (Sept. 3, 1914). 2nd Lt. 1/8th Middlesex Regt., afterwards Lt. R.N.V.R., attd. Admiralty Staff. Gibraltar, 1914–15; France, 1915.
1906 Legard, C. (Oct. 13, 1914). Capt. General List, A.D.C. France and Belgium. *M.C.*, Mar. 30, 1916.
1891 Legard, D'A. (Serving Aug. 4, 1914). Lt.-Col. 17th Lancers, temp. Brig.-Gen. France and Belgium. *C.M.G.* *C.B.E.* (Mil.). *D.S.O.*, June 22, 1918. Croix de Chevalier de la Légion d'Honneur. *D.* France, 1916, 1918.
1896 Legg, L. G. W., M.A. (Dec. 1914). 2nd Lt. 12th Worcestershire Regt., afterwards Lt. R.N.V.R., attd. Admiralty, Intelligence Dept.
1899 Leigh-Bennett, H. W., B.A. (May 23, 1916). Lt. 2nd Coldstream Guards. France and Belgium, 1916–19.
1908 Leitch, R. (1914). Staff-Officer, Artillery Division, Serbian Army. Serbia, 1914–16.
1908 Lennard, E. S., B.A. (June 23, 1916). Lt. 6th Tank Corps. France, 1917. *M.C.*, Jan. 1, 1918.
1904 [Lennard, R. V., M.A.] (Aug. 13, 1917). ‡Paymaster Sub-Lt., R.N.V.R. H.M.S. *President.*
1890 Lever, H. R., B.A. (Serving Aug. 4, 1914). Maj., temp. Lt.-Col., R.A.S.C. France. *O.B.E.* (Mil.). *D.* § Feb. 1917.
1915 Levy, M., B.A. (July 16, 1916). Croix rouge française, afterwards Qr.-Master Corps, U.S. Army. France, 1916–18.
1898 Lewis, G. D., M.A. (Oct. 4, 1916). Lt. Shropshire L.I. Lt. General List, attd. War Office. (Discharged on account of ill health.)
1906 Lewis, V. A., B.A. (Aug. 15, 1914). Capt. 1/2nd London Hy. Batt., R.G.A. (Maj.). France, 1917–19. *M.C.*, Nov. 19, 1917.
1917 Lindsay, K. G. (Dec. 1917). 2nd Lt. 3rd Rifle Brigade. France, 1918–19.
1906 Lindsey-Renton, R. H., B.A. (Mobilized Aug. 1914). Maj. 9th London Regt. (Queen Victoria's Rifles) (Lt.-Col.). France and Belgium, 1914–19. *D.S.O.*, Feb. 1, 1919. Belgian Croix de Guerre. *D.* France, 1916, 1917, 1918, 1919.
1889 Little, C. W., M.A. (Aug. 1914). Capt. Unattached List, T.F., Winchester College O.T.C.
1901 Little, J. O., B.A. (Serving Aug. 4, 1914). Capt. and Adjt. Northern Bengal Mounted Rifles. Capt. I.A.R.O., Cavalry Branch. India, 1914; S. Waziristan and N.W. Frontier, 1917–19.
1903 Little, W. O. (Mobilized Aug. 1914). Maj. Westmorland & Cumberland Yeomanry. Palestine, Belgium.
1909 Littlejohn, C. W. B., B.M. (Aug. 8, 1914). Capt. R.A.M.C., attd. 140th Field Ambulance and 3rd Lowland Bde., R.F.A. France, 1914, 1917–19; Salonika, 1916. *M.C.*, Feb. 15, 1919. Belgian Croix de Guerre.
1918 Litton, E. F., B.A. (Sept. 16, 1914). Lt. R.F.A. (Invalided.)
1904 Llewellyn, G. R. P. (Mobilized Aug. 1914). Capt. 1/1st Glamorganshire Yeomanry (Maj.). Egypt, Sinai, Syria, Palestine. *D.* Palestine, 1918.
1912 **Lloyd,* W. H.** (Sept. 1, 1914). Capt. Herefordshire Regt. Gallipoli, 1915. Accidentally killed at Oswestry on Mar. 19, 1916.
1902 Lloyd-Baker, A. B., M.A. (Mobilized Aug. 1914). Lt.-Col. Bucks. Bn.

Oxf. & Bucks. Lt. Infty. France and Belgium, 1915–17; Italy, 1917–18. *D.S.O.*, Jan. 1, 1918. Croce di Guerra. *D.* France, 1917; Italy, 1918, 1919.

1903 Lockwood, C. M., M.A. (Apr. 5, 1916). ‡Lt. 4/14th London Regt. (London Scottish). Lt. 14th Bn. Tank Corps (Capt.). France. *M.C.*, Mar. 8, 1919.

1899 Long, A. de L. (Serving Aug. 4, 1914). Capt., Bt.-Maj., Acting Maj., Gordon Highlanders. (Lt.-Col. R. Welch Fusiliers.) France. *D.S.O.*, June 3, 1918. *D.* France, 1916 twice, 1918.

1913 Longden, D. J., B.A. (Sept. 16, 1914). Lt. Middlesex Regt., attd. 23rd Sikh Pioneers, Indian Army. France, Salonika, India.

1897 Longstaff, R. (Serving Aug. 4, 1914). Maj., Acting Lt.-Col., 291st Bde., R.F.A. France, 1914–16, 1918. *D.S.O.*, Jan. 14, 1916. Croix de Chevalier de la Légion d'Honneur. *D.* France, 1914, 1915 twice.

1904 Lowe,* A. H., B.A. (Oct. 8, 1914). Capt., temp. Maj., 8th Oxf. & Bucks. Lt. Infty., attd. Ministry of Munitions. Salonika, Italy.

1911 Lowe, W. H., B.A. (Oct. 5, 1914). Maj. 20th Lancashire Fusiliers. France and Belgium. *D.* France, 1917. (Invalided on account of wounds.)

1902 Lucas, N. S., B.M., M.A. (Mar. 15, 1917). Capt. R.A.M.C. France, Italy.

1908 Lunn, H. K. (Nov. 6, 1914). Sub-Lt. R.N.V.R. France. (Prisoner of war.)

1890 Luxmoore, L. A., M.A. (Mobilized Aug. 1914). Capt., Acting Maj., R.F.A.

1893 **Lyell, Hon. C. H.,** B.A., *M.P.* (Sept. 1914). Lt. Res. of Officers. Asst. Mil. Attaché, U.S.A. G.S.O. 2. France, 1915–18. Died of pneumonia in Washington on Oct. 18, 1918.

1913 **Lyon, F. C.** (1915). Lt. Grenadier Guards. France. Killed in action, on Apr. 13, 1918.

1910 **Macandrew,* I. M. McL.** (Serving Aug. 4, 1914). Lt. 1st Seaforth Highlanders. India, France. *D.* France, 1914 twice. Killed in action at Festubert on Dec. 23, 1914.

1890 McClintock, H. F., B.A. (Mobilized Aug. 1914). Maj. 8th London Regt. (Post Office Rifles). Staff-Captain (Director of Postal Services). France. T.D. *D.* France, 1919.

1906 McCormick-Goodhart, F. H., B.A. (Oct. 19, 1914). Lt. R.N.V.R.

1903 McCormick-Goodhart, L. (Mobilized Aug. 4, 1914). Lt.-Commdr. R.N.V.R., Trade Div. Naval Staff, Admiralty, attd. Naval Section, Peace Delegation, Paris. *O.B.E.* (Mil.). *D.* Naval Dispatch, 1919.

1894 Macculloch, A. J., B.A., *D.C.M.*, (Mobilized Sept. 14, 1914). Capt., Bt.-Lt.-Col., 7th Dragoon Guards. Temp. Brig.-Gen. 62nd Inf. Bde. France, Belgium. *D.S.O.*, July 20, 1918; *Bar*, Sept. 16, 1918; *2nd Bar*, Jan. 11, 1919. Croix de Chevalier de la Légion d'Honneur. *D.* France, 1916, 1917, 1918.

1919 McDermot, T. W. L. (May 5, 1916). Cadet Canadian G.A. (Sergt.). France, 1917–18.

1909 Macdonald,* W. I. F., B.A. (Sept. 23, 1914). Capt. Leicestershire Yeomanry, attd. 16th Lancers (Adjt.). France, 1914–19. *D.* France, 1918.

1909 Macdonell, J. F. (Mobilized Aug. 1914). Capt., Acting Maj., B Batt., 83rd Bde., R.F.A. France, 1915–19. *M.C.*, June 18, 1917.

1909 **MacDougall, A.,** B.A. (Aug. 1914). Capt. 22nd R. Fusiliers. France. Killed in action on Aug. 2, 1916.

1903 **Macduff, A.** (Serving Aug. 4, 1914). Capt. 2nd Q.O. Cameron Highlanders. France and Belgium. Killed in action near Ypres on Apr. 23, 1915.

1893 Macduff, W. A. (Nov. 23, 1915). Lt. Highland Cyclist Bn., attd. 9th Seaforth Highlanders.

1911 **Macfie, C. W.** (Nov. 11, 1914). 2nd Lt. 3rd S. Staffordshire Regt., attd. 2nd Bedfordshire Regt. France and Belgium. *D.* France, 1915. Killed in action at Givenchy on June 16, 1915.

1913 Machin, L. F. (Feb. 15, 1915). Lt., temp. Capt., K.O. Scottish Borderers (Maj.). France, 1917, 1919; Italy, 1917–18. *M.C.*, Nov. 26, 1917. *D.* France, 1917.

1905 Mackay, J. B. I., M.A. (1914). ‡Lt. Special Lists, whilst empld. W.A.A.F. W. Africa.

1919 McKechnie, H. (Dec. 28, 1917). 2nd Lt. 5th Northumberland Fusiliers.

1912 Mackenzie, G. B., B.A. (Sept. 18, 1914). Capt. 3rd Q.O. Cameron Highlanders. Salonika, 1915.

1912 Mackenzie,* W. N. (Oct. 10, 1914). Lt., Acting Maj., 80th Bde., R.F.A. France. *M.C.*, Sept. 22, 1916; *Bar*, Feb. 15, 1919.

1911 Mackinnon, D. (Mobilized Aug. 1914). Capt. King Edward's Horse. France.

1909 Mackinnon, M., B.A. (Apr. 9, 1915). Capt. 4th Highland L.I., attd. War Office (Staff-Captain). France and Belgium, 1915–16. *M.C.*, Oct. 20, 1916. *D.* France, 1916.

1900 Mackirdy, E. M. S., M.A. (Mobilized Aug. 1914). Capt. Lanarkshire Yeomanry, attd. R. Horse Guards. France. T.D.

1892 McLachlan, D. (July 8, 1918). Lce.-Cpl. 2/1st Hampshire Yeomanry.

1880 McLean, N., B.A. (Oct. 12, 1914). Maj. 2/1st Dorset Yeomanry (T.F. Res.) (Hon. Lt.-Col.).

MacLehose, J. C. (1915). 2nd Lt. 16th Rifle Brigade. France and Belgium, 1916–17. Killed in action at Ypres on Feb. 14, 1917.

1913 Macnaghten, R. F. (Nov. 1915). Capt. Manitoba Regt., 27th Bn. Canadian Inf. France. *D.S.O.*, Jan. 18, 1918. *D.* France, 1918.

1905 McNair, G. D., B.A. (July 28, 1916). Lt. I.A.R.O. Mesopotamia. *M.B.E.* (Mil.). *D.* Mesopotamia, 1918, 1919.

1911 **Macnamara,* G. F.**, B.A. (1915). 2nd Lt. 4th, attd. 8th, R. Dublin Fusiliers. France. Killed in action near Loos on Aug. 18, 1916.

1896 Maitland, A., B.A. (Sept. 11, 1914). Lt. R.G.A. (T.F.) (Staff-Capt.). France, 1915, 1918–19; Salonika, 1915–16.

Maitland, A. J. (July 19, 1917). 2nd Lt. R.F.C. France. Killed in flying accident on Sept. 22, 1917.

1895 Malan, A. G., B.A. ‡2nd Lt. Labour Corps. France.

1904 Manger, C. H., M.A. (Serving Aug. 4, 1914). Capt., Bt.-Maj., 1st S. Staffordshire Regt. D.A.A. and Q.M.G., III Corps. France. *M.C.*, June 4, 1917. Croix de Chevalier de la Légion d'Honneur. *D.* France, 1918 twice.

1909 Mann, J. E. F., B.A. (Aug. 24, 1914). Lt. 6th D.C.L.I. Capt. 8th K.O.Y.L.I. Capt. General List. France, 1915–17; Italy, 1917–19. *M.C.*, June 3, 1918. *D.* Italy, 1918.

1919 Mann, J. G. (Aug. 30, 1916). Lt. R.A. Staff-Lt. (1st Class), 23rd Div., H.Q. France, 1917; Italy, 1917–19.

1898 **Manning, C. E.,** B.A. (1915). Maj. 24th Bn. A.I.F. Egypt, Gallipoli, France, 1915–16. *D.* France, 1916. Killed in action in France on Aug. 7, 1916.

1919 Manning, C. J. (Aug. 9, 1918). 2nd Lt. Oxf. & Bucks. Lt. Infty. (on demobilization).

1888 **Manning, P.,** M.A. Protection Coy., R. Defence Corps. Died on service on Feb. 27, 1917.

1902 Mannooch, E. M., B.A. Calcutta Light Horse. India.

1907 Manson, N. B., B.A. (Aug. 29, 1914). Capt. 22nd London Regt. (The Queen's).

1887 Marindin, A. H. (Serving Aug. 4, 1914). Lt.-Col., Bt.-Col., The Black Watch. Maj.-Gen. 35th Div. France, 1914–18. *C.B.*, Jan. 1, 1919. *D.S.O.*, Jan. 1, 1918. Croix d'Officier de la Légion d'Honneur. Commandeur de l'Ordre de la Couronne. Croix de Guerre with palm. Belgian Croix de Guerre with palm. *D.* France, 1915, 1916 twice, 1918 twice, 1919.

1919 Marrot, H. V., B.A. (Feb. 1917). Lt. 16th S. Lancashire Regt., attd. D.A.D.C., Italy. Italy.

1914 **Marshall, A. H. B.** (Nov. 24, 1914). Lt. 3rd Rifle Brigade. France. Killed in action near Lens on May 22, 1918.

1887 Marshall, Rev. C. B., M.A. (Oct. 1, 1915). Chaplain R.N. (Resigned.)

1901 Marshall, G., B.A. (Oct. 24, 1914). Lt. 9th Hampshire Regt. (Capt. and Adjt.). India, 1916–19.

1903 Martin, E. G., B.A. (1914). Lt., Acting Lt.-Commdr., R.N.V.R. *O.B.E.* (Mil.).

1909 Martin, P. A., B.A. (Feb. 26, 1916). Sub-Lt. R.N.V.R. H.M.S. *Hilary*, 10th Cruiser Squadron. (Invalided, Mar. 1917.)

1909 Martin, P. H. (June 4, 1916). Sub-Lt. R.N.A.S. Capt., Flying Officer, R.A.F. H.M.S. *Cleopatra*, 1916; France, 1917–19. *A.F.C.*, Jan. 1, 1919.

1913 Mason,* P. R. F., B.A. (Aug. 15, 1914). Capt. 4th King's (Liverpool Regt.), attd. 9th K.R.R.C. France, 1915–16, 1917–19.

1904 Mathews, J. S., B.A. (Jan. 13, 1915). Lt. S. Irish Horse (S.R.), attd. 7th R. Irish Regt. (Capt.). France.

1905 [Mathews, P. D., B.A.] (Oct. 10, 1914). Lt. 5th Connaught Rangers, attd. 12th R. Irish Rifles.

1912 Maude, A. A. J. P. (Aug. 1914). ‡Lt. Rifle Brigade, empld. R.A.O.C. France (attd. 7th Rifle Brigade), 1915–16.

1900 Maude, H. O. H., B.A. (Oct. 4, 1914). Lt. 1st Home Counties Bde., R.F.A. (T.F.)

1913 Mauleverer, W. M. M. G., B.A. (Oct. 3, 1914). Lt. 2/4th Dorsetshire Regt., empld. R.E. India, 1914–19.

1896 **Maxwell, E. L.** (Serving Aug. 4, 1914). Maj. 11th K.E.O. Lancers, Indian Army. Lt.-Col. 23rd Manchester Regt. Mesopotamia. Missing, presumed killed in action on Mar. 9, 1916.

1919 Maxwell, H. H. (Jan. 27, 1916). Lt. 1st Irish Guards. France, 1916–17. (Invalided on account of wounds.)

May, H. C. (Oct. 5, 1917). 2nd Lt. 6th, attd. 18th, K.R.R.C. France and Belgium, 1918. Died on Sept. 29, 1918, of wounds received in action near Ypres.

1910 Medley, J. D. G. (Sept. 4, 1914). Lt. 6th Welsh Regt. Maj. General List. D.A.D., R.T.O. France, 1914–19.
1912 Meier, E. S. French Foreign Legion, attd. Corps d'Aviation. France.
1919 Meldrum, A. F. (Aug. 10, 1914). ‡Lt. N.Z. Mounted Rifles Bde., 6th Squadron. Samoa, 1914–15; France, 1916; Palestine, 1916–18.
1908 **Melland,* E. G.,** B.A. (Aug. 8, 1914). ‡Lt. 8th Cheshire Regt., attd. 1st W. Yorkshire Regt. France and Belgium, 1914–15. Killed in action at St. Jean on July 1, 1915.
1912 Mellor,* J. S. P., B.A. (Aug. 1914). Capt. 5th Somerset L.I., attd. Oxf. & Bucks. Lt. Infty. Burmah, Mesopotamia. (Prisoner of war at Kut-el-Amara, Apr. 29, 1916.)
1898 Melvill, M. G. D. (Mobilized Aug. 1914). Capt., Acting Lt.-Col., 6th, attd. 5th, Manchester Regt. France. *M.C.*, Sept. 26, 1917.
1901 **Merriman, W. R. H.,** B.A. (Aug. 4, 1914). ‡2nd Lt. 8th Rifle Brigade. France and Belgium, 1914–16. *D.* France, 1915. Killed in action near Longueval on Aug. 15, 1916.
1909 Methuen, Hon. A. P., B.A. (Aug. 1914). Capt. Scots Guards, empld. Admiralty. France, 1915; Malta Base, 1916–17.
1906 Methuen, Hon. P. A., M.A. (Aug. 1914). Lt. R. Wiltshire Yeomanry. Lt. Scots Guards (S.R.). A.D.C. France.
1905 Meyer, F. C., B.A. (Aug. 26, 1914). Lt. Essex Yeomanry. Lt. Administrative Officer, R.A.F.
1900 Micholls, M. G., B.A. (Serving Aug. 4, 1914). Capt. 17th Lancers (Maj. School of Instruction).
1913 Micklem, E. R., M.A. (Jan. 1916). Lt. 478th Siege Batt., R.G.A. France and Belgium, 1917–18. (Commission relinquished on account of ill health.)
1909 Micklem, T. E., B.M., M.A. (Nov. 20, 1916). Capt. R.A.M.C. (S.R.).
1912 Miclesco-Prajesco, J. 2nd Lt. 9th Hussars, Rumanian Army. Lt. Rumanian Flying Corps. Rumania, France.
1894 Middleton, N., B.A. (Dec. 1916). Lt. Garr. Bn. Highland L.I. Staff-Lt. (1st Class).
1884 Milford, R. S., B.A. Lt., temp. Capt., 7th Vol. Bn. Cheshire Regt.
1901 Mill, T. R. S. V. Barker-, M.A. (Dec. 1914). ‡2nd Lt. 6th Rifle Brigade. France. (Placed on Retired List on account of ill health caused by wounds, May 1917.)
1893 **Mill, W. C. F. V. Barker-,** B.A. (1914). ‡Capt. 8th Rifle Brigade. France, 1915–16. *D.* France, 1916. Killed in action near Delville Wood on Sept. 15, 1916.
1897 Miller, A. B., B.A. (Jan. 23, 1915). Lt., Acting Capt., R.A. G.S.O. 3. *D.* § Aug. 1918.
1902 **Miller, J. L.,** B.A. (Apr. 22, 1915). Lt. 8th London Regt. (Post Office Rifles). France. Killed in action, May 21–2, 1916.
1920 Mills, H. C. (May 24, 1917). ‡Lt. R.E. France, 1918–19; Germany, 1919. *D.* France, 1919.
1919 Minot, H. W. (May 14, 1917). Lt. U.S. Infantry. France.
1905 Mirfield, F. G., B.A. (Dec. 28, 1912). Capt. R.A.S.C. Italy, 1916. *D.* § Mar. 1919, § Aug. 1919.
1888 Mitchell, A. I. (Mobilized Aug. 1914). Capt. 3rd Dragoon Guards, Res. of Officers.

1903 Mitchell, E. G. H., B.A. (Nov. 15, 1915). Capt. 5th, attd. 3rd, Rifle Brigade. France and Belgium.

1909 Mitchison, G. R., M.A. (Aug. 15, 1914). Capt., temp. Maj., 2nd Dragoon Guards. G.S.O. 2. France and Italy. Croix de Guerre.

1911 **Mitchison, W. A.** (Aug. 3, 1914). ‡Lt. R.E. (Signal Service). France and Belgium, 1914–17. Killed in action near Ypres on Sept. 20, 1917.

1903 Moberly, Rev. R. H., M.A. (Aug. 1917). Chaplain to the Forces (4th Class), attd. 57th Div. France.

1900 [Moberly, W. H., M.A.] (July 12, 1915). Lt. 2/4th Oxf. & Bucks. Lt. Infty. (Capt.). France, 1915–16, 1917. *D.S.O.*, Oct. 18, 1917. *D.* France, 1916, 1917.

1896 Moberly-Bell, E. S. (July 19, 1916). Lt. R.G.A. (S.R.), attd. Labour Corps.

1919 Mold, C. E. (July 6, 1918). Rfln. 16th London Regt. (Queen's Westminster Rifles).

1919 Monck-Mason, A. T. McC. (Sept. 5, 1914). ‡Capt. R.F.A. (graded as R.E.), Forestry Officer, G.H.Q., Constantinople A.B.S. France, Belgium, Salonika, Constantinople.

1895 Money-Coutts, Hon. H. B., B.A. (Mobilized Aug. 1914). Capt. R. N. Devon Yeomanry (Staff-Captain). Gallipoli, 1915; Egypt, 1916–17. T.D. (Invalided on account of ill health, Aug. 1918.)

1888 Monk-Bretton, J. W., Lord, *C.B.* (Mobilized Aug. 1914). Capt., temp. Maj., Sussex Yeomanry (T.F. Res).

1886 Montagu of Beaulieu, J. W. E., Lord, *C.S.I.*, V.D. (Mobilized Aug. 1914). Lt.-Col. and Hon. Col. Hampshire Regt. (T.F. Res.) (Temp. Brig.-Gen.).

1902 Montague, Hon. L.S., M.A. (Sept. 24, 1914). Capt. R. Marines, attd. Hood Bn., R.N. Div. France, 1914, 1916–17; Gallipoli, 1915. *D.S.O.*, Apr. 17, 1917. *D.* France, 1917.

1901 Moon, A., B.A. (Apr. 1915). Capt. 8th London Regt. (Post Office Rifles), attd. 17th Inf. Bde. France. *M.C.*, Jan. 1, 1919.

1894 Moon, R. O., D.M. (Mar. 1917). Maj. R.A.M.C. Salonika and France.

1913 Moresby-White, J. M., B.A. (Aug. 18, 1916). Lt. A Batt., 112th Bde., R.F.A. (Capt.). France. (Civilian prisoner of war, 1914–16.)

1897 Morgan, A. C., M.A. (Nov. 1915). Lt. 12th A.A. Mobile Batt., R.G.A.

1909 Morkill,* A. G., B.A. (Aug. 24, 1917). 2nd Lt. 81st Siege Batt., R.G.A. France and Belgium, 1918–19.

1919 Morley, F. M. (1916). Friends Amb. R.A.M.C., afterwards U.S. Field Artillery. France, 1916–17.

1914 Morrah, D. M., B.A. (Sept. 13, 1915). Lt. R.E. (Signals). O.C. Kantara Military School. Sinai and Palestine.

1905 Morris, R. O., B.A. (Oct. 13, 1914). Lt. 13th Durham L.I. Lt. General List, empld. Ministry of Munitions.

1904 Morrison, D. C., B.A. (Sept. 1914). Lt. R.G.A. (S.R.), attd. R.E. France, 1916–17.

1892 Morrison, J. A. (Serving Aug. 4, 1914). Capt. Grenadier Guards (Res. of Officers) (Maj.). France. *D.S.O.*, June 3, 1916. *D.* France, 1915, 1916.

1902 Morton, H. H. P. (Aug. 11, 1914). Capt. 32nd Amb. Train, R.A.M.C. France and Belgium, 1914–19. *D.* France, 1918, 1919.

1910 **Moss-Blundell,* C. B.** (Oct. 23, 1914). Lt. 14th Durham L.I. France. Missing, believed killed in action at Loos on Sept. 26, 1915.

1891 **Mount, F.**, M.A. (Sept. 14, 1914). Capt. 5th R. Berkshire Regt. France. Killed in action at the Quarries, Hulluch, on Oct. 13, 1915.
1885 Mount, W. A., M.A., *M.P.* Lt.-Col. Unattached List, Claims Commission. *C.B.E.* (Civil). Croix de Chevalier de la Légion d'Honneur.
1919 Mowbray, Sir G. R., Bt. (Feb. 6, 1918). 2nd Lt. D/36th Bde., R.F.A. France and Germany.
1907 **Moyes, W. B.** (Sept. 2, 1914). Sergt. Queen's (R. W. Surrey Regt.). France, 1915–18. *M.M.* Died on Mar. 25, 1918, of wounds received in action near Amiens.
1899 **Moyna, E. G. J.**, B.A. (Jan. 1915). Capt. 7th R. Scots Fusiliers. France. Killed in action at the Battle of Loos on Sept. 26, 1915.
1908 Munro,* E. A., B.A. (Feb. 26, 1915). Lt. R.G.A. (S.R.). Salonika.
1910 Murray, D. G. (Aug. 5, 1914). Sub-Lt. R.N.A.S. Capt. Seaplane Officer, R.A.F. Dunkirk, 1914–15. (Interned in Holland, 1915–19.)
1910 Murray, K., B.A. (Mobilized Aug 4, 1914). Capt. 2nd Lovat's Scouts, attd. R.A.O.C. Gallipoli, 1915; Egypt, 1916; Salonika, 1916–17. (Invalided, Nov. 1918.)
1913 Murray, W. E. G. (Nov. 14, 1914). Lt. 12th Highland L.I. Maj., Flying Officer, R.A.F. Italy. *M.C.* *D.F.C.* Croix de Guerre. Italian Silver Medal for Military Valour. Order of the Crown of Italy.
1897 Murray-Graham, A. J. G., B.A. (Aug. 8, 1914). Capt., Bt.-Maj., 3rd The Black Watch. D.A.A.G. *D.* § Aug. 1918.
1912 Muspratt,* C. K., B.A. (Aug. 29, 1914). Capt. 7th Hampshire Regt. India and Mesopotamia.
1888 Myres, J. L., M.A. (Apr. 1, 1916). Lt.-Commdr., Acting Commdr., R.N.V.R. Military Control Officer, Athens. Greece, 1915–19. *O.B.E.* (Mil.). Commander of the Order of George I of Greece. *D.* Naval Dispatch, July, 1917.
1919 Myres, M. C. (June 27, 1918). 2nd Lt. 4th Res. Regt. of Cavalry.
1893 Mytton, G. H., B.A. (Mobilized Aug. 1914). Lt.-Col., Bt.-Col., 2/1st Montgomeryshire Yeomanry T.D. *D.* § Feb. 1917.
1914 Nelson, D. T. (May 14, 1917). Lt. Intelligence Div., Gen. Staff, U.S. Army. France.
1889 Neve, E. J. (Serving Aug. 4, 1914). Lt.-Col. Staff Paymaster, A.P.D. (Col.). *D.* § Feb. 1917; Mar. 1919.
1911 Newbolt,* A. F., B.A. (Serving Aug. 4, 1914). Capt. and Adjt. 3rd Oxf. & Bucks. Lt. Infty., attd. No. 4 O.C.B. Belgium, 1915.
1894 **Newstead, G. P.** (Serving Aug. 4, 1914). Maj. Suffolk Regt. Lt.-Col. Sierra Leone Bn., W. African Frontier Force. W. Africa. *D.* Africa, 1915. Died on Mar. 4, 1915, of wounds received in action at Paro.
1894 Newton, H. K., M.A., *M.P.* (Nov. 8, 1914). Maj. R.A.S.C. D.A.D. Supply and Transport. *O.B.E.* (Mil.). *D.* § Feb. 1917.
1909 Niblett, B. M., B.A. (Sept. 4, 1914). Capt. Worcestershire Regt. France and Belgium. *D.* France, 1917.
1885 Nicholson, H. B. (Mobilized Aug. 1914). Maj. 3rd K.R.R.C. France, 1915; Salonika, 1916–17. *D.S.O.*, Jan. 1, 1918. *D.* France, 1915, 1917.
1896 Nickalls, C. P. (Mobilized Aug. 1914). Maj. 4th (S. Mid.) Howitzer Bde., R.F.A. (T.F.). France. *D.S.O.*, Jan. 1, 1918. *D.* France, 1915, 1917
1898 Nickalls, M. (Aug. 26, 1914). Capt. Northamptonshire Yeomanry. A.D.C. France. *M.C.*, Jan. 1, 1918.

1883 **Nickalls, N. T.** (Serving Aug. 4, 1914). Col. Lancers. Brig.-Gen. France, Belgium. Missing, presumed killed in action on Sept. 27, 1915.

1894 Nickalls, P. W., B.A. (Mobilized Aug. 1914). Maj. Northamptonshire Yeomanry. France, Italy. *D.S.O.*, June 3, 1918. Italian Silver Medal for Valour. *D.* France, 1917; Italy, 1918.

1892 Nicol, A. P. (Dec. 14, 1914). Capt., Acting Maj., R.F.A. France and Belgium. *M.C.*, June 3, 1918.

1901 **Nolan, R. P. D.,** B.A. (Serving Aug. 4, 1914). Lt. The Black Watch. France. Killed in action in France on Nov. 3, 1914.

Norcross, F. (July 7, 1916). 2nd Lt. 23rd Manchester Regt. France. Missing, presumed killed in action on July 29, 1916.

1911 Norris, T. P., B.A. (Aug. 6, 1914). ‡Capt. R.E. (Signal Service). France, 1914–15; E. Africa, 1916–18. *M.C.*, Jan. 1, 1918. *D.* France, 1914, 1915; E. Africa, 1917.

1900 North, S. T. F. (Sept. 10, 1917). 2nd Lt. R.A.S.C.

1919 Norton, W. C. (Sept. 16, 1914). Capt. 9th Sussex Regt. Staff-Captain. France and Belgium, 1915–16. *M.C.*, Sept. 27, 1915. *D.* § Mar. 1918.

1912 O'Connor,* T. J. (Aug. 14, 1914). Capt. 4th Highland L.I. France, Cameroons, Nigeria, Sudan.

1908 Ogg, D., M.A. (Feb. 10, 1915). Paymaster Lt. R.N.R. Mediterranean, Adriatic, Red Sea.

Ogilvie, A. M. (July 7, 1916). 2nd Lt. 3rd, attd. 2nd, Gordon Highlanders. France and Belgium. Killed in action on Oct. 5, 1917.

1909 Ogilvie, G. H. (Jan. 15, 1915). Lt., Acting Capt., 2/3rd Gurkha Rifles (Adjt.). Gallipoli, 1915; Egypt, 1915–16; Mesopotamia, 1916; Palestine, 1917–18. *M.C.*, June 3, 1919. *D.* Palestine, 1918.

1918 Ogilvie, W. F. (Dec. 14, 1915). Lt. 9th London Regt. (Queen Victoria's Rifles). (Commission relinquished on account of ill health.)

1906 Ogilvie, W. H., B.M., M.A., M.Ch. (1914). Capt. R.A.M.C. France.

1910 Ogilvie-Forbes,* G. A. D., B.A. (Mobilized Aug. 1914). Capt. Scottish Horse. A.D.C. Gallipoli, Egypt, Mesopotamia. *D.* Mesopotamia, 1917.

1885 Oldfield, C. B. (Sept. 28, 1914). Capt. (Hon. Maj.) 2/5th Devonshire Regt. (T.F. Res.). Egypt, 1915–16.

1889 Oldfield, F. B., M.A. (Sept. 1914). Maj. 13th R. Fusiliers. Maj. Training Res.

1895 Oldham, F. H. L., B.A. (Serving Aug. 4, 1914). Maj., Bt.-Lt.-Col., Acting Lt.-Col., 35th Bde., R.F.A. D.A.A.G. France, Italy. *D.S.O.*, June 4, 1917. Order of St. Maurice and St. Lazarus. *D.* France, 1916 twice, 1917; Italy, 1918 twice, 1919.

1901 **Oliver, R. M.,** B.A. (Aug. 1914). Lt. 2nd Grenadier Guards (S.R.), attd. as Capt. and Adjt. 5th The Buffs (E. Kent Regt.). France. Killed in action near St. Léger on Aug. 27, 1918.

1919 Olivier, M. J. (Sept. 4, 1918). 2nd Lt. R. W. Kent Regt. (on demobilization).

1902 O'Neill, Hon. R. W. H. (Sept. 17, 1914). Capt. 12th R. Irish Rifles. Maj. General List. Deputy Judge Advocate-General. France, 1915–17; Palestine, 1918–19. Chevalier de l'Ordre du Mérite Agricole.

1895 Onslow, R. W. A., Earl of, M.A. (June 15, 1915). Col. Intelligence Corps. A.D. Staff Duties, G.H.Q. France. *C.M.G. O.B.E.* (Mil.). Croix de Chevalier de la Légion d'Honneur. *D.* France, 1916, 1918; § Feb. 1917.

1899 **Oppé, H. S.,** M.A. (Feb. 21, 1915). Lt. 11th Yorkshire Regt., attd. 8th W. Riding Regt. Gallipoli. Killed in action in Gallipoli on Nov. 6, 1915.

1919 Oppenheimer, E. H. (Sept. 9, 1918). Cadet 212th Batt., R.F.A.

1919 Oppenheimer, P. H. M. (Aug. 1915). Lt. 2nd Dorsetshire Regt. Mesopotamia, 1916–18; Palestine, 1918.

1889 Ormerod, A. L., D.M. (Mobilized Aug. 5, 1914). Capt. R.A.M.C., attd. 3rd S. Gen. Hospital.

1917 Ormond, C. E. Cadet R.E.

1903 Ormsby-Gore, Hon. W. G. A., B.A. (Mobilized Aug. 4, 1914). Capt. Shropshire Yeomanry. Maj. War Cabinet Staff. Egypt, 1916; Hedjaz, 1917; Palestine, 1918.

1917 Osborn, H. A. S. African Horse. Africa. (Discharged on account of ill health.)

1911 Overton,* A. E., B.A. (June 16, 1916). Lt. R.E. France. *M.C.*, Apr. 11, 1918.

1913 **Overton,* T. D.** (Sept. 8, 1914). Lt. 6th Lincolnshire Regt. Gallipoli. Killed in action in Gallipoli, near Cape Helles, on July 30, 1915.

1902 Page, R. (Feb. 11, 1915). Lt. 13th Hampshire Regt. Lt., Acting Capt., M.G.C.

Paget, S. J. (Sept. 1914). Capt. 8th Norfolk Regt. Capt. General List, G.S.O. 3. (Bde. Maj. 149th Bde.). France, 1915–18. *D.* France, 1916. Killed in action at Famesville sur Somme on Mar. 31, 1918.

1910 Paine,* A. T. W., B.A. (Aug. 4, 1914). Capt. Northumberland Fusiliers. France and Belgium, 1915–16. *D.* § Mar. 1919.

1919 Painter, H. F. (Sept. 5, 1914). ‡Lt., temp. Capt., Northumberland Hussars. Staff-Captain. France and Belgium. Croix de Guerre. *D.* France.

1911 Palmer, E. H. G., B.A. (Mar. 1, 1915). Lt. Derbyshire Yeomanry, attd. 8th Sherwood Foresters. D.A.A.G.

1896 Palmer, Rev. H. H., M.A. (1914). Naval Chaplain and Instructor. (Retired.)

1919 Palmer, J. A. B. (Mar. 1, 1918). 2nd Lt. Guards M.G. Regt.

1907 Parish, C. W., B.A. (Aug. 1914). Capt. General List. (Maj.). A.P.M. I Corps. France, 1915–18. *D.* France, 1916.

1904 Parish, J. B. A., B.A. (Mobilized Aug. 1914). Capt. 2nd London Bde., R.F.A. (Adjt.).

1907 Parker,* Sir W. L., Bt., B.A. (Aug. 4, 1914). ‡Capt. 1/9th Hampshire Regt. India, 1916–18; Siberia, 1919. *O.B.E.* (Mil.). *D.* Siberia, 1919.

1910 Parr,* J. W., M.A. (Sept. 7, 1914). A.B., R.N.V.R. ‡Lt. 3rd, attd. 5th, Highland L.I. Egypt, Palestine, France. (Prisoner of war, Aug. 1918.)

1911 **Parson,* E. E.** (Jan. 1915). Lt. R.F.A. France. *M.C.*, July 26, 1917. Died on June 1, 1917, of wounds received in action at Arras.

1908 Parsons,* N. M., B.A. (Sept. 11, 1914). Lt. 15th Mountain Batt., R.F.A. (T.F.). India, 1914–17; Mesopotamia, 1917–18.

1903 Paul, H. M., B.A. (Dec. 15, 1916). Capt. General List. Staff-Captain.

1905 Paulin, N. G., B.A. (Mobilized Aug. 1914). Capt. 86th Bde., R.F.A. (T.F.). France, 1915–18.

1906 Pawling, C. H. (Mobilized Aug. 1914). Capt. 1st County of London Yeomanry, attd. M.G.C. (Maj.).

1912 Payne,* E. G., B.A. (Oct. 26, 1914). Capt. 1/7th R. Welch Fusiliers. Gallipoli, 1915; Egypt, 1916; Palestine, 1917–18.

1910 Peachell, G. P. (Aug. 4, 1915). Lt. 2/1st Monmouthshire Regt. (Capt. & Adjt.).

1919 Peake, L. S. (May 4, 1918). Midshipman R.N.V.R., H.M.S. *Parker*. North Sea.

1912 Peareth,* W. F. E., B.A. (Mobilized Aug. 4, 1914). Capt. 4th R. W. Kent Regt. Gallipoli, 1915; Afghanistan, 1919.

1911 **Pearse, W. J.,** B.A. (Aug. 1914). ‡2nd Lt. R.H.A. France and Belgium, 1915. *M.C.*, June 4, 1917. Killed in action at Vimy Ridge on Apr. 9, 1917.

Pearson, C. T. (Jan. 1917). 2nd Lt. 14th R. Warwickshire Regt. France. Died on Aug. 29, 1918, of wounds received in action at Grévillers.

1903 Pearson, J. M., B.A. (Serving Aug. 4, 1914). Capt. Indian Cavalry, attd. Supply and Transport, later E. Africa Transport Corps and Intelligence Dept. British and German E. Africa.

1910 **Pease, C.,** B.A. (Serving Aug. 1914). Capt. 1st Irish Guards. France, 1914, 1915, 1916. *D.* France, 1916. Died on Sept. 18, 1916, of wounds received in action near Martinpuich.

1886 Peel, Hon. A. G. V., M.A. (Mobilized Aug. 4, 1914). Maj. Bedfordshire Yeomanry (T.F. Res.), afterwards Maj. (A.P.M.), General Staff E.E.F. Gallipoli, 1915; Egypt, 1915–17. *D.* Gallipoli, 1915; Egypt, 1917.

1890 Peel, J. G., M.A. Maj. 6th Vol. Bn. Cheshire Regt.

1891 **Peel, Rev. the Hon. M. B.,** B.A. (Sept. 22, 1914). Chaplain to the Forces (4th Class). France, 1914–15, 1917. *M.C.*, Feb. 18, 1915; *Bar*, Apr. 17, 1917. *D.* France, 1914. Killed in action in France on May 14, 1917.

1900 Peel, R., M.A. (Sept. 12, 1914). Capt., Bt.-Maj., 16th London Regt. (Queen's Westminster Rifles). D.A.A.G. Macedonia and Turkey, 1915–19. *O.B.E.* (Mil.). Order of the White Eagle (4th Class) (with swords). *D.* Salonika, 1916, 1917.

1889 [Peel, Hon. S. C., M.A.] (Mobilized Aug. 4, 1914). Lt.-Col. Bedfordshire Yeomanry. France and Belgium. *D.S.O.*, June 2, 1917. T.D. Commdr. Hafidian Order. *D.* France, 1917.

1906 Peer, S. S. (Apr. 9, 1917). Maj. 313th Inf., U.S. Army.

1905 Peirs, H. J. C., M.A. (Sept. 1914). Lt.-Col. 8th Queen's (R. W. Surrey Regt.). France and Belgium. *C.M.G.* 1919. *D.S.O.*, June 3, 1916; *Bar*, Sept. 26, 1917; *2nd Bar*, Sept. 16, 1918. *D.* France, 1916 twice, 1917, 1918, 1919.

1897 **Pember, H. C.** (Sept. 1914). Lt. Q.O. Oxfordshire Hussars. Capt. The Household Bn. (Maj.). France. Killed in action at Rœux on May 3, 1917.

1909 Pemberton, R. L. S., B.A. (Aug. 1914). Maj. 11th Durham L.I. France, 1915–19. *M.C.*, Jan. 1, 1918; *Bar*, Sept. 16, 1918. *D.* France, 1916.

1919 Pennycuick, J. (May 1918). 2nd Lt. Coldstream Guards (on demobilization).

1919 Perrott, T. H. H. (June 1917). 2nd Lt. 1st (Res.) Bn. Worcestershire Regt. 2nd Lt. Labour Corps (P./W. Staff) (Lt.). France, 1917–18.

1907 Pery,* Hon. E. C., B.A. (Mobilized Aug. 1914). Maj. City of London Yeomanry. Bde. Maj. Egypt, Sinai, Gallipoli, 1915; France, 1916–19. *D.S.O.*, July 26, 1918. *D.* France, 1918.

1903 Pharo, A. C., M.A. (Sept. 24, 1914). Capt. R.A.S.C. Belgium, France, Salonika, Black Sea.
1919 Phelips, D. C. P. (July 21, 1918). Cadet O.C.B. (R.E.).
1893 Philips, F. G. P., M.A. (Aug. 9, 1914). Maj. 3rd Shropshire L.I. France, Belgium, Salonika. *M.C.*, Mar. 13, 1915. *D.* France, 1915.
1897 Philips, J. L. (Oct. 4, 1914). Maj., Bt.-Lt.-Col., 8th Bde., R.F.A. (Lt.-Col.). France, Mesopotamia, Palestine. *D.S.O.*, Aug. 25, 1917. *D.* Mesopotamia, 1917 twice.
1908 **Philipps,* Hon. R. E.,** M.A. (Sept. 1914). Capt. 9th R. Fusiliers. France. *M.C.*, Apr. 15, 1916. Killed in action at Ovillers on July 7, 1916.
1913 Phillips,* R. Y. (Nov. 16, 1914). Capt. Lanarkshire Yeomanry.
1888 Phillips, W. W. (Apr. 1, 1917). Maj. I.A.R.O., 10th S. Provinces Mounted Rifles. India.
1898 Philpot, H. A., D.M. (Aug. 16, 1915). Capt. R.A.M.C. France, 1916, 1918–19; Salonika, 1916–17; Palestine, 1918–19.
1899 Pidcock, R. G., M.A. (June 1917). 2nd Lt. 1st K.R.R.C. France.
1893 Pile, T. A. J., B.A. (Oct. 29, 1915). A.B., R.N.V.R., Anti-Aircraft Corps, afterwards Lt. R.G.A. (S.R.).
1911 Pitman, F. A. H. (Mobilized Aug. 5, 1914). Capt. 3rd R. Scots. France. (Commission relinquished on account of ill health.)
1895 Pitman, R. O., B.A. (May 25, 1916). ‡Lt. 11th Hussars (S.R.). A.D.C. France and Belgium, 1916–18.
1909 Pitt,* S. H., B.A. (Sept. 1, 1914). Lt. R.F.A. (Capt. and Adjt.). France, Salonika. *M.C.*, June 3, 1919. *D.* Salonika, 1919.
1909 Pixley,* S. E., B.A. (Mobilized Aug. 5, 1914). Maj. A/235th Bde., R.F.A. (T.F.). France, 1917–18.
1906 Platnauer, M., B.Litt., M.A. (Aug. 16, 1915). Capt. R.G.A. Staff-Lt. (2nd Class), XV Corps. France.
1889 Playne, W. H., B.A. (Mobilized Aug. 1914). Lt.-Col. R. Gloucestershire Hussars (T.F. Res.). T.D.
1906 **Plunkett, G.** (1914). Sub-Lt. R.N.V.R., Collingwood Bn., R.N. Div. Gallipoli. Killed in action in Gallipoli on June 7, 1915.
1911 **Pocock, T. G.** (Sept. 9, 1914). 2nd Lt. 4th King's (Liverpool Regt.). France, 1915. Died on Apr. 3, 1915, of wounds received at Neuve Chapelle.
1897 Pollock, D. W., M.A. (June 16, 1915). Lt. R.E. Salonika, Balkans. *M.B.E.* (Mil.).
1910 **Polson,* G. W.** (Serving Aug. 4, 1914). Lt. 1st The Black Watch. France. Killed in action at Battle of the Aisne on Sept. 15, 1914.
1900 **Pope, H. E.,** B.A. (Mar. 18, 1915). Lt. 1/2nd Lancs. Heavy Batt., R.G.A. (Capt.). France. *M.C.*, Aug. 16, 1917; *Bar*, Feb. 5, 1918. Killed in action in France on Aug. 24, 1918.
1901 **Pope, P. P.,** B.A. (Mar. 8, 1915). 2nd Lt. 3rd Welsh Regt. France. Killed in action at the Hohenzollern Redoubt on Oct. 2, 1915.
1910 **Porter,* A. B.** (Aug. 15, 1914). Lt. 4th, attd. 2nd, Highland L.I. France, 1915. Killed in action in France, near the Versailles–Hulich Road, on Oct. 3, 1915.
1908 Portman,* G. M. B., B.A. (Sept. 15, 1914). Capt. 8th London Regt. (Post Office Rifles). France. (Prisoner of war.)
1913 Post, L. A. (May, 1918). Cpl. 2nd Pioneer Bn., U.S. Infantry. Sergt. 1st Censor Press Coy.

1919 Potter, K. B. (Jan. 17, 1916). Lt. D/93rd Bde., R.F.A. (Staff-Lt.). Belgium and France. *M.C.*, Nov. 20, 1917. *D.* France, 1917.

1907 Potter, R. W. (Serving Aug. 4, 1914). Maj. 4th Queen's (R. W. Surrey Regt.) (Lt.-Col.).

1907 Powell, R. A., B.A. (Dec. 1914). Capt. 13th Hampshire Regt. Salonika.

Powell, T. C. (Aug. 10, 1916). 2nd Lt. 12th Heavy Batt., R.G.A. France and Belgium. Died on July 15, 1917, of wounds received in action.

1912 **Power,* G. H. F.** (Aug. 15, 1914). Lt. 6th, attd. 3rd, Middlesex Regt. France and Belgium. Died on May 9, 1915, as a prisoner at Zonnebeke, of wounds received in action at 2nd Battle of Ypres.

1880 Prescott, F. E., M.A. (Sept. 21, 1914). Capt., temp. Maj., 7th Worcestershire Regt. (T.F.). Capt. Garr. Bn. R. W. Kent Regt.

1912 Prescott,* W. R., B.A. (Sept. 5, 1914). Capt. 1/7th Worcestershire Regt. France, 1915–17; Italy, 1917–18. *M.C.*, May 5, 1917; *Bar*, Aug. 16, 1917; *2nd Bar*, Apr. 2, 1919. *D.* France, 1917.

1919 Price, H. H. (Aug. 1917). 2nd Lt., Pilot Officer, 31st T.S., R.A.F. (Lt.).

1901 **Primrose, Rt. Hon. N. J. A.**, M.A., *M.P.* (Mobilized Aug. 1914). Capt. R. Bucks. Hussars. Egypt and Palestine. *M.C.*, June 3, 1916. *D.* Egypt, 1915. Died on Nov. 15, 1917, of wounds received in action at 3rd Battle of Gaza.

1908 Pritchard,* I. T., B.A. (Mobilized Aug. 1914). Capt. 3rd Worcestershire Regt. France. *M.C.*, Feb. 4, 1916.

1919 Pullar, L. J. L. (Serving Aug. 4, 1914). Maj. 1st Seaforth Highlanders, attd. M.G.C. Gallipoli, 1915–16; France and Belgium, 1917–19. *M.C.*, June 3, 1918; *Bar*, July 26, 1918.

Pusch, E. J. (Sept. 1915). 2nd Lt. 4th, attd. 11th, R. Warwickshire Regt. France, 1916. Killed in action in Battle of the Somme on Aug. 8, 1916.

1910 Pye, D. R., M.A. (Jan. 1917). Capt., Experimental Officer, R.A.F.

1919 Pye, D. W. (Aug. 19, 1917). 2nd Lt. 1st (Garr.) Bn. Worcestershire Regt., attd. 1st R. Warwickshire Regt. Egypt, 1918–19.

1919 Pyne, P. R. (June 25, 1917). ‡1st Lt. U.S. Air Service (Flight Commdr.). France, 1917–18. *American D.F.C.*, Oct. 25, 1918.

1911 Quinn,* J. W. (Aug. 15, 1914). Lt. 3rd Oxf. & Bucks. Lt. Infty.

1919 Radcliffe, C. J. (Nov. 30, 1917). 2nd Lt. Labour Corps. France, 1918–19.

1894 Ralli, A. L., B.A. 2nd Lt. Lancs. Motor Vol. Corps.

1895 Ralli, E. L., B.A. (Dec. 25, 1915). Capt. and Adjt. R.F.A. (T.F.). France and Belgium. *M.C.*, Dec. 4, 1917.

1904 **Ralli, L. L.** (May 1915). Capt. R.A.S.C. France. Died on Apr. 20, 1917, of illness contracted while on active service.

1919 Ralli, R. P. (Mar. 27, 1918). ‡2nd Lt. Grenadier Guards (S.R.).

1895 Ramsden, J. V., M.A. (Serving Aug. 4, 1914). Lt.-Col. R.A. A.D.D.G. Ministry of Munitions. France. *C.M.G.* *D.S.O.*, June 23, 1915. *D.* § Feb. 1917, Mar. 1918.

1909 Randall,* B. FitzH. (Serving Aug. 4, 1914). Capt. 3rd Skinner's Horse, Indian Army. France, 1914–16; India, 1916–19; Afghanistan, 1919.

1903 **Ranking, Rev. G. H.** (Mar. 12, 1917). Chaplain to the Forces (4th Class). France and Belgium. Killed in action nr. Cambrai on Nov. 20, 1917.

1919 Rannie, J. A. M. (Oct. 1, 1914). Lt. R. Monmouthshire R.E. (T.F.).

1913 **Rapoport, J. L.** (Jan. 20, 1916). 2nd Lt. 6th, attd. 12th, Rifle Brigade. France. Killed in action at Berry au Bac on May 27, 1918.

1903 Rawle, T. F., M.A. (Feb. 1915). Lt. S. Wales Borderers (S.R.), attd. 1st Bn. France and Belgium. *M.C.*, Jan. 1, 1919.
1915 Redfern, R. A. (Jan. 23, 1916). Lt. R.M.L.I., afterwards Lt. R.A.F. France.
1897 Reeve, W. F., M.A. (Aug. 4, 1915). ‡Lt. 19th Durham L.I. France.
1914 Reford, R. B. S. (Jan. 3, 1915). 2nd Lt. 13th Sherwood Foresters. Lt. Irish Guards (Capt. A.D.C.). France. *M.C.*, Dec. 17, 1917.
1888 Reiss, J. A., B.A. (Mar. 24, 1916). Capt. General List. A.D.C. France and Belgium. Belgian Croix de Guerre. *D.* France, 1917.
1906 Rennie, J. G. (Nov. 30, 1916). Lt. R.G.A. (S.R.).
1881 Rennie, J. H. W. (Mobilized Aug. 1914). Maj. Lancashire Yeomanry. (Resigned on account of ill health.)
1898 Reynolds, A. B. (Serving Aug. 4, 1914). Maj. 12th Lancers. Lt.-Col. 1/1st Northumberland Hussars. France and Belgium. *D.S.O.*, June 3, 1919. *D.* France, 1918, 1919.
1904 Reynolds,* G. F. (Serving Aug. 4, 1914). Capt., Bt.-Maj., 9th Lancers. G.S.O. 2 (Maj.). France and Belgium, 1914–19; Germany, 1919. *M.C.*, July 3, 1915. *D.* France, 1915, 1919.
1915 Rhodes, H. G. (Oct. 1915). Lt. 7th King's (Liverpool Regt.). France. *M.C.*, Dec. 2, 1918.
1903 Richards, B. S., M.A. (Serving Aug. 4, 1914). Lt. Unattached List, T.F., Bury St. Edmunds Grammar School O.T.C.
1899 Richards, F. A., M.A. (Aug. 19, 1914). Lt. R.N.V.R.
1903 Richards, G. B., B.A. (Nov. 13, 1914). Lt. 1st London Regt. Lt. R.A.S.C.
1892 Richards, O. W., D.M. (Sept. 30, 1914). Capt. R.A.M.C. Col. A.M.S. France, 1914–18. *C.M.G.*, June 3, 1918. *D.S.O.*, June 23, 1915. *D.* France, 1915, 1916, 1918.
1913 Richards, R. W. St. J. W., B.A. (Mobilized Aug. 1914). Capt., temp. Maj., 3rd Shropshire L.I. (Lt.-Col.). France, Belgium, Salonika, Germany. Croix de Guerre. *D.* France, 1919.
1897 Richmond, A. H. R. (Jan. 19, 1916). Maj. 3rd, attd. 5th, R. Irish Rifles. Belgium, France.
1908 Richter,* F. J. P., B.A. (Nov. 5, 1917). Lce.-Cpl. R.A.O.C.
1919 Riding, G. A. (July 1915). Lt. Northumberland Fusiliers. France, 1916–17.
1912 Riley,* F. B., M.A. (Aug. 15, 1914). Lt. 3rd Wiltshire Regt. France, 1914. *D.* May 5, 1919. (Prisoner of war, 1914–18.)
1919 Robbins, C. R. (Sept. 1, 1914). ‡2nd Lt. R.F.A. Capt. 35th Squadron, R.A.F. Belgium and France. *M.C.*, Jan. 1, 1917. *D.F.C.*, Feb. 8, 1919. *D.* France, 1918.
1900 Roberts, A. B., M.A. (Feb. 27, 1915). Lt. Unattached List, T.F., Uppingham School O.T.C. (Commission relinquished.)
1894 Roberts, R. A., M.A. 125th S.A. Siege Batt.
1910 **Robertson, A.,** B.Litt. (Sept. 1914). Cpl. 12th York & Lancaster Regt. Egypt, 1916; France, 1916. Missing, presumed killed in action near Serre on July 1, 1916.
1913 Robertson,* F. J., B.A. (Sept. 30, 1914). Capt. 13th London Regt. (Princess Louise's Kensington Bn.) (Maj.). France.
1900 **Robertson, H. M.,** M.A. (Jan. 13, 1915). Capt. 3rd, attd. 2nd, R. Welch Fusiliers. France. Killed in action in France on Jan. 26, 1916.

1905 Robertson, J. A. St. G. Fitzwarrenne-Despencer, B.A. (Nov. 7, 1914). Capt., Bt.-Maj., S. Bn. R. Welch Fusiliers. Asst. Mil. Secretary. *O.B.E.* (Mil.). *D.* § Feb. 1917, Mar. 1919.

1901 Robins, Rev. H. C., M.A. (July 11, 1918). Chaplain to the Forces (4th Class). France.

1902 Robinson, Rev. J. H., M.A. (Jan. 18, 1918). Chaplain, R.N., H.M.S. *Blake.*

1913 Robinson, L. G., B.A. (Jan. 20, 1916). ‡2nd Lt. 305th Siege Batt., R.G.A. France, 1916–17, 1918–19.

1913 Robinson, W. V., B.M. (Nov. 1918). Lt. R.A.M.C. Copenhagen, 1918–19; Belgium, 1919.

1906 Robson, G. C., B.A. (Oct. 12, 1916). Lt. R.G.A. (Commission relinquished on account of ill health.)

1906 Robson, Hon. H. B., B.A. (Mobilized Aug. 1914). Capt. Northumberland Yeomanry. Belgium, France, 1914–17; Italy (attd. H.Q. 7th Inf. Div.), 1917–18. Belgian Croix de Guerre. *D.* Italy, 1918.

1919 Robson, L. C. (Aug. 1915). ‡Lt. and Adjt. 18th Bn. A.I.F. Egypt, 1915–16; France, 1916–18. *M.C.*, June 3, 1918. *D.* France, 1918.

1883 Rolt, Rev. C. H., M.A. (Mobilized Aug. 1914). Chaplain (4th Class), attd. W. Riding Regt.

1909 **Romilly, C. G.,** B.A. (Sept. 17, 1914). Lt. 13th Sherwood Foresters, attd. 1st R. Inniskilling Fusiliers. Gallipoli. Killed in action in Gallipoli on Aug. 11, 1915.

1911 **Rooper, R. B.,** B.A. (1914). Croix rouge française. France. Croix de Guerre avec palme. Killed in action at Gueux on May 29, 1918.

1919 Ross, H. C. M. (Mar. 9, 1917). Lt. 71st Siege Batt., S.A. Horse Art. France, 1917–18.

1919 Ross-Lewin, F. H. W. (Nov. 4, 1916). Lt. 3rd R. W. Kent Regt. Lt. I.A.R.O., attd. 2/150th Infantry France, 1917; India, 1918–19.

1919 Rousseau, I. J., B.A. (June 25, 1917). ‡2nd Lt. R.G.A. S. Africa.

1911 Routledge,* F. J., B.Litt. (Mar. 25, 1915). Lt. 4th King's (Liverpool Regt.). France, 1916–17.

1907 Rowden, A. C., B.A. (Oct. 5, 1914). Lt. 4th R. Sussex Regt. Lt., Acting Maj., Administrative Officer, R.A.F.

1910 Rowe,* V. B., B.A. (Aug. 29, 1914.) Maj. 230th Bde., R.F.A. France and Belgium, 1915–19. *M.C.*, Oct. 18, 1917. *D.* France, 1917, 1918.

1913 Rowsell, H. W. (Feb. 18, 1915). Capt. 1/6th Manchester Regt. Gallipoli, 1915; Sinai, 1915–17; France, 1917–18.

1919 Royce, A. B. (May 8, 1917). Maj. 320th Field Artillery, U.S. Army. France.

1908 Russell, A. D. C., B.A. (Aug. 14, 1914). Capt. Special Lists, attd. Intelligence Corps. R.T.O. Belgium, France, Germany.

1914 **Russell, H. B.** (Nov. 1914). Lt. 1st Essex Regt. Gallipoli, Egypt, France, 1915–16. Died on July 11, 1916, of wounds received in action at Gézincourt.

1919 Russell, J. N. (Mar. 25, 1918). ‡2nd Lt. 4th Dorsetshire Regt., attd. 43rd (Garr.) Bn. R. Fusiliers. France.

1912 Russell, J. W., M.A. (July 26, 1914). ‡Lt. 98th Bde., R.F.A. Acting Capt., R.G.A., Anti-Aircraft. France, Salonika.

1916 Russell, T. T., B.A. (Sept. 26, 1917). 2nd Lt. 4th Loyal N. Lancashire Regt.

1893 Russell, Hon. V. A. F. V., B.A. (Mobilized Aug. 1914). Lt.-Col. 5th Bedfordshire Regt. (T.F.). Hon. Lt.-Col. Administrative Officer, R.A.F. *O.B.E.* (Mil.). *D.* France, 1918 ; § Feb. 1917 ; § Air Ministry, Jan. 1919.

1907 Ryan, G. E., M.A. (Aug. 1, 1915). Lt. R.A.S.C.

1919 Sale, G. S. (Feb. 17, 1915). Lt. 11th Hussars, Res. of Officers, attd. H.Q. Cavalry Corps, Signal Service (Capt.). France. *M.C.*, Nov. 20, 1917. *D.* France, 1919.

1904 Saltoun, Master of, M.A. (Hon. A. A. Fraser) (Mobilized Aug. 1914). Capt. 3rd Gordon Highlanders. France, 1914. *M.C.*, May 5, 1919. (Prisoner of war, 1914–18.)

1900 Samuel, W. H. (Mobilized Aug. 4, 1914). Capt. W. Kent Yeomanry (Staff-Captain). Gallipoli, Egypt, France, Belgium. *M.C.*, June 3, 1918. *D.* France, 1917.

1898 Sands, M. A., B.A. (Aug. 1914). Lt. R. Gloucestershire Hussars. Capt. R. Horse Guards. D.A.P.M. (50th Div.). Egypt, 1915–16 ; Gallipoli, 1915 ; France, 1917–19.

1904 Sands, M. H., B.A. (Apr. 2, 1915). Lt. 1st London Regt. (R. Fusiliers) (Commission relinquished on account of ill health.)

1901 Savage, A. H., B.M., M.A. (Feb. 1915). Capt. R.A.M.C.

1910 **Savage,* C. F.,** B.A. (Aug. 11, 1914). ‡Lt. 10th Northumberland Fusiliers. France and Belgium. Died on June 20, 1917, of wounds received in action at Dickebusch.

1911 Schlesinger, A. L. (Aug. 18, 1915). Lt. 5th Sherwood Foresters. Lt. R. Defence Corps, temp. Capt., Commandant P. of W. Camp.

1891 Scholefield, E. H., B.M., M.A. (Oct. 14, 1915). Capt. R.A.M.C., attd. 2nd Wessex Field Ambulance.

1898 Schomberg, R. C. F., B.A. (Serving Aug. 4, 1914). Maj., Bt.-Lt.-Col., 1st Seaforth Highlanders (Lt.-Col.). Mesopotamia. *D.S.O.*, Dec. 22, 1916 ; *Bar*, Jan. 11, 1919. *D.* Mesopotamia, 1916, 1918.

1901 **Schuster, A. F.,** M.A. (Serving Aug. 4, 1914). Lt. 4th Hussars (S.R.). France and Belgium, 1914. Killed in action near Ypres on Nov. 20, 1914.

1897 Schuster, E. H. J., M.A., D.Sc. (Oct. 1914). Capt. Wessex R.G.A. (T.F. Res.) (Staff-Captain). France, 1915 ; Salonika, 1915–16.

1904 Schuster, F. V., B.A. (Jan. 19, 1915). Capt. 2nd Highland Cyclist Bn. Staff-Captain. Belgium and France, 1917 ; Italy, 1917–19. *D.* Italy, 1918, 1919.

1899 Schuster, G. E., M.A. (Aug. 1914). Capt. Q.O. Oxfordshire Hussars. Lt.-Col. D.A.A.Q.M.G. France, 1915–18 ; North Russia, from Nov. 1918. *C.B.E.* (Mil.). *M.C.*, June 3, 1918. *D.* France, 1916, 1917, 1918 ; *D.* Murmansk, 1919.

1911 Schwerdt, G. F. I., B.A. (Mobilized Aug. 1914). Capt. 1/1st Hampshire Yeomanry. Maj. 15th Hampshire Regt. France, Italy.

1893 Scoones, P., M.A. (July 2, 1915). Lt. R. Defence Corps.

1912 Scott,* S. S., B.A. (Sept. 1914). Capt. 16th K.R.R.C. France, 1915–16, 1917–18 ; Germany, 1919.

1907 [Scott, Rev. W. F., B.A.] (Serving Aug. 4, 1914). Chaplain R.N., H.M.S. *Renown*. Grand Fleet.

1919 Scott-Stokes, H. F. (Dec. 12, 1914). Lt. 1/4th Hampshire Regt. (Capt. G.S.O. 3.) India, 1915–16, 1917–18 ; Mesopotamia, 1918–19 ; N. Persia, 1918 ; Cameroons, 1918–19. *M.C.*, Feb. 1, 1919.

1902 Scrimgeour, H. C. (Sept. 1914). ‡Lt. N. Somerset Yeomanry. Lt. Coldstream Guards (Capt.). France.

1904 Scrimgeour, S., B.A. (Aug. 1914). Lt. 6th, attd. 4th, Suffolk Regt. (Maj.). France, from 1916. *M.C.*, Sept. 26, 1917 ; *Bar*, June 3, 1919.

1906 Searle, H. F., B.A. (Jan. 15, 1918). Lt. I.A.R.O., attd. 4/70th Burma Rifles (Capt.). India.

1901 Sechiari, T. E., B.A. (Mar. 2, 1915). 1st A.M. 150th Squadron, R.A.F. Egypt, 1915–16 ; Macedonia, 1916–19.

1911 Segar, B. G., M.A. 2nd Lt. 5th Northamptonshire Regt. France. (Commission relinquished on account of ill health.)

1908 **Selby,* G. P.,** B.M., M.A. (July 29, 1914). Capt. R.A.M.C., attd. 9th Lancashire Fusiliers. France and Belgium, 1914–15, 1916. Killed in action near Thiepval on Sept. 26, 1916.

1892 Selby, P. R., B.A. (Mar. 27, 1915). Capt. R. Marines.

1919 Seligman, V. J. (May 1915). Lt. R.A.S.C. France, 1916 ; Salonika, 1916–18.

1906 Senneck, F. H., B.A. (Mobilized 1914). ‡Lt. S. Provinces Mounted Rifles, I.D.F. A.P.M. India.

1894 Serocold, C. P. (Dec. 3, 1914). Commander R.N.V.R., attd. Admiralty. *O.B.E.* (Mil.). Croix d'Officier de la Légion d'Honneur. Officer of the Order of St. Maurice and St. Lazarus. Officer of the Order of Leopold. Order of St. Anne (3rd Class). Order of the Sacred Treasure (3rd Class).

1894 **Sewell, H. E.,** B.A. (Serving Aug. 4, 1914). Maj. R.G.A. Gibraltar, France. Killed on June 4, 1918, as the result of an explosion.

1919 Seymour, E. W. (June 22, 1915). Lt. 2nd Grenadier Guards. France.

1907 Seymour, L. (Sept. 1914). Lt. Hertfordshire Regt. Dep. Asst. Mil. Sec. E. Command (Capt.). *O.B.E.* (Mil.). *D.* § Mar. 1919.

1912 Shaw, M. E., B.A. (Apr. 12, 1915). Lt., temp. Capt., 10th Gloucestershire Regt. Gallipoli, 1915 ; France, 1916–17.

1882 Shearer, D. F., B.M. (Feb. 18, 1915). Capt. R.A.M.C.

1901 Shedden, Rt. Rev. R. G., D.D. (Serving Aug. 4, 1914). Chaplain to the Forces (4th Class) (T.F.), attd. 1st London Regt.

1909 **Sheepshanks, W.,** B.A. (Sept. 5, 1916). 2nd Lt. 6th, attd. 2nd, K.R.R.C. France and Belgium. Died on July 10, 1917, of wounds received in Belgium.

1905 Shephard, J. W., B.A. (Feb. 8, 1915). Capt. R.A.S.C. France. *M.C.*, Jan. 14, 1916. Croix de Guerre. *D.* France, 1915.

1908 Siepmann, H. A., B.A. (Aug. 5, 1915). Lt., Acting Capt., 400th Batt., R.F.A. Egypt, Belgium, France, Italy, 1917–18 ; Germany. *D.* Italy, 1918.

1909 **Sievers,* N. J.,** B.A. (Aug. 22, 1914). Capt. 9th Essex Regt. France and Belgium. *D.* France, 1915. Killed in action at Villars Guislain on Nov. 30, 1917.

1899 [Simcox, A. H. A., B.A.] (Apr. 1, 1917). Maj. 4th Bombay Group Garr. Artillery, I.D.F. India.

1900 Simonds, G. F., B.A. (Jan. 1915). Lt. 2/4th R. Berkshire Regt., attd. M.G.C. (Invalided Aug. 1916.)

1919 Simpson, A. A. le M. (Feb. 4, 1917). Lt. 6th K.R.R.C. 2nd Lt. (Hon. Lt.) Administrative Officer, R.A.F. (Resigned). France, 1917, 1918, 1919 ; Italy, 1917, 1918.

1908 Simpson, G. W. Ackroyd, B.A. (Oct. 6, 1914). Lt. R.A.O.C. Gallipoli, 1915; Egypt, 1918. Died on Jan. 25, 1919.
1919 Singer, C. M. (1918). 2nd Lt. R.E. (on demobilization).
1911 Skinner,* O. C., B.A. (Aug. 20, 1914). Lt. 16th Lancers (S.R.) (A.D.C.). Lt., Administrative Officer, R.A.F. France.
1919 Sladen, J. M. (May 1915). Lt. 2nd K.R.R.C. (Capt.). France.
1878 Slee, F. E., M.A. (Oct. 12, 1914). Sub-Lt. R.N.V.R. Lt. R.G.A., 1st A.A. Mobile Bde.
1913 Slingsby, F. H., B.A. (Apr. 8, 1915). Lt. 3rd, attd. 2nd, S. Staffordshire Regt. France, 1915–16, 1918; Belgium, 1917. *M.C.*, Dec. 2, 1918.
1909 Smale, W. R., M.A. (Sept. 13, 1917). Signaller (1st Class) R.G.A.
1914 Small, G. Lothian (Mar. 24, 1915). Lt. 3rd S. Staffordshire Regt. Staff-Lieutenant (2nd Class).
1919 Smart, P. H. (May 12, 1917). Lt. 101st Field Artillery, U.S. Army. France, 1917–19. *D.* France, 1918.
1900 Smith, D. M., B.A. (July 1, 1915). Lt. Sussex R.G.A.
1899 Smith, Rev. G. V., M.A. (Oct. 1914). Chaplain to the Forces (4th Class). France, 1917; Salonika, 1918. *M.C.*, Aug. 25, 1917. Officier, Order of the Redeemer.
1899 **Smith, G. W.,** M.A. (Aug. 1914). Capt. 13th Rifle Brigade. France, 1915–16. Killed in action near Pozières on July 10, 1916.
1890 Smith, N. C., M.A. 2nd Lt. Vol. Bn. Dorsetshire Regt. (Commission relinquished.)
Smithers, E. H. K. (Sept. 14, 1914). Lt. 11th, attd. 16th, Manchester Regt. Gallipoli, France, 1915–16. Killed in action in Trônes Wood on July 11, 1916.
1911 **Snead-Cox, R. M.** (Aug. 7, 1914). 2nd Lt. 3rd R. Scots. France. Killed in action at Neuve Chapelle on Oct. 28, 1914.
1919 Snow, G. R. S. (Aug. 28, 1915). Lt. R.F.A.
1894 Soames, A. F. (Aug. 1914). ‡Lt. 2nd Dorset Yeomanry. A.D.C. Egypt and France, 1915–18. *D.* France, 1917.
1905 Somers, A. H. T., Lord (Serving Aug. 4, 1914). Capt. 1st Life Guards. Maj., Acting Lt.-Col., 6th Bn. Tank Corps. Belgium, France. *D.S.O.*, June 4, 1917. *M.C.*, June 4, 1917. Croix de Chevalier de la Légion d'Honneur. *D.* France, 1918.
1912 Somerville-Smith, H. (Mobilized Aug. 1914). ‡Lt., Acting Maj., 113th Bde., R.F.A. France. *D.S.O.*, June 3, 1919. *M.C.*, June 3, 1918. *D.* France, 1917, 1919.
1919 Sparshott, F. B. (Apr. 6, 1916). Corpl. 3rd Queen's (R.W. Surrey Regt.), (Sergt.-Instr.). France, 1916–17.
1899 Spencer-Phillips, J. C., M.A. (Aug. 4, 1914). Capt., temp. Maj., R.A.S.C. France, 1915–19. *D.S.O.*, June 4, 1917. *D.* France, 1917.
1901 Spencer-Phillips, P. T., B.M. (Dec. 15, 1914). Capt. R.F.A. (T.F.), (Maj.), and Capt. R.A.M.C. France. *D.* France, 1917.
1896 Spencer-Smith, D. C. (Serving Aug. 4, 1914). Maj., Acting Lt.-Col., R.A. France. *D.* France, 1915.
1900 Spencer-Smith, M. S., B.A. (Feb. 22, 1915). Capt. 15th K.R.R.C. Temp. Lt.-Col. General List, attd. Canadian Heavy Artillery. A.A. & Q.M.G. France. *D.S.O.*, Jan. 1, 1919. *M.C.*, Jan 1, 1918. *D.* France, 1916, 1918.

1897 Spender, R. E. S., B.A. (Jan. 28, 1915). 2nd Lt. 17th R. Irish Rifles. Lt., R.A.S.C. (Capt.).

1904 Spens, W. P., B.A. (Mobilized Aug. 1914). Capt. 1/5th Queen's (R.W. Surrey Regt.) D.A.A.G. India, 1914–15, and 1918–19; Mesopotamia, 1915–18. *O.B.E.* (Mil.). *D.* Mesopotamia, 1917, 1918, 1919.

1912 Spicer,* W. N., B.A. (Sept. 28, 1914). Lt. R.F.A. (Capt.). Belgium and France. *M.C.*, Aug. 24, 1916.

1911 **Sprunt,* A. D.,** B.A. (Aug. 1914). 2nd Lt. 4th Bedfordshire Regt., attd. 2nd S. Staffordshire Regt. France. Died on Mar. 17, 1915, of wounds received in action near Neuve Chapelle.

1893 Spurling, Rev. H. W., M.A. (Dec. 1915). Pte. 1/9th Hampshire Regt. ‡2nd Lt. E. African Local Forces. Chaplain to the Forces (4th Class). Wazaristan F.F. 1917; E. Africa, 1918.

Squire, E. W. (Aug. 1914). Pte. 13th London Regt. France. Killed in action at Neuve Chapelle on Mar. 11, 1915.

1905 **Stables, H. R.,** B.A. (Aug. 15, 1914). Lt. 5th R. Fusiliers, attd. 1st Cheshire Regt. France and Belgium. Killed in action in Belgium on Nov. 15, 1914.

1917 Stacey, H. R. (July 4, 1918). 2nd Lt. Tank Corps (on demobilization).

1918 Stacpole, F. A., B.A. (Aug. 1914). ‡Lt. 7th E. Yorkshire Regt. Capt. R.A.F. France. (Invalided, 1918.)

1904 Stairs, G. S., M.A. (Sept. 29, 1915). Capt., temp. Maj., 87th Canadian Infantry. France and Belgium, 1917–19. *M.C.*, Sept. 30, 1918.

1919 Stamford, R., Earl of (Feb. 1916). 2nd Lt. Gen. List, T.F. Res. (A.D.C.).

1916 Stanley, D. R. (May 1, 1917). Lt. 1/128th Pioneers, Indian Army. Mesopotamia, Persia. *D.* Kurdistan, 1919.

1919 Steel, A. B. (Sept. 9, 1918). ‡2nd Lt. Northern (3rd) Div. M.T. Coy. R.A.S.C. France, Germany.

1899 Steer, Rev. C., M.A. (Oct. 31, 1915). Pte. S. African Medical Corps. ‡Chaplain to the Forces (2nd Class), D.A.C.G., XIX Corps. E. Africa, France. (Prisoner of war, 1918.) *M.C.*, Sept. 26, 1917. *D.* E. Africa, 1917; France, 1918.

1908 Steer, Rev. E. A., M.A. (Oct. 7, 1918). Chaplain, R.N., H.M.S. *Vindictive.*

1910 Steer,* W., M.A. (Mobilized Aug. 1914). Pte. 28th London Regt. (Artists' Rifles), afterwards Lt. Flying Officer, R.A.F. France, 1914–17; Egypt, 1917–18.

1912 Stephenson,* J. E., B.A. (Aug. 28, 1914). Capt. 1/4th Somerset L.I. India, 1915–16; Mesopotamia, 1916–19.

1897 Stevens, F. G., B.A. (Sept. 1916). Lt., Acting Maj., 352nd Siege Batt. France and Belgium.

1883 Steward, H. A. H., B.A. (Dec. 30, 1914). Capt. 8th London Regt. (Post Office Rifles), (T.F. Res.).

1910 Stewart, C. W., B.A. (July 1, 1916). Lt. I.A.R.O. Supply and Transport Corps. India, N.W. Frontier; Persia; Mesopotamia.

1909 **Stewart, H. E.,** B.A. (Sept. 1914). Capt. 8th R. Sussex Regt. France. Croix de Chevalier de la Légion d'Honneur. *D.* France, 1917. Killed in action near Arras on June 1, 1917.

1917 Stewart, R. B. (May 1, 1916). Sergt. Observer, R.A.F. France, 1916–19.

1917 Stirling, D.A. (Apr. 5, 1918). 2nd Lt. Coldstream Guards (S.R.).

1914 Stisted, J. L. H. (1915). Orderly, Serbian Relief Unit. 2nd Lt. Seaforth Highlanders (on demobilization). Serbia.
1896 Stocks, F. W., M.A. (Nov. 28, 1914). 2nd Lt., Unattached List, T.F., Framlingham College O.T.C. Capt. 6th Vol. Bn. Suffolk Regt.
1905 Stormonth-Darling, P., B.A. (Oct. 16, 1914). Maj., Acting Lt.-Col., 10th The Black Watch. Salonika. *D.* Salonika, 1917.
1898 Strangeways, L. R., M.A. (Dec. 12, 1914). Lt., Unattached List, T.F., Nottingham School O.T.C.
1919 Stratford, J. R. F. (July 1917). 2nd Lt. Coldstream Guards. France, Germany.
1911 **Strauss, B. L.** (Oct. 8, 1914). Lt., Acting Maj., 9th The Buffs (E. Kent Regt.). France. *M.C.*, Jan. 1, 1918. Killed in action on Dec. 1, 1917.
1918 Strauss, E. B. (Oct. 22, 1914). Capt. Middlesex Regt., attd. O.C.B. France. (Commission relinquished on account of ill health.)
1912 Stuart-Maclaren, C. W., B.A. P. of W. Escort Coy.
1888 Style, G. M., B.A. (Mobilized Aug. 1914). Capt. R. E. Kent Yeomanry (T.F. Res.) (Maj.).
1905 Sutton, H., B.Sc. (Dec. 12, 1915). Capt. Australian A.M.C. Capt., temp. Maj.. D.A.D.M.S. Anzac Mounted Div. Egypt, Sinai, Palestine, 1916–19. *D.* Palestine, 1918, 1919.
1890 Swifte, L. C. (Mobilized Aug. 1914). Maj. 5th R. Dublin Fusiliers (Lt.-Col.). France, Italy, Austria, Poland, Serbia, Germany. Croce di Guerra. *D.* Italy, 1918.
1904 Swire, D. W., B.A. (Aug. 4, 1914). Capt. Shropshire Yeomanry. Egypt, Palestine. *D.* Egypt, 1917.
1908 Swithinbank, C. (Sept. 28, 1914). 2nd Lt. 1st London Regt. (T.F. Res.).
1871 Sylvester, Rev. Canon S. A. K., M.A. (Serving Aug. 4, 1914). Chaplain to the Forces (4th Class).
1908 Symonds, C. P., D.M. (Aug. 4, 1914). ‡Capt. R.A.M.C. France, Aug. 1914; Egypt; Malta. Médaille Militaire. (Commission relinquished on account of ill health.)
1903 Symons-Jeune, B. H. B. (Apr. 24, 1915). Capt. R.A.S.C.
1901 Talbot, H. E. (Serving Aug. 4, 1914). Capt. 11th Hussars. Capt. R.A.F. France. (Prisoner of war.)
1903 Tallents, H., B.C.L., M.A. (Aug. 4, 1914). Maj. Nottinghamshire Yeomanry. Gallipoli, 1915; Egypt, 1915; Salonika and Palestine, 1916–18. *D.S.O.*, June 4, 1917. *D.* Salonika, 1917.
1913 Tamworth, R. W. S., Viscount. A.B., R.N.V.R.
1913 **Tate, *F. H.** (Nov. 7, 1914). Capt. 10th K.R.R.C. France and Belgium. *D.* France, 1917. Died on Aug. 12, 1917, of wounds received in action near Langemarck.
1905 **Tatham, C.,** B.A. (Mobilized Aug. 1914). ‡Lt., temp. Capt., 11th H.A.C. France and Belgium, 1914–15. Died on June 18, 1915, of wounds received in action at Hooge.
1911 **Tayler, J. G.** (Mobilized Aug. 4, 1914). ‡2nd Lt. 2nd Leicestershire Regt. France. Killed in action at Richebourg l'Avoué on May 16, 1915.
1898 Taylor, L. W., M.A. (Mobilized Aug. 1914). Capt. 5th Durham L.I. France. (Prisoner of war, Mar.–Dec. 1918.)

1903 Taylor,* T. G. (Serving Aug. 4, 1914). Capt., Bt.-Maj. Gordon Highlanders (Lt.-Col.). France and Belgium. *D.S.O.*, Jan. 1, 1917. *D.* France, 1916, 1917.

1910 **Tennant, M.** (Nov. 5, 1914). Lt. Scots Guards (S.R.). France. Killed in action near Ginchy on Sept. 16, 1916.

1919 Tennant, M. F. (Jan. 1917). Lt. Scots Guards. France, 1918–19. *D.S.O.*, Sept. 2, 1918. *D.* France, 1918.

1898 Thomas, J. R. L., M.A. (1914). Lt. R.E. (Commission relinquished on account of ill health, 1915.)

1919 Thomas, R. W. (Sept. 2, 1917). 2nd Lt. R.F.A.

1905 **Thompson, A. B.,** B.M., M.A. (April 1915). Capt. R.A.M.C., 3rd E. Lancashire Field Amb. Gallipoli. Killed in action in Gallipoli on Dec. 25, 1915.

1919 Thompson, A. D. F. (June 9, 1917). 2nd Lt. R.F.A. (S.R.) (46th T.M.B.). France.

1916 Thompson, E. L. G. Trooper 2/1st Essex Yeomanry. Pte. 6th Leicestershire Regt.

1908 Thompson, R. S., M.A. Cadet R.A.F. Italy (with B.R.C.S.).

1909 Thompson,* S. G., M.A. (Aug. 1914). Capt. 8th (Yeomanry Bn.) R.W. Kent Regt. (Maj.) France. *M.C.* Sept. 16, 1918.

1913 **Thomson, P. W.,** B.Litt. (July 17, 1915). 2nd Lt. R.G.A., N. Scottish G.A. (T.F.). France. Killed in action on July 24, 1916.

1919 Thornewill, A. S. (Aug. 18, 1914). ‡Capt. N. Staffordshire Regt. Capt. I.A.R.O., Supply and Transport Corps. N.W. Frontier, India, 1915; Mesopotamia, 1918–19.

1906 Thornewill, J. M. H., B.A. (Jan. 1915). Lt., Acting Capt., 'E' Batt. R.H.A. France and Belgium.

1910 Thornton,* H. G., B.A. (Oct. 3, 1914). Lt. 4th Northamptonshire Regt. Lt., Acting Capt. Technical Officer, R.A.F. Salonika. *D.* Salonika, 1916.

1919 Thorold, E. L. (Jan. 5, 1917). ‡Lt. R.G.A. Palestine, 1917–19.

1919 Thorold, G. F. (Jan. 23, 1917). Lt. C/348th Bde., R.F.A. Belgium 1917.

1911 Thorold,* W. G. P., M.A. (Sept. 23, 1914). Capt. Berkshire Yeomanry, attd. Signal Service R.E.

1894 Thorpe, H., B.A. (Aug. 1914). Lt.-Col. Nottinghamshire Yeomanry. Gallipoli, 1915; Salonika, 1916–17; Egypt, 1915–17; Palestine, 1917. *D.S.O.*, Jan. 1, 1917. *D.* Gallipoli, 1916; Salonika, 1916, 1917.

1910 Thorson, J. T., B.A. (May 3, 1917). Capt. Manitoba Regt., 223rd Canadian Inf. Staff-Lt. (1st Class). France 1917–19.

1896 Tidy, H. L., D.M. (Oct. 2, 1914). Maj. R.A.M.C. France.

1899 Tiverton, H. G., Viscount (Dec. 1914). ‡Lt.-Commdr. R.N.V.R. Maj. R.A.F. Dover Patrol, 1915; France, 1916–18.

1911 Tollemache, L. de O., B.A. (Mar. 29, 1916). Lt. Unattached List, T.F., Bradfield School O.T.C.

1890 Tomlin, Rev. J. W. S., M.A. (Mar. 22, 1916). Chaplain to the Forces (4th Class). France, 1916–17. (Invalided May, 1917.)

1881 Tomlin, M. J. B., M.A. (Mobilized Aug. 4, 1914). Lt.-Col. 1/21st, attd. 3/19th, London Regt. Belgium, 1915. *O.B.E.* (Mil.). Cavalier, Military Order of Savoy. *D.* § Feb. 1917.

1885 Tomlin, T. J. C., B.C.L., M.A. (Oct. 19, 1916). Lt. 2nd Vol. Bn. County of London Regt.

1897 Tomlinson, E. H., B.A. (Mobilized Aug. 1914). Maj. 6th N. Staffordshire Regt. Belgium and France, 1915–17. T.D.

1914 Torr, C. J. W. (May 11, 1915). Lt. R.F.A. Staff-Lt. (2nd Class). Belgium and France.

1907 Torr,* J. H. T., B.A. (Mobilized Aug. 4, 1914). Capt. Lincolnshire Yeomanry (Maj.). Egypt and Palestine. *D.* Egypt; Palestine, 1918.

1908 **Torry, J. S. A.,** B.A. (Aug. 1914). 2nd Lt. 12th Rifle Brigade. France. Killed in action at Merville on Sept. 19, 1915.

1901 Townsend, J. S. E., M.A. (Mar. 30, 1915). Lt. R.N.V.R. Maj., Special Lists, attd. R.A.F. Croix de Chevalier de la Légion d'Honneur.

1905 **Townsend,* T. A.,** B.A. (June 25, 1915). Capt. R.A.M.C., attd. 20th London Regt. France and Belgium. *M.C.*, Nov. 25, 1916; *Bar*, Feb. 18, 1918. Gold Medal of Order of St. Sava. Missing, presumed killed in action near Rocquigny on Mar. 24, 1918.

1911 Tozer,* A., B.A. (Aug. 7, 1914). ‡Lt. Acting Capt. R.E. France, 1914 and 1916–19. *M.C.*, June 4, 1917.

1908 **Traill,* A.,** B.M. (Feb. 1916). Capt. R.A.M.C., attd. 2/4th W. Riding Field Amb. France. Died on Aug. 25, 1917, of illness contracted on active service.

1898 **Trefusis, Hon. J. F. Hepburn-Stuart-Forbes-** (Serving Aug. 4, 1914). Maj. Irish Guards, temp. Brig.-Gen. France. *D.S.O.*, Feb. 18, 1915. *D.* France, 1915. Died on Oct. 24, 1915, of wounds received in action in France.

1893 Tritton, C. H. (Nov. 30, 1914). Maj. R.A.S.C.

1908 Trower,* W. G., B.A. (Mobilized Aug. 1914). Lt., Acting Capt., 2nd E. Anglian Bde., R.F.A. Egypt and Palestine. *D.* Palestine, 1919.

1912 Trubshawe,* W. V., B.A. (Mar. 3, 1915). Lt., 1st King's (Liverpool Regt.), 2nd Lt. (Hon. Lt.), Flying Officer, R.A.F. France and Belgium, 1915–18.

Tudor, P. B. (May 20, 1917). 2nd Lt. R.F.A., attd. 26th Jacob's Mounted Batt., R.G.A. India, Mesopotamia. Died in Mesopotamia on Nov. 1, 1918, of illness contracted while on active service.

1906 Turberville, A. S., B.Litt., M.A. (Oct. 1, 1915). Lt., temp. Capt., 20th K.R.R.C. Educational Officer. France and Belgium. *M.C.*, July 18, 1917. *D.* France.

Turner, R. R. (Jan. 20, 1915). 2nd Lt. 3rd, attd. 12th, R. Sussex Regt. France. Killed in action on Feb. 3, 1917.

1897 Twisleton-Wykeham-Fiennes, Hon. G. R. C. (Mobilized Aug. 1914). Capt. Q.O. Oxfordshire Hussars. (Maj.)

1906 Tyndale, H. E. G., B.A. (Aug. 31, 1914). Lt. 8th K.R.R.C., attd. W.O. Intelligence Dept. France and Belgium, 1915. *M.B.E.* (Mil.). *D.* § Aug. 1917.

1894 Unthank, J. S. (Serving Aug. 4, 1914). Maj. Durham L.I. (Lt.-Col. 4th Seaforth Highlanders.) France, 1915–18. *D.S.O.* Jan. 1, 1918. *D.* France, 1916, 1917.

1919 Upton, J. H. (Aug. 4, 1914). Lce.-Cpl. 1/3rd S. Midland Field Amb., R.A.M.C. France, 1915–17; Italy, 1917–19. *M.M.*, Apr. 1917.

1910 Urwick,* L. F., M.A. (Serving Aug. 4, 1914). Capt., temp. Maj., 3rd Worcestershire Regt. D.A.A.G. France, 1914–16, 1917–18. *O.B.E.* (Mil.). *M.C.*, Jan. 1, 1917. *D.* France, 1918.

1895 Utterton, Rev. E. E. S., M.A. (July 5, 1918). Chaplain to the Forces (4th Class).
1904 Vale, W. S. (May 12, 1917). Lt. R.A.F.
1889 Venables-Llewelyn, C. L. Dillwyn (Mobilized Aug. 1914). Lt.-Col. Glamorganshire Yeomanry, attd. Labour Corps. *D.* § Feb. 1917.
1898 Venning, J., M.A. (Sept. 28, 1914). Capt. 1st, attd. 6th, London Regt. (Rifles) (Maj.). France. *M.C.*, Feb. 15, 1919. *D.* France, 1918.
1911 Vernon, H. A. (Aug. 15, 1914). Capt. 4th Irish Fusiliers. Salonika, 1916–17; Egypt, 1917–19.
1904 **Vickers, H. G. M.,** B.A. (July, 1915). Lt. I.A.R.O., attd. 13th Lancers. Mesopotamia. Killed in action at Quaiaragh on Oct. 30, 1918.
Villiers, W. E. (Aug. 14, 1915). Lt., Acting Capt. 5th, attd. 9th, K.R.R.C. France and Belgium. Killed in action on Nov. 10, 1917.
1909 Vines,* W. S., M.A. (Aug. 22, 1914). Lt. 11th Highland L.I. Capt. Labour Corps. France, 1918. (Invalided.)
1896 Vlasto, J. A., B.M. (Apr. 7, 1916). Capt. R.A.M.C. France. *M.C.*, Oct. 18, 1917.
1886 [Wace, Rev. H. C., M.A.] (Aug. 5, 1914). Capt., temp. Maj., Unattached List, T.F., attd. No. 4 O.C.B. France, 1916, as Camp Commandant.
1907 [Wade-Gery, H. T., M.A.] (Sept. 1914). Maj. 19th Lancashire Fusiliers. (G.S.O. 3.) France, 1915–18. *M.C.*, June 3, 1918.
1904 Wagstaffe, W. W., B.M. (Aug. 5, 1914). Capt. R.A.M.C., attd. 33rd C.C.S. (Maj.). France. *O.B.E.* (Mil.). *D.* France, 1918.
1891 Walden, A. F., M.A. Maj. 1st Vol. Bn. Oxf. & Bucks. Lt. Infty.
1912 **Wale,* A.** (Oct. 14, 1914). ‡Capt. 186th Bde., R.F.A. France. Killed in hospital at Doullens by a bomb on May 30, 1918.
1888 Walker, A. J. (May 1915). Capt. 155th Protection Coy., R. Defence Corps.
1898 Wallace, R. F. H., M.A. (Serving Aug. 4, 1914). Maj., Bt.-Lt.-Col., The Black Watch. G.S.O. 1. France. *C.M.G.* Officier, Ordre de Léopold. Croix de Guerre. Belgian Croix de Guerre. *D.* § Aug. 1917; France, 1914, 1918.
1907 Waller, W. W., B.M. (Sept. 22, 1914). Capt. R.A.M.C., attd. 8th Border Regt. (Commission relinquished on account of ill health, Sept. 22, 1916.)
1900 **Walpole, H. S.,** B.A. (Mar. 25, 1916). Lt. Coldstream Guards (S.R.). France. Killed in action on April 9, 1918.
1894 Walpole, R. H., B.A. (1918). 2nd Lt. 12th Rifle Brigade.
1893 Walter, R., M.A. (Sept. 1914). Lt. 9th Hampshire Regt. (T.F. Res.).
1909 Wann, J., B.A. (June 1915). Capt., Acting Maj., R.A.F. Dover Patrol; Belgian Coast, 1915–16; Grand Fleet, 1916–19. *D.* § Air Ministry, Jan. 1919.
1914 **Ward, E. L.** (Mar. 25, 1915). 2nd Lt. 3rd S. Staffordshire Regt. France and Belgium. Killed in action in the Bois de Foureaux on July 14, 1916.
1911 Ward,* H. K. (Mobilized Aug. 5, 1914). Capt. R.A.M.C. (S.R.), attd. 2nd K.R.R.C. France. *M.C.*, Oct. 20, 1916; *Bar*, July 10, 1918; *2nd Bar*, Jan. 1, 1919. *D.* France, 1915. (Prisoner of war, 1917.)
1894 Ward, H. R., B.A. (Mobilized Aug. 4, 1914). Capt. 1st R. Wiltshire Yeomanry, attd. as Staff Capt. H.Q. XV Corps. France. *D.* France, 1917, 1918.

1919 Warner, R. (May 15, 1917). 2nd Lt. 303rd Infantry, U.S. Army. France.
1893 Warren, R., D.M., M.Ch. Capt. R.A.M.C.
1893 Waterfield, A. W., B.A. (1914). ‡2nd Lt. Northamptonshire Yeomanry. Temp. Capt., Town Maj. Italy.
1883 Waterfield, N., M.A. (June 14, 1916). Ambulancier, Croix rouge française (1915). Lt. 1st Vol. Bn. Oxf. & Bucks. Lt. Infty. France, 1915.
1892 **Waters, G. T.,** M.A. (Nov. 1, 1914). Capt. Unattached List, T.F., attd. 7th Suffolk Regt. France and Belgium. Died on Mar. 29, 1918, of wounds received in action at Albert.
1902 Watts, H. L., B.A. (Mar. 18, 1915). Lt. 11th London Regt. (Finsbury Rifles). Staff-Lt. (2nd Class).
1897 Watts, J., B.A. (Apr. 20, 1915). ‡2nd Lt. 1st Vol. Bn. Lancashire Regt.
1905 Watts, M. B., B.A. (June 30, 1916). Signaller 2nd Grenadier Guards. France, Belgium, Germany, 1917–19. Croix de Guerre avec Palme.
1892 Way, B. G. V., *M.V.O.* (Serving Aug. 4, 1914). Lt.-Col. Sherwood Foresters. Asst. Director of Movements. *C.B.E.* (Mil.). Croix d'Officier de la Légion d'Honneur. Officier, Ordre de la Couronne. Belgian Croix de Guerre. *D.* § Feb. 1917.
1898 Webster, Rev. Dom. D. R., M.A. (July 5, 1915). Chaplain to the Forces (4th Class), attd. 12th K.R.R.C. France. (Invalided, July 5, 1917.)
1910 Webster, *F. (June 21, 1916). Gunner 64th Coy. R.G.A. (Bomdr.). Burma.
1897 Weech, W. N., M.A. (Serving Aug. 4, 1914). Capt., Bt.-Maj., Unattached List, T.F., Sedburgh School O.T.C. Asst. Commdt. School of Musquetry, Tyneside.
1907 **Weekes, A. N. H.,** B.A. (Mobilized Aug. 1914). Capt. 4th R. Sussex Regt. Gallipoli, Palestine, France, 1915–18. *M.C.*, Feb. 18, 1918. *D.* Palestine, 1917. Killed in action at Ouchy le Chateau on July 29, 1918.
1919 Welsford, F. M. (May 17, 1918). 2nd Lt. R.E. (Signals).
1883 West, Rev. A. G. B., M.A. (May 5, 1915). Chaplain to the Forces (4th Class).
1912 **Westlake,* A. N.,** B.A. (Feb. 6, 1915). Lt. 4th N. Staffordshire Regt., attd. R.F.C. France. *M.C.*, Sept. 26, 1917. Missing, presumed killed in action on Jan. 4, 1918.
1910 Wharry,* H. M. (Aug. 7, 1916). Capt. R.A.M.C.
1902 Whately, E. G., M.A. (Sept. 1914). ‡Capt., Bt. Maj., 2/1st Hertfordshire Regt. D.A.A.G. France and Belgium, 1915–18; Italy, 1917–18. *M.C.*, Jan. 1, 1917. Belgian Croix de Guerre. *D.* France, 1916, 1917, 1919. *D.* Italy, 1918.
1908 **Wheatcroft, R. D.,** B.A. (Sept. 1914). Lt. 6th Sherwood Foresters (T.F.). France, 1915–16. Died on July 2, 1916, of wounds received in action at Gommecourt.
Whetstone, W. H. (Dec. 24, 1916). Lt. 3rd Coldstream Guards. France. Killed in action south of Arras on March 28, 1918.
1919 Whineray, R. W. (Sept. 21, 1917). Lt. R.F.A. (T.F.). France, 1918–19.
1909 Whitcombe, D. M. P., B.A. (Dec. 23, 1915). Surgeon Lt. R.N. Mediterranean, 1916–18.
1881 Whitcombe, Rt. Rev. R. H., D.D. (Oct. 1918). Chaplain to the Forces (2nd Class). Belgium and France.

1883 White, R. E., B.A. (Mobilized Aug. 1914). Maj. 4th Suffolk Regt. (T.F.) Res. (Hon. Lt.-Col.). *D.* § Feb. 1917.
1906 Whitfield, G. E., B.A. (Mobilized Aug. 4, 1914). Capt. 1st Hertfordshire Regt. (Lt.-Col.). France. *M.C.* June 3, 1916. *D.* France, 1915, 1916.
1912 Whitley, P. N., B.A. Y.M.C.A. France, Salonika. *D.* Salonika.
1895 Whitty, J. T. 2nd Lt. Behar Light Horse. India.
1919 Wickham, D. H. 2nd Lt. 8th R. Scots. France.
1901 Wickham, Rev. E. S. G., M.A. (July 3, 1918). Chaplain to the Forces (4th Class), attd. Tank Corps. France, Germany.
1904 Wickham, J. B., B.A. (Mobilized Aug. 1914). Capt. 4th Dragoon Guards (S.R.). Staff-Captain. France, Belgium, Germany. Belgian Croix de Guerre.
1911 Wicks,* C. L., B.A. (Sept. 19, 1914). Lt., temp. Capt., 7th Oxf. & Bucks. Lt. Infty. Staff-Lt. (1st Class). Capt. General List. France, 1915, 1918; Salonika, 1915–1917.
1911 Wiggins,* A. F. R. (Aug. 26, 1914). Capt. and Adjt. 2nd Grenadier Guards. France and Belgium. *D.* France, 1916, 1918.
1898 Wightwick, N. H., B.A. (Apr. 6, 1915). Capt. R.E. Kent Yeomanry.
1913 Wilder, H. A. J., B.A. (July 6, 1915). Driver, Section Sanitaire Anglaise, attd. 163rd Div. French Army. France. Croix de Guerre. Médaille Militaire.
1891 **Wilkinson, B. K. R.,** M.A. (Feb. 1915). Capt. N. Staffordshire Regt. (attd. 7th Bn.). Mesopotamia. Died in hospital in London on Jan. 24, 1918.
1906 Wilkinson, F. H. J., M.A. (Aug. 1915). Lt. R.F.A. (S.R.) (Capt.). France, 1916–18.
1875 Willett, E. W., D.M. (Apr. 1915). Capt., Acting Maj., R.A.M.C.
1890 Williams, A., D.Mus., *M.V.O.* (Serving Aug. 4, 1914). Hon. Lt., Bandmaster, Grenadier Guards.
1886 Williams, A. F. B., M.A. (July 30, 1915). Capt., temp. Maj., General List. G.S.O. 2. *O.B.E.* (Mil.). *D.* § Feb. 1917.
1914 Williams,* B. T., B.A. (July 1915). 2nd Lt. 9th S. Wales Borderers. Capt. 1/7th Gurkha Rifles (Adjt.). India and Afghanistan, 1917–19.
1914 Williams, C. R. (May 1918). 2nd Lt. R.A.F. Egypt.
1909 Williams,* Rev. D. H. A., M.A. (June 1, 1915). Chaplain R.N., attd. R.A.F. North Sea; German E. Africa.
1909 Williams,* H. R. (Aug. 5, 1914). ‡Lt. 61st Bde., R.F.A. France, 1915–19. *M.C.*, June 3, 1919. *D.* France, 1918.
1897 **Williams, J. N.,** M.A. (Aug. 1914). Pte. Auckland Bn., N.Z.E.F. Gallipoli. Killed in action in Gallipoli on April 25, 1915.
Williams, L. (Nov. 11, 1914). Lt. S. Wales Borderers. Killed in action on Sept. 11, 1915.
1895 Williams, M. P., M.A. (May 1, 1916). Pte. 1st Can. Inf. Works Coy. France and Belgium, 1916–18.
1919 Willis, E. I. (Mar. 2, 1917). Lt. 440th Siege Batt., R.G.A. (Staff-Lt.). Egypt and Palestine.
1902 **Willoughby, J. G.** (Serving Aug. 4, 1914). Capt. 33rd Q.V.O. Light Cavalry, Indian Army. Mesopotamia, 1914–15. Killed in action at Shaiba on Mar. 3, 1915.
1888 Willoughby de Broke, R. G., Lord (Mobilized, Aug. 1914). Maj. Warwickshire Yeomanry (T.F. Res.) (Lt.-Col.).

1905 Wilmott, F. A. N., M.A. (Feb. 25, 1916). Lt. 4th R. Berkshire Regt. France, 1916–17. *M.C.*, Jan. 1, 1918.

1893 **Wilson, D. D.** (Aug.6, 1914). Capt. 17th Cavalry, Indian Army. Lt.-Col. 5th Sherwood Foresters. France and Belgium. *M.C.*, June 3, 1916. *D.* France, 1915. Killed in action at Gommecourt on July 1, 1916.

1910 Wilson,* F. W. Lt. Coldstream Guards.

1897 Wilson, H. C. B., B.A. (Mobilized Aug. 3, 1914). Lt.-Col. 3rd York & Lancaster Regt. France, 1914, 1915. *O.B.E.* (Mil.). *D.* § Feb. 1917.

1901 Wilson, H. S., B.A. (Aug. 1914). Lt. 3rd, attd. 1st, Somerset L.I. Staff-Lt. (1st Class). Belgium and France, 1915–19. Chevalier, Ordre du Mérite Agricole.

1919 Wilson, J. M. H. (Apr. 2, 1917). 2nd Lt. Coldstream Guards.

1919 Wilson, J. O. (Nov. 25, 1914). Lt. 8th Durham L.I. (Commission relinquished on account of ill health.)

Wilson, P. J. C. (Aug. 15, 1914). Lt. 1st Q.O. Cameron Highlanders. France. Killed in action near Richebourg l'Avoué on May 9, 1915.

1915 Wilson, W. C. (Oct. 8, 1915). Lt., Acting Capt., 17th London Regt., attd. 2/4th The Buffs (E. Kent Regt.), and 202nd T.M.B. Egypt, Palestine, France, 1917–19.

1905 Wilson-Fitzgerald, F. W. (Serving Aug. 4, 1914). Capt. 1st Dragoons. Staff-Captain (Bde. Maj.). France and Belgium, 1914–18. *D.S.O.*, Jan. 1, 1919. *M.C.*, Jan. 1, 1917. *D.* France, 1915, 1916, 1918.

1910 Wilton, E. W., B.A. (June 2, 1916). ‡Lt. E. Surrey Regt.

1909 Winn, H. E., M.A. (Nov. 27, 1914). Capt. 2/6th Gurkha Rifles. Gallipoli, 1915; Egypt, 1916; Mesopotamia, 1916–18; Salonika, 1918; Caucasus, 1919. *D.* Mesopotamia, 1918.

1902 [Winterton, E., Earl, *M.P.*] (Mobilized Aug. 4, 1914). Maj. Sussex Yeomanry (T.F. Res.), attd. Imperial Camel Corps. Gallipoli, Egypt, Sinai, Syria, Arabia. Order of the Nile (4th Class). *D.* Egypt, 1917; Palestine, 1919.

1889 Wise, H. E. D., B.A. (Mobilized Aug. 1914). Lt.-Col. 3rd Sherwood Foresters. *C.B.E.* (Mil.). *D.* § Feb. 1917.

1912 Wiseman, A. M., M.A. (Sept. 4, 1914). ‡2nd Lt. 13th Rifle Brigade. France, 1916–17. *M.C.*, Nov, 14, 1916. (Commission relinquished on account of ill health caused by wounds, June, 1918.)

1895 Wolfe-Barry, B. J., B.A. (Jan. 26, 1915). 2nd Lt. R.G.A. Capt. General List, Staff-Captain. Lt.-Col. R.A.F. France. *O.B.E.* (Mil.). *D.* § Mar. 1918.

1909 Wood, E. C., B.A. (Sept. 22, 1916). Lt. I.A.R.O., attd. 7th Hariana Lancers (Capt.). India.

1916 Wood, R. W. (June 5, 1917). 2nd Lt. R.G.A. (S.R.). France, 1917–18.

1895 Woodd-Smith, N. B., M.A. (Sept. 1, 1916). Lt. 2nd Vol. Bn. Hertfordshire Regt. (Commission relinquished.)

1874 Woodford, E. F., M.A. (Sept. 15, 1914). Maj. 7th York and Lancaster Regt. Maj. 1st (Garr.) Bn. Yorkshire Regt.

1905 **Woodhead, R. C.** (Oct. 1914). Capt. 12th Durham L.I. France. Killed in action on July 17, 1916.

1897 Wooll, E., B.A. (Oct. 19, 1914). Lt., Acting Capt., Cheshire Yeomanry, attd. Cavalry Corps H.Q. France, 1916–19. *O.B.E.* (Mil.). *D.* France, 1918, 1919.

1899 Woolley, C. L., M.A. (Sept. 24, 1914). Capt. R.F.A., temp. Maj. Asst. Political Officer. Egypt, 1914–16; Syria, 1919. (Prisoner in Turkey, Aug. 1916–Nov. 1918.) Croix de Guerre. *D.* Egypt, 1915.

1909 Worsley, W. A. (Serving Aug. 4, 1914). Capt. Yorkshire Regt. France. (Prisoner of War, 1915.)

1880 Worsley, Sir W. H. A., B.A. Lt. 2nd Vol. Bn. Yorkshire Regt. Maj. York (N. Riding) T.F. Association.

1890 Worthington, W. W., M.A. R.A.S.C. (M.T.).

1904 **Wright, E. L.,** B.A. (Sept. 3, 1914). Capt. Bucks. Bn. Oxf. & Bucks. Lt. Infty. Bde.-Maj. France. *M.C.* Jan. 1, 1918. *D.* France, 1916. Killed in action on May 11, 1918.

1919 Wright, P. L. M. (Apr. 1917). Lt. B/242nd Bde., R.F.A. France and Belgium.

1900 Wyatt-Edgell, C. S. C., M.A. (Mobilized Aug. 1914). Maj. 6th Devonshire Regt., attd. Labour Corps.

1890 Wykeham-Musgrave, H. W. (May 29, 1915). 2nd Lt. 1/1st R. Gloucestershire Hussars (T.F. Res.). Gallipoli, 1915.

1901 Wyndham, Hon. E. S. (Serving Aug. 4, 1914). Maj., Bt.-Lt.-Col. 1st Life Guards. Temp. Lt.-Col. Guards M.G. Regt. France and Belgium, Aug.–Nov. 1914 and 1915–19. *D.S.O.*, Dec. 1, 1914. *D.* France, 1914, 1915.

1895 Wyndham, Hon. H. A. (Sept. 1914). Lt.-Col. Intelligence Officer, Staff, S.W. Africa. German S.W. Africa. *D.* S.W. Africa.

1919 Wynn-Parry, H. (Aug. 27, 1917). 2nd Lt. 3rd Worcestershire Regt. France.

1899 Yeames, A. H. S., M.A. (May 26, 1916). Hon. Capt. Special Lists. Croix de Chevalier de la Légion d'Honneur. Cavalier, Order of the Crown of Italy.

1900 Yerburgh, Rev. W. H. B., M.A. (Feb. 20, 1916). Chaplain R.N. H.M.S. *Drake*, H.M.S. *Companion*, H.M.S. *Queen*, 1917–19.

1892 Young, J. W. A., B.A. (Oct. 29, 1916). Capt. Special Lists. Hedjaz, Palestine. Order of the Nile (4th Class). *D.* Palestine, 1917.

1904 **Younger, C. F.,** B.A. (Aug. 29, 1914). Lt. Lothians and Border Horse. France. Died on Mar. 21, 1917, of wounds received in action.

1899 Younger, J., B.A. (Mobilized Aug. 4, 1914). Lt.-Col. 1/1st Fife and Forfar Yeomanry. Gallipoli, Egypt, Palestine, France. *D.S.O.*, Feb. 15, 1919. *D.* Egypt, 1916.

LINCOLN COLLEGE

1905 Abell, Rev. R. B., M.A. (Feb. 12, 1917). Chaplain to the Forces (4th Class). Egypt, Palestine.

Ackroyd, T. N. (Apr. 1914). 2nd Lt. 10th Res. Cavalry, afterwards 9th, attd. 1st, Bedfordshire Regt. Egypt, 1916; France, 1916–17. Killed in action at La Coulotte on Apr. 23, 1917.

1904 Adams, W. G., B.A. E. African E.F.

1902 Adkin, G. T., M.A. (May 1916). Paymaster Lt. R.N.R. France. *M.B.E.* (Mil.).

1912 Aldous, W. M., B.A., B.Sc. (Nov. 16, 1915). Lt. E. Yorkshire Regt. Lt., Acting Capt., R.E.

1907 **Algeo,* W. B.,** B.A. (Serving Aug. 4, 1914). Capt. 1st Dorsetshire Regt. France and Belgium. *M.C.*, Jan. 14, 1916. *D.* France, 1915, 1916. Killed in action near Thiepval on May 17, 1916.

1910 Allen, W. C., B.A. E. African Defence Force. E. Africa.

1895 Alston, R. S., M.A. (May 1915). Capt. 1st S. Midland Field Coy., R.E.

1910 Anthony,* E. H. H., B.A. (Feb. 10, 1915). Lt. 9th Norfolk Regt., attd. War Office.

1910 Apperly, F. L., D.M. (July 1, 1915). Capt. R.A.M.C. Gallipoli, Egypt, Malta.

1912 **Atkinson-Jowett, J.** (Aug. 1914). Lt. 6th K.O.Y.L.I. France and Belgium. Killed in action at Guedecourt on Sept. 16, 1916.

1903 Attlee, L. G., B.A. (Oct. 9, 1914). Lt. R.A.S.C. France, 1916–17; Salonika, 1918–19.

1880 Auden, Rev. J. E., M.A., T.D. (Dec. 1915). Chaplain to the Forces.

1898 Badcock, Rev. W. J., M.A. (Nov. 1, 1916). Chaplain to the Forces (4th Class), attd. 17th Div. France, 1918–19.

1912 Baker, F. R., B.A. (Oct. 14, 1914). Lt. 351st Bde., R.F.A. France, 1915–16.

1891 Barkley, M., B.A. (Mobilized Aug. 4, 1914). Lt.-Col. 2/1st Huntingdonshire Cyclist Bn. *D.* § Aug. 1919.

1900 Barne, H. H., B.A. (Sept. 15, 1914). Maj. R.A.S.C. Maj. General List. France, 1914–18. Chevalier, Ordre du Mérite Agricole. *D.* France, 1916, 1918.

1919 Barnes-Lawrence, C. H. F. (Jan. 8, 1916). Lt. R.G.A. France, 1918.

1919 Barr, P. M. (Apr. 15, 1918). Pte. 2/28th London Regt. (Artists' Rifles O.T.C.).

1894 Barrow, C. D. (Serving Aug. 4, 1914). Lt.-Col. 3rd R. W. Kent Regt.

1907 Basden, E. D., M.A. (Oct. 29, 1915). Lt. 9th Sherwood Foresters. Lt.-Col. M.G.C. Gallipoli. *M.C.*, Mar. 15, 1916. *D.* France, 1916.

1910 Battiscombe,* C. F., B.A. (Dec. 24, 1914). 2nd Lt. R. Berkshire Regt. Lt. Grenadier Guards.

1894 Batty, Rev. W. G., M.A. (Mar. 12, 1917). Chaplain to the Forces (4th Class).

1893 Belcher, E. A., M.A. (Jan. 1915). Maj. 9th D.C.L.I. Maj. General List (Specially empld.). France. *C.B.E.* (Civil).

1914 Belgrave, C. D. (Feb. 8, 1915). 2nd Lt. 9th R. Warwickshire Regt. Lt. Special Lists, empld. Egyptian Government. Egypt, Sudan, Palestine.

1920 Bennett, S. M. (Jan. 16, 1917). Lt. R.H. and R.F.A., empld. Records. Belgium, 1917.

1885 Bere, Rev. M. A., M.A. (Mar. 28, 1916). Chaplain to the Forces (4th Class). France. *D.* France, 1917.

1910 Bestall, P. G., B.A. Cavalry (S.R.).

1910 **Bigsby,* E. A.,** B.A. (Nov. 19, 1914). 2nd Lt. 9th R. W. Kent Regt. France. Killed in action at the Battle of Loos on Sept. 25, 1915.

1919 Birks, G. A. (July 24, 1916). Gnr. 208th Siege Batt., R.G.A. France, 1916–19.

1913 Blackstock, G. (1914). Pte. 19th R. Fusiliers (P.S. Bn.).

1919 Blagden, C. F. V. (Aug. 28, 1918). 2nd Lt. Guards M.G. Regt.

1910 **Bland, W. J.,** B.C.L. (1917). Capt. U.S. Infantry. France. Killed in action on Sept. 13, 1918.

1915 Boone, W. B., B.A. (Dec. 23, 1915). Capt. R.F.A. (T.F. Res.). France and Belgium.

1908 Brandon,* R. V., B.A. (Serving Aug. 4, 1914). Capt. Indian Army, Acting Maj. 1/4th Gurkha Rifles. France, 1915; Gallipoli, 1915; Egypt, 1915–16; Wazaristan, 1917; Afghanistan, 1919.

1898 Bretherton, C. H., B.C.L., M.A. (Feb. 29, 1916). ‡Lt. R.A.O.C.

1910 Brice, C. S., B.A. (1917). Capt. 49th Coast Artillery, U.S. Army. France, 1918–19.

1919 Bromet, H. A. (Sept. 28, 1917). 2nd Lt. 19th R. Hussars. France and Germany.

1899 [Brook, Rev. R., M.A.] (Aug. 3, 1916). Chaplain to the Forces (4th Class). France, 1915–16 (as Acting Chaplain). *D.* § Mar. 1918.

1914 **Brooke, L. S.** (Mar. 24, 1915). Lt. Army Cyclist Corps. Lt. R.A.F. (Flying Officer). France. Killed in aerial action in Vosges Mountains on Sept. 25, 1918.

1919 Brown, F. N. (Sept. 16, 1914). Lt. R.F.A. (Capt.). France, 1916.

1920 Browne, C. (Aug. 20, 1914). ‡Lt. R.A.F. (Capt.). France.

1920 Bullocke, J. G. (May 12, 1916). ‡Lt. 2/81st Pioneers, Indian Army (Capt.). India, N.W. Frontier, Afghanistan.

1908 Burgess, R. W., B.A. (Oct. 1917). Lt. U.S. Ordnance Dept. Capt. Statistical Branch, U.S. Army.

1897 Burgis, E. C., B.C.L., M.A. (June 1915). Maj. 349th Siege Batt., R.G.A. Italy, Mesopotamia, Palestine.

1910 Bury, H. V., B.A. (Feb. 10, 1915). Lt. 5th Middlesex Regt.

1908 Butler, C. J. (Dec. 16, 1914). Lt. R. W. Kent Regt.

1910 Cade,* C. M. D., B.A. (Aug. 5, 1914). Capt. I.A.R.O. India, 1916–17.

1912 Calthrop, C. D. U., B.A. (Nov. 14, 1914). 2nd Lt. 6th Border Regt. (Invalided.)

1909 Campbell,* C. B., B.A. (Aug. 29, 1914). Lt. 10th Highland L.I. Capt. General List. Staff-Captain. France. *D.* France, 1916.

1894 Careless, Rev. W. E., M.A. (Serving Aug. 4, 1914). Chaplain to the Forces (Indian Service). India, 1915–18.

1908 [Casson,* S., M.A.] (May 1, 1915). Capt. 3rd E. Lancashire Regt. G.S.O. 3. Salonika. Chevalier, Order of the Redeemer (5th Class). *D.* Salonika, 1918.
1900 Cathie, L. R. (Dec. 18, 1917). Lt. R.A.S.C.
1890 Cave-Moyles, Rev. T. H., M.A. Chaplain to the Forces (4th Class).
1919 Cazalet, P. C. (June 7, 1918). 2nd Lt. R. Fusiliers (on demobilization).
1903 Charles, M. de B. Capt. General List.
1908 Chave,* P. G. E. Pte. R. Fusiliers. (Discharged, medically unfit.)
1898 Clarke, S. A., B.C.L., M.A. (Sept. 25, 1915). Maj. R.A.S.C., Deputy Asst. Director of Supplies. *D.* § Mar. 1919.
1919 Coates, D. I. (Sept. 7, 1918). 2nd Lt. Devonshire Regt. (on demobilization).
1908 **Coleman,* H. E. E.** (July 7, 1916). 2nd Lt. 3rd, attd. 2nd, R. Sussex Regt. France. Killed in action on Sept. 9, 1916.
1919 Connolly, J. D'A. (Sept. 3, 1914). ‡Lt. Cheshire Regt. (Capt.). France, N. Russia.
1905 Cook, H. C., M.A. (Dec. 12, 1915). Sergt. 28th London Regt. (Artists' Rifles). Sergt.-Instructor V Corps Gas School. France, 1916–18.
1890 Cookson, G. H. F., M.A. (Mar. 1, 1915). Capt. 9th D.C.L.I. Capt. Administrative Officer, R.A.F. (since Apr. 1, 1918). France, Belgium.
1913 Copner, E. C. L. (Apr. 2, 1915). Lt. 8th Devonshire Regt. France.
1898 Cornish, L. J., M.A. (Sept. 27, 1915). Lt. 3/1st E. Lancashire R.A.S.C.
1920 Cox, A. F. (Jan. 18, 1916). 1st Class Petty Officer (Artisan), R.N., H.M.S. *Bellerophon*. North Sea.
1909 Coxwell,* E. C. (June 24, 1915). Lt., Acting Capt., 1st Worcestershire Regt. France. *M.C.*, June 3, 1919.
1912 **Craig, H. D. C.** (Aug. 15, 1914). Capt., temp. Maj., 3rd Highland L.I. France, Finland. *M.C.*, June 3, 1919. *D.* Finland, 1919. Died on Feb. 13, 1920, at Reval, of illness contracted while on active service.
1919 Crew, A. E. (Aug. 21, 1914). ‡Lt. 1/4th Oxf. & Bucks. Lt. Infty. (Capt.). France, 1917. *M.M.*, July 16, 1916. *D.* France, 1917.
1890 Currie, J. R., M.A. (Mar. 21, 1916). Capt. R.A.M.C. Italy, France.
1902 Cuthbertson, W. R. D., B.A. (Aug. 1914). Capt. Sussex Yeomanry, attd. 16th R. Sussex Regt. (Maj.). Gallipoli, 1915; Egypt and Palestine, 1916–17; France, 1918. *M.C.*, Feb. 15, 1919.
1913 Dalton, W. P. (Apr. 7, 1915). Lt. 6th Norfolk Regt., empld. Ministry of Labour. France, Belgium.
1913 Daniel, R. Y., B.A. (Sept. 9, 1914). ‡Lt. R. Fusiliers. France.
1919 Darley, R. G. (Dec. 12, 1916). Pte. Oxf. & Bucks. Lt. Infty., attd. No. 646 Agricultural Coy.
1919 Darrington, V. G. (Dec. 21, 1915). Lt. R.F.A. Lt. R.A.F., attd. Air Ministry. France and Belgium.
1919 Dartford, R. C. G. (Sept. 15, 1914). Capt. 19th London Regt. (Liaison Officer). France and Belgium, 1915–19. *M.C.*, Jan. 1, 1918. Order of Aviz (Portuguese). *D.* France, 1918.
1919 Dash, W. M. (Aug. 15, 1917). 2nd Lt. 259th Siege Batt., R.G.A. France and Belgium, 1918–19.
1899 Davies, D. E., M.A. R.N.A.S.
1919 Davies, H. (Feb. 1917). Rfln. 5th London Regt. (London Rifle Brigade). ‡2nd Lt. R.A.F. (since Feb. 1918). France, 1918.

1908 Davies, L. M., D.M. (Aug. 10, 1914). Surgeon Probationer R.N.V.R. Capt. R.A.M.C. North Sea, 1914; France, 1914; Salonika, 1916.

1897 Davison, Rev. F. D. P., M.A. (Apr. 28, 1916). Chaplain to the Forces (4th Class).

1919 Day, R. G. (Sept. 19, 1917). ‡2nd Lt. (Pilot) Air Service, U.S. Army. France, 1918.

1895 Deas, G. F., B.A. (Oct. 1, 1914). Capt. 2/9th R. Scots.

1888 de Lisle, Rev. H. F., M.A. (Oct. 26, 1914). Chaplain, Capt. S. African Forces. E. Africa. *M.B.E.* (Mil.). *D.* E. Africa, 1917 twice.

1920 Dent, J. C. (Apr. 1915). 2nd Lt. 12th W. Yorkshire Regt. France.

1919 Dix, F. H. R. (July 5, 1917). Lt. 8th Sherwood Foresters. France, 1918.

1920 Dodd, T. C. (Dec. 1914). Capt. Northumberland Fusiliers. France, Salonika, Italy.

1916 [Dolley, S. P. B.] (Sept. 5, 1914). Pte. 7th Oxf. & Bucks. Lt. Infty. France, 1915–17; The Balkans, 1917–19.

1913 Douglas,* W. S. (Aug. 15, 1914). Capt. R.F.A. (S.R.). Maj., Acting Lt.-Col., Squadron Commdr., 59th Wing, R.A.F. France. *M.C.*, Jan. 14, 1916. *D.F.C.*, Feb. 8, 1919. Croix de Guerre with palms. *D.* France, 1918 twice.

1899 Douglas-Hamilton, K. (Oct. 3, 1914). Capt. 11th Lancashire Fusiliers. Capt. Labour Corps.

1919 Doulton, R. F. (Jan. 5, 1918). 2nd Lt. 6th Queen's (R. W. Surrey Regt.). France, 1918–19.

1919 Draper, H. M. (Apr. 20, 1917). 2nd Lt. R.G.A. (T.F.).

1907 Drewe,* F. S., M.A. (Oct. 11, 1918). Lt. R.A.F. Medical Service.

1907 Dreyer, G., M.A. (July 1915). Hon. Lt.-Col. R.A.M.C. Lt.-Col. R.A.F. France, 1915–19. *C.B.E.* (Mil.). *D.* France, 1918, 1919.

1912 Edenborough, E. J. H., B.A. (Sept. 10, 1914). ‡Lt. 16th Queen's (R. W. Surrey Regt.). Belgium, 1915, 1916, 1917; France, 1916.

1895 **Edmonds, W. J.** (Aug. 13, 1915). Capt. 6th Devonshire Regt., attd. Staff. Died on May 19, 1919, of illness contracted on active service.

1919 Edwards, I. ab O. (Feb. 10, 1916). ‡2nd Lt. R.G.A. France.

1919 Eeles, G. N. (Aug. 17, 1915). ‡Lt. K.R.R.C. Belgium and France.

1919 Elliott, C. M. W. (June 20, 1916). ‡2nd Lt. 3/5th E. Lancashire Regt. 2nd Lt. R.A.F. France.

1913 **Elsworth,* H.** (Jan. 25, 1915). Lt. 4th R. Scots Fusiliers. France. Missing, believed killed in action on Aug. 21, 1918.

1905 Embling, Rev. H. J., M.A. (Aug. 4, 1914). Chaplain R.N. H.M.S. *Agincourt*, Grand Fleet; Aegean Sea; Asia Minor. *O.B.E.* (Mil.).

1907 Emden, A. B., M.A. (Nov. 29, 1915). A.B. H.M.S. *Parker* (P.O.). Grand Fleet, 1916–19.

1919 Emsley, S. J. (Apr. 20, 1915). ‡Lt. R.G.A. France and Belgium, 1915–18.

1897 **Evans, A.,** B.A. (1914). ‡2nd Lt. Essex Regt. France. Killed in action on Oct. 18, 1916.

1901 Evans, C. J. M., B.A. (1915). ‡Lt., Flying Officer, R.A.F.

1899 Evans, E. M. F., B.A. R.A.F.

1911 Evans, M. P., B.A. (Oct. 7, 1914). Lt. 5th Lancashire Fusiliers. Capt. I.A.R.O. France, 1915–16; India, 1916–19; Mesopotamia, 1919.

1920 Evans, N. D. H. (Mar. 5, 1917). ‡2nd Lt. R.A.F.

1903 Evans, R. S., M.A. (July 26, 1915). Lt. 5th Welsh Regt. Capt. Special Lists. Courts Martial Officer.

1901 **Fairbairns, A.,** B.A. (Apr. 10, 1916). ‡Capt. 13th W. Riding Regt. France. Killed in action near Fleurbaix on Oct. 14, 1918.

1881 Fairbrother, W. H., M.A. (Oct. 12, 1914). Capt. 4th R. Warwickshire Regt. *D.* § Feb. 1917.

1910 Farley, L. E., B.C.L. (Apr. 6, 1917). ‡Capt. U.S. Infantry.

1912 Fergusson,* H. W. E. (Aug. 22, 1914). Lt. 10th Highland L.I. Lt. Coldstream Guards (S.R.).

1907 **Filleul,* L. A.,** B.A. (Aug. 14, 1914). 2nd Lt. Oxf. & Bucks. Lt. Infty. (S.R.). France. Killed in action on Oct. 21, 1914.

1912 Filleul,* R. R., B.A. (Oct. 31, 1914). Lt. 4th Dorsetshire Regt.

1888 Firmstone, J. A. L. (Mobilized Aug. 4, 1914). Maj. R.A. (Res. of Officers.)

1906 Fisher, G. T., B.A. (Serving Aug. 4, 1914). Capt. 1/3rd Gurkha Rifles, attd. Political Dept. France, 1914–15; Mesopotamia, 1917–19. *D.* Mesopotamia, 1919.

1919 Florey, E. H. (July 5, 1915). Sergt. 16th Bn. M.G.C. France, 1916–19. *D.* France.

1913 Foster, R. B., M.A. (Dec. 1915). American Ambulance (1915–16). Sergt. Intelligence Police (1918). France, 1915, 1917–18; Egypt, 1916–17 (with Y.M.C.A.).

1894 Fowler, R. C. (Sept. 12, 1914). Capt. 7th Northamptonshire Regt. France and Belgium. *D.* France, 1916.

1906 Francis, C. C. (Mar. 31, 1915). Capt. E. Surrey Regt.

1908 Frazer, K. G. (July 7, 1916). Lt. K.R.R.C., attd. M.G.C. (Capt. and Adjt.). France, Germany, 1917–19.

1907 Freeman, A. C. (July 12, 1917). 2nd Lt. Labour Corps. (Invalided, Nov. 6, 1918.)

1897 Freeman, A. M., B.A. (Nov. 2, 1916). Pte. R.A.S.C. Salonika, 1917–19.

1904 Freeman, M., M.A. (Mobilized Aug. 1914). Maj. 6th (Res.) Worcestershire Regt. Lt.-Col. R.A.F. Belgium. *O.B.E.* (Mil.). *D.* § June, 1918.

1896 [**Frost, K. T.,** B.Litt., M.A.] (Serving Aug. 4, 1914). Lt. 3rd Cheshire Regt. France. Killed in action on Aug. 25, 1914.

1902 Garden, A. W., M.A. (Sept. 25, 1914). Lt. 854th Coy., R.A.S.C. Salonika.

Garraway, W. F. (Apr. 1915). 2nd Lt. 82nd Punjabis, Indian Army. India, Mesopotamia, 1915–16. Drowned on duty on Nov. 5, 1916.

1905 Geerdts, C. E., B.C.L. ‡2nd Lt. General List. German S.W. Africa, E. Africa. (Invalided, Dec. 1916.)

1909 Gillbert,* J. G., B.A. (Aug. 29, 1914). Lt. 6th E. Lancashire Regt. Lt. General List.

1919 Gillett, E. W. (Nov. 4, 1914). Capt. 7th Lancashire Fusiliers. France and Belgium.

1904 Gipson, L. H., B.A. (1917). Pte. U.S. Army.

1900 Glass, D. J. C., B.A. (Sept. 1914). Capt. Coldstream Guards (S.R.). France.

1919 Gluckstein, L. H. (Dec. 20, 1915). ‡Lt. 2/5th Suffolk Regt., attd. Intelligence Corps. Italy. *D.* Italy, 1918.

1919 Godfrey, E. G. (Apr. 5, 1915). ‡Lt., Acting Capt., 6th London Regt. (Rifles.) France. *M.C.*, Jan. 1, 1918.

1914 **Gonner, E. M.** (Mar. 29, 1915). Capt. 16th K.R.R.C. France. *M.C.*, June 4, 1917. Missing, believed killed in action on Apr. 23, 1917.

1914 Good, P. F., B.A. (Aug. 28, 1917). Ensign U.S. Naval Reserve. France, 1917–18.

1919 Gotto, B. D. (Sept. 28, 1914). Pte. 2nd E. Surrey Regt. (Lce.-Cpl.). Salonika.

1904 Green,* A. M., M.A. (Aug. 10, 1914). Capt. 4th Bombay Garrison Artillery, I.D.F. India.

1908 **Green, C. W.** (Aug. 14, 1914). Capt. 1st R. Berkshire Regt. France. Died on June 27, 1915, of wounds received in action.

1911 **Greenhill, F. W. R.** (Aug. 26, 1916). 2nd Lt. Grenadier Guards, attd. 3rd Bn. France and Belgium. Killed in action on Oct. 10, 1917.

1897 Grimshaw, C. H., B.A. (Sept. 23, 1914). Capt. W. Yorkshire Regt. France. *M.C.*, Aug. 25, 1917.

1905 Groves, Rev. S., M.A. (Dec. 10, 1914). Chaplain to the Forces (4th Class), attd. 51st Div. France. *M.C.*, June 3, 1919. *D.* France, 1918.

1905 Grundy, F. D., M.A. (Sept. 1, 1915). Lt. K.R.R.C. France.

1919 Guest, A. W. (Mar. 1916). Ordinary Telegraphist R.N. Warrant Schoolmaster. H.M.S. *Dominion*, 1916–17 ; H.M.S. *Caledon*, 1917–18.

1905 Gummer, H. I., M.A. (June 1915). Pte. 1st H.A.C. France.

1896 Gwynne-Evans, E. G., B.A. (July 4, 1916). Lt. R.A.S.C.

1907 Hall,* E. C. H., B.A. (Aug. 8, 1914). Capt. 3rd Devonshire Regt. Palestine. *D.* Palestine, 1918.

1910 Hall, G. F. E., B.A. (1918). 2nd Lt. R.A.F.

1913 Hall,* J. H., B.A. (Sept. 28, 1914). Capt. 1st Munster Fusiliers. Bde. Maj. France. *D.S.O.*, June 3, 1919. *M.C.*, June 4, 1917.

1919 Hamilton, A. P. F. (Mobilized Aug. 4, 1914). Capt. 8th Sherwood Foresters (T.F.). Maj. 16th Bn. Tank Corps. France and Egypt. *M.C.*, Oct. 8, 1918.

1910 Hamilton, C. K. J., B.A. (Dec. 11, 1914). Lt. R.F.A.

1907 Hancock,* E., B.A. (Oct. 17, 1916). ‡Lt. R.G.A. (S.R.) (Capt.). France. *M.C.*, Sept. 16, 1918.

1914 **Hankinson, R. H.** (Dec. 22, 1914). Lt. 1/6th Manchester Regt. Egypt and France. Killed in action at Havrincourt on June 21, 1917.

1910 Hargreaves-Mawdsley, R. (1915). ‡2nd Lt. 6th R. Fusiliers.

1895 **Hattersley-Smith, J. H.,** B.A. (Sept. 25, 1914). Lce.-Cpl. 9th Norfolk Regt. France, 1915. Died on Oct. 7, 1915, of wounds received in action at Loos on Sept. 25.

1913 Hay,* C. C., B.A. (Oct. 20, 1914). Lt., Acting Capt., 7th Seaforth Highlanders (A.D.C.). France, 1915–18.

1895 Heaslop, A. C., B.A. (Serving Aug. 4, 1914). Maj. R.A. Bde. Maj. France, Mesopotamia. *O.B.E.* (Mil.). *M.C.*, Jan. 14, 1916. *D.* France, 1916 ; Mesopotamia, 1918, 1919.

1920 Heather, H. G. (Sept. 1914). ‡Lt. R.A.F. (Capt.). German S.W. Africa, France.

1919 Heawood, B. E. (Sept. 16, 1918). Pte. Queen's (R. W. Surrey Regt.). Cadet No. 21 O.C.B.

1904 Hepburn, D. H. (May 1916). ‡Lt. R.A.O.C. France.

1895 Hepworth, Rev. C. L., M.A. (Nov. 1914). Capt. 3/4th Leicestershire Regt.

1902 **Hess, A. F.,** B.A. (Serving Aug. 4, 1914). Capt., temp. Maj., 7th W. Yorkshire Regt. France. Died on July 14, 1916, of wounds received in action in the Battle of the Somme.

1901 Hewett, H. P., B.A. (Apr. 23, 1915). Capt. I.A.R.O., attd. 23rd Cavalry. Mesopotamia, 1916–19. *D.* Mesopotamia, 1918.

1891 Hill, W. H., M.A. (Mar. 1919). Lt.-Col. Special Lists. Legal Adviser, 10th Div. Egypt.

1919 Hills, J. D. (Sept. 14, 1914). Maj. 1/5th Leicestershire Regt. France and Belgium, 1915–19; Egypt, 1915. *M.C.*, Feb. 15, 1919; *Bar*, Jan. 1, 1919. Croix de Guerre. *D.* France, 1916, 1918.

1919 Hodgkinson, J., B.A. (Mar. 3, 1917). Lt. 1/4th K.O.Y.L.I. (Capt.). France and Belgium, 1917–19. *M.C.*, Sept. 16, 1918.

1911 **Hodgson, A. D.** (Sept. 23, 1914). Lt., Bombing Officer, 15th Sherwood Foresters. France. Killed in action at Trônes Wood on July 20, 1916.

1906 Hodson, Rev. H. V., M.A. (Nov. 1916). Pte. A.I.F. ‡Chaplain to the Forces (4th Class), attd. Coldstream Guards. Salonika, 1917–18; France, 1918–19. *M.C.*, Sept. 16, 1918.

1906 Holden,* Rev. P. G., M.A. (June 1915). Pte. R.A.M.C. ‡Chaplain to the Forces (4th Class), attd. R.F.A. France, 1915–19. *O.B.E.* (Mil.). *D.* France, 1919.

1914 Homan, P. T., B.A. Lt. U.S. Aviation Service.

1905 Hookham,* G. R., B.A. (Nov. 1916). Lt. 3rd (Res.) R. Welch Fusiliers (Capt.). France. *D.* France, 1917.

1902 Hopkins, U. S. (Serving Aug. 4, 1914). Capt. R. Berkshire Regt.

1897 Housman, Rev. A. O. V., B.A. (June 5, 1917). Chaplain to the Forces (4th Class), attd. R.A.O.C. France and Belgium, 1917–19.

1911 Hudson, C. N., M.A. (June 24, 1918). Rfln. 5th London Regt. (London Rifle Brigade).

1908 Hudson,* Rev. W. N., M.A. (1915). Chaplain to the Forces (4th Class).

1895 Hughes, Rev. J. A., M.A. (Dec. 29, 1915). Chaplain to the Forces (4th Class). Salonika, 1916–17; Italy, 1917–18.

1907 **Humfrey,* D. H. W.,** B.A. (1914). Lt. 3rd, attd. 2nd, Oxf. & Bucks. Lt. Infty. France. Killed in action, May 13–14, 1915.

1889 [Hunt, A. S., M.A., D.Litt.] (May 1, 1915). Lt. 4th Oxf. & Bucks. Lt. Infty., attd. War Office.

1912 **Hunt,* R. L. G.** (Sept. 12, 1914). Capt. 6th Oxf. & Bucks. Lt. Infty. France. Killed in action on Oct. 7, 1916.

1913 Hunter,* P. C. (Oct. 14, 1914). Capt. 6th The Black Watch. France.

1895 Hurst, G. B., B.C.L., M.A., *M.P.* (Mobilized Aug. 4, 1914). Maj. 1/7th Manchester Regt. Sudan, Gallipoli, Egypt, Sinai, Belgium.

1908 Hyde-Thomson, R. H., B.A. (Sept. 6, 1914). ‡2nd Lt. 5th Rifle Brigade. France. (Placed on retired pay on account of wounds, Sept. 1916.)

1919 Ife, A. E. (Aug. 27, 1917). 2nd Lt. 2/1st W. Somerset Yeomanry.

1914 **Ireland, J. B.** (Sept. 22, 1914). Lt. 12th Gloucestershire Regt. France. Killed in action on May 5, 1917.

Irving, A. D. (Sept. 21, 1917). 2nd Lt. R.F.A. France. Killed in action on Sept. 16, 1918.

1919 Isaacs, C. M. (Mar. 8, 1918). 2nd Lt. 3rd Irish Guards.

1902 Ivens, Rev. A. L., M.A. (May 22, 1915). Chaplain to the Forces (4th Class.)

1895 **Jack, J. C.,** M.A. (Aug. 26, 1914). Lt., Acting Maj., R.F.A. (S.R.) France. *D.S.O.*, July 26, 1918. *M.C.*, Sept. 26, 1917 ; *Bar*, Jan. 18, 1918. *D.* France, 1918. Died on May 31, 1918, of wounds received in action.

1907 **Jalland,* S.,** M.A. (Sept. 29, 1914). Lt. 6th E. Yorkshire Regt. Gallipoli. Killed in action on Aug. 9, 1915.

1892 James, Rev. C. W., M.A. (Apr. 26, 1918). Chaplain to the Forces (4th Class).

1898 James, N. G. B., M.A. (Mar. 1911). Capt. Unattached List, T.F., Mill Hill School O.T.C.

1911 Jameson,* J. B. (Sept. 22, 1914). Lt. 15th King's (Liverpool Regt.).

1914 Jee, R., B.A. (Jan. 11, 1915). ‡Capt. 11th Durham L.I. France and Belgium, 1915–18. *M.C.*, Jan. 1, 1919.

1902 John, R. B., B.A. (1916). Capt. R.A.M.C.

1919 Johnson, A. (Feb. 1917). ‡Lt. Leicestershire Regt. France and Germany.

1908 Jones, A. G., M.A. (Nov. 4, 1917). Capt. 346th Bde., R.F.A. France and Belgium.

1912 Jones, R. B. (Mar. 17, 1915). Capt. 8th R. Welch Fusiliers. France. *M.C.*, 1919.

1919 Jones, T. J. (June 16, 1915). Capt. 4th S. Wales Borderers. India, 1916–17 ; Mesopotamia and Kurdistan, 1917–19.

1906 Joseph,* E. G., B.Sc., M.A. (Aug. 26, 1914). Lt. Army Cyclist Corps. France. *M.C.*, Sept. 16, 1918.

1907 Judy, C. K., M.A. (June 24, 1918). Capt. C.A. Res. Corps.

1919 Kemp, W. W. (Sept. 21, 1917). Lce.-Cpl. 6th London Regt. (Rifles).

1912 **King,* E. R.** (Aug. 15, 1914). Capt. 3rd, attd. 1st, Norfolk Regt. France and Mesopotamia. Died on Apr. 25, 1916, of wounds received in action at Sanna-i-Yat.

1893 Kirkby, W. H., M.A. (Aug. 4, 1914). Capt. Unattached List, T.F., King Edward's School, Birmingham, O.T.C.

1919 Knight, J. H. (Nov. 18, 1917). 2nd Lt. R.A.F. France.

1904 **Knowles, A. B.,** B.A. 2nd Lt. I.A.R.O., attd. Indian Cavalry. Mesopotamia. Killed in action on June 11, 1916.

1919 Kyle, S. H. (Dec. 2, 1915). Capt. General List, attd. W. Command Staff.

1900 Kyrke, G. V., B.A. (Apr. 1916). Paymaster Sub-Lt. R.N.R. Auxiliary Patrol, North Sea.

1911 Lang, R. L. F. (Apr. 13, 1915). Lt. R.A.S.C. France and Belgium.

1913 Lassen, E. J., B.A. (Jan. 2, 1915). 2nd Lt. 11th W. Riding Regt., afterwards Capt. General List, attd. 60th Inf. Bde., H.Q. France, 1916–19.

1914 **Lee, A. A. D.** (Dec. 1914). Capt. 9th Leicestershire Regt. France and Belgium. *M.C.*, Jan. 1, 1917. Killed in action at Polygon Wood on Oct. 1, 1917.

1893 Leslie-Jones, F. A., M.A. Punjab Light Horse. *C.B.E.* (Mil.).

1920 Lewis, C. (Aug. 25, 1917). Sergt. R.A.M.C., attd. No. 36 C.C.S. Germany, 1919.

1919 Lole, A. G., B.A. (Sept. 1915). Lt. 4th Rifle Brigade. Lt., Acting Capt., 11th Bn. Tank Corps. France, 1916–17, 1917–19. *M.C.*, Dec. 2, 1918. *D.* France, 1917.

1895 Lomas, H. A., M.A. (Apr. 1, 1917). Maj. 8th United Provinces Horse, I.D.F. India. *O.B.E.* (Civil).

1919 Lord, L. (Dec. 1914). Lt. R.F.A. France.
1900 Lorimer, R., B.A. (Oct. 1914). ‡Lt. 4th (Res.) Arg. & Suth'd. Highlanders (Capt. and Adjt.). France.
1912 Luxmoore,* E. C. L. (Aug. 22, 1914). Capt. 6th Queen's (R. W. Surrey Regt.), attd. No. 19 O.C.B. France.
1920 McBride, D. R. (Dec. 6, 1917). Lt. Aviation Corps, U.S. Army.
1919 Macdonald, A. D. (Oct. 1, 1914). Lt. 2nd Lancashire Fusiliers (Capt.). France, 1915–18. *M.C.*, June 4, 1917 ; *Bar*, Nov. 8, 1918.
1913 MacEwen,* A. R. (Oct. 19, 1914). Capt. 5th Highland L.I. Gallipoli, 1915 ; Egypt, 1916–17 ; Palestine, 1917–18. *M.C.*, Apr. 17, 1917.
1896 Mann, H. E., M.A. (Dec. 22, 1915). ‡Capt. A.S.C. Capt. Special Lists. G.S.O. 3, General Staff, 1st Army. France, 1916–19. *D.* France, 1917.
1919 Marks, A. H. (Mar. 7, 1918). ‡2nd Lt. 4th Middlesex Regt. France, 1918.
1914 Marshall, J. F., M.A. (Mar. 25, 1915). Capt. and Adjt. 10th Highland L.I. France, 1915–19. *M.C.*, June 3, 1918. *D.* France, 1917.
1919 Martin, H. R. C. (Aug. 15, 1914). Capt. 3rd E. Lancashire Regt., empld. Recruiting Duties.
1914 Martin, R. R., B.A. (Nov. 27, 1914). Lt. 7th Bedfordshire Regt.
1913 **Meares,* G. P. S.** (Mar. 1, 1916). Rfln. 1st Monmouthshire Regt. Died on Mar. 16, 1916, of illness contracted on active service.
1882 Merry, Rev. W. M., M.A. (June 1917). Hon. Chaplain (4th Class).
1919 Meyer, J. C. (May 9, 1917). Cpl. 3rd Labour Bn., Southern Command Labour Centre.
1910 Michael,* G. C. (Feb. 15, 1915). 2nd Lt. 11th Devonshire Regt.
1909 Millar,* E. F., M.A. (Aug. 7, 1914). ‡Lt. 1st Sherwood Foresters. Lt. R.A.F. France, 1914–16 ; Egypt, 1918–19.
1920 Mills, J. D. (Jan. 1917). Lt. 6th British West Indies Regt. France, Belgium, 1917–18, 1918–19 ; Italy, 1918. *D.* Italy, 1918.
1902 Mitchell-Dawson, H. C., M.A. (Sept. 5, 1914). ‡Lt. 12th Hampshire Regt. (Capt.). France.
1913 Moat, C. A., M.A. (Dec. 27, 1917). Lt. Somerset L.I., attd. 1st Yorkshire Regt. India, 1917–19.
1900 Moberly, W. H., M.A. (July 12, 1915). Lt. 2/4th Oxf. & Bucks. Lt. Infty. (Capt.). France and Belgium, 1916, 1917–18. *D.S.O.*, Oct. 18, 1917. *D.* France, 1916, 1917.
1911 Monier-Williams, C. F., B.A. (Aug. 10, 1914). ‡Lt. 12th London Regt. (The Rangers). France, 1915–16. (Invalided on account of wounds, Feb. 21, 1919.)
1904 Monk, F. F., M.A. (May 5, 1917). Lt. I.A.R.O., attd. 1/54th Sikhs (Frontier Force). Capt. Intelligence Corps. Egypt.
1911 Moody, S. (Sept. 1914). ‡Lt. 1st (Garr.) Bn. King's (Liverpool Regt.). Capt., Deputy Military Governor, Tiberias. Belgium, 1915 ; Egypt, 1916–17 ; Palestine, 1917–19.
1908 **Morant,* W. H.,** B.A. (Sept. 9, 1914). 2nd Lt. 15th Northumberland Fusiliers. France. Killed in action on Oct. 25, 1916.
1906 Morgan, H. W., M.A. (Nov. 12, 1916). 2nd Lt. R.F.A. France and Belgium.
1902 Mortimer-Booth, T. K., M.A. (Serving Aug. 4, 1914). Capt. Unattached List, T.F., Christ's Hospital O.T.C.
1909 Morton,* J. B., M.A. (Sept. 5, 1914). Capt. R.A.S.C. France.

1906 Moses, L., B.A. (Mar. 17, 1915). 2nd Lt. 10th Leicestershire Regt. (Resigned.)
1902 Mounsey, J. J. (May 27, 1915). Lt. 2nd Lovat's Scouts.
1911 Naish, W. V. J., B.A. (Apr. 3, 1915). Lt. 2nd Hampshire Regt.
1919 Neill, J. A. (Sept. 7, 1914). ‡Lt. R.F.A. Lt. R.A.F. Egypt and Palestine. *D.* Egypt, twice.
1909 Newhall, D. V., B.A. (May 26, 1917). 1st Lt. 9th Inf., U.S. Army.
1904 Newman, F. F. (Oct. 4, 1915). Capt. 180th Bde., R.F.A. France. *M.C.*, Sept. 16, 1918.
1910 Newton, G. F. (Jan. 7, 1915). Lt. R.A. *M.B.E.* (Mil.).
1906 Newton, N. (1914). ‡2nd Lt. 10th W. Yorkshire Regt. Lt. 85th Training Res. Bn. France, 1916–17.
1919 Nicholls, L. (Sept. 9, 1914). ‡Capt. Bedfordshire Regt., attd. Loyal N. Lancashire Regt. Lt. Army Signal Service. France and Belgium, 1916–18. *M.C.*, June 3, 1918.
1919 Nicholson, G. A. (Nov. 1915). ‡2nd Lt. 10th King's (Liverpool Regt.). 2nd Lt. 2/98th Inf., Indian Army. France, India.
1913 Nicholson,* T. (Serving Aug. 4, 1914). Lt. R. Irish Regt. France, 1914. (Prisoner of war in Germany, Oct. 1914–Feb. 1918. Interned in Holland, Feb. 1918–Aug. 1918.)
1919 Nitch, St. J. B. (Apr. 21, 1917). Lt. 303rd Siege Batt., R.G.A. France, Belgium, Germany.
1902 Noble, R. S. H., M.A. (Jan. 28, 1915). 2nd Lt. 2nd R. Irish Rifles. Belgium and France, 1915, 1917. (Placed on Retired List on account of wounds, Mar. 1918.)
1919 Norwood, L. R. O. (Aug. 4, 1914). ‡Lt. 4th Q.O. Cameron Highlanders. France, 1916–17.
1906 **Nuttall, H. N.,** B.A. (Oct. 8, 1915). 2nd Lt. A.S.C. France. Died on July 5, 1917, of wounds received in action.
1882 O'Connor, E., B.M., M.A. (Aug. 14, 1914). Capt. R.A.M.C. France, 1915 ; Mudros, 1915–16 ; Egypt, 1916.
1890 Odgers, A. W., B.A. (Sept. 1914). Capt. 2/8th Worcestershire Regt., specially empld. France, 1916–19.
1894 Odgers, P. N. B., B.M., M.A., M.Ch. (Mar. 5, 1916). Capt. R.A.M.C., (T.F.) Temp. Maj. 1st Eastern General Hospital. France, 1918.
1908 [Ogg, D., M.A.] (Feb. 10, 1915). Paymaster Lt. R.N.R. Mediterranean, Adriatic, Red Sea.
1903 **Oldfield, L. C. F.,** M.A. (Mar. 3, 1915). Capt. 12th Rifle Brigade. France. Killed in action at Loos on Sept. 25, 1915.
1909 Oliver, C. H. (Oct. 31, 1914). Lt. King Edward's Horse. Lt. R.A.S.C. (S.R.).
1910 Oliver, G. M. (Mar. 30, 1915). Lt. Scots Guards (S.R.).
1913 **O'Rorke,* D. C.** Lt. 3rd, attd. 11th, K.R.R.C. France. *M.C.*, June 18, 1917. *D.* France, 1915. Killed in action on Mar. 24, 1918.
1919 Paget-Wilkes, A. H. (June 21, 1917). 2nd Lt. R.F.A. (T.F.). France. (Prisoner of war in Germany, Mar.–Dec. 1918.)
1909 Parry,* R. F. S., M.A. (June 8, 1915). Lt. 3rd, attd. 6th, Shropshire L.I. France, 1916–19.
1888 Paton, Rev. F. H. V., M.A. (Aug. 1917). Chaplain to the Forces (4th Class), A.I.F. France.

1911 **Pearson,* A. C.,** B.A. (Aug. 26, 1914). Capt. 9th R. Warwickshire Regt. Asst. Political Agent at Zakho in Mosul. Gallipoli, 1915; Mesopotamia, 1916–19. Killed on the frontier on Apr. 4, 1919.
1919 Pedder, J. T. (May 8, 1916). Pte. 1/8th Middlesex Regt. France, 1918.
1919 Pegrum, H. B. (Nov. 16, 1914). Lt. 9th Lancashire Fusiliers. Capt. General Staff, V Corps. Gallipoli, 1915; France, 1916–19. *M.C.*, Jan. 1, 1918. *D.* Gallipoli, 1916.
1892 Petit, Rev. O. S., M.A. (Aug. 12, 1915). Chaplain to the Forces (4th Class).
1906 Pickford, P., M.A. (Aug. 1914). Maj. 1/4th Oxf. & Bucks. Lt. Infty. (Lt.-Col.). Belgium, 1915; France, 1917; Italy, 1917–19. *D.S.O.*, Sept. 24, 1918. *M.C.*, Jan. 1, 1916. Italian Silver Medal for Valour. *D.* France, 1915; Italy, 1918.
1919 Pierce, H. F. (Nov. 23, 1917). Maj. Sanitary Corps., U.S. Army. France, 1918–19.
1904 **Pipe, A. D.** Pte. B.E.F. France. Killed in action on Oct. 26, 1917.
1903 Pope, H. M., B.M. (Sept. 9, 1914). Capt. R.A.M.C. (S.R.).
1906 **Popplewell,* H. B.,** B.A. (Apr. 1917). Capt. 3rd R. Irish Rifles (S.R.), attd. King's African Rifles. British, German, and Portuguese E. Africa. Killed in action in Portuguese E. Africa on July 22, 1918.
1908 **Prain,* T.,** B.A. (Serving Aug. 4, 1914). Lt. 1st Leicestershire Regt. France, 1914. Killed in action at Rue de Bois, near Armentières, on Oct. 22, 1914.
1911 Pringle, G. T., M.A. (Oct. 19, 1916). 2nd Lt. R.F.A.
1907 **Pringle,* N. D.,** M.A. (May 1915). Capt. 6th E. Yorkshire Regt. Gallipoli. Killed in action in Gallipoli, Aug. 7–11, 1915.
1885 Probert, W. G., B.A. (Serving Aug. 1914). Lt.-Col. R.A.S.C. France, 1914–15; Salonika, 1916; France, 1917–18. *O.B.E.* (Mil.).
1907 **Purdon, T. O.,** B.A. (Sept. 26, 1914). Capt. 7th Leinster Regt. France. *M.C.*, Sept. 26, 1916. Killed in action on Sept. 9, 1916.
1915 Purdy, J. K., B.A. Sergt. 10th R. Fusiliers, attd. Intelligence Corps. France.
1911 Puttock, J. S., B.A. (Oct. 31, 1914). Lt. 7th Devonshire Regt., attd. R. Defence Corps.
1919 Quin, G. P. C. (Dec. 4, 1916). Lce.-Cpl. R. Inniskilling Fusiliers. France and Belgium. *M.M.*
1900 Rankine, J. L. (Apr. 2, 1917). Capt. R.A.M.C. (Maj.).
1888 Ravenshaw, Rev. T., M.A. (Serving Aug. 4, 1914). Chaplain R.N., attd. R.M.A.
1914 Reah, G. P. G. (Nov. 1914). Capt. 8th E. Surrey Regt., attd. H.Q. 122nd Inf. Bde. France, 1916–17; Italy, 1917–18; France, 1918. *D.* Italy, 1918.
1919 Rees, G. (Nov. 16, 1915). Pte. 24th Field Amb., R.A.M.C. H.M.H.S. *Aquitania*, Mudros; France and Belgium. (Prisoner of war, May–Nov. 1918.)
1905 Reeves, R. M. E., M.A. (Mobilized Aug. 4, 1914). ‡Capt. 3rd Leicestershire Regt. France and Belgium, 1914–15; Gallipoli, 1915.
1899 Rew, H., B.C.L. (1914). Pte. 20th R. Fusiliers.
1912 Reynolds,* F. L. (Feb. 16, 1915). 2nd Lt. 11th Sherwood Foresters.
1913 Richardson,* W. R. (Sept. 30, 1914). ‡Lt. 21st W. Yorkshire Regt. France, 1915, 1916, 1917, 1918–19.
1913 Riggs, L. H. (July 22, 1918). Sergt. 11th Bn. 163rd Depot Bde.

1907 Rivett, A. C. D., B.Sc., M.A. Capt. Australian A.M.C.
1912 Robertson, R. A. F. S. (Dec. 6, 1915). Lt. R.A.S.C. Salonika.
1913 Robinson, B. S. (Dec. 15, 1914). Lt. 1st Bn. Canadian E.F. Lt. D.C.L.I. Capt. M.G.C. France.
1919 Robinson, J. W. (Aug. 11, 1917). Pte. 1st H.A.C. 2nd Lt. Res. of Officers (on demobilization). France.
1906 Rogers,* G. S., B.A. (Serving Aug. 4, 1914). Maj. 2/50th Kumaon Rifles, Indian Army. France, 1914–15; India.
1919 Roper, D. (Nov. 1915). ‡Warrant Schoolmaster R.N. Dover Patrol, 1916.
1910 Rosedale,* W. O. P., M.A. Cameroons E.F. W. Africa.
1901 Rowe, M., B.A. (Jan. 20, 1916). Cpl. 1/3rd Northumberland Field Amb. France and Belgium. *M.M.*, Feb. 1918.
1912 **Rutherford,* R. B.** (Aug. 22, 1914). Capt. 6th Queen's (R. W. Surrey Regt.). France. Killed in action at Ovillers la Boisselle on July 3, 1916.
1895 Ryland, A. (July 8, 1918). Pte. R.A.M.C.
1904 Rylett, S. H. (Mobilized Aug. 1914). Capt. 17th London Regt., empld. Ministry of Munitions.
1908 Sanctuary,* W. T., B.A. (Sept. 23, 1914). Capt. 8th Suffolk Regt.
1914 **Sant, W. W.** Y.M.C.A., Egypt. Died in Egypt in June, 1917.
1915 Sarson, Rev. A. W., M.A. (June 12, 1916). Chaplain to the Forces (4th Class).
1911 **Sculthorpe,* W. V.,** B.A. (Nov. 22, 1915). 2nd Lt. 22nd London Regt. (The Queen's). France and Belgium. Killed in action at Messines on June 8, 1917.
1896 **Sellman, E. N. N.,** M.A. (Apr. 16, 1915). Lt. 3rd Gloucestershire Regt., attd. 5th Oxf. & Bucks. Lt. Infty. France. Killed in action on Apr. 4, 1918.
1904 Shaw, F. A. (Sept. 19, 1914). Lt. Cameronians.
1905 Sheppard, Rev. F. L., M.A. (June 27, 1917). Chaplain to the Forces (4th Class). France.
1902 Shewell, Rev. M. W., M.A. (Mobilized Aug. 1914). Chaplain to the Forces (4th Class) (C.F. 2nd Class). France and Belgium. *D.* France, 1917.
1919 Short, W. P. (June 10, 1915). Lt. 2/6th N. Staffordshire Regt. France.
1908 Sinclair, J. H., M.A. (May 11, 1917). Capt. U.S. Inf., Intelligence Section. France and Germany, 1918–19.
1911 Single,* H. S., M.A. (June 29, 1915). Lt. 8th E. Surrey Regt.
1888 Smith, Rev. E. F., M.A. (Serving Aug. 4, 1914). Chaplain to the Forces (4th Class), attd. 4th Oxf. & Bucks. Lt. Infty.
1914 **Smith,* F. F.** (Nov. 2, 1914). Lt. 4th Hussars. France. Killed in action on Nov. 28, 1917.
1919 Smith, G. M. (Aug. 1917). 3rd Clerk R.A.F.
1911 Smith, H. A., M.A. (Aug. 15, 1914). ‡Lt. 2nd Oxf. & Bucks. Lt. Infty. France and Belgium. *M.C.*, Dec. 2, 1918.
1904 **Smyth, J.** (Serving Aug. 4, 1914). Capt. 2nd Lancashire Fusiliers. France and Belgium. Killed in action at Pilkem on July 8, 1915.
1912 Somers-Smith, E. (Aug. 15, 1914). Capt. R.E. (S.R.). France. *D.* France, 1917.
1896 Sparrow, R. B. (Oct. 29, 1914). Lt. S. Wales Borderers, attd. M.G.C.

1911 Spurrell,* W. J., B.A. (Sept. 2, 1914). Maj. 9th Norfolk Regt. (Lt.-Col.). France, 1915–16, 1917–18. *D.S.O.*, Sept. 16, 1918. *M.C.*, Nov. 14, 1916. *D.* France, 1916, 1918.

1919 Stallard-Penoyre, S. B. (Apr. 12, 1917). Midshipman R.N., H.M.S. *Marlborough.* Grand Fleet.

1904 Stanford, E. F. (1914). ‡2nd Lt. R.F.A.

1903 Stanger, G., B.M. (June 1915). Capt. R.A.M.C. France, 1915–19.

1914 Stansbie, E. H. (Jan. 17, 1916). Capt. Special Lists. *D.* § Aug. 1918.

1912 Steel,* F., B.A. (Aug. 15, 1914). Capt. 3rd Essex Regt. Acting Maj. R.A.F. France, 1915. *O.B.E.* (Mil.). *D.* France, 1915; § Mar. 1918.

1919 Steinthal, L. R. (Mar. 1917). Lt. 129th B.A.C., 27th Div., R.F.A. France, Belgium, Salonika.

1911 **Stephenson,* D. P.** (1915). 2nd Lt. N. Staffordshire Regt. France. Died in hospital at Boulogne on May 24, 1915, of wounds received in action.

1902 Stevens, J. R., M.A. (Feb. 8, 1915). Capt. I.A.R.O., Supply and Transport Corps. Egypt.

1896 Stewart-Wallace, J. S., M.A. (Nov. 1914). Lt.-Col. R.A.O.C. A.D. of Ordnance Services. France. *D.* France.

1906 **Styer,* W. H.,** B.A. (Aug. 8, 1914). ‡2nd Lt. 19th London Regt. France. Accidentally killed at Blandugue on Nov. 3, 1916.

1919 Sudbury, E. R. (Jan. 10, 1916). ‡Lt. 13th York & Lancaster Regt. France.

1913 Surridge,* S. O., B.A. (Oct. 9, 1914). Capt. 1/5th York & Lancaster Regt. (Adjt.). France. *M.C.*, Feb. 4, 1918.

1890 Sutton, F. F., M.A. (Aug. 23, 1915). 2nd Lt. Unattached List, T.F., St. Lawrence School O.T.C.

1910 **Sutton, G. N.** (Aug. 1914). 2nd Lt. R.F.A. France. Died on Oct. 14, 1916, of illness contracted while on active service.

1902 **Swallow, L. J.,** B.A. (June 14, 1915). Lt. 11th N. Staffordshire Regt. France and Belgium. Missing, presumed killed in action on July 31, 1917.

1919 Sykes, G. (Apr. 7, 1917). ‡2nd Lt. K.O.Y.L.I. Balkans, France.

1910 Symes,* G. G. H., M.A. (Mobilized Aug. 3, 1914). Lt. R.G.A. (T.F.). France, 1916–19.

1912 Tate, A. L., B.A. (Aug. 23, 1914). ‡Lt. 1st R. W. Kent Regt. India, Mesopotamia, France.

1919 Taylor, F. S. (Apr. 20, 1917). Pte. H.A.C. France.

1903 Thomas, Rev. A. F. W., M.A. (May 1918). Chaplain to the Forces (4th Class), attd. 16th Devonshire Regt. France.

1919 Thomas, J. B. (Jan. 28, 1916). Cpl. R.A.M.C., attd. 37th General Hospital. Salonika.

1897 **Thomas, P. E.,** B.A. (1915). ‡2nd Lt. R.G.A. France. Killed in action on Apr. 9, 1917.

1919 Thomas, R. H. (Sept. 11, 1914). Maj. R.E. Belgium and France, 1914–19. *M.C.*, Jan. 1, 1917. *D.* France, 1916.

1912 Thompson,* J. F. (Apr. 22, 1916). Lt. 3rd Dragoon Guards (S.R.). Temp. Capt. attd. Tank Corps. France, S. Russia. *O.B.E.* (Mil.). *D.* S. Russia, 1919.

1919 Tobin, H. J. (Dec. 1915). ‡Lt. M.G.C. France, 1917–19.

1919 Tomsen, J. H. N. (Jan. 8, 1916). Lce.-Cpl. R.E. Salonika, Macedonia, Turkey.

1919 Townley, G. F. (Sept. 9, 1914). Sergt. 4th Northamptonshire Regt. ‡2nd Lt..Bedfordshire Regt. (on demobilization). Gallipoli, Egypt.

1909 Triefus,* P., B.A. (Aug. 6, 1914). ‡Capt. and Adjt. R.F.A. France and Belgium, 1914–18. *M.C.*, June 3, 1918.

1920 Tucker, F. G. (Oct. 13, 1915). ‡Lt. D.C.L.I. France, 1916; India, 1917–19.

1908 Tunbridge, W. S., B.A. (Mobilized Aug. 4, 1914). Lt. R.F.A. (T.F.). (Resigned.)

1920 Turner, S. L. (Dec. 20, 1915). Lt. R.G.A. France.

1900 Ure, S. N., M.A. (Jan. 11, 1915). ‡Lt. 65th Coy., M.G.C. Gallipoli, Imbros, 1915–16; France, 1916; Salonika, 1917–19. *M.C.*, Jan. 1, 1919.

1907 Vaughan-Stevens,* D. L., B.A. (Sept. 21, 1916). Capt. Special Service Officer, Hyderabad I.S. Lancers, Indian Army. Palestine and Syria, 1918.

1914 Venn, R. T., B.A. (Mar. 25, 1915). Lt. 19th Middlesex Regt. France, 1916–19; Italy, 1917–18; Germany, 1919. *D.* Italy, 1918.

1912 Wainwright,* C. B.(Serving Aug. 4, 1914). Capt. 27th Bde., R.F.A. France, 2 years.

1906 Wall, B. E., B.M. (Jan. 12, 1915). Capt. R.A.M.C.

1920 Walton, H. B. (1915). Lt. R.G.A. France, Gibraltar.

1900 Warner, S. A., M.A. (1914). ‡2nd Lt. 9th Essex Regt. France. *M.C.*, Mar. 26, 1918.

1894 Warren, C. R., B.C.L., M.A. (1915). ‡2nd Lt. Devonshire Regt. Lt. Labour Corps.

1909 Watkins, Rev. W. E., M.A. (Mar. 31, 1916). Chaplain to the Forces (4th Class).

1913 Watson,* O. E., B.A. (Sept. 29, 1914). ‡2nd Lt. 7th Middlesex Regt. France and Belgium. *M.M.*, June 1917.

1907 **Watson, O. H.** (May 30, 1917). 2nd Lt. 8th London Regt. (Post Office Rifles). Belgium. Missing, believed killed in action, Aug. 1917.

1919 Weatherill, J. (June 20, 1917). Pte. 52nd W.Yorkshire Regt., afterwards Flight Cadet R.A.F.

1914 **Weatherill, W. B.** (Apr. 1916). ‡2nd Lt. Loyal N. Lancashire Regt. France. Presumed killed in action at Givenchy on June 17, 1918.

1913 West, G. A., M.A. (Apr. 10, 1917). ‡2nd Lt. 435th Siege Batt., R.G.A. France. *M.M.*

1919 West, J. D. F. (Aug. 11, 1914). ‡2nd Lt. 1/9th Middlesex Regt. Lt., Flying Officer, R.A.F. India, Egypt.

1892 Whitelocke, R. H. A., Hon. M.A. (Mobilized Aug. 4, 1914). Lt.-Col. R.A.M.C. (T.F.)

1895 Wigan, E. C. (Sept. 14, 1916). Lt. R. Defence Corps.

1905 Wilding,* T. S., M.A. (Aug. 26, 1914). Major 4th Loyal N. Lancashire Regt., attd. M.G.C. France (with 63rd (R.N.) Div.).

1910 Williams, H. L., M.A. (Aug. 6, 1915). Lt. and Adjt., 'P' Siege Park, XV Corps., R.A.S.C. France and Belgium, 1917–19.

1899 Williams, S. F., B.A. (Feb. 1917). Lt. 1st (Res. Garr.) Bn. Worcestershire Regt. (Capt.).

1909 Williams, V. E. G., B.C.L., M.A. (June 16, 1915). Lt. 4th Yorkshire Regt. France and Belgium, 1916–19.

1894 Williams, Rev. W. C. B., B.A. (Oct. 10, 1914). Chaplain to the Forces (4th Class), attd. 4th Northumberland Fusiliers.

1909 **Wilmot, P. D.** (Dec. 4, 1915). Lt. 4th, attd. 12th, R. Sussex Regt. France. Killed in action on Apr. 25, 1918.

1911 Wilson, F. P., B.Litt. (Mar. 10, 1915). Lt. 14th R. Warwickshire Regt. France.

1920 Wilson, R. T. (Apr. 28, 1918). 2nd Lt. Air Service, U.S. Army.

1913 Wilson, W. F. P. (Sept. 4, 1914). ‡2nd Lt. 8th Hampshire Regt. (T.F. Res.). France.

1906 **Winterbotham,* C. W.,** B.A. (Sept. 1914). Lt. 1/5th Gloucestershire Regt. Belgium and France. *D.* France, 1916. Killed in action near Ovillers la Boisselle on Aug. 27, 1916.

Wise, G. E. F. (Dec. 15, 1914). Lt. 7th R. Warwickshire Regt. France. Killed in action on June 4, 1916.

1899 Wood, H. J., M.A. (Dec. 1915). Lt. Border Regt., empld. War Office.

1908 **Woodhouse, G. S.** (Oct. 17, 1914). 2nd Lt. R.F.A. France. Killed in action on Oct. 13, 1915.

1915 Woodruff, E. P., B.A. (Aug. 24, 1917). Capt. Field Artillery, U.S. Army (Maj.).

1904 Worthington, G. J., B.A. (Serving Aug. 4, 1914). Capt. 5th N. Staffordshire Regt. France. *D.* France, 1916.

1919 Wright, B. A. (Sept. 20, 1914). Pte. R.M.L.I. Gallipoli, 1915.

1911 **Wright,* S. K.** (Oct. 17, 1914). Lt. 8th W. Riding Regt. Gallipoli. Killed in action, Aug. 7–11, 1915.

1899 Wrottesley, F. J., B.A. (Serving Aug. 4, 1914). Maj. R.F.A., empld. Ministry of National Service. France. *D.* France, 1915.

1911 Yates, S., B.A. (June 27, 1917). 'Sergt. R.A.M.C., attd. 163rd Field Hospital. France, Germany.

1919 Yonge, C. M. (July 2, 1918). 2nd Lt. Yorkshire Regt.

1901 Young, O. L., B.A. (May 31, 1915). Capt. R. Marines.

1908 Young,* R. de M., B.A. 2nd Lt. Lagos Coy., Nigerian Land Contingent.

ALL SOULS COLLEGE

1911 Abel Smith, L. R., M.A. (Dec. 20, 1915). Lt. 5th Grenadier Guards. France and Belgium, 1916, 1917.

1892 Amery, L. C. M. S., M.A. (Oct. 6, 1914). Hon. Capt. 14th R. Warwickshire Regt. and Intelligence Corps. Temp. Lt.-Col. General List. G.S.O. 1, War Office. Belgium, France, 1914–15; Balkans, 1915; Dardanelles, 1915; Salonika, 1916; Supreme War Council, Versailles, 1917–18. Serbian Order of the White Eagle (4th Class) (with swords). Officier, Greek Order of the Redeemer.

1908 **Anderson, G. R. L.,** B.A. Lt. 3rd, attd. 1st, Cheshire Regt. (Capt.). France and Belgium, 1914. *D.* France, 1914. Killed in action near Hooge on Nov. 8, 1914.

1897 **Asquith, R.,** M.A. (Dec. 1914). Lt. 3rd Grenadier Guards. France. *D.* France, 1916. Killed in action in Battle of Somme on Sept. 15, 1916.

1912 **Bath,* J. E. W.** (Aug. 29, 1914). Capt. 5th R. Berkshire Regt. France. Killed in action on Dec. 22, 1915.

1903 [Bell, K. N., M.A.] (Aug. 3, 1914). Lt. 99th Siege Batt., R.G.A. (Maj.). France and Belgium. *M.C.*, Dec. 17, 1917.

1902 Butler, H. B., M.A. (Oct. 1, 1914). Capt. Inns of Court O.T.C., attd. Home Office. *C.B.*

1889 Chaytor, Rev. H. J., M.A. (Sept. 1914). Chaplain to the Forces (4th Class), attd. Devon Fortress R.E. (T.F.) (Chaplain, 3rd Class). France, 1916–17.

1887 Chelmsford, Lord, M.A., *G.C.M.G.*, *G.C.S.I.*, *G.C.I.E.* (Aug. 5, 1914). Viceroy of India. Capt. 4th Dorsetshire Regt. India. *G.B.E.*

1908 [Clark, G. N., M.A.] (Aug. 1914). Lt. 8th London Regt. (Post Office Rifles) (Capt.). France. (Prisoner of war, May 1916.)

1907 Cowgill,* J. V., B.A. (Mar. 5, 1915). Lt. 4th Sherwood Foresters, attd. 4th Div. Signal Coy., R.E. France, 1916–19. *M.C.*, Aug. 16, 1917. *D.* France, 1918.

1898 Craster, H. H. E., M.A., D.Litt. (Mar. 28, 1917). Lt. Special Lists, empld. War Office (Intelligence Directorate).

1906 [Cruttwell, C. R. M. F., M.A.] (Aug. 19, 1914). Capt. 1/4th R. Berkshire Regt., attd. General Staff, War Office (Mil. Intelligence). France and Belgium, 1915.

1894 **Cunliffe, Sir F. H. E., Bt.,** M.A. (Dec. 1914). Maj. 13th Rifle Brigade. France. Killed in action in the Battle of the Somme on July 10, 1916.

1897 de Zulueta,* F., M.A., D.C.L. (Dec. 30, 1914). Capt. 2nd Worcestershire Regt. France, 1918–19.

1908 Faber, G. C., M.A. (Oct. 1914). Capt. 8th London Regt. (Post Office Rifles) (Maj.). France and Belgium, 1917–18.

1902 Greene, W. A., M.A. (Nov. 1914). Capt., temp. Maj., 2/1st Bucks. Bn. Oxf. & Bucks. Lt. Infty. G.S.O. 2. France, Italy. *O.B.E.* (Mil.). *M.C.*, Jan. 1, 1918. Cavalier, Order of the Crown of Italy. Croix de Guerre.

1900 Grundy, W. M., M.A. (Serving Aug. 4, 1914). Lt. Unattached List, T.F., Roysse's School O.T.C.

1912 Hancock, C. V., M.A. (Sept. 20, 1915). Lt. 4th Oxf. & Bucks. Lt. Infty., attd. M.G.C. France.

1881 Henson, Rt. Rev. H. H., D.D. (Serving Aug. 4, 1914). Chaplain to the Forces (1st Class).

1904 **Hulton, A. E. G.,** M.A. (Sept. 14, 1914). ‡Lt. A.S.C. France and Belgium, 1915. Died on June 6, 1915, of wounds received at St. Jean, near Ypres, on Apr. 25, 1915.

1894 Hunter, M. H. M., M.A. (Aug. 1914). ‡Capt. 23rd R. Fusiliers. France, 1916–18; Germany, 1919.

1914 Kenney, H. B. F. (May 6, 1915). Lt. 4th, attd. 8th, R. Berkshire Regt. France, 1916, 1917–18.

1907 Lawrence, T. E., B.A. (Oct. 1914). Col. Special Lists. Egypt and Arabia. *C.B. D.S.O.*, May 13, 1918. Croix de Chevalier de la Légion d'Honneur. Croix de Guerre. Italian Silver Medal for Military Valour. *D.* Egypt, 1915; Hedjaz, 1918.

1902 Legh, A. H. (Aug. 5, 1916). Lt. Cheshire Regt. Staff-Lt. (3rd Class). France. *M.C.*, June 3, 1919.

1903 Lindsell, H. O., B.A. Nigerian Naval Contingent.

1903 Marsden, G., M.A. (Nov. 1915). Sub-Lt. R.N.V.R. H.M.S. *President.* North Sea. Order of the Sacred Treasure (5th Class).

1910 Meredith,* H. T. D., B.A. (Aug. 15, 1914). Capt. 4th King's (Liverpool Regt.), attd. Dept. of Aircraft Production. France, Aug. 1914. (Wounded and prisoner of war, Aug. 21, 1914.)

1911 **Neale, A. C.** (July 11, 1916). 2nd Lt. Cameronians, attd. 10th Bn. France and Belgium, 1917. Killed in action near Ypres on Aug. 1, 1917.

1904 **Radcliffe, J. D. H.,** B.C.L., M.A. (Aug. 5, 1914). Capt. 7th K.R.R.C. France and Belgium. Died on July 30, 1915, of wounds received in action near Hooge.

1875 [Reichel, Sir H. R., M.A.] (Serving Aug. 4, 1914). Capt. Unattached List, T.F., Bangor University O.T.C.

1907 **Shaw-Stewart, P. H.,** M.A. (Sept. 25, 1914). Lt.-Commdr. R.N.V.R. G.S.O. 3. France, Gallipoli, Salonika, France. Croix de Chevalier de la Légion d'Honneur. Croix de Guerre. Killed in action in France on Dec. 30, 1917.

1907 Somervell, D. B., B.A. (Aug. 4, 1914). Capt. 1/9th Middlesex Regt. (Staff-Captain 53rd Brigade, M.E.F.). India, 1914–17; Mesopotamia, 1917–19. *O.B.E.* (Mil.). *D.* Mesopotamia, 1918.

1911 **Stonex,* F. H. T.,** B.A. (June 1915). Lt. 4th R. Dublin Fusiliers. France. Died on Feb. 1, 1918, of illness contracted on active service.

1912 Sumner, B. H., M.A. (Aug. 15, 1914). Capt. 6th K.R.R.C., attd. War Office. France, 1914–17; Paris (Peace Conference), 1919. *D.* § Mar. 1919.

1914 Symes, C. L., B.A. (June 1917). 2nd Lt. 1st (Res. Garr.) Bn., Worcestershire Regt.

1908 Warris,* M. W., B.A. (Mobilized Aug. 1914). Capt. 9th (Cyclist) Hampshire Regt., attd. Labour Corps.

1897 Watkins, O. F., M.A. (1914). Lt.-Col. Director of Military Labour, E. African Command. E. Africa. *C.B.E.* (Mil.). *D.S.O.*, June 26, *D.* E. Africa, 1916, 1917.

1899 Wood, Hon. E. F. L., M.A., *M.P.* (Serving Aug. 4, 1914). Maj. Yorkshire Dragoons, empld. Ministry of National Service. France, 1915. *D.* France, 1916.

1893 Wood, Rev. J. D., M.A. (Jan. 1, 1917). Chaplain to the Forces (4th Class).

1908 Woodward, E. Ll., M.A. (Oct. 1914). Lt. R.F.A. Staff-Lt. (2nd Class), empld. Foreign Office. France, 1915–16; Salonika, 1916–18.

MAGDALEN COLLEGE

1919 Acheson-Lyle, A. M. (Jan. 12, 1917). ‡2nd Lt. 6th Shropshire L.I. France, 1918. (Prisoner of war in Germany, Mar.–Dec. 1918.)

1901 Ackers, C. P., M.A. (Sept. 9, 1914). Maj. VI Corps Troops, M.T. Coy., R.A.S.C. France, Belgium, and Germany. *D.* France, 1918 twice.

1909 Acland, L. H. D., B.A. (Aug. 25, 1914). ‡Capt. Special Bde., R.E. France, 1915–17. *M.C.*, Jan. 1, 1918.

1916 **Acworth, J. A.** (Apr. 26, 1917). 2nd Lt. 1/7th Worcestershire Regt. France. Died on Oct. 13, 1917, of wounds received at Passchendaele on Oct. 9.

Adams, G. H. C. (Sept. 1915). 2nd Lt. 3/4th Suffolk Regt. France, 1916. Killed in action at Les Bœufs on Nov. 1, 1916.

1911 Adams,* R. E. C., B.A. (Serving Aug. 4, 1914). Capt. 1st E. Surrey Regt. G.S.O. 3 (1916–17); Bde. Maj. (1917–19). France, Belgium, Egypt, Palestine. *M.C.*, Feb. 15, 1919. *D.* Egypt, 1916.

1894 Adams, W. G., B.A. (Mobilized Aug. 1914). Capt. 7th King's (Liverpool Regt.) (T.F.).

1898 Addison, J., B.A. (Aug. 6, 1914). Lt. Special Lists (Interpreter).

1907 Aitken, I. W., B.A. (Sept. 9, 1914). Lt. 6th Dragoon Guards. France and Belgium. *M.C.*, Jan. 18, 1918.

1907 Alexander, R. (Dec. 16, 1914). Capt. 11th The Black Watch, attd. M.G.C. France and Belgium. Croix de Guerre.

1919 Alington, A. F. (June 8, 1917). Lt. 5th Grenadier Guards. France, 1918; Germany, 1918–19.

1919 Alington, A. R. (Sept. 1914). ‡Lt. 6th Wiltshire Regt. (Capt.). France, 1915–18.

1907 **Alington, G. H.,** M.A. (May 5, 1915). 2nd Lt. 2/5th R. Sussex Regt. France. Killed in action in Aveluy Wood on Aug. 9, 1916.

1910 **Alington,* G. W. S.,** B.A. (Sept. 6, 1917). Cpl. 1/17th London Regt. France and Belgium. *M.M. with Bar.* Killed in action at Tournai on Nov. 9, 1918.

1872 Allanby, H. C. H., M.A. (Oct. 5, 1914). Maj. 3rd Seaforth Highlanders (Depot). *D.* § Feb. 1917.

1895 Allen, A. L. (Serving Aug. 4, 1914). Maj., temp. Staff Paymaster, A.P.D.

1875 Anderson, A. J., B.M., M.A. (Serving Aug. 4, 1914). Maj., Bt. Lt.-Col., temp. Lt.-Col., R.A.S.C.; A.D. of Supplies. Salonika. *D.* Salonika, 1916.

1919 Anderson, H. B. (May 27, 1915). Lt. 2/7th W. Yorkshire Regt. France.

1911 Anderson,* R. G. F., B.A. (Serving Aug. 4, 1914). Capt., Bt. Major, R. Welsh Fusiliers. N. Russia.

1911 Angas, L. L. B., M.A. (Aug. 1914). Capt. 1st, attd. 1/4th, Cheshire Regt. France, Italy. *M.C.*, Mar. 8, 1919. Belgian Croix de Guerre. *D.* France, 1918, 1919.

1908 Angas, R. F., B.A. (Sept. 1915). Lt. R.H.A. (S.R.). Lt. R.A.F., No. 1 T. Wireless School. France and Belgium, 1915–18. *D.* France, 1917.

1862 Anstice, Sir R. H., M.A., *K.C.B.* Hon. Col. R.E.

1900 Argles, R. M., B.A. (Dec. 22, 1914). Lt. 19th Divl. Train, R.A.S.C. France and Belgium.

1890 Armstrong, F. P., B.A. (Aug. 10, 1914). Commdr. R.N.V.R. (Motor Boat Service). *O.B.E.* (Mil.).

1919 Armstrong-Jones, R. O. L. (Jan. 1, 1918). 2nd Lt. R.F.A.

Arnold, T. S. (May 10, 1916). 2nd Lt. E. Surrey Regt., attd. 2/7th Lancashire Fusiliers. France and Belgium, 1917. Died on Oct. 11, 1917, of wounds received in action at Passchendaele.

1912 Ashley,* A. H. E. (Aug. 1914). Capt. Coldstream Guards. France and Belgium.

1885 Ashley, W. W. (Oct. 11, 1914). Hon. Capt. Res. of Officers, Lt.-Col. 20th King's (Liverpool Regt.). (Resigned Commission through ill health.)

1890 Aspinall, A. E., B.A. Anti-Aircraft Corps, R.N.V.R. *C.M.G.*

1909 Asquith, C., M.A. (Nov. 18, 1914). Capt. 3/16th London Regt. (Queen's Westminster Rifles), empld. Ministry of Labour.

1893 [Atkinson, C. T., M.A.] (Serving Aug. 4, 1914). Capt. O.U.O.T.C., attd. Imp. General Staff, War Office (1914–15), attd. Mil. Branch, Hist. Section, Committee of Imp. Defence (1915–19).

1907 Atkinson,* R. L., M.A. (Mobilized Aug. 1914). Capt. 5th Queen's (R. W. Surrey Regt.). India, 1914–15; Mesopotamia, 1915–16; France and Belgium, 1917. *M.C.*, July 18, 1917.

1908 **Babington, T. Z. D.,** B.A. (1914). Capt. I.A.R.O. India. Died on Oct. 16, 1918.

1890 Bailey, Hon. H. C. (Mar. 19, 1916). Lt. General List (T.F. Res.).

1901 **Bailey, R. N. M.,** M.A. (Sept. 1914). Lt. E. Riding of Yorkshire Yeomanry. Egypt and Palestine, 1915–17. Died at Cairo on Dec. 1, 1917, of wounds received on Nov. 14 at Naame.

1911 Baillieu,* C. L., M.A. (Dec. 1915). Maj., D.A.A.G., Australian Flying Corps. *O.B.E.* (Mil.).

1905 Baker, K. W. H. (Oct. 5, 1916). 2nd Lt. R.G.A.

1898 Baker, Sir R. L., B.A. (Mobilized Aug. 4, 1914). Lt.-Col. Dorset Yeomanry and Tank Corps. Egypt, Gallipoli, Palestine, France. *D.S.O.*, Jan. 1, 1918; *Bar*, Mar. 5, 1918. *D.* Palestine, 1918.

1908 **Balfour,* I. B.,** B.A. (Nov. 24, 1914). Lt. 14th R. Scots, attd. 1st K.O. Scottish Borderers. Gallipoli. Killed in action in Gallipoli on June 28, 1915.

1898 Balfour-Browne, V. R., B.A. (Nov. 8, 1915). Lt. attd. 5th R. Fusiliers. (Maj. whilst D.R.O., No. 2 Dist., 1916–18.) *D.* § Feb. 1917, Aug. 1917.

1893 Balfour-Browne, W. A. F., M.A. (June 1916). Capt. Sanitary Service, R.A.M.C. (T.F. Res.).

1907 Barnes,* H. D. (Dec. 6, 1916). 2nd Lt. R.A.S.C. *D.* § Mar. 1919.

1907 Barnes,* T. D., B.A. (Nov. 19, 1914). Capt. and Adjt. 25th D.A.C., R.F.A. France and Belgium, 1915–19. *D.* France, 1919.

1899 Barnett, G. A., B.A. (Nov. 12, 1914). Lt. Hertfordshire Yeomanry. (Maj. whilst D.A.A.G., G.H.Q., E.E.F.) Mesopotamia and Egypt, 1915–18. *M.B.E.* (Mil.).

Barratt, J. L. (Sept. 27, 1916). ‡2nd Lt. 13th King's (Liverpool Regt.). France and Belgium. Killed in action near Zonnebeke on Sept. 27, 1917.

1904 Barton, W. A., B.A. (May 12, 1915). Capt. 19th King's (Liverpool Regt.). Temp. Capt. Class F.F., attd. G.H.Q. France. *D.* France, 1916.

1900 Bassett, J. C., B.A. (Mobilized Aug. 1914). Lt.-Col. 5th Hampshire Regt. India, 1914–15. *D.* § Feb. 1917.

1907 Bate, L. R. A., B.A. (Oct. 27, 1914). Capt. 12th K.R.R.C. Capt. General List. *D.* § Aug. 1918, Aug. 1919.

1913 Bateson, W. L., B.A. (Apr. 21, 1915). Capt. 58th Divl. Signal Coy., R.E. France. *M.C.*, June 3, 1918.

1919 Bathurst, Hon. B. L. (Mar. 1918). 2nd Lt. R.G.A.

1893 Bayley-Worthington, A. B., B.A. (Mobilized Aug. 1914). Maj. S. Nottinghamshire Hussars. Maj. attd. H.Q. 3rd Canadian Divl. Artillery. France, 1917–18.

1904 Bazett, H. C., D.M. (Mobilized Aug. 4, 1914). Capt. R.A.M.C. Capt. R.A.F. Medical Service, attd. No. 14 General Hospital. France. *O.B.E.* (Mil.). *M.C.*, Jan. 14, 1916. *D.* France, 1915 twice.

1898 Beachcroft, P. M., M.A. (Mar. 1, 1916). Lt. R.F.A. Capt., temp. Staff Maj., Air Ministry, attd. R.A.F. France, 1916–17. *O.B.E.* (Mil.). *D.* § Air Ministry, Jan. 1919.

1888 Beckwith, E. G. A., M.A. (1914). 2nd Lt. Imperial Services College O.T.C.

1903 Beevor, C. F., B.M., M.A. (Apr. 9, 1917). Lt. R.A.M.C.

1898 **Bell, H. R.,** B.A. (Sept. 2, 1915). 2nd Lt. Motor Machine Gun Service. Maj. Tank Corps. France. *D.* France, 1918. Killed in action in France on Sept. 3, 1918.

1908 **Benison, E. W.,** B.A. (Mar. 1915). 2nd Lt. R.G.A. Died on Aug. 13, 1915, of illness contracted on active service.

1913 Bennett,* B. H. (Jan. 29, 1915). Capt. 8th Rifle Brigade, empld. Ministry of Munitions.

1911 Bennett, G., B.A. (Nov. 13, 1914). Capt. Special Lists. France. *D.* France, 1918.

1902 Bennett, G. G. M., B.A. (Sept. 3, 1914). ‡2nd Lt. 4th R. Irish Rifles. Acting Maj. 3rd Bn. M.G.C., Northern Div. France and Belgium, 1915–16, 1917–19; Germany, 1919. *M.C.*, June 3, 1919. *D.* France, 1918.

1904 Bennett, J. H., B.A. (Sept. 1914). ‡Lt. 4th R. Warwickshire Regt. France.

1894 **Beresford, P. W.,** M.A. (Mobilized Aug. 1914). Lt.-Col. 3rd London Regt. (R. Fusiliers). France and Belgium. *D.S.O.*, July 18, 1917. *D.* France, 1916. Killed in action on Oct. 26, 1917.

1919 Berkeley, R. G. W. (Feb. 1917). Lt. Westminster Dragoons, attd. M.G.C. France, Belgium, Palestine, Germany.

1913 Berners,* G. H. (Aug. 15, 1914). Lt. 3rd Norfolk Regt.

1902 Bethell, Hon. R. (Aug. 15, 1914). Capt. 3rd Scots Guards (S.R.).

1919 Bickmore, A. F. (Dec. 17, 1917). 2nd Lt. 52nd D.A.C., R.F.A. France.

1896 **Birchall, A. P. D.** (Serving Aug. 4, 1914). Capt. R. Fusiliers. Lt.-Col. 4th Canadian Infantry. France and Belgium, 1915. *D.* France, 1915. Killed in action on the Pilkem Ridge, Ypres, on Apr. 23, 1915.

1903 **Birchall, E. V. D.,** B.A. (Mobilized Aug. 1914). Capt. Bucks. Bn. Oxf. & Bucks. Lt. Infty. France, 1915–16. *D.S.O.*, Aug. 25, 1916. *D.* France, 1916. Died on Aug. 10, 1916, of wounds received in action at Pozières on July 23.

1912 Bird, A. H. (Sept. 4, 1914). ‡Capt. 1st Lincolnshire Regt., D.A.A. and Q.M.G. Gallipoli, 1915; France, 1916, 1917.

1905 Birkbeck, B. (Serving Aug. 4, 1914). Maj. Coldstream Guards, attd. Guards M.G. Regt. France and Belgium. *D.S.O.*, Jan. 1, 1918. *M.C.*, June 3, 1916. *D.* France, 1917.

1873 Blagrove, H. J. (Re-employed 1916). Lt.-Col. and Bt.-Col. 13th Hussars, Col. Commandant P. of W. Camp. *C.B.* *C.B.E.* *D.* § Mar. 1918.

1893 Blaine, G. (Aug. 15, 1914). Capt. 3rd, attd. 1st, Somerset L.I. France. *M.C.*, Jan. 1, 1917.

1899 Blair, J. M. (Serving Aug. 4, 1914). Lt.-Col. Gordon Highlanders (Mil. Attaché at Petrograd). Russia. *C.M.G.* *D.S.O.*, Jan. 1, 1917. Order of St. Stanislas (2nd Class). Order of St. Vladimir (4th Class) (with Swords and Bow). *D.* § Jan. 1917; Russia, 1918, 1919.

1897 Blake, M. B., B.A. (Serving Aug. 4, 1914). Capt. R.A.F.

1911 Blake, M. C., B.A. (1917). 1st Lt. U.S. Artillery. France.

1883 **Blakeway, Rev. P. J. T.,** M.A. (Sept. 1914). Chaplain (1st Class), attd. London Mounted Bde. Egypt. Died of heat-stroke at Ismailia, Egypt, on June 16, 1915.

1919 Blenkinsop, E. S. (Oct. 30, 1914). Lt. 2/6th Gloucestershire Regt. (Capt.). France.

1888 Blood, J. N., B.C.L., M.A. (Mar. 19, 1915). Maj. R. Defence Corps.

1895 Blunt, J. W., M.A. (Mobilized Aug. 1914). Capt. Leicestershire R.H.A. (Resigned.)

1919 Boase, T. S. R. (Apr. 8, 1917). Lt. 2/4th Oxf. & Bucks. Lt. Infty. (Capt.). France. *M.C.*, Sept. 16, 1918.

1914 Bobrinskoy, Count A. (Aug. 11, 1914). ‡Lt. Hussar Regt., Russian Guards. E. Prussia, 1914; Poland, 1915; Russia, 1915–17. Order of St. Stanislas (3rd Class). *D.* Russian Dispatches, 1915.

1878 Bogle-Smith, S., *C.B.* (Oct. 31, 1914). Col. 4th Base Remount Depot. France. *C.B.E.* (Mil.). *D.* France, 1919.

1902 **Bonham-Carter, G.,** B.A. (Mobilized Aug. 1914). Capt. and Adjt. Q.O. Oxfordshire Hussars. France and Belgium, 1914–15. *D.* France, 1915. Killed in action near Ypres on May 14, 1915.

1914 Bonner, G. H. (Nov. 27, 1914). 2nd Lt. 7th S. Staffordshire Regt. Lt. 'K' A.A. Batt., R.F.A. France, 1915–16.

1919 Boothby, R. J. G. (May 1918). 2nd Lt. Scots Guards (S.R.).

1906 Bosville Macdonald, G. M. Driver A.S.C. O.C., B.R.C. Stores Transport.

1901 Bouch, T. (Aug. 1914). Maj. 3rd County of London Yeomanry. France.

1902 Boulenger, C. R., B.A. (Jan. 5, 1915). Lt. 8th Lancashire Fusiliers (Capt.). Egypt, 1915, 1918–19; Gallipoli, 1915; Palestine, 1917.

1917 Boulter, S. (Jan. 30, 1918). 2nd Lt. 4th Bn. Tank Corps. France. *M.C.*, Feb. 15, 1919.

1885 **Boulton, C. P.,** B.A., *D.S.O.* (Serving Aug. 4, 1914). Maj. 4th (Res.) Bedfordshire Regt. Died on Feb. 24, 1916.

1920 Bower, L. T. (Jan. 15, 1917). Lt. 3rd Coldstream Guards. France, 1917–19.

1912 Bowhill, A. H., B.A. (Mobilized Aug. 1914). Capt. and Adjt. 10th (Lovat's Scouts Bn.) Q.O. Cameron Highlanders. Gallipoli, Egypt, Macedonia, France. *D.* France, 1919.

Bowring, J. G. C. (Sept. 1916). Lt. 2nd S. Wales Borderers. France. Died on Nov. 22, 1917, of wounds received in action at Cambrai.

1894 [Boycott, A. E., B.Sc., D.M.] (June 25, 1917). Capt., Bt.-Maj., R.A.M.C. *D.* § Aug. 1918.

1896 Boyle, R. C., M.A. (Mobilized Aug. 4, 1914). Capt. W. Somerset Yeomanry (Bde. Maj.). Gallipoli, 1915; Egypt, 1916–17; Palestine, 1917–18; France, 1918. *M.C.*, June 3, 1919. *D.* Egypt, 1916; Palestine, 1918.

1888 Bremridge, R. H., B.M., M.A. (Dec. 1, 1915). Maj. R.A.M.C. *O.B.E.* (Mil.). *D.* § Sept. 1917.

1911 Bridges,* E. E., M.A. (Sept. 14, 1914). Capt. 1/4th Oxf. & Bucks. Lt. Infty. (Capt. and Adjt.). France, 1915–17; Italy, 1918–19. *M.C.*, Jan. 1, 1917.

1912 Briscoe, R. G. (Aug. 24, 1916). Lt. Grenadier Guards. France and Belgium. *M.C.*, Sept. 26, 1917.

1912 Britten-Jones, E. (Sept. 30, 1914). Capt. R.A.M.C. (S.R.). India.

1919 Broadbent, J. G. (Oct. 25, 1916). Lt. 16th, attd. 9th, K.R.R.C. France, Belgium, from 1916.

1899 Brocklebank, R. H. R. (Serving Aug. 4, 1914). Capt., Acting Lt.-Col., 9th Lancers, attd. M.G.C. (D.A.A. and Q.M.G.). Egypt, Gallipoli, France, and Germany. *D.S.O.*, June 3, 1919. *D.* France, 1919.

1907 Brodie, B. C., B.A. (Oct. 1914). Capt. Surrey Yeomanry. Staff-Captain H.Q. 1st Highland Bde. (Capt. and Adjt. attd. 4th Gordon Highlanders, 1918–19). France. *M.C.*, Jan. 1, 1919; *Bar*, Mar. 8, 1919. *D.* France, 1918.

1881 Brodie, Sir B. V. S., M.A. (Mar. 12, 1916). 2nd Lt. Unattached List, T.F., Reigate Grammar School O.T.C.

1894 Brooke, T., M.A. (Aug. 1914). Maj. Q.O. Yorkshire Dragoons. France.

1891 Bros, H. A., B.A. (Re-employed May 1, 1916). Maj. R.A. (Res. of Officers), empld. Recruiting Duties.

1895 Brown, A. C., B.A. (Nov. 6, 1914). ‡Lt. 4th Q.O. Cameron Highlanders, attd. M.G.C. France, 1916–17.

1902 **Brown, E. F. M.,** B.A. (Feb. 1, 1916). Lt. 1st Hertfordshire Regt. France. Died on Jan. 8, 1918, of wounds received in action.

Brown, K. E. (Sept. 1914). Capt. 2/4th Oxf. & Bucks. Lt. Infty. France, 1915–18. *M.C.*, Oct. 20, 1916; *Bar*, June 18, 1917. Died as a prisoner on Apr. 13, 1918, of wounds received in action at St. Quentin on Mar. 21.

1898 Browne, J. G. (Serving Aug. 4, 1914). Maj., Bt. Lt.-Col., 14th Hussars. G.S.O. 1. France, Arabia. *C.M.G.* *D.S.O.*, Jan. 1, 1917. Order of the Nile (3rd Class). *D.* France, 1915, 1916, 1917; Hedjaz, 1918.

1919 Browne, P. A. (Sept. 18, 1916). ‡Lt. The Black Watch. India, Egypt, France, Mesopotamia.

1912 Browne,* W. L. F., M.A. (Dec. 16, 1914). Capt. 80th Batt., 5th Div., R.F.A. Belgium, France, Italy.

1889 Browning, F. H. (July 1, 1915). Lt.-Col. Special Lists. G.S.O. 1, War Office. *C.B.E.* (Mil.). Order of St. Anne (3rd Class). Officier de l'Ordre de la Couronne. *D.* § Feb. 1917.

1883 Brownrigg, C. E., M.A. (Sept. 1, 1916). 2nd Lt. Vol. Bn. Oxf. & Bucks. Lt. Infty.

1886 Budworth, Rev. R. T. D., M.A. (Oct. 26, 1914). 2nd Lt. Unattached List, T.F., Durham School O.T.C.

1908 Bulley, F. G. (June 19, 1916). 2nd Lt. R.A.S.C.

1886 Burges, F. (Serving Aug. 1914). Capt. Gloucestershire Regt., Res. of Officers, empld. under Sudan Government. Sudan.

1910 Burgess,* E. R., M.A. (1918). Egyptian Civil Service, attd. as Capt. to Palestine E.F. Palestine, 1918.

1908 Burgess,* R. E., B.A. (Mobilized Aug. 1914). Capt. 149th Bde., R.F.A., attd. War Office. France.

1892 Burnaby Atkins, J., M.A. (Mobilized 1914). Capt. 3rd S. Staffordshire Regt., Res. of Officers, empld. War Office. *D.* § Mar. 1919.

1895 Burnell, C. D., B.A. (Mobilized Aug. 1914). Maj., Acting Lt.-Col., 1/5th London Regt. (London Rifle Brigade). France and Belgium. *D.S.O.*, June 3, 1919. *D.* France, 1918.

1897 Burns, W. A. (Mobilized Aug. 1914). Maj. R.A.M.C. (T.F.).

1913 Burton,* G. S. M., B.A. (Jan. 21, 1915). Lt. 6th The Black Watch (T.F.). France. *M.C.*, Sept. 16, 1918.

1908 Busk,* J., B.A. (Mobilized Aug. 1914). Capt. Dorset Yeomanry. Gallipoli, Egypt, Palestine.

1919 Butler, L. T. (Aug. 2, 1914). Lt. 12th Bn. A.I.F. Egypt, Belgium, France.

1895 Butter, C. A. J. (Aug. 25, 1914). Capt. Scottish Horse. Col. R.A.F. Gallipoli, 1915. *O.B.E.* (Mil.). *D.* § Mar. 1918, June 1918, Aug. 1919.

1890 Buzzard, E. F., D.M. (Sept. 1915). Col. A.M.S. France, 1918.

1905 Byng-Stephens, F. G. R. (Nov. 1914). Capt. 12th Rifle Brigade (A.D.C.). France, 1915–17; Italy, 1917–18. *M.C.*, June 3, 1919.

Byron, C. J. (Oct. 1914). ‡2nd Lt. H.A.C. France. Killed in action at Beaumont Hamel on Jan. 10, 1917.

1911 **Cable,* G. P.** (Aug. 7, 1914). 2nd Lt. 2nd Rifle Brigade. France and Belgium. Killed in action at Fromelles on May 9, 1915.

1911 **Cadenhead,* G.** (Aug. 4, 1914). 2nd Lt. 2nd Q.O. Cameron Highlanders. France and Belgium, 1915. Killed in action at Ypres on May 10, 1915.

1886 Caldwell, Rev. W. H. McK., B.A. (Nov. 19, 1917). Chaplain to the Forces (4th Class).

1885 Campbell, A. J. (Mobilized Aug. 4, 1914). Maj. Arg. & Suth'd. Highlanders. France. *D.* France, 1915.

1910 Campbell, J. M. H., B.M. (Aug. 1916). Capt. R.A.M.C. Mesopotamia and Persia. *O.B.E.* (Mil.). *D.* Mesopotamia, 1918, 1919.

1909 **Campbell,* K. J.,** B.A. (Sept. 1914). 2nd Lt. 1/9th Arg. & Suth'd. Highlanders. France and Belgium. Killed in action near Ypres on May 10, 1915.

1913 Campbell,* Hon. L. S. (Sept. 1, 1914). Lt. R.F.A. (Capt.). France and Belgium. *M.C.*, June 10, 1915. *D.* France, 1919.

1909 Campbell, W. L. W., B.A. (June 22, 1916). Capt. 6th, attd. 1st, The Black Watch. *D.* § Aug. 1919.

1895 **Cardwell, H. B.** (Aug. 5, 1914). Lt. R.F.A. (Capt.). France. Died on Aug. 9, 1918, of wounds received in action.

1906 Cardwell,* R. McK., B.A. (Mobilized Aug. 1914). Capt. Sussex Yeomanry, attd. Lincolnshire Yeomanry. France and Belgium. *D.* France, 1916.

1901 Carlisle, K. M., B.A. (Mar. 10, 1918). 2nd Lt. R.F.A.

1911 Caröe,* O. K. K., M.A. (Aug. 29, 1914). Capt. 4th Queen's (R. W. Surrey Regt.). India.

1912 Carr,* J. L., B.A. (Serving Aug. 4, 1914). Capt. R. Berkshire Regt.
1895 [Carr, R.] (Oct. 12, 1914). Lt. Interpreter. Maj. King's African Rifles. Africa.
1904 Carr-Saunders, A. M., M.A. (Aug. 30, 1914). ‡Capt. R.A.S.C. France, Egypt, Palestine.
1912 **Carver,* F. M.** (Aug. 26, 1914). Lt. 8th Devonshire Regt. France. Killed in action at the Battle of Loos on Sept. 25, 1915.
1919 Carver, J. E. A. (Nov. 1, 1917). Midshipman R.N.V.R. Channel Patrol; Destroyer Flotilla, Grand Fleet.
1913 **Cash,* G. E.** (Oct. 5, 1914). Lt. 6th Loyal N. Lancashire Regt. France. Killed in action near Thiepval on Aug. 26, 1916.
1907 **Cattley,* C. F.** (Sept. 1914). Maj. 6th The Buffs (E. Kent Regt.) (Col.). *M.C.*, June 3, 1916. *D.* France, 1915. Killed in action at Cambrai on Nov. 30, 1917.
1908 **Cattley, G. W.** (1914). Nigerian Land Contingent. West Africa. Died of illness on Aug. 1, 1918.
1906 **Cave, T. B.** Sergt. Canadian Infantry. France and Belgium. (Recommended for a Commission on account of gallant service in action.) Killed in action on Nov. 11, 1916.
1908 Cavenagh,* J. B., B.M. (Nov. 18, 1915). Capt. H.Q. Douai Cadres, R.A.M.C. (Maj. R.A.M.C., attd. 113th Field Amb.). France, Belgium. *M.C.*, Sept. 17, 1917; *Bar*, Feb. 15, 1919.
1900 Cely-Trevilian, M. F., B.A. (Mobilized Aug. 1914). Maj. 1/1st W. Somerset Yeomanry. Gallipoli, Egypt.
1902 **Chamberlain, N. G.** (Sept. 1914). Lt. 6th R. Warwickshire Regt. Capt. Grenadier Guards. France and Belgium. Killed in action near Cambrai on Dec. 1, 1917.
1907 Chambers, R. S. (Sept. 26, 1914). Capt. 3rd Highland L.I., attd. R.E. (Signals). France and Belgium.
1899 **Chamier, F. C.,** M.A. 2nd Lt. Indian Light Horse. India. Died, July 1916.
1911 Chapman, E. F., B.A. (Dec. 1915). Lt. 20th R. Fusiliers, attd. 53rd R. Sussex Regt. (Capt.). France, 1916–17.
1893 Chapman, E. H., M.A. (Apr. 26, 1915). Capt. T.F. Res. (Maj. D.A.A.G.). France. *D.* France, 1918.
1895 Chapman, G. D. E. (Aug. 6, 1914). Lt. Special Lists. Staff-Lt. (1st Class) (Capt.). France. *D.* France, 1914.
1912 **Charlesworth, F. R.** (Mar. 1915). Lt., Acting Capt., Montgomeryshire Yeomanry, attd. 25th R. Welsh Fusiliers. Egypt, Palestine, France. Died on Sept. 19, 1918, of wounds received in action at Roussy (Hindenburg Line) on Sept. 18.
1907 Charrington, N. A. (July 16, 1915). Capt. 4th, attd. 7th, R. W. Kent Regt.
1887 [Chelmsford, Lord, M.A., *G.C.M.G., G.C.S.I., G.C.I.E.*] (Aug. 5, 1914). Capt. 4th Dorsetshire Regt. Viceroy of India. India. *G.B.E.*
1908 Cholmeley,* G. H., B.A. (Mobilized Aug. 1914). Capt. 5th London Regt. (London Rifle Brigade). Instructor, O.C.B. France and Belgium, 1914–15, 1915–16.
1912 **Cholmeley,* H. L.** (Sept. 1914). ‡Lt. The Border Regt. France, 1915, 1916. Killed in action at Beaumont Hamel on July 1, 1916.
1905 Christie,* B., B.A. (Serving Aug. 4, 1914). Capt. 32nd Sikh Pioneers, Indian Army, attd. 1/155th Indian Pioneers. India.

1903 Chute, Rev. A. W., M.A. (Mar. 1916). Chaplain to the Forces (4th Class), attd. 103rd Bde., R.F.A. France and Belgium, 1916–17; Italy, 1917–19. *O.B.E.* (Mil.). *D.* France, 1917; Italy, 1918, 1919.

1898 Chute, C. L., M.A. (Sept. 15, 1914). Capt. 16th Middlesex Regt. Capt. General List. Bde. Maj. 164th Inf. Bde. France. *M.C.*, Mar. 8, 1919.

1903 Clarke, A. C., B.A. (Aug. 1914). 2nd Lt. 3rd D.C.L.I. (until Jan. 1915). Maj., Squadron Commdr., R.A.F. France. *D.* § Mar. 1918.

1889 Clarke, A. H. P. (Dec. 3, 1914). Lt. R.F.A. (Capt.).

1910 Clarke, D. A., M.A. (Sept. 19, 1914). Capt. and Adjt. 5th S. Staffordshire Regt. *M.B.E.* (Mil.). *D.* § Aug. 1918.

1899 Clarke, O. B., B.A. (Feb. 15, 1915). Lt. R.F.A. (T.F.) (Capt. and Adjt.). Egypt, Palestine. *D.* § Mar. 1918; Palestine, 1919.

1902 Clarke, W. F. (Feb. 5, 1915). Lt.-Commdr. R.N.V.R., empld. Intelligence Div., Admiralty, 1916–18. *O.B.E.* (Mil.).

1888 Clegg, W. G. (Mar. 1916). Lt., Acting Capt., Manchester Regt.

1907 Clements-Finnerty, H., B.A. (Serving Aug. 4, 1914). Lt. 17th Lancers. Lt. Observer R.A.F. France. (Prisoner of war.)

1908 Clemes, A. W., B.A. (1915). Friends Ambulance Unit, afterwards Lt. 12th Bn. A.I.F. France, 1915–18.

1905 **Clerke, F. W. T.** (Sept. 14, 1915). Lt. 2nd Coldstream Guards. France. Killed in action near Les Bœufs on Sept. 26, 1916.

1919 Cleverly, G. C. (Mobilized Aug. 4, 1914). Lt. 1/5th Queen's (R.W. Surrey Regt.) (Capt.). India, 1914–15; Mesopotamia, 1915–19. *D.* Mesopotamia, 1918.

1910 Cleverly,* O. S., M.A. (Mobilized Aug. 1914). Capt. 1/5th Queen's (R. W. Surrey Regt.). India, 1914–15; Mesopotamia, 1915–18. *D.* Mesopotamia, 1919.

1905 Clover, A. (Aug. 31, 1914). Lt. 3rd King's (Liverpool Regt.). France, 1916.

1900 Clowes, G. C. K. (Mobilized Aug. 1914). Lt.-Col. 1/14th London Regt. (London Scottish). D.A.Q.M.G. 1st Div., 1917–18. France, 1914–18. *D.S.O.*, Jan. 1, 1917. *D.* France, 1916 twice.

1904 Clutterbuck, T. R. (Serving Aug. 4, 1914). Maj. Coldstream Guards and Guards M.G. Regt. France and Belgium. *D.* § Mar. 1918, Mar. 1919.

1913 Coats,* J. S. (Oct. 10, 1914). Capt. 2nd Coldstream Guards. France, 1915–18. *M.C.*, Jan. 1, 1918. *D.* France, 1916.

1898 Coe, F. A., B.A. (Sept. 19, 1914). Capt. 7th S. Wales Borderers.

1902 Coke, Hon. R., B.A. (Aug. 28, 1914). Capt. 1st Scots Guards. Maj. Airship Service, R.A.F. France and Belgium. *D.S.O.*, Jan. 1, 1915. *A.F.C.*, Jan. 1, 1919. *D.* France, 1915, 1919; § Aug. 1919.

1901 Coles, E. L., B.A. (Sept. 1, 1914). ‡Lt. 7th Queen's (R. W. Surrey Regt.) (Capt.). France. *M.C.*, Feb. 1, 1919.

1908 Collins,* R. L. H., B.A. (Serving Aug. 4, 1914). Capt. Rifle Brigade. Egypt, Sudan, India, France, Italy. *D.* France, 1915 twice; Hedjaz, 1918.

1907 Colville,* A. R., B.A. (Sept. 2, 1914). ‡Capt. 3rd King's African Rifles. France, 1915–16; E. Africa, 1916–19. *D.* E. Africa, 1917, 1919.

1897 Colville, J. R. (Serving Aug. 4, 1914). Maj., Bt. Lt.-Col., Acting Lt.-Col., 241st S. Midland Bde., R.F.A. France and Belgium, 1914–15, 1915–17; Italy, 1917–18. *D.S.O.*, July 3, 1915. Croce di Guerra. *D.* France, 1914, 1915 twice, 1916, 1917; Italy, 1918.

1910 Compton, E. R. F. (Serving Aug. 4, 1914). Lt. 2nd Dragoons. Capt. M.G.C. (Cavalry). France and Belgium. Order of St. Stanislas (3rd Class). *D.* France, 1914.

1910 Congreve-Pridgeon,* R., B.A. (Nov. 28, 1914). Lt. 2/7th Hampshire Regt., attd. M.G.C. India.

1910 Cooke, R. C., B.A. (Aug. 1914). Capt. 3rd Norfolk Regt., attd. Egyptian Army. Mesopotamia, 1915–16. *M.C.*, June 24, 1916.

1913 **Copeman,* R. G. H.** (Aug. 1914). 2nd Lt. 9th Essex Regt. (Lt.). France, 1915–16. Died on Jan. 12, 1916, of wounds received in action on the previous day near Bethune.

1913 Courage,* R. E. F. (Aug. 26, 1914). Lt. N. Somerset Yeomanry. France and Belgium, 1915, 1916–19.

1892 Corbet, H. D. (Oct. 1, 1914). Lt. 4th, attd. 5th, Shropshire L.I. (Capt.).

1907 Coventry,* A. F., B.A. (1915). Canadian Contingent.

1905 Cox, C. E. C. (Nov. 1915). Lt. 12th Cavalry, Indian Army. Mesopotamia, 1915–16.

1900 Cox, C. M., M.A. (Dec. 31, 1915). 2nd Lt. Unattached List, T.F., Lt. Berkhamsted School O.T.C.

1910 Craigie, J. C. (Aug. 5, 1914). Capt. Grenadier Guards (Gen. Res. of Officers). France. *M.C.*, Jan. 14, 1916. Croix de Guerre. *D.* France, 1915, 1917.

1890 Crawford and Balcarres, Earl of. ‡2nd Lt. Special Duties.

1895 Crawley, Rev. A. S., M.A. (Sept. 1915). Chaplain to the Forces (3rd Class), attd. H.Q. 48th Div. France and Italy. *M.C.*, Nov. 14, 1916; *Bar*, Sept. 26, 1917. *D.* Italy, 1919.

1900 **Cree, A. T. C.,** B.A. (Aug. 14, 1914). Lt. 7th Durham L.I. France and Belgium, 1915. Killed in action at Ypres on May 12, 1915.

1905 **Cree, C. E. V.,** B.A. (Sept. 1914). Lt. 8th Sherwood Foresters. France, 1915–16. Killed in action on the Somme on July 20, 1916.

1901 Cree, J. F. G., B.A. (Dec. 6, 1914). Lt. 23rd Welsh Regt. Capt., Courts Martial Officer.

1919 Crewdson, H. A. F. (Sept. 18, 1916). Lt. Coldstream Guards. France, 1917–18.

Crick, W. H. R. (Apr. 9, 1915). Lt., Acting Capt., 2/4th Dorsetshire Regt. Egypt and Palestine. Killed in action in the attack on Three Bushes Hill, Palestine, on Apr. 9, 1918.

1919 Crisp, G. H. (Apr. 23, 1917). 2nd Lt. 23rd London Regt. France, 1917–18.

1912 Crookshank, H. F. C., B.A. (Sept. 19, 1914). Capt. Grenadier Guards (S.R.). France, 1915, 1916. British Mission to Serbian Army, Salonika, 1917–18. Serbian Order of the White Eagle (5th Class) (with swords). Serbian Gold Medal for Valour.

1901 Cruickshank, F. C. M., B.A. (June 11, 1915). Lt., temp. Maj., I.A.R.O. India.

1905 Cudmore, C. R., B.A. (Aug. 11, 1915). Lt. 86th Bde. R.F.A., (Capt.). France.

1908 **Cudmore, M. M.,** B.A. (Jan. 12, 1915). Lt., Acting Capt., R.F.A. D.T.M.O., 3rd Div. France and Belgium. *M.C.*, Jan. 14, 1916. *D.* France, 1915. Killed in action at St. Eloi on Apr. 5, 1916.

1906 Cundy-Cooper, O. S. (Serving Aug. 4, 1914). Capt. R. Fusiliers. France. *M.C.*, Feb. 18, 1915. *D.* France, 1915.

1904 Cunliffe, J. R. E. (Aug. 27, 1914). Lt. R.F.A. (Res. of Officers).
1906 Cunningham,* G., B.A. Punjab Light Horse. India.
1896 Curling, B. J., B.A. (Serving Aug. 4, 1914). Maj., Bt.-Lt.-Col., Acting Lt.-Col., K.R.R.C., attd. Durham L.I. (Brig.-Gen. commdg. 189th Inf. Bde.). Gallipoli, 1915; Salonika, 1915–16; France, 1917–18. *D.S.O.*, Nov. 8, 1915. Croix de Chevalier de la Légion d'Honneur. *D.* France, 1915, 1917, 1919.
1902 **Curwen, W. J. H.,** B.A. (Mobilized Aug. 1914). Capt. 6th London Regt. (Rifles). France and Belgium. Killed in action in Belgium in May 1915.
1881 Cust, R. H. H., M.A. (June 28, 1915). A.B., R.N.V.R., R.N.A.S. France (with Y.M.C.A.).
1913 **Daman,* G. W.,** M.A. (Aug. 1914). Lt. 4th Seaforth Highlanders. France and Belgium. Killed by a sniper near Richebourg l'Avoué on May 24, 1915.
1919 Dams, K. L. (Jan. 12, 1916). Lt. 8th Sherwood Foresters (attd. War Office Staff). France, 1916–17.
1920 Darlington, J. (Mar. 1, 1918). 2nd Lt. R.G.A.
1911 Dashwood,* G. P. (Mar. 11, 1916). Capt. R.A.S.C.
1919 Dashwood, Sir J. L., Bt. (Sept. 12, 1914). Capt. 10th Arg. & Suth'd. Highlanders. Capt., Acting Maj., 3rd Bn. Tank Corps. France, 1915–19.
1907 Davidson,* D. G., B.A. (Serving Aug. 4, 1914). Capt. 2nd Q.O. Cameron Highlanders. France.
1911 Davidson, R. E. M., B.A. (Aug. 22, 1914). Capt. 6th Queen's (R. W. Surrey Regt.). Capt. General List. France, 1915–16; Salonika, 1916–18. *D.* Salonika, 1917.
1889 Davidson, W. D., B.A. 2nd Lt. City of Aberdeen Vol. Regt.
1905 **Davies,* C. H.,** B.A. (1916). 2nd Lt. 9th Welsh Regt. France. Killed in action on Jan. 17, 1916.
1918 Davies, D. S. (Aug. 24, 1914). ‡Lt. 7th S. Wales Borderers. Lt. R.E. France, Salonika.
1913 Davies,* T. E. H. (Nov. 11, 1914). Lt. 4th K.R.R.C., attd. R.F.C. France and Belgium, 1914–15. (Shot down and taken prisoner, Mar. 1915.)
1906 Dawkins, C. G. H., B.A. (Nov. 7, 1914). Maj. Special Lists. D.A.Q.M.G., G.H.Q. France. *D.* France, 1917, 1919.
1905 Dawnay, A. G. C., B.A. (Serving Aug. 4, 1914). Capt., Bt.-Maj., temp. Lt.-Col., Coldstream Guards. Egypt, Palestine, Arabia. *C.B.E.* (Mil.). *D.S.O.*, Jan. 1, 1917. Croix de Chevalier de la Légion d'Honneur. Order of the Nile (4th Class). Italian Silver Medal for Military Valour. Order of El Nahda (2nd Class). *D.* Egypt, 1915, 1916, 1917; Palestine, 1918, 1919; Hedjaz, 1918.
1897 Dawnay, G. P., *M.V.O.*, *D.S.O.* (Mobilized Aug. 1914). Maj., Bt.-Lt.-Col., Coldstream Guards (Res. of Officers), temp. Maj.-Gen. Gallipoli, 1915; Egypt and Palestine, 1916–17; France, 1918–19. *C.B. C.M.G.*, Jan. 1, 1918. Croix d'Officier de la Légion d'Honneur. Order of St. Anne (2nd Class) (with swords). Officer of the Order of St. Maurice and St. Lazarus. *D.* Gallipoli, 1915 twice, 1916; Egypt, 1916 three times, 1917; France, 1918 twice, 1919.
1902 Daynes, J. N., B.C.L., M.A. (Feb. 5, 1918). Lt. R.A.O.C.

1917 de Beer, G. R. (Dec. 7, 1917). 2nd Lt. 2nd Grenadier Guards. France, Belgium, Germany.

1912 **De Fontaine, E. H.** (Apr. 15, 1915). Lt. 19th London Regt. (Capt.). France and Belgium. Died on Nov. 17, 1915, of wounds received at Loos on Sept. 25.

1899 de Hoghton, C. (Mar. 28, 1916). Lt. R.N.V.R.

1899 de la Rue, I. A., B.A. (Mar. 15, 1915). Lt. 19th R. Fusiliers, empld. War Office. France. *D.* France, 1917.

1919 de la Warr, H. E. D. B. S., Earl (May 1, 1918). Deck-Hand Signalman, R.N.R. Irish Channel and North Sea, 1918–19.

1912 Delius,* J. D., B.A. (Sept. 16, 1914). Lt. 4th Hussars (Capt.). France, 1915–19. *D.* France, 1919.

1916 Denning, A. T., B.A. (Aug. 19, 1917). 2nd Lt. 151st Field Coy., R.E. France, 1918–19.

1917 Derry, W. (May 1918). 2nd Lt. Loyal N. Lancashire Regt. (after demobilization).

1906 de Stein,* E., B.A. (Aug. 1914). Capt. K.R.R.C. Maj. M.G.C. (Corps M.G. Officer, Staff). France.

1913 Dewhurst, R. C. (Nov. 22, 1914). Lt., Acting Capt., General List, attd. H.Q. 14th Div. France and Belgium, 1915–19. *M.C.*, June 3, 1919.

1919 Disney, S. C. W. (Mobilized Aug. 5, 1914). Maj. 5th Lincolnshire Regt., attd. No. 8 O.C.B. (Lt.-Col.). France, 1915, 1916–18. *M.C.*, Jan. 1, 1918.

1886 Dodds-Parker, A. P., B.M., M.A. (Mobilized Aug. 5, 1914). Lt.-Col. R.A.M.C., attd. 3rd Southern General Hospital. *D.* § Sept. 1917.

1906 Donkin, A. W. F., B.A. (1914). Capt. Antrim R.G.A., attd. R.E. France.

Donner, E. R. (Aug. 1914). ‡Capt. 11th Rifle Brigade. France and Belgium, 1915–16. *D.* France, 1916. Killed in action in Battle of the Somme on Sept. 3, 1916.

1900 [Douglas, C. G., B.Sc., D.M.] (Oct. 10, 1914). Lt.-Col. R.A.M.C. France. *C.M.G.*, June 3, 1919. *M.C.*, Jan. 1, 1916. *D.* France, 1915, 1917, 1919.

1919 Drake, R. H. M. (Feb. 1, 1917). 2nd Lt. 1/1st Leicester R.H.A. Palestine.

1911 Driver, G. R., M.A. (Feb. 9, 1915). Capt. Graves Registration Commission. Capt. Intelligence Corps (Maj. D.A.A.G.). Serbia, France, Belgium, Egypt, Palestine. *M.C.*, Jan. 3, 1918. *D.* France, 1917.

1895 Duckworth, R., B.A. (Aug. 12, 1914). Maj., Bt.-Lt.-Col., S. Staffordshire Regt. Temp. Lt.-Col. Staff. France and Belgium. *D.S.O.*, Jan. 1, 1918. *D.* France, 1915, 1917, 1919.

1904 Dumaresq, L. S., B.A. (Aug. 21, 1916). Lt. Coldstream Guards (S.R.).

1912 Dunne,* L. R. (Aug. 15, 1914). Capt. 6th K.R.R.C. Maj. H.Q. 27th Div. (D.A.A.G., H.Q. 22nd Div.). France, 1914–15; Salonika, 1916–19; Caucasus, 1919. *M.C.*, June 3, 1918. Croix de Guerre avec palme. *D.* Salonika, 1918, 1919.

1895 Dunlop, D. O. (Jan. 1915). Capt. and Adjt. 6th (Res.) Lancashire Fusiliers. *D.* § Aug. 1919.

1912 Dunstan, E. C., B.A. (Oct. 3, 1914). Lt. 7th The Buffs (E. Kent Regt.). France. (Resigned on account of ill health.)

1896 Du Pre, C. H., B.A. (Dec. 1, 1914). Lt. R.A.S.C. (T.F.) (Capt.). France. *M.C.*, June 3, 1918. *D.* France, 1917.

1919 Durand, A. T. M. (Aug. 9, 1918). 2nd Lt. Coldstream Guards (S.R.) (after demobilization).

1903 Dutton, F. B., M.A. (Sept. 17, 1917). Surgeon Lt. R.N., H.M.S. *Commonwealth*. Grand Fleet.

1897 Edwards, A. H., M.A. (Aug. 1914). Capt. R.F.A. (Res. of Officers). France. *D.* § Mar. 1919.

1911 **Edwards, C.,** B.A. (Sept. 19, 1914). ‡Capt. R.A.S.C. France and Belgium. *D.* France, 1916. Died on Apr. 17, 1918, of wounds received in action at Gentelles on Apr. 12.

1900 Eggar, T. M., M.A. (Aug. 25, 1914). ‡Capt. 14th London Regt. (London Scottish). Temp. Lt.-Col. R.A.F. France. *O.B.E.* (Mil.). *D.* France, 1918.

1896 Eliot, E. G., B.A. (Oct. 1914). ‡Capt. R.G.A. France, 1917–18.

1911 **Ellwood, G. T. L.** (Aug. 28, 1914). Lt. 6th Leicestershire Regt. France and Belgium, 1914, 1916. Killed in action at Bazentin, July 14–19, 1916.

1914 Eltham,* Earl of (May 27, 1916). Lt. Res. Regt. 1st Life Guards.

1919 Encombe, J. S., Viscount (June 3, 1917). Lt. Scots Guards. France.

1902 **English, R. E.,** B.A. (Mobilized Aug. 1914). Capt. N. Somerset Yeomanry. France and Belgium. Killed in action in Belgium on May 13, 1915.

1910 Evans,* G. I., B.M. (May 1914). Capt. R.A.M.C. France and Belgium, 1917–19.

1900 Evans, G. P., B.A. (Aug. 24, 1915). Lt. R.N.V.R. Belgium, 1915; Russia, 1916–17; Rumania, 1917–19. Croix de Guerre avec palme. Officier of the Crown of Rumania. Chevalier of the Order of the Star of Rumania. Order of St. Stanislas (2nd and 3rd Classes).

1900 Evans, J. D. D. (Mobilized Aug. 1914). Capt. 2/1st Montgomeryshire Yeomanry. (Discharged on account of ill health, Feb. 1918.)

1906 **Evans, R. T.,** B.A. (Mobilized Aug. 4, 1914). Capt. 1/5th Welsh Regt. (Staff-Captain). Gallipoli, 1915. Presumed to have died on Aug. 10, 1915, of wounds received in action at Suvla Bay.

1914 **Eyre, C. A.** (July 1915). Flight Lt. R.N.A.S. (Flight Commdr.). France and Belgium, 1916–17. Killed in action near Bailleul on July 7, 1917.

1887 Fair, J. St. F., M.A. (Mar. 19, 1916). Maj. Special Lists. D.A.D. of Graves Registration and Inquiries. France. *M.C.*, June 3, 1917. *D.* France, 1916.

1887 Fairbairn, J. S., B.M., M.A. (Aug. 1915). Capt. R.A.M.C., attd. 5th London General Hospital.

1894 Fane, F. L., B.A. (Sept. 8, 1914). Capt. 2/7th W. Yorkshire Regt. France. *M.C.*, June 18, 1917.

1901 Fane, H. N., B.A. (Mobilized Aug. 5, 1914). Capt. Coldstream Guards (S.R.). A.D.C.

1912 Farquhar,* H. L. (Aug. 15, 1914). Lt. Coldstream Guards. G.S.O. 3 France. *M.C.*, June 3, 1919.

1913 **Farrar,* V. A.** (Sept. 1914). ‡2nd Lt. Lancashire Fusiliers. France. Died on Mar. 16, 1916, of wounds received in action at Bethune.

1890 Fennell, C. H., D.M. (Nov. 21, 1914). Capt. R.A.M.C.

1905 Fenwick, C. B., M.A. (Nov. 5, 1914). Capt. Northern Cyclist Bn.

1910 Fergusson,* J. D. B., M.A. (Aug. 22, 1914). Lt. Hertfordshire Regt.

1901 Fisher, K., M.A. (Serving Aug. 4, 1914). Lt. Unattached List, T.F., Clifton College O.T.C.

1902 **Fitzwygram, Sir F. L. F.,** Bt., M.A. (Serving Aug. 4, 1914). Capt. Scots Guards. France, Belgium, 1914–15. *M.C.*, May 5, 1919. *D.* France, 1915. (Wounded prisoner of war, May 16, 1915.) Died on May 5, 1920.

1914 **Fleet, W. A.,** M.A. (Oct. 1916). ‡2nd Lt. 1st Grenadier Guards. France. Killed in action near Arras on May 18, 1918.

1920 Fleming, J. F. (June 6, 1917). Lt. 'U.' Batt., R.H.A. France, 1917–18; Germany, 1918–19. *D.* France, 1918.

1908 Fleming, P. (Mobilized Aug. 1914). Maj. Q.O. Oxfordshire Hussars France, 1914–18.

1900 **Fleming, V.,** B.A., *M.P.* (Mobilized Aug. 1914). Maj. Q.O. Oxfordshire Hussars. France, 1914–17. *D.S.O.*, June 4, 1917. *D.* France, 1915, 1917. Killed in action at Guillemont Farm on May 20, 1917.

1902 Flower, C. H. (Mobilized Aug. 1914). Capt. 16th London Regt. (Queen's Westminster Rifles) (Maj. 22nd London Regt. (The Queen's)). France. *M.C.*, Mar. 27, 1918.

1919 Foster, R. A. C. (Sept. 1914). Capt. 51st Rifle Brigade. France, Belgium, Germany.

1888 Foxcroft, C. T., *M.P.* (Rejoined Sept. 1914). Capt. 2/4th Somerset L.I. India, 1914–15. (Invalided, 1916.) Asst. Adjt. Vol. Bn. (1917–20).

1901 Francis, H. D. P., M.A. (Mobilized Aug. 3, 1914). Capt. E. Riding Yeomanry, attd. M.G.C. (Adjt.). Egypt, 1915–16; Palestine, 1916–18; France, 1918–19. *M.C.*, Jan. 1, 1918. *D.* Palestine, 1917.

1898 Frank, N. G., B.A. (Aug. 5, 1914). Maj. 6th Manchester Regt. France.

1895 Fraser, Hon. A. T. J., B.A. (Mobilized Aug. 4, 1914). Maj. 1st Lovat's Scouts (Lt.-Col.). Gallipoli, Macedonia, France. *D.S.O.*, Jan. 1, 1918. *D.* Salonika, 1917.

1920 Fraser, H. A. H. (Mar. 27, 1915). 2nd Lt. R. N. Devon Yeomanry. Lt., Acting Capt., 21st Lancers. N.W. Frontier, India.

1915 Fraser, H. D. F. (1916). 2nd Lt. R.F.C. Lt. Grenadier Guards. France.

1911 Fraser, J. N., B.A. (Aug. 27, 1914). ‡Lt. R.F.A. (Capt.). France.

1896 Fremantle, A. F., B.A. (May 8, 1915). Capt., Asst. Recruiting Officer, I.A.R.O., late 28th Light Cavalry, Indian Army. E. Persia, 1915–16; N.W. Frontier, 1917.

1900 **Frere, E.,** B.A. (June 8, 1915). 2nd Lt. 8th London Regt. (Post Office Rifles). France. Died on May 22, 1916, of wounds received in action at Vimy.

1903 Fry, H. J. B., B.Sc., D.M. (Sept. 20, 1914). Capt. R.A.M.C., attd. No. 2 Stationary Hospital. France. *D.* France, 1917.

1902 Fulford, R. L., B.A. (June 17, 1915). Capt. R.A.S.C. Chevalier, Ordre du Mérite Agricole.

1892 Fuller, Rev. A. R., M.A. (Mobilized Aug. 1914). Chaplain to the Forces (4th Class), attd. R. N. Devon Yeomanry. Gallipoli, 1915; Egypt, 1916. *D.* Egypt, 1916.

1914 Furniss, A. E. (Dec. 2, 1914). Capt. 5th York & Lancaster Regt. France and Belgium.

1899 Galloway, J. A., B.A. (Mar. 15, 1915). Capt. 20th Manchester Regt.

1920 Gardiner, G. A. (Sept. 6, 1918). 2nd Lt. Coldstream Guards (after demobilization).

1914 **Gardner, M. R. G.** (Jan. 1916). ‡2nd Lt. 1st Worcestershire Regt. France. Killed in action at Berry-au-Bac on May 27, 1918.

1908 Garton, A. S., B.A. (Oct. 20, 1914). Lt. R.N.V.R. Eastern Mediterranean, Greece, Egypt, France.

1904 Garton, C. L., B.A. (July 24, 1915). Capt. Special Lists. *D.* § Feb. 1917.

Garton, E. C. (Apr. 24, 1918). 2nd Lt. Rifle Brigade. France. Died on Sept. 2, 1918, of wounds received in action at Arras.

1911 **Garton, H. W.,** B.A. (Aug. 26, 1914). Capt. 9th Rifle Brigade. France. Killed in action in the Battle of the Somme on Sept. 15, 1916.

1904 Gatehouse, L. R. A., B.A. (Mobilized Aug. 1914). Capt. 10th King's (Liverpool Regt.).

1911 Gelderd-Somervell, R. C., B.A. (Aug. 1914). Capt. 7th K.R.R.C. Lt. (Hon. Capt.) 190th N.T. Squadron, R.A.F. (Transferred on account of wounds). France, 1915.

1908 Gery,* R. V., B.A. (Aug. 9, 1914). Capt. 4th London Regt. (R. Fusiliers), attd. M.G.C.

1911 Gibbons, G. S. (Sept. 11, 1914). ‡2nd Lt. 13th R. Fusiliers, attd. H.Q. 3rd Army. France and Belgium.

1903 **Gibbs, E. L.** (Mobilized Aug. 1914). Capt. N. Somerset Yeomanry. France and Belgium. *D.* France, 1914. Died on Feb. 11, 1915, of wounds received in action.

1906 Gibbs,* Rev. F. A. W., B.A. (April 15, 1916). Chaplain (4th Class), attd. 1st Hertfordshire Regt. France, Belgium. *M.C.*, Oct. 15, 1918; *Bar*, Feb. 15, 1919.

1910 Gibbs, R. C. B. (Mobilized Aug. 1914). Capt. N. Somerset Yeomanry, attd. 7th Dragoon Guards. France. *D.* France, 1914.

1896 Gibbs, W., M.A. (Serving Aug. 4, 1914). Maj., Acting Lt.-Col., 7th Hussars. Gallipoli, Egypt, France, Mesopotamia. Croix de Guerre. *D.* France, 1916; Mesopotamia, 1919.

1912 Gielgud, L. E., B.A. (Sept. 15, 1914). Capt. 6th Shropshire L.I. Capt. (Staff-Lt.) General Staff. France. *M.B.E.* (Mil.). Croix de Chevalier de la Légion d'Honneur. Officer of the Order of the Crown of Rumania.

1907 Gilbey-Rivière, H., B.A. (Oct. 8, 1914). ‡Lt. R.N.V.R.

1905 Gillan,* J. A., B.A. Soudan C.S., attd. Soudan W. Frontier Force. Order of the Nile (4th Class). *D.* Egypt.

1909 Gillan,* J. R. W., B.A. (Nov. 7, 1914). Capt. 6th Gordon Highlanders (T.F.), attd. Egyptian Army. Egypt.

1911 Gilmour,* C. D., B.A. (Serving Aug. 4, 1914). Capt. 2nd The Black Watch, empld. War Office. France and Mesopotamia. *M.C.*, Dec. 22, 1916. *D.* Mesopotamia, 1916.

1908 **Gilroy, G. B.** (Aug. 1914). Capt. 8th The Black Watch. France and Belgium. *M.C.*, June 3, 1916. Died on July 15, 1916, of wounds received in action at Longueval.

1898 **Girdlestone, M. A.** (Serving Aug. 4, 1914). Capt. 41st Dogras, Indian Army. France. Killed in action at Neuve Chapelle on Mar. 25, 1915.

1902 Glen Coats, A. H., B.A. (Mobilized Aug. 4, 1914). Maj. Q.O. R. Glasgow Yeomanry, attd. XXI Corps Cavalry Regt. Gallipoli, Egypt, Palestine, Syria, Cilicia. *D.* Palestine, 1917, 1919.

1904 Glover, H. M., B.A. (Jan. 1915). Tpr. Punjab Light Horse, I.D.F. India. *D.* India, 1919.

1874 Godley, A. D., M.A., Hon. D.Litt. (1914). Lt.-Col. and County Commandant Vol. Bn. Oxf. & Bucks. Lt. Infty. *O.B.E.* (Mil.). *D.* § Mar. 1919.

1906 **Gold, C. A.,** B.A. (Nov. 1914). Lt. and Adjt. 5th R. Berkshire Reg. France, 1915–16. *D.* France, 1916. Killed in action at Ovillers on July 3, 1916.

1895 Gold, H. G., B.A. (Sept. 3, 1916). Capt., Acting Lt.-Col., R.A.F. *D.* § Mar. 1918.

1897 Goldsmith, F. B., M.A. (Mobilized Aug. 4, 1914). Maj. Suffolk Yeomanry. Gallipoli, Egypt, Palestine, France. *O.B.E.* (Mil.). Croix de Chevalier de la Légion d'Honneur.

1896 Golla, F. L., B.M., M.A. (Sept. 5, 1914). Capt. R.A.M.C. (T.F.). *O.B.E.* (Mil.). *D.* § Aug. 1917.

1902 Goodliffe, G. V., B.A. (Serving Aug. 4, 1914). Capt., Bt.-Maj., R. Fusiliers. G.S.O. 2. France and Belgium. *M.C.*, Jan. 1, 1917. *D.* France, 1917, 1918.

1908 **Goodyear, K. C.,** B.A. (Sept. 1914). Pte. R.A.M.C. France. Killed in action at Vermelles on Sept. 28, 1915.

1902 Gordon, G. S., M.A. (Aug 1, 1914). Capt. 6th W. Yorkshire Regt. (T.F.). G.S.O. 3. France. *D.* § Mar. 1919.

1905 Gordon, J. H. (Feb. 3, 1915). 2nd Lt. Royal 1st Devon Yeomanry. (Resigned.)

1891 Gore, Rev. G. H., M.A. (Nov. 24, 1916). Chaplain to the Forces (4th Class). *D.* § Aug. 1919.

1906 Goschen, G. G. (Aug. 28, 1914). Lt. 2nd Grenadier Guards. France.

1882 Gossage, A. M., D.M. (Mobilized Aug. 1914). Maj. R.A.M.C., attd. Base Hospital, London. *C.B.E.* (Civil). *D.* § Sept. 1917.

1894 Graham, H. H., B.A. (July 21, 1917). 2nd Lt., Acting Capt., 232nd P. of W. Coy., Labour Corps. France and Belgium, 1918–19.

1912 Graham, H. L. (Sept. 3, 1914). Capt. Scots Guards. France, 1915, 1917, 1918. *M.C.*, Dec. 2, 1918.

1904 Grant, J. P., M.A. (Mobilized Aug. 1914). Maj. 10th (Lovat's Scouts) Bn. Q.O. Cameron Highlanders. Egypt, Salonika. *M.C.*, June 4, 1917. *D.* Egypt, 1916 ; Salonika, 1918.

1904 Gray, C. B., M.A. (Serving Aug. 1914). Lt. Unattached List, T.F., Clifton College O.T.C. (Relinquished Commission on account of ill health.)

1906 Greene, B. S. C. (Feb. 2, 1915). Lt. R.N.V.R.

1907 Greene, G. G. R., M.A. (Dec. 15, 1914). Pte. R.A.M.C., afterwards Gnr. 262nd Bde., R.F.A. Egypt and Syria.

1901 Greenlees, W. L., B.A. (Mobilized Aug. 4, 1914). Lt., temp. Ma., Scots Guards. Gallipoli, Egypt, France. *D.* § Mar. 1919.

1919 Greenway, J. D. (Apr. 22, 1915). Lt. 5th Rifle Brigade. France, Belgium, Salonika, Serbia.

1897 Green Wilkinson, Rev. L. C., M.A. (Sept. 29, 1914). Chaplain (4th Class), attd. 41st Inf. Bde. France and Belgium. *D.* France, 1915. (Resigned.)

1893 Gretton, R. H., M.A. (Aug. 27, 1917). ‡Capt. General List (G.S.O. 3). France. *O.B.E.* (Mil.).

1881 Grey, T. R., M.A. (Oct. 1915). Sub-Lt. R.N.V.R.

1909 Grierson-Jackson,* H. C. (Nov. 17, 1914). Lt., Acting Capt., 4th Border Regt.

1907 Grisewood, F. H. (Sept. 12, 1914). Lt. 1/4th Oxf. & Bucks. Lt. Infty. France, 1914–15.

Gunther, G. R. (Apr. 1917). 2nd Lt. 3rd Grenadier Guards. France. *M.C.*, Feb. 1, 1919. Killed in action on Nov. 4, 1918.

1919 Gunther, R. J. (Aug. 1914). ‡Lt. 2nd Life Guards. France. Star of Rumania.

1909 **Haggie,* G. E.,** B.A. Pte. Yorkshire Regt. France. Killed in action on Oct. 2, 1917.

1883 Hall, C. O., B.A. (Oct. 15, 1914). Capt. E. Riding of Yorkshire Yeomanry (T.F. Res.).

1913 **Halsey,* F. W.** (Aug. 4, 1914). 2nd Lt. R.G.A. France. Killed in action on Nov. 15, 1915.

1899 Halsey, Rev. G., M.A. (Aug. 2, 1916). Chaplain R.N., H.M.S. *Emperor of India*. Grand Fleet.

1887 Halsey, W. J., B.A. (Mobilized Aug. 1914). Lt.-Col. 4th Bedfordshire Regt. A.A.G. Gallipoli, Egypt, and Palestine. *O.B.E.* (Mil.). *D.* Gallipoli, 1916; Palestine, 1918 twice.

1888 Hamersley, Rev. H., M.A. (Dec. 10, 1914). Chaplain to the Forces (4th Class). France.

1919 Hamerton, B. J. C. (Oct. 1917). 2nd Lt. 12th Rifle Brigade, attd. 10th R. Fusiliers. France and Belgium, 1918, 1919.

1908 Hamilton, I. B. M., B.A. (Serving Aug. 4, 1914). Capt. 1st Gordon Highlanders. France. (Prisoner of war, Feb. 1915–Nov. 1918.)

1894 Hamilton, L. G., B.A. (Mar. 26, 1915). Lt. 1st Dorsetshire Regt. France. *M.C.*, Sept. 16, 1918; *Bar*, Nov. 6, 1918.

1906 Hammick,* D. L., B.A. (Serving Aug. 1914). Capt. Unattached List, T.F., Gresham's School O.T.C.

1907 **Hamnett, F. G.** ‡2nd Lt. R. Fusiliers. Russia, Mesopotamia, France. Died in France on Nov. 15, 1918.

1905 Handover, Rev. S. J., M.A. (Oct. 1915). Chaplain to the Forces (4th Class), attd. H.M.H.S. *Goorkha*.

1919 Hanham, Sir J. L., Bt. (Oct. 5, 1916). Lt. Grenadier Guards. France, 1917.

1889 Hankey, S. T. Maj. 2nd Life Guards, Res. of Officers.

1908 Hankey,* T. B., B.A. (Dec. 13, 1914). ‡Lt. 12th K.R.R.C. Capt. General List. Bde. Maj. 72nd Inf. Bde. France. *M.C.*, Sept. 16, 1918. Albert Medal (1st Class). Croix de Chevalier de la Légion d'Honneur. *D.* France, 1916, 1917, 1918.

1882 Hansell, H. P., M.A. (Feb. 1915). A.B., Anti-Aircraft Corps, R.N.V.R. (until Apr. 1917). G.S.O. 3, G.S. Training, G.H.Q. France. *C.V.O.*

1910 **Hardinge,* P. R.,** B.A. (Serving Aug. 4, 1914). Maj. 10th Cameronians. France. *M.C.*, June 3, 1916. Died on June 17, 1916, of wounds received in action.

Harford, J. H. (Sept. 16, 1914). Lt. 3rd, attd. 1st, S. Wales Borderers. Gallipoli and France. Killed in action at Guedecourt on Oct. 26, 1916.

1900 Hargreaves, G. de la P., B.A. (Mobilized Aug. 1914). Capt. Bedfordshire Yeomanry. France. *D.* France, 1919.

1908 **Harper, A. G.,** B.Sc., M.A. (1914). ‡2nd Lt. R.F.A. (Lt. i/c Bde. Trench Mortars, 1915–16. India, France, Belgium. Killed in action at Brasserie, Dickebusch, on June 1, 1917.

1901 **Hartford, H. I. St. J.,** B.A. (Serving Aug. 4, 1914). Capt. 1st Cheshire Regt. France and Belgium. Killed in action on Oct. 22, 1914.

1903 Hartshorne, J. F. B., B.A. (1914). Sergt. 35th Poona Bn., I.D.F. India.

1914 Harvey, R. A. (Sept. 1915). Lt. R.N.V.R., H.M.S. *Assistance*. Grand Fleet, 1916.

1895 Hastings, Rev. J. H., M.A. (Aug. 17, 1917). Chaplain to the Forces (4th Class).

1914 Hawke, E. A. (Feb. 4, 1915). Lt., Acting Capt. and Adjt., 29th Bde., R.F.A. France.

1897 Hawkes, Rev. F. O. T., M.A. (May 21, 1918). Chaplain to the Forces (4th Class).

1895 Hawley, Sir H. C. W., Bt., B.A. (Nov. 1914). Capt. 8th R. W. Kent Regt. Capt. Labour Corps. France, 1915–18.

1909 Hay,* Lord E. D. J. (Mobilized Aug. 1914). Capt. Lothians & Border Horse. Lt. Grenadier Guards. France.

1910 Hay, L. F., B.A. (Serving Aug. 4, 1914). Capt. The Black Watch. France, Salonika. *D.* Salonika, 1917.

1914 Hayward, C. C. (Jan. 8, 1915). 2nd Lt. 9th Rifle Brigade. Capt., Flight Commdr., R.A.F. France, 1915–16. *D.* § Air Ministry, Jan. 1919.

1891 Hazell, E., M.A. (May 12, 1915). Lt. 7th R. Fusiliers.

1895 Headlam, C. M., B.A. (Mobilized Aug. 5, 1914). Capt. Bedfordshire Yeomanry. Temp. Lt.-Col. General Staff. France and Belgium, 1915–18. *O.B.E.* (Mil.). *D.S.O.*, Jan. 1, 1918. *D.* France, 1916 twice, 1917, 1918, 1919.

1900 Heard, W. B. (Apr. 5, 1917). Capt. Special Lists. *D.* § Mar. 1918.

1907 **Heath, P. V.,** B.A. (Serving Aug. 4, 1914). Lt. R. Horse Guards. France. Died on Sept. 5, 1914, of wounds received at Néry on Sept. 1.

1880 Heaton, G., M.A. (Mobilized Aug. 1914). Maj. R.A.M.C. (T.F.), 1st Southern General Hospital.

1911 Heilgers, F. J. F. A. (Aug. 31, 1914). Lt. 11th London Regt. (Finsbury Rifles). A.D.C. Gallipoli, Egypt, Palestine. *D.* Palestine, 1919.

1902 **Helme, T. H.,** B.A. (Nov. 23, 1914). Capt. and Adjt. 2/16th London Regt. (Queen's Westminster Rifles). France, Salonika, Palestine. Died on Nov. 3, 1918, of wounds received at Es Salt on Apr. 30, 1918, followed by influenza and pneumonia.

1912 Henderson, J. E. (Sept. 16, 1914). Capt. R.A., Staff-Captain, H.Q. II Corps. France, Belgium, Germany. *M.C.*, June 3, 1918. *D.* France, 1916 twice, 1919.

1906 [Herbert, Hon. G. S.] (Mobilized Aug. 1914). Maj. 1/4th Wiltshire Regt. India.

1904 Hermon Hodge, Hon. H. B., B.A. (Aug. 1914). Lt. Nigerian Land Contingent (Transport and Intelligence Officer). W. Africa, Cameroons.

1897 Herschell, Lord, B.A., *G.C.V.O.* (Nov. 23, 1914). Commdr. R.N.V.R. Croix d'Officier de la Légion d'Honneur.

1900 Hewitt, C. J., B.A. (Oct. 10, 1914). 2nd Lt. 3rd S. Wales Borderers. Lt. Grenadier Guards. France.

1886 Hichens, Rev. A. S., B.D. (Apr. 7, 1915). Chaplain to the Forces (4th Class), attd. 42nd Div. Gallipoli, Egypt, Palestine.

1891 **Hichens, J. B.,** B.A. (Sept. 1914). Lt. 16th K.R.R.C. France. Killed in action near High Wood on July 15, 1916.

1888 Hichens, P. S., D.M. (Feb. 1915). Lt.-Col. R.A.M.C., O.C. No. 35 General Hospital. France.

1912 Higham, R. H., B.A. (Sept. 12, 1914). Capt. R. Welch Fusiliers.

1911 Hill, J. C. H., B.A. (Sept. 1914). Lt. 1/7th Worcestershire Regt. France. *D.S.O.*, Sept. 26, 1916. Italian Silver Medal for Military Valour. *D.* France, 1916.

1904 Hill, J. S. B. (Sept. 1914). Capt. 1st Bucks. Bn. Oxf. & Bucks. Lt. Infty., attd. 144th Inf. Bde. France, Italy. *O.B.E.* (Mil.). *M.C.*, June 4, 1917. Croce di Guerra. *D.* France, 1917; Italy, 1918 twice, 1919.

1910 **Hine-Haycock,* R. H.** (Sept. 16, 1914). Capt. 1st K.O.Y.L.I. France and Belgium. Killed in action near Henin-sur-Cojeul on May 3, 1917.

1912 Hinmers,* W., B.A. (Oct. 24, 1914). Capt. 2/7th King's (Liverpool Regt.). France, 1917–18. *M.C.*, Mar. 26, 1918.

1911 **Hobson,* A. C.** (Aug. 1914). Lt. 2nd Life Guards. France and Belgium. Killed in action near Ypres on May 13, 1915.

1901 Hodgkinson, G. W. (Mar. 9, 1915). Capt. 2nd County of London Yeomanry, attd. R.A.F. France. *M.C.*, Feb. 1, 1917; *Bar*, Jan. 1, 1918.

1910 Hodgkinson, I. T. (Aug. 28, 1914). Lt. 2/4th Somerset L.I. (Capt.). India.

1911 Hodgkinson, N. A., B.A. (1914). Capt. 3rd, attd. 10th, R. Warwickshire Regt., empld. O.C.B. France.

1901 **Hodgson, C. B. M.,** B.A. (Mobilized Aug. 1914). Capt. 3rd Queen's (R. W. Surrey Regt.), attd. 24th London Regt. Egypt and Palestine. Croix de Guerre. *D.* Egypt, 1915. Died at Cairo on Apr. 1, 1918, of wounds received in action in Palestine.

1914 **Hodgson, F. H.** (Jan. 1916). Capt. R.A.F. France. *D.* France, 1918. Accidentally killed at Elincourt on Nov. 16, 1918.

1908 Hodgson, Rev. L., M.A. (Jan. 1918). 2nd Lt. Unattached List, T.F., O.U.O.T.C.

1881 Hogarth, D. G., M.A., D.Litt. (Oct. 25, 1915). Commdr. R.N.V.R. Egypt, Arabia, Palestine. *C.M.G.*, Jan. 1918. Order of the Nile (3rd Class). Order of El Nahda (2nd Class). Egypt, 1916, 1917; Hedjaz, 1918.

1919 Hogarth, J. U. (July 1917). 2nd Lt. R. Horse Guards. France, 1918.

1911 Hogg,* R. J. J. (Oct. 15, 1915). Lt. 5th, attd. 7th, E. Surrey Regt. France. *M.C.*, Nov. 6, 1918.

1907 Holcroft, C. W., M.A. (Sept. 5, 1914). Capt., Acting Maj., 1st R. Warwickshire Regt. France, Belgium. *D.S.O.*, Feb. 4, 1918. *D.* France, 1918.

1919 Holden, Hon. A. W. E. (Nov. 15, 1916). 2nd Lt. 4th Coldstream Guards.

1896 Hollins, F. H., M.A. (Dec. 7, 1914). Capt. 9th Rifle Brigade (Maj.). France and Belgium.

1910 Hollins, J. C. H. L. (Nov. 6, 1914). Lt. 4th Loyal N. Lancashire Regt. (T.F.).

1914 **Holmes, G.** (Apr. 9, 1915). 2nd Lt. 1st E. Yorkshire Regt. France. Killed in action at Arras on Apr. 9, 1917.

1882 Holt, H. E. S., M.A. (Dec. 1914). Maj. Hampshire Yeomanry. Temp. Maj. Instructor to French Corps d'Aviation. Hon. Lt.-Col. R.A.F. France. *C.B.E.* (Mil.). Officier de l'Ordre de la Couronne.

1906 Holt, V. H., B.A. (Aug. 1914). ‡Capt. R.A., XIX Corps (Staff-Captain). British E. Africa, France. *M.C.*, June 3, 1919. Belgian Croix de Guerre. *D.* France, 1918.

1901 Hood, A. J. F., B.A. (Sept. 1914). Capt., Bt.-Maj., 3rd K.O. Scottish Borderers, attd. Ministry of Munitions. France. *D.* § Feb. 1917, § Mar. 1918.

1905 **Hood,* Rev. C. I. S.,** B.A. (Oct. 3, 1915). Chaplain to the Forces (4th Class), attd. 41st Bde., R.G.A. Gallipoli, Egypt, France, Belgium. Died on Apr. 15, 1918, of wounds received near Mt. Kemmel.

1914 Hopkins, H. O. (Feb. 5, 1915). Lt. 7th King's (Liverpool Regt.) (T.F.). France.

1911 Hopper, A. A., M.A. (Sept. 15, 1914). ‡Lt. 3rd E. Yorkshire Regt. France and Belgium. (Placed on retired list on account of ill health caused by wounds, July 7, 1918.)

1907 Hornby,* H. R., B.A. (Mobilized Aug. 1914). Lt. Duke of Lancaster's Own Yeomanry. A.D.C. (Resigned on account of ill health.)

1911 Horsfall, E. D., M.A. (Aug. 1914). 2nd Lt. Rifle Brigade (until Nov. 1914). Maj. R.A.F. (Lt.-Col.). France. *D.F.C.*, 1918. *M.C.*, Jan. 1, 1916. Croix de Chevalier de la Légion d'Honneur. *D.* France, 1915; § Aug. 1919.

1903 **Horsfall, H. F. C.** (Sept. 1914). ‡Capt. 6th Loyal N. Lancashire Regt. (Maj.). Egypt, 1914–15; Gallipoli, 1915; Mesopotamia, 1916. Died on Apr. 22, 1916, of wounds received in action near Kut.

1909 Hosie,* A. L. (Mar. 15, 1917). Lt. I.A.R.O. India.

1919 Hoskyns, H. W. W. (Mar. 28, 1918). 2nd Lt. R.G.A.

1895 Hotson, J. E. B., M.A. (Mar. 19, 1915). Capt. (local Lt.-Col.) I.A.R.O., attd. 23rd Sind Bn., I.D.F. (Asst. Political Agent). Persia and Baluchistan, 1916–19. *O.B.E.* (Civil).

1910 **Houldsworth,* W. G.,** B.A. (Serving Aug. 4, 1914). Lt. Scots Guards. France and Belgium, Aug. 1914. Died on Sept. 12, 1914, of wounds received in action.

1914 Howard, Hon. A. J. P. (Mar. 7, 1915). Capt. Scots Guards. France. Croix de Guerre. *D.* France, 1917.

1911 **Howard,* Hon. R. H. P.,** B.A. (Aug. 22, 1914). 2nd Lt. E. Surrey Regt. France and Belgium. Killed in action near Ypres on May 9, 1915.

1907 Hubbard, Hon. F. S. R. Fusiliers.

1912 **Hudson,* A. J. B.** (Nov. 4, 1914). Lt. 3rd Worcestershire Regt. France, Salonika, Belgium. *M.C.*, July 26, 1917. Killed in action at the Battle of Messines on June 7, 1917.

1907 **Hudson, J. H.,** B.A. (Oct. 1, 1914). Lt. R.F.A. (T.F.). France. Died on Jan. 12, 1916, of wounds received in action.

1906 Hudson, R. S., B.A. (Oct. 31, 1914). 2nd Lt. 5th Res. Regt. of Cavalry. (Resigned.)

1913 Hughes, A. H., B.A. (Sept. 28, 1914). Capt. A Batt., 306th (S. Midland) Bde., R.F.A. (Maj.). France, 1916–19. *M.C.*, June 3, 1919.

1909 Hughes, G. A. (Aug. 24, 1914). Lt., Acting Capt., 6th S. Lancashire Regt., attd. No. 6 O.C.B. Gallipoli, 1915. (Discharged on account of wounds, Dec. 4, 1918.)

1881 Hulbert, H. H., M.A. (July 6, 1915). Capt. R.A.M.C.

1896 Hulton, C. B., M.A. (June 1916). Lt. Section Sanitaire Anglaise, No. 5, Croix rouge française. France.

1905 [**Hunter, L. W.,** M.A.] (Apr. 1915). Lt. 1/4th Oxf. & Bucks. Lt. Infty. France, 1916. Killed in action near Pozières on Aug. 13, 1916.

1897 Hurst, A. F., D.M. (Oct. 1915). Maj. R.A.M.C. *O.B.E.* (Mil.).

1899 [Hutchinson, G. T., M.A.] (Mobilized Aug. 4, 1914). Lt. Q.O. Oxfordshire Hussars. Staff-Captain. France. *M.C.*, Jan. 1, 1917.

1902 Hutchinson, St. J., B.A. (1914). Anti-Aircraft Corps, R.N.V.R.

1903 **Huth, A. H.,** B.A. (Sept. 1914). ‡Capt. 4th E. Surrey Regt. France and Belgium. Killed in action at Hill 60 on Apr. 20, 1915.

1897 Huth, G. E. (Aug. 4, 1914). Maj. 4th E. Surrey Regt. France.

1879 Hutton, E. E., M.A. (1915). Maj. 11th Canadian Mounted Rifles, empld. War Office. *D.* § Mar. 1919.

1905 im Thurn, R. F. (Aug. 4, 1914). Lt. 18th Hussars (S.R.). France and Belgium, 1916–19.

1883 Ingram, F. M., M.A., T.D. (Serving Aug. 4, 1914). Capt., Hon. Maj., Shrewsbury School O.T.C. *D.* § Mar. 1918.

1909 **Inigo Jones,* H. R.,** B.A. (Aug. 1914). 2nd Lt. Scots Guards. France and Belgium, 1914. Killed in action on Sept. 12, 1914.

1904 **Irvine, H.** (Sept. 9, 1914). Lt. 13th WorcestershireRegt., attd. R. Munster Fusiliers. Gallipoli. Died on June 28, 1915, of wounds received in action at Gully Ravine, Gallipoli.

1919 Irvine, H. C. (Aug. 10, 1917). 2nd Lt. A Batt., 255th Bde., R.F.A. France, 1918–19.

1919 Ivimey, W. M. (June 17, 1917). 2nd Lt. 1st (Garr.) Bn. R. Welch Fusiliers. Gibraltar.

1911 Jack, W. L. (Mar. 1916). Lt. 29th Bn. A.I.F. France.

1911 Jackson, M. K., B.A. (Sept. 5, 1914). ‡Lt. 2/6th R. Warwickshire Regt. (Capt.). France. *M.C.*, Feb. 18, 1918; *Bar*, Jan. 11, 1919.

1919 Jalland, T. G. (Aug. 21, 1915). Pte. R.A.M.C. ‡Capt. 2/1st Leicestershire Yeomanry.

1890 James, Hon. C. (Aug. 1914). Capt. 7th E. Surrey Regt. (until Apr. 1916). Lt.-Col. R. Marines, Inspector Admiralty Motor Transport. Belgium and France, 1915–16. *C.B.E.* (Mil.).

1902 **James, G. C. B.,** B.A. (Mar. 28, 1917). Lt. 3rd, attd. 2nd, S. Wales Borderers. France and Belgium. Died on Nov. 23, 1917, of wounds received in action.

1919 James, W. E. C. (Dec. 15, 1914). Lt. 2/4th Northumberland Fusiliers, afterwards Lt. 10th Bn. M.G.C. Salonika, 1917; Palestine, 1917–19. *D.* Palestine, 1918.

1887 James, Hon. W. J., M.A. (Feb. 11, 1915). ‡Lt. R.N.V.R., Admiralty special service.

1916 Jellicoe, J. B. L. (Nov. 1917). Paymaster Sub-Lt. R.N.V.R., H.M.S. *Iron Duke*. Mediterranean, Constantinople, Black Sea, 1919.

1892 Jex-Blake, A. J., D.M. (Aug. 26, 1914). Capt., Acting Lt.-Col., R.A.M.C., 54th General Hospital, B.E.F. France, 1917–19. *D.* France, 1919.

1897 **Johnson, G. M.,** M.A., B.M. (1915). Surgeon R.N., H.M.S. *Defence*. Grand Fleet. Killed in action at Battle of Jutland on May 31, 1916.

1909 Johnson,* M. K., B.A. (Aug. 29, 1914). Lt. R.G.A. Malta, France. (Invalided, Oct. 8, 1918.)

1908 Johnston,* H. L., M.A. (Aug. 26, 1914). Capt. 1/5th London Regt. (London Rifle Brigade) (Maj.). France, 1914–16, 1918–19. *M.C.*, June 3, 1916.

1904 **Johnston,* J. L.,** M.A. (Aug. 1914). 2nd Lt. 3rd, attd. 2nd, Oxf. & Bucks. Lt. Infty. (Capt.). France. Missing, presumed killed in action at Festubert on May 12, 1915.

1913 **Jones,* D. W. Ll.** (Aug. 1914). Lt. 1/3rd London Regt. (R. Fusiliers) (Adjt.). Malta, 1914–15; France, 1915–16. Died on July 1, 1916, of wounds received at Gommecourt.

Jones, J. T. (Oct. 1915). 2nd Lt. 20th London Regt. France and Belgium. Died on Aug. 24, 1917, of wounds received in action at Westhoek.

1894 Jones, R. P., M.A. (Serving Aug. 4, 1914). Maj., temp. Lt.-Col., R.A.O.C., A.D. of Ordnance Services.

1904 Jones, T. A., M.A. (Oct. 5, 1914). Lt. R.A.

1873 Jones, W. W. (Aug. 1914). Maj. R.A.M.C. (T.F. Res.). *D.* § Aug. 1919.

1882 **Jones-Parry, J. J. B.** (Rejoined Oct. 4, 1914). Maj. 6th D.C.L.I. France. Died on Aug. 1, 1915, of wounds received in action.

1913 Jury, C. R., B.A. (Oct. 8, 1914). Lt. 5th Oxf. & Bucks. Lt. Infty. France and Belgium.

1894 Kaye, H. W., D.M. (Aug. 20, 1914). Capt. R.A.M.C. (D.C.M.S., Jan. 1918). Belgium and France, 1914–16.

1890 Kaye, W. A., B.A. (1914). Anti-Aircraft Corps, R.N.V.R.

1910 Kelly, D. V., B.A. (Dec. 7, 1914). Lt. 7th Leicestershire Regt. Temp. Capt., Education Officer. France. *M.C.*, June 4, 1917.

1899 **Kelly, E. D. F.** (Serving Aug. 4, 1914). Capt. 1st Life Guards. Belgium. Missing, presumed killed in action, 1915.

1900 Kemp, E. S., B.A. (Nov. 4, 1914). ‡2nd Lt. 7th Lincolnshire Regt. Capt. General List. Staff-Captain, Boulogne. France and Belgium. *O.B.E.* (Mil.). *D.* France, 1919.

1903 Kennedy, A. L., B.A. (Dec. 1914). 2nd Lt. 10th K.O.Y.L.I. Lt. Scots Guards (S.R.). France. *M.C.*, Mar. 15, 1916. Croce di Guerra. *D.* France, 1917.

1909 **Kennedy,* J. P. F.,** B.A. (Oct. 8, 1914). Capt. Rifle Brigade. France. *D.* France, 1916. Killed in action in France on Apr. 24, 1918.

1882 Kent, A. F. S., M.A., D.Sc. (Aug. 1914). 2nd Lt. Unattached List, attd. Bristol University O.T.C.

1915 Kent, P. C. (Jan. 1916). Lt. R.A.S.C. Salonika. Serbian Gold Medal for Zealous Service. *D.* Serbian 3rd Army Dispatches, Dec. 1916.

1882 Kenyon, Sir F. G., *K.C.B.*, M.A. (Mobilized Aug. 5, 1914). Lt.-Col. Inns of Court O.T.C., attd. Imperial War Graves Commission. France, 1914. T.D. *D.* § Mar. 1918.

1911 **Kersey, W. H. M.,** B.A. (Feb. 6, 1915). Capt. 166th Siege Batt., R.G.A. France and Belgium. Killed in action near Ypres on Oct. 17, 1917.

1913 Kingdom, S. St. G. S., B.A. (Aug. 1914). Capt. 10th R. Warwickshire Regt. Gallipoli, 1915; France, 1916–18. (Prisoner of war, 1918.)

1893 Kingsley, Rev. H. W. (Jan. 3, 1917). Chaplain to the Forces (4th Class).

1905 **Kirby, A. G.,** B.A. (Aug. 26, 1914). Capt. 3/5th London Regt. (London Rifle Brigade). Staff-Captain 2nd Divl. Art. France. Died at Marseilles on Mar. 29, 1917, of illness contracted on active service.

1901 Kirby, C. A. (1914). Petty Officer A.A. Corps, R.N.V.R. Lt.-Col. R.A.F.

1904 Kirk, Rev. K. E., M.A. (Sept. 1914). Chaplain to the Forces (3rd Class). France, 1915–17.

1908 **Knight, A. G.,** B.A. (Aug. 22, 1914). Lt. 9th R. Fusiliers. France and Belgium. Killed in action on June 29, 1915.

1900 **Knight, A. Tait,** B.A. (Aug. 15, 1915). ‡Capt. 22nd Durham L.I. France. Died on Oct. 27, 1916, of wounds received in action at Guedecourt.

1900 Knight, E. E. (Dec. 15, 1914). Lt. R.F.A. France. *M.C.*, June 24, 1916.

1900 Knight, J. G. D. (Apr. 13, 1915). ‡Lt., Hon. Capt. and Qr.-Master, The R. Highlanders of Canada (The Black Watch). France, Belgium, Germany.

1894 Knight, Rev. O. H., M.A. (Jan. 12, 1916). Chaplain to the Forces (4th Class). Egypt and Palestine.

1881 Laing, C. M., B.C.L., M.A. (Mar. 1916). Lt. Recruiting and Demobilization Officer.

1895 Laird, R. H., B.A. (Aug. 29, 1914). Capt. 20th King's (Liverpool Regt.). France.

1890 Lake, Rev. K. A., B.A. (Apr. 24, 1917). Chaplain to the Forces (4th Class).

1897 Lambart, Ven. Hon. H. E. S. S., M.A. (Mobilized Aug. 4, 1914). Chaplain (4th Class), Shropshire Yeomanry. Egypt.

1892 Lambert, G. B., B.A. (1914). United Provinces Horse, I.D.F. India.

Lambert, J. E. D. (Sept. 1914). Lt. 6th Northamptonshire Regt. France. Killed in action near Fricourt on Nov. 1, 1915.

1914 Langstaff, J. B., B.Litt. (Sept. 1918). Pte. 28th London Regt. (Artists' Rifles).

1906 Latham,* G. C., B.A. (Aug. 15, 1914). Capt. N. Rhodesia Police. E. Africa. Croix de Guerre. *D.* E. Africa.

1913 Lawford, A. B. (Sept. 1914). 2nd Lt. Grenadier Guards. France. (Resigned on account of ill health.)

1888 Lawrence, H. S. (July 25, 1915). Lt. I.A.R.O., attd. Sappers and Miners. India.

1907 [Lawrence, T. E., B.A.] (Oct. 1914). Col. Special Lists. Egypt, Arabia, Syria. *C.B.* *D.S.O.*, May 13, 1918. Croix de Chevalier de la Légion d'Honneur. Croix de Guerre. Italian Silver Medal for Military Valour. *D.* Egypt, 1915; Hedjaz, 1918.

1908 Lee,* S. G., M.A. (Oct. 2, 1914). Capt. 6th Rifle Brigade, empld. School of Musketry.

1884 [Lee, W. L. Melville, M.A.] Late Maj. Queen's (R. W. Surrey Regt.). Sec. Oxfordshire T.F. Association. *D.* § Aug. 1917.

1908 Legh, Hon. R. W. D. (Mobilized Aug. 4, 1914). Capt. Lancashire Hussars, Staff Officer. Belgium and France. *D.* France, 1917.

1910 Leigh,* G. H., B.A. (Aug. 29, 1914). Capt. 13th London Regt. Acting Lt.-Col. 17th S. Lancashire Regt. Egypt and Palestine. *O.B.E.* (Mil.).

1912 Leir, R. M., B.A. (Apr. 17, 1915). 2nd Lt. 15th Hussars. (Resigned.)

1908 Leng,* D. C., M.A. (Mobilized Aug. 1914). Capt. 1/1st Yorkshire Dragoons. France, 1915–19.

1910 Leverson,* B. D. A., B.A. (Aug. 1914). Capt. 9th Loyal N. Lancashire Regt. France.

1890 Leveson-Gower, Rev. F. A. G., M.A. (Oct. 16, 1917). Chaplain to the Forces (4th Class).

1892 Leveson-Gower, H. D. G. (Oct. 30, 1914). Maj. R.A.S.C. France. *D.* France, 1919.

1915 **Levett, R. W. B.** (July 1916). 2nd Lt. 1st K.R.R.C. France. Killed in action on Mar. 10, 1917.

1909 Lewis,* H. G. C. T., B.A. (Mobilized Aug. 1914). Capt. 15th London Regt. (Civil Service Rifles). France. *D.* France, 1916, 1917.

1895 **Lewis, J. W.,** M.A. (Aug. 10, 1914). Lt. Welsh Guards (Capt.). Egypt, France, Belgium. Killed in action at Ypres on June 6, 1916.

1914 Lewthwaite, R. (Jan. 2, 1916). Lt. 1/4th Border Regt. India.

1886 Lindley, Hon. L. H., B.M., M.A. (Sept. 22, 1914). Capt. R.A.M.C. France, Palestine, Egypt. *D.* Palestine, 1918.

1895 Lindsay, Rev. Hon. E. R., M.A. (May 28, 1917). Gnr. 211th Siege Batt., R.G.A. (Bomdr.). France, Belgium, 1917–18. *M.M.*

1878 Lister, J. J., B.A., V.D. (1915). Capt., Hon. Maj., 3rd Vol. Bn. R. Sussex Regt.

1894 Lloyd, D. R. L., B.A. (Nov. 13, 1916). Lt. R.A.S.C.

1916 Lloyd, L. W. (Sept. 1915). Cadet Inns of Court O.T.C. (Invalided). Died on Nov. 11, 1918.

1904 Lock, C. F., B.A. (Sept. 1914). Lt. Hertfordshire Yeomanry. Mudros, 1915; Egypt, 1915–16; Mesopotamia, 1916–18.

1912 **Lockhart,* G. B.** (Sept. 5, 1914). Lt. 6th Loyal N. Lancashire Regt. Gallipoli. Killed in action at Sari Bair, Gallipoli, on Aug. 10, 1915.

1907 Loder, H. S., B.A. (Sept. 23, 1914). Lt. R. E. Kent Yeomanry. Gallipoli, Palestine.

1910 Long, F. A. (June 14, 1915). Lt. R.A.S.C.

1888 Long, S. C., B.A. (Aug. 5, 1914). Maj., Bt.-Lt.-Col., Rifle Brigade. Asst. Director-General of Transportation (A.Q.M.G.). France. *D.* France, 1915, 1916, 1917.

1913 Long,* W. H. T. (Aug. 26, 1914). Lt., Acting Capt., Labour Corps, attd. H.Q. Australian Corps. France, Belgium. *D.* France, 1918.

1890 Lovat, Lord, *K.T.*, *K.C.V.O.*, *C.B.*, *D.S.O.* (Mobilized 1914). Col. 1st and 2nd Lovat's Scouts and 4th Gordon Highlanders. A.D.C. to the King. Temp. Brig.-Gen., Director of Forestry. France. Croix d'Officier de la Légion d'Honneur. Commandeur, Ordre du Mérite Agricole. *D.* § Feb. 1917; France, 1917, 1918.

1902 Low, S. P., B.A. (Aug. 15, 1914). Maj. 1/9th Hampshire Regt. India, Siberia.

1913 Loyd,* E. W. (Apr. 17, 1915). Lt. Yorkshire Regt., attd. M.G.C. Salonika. *D.* Salonika, 1918.

1909 **Loyd, G. A.** (Serving Aug. 4, 1914). Lt. Scots Guards. France and Belgium. Croix de Chevalier de la Légion d'Honneur. *D.* France, 1914. Killed in action on Nov. 13, 1914.

1907 Loyd,* R. L., B.A. (Serving Aug. 4, 1914). Lt. 16th Lancers (Maj.). France. *O.B.E.* (Mil.). *M.C.*, Jan. 14, 1916. *D.* France, 1915 twice, 1918.

1914 Lucas, R. S. C. (Jan. 9, 1915). 2nd Lt. K.R.R.C., Lt. R.F.A. (T.F.), O.C. Signal Subsection, R.E., 34th Army Bde. France, Belgium, Germany.

1919 Lumley, L. R. (Jan. 1916). Lt. 11th Hussars. France.

1886 Luttrell, C. M. F., B.A. (Dec. 11, 1914). Capt. 2nd N. Somerset Yeomanry.

1902 Lygon, Hon. H., M.A. (Mobilized Aug. 1914). Capt. Suffolk Yeomanry, attd. Intelligence Corps. (Maj.). France, 1915–16; France and Italy, 1916–18. Chevalier of the Order of St. Maurice and St. Lazarus.

1904 Lyon, F. H., B.A. (July 28, 1915). 2nd Lt. Special Lists. Staff-Lt. (2nd Class). France. *D.* France, 1916, 1917.

1913 Lyon, Hon. M. C. H. Bowes (Aug. 15, 1914). Lt. 3rd, attd. 2nd, R. Scots. France. (Prisoner of war.)

1913 McAndrew,* G. A. (Oct. 5, 1914). Lt. 5th Hampshire Regt., attd. 4th Wiltshire Regt.

1896 **Macarthur Onslow, A. W.,** B.A. (Serving Aug. 4, 1914). Capt. 16th Lancers. France. *D.* France, 1914. Killed in action on Nov. 7, 1914.

1894 **McClure, C. R.,** B.A. (Serving Aug. 4, 1914). Maj. 19th Hussars. France, 1914. *D.* France, 1914. Killed in action at Le Gheer on Oct. 21, 1914.

1897 McCreagh Thornhill, M. C., M.A. (Aug. 5, 1914). Lt.-Col. 5th London Regt. (London Rifle Brigade). Asst. Adjt.-Gen. War Office. France, Belgium. *C.B.E.* (Mil.). *D.* France.

1892 MacDermot, E. T., M.A. (Jan. 17, 1916). Capt. Special Lists. R.T.O. *D.* § Aug. 1919.

1876 Macfarlane, D. A., B.A., *D.S.O.* (Serving Aug. 4, 1914). Brig.-Gen. Seaforth and Cameron Inf. Bde., afterwards Member of Inverness T.F. Association. *C.B.* *D.* § Feb. 1917.

1902 McGeagh, H. D. F. (Mobilized Aug. 1914). Capt., Bt.-Maj., temp. Lt.-Col., 5th London Regt. (London Rifle Brigade). *C.B.E.* (Mil.). *D.*

1909 [Macgregor, D. C., M.A.] (Aug. 1914). ‡Lt. 8th Q.O. Cameron Highlanders. Lt. General List (Intelligence Corps). France. *D.* France, 1919.

1907 Macgregor,* E. D. (June 29, 1915). 2nd Lt. 7th Highland L.I. (T.F.) (Lt.).

1910 Machon,* R. E., M.A. (Sept. 18, 1914). Capt. 10th (Yeomanry) Bn. Devonshire Regt. France and Belgium, 1916–17, 1918–19. *M.C.*, Feb. 15, 1919.

1908 Mackenzie,* D. W. A. D., B.A. (Serving Aug. 4, 1914). Capt., Bt.-Maj., 1st Seaforth Highlanders. France. *D.S.O.*, June 4, 1917. Chevalier de l'Ordre de Léopold. Belgian Croix de Guerre. *D.* France, 1916, 1917.

1901 Mackenzie, E. M. Compton, B.A. (1915). War Correspondent. Capt. R. Marines. Gallipoli, Salonika. Croix de Chevalier de la Légion d'Honneur. Order of the White Eagle (4th Class) (with swords). Chevalier of the Order of the Redeemer. *D.* § Feb. 1917.

1888 Mackenzie, H. G. G., M.A. (Mobilized Aug. 1914). Capt. R.A.M.C. (T.F.) (Lt.-Col.). France, Salonika. *D.S.O.*, June 3, 1918. *D.* France, 1915; Salonika, 1918.

1907 **Mackenzie,* M. K.,** B.A. (Serving Aug. 4, 1914). Lt. 4th K.R.R.C., attd. 3rd Rifle Brigade. India, France. Killed in action at Soupir, near River Aisne, on Sept. 25, 1914.

1906 **Mackinnon,* D.,** B.A. (Mar. 18, 1915). Lt. Scots Guards. India, Gallipoli, Egypt, France, Belgium. Killed in action at Ypres on Oct. 9, 1917.

1902 **Mackinnon, W.,** B.A. (Sept. 1, 1914). Capt. 14th London Regt. (London Scottish). France. Killed in action near Arras on May 11, 1917.

1905 **Mackworth, A. C. P.,** M.A. (Nov. 1914). Lt. Rifle Brigade, attd. Intelligence Dept., War Office. France, 1915–16. Died on Nov. 25, 1917.

1894 **Maclachlan, A. F. C.,** B.A., *D.S.O.* (Serving Aug. 4, 1914). Maj., Bt.-Lt.-Col., Acting Lt.-Col., 12th Rifle Brigade (Brig.-Gen.). Salonika, France. *Bar to D.S.O.*, Jan. 1, 1918. Serbian Order of Karageorge (4th Class) (with swords). *D.* France, 1915; Salonika, 1917. Killed in action near St. Quentin on Mar. 22, 1918.

1898 **Maclagan, G. S.,** B.A. (Sept. 1914). Lt. 1st R. Warwickshire Regt. France and Belgium. Killed in action at Pilkem Wood on Apr. 25, 1915.

1907 Maclane, J. R., B.A. (1917). New Hampshire State Guard.

1895 Macmillan, Rev. J. V., M.A. (Oct. 26, 1915). Chaplain to the Forces (3rd Class). France. *O.B.E.* (Mil.). *D.* France, 1917, 1919.

1906 McMinnies, W. G., B.A. (1916). Flight Commdr. R.N.A.S. Capt., Acting Maj., R.A.F. *A.F.C.*, Jan. 1, 1919. *D.* Naval Dispatches.

1913 **McNair, E. A.** (Oct. 8, 1914). Capt. 9th R. Sussex Regt. Capt. General List. G.S.O. 3. France, Belgium, Italy. Died at Genoa on Aug. 12, 1918, of illness contracted while on active service. **V.C.** won at Hooge on Feb. 4, 1916.

For most conspicuous bravery. When the enemy exploded a mine, Lieutenant McNair and many men of two platoons were hoisted into the air, and many men were buried. But, though much shaken, he at once organized a party with a machine-gun to man the near edge of the crater and opened rapid fire on a large party of the enemy, who were advancing. The enemy were driven back, leaving many dead.

Lieutenant McNair then ran back for reinforcements, and sent to another unit for bombs, ammunition, and tools, to replace those buried.

The communication trench being blocked, he went across the open under heavy fire and led up the reinforcements the same way. His prompt and plucky action and example undoubtedly saved the situation.

1914 Madigan, C. T., B.A. (Sept. 5, 1914). Capt. 76th Field Coy., R.E. France, 1915–17. *D.* France, 1917.

1891 Magnus, L., M.A. (Sept. 10, 1915). Maj. R. Defence Corps. *D.* § Aug. 1918.

1904 Maidstone, Viscount (Nov. 1914). Lt.-Commdr. R.N.V.R. Lt.-Col. R.A.F. Belgium. *O.B.E.* (Mil.). *D.S.C.* (for services in Flanders, 1915–17). Croix de Guerre.

1888 Mallam, E., D.M. (Mobilized Aug. 1914). Maj. R.A.M.C. (T.F.), 3rd Southern General Hospital.

1912 Mander, H. V., B.A. (Aug. 26, 1914). Capt. 1/6th S. Staffordshire Regt., attd. No. 8 O.C.B. France and Belgium, 1915–17. *M.C.*, Jan. 14, 1916. *D.* France, 1915.

1919 Mansel-Carey, D. V. M. (Jan. 15, 1916). Lt. 3rd Devonshire Regt. France.

1913 **Mansel Carey,* S. L. M.** (Jan. 1915). 2nd Lt. 8th Devonshire Regt. France. Died on Feb. 24, 1916, of wounds received in action at Fricourt.

1906 Margoliouth, H. M., M.A. (Sept. 16, 1914). ‡Capt. 6th Northamptonshire Regt. France and Belgium.

1900 **Martin,* C. H. G.,** M.A. (Mobilized Aug. 1914). Lt. 3rd Monmouthshire Regt. France and Belgium. Killed in action near Ypres on Apr. 24, 1915.

1907 Martin, H. T. (Aug. 5, 1916). Lt. 4th, attd. 8th, King's Own (R. Lancaster Regt.).

1919 Martin, R. A. (Sept. 13, 1915). 2nd Lt. 2/3rd Home Counties Bde., R.F.A. Lt. R.A.F. France, 1917–18.

1883 Marwood Tucker, C. (Sept. 23, 1914). Lt.-Col. 2/4th Devonshire Regt. (T.F. Res.). India, 1914–17; Palestine, 1917–18. *D.* Palestine, 1918.

Mason, A. E. G. (Aug. 1914). ‡2nd Lt. 7th Leicestershire Regt. France. Died on June 30, 1916, of wounds received in action at Bienvillers.

1900 Masters, F. N. D., M.A. (Feb. 1915). 2nd Lt. R.F.A. Capt. R.A.F. France and Belgium, 1916.

1898 Mathews, G. A. A., B.A. (Oct. 21, 1916). Lt. County of London Vol. Regt.

1909 Mathieson,* D. (Dec. 1, 1914). Lt. 10th The Black Watch. Camp Comdt. H.Q., 74th Div. France, 1915; Salonika, 1915–17; Palestine, 1917–18; France, 1918. *D.* Palestine, 1918.

1907 Mawson,* G. H., B.A. (Sept. 5, 1914). Lt. R.E. (Signals) (T.F.). France. *M.C.*, July 26, 1918.

1906 Maxwell,* H. St. G. H., B.A. (Mobilized Aug. 1914). Capt. 6th (Cyclist) Suffolk Regt. (T.F.).

1888 Medlicott, Rev. R. S., M.A. (May 1, 1918). Chaplain (4th Class), 6th Hampshire Regt. France.

1898 Medlicott, W. S. (Nov. 22, 1914). Lt. Northumberland Hussars (T.F. Res.) (Capt.).

1910 Meikle,* R., M.A. (Mobilized Aug. 1914). Capt., Acting Maj., 2/7th Hampshire Regt. India, 1915–17; Mesopotamia, 1917–19.

1911 Mellows, A. H., B.A. (Mobilized Aug. 5, 1914). Capt. 1/1st Huntingdonshire Cyclist Bn. (till Apr. 1918). Capt. R.A.F. (Staff-Captain). Mesopotamia. *D.* Mesopotamia, 1918, 1919.

1910 **Menzies,* A. Graham** (Serving Aug. 4, 1914). Lt. Scots Guards. France. Killed in action at Givenchy on Jan. 1, 1915.

1892 Mercer, E. G., M.A. (Mobilized Aug. 4, 1914). Lt. 1st London Regt. Lt.-Col. 58th Bn. M.G.C. France, Belgium. *C.M.G.* *D.* France, 1915, 1916.

1919 Meyer, J. V. (Sept. 2, 1916). 2nd Lt. 4th Suffolk Regt. France and Belgium, 1917, 1918. (Wounded and prisoner of war, Oct.–Dec. 1918.)

1908 Meyerstein, E. H. W., M.A. (Oct. 20, 1914). Pte. 3rd R. Dublin Fusiliers. (Discharged unfit, Dec. 1914).

1898 Middleton, W. (Serving Aug. 4, 1914). Maj. Shropshire L.I. Egypt. *O.B.E.* (Mil.). Order of the Nile (4th Class). *D.* Egypt, 1916; Sudan, 1919.

1919 Milford, T. R. (Sept. 17, 1914). ‡Lt. Oxf. & Bucks. Lt. Infty. Mesopotamia, 1916–19.

1900 Miller, A. G., B.A. (June 15, 1915). Capt. and Adjt. 16th R. Sussex Regt. Gallipoli, Egypt, Palestine, France.

1912 Mills,* Hon. A. R. (Mobilized Aug. 4, 1914). Lt. 1/1st W. Kent Yeomanry, attd. 4th R. W. Kent Regt. Gallipoli, 1915.

1905 **Mills, Hon. C. T.,** B.A. (Serving Aug. 4, 1914). 2nd Lt. 2nd Scots Guards. France, 1915. Killed in action at Hulluch on Oct. 6, 1915.

1896 Mills, T. P., B.A. (Oct. 1914). Capt. 1st London Regt. (R. Fusiliers). (Resigned on account of ill health.)

1908 **Miln, G. G.,** M.A. (Dec. 1914). Capt. 15th Cheshire Regt. (Maj.). Gallipoli, 1915; France, 1916–18. *M.C.*, July 26, 1918. *D.* France, 1918. Killed in action at Honnecourt Wood on Apr. 22, 1918.

1914 Milne, H. V. R., B.A. (1917). ‡2nd Lt. 1st (Garr.) Bn. Worcestershire Regt.

1901 Mitchell, C. (Serving Aug. 4, 1914). Capt. Grenadier Guards (Maj.). France, Belgium, Italy. *O.B.E.* (Mil.). *D.S.O.*, Jan. 1, 1918. Croce di Guerra. *D.* France, 1915, 1917 twice; Italy, 1919.

1907 **Molineux, G. K.** (Serving Aug. 4, 1914). Capt. 2nd Northumberland Fusiliers. France, Belgium. Killed in action at Ypres on May 8, 1915.

1899 Monck, G. S. S. (Jan. 11, 1915). Lt., Acting Maj., R.E. (T.F.).

1892 Monson, W. J., M.A. Hon. Col. Chief Political Officer, E. African Protectorate. E. Africa. *D.* E. Africa.

1897 **Monteith, W. N.,** B.A. (Sept. 8, 1914). ‡Lt. 6th Rifle Brigade. France. *D.* France, 1915. Killed in action at Loos on Sept. 25, 1915.

1902 **Moon, B. O.,** B.A. (Aug. 1914). 2nd Lt. 8th London Regt. (Post Office Rifles). France. *D.* France, 1915. Killed in action at Festubert on May 25, 1915.

Moore, E. P. A. (Nov. 28, 1917). 2nd Lt. 1st Coldstream Guards. France. *M.C.*, Apr. 2, 1919. Killed in action at Maubeuge on Nov. 4, 1918.

Moore, W. H. H. (Oct. 3, 1914). 2nd Lt. 10th K.R.R.C. Accidentally killed on Oct. 19, 1915.

Morey, A. W. (Oct. 22, 1914). Lt. 11th R. Scots. Flying Officer, R.F.C. France. *M.C.*, Nov. 4, 1915. *D.* France, 1915. Killed in action in Feb. 1918.

1901 Morrell, J. H., M.A. (Oct. 5, 1914). Capt. O.U.O.T.C., attd. No. 4 O.C.B.

1892 Morres, E. R., B.A. (Aug. 6, 1914). Maj. R.A.S.C. France, Belgium, Germany. *D.* France, 1916.

1913 Morrieson,* D. B., B.A. (Nov. 11, 1914). Capt. K.R.R.C. France.

1894 Morris, H. S., B.A. (Oct. 1914). Maj. 8th E. Yorkshire Regt.

1919 Morris, W. R. (May 5, 1915). ‡2nd Lt. M.G.C. France and Belgium.

1913 Morrison,* C. E. (Aug. 14, 1914). Maj. Leicestershire Regt., attd. G.H.Q. France, Belgium, Germany. *M.C.*, Jan. 1, 1918. *D.* France, 1915.

1908 **Morrison,* G. H.,** B.A. (Mobilized Aug. 1914). Capt. 1/5th London Regt. (London Rifle Brigade). France and Belgium. Killed in action at Ploegsteert Wood on Mar. 31, 1915.

1894 Mort, M., M.A. (Mar. 20, 1915). Lt. 3rd Northumberland Fusiliers, empld. Ministry of National Service.

1905 Moulton, J. C., B.Sc., M.A. (Mobilized Dec. 16, 1914). Capt. 1/4th Wiltshire Regt. Capt., temp. Maj., G.S.O. 2. Straits Settlements Command. India, 1915–16; Straits Settlements, 1916–19. *O.B.E.* (Mil.). *D.* India, 1919.

1910 Mudie, D. C. (Oct. 1, 1914). Capt. 89th Bde., R.F.A. (Ma.). Belgium, 1914; France, 1915; Egypt, 1915–16; Salonika, 1916–18.

1912 Muirhead,* A. J. (Mobilized Aug. 1914). Capt., Bt.-Maj., Q.O. Oxfordshire Hussars. France and Belgium, 1914.–17, 1918; Italy, 1917–18. *M.C.*, June 4, 1917; *Bar*, Feb. 1, 1919. *D* France 1915, 1918; Italy, 1918.

1902 Murray, J., M.A. (Mobilized Aug. 1914). Maj. Scottish Horse, attd. 12th R. Scots (Lt.-Col.). Gallipoli, 1915; Egypt, 1916; France, 1917–18; Germany, 1918–19. *D.S.O.*, Feb. 15, 1919; *Bar*, June 3, 1919. Belgian Croix de Guerre. *D.* France, 1918, 1919.

1885 Murray, W., B.A. (Oct. 14, 1914). Capt. Special Lists, empld. Recruiting Duties.

1909 Myers, L. W., B.A. (May 19, 1916). Pte. H.A.C. 2nd Lt. (on demobilization). France, 1916–18.

1888 [Myres, J. L., M.A.] (Apr. 1, 1916). Lt.-Commdr., Acting Commdr., R.N.V.R. Military Control Officer, Athens. Greece, 1915–19. *O.B.E.* (Mil.). Commander of the Order of George I of Greece. *D.* Naval Dispatch, July, 1917.

1903 Nalder, H. G. (Dec. 4, 1914). Lt.-Commdr. R.N.V.R.

1902 Napier-Martin, J. G. F. N. (Mobilized Aug. 4, 1914). Capt. 3rd R. Dublin Fusiliers. Inland Water Transport Officer (D.A.Q.M.G.).

1899 Nevile, G. C. (Serving Aug. 4, 1914). Bde. Maj. R.A. France, 1914–16; Salonika, 1916–18. *D.S.O.*, Jan. 1, 1918. *D.* Salonika, 1917 twice; § Aug. 1919.

1897 Newbold, W., M.A. (Dec. 1, 1914). Capt., Acting Maj., 13th Batt., R.G.A. France, 1915–19. *O.B.E.* (Mil.). *D.* France, 1916, 1917, 1918.

1916 Newhall, P., B.A. (Dec. 1, 1917). 2nd Lt. R.F.A.

1899 Nicholl, C. R. I., B.A. (Mobilized Aug. 4, 1914). Lt.-Col. Q.O. Oxfordshire Hussars. France. *D.* France, 1915; § Feb. 1917.

1903 Nicholl, K. I. (Serving Aug. 4, 1914). Maj. R. Welch Fusiliers. France. *D.* France, 1916, 1918.

1907 **Nicholson, W. D.,** B.A. (Serving Aug. 4, 1914). Lt. 2nd Q.O. Cameron Highlanders. France and Belgium, 1914–15. Killed in action near St. Eloi on Feb. 23, 1915.

1886 Nickalls, G. (Nov. 1, 1917). Capt. 23rd Lancashire Fusiliers. France.

1920 Nickalls, G. O. (Oct. 1917). 2nd Lt. 5th Rifle Brigade. Salonika, 1918.

1890 Nickalls, V., M.A. (Aug. 26, 1915). Lt., Acting Maj., R.F.A. (S.R.).

1919 Nokes, M. C. (May 1916). 2nd Lt. R.G.A. Lt. (Observer) R.A.F. France, 1916–18. *M.C.*, Aug. 16, 1917.

1898 Norton, J. H., B.A. (Mobilized Aug. 1914). Capt., temp. Maj., Hampshire Yeomanry and Res. of Officers. France, 1917–18. *D.* § Feb. 1917.

1903 **Norton, T. E.,** M.A. (Oct. 14, 1914). 2nd Lt. 1st E. Surrey Regt. France, Belgium. Killed in action at Hill 60, near Ypres, on Apr. 20, 1915.

1914 Nugee, A. C., B.A. (Nov. 19, 1914). Lt. 14th Rifle Brigade. France and Belgium. (Invalided on account of wounds, Nov. 29, 1916.)

1910 Nugee,* F. J., M.A. (Oct. 5, 1914). Capt. 1/4th Leicestershire Regt. (Maj.). France, 1915–18, 1918–19. *M.C.*, Jan. 1, 1918.

1919 O'Brien, Hon. P. L. (Sept. 25, 1918). Cadet 212th Batt., R.F.A.

1881 O'Donovan, M. W., B.A., *C.B.* Hon. Col. R. Munster Fusiliers.

1900 O'Hagan, H. O., B.A. (November 1914). Lt. R.N.V.R. France, 1914–15; at sea, 1916–18.

1890 Otto, J. E., B.A. (Oct. 14, 1914). Capt. 3rd Highland L.I. (Maj.). A.P.M.

1906 Ogilvie,* A. G., B.Sc., M.A. (Serving Aug. 4, 1914). Capt. R.F.A. France, 1915; Gallipoli, 1915; Salonika, 1916–18. *O.B.E.* (Mil.). Serbian Order of the White Eagle (5th Class). *D.* Salonika, 1916.

1896 Ovey, R. L. (Mobilized Aug. 4, 1914). Maj. 4th Oxf. & Bucks. Lt. Infty. (Lt.-Col.). France, Belgium. *D.S.O.*, Jan. 14, 1916. *D.* France, 1915.

1895 Page, A., B.A. (Apr. 1915). ‡Lt. R.M.A. (Capt.). Belgium, France.

1919 Pallemaerts, F. A. F. (June 15, 1916). ‡Sous-Lt. de Réserve, Con. I.D.A., Belgian Army. Belgium, France. Croix de Guerre.

1909 Pardington,* G. E. L., B.A. (Mobilized Aug. 1914). Capt. 1/4th R. W. Kent Regt. Capt. and Adjt. M.G.C. India, 1914–19.

1902 Parham, Rev. A. G., M.A. (Oct. 28, 1914). Chaplain to the Forces (4th Class) (Deputy Asst. Chaplain-General). Egypt, 1915; Gallipoli, 1915; Egypt, 1916; France, 1917–19. *M.C.*, June 3, 1916. *D.* Gallipoli, 1916; France, 1918.

1911 Park,* M. E. (Sept. 26, 1914). Capt. 2nd The Black Watch. France, Mesopotamia. *D.S.O.*, Nov. 4, 1915. Italian Silver Medal for Military Valour. *D.* France, 1915; Mesopotamia, 1917.

1884 Parker, C. J. E., B.A. (Mobilized Aug. 1914). Capt. 3rd Lincolnshire Regt.

1903 Parkinson, A. C. C., M.A. (1914). Capt., temp. Maj., Inns of Court O.T.C., attd. King's African Rifles. D.A.A.G. *O.B.E.* (Mil.). E. Africa.

1913 **Parnell,* J. A. P.** (Dec. 23, 1914). Lt. 1st Gloucestershire Regt. France. Killed in action in the Battle of the Ancre on Sept. 8, 1916.

1913 Parr, E. R. (Dec. 28, 1915). Lt. A.S.C. Lt. Special Lists, Interpreter. Salonika. Gold Medal for Valour (Serbia).

1906 **Parry-Jones,* O. G.,** B.A. (Mobilized Aug. 1914). Lt. 3rd Lancashire Fusiliers. Capt. R.A.M.C. (S.R.). France, 1915–16. *D.* France, 1917. Died on Sept. 29, 1916, of wounds received in action.

Parsons, A. O. (July 21, 1916). ‡2nd Lt. 5th Durham L.I. France, 1917; Italy, 1917–18; France, 1918. Died on Mar. 26, 1918, at No. 6 Stationary Hospital, Frevent, of wounds received in action.

1914 **Parsons, E. K.** (Dec. 1914). Capt. 9th Rifle Brigade. France, 1915–16. Killed in action in the Battle of the Ancre on Sept. 15, 1916.

1904 Parsons, J. R., B.A. (Jan. 1915). Lt. Unattached List, T.F., Epsom College O.T.C.

1901 [Parsons, Rev. R. G., M.A.] (Aug. 15, 1916). Chaplain to the Forces (4th Class).

1909 Paterson,* H. S., B.A. (Mar. 19, 1915). Lt. 9th Queen's (R. W. Surrey Regt.). Maj. 18th Bn. M.G.C. France, 1916–17, 1918. *D.* France, 1919.

1910 Paterson,* J. C., B.A. (Mobilized Aug. 4, 1914). Capt. 7th King's (Liverpool Regt.) (T.F.). Lt., Acting Capt., R.F.A. France and Belgium, 1915–19. *D.* France, 1917.

1912 Paton,* R. D. (Aug. 1914). Lt. 3rd R. Scots Fusiliers (Capt.). France.

1911 **Pawle, B.** (Aug. 26, 1914). Capt. 8th Rifle Brigade. France and Belgium. Killed in action near Hooge on July 30, 1915.

1919 Payne, A. F. (Jan. 10, 1916). Lt. 4th Pioneer Bn., A.I.F. Lt. Australian Flying Corps. Egypt, 1916; France, 1916–17.

1919 Peake, C. P. P. (Oct. 6, 1914). Capt. 4th Leicestershire Regt. France. *M.C.*, Aug. 26, 1916.

1911 Pearse,* H. A. W., B.A. (Aug. 15, 1914). Capt. 3rd Bedfordshire Regt. France. *M.C.*, Sept. 17, 1917.

1894 Pearson, G. S. H., B.A. (Re-employed Mar. 10, 1915). Col. G.S.O. 1 at War Office. *C.M.G.* Croix d'Officier de la Légion d'Honneur. *D.* § Jan. 1917.

1905 Penny, J. D., B.A. (1914). ‡Capt. I.A.R.O., attd. 1/124th Balluchis. G.S.O. 3, Army H.Q., Simla. India.

1901 Perkins, B. W., B.A. (Oct. 1915). ‡2nd Lt. 14th (Tenasserim) Bn., I.D.F. India. *D.* § India, 1919.

1885 Perks, B., M.A. (Serving Aug. 4, 1914). C.S.M. Inns of Court O.T.C. *D.* § Feb. 1917.

1901 Perry, W., B.A. (Dec. 4, 1914). Capt. R.A.S.C. France, 1916–18.

1912 **Perssé,* R. A.** (Aug. 26, 1914). 2nd Lt. 2nd K.R.R.C. France, 1914–15. *D.* France, 1914. Killed in action at Cuinchy on Jan. 1, 1915.

1885 Phelps, E. J., B.A. Pte. Middlesex Regt.

1903 Phillips, E. G. M., B.A. (Dec. 1914). Capt. 8th The Black Watch. France, 1915; Salonika, 1915–18; Belgium, 1918; Germany, 1918–19. *M.C.*, Jan. 1, 1918. *D.* Salonika, 1917.

1904 Phillips, H. L. (Nov. 11, 1914). Maj. R.A.S.C.

1912 **Philpott, J. R.** (Sept. 1, 1914). Lt. 7th Suffolk Regt. Capt. 63rd Squadron R.F.C. France, 1915–16; Mesopotamia, 1917–18. *M.C.*, Oct. 20, 1916. (Prisoner of war, Sept. 1917.) Died as a prisoner at Asion Kara, Hissar, on Jan. 15, 1918.

1901 Pierce, Rev. C. F., M.A. (Serving Aug. 4, 1914). Capt. Unattached List, T.F., Haileybury College O.T.C.

1909 **Pigot-Moodie,* C. A.** (Aug. 15, 1914). 2nd Lt. 6th Rifle Brigade, attd. 2nd R. Irish Rifles. France and Belgium. Killed in action at Kemmel on Jan. 13, 1915.

1887 Pilkington, E. S., M.A. (Mobilized Aug. 1914). Maj. Lancashire Hussars. T.D.

1904 Pilkington, G. L. (Aug. 4, 1914). Capt. Lancashire Hussars (Maj.). Capt. R.A.F. Egypt, 1916; France, 1916; Belgium, 1916.

1898 Pilkington, H. C. (Nov. 19, 1914). Lt. Hertfordshire Yeomanry. Lt. Guards M.G. Regt. France.

1902 Pirie-Gordon, C. H., M.A. (Nov. 10, 1914). Lt.-Commdr. R.N.V.R. Lt.-Col. General List. Syrian Coast, 1914–15; Anzac Cove, 1915; Aegean, 1915–16; Macedonia, 1916–17; Palestine, 1917–19. *D.S.C.*, June 30, 1915. Croix de Chevalier de la Légion d'Honneur. *D* E. Indies; Palestine, 1919.

1909 **Platt, J. R.** (Oct. 5, 1914). Lt. R.F.A. (T.F.). France, Belgium. Killed in action at Ypres on Mar. 27, 1916.

1904 **Platt, L. S.** (Serving Aug. 4, 1914). Capt. 17th Lancers. Flight Commdr. R.F.C. France. Killed in action on Apr. 13, 1917.

1919 Pocklington-Senhouse, R. H. (May 1918). ‡2nd Lt. Coldstream Guards (S.R.).

1901 Pope, A. N. (Serving Aug. 4, 1914). Capt. R. Fusiliers (Maj.). France, Belgium, Germany. *O.B.E.* (Mil.). *D.* France, 1916, 1918.

1897 Porch, M. P., M.A. (Sept. 1914). Intelligence Officer, Nigeria Regt., W.A.F.F. W. Africa, Cameroons, 1914–15.

1909 **Porter,* A. M. F. W.** (Serving Aug. 4, 1914). Lt. 1st Lancashire Fusiliers. Gallipoli. Killed in action at 'Lancashire Landing' on Apr. 24, 1915.

1893 Powell, D., B.A. (Serving Aug. 1914). Maj., Bt.-Lt.-Col., R. W. Fusiliers. Lt.-Col. Staff Officer (1st Class) to Director of Manning, R.A.F. *C.B.E.* (Mil.). *D.* § Feb. 1917, § Mar. 1918.

1910 **Powell,* E. I.,** B.A. (Aug. 28, 1914). Capt. 13th R. Sussex Regt. France, Belgium. Died on Mar. 22, 1918, of wounds received in action at Villers Faucon.

1910 **Powell, G. F. W.,** B.A. (Mobilized Aug. 1914). Capt. Kent Cyclist Bn. Maj. 8th R. W. Kent Regt. France and Belgium. Killed in action at Hill 60 on July 29, 1917.

1904 **Powell, M.,** B.A. (Aug. 4, 1914). Lt. 68th Batt., R.F.A. France. Killed in action near Lens on July 5, 1917.

1903 Pratt Barlow, R. F. (Jan. 23, 1915). Lt. Coldstream Guards (S.R.) (A.D.C.).

1899 Prescott, C. W. B., B.A. (Sept. 1914). 2nd Lt. 2nd Life Guards. France and Belgium. *O.B.E.* (Mil.).

1912 Prevett,* R.A.C., B. A. (Aug. 26, 1914). Lt. E. Yorkshire Regt. Belgium and France.

Price, S. J. (Aug. 1914). ‡2nd Lt. 10th Norfolk Regt. France. Killed in action in the Battle of the Somme on Sept. 15, 1916.

1919 Price, V. R. (Sept. 1, 1914). ‡Capt. 3rd R. Berkshire Regt. France.

1905 **Priest, C. R.,** B.A. (Jan. 4, 1915). Pte. 18th R. Fusiliers. France and Belgium. Died on Jan. 22, 1916, of wounds received in action at Cuinchy.

1914 **Pye-Smith, P. H. G.** (Jan. 1, 1915). Lt. 11th King's (Liverpool Regt.). France and Belgium, 1915–17. Killed in action near Arras on May 15, 1917.

1897 Pym, C. E. (Mobilized Aug. 5, 1914). Maj. Suffolk Yeomanry. A.P.M. Gallipoli, 1915; Egypt, 1916; France, 1917–19. *O.B.E.* (Mil.). *D.* France, 1918, 1919.

1910 Railton, G. N., B.A. (Sept. 15, 1914). 2nd Lt. 23rd London Regt. (Resigned on account of ill health.)

1899 Ramsbotham, R. B., M.A. (Aug. 17, 1915). Capt. I.A.R.O., attd. 45th Rattray's Sikhs. India, N.W. Frontier, 1916–17; Mesopotamia, 1917–19. *M.B.E.* (Mil.).

1898 Rattigan, W. F. A. (Aug. 8, 1914). Capt. General Staff. France, Belgium, Rumania.

1909 Rattray,* Rev. E. A. C., M.A. (Jan. 1, 1918). Chaplain to the Forces (4th Class).

1913 **Rawdon-Hastings, E. H. H.** (Aug. 1914). 2nd Lt. The Black Watch. France, 1915. Died on Sept. 15, 1915, of enteric contracted on active service.

1911 Rawnsley, J. R. C., B.A. (Serving Aug. 4, 1914). Lt. 12th Lancers (Capt.). France, 1914–19. *M.C.*, July 26, 1918. *D.* France, 1918.

1898 **Rawstorne, T. G.** (Mobilized Aug. 4, 1914). Maj. Lancashire Hussars. France and Belgium. Killed in action on July 31, 1917.

1919 Read, H. S. H. (Mar. 8, 1917). Lt. R.A.F. France and Belgium, Independent Air Force.

1915 Read, W. D. B. (July 7, 1916). Lt. 1/4th Queen's (R. W. Surrey Regt.).

1919 Reid, T. L. G. (Feb. 20, 1918). 2nd Lt. R.G.A.

1880 Remnant, Sir J. F., B.A. (Dec. 14, 1914). Lt.-Col. R.A.S.C. *C.B.E.* (Mil.). *D.* § Feb. 1917, § Mar. 1918, § Mar. 1919.

1911 Renton,* A. F. G., M.A. (Aug. 15, 1914). Lt. 11th Hussars (Capt.). France and Belgium. *M.C.*, Jan. 1, 1919. *D.* France, 1918.

Renton, H. N. L. (Sept. 15, 1914). Lt. 9th K.R.R.C. (Capt.). Belgium and France. Killed in action near Hooge on July 30, 1915.

1919 Renton, R. K. D. (Nov. 10, 1915). Lt. Hussars (S.R.). Intelligence Officer, 1st Cavalry Bde. H.Q. France and Germany, 1917–19.

1912 Reynolds,* E. B. (Oct. 2, 1914). Lt. 2/8th Middlesex Regt. Capt. and G.S.O. 3, G.H.Q., Great Britain. Gibraltar, 1915; France, 1915–16, 1917.

1906 Rice, G. V., M.A. (Serving Aug. 4, 1914). Capt. R.F.A. Maj. R.A.F. France. *D.* France, 1916.

1902 Richards, R. P. E., M.A. (July 5, 1915). Lt. R.A.S.C.

1901 Riley, H. L., B.A. (Serving Aug. 4, 1914). Capt. 1st Rifle Brigade. Temp. Lt.-Col. M.G.C. India, 1914; France, 1914–19. *D.S.O.*, Feb. 18, 1915. Bt.-Maj., June 1916. Order of Danilo (4th Class). *D.* France, 1914, 1915, 1916, 1917 twice.

1912 Ritchie, A. P., B.A. (Sept. 7, 1914). 2nd Lt. 3rd R. Scots Fusiliers.

1909 Ritchie, A. T. A., B.A. (June 2, 1915). Lt., Acting Capt., Grenadier Guards. France and Belgium. *M.C.*, Nov. 4, 1915. Croix de Chevalier de la Légion d'Honneur. *D.* France, 1915.

1919 Rivington, J. M. (May 27, 1915). Capt. 5th W. Yorkshire Regt. France.

1898 Robarts, G. (Mobilized Aug. 1914). Capt. Northamptonshire Yeomanry. Lt. Res. Regt. of Cavalry. France. *D.* France, 1915.

1899 Roberts, M. O. (Mobilized Aug. 1914). Capt. Welsh Guards. France.

1897 **Robins, G. U.** (Feb. 1915). Capt. 3rd E. Yorkshire Regt. Belgium. Killed in action at Hill 60 on May 5, 1915.

1918 Rogers, A. J. Lt. R.N.V.R.

1899 Rogers, J. L., B.A. (Mar. 1, 1915). Capt. Cornwall Fortress R.E.

1912 **Romanes, E. G. R.** (Sept. 1914). Lt. Worcestershire Regt. Gallipoli. Died on June 8, 1915, of wounds received in action.

1912 Ronald, N. B., B.A. (Oct. 14, 1914). Lt. 6th King's (Liverpool Regt.) (T.F.). Lt. Grenadier Guards (S.R.). France.

1901 Rose, H. G. St. C., B.A. (Sept. 11, 1914). Capt., Staff-Captain, Hertfordshire Regt., empld. under Foreign Office. Gallipoli, 1915. Croix de Chevalier de la Légion d'Honneur.

1909 **Rose,* R. H. I.,** B.A. (Sept. 1914). Lt. 6th Bedfordshire Regt. France. Killed in action at Arras on Apr. 28, 1917.

1887 Rowe, R. P. P., M.A. (Dec. 3, 1914). Capt. 6th R. W. Kent Regt. *D.* § Feb. 1917.

1896 **Rowley, C. P.,** B.A. (Serving Aug. 4, 1914). Maj. R.G.A. India, Belgium, 1914–15. Accidentally killed at Botley, Hants, on Oct. 29, 1916.

1913 Rubie, H. E., B.A. (Aug. 14, 1918). 2nd Lt. Flying Officer, R.A.F.

1910 **Russell,* H. R.** (Mobilized Aug. 1914). Lt. 3rd Gloucestershire Regt. (Capt.). France, Belgium, 1915. Killed in action at Hulluch on Oct. 13, 1915.

1897 Ryder, C. F., M.A. (Mobilized Aug. 1914). Lt. Yorkshire Hussars. Soudan C.S., attd. Intelligence Dept., Egypt. Egypt and Palestine. *O.B.E.* *D.* § Mar. 1918; Palestine, 1918.

1912 St. Audries,* A. P., Lord (Oct. 3, 1914). Lt. 5th Somerset L.I. (T.F.). India.

1907 St. John,* G. R. (Nov. 12, 1914). Capt. R. Fusiliers. France. *M.C.*, June 4, 1917. *D.* France, 1917.

1892 Salmon, Rev. T., M.A. (July 5, 1917). Chaplain to the Forces (4th Class).

1900 Samson, W. L., B.A. (Aug. 21, 1914). Lt. R.N.V.R. Capt. R.A.F. *D.F.C.*, Jan. 1, 1919.

1901 **Sanders, H. S.,** M.A. (Sept. 2, 1914). ‡Lt. 6th R. Warwickshire Regt. (T.F.). France, 1918. Killed in action at Achiet-le-petit on Aug. 21, 1918.

1914 Sandford, V. H., B.A. (Dec. 18, 1914). Lt. Q.O. Oxfordshire Hussars. Lt. 2nd Life Guards. France.

1920 Saunders, J. M. (Nov. 27, 1917). ‡2nd Lt. Air Service, U.S. Army.

1904 Savory, R. C., B.A. (Dec. 1, 1914). Maj. and D.A.D.R., Remount Service. France, 1916–19. *D.* France, 1918.

1907 Scanlan, Rev. G. E. B., B.A. (June 1915). Sergt. R.A.M.C., No. 2 Base Depot. France, 1915–18.

1919 Scott, E. (Jan. 2, 1916). ‡Lt. 5th Canadian Siege Batt. France, 1917–18.

1910 Scott, J. B., B.A. (Serving Aug. 4, 1914). Capt. 7th Hussars (Lt.-Col.). India, 1914–17; Mesopotamia, 1917–19.

1912 Scott,* O. A. (Aug. 22, 1914). Maj. 10th Hampshire Regt. Salonika. *D.S.O.*, June 3, 1918. *D.* Salonika, 1918.

1906 Scott,* R. A., B.A. (Serving Aug. 4, 1914). Capt. W. Riding Regt. (Invalided.)

1898 **Scott, S. G.,** B.M., M.A. (July 1, 1916). Capt. R.A.M.C. France, 1917; Italy, 1917–18. Died on Jan. 6, 1918, of illness contracted while on active service.

1884 Scrivener, H. S., M.A. (May 15, 1916). Capt. R.A.S.C. *M.B.E.* (Mil.). *D.* § Mar. 1919.

1918 Segar, R., B.A. (Aug. 1916). Capt. and Adj. Worcestershire Regt. Capt. General List. Courts Martial Officer. Chief Nat. Service Representative, No. 8 Area (1918). France, 1917.

1899 Semon, S. C. G., D.M. (Jan. 7, 1915). Capt. R.A.M.C. Médaille de l'Assistance Publique (en argent).

1896 Seymour, B. (Serving Aug. 4, 1914). Maj. 1st K.R.R.C. France. (Invalided on account of wounds, July 1918.)

1901 Seymour, C. E. (Sept. 4, 1914). Lt., temp. Capt., 2nd Dragoons (S.R.). G.S.O. 3. Egypt and Palestine. Croix de Chevalier de la Légion d'Honneur. *D.* Palestine, 1918, 1919.

1899 Seymour, M. H., M.A. (Serving Aug. 4, 1914). Maj. 2/10th Gurkha Rifles. Staff-Captain. Mesopotamia. *D.* Mesopotamia, 1917.

1903 Shiel, G. G., M.A. (Apr. 18, 1915). Maj. 3rd Northumberland Fusiliers, attd. M.G.C. Salonika. *M.C.*, June 3, 1918. *D.* Salonika, 1917, 1918.

1912 Shorthose, D. N. (Dec. 12, 1914). Lt., Acting Capt., R.F.A. France, Mesopotamia.

Shrapnel, V. G. F. (Sept. 1915). Capt. 8th E. Surrey Regt. France and Belgium, 1917–18. Killed in action on Mar. 23, 1918.

1919 Shute, D. A. F. (May 12, 1917). 2nd Lt. 3rd Dorsetshire Regt., attd. 11th Somerset L.I. France and Belgium.

1919 Sich, G. W. (Apr. 1917). 2nd Lt. Grenadier Guards. France.

1889 Simcox, A. H. A., B.A. (Mobilized 1914). Maj. Bombay Artillery, I.D.F. India. *D.* India, 1919.

1899 Simonds, F. A. Hon. Lt. R.A.M.C.

1897 Simonds, J. H., B.A. (Dec. 10, 1914). Maj. 2/4th R. Berkshire Regt. France.

1898 Simpson, A. R., B.A. (Oct. 6, 1915). Capt. N. Scottish R.G.A.

1911 Simpson,* T. B., M.A. (Aug. 6, 1915). Lt. 3rd R. Scots. France and Belgium, 1916–18.

1896 Singer, C. J., D.M. (Nov. 23, 1914). Capt. R.A.M.C. Malta, Salonika.

1919 Slade, G. P. (Jan. 5, 1918). 2nd Lt. 6th Corps Signal Coy., R.E. France, 1918; Germany, 1918–19.

1899 Smith, A. L. F., M.A., *M.V.O.* (Dec. 20, 1914). Capt. 9th (Cyclist) Hampshire Regt. India, Mesopotamia.

1908 Smith, G. H. G., B.A. (Mar. 9, 1917). Lt., Acting Maj., R.E. (Postal Section). Salonika. *M.B.E.* (Mil.). *D.* Salonika, 1919.

1901 Smith, G. M. (Serving Aug. 4, 1914). Capt. 1st E. Lancashire Regt. S. Africa, 1914; France, 1914–15. (Prisoner of war, May 1915–Dec. 1918.)

1904 Smith,* H. A., M.A. (Dec. 12, 1914). Lt. 8th Oxf. & Bucks. Lt. Infty. Capt. M.G.C., attd. Ministry of Information. France, 1915–16.

1904 **Smith, H. H.,** B.A. (Aug. 1914). ‡Capt. 8th K.O. Scottish Borderers. France. Killed in action at Loos on Sept. 25, 1915.

1869 Smith, Rev. H. R. C., D.D. (Serving Aug. 4, 1914). Chaplain (3rd Class), 7th London Regt. T.D.

1913 **Smith,* L. L. de B.** (Aug. 1914). Lt. 6th Rifle Brigade. France and Belgium, 1914. Killed on duty in Sheppey on Sept. 2, 1916, during an air raid.

1890 [Smith, N. C., M.A.] 2nd Lt. Dorsetshire Vol. Regt. (Commission relinguished.)

1893 Smith, P. G., M.A. (Mobilized Aug. 4, 1914). Maj. Q.O. Yorkshire Dragoons. France and Belgium, 1915–16.

1909 Smith, R. C., B.A. (Aug. 11, 1914). ‡Lt. 251st Bde., R.F.A. (Maj.). France and Belgium, 1915–17. *M.C.*, June 18, 1917. (Invalided on account of wounds, 1918.)

1910 Smyth, G. M., B.A. (Sept. 13, 1914). Capt. 6th Loyal N. Lancashire Regt. Capt. 31st Wing H.Q., R.A.F. Gallipoli, Suez Canal, Mesopotamia, Persia.

1913 Snow, C. E., B.A. (Aug. 1917). Capt. A.D.C. to O.C. 4th F.A. Bde., U.S. Army. France, 1918; Germany, 1918–19.

1906 **Somers-Smith,* J. R.,** B.A. (Mobilized Aug. 4, 1914). Capt. 5th London Regt. (London Rifle Brigade). France and Belgium. *M.C.*, Jan. 14, 1916. *D.* France, 1915. Killed in action at Gommecourt on July 1, 1916.

1907 [Somervell,* D. B., M.A.] (Mobilized Aug. 4, 1914). Capt. 1/9th Middlesex Regt. (Staff-Captain). India, 1914–17; Mesopotamia, 1917–19. *O.B.E* (Mil.). *D.* Mesopotamia, 1918.

1904 **Southwell, E. H. L.,** B.A. (Apr. 24, 1915). Lt. 9th Rifle Brigade (Capt.). France. Killed in action near Flers on Sept. 15, 1916.

1872 Southwell, Rt. Rev. H. K., D.D. (Mobilized Aug. 4, 1914). Chaplain to the Forces (1st Class) (Asst. Chaplain-General). France and Belgium. *C.M.G.*, June 1916. *D.* France, 1915, 1916.

1908 Sparrow,* R. W., B.A. (Serving Aug. 4, 1914). Capt. 20th Hussars. France, Belgium, 1914–18; Germany, 1918. *M.C.*, Jan. 1, 1917.

1905 Sparrow, W. G. K., B.A. (Mobilized Aug. 1914). Capt. Cheshire Yeomanry. Egypt, Palestine, France.

1894 Spencer-Churchill, E. G., B.A. (Sept. 15, 1914). Capt. Grenadier Guards. France, 1914–18. *M.C.*, Oct. 16, 1918. Croix de Guerre. *D.* France, 1917.

1919 Spencer-Churchill, Lord I. C. (July 1917). 2nd Lt. R.A.S.C.

1892 Spranger, F. J. G., B.A. (Oct. 6, 1914). Lt.-Col. R.A.O.C. France and Belgium, 1916–17, 1918–19; Italy, 1917–18. *O.B.E.* (Mil. and Civil). *D.* France, 1916, 1917, 1918; Italy, 1918.

1912 **Sproat, G. M.** (Sept. 1, 1914). Lt. 11th, attd. 17th, Manchester Regt. Gallipoli, France. Killed in action in the Battle of the Somme on July 1, 1916.

1919 Squance, T. C. (Nov. 1916). Lt. 1/7th Durham L.I. (Capt. and Adjt.). France and Belgium, 1917–19.

1885 Stainer, J. F. R., B.C.L., M.A. (Sept. 19, 1914). Sergt. E. Surrey Regt.

1899 Stanhope, Earl (Serving Aug. 4, 1914). Lt.-Col. 1st Grenadier Guards. G.S.O. 1, General Staff, afterwards Parliamentary Secretary to War Office. France. *D.S.O.*, June 4, 1917. *M.C.*, Jan. 14, 1916. Croix de Chevalier de la Légion d'Honneur. *D.* France, 1915, 1917.

1903 **Stanhope, Hon. R. P.,** M.A. (Aug. 5, 1914). Capt. 3rd Grenadier Guards. France and Belgium. Killed in action during attack on Les Bœufs on Sept. 15, 1916.

1912 Stanley,* Lord (Aug. 1914). Capt. Grenadier Guards (Bde. Maj.). France, Italy. *M.C.*, June 3, 1919. Croce di Guerra.

1904 **Steer, G. P.,** B.A. (Serving Aug. 4, 1914). Capt. Somerset L.I. India, France, 1915. Died on Dec. 26, 1915, at Wimereux of wounds received in action on Nov. 25, 1915.

1899 **Stephenson, C. S.** (Sept. 1914). ‡Lt. 9th Lancers. France. Died on Dec. 6, 1916, of illness contracted on active service.

1914 Stevens, T. E. A. (Oct. 1914). Capt. Berkshire Yeomanry. Egypt, Sinai, Palestine.

1902 **Steward,* Rev. A. A.,** B.A. (Oct. 11, 1915). Lt. R.F.A. and R.F.C. France and Belgium. Killed in action in 2nd Battle of Ypres on Oct. 6, 1917.

1897 Stewart, D. M. (Aug. 6, 1915). Lt. I.A.R.O., attd. 2/154th Indian Infantry. India.

1890 Stewart, Sir F. H., M.A. (Aug. 8, 1914). Maj. Calcutta Scottish, I.D.F. India. *K.C.I.E.*

1901 Stewart, R. H. R., B.A. (Oct. 1914). ‡Paymaster Lt. R.N.R. North Sea and West of Scotland patrols.

1884 Stilwell, G. H., M.A. (Mobilized Aug. 1914). Lt. 4th Hampshire Regt. (T.F. Res.). V.D.

1913 Stilwell, J. G., M.A. (Mobilized Aug. 4, 1914). Capt. 1/4th Hampshire Regt. India, 1914–15; Mesopotamia, 1915–16. (Prisoner in Turkey, Jan. 1916–Nov. 1918.)

1899 Stilwell, W. B. (Mobilized Aug. 1914). Lt.-Col. 1/4th Hampshire Regt. Mesopotamia and India. *D.S.O.*, Apr. 15, 1916. *D.* Mesopotamia, 1915.

1904 Stinton, T., M.A. (Mar. 31, 1915). Capt. 1/8th Worcestershire Regt. France, Italy. Italian Bronze Medal for Military Valour.

1913 Stirling,* J. (Aug. 15, 1914). Capt. 1/2nd Lovat's Scouts. Gallipoli, Egypt, Macedonia, Russia. *M.B.E.* (Mil.). *D.* Salonika, 1918, 1919.

1902 Stobart, H. M., B.A. (Mobilized Aug. 4, 1914). Hon. Lt.-Col. T.F. Res. (Lt.-Col. Asst. Director of Light Railways, 1916). France, Belgium. *C.B.E.* (Mil.). *D.S.O.*, Jan. 1, 1918. *D.* France, 1917.

1902 Stobart,* J. D., B.A. (Dec. 23, 1914). Capt. Hampshire Yeomanry.

1910 Stobart, R. L. (Mobilized Aug. 1914). Capt. and Adjt. 1/1st Northumberland Hussars (Maj.). France, 1914–18. *M.C.*, Jan. 1, 1919.

1911 Strange,* V. C., B.A. (Aug. 29, 1914). Capt. 8th Devonshire Regt. France, Italy.

1896 Strong, A. T., B.A. (Mar. 11, 1917). Lt. 1st (Garr.) Bn. Worcestershire Regt.

1897 Strutt, G. A. (Mobilized Aug. 4, 1914). Maj. Derbyshire Yeomanry (Lt.-Col.). Egypt, 1915; Gallipoli, 1915; Salonika, 1916; France, 1917; Italy, 1918. *D.* Gallipoli, 1916; France, 1919.

1907 Strutt, G. St. J., B.A. (Sept. 5, 1914). ‡Capt. 5th Essex Regt. France.

1882 Stuart, Sir S. H. Lechmere (Aug. 31, 1914). Lt.-Col. 2nd County of London Yeomanry. France. *D.* France, 1917.
1919 Studholme, H. G. (Aug. 10, 1917). Lt. Scots Guards. France and Belgium, 1918.
1919 Studholme, J. M. R. (May 1, 1917). Lt. Canterbury Mounted Rifles, N.Z.E.F. Egypt, Palestine, Syria, 1917–19.
1899 Sturrock, W. D., D.M. (Dec. 10, 1914). Lt.-Col. R.A.M.C. (T.F.). Belgium, France, Macedonia, Caucasia. *D.S.O.*, Jan. 11, 1919. *D.* Salonika, 1917.
1899 Sugden, K. A. R., M.A. (Serving Aug. 1914). Capt. Unattached List, T.F., Rossall School O.T.C.
Swallow, E. H. (July 14, 1916). ‡2nd Lt. 6th Middlesex Regt. France and Belgium. Killed in action at Zillebeke on Oct. 11, 1917.
1874 Swan, C. A., M.A., *C.M.G.* Hon. Col. 3rd Lincolnshire Regt.
1908 Sweet-Escott, W. W., B.A. (Oct. 29, 1914). Lt. 15th Hampshire Regt. (Capt.). India, 1914–16 ; Mesopotamia, 1916 ; France and Germany, 1918–19.
1905 Symon, C. J. B., M.A. (Sept. 1, 1914). Lt. Coldstream Guards. France and Belgium, 1916–18. *M.C.*, Feb. 18, 1918.
1909 Symon, O. S. (June 30, 1915). ‡Lt. Cyclist Corps, A.I.F. Egypt, France.
1905 Tallents, P. C., M.A. Chota Nagpur Light Horse. India.
1912 Tankerville-Chamberlayne, C. H. L. F. M. T. (Jan. 16, 1915). 2nd Lt. 5th Leinster Regt. Lt. Scots Guards. France.
1909 Taylor,* J. (Nov. 16, 1914). 2nd Lt. R.F.A. (S.R.). France. *M.C.*, Sept. 26, 1916.
1900 Thomas, B. (Nov. 22, 1914). Maj. 8th Gloucestershire Regt. France and Belgium. *D.S.O.*, Jan. 1, 1918. *D.* France, 1917.
1900 Thomas, H. J., B.A. (Sept. 18, 1914). ‡Lt. 2nd Life Guards and Guards M.G. Regt. Belgium and France.
1906 Thomson, C., B.A. (Aug. 1, 1914). Maj. 202nd Heavy Batt., R.G.A. France, 1916 ; Palestine, 1917–18.
1896 Thornton, C. F. (Mobilized Aug. 18, 1914). Maj. 3rd Wiltshire Regt. (Bde. Maj.). *D.* § Feb. 1917, § Aug. 1919.
Thornton, D. S. (July 1915). 2nd Lt. 11th Sherwood Foresters. France. Killed in action at Le Sars on Oct. 1, 1916.
1901 **Tillard, P. A.,** B.A. (Aug. 1914). Capt. 6th E. Surrey Regt. France. Killed in action on the Somme on Nov. 18, 1916.
1919 Timothy, D. R. G. (Oct. 1916). 2nd Lt. 3rd, attd. 9th, R. Sussex Regt.
1900 Tindal-Carrill-Worsley, P. E., B.A. (Mar. 1915). Capt. Shropshire Yeomanry (Maj.). *D.* § Mar. 1919.
1904 [Tizard, H. T., M.A.] (Oct. 1914). Lt.-Col. Technical Officer, R.A.F. *A.F.C.*, Nov. 2, 1918. *D.* § Mar. 1918.
1900 Todd, R. G. (Aug. 28, 1914). Lt. R.N.V.R. Motor Boat Patrol. *D.* Admiralty, Nov. 1918.
1888 Tomlinson, R. G., B.A. (Mobilized Aug. 1914). Capt. R.F.A. (T.F.).
1919 Topping, C. (Sept. 20, 1918). Cadet No. 8 O.C.B.
Tredgold, J. C. (1914). ‡Lt. R. Scots (S.R.). German S.W. Africa, France, and Belgium. *M.C.*, May 26, 1917. Killed in action on Apr. 12, 1917.
1913 **Trench,* Hon. F. S.** (Nov. 11, 1914). Lt. K.R.R.C. France and Belgium. Killed in action on Nov. 13, 1916.

1906 Trevelyan,* C. W., M.A. (Oct. 1914). Capt. 5th London Regt. (London Rifle Brigade). D.A.P.M. 55th Div. France and Belgium. *M.C.*, July 3, 1915. *D.* France, 1915, 1917, 1919.
1910 Tristram, R., B.A. (Jan. 25, 1916). Lt. 3rd Northumberland Fusiliers. France, 1917.
1908 Trotter,* A. M. G., B.A. (Sept. 1914). ‡Lt. A/250th Bde., R.F.A. (Maj.). Egypt, France. *M.C.*, Jan. 1, 1918.
1910 Trower,* A. K., B.A. (Aug. 22, 1914). Capt. 7th R. Sussex Regt. France. (Invalided on account of wounds, Jan. 1918.)
1904 Tudhall, T. B. D., M.A. (May 20, 1916). Lt. Quebec Regt., C.E.F. France.
1901 **Turbutt, G. M. R.,** B.A. (Mobilized Aug. 1914). Lt. 3rd, attd. 2nd, Oxf. & Bucks. Lt. Infty. France, 1914. Killed in action in Oct. 1914.
1898 Turner, C. W. A., B.A. Bombay Light Horse. India.
1910 Turner,* G. C., M.A. (Oct. 7, 1914). Capt. 2/23rd London Regt. G.S.O. 3, 47th Div. France, 1915–18. *M.C.*, June 3, 1918. *D.* France, 1918, 1919.
1907 Turner, G. McD. (Sept. 9, 1914). Lt. 5th Yorkshire Regt. Lt., Hon. Capt., Staff Officer, R.A.F.
1909 Twining,* R. H. (Oct. 1914). Capt., Bt.-Maj., 2/5th Queen's (R. W. Surrey Regt.). Gallipoli, 1915; France, 1918. *D.* §Aug. 1917; France, 1918.
Tyson, A. B. (Aug. 1914). Capt. 2nd Arg. & Suth'd. Highlanders. France, 1915–17. Killed in action at Fontaine-lez-Croiselles on Apr. 23, 1917.
1919 Tyson, H. A. M. (July 29, 1915). Lt. 4th Arg. & Suth'd. Highlanders (A.D.C. to G.O.C. Scottish Command). France, 1916–17.
1912 Tyson,* J. D., B.A. (Aug. 15, 1914). Capt. 4th Arg. & Suth'd. Highlanders. France, 1915, 1917. (Prisoner of war, Dec. 1917–Nov. 1918.)
1878 Underhill, G. E., M.A. Maj. 1st Vol. Bn. Oxf. & Bucks. Lt. Infty.
1913 Upton,* Hon. H. A. G. M. H. (Aug. 29, 1914). Lt. R.E. Kent Yeomanry.
1919 Van Oss, M. D. (Sept. 29, 1916). 2nd Lt. R.F.A. France, 1917–18. (Invalided Sept. 1918.)
1905 [Vaux, F. G., B.A.] (Aug. 5, 1914). ‡Lt. 5th Durham L.I. France, 1916–19.
1903 Venables,* Rev. E. M., M.A. (July 27, 1915). 2nd Lt. Unattached List, T.F., Felsted School O.T.C.
1906 Venables, J. F., B.M. (Jan. 21, 1915). Capt., Acting Maj., R.A.M.C. Egypt.
1891 Venables, W. A., B.A. (Aug. 19, 1914). Capt. Remount Service.
1895 Verdin, R. N. H. (Mobilized Aug. 1914). Maj., temp. Lt.-Col., 2/1st Cheshire Yeomanry. *D.* § Feb. 1917.
1914 Vernon, H. B. (June 1, 1915). Lt. 1st Grenadier Guards (S.R.). France. *M.C.*, Jan. 11, 1919.
1912 **Vernon, H. D.** (Aug. 1914). 2nd Lt. 7th King's (Liverpool Regt.). Lt. Grenadier Guards. France, 1915–16. Killed in action on the Somme on Sept. 15, 1916.
1903 **Villiers, A. H.,** B.A. (Aug. 30, 1914). ‡Lt. Lothians & Border Horse, attd. M.G.C. (Capt.). Egypt, 1914–15; France, 1917. Killed in action at Bourlon Wood on Nov. 28, 1917.
1910 Villiers, G. J. T. H. (Sept. 1914). Lt. Grenadier Guards. France, 1915.

1909 **Vince,* W. L.,** B.A. (Aug. 29, 1914). Capt. 14th R. Warwickshire Regt. France. Killed in action near Oppy on May 8, 1917.
1919 Vivian, A. H. S. (Feb. 4, 1918). 2nd Lt. R.F.A.
1912 Wales,* H.R.H. the Prince of, D.C.L., *K.G.*, (Aug. 8, 1914). Capt., temp. Maj., Grenadier Guards. G.S.O. 2. Col.-in-Chief 12th Lancers, R. Scots Fusiliers, and D.C.L.I. Col. Welsh Guards. France, Belgium, Egypt, Italy, 1914–19. *G.C.M.G. G.C.V.O. G.B.E. M.C.*, June 3, 1916. Croix de Guerre. Order of St. George (3rd Class). *D.* France, 1916.
1899 Walker, B. J. (Oct. 16, 1914). Lt.-Col. 8th R. Sussex Regt. France. *D.S.O.*, June 3, 1918. *D.* France, 1918, 1919.
1902 Walker, C. F. A., M.A. (Serving Aug. 4, 1914). Capt., temp. Lt.-Col., Grenadier Guards. France and Belgium, 1914–18. *M.C.*, Jan. 14, 1916. Croix de Chevalier de la Légion d'Honneur. *D.* France, 1915, 1918.
1909 **Walker,* F. C.,** B.A. (Aug. 1915). Lt. 1/5th King's (Liverpool Regt.). France and Belgium. Killed in action at Ypres on Sept. 20, 1917.
1891 Walker, J. A., M.A. (Mobilized Aug. 5, 1914). Capt. 6th Essex Regt. Maj. M.G.C. Egypt and Palestine. *D.* Egypt, 1917.
1905 Waller, Rev. C. L., M.A. (Serving Aug. 4, 1914). Chaplain R.N. Grand Fleet. France, 1917–18.
1904 **Walling, E.,** M.A. (Mobilized Aug. 1914). Capt., Acting Maj., 7th W. Yorkshire Regt. France and Belgium. *M.C.*, Jan. 1, 1918. Croix de Guerre. *D.* France, 1917. Killed in action at Kemmel Hill on Apr. 25, 1918.
1895 Walton, F. J. (Mobilized Aug. 1914). Maj. Montgomeryshire Yeomanry. Egypt, 1916.
1919 Warner, C. F. A. (Oct. 5, 1914). Capt. 14th R. Fusiliers. France, 1915–17.
1915 Warren, A. P. (July 8, 1916). Lt., Flying Officer, R.A.F. France. (Prisoner of war.)
1907 Warren, J. R., M.A. (Mobilized Aug. 1914). Capt. 4th R. Sussex Regt. (Maj.). Gallipoli, France, Palestine, Egypt, Belgium. *M.C.*, Feb. 1, 1919.
1895 Waterhouse, P., B.A. (Aug. 26, 1914). Lt. R.E. (T.F.).
1899 Watkins, H. G. (Mobilized Aug. 3, 1914). Col. Coldstream Guards, attd. Staff, XIII Corps. France, 1914, 1916–19; Egypt, 1915. *C.B.E.* (Mil.). Chevalier du Mérite. *D.* France, 1917, 1919.
1911 Watterson, J. W., M.A. (Feb. 19, 1915). Capt. 2/4th Somerset L.I. India, 1916; Palestine, 1917; France, 1918.
1910 Wavell-Paxton, R. G., B.A. (Serving Aug. 4, 1914). Capt. Coldstream Guards. France and Belgium, 1914. (Prisoner of war, Oct. 1914.) *D.* May 5, 1919.
1903 Weatherby, F. (Aug. 1914). ‡Capt. Q.O. Oxfordshire Hussars. France. *M.C.*, July 26, 1918.
1896 Weatherby, J. T. (Serving Aug. 4, 1914). Maj., temp. Lt.-Col., Oxf. & Bucks. Lt. Infty. France. *D.S.O.*, June 3, 1915. Croix de Chevalier de la Légion d'Honneur. *D.* France, 1914; § Mar. 1918; France, 1919.
1896 Webster, J. A., B.A. (Sept. 1914). Capt., Bt.-Maj., 8th London Regt. (Post Office Rifles). France. *D.S.O.*, Mar. 8, 1919. Cavalier of the Order of St. Maurice and St. Lazarus. *D.* France, 1918.
1894 Welch, F. B., M.A. (Feb. 20, 1916). Lt. Interpreter, Special Lists. Salonika. *D.* Salonika, 1918.

1919 Weldon, T. D. (Sept. 17, 1915). Lt., Acting Capt., 57th Batt., R.F.A. France. *M.C.*, Feb. 15, 1919; *Bar*, Jan. 1, 1919. *D.* France, 1918.

1904 Wellesley, G. V. (Mar. 7, 1915). Capt. Q.O. Oxfordshire Hussars. France. *M.C.*, June 3, 1916.

1919 Wellesley-Wesley, C. M. St. M. (Sept. 10, 1916). Gentleman Cadet, R.M.C., Sandhurst. (Discharged unfit, 1918.) Enlisted as 3rd Air Mechanic, R.A.F., June 1918.

1909 Wells,* H. B., B.A. (Nov. 16, 1914). Lt. R.F.A., Mobilization Directorate, War Office. France, 1915. *M.B.E.* (Mil.). *D.* § Aug. 1918.

1907 **Wells, H. M. V.,** B.A. (Oct. 1914). 2nd Lt. 1/4th R. Berkshire Regt., attd. R.A.F. Belgium and France, 1915. Missing, believed killed in action in Sept. 1916.

1911 Westmacott,* R. B., M.A. (Oct. 10, 1914). Lt. R.G.A., empld. Ministry of Munitions.

1909 Wharton, A. F., B.A. (Mobilized Aug. 1914). Capt. 5th Hampshire Regt. India and Burma, 1914–19.

1907 Wheatley, C. J. H. (Mobilized Aug. 1914). Capt., Acting Maj., 1/1st Warwickshire Yeomanry, attd. M.G.C. Egypt, Sinai, Palestine, France. *D.* France, 1919.

Whinney, J. A. P. (Oct. 1915). 2nd Lt. Q.O. Oxfordshire Hussars. France. Killed in action at Guillemont Farm, Lempire, on June 22, 1917.

1903 Whitaker, H. S. (Aug. 2, 1915). Lt. R.N.V.R. Italy.

1897 Whitaker, W. H. B., B.A. (Mobilized Aug. 4, 1914). Maj. Montgomeryshire Yeomanry. France, 1918–19.

1908 Whiteley, Hon. R. G., B.A. (Dec. 2, 1915). Lt. R.G.A. (Maj.). *O.B.E.* (Mil.).

1897 Whitnall, S. E., D.M. (Sept. 1915). Capt. R.A.M.C. (T.F.). France.

1912 Wigan,* D. G. (Aug. 5, 1914). Capt. K.R.R.C. France.

1904 Wight, A. N. (Sept. 15, 1915). Lt. 4th Q.O. Cameron Highlanders (T.F.).

1919 Wightman, W. A. (May 22, 1916). Lce.-Cpl. Q Special Coy., R.E. France, 1916–19.

1907 Wilkie, A. H. (Serving Aug. 1914). Capt. K.R.R.C. (Maj.). France, Italy. *D.* France, 1917; § Mar. 1919.

1912 Wilkinson,* W. D., M.A. (Dec. 1914). Capt. 7th Yorkshire Regt. France, 1915–18; India, 1918–19. *D.S.O.*, Feb. 8, 1917. *M.C.*, Aug. 25, 1916. *D.* France, 1917.

1903 Willey, F. V., M.A. (Aug. 1914). Lt.-Col. Sherwood Rangers, attd. R.A.O.C. Egypt and Gallipoli, 1915. *C.M.G.*, Jan. 1, 1918. *C.B.E.* (Mil.). *M.V.O.* *D.* § Feb. 1917, Feb. 1918.

1919 Williams, E. S. (Apr. 14, 1916). Lt. R.A.F. (Flight Commdr.). France.

1916 Williams-Vaughan, E. A. (Sept. 25, 1915). 2nd Lt. 3rd Shropshire L.I. (Invalided, 1916.)

1900 Willis, C. A., B.A. (Mar. 1, 1916). Capt. Special Lists, attd. Intelligence Dept., Sudan. Sudan. *O.B.E.* (Civil). Order of the Nile (4th Class). *D.* Egypt, 1916; Sudan, 1919.

1917 Willis, R. H. (Mar. 1918). 2nd Lt. R.G.A. (on demobilization).

1900 **Willoughby, E. C.,** B.A. (Sept. 25, 1914). Capt. 7th Gloucestershire Regt. France. Died on Aug. 8, 1915.

1906 Wills, F. N. H., B.A. (Mobilized Aug. 1914). Capt. R. N. Devon Yeomanry, attd. M.G.C.

1900 Wills, Sir G. A. H., Bt., M.A. (Mobilized Aug. 1914). Maj. R. N. Devon Yeomanry. Lt.-Col. M.G.C. Gallipoli, Egypt, France. *O.B.E.* (Mil.). *D.* France, 1918; § Mar. 1918.

1915 Wilson, L. G. (July 5, 1916). Gnr. 128th Batt., R.F.A. France, 1916–19.

1898 Wingfield, M. ff. R. (Mobilized Aug. 1914). Lt. 3rd Oxf. & Bucks. Lt. Infty. (Placed on Half-Pay List on account of ill health.)

1900 Winser, Rev. A. A. P., M.A. (Oct. 23, 1917). Chaplain to the Forces (4th Class).

1901 Wolryche-Whitmore, G. C., B.A. (Mobilized Aug. 1914). Capt. 1/1st Shropshire Yeomanry. Egypt.

1899 Wood, W. T., B.A. (Aug. 18, 1915). Lt.-Col. R.A.S.C.

1919 Woodcock, H. H. W. W. (Dec. 1915). Lt. B Batt., A.A., Parkhurst, R.G.A. France and Belgium, 1917.

1906 Woodhead, S., M.A. (Oct. 28, 1914). ‡Sub-Lt. R.N.V.R., H.M.S. *Changuinola*. German S.W. Africa, 1914–15; North Sea, N. American Waters, W. Coast of Africa, 1916–19.

1902 Woodward, A. M., M.A. (Nov. 24, 1915). Lt. Intelligence Corps (Staff-Lt.). Salonika, 1915–18. *D.* Salonika, 1916, 1918.

1909 Wormald,* L. G., B.A. (Sept. 17, 1914). Capt., Acting Maj., R.F.A. France. *M.C.*, Jan. 1, 1918.

1905 **Worsley, E. G.,** B.A. (Feb. 3, 1916). 2nd Lt. 3rd Grenadier Guards (S.R.). France, 1916. Died on Sept. 17, 1916, of wounds received in action on the Somme.

1904 Worsley, H. H. K., B.A. (Aug. 1914). Lt. Nigeria Regt. Cameroons, Nigeria.

1900 Worsley, H. M., B.A. (Sept. 1, 1914). ‡Lt. Q.O. Oxfordshire Hussars (Capt.). France. *M.C.*, Sept. 17, 1917.

1907 **Worsley,* J. F.,** B.A. (Oct. 1915). Lt. 3rd Grenadier Guards. France. Killed in action at Fontaine Notre Dame on Nov. 27, 1917.

1919 Wright, J. B. (June 18, 1916). Driver, Section Sanitaire Anglaise, No. 20, French Army. France, 1916–19. Croix de Guerre.

1885 Wright, P. C., B.A. (Sept. 17, 1914). Capt. 36th Northumberland Fusiliers. France, 1916, 1918.

1911 Wrong, E. M., M.A. (Jan. 22, 1918). 2nd Lt. Unattached List, T.F.

1899 Wyld, H. J., B.A. (Mobilized Aug. 4, 1914). Maj. Hertfordshire Yeomanry. D.A.P.M., 5th Div. Egypt, Gallipoli, France. *D.* France, 1919.

1904 Wylly, H., Port Defence Volunteers, Calcutta. India.

1898 Wynyard, H. B. W., B.A. (1914). Air Defence Corps, R.N.V.R.

1898 **Yeatman, H. F.,** B.A., B.C.L. (Aug. 4, 1914). Capt. 1st Dorset Yeomanry. Egypt, Palestine. Killed in action at Beitunia on Nov. 21, 1917.

1910 **Young, E. T.,** B.A. (Mobilized Aug. 1914). Capt. 8th Cameronians. Gallipoli. Killed in action in Gallipoli on June 28, 1915.

BRASENOSE COLLEGE

1892 **Abell, W. H.** (Serving Aug. 4, 1914). Maj. 4th Middlesex Regt. France, Aug. 1914. Killed in action at Obourg on Aug. 23, 1914.

1919 Adams, C. K. (1918). 2nd Lt. E. Surrey Regt. France, 1918.

1906 Agar-Robartes, Hon. A. V. (Serving Aug. 4, 1914). Lt., Acting Maj., Grenadier Guards, attd. Guards M.G. Regt. France. *M.C.*, Sept. 26, 1917.

1914 Agnew, E. K. (Dec. 17, 1914). Lt. 20th Manchester Regt. Lt. 36th Bn. M.G.C. France, 1915–16, 1917–19.

1914 Agnew, N. M., B.A. (Sept. 20, 1915). Lt. 73rd A.A.S., R.F.A. France, Salonika.

1913 Alchin,* G. (Aug. 12, 1914). Capt. R.F.A. (S.R.). Maj. R.A.F. France, 1914. *A.F.C.*, June 3, 1919.

1912 Alcock,* J. E., B.A. (Sept. 29, 1914). Capt. 5th London Regt. (London Rifle Brigade). France, 1914–15.

1890 **Allan, W. L. C.** (Serving Aug. 4, 1914). Maj. 3rd K.O. Scottish Borderers. France, 1914. Killed in action at Givenchy on Oct. 13, 1914.

1910 **Allies, A. E.,** B.A. (Aug. 1914). Lt. 8th R. Welch Fusiliers. Gallipoli. Killed in action at Anzac on Aug. 16, 1915.

1906 [Amery, G. D., M.A.] (Dec. 11, 1914). Maj. 15th Hampshire Regt. France. *M.C.*, Jan. 1, 1917.

1889 Anderson, J. F., M.A. (Mobilized Aug. 1914). Lt.-Col. 3rd Highland L.I. *D.* § Aug. 1919.

1893 Andrew, G. P., B.A. (Mar. 1915). Lt. I.A.R.O., 8th Gurkha Rifles, attd. Staff. India.

1885 Ashby, Rev. P. O., M.A. (Mobilized Aug. 1914). Chaplain to the Forces (4th Class), attd. 14th Div. (S.C.F.). France, 1915, 1916, 1917 ; Egypt, 1915. *M.C.*, Jan. 14, 1916. *D.* France, 1915.

1919 Ashwell, T. G. L. (Aug. 2, 1916). Capt. 10th Rifle Brigade. France. *M.C.*, Oct. 27, 1917 ; *Bar*, Feb. 4, 1918.

1905 Atkinson, D., B.A. (Oct. 29, 1917). Gunner Signaller 2/1 S.M. (Warwick) Heavy Batt. R.G.A.

1903 Aubertin, T., B.A. (Mobilized Aug. 4, 1914). Maj. 5th The Black Watch, Embarkation Staff Officer, Cologne (Lt.-Col.). France, Belgium, Germany.

1899 **Back, H. A.,** M.A. (Nov. 1915). 2nd Lt. 3rd, attd. 1st, Gloucestershire Regt. France. Killed in action at Mametz on Sept. 22, 1916.

Badcock, F. M. (Oct. 3, 1914). Capt. 5th Gloucestershire Regt. France, 1916, 1917–18. *M.C.*, Dec. 17, 1917. Killed in action during German advance on Mar. 27, 1918.

1910 **Bailey,* G. H.** (July, 1914). Capt., Acting Maj., R.H.A. Gallipoli, Egypt, France. *M.C.*, Feb. 2, 1916. *D.* Gallipoli, 1915. Killed in action at Morval on Feb. 28, 1917.

1912 Bailey,* V. H., B.A. (Serving Aug. 4, 1914). Capt. 53rd Bde., R.F.A. (3rd Lahore Div.). France, 1915–16; Egypt and Palestine, 1916–19. *M.C.*, June 3, 1919.

1911 **Baillie, E. H.** (Aug. 1914). Capt. 10th Cameronians. France. Killed in action at Hill 70, near Loos, on Sept. 26, 1915.

1896 Baker-Cresswell, H. G., M.A. (Mobilized Aug. 1914). Capt. London Signal Coy. R.E. (T.F.).

1886 Barker, F. G., M.A. (Mobilized Aug. 1914). Lt.-Col. 3rd Berkshire Regt. and Special Lists. France. *C.B.E.* (Mil.). *D.* § Feb. 1917.

1888 Barker, G. E. (Serving Aug. 4, 1914). Lt.-Col. 6th Middlesex Regt. *D.* § Feb. 1917. (Resigned.)

1919 Barlow, M. M. (Apr. 7, 1917). Lt. King's Own (R. Lancaster Regt.). Salonika.

1919 Barlow, V. H. (May 5, 1918). 2nd Lt. R.G.A.

1919 Barnes, A. G. (Jan. 2, 1918). 2nd Lt. 1st Somerset L.I. France.

1900 Barrow, Rev. A. E. J. B., M.A. (Nov. 11, 1918). Chaplain to the Forces (4th Class). Belgium and France, 1918–19.

1910 Barrow, H. P. (Oct. 1, 1914). Lt. 26th London Bde., R.F.A. France and Belgium.

1881 Barry, L. E. (Aug. 1914). Maj. 1st Life Guards (Res. Regt.). France, 1914–16. *D.* France, 1915.

1920 Barstow, J. M. O. (Apr. 3, 1917). Lt. 17th Lancers. France, Belgium.

1897 Batchelor, G. J. L., M.A. (Nov. 18, 1914). Capt. 2/1st Kent Cyclist Bn. (Education Officer). France. *D.* § Aug. 1918.

1888 **Bayly, J.**, M.A. (Mobilized Aug. 1914). Maj. R.N. Devon Yeomanry. Gallipoli. T.D. Died of illness on Feb. 26, 1918.

1912 Beard, E. C., B.A. (Oct. 1, 1914). Lt. 2nd R. Irish Rifles (Maj.). Gallipoli, Salonika, Palestine, France. *M.C.*, Apr. 11, 1918. *D.* Salonika, 1917.

1913 **Benn,* A. M.** (Aug. 22, 1914). Lt. 9th W. Yorkshire Regt. (Capt.). Gallipoli, Egypt, France, 1915–16. Killed in action at Stuff Redoubt on Sept. 27, 1916.

1873 Benson, H. W., *D.S.O.* (Serving Aug. 4, 1914). Lt.-Col. 14th Welsh Regt.

1909 Beresford-Peirse, A. C. P. de la P. (Mobilized Aug. 4, 1914). Capt. 5th Durham L.I. (Maj.). France. *M.B.E.* (Mil.). *D.* § Aug. 1918.

1919 Binnie, T. G. J. (May 5, 1917). Lt. 6th K.R.R.C. France, Germany.

1919 Binns, B. O. (Apr. 3, 1917). Lt. I.A.R.O., attd. 37th Dogras (Capt.). Mesopotamia, India, N.W. Frontier.

1916 Binns, J. H. (Aug. 26, 1917). 2nd Lt. U.S. Infantry, Res. Corps.

1913 **Blackett,* C. R.** (Aug. 15, 1914). 2nd Lt. 2nd Shropshire L.I. France, Belgium. Missing, believed killed in action at Zonnebeke on April 26, 1915.

1883 Blair, A. S. (Mobilized Aug. 4, 1914). Lt.-Col. 9th R. Scots (T.F.). France and Belgium, 1915–17. *C.M.G.* 1915. T.D. *D.* France, 1915, 1917.

1913 Blair, J. R. (Mar. 1915). Lt. 10th Middlesex Regt. Capt. 30th Lancers, Indian Cavalry. India.

1905 Bleaden, W. H., B.M., M.A. (Mobilized Aug. 1914). Surgeon Lt., R.N.V.R. North Sea.

1879 Blencowe, J. I. (Oct. 1914). Capt. Sussex Yeomanry, attd. W.D. Lands Branch (Maj.).

1897 Bloxsom, C. W. (1916). Sergt. A.P.D. Asst. Bond Officer, Ministry of Munitions.

1896 **Blyth, R. C. P.** (Serving Aug. 4, 1914). Capt. 1st Gloucestershire Regt. Gallipoli. Killed in action in Gallipoli on June 4, 1915.

1896 Blyth, T. T., M.A. (Aug. 7, 1914). Capt. R.A.S.C., attd. D.A.A.G.'s Office, 5th Army H.Q. France.

1881 Bodington, Ven. Archdeacon E. J., M.A. (Serving Aug. 4, 1914). Chaplain (3rd Class), 4th Wiltshire Regt.

1919 Bolton, A. (Mar. 4, 1917). ‡2nd Lt. R.F.A. France, 1917–18.

1913 **Bolton,* H. F.** (July, 1915). Lt. 103rd Bn. M.G.C. France. Died on May 3, 1917, of wounds received in action at Fampoux, near Arras.

1919 Booker, R. E. E. (July 2, 1917). 2nd Lt. 4th, attd. 7th, The Buffs (E. Kent Regt.). France.

1913 **Boor, A. P.** (Dec. 28, 1914). Lt. 7th Oxf. & Bucks. Lt. Infty. Lt., Flying Officer, R.F.C. France, Salonika, Italy, Egypt. Died, Nov. 1917, of wounds received in action.

1911 Bostock, L., B.A. (Dec. 2, 1914). Capt. 7th Northamptonshire Regt. France. *D.S.O.*, Sept. 16, 1918. *D.* France, 1918.

1885 Boswell, J. D., B.A. (Mobilized Aug. 4, 1914). Lt.-Col. 12th (Ayrshire Yeomanry Bn.) R. Scots Fusiliers. Gallipoli, Egypt, Palestine, France. T.D. Order of the White Eagle (4th Class) (with Swords).

1919 Bowen, C. L. J. (Aug. 5, 1914). ‡Lt. King's Own (R. Lancaster Regt.) (Capt.). France and Belgium, 1915–19.

1898 Bowly, W. A. T., M.A. (Serving Aug. 4, 1914). Maj. Warwickshire Regt. Temp. Lt.-Col. G.S.O. 1. Mil. Sec. to Sec. of State for War. France and Belgium, Aug. 1914–18. *C.B.E.* (Mil.). *M.C.*, Jan. 1, 1915. Bt.-Maj. 1916. Chevalier de l'Ordre de Léopold. Belgian Croix de Guerre. *D.* France, 1914, 1915 three times, 1917, 1918.

1894 Boycott, A. E., D.M. (June 25, 1917). Capt., Bt.-Maj. R.A.M.C. *D.* § Aug. 1918.

1919 Bozman, G. S. (Oct. 2, 1915). ‡Lt., Flying Officer, R.A.F. France, 1916–17.

1920 Bradley, F. I. (May 3, 1917). Lt. R.A.F. (Flight Commdr.).

1919 Bradnack, B. O. (Jan. 26, 1917). Lt. R.G.A. France. *M.C.*, July 26, 1918.

1897 Brakspear, F. G. (Dec. 13, 1915). Capt. R.A.S.C.

1906 **Brandt, D. R.,** B.A. (Aug. 4, 1914). Lt. 6th, attd. 1st, Rifle Brigade. France and Belgium. Killed in action in Belgium on July 6, 1915.

1906 Bray, H. R., B.A. (Aug. 4, 1914). R. Canadian Navy. ‡Lt. Canadian Garrison Artillery (Capt.). Pacific and Atlantic Oceans; France.

1914 **Brewis, A. P.** (Oct. 1914). Capt. 1st Northumberland Fusiliers. Gallipoli, 1915–16; Sinai, 1916–17; France, 1917. *D.* France, 1917. Killed in action in Havrincourt Wood on June 1, 1917.

1919 Brewis, N. H. (June, 1918). Cadet R.A.F.

1900 [Brierly, J. L., B.C.L., M.A.] (Oct. 1914). 2nd Lt. 7th Wiltshire Regt. Capt., Bt.-Maj., General List. D.A.A.G., G.H.Q., Constantinople. *O.B.E.* (Mil.). *D.* § Feb. 1917.

1910 Broadbent,* H., M.A. (Aug. 6, 1914). Capt. 7th Lancashire Fusiliers; Staff-Capt. Egypt, 1914–15; Gallipoli, 1915; Macedonia and Turkey, 1918–19. *D.* § Mar. 1919.

1894 Brocklehurst, E. (Feb. 1915). Maj. Special Lists, empld. Remount Depot.

1901 Bromilow, H. A., B.A. (Mobilized Aug. 1914). Maj. Lancashire Yeomanry, attd. 1/4th Shropshire L.I. (Lt.-Col.). France, 1915–19. *D.* France, 1918, 1919.

1880 Brooke, F. W. (Jan. 22, 1915). Capt. 10th Suffolk Regt., attd. 118th Coy. Labour Corps. France and Belgium, 1917.

1907 Broom, C. G. M., M.A. (Dec. 3, 1914). Lt. Unattached List, T.F., City of London School O.T.C.

1907 Brougham,* H., B.A. (Sept. 1914). Maj. R.F.A. France.

1909 **Brown,* E. F.,** B.A. (Aug. 1914). ‡Capt. 5th Wiltshire Regt. Gallipoli, 1915; Mesopotamia, 1915–17. Died on April 1, 1917, of wounds received in action in Mesopotamia on Mar. 29, 1917.

1906 Brown, O. F., M.A. (Mar. 17, 1915). Lt. R.N.V.R.

1895 Buchan, J., M.A. (June 1, 1916). Lt.-Col. Special Lists (Director of Information). France, 1916–17. Officier de l'Ordre de la Couronne. Officer of the Order of the Crown of Italy.

1912 **Buckley, F. G.** (Aug. 29, 1914). Capt. 8th Northumberland Fusiliers. Gallipoli, 1915; Egypt, France, and Belgium, 1916–17. *M.C.*, June 4, 1917. *D.* France. Killed in action near Poelcappelle on Aug. 16, 1917.

1897 Bucknall, B. E. (Oct. 1914). ‡Capt. 3rd Inniskilling Fusiliers. France, Belgium.

1906 Bullough, I. (Serving Aug. 4, 1914). Capt. Coldstream Guards (Maj.). France, Belgium, Germany. *M.C.*, Sept. 27, 1918. *D.* France, 1918 twice.

1908 Burn, P., B.A. Hong-Kong Vol. Corps.

1907 Burne, C. H., B.A. (Nov. 1914). Lt. A.S.C. Lt. R. Defence Corps. Capt. General List, T.F. Res., attd. General Staff (Intelligence). France.

1910 Burton, R. C., B.A. (Oct. 17, 1914). Capt. K.R.R.C. France.

1904 Bush, C. W., B.A. (1917). 2nd Lt. U.S. Army Y.M.C.A.

1901 **Bussell, Rev. J. G.,** M.A. (Sept. 9, 1914). Capt. 7th R. Sussex Regt. France and Belgium. Killed in action in Belgium on June 28, 1915.

1913 Caccia, A. M., M.A., *M.V.O.* (July, 1915). Maj., General List, G.S.O. 3. France, 1915–17, 1918–19 (with Supreme War Council). *C.B.* Croix de Chevalier de la Légion d'Honneur. Chevalier of the Order of S. Maurice and S. Lazarus. *D.* § Feb. 1917.

1910 **Cairns, H.,** B.A. (Nov. 1915). 2nd Lt. 13th K.R.R.C. France and Belgium. Killed in action near Ypres on Oct. 4, 1917.

1903 [Calder, W. M., B.A.] (Nov. 16, 1914). 2nd Lt. Unattached List, T.F., Manchester University O.T.C.

1913 Cameron, G. F. (Aug. 4, 1914). ‡2nd Lt. 6th Q.O. Cameron Highlanders. France. (Relinquished Commission on account of ill health caused by wounds, July 27, 1917.)

1906 Campbell, Rev. H. C. M., M.A. (Oct. 1915). Chaplain to the Forces (3rd Class). Gallipoli, Egypt, France. *M.C.*, Sept. 22, 1916. *D.* France, 1917 twice.

1910 **Campbell, J.,** B.A. (Oct. 1915). Capt. R. Marines. France. Killed in action at Oppy Wood on Apr. 28, 1917.

1919 Campbell, P. J. (Sept. 1, 1916). Lt., Acting Capt., C/150th Bde., R.F.A. France and Belgium. *M.C.*, July 26, 1918.

1890 Carr, D. W., B.A. (Sept. 1915). Lt. R.A.O.C. Egypt, 1915–17.

1881 Casson, A. C. B., M.A. Lt. R.N.V.R.

1909 Chamberlen, Rev. L. G., M.A. (Jan. 9, 1917). Chaplain to the Forces (4th Class), attd. Tank Corps H.Q. (Chaplain, 3rd Class). France, 1917–19; Germany, 1919. *M.C.*, Jan. 1, 1919.

1919 Chamberlen,* L. S. (May 15, 1915). Lt. 6th Rifle Brigade. France, 1916, 1917, 1918. *M.C.* Apr. 12, 1917.

1890 Chapman, M. H. (Mobilized Aug. 1914). Capt. 3rd Sherwood Foresters.

Chester, R. H. V. (Mar. 3, 1917). Lt., Instructor, R.A.F. Accidentally killed at Stamford, Lincolnshire, on July 13, 1918.

1906 **Chinnery, E. F.** (Serving Aug. 1914). Capt. Coldstream Guards, attd. R.F.C. France, Belgium, 1914–15. *D.* France, 1914. Killed while testing an aeroplane near Paris on Jan. 18, 1915.

1894 Chinnock, H. S. (Apr. 29, 1915). Capt. Special Lists, empld. Remount Depot.

1913 **Christian,* E. C.** (Aug. 14, 1914). Capt. 7th S. Staffordshire Regt. Gallipoli, Suvla Bay, Egypt, France. Killed in action in France on Sept. 11, 1916.

1900 Cleave, J. R. Sub-Lt. R.N.V.R.

1907 **Clegg,* F. C.**, B.A. (Aug. 1914). Capt. 6th Border Regt. Gallipoli. Killed in action at Suvla Bay on Aug. 22, 1915.

1912 **Coats, E. R.** (Dec. 1914). Lt. 1st Scots Guards (Capt.). France. Killed in action near Arras on May 17, 1918.

1889 Cockcroft, E. F. (Aug. 4, 1914). Maj. 1/1st Brecknockshire Bn. S. Wales Borderers. Aden and India, 1914–15.

1906 Coe,* T. P., B.A. (Mar. 11, 1915). Capt. 7th Norfolk Regt. Capt., General List. Bde.-Maj. 43rd Inf. Bde. France and Belgium. *M.C.*, Mar. 30, 1916.

1919 Coffey, T. M. (Oct. 7, 1914). Lt. 5c. Res. Bde., R.F.A. France.

1919 Collenette, C. B. R. (Sept. 17, 1914). ‡Capt. 2/18th London Regt. (London Irish Rifles). France, 1915, 1916; Salonika, 1916–17. *M.C.*, Jan. 1. 1918. *D.* Salonika, 1917. (Relinquished Commission on account of ill health caused by wounds.)

1878 Collis, G. R. H., M.A. (Sept. 22, 1914). Maj., Hon. Lt.-Col. 11th Gloucestershire Regt. France.

1893 Comyns-Carr, P. A. V. (Oct. 23, 1915). Capt. Intelligence Corps. Maj., Staff-Officer R.A.F. France. Croix de Guerre. *D.* France, 1917.

1900 Connop, G. R., B.A. (Dec. 1, 1914). Lt. County of London Yeomanry, attd. 24th London Regt. (The Queen's).

1905 Cooper, C. M., M.A. (Aug. 15, 1914). Lt. 3rd Durham L.I. (Capt. 1st Northumberland Fusiliers.) France 1915–17. *M.C.*, Oct. 20, 1916. *D.* France, 1916. (Retired on account of wounds, Oct. 1918.)

1888 Coventry, R. G. T., B.A. (Jan. 9, 1915). Capt. 6th Worcestershire Regt. (Resigned.)

1891 Cowan, C. H., B.A. (Aug. 1914). ‡Capt. 1/4th Hampshire Regt. (Maj. and A.P.M.). India, Mesopotamia.

1908 **Coxhead,* M. E.**, B.A. (Serving Aug. 4, 1914). Maj. R. Fusiliers, i/c 9th Bn. France. *D.* France, 1917. Killed in action near Monchy on May 3, 1917.

1895 Crawshay, L. R., M.A. (May 1, 1915). Trooper 1st King Edward's Horse; Cpl. Field Survey Coy. R.E.; Cadet R.A.F. France, 1915–18.

1911 Creery,* L. (May 12, 1915). Lt. 4th R. W. Kent Regt.

1912 Creese,* H. R., B.A. (Oct. 1, 1914). Lt. 16th Div. Signal Coy., R.E. France, 1917–18. (Relinquished Commission on account of wounds.)

1904 Crick, Rev. T., M.A. (June 14, 1917). Chaplain R.N.

1919 Crimmins, R. G. (Dec. 14, 1917). ‡2nd Lt. Ordnance Corps U.S. Army.
1913 Croft, G. C. (Oct. 1914). 2nd Lt. Yorkshire Hussars; Lt. Coldstream Guards (S.R.). France.
1909 **Crooke,* E. H.,** B.A. (Aug. 5, 1914). Capt. 8th Gloucestershire Regt. France, 1915–16. Killed in action at La Boisselle on July 3, 1916.
1885 Crowdy, W. M., B.A. (Mobilized Aug. 1914). Capt. 3rd Devonshire Regt. G.S.O. 3. France.
1901 Crundall, E. R., B.C.L. (Oct. 30, 1914). Maj. 2nd R. E. Kent Yeomanry, attd. Ministry of Munitions. (Resigned.)
1909 **Cuninghame,* A. K. S.** (Serving Aug. 4, 1914). Capt. Grenadier Guards. Belgium and France, 1914–16. *D.* France, 1915. Killed in action near Les Boeufs on Sept. 25, 1916.
1912 Cunningham,* St. C. U. (Aug. 15, 1914). Capt., Bde.-Maj. R.A., 27th Div. France, 1914–15; Salonika, 1915–18; Caucasus, 1918–19. *M.C.*, June 4, 1917. *D.* Salonika, 1917, 1919.
1915 Currie, A. McL., B.A. (Jan. 30, 1916). Lt. 4th Loyal N. Lancashire Regt. France.
1902 **Dacres, L. S. L.,** B.A. (Jan. 1915). Capt. I.A.R.O., attd. 21st Cavalry F.F. Mesopotamia. *D.* Mesopotamia, 1918. Died at Baghdad on April 20, 1919, of illness contracted while on active service.
1897 Davidson, D., D.M. (Aug. 1914). Capt. R.A.M.C. (T.F.). France, 1915–17; Italy, 1917–18. *M.C.*, Jan. 1, 1917.
1914 **Davies, C. B.** (Mar. 10, 1915). Lt. 3rd Dublin Fusiliers. France. Killed in action on June 9, 1916.
1909 Davies,* J. H., B.A. (July 8, 1916). Lt. I.A.R.O. India.
1908 Davis,* G. H., M.A. (Aug. 1914). Lt. 4th London Regt. (R. Fusiliers). France.
1910 Dawe, A. J., B.A. (Dec. 10, 1914). Lt. R.N.V.R.
1919 Dawson, C. W. (Mar. 9, 1915). Lt. 15th E. Surrey Regt. (Capt.). India, N.W. Frontier, Mesopotamia.
1912 de Freitas, S. M., B.A. (Oct. 19, 1915). ‡Lt. R.A.F. France, 1916–17; Egypt, 1917–19.
1906 De la Bere,* R., M.A. (Dec. 1916). Capt. R.G.A., attd. R.F.A. France.
1893 Denning, H. F. (June 21, 1916). 2nd Lt. Lancashire Hussars.
1903 Denison, Rev. H. B. W., M.A. (Nov. 25, 1915). Chaplain to the Forces (4th Class).
1913 de Vere,* A. A., M.A. (Serving Aug. 4, 1914). Lt. Gloucestershire Regt., empld. Min. of Munitions.
1913 Devereux,* R. G. de B., M.A. (Mar. 17, 1915). Lt. Welsh Guards. France.
1890 Dewhurst, W. A. (Nov. 30, 1914). Lt. R. Defence Corps.
1908 Digby, A. E. H., B.A. (Feb. 25, 1915). 2nd Lt. R. Marines. (Invalided.)
1908 Dixey, J. C., B.M. (Mobilized Aug. 1914). Capt. 241st Bde., R.F.A. (T.F. Res.). France and Belgium.
1898 Dixon, G. F., B.A. (April, 1916). ‡Lt. R.A.S.C. *D.* § Aug. 1919.
1886 [Dodds-Parker, A. P., B.M., M.A.] (Aug. 5, 1914). Lt.-Col. R.A.M.C., attd. 3rd Southern General Hospital. *D.* § Sept. 1917.
1891 Donaldson, W. P. (Oct. 5, 1914). Maj. K.O. Scottish Borderers.
Douglas, A. H. (Sept. 1914). Lt. 9th R. Scots Fusiliers. France. Killed in action at Armentières on Sept. 16, 1916.
1907 Downing, W. N., B.A. (Sept. 1914). Lt. Welsh Guards. France.

1879 Drummond, M. P. D. G. (Oct. 4, 1914). ‡Capt. Special Lists; Remount Service. France and Belgium. *D.* France, 1917.

1912 Dubash, J. K., M.A. (Aug. 13, 1915). Petty Officer R.N.V.R. (Chief Petty Officer).

1891 Duff, R. W. (Mobilized Aug. 1914). Maj. R.F.A.

1876 Dugdale, F., *C.V.O.* (Mobilized 1914). Lt.-Col. Warwickshire Yeomanry (T.F. Res.). T.D. *D.* § Feb. 1917.

1909 Duke,* L. G., M.A. (Sept. 1914). Lt. 8th Queen's (R. W. Surrey Regt.). (Wounded and prisoner of war, Sept. 1915.) France.

1889 Dunn, W. S. (Sept. 28, 1914). Capt. Remount Service. France, 1914. *D.* § Aug. 1918.

1902 Dunston, T. F. G. W., B.A. (June 25, 1915). Sergt. R.A.S.C. (M.T.) (Coy. Sergt.-Maj.). France, Belgium, E. Africa.

1896 du Vallon, H. C. de J., B.A. (Jan. 18, 1915). Capt. 11th W. Yorkshire Regt. Capt. General List, empld. as Interpreter. (Relinquished Commission on account of ill health contracted on active service.)

1900 Dyott, R. A., B.C.L., M.A. (Nov. 7, 1914). Maj. H.A.C. (T.F. Res.). France. *D.* France, 1917.

1875 Eckersley, N. ff., M.A. Lt. Shropshire Vol. Regt. Hon. Col. Manchester Regt.

1919 Edmonds, H. R. O. (Oct. 7, 1918). Cadet R.E.

1904 Edwardes-Ker, D. R., M.A. (Aug. 14, 1914). Capt. 5th The Buffs (E. Kent Regt.) Lt.-Col. R.E. France, Belgium. *O.B.E.* (Mil.). *D.* France, 1918 twice.

1889 Edwards, E., M.A. (Dec. 24, 1914). Paymaster Lt. R.N.R.

1910 **Egerton-Green,* J. W. E.,** M.A. (Aug. 4, 1914). Capt. 1st Rifle Brigade. France and Belgium. Died at Boulogne on Oct. 9, of wounds received in action near Langemarck on Oct. 5, 1917.

1902 Eiffe, L. G. P., B.A. (Mar. 26, 1917). ‡Lt. Special Lists, empld. Recruiting Duties.

1910 Ellis,* A. E., B.A. (Aug. 1914). Capt. 12th London Regt. (The Rangers). France and Belgium.

1884 Ellis, F. H. B., M.A. (Oct. 25, 1915). Sergt. Instructor 23rd Rifle Brigade School of Musketry. *D.* § Mar. 1919.

1919 Ellis, J. P. M. (May 13, 1918). Lce.-Cpl. 1st K.R.R.C. (Cpl.).

1908 Emsley, C. H., M.A. (Mobilized Aug. 3, 1914). Maj., 150th Batt., R.F.A. Belgium, France, 1915–19. *D.* France, 1918.

1908 English, G. C., B.A. (Sept. 29, 1914). Lt. 7th N. Staffordshire Regt. Lt. General List (Capt.). Gallipoli, Mesopotamia, Salonika. *D.* Salonika, 1919.

1919 Evans, C. H. (Jan. 3, 1917). Lt. 5th Rifle Brigade. France, 1917.

1920 Evans, E. (July 20, 1917). 1st Lt. Camp Ordnance Officer, Camp Shirman, Ohio, U.S. Army.

1900 Eveleigh, E. C. (Dec. 1915). ‡Capt. R.A.S.C., attd. 18th Bde., R.G.A. Belgium, France, Germany.

1899 Evetts, E. F., B.A. (Sept. 21, 1914). Capt. 1/5th Queen's (R. W. Surrey Regt.). A.D.C. to G.O.C. 15th Indian Div., M.E.F. India, 1914–15; Mesopotamia, 1915–19. *D.* Mesopotamia, 1918 twice.

1919 Facey, R. V. (Sept. 1916). ‡Lt. 143rd Squadron R.A.F. Belgium, 1917–18.

1905 Fairburn, C. E., M.A. (Jan. 24, 1915). Capt., Acting Maj., Technical Officer, R.A.F.

1894 Fellows, L. E., B.A. (Oct. 4, 1915). Capt. R.A.S.C.

1907 Fenwick, G. C. D. (Nov. 25, 1916). Lt. R.G.A. (S.R.).
1905 **Fenwicke-Clennell, T. P. E.,** B.A. (Oct. 1914). Capt. Lothians and Border Horse. Salonika, 1917–19. Died on Feb. 20, 1919, from injuries received at Salonika.
1900 Ferguson, Rev. W. A., M.A. (June 2, 1916). Chaplain (Capt.), Canadian E.F.
1911 Ferreira,* H. M. F. (Aug. 7, 1914). ‡Lt. Northumberland Fusiliers. Capt. R.A.F. France and Belgium. Croix de Guerre.
1919 Fielden, L. (Dec. 4, 1914). Lt. R.G.A.
1907 Finch-Hatton, Hon. D. G., B.A. (Sept. 1914). Lt. General List, attd. R.A.F. (Capt.). E. Africa, Mesopotamia. *M.C.*, Feb. 1, 1917.
1905 Finnigan, J. Manchester Regt.
1887 Fisher, J. C., B.M., M.A. (July 17, 1915). Capt. R.A.M.C.
1919 Flecker, H. L. O. (Dec. 21, 1914). Capt. Unattached List, T.F. Mesopotamia.
1902 Fletcher, H. F. (Mobilized Aug. 1914). Maj. Denbighshire Yeomanry. Maj., Commandant Western Command, R.G.A., Signal Depot. Egypt.
1885 Force, C. F. B., M.A. 2nd Lt. Special Lists ; Staff-Lt. 2nd Class. (Resigned on account of ill health.)
1888 Ford, J. A., B.A. (Mobilized Aug. 1914). Maj. Cornwall Fortress Engineers. *D.* § Feb. 1917.
1905 Foster, C. H., M.A. (1917). Instructor of Midshipmen at Naval Academy, Annapolis.
1919 Fox, C. (Sept. 21, 1917). 2nd Lt. 145th Heavy Batt. R.G.A. France, Germany.
1909 Fox,* E. T. Driver R.A.S.C.
1919 Fox, H. F. B. (Mar. 19, 1917). Lt. Suffolk Regt., attd. 10th Highland L.I. France.
1894 Fox, P. P., B.A. (Nov. 12, 1915). Pte. 2/7th Devonshire Regt.
1918 Franklin, J. A. (Jan. 23, 1916). Pte. 28th R. Fusiliers.
1907 **Frere, G. R.** (Sept. 1914). Capt. and Adjt. 10th Rifle Brigade. France. Died on Oct. 26, 1915, of wounds received in action at Laventie.
1910 Frere, P. R., B.A. (May 22, 1915). Paymaster Lt. R.N.R. H.M.S. *Queen*, Italy, 1918 ; H.M.S. *Europa*, Mudros, 1918–19.
1896 **Frost,* K. T.,** B.Litt. (Serving Aug. 4, 1914). Lt. Cheshire Regt. France, Aug. 1914. Killed in action on Aug. 25, 1914.
1894 Frost, M., B.A. (Dec. 18, 1914). Capt. Cheshire Regt. France. *M.C.*, July 26, 1918.
1920 Fry, W. M. (Aug. 4, 1914). ‡2nd Lt. Somerset L.I. Capt. R.A.F. (Maj.). France, 1914–18 ; Egypt and Palestine, 1918–19 ; Germany, 1919. *M.C.*, Aug. 16, 1917.
1903 **Fulton, G. K.** (Feb. 1915). Lt.-Col. 9th Cheshire Regt. France. *D.S.O.*, Sept. 16, 1918. *D.* France 1918 twice. Killed in action on Apr. 15, 1918.
1912 Gadd,* C. J., B.A. (Jan. 20, 1916). Pte. 1st (Garr.) Bn. Worcestershire Regt. Sapper R.E.
1918 Gallaway, P. H., B.A. (Feb. 1915). Staff-Sergt. 3rd Canadian Res. Bn., C.E.F. France.
1910 **Garnett, L. H.** (Aug. 1914). ‡Lt. R.F.A. France and Belgium. Killed in action at Messines Ridge on June 7, 1917.
1879 Gascoyne, W. W., B.A. (Sept. 16, 1914). Capt. 7th The Buffs (E. Kent Regt.). France, 1915–18.

1894 Gibbes, A. M. (Re-employed Feb. 1915). Maj. Res. of Officers. G.S.O. 3, empld. War Office. *D.* § Feb. 1917, Aug. 1918.

1891 Gibbes, F. D. (Mobilized Aug. 1914). Maj. Lincolnshire Yeomanry, afterwards Lt.-Col., T.F. Res. Egypt, Palestine. *D.* Egypt, 1916.

1913 Gibbs, A., B.A. (Feb. 26, 1915). Lt. Welsh Guards (Capt.). France and Belgium, 1915–18. *M.C.*, Jan. 1, 1918.

1918 Gibson, A. H. (Aug. 5, 1914). Lt. 3rd Essex Regt., attd. R.F.C. France, Belgium, 1916. (Discharged Nov. 1917.)

1913 Gilbert, C. G. G. (Mar. 15, 1915). 2nd Lt. 8th R. W. Kent Regt. Lt., Acting Maj. 24th Bn. M.G.C. France and Belgium, 1916–19. *M.C.*, Jan. 1, 1918.

1900 Gilliat, Rev. H. M. E., M.A. (Dec. 20, 1915). Chaplain to the Forces (4th Class). Egypt and Palestine. *D.* Palestine, 1918.

1910 Goldingham, G. R. (Aug. 1914). ‡Capt. R.M.L.I., attd. 223rd Coy. M.G.C. (Prisoner of war.) *M.C.*, Jan. 13, 1918; *Bar*, Feb. 18, 1918. *D.* France, 1917.

1901 Good, C. H. B., B.A. (Aug. 1914). Capt. 15th Hampshire Regt. (Maj.). France, 1917; Italy, 1917–18; France, 1918–19. Belgian Croix de Guerre. *D.* France, 1919.

1905 **Goodyear, F.**, B.A. (Feb. 1915). ‡2nd Lt. 2nd Essex Regt. France, 1915–17. Died at 1st Canadian C.C.S. on May 23, 1917, of wounds received in action.

1907 Gordon,* C. (Dec. 21, 1914). Lt. R.F.A. (Capt.). France, Salonika, Palestine.

1911 **Gordon, S. E. L.** (Aug. 1914). Lt. 4th R. Fusiliers. France and Belgium. Killed in action at Ypres on Mar. 13, 1915.

1893 Gorringe, L. (Sept. 16, 1914). Capt. R.A.S.C. (A.P.M.). E. Africa. *M.C.*, June 4, 1917. *D.* E. Africa, 1916, 1917.

1893 Gorringe, Rev. R. E. P., M.A. (Aug. 22, 1916). Chaplain to the Forces (4th Class). France.

1906 Gould, H. R., B.A. (July 22, 1916). Lt., temp. Capt. I.A.R.O. India.

1892 Graham, J. D. (Aug. 20, 1915). Maj. Lothians and Border Horse. Salonika.

1918 Grant, J. R. (Sept. 29, 1918). Midshipman, H.M.S. *Victory VI.*

1910 Grasett,* G. W., B.A. (Sept. 30, 1914). Maj. R.A.S.C. (M.T.). France. *O.B.E.* (Mil.). *D.* France, 1916, 1917, 1918.

1902 **Green, A.**, B.A. (June, 1915). Lt. Manchester Regt. France. Killed in action on Mar. 26, 1918.

1919 Green, G. E. J. (Oct. 5, 1918). ‡2nd Lt. R.E. (on demobilization).

1895 Green, J. G., B.A. (Serving Aug. 4, 1914). Instructor Commander R.N.

1907 **Greenall, J. E.** (Mobilized Aug. 1914). Capt. Duke of Lancaster's Own Yeomanry, attd. R.F.C. France. Killed in action on Mar. 31, 1918.

1899 Greenhill, C. B., B.A. (Oct. 7, 1914). Capt. W. Somerset Yeomanry, attd. 2/4th Somerset L.I. France.

1901 Grey, W. A. S. (Serving Aug. 4, 1914). Capt. Indian Army. India.

1898 Griffith, I. O., M.A. (Sept. 5, 1915). Maj. Technical Officer, R.A.F. *A.F.C.*, Nov. 2, 1918.

1914 Griffiths, T. S. (Dec. 22, 1914). Lt. 2nd R. Welch Fusiliers (Capt.) (attd. R.F.C. and R.A.F. 1917–19). Gallipoli, Egypt, Mesopotamia, France, India.

1899 Grischotti, W. (Serving Aug. 4, 1914). Capt. 1st Shropshire L.I., attd. R.A.F. France and Belgium.

1890 Grotrian, H. H., M.A. (Oct. 17, 1914). Maj. 11th York and Lancaster Regt. Maj., General List.

1911 **Grubb,* L. E. P.** (Aug. 1914). ‡2nd Lt. 2nd K.O.Y.L.I. France and Belgium. Killed in action at Hooge on Nov. 15, 1914.

1902 **Grundy, G. E.**, M.A. (Sept. 4, 1914). Lt. 9th R. Warwickshire Regt. Gallipoli, 1915. Killed in action in Gallipoli on July 22, 1915.

1897 Gullick, F. W., B.C.L. (July 5, 1915). Capt. Army Pay Dept. *D.* § 1918.

1912 **Gunter,* F. J.** (Aug. 1914). Lt. 11th Hussars. France, Belgium. Killed in action at Ypres on May 24, 1915.

1882 Gwynn, S. L., B.A. (Jan. 15, 1915). ‡Capt. 6th Connaught Rangers. France 1915–16, 1916–17. Croix de Chevalier de la Légion d'Honneur.

1880 Haig, Field-Marshal Douglas, Earl, Hon. D.C.L., *K.C.I.E.* (Serving Aug. 4, 1914). Col. 17th Lancers; Lt.-Gen., Commander, 1st Army Corps, B.E.F.; Commander-in-Chief, B.E.F., 1916–18; Commander-in-Chief, Forces in Great Britain, 1918–19. **A.D.C.** France and Belgium, Aug. 1914–18; Germany, 1918. *K.T., G.C.B., O.M., G.C.V.O.* Grand Officier de la Légion d'Honneur, Grand Croix de la Légion d'Honneur, Grand Cordon de l'Ordre de Léopold, Knight Grand Cross of the Order of St. Maurice and St. Lazarus, Obilitch Medal (Gold), Order of Danilo (4th Class), Order of St. George (4th Class), Rumanian Order of St. Michael the Brave, Serbian Order of Karageorge (1st Class) (with swords), Grand Cordon of the Order of the Rising Sun with Paulowina, Order of Chia-Ho (1st Class), 'Ta-Shou Pao-Kuang,' Order of Rama for Military Merit (1st Class) (Siam), Grand Cross, Order of Tower and Sword, American Cross of Honour, Médaille Militaire, Croix de Guerre, Belgian Croix de Guerre, Medal of 'La Solidaridad' (1st Class) (in gold). *D.* France, 1914 twice, 1915 four times.

1890 Haldane, H. C., B.A. (Dec. 5, 1914). Capt. Lothians and Border Horse; A.D.C. (Courts Martial Officer). France. *O.B.E.* (Mil.). *D.* France, 1916, 1917, 1918, 1919.

1906 Hall, K. L. (1914). Nigerian Land Contingent. Cameroons.

1919 Hall, R. O., B.A. (Sept. 4, 1914). ‡Capt. 18th Northumberland Fusiliers. Maj., General List (Bde.-Maj., attd. H.Q., II Corps.). France, Belgium, Germany, 1916–19. *M.C.*, Jan. 1, 1918; *Bar*, Jan. 1, 1919. *D.* France, 1917.

1903 Halliday, H. E., M.A. (July 11, 1916). Lt. 1/7th Worcestershire Regt. France, Italy. *M.C.*, Feb. 1, 1919.

1919 Hamilton, E. A. D. (May 28, 1917). 2nd Lt. 4th King's Labour Bn., Labour Corps (Coy. Commdr.). France, 1918–19.

1890 **Hammick, S. F.** (Serving Aug. 4, 1914). Capt. Oxf. & Bucks. Lt. Infty. France, 1914–15; Mesopotamia, 1915–16. *D.* Mesopotamia, 1916. Died on Apr. 18, 1916, of wounds received in action at Sanna-i-Yat.

1903 Hammond-Chambers-Borgnis, J. A. (Oct. 6, 1914). Capt. R. Defence Corps (Adjt. and Q.M.). *D.* § Feb. 1917.

1919 Hanbury, H. G. (Nov. 1, 1916). ‡Lt. 3/1st Warwickshire Yeomanry.

1906 Harley,* T. R., M.A. (Serving Aug. 4, 1914). Capt. Unattached List, T.F., St. Alban's School O.T.C.

1919 Harlow, V. T. (Feb. 1917). Lt. 'B' Batt. 285th Bde., R.F.A. Belgium and France, 1917–19. *D.* France, 1919.

1913 Harris,* D.'A. F. H. (Sept. 15, 1914). Lt. 1st Dragoons. France. *M.C.*, July 26, 1918.

1911 Harris,* H. T. T., B.A. (Sept. 14, 1914). Capt. 4th Oxf. & Bucks. Lt. Infty. G.S.O. 3. (Bde.-Maj. 23rd Inf. Bde.) France. *M.C.*, Feb. 15, 1919.
1912 Harris,* L. H. H. (Sept. 15, 1914). Lt. 9th Lancers.
1902 Harris, M. R., B.A. (Jan. 28, 1915). Maj. 13th London Regt. France. *M.C.*, Nov. 14, 1916.
1919 Harrison, A. (Sept. 1914). Capt. 8th Loyal N. Lancashire Regt., attd. 7th T.M. Batt. France, Belgium. *D.S.O.*, Aug. 25, 1916. *D.* France, 1916 twice, 1917. (Wounded and prisoner of war.)
1919 Harrison, G. (Apr. 14, 1917). ‡2nd Lt. R.A.F. France.
1913 Harrison,* R. B., M.A. (July 6, 1915). Lt. R.F.A. Gallipoli, 1915; Egypt, 1916; France and Belgium, 1916–18.
1914 **Hartley,* E.** (Nov. 1914). Lt. 2nd Lancashire Fusiliers. France and Belgium, 1915, 1916, 1917, 1918. Killed in action on May 18, 1918.
1893 Hartley, J. C., B.A. (Sept. 25, 1914). Maj., Acting Lt.-Col. R. Fusiliers. France. *D.S.O.*, Jan. 1, 1919. *D.* France, 1918 twice.
1913 **Harvey, E. H.** (Aug. 1914). ‡Capt. 2/5th Gloucestershire Regt. France. *M.C.*, Sept. 26, 1916; *Bar*, Jan. 11, 1919. Killed in action near Fleurbaix on Sept. 30, 1918.
1911 Harvey, G. M. (1914). ‡Paymaster Sub-Lt. R.N.V.R.
1884 Harvey, R. K. (Mobilized Aug. 1914). Lt.-Col. 5th E. Surrey Regt. T.F. Res. T.D.
1903 **Hatfield, R. B.**, B.A. (Mobilized Nov. 1914). Lt. 8th London Regt. (Post Office Rifles). France and Belgium. Died at Bethune on May 24, 1915, of wounds received in action at Festubert.
1907 Hawker, C. W. S. (Oct. 23, 1914). Lt. 13th Hampshire Regt. Died on Mar. 13, 1918.
1886 Hay, R. N. E. (Aug. 14, 1915). Lt. 6th (Res.) Middlesex Regt.
1885 Hayne, R., B.A. (Oct. 1914). ‡Lt. 157th Coy. Labour Corps (Capt.). France, 1916–18. *D.* France, 1918.
1906 Heale, Rev. T. W., M.A. (Dec. 4, 1917). Chaplain to the Forces (4th Class).
1875 Heath, A. H., M.A. (Dec. 31, 1914). Lt.-Col. R.F.A. (T.F. Res.). T.D. *D.* § Feb. 1917.
1898 Heath, J. G., M.A. (Jan. 1, 1917). Maj. R.A.M.C. English Channel, 1917–18; N. Russia, 1918–19.
1905 Heath, R. A., B.A. (Aug. 5, 1914). Capt. Leicestershire Yeomanry, attd. 5th Lancers (Maj.). France. *M.C.*, Apr. 2, 1919.
1912 Hebbert,* F. L. B., B.A. (Aug. 4, 1914). ‡Lt. R.F.A.; Lt., Acting Capt., Flight Commdr. R.A.F. France and Belgium, 1915–17.
1899 **Hedley, J. W.**, B.A. (Dec. 15, 1914). 2nd Lt., Acting Capt., 2/5th Lancashire Fusiliers. France, 1915–16. Died on Sept. 12, 1916, of wounds received in action at Ginchy.
Hemus, C. H. (Sept. 1916). 2nd Lt. B/87th Bde. R.F.A. France, 1917–18. *M.C.*, June 22, 1918. Died at Doullens on Mar. 27, 1918, of wounds received in action at Bouzincourt, near Albert.
1899 Henderson, H. A., M.A. (Dec. 24, 1915). Lt. Unattached List, T.F., Bedford Grammar School O.T.C.
1901 Henderson, P. C., M.A. (June 17, 1917). 2nd Lt. 1st (Garr.) Bn. Worcestershire Regt.
1906 Henniker-Gotley,* A. L., B.A. (Aug. 1915). Lt. Northern Rhodesia Police (Capt.); Asst. Political Officer. German E. Africa.

1920 Henniker-Gotley, G. R. (Aug. 22, 1914). Capt. 9th N. Staffordshire Regt. Maj. M.G.C. France, Belgium, 1915–16, 1916–17; Italy, 1917–19. *D.S.O.*, June 3, 1918. *D.* France, 1916, 1917; Italy, 1918.

1906 Henry, L. W., M.A. Inns of Court O.T.C.

1912 Herapath,* J. N., M.A. (Nov. 7, 1914). ‡Lt. 10th Devonshire Regt. Salonika.

1890 Heriot, E. A. (Serving Aug. 4, 1914). Capt. S. Wales Borderers, empld. W.A.F.F. W. Africa.

1919 Hill, C. V. (June 13, 1917). 2nd Lt. R.F.A. France.

1911 Hill, F. E., B.A. (Aug. 28, 1914). Lt. 5th Wiltshire Regt. Lt., General List, empld. Min. of National Service. Gallipoli, 1915.

1919 Hill, H. R. (Sept. 3, 1918). Cadet R.E.

Hobart Hampden, G. M. A. (Sept. 2, 1914). Lt. Oxf. & Bucks. Lt. Infty., and R.F.C. France, Belgium, 1915–17. Killed accidentally while flying at Upavon on Sept. 17, 1917.

1914 Hodgson, H. B., B.A. (Jan. 25, 1917). ‡2nd Lt. Worcestershire Regt. France.

1900 Hoghton, C. K., M.A. (Oct. 1915). Lt. R.A.S.C. Egypt, France. *D.* France, 1918.

1893 Holder, H. C., B.A. (Feb. 13, 1915). Capt. R.F.A.

1911 Holdsworth, B. G., B.A. (Nov. 5, 1917). Lt. 1/155th Pioneers, Indian Army. Mesopotamia and Palestine.

1896 Hole, W. S. K. (Mar. 20, 1915). Capt. R.A.S.C.

1919 Holland, E. W. (Jan. 21, 1918). 2nd Lt. 256th Siege Batt. R.G.A. France.

1866 **Holland, W. F. C.,** B.A. (June 28, 1915). Capt. Durham L.I.; Draft Conducting Officer (graded as Staff-Lt.). Died on Nov. 8, 1917, at Seaham Harbour, of frostbite, contracted while on active service.

1887 Holmes, C. J., M.A. R.N.A.S. (Anti-Aircraft). (Resigned.)

1911 Holroyd,* M., M.A. (Aug. 17, 1914). Capt. 3rd Hampshire Regt., empld. War Office (Intelligence Dept.). France, 1915.

Honey, A. C. (May, 1917). 2nd Lt. Worcestershire Regt. Belgium and France. Died on Feb. 10, 1918, of wounds received in action at Cambrai on Nov. 30, 1917.

1907 Hooman, C. V. L. (Feb. 4, 1915). Paymaster Sub-Lt., Acting Paymaster Lt. R.N.R.

1908 Hooper, R. S., B.A. (Sept. 22, 1914). Capt. Herefordshire Regt. (Lt.-Col. while A.A. and Q.M.G.).

1900 **Hopkyns, Rev. T. G.,** M.A. (Apr. 19, 1917). Pte. S.A. Medical Corps. (Sergt.). France and Belgium. Killed in action at Menin Road on Sept. 20, 1917.

1906 **Horlick G. N.** (Jan. 1915). Maj. R. Gloucestershire Hussars, attd. 19th Sqdn. M.G.C. Gallipoli, Egypt and Palestine. *D.* Gallipoli, 1916; Palestine, 1918. Died on July 5, 1918, at Alexandria, of malaria contracted on active service.

1919 Hort, A. V. D. (Sept. 18, 1916). ‡Lt. R.E. (Signals). Egypt and Palestine.

1913 Hoskins, W. L. (Sept. 26, 1916). Capt. Glamorganshire Yeomanry.

1906 Houlder,* A. C., M.A. ‡2nd Lt. 4th Queen's (R.W. Surrey Regt.).

1905 Huggins, C. R., M.A. (1914). Sub-Lt. R.N.V.R.; Maj., Technical Officer, R.A.F.

1918 Huggins, W. J. (Feb. 13, 1917). Pte. H.A.C. (Discharged, Nov. 1917, on account of ill health.)

1879 Hughes, R. G. H. (Sept. 18, 1914). Lt.-Col. Res. of Officers; Draft Conducting Officer.

1919 Hulley, J. J. (July 10, 1918). Cadet No. 23 O.C.B.

1906 **Hunter,* R. J.,** M.A. (Jan. 16, 1915). Capt. 5th London Regt. (London Rifle Brigade). France, 1917–18. Died on Aug. 25, 1918, of wounds received in action.

1903 Hutchinson, W. H. H. (Mobilized Aug. 5, 1914). Maj. R.F.A. (T.F.). France and Belgium. (Wounded and Prisoner of war, 1918.) *M.C.*, Jan. 14, 1916. *D.* France, 1915.

1909 **Hutchison, R. H.,** B.A. (Sept. 1914). Lt. 8th, attd. 1st, The Black Watch. France. Killed in action near Hulluch on Oct. 13, 1915.

1903 Icely, H. E. McL., M.A. (Serving Aug. 4, 1914). Capt. Unattached List, T.F., Bromsgrove School O.T.C.

1904 Ingram, A. I., M.A. (Oct. 1914). Capt. 2/4th Somerset L.I. (Maj.). India, Burmah, Palestine, Egypt, Sudan, 1914–19.

1903 Iredell, Rev. E. O., B.A. (Oct. 4, 1918). Chaplain to the Forces (4th Class).

1889 Irish, H. J. H., B.A. (1914). Anti-Aircraft Corps, R.N.V.R.

1897 Ironside, R. A., B.A. (1914). Capt. Remount Service (Adjt. and Q.M.). E. Africa, 1916–17; France, 1917; Italy, 1918–19. *D.* E. Africa.

1919 Isherwood, T. W. (Aug. 3, 1917). Pte. 4th (Res.) S. Lancashire Regt. (T.F.).

1910 Jackson, A. N. S., B.A. (Oct, 12, 1914). Capt., Bt.-Maj., Loyal N. Lancashire Regt. Temp. Lt.-Col. 13th K.R.R.C., attd. British Delegation, Paris (Brig.-Gen.). France. *C.B.E.* (Civil). *D.S.O.*, June 4, 1917; *1st Bar*, July 18, 1917; *2nd Bar*, May 13, 1918; *3rd Bar*, Dec. 2, 1918. *D.* France, 1916, 1917 twice, 1918 twice, 1919.

1914 Jackson, E. B., B.A. (Dec. 1915). ‡Maj. Heavy Artillery, U.S. Army. France. Croix de Guerre. *D.* American Divisional Orders.

1910 **Jackson, H. H.,** M.A. (Mobilized Aug. 1914). Capt. 15th Hussars, attd. R.A.F. France and Belgium, 1914–17. *M.C.*, Jan. 1, 1917. Died on Nov. 28, 1918, of illness contracted while on active service.

1896 Jackson, J. B. (Jan. 29, 1915). Lt. 5th Sherwood Foresters. Capt. and Adjt. R.A.F. *D.* § Aug. 1919.

1914 Jacobs, A. R. (Aug. 23, 1915). Lt. 9th Yorkshire Regt., attd. 2nd King's Own (R. Lancaster Regt.). France, 1916; Salonika, 1916–18; Turkey, 1918–19.

1913 **Jacques,* E. W. R.** (Sept. 2, 1914). Lt. 1st Northamptonshire Regt. France. Killed in action at High Wood, Foureaux, on Aug. 16, 1916.

1908 Jenkin, C. F., M.A. (April 27, 1915). Lt. R.N.V.R. Lt.-Col. R.A.F. *C.B.E.* (Mil.).

1894 Jenkins, C. E. (Aug. 4, 1914). Maj. Shropshire Yeomanry. Administrative Officer, Tank Corps.

1893 Jenkinson, A. G., M.A. (Dec. 17, 1914). ‡Maj. R.A.O.C. France, 1915–17; Italy, 1917–19.

1910 Jenks,* E. H. (Oct. 1914). Capt. 10th Cameronians. France. *D.* France, 1916, 1919.

1907 Jennings-Bramley, B. (Sept. 18, 1914). 2nd Lt. Interpreter Corps, Indian Army, attd. 19th Lancers. Capt. R.F.A. Staff-Capt. 16th Corps H.Q. Salonika Army. France and Salonika. *M.C.*, June 3, 1918. *D.* Salonika, 1917, 1918.

1888 Johnson, E., M.A. (Mobilized Aug. 1914). Maj. Duke of Lancaster's Own Yeomanry, attd. H.Q. 62nd Div. France.

1919 Johnson, H. S. (Mar. 1, 1916). Lt. R.F.A. France.

1904 Johnson, J. M. O., B.A. (Apr. 30, 1915). Capt. 3rd Cheshire Regt. (Staff-Lt.). Mesopotamia, 1916–19. *D.* Mesopotamia, 1918.

1914 Johnston, C. M. (May 14, 1915). Lt. 8th Arg. & Suth'd. Highlanders.

1913 **Johnston, D. C.** (Oct. 9, 1914). Capt. Cameronians. France. Died at Rouen on Sept. 13, 1918, of wounds received in action.

1894 Jones, Ellis, M.A. (Nov. 20, 1914). Lt. Unattached List, T.F., Bradford Grammar School O.T.C.

1907 **Jones, G. St. J.**, B.A. (Jan. 1915). 2nd Lt. 5th, attd. 4th, Middlesex Regt. France and Belgium, 1915–16. Killed in action on June 14, 1916.

1906 Juett, A., B.M. (Mar. 1, 1916). Capt. A.M.C., A.I.F. France. *D.* France, 1917.

1919 Keay, G. A. (Mar. 1, 1916). Staff-Lt. H.Q. 25th Divl. Artillery, R.A. France, 1916–18. *M.C.*, June 3, 1919.

1883 [Keeling, J. H., M.A.] (Dec. 27, 1914). Capt. 5th London Regt. (London Rifle Bde.), attd. R.E.

1911 Kelly, M. H. (Sept. 3, 1914). ‡Capt. 5th Queen's (R.W. Surrey Regt.). Gallipoli, 1915; France, 1918.

1891 Kennard, C. H. (Nov. 3, 1914). Capt. R.A.S.C.

1911 Ker,* A. M. (July 21, 1914). Capt. 1st Loyal N. Lancashire Regt. Temp. Maj. D.A.D.A. War Office. France and Belgium.

1907 Kewley, E. R., M.A. (Serving Aug. 4, 1914). Capt., Bt.-Maj., temp. Lt.-Col., 3rd Rifle Brigade. France. *D.S.O.*, Sept. 26, 1917; *Bar to D.S.O.*, July 26, 1918. *M.C.*, June 3, 1916. Croix de Guerre. *D.* France, 1916, 1917, 1918 twice.

1910 **Kewley, J. T.** (Aug. 22, 1914). Lt. 6th Loyal N. Lancashire Regt. (Capt.). Gallipoli, Egypt, Mesopotamia. Died on Jan. 16, 1917, of wounds received in action near Kut el Amara.

1876 King, A. C. Maj. (Ret. Pay), General Staff. *D.* § Feb. 1917.

1881 Kirkpatrick, H. P., *D.S.O.* (Mobilized Aug. 1914). Maj. 16th Lancers, Res. of Officers. Died on Aug. 30, 1919.

1904 Knight-Bruce, J. H. W. (Serving Aug. 4, 1914). Capt. 2nd R. Warwickshire Regt. attd. O.C.B. (Staff-Capt.). France and Belgium.

1910 Knott, F. H., B.A. (Dec. 14, 1914). Capt. 3rd Wiltshire Regt. France, 1915; Salonika, 1915–17. *M.C.*, Jan. 1, 1918. *D.* Salonika, 1917. (Relinquished Commission on account of ill health caused by wounds.)

1905 Knox, J. H. (Aug. 4, 1914). ‡Lt., Acting Maj., H.A.C., 309th Siege Batt. Egypt, France. *M.C.*, Dec. 17, 1917. (Invalided, Aug. 1919.)

1908 Laing, T. E. (Nov. 11, 1914). Capt. R.A.S.C. Lt., Hon. Capt., Flying Officer, R.A.F. France. *D.* France, 1915.

1896 Lancashire, J. K., B.A. (Jan. 1918). ‡2nd Lt. I.A.R.O., attd. Supply and Transport Corps. India.

1906 Landon, P. A., M.A. (Aug. 1914). Capt. 4th Essex Regt. France. *M.C.*, June 4, 1917. *D.* France, 1916.

1882 Lane, S. E. R., B.A. (Oct. 1914). Capt. 6th The Black Watch (T.F.). (Resigned.)

1891 Latham, A. M. (Mobilized Aug. 1914). Capt. R.F.A. (T.F. Res.).

Latimer, H. (Jan. 1915). 2nd Lt. 3rd R. W. Kent Regt. France. Killed in action at Ovillers on July 3, 1916.

1912 Lawrence,* E. H. (Aug. 15, 1914). ‡Lt., Acting Capt., 21st Batt. 2nd Bde., 6th Div., R.F.A. France, Belgium, 1915–18; Germany, 1918–19.

1898 **Layton, R. C.** (Mobilized Aug. 1914). Capt. Sherwood Rangers. Salonika, 1916–17; Egypt, Palestine, 1918. Croix de Chevalier de la Légion d'Honneur. Croix de Guerre. Killed in action at Es Salt on April 30, 1918.

1919 Lea, R. S. (July 8, 1916). Lt. 4th Rifle Brigade, attd. 4th R. Fusiliers. Salonika, 1917–18; Germany, 1918–19.

1912 Leask, J. A. G. (Oct. 3, 1914). Capt. King's Own (R. Lancaster Regt.). France and Belgium. *M.C.* Jan. 1, 1918.

1888 Leith, Sir A. (Mobilized 1914). Lt.-Col. Northumberland Hussars. D.A.A. and Q.M.G., Suvla Bay, Mudros East. Lt.-Col. 2nd, 3rd, and 4th Vol. Bn. Durham L.I. France, 1914–15; Gallipoli, Mudros, 1915–16. *M.C.*, June 3, 1916. *D.* Gallipoli, 1916.

1890 Leslie-Jones, L. H., B.A. (Nov. 1914). ‡Lt.-Col. A.A.G., I.A.R.O. India. *O.B.E.* (Mil.).

1893 Lewis, C. A. L., B.A. (Mobilized Aug. 1914). Maj. 4th R. Berkshire Regt. (T.F. Res.), empld. Min. of Reconstruction. France. (Relinquished Commission on account of ill health due to wounds.)

1910 **Lewis, E. R. H.,** B.A. (Nov. 1915). 2nd Lt. 4th Worcestershire Regt. France. Died on Apr. 25, 1917, of wounds received in action near Arras.

1911 **Lewis, L. W.,** B.A. (Aug. 5, 1914). 2nd Lt. K.R.R.C., attd. 165th Bn. M.G.C. France and Belgium. Killed in action at Guillemont on Aug. 9, 1916.

1914 Liddle, D. G. (Aug. 10, 1914). Lt. 8th The Buffs (E. Kent Regt.) (Capt.). France.

1919 Liesching, P. (Aug. 25, 1914). ‡Capt. Tank Corps. France, German E. Africa.

1911 Lindsay,* D. C. M., M.A. (Mobolized Aug. 4, 1914). ‡Lt. 1st The Black Watch. (Asst. Staff-Capt. 205th Inf. Bde.) France, 1914–15, 1916.

1919 Lingeman, P. D. M. (Sept. 23, 1917). Lt. R.A.F. (attd. R.N.). Grand Fleet, 1917–18.

1919 Little, J. C. (May 1, 1917). 1st Lt. Field Artillery, U.S. Army (Capt.).

1919 Llewellyn, P. (Aug. 6, 1916). Lt. 1st Welsh Guards. France, from 1917. *M.C.*, May 13, 1918.

1915 Logan, A. C. (Apr. 12, 1916). Pte 2/4th R. Welch Fusiliers. Clerk R.A.F. (Cpl.).

1908 Logan, W. M., B.A. Lt. A.S.C. (Resigned.)

1919 Lomas, J. E. W. (June 7, 1915). Lt. 5th Rifle Brigade. France.

1901 Lord, J. C. (Jan. 17, 1916). Lt. 5th Lancashire Fusiliers (T.F.). France. (Relinquished Commission on account of ill health caused by wounds.)

1900 Lord, J. E. (Jan. 2, 1915). 2nd Lt. 7th Loyal N. Lancashire Regt. Lt. Training Reserve. France.

1919 Lowe, G. O. (Aug. 28, 1915). ‡Lt. R.A.F. E. Africa, Egypt.

1900 Lowe, R. M., B.A. (Jan. 3, 1916). Lt., Acting Capt., R.G.A. France, 1916–17, 1918.

1896 Lucena, J. L., B.A. (Nov. 24, 1914). Capt. R.G.A. Capt. R.A.F. France, 1915–17.

1896 Lyall, W. H., M.A. (Feb. 3, 1916). Acting Paymaster, A.P.D., afterwards Lt., Acting Capt., R.A.F. *M.B.E.* (Mil.).

1908 **Macdonald,* C. K.,** B.A. (Sept. 10, 1914). Lt. 10th Arg. & Suth'd. Highlanders. France. Killed in action at Loos on Sept. 27, 1915.

1900 Macdonald, R. L., B.A. (June 16, 1915). Lt. Scots Guards. France and Belgium.

1919 Macfadyen, J. A. (Feb. 20, 1917). Driver, S. African A.S.C. German E. Africa, Nyasaland, Portuguese E. Africa. *D.* E. Africa.

1911 Macfarlane,* R. C., B.A. (Sept. 23, 1914). Maj. 12th Arg. & Suth'd. Highlanders. France, 1916; Salonika, 1916–19. *M.C.*, Apr. 22, 1918.

1920 McGowan, F. P. (July 19, 1918). 2nd Lt. F.A., U.S. Army.

1913 McKay,* G. M. (Dec. 12, 1914). Capt. 21st London Regt. (1st Surrey Rifles). France. *M.C.*, June 24, 1916; *Bar*, Nov. 14, 1916. *D.* France, 1916 twice.

1919 Mackenzie, C. A. (Feb. 19, 1917). Lt. 3rd Seaforth Highlanders. Egypt, 1918; France, 1918.

1908 Mackie, J. H., B.A. (1914). ‡Lt. Technical Officer R.A.F.

1919 McKie, J. I. (Aug. 8, 1918). 2nd Lt. King's (Liverpool Regt.) (on demobilization).

1896 Mackintosh, D. E. (Mobilized Aug. 1914). Maj. 3rd Q.O. Cameron Highlanders.

1906 Mains, A., B.A. (Mobilized Aug. 1914). Lt. 3rd County of London Yeomanry. Capt. R.F.A. (T.F.).

1901 Mannering, Rev. E., M.A. (Aug. 1915). Chaplain to the Forces (3rd Class). France, 1915–19.

1899 Manners, R. H. H. (Serving Aug. 4, 1914). Maj. 106th Hazara Pioneers, Indian Army; Bde.-Maj. India.

1919 Manning, C. A. W. (Sept. 1, 1914). ‡Lt. 7th Oxf. & Bucks. Lt. Infty. (Capt.). France, 1915; Salonika, 1915–17. *D.* Salonika, 1916, 1917.

1912 **Marriott, F. E.** (Sept. 1914). 2nd Lt. 7th Rifle Brigade. France and Belgium, 1915. Killed in action at Hooge on July 30, 1915.

Marriott, H. D. (Oct. 1914). 2nd Lt. 8th Rifle Brigade. France and Belgium, 1915. Killed in action in Belgium on Oct. 9, 1915.

1898 **Marriott, H. N.,** M.A. (Dec. 1914). Capt. 12th E. Yorkshire Regt. France. Killed in action on the Ancre on Nov. 13, 1916.

1919 Marriott, R. A. (Oct. 5, 1918). 2nd Lt. 4th Rifle Brigade. Salonika, Trans-Caucasia.

1896 Marsden, Rev. R. S., M.A. (Apr. 20, 1915). Chaplain to the Forces (4th Class). France.

1906 Marshall, C. (Feb. 13, 1915). Capt. 5th Loyal N. Lancashire Regt. (T.F.).

1884 Marshall, E. T., B.A. Maj. (Ret.) E. Yorkshire Regt.

1908 Martin,* E., B.A. (Apr. 12, 1915). Capt. 6th London Regt. (Rifles). France.

1909 Martin, J. H. (Dec. 31, 1914). Capt. 16th London Regt. (Queen's Westminster Rifles).

1901 Master, A., B.A. (Apr. 1, 1917). Capt. 1/17th Bombay, Baroda, and Central India Rly. Bn. Major I.A.R.O. India.

1919 Masterman, K. C. (Nov. 1914). Cpl. 40th Bn. A.I.F. France, 1917–18. (Prisoner of war, Sept. 1918–Jan. 1919.)

1900 Maude, C. R., B.A. (Nov. 5, 1914). Capt. 10th Loyal N. Lancashire Regt. Maj., General List. France. *O.B.E.* (Mil.). *M.C.*, Jan. 1, 1917. *D.* France, 1918, 1919.

1893 May, F. M., M.A. (Sept. 14, 1914). Capt. 20th Divl. Train, R.A.S.C. France and Belgium, 1915–18. *D*. France, 1918.

1913 **May,* R. W.** (Aug. 1914). Lt. 2nd Durham L.I. Belgium. Killed in action at Hooge on Aug. 9, 1915.

1906 Meek, C. K., B.A. (1914). Nigerian Land Contingent. Cameroons.

1912 Mellé, B. G. von B., B.M. (Mobilized Aug. 1914). ‡Capt. R.F.A. (Staff-Capt.). France, 1915–18.

1919 Mellé, H. A., B.A. (Oct. 30, 1914). ‡Lt. 7th Middlesex Regt. German S.W. Africa, German E. Africa.

1905 Mellows, C., M.A. (Nov. 3, 1914). Capt. 1/5th Bedfordshire Regt., attd. Staff E.E.F. (1918). France, Egypt, Palestine.

1901 **Merewether, J. A.,** B.A. (Feb. 1915). ‡Capt. 9th Rifle Brigade. France. Killed in action in the Battle of the Ancre on Sept. 15, 1916.

1912 Meyrick,* R. O. (Feb. 17, 1915). Lt. 1st K.R.R.C. (Capt.). France and Belgium.

1913 **Miles, H. F.** (Aug. 1914). ‡Capt. 2nd K.O. Scottish Borderers. France, Belgium, 1914–16. Killed in action at Falfemont Farm on Sept. 3, 1916.

1905 Miley, J. F. O., B.A. (June 22, 1915). Lt. R.F.A. Courts Martial Officer. France.

1919 Milford, C. S. (July 31, 1915). Lt. 3rd R.W. Kent Regt. (Capt.). Mesopotamia, 1916; France, 1917, 1918; Italy, 1917, 1918. *M.C.*, Dec. 2, 1918.

1904 Milton, E. S. R., M.A. (Nov. 20, 1914). Capt. R.G.A. (T.F.) (Anti-Aircraft duties).

1919 Mincovitch, R. I. (Nov. 30, 1917). Pte. Northumberland Fusiliers.

1911 Mitcalfe,* W. S., B.A. (Aug. 31, 1914). Lt. 251st Bde. R.F.A. (Maj.). France and Belgium. *M.C.*, Sept. 16, 1918.

1910 Monk-Jones,* R., B.A. (Oct. 8, 1914). Lt. 9th S. Lancashire Regt. Egypt, Macedonia.

1906 Mooney, E. W. B., B.A. (May, 1915). Lt. R.A.S.C. (H.T.). Salonika, 1915–16; France and Belgium, 1918–19.

1908 Mooney,* W. McC., B.A. (Aug. 13, 1914). Capt. 1st D.C.L.I. France.

1911 Moore, H. B., M.A. (Aug. 20, 1914). Capt. 9th Rifle Brigade. Maj., General List, attd. 14th Div. France, Belgium, 1915–19. *M.C.*, June 3, 1916. Belgian Croix de Guerre. *D*. France, 1916, 1917, 1918, 1919.

1919 Morgan, C. L. (Aug. 1914). Sub-Lt. R.N.V.R., attd. R.N.D. Antwerp, 1914. (Interned in Holland, Oct. 1914–Nov. 1918.)

1888 Morris, Rev. A. J. (Serving Aug. 4, 1914). Chaplain (4th Class), attd. 1st E. Lancs. Bde. R.F.A. (T.F.).

1919 Morris, L. F. (Oct. 19, 1917). Lce-Cpl. 2/28th London Regt. (Artists' Rifles). France.

1909 Morris-Eyton, C. R. (Mobilized Aug. 1914). Maj. R.F.A. (T.F.). France. *M.C.*, Apr. 26, 1917.

1901 Moseley, F. A., B.A. (1916). Lt. 16th Bn. A.I.F. France.

1914 Mosley, J. I. (Mar. 16, 1915). Lt. 4th D.C.L.I. (Capt.). France and Belgium, 1918–19.

1914 Motion, A. K. (Aug. 4, 1914). Capt. Warwickshire Yeomanry, attd. 62nd Bn. M.G.C. Sinai, Palestine, Senussi, 1915–18; France, 1918–19.

1915 Munday, W. H. (Aug. 27, 1917). Rfln. 3rd Rifle Brigade (Cpl.). France, 1918–19.

1917 Munroe, M. M. (Jan. 1918). Gnr. B. Batt. 17th F.A., U.S. Army. France, 1918.
1898 Murphy, F. P. (Nov. 1915). Lt. A.I.F. Capt. R.G.A. France.
1909 [Murphy, N. R., M.A.] (Oct. 2, 1914). ‡Captain, 3rd R. Irish Fusiliers, attd. Tank Corps. France, Salonika.
1919 Mylius, E. N. (July 1916). Lt. 1/4th Leicestershire Regt. France.
1919 Natestad, H. D. (Oct. 4, 1918). Pte. Unassigned, U.S. Army. (Serving on Draft Board, S. Dakota.)
1910 Nathan, C., B.A. (Sept. 5, 1916). Lt. 7th Wiltshire Regt., empld. Min. of Munitions. Cavalier of the Order of the Crown of Italy.
1899 Neale, F. T., B.A. (Nov. 3, 1914). Maj. R.A.S.C. Maj., General List, D.A.Q.M.G. France, Belgium, Germany. *M.C.*, Sept. 15, 1916. Belgian Croix de Guerre. Chevalier de l'Ordre de Léopold. Croix de Guerre. *D.* France, 1918.
1908 Neild, R., B.A. (Apr. 9, 1915). Capt. I.A.R.O. India, Mesopotamia. *D.* Mesopotamia, 1917, 1919.
1919 Neser, V. H. (Oct. 6, 1914). ‡2nd Lt. R.F.A. German S.W. Africa, 1914–15; German E. Africa, 1915–17; France, 1918. *M.C.*, Sept. 16, 1918.
1911 Neville, H. A. G. (Aug. 17, 1914). ‡Capt. 10th W. Yorkshire Regt. (Capt. and Adjt.). India and Egypt, 1914–15; France, 1916–18. *M.C.*, July 18, 1917.
1908 **Newton, C. H. F. A.** (Nov. 1914). Lt. 10th K.R.R.C. France and Belgium, 1915–16. Killed in action near Ypres on Mar. 13, 1916.
1902 Nicholls, E. P. (Mobilized Aug. 1914). Maj. 42nd Batt., 2nd London Bde., R.F.A. France, Belgium, Italy, Egypt, 1914–18. *D.S.O.*, Sept. 16, 1918. T.D. *D.* France, 1918.
1919 North, C. F. (June 25, 1918). Flight Cadet R.A.F.
1904 Nott, F. T., M.A. (Mobilized Aug. 4, 1914). Capt. 1st Herefordshire Regt. (Maj.). Egypt, Gallipoli, 1915; France and Belgium, 1917–18; Germany, 1919.
1909 Nott-Bower,* W. G., B.A. Ceylon Planters' Rifle Corps. Inns of Court O.T.C. (Resigned.)
1894 Nunneley, F. P., D.M. (Nov. 2, 1914). Maj. R.A.M.C. France.
1889 Nutter, A. B., M.A. (Dec. 2, 1915). A.B., R.N.V.R. (Anti-Aircraft).
1881 Ormsby-Gore, Hon. S. F. (Sept. 1914). Capt. Draft Conducting Officer. France. (Resigned on account of ill health, Nov. 1917.)
1913 O'Rorke, M. H., B.A. (Aug. 25, 1914). Lt. 12th Lancers. France. *M.C.*, June 3, 1919. *D.* France, 1918.
1897 Orr, F. W., M.A. (June 14, 1916). Captain R.G.A.
1904 Paget, F. E. H. (Sept. 4, 1914). ‡Lt., Acting Capt., 1st Grenadier Guards. France, 1915–16.
1911 **Panes,* E. P. M.,** B.A. (Sept. 1914). 2nd Lt. 12th K.R.R.C. France and Belgium, 1915. Killed in action near Ypres on Sept. 25, 1915.
1905 **Papineau, T. M.,** B.A. (Sept. 22, 1914). Maj. Princess Patricia's Canadian L.I., C.E.F. France and Belgium, 1915–17. *M.C.*, April 15, 1915. *D.* France, 1915. Killed in action in Belgium on Oct. 30, 1917.
1885 Parker, H. R., B.A. (Dec. 1914). Capt. 8th Hampshire Regt. (T.F.).
1899 Parker-Jervis, E. M. (Oct. 1914). Capt. 3rd N. Mid. Bde. R.F.A. (T.F.). Maj. H.Q., R.A., 59th Divl. Artillery. France. *M.C.*, June 3, 1918. *D.* § Feb. 1917.

1912 Parkin,* C. L., B.A. (Aug. 26, 1914). Capt. R.F.A. France. *M.C.*, Jan. 1, 1917.

1911 Parr,* M. W., B.A. (Aug. 15, 1914). Capt. 3rd, attd. 1/5th, Highland L.I. (Staff-Captain). France, 1914–15, 1918; Palestine, 1917–18.

1912 Paton,* J. A., B.A. (Serving Aug. 4, 1914). Lt. 6th Dragoon Guards, attd. R.E. (Signals). France and Belgium, 1914–15, 1916–18. *D.* France, 1918 twice, 1919.

Paton, J. M. (Nov. 5, 1917). 2nd Lt. R.E. (Signals). France. Killed in action at Arras on Mar. 21, 1918.

Paul, E. K. M. (Dec. 1916). 2nd Lt. 252nd Heavy Batt., R.G.A. France and Belgium. *M.C.*, May 25, 1918. Died at No. 13 C.C.S. on Apr. 18, 1918, of wounds received in action.

1913 Pearse, G. V., B.A. (Aug. 4, 1914). ‡Maj. 'B' Batt., 95th Bde., R.F.A. France. *M.C.*, Jan. 1, 1917.

1915 Pearson, H. W. (Oct. 18, 1915). Lt. 159th Heavy Batt., R.G.A. France and Belgium, 1917–18; Germany, 1918–19.

1906 Pearson-Gregory, P. J. S. (Aug. 1914). Capt., Acting Maj., 3rd Grenadier Guards. France. *M.C.*, Jan. 1, 1918.

1894 Pechell, H. R. K. (Sept. 20, 1914). ‡Lt. 18th R. Fusiliers. Lt., Acting Capt., R.E. France, 1916.

1912 Peck, R. H., B.A. (Dec. 22, 1914). Lt. 11th E. Surrey Regt. Maj. Squadron Commdr., R.A.F. France, 1916. *O.B.E.* (Mil.). *D.* § Air Ministry, Jan. 1919.

1919 Pedder, R. W. (Sept. 22, 1914). Capt. 8th N. Staffordshire Regt. France and Belgium, 1915–19.

1904 [Peel, R., M.A.] (Dec. 18, 1914). 2nd Lt. 9th Oxf. & Bucks. Lt. Infty. Lt. R.A.F.

1890 Pennyman, Rev. W. G., M.A. (Serving Aug. 4, 1914). Chaplain (4th Class), Yorkshire Hussars.

1911 Pepys, C., M.A. (Aug. 24, 1914). Maj. 8th Devonshire Regt. France, 1915–17; Italy, 1917–19. *D.S.O.*, Dec. 19, 1918. *M.C.*, June 4, 1917. Croce di Guerra. *D.* France, 1916; Italy, 1918, 1919.

1913 Pethick, J. E. S. (Aug. 10, 1914). Capt. 3rd S. Lancashire Regt. (Maj.). France, 1916–18. *M.C.*, July 26, 1918.

1902 Phillips, E. C. M. (Mobilized Aug. 1914). Lt.-Col. 1st Hertfordshire Regt. France and Belgium, 1914–18. *D.S.O.*, May 5, 1919. *D.* France, 1918. (Prisoner of war, Mar.–Nov., 1918.)

1917 Phillips, G. A. (June 6, 1918). Pte. N. Staffordshire Regt.

Pickop, W. B. A. (1915). Lt. R. Fusiliers. France. Died on Oct. 24, 1918, of wounds received in action near Valenciennes.

1913 Pink,* F. W. (Nov. 10, 1914). Lt. 18th Hussars. France, 1915–19.

Platnauer, L. M. (Aug. 1914). Cpl., Cape Peninsula Rifles. ‡2nd Lt. 16th W. Yorkshire Regt. German S.W. Africa, 1914–15; France and Belgium, 1916–17. Presumed to have died of wounds on May 3, 1917, as a prisoner.

1872 Pollock, A. W. A. (Serving Aug 4, 1914). Lt.-Col. 10th K.O.Y.L.I. France, 1915, 1917–19. *D.* § Feb. 1917; France, 1919.

1907 **Pope,* C. M.,** B.A., B.C.L. (Mobilized Aug. 4, 1914). Lt. 1st Worcestershire Regt. France and Belgium, Aug.–Oct. 1914. Died on Oct. 24, 1914, of wounds received in action.

1906 **Pope, P. G.** (Dec. 1915). Lt. R.F.A. (Adjt.). France and Belgium. Killed in action at Passchendaele on Oct. 16, 1917.

1905 Prescot, C. P., B.A. (Apr. 21, 1915). Maj. R.E. i/c 34th Divl. Signal Coy. Indian Army. Gallipoli, 1915; Egypt, 1916; Mesopotamia, 1916; India, 1916–19.

1907 Prescot,* R. W. K., M.A. Cpl. E. Surrey Regt., serving under R.T.O.

1893 Preston, J. H., M.A. (Mar. 30, 1915). Lt. 1st (Garr.) Bn. Devonshire Regt. (Capt. and Adjt.). Mudros, 1915; Egypt, 1915–1916.

1903 Preston, W. B. (Dec. 24, 1914). 2nd Lt. 8th K.O.Y.L.I. Lt. General List, attd. W. African Frontier Force. W. Africa. (Relinquished Commission on account of ill health contracted while on active service.)

1905 Prichard, H. M., M.A. (Oct. 1, 1918). 2nd Lt. I.A.R.O. India.

Prichard, R. G. (Aug. 14, 1914). Lt. 1st Suffolk Regt. France, 1915. Killed in action on Apr. 27, 1915.

1908 Pritchard, C. T., B.A. (Sept. 21, 1914). Lt. 5th S. Staffordshire Regt. (T.F.).

1913 Pritchard,* J. M. (Aug. 22, 1914). Capt. 5th Royal W. Kent Regt. (T.F.). Staff-Captain. *O.B.E.* (Mil.).

1897 Pritchard, P. A. R., B.A. (Serving Aug. 4, 1914). Maj. 1/2nd Gurkha Rifles, Indian Army (Lt.-Col.). India, 1914–16; Mesopotamia, 1916–18.

1920 Pritchard Gordon, H. (Dec. 21, 1916). Lt. Grenadier Guards. France, Belgium.

1886 Puxley, F. L. L., B.A. (Sept. 21, 1916). Capt. 31st (Works) Bn. Middlesex Regt.

1919 Radcliffe, E. R. W. (Jan. 1918). 2nd Lt. Coldstream Guards.

1907 Radice,* F. R., B.A. (Mobilized Aug. 4, 1914). Capt. 2/15th London Regt. (Civil Service Rifles). France, 1915, 1916; Macedonia, 1916–17; Egypt, 1918; Italy, 1918–19.

1895 Ralston-Patrick, R., B.A. (Mobilized Aug. 1914). Maj. Ayrshire Yeomanry, attd. 1st Aust. Div. Gallipoli, Egypt, France, 1915–18. T.D.

1904 Rambaut, A. E., B.A. (June 29, 1915). Lt. 7th Northumberland Fusiliers, attd. Intelligence Corps (Capt.). France, 1916–17, 1918.

1898 Ramsbotham, H. R., B.M., M.A. (Oct. 11, 1915). Capt. R.A.M.C. (Relinquished Commission on account of ill health.)

1903 **Randolph, A. B.** (Apr. 1915). Lt. Welsh Guards. France. Killed in action at Hill 70, Loos, on Sept. 27, 1915.

1904 Ravenhill, M. H., B.A. (Aug. 5, 1915). Lt., temp. Capt., I.A.R.O., 26th Punjabis, afterwards attd. Dacca Military Police, Bengal. India, N.W. Frontier, 1915; Mesopotamia, 1916; Bengal, 1917–19.

1898 **Raw, R. G.,** *D.S.O.* (Serving Aug. 4, 1914). Capt. 8th Northumberland Fusiliers. Gallipoli. Killed in action in Gallipoli on Aug. 10, 1915.

1897 Rawlence, C. V., B.A. (Oct. 20, 1914). ‡Lt. R.N.V.R., H.M.M.L. 341. Gallipoli, 1915; Belgian Coast, 1916–17.

1870 Rawnsley, E. P., B.A. (Nov. 1914). Capt. Vol. Bn. Lincolnshire Regt.

1911 Raworth,* K. L., B.A. (Oct. 1, 1914). Lt. B/302nd Bde., R.F.A. France, Salonika, Palestine.

1881 **Rawson, R. H.,** *M.P.* (Mobilized Aug. 1914). Lt.-Col. Sussex Yeomanry. T.D. Died on Oct. 18, 1918.

1912 Rednall, F. G., B.A. (Sept. 1, 1915). Instructor Lt. R.N., H.M.S. *Thunderer*. Grand Fleet.

1908 Reed, C. G., B.A. (Nov. 1914). ‡Lt. 6th K.R.R.C. (Capt.). France. *M.C.*, Jan. 1, 1918.
1909 **Reid,* J. G.,** B.A. (Sept. 1914). Capt. 11th Worcestershire Regt. France, Macedonia. Killed in action in Macedonia on Sept. 8, 1916.
1902 Reid, R. N., M.A. (Aug. 19, 1916). Lt. I.A.R.O., attd. 1st D.Y.O. Lancers, afterwards Maj. Adm. Comdt. L. of C., E. Persia F.F. E. Persia.
1908 Rhodes, C. K., B.A. (May 21, 1915). Lt. I.A.R.O., attd. 123rd Outram's Rifles. India, Egypt, and Palestine. *D.* Palestine, 1918.
1880 Rhodes, F. J. M. (June 13, 1915). Lt. 1st (Res. Garr.) Bn. Suffolk Regt. Lt. General List. W. Africa.
1920 Rhodes, F. W. (Sept. 1916). Lt. R. Dragoons. France, Belgium, Germany.
1911 Rhodes, J., B.A. (Sept. 27, 1915). Lt. 1/7th W. Yorkshire Regt. (Capt.). Belgium and France.
1880 Rhodes, Hon. R. H. (Sept. 1915). Col. Hdqrs., N.Z.E.F. Col. N.Z. Red Cross Commission. Egypt, Gallipoli. Croix de Chevalier de la Légion d'Honneur.
1898 Richards, A. J., M.A. (Feb. 25, 1915). Capt. R. Welch Fusiliers.
1909 **Richmond,* H. S.,** B.A. (Dec. 1914). Capt. 9th K.R.R.C. France. Killed in action at Delville Wood on Aug. 24, 1916.
1889 Rickards, E. (Mobilized Aug. 1914). Maj. 4th Dragoon Guards, Res. of Officers. Maj. 6th Res. Regt. of Cavalry. Egypt and Palestine. *D.* Palestine, 1917.
1912 Roberts,* W. St. C. H., B.A. (Dec. 1916). Lt. 149th Bde., R.F.A. France, 1917–18, 1918–19. *M.C.*, Sept. 16, 1918. (Civil prisoner of war in Germany, 1914–16.)
1910 Robertson, W. C., B.A. (Aug. 1915). ‡Lt. 2nd Rhodesia Regt. Lt. 1st K.R.R.C., attd. S.A. Inf. German E. Africa, France. (Wounded and prisoner of war, Mar. 1918.)
1879 Robertson-Aikman, T. S. G. H. (Apr. 15, 1915). Colonel R. Defence Corps, No. 1 District.
1914 **Rodakowski, R. J. P.** (Dec. 1914). Capt. Irish Guards (S.R.). France and Belgium. *D.* France, 1917. Killed in action on Oct. 9, 1917.
1912 **Rogers,* S. D. K.** (Aug. 4, 1914). 2nd Lt. 4th R. Fusiliers. France and Belgium. Killed in action at Ypres on June 14, 1915.
1920 Rogerson, C. M. (Aug. 5, 1914). ‡2nd Lt. 57th Coy. M.G.C. Singapore, France.
1908 **Rooke,* W. M.,** B.A. (Mobilized Aug. 1914). Capt. R. Wiltshire Yeomanry, attd. 2nd Wiltshire Regt. France and Belgium, 1916–18. *D.* France, 1917. Died on Oct. 8, 1918, of illness contracted while on active service.
1879 Rothwell, R. R., M.A. (Dec. 19, 1914). Maj. 2/7th Manchester Regt.
1914 Row, A. W. L., B.A. (Dec. 10, 1915). Lt. 189th Heavy Batt., R.G.A. Palestine, 1917–18.
1878 **Ruffer, Sir M. A.,** M.A. Red Cross Commissioner. Egypt. Drowned in the sinking of H.M.T. *Arcadian* on Apr. 15, 1917.
1901 Rundell, W. W. O., B.A. (Mobilized Aug. 1914). Maj. Scottish Horse.
1911 Russell, F. F., B.A., B.C.L. (Mar. 14, 1918). Lt. Rly. Transportation Corps, U.S. Army. France, 1918.
1912 Sadler, G. F., B.A. (Aug. 23, 1914). ‡Capt. 88th Batt., R.F.A. France, 1914–15, 1916–18.
1903 Samson, F. R., B.A. (Feb. 4, 1916). Lt.-Commdr. R.N.V.R. Maj. R.A.F.

1900 Sanderson, G.B., M.A. (Dec. 20, 1916). 2nd Lt. Res. Regt. of Cavalry. Lt. Special Lists ; Staff-Lt.

1891 Sargent, A. J., M.A. (Sept. 1, 1916). 2nd Lt. Surrey Vol. Regt.

1911 Savage, J. J., B.M. (June 8, 1918). Lt. (Med. Officer), R.A.F.

1897 Scott-James, R. A., B.A. (June 1916). ‡Capt. R.G.A. France, 1917, 1918. *M.C.*, June 22, 1918.

1905 Scudamore, H. F. (Sept. 9, 1914). ‡Capt., Acting Maj., A/92nd Batt., R.F.A. France, 1915–19. *D.* France, 1916, 1917.

1919 Sears, L. B. (Mar. 1, 1916). Sergt. 7th Can. Siege Batt., C.E.F. 2nd Lt. R.A.F. (on demobilization). France, Belgium, 1917–18.

1914 Selbie, W. H., B.A. (Nov. 17, 1915). Lt. Cambridgeshire Regt., attd. 100th P. of W. Coy. France, 1918–19.

1907 Seth-Smith, H. E., M.A. (Oct. 21, 1914). Capt. 4th R. Irish Rifles. Staff-Captain 25th Inf. Bde. Belgium, 1915 ; France, 1916–19. *M.C.*, Jan. 1, 1917.

1913 Sharp, W. D., B.A. (July 8, 1915). Lt. 7th S. Lancashire Regt. France and Belgium.

1877 Sharpe, Rev. H. E., M.A. (Serving Aug. 4, 1914). Chaplain to the Forces (2nd Class), attd. R.G.A. (T.F.). T.D.

1911 **Shaw, E. A.** (Aug. 1914). Capt. 6th Oxf. & Bucks. Lt. Infty. France. Killed in action in the Battle of the Somme on Oct. 7, 1916.

1867 Shephard, C. S., *D.S.O.* (Rejoined Nov. 12, 1914). Lt.-Col. Labour Bn. Devonshire Regt. France, 1915.

1892 Shepherd-Cross, T. A. S., B.A. (Mobilized Aug. 1914). Maj. Duke of Lancaster's Own Yeomanry. T.D.

1910 Sherwell, A. G., M.A. (Aug. 16, 1914). Lt. King's African Rifles. E. Africa, (Resigned.)

1910 Shields, F. R., B.A. (May 15, 1917). 2nd Lt. 10th R. Fusiliers. France.

1910 **Shurey, C.** (Sept. 9, 1914). Capt. 10th R. Fusiliers. France. Died on July 22, 1916, of wounds received in the Battle of the Somme.

1913 Simpson, R. H. (1917). Lt. 115th Mobile Ordnance Repair Shop, U.S. Army. France.

1919 Sinker, G. (Aug. 20, 1918). Gunner R.F.A.

1905 **Slaney, J. C.** (Dec. 8, 1914). Lt. R.F.A. France. Killed in action on Feb. 17, 1916.

1919 Slarke, C. W. (Nov. 1914). S. African Field Telegraphs. ‡Lt. R.A.F. German S.W. Africa.

1901 Sleigh, C. H., B.A. (Sept. 16, 1914). Capt. Special Lists (Intelligence Corps). France, 1914, 1915, 1916, 1917, 1918 ; Germany, 1918, 1919. *M.C.*, June 4, 1917. *D.* France, 1916.

Slicer, P. S. (Aug. 6, 1916). Lt. R.G.A., attd. 319th Siege Batt. France, Belgium. *D.* France, 1918. Died on Sept. 30, 1918, of wounds received in action.

1901 Smith, J. H., B.A. (Sept. 28, 1916). Lt. R.G.A. (Capt. and Adjt.). France. *M.C.*, Oct. 18, 1917.

1919 Smith, S. R. H. (June 7, 1918). 2nd Lt. Worcestershire Regt. (on demobilization).

1912 Speed,* D. C. L. (Serving Aug. 4, 1914). Capt. K.R.R.C. Capt., temp. Maj., R.A.F. *O.B.E.* (Mil.).

1897 Spencer, Rev. F. A. M., M.A. (1917). Pte. Australian A.M.C. ‡Chaplain to the Forces (4th Class), attd. 2nd Bde., Australian Light Horse. Egypt, Palestine, 1917–19.

1899 **Spencer, H. B.,** B.A. (Sept. 1914). ‡Lt. W. Somerset Yeomanry. Lt. Tank Corps. France, Killed in action on Sept. 2, 1918.

1913 **Spencer,* J. H.** (Aug. 1914). Capt. 1st Lancashire Fusiliers. Gallipoli, 1915; France, 1917. Died on July 15, 1918, while prisoner of war at Limberg, of wounds received in action.

1911 Spencer, R. P., B.A. (Dec. 21, 1916). Lt. 12th Lancers.

1899 Spooner, A. H. (Serving Aug. 4, 1914). Maj. Bt. Lt.-Col. Lancashire Fusiliers. Temp. Brig.-Gen. France and Belgium, Aug. 1914–18. *C.M.G.* *D.S.O.*, Feb. 18, 1915; *Bar*, July 26, 1918. Croix de Chevalier de la Légion d'Honneur. *D.* France, 1914, 1915, 1916, 1917 twice, 1918 twice.

1901 Spooner, G., M.A. (Oct. 22, 1914). Lt. York and Lancaster Regt.

1919 Standring, D. A. T. (May, 1916). Lt. 75th Batt., A/263rd Bde., R.F.A. (Capt.). Salonika, 1917; Palestine, 1917–18; Egypt, 1918–19.

1919 Stanger, D. H. (Aug. 8, 1918). 2nd Lt. Army Res. (on demobilization).

1919 Staynes, T. A. (Oct. 4, 1917). Lt. 2nd W. Yorkshire Regt. France, 1918–19; Germany, 1919. *M.C.*, Feb. 15, 1919.

1889 Steedman, H. P. G. (Apr. 3, 1916). Capt. R.A.S.C.

1902 Steel, J. D. (Aug. 5, 1918). Hon. Capt. R. Marines.

1880 Steele, F. A. S., B.A. (Nov. 28, 1914). Capt. R. Defence Corps. *D.* § Mar. 1919.

1919 Steemson, C. H. (Mov. 10, 1916). 2nd Lt. 10th Lincolnshire Regt. France and Belgium, 1917–18.

1902 Stelling, C. D. (May 27, 1915). Lt. 19th London Regt. *M.B.E.* (Mil.). (Relinquished Commission on account of ill health contracted while on active service.)

1889 Stenhouse, V. D. (Mobilized Aug. 1914). Lt.-Col. W. Somerset Yeomanry.

1905 **Stewart, C. E.** (Sept. 1914). ‡Capt. 10th Durham L.I. (Adjt.). France and Belgium, 1915–17. *M.C.*, June 4, 1917. Died on April 10, 1917, of wounds received in action.

1916 Stewart, C. E. (July 2, 1917). ‡2nd Lt. R. Fusiliers. France, 1918.

1891 Stewart, W.B., B.A. (Aug. 4, 1914). Maj. Lothians and Border Horse (D.A.Q.M.G.) (Lt.-Col. K.O.Y.L.I.). France. T.D. *D.* France, 1916.

1909 Stock,* J. R. W., B.A. (Oct. 4, 1914). Lt. W. Somerset Yeomanry. France and Belgium, 1916–18. (Relinquished Commission on account of ill health, Mar. 1918.)

1870 Stock, T., M.A., *C.M.G.* (Feb. 1, 1916). Col. D.A.D. of Remounts, No. 2 Circle, Eastern Command.

1900 Stone, B. A. W., B.M., M.A. (Dec. 18, 1915). Capt. R.A.M.C.

1883 Stone, H. J. (Mobilized Aug. 1914). Lt.-Col. 4th Highland L.I. (Resigned.)

1910 Strickland,* A. W. (Mobilized Aug. 4, 1914). Capt. 1/1st R. Gloucestershire Hussars. Gallipoli, 1915. Egypt, 1915–16; Sinai Peninsula, 1916. (Prisoner of war in Turkey, 1916–18.)

1903 Stuart, R. W., B.A. (Jan. 1917). Pte. 2nd (Garr.) Bn. King's (Liverpool Regt.). Macedonia, 1917–18; Bulgaria and Turkey, 1919.

1919 Sundius-Smith, W. F. (Jan. 17, 1916). ‡Lt. 2nd H.A.C. (Inf.). France, Italy.

1919 Swayne, A. C. C. (Nov. 3, 1918). 2nd Lt. 5th Res. Cavalry Regt.

1895 Swinburne, G. W. P., M.A. (Dec. 28th, 1916). Lt. General List.
1894 **Sykes, O. J.,** B.A. (Apr. 27, 1916). Capt. 23rd Siege Batt., R.G.A. France. Killed in action at Pozières on Oct. 17, 1916.
1912 Symon, C. H. N., B.A. (Sept. 4, 1914). ‡Lt. 2nd S. Lancashire Regt. France, Belgium, 1916–19.
1885 Tabberer, H. B., M.A. (Dec. 4, 1917). Lt. Army Pay Dept. Italy.
1913 Taylor,* C. de W. (Serving Aug. 4, 1914). Lt. 20th Hussars (attd. R.F.C., 1916). France and Belgium. *M.C.*, July 26, 1918.
1894 Taylor, C. R. (Aug. 1914). Lt. 5th London Regt. (London Rifle Brigade). France, 1917–19.
1894 Taylor, F. H., M.A. (Sept. 22, 1916). Lt. R. Defence Corps.
1913 Taylor,* T. W. J., M.A. (Aug. 1914). Lt. Essex Regt., attd. Field Survey Coy., R.E. Gallipoli, 1915; France, 1917–19.
1849 Teale, T. P., B.M., M.A. (Mobilized Aug. 1914). Lt.-Col. R.A.M.C. (T.F. Res.).
1879 Tennyson d'Eyncourt, A. L. (Rejoined Sept. 18, 1914). Maj. 6th R. Berkshire Regt. Maj. Garr. Bn. Norfolk Regt. India, 1915–16. (Relinquished Commission on account of ill health.)
1903 **Terrell, C. à B. R.,** B.A. (Apr. 1916). 2nd Lt., Acting Capt., 460th Batt., 15th Bde., R.H.A. France. *M.C.*, July 18, 1917. Died on June 10, 1917, of wounds received in action at Arras.
1913 **Thomas, A. L.** (Aug. 5, 1914). Capt. 20th London Regt. France. Died on Aug. 30, 1918, of wounds received in action at Maurepas, near Peronne.
1905 Thomas, F. E., M.A. (Sept. 12, 1914). ‡Lt. 51st (H.) Div. Signal Coy., R.E. Belgium, France, 1914–18.
1892 Thomas, R. J. F. D., M.A. (Oct. 12, 1914). Maj. 7th London Regt. France, 2½ years. T.D.
1910 Thomas, W. E., B.A. (Dec. 15, 1914). ‡Capt. 2nd Rhodesia Regt. Capt. 1st K.R.R.C. E. Africa, 1914–17; France, 1917–18; Germany, 1918–19. *M.C.*, June 3, 1919.
1909 **Thomas, W. H.** (Jan. 1915). Lt., Acting Capt., Berkshire Yeomanry. Egypt and Palestine. *M.C.*, Jan. 1, 1918; *Bar*, Mar. 26, 1918. *D.* Palestine, 1917. Killed in action at Kantara on Nov. 28, 1917.
1903 Thomas, W. J., B.A. (Serving Aug. 4, 1914). 2nd Lt. University College O.T.C. Lt. 18th London Regt. (London Irish Rifles). (Staff-Lt., Class H.H.) Salonika, 1916–17; Egypt and Palestine, 1917–19.
1919 Thompson, J. H. (Sept. 3, 1916). Capt. R.A.F. France and Belgium, 1917–18.
1912 Thompson,* P. G., M.A. (Aug. 26, 1914). Capt. 4th R. W. Kent Regt. (T.F.). Mesopotamia. (Prisoner of war in Turkey.)
1903 Throssell, A. G., B.A. (1914). ‡Lt. 6th Rifle Brigade, empld. War Office. France.
1885 Tilney, R. H. (Mobilized Aug. 4, 1914). Lt.-Col. Duke of Lancaster's Own Yeomanry, attd. Labour Corps (Col. Labour Commandant). France and Belgium. *D.S.O.*, June 4, 1917. T.D. Croix de Guerre. *D.* France, 1917, 1918.
1909 Tomlin, J. O. 2nd Lt. Grenadier Guards. (Relinquished Commission on account of ill health.)
1919 Tompson, B. E. (Sept. 1916). Lt. 11th Worcestershire Regt. Salonika.

1888 Tonge, Rev. A. W., M.A. (June 9, 1917). Chaplain (3rd Class), 2nd Div. Art., A.I.F. France, Belgium, 1917–19.

1896 Torrens, J. R. (Nov. 21, 1914). Maj. 13th R. Sussex Regt. Maj. Transport Officer.

1919 Tosswill, J. T. (June 16, 1918). 2nd Lt. R.A.F. (on demobilization).

1919 Towers, L. T. (Oct. 28, 1918). Gunner 211th Batt., R.G.A.

1901 Towle, E., M.A. (Sept. 1915). ‡Lt. 4th, attd. 1st, Border Regt. (Capt.). Belgium, France.

1920 Tracey, H. A. (Aug. 1915). Lt. S. Wales Borderers (attd. R.F.C.). France, 1916; E. Africa, Egypt, 1917; Salonika, 1917–18.

1898 Trappes-Lomax, E. N., M.A. (Oct. 4, 1915). Lt. King's Own (R. Lancaster Regt.).

1887 Tristram, C. E. (Sept. 9, 1914). Maj. 9th Lancashire Fusiliers.

1876 Tristram, L. S. B. (Serving Aug. 4, 1914). Maj. Welsh Regt. Gibraltar, Egypt, Malta.

1899 Trollope, C. C. (Sept. 1914). Capt. 2/16th London Regt. (Queen's Westminster Rifles). France, Macedonia, Palestine. *D.* Palestine, 1918.

1907 Trotter, B. A. (May 16, 1915). Capt. 411th Batt., 126th Bde., R.F.A. France, Germany.

1903 Trotter, M. A., B.A. (Mobilized Aug. 1914). Capt. 6th (Cyclist) Norfolk Regt. (T.F.), attd. R.A.F.

1905 Trotter, S. E., B.A. (Dec. 28, 1915). ‡Lt. 16th London Regt. (Queen's Westminster Rifles) (Capt.). France.

1909 Trotter, W. A. (Apr. 9, 1917). Lt. R.G.A. France.

1908 **Tuff, F. N.** (June 1, 1915). 2nd Lt. R. E. Kent Yeomanry. Gallipoli. Died on Nov. 5, 1915, at Malta, of wounds received in action.

1897 Tupper, G. W. H., B.A. (Mobilized Aug. 1914). Capt. 1/9th Middlesex Regt. (Maj.). India, 1914–17; Mesopotamia, 1917–19. *D.* Mesopotamia, 1919.

1912 Twycross, B. G., B.A. (Dec. 8, 1915). Maj. R.F.A. France. *M.C.*, Dec. 21, 1916; *Bar*, Sept. 16, 1918.

1875 Tylden-Pattenson, A. H., *D.S.O.* (Serving Aug. 4, 1914). Maj. and Adjt. The Buffs (E. Kent Regt.). *D.* § Feb. 1917.

1897 Tyrer, A. K. (Oct. 24, 1914). 2nd Lt. Cheshire Yeomanry. Lt. R.A.S.C., No. 7 Aux. M.T. Coy. France and Belgium.

1909 Underhill,* S. W. F., B.M., M.A. (Aug. 14, 1914). Pte. R.A.M.C., 3rd Southern General Hospital. ‡Surgeon Lt. R.N. N. Atlantic and W. Coast of Africa.

1913 **Van den Bergh,* J. H.** (Aug. 29, 1914). Lt. 6th London Bde., R.F.A. France. *D.* France. Killed in action at Vimy Ridge on May 21, 1916.

1911 **Verner,* F. C.** (Aug. 7, 1914). Lt. Shropshire L.I. France. Killed in action at Bois Grenier on Oct. 25, 1914.

1906 **Vidal,* L. A.,** B.A. (Aug. 15, 1914). 2nd Lt. 3rd Oxf. & Bucks. Lt. Infty. Temp. Capt. attd. D.C.L.I. France and Belgium. Killed in action at the Battle of Loos on Sept. 25, 1915.

1910 Wace,* F. B., B.A. (Aug. 28, 1916). Lt. I.A.R.O., attd. 2/72nd Punjabis (Capt.). India; Mohmand Blockade, 1916–17; Wazaristan, 1917; Marri Punitive Expedition, 1918.

1886 Wace, H. C., M.A. (Mobilized Aug. 5, 1914). Maj. Unattached List, T.F., attd. No. 4 O.C.B. France, 1916 (as Camp Commandant).

1890 Walker, Rev. J. M. S., M.A. (Dec. 5, 1915). Chaplain to the Forces (4th Class) (attd. 21st C.C.S.). France, 1916.

1912 Wallace,* E. G. (Mobilized Aug. 1914). Lt. 5th Dragoon Guards, attd. M.G.C. France and Belgium, from 1914.

1880 Wallace, R. H., M.A., *C.B.* (Sept. 11, 1914). Lt.-Col. 19th R. Irish Rifles. *C.B.E.* (Mil.). (Relinquished Commission on account of ill health.)

1894 Wallroth, R. C., M.A. (Jan. 17, 1917). Canadian Engineers. ‡Lt. R.N.V.R.

1911 Walsh, J. N., B.A. (Feb. 27, 1917). 2nd Lt. 6th York and Lancaster Regt. France. (Resigned on account of wounds.)

1911 Walters, D. J., B.A. (Dec. 4, 1915). Lt. R.G.A. (S.R.), attd. H.Q. 49th Bde. France. *M.C.*, Jan. 1, 1919. *D.* France, 1917.

1904 Walton, J. C., B.A. (May 12, 1916). Lt. 173rd Siege Batt., R.G.A. (Capt.). France. *M.C.*, June 3, 1919.

1915 **Wanklyn, J. E.** (Jan. 1916). Lt. 128th Batt., 29th Bde., R.F.A. France. *M.C.*, July 26, 1918. Killed in action on the Scarpe on May 28, 1918.

1896 **Ward, A. E. M.,** B.A. (Mobilized Aug. 1914). Capt. and Adj. 5th Norfolk Regt. Gallipoli. Missing, believed killed in action in Gallipoli in Aug. 1915.

1888 Waters, W. A. P., D.M. (Mobilized Aug. 1914). Maj. R.A.M.C. (T.F.).

1919 Wathen, M. W. (May 14, 1917). 2nd Lt. R.F.A., attd. A.A. Batt., R.H.A. France.

1919 Watkins, J. C. S. (Sept. 25, 1916). Lt. 3rd, attd. 2/8th, Essex Regt. France.

1903 Watson, C., B.A. (Aug. 26, 1915). 2nd Lt. 2/4th Yorkshire Regt. Capt. and Adjt. Labour Corps.

1890 Watson, W. D. P. (Mobilized Aug. 1914). Capt. Res. of Officers; D.A.A.G. E. Africa. *M.C.*, June 4, 1917. *D.* E. Africa, 1916.

1898 Watts, H., B.A. (Mobilized Aug. 1914). Maj. 5th Cheshire Regt. France, 1915. *O.B.E.* (Mil.).

1886 Wearing, J. W., M.A. (Sept. 1914). Capt. 2/5th King's Own (R. Lancaster Regt.), attd. 41st Provisional Bn. (Invalided on account of ill health.)

1907 **Webster, A. H. B.,** B.A. (Sept. 1914). 2nd Lt. 7th Northamptonshire Regt. France. Accidentally killed at Bray on April 25, 1916.

1913 Westlake,* A. R. C. (Oct. 8, 1914). Lt. 2/4th D.C.L.I., attd. Political Dept., Mesopotamia. Capt. 31st Kurdish Labour Corps, 1918–19. India, N.W. Frontier, 1914–17; Mesopotamia, 1917–19.

1909 Whadcoat,* C. C., B.A. (Nov. 13, 1914). Lt. 14th Hussars. Mesopotamia.

1919 White, H. S. (May 14, 1917). 2nd Lt., Asst. Intelligence Officer, H.Q. 76th Div., U.S. Army. France, 1918.

1912 White, R. S. M. (Sept. 15, 1914). Capt. 1st (Garr.) Bn. Lincolnshire Regt. (Staff-Captain). India.

1897 Whitehead, Rev. W., M.A. (Jan. 1916). Chaplain to the Forces (4th Class). Chaplain R.N., H.M.S. *Furious*. France, 1916–18; Eastern Mediterranean, 1918; North Sea, 1919.

1909 Whitley,* H. C., B.A. (Mobilized Aug. 1914). Lt. W. Yorkshire Regt., attd. Indian Army. France, India. *D.* France, 1917.

1909 Wigzell, H., B.A. (1914.) ‡Lt. Suffolk Regt. France.

1912 Wilkie, H. G., B.A. (Aug. 4, 1914). ‡Lt., Acting Capt. and Adj., 336th Bde. R.F.A. France, 1915–16; Mesopotamia, 1917–19. *D.* Mesopotamia, 1918, 1919.

1919 Wilkie, J. (Sept. 22, 1914). 2nd Lt. 8th Queen's (R. W. Surrey Regt.). Capt. and Adj. 12th Bn. M.G.C. France. Chevalier, Order of the Crown of Rumania. *D.* France, 1916, 1917.
1877 Wilkinson, Rev. J., M.A. (Serving Aug. 4, 1914). Chaplain to the Forces (1st Class). T.D.
1894 Williams, G. C., B.A. (Aug. 21, 1915). Lt. Lothians and Border Horse (Capt.).
1919 Williams, H. (Oct. 19, 1915). Lt. R.G.A. China, 1917–19.
1911 **Williams, H. E. E.** (Sept. 1914). ‡2nd Lt. Rifle Brigade. Belgium and France. Killed in action at Laventie on Sept. 30, 1915.
1901 Williams, Rev. H. H., M.A. (Sept. 25, 1916). Chaplain to the Forces (4th Class). Egypt, Palestine. *D.* Palestine, 1918.
1911 Williamson, A. C. (Sept. 1, 1914). Sub-Lt. R.N.V.R. Antwerp, 1914. (Interned in Holland, 1914–18.)
1910 Willink, F. A., B.A. (Mobilized Aug. 4, 1914). Capt. 1/4th R. Berkshire Regt. France, Belgium, 1915. (Relinquished Commission on account of ill health, June, 1918).
1909 **Willmer, A. F.,** B.A. (Oct. 1914). Capt., Acting Maj., 9th Rifle Brigade. France, 1915–16. Died on Sept. 20, 1916, of wounds received in attack on Flers and Gueudecourt.
1918 Wills, W. A. (Oct. 1915). Lt. 5th London Regt. (London Rifle Brigade). (Capt.). France.
1920 Wilson, A. G. (Aug. 4, 1914). ‡Lt. 5th W. Yorkshire Regt. Lt. Flying Officer, 12th Sqdn. R.A.F. France, Belgium, 1915, 1916, 1917, 1918; Germany, 1919. *M.C.*, July 26, 1918.
1881 Wilson-Farquharson, D. L., *D.S.O.* (Serving Aug. 4, 1914). Maj., temp. Lt.-Col., The Black Watch, empld. Records. *D.* § Feb. 1917, § Nov. 1918, § Aug. 1919.
1910 Wingfield,* A. E. F. (Mobilized Aug. 4, 1914). Capt. 3rd Bedfordshire Regt., R.T.O.
1885 Wood, A. H., M.A. (Mobilized Aug. 1914). Capt. 5th R. Sussex Regt. (T.F.). France. *D.* France, 1916.
1919 Wood, B. G. J. (Oct. 29, 1917). 2nd Lt. (Observer Officer), 8th Sqdn., R.A.F. France.
1904 **Wood, H. K.,** B.A. (1915). Lt. 1st King's African Rifles. E. Africa. Died at Morogoro, E. Africa, on May 16, 1917, of illness contracted on active service.
1904 Wood, J. H., B.A. (Nov. 11, 1914). Capt. R.A.S.C.
1903 Wood, J. T., B.A. (Sept. 17, 1914). ‡Capt. R.A.S.C. France, Belgium, Italy.
1917 Wood, R. S. (Apr. 8, 1918). Pte. 28th London Regt. (Artists' Rifles O.T.C.) (Cadet).
1859 Woodgate, W. B., M.A. (July 1916). Pte. 7th City of London Regt. (Veteran Athletes Corps).
1903 Woodhouse, C. A., B.A. (1914). Nigerian Land Contingent. W. Africa.
1883 [Wootten, H. E.] (Serving Aug. 4, 1914). Maj., Hon. Lt.-Col., 9th Border Regt. Temp. Lt.-Col. President, Area Quartering Committee. France. *D.S.O.*, June 3, 1917.
1892 Worsley-Taylor, J. (Mobilized Aug. 1914). Lt.-Col. King's Own (R. Lancaster Regt.). France (attd. 7th Bn.).
1914 Wright, C. P. (Dec. 25, 1915). Lt. R.G.A. France.

1899 Wright, T. S., D.M. (Oct. 10, 1914). Capt. R.A.M.C. France and Belgium, 1915–19.

1911 Wrigley,* T., B.A. (Aug. 1914). Capt. 1st King's (Liverpool Regt.), attd. R.E. Signal Service. France, 1917–18; Germany, 1919.

1884 Wylie, F. J., B.A. (June 5, 1915). Capt. Unattached List, T.F., attd. No. 4 O.C.B.

1879 Yardley, G. W., B.A. (Oct. 1914). Capt. 2nd Army Field Remount Section. France, Belgium, Germany. *D.* France, 1917.

1911 **Yeomans,* H. W.** (Sept. 1, 1914). Capt. 1st Herefordshire Regt., attd. M.G.C. France. Killed in action at Onde Kenescik, nr. Gheluvelt, on Oct. 8, 1917.

1915 **Yorke-Lodge, B. W.** (Jan. 1, 1916). 2nd Lt. 12th Lancashire Fusiliers. Egypt and Macedonia. *M.C.*, Mar. 12, 1917. Killed in action in Macedonia on Sept. 13, 1916.

CORPUS CHRISTI COLLEGE

Abel, J. D. (Dec. 19, 1916). 2nd Lt. Seaforth Highlanders. France. Killed in action, 1918.

1901 **Addenbrooke, A.,** B.A. (Mobilized Aug. 1914). Capt. 14th R. Warwickshire Regt. France, 1915, 1916. *D.* France, 1916. Died on Oct. 5, 1916, of wounds received in action on the Somme.

1905 **Aglionby,* A. H.,** M.A. (Aug. 4, 1914). Lt., Acting Maj., 219th Siege Batt., R.G.A. France, 1916–18. *M.C.*, Jan. 1, 1919. Died on Nov. 7, 1918, of wounds received in action at Moen.

1897 Aglionby, F. B., B.C.L., M.A. (1916). ‡2nd Lt. R.G.A. France, 1916–17.

1908 Aglionby, Rev. W. H., M.A. (June 14, 1916). Chaplain to the Forces (4th Class). Palestine, 1916–18; France, 1918–19. *M.C.*, Feb. 18, 1918.

1897 **Alexander, H.,** B.A. (Aug. 1, 1915). 2nd Lt. Grenadier Guards. France and Belgium. Killed in action at Hulluch on Oct. 17, 1915.

1889 Allen, B. C., B.A. (April 1, 1917). Lt.-Col. I.A.R.O., attd. Labour Corps. France.

1901 Anderson-Morshead, P. E., M.A. (Aug. 20, 1914). ‡Capt. 152nd Batt., R.F.A., attd. London Div. H.Q. France, Germany.

1895 Ascroft, W. F., M.A. (April 20, 1915). Capt., Bt.-Maj., 3/4th Loyal N. Lancashire Regt. (T.F. Res.); R.T.O. France.

1920 Bailey, K. H. (Jan. 25, 1918). Gnr. 105th Howitzer Batt., A.I.F. (Cpl.). Egypt, France, 1918–19.

1898 Baines, C. E., B.A. (July 23, 1916). ‡2nd Lt. General List. France.

1906 Baker, P. M., B.A. Trooper, Nagpur Vol. Rifles. India.

1913 **Ballard,* G. A.** (Sept. 1, 1914). ‡2nd Lt. 23rd London Regt. France. Missing, believed killed in action at Loos on Sept. 26, 1915.

1910 Bamford,* E. St. J., B.A. (Sept. 28, 1914). Lt., Acting Capt., 5th Rifle Brigade. France.

1910 **Barker, A.,** B.A. (June 5, 1917). 2nd Lt. 150th Heavy Batt., R.G.A. France, Belgium. Died at Schlebusch on Dec. 20, 1918, as the result of an accident.

1906 Barker, Rev. T. H. W., M.A. (July 27, 1916). Chaplain to the Forces (4th Class). Mesopotamia. *D.* Mesopotamia, 1919.

1894 Barnsley, Rev. G., M.A. (Jan. 29, 1916). Chaplain to the Forces (4th Class). *D.* § Feb. 1917.

Bartholomew, G. H. F. (Jan. 4, 1915). Lt., Acting Capt., 14th Arg. & Suth'd. Highlanders. France. *D.* France, 1917. Died on Oct. 2, 1917, of wounds received in action.

1899 **Beachcroft, G. W.,** B.A. (May 29, 1915). 2nd Lt. 3rd, attd. 7th, King's Own (R. Lancaster Regt.). France and Belgium. Killed in action at Oostaverne on July 31, 1917.

1904 Beattie, I. H., M.A. (Nov. 17, 1916). Surgeon Lt. R.N.

1919 Behrens, M. (Apr. 1915). Lt. S. Wales Borderers, Salonika.

1898 Benton, P. A., B.A. Nigerian Land Contingent. W. Africa.

1901 Binney, C. N., B.M., M.A. (Aug. 10, 1914). Capt. R.A.M.C. Medical Officer, 5 C. Res. Bde. R.F.A. France.

1896 **Blathwayt, H. W.,** B.A. (Serving Aug. 1914). Maj. and Adjt. R.F.A. France. Killed in action on Nov. 30, 1917.

1912 Bonar, J. J., B.A. (Nov. 19, 1914). Capt. 6th R. Scots, attd. Tank Corps. France, 1916–18.

1913 Boulton, D. H. (Mar. 15, 1915). Lt. 6th E. Surrey Regt. Aden, India.

1906 **Bourdillon, T. L.,** B.A. (Mar. 1915). Maj. 8th K.R.R.C. France, Belgium. *M.C.*, Sept. 15, 1916. Killed in action at Stirling Castle, near Ypres, on Aug. 24, 1917.

1898 Bowen, A. P. (Mobilized Aug. 1914). Maj. Shropshire L.I. Bde.-Maj. France. *M.C.*, Jan. 1, 1917. *D.* § Aug. 1919.

1919 Bowen, C. A. (Feb. 9, 1917). Lce.-Cpl. 1st Field Survey Bn. R.E. France.

1905 Boyd, L. C., B.A. (Nov. 25, 1915). Lt. 31st Squadron R.A.F. (Capt. Flying Officer). N.W. Frontier, India, 1916–19.

1899 Boyle, E. A., M.A. (Sept. 7, 1914). ‡Lt. 2/1st Kent Cyclist Bn., attd. 1st R.W. Kent Regt. France.

1887 Brackenbury, H. L. (Dec. 1914). Capt. 3rd Lincolnshire Regt.

1909 Bradford,* W. G., B.A. (Jan. 27, 1915). Lt., Acting Capt., T.F. Res., attd. 1/5th Somerset L.I. India, 1915–17; Egypt, Palestine, 1917–19. *D.* Palestine, 1919.

1898 Brentnall, H. C., M.A. (Nov. 1917). 2nd Lt. Unattached List, T.F., Marlborough College O.T.C.

1901 Brooke, J. R., B.A. (May 23, 1915). Capt. Special Lists. Staff Captain. A.A.G.

1896 Brooke, N. P. (Serving Aug. 4, 1914). Lt.-Col. Leinster Regt. G.S.O. 2. France. *D.S.O.*, Jan. 1, 1918. *D.* France, 1917, 1918.

1905 **Brown, G. D.,** B.A. (Sept. 1914). ‡Maj. 1st Wiltshire Regt., attd. 11th Lancashire Fusiliers. Egypt, 1914; France, 1915–18. *M.C.*, Oct. 20, 1916. Missing, believed killed in action, Sept. 1918.

1909 **Buckell,* C. J. A.,** B.A. (Dec. 1914). ‡2nd Lt. 3rd Norfolk Regt. France, Palestine. Killed in action at Gaza on April 19, 1917.

1919 Burge, S. F. M. (April 5, 1918). 2nd Lt. Scots Guards.

1888 Burnaby, R. B., M.A. (Oct. 27, 1915). Lt. Unattached List, T.F., Uppingham School O.T.C.

1913 Burnett-Brown,* A. D. (Sept. 1, 1914). Capt. 2nd Oxf. & Bucks. Lt. Infty. France and Belgium, 1915–16. *M.C.*, Jan. 14, 1916. *D.* France, 1915.

1915 Burrowes, A. B., B.A. (Mar. 31, 1916). ‡Lt., Acting Capt., 4th R. Irish Fusiliers. France, 1916.

1910 Burt, A. L., M.A. (Apr. 22, 1918). Lt. 1st Canadian Tank Bn.

1906 **Bushell, C.,** B.A. (Mobilized Aug. 4, 1914). Lt.-Col. 7th Queen's (R.W. Surrey Regt.). France, Aug.–Sept. 1914, 1915–18. *D.S.O.*, Jan. 1, 1918. *D.* France, 1916, 1917. Killed in action on Aug. 8, 1918, near Morlancourt. **V.C.** won on Mar. 23, 1918, W. of St. Quentin Canal and N. of Tergnier.

For most conspicuous bravery and devotion to duty when in command of his battalion.

Lt.-Col. Bushell personally led C Company of his battalion, who were co-operating with an Allied regiment in a counter-attack, in face of very heavy machine-gun fire. In the course of this attack he was severely wounded in the head, but he continued to carry on, walking about in front of both English and Allied troops, encouraging and reorganizing them. He refused even to have his wound attended to until he had placed the whole line in a sound position and formed a defensive flank to meet a turning movement by the enemy. He then went to brigade headquarters and reported the situation, had his wound dressed, and returned to the firing line, which had come back a short distance. He visited every portion of the line, both English and Allied, in the face of terrific machine-gun and rifle fire, exhorting the troops to remain where they were, and to kill the enemy.

In spite of his wounds this gallant officer refused to go to the rear and had eventually to be removed to the dressing station in a fainting condition.

To the magnificent example of energy, devotion, and courage shown by their commanding officer is attributed the fine spirit displayed and the keen fight put up by his battalion, not only on the day in question, but on each succeeding day of the withdrawal.

1909 Cadell, A. E., B.A. (Aug. 20, 1917). Lt. 3rd Nigeria Regt. W. African Service Bde. E. Africa, 1917–18.

1912 **Calder, K.W.** (Sept. 30, 1914). ‡2nd Lt. R.F.A. Egypt, 1915; Gallipoli, 1915. Died on Dec. 21, 1915, of wounds received in action at Cape Helles.

1907 Calder, O. V., B.A. (Oct. 5, 1917). 2nd Lt. I.A.R.O.

1886 Caldicott, Rev. A. H., B.A. (July 1917). Chaplain to the Forces (4th Class), attd. 2nd London Res. Bde.

1891 **Callaway, Rev. R. F.,** B.A. (Oct. 2, 1914). Chaplain to the Forces (4th Class), afterwards 2nd Lt. Sherwood Foresters. France, Belgium, 1914, 1915, 1916. Killed in action on Sept. 18, 1916.

1918 Campbell, I. V. H. (Oct. 8, 1914). Lt. 17th King's (Liverpool Regt.). France and Belgium, 1915–16. (Invalided on account of wounds.)

1919 Campbell, T. A. 9th Siege Batt., Canadian G.A.

1903 Carden, P. T., B.C.L., M.A. (Sept. 1914). ‡Capt. and Flight Commdr. 120th Squadron, R.A.F. France. *M.C.*, Jan. 18, 1918.

1913 Carruthers, C. H., B.A. (Apr. 29, 1918). 2nd Lt. R.G.A. Palestine.

1911 Carter, E. C. D. S., B.A. (Serving Aug. 1914). Capt., Acting Maj., R.A.S.C. D.A.Q.M.G. France. Order of St. Stanislas (3rd Class) (with swords). *D.* France, 1916; § Mar. 1919.

1901 Cartwright, V. H., B.A. (Sept. 20, 1914). Maj. R. Marines. Belgium and France. *D.S.O.*, Jan. 1, 1918. Croix de Guerre. *D.* France, 1916.

1919 Carver, M. F. (Oct. 5, 1917). ‡2nd Lt. 52nd K.R.R.C. France, 1918.

1899 Cary, M. O. B., M.A. Pte. R. Fusiliers.

1888 Cassel, Sir F. M. S., M.A., *M.P.* (Aug. 20, 1914). Capt. 19th London Regt. France. *K.B.E.* American Distinguished Service Medal.

1910 **Chavasse,* A.,** B.A. (Aug. 1915). Lt. 17th King's (Liverpool Regt.). France, Belgium. Wounded and missing, presumed killed in action near Zillebeke on July 5, 1917.

1901 Chettle, H. F., B.A. (Sept. 3, 1914). Maj. R.A.S.C. (Staff-Captain), attd. War Office. France. *O.B.E.* (Mil.). *D.* § Feb. 1917.

1911 Chittenden, H. F., B.A. (Sept. 29, 1914). Capt. 1st Field Survey Bn. R.E. France, Belgium, 1915–19. *M.C.*, Jan. 1, 1917. *D.* France, 1918.

1890 **Cholmeley, R. J.,** B.A. (Aug. 9, 1915). Capt. 13th Cheshire Regt. France, N. Russia. *M.C.*, Sept. 27, 1917. Drowned on active service in N. Russia on Aug. 16, 1919.

1913 **Clarke,* E. F.** (Aug. 20, 1914). Capt. 3rd, attd. 13th, London Regt. (Maj.). Malta, 1914; Gallipoli, 1915; Egypt, 1915, 1916; France, 1916–17. Killed in action at Neuville Vitasse on Apr. 9, 1917.

1910 Clauson,* G. L. M., B.A. (Aug. 21, 1914). Capt. Somerset L.I. Capt. General List (Staff Officer). Egypt, Mesopotamia, Palestine, Syria, Gallipoli. *O.B.E.* (Mil.). Croix de Guerre. *D.* Mesopotamia, 1917; Palestine, 1918.

1919 Clemons, H. S. (Oct. 26, 1916). Lt. A.S.C. Lt. R.A.F. France.

1900 Clough-Taylor, E. L. F., B.A. (June 5, 1917). 2nd Lt. 3rd Grenadier Guards. France and Belgium, 1918; Germany, 1918–19.

1911 Cochrane, C. N., M.A. (Oct. 15, 1914). Lt. 1st Bn. Canadian Tank Corps.

1902 Cohen, D. H., B.C.L., M.A. (Apr. 1, 1915). Capt. Sherwood Foresters. France.

1900 Coldwell, Rev. C. S., M.A. (June 1, 1915). Chaplain to the Forces (4th Class).

1910 **Coles,* A. N.,** B.A. (Aug. 29, 1914). Lt. 8th Rifle Brigade. France. Killed in action on Aug. 24, 1916.

1898 Collins, S. M., M.A. (Serving Aug. 4, 1914). Capt. R.E. (Signal Service).

1907 Collis, M. S., B.A. (Nov. 20, 1917). Lt. I.A.R.O., attd. Scinde Horse, Indian Army. India.

1906 Colmer, G. J., B.A. (Sept. 30, 1914). Capt. 22nd London Regt. (The Queen's). France. *M.C.*, Nov. 25, 1916.

Connop, H. A. (Aug. 1, 1917). Flight Lt. R.N.A.S. France, 1918. Died on Mar. 31, 1918, from injuries received in aerial action.

1911 **Coombs, H. W.,** B.A. (Jan. 1915). Lt. Northumberland Fusiliers. France, 1916. Died on July 2, 1916, of wounds received in action on the Somme.

1891 **Coupland, H.** Capt. Chota Nagpur Light Horse. India. Died.

1903 Cowie, W. P., B.A. (Nov. 1918). 2nd Lt. 28th Indian Light Cavalry. Quetta.

1919 Crosfield, L. M. (Dec. 1917). 2nd Lt. 2nd Oxf. & Bucks. Lt. Infty. France, Germany.

1906 Crump, R. H., B.A. (Serving Aug. 4, 1914). ‡Capt. I.A.R.O. (Infantry). India.

1910 d'Albon, Marquis, M.A. Lt. Lancashire Fusiliers (Liaison Officer). France.

1896 Davis, H. Summersell, M.A. (Oct. 5, 1914). Maj. 2/5th Gloucestershire Regt. G.S.O. 3. France, 1916–17.

1919 Davy, C. B. (Nov. 1916). Driver, Section Sanitaire Anglaise, No. 10, Croix rouge française. France. Croix de Guerre.

1911 **de Pass,* W. H. D.** (Aug. 1914). Lt. 13th Middlesex Regt. (Capt.). France and Belgium. Missing, believed killed in action at Pouzeau-Chaulnes on Mar. 25, 1918.

1901 **Devas, B. W.,** M.A. (Nov. 1914). Lt. 2nd Suffolk Regt. (Capt.). France. Killed in action at Serre on Nov. 13, 1916.

1901 de Wesselow, O. L. V., B.M. (Aug. 5, 1914). Capt. R.A.M.C. France. *D.* France, 1916.

Dewhurst, R. W. M. (Aug. 26, 1914)., Lt. 5th Wiltshire Regt. Mesopotamia. *D.* Mesopotamia, 1916. Died on Apr. 25, 1916, of wounds received in action.

1897 Digby, A. K., B.A. (Serving Aug. 4, 1914). Capt., Acting Lt.-Col., 99th Bde. R.F.A. France, 1914–15, 1916–17; Salonika, 1918–19; Caucasus, 1919. *D.S.O.*, May 8, 1915. *D.* France, 1915 twice.

1902 **Digby, Rev. L. K.,** M.A. (May 15, 1918). Pte. 7th Norfolk Regt. France. Killed in action at Faumont on Oct. 18, 1918.

1910 Dixon, J. W., B.A. (Sept. 5, 1914). ‡Lt. 6th Middlesex Regt., attd. 48th Bn. M.G.C. (Capt.). France, 1916–17; Italy, 1918. *D.* France, 1917.

1919 Donnison, F. S. V. (Jan. 31, 1917). Lt. 3rd Grenadier Guards. France, 1917–18, 1918–19.

1896 Downes, Rev. R. D., M.A. (Aug. 5, 1915). Acting Chaplain to Australian Hospital (Chaplain, attd. 230th Bde.). Egypt and Palestine.

1915 Drew, A. O'Neil, B.A. (Jan. 5, 1916). Lt. 4th Border Regt. France.

1908 **Dugdale,* Rev. R. W.,** M.A. (June 1915). Chaplain to the Forces (4th Class), attd. 5th Div. France, 1915–18. *M.C.*, Mar. 3, 1917. Killed in action at Beaurain on Oct. 23, 1918.

1912 Duke,* R. N., B.A. (Aug. 21, 1914). Capt. 8th The Black Watch. Bde. Maj., Staff. France, Belgium, Germany. *D.S.O.*, June 3, 1918. *M.C.*, Jan. 1, 1917. *D.* France, 1915, 1917, 1918.

1903 Dunkley, Rev. E. H., M.A. (Mar. 20, 1916). 2nd Lt. 91st Punjabis, I.A.R.O. Chaplain to the Forces (4th Class). Mesopotamia, 1916–18; Egypt, 1918–19. *D.* Mesopotamia, 1918.

1915 Dyson, A. D. (July 20, 1916). Pioneer R.E. (Special Bde.). France.

1908 Earle,* J. W. A., B.A. (Oct. 18, 1916). Lt. Irish Guards, Acting Capt. attd. O.C.B.

Edkins, H. (Sept. 1915). 2nd Lt. 21st London Regt. (1st Surrey Rifles). France, 1916. Killed in action at High Wood on Sept. 15, 1916.

1886 Ellis, P. J., M.A. (Aug. 26, 1915). 2nd Lt. 13th Worcestershire Regt. Lt., Acting Capt., Labour Corps.

1909 Evans, E. W., B.A. (Mar. 3, 1918). 2nd Lt. 3rd King's Own (R. Lancaster Regt.). 2nd Lt. King's African Rifles. E. Africa.

1908 Eyre-Matcham, J. St. L. (June 1918). Rfln. 25th K.R.R.C. France, 1918–19.

1916 Facer, G. S. (July 17, 1916). 2nd Lt. 8th E. Surrey Regt. France, 1917. (Wounded and prisoner of war, 1917–18.)

1919 Fallows, T. H. (Jan. 22, 1918). Cadet O.C.B., R.E.

1905 Farrow, B. A., M.A. (Mar. 10, 1916). ‡Lt. R.G.A. (Capt. and Adjt.). Palestine, 1917–18.

1904 Fletcher, B. L., M.A. (Aug. 5, 1914). ‡Maj. 5th Manchester Regt. Egypt, Gallipoli, 1915; Sinai, 1916; France, 1918. *M.C.*, Jan. 1, 1918.

1908 Flynn, T. H., B.A. (Aug. 1914). Maj. R.F.A. (T.F.). France, 1914, 1916; India, Mesopotamia, 1915.

1910 **Forrest, E. A. A.,** B.A. (Sept. 1914). ‡Lt. 11th, attd. 7th, Gloucestershire Regt. Gallipoli. Died at Malta on Dec. 9, 1915, of illness contracted while on active service.

1920 Freston, T. A. (Dec. 1916). Lt. 17th Indian Cavalry. India, N.W. Frontier.

1878 Furneaux, L. R., M.A. (Mobilized Aug. 4, 1914). Maj. Unattached List, T.F., Rossall School O.T.C. T.D.

1899 Furtado Abraham, E., B.A. (Nov. 10, 1915). Capt. R.G.A. Lt. Special Lists. G.S.O. 3 (War Cabinet).

1905 Geary, F. C., M.A. (Dec. 1914). 2nd Lt. Unattached List, T.F., St. Bees School O.T.C.

1911 Geidt, F. B., B.A. (Aug. 20, 1914). Capt., Acting Maj., 94th Bde., R.F.A. France, Belgium. *M.C.*, Dec. 17, 1917.

1903 Gidney, A. R., M.A. (Dec. 18, 1914). 2nd Lt. Grenadier Guards.

Girling, C. J. (Dec. 1915). 2nd Lt. 1st Hampshire Regt. France, Belgium. Died on Oct. 23, 1916, of wounds received in action on the Somme.

1896 **Goldie, B. H.,** M.A. (Jan. 1915). 2nd Lt. I.A.R.O., attd. 32nd Lancers. Egypt. Died on Apr. 29, 1915, of wounds received in action in Egypt.

1912 **Goodwin,* W. A. D.** (Nov. 1914). Lt. 8th York & Lancaster Regt. France, 1916. Killed in action at Ovillers on July 1, 1916.

1902 Goring, F., B.A. (Oct. 8, 1914). Capt. 4th R. Sussex Regt. (Adjt.). Gallipoli, 1915; Egypt, 1916; France, 1918; Germany, 1919.

1914 **Grantham, R. A. F.** (Oct. 1915). 2nd Lt. 2nd Lincolnshire Regt. France, 1916. Killed in action near Bouchesvesnes Farm on Mar. 4, 1917.

1909 Gregory,* R. H. (Dec. 14, 1914). Capt. 49th Canadian Regt. France.

1900 Gregson, R. E. S., B.A. (June 10, 1915). Lt. 3rd Hampshire Regt., attd. T.M.B.

1897 **Griffin, R. H.,** B.A. (Nov. 11, 1915). Capt. 21st Siege Batt., R.G.A. France and Belgium. Died on July 7, 1917, of wounds received in action near Proven.

1914 **Griffiths, W. H.** (1914). ‡2nd Lt. 12th, attd. 7th, R. W. Kent Regt. France. Killed in action, Oct. 1916.

1895 Grimley, H. C., B.A. (Serving Aug. 4, 1914). Capt. 5th Worcestershire Regt. Commdt. Prisoner of War Camp.

1900 Grimshaw, W. E., M.A. (May 25, 1915). Capt. R.G.A., attd. Ministry of Munitions. *O.B.E.* (Mil.). *D.* § Mar. 1918.

1898 Gwynn, G. C., M.A. (Sept. 1914). Capt. 4th Gloucestershire Regt. Staff-Captain, 17th Corps (Maj.). France. *D.* France, 1918.

1894 Haig Brown, H. E., M.A. (Oct. 24, 1914). Maj. 5th Queen's (R. W. Surrey Regt.). Instructor No. 19 O.C.B.

1911 Haigh, A. D., B.A. (Sept. 22, 1914). Lt. 5th R. Sussex Regt. France, 1915, 1916–17; Italy, 1917–18. *M.C.*, Apr. 2, 1919.

1907 **Haigh, C. R.,** B.A. (Serving Aug. 4, 1914). Lt. and Adjt. Queen's (R. W. Surrey Regt.). Belgium, 1914. Killed in action near Ypres on Nov. 7, 1914.

1917 Hale, E. (Oct. 17, 1914). Lt. 7th E. Lancashire Regt. France, 1915–16.

1900 **Hales, A. J. S. H.,** M.A. (Aug. 10, 1914). ‡Capt. 1st Wiltshire Regt. France, 1914–16. *M.C.*, Apr. 15, 1915. *D.* France, 1915. Killed in action on the Somme on July 5, 1916.

1919 Hall, C. S. (Nov. 4, 1915). Lt. 4th York & Lancaster Regt., attd. Ministry of Labour. (Invalided.)

1919 Hancock, D. S. (Nov. 2, 1916). Lt. 3rd The Buffs (E. Kent Regt.); Acting Capt., attd. R.E. (Signals). France, 1917; N. Russia, 1918–19.

1915 Hancock, W. C., B.A. (Apr. 24, 1917). ‡Lt. 21st London Regt. France, Belgium.

1907 **Hankey, D. W. A.,** B.A. (Aug. 1914). ‡2nd Lt. 3rd R. Warwickshire Regt. France and Belgium, 1915–16. Killed in action near Morval on Oct. 12, 1916.

1919 Hargreaves, E. L. (June 1917). Pte. 11th E. Surrey Regt. France. (Wounded and prisoner, Apr. 1918.)

1918 Harris, C. R. S., B.A. (Sept. 1915). Lt. 433rd Siege Batt., R.G.A. Malta, 1916–17. (Invalided, Jan. 1918.)

1909 Harvey,* R. H. M. (Nov. 11, 1916). Lt. 9th N. Bengal Mounted Rifles, I.A.R.O., attd. Supply & Transport Corps. India.

1906 Hay, G. F. A., B.A. (1914). ‡Lt., Acting Capt., 1/70th Burma Rifles. India, Palestine.

1898 Heape, B., B.A. (Mar. 1915). Driver, Croix rouge française. France, 1915–19. Croix de Guerre. *D.* French Dispatches, 1917 twice, 1918.

1898 Heape, J. M. (1914). ‡Capt., Flight Commdr., R.A.F.

1908 Hemelryk,* C. J., M.A. (Aug. 5, 1914). Pte. A Coy. H.T., A.S.C. (Lce.-Cpl.). France, 1915–17. (Discharged on account of injuries received on active service.)

1895 Hemmant, D. G., B.A. (Aug. 11, 1916). Lt. R.G.A. (S.R.).

1911 Hemming,* A. F., B.A. (Aug. 15, 1914). Capt. 3rd, attd. 2nd, W. Riding Regt. France, 1914–16. (Retired on account of wounds, Dec. 3, 1918.)

Henderson, W. J. (Oct. 8, 1914). Capt. Loyal N. Lancashire Regt. France. *M.C.*, June 24, 1916. *D.* France, 1916. Killed in action on July 6, 1916.

1905 **Herdman, A. W.,** B.A. (Serving Aug. 4, 1914). Capt. 1st Shropshire L.I. France. Killed in action near Lille on Oct. 25, 1914.

1914 Herold, J. C. E., B.A. (Mar. 30, 1916). ‡2nd Lt. 2/11th London Regt. (Finsbury Rifles). France, 1916–18. (Prisoner in Germany, 1918.)

1900 Hicks, E. R., M.A. (Sept. 1914). Lt. 9th Lincolnshire Regt. Gallipoli, 1915 ; Egypt, 1915–16 ; France, 1916.

1915 Hignett, C. (Mar. 6, 1916). Gnr. R.G.A. (Invalided, 1917.)

Hitchcock, R. F. (1916). 2nd Lt. M.G.C. Killed in action.

1911 Hobhouse, R. O. (Aug. 30, 1914). ‡2nd Lt. 2/5th Somerset L.I. Lt. R.A.F. (Capt.). France, Egypt, India.

1909 **Holms,* J. C.,** B.A. (Aug. 1914). Capt. 1/9th London Regt. (Queen Victoria's Rifles). France, 1915. Died on Sept. 10, 1915, of wounds received in action at Carnoy.

1889 Hore, L. F. S., B.A. (Serving Aug. 4, 1914). Capt. Australian Light Horse. Maj. M.G.C. France. *M.C.*, Sept. 22, 1916. *D.* France, 1917.

1895 Hose, H. F., M.A. (Nov. 1914). Capt. Unattached List, T.F., Dulwich College O.T.C.

House, M. H. (July 1916). 2nd Lt. 8th Rifle Brigade. France, 1916–17. Killed in action at Chèrisy on May 3, 1917.

1913 **Hurd, D. W.** (Aug. 1914). Capt. 7th Middlesex Regt. Gibraltar, 1914 ; France, 1915 ; Belgium. Killed in action near Leuze Wood on Sept. 15, 1916.

1912 Hussey, D. (Oct. 31, 1914). Lt. 13th Lancashire Fusiliers. (Invalided. Aug. 17, 1917.)

1896 **Innes-Hopkins, J. R.,** B.A. (Sept. 22, 1914). Capt. 5th Canadian L.I. France. Killed in action near Festubert on May 24, 1915.

1919 Jack, A. C. (Sept. 6, 1917). 2nd Lt. B/256th Bde., 51st Div., R.F.A. France, 1918–19.

1908 Jackson, A. H. C., B.A. (Aug. 14, 1916). 2nd Lt. I.A.R.O. Staff-Captain Bombay Bde. India.

1891 Jackson, G. E., B.A. (Mobilized Aug. 4, 1914). Maj. Fife & Forfar Yeomanry. (D.A.A.G. Australian Mounted Div.) Gallipoli, 1915 ; Egypt, 1916–17 ; Palestine, 1917–18 ; Syria, 1919 ; Upper Egypt, 1919. *O.B.E.* (Mil.). *M.C.*, June 3, 1918. *D.* Egypt, 1917.

1912 **Janasz, J. G. G.** (Nov. 4, 1914). 2nd Lt. 3rd Dorsetshire Regt., attd. 2nd Wiltshire Regt. France. Killed in action on June 15, 1915.

1909 Jardine,* Sir J. E. B., Bt., B.A. (Mobilized Aug. 4, 1914). Capt. and Adjt. 1/5th Queen's (R. W. Surrey Regt.). India, 1914–15; Mesopotamia, 1915–19. *D.* Mesopotamia, 1919.

1919 Jardine, K. W. S. (Jan. 4, 1918). 2nd Lt. R.F.A. Italy.

1896 Jenkins, J. A., B.A. (Apr. 1, 1915). Lt. R.N. Div. Lt.-Col. 17th E. Yorkshire Regt. *O.B.E.* (Mil.).

1913 Joblin, B. E., M.A. (Apr. 11, 1917). ‡2nd Lt. 111th Labour Coy. France, 1918–19.

1893 Jones, D. W. C., D.M. (Serving Aug. 4, 1914). Col. A.M.S. France, 1915–18; Egypt and Palestine, 1918–19.

1887 Jones, E. B., B.A. (Serving Aug. 4, 1914). Maj. 3rd R. Welch Fusiliers, attd. R. Irish Rifles.

1911 Jones, M. H. (Feb. 23, 1915). Lt. R. Scots Fusiliers, attd. War Office.

1895 Kent, P. H. B., M.A. (June 11, 1916). Capt. 4th Scots Guards, attd. Guards M.G. Regt. (Maj.). France, 1916–18. *M.C.*, Sept. 26, 1917.

1908 King,* A. H., B.A. (Aug. 5, 1914). Lt. 4th E. Surrey Regt., empld. Ministry of National Service. France, 1914. (Placed on Retired List on account of wounds.)

1911 King, C. S., M.A. (Dec. 7, 1914). Lt. R.F.A. France. *M.C.*, Jan. 22, 1916. *D.* France, 1915.

1893 Kitcat, Rev. W. P. de W. (1914). Chaplain S.A. Forces.

1900 Klein, B. G., D.M. (Oct. 25, 1914). Capt. R.A.M.C. France.

1900 Knox, E. G. V. (Dec. 14, 1914). Lt. 4th Lincolnshire Regt., empld. 115th Training Res. Bn.

1898 Knox, F. P., B.A. (Oct. 1914). Maj. R.A.S.C. France. *D.S.O.*, June 3, 1918. *D.* France, 1916, 1917, 1918.

1884 Langridge, A. B. (Serving Aug. 4, 1914). Q.M.S. Inns of Court O.T.C. (1914–18). ‡2nd Lt., Acting Capt., Flying Officer, R.A.F.

1909 Laski,* N. J., B.A. (Mobilized Aug. 4, 1914). Capt. 1/6th Lancashire Fusiliers. Gallipoli, 1915; Sinai, 1916; France, 1917. (Invalided.)

1919 Lindsay, J. St. C. L. (Dec. 17, 1917). 2nd Lt. R.F.A. France, 1918–19.

1865 Liverpool, Bishop of, D.D. (Mobilized Aug. 4, 1914). Hon. Chaplain R.N.V.R.

1908 Llewellyn, R. A., B.A. (Sept. 8, 1915). Capt. 67th Siege Batt., R.G.A. France, 1916–19.

Lushington, S. E. J. C. (Sept. 9, 1914). 2nd Lt. 11th Hampshire Regt. Lt. General List. A.D.C. to G.O.C., R.A., 41st Div. France and Belgium, 1916. Died on Sept. 25, 1916, of wounds received in action in the Battle of the Somme.

1907 McDougall, W., M.A. (June 1, 1915). Maj. R.A.M.C. France.

1895 Machell, H. W. (Feb. 2, 1917). Paymaster Sub-Lt. R.N.V.R., H.M.S. *Blenheim*. Mudros, Brindisi, Ismid, Malta.

1906 Mackworth,* J. D., B.A. (Serving Aug. 4, 1914). Capt. 2nd Queen's (R. W. Surrey Regt.). Lt.-Col. R.A.F. Dep. Director Kite Balloons (Col.). France, Belgium, Gallipoli. *C.B.E.* (Mil.). Croix d'Officier de la Légion d'Honneur.

1912 Macrae,* E. H., B.A. (Aug. 29, 1914). Capt. 11th Highland L.I. Instructor No. 21 O.C.B. France and Belgium, 1915, 1916, 1917.

1913 **Malcolm,* P.** (Aug. 29, 1914). Lt. 1st Grenadier Guards (Capt. King's Coy.). France. Killed in action at Mory St. Leger on Aug. 25, 1918.

1919 Markham, H. V. (Dec. 31, 1915). Lt., Acting Capt. and Adjt., 2nd Bde., R.G.A. France, 1916–19. *M.C.*, Jan. 1, 1919. Croix de Guerre. *D.* France, 1918.
1910 **Maude,* L. E. J.,** B.A. (May 1915). 2nd Lt. K.O.Y.L.I. France. Killed in action at Fricourt on July 1, 1916.
1895 Menneer, E. A., M.A. (Aug. 10, 1917). ‡2nd Lt. R.A.S.C.
1875 Mildmay, G. St. J., B.A. (Oct. 6, 1914). Capt. 6th Somerset L.I. Capt. General List, Staff-Captain. Maj. Labour Corps. *D.* § Aug. 1919.
1906 Millar, E. G., B.A. (Sept. 14, 1915). Lt. 4th The Buffs (E. Kent Regt.). India.
1885 Milliken, K. E., M.A. (Oct. 29, 1914). Capt. 6th E. Surrey Regt., empld. R.E.
1900 **Mills, H. V.,** B.A. (Oct. 1915). 2nd Lt. R.G.A. France and Belgium. Killed in action at Vlamertinghe on June 25, 1917.
1909 Mills,* J. P., B.A. Tpr. Jumna Valley Light Horse. India.
1911 **Mocatta,* R. M.,** B.A. (July 1914). 2nd Lt. 5th R. Welch Fusiliers. Gallipoli. Killed in action on Aug. 10, 1915.
1898 Moggridge, H. W., B.A. (Jan. 29, 1916). Lt.-Col. 2nd County of London Yeomanry. (Pte. Sec. C.I.G.S., War Office, 1914–16.) France, 1916–18. *O.B.E.* (Mil.). Croix de Chevalier de la Légion d'Honneur *D.* France, 1916, 1917, 1918.
1902 Monk, G. L., M.A. Nigerian Land Contingent.
1919 Monk-Jones, A. (July 4, 1917). 2nd Lt. 5th Cheshire Regt. France, 1918–19.
1902 Morgan, C. L., M.A. (Nov. 9, 1914). Maj. 11th Suffolk Regt. France. (Relinquished Commission on account of wounds.)
1918 Morrice, Rev. J. C., B.Litt. (Oct. 1914). Chaplain to the Forces (4th Class), attd. W. Lancashire R.E.
1912 **Morris, H.** (Jan. 9, 1915). 2nd Lt. 6th, attd. 3rd, Middlesex Regt. France. Killed in action at the Hohenzollern Redoubt on Sept. 28, 1915.
1903 Murray-Graham, W., B.C.L., M.A. (Mar. 10, 1917). ‡2nd Lt. R.G.A. (S.R.). France. *M.M.* Croix de Guerre.
1919 Mylne, A. F. (Jan. 4, 1918). 2nd Lt. 5th Worcestershire Regt. France.
1906 Nalder,* L. F., B.A. (May 1916). Lt. R.N.V.R. Maj. Special Lists. Red Sea Patrol, Hedjaz, Mesopotamia. *C.I.E.* *D.* Naval Dispatches.
1919 Nelson, H. G. (Jan. 8, 1917). Lt. 310th Bde., R.F.A. France, 1917; France and Germany, 1918–19. *M.C.*, June 3, 1919.
1879 **Newton, W. J.,** M.A. (Serving Aug. 4, 1914). Maj. 4th Cheshire Regt. Died on Feb. 16, 1915, of illness contracted while on active service.
1915 Nickson, P. (Jan. 27, 1916). Capt. 2/5th King's Own (R. Lancaster Regt.). France.
1898 Noad, C. H. Carden, B.A. (Oct. 24, 1914). Lt. 9th Middlesex Regt. Capt. Special Lists. Adjt. 4th Simla Rifles, I.D.F. India.
1913 **Norris, F.** (July 6, 1915). Capt. 23rd Middlesex Regt. France. Killed in action on June 7, 1917.
1919 Oakley, A. S. (May 1, 1918). Cadet, O.C.B.
1911 Oakley, H. C., M.A. (July, 1915). Y.M.C.A. Malta, Salonika, Turkey. *D.* 1917, 1919.
1887 Oakshott, Rev. G. H., D.D. (1915). Chaplain R.N.

1899 O'Brien, R. F. C., M.A. (Mobilized Aug. 1914). Lt.-Col. 2nd City of London Yeomanry. France. *D.* France, 1918; § Aug. 1919.

1908 Ogle,* W. M., M.A. (Aug. 17, 1914). Capt. 3rd R. W. Kent Regt. France. *D.* § Feb. 1917. (Placed on Retired List on account of wounds, Aug. 1918.)

1904 O'Hanlon, G., M.A. (Aug. 4, 1914). Capt. 6th Dorsetshire Regt., attd. XVIII Corps School. France, 1915–18. *M.C.*, Aug. 19, 1916.

1901 **Oliver, J. M.**, B.A. (Sept. 1914). Lt. 16th Manchester Regt. France. Killed in action in Trônes Wood on July 1, 1916.

1903 Oliver, R. G., B.A. (May 6, 1917). Lt. R.F.A. (S.R.). France. *M.C.*, Nov. 19, 1917. (Invalided.)

1905 Ovens, A. R., B.A. (Jan. 8, 1916). 2nd Lt. R.G.A. Lt., Acting Capt., R.A.F. (Staff). *M.B.E.* (Mil.).

1913 **Owen, F. W.** (Sept. 1914). Pte. 18th R. Fusiliers, attd. R.E. France. Killed in action on Mar. 31, 1916.

1903 Owen, J. P., B.A. (Nov. 22, 1915). Lt. 3rd R. Welch Fusiliers. France. *M.C.*, Jan. 14, 1916.

1907 Patrick,* P. J., M.A. (Mar. 11, 1916). Lt. 4/11th Gurkha Rifles (Maj.). India, Palestine.

1903 Pattinson, H. D., B.A. (Sept. 21, 1916). Cpl. R.A.V.C. (Sergt.). France.

1902 Peckham, W. D., M.A. (June 28, 1916). Lt. Special Lists (Interpreter). Salonika. *D.* Salonika, 1918.

1914 **Peel, A.** (Aug. 14, 1915). 2nd Lt. 6th, attd. 2nd, R. Berkshire Regt. France. Killed in action on May 5, 1917.

1910 Peele,* C. R. de C., B.A. (Oct. 2, 1914). Capt. I.A.R.O., attd. 1/153rd Punjabis. India, Mesopotamia, Palestine. *D.* Mesopotamia, 1917.

1919 Pells, L. (Jan. 22, 1918). 2nd Lt. 21st D.A.C., R.F.A. France, 1918–19.

1907 Pembleton, E. S., B.A. Nigerian Land Contingent.

1914 Petrie, C. A., B.A. (Dec. 10, 1915). Lt. R.G.A., attd. Historical Section, War Cabinet.

1901 Phelps, W., M.A. (Oct. 10, 1914). Maj. 20th Lancashire Fusiliers. France, 1916–17.

1907 Phythian-Adams, W. J. T. P., B.A. (Sept. 1914). Lt.-Col. 22nd R. Fusiliers. Chief Instructor 2nd Army School. France, 1915–19. *D.S.O.*, Jan. 1, 1918. *M.C.*, Feb. 3, 1917. *D.* France, 1917 twice.

1893 Pipon, P. J. G., B.A. (Oct. 1914). Capt. Special Lists. G.S.O. 3. France. *C.I.E.* *M.C.*, Feb. 18, 1915. *D.* France, 1915.

1914 Platt, C. L. (July 8, 1915). Lt. 19th Lancashire Fusiliers. France and Belgium, 1915–18.

1908 [Poole,* A. L., M.A.] (Dec. 10, 1914). Lt. 8th Gloucestershire Regt., attd. No. 6 O.C.B. France, 1915–16, 1917.

1901 Pope, J. A., M.A. (July 22, 1916). 2nd Lt. Indian Cavalry, I.A.R.O. India.

1919 Porter, A. E. (Aug. 16, 1915). Lt. 36th Bn. M.G.C. France. *D.* France, 1918.

1905 Porter, H. E. L., M.A. (Nov. 1915). Lt. 20th Div. Survey Coy., R.E. (Capt.). France, 1916–19. *M.C.*, Jan. 1, 1918. *D.* France, 1916, 1919.

1913 Porter,* N. T. (Aug. 24, 1914). Capt. 5th Shropshire L.I. Capt. General List. France, 1915–19. *D.* France, 1919.

1881 Powell, H. A., D.M., M.Ch. (Mar. 14, 1916). Hon. Lt.-Col. R.A.M.C.

1913 Powell, I. (Sept. 17, 1914). ‡Capt. 6th Leinster Regt. Gallipoli, Serbia, Salonika, Palestine, France.

1907 Powell, L., B.A. (Nov. 16, 1914). ‡Lt. 121st Bde., R.F.A. (Capt.). France, 1915, 1916, 1919. *M.C.*, Jan. 1, 1919. *D.* France, 1917.

1897 Powers, Rev. C. S., M.A. (Sept. 3, 1915). Chaplain to the Forces (4th Class), attd. 15th Labour Coy. France, Belgium.

1913 Preedy,* B. (Sept. 1914). Lt. 1st London Regt. (R. Fusiliers). Belgium, France, 1914, 1917, 1918. *M.C.*, July 17, 1917.

1919 Price, D. W. M. (Feb. 8, 1918). 2nd Lt. 11th Queen's (R. W. Surrey Regt.). France, 1918; Germany, 1919.

1919 Price, H. L. (Jan. 11, 1918). Cadet No. 4 O.C.B.

1901 Prideaux, Rev. W. A., M.A. (Oct. 2, 1917). Chaplain to the Forces (4th Class). Egypt, Mesopotamia.

1904 Quick, Rev. O. C., M.A. (Feb. 13, 1917). Chaplain to the Forces (4th Class). France.

1913 **Radcliffe,* D.** (Dec. 1914). ‡Lt. 24th R. Fusiliers (Capt.). France. Killed in action near Bully-Grenay on Mar. 18, 1916.

Radcliffe, W. Y. (Aug. 26, 1914). 2nd Lt. 5th Wiltshire Regt. Gallipoli. Died on Aug. 15, 1915, of wounds received in action at Chunuk Bair.

1891 **Raikes F. M.,** B.A. (Sept. 25, 1915). 2nd Lt. Brecknockshire Bn. S. Wales Borderers, attd. M.G.C. France. Killed in action on Feb. 22, 1917.

Raikes, J. F. (Oct. 1914). ‡2nd Lt. 3rd Essex Regt. France, 1915–16. Killed in action on Oct. 10, 1916.

1912 **Ramsbotham,* G. B.** (Aug. 15, 1914). Lt. 3rd R. Sussex Regt., attd. 1st S. Staffordshire Regt. France, Belgium. *D.* France, 1915. Killed in action at Festubert on May 16, 1915.

1903 Ranger, C. L. A., M.A. (Sept. 1914). Capt. I.A.R.O., attd. 1/32nd Sikh Pioneers. India.

1897 Rankin, Sir J. R. L., Bt., M.A. (Apr. 1915). Maj. W. Kent Yeomanry. T.D.

1903 [Rawlinson, Rev. A. E. J., M.A.] (Oct. 1, 1915). Chaplain to the Forces (4th Class).

1909 **Rayner,* H. L.,** B.A. (Dec. 22, 1914). 2nd Lt. 9th Devonshire Regt. France, 1915–16. Killed in action on the Somme on July 1, 1916.

1911 **Read, H. E.** (Nov. 25, 1914). Lt. Lincolnshire Yeomanry. Capt. R.F.C. France. Killed in action near Crevecœur on Aug. 10, 1917.

1912 Rees, R. G., M.A. (Feb. 23, 1915). 2nd Lt. 12th R. Welsh Fusiliers. Capt. General List. Gallipoli.

1919 Regan, M. A. (Apr. 17, 1918). 2nd Lt. R.G.A.

1907 Reid, C. L., B.A. (Nov. 3, 1914). Capt. King George's Own Indian Cavalry, I.A.R.O. India.

1902 Rhodes, G. P., M.A. (Feb. 1916). Lt. R.A.S.C. France, 1916–19.

1904 Rhodes, H., M.A. (Dec. 1914). Capt. R.F.A. France and Belgium, 1915–19.

1919 Rhodes, K. (July, 1915). Lt. R.F.A. Egypt and Palestine, 1917–19.

1904 Richards, P. S., M.A. (Nov. 1915). Pte. attd. 2nd S. African Inf. Bde. German E. Africa, 1915–17; Nyasaland F.F., 1917–19.

1895 Roberts, W. M., M.A. (Feb. 28, 1916). Lt., Acting Capt., R.G.A. (S.R.). France.

1911 **Robinson,* T.** (Sept. 1914). ‡Lt. 26th R. Fusiliers. France and Italy. *M.C.*, Mar. 8, 1919. Killed in action at Courtrai on Oct. 25, 1918.

1913 Robley,* C. H. 2nd Lt. R.N. Div. (Invalided.)

1904 **Rodger, M. F.,** B.A. (Sept. 26, 1914). Lt. 4th Cameronians. France. Killed in action near Le Transloy on Oct. 23, 1916.

1906 Ross Hume, P. G., B.A. (Aug. 23, 1914). Maj. No. 2 Squadron, R.A.F. France. *M.C.*, Jan. 1, 1917.

1907 Rowlands, W. S., B.A. (Apr. 1, 1917). 2nd Lt. I.A.R.O., attd. 2nd Nagpur Rifles.

1903 **Royal Dawson, O. S.** (Nov. 5, 1914). Capt. 5th Oxf. & Bucks. Lt. Infty. France, 1917; Salonika, 1915–16. Died on Aug. 25, 1917, of wounds received in action.

1894 Rutherfurd, J. E., B.M. (Jan. 5, 1915). Capt. R.A.M.C., attd. R. Irish Rifles. Gallipoli, France, Belgium. *M.C.*, Feb. 13, 1917. *D.* France, 1917.

1915 Salmon, E. C. H. (July 24, 1916). Lt., Acting Capt., R. W. Kent Regt. Education Officer, 123rd Inf. Bde. Belgium, France, Italy, 1917–18; Germany, 1919. *M.C.*, Sept. 26, 1917.

1908 Sampson,* J. S., B.A. (Sept. 26, 1914). Capt. 5th Sherwood Foresters. France, 1915–17. *M.C.*, Feb. 18, 1918.

1902 Samuel, H. B., M.A. (Sept. 1914). ‡Capt. 42nd R. Fusiliers. France, Palestine.

1912 Sayer,* M. M. (Aug. 1914). ‡Lt. 19th Queen's (R. W. Surrey Regt.).

1902 Scott, E. T. (1914). Lt. R.F.A. France. (Prisoner of war, Mar. 1918.)

1913 Seel,* G. F. (Nov. 20, 1914). Lt. 7th Cheshire Regt. Lt. M.G.C. Palestine.

1904 Sharp, C. H. C., M.A. (Sept. 18, 1914). Maj. S. Wales Borderers (Lt.-Col.). Bde. Maj. Central Instruction School, Berkhamsted. France, 1915; Salonika, 1915–17. *D.* Salonika, 1917.

1906 **Shaw, A. M.,** B.A. (Sept. 1914). Capt. 12th Yorkshire Regt. France, 1916–18. Killed in action near Sailly sur Lys on Apr. 11, 1918.

1906 **Simpson, A. H.,** B.A. (Aug. 4, 1914). 2nd Lt. 1st R. Warwickshire Regt. France. Died on Feb 1, 1915, of illness contracted on active service.

1897 Sinclair, T. C., *D.S.O.* (Serving Aug. 4, 1914). Maj., Bt.-Lt.-Col., A.A. Res. Bde., R.A. Instructor in Gunnery. France and Belgium, 1914. *D.* France, 1914.

1896 Slater, E. V., M.A. (Dec. 26, 1914). Lt. Yorkshire Regt. Capt. R.E. France, 1915–18. *M.C.*, Jan. 1, 1917.

1909 Smith,* E. C., B.A. (Jan. 26, 1915). Lt. 2/4th Devonshire Regt. Acting Capt., attd. Staff 21st Corps H.Q., E.E.F. Egypt, Palestine, Syria, India. *D.* Palestine, 1919.

1913 **Smith, G. B.** (Jan. 1915). Lt. 19th Lancashire Fusiliers (Adjt.). France. Died on Dec. 3, 1916, of wounds received in action near Warlincourt.

1895 Smith, G. O., M.A. Lt. Toronto University O.T.C.

1911 **Smith, H. M.** (Oct. 1914). Lt. 11th, attd. 1st, Loyal N. Lancashire Regt. France. Died as a prisoner at St. Quentin on Feb. 27, 1917, of wounds received in action.

1908 **Smith,* H. S.,** B.A. (Apr. 1915). Capt. 2nd Arg. & Suth'd. Highlanders. France, 1915–16. Killed in action at High Wood on Aug. 18, 1916.

1908 Smith, L., M.A. (Aug. 30, 1914). ‡2nd Lt. 7th Lancashire Fusiliers. Egypt, 1914; Gallipoli, 1915; France, 1916.

1919 Somerset, H. F. V. (June 7, 1917). 2nd Lt. Coldstream Guards. France, 1918.

1898 Southorn, W. T., B.A. (Sept. 5, 1918). 2nd Lt. General List.

1919 Spence, H. (Dec. 29, 1915). Lt. 3rd The Buffs (E. Kent Regt.), attd. War Office. France, 1916.

1912 **Squire, S. C.** (Aug. 28, 1914). Lt. 7th Gloucestershire Regt. Gallipoli. Killed in action at Chanuk Bair on Aug. 9, 1915.

1897 Stansfield, R., B.A. (Dec. 1917). Capt. R.A.M.C. France. *M.C.*, Mar. 26, 1918.

1914 **Stewart, C. H.** Pte. Border Regt. France. Killed in action, 1916.

1901 [Stocks,* J. L., M.A.] (Nov. 21, 1914). Capt. 13th K.R.R.C. Capt. General List, attd. No. 19 O.C.B. France, 1915–16. *D.S.O.*, Mar. 3, 1917. *D.* France, 1917 ; § Aug. 1918.

1914 Stokes, R. H. C., B.A. (June 1916). Lt. R.G.A. Gibraltar, 1917–19.

1912 **Stokoe,* J. C.** (Mar. 25, 1915). 2nd Lt. 14th Manchester Regt., attd. 6th Loyal N. Lancashire Regt. Gallipoli. Killed in action in Gallipoli on Dec. 11, 1915.

1891 Stowell, V. A., B.A. (Sept. 1914). Pte. Naini Tal Rifles, I.D.F. (Lt.). Sec. United Provinces War Board. India. *O.B.E.* (Civil).

1910 Strong, E. N., M.A. (July 1915). Instructor Lt. R.N., H.M.S. *Princess Royal*, 1st Battle Cruiser Squadron. North Sea, Jutland.

1899 **Stuart, Viscount** (Oct. 8, 1914). Lt. 6th R. Scots Fusiliers. France. Killed in action at the Battle of Loos, Sept. 25–7, 1915.

1915 Tarrant, R. E. (Aug. 26, 1915). Lt. 11th Devonshire Regt. France, Italy.

1909 **Tate,* W. L.,** B.A. (Serving Aug. 4, 1914). Lt. R. Fusiliers. France and Belgium. Killed in action near St. Eloi on Mar. 13, 1915.

1913 **Taunton, C. P.** (Jan. 27, 1915). 2nd Lt. S. Staffordshire Regt. Gallipoli. Killed in action in Gallipoli on Aug. 9, 1915.

1913 Thomas, E. V. S. (Aug. 4, 1914). ‡Lt. R.H. and R.F.A. Signalling Training Centre. Belgium and France, 1915–17.

1908 Thomas, Rev. T. W., M.A. H.A.C.

1888 Thompson, A. T., M.A. (Feb. 1915). ‡2nd Lt. 1st Huntingdonshire Vol. Regt.

1903 Thompson, M. S., M.A. (Aug. 6, 1914). Capt., Acting Maj., 14th Durham L.I. G.S.O. 2 (Intelligence), G.H.Q., B.S.F. France, 1915–16 ; Salonika, 1916–19. *O.B.E.* (Mil.). *D.* France, 1916 ; Salonika, 1917 twice, 1919.

1900 **Thomson, A. G.,** B.A. (June 19, 1915). Capt. 7th R. Scots. France and Belgium. Missing, believed killed in action on Sept. 26, 1917.

1911 Thomson, G. R., B.A. (Nov. 9, 1914). ‡Capt. 1/5th Arg. & Suth'd. Highlanders. Egypt, Palestine, France. *D.* France, 1919.

1914 **Thomson, P. G.** (June 1917). Cpl. 1st Wiltshire Regt. France. Died on Nov. 29, 1918, of illness contracted while on active service.

1904 Thornton, Rev. C. T., B.A. (Nov. 26, 1916). Lt. 17th R. Scots.

1889 Thorold, H. G., B.A. (Serving Aug. 4, 1914). Maj. 3rd Northamptonshire Regt. France.

1890 Tombleson, J. B., B.M. (Aug. 5, 1915). Capt. R.A.M.C. (Maj.). Malta, 1915–17 ; Salonika, 1917 ; Mesopotamia, 1917–19 ; India, 1919.

1909 Upcott,* J. D., B.A. (Aug. 1914). Capt. 9th Devonshire Regt. France, 1915, 1916.

1897 **Vaughan, P. C.** (Sept. 1914). ‡2nd Lt. R.G.A. (S.R.). France and Belgium, 1917. Killed in action on Sept. 25, 1917.

1910 Veale, D., B.A. (Mobilized Aug. 4, 1914). Capt. 4th Gloucestershire Regt. France and Belgium, 1915.

1896 Venning, C. E., B.A. (Sept. 3, 1914). ‡Capt. Royal 1st Devon Yeomanry, attd. 1/1st Q.O. Oxfordshire Hussars (Maj.). France, 1916–19.

1913 Wace,* R. C. (Aug. 30, 1914). Lt. 4th Shropshire L.I., attd. M.G.C. Burmah, Hong-Kong, 1914–16; France, 1916–17, 1918. *M.C.*, Sept. 26, 1918.

Wake, C. B. D. (June, 1918). 2nd Lt. 2nd K.R.R.C. France, 1918. Killed in action near St. Quentin on Sept. 25, 1918.

1910 Walker, C. R., B.A. Lt. Nigeria Regt. W. Africa.

1905 Walker, E., M.A. (May 1916). Lt. R.A.S.C.

1896 Walker, H., M.A. (Nov. 10, 1914). Capt. 3rd Hertfordshire Vol. Regt.

1919 Walker, R. P. S. (July 21, 1917). Lce.-Cpl. The Buffs (E. Kent Regt.). France.

1905 Wall, J., M.A. (Aug. 4, 1914). Capt. 5th Manchester Regt. Salonika, 1915; Egypt, 1916–17; France, 1917–18.

1919 Ward, F. H. (Aug. 1, 1918). ‡2nd Lt. R.G.A.

1912 **Waters,* R. R.** (Dec. 1914). 2nd Lt. 1st R. Warwickshire Regt. (Capt.). France. Killed in action near Le Transloy on Oct. 24, 1916.

1911 **Watts, S.** (1914). ‡Lt. 20th Manchester Regt., attd. T.M.B. France. Died on Oct. 28, 1918, of illness contracted while on active service.

1913 **Wearne,* F. B.** (Sept. 1914). ‡2nd Lt. 3rd, attd. 11th, Essex Regt. France. *D.* France, 1916. Killed in action at Loos on June 28, 1917. **V.C.** won at Loos on June 28, 1917.

For most conspicuous bravery when in command of a small party on the left of a raid on the enemy's trenches. He gained his objective in the face of much opposition and by his magnificent example and daring was able to maintain this position for a considerable time according to instructions. During this period 2nd Lt. Wearne and his small party were repeatedly counter-attacked. Grasping the fact that if the left flank was lost his men would have to give way, 2nd Lt. Wearne at a moment when the enemy's attack was being heavily pressed and when matters were most critical, leapt on the parapet and followed by his left section ran along the top of the trench firing and throwing bombs. This unexpected and daring manœuvre threw the enemy off his guard and back in disorder. Whilst on the top of the trench, 2nd Lt. Wearne was severely wounded, but refused to leave his men. Afterwards he remained in the trench directing operations, consolidating his position, and encouraging all ranks. Just before the order to withdraw was given this gallant officer was again severely hit for the second time, and while being carried away was mortally wounded. By his tenacity in remaining at his post though severely wounded, and his magnificent fighting spirit he was enabled to hold on to the flank.

1905 Wells, Rev. A. R. K., M.A. (July 1915). Chaplain to the Forces (4th Class), attd. 5th Div. Chaplain R.N. France, 1915–16; Salonika, 1918–19.

1897 Wells, Rev. E. G., M.A. (Sept. 5, 1915). Chaplain to the Forces (4th Class). France, Italy. *M.C.*, Nov. 19, 1917; *Bar*, Oct. 16, 1918; *2nd Bar*, Apr. 2, 1919. Italian Bronze Medal for Valour.

1919 White, C. M. (July 29, 1916). Lt. R.A.F. (Capt. 258th Squadron). France.

1912 White, H. W., M.A. (July 1916). Signalman R.N.V.R. ‡Lt. R.A.F. Belgian Coast, 1917. (Prisoner of war, Nov. 1917–Dec. 1918.)

1912 Wight,* A. J. L. (Nov. 1, 1914). Capt. 2/9th (Cyclist) Hampshire Regt. France, 1918–19.

1915 Wight, C. H. (Nov. 26, 1916). Lt. 18th Middlesex Regt. France. *M.C.*, July 26, 1917.

1915 **Wilding-Jones, H. W.** (July 6, 1916). Lt. 3rd, attd. 11th, R. Welch Fusiliers. France, 1916–17; Salonika, Aug. 1918. Died on Sept. 22, 1918, of wounds received in action near Lake Doiran.

1903 Wilkinson, G. H., M.A. (June 1916). Lt. Hants R.G.A. France, 1917–18. (Invalided.)

1916 Wilkinson, M. (Aug. 3, 1917). ‡Lt. 20th Supply Coy., R.A.S.C. Egypt, Palestine, Syria.

1913 **Williams, P. J.** (June 1915). 2nd Lt. 6th E. Surrey Regt., attd. R. Berkshire Regt. France, 1917. Died on May 17, 1917, of wounds received in action.

1907 **Willink,* G. O. W.,** B.A. (Mobilized Aug. 4, 1914). Capt. 2/4th R. Berkshire Regt. France. *M.C.*, Oct. 18, 1917. *D.* France, 1917. Killed in action at Lamotte on Mar. 28, 1918.

1919 Willmer, H. G. (Feb. 22, 1918). 2nd Lt. R.G.A.

1906 Winser, Rev. R. B., M.A. (Sept. 6, 1914). Chaplain to the Forces (4th Class). Asst. A.C.G., 1st Army. France, 1915–17.

1898 Wodehouse, E. A., M.A. (May 2, 1916). Lt. Scots Guards (S.R.), attd. Foreign Office.

1919 Woodcock, P. (Sept. 11, 1916). Pte. 79th Field Amb., R.A.M.C. Egypt, Salonika. Died on Nov. 17, 1919.

1910 Woodman-Smith,* J., B.A. (Mobilized Aug. 4, 1914). Maj. Scottish Horse (Maj.). Gallipoli, 1915; Egypt, 1915–19.

1908 [Woodward, E. Ll., M.A.] (Oct. 1914). Lt. R.F.A. Staff-Lt. (2nd Class), empld. Foreign Office. France, 1915–16; Salonika, 1916–18.

1919 Woollerton, E. N. C. (Sept. 1914). Capt. 1/4th Oxf. & Bucks. Lt. Infty. Belgium, France, Italy.

1913 Yonge, C. D., B.A. (Apr. 8, 1915). Lt. 3rd E. Surrey Regt. France. (Invalided.)

1902 **Young, G. E. S.,** B.A. (Serving Aug. 4, 1914). Maj. Irish Guards. France. Died at No. 34 C.C.S. on Mar. 31, 1917, of wounds received in action.

1910 Young, L. E., B.A. (1915). ‡Lt. 38th Dogras, Indian Army (Adjt.). India.

1911 Young, N. E., B.A. (Sept. 13, 1914). ‡Capt. 9th R. Sussex Regt. France, 1915–18. *M.C.*, May 5, 1919. *D.* France, 1918. (Prisoner of war, Mar.–Dec. 1918.)

1908 Young, W. W., B.A. (Oct. 1914). Capt. 5th Rifle Brigade. France. (Prisoner of war.)

CHRIST CHURCH

Abrahams, A. C. L. (Aug. 1916). Lt. 3rd Coldstream Guards. France, Belgium. Killed in action on Apr. 13, 1918.

1917 Abrahams, D. A. (June 1918). Cadet R.F.A.

1870 Acland, T. D., D.M. (Mobilized Aug. 13, 1914). Maj., Bt.-Lt.-Col., R.A.M.C. Consulting Physician to the London Command, 1917–18.

1906 Acland,* W. H. D., B.A. (Mobilized Aug. 1914). Capt. Royal 1st Devon Yeomanry. Maj., Flying Officer, R.A.F. France, Belgium. *M.C.*, Jan. 14, 1916. *A.F.C.*, Feb. 8, 1919. Order of St. George (4th Class). *D.* France, 1915.

1918 Acton, W. E., B.A. (May 31, 1915). Rfln. N.Z. Rifle Brigade. Egypt, France.

1890 Adair, A. C. (Serving Aug. 4, 1914). Maj. R. Scots Fusiliers. Temp. Lt.-Col. whilst Commdt. Repatriated P. of W. Camp. France, Belgium, 1914. *O.B.E.* (Mil.). *D.* § Aug. 1919.

1877 Adam, Sir C. E., Bt., M.A. (July, 1915). ‡Lt. Special Lists. Staff-Lt. 2nd Class, R.T.O. France, 1916–18.

1911 Adams, H. M., M.A. (Aug. 30, 1914). Lt. 2/8th Worcestershire Regt. and M.G.C. (Capt.). France, 1916–18; Italy, 1918–19. *M.C.*, Feb. 4, 1918.

1872 Adderley, Hon. H. A., B.A. (Rejoined Apr. 1915). Capt. Warwickshire Yeomanry (T.F. Res.).

1902 Addington, Lord, B.A. (Mobilized Aug. 4, 1914). Capt., temp. Maj., Bucks. Bn. Oxf. & Bucks. Lt. Infty. Officer i/c Base Records, N.R.E.F. N. Russia. *O.B.E.* (Mil.). *D.* N. Russia, 1919.

1899 **Agar-Robartes, Hon. T. C. R.,** *M.P.* (Mobilized Aug. 1914). Capt. Coldstream Guards. France. *D.* France, 1915. Died on Sept. 30, 1915, of wounds received in action at the Battle of Loos.

1878 Alexander, H. B., B.A. Motor Ambulance Convoy (French Army). France.

1914 Alington, Lord N. G. H. (1914). Capt., Airship Officer, R.A.F.

1874 Altham, Sir E. A., *C.M.G.* (Rejoined July 15, 1915). Lt.-Gen. Q.M.G. Indian Headquarters Staff, East Indies. Gallipoli, Egypt, India. *K.C.B.* Order of the White Eagle, Grand Cross (1st Class) (with swords). Grand Cordon of the Order of the Sacred Treasure. *D.* Gallipoli, 1915 twice, 1916 twice; Egypt, 1916 twice, 1917.

1912 Amarjit Singh of Kapurthala, Prince (Dec. 31, 1914). Capt. Unattached List, Indian Army. France.

1919 Amory, D. Heathcoat (July 12, 1918). 2nd Lt. R.F.A.

1913 Amory, J. Heathcoat (Aug. 15, 1914). Capt. 1/4th Devonshire Regt. India, 1914–15; Mesopotamia, 1916–17; Persia, 1918; Caucasus, 1918. *D.* Mesopotamia, 1918.

1900 **Amory, L. Heathcoat,** B.A. (Oct. 1914). Capt. Royal 1st Devon Yeomanry. Staff-Captain R.A. France, Belgium. *D.* France, 1917. Died on Aug. 25, 1918, of wounds received in action.

1906 Anderson, G. D., B.A. (Sept. 1, 1914). Lt. R.F.A. (T.F.). Temp. Maj., Deputy Judge Advocate General. Serbia, 1915; Macedonia, 1916–17; Palestine, 1917–19.

Anderson, G. W. (May 14, 1917). Capt. and Adjt. 313th Field Artillery, U.S. Army. France, 1918. Killed in action at Le Grand Carré Ridge, Argonne, on Nov. 1, 1918.

1892 **Anderson, L.,** B.A. (Sept. 9, 1914). 2nd Lt. 4th Lincolnshire Regt. (T.F.). France. Killed in action in France on Oct. 12, 1915.

1894 Anderson, W. B., B.A. (Mobilized Aug. 1914). Lt.-Col. 1/8th Essex Regt.

1878 Andrewes, F. W., D.M. (Mobilized Aug. 1914). Maj. R.A.M.C., 1st London General Hospital.

1896 **Angel, A.,** B.Sc., M.A. Chief Chemist, Munitions Factory. Edward Medal (1st Class). Killed in explosion at Silvertown on Jan. 19, 1917.

1880 Anstice, J. C. A. Maj. 6th Dragoons (Res. of Officers).

1919 Apsley, Lord (Mobilized Aug. 1914). Capt. R. Gloucestershire Hussars. Egypt, 1915; Sinai, 1916; Palestine, 1917; Syria, 1918. *D.S.O.*, Mar. 8, 1919. *M.C.*, June 4, 1917. *D.* Egypt, 1917; Palestine, 1918.

1904 **Archer, T.,** B.A. (Aug. 1914). ‡2nd Lt. A.O.D. Lt. 6th K.O. Scottish Borderers. France, Belgium, 1914, 1916, 1917, 1918. Missing, presumed killed in action at Mt. Kemmel on Apr. 25, 1918.

1895 Archer-Houblon, H. L. (Oct. 27, 1914). Capt. 3rd, attd. 1st, The Buffs (E. Kent Regt.) (Maj.). France, Salonika. *D.* France, 1915.

1900 Argenti, L. P., M.A. (Aug. 1916). Lt., Acting Capt., Labour Corps. Capt. Intelligence Corps. Salonika. Order of the Redeemer.

1910 Argenti, P. P., M.A. (Sept. 1916). ‡Lt. 3rd Greek Cavalry Regt. (A.D.C.). Salonika. Greek Medal for Military Merit. Serbian Medal of Bravery.

1893 Argyll, Duke of. Hon. Col. 8th Arg. & Suth'd. Highlanders.

1911 Armistead,* J. H., B.A. (Sept. 12, 1914). Capt. 5th W. Yorkshire Regt., attd. No. 1 Reception Bn. France, Belgium, 1915–16.

1887 Armitstead, Rev. J. H., M.A. (Serving Aug. 4, 1914). Chaplain (4th Class) Cheshire Yeomanry.

1912 Armstrong, A. H. (Oct. 3, 1914). Lt. 5th Somerset L.I., attd. M.G.C.

1919 Arnold, F. T. (Mar. 1918). 2nd Lt. R.F.A.

1876 Arthur, Sir G. C. A., Bt., *M.V.O.* (1914). Capt. Special Lists. (Private Secretary to Lord Kitchener) (Staff-Captain). Officier de l'Ordre de la Couronne.

1902 Arthur, J. C. (Sept. 19, 1914). Capt. Ayrshire Yeomanry.

1907 Ashton, S. E., B.A. (Mobilized Aug. 1914). Capt. Cheshire Yeomanry. Egypt, Palestine.

1904 Ashworth, P. H., M.A. (Aug. 15, 1914). Lt. Grenadier Guards. Capt. Special Lists. A.D.C. to H.R.H. The Duke of Connaught. Cavalier of the Order of the Crown of Italy.

1904 Aston, H. W., B.A. (Aug. 6, 1914). Capt. 1/1st Surrey Yeomanry, attd. 7th Queen's (R. W. Surrey Regt.). France, Belgium, 1915; Macedonia, 1915–17; France, 1918–19.

1898 Aston, J., M.A. (Nov. 1915). ‡Lt. 3rd, attd. 12th, E. Surrey Regt. France, Belgium, 1916–17.

1919 Atkinson, D. J. (Dec. 30, 1914). Capt. 4th R. Dublin Fusiliers. Capt. 2/4th Gurkhas. France, 1916, 1917; India, 1918–19.

1916 Atkinson, G. L. (Apr. 1, 1917). Pte. R.A.M.C. (Radiographer).

1899 **Attwood, A. F.** (Serving Aug. 4, 1914). Capt. 4th R. Fusiliers. Belgium, France. Killed in action at Vailly on Sept. 14, 1914.

1907 **Bagshawe, G. H.,** B.A. (Sept. 22, 1914). 2nd Lt. 1st Dragoons. France, Belgium. Killed in action near Ypres on May 13, 1915.

1896 **Bagshawe, L. V.,** B.A. (Sept. 4, 1914). Capt. 3rd K.O. Scottish Borderers, attd. 1st Northumberland Fusiliers. France, Belgium. Killed in action at Hooge on June 16, 1915.

1913 Bain,* C. W. C., B.A. (Aug. 29, 1914). Capt., Hon. Maj., W. Riding Regt. (T.F. Res.). Maj. M.G.C. France. *M.C.*, Dec. 17, 1917. *D.* France, 1917.

1910 Bain, I. M. (Oct. 27, 1914). Lt. 5th The Black Watch, attd. R.E. Signals (Capt.). France.

1892 Baird, J. L., *M.P.*, *C.M.G.*, *D.S.O.* (Mobilized Aug. 1914). Maj. Scottish Horse (T.F. Res.). Vice-President of the Air Council. Croix de Chevalier de la Légion d'Honneur. Officier de l'Ordre de Léopold. Order of the Crown of Italy, Grand Officer. Belgian Croix de Guerre.

1893 Baker, H. A., B.A. (June 10, 1915). Lt. Army Pay Dept., Field Cashier, B.E.F. France.

1892 Baker, R. J. E., B.A. (Nov. 16, 1914). Capt. 2/4th R. Sussex Regt.

1901 Ballantine-Dykes, F. H. (Mobilized Aug. 1914). Capt. Scots Guards (Res. of Officers). France. *D.S.O.*, June 4, 1917. *D.* France, 1916, 1917, 1918.

1902 Bankes, Rev. C. D. R. O., B.A. (May 3, 1917). Chaplain to the Forces (4th Class), attd. R.A.F. France, 1917–19.

1899 Banks, R. M., B.A. (Aug. 7, 1915). Lt. I.A.R.O. (Infantry). India.

1914 Bannerjea, D. N. (1914). ‡Lt. Indian Field Ambulance Corps. India.

1877 Barclay, H. T. (Mobilized Aug. 1914). Maj. Leicestershire Yeomanry (T.F. Res.).

1908 Barclay-Harvey,* C. M. (Mobilized Aug. 1914). Capt. 7th Gordon Highlanders. Bde. Maj. 192nd Inf. Bde. (Invalided, May 1916.)

1900 Baring, Hon. W. (June 8, 1915). Lt. R.N.V.R.

1905 Barker, H. R., B.A. (Sept. 1914). Capt. 2/5th Yorkshire Regt.

1919 Barnard, T. T. (Jan. 15, 1917). Lt. Coldstream Guards. France, 1917–18; Germany, 1918–19. *M.C.*, Jan. 11, 1919.

1897 Barnes, K. R., M.A. (Mobilized Aug. 1914). Capt. 1/9th Hampshire Regt. India, Siberia. *D.* Siberia, 1919.

1899 Barnes, L. H., B.A. (July 18, 1916). Lt. Grenadier Guards (S.R.), attd. Guards M.G. Regt. Temp. Capt. whilst Courts-Martial Officer. France, 1917–18; Germany, 1919.

1907 **Barnes, R. G.** (Nov. 23, 1916). 2nd Lt. 8th London Regt. (Post Office Rifles). France, Belgium. Missing, presumed killed in action, Nov. 1917.

1903 Barnes, Rev. R. L., B.A. (Apr. 10, 1916). Chaplain to the Forces (4th Class), attd. 6th Lincolnshire Regt. France, 1916–19. *M.C.*, June 3, 1919.

1895 Barnes, W. C. (July 24, 1915). Lt. Royal 1st Devon Yeomanry (Capt.).

1899 **Barnett, C. F. R.** (Sept. 2, 1914). 2nd Lt. 5th Gloucestershire Regt. (T.F.). France. Killed in action on Apr. 19, 1915.

1912 Barnett, J. C. L., B.A. (Sept. 10, 1914). Capt. 1/4th Oxf. & Bucks. Lt. Infty., attd. R.A.F. (Flight Commdr.). France. *M.C.*, Feb. 4, 1918.
1890 Barnston, H., M.A. (Rejoined Oct. 1914). Maj. Cheshire Yeomanry, attd. Labour Corps.
1911 **Barr,* J. Y.,** B.A. (Feb. 5, 1915). Lt. 7th Arg. & Suth'd. Highlanders. France. Killed in action on Apr. 25, 1915.
1912 Barrington-Ward, J. G., M.A. (Sept. 20, 1914). Capt. Howitzer Bde., R.M.A. France, 1915; Salonika, 1915; Egypt, 1915–16; France, 1916–18.
1919 Barton, A. K. (May 14, 1917). 2nd Lt. 83rd Field Artillery, U.S. Army. France.
1919 Bates, W. E. (Mar. 27, 1918). 2nd Lt. R.G.A.
1883 Bathurst, Earl. Hon. Col., late Lt.-Col., 4th Gloucestershire Regt. Commdt. on Lines of Communication. France. *C.M.G.*
1919 Baty, C. W. (Sept. 28, 1918). Cadet R.A.F.
1919 Bayne, C. L. (Sept. 17, 1917). 2nd Lt. R.G.A.
1908 Baynes, E. R., M.A. (July 15, 1915). Lt. R.A.S.C.
1911 Beart, R. B. (Oct. 17, 1914). Lt. 18th Hussars. France.
1903 Beazley, J. D., M.A. (July 8, 1917). Lt. R.N.V.R., attd. Admiralty, Intelligence Dept.
1890 Beauchamp, Earl, *K.G., K.C.M.G.* Hon. Col. R.A. (T.F.). Hon. Col. 6th Sussex Regt.
1902 **Beaufort, F. H.,** B.A. (Serving Aug. 4, 1914). Capt. 2nd Oxf. & Bucks. Lt. Infty. India, France. Killed in action near Richebourg l'Avoué on May 15, 1915.
1919 Beckingham, R. H. H. (Nov. 25, 1915). Lt. 103rd Bde., R.F.A. France, 2 years.
1909 Beckwith-Smith,* M. (Serving Aug. 4, 1914). Capt. Coldstream Guards. G.S.O. 2. France, 1914, 1915–19. *D.S.O.*, Nov. 9, 1914. *M.C.*, June 4, 1917. Croix de Guerre. *D.* France, 1916.
1919 Beddington-Behrens, E. (Feb. 1915). ‡Capt. 189th Bde., R.F.A. (Maj.). France, 1916–18. *M.C.*, Aug. 16, 1917; *Bar*, June 22, 1918. *D.* France, 1916.
1919 Beer, R. M. H. (Jan. 29, 1916). Lt. B/290th Bde., R.F.A. France, Belgium, 1918.
1919 Beighton, T. P. D. (Oct. 16, 1916). Lt. 146th Siege Batt., R.G.A. France, 1917, 1918.
1900 Belfour, A. O., M.A. (1914). Motor Cyclist Dispatch Rider, R.E. France. (Prisoner of war.)
1916 Bell, A. M., B.A. (Apr. 23, 1917). ‡Lt. 15th Bn. Tank Corps. France.
1903 Bell, E. A., M.A. (Mar. 2, 1915). Lt. 9th Norfolk Regt. (Maj.). France,
1920 Bell, W. C. (Aug. 28, 1915). ‡Lt. I.A.R.O., attd. 1st Brahmans. India, Aden Field Force.
1911 Belser, I. F., B.A. (Apr. 26, 1917). Maj. Field Artillery, U.S. Army.
1900 Bennett, L. H., B.A. (Sept. 14, 1914). Capt. 1st Queen's (R. W. Surrey Regt.). France, Belgium.
1891 Bennett, R. A., B.A. (Sept. 22, 1914). Capt. R. Gloucestershire Hussars, empld. War Trade Intelligence Dept.
1895 Benson, P. G. R., B.A. (Mobilized Aug. 1914). Capt. W. Somerset Yeomanry. Adjt. Remount Depot. France. *D.* France; § Aug. 1918.

1919 Bentliff, E. D. (Nov. 5, 1914). ‡Lt. 1/6th Essex Regt. France, 1915; Gallipoli, 1915; Egypt, Palestine, 1916–19. *D.* Egypt, 1917.

1909 Benvenisti, J. L., B.A. (Mar. 5, 1915). Lt. R.G.A. (T.F.). Lt., Observer Officer, R.A.F.

Bertie, N. M. K. (Dec. 22, 1914). 2nd Lt. K.R.R.C. Belgium. Killed in action at Hooge on May 8, 1915.

1913 Bevan, J. H. (Mobilized Aug. 1914). Capt., temp. Maj., Hertfordshire Regt. G.S.O. 2, XI Corps. France, 1914–19. *M.C.*, June 4, 1917. *D.* France, 1916, 1917.

1899 Beveridge, H. W., B.A. (July 5, 1915). Capt. R.A.S.C.

1911 Bibby,* F. B. F., M.A. (Aug. 12, 1914). Capt. 1st Life Guards. France. *D.* France, 1919.

1908 Bickersteth, E. R., B.A. (Aug. 27, 1914). Lt. R.G.A., empld. Ministry of Labour. (Invalided on account of ill health contracted on active service, Feb. 1919.)

1903 Bickersteth, G. L., M.A. Capt. R. Marines.

1907 Bickersteth, J. B., M.A. (Aug. 1914). Lt. 1st Dragoons. France, 1915–19. *M.C.*, Feb. 1, 1919; *Bar*, Jan. 1, 1919.

1904 Bickersteth, Rev. K. J. F., B.A. (Feb. 21, 1916). Chaplain to the Forces (3rd Class). Senior Chaplain D.C.G.'s Dept., 56th Div. France, 1916–19. *M.C.*, Jan. 1, 1918. *D.* France, 1917, 1919.

1913 Bickersteth, R. M. (Aug. 4, 1914). Capt. W. Yorkshire Regt. France.

1910 **Bickersteth, S. M.,** B.A. (Sept. 1914). Lt. 15th W. Yorkshire Regt. (Capt.). Egypt, 1915; Salonika, 1916; France, 1916. Killed in action at Serre on July 1, 1916.

1888 Bicknell, Rev. N. L., M.A. (Nov. 29, 1918). Chaplain (Capt.) R.A.F.

1913 Binney,* A. L. (Mar. 15, 1915). Lt. 'M' Batt., R.H.A. (Maj.). Mesopotamia, 1916–17; Afghanistan, 1919.

1919 Binney, W. M. (May 10, 1918). 2nd Lt. Grenadier Guards (on demobilization).

1910 Birch-Reynardson,* H. T., B.A. (Serving Aug. 4, 1914). Capt. 1st Oxf. & Bucks. Lt. Infty. Mesopotamia.

1908 Birley, C. F., B.A. (Mobilized Aug. 1914). Capt. Duke of Lancaster's Own Yeomanry. Lt. Grenadier Guards (S.R.), attd. M.G.C. France.

1895 Biss, H. C. J. (Serving Aug. 4, 1914). Capt., Acting Maj., 2nd R. Irish Regt.

1893 Blaauw, H. T. G., B.A. (Dec. 21, 1914). Lt. 32nd R. Welsh Fusiliers.

1908 **Black,* G. B.,** B.A. (Serving Aug. 4, 1914). Capt. 17th Lancers and Tank Corps. France, Belgium. Montenegrin Order of Danilo (5th Class). *D.* France, 1915, 1917. Died on Aug. 23, 1918, of wounds received in action.

1920 Blackburn, G. D. (Jan. 1918). Pte. 28th London Regt. (Artists Rifles). France, Belgium.

1892 Blackett, Sir H. D. (Oct. 1, 1914). Capt. Montgomeryshire Yeomanry, attd. Labour Corps.

1900 Blackwood, R. T., M.A. (Jan. 18, 1916). Lt. R.G.A., empld. Ministry of Labour. Asst. Director No. 7 District. Salonika.

1897 Blakiston, C. H., M.A. (Dec. 19, 1914). Lt. Unattached List, T.F., Eton College O.T.C.

1919 Blanch, A. T. H. (Dec. 26, 1914). ‡Lt. R.E. France, Belgium. *M.C.*, July 26, 1918. *D.* France, 1917.

1911 **Blane,* M. G. S.,** B.A. (Mobilized Aug. 4, 1914). Lt. 5th Q.O. Cameron Highlanders. France. Killed in action at the Battle of Loos on Sept. 25, 1915.

1909 Bleaden, C. L., B.A. (Dec. 22, 1914). Capt. 8th York & Lancaster Regt. Belgium, France, Italy. *M.C.*, Aug. 25, 1916.

1876 Blencowe, R. C. (Oct. 8, 1914). Lt. R. Defence Corps.

1898 Blundell, C. L. Blundell-Hollinshed (Mobilized Aug. 18, 1914). Maj. Grenadier Guards (Res. of Officers). D.A.Q.M.G. France, Belgium, 1914, 1916. *O.B.E.* (Mil.).

1915 Blunt, B. G. (Feb. 3, 1916). ‡Lt. R.G.A. (S.R.) (Capt.). France, Belgium.

1883 Blunt, E. H. (Aug. 5, 1914). Capt. Res. of Officers. Capt. Asst. Embarkation Staff Officer. *D.* § Aug. 1918.

1915 Boas, G. H. S. (Jan. 26, 1916). Lt. 1st Q.O. Oxfordshire Hussars. France.

1911 Bodkin, H. W. A., B.A. (May 16, 1917). Lt. Special Lists. Staff-Captain.

1892 Bolton, H. E. L., B.A. (Oct. 2, 1914). Capt. 2/1st Surrey Yeomanry. (Invalided, July 16, 1918.)

1890 Bone, G. H. K., B.A. (Mar. 1915). ‡Acting Lt.-Commdr. R.N.V.R. Capt., temp. Maj., R.A.F. France.

1908 Border, G. W., M.A. (Dec. 22, 1915). Capt. 4th Lincolnshire Regt. France.

1909 Borough, J. G. B. (Mobilized Aug. 1914). Capt. 1/1st Staffordshire Yeomanry. Egypt, Palestine, Syria, 1915–19.

1912 **Bosanquet, A. P.** (Mobilized Aug. 1914). Capt. 3rd D.C.L.I., attd. 5th Wiltshire Regt. France, Belgium, Mesopotamia, 1914–17. *M.C.*, Dec. 22, 1916. *D.* Mesopotamia, 1916. Killed in action in Mesopotamia on Feb. 8, 1917.

1897 Bosanquet, E. M. (Serving Aug. 4, 1914). Lt. R.G.A., empld. Recruiting Duties.

1919 Bouch, C. M. L. (Mar. 31, 1916). ‡2nd Lt. Worcestershire Regt. Lt. 32nd Labour Coy., Labour Corps. France, Belgium, Germany.

1896 Boughton-Leigh, H. A. W. (1914). Capt. R.A. (T.F.).

1908 Boult,* A. C., B.Mus., M.A. (1915). Hon. Lt. 16th King's (Liverpool Regt.).

1908 Boumphrey,* R. (Mobilized Aug. 1914). Capt. Lancashire Hussars, attd. R.A.F. Egypt, France.

1910 Bourne, F. C., B.A. (Mobilized Aug. 1914). Capt. 4th R. W. Kent Regt. Bde. Maj. E. Indies Northern Command. India, 1914–19.

1913 Bovey, Q. C. D. (Sept. 7, 1914). Lt. 8th Gordon Highlanders. Capt. General List. A.D.C. to C.-in-C. British Army of the Rhine. France, Germany. *D.* France, 1915.

1891 Bovill, F. H., M.A. (1914). Pte. 23rd R. Fusiliers.

1898 **Bowring, F. H.,** B.A. (Aug. 1914). ‡Maj. 17th King's (Liverpool Regt.). France. Killed in action at Hendecourt on Aug. 28, 1918.

1919 Box, P. H. (Mar. 29, 1917). Sergt. R.A.O.C. Egypt, 1918–19. *D.* Egypt and Palestine, 1919.

1919 Boyle, M. (May 1, 1917). Lt.-Col. 328th Infantry, U.S. Army. France. *D.* American Orders.

1919 Bradford, L. G. (May 11, 1917). 2nd Lt. 55th Coast Artillery Corps. France.

1919 Bradley, W. H. (June 6, 1916). Rfln. 16th London Regt. (Queen's Westminster Rifles). France, Belgium, 1917.
1909 Brady, F. B., B.A. (1918). Sergt. 10th R. Fusiliers (Intelligence Corps). France, Germany, 1918–19.
1898 Branston, W. B. (Serving Aug. 4, 1914). Capt. 5th Rifle Brigade. *D.* § Aug. 1919.
1919 Brasnett, L. S. (May 19, 1918). Sub-Lt. R.N.V.R. H.M.S. *Tactician.*
1888 Brassey, H. L. C., *M.P.* (Sept. 1914). Maj. Northamptonshire Yeomanry (T.F. Res.).
1919 Brettle, L. (Dec. 11, 1915). ‡Lt. Labour Corps, Labour Central Establishment, G.H.Q. France, Belgium.
1904 Brichta, S. K. J., B.A. (Dec. 5, 1915). Lt. 13th Lancashire Fusiliers. Capt. General List. Adjt. Prisoners of War Camp.
1895 Bridge, P. S. R., M.A. (Sept. 22, 1915). ‡Lt. R.A.S.C. (Relinquished Commission on account of ill health, Feb. 1919.)
1909 **Brine, E. L.,** B.A. (Aug. 17, 1915). Lt. 1/4th Hampshire Regt. Mesopotamia, 1915; Persia, 1917. Died on Sept. 24, 1918, of illness contracted whilst on active service.
1913 Bristowe, O. C. (Sept. 8, 1914). ‡Lt. R.E. France.
1890 Britten, F. C., M.A. R. Defence Corps., Prisoners' Camp.
1909 Broadhurst, A. F. B., M.A. (Oct. 10, 1914). Capt. 3rd Highland L.I. Capt. R.A.F. France, 1915; Mesopotamia, 1916–17; Egypt, 1918–19. *D.* Mesopotamia, 1918.
1912 Broadmead, P. M., B.A. (Sept. 29, 1914). Lt. 12th K.R.R.C. Capt. General List. Staff-Captain, 3rd Inf. Bde. France, Belgium. *M.C.*, June 4, 1917. Croix de Guerre. *D.* France, 1918.
1911 Brocklebank, C. G. (Aug. 6, 1914). ‡Capt. R.E. Signals. France, Belgium, 1914–19. *M.C.*, June 4, 1917. Médaille Militaire. *D.* France, 1914.
1890 Brodrick, H. G. (Feb. 27, 1915). Lt. R. Defence Corps.
1907 Brooke, R. C. (Mobilized Aug. 1914). Lt. Scots Guards (S.R.). (Invalided.)
1908 Brooks, J. B., B.A. (1915). ‡Capt. I.A.R.O., attd. 2/2nd Gurkha Rifles. India.
1884 Brooks, W. T., M.A. (Mobilized Aug. 1914). Lt.-Col. R.A.M.C., 3rd S. General Hospital. *D.* § Aug. 1919.
1908 Brown, C. A., B.A. (May 19, 1915). Lt., Acting Capt. and Adjt., R.A.
1914 Brown, L. N., M.A. (Oct. 23, 1916). 2nd Lt. R.E., empld. Ministry of Food.
1900 Brown, W., D.M. (Dec. 15, 1914). Capt. R.A.M.C. (Maj.). Egypt, 1915; France, 1916–18. *O.B.E.* (Mil.). *D.* § Aug. 1919.
1913 **Brown, W. N. S.** (Jan. 28, 1915). Lt. 4th Somerset L.I. (T.F.). France. Died in hospital on Aug. 1, 1919, of meningitis as a result of wounds.
1919 Browne, E. M. (Aug. 8, 1918). Cadet Household Bde. O.C.B.
1919 Browning, R. S. (July 31, 1915). Lt. 7th R. Sussex Regt. France, 1916, 1917, 1918, 1919.
1908 **Bruce, N. M.,** B.A. (Sept. 1914). Lt. 6th Yorkshire Regt. Gallipoli. Killed in action in Gallipoli on Aug. 6, 1915.
1920 Bruce-Kingsmill, J. C. de K. (Oct. 1914). Lt.-Col. R.F.A. France, Italy, Mesopotamia, India.
1913 **Bryan, W. J.,** B.A. (Sept. 26, 1914). 2nd Lt. 15th R. Fusiliers.
1911 Bryans, J. G., B.A. Pte. 28th London Regt. (Artists' Rifles), attd. Intelligence Dept.

1897 [Buchanan-Riddell, W. R., M.A.] (Aug. 24, 1914). ‡Lt. 1/9th Hampshire Regt. (Capt.). India, Siberia.

1909 Buckmaster, Hon. O. S., B.A. (Sept. 14, 1914). Capt. D.C.L.I. Capt. General List, empld. O.C.B. France.

1911 Burchnall,* J. L., B.A. (Feb. 15, 1915). Capt. R.G.A. Staff-Captain, Special Educational Appointment. France, Belgium. *M.C.*, June 22, 1918.

1914 Burford, F. R. R. (Jan. 16, 1915). Lt. 4th R. Fusiliers, attd. O.C.B.

1911 **Burn,* A. H. R.** (Serving Aug. 4, 1914). 2nd Lt. 1st R. Dragoons. France, Belgium, 1914. Killed in action at Hollebeke on Oct. 30, 1914.

Burn, H. H. (Aug. 1914). Capt. 2nd Coldstream Guards. France, 1914–16. *M.C.*, June 3, 1916. Died on Sept. 16, 1916, of wounds received in action in the Battle of the Ancre.

1878 Burns, T. G. A., M.A. (Sept. 1914). Capt. R.A.M.C., 3rd London General Hospital.

1888 Burns-Lindow, I. W. (Mobilized Aug. 1914). Lt.-Col. S. Irish Horse. France, Belgium, 1914. *D.S.O.*, Feb. 18, 1915. *D.* France, 1914, 1915 twice, 1916.

1904 Burridge,* W., B.M., M.A. (Jan. 1, 1917). Capt. R.A.M.C., O.C., P. of W. Hospital, Damascus. Malta, 1917; Salonika, 1918; Egypt and Palestine, 1918–19.

1915 Burrowes, A. B. (Aug. 5, 1916). Lt. 4th R. Irish Fusiliers. Capt. Special Lists (whilst at Gas School).

1891 Burton, E. G. (Jan. 23, 1915). Maj. R.A.S.C. *O.B.E.* (Mil.). *D.* § Feb. 1917, Mar. 1918, Mar. 1919.

1908 Bury,* C. O. H., B.A. (Mobilized Aug. 1914). Capt. 1/1st Hertfordshire Yeomanry. Egypt, Gallipoli, Mesopotamia, Persia, Suez Canal. *M.C.*, Feb. 7, 1918.

1912 Bushell, H. S., B.A. (Sept. 1914). Capt. 24th London Regt. (The Queen's). France, Italy.

1877 Butler, A. H. (Oct. 11, 1914). Maj. 2nd R. Gloucestershire Hussars (T.F. Res.).

1873 Butler, F. J. P. (Sept. 28, 1914). Lt.-Col. Asst. Commandant, Remount Depot. *D.* § Aug. 1917.

1875 Butler, L. W. G. (Mobilized Aug. 1914). Capt. Res. of Officers. Temp. Lt.-Col., G.S.O. 1.

1882 Butler, W. J. C., B.A. (Mobilized Sept. 1914). Col. Res. of Officers. Temp. Brig.-Gen. Gallipoli, Egypt, Palestine. *C.B.*, 1918. *D.* Gallipoli, 1915; Palestine, 1917.

1896 Buxton, Rev. L., M.A. (Sept. 11, 1917). Chaplain to the Forces (4th Class). France, Belgium.

1901 Cain, R. C. (May 2, 1916). Lt. 5th Grenadier Guards. France, Belgium.

1919 Calburn, C. C. R. (Nov. 30, 1917). 2nd Lt. 5th Highland L.I.

1903 Calder, W. M., B.A. (Nov. 16, 1914). 2nd Lt. O.T.C., empld. under Admiralty.

1919 Calvert, J. C. (Mar. 8, 1918). 2nd Lt. R.F.A.

1914 Cameron, D. J. Pte. Devonshire Regt.

1913 Campbell,* G. I. (Aug. 15, 1914). Capt. Arg. & Suth'd. Highlanders, now Capt. Half-Pay List. France, Belgium.

1908 **Campbell, Ivar** (Feb. 1915). Lt. 3rd Arg. & Suth'd. Highlanders, attd. 1st Seaforth Highlanders (Capt. and Adjt.). France, 1915; Mesopotamia, 1915–16. Died on Jan. 8, 1916, of wounds received in action at Sheikh Saad.

1895 Campbell, J. E. F., B.A. (Feb. 25, 1916). Capt., Acting Maj., R.F.A. Egypt, Palestine. Order of the Nile (4th Class). *D.* Palestine, 1918 twice.

1894 Campbell, W. F. (Oct. 1914). Capt. 4th R. Sussex Regt., attd. 14th Suffolk Regt.

1909 Campbell-Davys, I. E., M.A. (Aug. 26, 1914). Lt. Glamorganshire R.H.A. (T.F.).

1909 Cantlie, K. (May 7, 1915). Lt., temp. Capt., I.A.R.O. Asst. Director of Labour. India.

1913 Cargill, R. E. D. (Aug. 8, 1914). ‡Lt. R.E. France, 1914–16.

1919 Carpenter, R. P. R. (Aug. 4, 1918). Cadet R.A.F.

1892 **Carpenter-Garnier, J. T.** (Serving Aug. 1914). Maj. Scots Guards. France. Died on Sept. 15, 1914, of wounds received in action near the Aisne.

1919 Carrington, C. E. (Sept. 8, 1914). ‡Lt. 5th R. Warwickshire Regt. (Capt.). France, 1916–17; Italy, 1918. *M.C.*, Nov. 26, 1917.

1913 Carrington,* N. L. (Aug. 15, 1914). Capt. 3rd Wiltshire Regt. (Staff-Captain). France. *O.B.E.* (Mil.). *D.* France, 1918, 1919.

1901 Carsley, W. E., M.A. Canadian A.M.C.

1915 Carson, G. (June 1916). Capt. 13th King's (Liverpool Regt.). France, Belgium, Germany. *M.C.*, July 26, 1918.

Cartwright, N. W. H. (Apr. 7, 1916). 2nd Lt. 20th Durham L.I. Belgium, France, 1916–17. Killed in action near Ypres on Sept. 21, 1917.

1912 **Casson,* R. A.** (Sept. 1915). 2nd Lt., Acting Adjt., R. Welch Fusiliers. France, Belgium. Killed in action at Polygon Wood on Sept. 26, 1917.

1909 Cavan, P. C. (Mobilized Aug. 1914). Capt. 4th Bedfordshire Regt., empld. Ministry of Labour.

1881 Cavendish-Bentinck, Lord H. C., *D.S.O.*, T.D. (Mobilized Aug. 1914). Lt.-Col. Derbyshire Yeomanry (T.F. Res.). Gallipoli, 1915. *D.* § Feb. 1917.

1919 Cazalet, V. A. (Aug. 4, 1915). 2nd Lt. W. Kent Yeomanry. Lt. 1st Life Guards. Capt. Household Bn., attd. British Mission to Siberia. France, Siberia. *M.C.*, Nov. 26, 1917.

1910 Cazenove, R. de L. (Mobilized Aug. 1914). Lt. Northamptonshire Yeomanry. (Resigned.)

1913 **Cecil, R. E. G.** (Aug. 1914). ‡Lt. 4th Bedfordshire Regt. France, Belgium. Killed in action near Ypres on July 11, 1915.

1908 Chalmers, R. W. S., B.A. (Sept. 14, 1914). Sergt. 52nd Middlesex Regt. France, Belgium.

1900 Chamberlayne, E. T., B.A. (Mobilized Aug. 4, 1914). Maj. 2/1st Warwickshire Yeomanry. Gallipoli, Egypt. *D.S.O.*, June 3, 1916. T.D. *D.* Gallipoli, 1916; § Aug. 1919.

1911 Chamberlayne, Tankerville (Oct. 8, 1914). 2nd Lt., temp. Lt., 1/7th Highland L.I. Gallipoli, Egypt, Sinai.

1919 Chance, E. S. J. (Sept. 8, 1918). 2nd Lt. Rifle Brigade (on demobilization).

Chancellor, R. A. B. (Aug. 1914). Capt. 7th R. Berkshire Regt. France, Salonika. *D.* Salonika, 1917. Died on Jan. 3, 1917, of wounds received in action on Salonika front.

1908 Chapman, G. P., B.A. (Nov. 27, 1914). Capt. and Adjt. 13th R. Fusiliers. France, Belgium. *O.B.E.* (Mil.). *M.C.*, Apr. 2, 1919. *D.* France, 1918.

1897 Chapman, J., B.A. (Dec. 13, 1916). Lt. 3rd Grenadier Guards. Belgium, France, Germany, 1917–19.

1909 Charles, N. H. H., B.A. (Sept. 21, 1914). Lt. 8th R. Fusiliers. Lt. General List. Staff-Captain Northern Res. Bde. France, 1915–18. *M.C.*, June 4, 1917. *D.* France, 1916, 1918.

1904 Charles, S. D., B.A. (Mobilized Aug. 1914). Capt. Lincolnshire Yeomanry. France, 1917–18. *M.C.*, Sept. 16, 1918.

1911 Charlesworth,* A. K. (Serving Aug. 4, 1914). Lt. 6th Dragoon Guards. France, Belgium. *M.C.*, Feb. 4, 1918.

Charlton, A. N. (Aug. 1914). Capt. and Adjt. 7th Norfolk Regt. France. *M.C.*, June 4, 1917. *D.* France, 1916. Killed in action at Cambrai on Nov. 30, 1917.

1892 Charlton, F. H., B.A. (Mobilized Sept. 1914). Capt. 1st Dragoon Guards (Res. of Officers), attd. War Office. *D.* § Feb. 1917, Mar. 1918.

1907 Charrington,* G. N. (Mobilized Aug. 1914). Capt. 1/1st Hertfordshire Yeomanry. Egypt, 1915–16; France, 1916–17; Palestine, 1917–19.

1898 Charteris, N. K. (Serving Aug. 4, 1914). Maj., Bt. Lt.-Col., R. Scots. Lt.-Col. M.G.C. France, Belgium. *C.M.G.* *D.S.O.*, Jan. 1, 1917. *D.* France, 1916, 1918, 1919.

1900 Charteris, R. L. (Mobilized Aug. 1914). Capt., Flying Officer, R.A.F.

Chattaway, P. S. (Apr. 14, 1915). 2nd Lt. 6th Cheshire Regt. France. Killed in action near Thiepval on Oct. 14, 1916.

1904 Cherry-Garrard, A. G. B., B.A. (Sept. 1914). ‡Lt.-Commdr. R.N.V.R. France.

1889 **Chester-Master, R.** (Mobilized Aug. 4, 1914). Lt.-Col. 13th K.R.R.C. France, Belgium. *D.S.O.*, June 4, 1917; *Bar*, Aug. 16, 1917. *D.* France, 1916, 1917 twice. Killed in action on Aug. 30, 1917.

1899 Child, Sir S. H., Bt., *M.V.O.* (Serving Aug. 4, 1914). Maj. Res. of Officers. Lt.-Col. R.A. Brig.-Gen. R.A., 46th Div. France, Belgium. *C.B.* *C.M.G.* *D.S.O.*, June 3, 1916. Croix de Guerre. *D.* France, 1915, 1916, 1917, 1918, 1919.

1910 Chippindale,* F. W. C., M.A. (Aug. 1914). Capt. 2nd Oxf. & Bucks. Lt. Infty. France, 1914, 1916, 1917, 1918.

1910 Christie,* A. H., M.A. (Aug. 15, 1914). Lt. and Adjt. 4th Hussars (S.R.) (Capt.). France, 1914–19. *M.C.*, July 18, 1917.

1893 Christie-Miller, S. R., M.A. (Nov. 16, 1914). Lt. R. Defence Corps.

1895 Christy, H. A., M.A. (Sept. 21, 1914). Capt. Glamorganshire Yeomanry, attd. Hood Bn. R.N. Div. France, 1917–18.

1898 **Christy, S. H.,** *D.S.O.* (Mobilized Aug. 1914). Capt. 20th Hussars. France, 1914. Killed in action at La Ferté sous Jouane on Sept. 3, 1914.

1903 **Churchyard, A. S.,** B.A. (Oct. 1914). Capt. 6th Rifle Brigade. Gallipoli, France. Died at Enfield, Middlesex, on Jan. 28, 1917.

1901 Churchyard, O. P., M.A. (Dec. 28, 1914). Capt. 7th Rifle Brigade. Maj. General List. G.S.O. 2, War Office. Belgium, France, 1915–16. *D.* § Aug. 1918.

1907 Clark, G. H. J., B.A. (Feb. 14, 1916). Lt. Special Lists. Staff-Lt. (2nd Class) Intelligence Corps. France. *D.* France, 1919.

1910 Clark, L. C. E. (Feb. 1, 1915). Lt. 2nd Dragoons, attd. Sherwood Rangers. Egypt.

1910 **Clarke, A. H. G.,** B.A. (Sept. 1914). ‡2nd Lt. 3rd Northamptonshire Regt. France, Belgium, 1914, 1915, 1916. *D.* France, 1915, 1916. Believed killed in action on the Somme on Sept. 9, 1916.

1896 Clarke, A. L. C. (Dec. 24, 1914). Lt., Acting Capt., Cheshire Regt. France, Belgium. *D.* France, 1915.

1912 Clarke, I. A., B.A. (Sept. 1, 1914). Maj. 4th Gordon Highlanders. Maj. M.G.C. France, Belgium, 1915–18.

1884 Clarke-Campbell-Preston, R. W. P. (Mobilized Aug. 1914). Lt.-Col. 3rd The Black Watch. *D.* § Feb. 1917.

1914 Clason, C. R., B.A. (June 19, 1918). Sergt.-Maj. Coast Artillery Corps, U.S. Army. Médaille du Roi Albert (for Belgian Relief Work, 1914–15).

1906 Cleaver, R. F., B.A. (1914). 28th London Regt. (Artists' Rifles).

1903 Cleveland-Stevens, E. C., M.A. (Oct. 5, 1914). Capt. R.E. Egypt, 1915–17; France, 1917–19.

1900 Cleveland-Stevens, W. C., B.C.L., M.A. (Aug. 1914). Lt. Commdr. R.N.V.R. Grand Fleet. *D.* Naval Dispatches, 1916.

1891 **Clifford, H. F.** (Mobilized Aug. 1914). Maj. R. Gloucestershire Hussars. Egypt, Sinai. *D.* Egypt, 1916. Killed in action at Rafa on Jan. 9, 1917.

1881 Clinton, Lord C. J. R. (Oct. 1914). Lt.-Col. 2/1st R. N. Devon Yeomanry (T.F. Res.). *D.* § Feb. 1917.

1903 Clowes, H. M., M.A. (Sept. 25, 1914). Capt., temp. Maj., 14th London Regt. (London Scottish). D.A.Q.M.G. France, Belgium. *D.S.O.*, Jan. 1, 1919. *D.* France, 1918 twice, 1919.

1919 Coade, T. F. (Sept. 17, 1915). Lt. 2nd Loyal N. Lancashire Regt. France, 1916.

1914 Coats, Hon. T. (Dec. 17, 1914). Lt. 6th The Black Watch. A.D.C.

1885 Cochrane, T. G. F., B.A. (Aug. 14, 1914). Capt., Acting Maj., The Black Watch (S.R.). France, Mesopotamia, Egypt, Palestine. *D.S.O.*, Jan. 1, 1919. *D.* France, 1916; Mesopotamia, 1917; Palestine, 1918.

1920 Cochrane Baillie, Hon. V. A. W. B. (Dec. 25, 1914). Lt., Acting Capt. and Adjt., 2nd Scots Guards. France, Belgium. *M.C.*, Sept. 26, 1917.

1885 Cockburn, N. C., B.A. (Rejoined 1914). Maj. Lincolnshire Yeomanry (T.F. Res.). Egypt, Palestine, 1915–17. *D.* Egypt, 1917.

1907 Cockburn, R. S., B.A. (Aug. 5, 1914). Maj. 10th K.R.R.C. Temp. Maj. General List, attd. H.Q. 63rd (R.N.) Div. France, Belgium. *M.C.*, June 25, 1916.

1906 Codrington, G. R., B.A. (Apr. 26, 1907). Maj. Leicestershire Yeomanry. D.A.Q.M.G. London District. France, 1914–17, 1918–19; Italy, 1917–18; Germany, 1919. *O.B.E.* (Mil.). *D.S.O.*, Jan. 1, 1918. Chevalier of the Order of St. Maurice and St. Lazarus. *D.* France, 1916, 1917 twice, 1919.

1885 Cole, E. H. (Serving Aug. 4, 1914). Lt.-Col. Nottinghamshire Yeomanry. Col. Indian Army. Administrative Commandant. Gallipoli, Mesopotamia. *C.B.* *C.M.G.*, Feb. 7, 1918. *D.* Gallipoli, 1915; Mesopotamia, 1917.

1875 Coleridge, W. R., B.A. (June 8, 1915). Maj. 4th Devonshire Regt. (T.F. Res.). T.D.

1897 Collard, C. L. (Apr. 23, 1918). Lt. R.N.V.R., attd. Staff.

1898 Colley, C. C. (Serving Aug. 4, 1914). Maj. R.A. Capt., Hon. Maj., Technical Officer, R.A.F. *D.* § Mar. 1918.

1905 Collier, J. V., B.A. (Oct. 14, 1914). Capt. Northamptonshire Yeomanry, attd. Labour Corps.

1898 Collier-Wright, J. R. C. (May 24, 1916). Pte. 102nd Canadian Infantry. France, Belgium, 1916.

1900 **Collings-Wells, J. S.** (Serving Aug. 4, 1914). Lt.-Col. 4th Bedfordshire Regt. (Brig.-Gen.). France. *D.S.O.*, July 18, 1917. *D.* France, 1917. Killed in action at Albert on Mar. 27, 1918. **V.C.** won at Albert, Mar. 22–7, 1918.

For most conspicuous bravery, skilful leading and handling of his battalion in a very critical situation during a withdrawal. When the rearguard was almost surrounded and in great danger of being captured, Lt.-Col. Collings-Wells realizing the situation, called for volunteers to remain behind and hold up the enemy whilst the remainder of the rearguard withdrew, and with his small body of men held them up for 1½ hours till they had expended every round of ammunition. During this time he moved freely amongst his men, guiding and encouraging them, and by his great courage undoubtedly saved the situation. On a subsequent occasion when his battalion was ordered to carry out a counter-attack he showed the greatest bravery. Knowing that his men were extremely tired after ten days' fighting he placed himself in front and led the attack, and even when twice wounded refused to leave them, but continued to lead and encourage his men until he was killed at the moment of gaining their objective. The successful results of the operation were without doubt due to the undaunted courage exhibited by this officer.

1897 Collins, E. A. D. (Mobilized Aug. 4, 1914). Maj. Yorkshire Hussars, empld. Ministry of National Service. France, Belgium, 1915–16. T.D. Chevalier de l'Ordre de la Couronne. Belgian Croix de Guerre.

1907 Collins, G. F. S. (July 22, 1916). Lt. 116th Mahrattas, I.A.R.O., temp. Capt. Asst. Recruiting Officer. India. *O.B.E.* (Civil).

1900 Collyer-Bristow, J. (Nov. 27, 1914). Capt. Northamptonshire Yeomanry, attd. Remount Service.

1911 Colman,* G. R. R. (Aug. 25, 1914). Capt. M.G.C. France, Belgium. *D.* France, 1916.

1904 Colt-Williams, E. W. D., B.A. (Mar. 23, 1915). Hon. Lt. R.A.S.C. (Capt.). France. *M.C.*, Jan. 1, 1917.

1898 Colville, E. F., B.A. (Aug. 1914). Capt. Political Officer, attd. Nyasaland Field Force. Nyasaland, 1914–15; German E. Africa, 1916–17.

1903 Colvile, K. N., M.A. (Oct. 29, 1915). Lt. R.G.A., attd. War Office (Capt.). France, 1916–17.

1908 **Combe, G. H. R.** (1914). ‡2nd Lt. 11th Rifle Brigade. France. Killed in action in the Battle of the Ancre on Sept. 16, 1916.

1919 Cooke, C. H. (Jan. 4, 1918). 2nd Lt. R.F.A.

1919 Cooke, D. R., B.A. (Dec. 24, 1914). ‡Lt. 6th Gordon Highlanders (T.F.). France, Belgium.

1902 Cooke, Rev. E. M., M.A. (Dec. 7, 1915). Chaplain to the Forces (4th Class).

1899 Cooke, Rev. H. E., M.A. (Sept. 11, 1917). Chaplain to the Forces (4th Class), attd. 1st King's Own (R. Lancaster Regt.). France, 1918.

1919 Cooper, H. R. L. (May 6, 1918). Cadet O.C.B. 2nd Lt. 5th Worcestershire Regt. (on demobilization).

1896 Corbett-Lowe, W. S., M.A. (June 2, 1916). Capt. and Adjt. Dock Bn., King's (Liverpool Regt.).

1897 Corbett-Smith, A., M.A. (Mobilized Aug. 1914). Maj. R.F.A. (S.R.), attd. British Navy. France, from Aug. 1914. *D.* France, 1914.

1894 Corbett-Winder, W. J., B.A. (Aug. 19, 1914). Maj. 7th R. Welch Fusiliers (T.F. Res.).

1909 Cornwallis,* F. W. M., B.A. (Serving Aug. 4, 1914). Lt. 17th Lancers. Acting Maj. M.G.C. France, 1914–19. *M.C.*, June 3, 1919. Croix de Guerre.

1911 Corrin, T. O. (Sept. 1914). ‡Lt. I.A.R.O., attd. 31st Punjabis (Capt.). Mesopotamia, Salonika.

1899 Cotesworth, C. H. (Serving Aug. 4, 1914). Capt. 21st Lancers. India.

1896 Courthope, G. L. (Mobilized Aug. 1914). Maj. 5th R. Sussex Regt. France, 1915, 1917. *M.C.*, June 3, 1915. T.D. *D.* France, 1915.

1909 Covington, C. K., B.A. (Oct. 25, 1916). Lt. 15th Sherwood Foresters. France. *M.C.*, July 26, 1918. Croix de Guerre.

1906 Craig, J., B.A. (1914). 2nd Lt. British Honduras Defence Force.

1912 Cranborne, Viscount (Aug. 15, 1914). Lt. Grenadier Guards (S.R.) A.D.C. France. Croix de Chevalier de l'Ordre de la Couronne. Croix de Guerre.

1891 Crane, G. P. (Sept. 23, 1914). Lt. Bedfordshire Yeomanry. Lt. R. Defence Corps.

1896 Cranstoun, C. J. E., B.A., T.D. (Mobilized Aug. 4, 1914). Maj. Lanarkshire Yeomanry, attd. 6th Gordon Highlanders (Lt.-Col.). Gallipoli, 1915; Egypt, 1916; France, 1918. *D.S.O.*, Jan. 1, 1919. Croix de Guerre avec palme. *D.* France, 1918, 1919.

1900 Cranstoun, G. H. H. E., B.A. (Mobilized Aug. 4, 1914). Capt. Lanarkshire Yeomanry, attd. Tank Corps (Engineers) (Maj.). Gallipoli, Egypt, Palestine, France.

1913 Cranswick, H. F., B.A. (Feb. 6, 1917). 2nd Lt. 2nd Rifle Brigade. France, Belgium. (Invalided, Sept. 1918.)

1919 Cranswick, R. L. (Aug. 19, 1918). Pte. 28th London Regt. (Artists' Rifles).

1911 **Creagh,* H. J. P.,** B.A. (Sept. 30, 1914). Lt., Acting Capt., 11th Suffolk Regt. France, 1915–18. *M.C.*, Mar. 8, 1919. *D.* France, 1916. Died at Le Tréport on Nov. 23, 1918, of wounds received in action.

1919 Crennell, J. T. (Sept. 3, 1918). Gnr. 211th Batt., R.G.A.

1899 Creyke, W. L. (May 1916). ‡Lt. R.G.A. (S.R.) (Staff-Captain). France, Belgium.

1895 Crichton, Hon. A. O. (Sept. 14, 1914). Capt. General List. Staff Officer (3rd Class), Air Staff, R.A.F. Belgium, France, Egypt. *D.* France, 1917; Egypt, 1917.

1910 **Crichton, J. D.,** B.A. (Aug. 26, 1914). Capt. 9th Loyal N. Lancashire Regt. France, Belgium. *D.* France, 1918. Killed in action on Mar. 22, 1918.

1901 **Crichton-Stuart, Lord N. E.,** *M.P.* (Mobilized Aug. 5, 1914). Lt.-Col. 6th Welsh Regt. France, Belgium. Killed in action at the Hohenzollern Redoubt on Oct. 2, 1915.

1902 Croft, P. R., B.A. (Aug. 1914). ‡Capt. R.F.A. (T.F.). France, Egypt, Palestine.

Crombie, J. E. (Sept. 1914). Capt. 4th Gordon Highlanders. France, Belgium, 1915–17. Died on Apr. 23, 1917, of wounds received in action at Rœux.

Crombie, J. M. (Dec. 1916). 2nd Lt. 10th R. W. Kent Regt. Belgium, France. Died on July 2, 1917, of wounds received in action at Messines Ridge.

1908 **Cross,* D. R.** (Serving Aug. 4, 1914). Lt. 16th Lancers. France, Belgium. *M.C.*, Feb. 18, 1915. *D.* France, 1914, 1915. Killed in action at Hooge on Feb. 21, 1915.

1909 Crowder,* J. F. E. (Aug. 28, 1914). Lt. Res. Regt. R. Horse Guards. Lt. Special Lists. A.D.C. to G.O.C. Aldershot Command.

1894 Crowe, H. W., D.M. (Aug. 1917). Capt. R.A.M.C. Egypt, 1917–18; Malta, 1918–19.

1913 Cubitt, C. C. R. (Aug. 28, 1914). Lt. 4th Grenadier Guards (Staff-Captain). Gallipoli, 1915; France, 1916, 1918; Italy, 1917. *M.C.*, Apr. 2, 1919.

1907 Cuff,* B., B.A. (Serving Aug. 4, 1914). Capt., Bt.-Maj., 2nd Cheshire Regt. Bde. Maj. 83rd Inf. Bde. India, 1914–15; Salonika, 1916–18; Turkey, 1918–19. Greek Military Cross (3rd Class).

1911 Cumberlege,* F. C. R., B.A. (1914). Pte., A.S.C. and R.F.A. (Invalided.)

1907 Cunningham, H. I. (1914). Pte. 5th Arg. & Suth'd. Highlanders.

1899 Currie, E. D. H. (July 29, 1915). Capt. R.A.S.C.

1880 **Curtis, Sir W. M.,** Bt. (Aug. 29, 1916). Capt. R. Defence Corps. Died on Dec. 19, 1916.

1903 Curzon, Viscount, *M.P.* (Mobilized Aug. 2, 1914). Commdr. R.N.V.R., H.M.S. *Queen Elizabeth*. Belgium, 1914; Dardanelles, North Sea from 1915.

1913 Dale-Harris, E. P., B.A. (Oct. 30, 1914). Lt. R.F.A. (T.F.). France, Italy.

1913 Dalkeith, Earl of (Sept. 16, 1914). Lt. Grenadier Guards. A.D.C. France.

1894 Darell, L. E. H. M. (Serving Aug. 4, 1914). Maj. 1st Life Guards. Bde. Maj. Egypt, Gallipoli, Sinai, Palestine. *D.S.O.*, June 4, 1917. *D.* Gallipoli, 1916; Egypt, 1917.

1899 Darley, C. F., B.A. (Sept. 2, 1916). Lt. R.H.A.

1909 Darley, T. B., B.A. (Oct. 7, 1914). Lt. R.H.A. (Capt.). Egypt, France.

1912 Darling, T. M., M.A. (Sept. 7, 1914). ‡Lt. 8th Seaforth Highlanders (Capt.). France, Belgium, 1914–15, 1915–16, 1916–17, 1918.

1905 Dash, A. J., B.A. (Aug. 4, 1915). Lt. I.A.R.O.

1901 Dashwood, S. L., B.A. (Sept. 9, 1914). Lt. R.E. Capt. Technical Officer, R.A.F. France. *M.B.E.* (Mil.). Belgian Croix de Guerre. *D.* France, 1917; § June 1919.

1907 David, E. J. C., M.A. (Mobilized Aug. 4, 1914). Capt. 1/1st Glamorganshire Yeomanry, attd. 24th Welsh Regt. Egypt, 1916–17; Palestine, 1917–18; France, 1918. *M.C.*, Feb. 4, 1918.

1897 Davis, E., M.A. (May 7, 1912). Maj. Unattached List, T.F., Sherborne School O.T.C.

1919 Davis, R. F. G. (Sept. 29, 1916). ‡Lt. R.G.A. (Capt.). France, Belgium, Germany.

Dawson, T. R. (Oct. 1, 1914). 2nd Lt. 19th London Regt. France. Died on Feb. 4, 1916, of wounds received on Sept. 25, 1915, at Loos.

1905 Day, F. P., M.A. (Sept. 1915). Lt.-Col. 25th Inf. Bn., C.E.F. France.

1900 **Day, H.**, B.A. (Aug. 1914). ‡2nd Lt. 11th, attd. 8th, Loyal N. Lancashire Regt. France. Killed in action on the Somme on July 10, 1916.

1919 Dean, W. G. (July 6, 1917). 2nd Lt. Scots Guards. France. *D.* France, 1919.

1913 **Dearmer, C.** (1914). ‡Lt. R.N.V.R., Armoured Car Div. Gallipoli. Died on Oct. 6, 1915, of wounds received in action at Suvla Bay.

1912 Dearmer, G. (Sept. 25, 1914). Lt. R.A.S.C. (Capt.). Gallipoli, Egypt, France. *D.* § Aug. 1919.

1888 de Capell Brooke, Sir A. R., Bt., B.A. (Feb. 15, 1915). Capt. 3rd Northamptonshire Regt.

1904 de Chassiron, Baron C. L. J. (Aug. 27, 1915). Capt. R.A.S.C. *D.* § Mar. 1919.

1897 de Forest, Baron (1914). Lt.-Commdr. R.N.V.R.

1899 Delap, J. O. K., B.A. (Aug. 25, 1914). Maj. 303rd Siege Batt., R.G.A. (T.F.). France, Belgium, Germany. *D.S.O.*, Jan. 1, 1919. *D.* France, 1918.

1899 Denis de Vitré, Rev. J. D., M.A. (Aug. 1914). Chaplain, R.N., H.M.S. *Canopus*. Falkland Islands, Dardanelles.

1909 de Poix, R. B. C. T., B.A. (Sept. 1, 1914). Capt. 1/4th Norfolk Regt. Bde. Maj. 9th Bde., R.A.F. Gallipoli, France, Egypt. *O.B.E.* (Mil.).

1919 de Uphaugh, R. G. D. (Oct. 1914). Lt. 5th R. Fusiliers, attd. No. 11 O.C.B. France, Belgium, 1915.

1911 Devan, Rev. S. A., M.A. (1918). Chaplain, Coast Artillery Corps, U.S. Army. France, 1918–19.

1894 de Watteville, H. G., B.A. (Serving Aug. 4, 1914). Maj., Bt. Lt.-Col., R.A. G.S.O. 2. *C.B.E.* (Mil.). Croix de Chevalier de la Légion d'Honneur.

1910 Dibdin,* A., M.A. (Aug. 1914). Capt. 4th Queen's (R. W. Surrey Regt.). India.

1919 Dick, A. C. (May 17, 1917). 1st Lt. Pershing's Guard, U.S. Army (Capt.). France, 1918–19.

1908 Dickinson, L. A. H., B.A. (Aug. 26, 1914). Lt. 6th King's Own (R. Lancaster Regt.). Gallipoli, 1915.

1880 **Digby, G. H.** (Mobilized Aug. 1914). Maj. Dorset Yeomanry (T.F. Res.). Accidentally killed on Oct. 20, 1914.

1892 Digby, K. E. J., B.A. (Mobilized Aug. 4, 1914). Capt. R. Monmouthshire R.E. Staff-Captain. France, Salonika, Egypt.

1913 **Dilbéroglue, A.** (Aug. 15, 1914). Lt. 3rd Hussars. France. Killed in action at Domart on Apr. 1, 1918.

1911 Dixon,* G. H. S., B.A. (Aug. 1914). Capt. R.H.A. France, Germany, 1915–19. *M.C.*, Feb. 4, 1918.

1897 **Dixon, H. B.** (Serving Aug. 4, 1914). Capt. 1st Sherwood Foresters (Maj.). France. *D.* France, 1915. Killed in action at Neuve Chapelle on Mar. 12, 1915.

Dixon, J. V. (Sept. 1915). 2nd Lt. 3rd N. Midland Bde., R.F.A. (T.F.), attd. T.M.B. France. Killed in action at Gommecourt on Mar. 6, 1917.

1900 Dobell, D. C., B.M., M.A. (May 1917). Capt. R.A.M.C. Macedonia, Italy.

1919 Dobson, G. de S. (May 10, 1918). 2nd Lt. Coldstream Guards.

1916 Dodd, K. S. (Jan. 3, 1917). ‡Lt. R.E. (T.F.). France, Belgium. *M.C.*, Sept. 16, 1918.

1903 Dodgson, A. D., B.A. (Oct. 9, 1915). Capt. R.A.S.C. Egypt, Palestine. *O.B.E.* (Mil.). *D.* Palestine, 1918, 1919.

1911 Doherty, F. C., B.A. (Oct. 18, 1915). Lt. 5th Essex Regt., empld. Ministry of Munitions. France, 1916. *M.B.E.* (Mil.). *D.* § Mar. 1919.

1898 Douglas, J. S. C., D.M. (July 19, 1915). Capt. R.A.M.C., 3rd Northern General Hospital. *D.* § Sept. 1917.

1885 Douglass, Rev. F. W., M.A. (May 1917). Acting Capt. I.A.R.O. Chaplain to the Forces (4th Class), attd. 12th King's (Liverpool Regt.). India, France, 1917–19. *O.B.E.* (Mil.). *M.C.*, Nov. 7, 1918. *D.* France, 1919.

1907 Dowding, K. T., B.A. (Aug. 7, 1914). ‡Lt. 4th Queen's (R. W. Surrey Regt.). Maj., Squadron Commdr., R.A.F. Belgium, France, 1916, 1918; Italy, 1917–18. *D.F.C.*, Jan. 1, 1919.

1914 **Downie, N.** (June 1916). 2nd Lt. I.A.R.O., attd. 1/4th Gurkha Rifles. Baluchistan, India. Died on May 17, 1917, of wounds received in action at Nili Kach, in S. Wazirstan.

1919 Drage, C. H. (Serving Aug. 4, 1914). Lt. R.N., H.M.S. *Thunderer*. Channel, 1914; Dardanelles, 1915; Adriatic, 1915–16; Atlantic, 1917; N. Russia, 1918.

1886 Drage, E. W., M.A. (Jan. 1915). Capt. 2nd Vol. Bn. Yorkshire Regt.

1879 Drage, G., M.A. (Oct. 1914). ‡Sub-Lt. R.N.V.R., attd. War Office.

1907 Drage,* R. L., B.A. (Oct. 19, 1914). Capt. General List. Maj. D.A.D. of Railway Transport. France, 1914–17; Belgium, 1918–19.

1917 Drake, G. L. (Oct. 4, 1918). Pte. 28th London Regt. (Artists' Rifles).

1909 **Draper, R. F.,** B.A. (Aug. 1914). Capt. 6th York & Lancaster Regt. Gallipoli. Killed in action at Suvla Bay on Aug. 21, 1915.

1913 Drewe, B. (Oct. 26, 1914). Capt. 191st Siege Batt., R.G.A. France, Belgium. *M.C.*, Nov. 19, 1917; *Bar*, Mar. 9, 1918.

1912 Driver,* C. E. (Aug. 22, 1914). Capt. 1/6th Devonshire Regt. India, 1914–15; Mesopotamia, 1915–19. *M.C.*, Aug. 26, 1918.

1910 Drummond, F. H. J. (Sept. 21, 1914). 2nd Lt. Warwickshire Yeomanry. Lt. Grenadier Guards (S.R.). France, Belgium. *M.C.*, Sept. 26, 1917.

1904 Drummond, G. H. (1914). Lt. 1st Life Guards. Lt.-Commdr. R.N.V.R. France; Dover Patrol. Croix de Chevalier de la Légion d'Honneur. Promoted for service in action. **V.C.** won at Ostend, May 9–10, 1918.

He volunteered for rescue work in command of M.L. 254. Following *Vindictive* to Ostend when off the piers a shell burst on board, killing Lt. Gordon Ross and Deckhand J. Thomas, wounding the coxswain and also severely wounding Lt. Drummond in three places. Notwithstanding his wounds he remained on the bridge, navigated his vessel, which was already seriously damaged by shell fire, into Ostend Harbour, placed her alongside *Vindictive*, took off 2 officers and 38 men, some of whom were killed and many wounded while embarking. When informed that there was no one alive left on board he backed his vessel out clear of the piers before sinking exhausted from his wounds. When H.M.S. *Warwick* fell in with M.L. 254 off Ostend half an hour later the latter was in a sinking condition. It was due to the indomitable courage of this very gallant officer that the majority of the crew of the *Vindictive* were rescued.

1910 Drummond,* L. (Sept. 19, 1914). Lt. 2nd Dragoons (S.R.), attd. M.G.C. France.

1888 Dugdale, A. (Mobilized Aug. 1914). Col. Q.O. Oxfordshire Hussars. France. *C.M.G.* *D.S.O.*, Jan. 1, 1919. T.D. *D.* France, 1915, 1918.

1892 Dugdale, J. G., B.A., *D.S.O.* (Mobilized Aug. 1914). Capt., Bt.-Maj., 18th Hussars, Res. of Officers. France. *M.V.O.* *M.C.*, June 3, 1916. Chevalier de l'Ordre du Mérite Agricole. *D.* France, 1915, 1916, 1917, 1918, 1919.

Dundas, H. L. N. (Aug. 7, 1915). Capt. 1st Scots Guards. France, Belgium, 1916–18. *M.C.*, Nov. 26, 1917; *Bar*, May 17, 1918; *2nd Bar*, Sept. 17, 1918. Killed in action at Canal du Nord on Sept. 27, 1918.

1903 Dundas, R. H., M.A. (Jan. 2, 1915). Capt. 3rd, attd. 2nd, The Black Watch. France, 1915; Mesopotamia, 1916; India, 1916–19. *D.* Mesopotamia, 1916; India, 1919.

1913 Dunlop, W. N. U., B.A. (Oct. 25, 1914). ‡Lt. 13th London Regt. Acting Capt. and Adjt. M.G.C. France, 1916–19. *D.* France, 1918.

1918 Dunne, F. P. N. (Mobilized Aug. 4, 1914). Maj. Westmorland & Cumberland Yeomanry. France, Belgium.

1910 **Dunnington-Jefferson,* W. M.,** B.A. (Aug. 15, 1914). 2nd Lt. 7th, attd. 3rd, R. Fusiliers. Belgium. Killed in action near Gravenstafel, in the 2nd Battle of Ypres, on Apr. 25, 1915.

1858 Dunraven, Rt. Hon. W. T., Earl of, *K.P.* (May 20, 1915). Hon. Col. 3rd County of London Yeomanry. Commdr. R.N.V.R. *C.M.G.* *O.B.E.* (Mil.).

1913 Durham, T. C., M.A. (1917). Lt. Field Artillery, U.S. Army.

1901 Dykes, F. H. B. (Mobilized Sept. 1, 1914). Lt. Scots Guards. D.A.A.G. (Maj.). France, 1915–18. *D.S.O.*, June 4, 1917. *D.* France, 1917 twice, 1918.

1919 Eden, R. A. (Sept. 29, 1915). Capt. 21st K.R.R.C. Capt. (Bde. Maj.) 198th Inf. Bde. France, Belgium. *M.C.*, June 4, 1917.

1912 Eden,* Sir T. C., Bt. (Apr. 1917). 2nd Lt. 15th K.O.Y.L.I. Acting Capt. T.M.B. France. (Civilian prisoner of war in Germany, 1914–16.)

1911 Edgar,* A. C., M.A. (Sept. 21, 1914). Capt. 6th, attd. 12th, E. Surrey Regt. France, Belgium, Italy, Germany. *M.C.*, Feb. 1, 1919.

1907 Edgar,* S. C., M.A. (Aug. 29, 1915). Lt. 6th E. Surrey Regt. (T.F.).

1912 Ednam, Viscount W. H. E. (Mobilized Aug. 1914). 2nd Lt. Worcestershire Yeomanry. Lt., temp. Capt., 10th Hussars. France. *M.C.*, June 18, 1917. Croix de Chevalier de la Légion d'Honneur.

1898 Edwards, F. W. L. (Serving Aug. 4, 1914). Maj. K.R.R.C. (Lt.-Col.). D.A.A.G. Headquarters Staff, Egyptian Army. Gallipoli, 1915; Egypt, 1916–19. *O.B.E.* (Mil.). Order of the Nile (4th Class). *D.* Egypt, 1916, 1917; Sudan, 1919.

1890 Edwards, H. P., B.A. (Mobilized Aug. 1914). Maj. 28th London Regt. (Artists' Rifles). T.D.

1907 **Egerton, E. B.,** B.A. (Serving Aug. 4, 1914). Capt. 17th Lancers. India, Belgium, France. Died on Sept. 1, 1916, of wounds received in action at Arras.

1914 **Egerton, J. F.** (Dec. 22, 1914). 2nd Lt. General List, attd. 8th K.R.R.C. France, Belgium. Killed in action on Apr. 3, 1916.

1900 **Egerton, L. E. W.** (Mobilized Aug. 5, 1914). Capt. R. Bucks. Hussars. Staff-Captain R.F.A. Egypt, Palestine. Killed in action on Aug. 1, 1917.

1906 Egerton-Warburton, G., B.A. (Mobilized Aug. 1914). Capt. Cheshire Yeomanry. Maj. M.G.C. Egypt, 1916–17; Palestine, 1917–18; France, 1918–19. *D.S.O.*, Apr. 12, 1918.

1902 **Egerton-Warburton, J.** (Serving Aug. 4, 1914). Capt. Scots Guards. France. Died on Aug. 30, 1915, of wounds received in action in France in May.

Eley, W. A. D. (Oct. 1916). 2nd Lt. 1st K.R.R.C. France. Killed in action near Miraumont on Feb. 17, 1917.

1912 Elliott, I. F. L. (June 26, 1915). Lt. 4th Suffolk Regt. attd. M.G.C. Lt. Administrative Officer, R.A.F., empld. Ministry of Labour.

1901 **Ellis, F. B.,** M.A. (Sept. 2, 1914). ‡Capt. 10th Northumberland Fusiliers. France, Belgium. Killed in action in the Battle of the Somme on Sept. 26, 1916.

1911 Elwes, R. P. (May 9, 1915). Lt., Acting Capt., Coldstream Guards. France. *M.C.*, June 3, 1918. (Prisoner of war.)

1919 Emmott, C. E. G. C. (June 7, 1917). 2nd Lt. R.F.A. (S.R.). France.

1880 Engleheart, H. L. D., M.A. (Jan. 10, 1915). Lt. 5th Suffolk Regt. (Vol.).

1900 English, C. R., M.A. (Nov. 28, 1914). Lt., Acting Capt., M.G.C. Lt. K.R.R.C., empld Ministry of Munitions. France, 1915–16.

1885 Ennismore, Viscount (Sept. 1914). Maj. 6th R. Munster Fusiliers. A.P.M., XV Corps. Maj. 1/6th County of London Vol. Regt. Salonika, Egypt. (Invalided.)

1913 Erle-Drax, J. C. W. (Dec. 7, 1914). Lt., Acting Capt., Rifle Brigade, empld. O.C.B. Belgium, France.

1913 Erskine, Lord (Feb. 12, 1915). Lt. 3rd Scots Guards.

1899 Evans, E. H., B.A. (Mobilized Aug. 1914). Capt. 6th R. Welch Fusiliers (T.F.). Egypt, Palestine. *M.C.*, Jan. 1, 1918; *Bar*, Mar. 9, 1918. *D.* Palestine, 1917.

1913 Evans, G. M., B.A. (Dec. 22, 1914). 2nd Lt. 9th S. Wales Borderers. (Invalided.)

1919 Evans, G. P. (June 12, 1917). Sergt. Field Artillery, U.S. Army. France.

1913 Eve,* A. M. T. (Sept. 2, 1914). Capt. and Adjt. 1/6th R. Welch Fusiliers. Bde. Maj. 159th Inf. Bde. Gallipoli, Egypt, Palestine. *M.C.*, June 3, 1918.

1894 Evelyn, J. H. C. (Sept. 5, 1914). ‡Lt. 11th Arg. & Suth'd. Highlanders. France, Belgium.

1908 [Faber, G. C., M.A.] (Oct. 1914). Capt. 8th London Regt. (Post Office Rifles) (Maj.). France, Belgium, 1917–18.

1919 Fabre-Luce, R. M. A. Interpreter, Franco-Greek Secret Service. France, Serbia.

Fair, J. G. (Oct. 23, 1915). 2nd Lt. Duke of Lancaster's Own Yeomanry. Lt. R.F.C. France, 1917. Killed in action near Hargicourt on Mar. 19, 1917.

1909 Fannière, E. (1914). Interpreter, French Army. France.

1919 Farquhar, G. W. J. (June 1917). Lt. 2nd Coldstream Guards. France.

1889 **Farquhar, J. E. M.,** M.A. (Aug. 1914). ‡Maj. 6th Q.O. Cameron Highlanders. France, 1915–16. Killed in action in the Battle of the Ancre on Sept. 15, 1916.

1885 Farquharson, A. H., B.A. (Oct. 8, 1914). Lt.-Col. 7th Gordon Highlanders. Maj. Labour Corps. France.

1919 Farquharson, M. G. (Nov. 9, 1917). 2nd Lt. 1st Grenadier Guards. France, 1918. *M.C.*, Apr. 2, 1919.

1899 **Farrar, J. G. K.** (Aug. 1914). ‡Capt. 12th Lancashire Fusiliers. France, Salonika. Killed in action on Sept. 14, 1916.

Faulkner, E. W. S. Rfln. 28th London Regt. (Artists' Rifles). France. Died on July 26, 1918, of wounds received in action at Aveluy Wood.

1904 Feilden, O. G. St. C., B.A. (June 30, 1915). ‡Lt. E. Yorkshire Regt. (Capt.). France, 1916–17.

1904 Feilding, Viscount R. E. A., B.A. (Mobilized Aug. 5, 1914). Maj., Bt. Lt.-Col., Coldstream Guards, attd. 3rd Bn. A.A. and Q.M.G. 8th Div. France, 1914–18. *C.M.G.*, 1918. *D.S.O.*, Oct. 21, 1914. Croix de Chevalier de la Légion d'Honneur. *D.* France, 1914, 1915, 1916 twice, 1917, 1918.

1903 Feiling, K. G., M.A. (Dec. 30, 1914). Capt. 3rd The Black Watch. Capt. A.H.Q. India. India, 1916–19. *O.B.E.* (Mil.).

1898 **Feversham, Earl of,** M.A. (Sept. 1, 1914). Lt.-Col. Yorkshire Hussars. Lt.-Col. 21st K.R.R.C. (Yeoman Rifles). France, Belgium, 1914, 1916. *D.* France, 1916. Killed in action at Flers on Sept. 15, 1916.

ffolkes, W. R. C. (Sept. 12, 1917). 2nd Lt. K.R.R.C. France. Killed in action on Dec. 30, 1917.

1898 ffrench-Blake, A. O'B. (Mobilized Aug. 1914). Lt.-Col. 1/4th Essex Regt. Gallipoli, Egypt, Palestine, Syria, 1915–19. T.D.

Field, R. G. (Sept. 28, 1914). 2nd Lt. 10th Hussars. France. Died on Apr. 9, 1918, of wounds received in action.

1904 Finlay, D. (July 30, 1915). Maj. Special Lists. G.S.O. 2. Italy. *D.S.O.*, Apr. 11, 1918. Cavalier, Order of St. Maurice and St. Lazarus. *D.* Italy, 1918.

1912 Firth, C. P. L., B.A. (Sept. 19, 1914). Capt. 6th Worcestershire Regt. Capt., Administrative Officer, R.A.F. France.

1909 Firth, D. G., M.A. (Mobilized Aug. 1914). Capt. 1/5th Hampshire Regt. India, 1914–15; Mesopotamia, 1915–16; India, 1916–19.

1919 Firth, J. D. E. (July 25, 1918). 2nd Lt. Scots Guards (S.R.).

1896 **Fisher, C. D.**, M.A. (1915). ‡Lt. R.N.V.R., H.M.S. *Invincible*. France, North Sea. *D.* Naval Dispatches, 1916. Killed in action in Battle of Jutland on May 31, 1916.

1912 Fisher, F. M. (Dec. 28, 1914). Capt. Coldstream Guards (S.R.), attd. Guards M.G. Regt. France.

1892 Fison, F. G., B.A. (Dec. 28, 1914). Lt. K.R.R.C. (Capt.). France. *M.C.*, Nov. 14, 1916. *D.* France, 1916, 1917. (Prisoner of war, Jan.–Dec. 1918.)

1912 Fison, F. G. C. (Oct. 26, 1914). Lt. 4th Suffolk Regt. Lt., Acting Maj., Administrative Officer, R.A.F. France and Belgium. *D.* France, 1916.

1909 **Fison, J. F. L.**, B.A. (Sept. 1914). Lt. 4th Suffolk Regt. Capt., Bde. Maj., 12th Inf. Bde. France. *M.C.*, June 24, 1916. *D.* France, 1916, 1917. Died of pneumonia after gas poisoning on Nov. 2, 1917.

1914 Fite, A. G., B.A. (1918). Artillery Officers' Training School, U.S. Army.

1919 Fite, F. B. (May 10, 1917). Lt. and A.D.C., H.Q. 80th Div., U.S. Army. France.

1908 **Fitzgibbon,* R. A.,** B.A. (Serving Aug. 4, 1914). Lt. 128th Pioneers, Indian Army. India, Egypt. *D.* Egypt, 1915. Died on Feb. 4, 1915, of wounds received in action on the Suez Canal.

1897 Fitzherbert, H. B., B.A. (May 1916). Capt. Technical Officer, R.A.F. France, 1916–18.

1896 **Fitzhugh, G.** (Mobilized Aug. 1914). Capt. 1/1st Montgomeryshire Yeomanry, attd. 25th R. Welch Fusiliers (Maj.). Egypt, Palestine. Killed in action at Gaza on Nov. 1, 1917.

1919 Fleming, A. R. C. (June 7, 1918). 2nd Lt. Q.O. Cameron Highlanders.

1894 Fletcher, H. J. (Aug. 1915). Capt. R. Wiltshire Yeomanry, attd. 2nd K.R.R.C. France, 1916–18. *M.C.*, Apr. 2, 1919.

1888 **Fletcher, W. A. L.,** *D.S.O.* (Aug. 1914). Capt., Bt.-Maj., temp. Lt.-Col., 2/6th King's (Liverpool Regt.). France. Croix de Chevalier de la Légion d'Honneur. *D.* France, 1917, 1918. Died of pneumonia after gas poisoning, on Feb. 14, 1919.

1919 Flux-Dundas, A. D. (Oct. 11, 1917). 2nd Lt. 136th Siege Batt., R.G.A. France, 1918–19; Germany, 1919.

1910 Foljambe,* E. W. S., B.A. (Serving Aug. 4, 1914). Capt. Rifle Brigade, attd. War Office. France, 1914. (Wounded and prisoner of war, 1914–18.)

1875 Foljambe, G. S., B.A., V.D. (Mobilized Aug. 1914). Lt.-Col. (Ret.), President of Area Quartering Committee, Northern Command. *C.B.* *D.* § Feb. 1917.

1902 Forbes, Lord A. L. C. (Aug. 26, 1905). Maj. Grenadier Guards. France, 1916.

1900 Forsyth, B., B.A. (Aug. 31, 1914). Pte. 9th London Regt. (Queen Victoria's Rifles). France, Belgium, 1914. (Discharged Nov. 5, 1915, joined Postal Censorship.)

1888 Fortescue-Brickdale,* J. M., D.M. (Mobilized Aug. 4, 1914). Capt. R.A.M.C., 2nd Southern General Hospital. France, 1915–17.

1909 Fortescue-Brickdale, M., B.A. (Sept. 7, 1914). Capt and Adjt. 8th London Regt. (Post Office Rifles). France.

1904 Foster, G. R., B.A. (Mobilized Aug. 1914). Lt. 13th Hussars. France.

1895 Fox, W. F., B.C.L., M.A. (Dec. 2, 1915). Lt. R.A.

1895 Franklyn, H. A. (Aug. 26, 1914). Capt. Hampshire Yeomanry (Staff Captain). Capt. Administrative Officer, R.A.F. *D.* § Feb. 1917.

1911 **Fraser,* A. K.** (Aug. 3, 1914). ‡Capt. 4th Seaforth Highlanders. France. *M.C.*, Jan. 1, 1918. Killed in action at Fontaine Notre Dame on Nov. 22, 1917.

1894 Fraser, B. N., B.A. (Oct. 12, 1914). Lt. R.H.A. (T.F.). Egypt, Palestine. *D.* Palestine, 1918, 1919.

1903 Fraser-Tytler, J. F., B.A. (Mobilized Aug. 1914). Maj. 1st Lovat's Scouts. Gallipoli, 1914; Egypt, 1916; Salonika, 1916–18; France, 1918. *D.S.O.*, Jan. 18, 1918. *D.* Salonika, 1918.

1906 Fraser-Tytler, W. K., B.A. (Serving Aug. 4, 1914). Capt. and Adjt. 25th Cavalry, Field Force, Indian Army. India, 1914–15; E. Africa, 1917–18. *M.C.*, Aug. 3, 1918.

1895 Freeman, G. H. H., B.A. (Oct. 1914). Lt. Res. of Officers. Maj. (S. Bn.) K.R.R.C. *D.* § Feb. 1917.

1919 Freeman, H. W. (Oct. 5, 1917). 2nd Lt. 7th Somerset L.I. France.

1912 **Freeman, R. H.** (Oct. 21, 1914). Capt. 6th Worcestershire Regt. Maj., Administrative Officer, R.A.F. France, 1915, 1918; Egypt and Palestine, 1916–17. *M.C.*, Jan. 26, 1917. Croix de Guerre. *D.* Egypt, 1917. Missing, presumed killed while flying near Belleau on July 21, 1918.

1918 Freer, R. C. (Serving Aug. 4, 1914). Capt., Acting Maj., A/70th Bde., R.F.A. France. *M.C.*, June 3, 1916. *D.* France, 1915.

1894 French, H. S., D.M. (May 1, 1916). Lt.-Col. R.A.M.C., Consulting Physician to Aldershot Command. France. *C.B.E.* (Mil.). *D.* § Aug. 1918.

1899 Friend, R. S. I. (Serving Aug. 4, 1914). Maj. The Buffs (E. Kent Regt.). Acting Lt.-Col. 24th London Regt. (The Queen's). France, Belgium. *D.S.O.*, Sept. 17, 1917. *D.* France, 1917.

1919 Fripp, A. T. (Oct. 5, 1917). 2nd Lt. 1st Life Guards. France, 1918–19.

1903 Frost, J. M., B.A. (Aug. 5, 1914). Lt.-Col. 303rd Bde., R.F.A. France, 1915, 1916, 1917; Egypt, 1916; Palestine, 1917–18. *D.S.O.*, Feb. 18, 1918.

1910 Frost, R. (Nov. 1914). Maj. 15th Cheshire Regt. France. *D.* France, 1918.

1903 Fry, B. H., M.A. (Feb. 27, 1915). Lt., Acting Capt., R.F.A. Staff-Lt. (1st Class). France, 1915–16; Salonika, 1916; France, 1916–19.

1894 Fuller, Rev. F. C., M.A. (Apr. 20, 1917). Chaplain to the Forces (4th Class), attd. R.A.V.C. Palestine, France.

1883 **Fuller, Sir J. M. F., Bt.,** M.A. (Mobilized Aug. 1914). Maj. R. Wiltshire Yeomanry. Died in England, 1915.

1912 Fuller, N. B., M.A. (Aug. 1914). Lt. 8th K.R.R.C. Capt., Flying Officer, R.A.F. France, 1916–17; Mesopotamia, 1918; Persia, 1918. *M.B.E.* (Mil.).

1919 Furber, A. R. (Aug. 12, 1918). Cadet R.E. Cadet Bn.

1883 Fyers, E. W. H., B.A. (Mobilized 1914). Lt. Rifle Brigade, Res. of Officers. Maj., empld. Recruiting Duties. T.D.

1919 Gage-Brown, C. L. (Sept. 23, 1914). Lt. Interpreter, attd. 1st Life Guards. Belgium, Oct. 1914. (Prisoner of war, Oct. 1914.)

1909 Gaisford-St. Lawrence,* T. J. E., M.A. (Sept. 15, 1914). Capt. 3rd Seaforth Highlanders (Maj.). France. *M.C.*, June 4, 1917; *1st Bar*, July 18, 1917; *2nd Bar*, Feb. 2, 1919.

1901 Galloway, T. L., B.A. (Mobilized Aug. 4, 1914). Maj. Q.O. Glasgow Dragoons. A.P.M. Belgium, France, Germany, 1915–19.

1896 Gamon, G. P., B.A. (Jan. 18, 1915). Capt. A.S.C. Maj. Labour Corps. Asst. Controller of Labour, Staff. *D.* France, 1917.

1900 Ganzoni, F. J. C., M.A., *M.P.* (Mobilized Aug. 4, 1914). Capt. 4th Suffolk Regt. Capt. IX Corps Staff. France, 1914–18.

1907 Gardner, O. J., M.A. (Oct. 18, 1914). ‡Lt. I.A.R.O., attd. 1/150th Infantry. India, 1914–19; Baluchistan, N.W. Frontier, 1918.

1908 Garnett, N. T. (1914). In charge of Commissariat Transport, and Press Censor, Togoland Expedition. Togoland.

1877 Garrod, Sir Archibald E., D.M. (Oct. 1914). Col. R.A.M.C. (Consultant to Forces). Malta, 1915–19. *K.C.M.G.*, 1918. *D.* Malta, 1916; § Feb. 1918.

Garvin, R. G. (Sept. 19, 1914). Lt., Acting Capt., 7th S. Lancashire Regt. France, Belgium, 1915–16. Killed in action near Bazentin-le-Petit on July 22, 1916.

1919 Gass, G. I. (Jan. 8, 1915). Capt. Worcestershire Regt. Capt. and Adjt., attd. 53rd Hampshire Regt. France, 1917.
1907 Gay, S. E. (Nov. 16, 1914). 2nd Lt. 9th Seaforth Highlanders. Lt. M.G.C. Lt., Acting Capt., Tank Corps. France, Belgium.
1904 Gay, W. G. M., B.A. (Aug. 15, 1914). Capt. 3rd The Buffs (E. Kent Regt.). A.D.C.
1877 Geary, Sir W. N. M., Bt., M.A. (Jan. 18, 1915). Capt. 25th Manchester Regt. Maj. (Courts Martial Officer) 9th R. Warwickshire Regt. India, 1916–18; Mesopotamia, 1918.
Gee, G. R. D. (July 31, 1915). 2nd Lt. 3rd R. Sussex Regt., attd. R.F.C. Presumed killed while flying on June 14, 1917.
1919 Gibbs, C. C. S. (Jan. 11, 1916). Lt. and Adjt. 4th Suffolk Regt. (Capt.). France, 1916–18. *M.C.*, July 26, 1917.
1892 Gibbs, G. A., M.A., *M.P.*, T.D. (Oct. 1914). Lt.-Col. 2/1st N. Somerset Yeomanry (T.F. Res.). *D.* § Feb. 1917.
1875 Gibbs, Ven. Hon. K. F., D.D. (Serving Aug. 4, 1914). Chaplain (4th Class) Hertfordshire Yeomanry.
1912 Gibbs, L. C. (Mobilized Aug. 1914). Lt. N. Somerset Yeomanry (T.F. Res.). A.D.C. 47th Div. France. *D.* France, 1915.
1897 Gibson, A. G., D.M. (Mobilized Aug. 5, 1914). Maj. R.A.M.C. (T.F.), 3rd Southern General Hospital. *D.* § Aug. 1919.
1896 Gibson, C. O. P., M.A. (Sept. 16, 1914). Capt. 1/4th Northumberland Fusiliers. Staff-Captain. France, 1915–18. *M.C.*, June 3, 1916. *D.* France, 1915, 1918.
1905 Gilbert, H. A., B.A. (Mobilized Aug. 4, 1914). Capt. 3rd S. Wales Borderers. France.
1896 Gilbert, J. C. W., B.A. (1916). Lt. R. Defence Corps. Capt. Provost Staff, Eastern Command.
1908 Gilbey,* G. H. (Sept. 22, 1914). Capt. 11th Rifle Brigade. Capt. General List. A.D.C. France, Belgium, from 1915. *M.C.*, Nov. 4, 1915. *D.* France, 1915, 1919.
1909 Gilbey-Rivière,* G., B.A. (Oct. 4, 1914). Capt. Rifle Brigade Capt. General List. France. *D.* France, 1916.
1912 Gilbey-Rivière, P. (Sept. 16, 1914). Capt. 11th Hussars. France.
1901 Giles, I. E., M.A. (Feb. 1916). ‡Capt. 183rd Siege Batt., R.G.A. France, 1916–18.
1919 Gilkes, H. A. (Sept. 8, 1914). ‡Lt. 1/21st London Regt. France, 1914–15, 1916–18. *M.C.*, Sept. 17, 1917; *Bar*, Mar. 4, 1918; *2nd Bar*, June 22, 1918; *3rd Bar*, Feb. 2, 1919.
1902 [Gill, W. B., B.Sc., M.A.] (Sept. 1915). Sergt. 9th Hampshire Regt. ‡Maj. R.E. Egypt, Palestine, Salonika, 1916–17. *O.B.E.* (Mil.). *D.* Palestine, 1918.
1908 Gillies, A. H. D., B.A. (Oct. 16, 1914). ‡Lt. 12th R. Scots. France and Belgium, 1917–18; Germany, 1918–19.
1919 Gillies, F. A. G. (Aug. 4, 1914). Capt. Gordon Highlanders (S.R.). Staff-Captain. France, 1915; Salonika, 1916.
1919 Gillmor, G. A. F. (Feb. 6, 1917). Lt. 4th R. Berkshire Regt. France, 1917.
1905 Gladstone, A. C., M.A. (Dec. 31, 1914). Capt. I.A.R.O., attd. 2/5th Gurkha Rifles. Gallipoli, 1915; Egypt, 1916; Mesopotamia, 1916–19. *M.B.E.* (Civil). *D.* Mesopotamia, 1917, 1918.

1907 Gladstone,* C. A., B.A. (Serving Aug. 4, 1914). Lt. General List. Lt., Observer Officer, R.A.F. France. (Prisoner of war.)

1870 Gladstone, Sir J. R., Bt. (May 1915). Lt.-Col. Commdt. of Prisoners' Camp. County Commdt. Kincardineshire Vol. Regt.

1913 Gladstone, N. W. H. (Aug. 29, 1914). Capt. Rifle Brigade, empld. O.C.B.

Gladstone, W. H. (Jan. 15, 1917). Lt. 1st Coldstream Guards (Capt.). France. *M.C.*, Apr. 22, 1918. Killed in action at Havrincourt on Sept. 27, 1918.

1892 Glancy, R. I. R., B.A., *C.I.E.* (Sept. 1914). Pte. 26th Bn. I.D.F.

1919 Glascodine, C. E. G. (Apr. 15, 1915). Lce.-Cpl. H.A.C. (Inf.). Belgium, France, 1916–17.

1914 Glyn, Hon. G. E. D. C. (Nov. 18, 1914). Lt. 10th Hussars. France.

1882 Godman, S. H., *D.S.O.* (Aug. 1914). Maj., Bt.-Lt.-Col., Scots Guards. Lt.-Col. A.A.G., A.H.Q., Mesopotamia. France, 1915–17; Mesopotamia, 1918. *D.* France, 1916; § Feb. 1917.

1899 Godsal, P., B.A. (Mobilized Aug. 1914). Capt. 3rd Oxf. & Bucks. Lt. Infty. (Maj.). France, 1914; Palestine, 1918. *M.C.*, May 5, 1919. (Prisoner of war in Germany, Aug. 1914, escaped Mar. 1917.)

1886 Goff, T. C. E. (Sept. 1914). Maj. 3rd R. Scots (attd. 2nd Bn. 1915). D.A.A.G. Commdt. on Lines of Communication. O.C. No. 31 Inf. Base Depot. France, Egypt, 1915–18.

1919 Goff, T. R. C. (Aug. 11, 1916). Lt. 1st Scots Guards. France and Poland.

1890 Gold, Sir A. G. (Nov. 27, 1914). Capt., Hon. Maj., Essex Yeomanry (T.F. Res.).

1919 Goldschmidt, E. C. (May 4, 1917). 2nd Lt. R.F.A. (S.R.).

1915 Gooch, R. K., B.A. (June 1917). Lt. U.S. Coast Artillery Corps. France.

1919 Goodenough, W. M. (Aug. 1917). ‡2nd Lt. 2nd Coldstream Guards. France.

1902 **Gooding, G. B.** (1914). Cpl. Rifle Brigade. France, Belgium. Killed in action near Hooge on July 24, 1915.

1875 Gordon-Gilmour, R. G., *C.B.*, *D.S.O.*, *C.V.O.* (Serving Aug. 4, 1914). Col. Grenadier Guards (Hon. Brig.-Gen.). France and Belgium, 1915, 1917, 1918, 1919. *D.* France, 1919.

1874 Gore, F. W. G., T.D. (Mobilized Aug. 1914). Lt.-Col. City of London Yeomanry.

1898 Goring, H., B.A. (Nov. 7, 1914). Lt., temp. Capt., 3rd Hussars (S.R.). Staff-Captain. France.

1882 Goring, W. (Mobilized Aug. 5, 1914). Lt.-Col., Bt.-Col., 2nd Res. Regt. of Cavalry. *D.* § Jan. 1917.

1912 **Goschen, Hon. G. J.** (Sept. 1914). Lt. 5th The Buffs (E. Kent Regt.). India, Mesopotamia. *D.* Mesopotamia, 1916. Died on Jan. 19, 1916, of wounds received in action at Amara.

1903 Gosselin, Rev. G. St. L. H., B.A. (Aug. 6, 1914). Chaplain R.N. H.M.S. *Caesar*, H.M.S. *Agincourt*, H.M.S. *Emperor of India*. Gibraltar, Malta, Bermuda, North Sea, Black Sea.

1900 Gouldesbrough, C., B.M., M.A. (Dec. 1914). Capt. R.A.M.C., 5th London General Hospital. France.

1909 Gow,* J. C., M.A. (Sept. 1914). Lt. 1/4th York & Lancaster Regt. (T.F. Res.). France, Belgium.

1898 **Graham, A. C.** (Sept. 1914). Lt.-Commdr. Hood Bn., R.N. Div. Capt. Grenadier Guards (S.R.), attd. 1st Bn. Antwerp, 1914; Gallipoli,

1915; France, 1916. Killed in action in the Battle of the Ancre on Sept. 12, 1916.

1891 Graham, A. S. (1914). Pte. P.S. Bn., R. Fusiliers.

1911 Graham, F. F., M.A. (Aug. 15, 1914). Capt. 3rd Irish Guards. France, Belgium. *D.* France, 1915.

1910 Grant-Hooper, G., B.A. (Aug. 12, 1914). ‡Lt. 3rd R. Scots, attd. Intelligence Corps (Capt.). Gallipoli, Egypt, Salonika, France, Turkey. *M.C.*, Oct. 8, 1917.

1889 Grant-Thorold, H., B.A. (Mobilized Aug. 1914). Maj. 3rd Northamptonshire Regt.

1902 [Greene, W. A., M.A.] (Nov. 1914). Capt., temp. Maj., 2/1st Bucks Bn., Oxf. & Bucks. Lt. Infty. G.S.O. 2. France, Italy. *O.B.E.* (Mil.). *M.C.*, Jan. 1, 1918. Cavalier, Order of the Crown of Italy. Croix de Guerre.

1910 Greenshields-Leadbetter,* J. G., B.A. (Mobilized Aug. 4, 1914). Capt. Lanarkshire Yeomanry, attd. M.G.C. (Cavalry). Cape Helles, 1915; Egypt, 1916–17; Palestine and Syria, 1917–18. *M.C.*, Sept. 16, 1918.

1906 Greenwood, V. J., B.A. (Serving Aug. 4, 1914). Capt. 10th Hussars. France, Belgium. *M.C.*, June 3, 1916.

1888 Gregorie, F. St. B. (Aug. 19, 1915). Lt. Special Lists. France. *D.* France, 1916, 1918.

1919 Greig, G. G. F. (Nov. 1916). Lt. Rifle Brigade. France, 1917–18. (Wounded and prisoner of war, Mar.–Nov. 1918.)

1912 Greig, J. Y., B.A. (Apr. 17, 1915). Lt. Cameronians, attd. M.G.C.

1919 Griffin, L. C. L. (June 1918). 2nd Lt. Coldstream Guards (S.R.).

1919 Griffin, R. L. (Nov. 15, 1916). Lt. Coldstream Guards (S.R.), attd. 5th Bn. France.

1914 Grigson, W. V., B.A. (Aug. 14, 1916). Lt. 30th Bn., M.G.C. France, 1917, 1918–19; Mesopotamia, 1917; Palestine, 1917–18.

1897 Grisewood, H. J. (Nov. 1, 1914). Lt.-Col. 11th R. Sussex Regt.

1908 **Gull,* F. W. L.,** B.A. (Serving Aug. 4, 1914). Maj. 13th Rifle Brigade. France, 1914–16, 1918. *D.* France, 1914, 1915, 1916. Killed in action at Favreuil on Aug. 25, 1918.

1913 Gull,* R. C. (Nov. 11, 1914). Capt. 4th Rifle Brigade, empld. Instructional duties. France. *D.* France, 1916.

1901 Gunther, F. A., B.A. (Nov. 2, 1915). Lt. General List (T.F. Res.), empld. Recruiting Duties. *M.B.E.* (Mil.). *D.* § Feb. 1917.

1899 Gurney, G. H. (Nov. 1914). Lt. Norfolk Yeomanry. Lt. R. Defence Corps. France.

1917 Guthrie, T. W. B. (Apr. 12, 1918). 2nd Lt. R.G.A. (on demobilization).

1904 **Gwyer, C.,** B.A. (Sept. 27, 1914). Lt. Grenadier Guards. France. Killed in action near St. Leger on Aug. 27, 1918.

1907 **Hadden, A. R.** (Mobilized Aug. 1914). Capt. 9th London Regt. (Queen Victoria's Rifles). France, 1917–18. Missing, now presumed killed in action at Hangard Wood on Apr. 25, 1918.

1908 **Hadden, E. W. R.** (Mobilized Aug. 1914). Maj. 4th Oxf. & Bucks. Lt. Infty. France, Belgium. Died on June 10, 1916, of illness contracted while on active service.

1912 **Haldinstein, F. W.,** B.A. (Sept. 1914). ‡Capt. 2nd London Divl. Sig. Coy., R.E. (T.F.). France. Died on Mar. 7. 1917, of wounds received in action at Bray sur Somme.

1886 Hall, D. B., *M.P.* (1914). Lt. R.N.R. Capt. R.E., empld. Ministry of Munitions. France.

1910 Hall, R. L., B.A. (1914). Headquarters Staff S. African E.F. S. Africa.

1905 Hallett, H. I. P., B.A. (Sept. 2, 1914). Capt. 24th London Regt. (The Queen's). Staff-Captain. France, 1915–17, 1917–18. *M.C.*, Jan. 14 1916. *D.* France, 1915.

1910 Hamer,* G. M., B.A. (Serving Aug. 4, 1914). Lt. 14th Hussars. Mesopotamia.

1919 Hamilton, A. S. L. (Feb. 25, 1916). Lt. 84th Batt., R.F.A. France, Belgium, 1916–18. *M.C.*, Sept. 16, 1918.

1903 Hamilton, C. A. M. B. (Jan. 30, 1915). Lt. Special Lists, empld. Recruiting Duties.

1893 Hamilton, F. A. C. (Serving Aug. 4, 1914). Maj. 1st Cameronians. Asst. Officer, Infantry Record Offices, Warwick. France, Belgium. *M.C.*, June 23, 1915. *D.* France, 1915; § Mar. 1919.

1910 Hammond, M., B.A. (Aug. 1914). Capt. The Buffs (E. Kent Regt.). Capt. Special Lists. Staff-Captain, empld. H.Q. Southern Command. France. Order of St. Stanislas (2nd Class) (with swords). *D.* France, 1916.

1919 Hampson, D. F. (Sept. 22, 1915). 2nd Lt. 5th Rifle Brigade. France, 1917–18.

1906 Hanbury, Rev. G. S., M.A. (June 5, 1917). Chaplain to the Forces (4th Class). France. *O.B.E.* (Mil.). *D.* France, 1919.

1902 Hanbury, R. F., B.A. (Mobilized Aug. 1914). Capt. 4th Bedfordshire Regt. France, 1915.

1911 Hanbury,* R. H. O., B.A. (Aug. 5, 1914). Capt. 15th Hussars. France, Belgium. *M.C.*, June 3, 1919. *D.* France, 1917, 1918.

1907 [Handover, Rev. S. J., M.A.] (Oct. 1915). Chaplain to the Forces (4th Class). Malta, H.M.H.S. *Goorkha.*

1888 Hanmer, Sir W. C. H., Bt. (May 24, 1915). Maj. Special Lists. Maj. Remount Depot. France, 1916–17.

1910 Harding,* R. A. C. (Aug. 5, 1914). Capt. R.A. India, 1914–16; Mesopotamia, 1916–19. *M.B.E.* (Mil.). *D.* Mesopotamia, 1917.

1905 **Harding, R. D. S.** (Mobilized Aug. 1914). Lt. 4th, attd. 1st, Bedfordshire Regt. France. Killed in action on Nov. 9, 1914.

1918 Harding, W. G. (1915). 2nd Lt. 1st Middlesex Regt. Egypt, France. (Invalided Feb. 1917.)

1893 Hardy, C. (Mobilized Aug. 1914). Capt. 12th London Regt. (The Rangers), Maj. 25th King's (Liverpool Regt.). France, Belgium. *D.S.O.*, Nov. 18, 1917. *D.* France, 1917.

1894 Hardy, F. H. (Serving Aug. 4, 1914). Maj., Bt.-Lt.-Col., temp. Lt.-Col., Coldstream Guards, attd. 5th Bn. France, Belgium. *D.* French Orders.

1870 Hardy, G. H., M.A. (Oct. 9, 1914). Maj. Staffordshire Yeomanry (T.F. Res.).

1906 Hargreaves, C. L., B.A. (Mobilized Aug. 1914). Capt. Scots Guards, Res. of Officers. G.S.O. 3 (Bde. Maj.). France. *D.* France, 1915, 1916, 1918.

1901 **Hargreaves, L. R.,** B.A. (Serving Aug. 4, 1914). Capt. 1st Irish Guards. France, 1914–16. *M.C.*, Nov. 14, 1916. Killed in action at Lesboeufs on Sept. 25, 1916.

1910 Harmsworth, A. L. St. B., B.A. (Jan. 18, 1915). 2nd Lt. 13th Gloucestershire Regt. Capt. General List. Asst. Embarkation Staff Officer.

1913 **Harmsworth, Hon. H. A. V. St. G.** (Aug. 1914). Capt. Irish Guards. France. *M.C.*, Feb. 18, 1918. Died on Feb. 12, 1918, of wounds received in action at Cambrai.

1915 Harmsworth,* H. C. A. (Oct. 28, 1916). 2nd Lt. R.G.A. Lt. R.M.A. Aegean Sea, Dardanelles, Bosphorus, S. Russia.

1891 Harris, Hon. A. C., B.A. (Mar. 25, 1916). Lt. R. Defence Corps. Lt., Acting Capt., T.F. Res. *D.* § Mar. 1919.

1895 Harris, Hon. A. F. W. (Serving Aug. 4, 1914). Maj., Bt.-Lt.-Col., K.R.R.C., attd. 51st Queen's (R. W. Surrey Regt.). France. *D.* § Mar. and Aug. 1919.

1909 Harris, Hon. G. St. V., B.A. (Mobilized Aug. 4, 1914). Capt. R. E. Kent Yeomanry. A.D.C. France. *M.C.*, June 4, 1917. *D.* France, 1916.

1919 Harris, R. A. M., B.A. (Oct. 1914). Capt. 11th Border Regt. France, Belgium, Germany, 1917–19.

1870 Harris, Baron, B.A., *G.C.S.I.*, *G.C.I.E.*, T.D. *A.D.C.* to the King. Late Col. E. Kent Yeomanry. *K.C.B.*

1919 Harrison, E. S. S. (Sept. 16, 1915). Lt. A/110th Bde., R.F.A. (Capt.). France, 1915–17.

1902 **Harrison, F. I.** (Nov. 2, 1915). Lt. 1st R. W. Kent Regt. (Capt.). France, 1916, 1918; Italy, 1917. Killed in action near Aire on May 8, 1918.

1904 Harrison, T. D., B.A. (Apr. 16, 1915). Lt. 9th Hampshire Regt.

1893 Hartley, E. G. J., M.A. (Jan. 28, 1916). Capt., Bt.-Maj., R.E. France. Cavalier of the Order of St. Maurice and St. Lazarus. *D.* France, 1917.

1919 Harwood, A. C. (Jan. 1917). ‡2nd Lt. 16th R. Warwickshire Regt. France.

1919 Harwood, J. E. G. (Apr. 9, 1918). 2nd Class Aircraftsman, M.T., R.A.F.

1913 Havens, V. B., B.A. (Aug. 1917). Lt. Junior Grade, U.S. Navy.

1908 **Hawarden,* Viscount,** B.A. (Mobilized Aug. 1914). Lt. 3rd Coldstream Guards. France, Belgium. Died on Aug. 25, 1914, of wounds received in action at Landrecies.

1904 Hayter, Rev. G. T. M. I., M.A. (Aug. 8, 1916). Chaplain to the Forces (4th Class), attd. 9th R. Welch Fusiliers. France.

1911 Hayter,* J. B. A. (Aug. 5, 1914). Lt. 15th Hussars. Capt. M.G.C. (Cavalry). France. *D.* France, 1919.

1910 Hayter,* M. C. (Oct. 1, 1914). Lt. 1st County of London Yeomanry. Capt., Flying Officer, R.A.F. France, 1915. *D.* § Aug. 1919.

1919 Hayter-Hames, G. C. (Aug. 20, 1916). Lt. 1st Life Guards. France.

1919 Heald, L. F., B.A. (Feb. 1916). Lt. 528th Field Coy., R.E. France, 1917; Italy, 1917–19. Italian Bronze Medal for Valour.

1905 Heaton,* T. B., D.M. (Sept. 28, 1914). Capt. R.A.M.C. (S.R.). N.W. Frontier, 1915; India, 1915–19. *O.B.E.* (Mil.).

1910 **Hellyer, G. E.** (Aug. 1914). Capt. 10th Hampshire Regt. Gallipoli. Died on Aug. 22, 1915, of wounds received in action in Gallipoli.

1892 Helme, E. (Mobilized Aug. 1914). Maj. Glamorganshire Yeomanry, attd. 15th Welsh Regt. (Lt.-Col.). France. *D.S.O.*, Dec. 2, 1918; *Bar*, Feb. 15, 1919. *D.* France, 1918, 1919.

1896 Henderson, Hon. F. (1914). Ermelo Commando S. African E.F. Lt. S. Irish Horse. Africa.

1896 [Henderson, H. L., M.A.] (Jan. 14, 1915). Lt. 1st Devonshire Regt. Lt. General List (Capt. G.S.O. 2). Egypt, 1915–16; Singapore, 1917–19.
1893 Henderson, P. B., B.A. (Oct. 1914). A.B., R.N.V.R. (till 1916). ‡2nd Lt. 7th County of London Vol. Regt.
1899 Henderson, R. E. (Sept. 1914). Lt. R. Horse Guards. Gallipoli, Egypt, France.
1907 Herbert, E. R. H., B.A. (Serving Aug. 4, 1914). Capt. K.R.R.C. (Maj.). D.A.Q.M.G. India, 1914; France, 1915–16. *D.* §Mar. 1918.
1919 Herbert, J. B. (Sept. 1917). 2nd Lt. 2/4th Queen's (R. W. Surrey Regt.). France, Belgium. *M.C.*, Dec. 2, 1918.
1902 Herbert, V. A., M.A. (May 5, 1915). Capt. and Adjt. I.A.R.O., attd. 29th Lancers (Bde. Maj.). India and N.W. Frontier, 1915; France, 1915–18; Palestine, 1918–19. *M.C.*, June 3, 1918. *D.* Palestine, 1919.
1886 Herdman, E. C. (Aug. 5, 1914). Maj. N. Irish Horse. France.
1898 **Hermon, E. W.** (Mobilized Aug. 1914). Maj. King Edward's Horse. Temp. Lt.-Col. 24th Northumberland Fusiliers. France and Belgium, 1915–17. *D.S.O.*, June 4, 1917. *D.* France, 1916 twice. Killed in action at the Battle of Arras on Apr. 9, 1917.
1919 Hersey, R. B. (May 11, 1917). Capt. 14th F.A., U.S. Army (Maj.).
1909 Hervey-Wyatt, R. B., M.A. Dresser, Hospital Ship, R.N.
1890 Heurtley, Rev. A. C., B.A. (Oct. 12, 1915). Chaplain to the Forces (4th Class). Salonika. *D.* Salonika, 1917, 1918, 1919.
1919 Hewins, M. G. (Feb. 24, 1917). 2nd Lt. 1st Middlesex Regt. 2nd Lt. T.F. Res., attd. Colonial Office.
1896 Hewitt, A. S. (Serving Aug. 4, 1914). Maj., temp. Lt.-Col., R. W. Kent Regt. P.M. France, Belgium, Italy. *O.B.E.* (Mil.). *D.S.O.*, Jan. 1, 1917. Croix de Guerre. *D.* France, 1915, 1916; Italy, 1918, 1919.
1911 **Hewitt, W. G.** (Aug. 7, 1914). 2nd Lt. R. Scots. France and Belgium. Croix de Chevalier de la Légion d'Honneur. Killed in action at Ypres on Oct. 13, 1914.
1903 **Heywood, R. M.** (Aug. 14, 1914). Lt. 2nd The Buffs (E. Kent Regt.). France, Belgium. Died on Feb. 15, 1915, of wounds received in action near St. Eloi.
1883 Higgins-Bernard, F. T. (Mobilized Aug. 1914). Lt.-Col. 3rd Oxf. & Bucks. Lt. Infty. Temp. Lt.-Col. Special Lists. Staff Appointment. France, 1918.
1882 Higson, W. (Nov. 1914). Capt. Remount Dept., District Remount Officer.
1892 Hill, Rev. E. St. C., B.A. (Sept. 1914). Chaplain S. African E.F. German S.W. Africa, 1914; Egypt (Senussi), 1915; France, 1916–18. *M.C.*, Jan. 1, 1917. (Prisoner of war, Mar.–Nov. 1918.)
1892 Hinckes, R. T. (Oct. 5, 1914). 2nd Lt. Herefordshire Regt. (T.F. Res.). Hon. Capt., empld. Recruiting Duties.
1906 **Hinckesman, R. B.,** M.A. (Aug. 15, 1914). Lce.-Cpl. 1st King Edward's Horse. France. Accidentally killed at La Bassée on Oct. 20, 1915.
1890 Hindley, G. D., B.M., M.A. (Apr. 24, 1915). Lt.-Col. 50th Field Amb., R.A.M.C. France, Belgium. *M.C.*, June 3, 1918. *D.* France, 1917 twice, 1919.
1897 Hoare, A. H. (Aug. 29, 1914). Lt. R.G.A., empld. War Office.
1897 Hoare, G. L. (Mobilized Aug. 5, 1914). Maj., Bt.-Lt.-Col., R.G.A. Res.

of Officers. France. *C.B.E.* (Mil.). Croix de Chevalier de la Légion d'Honneur. *D.* § Feb. 1917.

1880 Hobhouse, Rt. Hon. C. E. H. Hon. Col. 6th Gloucestershire Regt.

1912 **Hobson, J. C.** (Aug. 1914). Lt. 12th R. Scots (Capt.). Lt. 116th Coy., M.G.C. France, Belgium. Killed in action near St. Julien on July 31, 1917.

1908 Hodder-Williams, R. W., M.A. (June 1915). ‡Lt. Princess Patricia's Canadian L.I. (Capt.). Belgium, France, 1915–16. *M.C.*, Nov. 14, 1916.

1901 Hodge, Rev. C. E. V., M.A. (Apr. 16, 1918). Chaplain to the Forces (4th Class).

1904 Hodges, C. S., B.A. (Aug. 24, 1915). 2nd Lt. Connaught Rangers.

1897 Hodgkinson, W. B., B.A. Lt. and Qr.-Master R. Sussex Regt.

1911 **Hodgson,* W. N.** (Sept. 1914). Lt. 9th Devonshire Regt. France, 1915–16. *M.C.*, Jan. 14, 1916. *D.* France, 1915. Killed in action on the Somme on July 1, 1916.

1919 Hoes, G. (May 14, 1917). Lt. Air Service, U.S. Army. France, 1918–19.

1896 **Hogarth, A. H.**, D.M., *D.C.M.* (Mobilized Aug. 5, 1914). Maj. R.A.M.C., attd. R.A.F. France, Belgium, 1914–16; Italy, 1918; Mediterranean, 1918. *C.B.E.* (Mil.). *D.* 1918. Died on Sept. 5, 1919, of illness contracted on active service.

1919 Hogg, A. R. (Dec. 2, 1914). Capt. 7th R. W. Kent Regt. France, Belgium, 1915–17.

1912 Hogg, K. W. (Oct. 5, 1914). 2nd Lt. 9th Gloucestershire Regt. Lt., Acting Capt., Irish Guards. France.

1883 Holden, E. C. S., *D.S.O.*, T.D. (Mobilized Aug. 1914). Maj., Hon. Lt.-Col., Derbyshire Yeomanry. (Resigned.)

1895 Holland, B. T. (Feb. 13, 1915). Qr.-Master, Hon. Lt., R.A.M.C. (T.F.).

1919 Holland-Martin, E. (Aug. 1918). 2nd Lt. 3rd Hussars (after demobilization).

1910 Holley, E. J. H., B.A. (Mobilized Aug. 1914). Capt. Royal 1st Devon Yeomanry, attd. 16th Devonshire Regt. (Lt.-Col.). Gallipoli, Egypt, Palestine, France. *M.C.*, Jan. 1, 1918. *D.* France, 1919.

1903 Holloway, G. J. W., B.A. (Oct. 1914). Lt. 9th W. Yorkshire Regt. Gallipoli, 1915; Egypt, 1916; France, 1916. (Prisoner of war, 1916, afterwards interned in Holland.)

1919 Holmes, R. E. (May 5, 1917). Lt. Grenadier Guards. France.

1919 Holmes, S. L. (July 15, 1915). Lt., Acting Maj., 327th Siege Batt., R.G.A. France, Belgium. *M.C.*, Sept. 16, 1918. *D.* France, 1918, 1919.

1889 Holroyd, G. W. F., M.A. (Aug. 4, 1914). Cpl. R.E. (Special Bde.), attd. War Office. France, 1915–16.

1911 [Holroyd,* M., M.A.] (Aug. 17, 1914). Capt. 3rd Hampshire Regt., empld. War Office (Intelligence Dept.). France, 1915.

1900 **Holt, J.** (Mobilized Aug. 1914). Capt. 6th Manchester Regt. (T.F.). Egypt, Gallipoli. Killed in action in Gallipoli on June 4, 1915.

1892 Home, Earl of, M.A. (Mobilized Aug. 1914). Lt.-Col. Lanarkshire Yeomanry. Gallipoli, 1915; Egypt, Palestine, 1916–17. *D.* Palestine, 1917.

1901 Hoole, F. W. (Oct. 5, 1914). Lt. 6th London Regt. (Rifles). (Resigned.)

1905 **Hope, G. E.** (Serving Aug. 4, 1914). Capt. Grenadier Guards. France,

Belgium. *M.C.*, Feb. 18, 1915. *D.* France, 1916, 1917. Died on May 9, 1918.

1919 Hope, H. J. (May 21, 1917). 2nd Lt. Scots Guards. France, 1918. *D.* France, 1918.

1920 Hope, W. (Feb. 12, 1918). Gnr. 211th Batt., R.F.A.

1897 Hope, W. G. I., B.A. (Dec. 14, 1914). Capt. 11th K.R.R.C. Capt. General List. France.

1887 Hordern, Rev. H. M., M.A. (Serving Aug. 1914). Chaplain (4th Class) 6th R. Sussex Regt.

1898 Horlick, E. B., B.A. (Dec. 12, 1915). Lt. R.A.F., 2nd Class Technical Officer (Capt.). France, 1917.

1905 Horlick, J. N., B.A. (Aug. 12, 1914). Capt., Bt.-Maj., Coldstream Guards (Lt.-Col. G.S.O. 1.). France, 1914, 1915, 1916; Salonika, 1916–18; Constantinople, 1918–19. *O.B.E.* (Mil.). *M.C.*, June 4, 1917. Croix de Chevalier de la Légion d'Honneur. Greek Military Cross. Order of the White Eagle (4th Class) (with swords). *D.* France, 1916; Salonika, 1917, 1918, 1919.

1906 Horn, K. K., M.A. (Aug. 1914). ‡Maj., Squadron Commdr., R.A.F. France, Belgium. *M.C.*, Jan. 1, 1918. Belgian Croix de Guerre.

1908 Horn, M. L., B.A. (Aug. 1914). ‡Capt. R.A.F. France, Belgium. Croix de Guerre. Belgian Croix de Guerre. *D.* France, 1918.

1908 Horner, B. S., B.A. (Mobilized Aug. 1914). Capt. 1/6th E. Surrey Regt., attd. 2/30th Punjabis. India.

1881 Horner, J. FitzL. Hon. Maj. late 3rd R. Devonshire Regt. Asst. Officer Record Offices. *D.* § Nov. 1918.

1912 **Horsley, O.** (Dec. 15, 1914). Capt. Gordon Highlanders and R.A.F. France, Belgium. *M.C.*, Oct. 2, 1916; *Bar*, June 22, 1918. *D.* France, 1915. Accidentally killed in England on Aug. 19, 1918.

1904 **Hosking, H. E.** (Serving Aug. 4, 1914). Capt. 66th, attd. 62nd, Punjabis, Indian Army. Mesopotamia. Killed in action on Feb. 3, 1917.

1887 Houldsworth, Sir H. H., M.A. (1915). Maj. 4th Arg. & Suth'd. Highlanders (Recruiting Duties).

1893 Houldsworth, W. T. R., M.A. (Mobilized Aug. 1914). Maj. 2nd Ayrshire Yeomanry. Egypt, Palestine. T.D. Order of the Nile (3rd Class).

1904 Howard, A., M.A. (July 13, 1915). Lt., Acting Capt., 17th R. Fusiliers.

1908 Howard, G., B.A. (Sept. 1914). Lt. 6th R. Fusiliers. France.

1919 Howard-Langton, C. M. (Jan. 15, 1915). Lt. 1st Gloucestershire Regt., attd. No. 3 Coy., M.G.C. (Capt.). France, 1915–16.

1919 Howe, G. W. (1918). Cadet R.M.C., Sandhurst.

1885 Howe, R. B. B. (Rejoined May 16, 1916). Maj. 25th (Works) Bn., Durham L.I.

1919 Howe, R. M. (July 29, 1915). Lt., Acting Capt., 3rd, attd. 7th, R. Sussex Regt. France, 1916–19. *M.C.*, Jan. 11, 1919.

1893 Howell, G. C. L., B.A. (Apr. 1, 1917). Lt., Acting Capt., I.A.R.O., attd. Jacob's Horse. India.

1903 Howes, S. G. (Serving Aug. 4, 1914). Capt., temp. Maj., 21st Lancers. G.S.O. 2, 3rd Cavalry Div. France, 1914–19. *D.S.O.*, Jan. 1, 1919. *M.C.*, Jan. 1, 1917. *D.* France, 1916, 1918 twice.

Hubbard, B. J. (June 2, 1915). 2nd Lt. Grenadier Guards. France, Belgium. *M.C.*, Sept. 26, 1917. Killed in action on Dec. 1, 1917.

1904 Hubbard, E. W. (Jan. 30, 1918). 2nd Lt. Welsh Guards, empld. Guards M.G. Regt.

1902 Hubbard, Rev. H. E., M.A. (Dec. 7, 1914). Chaplain to the Forces (4th Class). France, 1914, 1916–18. *D.S.O.*, Feb. 18, 1918. *M.C.*, Sept. 16, 1918. *D.* France, 1917, 1918.

1902 Hughes, G. S. (Mobilized Aug. 1914). Capt. R.A.M.C. (T.F.).

1919 Hulley, B. M. (Oct. 2, 1918). Cpl. Harvard Naval Unit, 1st District.

1898 Humphrys, F. H. (Serving Aug. 4, 1914). Maj. Indian Political Service. Temp. 2nd Lt., Hon. Maj., Pilot Officer, R.A.F. India, N.W. Frontier, 1914–17; France, 1918. *D.* Mahsuds, 1918.

1902 Hunt, G. H., D.M. (Nov. 25, 1914). Capt., Bt.-Maj., R.A.M.C. (T.F.), empld. Ministry of Munitions. France. *D.* France, 1915.

1906 Hunter, E. A., B.A. (Sept. 30, 1914). Lt., temp. Capt., R.A.S.C. Staff-Captain, War Office (Q.M.G. 3). France, Belgium. *O.B.E.* (Mil.). *D.* § Mar. 1919.

1898 Hunter, P. H. R., M.A. E. African Mounted Rifles. E. Africa.

Hurley, F. S. G. (Sept. 1917). Lt. R.A.F. Died on Mar. 4, 1919, of illness contracted while on active service.

1913 **Hurst-Brown, C.** (Dec. 16, 1914). 2nd Lt. 2nd Oxf. & Bucks. Lt. Infty. France. Died on Sept. 26, 1915, of wounds received in action at Givenchy.

1919 Hussey, C. E. A. (May 1, 1918). ‡2nd Lt. R.F.A.

1899 Hutchinson, G. T., M.A. (Mobilized Aug. 4, 1914). Lt. Q.O. Oxfordshire Hussars. Staff-Captain. France. *M.C.*, Jan. 1, 1917.

1892 Ilchester, Earl of (Aug. 4, 1914). Capt. Coldstream Guards Res. of Officers. Graded as G.S.O. 3. France, Gallipoli, Egypt, Russia. *O.B.E.* (Mil.). Croix de Chevalier de la Légion d'Honneur. *D.* France, 1916.

1901 Illingworth, D. (Oct. 19, 1914). Lt.-Commdr. R.N.V.R. Maj. R.A.F. Gallipoli, 1915; Egypt, 1915.

1896 Illingworth, W. L., B.A. (Nov. 3, 1914). Capt. 7th W. Yorkshire Regt. Lt., Acting Capt. and Adjt., R.E.

1911 Ince, N. S. (Sept. 1914). ‡Capt. 19th Manchester Regt. France, 1915–18. *M.C.*, Jan. 1, 1918.

1909 **Ingram,* G. S.,** B.A. (Serving Aug. 4, 1914). Lt. 2nd Queen's (R. W. Surrey Regt.). France, Belgium, 1914. Killed in action near Ypres on Oct. 21, 1914.

1900 Irvine, A. L., M.A. (Serving Aug. 4, 1914). Capt. Unattached List, T.F., Charterhouse O.T.C.

1897 Irvine, L. H., M.A. (Mar. 21, 1916). Capt. General List (T.F. Res.), empld. Ministry of National Service. *M.B.E.* (Mil.).

1874 Irwin, Hon. G. R., *C.S.I.* (Sept. 1914). Capt. 9th R. Irish Fusiliers. Capt. Special Lists (A.P.M.).

1913 Iswolsky, G. (1914). Russian Army. Russia.

1897 Jacomb-Hood, Rev. F. E. S., M.A. (May 1918). Chaplain to the Forces (4th Class). France, Belgium, 1918–19.

1912 James, H. H., B.A. (Sept. 1, 1914). 2nd Lt. 6th Somerset L.I. Capt., Flight Commdr., R.A.F. France, 1915; Egypt, 1915–16; Palestine, 1916–17; Aden, 1917; Italy, 1918–19. Croce di Guerra.

1908 James, R. B., B.A. (Aug. 1914). Capt. R. Horse Guards. France, 1915–18. *D.* France, 1917.

1901 Jelf, H. W., M.A. (June 8, 1916). Sub-Lt. R.N.V.R., H.M.S. *Kildonan Castle*. Grand Fleet, White Sea Station, North American and West Indies Station, E. Coast of Africa, S.E. Coast of America.

1895 Jerome, A. J. Smith, B.A. (Dec. 1, 1915). Lt. Interpreter, Special Lists.

1919 Jerome, J. S. (Jan. 9, 1915). Lt. 11th Rifle Brigade. Lt. General List, attd. Signal Service. France. *M.C.*, June 3, 1919.

1892 Jervoise, F. H. T. (Mobilized Aug. 1914). Capt., Acting Maj., Hampshire Yeomanry, attd. Labour Corps. *D.* § Aug. 1919.

1909 **Johnson, C. B.,** B.A. (Mobilized Aug. 1914). Lt.-Col. 6th Sherwood Foresters. France, Belgium. *D.* France, 1916, 1917 twice. Killed in action on Sept. 21, 1917.

1919 Johnson, M. M. (Aug. 10, 1917). Lt. 2nd Scots Guards. France, 1918.

1898 Johnson, P., M.A. (Dec. 20, 1915). Maj. R.A.O.C. D.A.D. Ordnance. France, 1917–19.

1903 Johnston, G. D., B.C.L., M.A. (Nov. 23, 1915). Lt. R.G.A. (S.R.) (Capt.), attd. H.Q. as Courts-Martial Officer. France, Belgium.

1919 Johnston, H. W. (Aug. 14, 1916). Sergt. 8th Canadian Engineers (C.S.M.). France, Belgium, 1918–19.

Johnstone, F. J. L. (Oct. 11, 1914). Capt. 2nd K.R.R.C. France, Belgium, 1915–17. *M.C.*, Oct. 20, 1916. Died on Aug. 29, 1916, of wounds received in action at High Wood.

1877 Jones, Very Rev. Ll. Wynne, M.A. (June 19, 1915). Chaplain to the Forces (4th Class).

1884 Jones, Rev. P. H., M.A. (Serving Aug. 4, 1914). Chaplain and Instructor Commander, R.N. Grand Fleet, H.M.S. *Vanguard*, 1914–16. *C.B.E.* (Mil.). *D.* Naval Dispatches, 1916.

1913 Jones-Bateman, R. (Sept. 2, 1914). ‡Capt. 3rd Welsh Regt. France, 1915–16; N. Russia, 1918.

1917 Jowitt, R. L. P. (Aug. 20, 1917). Pte. 2/28th London Regt. (Artists Rifles).

1907 Joynson, W. O. H., B.A. (Mobilized Aug. 5, 1914). ‡Lt., Acting Capt. R.F.A. Egypt, 1915–16; France, 1916–19; Germany, 1919.

1919 Karminski, J. M. (Apr. 20, 1917). 2nd Lt. R.G.A. (S.R.). France, 1917–18.

1903 Keeling, E. A., B.A. Lt. R.N.V.R.

1905 **Kekewich, A. St. J. M.,** M.A. (Serving Aug. 4, 1914). Capt. Devonshire Regt., attd. 8th Bn. (Adjt.). France. *D.* France, 1915. Killed in action at the Battle of Loos on Sept. 25, 1915.

1872 Kemble, H. W. (Apr. 1, 1915). Maj. 4th Q.O. Cameron Highlanders (T.F.).

1919 Kendall, R. Y. T. (Aug. 5, 1915). Lt. Grenadier Guards. France, Germany.

1912 Kendrew, A. (Feb. 2, 1916). Sergt. 21st M.T., Vehicle Reception Park, R.A.S.C. France.

1919 Kent-Hughes, W. S. (Aug. 1914). ‡Maj. Australian Light Horse, attd. Educational Dept. A.I.F. Egypt, Gallipoli, Sinai, Palestine, Syria, 1914–19.

1882 Kenyon, Lord, *K.C.V.O.*, T.D. (Sept. 1914). Col. *A.D.C.* to the King. Col. 2/1st Welsh Horse (T.F. Res.). *D.* § Feb. 1917.

1898 Kenyon, H. M. (Mobilized Aug. 1914). Maj. R.A.S.C., E. Lancs. Divl. Train (T.F. Res.).

1901 Kenyon, J. R., B.A. (Mobilized Aug. 4, 1914). Maj. A/191st Bde., R.F.A. France, Egypt, Palestine, Syria. *M.C.*, Jan. 1, 1918. *D.* Palestine, 1917.

1920 Kenyon-Slaney, G. W. (Jan. 4, 1918). 2nd Lt. 1st Grenadier Guards. France, Belgium, Germany, 1918–19.

1909 Kenyon-Slaney, R. O. R. (Serving Aug. 4, 1914). Capt. Grenadier Guards. A.D.C. to Governor-General of Canada.

1895 Keppel, B. W. A. (Sept. 1914). Maj. Staffordshire Yeomanry (T.F. Res.). France, 1917–18.

1881 Kerr, R. J., B.A. (Oct. 1, 1914). Lt.-Col. 94th Training Res. Bn. *D.* § Feb. 1917.

1903 Kershaw, H. O., B.A. (Aug. 1, 1918). 2nd Lt. 1st Madras Guards, I.D.F. India.

1919 Kinchin-Smith, A. E. (Oct. 7, 1916). Capt. 6th Shropshire L.I. France. *M.C.*, Sept. 16, 1918. *D.* France, 1917, 1918.

1907 King, C., B.A. (Feb. 7, 1917). Lt., temp. Capt., I.A.R.O. (Cavalry). India.

1897 King, E. J., B.A. (Mobilized Aug. 5, 1914). Lt.-Col., temp. Col., 7th Middlesex Regt. Mediterranean, 1914; France, Belgium, 1915–19. *C.M.G.*, June 3, 1916. T.D. *D.* France, 1915, 1916 twice.

1919 King, L. M. (Jan. 1, 1917). 2nd Lt. 2/5th Gloucestershire Regt. France, 10 months.

1902 Kingdon, J. (Serving Aug. 4, 1914). Capt., Bt.-Maj., 86th Carnatic Inf., Indian Army. Balkans, Black Sea.

1900 Kingsmill, A. de P. (Mobilized Aug. 4, 1914). Capt. Grenadier Guards Res. of Officers. Temp. Lt.-Col. 7th The Buffs (E. Kent Regt.). France. *D.S.O.*, June 4, 1917. *M.C.*, June 3 1916. *D.* France, 1917.

1918 Kirby-Smith, C. M. (June 15, 1918). Cadet R.F.A. Reception Bde.

1897 **Kirkpatrick, E. H.** (Serving Aug. 4, 1914). Capt., Bt.-Maj., 2nd Oxf. & Bucks. Lt. Infty. France. *D.* France, 1915. Killed in action at Richebourg on May 16, 1915.

1897 Kirlew, T. O., M.A. (July 23, 1915). Capt. 11th Sherwood Foresters.

1897 Knox-Little, W. L. W. (Sept. 1, 1914). ‡Maj. M.G.C. (Cavalry). France, 1915–19. *M.C.*, Nov. 20, 1917; *Bar*, Sept. 16, 1918. Belgian Croix de Guerre.

1920 Kyle, A. G. (Serving Aug. 4, 1914). Capt. R.M.L.I. Egypt, Gallipoli, Balkans, France. *D.* France, 1917.

1893 Kynaston, W. R. O., B.A. (Mobilized Aug. 5, 1914). Maj. Shropshire Yeomanry. Egypt, Palestine.

1877 Lamington, Baron, B.A., *G.C.M.G.*, *G.C.I.E.*, T.D. (Mobilized Aug. 1914). Lt.-Col. Lanarkshire Yeomanry. County Commandant, King's Bodyguard for Scotland.

1918 Lance, G., B.A. (Oct. 29, 1914). Capt. Border Regt. (Lt.-Col.). France, 1915, 1916.

1898 Landale, H. R., B.A. (Feb. 12, 1915). Capt. I.A.R.O., attd. 36th Jacob's Horse, Indian Remount Depot. France, 1915.

1891 Lane, A. E. C., M.A. (Oct. 1, 1915). Lt. Manitoba Regt.

1898 Langford-James, J. W. L., M.A. Barrister-at-Law, Ecclesiastical Establishment, Bengal. India.

1913 Langley, H. F. G. Inns of Court O.T.C. (Resigned.)

1908 Lascelles, F. W., B.A. (Mobilized Aug. 1914). Capt. Sussex Yeomanry, attd. 16th R. Sussex Regt. Gallipoli, 1915; Egypt and Palestine, 1916–18; France, 1918. *M.C.*, Feb. 15, 1919.

1905 Lascelles, H. F., B.A. (Aug. 16, 1916). ‡Lt. 1st Welsh Guards. British E. Africa, 1914–16; France, Belgium, 1916–17. Croix de Guerre (with gold star).

1911 Lasseter, F. M., M.A. (Aug. 5, 1914). ‡Capt. 4th K.O.Y.L.I. Staff-Captain D.A.A.G. France, 1914, 1917, 1918. (Invalided Apr. 1918.)

1906 Lattey, J. T., B.A. (Aug. 5, 1914). ‡Lt. I.A.R.O., attd. 14th K.G.O. Sikhs. Egypt, Palestine.

1887 Laurie, R. M., B.A. (Mobilized Aug. 1914). Lt.-Col. R.F.A. (T.F.). Egypt, Palestine. *D.S.O.*, Aug. 15, 1917. Order of the Nile (3rd Class). *D.* Egypt, 1917.

1919 Laurie, V. S. (Nov. 28, 1914). Lt., Acting Capt., R.F.A. France, Palestine. *D.* Egypt, 1917; Palestine, 1918.

1907 **Laurie, W. J. C.** 2nd Lt. I.A.R.O., attd. 124th Duke of Cornwall's Baluchistan Inf. Mesopotamia. Killed in action on Jan. 6, 1917.

1901 Lavender, P., B.A. (Dec. 14, 1915). Lt. 6th Devonshire Regt.

1906 **Lawrence, H. R. L.,** B.A. (Serving Aug. 4, 1914). Capt. Indian Infantry. Drowned in the sinking of the *Persia* on Dec. 30, 1917.

1909 **Lawson, F. H. R.** (Aug. 1914). 2nd Lt. R. Bucks. Hussars. Accidentally killed on Nov. 19, 1914.

1911 Ledward, P. A., B.A. (Aug. 31, 1914). ‡Lt. 9th Hampshire Regt. Staff-Captain 23rd Inf. Bde. France. *M.C.*, Sept. 22, 1918. *D.* France, 1918.

1911 **Lee, M. P. E.** (Serving Aug. 4, 1914). Lt. 6th Dragoon Guards. France. *M.C.*, Feb. 1, 1919. Killed in action on Mar. 26, 1918.

1910 Lees, B. P. T. (Mobilized Aug. 4, 1914). Capt. 1/1st Dorset Yeomanry. Egypt, Palestine, Syria. *M.C.*, Mar. 8, 1919.

1910 Lees, G. W. M., B.A. (Serving Aug. 4, 1914). Lt. 17th Lancers. France.

1905 **Lees, Sir T. E. K., Bt.,** B.A. (Mobilized Aug. 1914). Lt. Dorset Yeomanry. Gallipoli. Died on Aug. 24, 1915, of wounds received in action at Suvla Bay.

1912 Le Fleming, J. N. (Dec. 1914). Lt. Kent Cyclist Bn. (T.F.). India, N.W. Frontier.

1898 Lefroy, A. L. M., M.A. (Mar. 24, 1915). Lt. 4th Devonshire Regt.

1901 **Legge, Hon. G.** (Sept. 4, 1914). Capt. 7th S. Staffordshire Regt. Gallipoli. Killed in action in Gallipoli on Aug. 9, 1915.

1909 Leigh, C. E. (Aug. 15, 1914). Lt., temp. Capt., 3rd The Buffs (E. Kent Regt.). R.T.O.

1912 **Leigh-Pemberton, T. E. G.** (Sept. 1914). Lt. 13th London Regt. France, 1914–15. Killed in action at Laventie on Jan. 11, 1915.

1888 **Leighton, Sir B. B. M., Bt.,** T.D. (Mobilized Aug. 4, 1914). Maj. Westmorland & Cumberland Yeomanry (T.F. Res.) (Lt.-Col.). Pilot R.F.C. France, 1915. Died, Jan. 1919, of illness.

1899 Leitrim, Earl of (Sept. 22, 1914). Maj. 11th R. Inniskilling Fusiliers. France.

1919 Lenanton, G. F. R. (Mar. 1915). Lt. R.H.A. (Capt.). France, 1915–18.

1919 Leng, B. (Jan. 15, 1917). Lt. Coldstream Guards. France, Belgium.

1877 Lennard, Sir H. A. H. F., Bt. (Sept. 16, 1914). Lt.-Col. 11th Cheshire Regt. Belgium, 1915–16; France, 1917–18. Belgian Croix de Guerre.

1913 Le Roy-Lewis, S. H. (Dec. 23, 1914). Lt. 9th Lancers, attd. M.G.C. France.

1893 Leschallas, J. H. P. (Aug. 1914). Maj. 4th Arg. & Suth'd. Highlanders. France, 1914. *D.* § Aug. 1918. (Relinquished Commission on account of ill health contracted on active service, Nov. 1918.)

1907 Lethbridge, M. H. B., B.A. (Aug. 14, 1916). Lt. I.A.R.O., Cavalry. India.

1901 **Leveson Gower, W. G. G.,** M.A. (Serving Aug. 4, 1914). Lt. Inns of Court O.T.C. Capt. G.S.O. 3. Eastern Command, Southern Army and 67th Div. (1915–17). Lt. 1st Coldstream Guards (S.R.). France, 1918. Killed in action at Awoingt, near Cambrai, on Oct. 9,1918.

1909 Lewis, O. (Mobilized Aug. 1914). Lt. 2nd County of London Yeomanry. Egypt, Sinai.

1900 Lewisham, Viscount (Mobilized Aug. 1914). Lt.-Col. Staffordshire Yeomanry. Egypt, Sinai, Palestine, Syria. Order of the Nile (4th Class).

1914 Ley, C., B.A. (Mar. 9, 1916). Pte. R.A.S.C. (M.T.). France, Belgium, 1916–18.

Ley, J. W. Pte. London Regt. France. Killed in action, Jan. 1918.

1918 Liddon, J. H. C., B.A. (Dec. 3, 1915). 2nd Lt. 5th Somerset L.I. France, Belgium, 1917. (Invalided on account of wounds, May 1918.)

1911 Lillingston, E. G. G., B.A. (Sept. 4, 1914). Lt. 4th Dragoon Guards. Belgium, France, Germany, 1914–18. *D.* France, 1917.

1913 Little, W. J. N. (Sept. 1, 1914). Maj. 3rd Bedfordshire Regt. Maj. M.G.C. France. *D.* France, 1917, 1918.

1888 Littledale, J. B., B.A. (1915). Capt. 24th Motor Amb. Convoy, R.A.S.C. France, Belgium. *D.* France, 1919.

1893 Livingstone, W. H. D. (Mar. 4, 1915). Capt. 3rd Northumberland Fusiliers, attd. Labour Corps. France. *D.* France, 1917.

1880 **Llangattock, Lord,** B.C.L., M.A. (Jan. 1915). Maj. 4th Welsh Bde., R.F.A. France. Died at Boulogne on Nov. 2, 1916, of wounds received in action.

1879 Lloyd, E. T., M.A. (Sept. 16, 1914). Capt. T.F. Res., attd. 2nd G.H.Q. Res. M.T. Coy., R.A.S.C. France. *D.* France, 1918.

1897 Lloyd, J. C. (Mobilized Aug. 1914). Capt. 3rd S. Wales Borderers. A.P.M. France. *M.C.*, Jan. 1, 1917. *D.* France, 1918, 1919.

1910 Lloyd, L. S., B.A. (Serving Aug. 4,1914). Lt., Acting Capt., 18th Hussars. France. *M.C.*, June 3, 1916.

1891 **Lloyd-Baker, M. G.** (Mobilized Aug. 1914). Capt. R. Gloucestershire Hussars. Gallipoli, Egypt. *D.* Egypt, 1917. Missing, presumed killed in action at Katia, Sinai, on Apr. 23, 1916.

1903 **Lluellyn, R. C.** (Dec. 5, 1915). Lt. 7th Lincolnshire Regt. France. Killed in action on Aug. 13, 1918.

Lockerbie, H. (Jan. 10, 1916). 2nd Lt. M.G.C. France. Killed in action at Courcelles on Aug. 21, 1918.

1897 Lomax, E. P. S. (Sept. 26, 1915). 2nd Lt. 12th Rifle Brigade. Lt., Acting Capt., General List (Asst. Area Gas Officer).

1881 **Longford, Earl of,** B.A., *K.P.*, *M.V.O.* (Serving Aug. 4, 1914). Brig.-Gen. 2nd S. Midland Mounted Bde. Gallipoli. Croix de Chevalier de la Légion d'Honneur. *D.* Gallipoli, 1915. Killed in action at Hill 60, near Suvla Bay, on Aug. 21, 1915.

1901 Longford, Rev. M. W. W., D.D. (Mar. 1917). Chaplain to the Forces (4th Class). S.C.F. XXI Army Corps. Egypt, Palestine. *D.* Palestine, 1918.

1894 Longstaff, C. Ll., M.A. (Mobilized Aug. 4, 1914). Maj. 1/6th N. Staffordshire Regt. (T.F. Res.). France, Belgium, 1915. T.D.

1893 Longstaff, T. G., D.M. (Mobilized Aug. 4, 1914). Capt. 1/7th Hampshire Regt. Asst. Commdt. Gilgit Corps of Scouts, A.H.Q., India. India, 1914–17.

1919 Lougheed, M. S. (Mar. 19, 1915). ‡Lt. Canadian A.M.C. France.

1919 Loughman, E. L. (Mar. 22, 1915). Leading Telegraphist, R.N.V.R.

1913 **Lowe, R. C.** (Aug. 1914). Capt. 1/6th R. Warwickshire Regt. France, 1915–16. *M.C.*, Nov. 18, 1915. *D.* France, 1916. Killed in action at Thiepval on Aug. 18, 1916.

Lowson, C. P. F. (Dec. 1915). Lt. Rifle Brigade, attd. R.F.C. (Adjt. and Flight-Commdr.). France. Accidentally killed while flying at Stow-on-the-Wold on Nov. 3, 1917.

1909 Loyd, E. E. F. (May 4, 1916). 2nd Lt. 4th Dragoon Guards. Lt., Flying Officer, R.A.F. France. (Prisoner of war.)

1901 Loyd, L. R. W. (1917). Lt., Technical Officer, R.A.F.

1888 Luard, C. E., M.A. (Serving Aug. 4, 1914). Lt.-Col. Supernumerary List, Indian Army. Political Agent, Central India.

1898 Luard, G. D., B.A. (Feb. 1916). Lt. R.A.S.C., empld. under Directorate of Requisitions and Hirings. France, 1916–18; Italy, 1918–19.

1907 Lucas, R. H. (Nov. 1, 1915). Maj. R.A.S.C. D.A.A.G. *O.B.E.* (Mil.). *D.* § Mar. 1919.

1898 **Lucas-Tooth, S.,** B.A. (Serving Aug. 4, 1914). Capt. Lancashire Fusiliers. France. Killed in action on Oct. 20, 1914.

1912 Lunn, B. H., B.A. (Nov. 14, 1914). 2nd Lt. 9th The Black Watch.

1907 Luscombe, W. O., B.A. (Mar. 1915). Capt. 19th Rifle Brigade. Staff-Captain. Egypt, Palestine. *M.C.*, June 3, 1918. *D.* Palestine, 1918.

1919 Lush, H. C. (Aug. 9, 1917). 2nd Lt. Coldstream Guards. France, Germany.

1919 Lush, M. A. (July 1, 1916). Pte. Motor Transport, B.R.C.S. France.

1911 Lush, R. W., B.M. (Sept. 4, 1914). ‡Capt. R.A.M.C. (S.R.). Salonika.

1893 Lutley, J. T., B.A. (Mobilized Aug. 1914). Maj., temp. Col., Worcestershire Yeomanry. *D.* § Feb. 1917.

1910 Lutyens, W. F., B.A. (Nov. 9, 1914). 2nd Lt. Lancashire Hussars (T.F. Res.).

1919 McCaffery, J. A. (May 12, 1917). Capt. 306th Machine Gun Bn., U.S. Army. France, 1918–19.

1907 Macclesfield, Earl of (Dec. 1, 1914). 2nd Lt. Q.O. Oxfordshire Hussars. Staff-Lt. (2nd Class). Lt. R.A.S.C.

1908 **McCowan, H.,** B.A. (Mobilized Aug. 1914). Lt. 1/8th Cameronians. Gallipoli. Killed in action on June 28, 1915.

1909 Macdonald, G. R., M.A. (June 14, 1915). 2nd Lt. A.S.C. Capt. Tank Corps. France, 1915, 1916, 1917, 1918. *M.C.*, Jan. 11, 1919. *D.* France, 1918.

1907 McGrath, E. H., M.A. (Aug. 1914). Lt. Special Lists, empld. War Office (Intelligence). France, Germany.

1903 **McIlwaine, A. A.,** B.A. (Apr. 27, 1915). 2nd Lt. 3rd, attd. 1st, Loyal N. Lancashire Regt. France. Killed in action on Mar. 5, 1916.

1913 MacIver, A. S. (Aug. 15, 1914). Lt. 4th Lancashire Fusiliers. France. *M.C.*, July 26, 1918.

1911 **MacIver, R. S.** (Aug. 31, 1914). Lt. 2nd Lancashire Fusiliers. Belgium, France, 1915–16. Killed in action on the Somme on July 1, 1916.

1898 McKenna, H., M.A. (Nov. 15, 1914). Capt., Bt.-Maj., R.A., empld. Ministry of Munitions. *D.* § Aug. 1918.

1884 Mackenzie, W. R. D. (Oct. 12, 1914). Maj. 6th Q.O. Cameron Highlanders, afterwards Maj. 51st Gordon Highlanders.

1906 Mackie, E. R., B.A. (July 20, 1915). Capt. R.A.S.C.

1912 **Mackintosh, E. A.** (Dec. 31, 1914). Lt. 5th, attd. 4th, Seaforth Highlanders (Capt.). France. *M.C.*, June 24, 1916. Killed in action at Fontaine on Nov. 21, 1917.

1893 Maclagan, N. (Feb. 6, 1915). Lt. 4th Somerset L.I. (Invalided.)

1897 Maclaverty, C. F. S. (Aug. 24, 1914). Maj., Acting Lt.-Col., R.F.A. Nigeria, Cameroons, 1914–15; France, Belgium, 1916–19. *D.S.O.*, June 23, 1915. *D.* France, 1916 twice, 1917 twice.

1912 Macmillan, J. E. (Aug. 19, 1914). Capt. 10th Arg. & Suth'd. Highlanders. Staff-Captain. France, Belgium, Germany. *M.C.*, Dec. 16, 1917.

1895 McNeile, Rev. R. F., M.A. (Oct. 1915). Chaplain to the Forces (4th Class). Egypt, Palestine.

1887 McPherson, J. W., M.A. (1915). 2nd Lt. Special Lists, attd. Egyptian Camel Transport Corps. Gallipoli, Sinai, Palestine, Syria.

1908 **Madan, N. C.,** B.A. (Sept. 19, 1914). Lt. 8th King's Own (R. Lancaster Regt.). France, Belgium, 1915–16. Killed in action near the Bluff, Ypres, on Mar. 2, 1916.

1899 Maffey, J. L. (Mobilized 1914). 2nd Lt. I.A.R.O. (Private Secretary to Viceroy). India. *C.I.E.*

1894 Mainwaring, W. R. K. (Mobilized Aug. 1914). Maj., Acting Lt.-Col., Denbighshire Yeomanry. A.Q.M.G. Gallipoli, Egypt, Palestine. *C.B.E.* (Mil.). Order of the Nile (3rd Class). Order of the White Eagle (5th Class) (with swords). Order of El Nahda (3rd Class). *D.* Egypt and Palestine, 1917, 1918, 1919; § Apr. and Sept. 1917.

1905 Mais, S. P. B., M.A. (Serving Aug. 4, 1914). Lt. Unattached List, T.F. Tonbridge School O.T.C.

1907 **Majolier, E.** (Sept. 9, 1914). Lt. 5th Yorkshire Regt. Died on Nov. 26, 1918, of illness contracted while on active service.

1907 Major, R. E., B.A. (Oct. 31, 1914). Capt. 4th R. Welch Fusiliers. France.

1888 Makins, E., *D.S.O.* (Serving Aug. 4, 1914). Col., temp. Brig.-Gen., Staff. France. *C.B.* Officer of the Order of St. Maurice and St. Lazarus. *D.* France, 1915, 1917.

1891 Malmesbury, Earl of, M.A. (Sept. 5, 1914). Maj. 3rd Hampshire Regt. (Specially empld.). France, 1915–18.

1913 **Manger, J. K.** (Nov. 11, 1914). 2nd Lt. attd. 2nd Northumberland Fusiliers. France, Belgium, 1915. Killed in action at Wieltje, near Ypres, on May 8, 1915.

1888 March, Earl of, *M.V.O.*, *D.S.O.* (Mobilized Aug. 1914). Maj. Irish Guards Res. of Officers. *D.* § Feb. 1917.

1919 Marjoribanks, E. (Aug. 8, 1918). 2nd Lt. Scots Guards.

1903 Marshall, M. H. (Mobilized Aug. 4, 1914). Maj. S. Midland Divl. Train, R.A.S.C. (T.F.). D.A.Q.M.G. France, 1916. *O.B.E.* (Mil.). T.D. *D.* § Mar. 1919.

1898 Marsham, C. H. B., B.A. (Mobilized Aug. 4, 1914). Capt. 1/1st W. Kent Yeomanry, attd. 10th The Buffs (E. Kent Regt.). Gallipoli, Senussi, Egypt, Palestine. (Invalided, 1917.)

1898 **Marsham-Townshend, F.,** B.A. (Feb. 3, 1915). 2nd Lt. Scots Guards (S.R.). France. Killed in action on May 16, 1915.

1897 Marsham-Townshend, H. S. (June 17, 1916). Lt. Scots Guards (S.R.). France.

1897 Martin, B. (Aug. 15, 1917). Maj. 153rd Inf. Bde., U.S. Army. France, 1918.

1912 Martin, O. M. (Aug. 14, 1916). Lt. I.A.R.O., Cavalry. India.

1896 Martin, Rev. W. K., M.A. (Apr. 4, 1918). Chaplain to the Forces (4th Class).

1919 Martin Harvey, J. S. E. (Feb. 3, 1915). Sergt. R.A.M.C., 31st General Hospital, Cairo. France, Salonika, Egypt, Palestine.

1907 Mason, E. R. (Sept. 9, 1914). Lt. 6th York & Lancaster Regt. Capt. General List. France. *M.C.*, Nov. 25, 1916.

1904 Mason, L., B.A. (Oct. 30, 1914). Capt., temp. Maj., R.A. D.A.A.G. France, 1915–19. *O.B.E.* (Mil.). *M.C.*, Jan. 1, 1917. Belgian Croix de Guerre. *D.* France, 1917, 1918.

1905 Mathews, J. R. T., B.A. (Mobilized Aug. 1914). Maj. R.F.A. (T.F.).

1901 Mavrogordato, T. M., B.A. (Sept. 2, 1914). ‡Maj. R.A.S.C. France, Italy.

1904 Maxwell, F. M., B.A. (Sept. 10, 1914). Capt., Acting Maj., City of London Yeomanry, attd. M.G.C. Gallipoli, Egypt, Salonika, Palestine, Syria.

1911 Mellor, A. R. I. (Aug. 29, 1914). Capt. Surrey Yeomanry, attd. 10th Queen's (R. W. Surrey Regt.). Egypt, Gallipoli, France, Italy, Belgium. *M.C.*, Sept. 16, 1918; *Bar*, Mar. 8, 1919. *D.* Italy, 1918.

1908 Mellor, E. L., B.A. (Jan. 21, 1916). Cadet R.E.

1914 Mellor, G. R. (Jan. 21, 1915). Capt. 2/1st Welsh Horse, attd. 1/1st Denbigh Yeomanry. Egypt, 1916; Palestine, 1916–17; France, 1918.

1896 Mercier, Rev. P. B., M.A. (June 2, 1916). Chaplain to the Forces (4th Class). Gibraltar, 1916–17.

1901 Meredith, H. C. (Mobilized Aug. 1914). Maj. Shropshire Yeomanry. A.D.C. France. *O.B.E.* (Mil.). *D.* France, 1919.

1910 **Meredith, W. M.,** B.A. (Serving Aug. 4, 1914). Capt. 1st King's (Liverpool Regt.). A.D.C. France, Belgium. Died on Dec. 7, 1918, of illness contracted while on active service.

1906 Merriman, F. V., M.A. ‡2nd Lt. Special Lists.

1887 Metcalfe, Rev. E. L., M.A. (Feb. 8, 1907). Chaplain to the Forces (4th Class), attd. 19th London Regt.

1919 Meyer, H. A. (June 6, 1917). Lt. 5th S. Lancashire Regt. India, 1918–19; Aden Field Force, 1919.

1903 Meynell, E. C. (Aug. 5, 1914). Lt., temp. Maj., R.F.A. D.A.Q.M.G. France. *O.B.E.* (Mil.). *M.C.*, Jan. 1, 1918. *D.* France, 1918, 1919.

1919 Middleton, J. A., B.A. (Oct. 21, 1914). Lt. R.F.A. (T.F.) (Capt.). France, Belgium, 1915–18. *M.C.*, June 3, 1918.

1876 Milborne-Swinnerton-Pilkington, Sir T. E., Bt. M.A. (Nov. 9, 1914). Lt.-Col. 14th K.R.R.C. Lt.-Col., Hon. Col., Staff Appointment, Class H.H.

1897 Millar, Rev. E. W., B.A. (May 16, 1916). Chaplain to the Forces (4th Class).

1884 Mills, Hon. E. J., *D.S.O.* (Sept. 14, 1914). Lt.-Col. 2/1st W. Kent Yeomanry. Lt.-Col. Special Lists, whilst Commandant. *D.* § Aug. 1918, Mar. 1919.

1919 Mills, G. R. A. (June 16, 1916). Pte. R.A.S.C. (Lce.-Cpl.).

Mills, W. R. G. (Feb. 1916). 2nd Lt. R.F.A. (S.R.). France, Belgium, 1916–17. Killed in action at Zillebeke on Feb. 17, 1917.

1877 Milner, E. (Oct. 22, 1914). Maj. (Ret. Pay) 12th K.R.R.C. Staff-Captain, Gentleman at Arms.

1912 Milner, W. F. V. M., B.A. (July 27, 1915). Lt. Lothians & Border Horse.

1893 Mitchell, A., M.A. (July 12, 1915). Lt. 2/1st Staffordshire Yeomanry. *D.* § Feb. 1917.

1907 Mitchell, F. A. (Mobilized Aug. 1914). Maj. R. Gloucestershire Hussars. Egypt, Sinai, Palestine. *M.C.*, Nov. 25, 1916. *D.* Egypt, 1916.

1888 Mitchell, P. Chalmers, M.A., D.Sc. (Jan. 1916). Capt. Res. of Officers, General List, attd. British War Mission, U.S.A. France. *C.B.E.* (Mil.). *O.B.E.* (Civil). *D.* § Feb. 1917.

1912 Moberley, H. W. (Aug. 10, 1914). ‡Lt. 1/4th D.C.L.I. India, 1914–16; Aden, 1916–17; Palestine, 1917–19. *M.C.*, Mar. 26, 1918.

1911 Moise, E. W. (May 14, 1917). Maj. U.S. Infantry. France, 1918.

1909 **Monckton, F. A.,** B.A. (Serving Aug. 4, 1914). Lt. 1st Scots Guards. France, Belgium. Killed in action at Hooge, near Ypres, on Nov. 8, 1914.

1900 Monckton-Arundell, Hon. G. V. A., M.A. (Serving Aug. 4, 1914). Maj., temp. Lt.-Col., 1st Life Guards. A.A.Q.M.G. 2nd Cavalry Div. France, Belgium. *O.B.E.* (Mil.). *D.S.O.*, June 3, 1917. Chevalier de l'Ordre du Mérite Agricole. *D.* France, 1915, 1916, 1917, 1919.

1884 Money, N. E., *D.S.O.* (Mobilized Aug. 1914). Maj. Shropshire Yeomanry. Lt.-Col. Queen's (R. W. Surrey Regt.) (Brig.-Gen.). Egypt, Palestine. *C.M.G.*, Jan. 1, 1919. *Bar to D.S.O.*, Jan. 1, 1918. *D.* Egypt, 1916; Palestine, 1917, 1918.

1910 Monier-Williams, R. H., B.A. (Aug. 10, 1914). ‡Lt. R.N.V.R.

1906 Montagu-Douglas-Scott, D. J., B.A. (Aug. 1914). Capt. 3rd R. Scots. G.S.O. 3. France, Belgium, 1914–15; Salonika, 1915–16. *O.B.E.* (Mil.). Croix de Chevalier de la Légion d'Honneur. *D.* Salonika, 1916; § Aug. 1918.

1898 Montagu-Douglas-Scott, Lord F. G. (Serving Aug. 4, 1914). Maj., Bt.-Lt.-Col., temp. Lt.-Col., Grenadier Guards. France, Belgium, 1914. *D.S.O.*, Dec. 1, 1914. *D.* France, 1915; § Aug. 1919.

1886 Montagu-Douglas-Scott, Lord G. W. (Mobilized Aug. 1914). Lt.-Col. 2/1st Lothians & Border Horse. *O.B.E.* (Mil.).

1886 Montagu-Douglas-Scott, Lord H. F. (Aug. 18, 1914). Hon. Col. 3rd R. Scots. Lt.-Col. 3rd Bedfordshire Regt. Temp. Col. Labour Corps, Labour Commandant. France, Belgium, 1915–19. *C.B.E.* (Mil.). *D.* France, 1916, 1917 twice, 1918, 1919.

1914 Montgomery, H. E. L. (Aug. 16, 1915). Lt. N. Irish Horse (S.R.) (Capt.). France, Belgium, 1916–18. *M.C.*, June 3, 1919.

1887 Moor, C. G. (Aug. 1914). Capt. R.A.M.C.

1881 Moore, E. J., B.M., M.A., *C.B.*, V.D. (Mobilized Aug. 1914). Lt.-Col. R.A.M.C. Lt.-Col. 20th London Regt. (T.F. Res.). *D.* § Feb. 1917.

1873 Moore-Stevens, R. A., M.A. (May 11, 1915). Maj. (Hon. Col.) R.A. (Ret.). Draft Conducting Officer, Special Lists. *D.* § Aug. 1919.

1919 Morgan, A. C. (Aug. 11, 1918). 2nd Lt. R.G.A.

1914 Morgan, Hon. E. F. (June 1916). Lt. Welsh Guards, empld. Ministry of Labour.

1911 Morgan, F. S. (Mobilized Aug. 4, 1914). Capt. 1/1st Pembrokeshire Yeomanry, attd. 24th Welsh Regt. Egypt, Sinai, Palestine, 1916; France, 1918–19.

1913 **Morgan, G. W. S.** (Serving Aug. 4, 1914). Capt. 1st R. Welch Fusiliers. France. Killed in action at Loos on Sept. 25, 1915.

1897 Morgan, H. W., B.A. (Dec. 31, 1914). Capt. I.A.R.O. (Infantry). India.

1919 Morgan, T. A. (May 12, 1917). Capt. 79th Div., U.S. Army. France, 1918–19.

1901 Morgan-Griffiths, C. V. P. (Nov. 3, 1914). Lt. K.O.Y.L.I. (Res. of Officers). (Capt. 10th Welsh Regt.)

1905 Moriarty, G. A. (Apr. 4, 1918). Capt. Mil. Intelligence Div., Gen. Staff, Washington, U.S. Army.

1889 Morland, S. (Sept. 18, 1914). Maj. 6th (Res.) Rifle Brigade. *D.* § Feb. 1917.

1897 Morrell, C. C. (Oct. 2, 1914). Capt. R.A.M.C.

1911 Morris, R. E. C., B.A. (Aug. 11, 1915). Lt. 1st R. Welch Fusiliers. France, 1916.

1908 Morton, E., M.A. (Nov. 1916). Capt. R.A.M.C., 3rd Southern General Hospital.

1914 **Morton, J. L. M.** (Apr. 3, 1915). Capt. 22nd Manchester Regt. France, Belgium. Killed in action at Houlthoust Forest on Oct. 22, 1917.

1909 **Morton, W. R.** (Sept. 2, 1914). ‡Capt. 8th R. Warwickshire Regt. France, 1916–17. Killed in action near St. Quentin on May 4, 1917.

1903 Moseley, G., B.A. (Sept. 28, 1914). Capt. 5th Yorkshire Regt. France. (Prisoner of war, 1917–18.)

1919 Moss, F. L. (Feb. 1917). ‡Lt. Sherwood Foresters. Palestine.

1905 Mosse, E. F. C., B.A. (Dec. 1915). Lt. R.G.A. (S.R.) (Capt.). France, 1916–17, 1918.

1915 Mostyn-Owen, H. L. (May 20, 1915). Lt. 1/1st Montgomeryshire Yeomanry. Lt., Acting Capt., 18th Lancers, Indian Army. Egypt, Palestine.

1905 **Motyer, A. J.,** B.A. (Sept. 1914). ‡Lt. Canadian Field Artillery. France. Killed in action at Contalmaison on Sept. 15, 1916.

1883 Mount-Edgcumbe, P. A. H., Earl of (Sept. 17, 1914). Maj. 3rd D.C.L.I. *D.* § Mar. 1919.

Muirhead, P. Q. (Oct. 28, 1914). Lt. R.F.A. France. Killed in action in the Battle of the Somme, July, 1916.

1902 **Mulholland, Hon. A. E. S.** (Serving Aug. 4, 1914). Capt. Irish Guards. France, Belgium. Killed in action at Ypres on Oct. 31, 1914.

1897 Mulligan, A. de W., B.A. (Oct. 30, 1914). Lt. R.N.V.R.

1910 Mumford, L. F., B.A. (Aug. 11, 1914). Lt., Acting Capt., 9th Middlesex Regt., attd. 7th Essex Regt. Palestine. *D.* Palestine, 1918.

1913 Munro, J. J., B.A. (Dec. 9, 1914). Capt., Acting Maj., R.E. Gallipoli, Egypt, Sinai, Palestine. *M.C.*, Jan. 3, 1918. *D.* Palestine, 1917.

1912 Munro-Faure, C. A., B.A. (Aug. 22, 1914). Lt. 7th E. Surrey Regt., attd. M.G.C. France, 1915–16. (Invalided, 1916.)

1919 Murphy, Du B. (May 14, 1917). Capt. 321st Field Artillery, U.S. Army. France, 1918.

1919 Murray, H. D. (Jan. 1918). 2nd Lt. R.G.A.

1911 **Murray, K. D.** (Dec. 22, 1914). 2nd Lt. 9th E. Surrey Regt. France, 1915. Killed in action at the Battle of Loos on Sept. 25, 1915.

Murray, L. (Jan. 1916). Lt. Lancashire Hussars, attd. R.F.C. Accidentally killed on Mar. 13, 1917.

1914 **Murray, R.** (Sept. 27, 1915). Lt. Q.O. Cameron Highlanders. France, Belgium. Died on Oct. 27, 1917, of wounds received in action.

1905 Musgrave, Rev. C., M.A. (Mar. 10, 1916). Chaplain to the Forces (4th Class), attd. 1st Bde. Tank Corps. France, 1916–18.

1888 Myburgh, A. M. (Dec. 4, 1915). Capt., Hon. Maj., 3rd (Res.) Regt. of Cavalry, empld. P. of W. Camp.

1888 [Myres, J. L., M.A.] (Apr. 1, 1916). Lt.-Commdr., Acting Commdr., R.N.V.R. Military Control Officer, Athens. Greece, 1915–19. *O.B.E.* (Mil.). Commander of the Order of George I of Greece. *D.* Naval Dispatches, July, 1917.

Nalder, F. S. (Aug. 1914). Capt. 8th Shropshire L.I. France, 1915; Greece, 1915–18. Killed in action at Pitt Ridge on Sept. 18, 1918.

1919 Needham, F. R. D. (Sept. 11, 1918). Pte. 53rd Hampshire Regt. (8th Tr. Res.).

1896 Nevill, P. L. (Aug. 5, 1916). Lt. Protection Coy., R. Defence Corps.

1906 Newman, E. W. P., B.A. (Serving Aug. 4, 1914). Capt. The Cameronians, attd. General Staff. Maj. R.A.F. France, 1914.

1880 Nicholl, J. I. D., B.A. (Mobilized Aug. 1914). Lt.-Col. Glamorganshire Yeomanry (T.F. Res.).

1915 Nicholl, R. I. Pte. R. W. Kent Regt.

1882 Nicholson, A. C., B.A. (Mobilized Aug. 1914). Lt.-Col. Hampshire Yeomanry (T.F. Res.). T.D. *D.* § Feb. 1917.

1908 Nicholson, J. H., B.A. (Aug. 15, 1915). ‡2nd Lt. R.G.A. France, Belgium. *M.M.*

1902 Nicol, R. J. (Mobilized Aug. 1914). Capt., temp. Maj., 4th Arg. & Suth'd. Highlanders. Camp Commandant. France, 1915, 1917–19. *O.B.E.* (Mil.). *D.* France, 1915, 1918, 1919.

1919 Niles, E. A. (July 2, 1917). ‡1st Lt. Res. Military Aviator, U.S. Army.

1912 Noakes, C. E. S., B.A. (Aug. 22, 1914). Capt. 9th Sherwood Foresters.

1911 North, D. W. J. (Aug. 1914). Lt. 19th Hussars. France. *M.C.*, Jan. 18, 1918.

1865 Northumberland, Duke of, *K.G.*, V.D. Hon. Col. Northumberland Fusiliers. *A.D.C.* to the King. Died on May 14, 1918.

1897 Northumberland, Duke of (Mobilized Aug. 1914). Hon. Col. R.E. and 7th Northumberland Fusiliers. Capt., Bt.-Lt.-Col., Grenadier Guards (S.R.) (Ret. Pay). France. *C.B.E.* (Mil.). *M.V.O.* Croix de Chevalier de la Légion d'Honneur. Order of St. Anne (3rd Class). Order of Medjidieh (4th Class). *D.* France, 1915.

1906 Nott-Bower, R. E., B.A. (Sept. 19, 1914). Capt. 12th Rifle Brigade. Maj. 20th Bn. Training Res.

1912 Nunn, R. L. H., B.A. (Nov. 4, 1914). 2nd Lt. R.A. A.D.C.

1912 Obolensky-Neledinsky-Meletzky, Prince Sergius (Aug. 3, 1914). ‡1st Lt. Cavilierguards, Russian Army. Russia. St. George's Cross (2nd, 3rd, and 4th Classes). Order of St. Anne (3rd and 4th Classes). Order of St. Stanislas (3rd Class).

1898 O'Brien, Hon. D., M.A. (Aug. 18, 1914). Flight-Lt. R.N.A.S. (Invalided.)

1908 Oddy, H. M., B.M., M.A. (Dec. 1915). Surgeon Lt. R.N. Grand Fleet.

Ogilvy, Hon. P. J. H. S. (Oct. 6, 1914). Capt. Irish Guards (S.R.). France, Belgium. *M.C.*, Nov. 14, 1916. Killed in action on Oct. 9, 1917.

1918 Okell, R. (Jan. 1918). Cadet, R.F.A.

1905 Oldham, Rev. G. M. S., M.A. (Feb. 8, 1917). Chaplain to the Forces (4th Class). France, Belgium, Germany, 1917–19. *O.B.E.* (Mil.). *D.* France, 1919.

1901 Oldham, J. B., M.A. (Feb. 1916). Lt. Unattached List, T.F., Shrewsbury School O.T.C.

1910 Openshaw, L. P., M.A. (Nov. 16, 1914). Maj., Flying Officer, R.A.F.

1911 Orr-Ewing, M. R. (Serving Aug. 4, 1914). Capt. R.A. Staff-Captain. France, Gallipoli, Palestine. *M.C.*, Jan. 14, 1916. *D.* France, 1915; Palestine, 1918.

1911 Osborne, J. I., B.A. (1918). Lt. Mil. Intelligence Branch, Gen. Staff., U.S. Army.

1914 **Osler, E. R.** (Feb. 23, 1915). Lt. Canadian A.M.C. 2nd Lt. R.F.A. France, Belgium. Died on Aug. 30, 1917, of wounds received in action in Belgium.

1905 Osler, Sir W., Bt., D.M., Hon. D.Sc. Hon. Col. R.A.M.C. Died on Dec. 29, 1919.

1903 Ottley, Rev. D. L. E. B., M.A. (Aug. 24, 1916). Chaplain to the Forces (4th Class), attd. R.G.A. France, Belgium, 1917–19.

1913 Overend, T. D. R.A.S.C.

1908 Owen, A. G. L., B.A. (June 14, 1914). Capt., Acting Maj., 3rd R. Sussex Regt. (S.R.). France, Belgium, 1914–17. *D.* France, 1916.

1919 Owen, R. E. (Aug. 8, 1917). Lt. R.M.A. France.

1912 Owtram, T. C., B.A. (Sept. 1914). Capt. 1/5th King's Own (R. Lancaster Regt.). France. *M.C.*, Apr. 4, 1916.

1892 Oxley, J. C. S. (Serving Aug. 4, 1914). Maj. Indian Medical Service. Acting Lt.-Col. 15th Casualty Clearing Hospital. India, Mesopotamia, Egypt, Palestine, Syria. *D.* Palestine, 1919.

1914 Page, T. S. (1914). 2nd Lt. R.A. Lt. Special Lists, whilst with Nyasaland Force. E. Africa.

1905 Paget, Rev. E. F., M.A. (Feb. 1916). Capt. and Chaplain, S. African Forces. British and German E. Africa. *M.C.*, Mar. 26, 1918.

1910 Paget, H. (Aug. 25, 1914). Capt. and Adjt. 15th Loyal N. Lancashire Regt. France, Belgium, 1915–19. *M.C.*, June 3, 1919. *D.* France, 1917, 1918.

1903 Paget, R. J. (Aug. 4, 1914). Capt. 8th Bn. C.E.F. Staff-Captain, A.D.C. to G.O.C. 3rd Canadian Div. France, Belgium, 1915–19.

1909 Paget-Cooke, O. D. P., B.A. (Sept. 3, 1914). ‡Lt. 5th Grenadier Guards. France, 1915–18.
1919 Pakenham-Walsh, G. P. (Aug. 19, 1917). Lt. R.A.F. *D.* § Jan. 1919.
1920 Palmer, T. M. (June 1, 1918). 2nd Lt. Inf., U.S. Army (Capt.).
1912 Palmer, Hon. W. J. L. (Sept. 6, 1914). Lt., temp. Capt., 6th Hampshire Regt. Staff-Captain. India, Mesopotamia, 1917–19.
1898 Palmer-Morewood, R. C. A., B.A. (Sept. 30, 1914). Capt. Sherwood Foresters.
1901 Pape, H. R., B.A. (Sept. 3, 1914). Capt., Acting Maj., 2nd County of London Yeomanry, attd. 13th Bn. Tank Corps. Egypt, Palestine. *M.C.*, Jan. 11, 1919. Egypt, 1916.
1902 [Parham, Rev. A. G., M.A.] (Oct. 28, 1914). Chaplain to the Forces (2nd Class). D.A.C.G. XVII Corps. Egypt, 1915; Gallipoli, 1915; Senussi, 1916; France, 1917–19. *M.C.*, June 3, 1916. *D.* Gallipoli, 1916; France, 1918.
1897 Parish, S. C., M.A. (1916). Cpl. H.A.C. France.
1919 Park, A. (Dec. 13 1915). ‡2nd Lt. R.F.A. France.
1905 Park, Rev. R., M.A. (July 3, 1917). Chaplain to the Forces (4th Class). France.
1905 **Parker, L.** (Aug. 12, 1914). Maj., Squadron Commdr., R.F.C. France, 1915, 1916, 1917. Killed in action while flying near Peronne on Mar. 22, 1917.
1913 Parker, R. C. O., M.A. (Aug. 15, 1914). Lt. 6th Dragoon Guards (S.R.). France.
Parker, R. H. (Oct. 21, 1914). Lt. 2nd Lincolnshire Regt. France. Killed in action on Dec. 2, 1917.
1901 Parker, Rev. W., M.A. (July 10, 1916). Chaplain to the Forces (4th Class), attd. 91st Inf. Bde. France, 1916–18; Italy, 1918–19. Croce di Guerra.
1906 Parker-Jervis, T. (Aug. 14, 1914). Lt. Grenadier Guards (S.R.). Capt., Administrative Officer, R.A.F. France, Belgium, 1914–15, 1916.
1897 Parkes, H. R. (Feb. 2, 1915). Capt. R.G.A. France.
1907 Parkinson, Rev. C. T., M.A. (Dec. 30, 1915). Chaplain to the Forces (4th Class).
1907 Parson, A. L., M.A. (July 29, 1915). Cpl. R.E. France.
1919 Parsons, G. L. (Aug. 16, 1916). Pte. H.A.C. Cadet 2 B Bde., R.F.A. France, 1917–18.
1913 Partridge, R. S., B.A. (Aug. 29, 1914). Maj. 1/6th R. Warwickshire Regt. France, Belgium, Italy. *M.C.*, Jan. 26, 1917; *Bar*, Oct. 18, 1917. Croce di Guerra.
1913 Paton, L. C. (Nov. 4, 1914). Lt. 10th Cameronians. Capt. General List. attd. Intelligence Corps. France, Belgium. *M.C.*, Nov. 4, 1915. *D.* France, 1915, 1916.
1913 Patrick, C. M. (Aug. 15, 1914). Lt. 16th Lancers, attd. R.F.C. France. *D.* France, 1917.
1901 Patten, J. MacD. (Feb. 21, 1916). Lt. R.A.F. France, 1916–18. *D.* France, 1917.
1919 Patterson, C. R. (May 1, 1918). 2nd Lt. R.F.A.
1919 Patterson, H. G. (May 3, 1917). 2nd Lt. R.F.A. Palestine, 1918; France, 1918.

1912 Pavière, H. D. (Feb. 17, 1915). Lt. 3rd Gloucestershire Regt. Lt., Acting Maj., M.G.C.

1900 Pawson, A. C., B.A. (Mobilized Aug. 4, 1914). Capt. 1/1st Nottinghamshire Yeomanry. R.T.O. Gallipoli, 1915; Egypt, Palestine, 1916–19.

1907 Pawson, A. G., B.A. (May 8, 1915). Lt. 17th W. Yorkshire Regt. Lt. 88th Bn. Training Res. (Invalided.)

1919 Payne, A. F. (Dec. 1917). Lt. Grenadier Guards. France.

1919 Peake, O. (Apr. 27, 1916). Lt. Coldstream Guards. France, Germany.

1893 Pearce, C. M., B.A. (Sept. 3, 1914). Instructor Artists' Rifles, transferred Naval Intelligence Dept.

1909 Pearce, C. M. H., B.A. (July 7, 1915). Lt. Coldstream Guards (S.R.). *D.* § Mar. 1919.

1913 **Pearce, C. S.** (Sept. 1914). Capt. 8th E. Surrey Regt. France, 1915–16. Killed in action near Montauban on July 1, 1916.

1918 Pearce, J. (Mobilized Aug. 1914). Maj. 6th Devonshire Regt. France, Mesopotamia, India.

1905 **Pearce-Gould, A. L.,** D.M., M.Ch. (Aug. 6, 1914). Surgeon-Lt. R.N.D. Gallipoli, France. Killed in action at Mesnil on May 19, 1918.

1904 Pearce-Gould, E. L., D.M. (Aug. 3, 1914). Surgeon Lt. R.N. Gibraltar, 1917–18.

1901 Pearson, Hon. W. H. (Mobilized Aug. 1914). Maj. Sussex Yeomanry. Gallipoli, Egypt.

1897 Peck, J. W. (Nov. 24, 1914). Capt. and Adjt. R.A.

1904 Pemberton, T. B. (Sept. 1915). Lt., Acting Capt., 11th Canadian Engineers. France, Belgium.

1913 Pendarves, J. S. (Sept. 25, 1914). Lt. 2nd Life Guards.

1905 Penrose, J., B.A. (Serving Aug. 4, 1914). Maj. R.A. Belgium, France. *M.C.*, June 3, 1915. *D.* France, 1914, 1915, 1916, 1917.

1907 Pepper, W. (Mobilized Aug. 1914). Capt. Q.O. Oxfordshire Hussars. France. *M.C.*, July 26, 1918.

1894 Percival, H. F. P., M.A., *D.S.O.* (Serving Aug. 4, 1914). Maj., Bt.-Lt.-Col., temp. Col., R.A.S.C. D.A.Q.M.G. *C.M.G.* *C.B.E.* (Mil.). Croix d'Officier de la Légion d'Honneur. Russian Order of St. Anne (3rd Class). Serbian Order of the White Eagle (4th Class). *D.* § Mar. 1918.

1896 Percival, P. M. P., M.A. (Feb. 14, 1917). Staff-Lt. Special Lists. *M.B.E.* (Mil.).

1904 **Percy, A. W.** (Sept. 1914). Sub.-Lt. R.N.R., H.M.S. *Queen Mary*. Grand Fleet. Killed in action at the Battle of Jutland, on May 31, 1916.

1900 Percy, Lord, W. R., B.A. (Sept. 23, 1914). Capt., Bt.-Maj., temp. Col. Grenadier Guards (S.R.). Asst. Director to Chief of General Staff. G.S.O. 1. France, 1914–15; Gallipoli, 1915; Egypt, 1916–17; Palestine, 1917–18. *C.B.E.* (Mil.). *D.S.O.*, June 4, 1917. Order of the White Eagle (4th Class) (with swords). *D.* Egypt, 1916, 1917.

1905 **Philips, M. H.,** B.A. (May 1916). 2nd Lt. 4th, attd. 1st, S. Staffordshire Regt. France, Belgium. Killed in action at Passchendaele on Oct. 4, 1917.

1898 Phillimore, G. W., M.A. (Aug. 31, 1914). Capt. 3rd Highland L.I. France, Egypt. *M.C.*, May 5, 1919. (Prisoner of war in Austria, 1916–18.)

1913 Phillimore, H. A. G. (July 22, 1915). Lt. 2/4th Hampshire Regt., attd.

Light Divl. College (Rhine Army). India and N.W. Frontier, 1915–17; Egypt, Palestine, 1917–18; Germany, 1919.

1914 **Phillimore, M. A.** (Apr. 23, 1915). 2nd Lt. 9th Essex Regt., attd. R.E. France. Killed in action on June 25, 1916.

1901 Phillimore, Rev. Hon. S. H., M.A. (Mar. 1917). Chaplain to the Forces (4th Class), attd. 3rd Grenadier Guards. France. *M.C.*, Nov. 26, 1917; *Bar*, Apr. 2, 1919.

1908 Phillips, A. (May 14, 1915). Lt. R.F.A.

1903 Phillips, G. W., B.A. (Sept. 14, 1914). ‡Lt., temp. Capt., Oxf. & Bucks. Lt. Infty. France.

1908 Pidgeon, G. D., B.A. (1914). Maj., Acting Lt.-Col., Staff Officer, R.A.F. Liaison Officer with U.S. Air Service. Belgium. *O.B.E.* (Mil.). *D.* § Mar. 1918.

1889 Pilkington, R. A., B.A. (May 25, 1916). 2nd Lt. 5th S. Lancashire Regt. (T.F. Res.).

1876 Pilkington, Sir T. E. M. S., M.A. (Rejoined Nov. 1914). Col. comdg. 14th K.R.R.C., attd. Staff, Army of Rhine. France, Belgium, Germany, 1917–19. *D.* § Dec. 1916.

1891 Pinckney, E. C. (Sept. 11, 1914). Capt. 4th Wiltshire Regt. (T.F. Res.). India.

1914 Pinto, V. de Sola (Apr. 14, 1915). Lt. 25th R. Welch Fusiliers. Gallipoli, 1915; Egypt, 1915–16; France, 1917–18.

1906 Pitt-Lewis, G. F., B.A. (Feb. 12, 1915). Lt., Acting Capt., 3rd Devonshire Regt. France, 1916–17; France, Belgium, Germany, 1918–19. *M.C.*, Feb. 15, 1919.

1895 Plant, H. N., M.A. (Mar. 2, 1916). ‡Lt. 240th Siege Batt., R.G.A. (S.R.). France, 1917; Italy, 1917–19. *D.* Italy, 1918, 1919.

1899 **Plaskitt, H.** A.S.C. France. Killed in action on Nov. 12, 1917.

1867 Pole-Carew, Sir R., *K.C.B.*, *C.V.O.* Col. (Ret.) D.C.L.I.

1919 Pollard-Urquhart, A. L. (Mar. 23, 1915). ‡Lt. 5th Leinster Regt. Gallipoli, 1915–16; Egypt, 1916–17; France, 1917–18. *D.* France, 1918.

1912 Portal, C. F. A. (Serving Aug. 4, 1914). Lt. R.E. Maj., Acting Lt.-Col., Flying Officer, R.A.F. France, 1914–19. *D.S.O.*, July 18, 1917; *Bar*, July 26, 1918. *M.C.*, Jan. 10, 1917. *D.* France, 1914, 1917, 1918.

1912 **Portal, O. S.** (Sept. 1914). Lt. 1st Life Guards (S.R.), temp. Capt. The Household Bn. France. Killed in action on May 3, 1917.

1903 Portal, W. R. (Serving 1914). Capt., Bt.-Maj., 1st Life Guards. Acting Lt.-Col. 47th Bn. M.G.C. France. *M.V.O.* *D.S.O.*, Nov. 25, 1917. *D.* France, 1917, 1918, 1919.

1879 Portman, Hon. H. B. (Mobilized Aug. 1914). Maj. Dorset Yeomanry (T.F. Res.).

1919 Potter, G. J. R. (July 25, 1915). Lt. R.F.A. (T.F.) and R.A.F. France, Belgium.

1908 Potter, H. W. M., B.A. (Aug. 15, 1914). Capt. and Adjt. 6th Middlesex Regt. France. *M.C.*, Dec. 21, 1916. *D.* France, 1915.

1903 **Powell, S.,** B.A. (Mobilized Aug. 3, 1914). Capt. 8th R. Welch Fusiliers. Gallipoli, Egypt, Palestine, Mesopotamia. *D.* Mesopotamia, 1916. Died on Apr. 5, 1916, of wounds received in action at Umm-el-Hannah, Mesopotamia.

1908 Pratt, O. B., B.A. (Feb. 7, 1915). Capt., Acting Maj., R.A.M.C.

1918 Prewitt, F. J. (Nov. 26, 1915). Lt. R.F.A. (S.R.). France.
1888 Price, B. G., *D.S.O.* (Serving Aug. 4, 1914). Lt.-Col., Bt.-Col., R. Fusiliers. Temp. Brig.-Gen. France. *C.B.* *C.M.G.* Officer of the Order of St. Maurice and St. Lazarus. *D.* France, 1916, 1917 twice.
Prideaux-Brune, E. N. (Dec. 20, 1917). 2nd Lt. 3rd Rifle Brigade. France. Killed in action at Maisnil Bouche, near Arras, on May 22, 1918.
1909 Priestley, A. G. B. (Oct. 14, 1914). ‡2nd Lt. 1st Worcestershire Regt. France, 1916–18.
1898 Priestley, J. G., D.M. (Sept. 1, 1914). Capt. R.A.M.C. Belgium, France. *M.C.*, Apr. 15, 1915. *D.* France, 1915.
1910 Priestman, J. L., M.A. (Mobilized Aug. 4, 1914). Capt., Acting Maj., R.F.A. (T.F.). France, Belgium, 1915–19. *M.C.*, Jan. 1, 1918.
1901 Prioleau, J. R. H. (June 17, 1915). Lt. R.N.V.R.
1875 Proby (formerly Hamilton), D. J., M.A. (Aug. 12, 1914). Lt.-Col., Bt.-Col., Irish Guards, i/c Regimental District, Irish Guards.
1895 Probyn, S. C., M.A. (Oct. 1, 1914). Capt. 9th London Regt. (Queen Victoria's Rifles). Staff-Lt. (2nd Class) R.T.O.
1896 Proctor, G., M.A. (Apr. 1916). Lt. D Batt., 18th Army Bde., R.F.A. France, 1916–19.
1919 Pryce, A. R. (1915). Driver, Motor Transport, A.I.F. France.
1887 Pulteney, K., B.A. (Mobilized Aug. 4, 1914). 2nd Lt., temp. Capt., Hampshire R.H.A. (T.F. Res.). Egypt, 1916.
1903 Purcell, R. J., M.A. (Serving Aug. 4, 1914). Capt., Acting Maj., 18th K.R.R.C., attd. R.F.C. France, 1914. *D.* France, 1914.
1919 Pyke, E. J. (Sept. 6, 1918). 2nd Lt. Grenadier Guards (on demobilization).
1895 **Quenington, Viscount,** M.A. (Aug. 1914). Lt. R. Gloucestershire Hussars. Gallipoli, Egypt. *D.* Egypt, 1916. Died on Apr. 23, 1916, of wounds received in action at Katia, Egypt.
1920 Quilter, D. V. C. (Nov. 17, 1916). Pte. 18th Coy. R.A.M.C. France.
1919 Quilter, E. G. C. (June 3, 1916). Lt. R.A.F. France. (Prisoner in Germany, Nov. 1917–Dec. 1918.)
1902 Radcliffe, E. J. R. H., B.A. (Aug. 1914). Lt. Yorkshire Hussars. G.S.O. 3.
1905 Radcliffe, G. R. Y., M.A. (Aug. 5, 1914). Capt., Bt.-Maj., 23rd London Regt. G.S.O. 3. France, 1915. *D.* § Aug. 1918.
1907 Radcliffe, W. I., M.A. (Aug. 2, 1915). Lt. Special Lists, empld. Recruiting Duties.
1920 Radermacker, D. A. (Jan. 4, 1918). 2nd Lt. Grenadier Guards. France, Germany.
1919 Raeburn, W. A. L. (Aug. 11, 1915). ‡Lt. R.A.F. Cadet Wing. France, 1916.
1906 Rae Fraser, G. G., B.A. Capt., Technical Officer, R.A.F. Grand Fleet, 1916–18. *M.B.E.* (Mil.).
1886 Ragg, P. M. (Nov. 1, 1915). Capt. R.A.M.C.
1908 Raikes, M. H., M.A. (Aug. 4, 1914). Capt. 1/4th Border Regt., attd. Supply and Transport Corps, Indian Army. Burma, India.
1912 Rains, J. C. T. (Mar. 26, 1915). Lt. R.G.A. Gibraltar, 1915–19.
1908 Ralli, J. R. (Aug. 1914). Capt., temp. Maj., Irish Guards (S.R.). France, Belgium. *D.* France, 1915.
1919 Ralli, P. C. (May 17, 1918). Cadet 28th London Regt. (Artists' Rifles O.T.C.).

1906 Rambaut, G. M., B.A. (Mobilized Aug. 1914). Capt. R.F.A. (T.F.). (Maj. 1916–17). France, 1915–17. *D.S.O.*, Jan. 1, 1918. *D.* France, 1917 twice.

1914 Ranger, V. W. G. (Sept. 1914). Capt. Bucks. Bn. Oxf. & Bucks. Lt. Infty. Staff-Captain R.A.F. France, 1916–17; Italy, 1917–18. *M.C.*, Jan. 1, 1917. Croce di Guerra.

1903 Ranken, L. D., B.A. (Sept. 4, 1914). Capt. 1st Seaforth Highlanders. France, 1915; Mesopotamia, 1916–18; Palestine, Egypt, 1918–19.

1910 Ransom, J. C. (1917). Lt. U.S. Field Artillery. France.

1915 Raphael, C. E. (Jan. 28, 1916). Lt. Coldstream Guards. France, 1917.

1908 **Rawdon-Hastings, P. C. J. R.,** B.A. (Mobilized Aug. 1914). Capt. 1/5th Leicestershire Regt. France, 1915. Killed in action in France on Oct. 13, 1915.

1903 Rawlinson, Rev. A. E. J., M.A. (Oct. 1, 1915). Chaplain to the Forces (4th Class).

1912 Rawstorne, R. A., B.A. (Sept. 1914). Lt. 6th E. Yorkshire Regt. Gallipoli. (Prisoner of war in Turkey, 1915–18.)

1914 Ray, J. V. (July 1917). Ambulance Driver, French Red Cross (1915–16). Lt. U.S. Coast Artillery. France, 1915–16.

1919 Rea, P. R. (Sept. 1918). 2nd Lt. Grenadier Guards.

1905 Reed, Rev. R. W., M.A. (July 5, 1918). Chaplain to the Forces (4th Class).

1919 Renshaw, T. A. (Sept. 25, 1918). 2nd Lt. Coldstream Guards (S.R.).

1903 Rentoul, G. S. C., M.A. (Jan. 19, 1918). Capt. Special Lists (Legal Adviser to Headquarters Staff, Eastern Command).

1919 Reynolds, J. F. R. (Nov. 1917). Lt. Irish Guards. Germany.

1919 Reynolds, L. F. (Nov. 8, 1916). Lt. Coldstream Guards. France.

1907 Rhodes, J. H., M.A. (Sept. 1914). Lt. R.A.S.C. Salonika, 1916–18.

1919 Rice, E. D. (Apr. 2, 1918). Lce.-Cpl. The Buffs (E. Kent Regt.).

1919 Richards, J. F. C. (July 29, 1916). Lt. R.E. (Cable Section). France, Germany, 1916–19. *D.* France, 1919.

1919 Richardson, A. S. (Aug. 10, 1914). ‡2nd Lt. 5th Bn. M.G.C. France, Belgium, Italy, Salonika.

1916 Richardson, R. M. D. (Aug. 28, 1917). Ensign U.S. Naval Res. A.D.C. France.

1895 Rickards, A. W., M.A. (Jan. 21, 1915). Lt., Acting Capt., R.G.A. (T.F.). France, 1918.

1902 Ridsdale, Rev. H. E., B.A. (Aug. 17, 1917). Chaplain to the Forces (4th Class).

1889 Robert, C. L. (Apr. 10, 1915). Capt. Warwickshre Yeomanry, specially empld.

1909 Roberts, R. G. (Serving Aug. 4, 1914). Capt and Adjt., temp. Maj., 7th Dragoon Guards. France, Belgium, 1914–18. *M.C.*, June 3, 1919. *D.* France, 1918 twice.

1919 Robertson, J. A. (June 7, 1916). ‡Lt. Guards M.G. Regt. France.

1891 Robertson, Hon. R. B. F. (Mobilized Aug. 29, 1914). Capt. 21st Lancers (S.R.).

1901 Robertson-Luxford, J. O., B.A. R.N.V.R.

1904 Robins, T. E. (Mobilized Aug. 4, 1914). Maj. City of London Yeomanry (Col.). A.P.M., E.E.F. Egypt and Sinai, 1915; Palestine and Syria, 1915–19. *D.S.O.*, Jan. 1, 1919. *D.* Egypt, 1917; Palestine, 1918.

1911 Robinson, E. S., B.A. (Aug. 29, 1915). Lt. 161st Bde., R.F.A. (T.F.). France.

1906 Robinson, E. S. G., B.A. (Nov. 1914). Lt. 3rd, attd. 1st, Northamptonshire Regt. France, 1915–16.

1901 Robinow, W., M.A. (Mar. 1916). ‡Lt. 3rd Bn. Tank Corps. France, Belgium, 1917–18. *M.C.*, Nov. 7, 1918; *Bar*, Jan. 11, 1919.

1907 Rodocanachi, T. E., B.A. (Feb. 27, 1915). Lt., temp. Capt., 3rd Hampshire Regt., attd. 5th Oxf. & Bucks. Lt. Infty. France, 1915–16, 1917, 1918–19. *D.S.O.*, June 18, 1917. *M.C.*, Nov. 18, 1915. *D.* France, 1915, 1916, 1917.

1911 Romanes, N. H., B.A. (Aug. 17, 1914). ‡Lt. 9th Worcestershire Regt., attd. G.H.Q. Mesopotamia, Persia, Baku, India.

1912 **Rose, F. A.,** B.A. (May 27, 1915). 2nd Lt. 4th Gordon Highlanders. France, Belgium. Killed in action at Ypres on Aug. 10, 1915.

1866 Rosebery, Earl of, Hon. D.C.L., *K.G.*, *K.T.*, V.D. Hon. Col. 10th R. Scots. Hon. Col. R.A.

1908 Rose-Troup, J. M., B.A. (Mobilized Aug. 1914). Capt. Queens (R. W. Surrey Regt.) (S.R.), attd. 1st Bn. France. (Prisoner of war.)

1891 **Rosse, Earl of,** B.A. (Serving Aug. 4, 1914). Maj. Irish Guards. France, Belgium. Died on June 10, 1918, of wounds received in action at Festubert on May 10, 1915.

1919 Routh, C. R. N. (Oct. 21, 1915). Lt. 6th Rifle Brigade, empld. at War Office. France, 1916.

1919 Rowlatt, J. (Aug. 29, 1917). 2nd Lt. Coldstream Guards (S.R.), attd. 1st Bn. France. *M.C.*, Dec. 2, 1918.

1908 Rudall, R. J., B.Litt. (July 1915). ‡Lt. 50th Bn., A.I.F. Capt. Educational Service, A.I.F. Egypt, France, 1916–18.

1913 Rudd, G. B. F. (Sept. 29, 1914). Lt., temp. Capt., Leicestershire Regt., attd. 6th Bn. France, 1915–18. (Prisoner of war, Apr.–Nov. 1918.)

Russell, F. W. (Jan. 1917). Lt. 16th London Regt. (Queen's Westminster Rifles). France. *M.C.*, June 22, 1918. Killed in action at Croisilles on Aug. 27, 1918.

1919 Russell, J. A. (Sept. 28, 1914). Capt. 2nd S. Staffordshire Regt., attd. 2nd Gloucestershire Regt. France, 1916; Macedonia, 1916–18. *M.C.*, Jan. 11, 1919.

1911 **Russell, W. E.** (Dec. 22, 1916). 2nd Lt. R.F.A. France. Killed in action near Arras on May 12, 1917.

1919 Russell-Parsons, J. C. (Dec. 1915). 2nd Lt., Equipment Officer, R.F.C. 2nd Lt. Grenadier Guards (S.R.). France, 1915–16 (with French Red Cross).

1905 Rycroft, N. E. O., B.A. (Sept. 2, 1914). 2nd Lt. 9th Rifle Brigade. 2nd Lt. Army Cyclist Corps. (Discharged on account of ill health, 1915.)

1919 Sachs, E. L. O. (July 6, 1917). Lt. 484th Batt., R.G.A. France, 1918.

1885 Sackville, Baron, M.A. (Mobilized Aug. 4, 1914). Lt.-Col. W. Kent Yeomanry. Gallipoli, Egypt, Palestine, France. T.D.

1858 Sackville, S. G. Stopford, M.A. Hon. Col. Northamptonshire Regt.

1891 Sackville-West, Hon. B. G., B.A. (Apr. 1915). Lt., Acting Lt.-Commdr., R.N.V.R. (Admiral's Staff). Maj. General List, attd. Ministry of National Service (1918). Gallipoli, Lemnos, Jerusalem. Croix de Chevalier de la Légion d'Honneur.

1895 Sadler, H. K., M.A. (Serving Aug. 4, 1914). Maj., Acting Lt.-Col., R.F.A. France, Belgium. *D.S.O.*, June 4, 1917. *M.C.*, June 4, 1917. *D.* France, 1914, 1915 twice, 1916 twice, 1917, 1918.

1919 Sainsbury, P. A. (Nov. 4, 1917). Lt. R.A.F. North Sea, 1918–19.

1888 St. John, E. F. St. J., M.A. (Oct. 10, 1914). Maj., Superintendent Remount Squadron, Remount Service.

1910 St. Leonards, Baron (Oct. 16, 1914). 2nd Lt. R. Horse Guards (Res. Regt.). (Resigned.)

1919 Salwey, H. J. (Sept. 3, 1918). 2nd Lt. Grenadier Guards (after demobilization).

1897 **Samuda, C. M. A.** (Mobilized Aug. 1914). Maj. Somerset L.I., attd. 13th R. Fusiliers. Belgium, France. Died on July 2, 1917, of wounds received in action at Messines.

1910 **Sandbach, G. R.,** B.A. (Mobilized Aug. 1914). Capt. Denbighshire Yeomanry, attd. 24th R. Fusiliers. Egypt, Palestine. Died on July 3, 1917, in Cairo, of wounds received in action near Gaza.

1897 **Sandbach, H. H.** (Aug. 1914). Capt. late 1st R. Dragoons, comdg. E. African Mounted Rifles. E. Africa. Killed in action in E. Africa on Nov. 4, 1914.

1901 Sandeman, C. A. W. (Aug. 4, 1914). ‡Capt. Special Lists. Staff-Captain (Intelligence). France, 1914–15. *D.* France, 1915.

1902 **Sandeman, G. A. C.,** M.A. (Sept. 1914). Capt. 3rd, attd. 1st, Hampshire Regt. France, Belgium. Killed in action near Ypres on Apr. 24, 1915.

1918 Sanderson, R. W. (Jan. 10, 1916). ‡2nd Lt. 7th E. Surrey Regt. France.

1911 Sandon, Viscount, B.A. (Mobilized Aug. 5, 1914). Capt., Acting Maj., R.F.A. (T.F.). France, Belgium, Germany, 1915–19.

1893 Sankey, R. H., B.M., M.A. (Aug. 8, 1914). Capt. R.A.M.C. (T.F.).

1907 Sassoon, Sir P. A. G. D., Bt. (Mobilized Aug. 1914). Capt. R. E. Kent Yeomanry. Private Secretary to Military Secretary. France. *C.M.G.* Croix de Chevalier de la Légion d'Honneur. Officier de l'Ordre de la Couronne. Belgian Croix de Guerre. L'Ordre de l'Étoile Noire. *D.* France, 1916, 1917.

1904 Sassoon, S. J., B.A. (Serving Aug. 1914). Capt. 6th Dragoons, attd. War Office. France, 1914–15.

1898 Saunderson, J. V. (Nov. 26, 1914). Capt. R.A. (Res. of Officers), empld. War Office.

1894 Sawyer, J. E. H., D.M. (Mobilized Aug. 4, 1914). Maj., Bt.-Lt.-Col., R.A.M.C. (T.F.). Administrator 1st Southern General Hospital. *D.* § Aug. 1919.

1898 Sawyer, R. FitzJ., M.A. (May 15, 1915). Capt. and Q.M. R.A.M.C. (T.F.). 1st Southern General Hospital.

1905 Scarisbrick, C. E. (Serving Aug. 4, 1914). Capt. 3rd R. Scots. France, 1914.

1908 Schellens, R., M.A. (1917). Lt. Intelligence Section, H.Q. U.S. Army. France.

1908 **Schill, E. M.,** B.A. (Nov. 1914). Lt. 17th Lancashire Fusiliers. France. Died on Aug. 25, 1916, of wounds received in action at Trônes Wood.

1890 Scofield, Rev. H. H., M.A. (Dec. 20, 1916). Chaplain to the Forces (4th Class).

1893 Scott, G. H. G., B.A. (Nov. 1914). C.P.O., R.N.V.R., A.A.C. Farrier-Sergt. Inns of Court O.T.C.

1911 **Scott, G. K.** (Sept. 28, 1914). Lt., Acting Capt., R.E. France, Belgium. Killed in action at Dickebusch on Feb. 24, 1917.

1919 Scott, K. C. (Sept. 15, 1914). Lce.-Cpl. 20th R. Fusiliers. France.

1914 Scott-Elliot, W. T. (Oct. 29, 1914). Capt. Coldstream Guards. France.

1901 Seale, H. D., B.A. (1915). Lt. R.N.V.R.

1911 **Seaverns, J. H.** (Mobilized Aug. 5, 1914). Lt. 1/1st London Regt. Malta, 1914–15; France, 1915. Died on May 10, 1915, of wounds received in action at Aubers Ridge.

1905 Secker, Rev. W. H. N., M.A. (Dec. 1916). Chaplain to the Forces (4th Class), attd. 1st Coldstream Guards. France. *M.C.*, Nov. 25, 1917. *D.* France, 1917.

1882 Selby-Bigge, D. L. (Mobilized Aug. 1914). Maj., Hon. Lt.-Col., Northumberland Yeomanry (T.F. Res.).

1911 Selby-Bigge, J. A. (Mar. 15, 1915). Lt. R.A.S.C.

1902 Senhouse, G. J. P. (Mobilized Aug. 5, 1914). Maj. Westmorland & Cumberland Yeomanry, attd. 34th Bde., R.F.A. France, Belgium, 1915–18; Germany, 1918–19.

1919 Sephton, A., B.A. (Oct. 18, 1916). Gnr. 12th (Army) F.A.B., A.I.F. (Sergt.). France.

1913 Serbia, Prince Paul of (Serving Aug. 1914). Lt. R. Serbian Horse Guards. Serbia, 1914–15. Order of Karageorge (1st Class). Order of the White Eagle (2nd Class).

1894 Severn, A. R., B.A. (Jan. 1915). C. P. O. R.N.V.R.

1913 Shaer, J., B.A. (June 23, 1915). ‡2nd Lt. R.A.S.C. France, Belgium, 1914.

1913 **Shann, J. W.** (Jan. 1, 1915). Lt., Acting Adjt., 10th W. Yorkshire Regt. France. Killed in action at Fricourt on July 1, 1916.

1900 Sharp, R. R., B.A. (June 1916). Lt., Acting Maj., A Batt., 173rd Bde., R.F.A. France, Belgium, 1916–18. *D.S.O.*, Sept. 16, 1918. *M.C.*, Jan. 9, 1918. Croix de Guerre (with palm). *D.* France, 1917, 1918.

1906 Shawcross, R. R.,B.A. (Serving Aug. 4, 1914). Capt. Sherwood Foresters.

1919 Sheffield, A. D. (July 11, 1916). Lt. 3rd, attd. 2nd, Shropshire L.I. Salonika, 1917–19. *D.* Salonika, 1918.

1902 Sheringham, C. J. de B., B.A. (Aug. 1914). Capt. 79th Cameron Highlanders of Canada. Temp. Lt.-Col. comdg. 8th Somerset L.I. France. *D.S.O.*, Feb. 1, 1919. *M.C.*, June 3, 1918. *D.* France, 1916, 1917, 1918, 1919.

1902 Shiell, A. G. (Oct. 27, 1915). Lt. 2/1st Highland Cyclist Bn. (T.F.), attd. 4th King's African Rifles. E. Africa.

1907 Shirley, A. C., B.A. (Mobilized Aug. 1914). Capt., Acting Maj., Warwickshire Yeomanry. Egypt, Gallipoli, N. Russia.

1919 Shoobert, W. H. (Jan. 18, 1915). Lt. 7th Rifle Brigade. France, 1915–19.

1880 Shortt, A. G., B.A. (Rejoined Aug. 1914). Capt., Acting Lt.-Col., R.F.A. Capt., Equipment Officer, R.A.F. France, 1916.

1919 Sidebottom, S. R. (Aug. 22, 1914). Lt. R.F.A. France, 1916; India, 1917–18; Mesopotamia, 1918–19.

1905 Simeon, Sir J. W. B., Bt. (Aug. 20, 1914). Lt. 8th Hampshire Regt. Capt., Technical Officer, R.A.F. France, Belgium.

1899 Simmons, G. A. (July 20, 1915). Capt. R.A.M.C.
1919 Simpson, C. A. (July 4, 1916). Capt. Canadian Army Pay Corps.
1919 Simpson, D. C. (Mar. 14, 1918). 2nd Lt. Scots Guards. Germany, 1918–19.
1919 Simson, J. (May 13, 1915). Flt.-Sub-Lt. R.N.A.S., afterwards Sub-Lt. R.N.V.R. First Battle Cruiser Squadron, 1917; Dunkirk, 1918; Malta, 1918–19.
1908 Sing, R. M. (Jan. 30, 1915). Lt. R.F.A. (T.F.). France. *M.C.*, June 3, 1918. *D.* France, 1917.
1878 Sitwell, F. Hurt, M.A. (Aug. 6, 1914). Lt.-Col. O.C. Remount Depot.
1899 Skelton, A. N., B.A. (Aug. 25, 1914). Lt. Scottish Horse.
1899 Skene, P. G. M. (Serving Aug. 4, 1914). Maj., temp. Lt.-Col., The Black Watch. G.S.O. 1. France, Russia, N. Russia. *O.B.E.* (Mil.). Croix de Guerre. Order of St. Stanislas (2nd Class). *D.* § Feb. 1917; France, 1918.
1909 Sladden, C. E., B.A. (Aug. 26, 1914). Maj. 9th Worcestershire Regt. Gallipoli, Egypt, Mesopotamia, Persia, Caucasus. *D.S.O.*, Mar. 8, 1919. *M.C.*, Feb. 6, 1918. *D.* Mesopotamia, 1917, 1918.
1883 Slessor, A. K., M.A. (Rejoined Nov. 1914). Maj. 1/4th Oxf. & Bucks. Lt. Infty., empld. Recruiting Service, 1916–18.
1895 **Smalley, R. F.,** M.A. (May 26, 1915). Lt. 4th S. Staffordshire Regt. France, Belgium. Killed in action at Ploegsteert on Apr. 14, 1918.
1864 Smith, Rev. Canon C., M.A., *M.V.O.* (Serving Aug. 4, 1914). Chaplain (2nd Class), Hampshire Regt.
1912 Smith, C. L., M.A. (Jan. 27, 1916). Sergt. R.A.M.C. France, 1916–18.
1919 Smith, E. C. (Sept. 1, 1917). Signaller, Lce.-Bdr., H.A.C.
1920 Smith, E. F. H. (Oct. 1916). Capt. 4th Rifle Brigade. France.
1877 Smith, H. F. (Oct. 27, 1914). Maj. Montgomeryshire Yeomanry (T.F. Res.).
1911 Smith, J. W. N., B.A. (1914). Pub. Schools Bde., R. Fusiliers. (Discharged on account of ill health.)
1894 Smith, M. T., B.A. (1914). ‡Maj. R.A.O.C. France, Mesopotamia, India, N.W. Frontier.
1872 Smith, W. A., *C.B.* (Aug. 6, 1914). Col. A.Q.M.G., Eastern Command. *C.M.G.* *D.* § Feb. 1917.
1917 Smith, W. L. (Jan. 1915). Lt. Worcestershire Regt.
1907 Smythe, P. C., B.A. (Jan. 18, 1915). Lt., Acting Capt., 6th The Black Watch, attd. Army Gymnastic Staff. France, Belgium. *O.B.E.* (Mil.). *D.* France, 1919.
1903 Snell, I. E., B.A. (Sept. 1, 1914). Lt. 14th London Regt. (London Scottish). Lt., temp. Capt., The Black Watch. Bde. Maj. France, Italy. *M.C.*, Jan. 14, 1916. *D.* France, 1915, 1916; Italy, 1918.
1913 Somers-Cocks, C. V. (Dec. 30, 1914). Capt. 3rd The Black Watch. France, 1915; Mesopotamia, 1915–16.
1905 Southam, A. H., B.M., M.Ch. (Apr. 1917). Capt. R.A.M.C. France.
1920 Southey, R. G. (Oct. 7, 1914). Capt. R.F.A. Staff-Captain R.A., G.H.Q., E.E.F. France, Belgium, 1915–16; Salonika, 1916–17; Palestine, Syria, 1917–19. *M.C.*, June 3, 1919. *D.* Palestine, 1918.
1896 **Sparrow, G. W. S.,** M.A. (Oct. 1914). Capt. Shropshire Yeomanry, attd. 10th Shropshire L.I. Palestine, France. Killed in action at Aubers Ridge on Oct. 4, 1918.

1899 Sparrow, J. A. G., B.M., M.A. (Aug. 1915). Capt. R.A.M.C. France, Belgium.
1907 Spencer, A. E. A. F., M.A. (Aug. 1914). ‡Capt. 6th E. Yorkshire Regt. Capt. General List, attd. G.H.Q. Gallipoli, 1915; Egypt, France, Siberia.
1890 Spender, A. E., B.A. (Nov. 14, 1914). Capt. 5th Devonshire Regt. (T.F.).
1908 Sprott, N. A., B.M., M.A., M.Ch. (May 1915). Surgeon Lt. R.N., H.M.S. *Marlborough*. Grand Fleet, 1916–18.
1913 Squire, G. F., B.A. (Aug. 26, 1914). Capt. 7th Gloucestershire Regt. (Staff-Captain). Gallipoli, 1915; Mesopotamia, 1916, 1918; India, 1917; Persia, 1918; S. Russia, 1918–19. *D.* Mesopotamia, 1917.
1907 Stable, W. N., B.A. (Mobilized Aug. 1914). Capt. Montgomeryshire Yeomanry, attd. 25th R. Welch Fusiliers. France. *M.C.*, Jan. 18, 1918. *D.* France, 1919.
1913 **Stables, J. H.** (Oct. 1914). ‡Lt. I.A.R.O., attd. 1/5th Gurkha Rifles. India, Mesopotamia. Missing, presumed to have died on Feb. 17, 1917, of wounds received in action at Sanna-i-yat.
1904 Stafford, W., B.A. (Oct. 1, 1914). Capt. R.A.S.C. France. *O.B.E.* (Mil.). *D.* France, 1918.
1889 Stainer, C. L., M.A. (May 6, 1915). Lt. 4th Oxf. & Bucks. Lt. Infty. (T.F. Res.).
1907 Stainton, J. A. (Aug. 15, 1914). Capt. 4th Arg. & Suth'd. Highlanders. Staff-Captain. *D.* § Mar. 1919.
1912 Staniforth, J. H. M. (Sept. 13, 1914). ‡Capt. 2nd Leinster Regt. France.
1898 Stanley, E. A. V. (Aug. 30, 1914). ‡Lt. 21st Lancers. France, Belgium, Italy.
1902 Stannard, H. M., M.A. (Dec. 9, 1915). Lt. 6th Hampshire Regt., empld. War Office.
1914 Stannard, R. W., B.A. (Apr. 12, 1915). Lt. Middlesex Regt. France, Belgium, Germany.
1879 Stanyforth, E. W. (Serving Aug. 4, 1914). Lt.-Col. Yorkshire Hussars (T.F. Res.). T.D. *D.* § 1915, § Feb. 1917.
1911 Stanyforth, R. T., B.A. (Serving Aug. 4, 1914). Lt., Acting Capt., 17th Lancers. France, Belgium, Germany, 1914–19. *M.C.*, June 3, 1919. *D.* France, 1918.
1878 Starkey, J. R. (Apr. 1915). Capt. Nottinghamshire Yeomanry (T.F. Res.).
1920 Starr, N. C. (May 15, 1917). 1st Lt. (Coy. Commdr.) 311th Inf., 78th Div., U.S. Army. France.
1897 Stern, Sir A. G., M.A. (1914). Lt. R.N.V.R. Temp. Lt.-Col. Special Lists, empld. Ministry of Munitions. *K.B.E.* *C.M.G.* Croix de Chevalier de la Légion d'Honneur. *D.* § Jan. 1917.
1903 Stern, F. C. (Mobilized Aug. 4, 1914). Capt., temp. Maj., 2nd County of London Yeomanry. D.A.Q.M.G. Eastern Command. Egypt, 1914; Gallipoli, 1915; France, 1915–16. *O.B.E.* (Mil.). *M.C.*, Jan. 1, 1918. *D.* Palestine, 1917, 1918.
1912 Stevens, A. L. B. (Oct. 13, 1914). Lt., Acting Capt., 6th R. Munster Fusiliers. Egypt, 1915; Salonika, 1916–17; Palestine, 1917–18; France, 1918–19. *D.* Palestine, 1918; France, 1919.
1918 Stevens, G. C. (Sept. 21, 1914). Capt. 2/1st Bucks. Bn. Oxf. & Bucks.

Lt. Infty. France, Belgium, 1916–17. (Invalided on account of wounds, Aug. 1918.)

1908 Stevenson, A. F. M. (Nov. 9, 1914). Lt. 17th Lancers (S.R.). France. *M.C.*, June 22, 1918.

1920 Stevenson, E. H. (Mar. 1, 1918). Petty Officer, U.S. Navy.

1890 **Stewart, B.** (Mobilized Aug. 1914). Capt. W. Kent Yeomanry. France, 1914. Killed in action on Sept. 16, 1914.

1902 Stewart, E. O., M.A. (Aug. 4, 1914). Capt. Grenadier Guards, attd. War Office. France.

1904 Stewart, J. A. (May 7, 1915). Lt. I.A.R.O. India, Mesopotamia. *M.C.*, June 4, 1917. *D.* Mesopotamia, 1917.

1905 Stewart-Liberty, I. (Sept. 2, 1914). Lt., Acting Capt., 2nd Bucks. Bn. Oxf. & Bucks. Lt. Infty. France, 1916. *M.C.*, Sept. 9, 1916.

1891 Still, A. L., B.A. (Sept. 2, 1917). 2nd Lt. R.G.A. (S.R.).

1910 **Stirling-Stuart, J.,** B.A. (Serving Aug. 4, 1914). Lt. 1st Scots Guards. France, Belgium, 1914. Died on Nov. 9, 1914, of wounds received in action at Ypres.

1901 Stock, J. E. K. (Dec. 28, 1914). Capt. Remount Service.

1914 Stockton, G. B. (1917). Lt. (Junior Grade) U.S. Naval Res. Chevalier de l'Ordre de la Couronne.

1907 **Stollery, J. C.,** B.A. (Mobilized Aug. 4, 1914). Lt. 5th R. Fusiliers. France, Belgium, 1914–15. Killed in action at Ypres on May 24, 1915.

1901 Stone, C. R., B.A. (Sept. 10, 1914). Maj. 22nd R. Fusiliers. Maj. General List. A.D.C. to G.O.C. 2nd Div. France, Germany, 1915–18. *D.S.O.*, June 3, 1918. *M.C.*, Nov. 25, 1916. *D.* France, 1916, 1917, 1918.

1903 Streatfeild, Rev. F., B.D. (Oct. 10, 1914). Chaplain to the Forces (4th Class), attd. 1/4th Oxf. & Bucks. Lt. Infty. France.

1889 **Street, F.,** M.A. (Aug. 1914). ‡Lt. 9th R. Fusiliers. France, 1915–16. Killed in action in the Battle of the Somme on July 7, 1916.

1918 Strover, C. H. (Feb. 25, 1915). Pte. 23rd Bn. A.I.F., attd. 6th Field Amb. Egypt, 1915; Gallipoli, 1915; Egypt, 1916; France, 1916–17.

1893 Strutt, E. L. (Serving Aug. 4, 1914). Maj., temp. Lt.-Col., 3rd R. Scots. G.S.O. 2. Salonika. *C.B.E.* (Mil.). *D.S.O.*, Jan. 1, 1918. Croix d'Officier de la Légion d'Honneur. Croix de Chevalier de l'Ordre de Léopold. Croix de Guerre, avec Palme. *D.* Salonika, 1917, 1918.

1919 Stuart, J. J. (Apr. 16, 1917). Lce.-Cpl. 4th Res. Cavalry Regt. (Cpl.).

1906 Stuart, P. P., B.A. (Mar. 19, 1915). Lt., temp. Capt., I.A.R.O. (Cavalry). India.

1920 Stubbs, W. B. (July 18, 1918). 2nd Lt. 36th Training Batt., F.A., U.S. Army.

1894 Stubbs, Rev. W. T., M.A. (June 1917). Chaplain to the Forces (4th Class). France, Belgium, 1917–18.

1883 Studholme, J., M.A., *D.S.O.* (Serving Aug. 4, 1914). Maj. New Zealand Military Forces. A.A.G. France. *M.B.E.* (Mil.). *D.* France, 1916.

1903 **Studholme, L. J. M.,** B.A. (Aug. 1914). Lt., Acting Capt., 7th Leinster Regt. France, 1915–16. *D.* France, 1916. Killed in action in the Battle of the Somme on Sept. 9, 1916.

1912 Sturges, R. S. M., M.A. (Sept. 2, 1914). ‡Lt. M.G.C., attd. War Office (Intelligence). France, 1915.

1910 Sturley, A. A. (Mar. 9, 1915). Maj. Nova Scotia Regt., attd. H.Q. 4th and 2nd Armies. France, Germany, 1917–19.

1906 Sturt, G. C. N., B.A. (Aug. 10, 1914). ‡Capt. Worcestershire Regt. Gallipoli, 1915; France, 1916–17.

1919 Surls, J. K. (Aug. 7, 1917). Capt. 103rd Amb. Coy., U.S. Army. France.

1919 Sutton, C. W. H. (Sept. 5, 1917). 2nd Lt. 1st Coldstream Guards. France, Germany.

1914 Sutton, N. E. P. (July 7, 1915). Capt. Coldstream Guards (S.R.). A.D.C. Croix de Chevalier de la Légion d'Honneur.

1919 Sutton, W. H. A. (May 8, 1918). Air Mechanic R.A.F.

1914 Swaine, Y. W. (Feb. 27, 1915). Lt. Grenadier Guards. France, Belgium, Germany, 1915–18.

1909 Swinden, B. A. (Nov. 29, 1915). Lt., Acting Capt., R.F.A., empld. Instructional Duties. Belgium, France, 1917–18.

1890 Sykes, H. R., M.A. (Mobilized Aug. 1914). Maj. Montgomeryshire Yeomanry, attd. Labour Corps.

1919 Sykes, J. A. (Mar. 23, 1917). Lt. R.F.A. France. (Prisoner of war, Sept.–Dec. 1918.)

1894 Symes-Thompson, Rev. F., M.A. (Feb. 20, 1917). Chaplain to the Forces (4th Class). France, Belgium.

1913 Symonds, R. F. (Dec. 22, 1914). Capt. and Adjt. Bucks. Bn. Oxf. & Bucks. Lt. Infty., attd. 2/4th Bn. Staff Appointment. France; Palestine, 1919. Belgian Croix de Guerre. *D.* France, 1919.

1889 Synge, M., B.A. (Serving Aug. 4, 1914). Maj. Supply & Transport Corps, Indian Army (Lt.-Col.). France, Belgium, East Persia, Transcaspia. *C.I.E.* *D.S.O.*, Jan. 1, 1917. *D.* France, 1916 twice, 1919.

1897 Talbot, Rev. E. K., M.A. (Aug. 30, 1914). Chaplain to the Forces (4th Class). France. *M.C.*, June 3, 1916.

1910 **Talbot, G. W. L.** (Aug. 1914). Lt. 7th Rifle Brigade. Belgium, 1915. Killed in action at Hooge on July 30, 1915.

1902 Talbot, H. J., B.A. (Sept. 16, 1914). ‡Lt. R.A.S.C. France, Belgium.

1903 [Talbot, Rt. Rev. N. S., D.D.] (Aug. 21, 1914). Chaplain to the Forces (1st Class) (Asst. Chap.-Gen.). France. *M.C.*, Jan. 14, 1916. *D.* France, 1915 twice, 1916.

1908 Talbot-Rice, H., B.A. (Serving Aug. 4, 1914). Capt. 1st Welsh Guards. France, Belgium.

1919 Talbot-Rice, M. G. (Jan. 4, 1918). 2nd Lt. Coldstream Guards.

1890 Tassell, D. S. M., M.A. (Serving Aug. 4, 1914). Maj. Unattached List, T.F., Malvern College O.T.C. *D.* § Mar. 1919.

1902 Tatton, R. H. G. (Mobilized Aug. 1914). Capt. 3rd Oxf. & Bucks. Lt. Infty., attd. O.C.B. France, 1915; Mesopotamia, 1915–16.

1887 Taylor, C. de B. (Mobilized Aug. 1914). Capt. 1st Bn. Channel Islands Militia. Capt. R. Irish Rifles.

1914 Taylor, R. T. (1916). Pte. U.S. Field Artillery. France.

1910 Taylor, Rev. W. A., M.A. (Jan. 1916). Chaplain to the Forces (4th Class). Egypt, 1916–17; Mesopotamia, 1917–19.

1886 Teale, M. A., M.A. (Mar. 1, 1917). Lt. R.A.M.C.

1915 **Terres, H.** (May 26, 1917). Lt. Foreign Legion. Ensign U.S. Res. Naval Air Service. France, Italy. Killed in action in Italy on Aug. 17, 1918.

1906 Tetley, G. S., B.C.L., M.A. (Sept. 2, 1914). ‡Capt. 9th E. Surrey Regt. France, 1915–17. *M.C.*, Mar. 30, 1916.

1912 Thompson, G. K. (Sept. 19, 1914). Lt., Acting Capt., Irish Guards. France. *M.C.*, Mar. 15, 1916 ; *Bar*, Sept. 2, 1916.

1908 Thomson, G. T., B.A. (Jan. 28, 1915). Lt. 8th R. Scots (T.F.).

1904 **Thomson, S.,** B.A. (Sept. 1914). Capt., Acting Maj., 2nd R. Fusiliers. Gallipoli, Egypt, France. *M.C.*, June 4, 1917. Killed in action at Monchy on Apr. 24, 1917.

1911 Thorne, F. O., B.A. (Jan. 28, 1915). Capt. 13th Manchester Regt. (Adjt.). Salonika. *M.C.*, Jan. 1, 1918. *D.* Salonika, 1917.

1907 Thorne, R. G. A., B.A. (Aug. 15, 1914). Capt. 3rd S. Lancashire Regt., attd. 234th Inf. Bde. H.Q., 76th Div. British E. Africa, 1915–17 ; Egypt, Palestine, 1917–19. *D.* Palestine, 1919.

1906 **Thorne, T. F. J. N.,** B.A. (Serving Aug. 4, 1914). Capt. and Adjt. 4th Grenadier Guards. France. Missing, believed killed in action at the Battle of Loos on Sept. 28, 1915.

1899 Thornton, B. M. (July 19, 1915). Capt. R.A.O.C. (Maj.). D.A.D. Ordnance Service. France, Belgium, Italy. *M.C.*, Jan. 1, 1918. *D.* France, 1917.

1900 Thornton, H. C., B.A. (1914). Maj. Training Res.

1884 Timmis, G. D., B.A. (Mobilized Aug. 1914). Lt.-Col. 5th Manchester Regt. (T.F. Res.). *D.* § Feb. 1917.

1885 Timmis, T. S., B.A. (Mobilized Aug. 1914). Maj. 3rd S. Staffordshire Regt.

1919 Tingey, A. H. (Aug. 6, 1916). 2nd Lt. R.F.A. (on demobilization).

1900 Todd, A. M., M.A. (Mobilized Aug. 1914). Maj. Worcestershire Yeomanry.

1907 Todd, E. E. E. (Nov. 27, 1916). Maj., temp. Lt.-Col., Paymaster, A.P.D. *O.B.E.* (Mil.).

1900 Todd, E. H., M.A. (July 9, 1915). Cpl. R.E. France.

1883 Toler, T. C., B.A. (Jan. 1915). Maj. 3/5th Sherwood Foresters (T.F. Res.).

1907 Tomlinson, B. (May 22, 1917). Capt. U.S. Field Artillery. France, 1918.

1903 **Tower, C. C.,** M.A. (Mobilized Aug. 4, 1914). Lt. Essex Yeomanry. A.D.C. to the Maj-Gen. of the 12th Div. France. Killed in action in France on Oct. 2, 1915.

1914 Toynbee, J. W. H. (Dec. 2, 1914). Lt. 3rd The Buffs (E. Kent Regt.). Maj. M.G.C. Belgium, France, 1916–17 ; Italy, 1917–19. *M.C.*, Jan. 1, 1917 ; *Bar*, Oct. 17, 1918. Belgian Croix de Guerre. *D.* Italy, 1918.

1913 Trask, C. S. L., B.A. (Oct. 1914). Capt. General List. Staff-Lt. (1st Class) Intelligence Corps. France. *O.B.E.* (Mil.). *D.* France, 1918.

1914 Trelawney-Ross, S. M. T. (July 15, 1917). Pte. 1/28th London Regt. (Artists' Rifles). Belgium and France, 1917–18. (Prisoner of war, Mar.–Dec. 1918.)

1903 Trench, J. R., B.A. (Mobilized Aug. 4, 1914). Capt. 6th King's (Liverpool Regt.). France.

1904 Trenchard, C., M.A. (Apr. 29, 1915). Lt. 5th Somerset L.I.

1909 Troutbeck, G. L., B.A. (Oct. 20, 1914). Capt. Bucks. Bn. Oxf. & Bucks. Lt. Infty. France, Italy. *D.* Italy, 1919.

1913 Troutbeck, J. M. (Sept. 1914). Lt. 12th London Regt. (The Rangers). A.D.C. Headquarters Staff, India. France, Gallipoli, India. *O.B.E.* (Mil.). *D.* France, 1915.

1898 [Truslove, R., M.A.] (Mobilized Aug. 1914). Maj. 4th Seaforth Highlanders. Staff-Captain in the 51st Div. France, 1914–15, 1916–18.

1905 Tucker, Rev. B. D., M.A. (1917). Lt. Chaplain, 17th U.S. Engineers. France.

1903 Tull, A. S. B. (May 1916). Lt. R.A.S.C., attd. R.G.A. France, Belgium. *D.* France, 1918.

1906 Turbutt, R. B., M.A. (Serving Aug. 4, 1914). Capt., Acting Maj., R.G.A. France, 1915–16; Italy, 1917; Egypt, 1917–18; Italy, 1918–19. Italian Bronze Medal for Valour.

1880 Turing, Sir J. W., Bt. (Oct. 8, 1914). Lt. General List (T.F. Res.).

1900 Turner, F. W., B.A. (Feb 3, 1915). Lt., Acting Capt., R.G.A. France, Gibraltar, Belgium.

1905 **Turnor, C. R.,** B.A. (Serving Aug. 4, 1914). Lt. 10th Hussars. Belgium, France. Killed in action at Zandevoorde, Belgium, on Oct. 26, 1914.

1904 Turnor, H. B., B.A. (Serving Aug. 4, 1914). Capt. 17th Lancers. France, Belgium, Germany, 1914–19. *M.C.*, June 3, 1918; *Bar*, Oct. 16, 1918. *D.* France, 1917.

1881 Turville-Petre, O. H. P., B.A. (Feb. 1915). Maj., Hon. Lt.-Col., Northamptonshire Yeomanry (T.F. Res.).

1903 Tweeddale, Marquis of (Mobilized Aug. 1914). Capt. 1st Life Guards.

1871 Twemlow, F. R., M.A., *D.S.O.* (Mobilized 1914). Hon. Col., late Lt.-Col., 4th N. Staffordshire Regt. O.C. 3/6th N. Staffordshire Regt.

1898 Twiss, C. C. H., B.A. (Nov. 14, 1914). Lt.-Col. 13th E. Yorkshire Regt. Mediterranean, 1915–16; France, 1916–18. *D.S.O.*, Jan. 1, 1918. *D.* France, 1917. (Prisoner of war, 1918.)

1888 Tyringham, R. W. G. (July 16, 1915). Lt. empld. Recruiting Duties. (Resigned.)

1884 Underwood, J. W. (Aug. 15, 1914). Maj. Res. of Officers, attd. 10th (Res.) Regt. of Cavalry.

1912 Usher, C. G. (Sept. 1, 1914). Lt. S. Wales Borderers. Mesopotamia. *M.C.*, Aug. 16, 1917; *Bar*, Aug. 25, 1917.

1919 Usher, P. C. A. (Oct. 8, 1917). 2nd Lt. R.G.A. (S.R.), Anti-Aircraft Section. Salonika.

1883 Valletort, Viscount (Sept. 17, 1914). Maj., Hon. Col., 3rd D.C.L.I. (S.R.).

1900 **Vane, Hon. H. C.** (Nov. 23, 1914). Lt., Acting Maj., Yorkshire Hussars. Lt., Acting Capt., R.F.A. (T.F.). France, Belgium. Killed in action on Oct. 9, 1917.

1907 **Vansittart, A. B.,** B.A. (Aug. 15, 1914). 2nd Lt. 11th Hussars. France. Died on May 12, 1915, of wounds received in action.

1898 Verney, R. (Serving Aug. 4, 1914). Maj., temp. Lt.-Col., Rifle Brigade. Military Secretary to Viceroy of India. India. Order of the Sacred Treasure (3rd Class).

1906 **Vernon, Lord** (Mobilized Aug. 1914). Capt. Derbyshire Yeomanry. Egypt, Gallipoli. Died at Malta on Nov. 10, 1915, of illness contracted on active service in Gallipoli.

1897 Vernon-Harcourt, B. F. (Serving Aug. 4, 1914). Maj. R. Welch Fusiliers. Maj., Squadron Commdr., R.A.F. France, 1915–19.

1892 Vesey, S. P. C., M.A. (Aug. 10, 1918). Capt. 20th K.R.R.C. A.D.C. to G.O.C. Light Div., Army of Occupation. Germany, 1919. *C.B.E.* (Civil).

1904 Vesey, Hon. T. E. (Serving Aug. 4, 1914). Lt.-Col. 1st Irish Guards. France, Belgium, from Aug. 1914. Croix de Guerre (with palm). *D.* § Mar. 1919.
1897 Vigors, E. C. (Jan. 21, 1916). Capt. Special Lists.
1891 Villiers, C. W. (Aug. 25, 1915). Lt., temp. Lt.-Col., Coldstream Guards (S.R.). Provost Marshal. Salonika. *C.B.E.* (Mil.). *D.S.O.*, Nov. 23, 1916. Order of the White Eagle (5th Class). Commander of the Order of the Redeemer. *D.* Salonika, 1917, 1918, 1919.
1907 Villiers, F. E. E. (May 3, 1917). Lt., Flying Officer, R.A.F.
1906 Visconti-Venosta, Marchese Enrico (1915). Italian Army. Italy.
1915 Voltos, C. P. (Oct. 1915). Volunteer, Monastir Divl. Cavalry, Serbian Army. 2nd Lt., Interpreter, Special Lists. Serbia, 1915–16; Salonika, Italy, France, 1917–19.
1900 Wade-Palmer, A. N. (Mobilized Aug. 1914). Capt. Sherwood Rangers.
1880 Waggett, Rev. P. N., M.A. (Sept. 8, 1914). Chaplain to the Forces (3rd Class), attd. Gen. Staff (Political Branch), E.E.F. France, 1914–18; Egypt, Palestine, 1918–19. *D.* France, 1916.
1895 Wake, D., B.A. (1914). ‡Capt. 10th Rifle Brigade. Capt. General List. France. Chevalier de l'Ordre du Mérite Agricole.
1911 Wakefield, H. B. (Mar. 18, 1916). Lt., Technical Officer, R.A.F.
1906 Wakeman, O., M.A. (Mobilized Aug. 4, 1914). Capt. Grenadier Guards (Res. of Officers). A.D.C. to Viceroy of India. France, 1915; India, 1918.
1919 Walding, T. W. (Sept. 12, 1914). ‡Lt. 2nd Oxf. & Bucks. Lt. Infty., attd. M.G.C. France, 1916, 1917–18. (Prisoner of war, 1918.)
1890 [Walker, E. W. A., D.M., D.Sc.] (Oct. 1914). Capt. O.U.O.T.C. (Medical Unit), attd. 3rd Southern General Hospital.
1902 **Walker, R.,** B.A. (Aug. 4, 1914). ‡2nd Lt. 2/5th Lancashire Fusiliers. France. Killed in action at Trônes Wood on Aug. 9, 1916.
1914 Wallace, A. R. (Aug. 14, 1916). Lt. I.A.R.O., attd. Patiala Lancers. Mesopotamia.
1919 Wallace, H. C. (July 2, 1918). Cadet, R.A.F.
1900 Wallace, H. F., B.A. (1914). Anti-Aircraft Corps, R.N.V.R.
1905 Wallace, R. S., M.A. (Feb. 23, 1917). ‡Lt. F.A., A.I.F. Lt. Educational Service, A.I.F. France.
1920 Wallis, T. H. (Sept. 29, 1917). 2nd Lt. 3rd, attd. 1st, K.R.R.C. France, Germany.
1912 Walmisley, G. H., M.A. (Sept. 1914). ‡Lt., Acting Capt., R.E. (Signals). France, 1915. *M.C.*, June 3, 1916.
1897 Walter, S., M.A. Lt. R.N.V.R. (Armoured Car Div.).
1919 Warburg, F. J. (June 6, 1917). 2nd Lt. 186th Siege Batt., R.G.A. France.
1912 **Ward, C. S.** (Sept. 1914). Lt., Acting Capt., 10th R. Warwickshire Regt. France, Belgium. Killed in action near Neuve Chapelle on Jan. 8, 1915.
1896 **Ward, J. S.** (Aug. 1914). Maj. Princess Patricia's Canadian L.I. France, Belgium, 1914–15. Died at Boulogne on Mar. 17, 1915, of wounds received in action.
1915 Ward, L. P., B.A. (May 23, 1917). 2nd Lt. 1st (Garr.) Bn. Worcestershire Regt., attd. War Office.

1919 Ward-Jackson, G. N. R. (Serving Aug. 4, 1914). Midshipman R.N., H.M.S. *Agincourt*. Grand Fleet.

1907 **Warner, C. J.** (Mobilized Aug. 1914). Lt. 3rd, attd. 2nd, Oxf. & Bucks. Lt. Infty. (Capt.). France. Killed in action at Festubert on May 16, 1915.

1904 Warner, E. C. T. (Serving Aug. 4, 1914). Capt., Bt.-Maj., Scots Guards. France, Belgium, 1914–18. *D.S.O.*, June 4, 1917. *M.C.*, June 3, 1915. Croix de Guerre. Order of Danilo (5th Class) (Montenegro). Military Order of Avis (Portuguese) (3rd Class). *D.* France, 1915 three times, 1916, 1917 twice, 1918.

1903 Warren, R. G. (Mobilized Aug. 4, 1914). Maj. 9th London Regt. (Queen Victoria's Rifles). D.A.Q.M.G. Belgium, 1914–15; N. Russia, 1919. *D.* N. Russia, 1919.

1905 Waterfield, W. F. H., B.A. (Apr. 23, 1917). Lt. R.G.A. (S.R.).

1911 **Waterton, J. C.** (Oct. 11, 1914). 2nd Lt. 5th Bedfordshire Regt. Killed in an accident on Feb. 18, 1915.

1893 Watson, H. G. (Oct. 23, 1914). Capt. 19th Divl. Train, R.A.S.C. France.

1912 Watts, H. G., B.A. (Sept. 5, 1914). ‡Lt. King's (Liverpool Regt.), attd. 14th Bn. France, 1915–16, 1918–19; Macedonia, 1916–18. *M.C.*, Jan. 1, 1918.

1895 Wayman, H. R. B., M.A. (Nov. 1914). Lt.-Col. 14th Northumberland Fusiliers. France, Belgium. *D.S.O.*, Jan. 1, 1918. *D.* France, 1917.

1894 Webb, W. H. (Mobilized Aug. 4, 1914). Maj. Staffordshire Yeomanry (T.F. Res.). Egypt, 1915–16. (Invalided.)

1906 **Welby, R. W. G.,** B.A. (Serving Aug. 4, 1914). Lt. 2nd Grenadier Guards. Belgium, France, Aug. 1914. Killed in action at Cour de Soupir, near the Aisne, on Sept. 20, 1914.

1918 Weldon, E. G. (Serving Aug. 4, 1914). Capt. 8th Hussars. France, Belgium.

1900 **Were, Rev. C. N.,** M.A. (Dec. 1917). Chaplain to the Forces (4th Class), attd. 12th Rifle Brigade. France, 1917–18. Died in France on Jan. 8, 1918.

1903 West, A. T. (Mobilized Aug. 1914). Maj. Berkshire Yeomanry.

1904 West, Rev. G. H. (Jan. 1918). Chaplain to the Forces (4th Class). France, Belgium, 1918–19.

1907 West, J. F., B.M., M.A. (May 17, 1915). Capt. R.A.M.C. France.

1910 Weston-Stevens, J. A. R. (Aug. 15, 1914). Capt. 3rd Dorsetshire Regt. Staff-Lt., War Office. France, Belgium, 1915.

1910 Westmacott, G. R. (Aug. 15, 1914). Capt. Grenadier Guards. France, from 1914. *D.S.O.*, Nov. 30, 1917. Croix de Guerre. *D.* France; § June, 1919.

1882 Wethered, F. O., M.A. (Mobilized Aug. 1914). Lt.-Col. R. Warwickshire Regt. (T.F. Res.). France, 1915–17. *C.M.G.*, June 3, 1916. V.D. *D.* France, 1915, 1916.

1885 Wethered, Rev. O. H., M.A., T.D. (Serving Aug. 4, 1914). Chaplain to the Forces (2nd Class).

1917 Wethered, R. H. (Aug. 13, 1917). 2nd Lt. R.G.A. (S.R.). France, Belgium.

1902 Whately, F. B., B.A. (Sept. 2, 1914). ‡Lt., Acting Capt., 6th K.R.R.C. France, 1915–16.

1913 **Whately, R. H.** (Nov. 1914). Lt., Acting Capt., 5th Rifle Brigade. France. Missing, presumed killed in action in France on Aug. 25, 1916.

1911 Whatmore, W. R. T., B.A. (Sept. 1914). ‡Maj., Acting Lt.-Col., 8th, attd. 2/7th, R. Warwickshire Regt. France, 1916–19. *M.C.*, Jan. 1, 1918; *Bar*, Sept. 16, 1918. *D.* France, 1918.

1905 Wheeler-Bennett, C. W., B.M., M.A. (Nov. 1914). Surgeon Lt. R.N.

1891 Wheler, G. B. H., M.A. (Serving Aug. 4, 1914). Maj. 21st Lancers. Bde. Maj., attd. H.Q. Gallipoli, 1915; Belgium, France, 1916–17; Palestine, Syria, 1917–19. *M.C.*, Jan. 1, 1919. *D.* France, 1917.

1891 Wheler, G. C. H., M.A., *M.P.* (Mar. 28, 1915). Lt.-Col. General List. D.A.Q.M.G. *C.B.E.* (Mil.). *D.* § Feb. 1917, § Mar. 1918, § Aug. 1918.

1919 Whinney, E. F. G. (May 1, 1917). Lt. 14th Divl. Train, R.A.S.C. France, Belgium.

1902 Whinyates, G., B.A. (May 27, 1916). Lt. General List. Staff-Lt. (2nd Class) Intelligence Corps.

1895 White, J. W. B. (Sept. 7, 1914). ‡Capt. 1st County of London Yeomanry. Egypt, 1915–16; Salonika, 1916–17; Palestine, 1917.

1907 **Whitehead, G. N.** (Dec. 1916). 2nd Lt. R.F.C. France, Belgium. Killed in action near Ypres on Oct. 15, 1917.

1908 Whitelock, H. A. B., B.M., M.A. (Nov. 5, 1915). Capt. R.A.M.C. Egypt.

1914 Whiting, H. N. (Dec. 11, 1914). Lt. 6th Somerset L.I.

1901 Whitmore, J. B., B.A. (Mobilized Aug. 1914). Maj. 16th London Regt. (Queen's Westminster Rifles). Staff-Captain. France.

1919 Widdowson, W. P. (Mar. 17, 1917). Sergt. R.E. (Anti-Gas Establishment).

1919 Wigan, T. H. (Jan. 24, 1918). 2nd Lt. Grenadier Guards.

1912 Wigan, T. K., B.A. (Aug. 12, 1914). Capt. 1/6th Devonshire Regt. Mesopotamia. *D.* Mesopotamia, 1918, 1919.

1896 Wilberforce, A. R. G., B.A. (Mobilized Aug. 1914). Capt. 3rd R. Sussex Regt., Res. of Officers. Staff-Captain. *O.B.E.* (Mil.). *D.* § Aug. 1918.

1913 **Wilcox, K. T. D.** (Sept. 13, 1914). 2nd Lt. 8th Queen's (R. W. Surrey Regt.). France, Belgium. Killed in action near Ypres on Nov. 8, 1915.

1905 Willes, H. W. H. (Aug. 5, 1914). ‡2nd Lt. Oxf. & Bucks. Lt. Infty. Lt. M.G.C. France, Belgium, Germany.

1902 Willett, A. T., M.A. (Serving Aug. 4, 1914). Capt. Unattached List, T.F., Westminster School O.T.C. *D.* § Mar. 1919.

1899 Willett, B. H., M.A. (Dec. 17, 1915). Lt. R.G.A. (S.R.), empld. R.E. France.

1908 Williams, Rev. C., M.A. (Jan. 10, 1917). Chaplain to the Forces (4th Class).

1909 Williams, G. G., B.A. (Nov. 14, 1914). Lt., temp. Capt., 4th Dorsetshire Regt. Staff Appointment.

1908 **Williams, H. L. J.,** B.A., B.Litt. (May 1917). Capt. 326th Infantry, U.S. Army. France. Killed in action at Albert on June 9, 1918.

1881 Williams-Wynn, R. W. H. W., B.A., *D.S.O.*, T.D. (Mobilized Aug. 4, 1914). Maj., Bt.-Lt.-Col., Montgomeryshire Yeomanry. Egypt, Palestine, 1916–18. *D.* Egypt, 1916; Palestine, 1918 twice.

1912 **Williamson, H. H. C.** (Sept. 26, 1914). Lt. Coldstream Guards. France. Killed in action in the Battle of the Ancre on Sept. 16, 1916.

1919 Willis, F. P. de L. (Mar. 5, 1916). Lt. R.A.S.C. France, 1916–18.

Willis, G. W. (Sept. 5, 1917). 2nd Lt., Flying Officer, R.A.F. France. Killed on active service at Marginse on Jan. 4, 1919.

1890 Willis, R. A. de A. (Nov. 6, 1914). Maj. N. Somerset Yeomanry.

1913 Willis-Fleming, J. B. P. (Aug. 1914). 2nd Lt. Hampshire Yeomanry. Lt. 6th Dragoons (S.R.).

Willis-Fleming, R. T. C. (1916). 2nd Lt. R.H.A. (T.F.). France. Died in July 1916 of wounds received in action on the Somme.

1919 Willock-Pollen, H. L. B. (Jan. 3, 1917). Lt. 1st Coldstream Guards. France.

1876 Willoughby, F., M.A. (Mobilized Aug. 1914). Hon. Lt.-Col. 2/4th Northamptonshire Regt. *O.B.E.* (Mil.). V.D. *D.* § Feb. 1917, § Mar. 1919.

1919 Wills, H. E. M. (Mar. 1916). Lt. Scots Guards. France, Belgium, Germany.

1913 **Wilmot-Sitwell, J. S.** (Feb. 1915). Lt. Coldstream Guards. France, Belgium. Died on July 9, 1916, of wounds received in action at Ypres.

1892 Wilson, C. C., B.A. (Mobilized Aug. 1914). Maj. Westmorland & Cumberland Yeomanry.

1895 **Wilson, C. E. A.,** B.M. (Sept. 15, 1916). Capt. R.A.M.C., attd. Rifle Brigade. France. Died on Apr. 8, 1918, of wounds received in action near St. Quentin on Mar. 28.

1885 **Wilson, G. C.,** *M.V.O.* (Serving Aug. 4, 1914). Lt.-Col. R. Horse Guards. France, Belgium. Killed in action on Nov. 6, 1914.

1899 Wilson, Rev. J. M., M.A. (Aug. 7, 1917). Chaplain to the Forces (4th Class). Palestine, Syria.

1919 Wilson-Fox, G. H. (Sept. 7, 1917). 2nd Lt. 1st Life Guards, Guards M.G. Regt. France.

1897 Wingate-Saul, N. W., B.A. (Serving Aug. 4, 1914). Capt., temp. Maj., R.A.O.C. Chief Ordnance Officer, N.Z.E.F. France.

1892 Wingfield-Digby, Canon S. H., M.A. (June 29, 1916). Chaplain to the Forces (4th Class), attd. 4th Cavalry Div. France.

1919 Winn, Hon. R. H. (Feb. 8, 1918). 2nd Lt. Grenadier Guards. Germany.

1919 Winterbotham, F. W. (Apr. 22, 1915). Capt. R.A.F. France, Belgium.

1883 Wintour, E. (Serving Aug. 4, 1914). Lt.-Col. Indian Army. India.

1919 Wiswell, D. M. (Mar. 7, 1916). Lt. Nova Scotia Highlanders, C.E.F. France. Belgian Ordre de la Couronne.

1910 Withington, T. E., B.A. (Jan. 1914). Lt. 2nd Oxf. & Bucks. Lt. Infty. Capt., Staff Officer, R.A.F. France, Belgium, 1915–18. *A.F.C.*, June 3, 1919.

1919 Wood, D. (Dec. 7, 1917). 2nd Lt. Grenadier Guards.

1899 [Wood, Hon. E. F. L., M.A.] (Mobilized Aug. 1914). Maj. Yorkshire Dragoons, empld. Ministry of National Service. France, 1915. *D.* France, 1916.

1916 Wood, J. (June 1917). 2nd Lt. S. Lancashire Regt. France, 1917–18.

1895 Wood, J. N. P. (Mobilized Aug. 1914). Lt.-Col. 2/1st Lanarkshire Yeomanry. *D.* § Feb. 1917.

1903 Wood, R. L. (Sept. 1, 1914). Capt. R.E. (T.F.) (Maj.). France, 1915–18. *M.C.*, July 26, 1917. *D.* France, 1917.

1899 Wood, W. J. C., M.A. (Mar. 1, 1917). 2nd Lt. Shropshire L.I.

1896 Woodard, G. H. (May 30, 1917). 2nd Lt. 1st (Garr.) Bn. Suffolk Regt.

1899 Woodhouse, J. D. F., M.A. (Serving Aug. 4, 1914). Capt. 14th Hussars (Maj.). Egypt, Gallipoli, Salonika, Mesopotamia, Persia. *D.S.O.*, Jan. 11, 1919. *D.* Gallipoli, 1915; Mesopotamia, 1917, 1918.

1900 Woodhouse, R. F., M.A. (Feb. 22, 1916). Cpl. Army Pay Corps. France.

1897 **Woodward, R.,** M.A. (Oct. 5, 1914). Lt., Acting Capt., 3rd, attd. 1st, S. Wales Borderers. France, 1915. Killed in action at Richebourg l'Avoué on May 9, 1915.

1905 Woosnam, R. W., B.A. (Mobilized Aug. 1914). Capt., Acting Lt.-Col., S. Wales Borderers. Aden, India, 1915–16; Mesopotamia, 1916–19. *D.* Mesopotamia, 1917.

1901 **Worsley-Worswick, B. H.** (1914). ‡2nd Lt. 2nd King Edward's Horse, (Cavalry S.R.). Killed in Irish Rebellion at Dublin on Apr. 29, 1916.

1898 Wray, H. C. (May 10, 1915). Maj., temp. Lt.-Col., R.F.A. France, Belgium. *D.S.O.*, June 4, 1917. *D.* France, 1916, 1917.

1913 **Wright, H. M.** (1914). Ambulance Driver, attd. French Army. 2nd Lt. Yorkshire Regt. France, 1915, 1917. Killed in action on Apr. 2, 1917.

1919 Wright, N. C. (Apr. 3, 1918). 2nd Lt. R. Berkshire Regt. (on demobilization).

1918 Wrisberg, F. G. (May 12, 1915). Capt. R.G.A. France, Belgium.

1913 **Wrong, H. V.** (Dec. 14, 1914). Lt. 15th Lancashire Fusiliers. France. Killed in action at Thiepval on July 1, 1916.

1910 **Wroughton, M. C.** (Aug. 1914). 2nd Lt. 12th Lancers. France, Belgium. *D.* France, 1914. Died on Oct. 30, 1914, of wounds received in action in 1st Battle of Ypres.

1906 **Wroughton, P. M. N.,** B.A. (Mobilized Aug. 4, 1914). Maj. Berkshire Yeomanry. Gallipoli, Egypt, Sinai, Palestine, Senussi. Killed in action in the 2nd Battle of Gaza on Apr. 19, 1917.

1897 Wurtzburg, Rev. J. A., M.A. (June 1915). Chaplain to the Forces (4th Class), attd. R.A.M.C.

1909 **Wyatt, H. G. P.,** B.A. (Mobilized Aug. 1914). 2nd Lt. 1st Sussex Yeomanry. Gallipoli. Died at Alexandria on Nov. 12, 1915, of illness contracted on active service.

1919 Wyatt, O. E. P. (Jan. 21, 1917). Lt. 'C' Batt., 75th Bde., R.F.A. France, Belgium, 1917–18; Germany, 1918–19. *M.C.*, Jan. 11, 1919.

1911 Wyatt, R. J. P., M.A. (Sept. 1, 1914). Capt. 8th W. Riding Regt. Capt., Bt.-Maj., General List. Bde. Maj. Egypt, 1916; France, Belgium, 1916–19. *M.C.*, Jan. 1, 1918; *Bar*, July 26, 1918. *D.* France, 1916, 1917, 1919.

1912 **Wynne, E. H. J.** (Jan. 1915). Lt. 3rd Grenadier Guards. Belgium, France. Died on Sept. 16, 1916, of wounds received in Battle of the Somme.

1882 Wynne-Edwards, Rev. J. R., M.A. (Serving Aug. 4, 1914). Capt. Unattached List, T.F., Leeds Grammar School O.T.C.

1919 Wynne-Edwards, R. M. (Aug. 11, 1914). ‡Capt. 13th R. Welch Fusiliers. France, 1915–19. *D.S.O.*, Jan. 11, 1919. *M.C.*, Jan. 1, 1917; *Bar*, Feb. 15, 1919.

1910 **Yeatherd, R. G. H.,** B.A. (Aug. 15, 1914). Lt. Dragoon Guards (S.R.), attd. 2nd Bn. France. *D.* France, 1917. Killed in action on the Somme on Sept. 15, 1916.

1898 Yeatman, L. L., B.A. (Dec. 7, 1915). Lt., Acting Capt. and Adjt., Dorset Yeomanry.

1897 Yeatman-Biggs, W. H. (Mar. 15, 1915). Lt.-Commdr. R.N.V.R., attd. R.N.A.S. (Armoured Cars). Maj., Administrative Officer, R.A.F. France, 1915; Russia, 1915–17. Order of St. Anne (3rd Class). Order of St. Stanislas (3rd Class). *D.* Air Ministry; § Jan. 1919.

1906 Young, B. W. M., M.A. (Jan. 10, 1915). Capt. 7th Wiltshire Regt. Bde. Maj. France, 1915; Salonika, 1915–18; France, Belgium, 1918.

1911 Young, M. C. B. K. (Mobilized Aug. 1914). Capt. 3rd W. Riding Regt. Belgium, France, Aug. 1914. (Prisoner of war, Aug. 1914–Nov. 1918.)

1919 Young, W. A. (Jan. 1916). Lt. R.M.A. Lt. Tank Corps. France, Belgium.

TRINITY COLLEGE

1913 Acland Hood, F. P. (Feb. 28, 1915). Capt. Coldstream Guards. France and Belgium. *M.C.*

1913 Adams,* O. P. (Aug. 29, 1914). Lt. 1/4th Dorsetshire Regt. Lt. A/75th Bde., R.F.A. (Capt.). India, 1914–15; Mesopotamia, 1916–17; France, Belgium, and Germany, 1918–19.

1873 Adamson, J. G. (Oct. 1914). Col. Special Lists. Officer i/c Record Office. *C.M.G.* *D.* § Feb. 1917; § Mar. 1918.

1912 Adkin, C. W., B.A. (Aug. 10, 1914). Lt. R.A.F. France, 1915–17; Italy, 1918–19.

1891 Alexander, E. B., B.A. (Sept. 9, 1914). Lt. 2nd Res. Regt. of Cavalry. Capt. and Adjt. 70th Labour Group. France.

1905 **Alington, G. H.,** B.A. (Apr. 10, 1915). 2nd Lt. I.A.R.O., attd, Indian Infantry. Mesopotamia. Killed in action on Feb. 25, 1917.

1907 **Allen,* T.,** B.A. (Sept. 24, 1914). 2nd Lt. Irish Guards. France and Belgium. Killed in action in Mar. 1915.

1911 Allsebrook, G. C., M.A. (Mobilized Aug. 5, 1914). Capt. 1/1st Derbyshire Yeomanry. Egypt, Lemnos, Senussi, 1915; Salonika, 1916. (Invalided Sept. 1916.)

1908 Altham,* H. S., B.A. (Aug. 19, 1914). Capt. 5th K.R.R.C. (Lt.-Col.). France, 1915–19. *D.S.O.*, June 3, 1918. *M.C.*, Jan. 1, 1917. *D.* France, 1916, 1918.

1908 **Anderson, G. R. L.,** B.A. (Aug. 7, 1914). 2nd Lt. 3rd Cheshire Regt. France and Belgium. *D.* France, 1914. Killed in action near Hooge on Nov. 9, 1914.

1915 Anderson, J. B. (June, 1915). 2nd Lt. Gordon Highlanders. Lt. R.A.F. France. *M.C.*, Nov. 25, 1916; *Bar*, July 18, 1917.

1913 Anderson,* R. C. B. (May 6, 1915). Lt., Acting Capt., Arg. & Suth'd. Highlanders. France. *M.C.*, Feb. 15, 1919; *Bar*, Mar. 8, 1919.

1911 Anson,* G. W., M.A. (Sept. 16, 1914). Capt. 7th Loyal N. Lancashire Regt. (Maj.). France, 1915–17. *M.C.*, Jan. 1, 1917. *M.B.E.* (Mil.).

1903 Arbuthnot-Leslie, G. R., M.A. (Oct. 29, 1914). Capt. Suffolk Yeomanry, attd. 15th Suffolk Regt.

1887 Armour, Rev. H. C., M.A. (July 20, 1915). Chaplain to the Forces (4th Class). France, 1915; Salonika, 1915–17; Hospital Ship, 1918.

1919 Arnold, C. (Jan. 16, 1918). Gnr. R.G.A. (Heavy Artillery).

1888 Arnold, R. A., B.A. (Serving Aug. 4, 1914). Maj. R.A.S.C. (till Oct. 1914). Maj. R.E. France and Belgium. *D.* France, 1917.

1896 Athelstan-Johnston, W., B.A. (Sept. 8, 1914). Lt. Interpreter, Special Lists. Asst. Provost-Marshal. France and Belgium. (Transferred back to Diplomatic Service, Jan. 1916.)

1888 Atherton, R. P., M.A. (Serving Aug. 4 1914). Lt. Unattached List, T.F., Haileybury College O.T.C.

1895 **Auchinleck, D. G. H.** (Serving Aug. 4, 1914). Capt. Inniskilling Fusiliers. France and Belgium. Killed in action on Oct. 21, 1914.

1906 Ayrton, B. F. (Sept. 28, 1914). Capt. 7th London Regt., attd. R.A.F.

1893 Bagwell, J. P., B.A. (Serving Aug. 4, 1914). Lt.-Col. Engineer and Rly. Staff Corps, R.E.

1910 **Bain,* D. M.** (Aug. 15, 1914). Capt. 3rd Gordon Highlanders. Egypt. Killed in action on the W. Frontier on June 3, 1915.

1908 **Baker,* A. H.,** B.A. (Mobilized Aug. 4, 1914). Capt. 1/4th Somerset L.I. India, 1914; Mesopotamia, 1916. Killed in action at Es-Sinn on Mar. 8, 1916.

1913 **Baker,* N. E.** (Aug. 7, 1914). ‡Lt. R.E. (Signals) (Capt.). France and Belgium, Aug. 1914–17. Killed in action at Voormezeele, in 3rd Battle of Ypres, on July 31, 1917.

1886 Baker, P. T., M.A. (Nov. 9, 1914). Lt. T.F. Reserve.

1902 Balfour, A., B.A. (Sept. 17, 1916). Lt. R.G.A. (S.R.).

1912 **Balfour, A. S.** (Aug. 6, 1916). 2nd Lt. R.G.A. France. Died on Jan. 13, 1917.

1892 Balfour, F. R. S., M.A. (Oct. 27, 1916). Hon. Lt.-Col. Special Lists, empld. War Office. Staff-Captain. France, 1916–18.

1919 Balfour, G. G. (Nov. 2, 1917). 2nd Lt. 1st F.A. Bde., 27th Div., R.F.A. Salonika, Caucasus.

1896 Ball, W. C., M.A. (Aug. 21, 1915). Maj. Anti-Gas Dept., R.E. France. *O.B.E.* (Mil.). *D.* § Mar. 1918.

1913 Banks, C. C., M.A. (Dec. 10, 1914). Capt. 2/5th R. Welch Fusiliers (till Oct. 1916). Capt. R.A.F. France, Italy. *M.C.*, Feb. 9, 1918. *D.F.C.*, Feb. 8, 1919. Croce di Guerra. *D.* France.

1919 Banks, K. B. (Sept. 1916). Midshipman, R.N. H.M.S. *Valiant* and H.M.S. *Raider*, North Sea.

1895 Banning, H. D., M.A. (Aug. 11, 1916). Lt. R.G.A. (S.R.).

1905 Baring, J. H., M.A. (Feb. 8, 1916). Capt. R. Irish Regt., R.T.O. Salonika, 1917–19; Italy, 1919.

1901 Barker, A. P., M.A. (Feb. 13, 1915). Lt. R. Defence Corps.

1907 **Barrow,* A. E.,** M.A. (Nov. 28, 1915). 2nd Lt. 4th Queen's (R.W. Surrey Regt). France. Killed in action on Oct. 4, 1917.

1896 Bartholomew, A. W. (Mobilized Aug. 15, 1914). Maj., Bt. Lt.-Col., R.A., G.S.O. 1. France and Belgium, Aug. 1914–17; Italy, 1917–19. *C.M.G.* *C.B.E.* (Mil.). *D.S.O.*, Feb. 18, 1915. Croix de Guerre. Croce di Guerra. *D.* France, 1914, 1915, 1916, 1917 twice; Italy, 1918.

1899 **Bartholomew, G. W.,** M.A. (Aug. 1914). ‡Capt. 7th K.R.R.C. France. Killed in action on Aug. 25, 1916.

1900 Batt, B. E. A., B.M. (Oct. 14, 1915). Capt. R.A.M.C. Mesopotamia, 1916–19. *D.* Mesopotamia, 1918, 1919.

1907 Batt, J. D., B.A. (May 4, 1915). Capt. R.A.M.C. Mesopotamia. *M.C.*, July 26, 1917. *D.* Mesopotamia, 1918.

1901 Battcock, G. A., B.A. (Mobilized Aug. 4, 1914). Maj. 4th R. Berkshire Regt. France. *D.* France, 1915, 1916.

1905 Beale, A. H. L., M.A. (Sept. 1914). ‡Lt. R.F.C. (Placed on retired list on account of injuries received.)

1909 **Beale, E. L.,** B.A. (Sept. 2, 1914). ‡Lt., Acting Capt., Cambridgeshire Regt. France and Belgium, 1915, 1917–18. Killed in action at Longavesnes on Mar. 22, 1918.

1894 Beale, S. W. P., M.A. (Mobilized Aug. 1914). Maj. 4th R. Sussex Regt. (Lt.-Col.). Suvla Bay, Egypt, Sinai, Palestine. *D.* Palestine, 1917.
1919 Beaumont, H. W. H. (Jan. 13, 1917). Lt. R.G.A. (S.R.). France. *M.C.*, Sept. 16, 1918.
1903 Beaumont, K. M., B.A. (Sept. 18, 1914). Capt., Acting Maj., R.A.S.C. *D.S.O.*, Apr. 11, 1918. *D.* Egypt, 1917; Palestine, 1919.
1898 Beeton, H. F., M.A. Sub-Lt. R.N.V.R.
1905 **Bell, J. M.** (Aug. 13, 1915). 2nd Lt. 10th, attd. 11th, Highland L.I. France. Killed in action on Apr. 24, 1917.
1920 Bennett, C. W. (Apr. 1916). Lt. 9th Lancers. France, Belgium.
1898 Berkeley-Hill, O. A. R., D.M. (Serving Aug. 4, 1914). Maj. Indian Medical Service. O.C. 'C' Section, 120th Indian Field Ambulance. E. Africa. *D.* E. Africa, 1917.
1900 Bernard, A. C. (Apr. 20, 1915). Lt. 5th Gloucestershire Regt.
1885 Bernays, Rev. S. F. L., M.A. (July, 1915). Chaplain to the Forces (4th Class). *O.B.E.* (Mil.). *D.* § Mar. 1919.
1896 Berwick, Lord, M.A. (Mobilized Aug. 4, 1914). Capt. Shropshire Yeomanry. Staff-Captain.
1919 Best, L. W. H. (Mar. 13, 1915). Lt. 478th Field Coy. R.E. France. *M.C.*, June 26, 1918.
1913 Bettington, J. B. (Feb. 15, 1915). Lt. Shropshire L.I. Salonika. *M.C.*, Jan. 1, 1919. *D.* Salonika, 1918.
1904 Beyfus, G. H. (Aug. 15, 1914). Lt. 3rd W. Riding Regt. France. (Prisoner of war.) *D.* May 5, 1919.
1899 Bischoff, Rev. P. W., M.A. (Feb. 14, 1917). Chaplain R.N.
1904 Bischoff, T. H., M.A. (Oct. 22, 1915). Capt. R.F.A. (Staff-Captain). France and Belgium, 1916–17, 1918; Italy, 1917–18. *M.C.*, June 3, 1918. *D.* France, 1917.
1904 Blackler, W. F. G., M.A. (Sept. 1917). 1st Lt. U.S. Army.
1902 **Blake, C. R.,** B.A. (Sept. 19, 1914). Capt. 10th K.R.R.C. France. Killed in action on Apr. 4, 1917.
1903 Blake, G. S., M.A. (Oct. 9, 1915). Lt., temp. Capt., 4th N. Staffordshire Regt. Staff Lt. Salonika. *M.B.E.* (Mil.). Greek Military Cross (3rd Class). *D.* Salonika, 1916, 1917, 1918, 1919.
1911 Boddington, R. A., B.A. (Mobilized Aug. 4, 1914). Lt. Duke of Lancaster's Own Yeomanry.
1908 Boldero,* H. E. A., B.M., M.A. (Feb. 10, 1915). Capt., Acting Maj., 29th Field Ambulance, R.A.M.C. France, 1915–19. *D.* France, 1915, 1919.
1881 **Bolitho, W. E. T.,** *D.S.O.* (Mobilized Aug. 1914). Lt.-Col. Royal 1st Devon Yeomanry. *D.* § Feb. 1917. Died on Feb. 21, 1919, after an operation, from illness contracted on active service.
1902 **Bolton, E. T.,** B.A. (Sept. 19, 1916). Lt. 11th Suffolk Regt. France. *D.* France, 1918. Killed in action on Apr. 10, 1918.
1899 Bolton, Rev. J. D., M.A. (July 30, 1915). Chaplain to the Forces (4th Class).
1884 Bond, R. C., *D.S.O.* (Serving Aug. 4, 1914). Lt.-Col. 2nd K.O.Y.L.I. France. (Prisoner of war.) *Bar to D.S.O.*, May 5, 1919. *D.* France, 1914.
1898 Borwick, G. O., M.A., *M.P.* (Mobilized Aug. 4, 1914). Maj. Surrey Yeomanry. Belgium, France, Salonika. *D.S.O.*, June 4, 1917. Croix de Chevalier de la Légion d'Honneur. *D.* Salonika, 1915, 1916, 1917.
1913 Bosworth, W. C., M.A. Sergt. 57th Pioneer Inf., U.S. Army. France.

1906 Bothwell, A. McP. (1916). Lt. 174th Bn. Cameron Highlanders of Canada, C.E.F.

1902 Botterell, J. D., B.A. (Mobilized Aug. 4, 1914). Capt. W. Kent Yeomanry. Staff-Captain.

1899 Botterell, P. D., B.A. Anti-Aircraft Corps, R.N.V.R. *O.B.E.*

1900 Bowers, B. A., M.A. (Feb. 12, 1917). 2nd Lt. R.A.S.C.

1895 Bowker, A. L., M.A. (Mobilized 1914). Maj. R.F.A. (T.F. Res.).

1912 Bown,* A. M., B.A. (Aug. 26, 1914). Lt. 7th London Bde., R.F.A. France. *M.C.*, June 18, 1917.

1910 Boyce, J. I., B.A. (June, 1917). Lt. U.S. Navy, U.S.S. ***Pennsylvania.***

1907 Boyd,* A. J., B.A. (Mobilized Aug. 3, 1914). Lt. 4th York and Lancaster Regt. France and Belgium.

1911 **Boyd, R. C.** (Sept. 1914). ‡2nd Lt. 8th Devonshire Regt. (Capt.). Mediterranean, France. Killed in action at Bazentin on July 14, 1916.

1909 Boyd, T. J. L. S., M.A. (Dec. 17, 1914). Asst. Paymaster, R.N.V.R. (till Mar. 1, 1918). Lt. R.A.F. France.

1904 Bradgate, L., B.A. (Nov. 14, 1914). 2nd Lt. 9th Bedfordshire Regt. Lt. General List.

1894 Brandt, H. E., B.A. (1915). Pte. 22nd London Regt. (The Queen's). France, Salonika, Egypt, Palestine.

1912 Brenan, E. H. (Oct. 17, 1914). Capt. 11th Essex Regt., attd. Sistan Levy Corps. France, 1915–16; Persia, 1916–18.

1901 Bridge, R. S., M.A. 2nd Lt. Unattached List T.F., Bristol Grammar School O.T.C.

1900 Brierly, J. L., B.C.L., M.A. (Oct. 1914). 2nd Lt. 7th Wiltshire Regt. Capt., Bt.-Maj., General List, D.A.A.G., Constantinople. *O.B.E.* (Mil.). *D.* § Feb. 1917.

1911 Briggs, D. H. C., M.A. (Serving Aug. 4, 1914). Capt., Acting Maj., R.F.A. France, 1915–16. Promoted for service in the field. *D.* France, 1915.

1908 Bright, A. J., M.A. (Apr. 5, 1917). Capt. R.A.F. France.

1885 Brinton, J. C., *M.V.O.*, *D.S.O.* (Mobilized Aug. 4, 1914). Maj. 2nd Life Guards (Res. of Officers). Staff-Captain. *D.* § Mar. 1918.

1908 Broadbent, Rev. H. S., M.A. (Dec. 9, 1914). Chaplain to the Forces (4th Class).

1907 Brocklebank, H. A., B.A. (Sept. 5, 1914). Capt. 4th King's Own (R. Lancaster Regt.).

1901 **Brocklebank, T. G.**, M.A. (Mobilized Aug. 4, 1914). Capt. 4th W. Lancs. Bde., R.F.A. France. Killed in action on Aug. 5, 1916.

1909 Broster, L. R., D.M. (Feb. 10, 1915). Lt. 44th Field Amb., R.A.M.C. Maj. Tank Corps. (D.A.D.M.S.). France. *O.B.E.* (Mil.). *D.* France, 1918.

1910 Brown, H. C., M.A. (Feb. 1915). ‡Lt., Acting Capt., 10th Queen's (R. W. Surrey Regt.). France.

1890 Brown, J. Hope, B.A. (Sept. 24, 1914). Maj. 5th Border Regt.

1909 Bruce,* J. C. (Oct. 10, 1914). Lt. 9th R. Scots.

1898 Bruce, K. H. (Serving Aug. 4, 1914). Maj., Bt.-Lt.-Col., Gordon Highlanders. A.A. & Q.M.G. France. *D.S.O.*, Jan. 1, 1917. *D.* France, 1916.

1899 Bruce, T. J. (Feb. 26, 1915). Lt. 16th London Regt. (Queen's Westminster Rifles). France. *M.C.*, Feb. 18, 1918.

1899 Bruce, W. W. (Feb. 26, 1915). Capt. 16th London Regt. (Queen's Westminster Rifles).

1916 Brunner, F. J. M. (July, 1916). Lt. 460th Batt. R.F.A., 15th Bde., R.H.A. Staff-Lt., 1st Class (1917–18). France and Germany, 1917–18.

1908 Buchanan, F. G., B.A. (Apr. 28, 1915). Capt. R.E. Staff-Captain, H.Q., Signal Section Training Centre. France, Belgium. *D.* France, 1917.

1919 Buchanan, K. G. (Feb. 1915). Lt. 2nd The Black Watch (Capt.). France, 1915; Mesopotamia, 1916–17; Palestine, 1918.

1902 **Buck, Rev. C. B. W.,** B.A. (May 17, 1916). Chaplain to the Forces (4th Class), attd. 1/5th Leicestershire Regt. France. *M.C.*, Mar. 8, 1919. *D.* France, 1917. Killed in action at Bellenglise on Sept. 29, 1918.

1900 Buckley, F., B.C.L., M.A. (May 10, 1915). Capt. 7th Northumberland Fusiliers. Capt. T.F. Res. France and Belgium, 1916–19. *D.* France, 1917.

1905 Bucknall, W. H., M.A. (Feb. 25, 1915). Lt. 11th W. Riding Regt. Lt. Intelligence Corps. Gallipoli, 1915–16; Egypt, 1916; France, 1916–18.

1899 Bucknill, A. T., M.A. (Nov. 4, 1914). Lt., temp. Capt., Surrey Yeomanry. Deputy Judge Advocate General. *D.* § Feb. 1917.

1902 Bucknill, T. D., B.A. (1914). Staff-Lt. R.A.F.

1910 **Buller,* F. E.** (Aug. 1914). Tpr. E. African Rifles. German E. Africa. Killed in action at Ingito Hills, German E. Africa, on Sept. 25, 1914.

1898 Burstal, E., D.M. (July 24, 1916). Capt., Acting Maj., R.A.M.C. Salonika.

1908 Bury, C. R., B.Sc. (Aug. 5, 1914). ‡Lt. 7th Gloucestershire Regt. Mesopotamia, 1916–18; Persia, 1918; Caucasus, 1918-19.

1910 **Bury, E. L.** (Aug. 4, 1914). ‡2nd Lt. R.E. Staff-Captain. France. *M.C.*, Jan. 1, 1917. *D.* France, 1916. Died on Nov. 9, 1918, at Bristol, of illness contracted while on active service.

1912 Bury, E. P., M.A. (Aug. 8, 1914). Capt. S. Wales Borderers. Temp. Maj. D.A.A.G. Gallipoli, 1915; France, 1916–17; India, 1919.

1906 **Butter,* H. J.** (Sept. 16, 1914). Capt. 8th The Black Watch. France. Killed in action in the Battle of the Somme on July 14, 1916.

1904 **Butterworth, G. S. K.,** M.A. (Aug. 1914). ‡Lt. Durham L.I. France. *M.C.* July, 1916. Killed in action on Aug. 4, 1916.

1902 Buxton, R. V., M.A. (Mobilized Aug. 4, 1914). Capt. W. Kent Yeomanry, empld. Imperial Camel Corps. Palestine. *D.S.O.*, Feb. 15, 1919. Officer of the Order of the Crown of Italy. Order of the Nile (3rd Class). *D.* Palestine, 1917.

1898 Cairns, A. G., B.A. (Sept. 1914). Lt. Lothians and Border Horse. Lt., Acting Capt. and Adjt., 32nd Bde. R.F.A., 4th Div. France.

1887 **Calderon, G. L.,** M.A. (Sept. 24, 1914). Lt. 9th Oxf. & Bucks. Lt. Infty., attd. 1st K.O. Scottish Borderers. Gallipoli. Believed killed in action in Gallipoli on June 4, 1915.

1899 Calmady Hamlyn, C. H. H., M.A. (Mobilized Aug. 1914). Capt. 1/1st R.N. Devon Yeomanry. Capt., temp. Maj., Asst. Political Officer. Damascus, Egypt, Palestine, Syria. T.D.

1910 **Cameron, R. A.** (1914). Pte. Q.O. Cameron Highlanders. France. Killed in action in Sept. 1915.

1886 Campbell, C. H. (Aug. 5, 1914). Maj. 8th Hussars (Res. of Officers).

1907 Campbell, J. H. (Serving Aug. 4, 1914). Lt. 5th The Black Watch. A.D.C. to the Governor of Newfoundland. Serbian Order of St. Sava (5th Class).

1893 Campbell-Colquhoun, A. J. (Oct. 14, 1914). ‡Capt. 6th Q. O. Cameron Highlanders. France, 1915–16. *D.* France, 1916.

1902 **Cane, M.** (July 5, 1915). 2nd Lt. R.F.A. France. Killed in action on Aug. 4, 1917.

1913 Capel,* A. J. (Aug. 14, 1914). Capt. Somerset L.I. Maj. No. 92 Sqdn. R.A.F. Belgium and France. *D.* France, 1915, 1917; § Mar. 1918.

1919 Carbutt, G. H. (Aug. 9, 1915). Midshipman R.N. Temp. Lt. R.A.F. (promoted for service, Jan. 1, 1919). North Sea.

1901 Carr, A. S. Comyns, B.A. (1914). Anti-Aircraft Corps, R.N.V.R.

1899 Carr, R. H., M.A. (Apr. 1917). Maj. Special Lists (Staff Officer). Russia.

1892 Carr-Birkbeck, L. H., B.M. (Feb. 20, 1915). Capt., Acting Maj., R.A.M.C.

1885 Carter, Sir E. E. (Serving Aug. 4, 1914). Maj.-General, Director of Supplies and Transport. France, Aug. 1914–19. *K.C.M.G., C.B., M.V.O.* Croix de Commandeur de la Légion d'Honneur. Commandeur de l'Ordre de la Couronne. Belgian Croix de Guerre. Order of St. Stanislas (2nd Class) (with Swords). Order of St. Anne. American Distinguished Service Medal. *D.* France, 1914, 1915, 1916, 1917, 1918, 1919.

1901 Cary, A. J. L., B.A. (April, 1915). Lt. Nigeria Regt. Cameroons.

1910 Cash, R. J., B.A. (Oct. 17, 1914). Capt. 8th Loyal N. Lancashire Regt. Capt. General List. Bde.-Maj. France. *M.C.*, Jan. 1, 1918. Croix de Guerre. *D.* France, 1918.

1914 Cathrall, T. H., B.A. (Dec. 12, 1914). 2nd Lt. 11th R. Welch Fusiliers (Capt.). France, 1915–16.

1911 Cattley,* G. A., B.A. (Aug. 15, 1914). Lt. 4th, attd. 6th, Dragoon Guards. Belgium, France, Germany.

1910 Chadwick, F. (Sept. 12, 1914). Maj. 13th K.R.R.C. Belgium, France, Germany. *D.S.O.*, Sept. 16, 1918; *Bar*, June 3, 1919. *M.C.*, Jan. 1, 1918. *D.* France, 1918.

1892 Chadwyck-Healey, G. E., M.A. (Mar. 10, 1915). Lt. R.N.V.R. Director of Materials, Admiralty. *C.B.E.* Commander of the Order of the Crown of Italy.

1905 Chadwyck-Healey, O. N., M.A. (Oct. 1914). Maj., General List. Bde.-Maj. *D.* § June 1916; § Aug. 1919.

1891 Chalmers-Hunt, D. R., B.C.L. (June 1917). 2nd Lt. (Hon. Lt.) R.A.F.

1899 Chalmers-Hunt, N. G., B.A. (Oct. 1914). ‡Capt. 61st Auxiliary Petrol Coy., R.A.S.C. (M.T.). France, 1915–18.

1905 Charteris, Hon. G. L., B.A. (Aug. 15, 1914). Lt. Scots Guards (S.R.), attd. Guards M.G. Regt. (Capt.). France, Balkans. Order of St. Sava (4th Class).

1904 Chavasse, Rev. C. M., M.A. (Aug. 18, 1914). Chaplain to the Forces (2nd Class). D.A.C.B. to 9th Corps. Belgium and France, Aug. 1914–19. *M.C.*, Aug. 25, 1917. Croix de Guerre.

1904 **Chavasse, N. G.,** B.M., M.A. (Mobilized Aug. 4, 1914). Capt. R.A.M.C., attd. 10th King's (Liverpool Regt.) (Liverpool Scottish). France, Belgium. *M.C.*, Jan. 14, 1916. *D.* France, 1915. Died on Aug. 4, 1917, of wounds received in action at Brandhoek. **V. C.** won at Guillemont on Aug. 9, 1916.

For most conspicuous bravery and devotion to duty.

During an attack he tended the wounded in the open all day, under heavy fire, frequently in view of the enemy. During the ensuing night he searched for wounded on the ground in front of the enemy's lines for four hours.

Next day he took one stretcher-bearer to the advanced trenches, and under heavy shell fire carried an urgent case for 500 yards into safety, being wounded in the side by a shell splinter during the journey. The same night he took up a party of twenty volunteers, rescued three wounded men from a shell hole twenty-five yards from the enemy's trench, buried the bodies of two officers, and collected many identity discs, although fired on by bombs and machine guns.

Altogether he saved the lives of some twenty badly wounded men, besides the ordinary cases which passed through his hands. His courage and self-sacrifice were beyond praise.

Bar to V.C. won at Wieltje, July 31–Aug. 2, 1917.

For conspicuous bravery and devotion to duty when in action.

Though severely wounded early in the action whilst carrying a wounded soldier to the dressing station, Captain Chavasse refused to leave his post, and for two days not only continued to perform his duties, but in addition went out repeatedly under heavy fire to search for and attend to the wounded who were lying out.

During these searches, although practically without food during this period, worn with fatigue and faint with his wound, he assisted to carry in a number of badly wounded men, over heavy and difficult ground.

By his extraordinary energy and inspiring example he was instrumental in rescuing many wounded who would have otherwise undoubtedly succumbed under the bad weather conditions.

This devoted and gallant officer subsequently died of his wounds.

1919 Chitty, F. J. P. (Jan. 1917). Lt. 2nd Coldstream Guards.

1912 Chitty, J. T., B.A. (Aug. 1914). Pte. H.A.C. ‡Capt. R.A.F. Gallipoli, 1915; Egypt, 1915. *D.* Gallipoli, 1915.

1918 Christie, J. T. (June 7, 1918). 2nd Lt. Coldstream Guards.

1886 Christie, O. F., M.A. (Sept. 1914). Maj. 19th London Regt. (Res. of Officers).

1905 Christie, W. M., B.A. (July 24, 1916). Lt. 7th R. Scots.

1900 Christie-Miller, G., M.A. (Mobilized Aug. 4, 1914). Capt., Acting Lt.-Col., Bucks. Bn., Oxf. & Bucks. Lt. Intfy., attd. 2/5th Gloucestershire Regt. France. *D.S.O.*, Mar. 8, 1919. *M.C.*, Jan. 1, 1918. *D.* France, 1917.

1904 **Chrystal, G. G.,** B.A. (Sept. 2, 1914). Lt. 9th Arg. & Suth'd. Highlanders. France. Killed in action on May 25, 1915.

1900 Chrystal, R. A. (Serving Aug. 4, 1914). Capt., Acting Maj., 51st Gordon Highlanders. France, 1915; Germany, 1919.

1902 **Church, H.,** B.A. (Oct. 31, 1914). Capt. Bucks. Bn. Oxf. & Bucks. Lt. Infty. France. Killed in action on July 21, 1916.

1895 Clark, W. C., B.A. (Oct. 30, 1914). Lt.-Col. 10th Queen's (R. W. Surrey Regt.). Belgium, France, Italy, 1916–18. *D.S.O.* Aug. 25, 1917; *Bar,* Nov. 19, 1917. *D.* France, 1917 twice.

Clarke, J. S. D. (Mar. 26, 1915). Lt. Arg. & Suth'd. Highlanders. Egypt, Palestine. Killed in action at Gaza on Nov. 10, 1917.

1895 Clarke, M. F. (Serving Aug. 4, 1914). Maj., Acting Lt.-Col. 1st Cheshire Regt. France. *D.S.O.*, Jan. 1, 1917. *D.* France, 1916.

1898 Clarke, R. C. L., B.A. (Sept. 2, 1914). ‡Lt. 13th Worcestershire Regt. Salonika, 1916–17.

1896 Clay, H. J., B.A. (Sept. 12, 1914). Lt. General List. France, Belgium.

1919 Clayton, C. H. (Aug. 31, 1914). Maj. 5th Dorsetshire Regt. Gallipoli, Egypt, France. *M.C.*, Aug. 23, 1917. *D.* France, 1917.
1897 Clayton, G. S., M.A. (Oct. 31, 1914). ‡Lt.-Col. 18th King's (Liverpool Regt.). France, 1914–18. *D.S.O.*, June 3, 1918. *D.* France, 1918.
1899 Clements, M. L. S. (Serving Aug. 4, 1914). Maj., Acting Lt.-Col., 4th K.R.R.C. France, 1914–15, 1915–16; Salonika, 1916–18. *D.* Salonika, 1917.
1900 Close, P. J. H., M.A. (Dec. 5, 1914). Lt. Irish Guards. France.
1902 Close, R. C. A., M.A. (Nov. 6, 1915). Lt. 2nd Irish Guards. Belgium and France, 1916.
1908 Clover, E. (Apr. 5, 1915). Maj. R.A.S.C. D.A.D. of Transport. *D.* § Mar. 1919.
1919 Clyde, J. L. M. (Mar. 1917). Lt. 20th Fire Command, R.G.A.
1916 Coffin, R. P., B.A. (Aug. 22, 1917). Lt. 72nd Artillery, U.S. Army (Adjt.). France, 1918–19.
1907 **Cohan, E. M.,** B.A. (Serving Aug. 4, 1914). 2nd Lt. R.F.A. Accidentally killed during mobilization on Aug. 5, 1914.
1910 Cohen, D. D. M., B.A. (Nov. 1914). Lt., Acting Capt., R.H.A. Staff-Captain. France, 1916–19.
1896 Coleridge, Hon. G. D., B.A. (May 21, 1915). Lt., Acting Capt., 4th Devonshire Regt.
1908 Coleridge, W. D., B.A. (Sept. 28, 1914). Capt. 7th London Regt.
1871 Collings, C. d'A., D.M. (Serving Aug. 4, 1914). Lt.-Col. R. Guernsey Militia.
1900 Collins, A. J. F., B.A. (Nov. 2, 1916). Lt. R.G.A. (S.R.).
1909 Collyer, H. O. (Sept. 28, 1914). Lt. 7th E. Lancashire Regt. Temp. Maj. M.G.C. France, 1915, 1917, 1918.
1919 Colquhoun, W. R. (Feb. 8, 1918). 2nd Lt. 2nd Scots Guards. France.
1903 Compton, Rev. C., M.A. (Oct. 8, 1917). Chaplain to the Forces (4th Class).
1891 Comyns, J. H., B.A. (Sept. 3, 1915). Lt. Hertfordshire Regt.
1907 Conder,* E., M.A. (Sept. 2, 1914). Capt. 1/5th Gloucestershire Regt. Belgium and France. *M.C.*, May 11, 1917. *D.* France, 1915.
1896 Connell, A. MacG. (Oct. 1914). Capt., Hon. Maj., Q.O.R. Glasgow Yeomanry (T.F. Res.).
1910 Coode, D. R., B.A. (Aug. 1914). Maj. 2/3rd Lowland Bde., R.A.
1910 **Copeman, H. G. H.,** B.A. (Sept. 1914). ‡2nd Lt. 6th Oxf. & Bucks. Lt. Infty. France, 1916. Killed in action at Guillemont on Sept. 3, 1916.
1919 Corsellis, D. H. (Dec. 30, 1914). Capt. M.G.C. Gallipoli, France.
1908 **Counsell, C. H.,** B.A. (1914). ‡2nd Lt. 3rd, attd. 2nd., Hampshire Regt. France. Killed in action on the Somme on July 6, 1916.
1892 Cowan, A. G. (Mobilized Aug. 4, 1914). Maj. Lothians and Border Horse. A.P.M. 21st Div. France. *D.* France, 1919.
1912 Cowper, J. E., B.A. (Dec. 14, 1914). Capt. 1st Hampshire Regt. (Bde. Signalling Officer). France, 1916; N. Russia, Murman Coast, 1918.
1908 Cox,* D. A., B.C.L. (Sept. 15, 1914). Capt. 2nd E. Yorkshire Regt. France, Egypt, Macedonia, Constantinople. *M.C.*, June 3, 1918. *D.* Salonika, 1917; § Mar. 1919.
1876 Cox, G. V., B.A. (1914). 2e Régiment étranger de l'armée française. France.

1906 Cox, K. T., B.A. (Sept. 17, 1914). 2nd Lt. Queen's (R. W. Surrey Regt.). Capt., attd. General Staff, War Office. France, 1915. *M.B.E.* (Mil.). *D.* § Mar. 1919.

1903 Cozens-Hardy, B., B.A. (Oct. 21, 1914). Lt., Acting Capt., 4th Norfolk Regt.

1913 Cranage, R. W. (Aug. 12, 1914). Capt. 4th Northumberland Fusiliers. France.

1901 Crawley-Boevey, M., B.A. (Sept. 14, 1914). Capt., Bt.-Maj., D.C.L.I. G.S.O. 2. Salonika, Palestine. *D.S.O.*, June 3, 1916. *M.C.*, Feb. 18, 1915. *D.* Salonika, 1917; Palestine, 1918.

1899 **Crawley-Boevey, T. R.,** M.A. (Aug. 11, 1915). Capt. 14th Gloucestershire Regt. France. *D.* France, 1915. Died on Aug. 30, 1916, of wounds received in action.

1898 Crawshay Williams, E. (Mobilized Aug. 4, 1914). Capt. R.H.A. (T.F.) (specially empld.).

1910 Creed,* E. ff., B.A. (Mar. 26, 1917). Capt. R.A.M.C. (S.R.). W. Africa, 1917–19.

1916 Creed, R. S., B.A. (June 27, 1917). 2nd Lt. 162nd Bde.; R.F.A. France and Belgium, 1918–19.

1887 Cripps, Rev. A. S., M.A. (June, 1915). Chaplain to I.E.F. E. Africa.

1907 Cronje, S. N., B.A. (1914). Capt. 1st S. African Rifles. E. Africa. *M.C.*, June 4, 1917. *D.* E. Africa, 1917.

1913 Crosby, L. A., B.C.L., M.A. (June, 1916). ‡1st Lt. U.S. Inf. G.H.Q. France, 1916–19.

1903 Cruickshank, R. G., B.A. (Nov. 12, 1914). Capt. Suffolk Yeomanry.

1904 Cumberbatch, H. C., B.A. (May 1918). Pte. 28th London Regt. (Artists' Rifles).

1912 Cumberbatch,* R. C., B.A. (Oct. 17, 1914). Capt. General List (specially empld.). Greece. Chevalier, Greek Order of the Redeemer.

1908 **Cumming, C. L.,** B.A. (1917). ‡Lt. Flying Officer R.A.F. France, Germany. Accidentally killed while flying at Cologne on Jan. 31, 1919.

1914 Currey, R. F. (Dec. 10, 1914). Lt. 13th Arg. & Suth'd. Highlanders. France, Belgium, 1915–18. *M.C.*, Jan. 26, 1917; *Bar*, Sept. 26, 1917.

1919 Dale, A. F. (Jan. 20, 1916). Pte. M.G.C. (2nd Lt.). France, 1917–18.

1903 Daniell, I. A. E. Lt. Canadian E. F.

1875 Daniell, O. J. (Oct. 1914). Maj. Queen's (R. W. Surrey Regt.) (retired). *D.* § Feb. 1917.

1910 **Danson, F. R.,** B.A. (Mobilized Aug. 4, 1914). Lt. 4th Cheshire Regt. Gallipoli. Killed in action in Gallipoli on Aug. 10, 1915.

1913 Danson,* J. F., M.A. (Aug. 4, 1914). ‡Lt. 38th Divl. Sig. Coy., R.E. France. *D.* France.

1912 Danson,* J. R., M.A. (Oct. 10, 1914). Lt., Acting Capt., 1/4th Cheshire Regt. Gallipoli, 1915; Egypt, Palestine, 1915–18; France, 1918–19. *M.C.*, Jan. 1, 1919.

1885 Darbishire, B. V., M.A. (July 12, 1915). Lt. Special Lists. Staff-Lt. (2nd Class).

1911 Darnley-Smith, G. (Sept. 1, 1914). ‡2nd Lt. 202nd M.G. Coy., Indian Army. India, 1914–19.

1913 Daunt, A. (Sept. 14, 1914). Lt., Acting Capt., 2/4th D.C.L.I. India, 1915–19.

1901 Davidson, M., D.M. (Sept. 10, 1915). Capt. R.A.M.C. Gallipoli, 1915; Sinai, 1916; Egypt, 1916–17; Palestine, 1917.

1892 Davidson, R. P., M.A. (Oct. 1, 1915). 2nd Lt. Unattached List, T.F., Winchester College O.T.C.

1898 Davidson, T. (Serving Aug. 4, 1914). Maj., Acting Lt.-Col., 255th Bde., R.F.A. France, 1915–19. *D.S.O.*, Oct. 28, 1917; *Bar*, Sept. 16, 1918. Croix de Guerre (with Palm). *D.* France, 1916, 1917, 1918.

1915 **Davies, D. J.** (Dec. 28, 1915). Lt. M.G.C. France. Killed in action on July 13, 1917.

1908 **Davies, W. B.,** B.A. (Dec. 15, 1916). 2nd Lt. 1st (Garr.) Bn. Somerset L.I. India. Died on Dec. 3, 1918.

1910 Dawson,* W. S., B.M., M.A. (Aug. 4, 1914). Capt. R.A.M.C. E. Africa.

1918 Dean, A. V. T. (May 10, 1918). 2nd Lt. The Buffs (E. Kent Regt.).

1907 Dean, C., D.M. (Dec. 30, 1917). Lt. R.A.M.C.

1905 Dean, C. W., M.A. (Aug. 14, 1916). Lt. R.A.S.C.

1898 De la Rue, Sir E. A., M.A. (Mobilized Aug. 4, 1914). Capt. R. E. Kent Yeomanry (T.F. Res.). France. *D.* France, 1917.

1898 de Liedekerke, Count C., B.A. Liaison Officer, Belgian Army.

1908 **Delmege,* E. B. M.,** B.A. (Serving Aug. 4, 1914). Capt. E. Lancashire Regt. France. *M.C.*, Feb. 18, 1915. Killed in action on Oct. 23, 1916.

1909 Delmege,* H. B. E., B.A. (Sept. 1914). ‡Lt. Bedfordshire Yeomanry.

1919 Dennys, C. G. (Aug. 31, 1916). Lt. R.G.A. (S.R.). France. *M.C.*, June 26, 1918.

1919 de Selincourt, O. (May 1917). 2nd Lt. R.F.A. France, 1917–18.

1896 Dewar, F. (May 7, 1915). Lt. I.A.R.O., attd. 2nd Nagpur Rifles. India.

1919 de Wet, J. C. (Oct. 1914). ‡1st Staff-Lt. 1st Mtd. Bde. E. African Forces. German S.W. Africa, German E. Africa.

1906 Dibben, Rev. H. L., M.A. (May 18, 1915). Chaplain to the Forces (4th Class).

1910 Dickinson,* F. H., B.A. (Aug. 6, 1914). Capt. 6th London Regt. France, 1915. (Invalided, Oct. 1917.)

1911 Diver,* C. R. P., M.A. (Aug. 26, 1914). Capt. 1st Loyal N. Lancashire Regt. (Adjt.). France.

1912 Dixey, A. G. N. (Sept. 4, 1914). ‡Capt. 20th Manchester Regt. France, Belgium, Italy. *M.C.*, Dec. 11, 1916.

Douglas, A. (June 1915). 2nd Lt. R.F.A. (S.R.), attd. R.F.C. France. Killed in action on Oct. 16, 1916.

1911 **Downes, A. C.** (Serving Aug. 4, 1914). 2nd Lt. Cheshire Regt. France and Belgium. Died at Poperinghe on Nov. 20, 1914, of wounds received in action at Bailleul.

1909 **Downes,* V. C.** (Serving Aug. 4, 1914). Lt. 1st Bedfordshire Regt. France, Aug.–Oct. 1914. Died at St. Omer on Oct. 18, 1914, of wounds received in action a few days previously.

1907 Doyne, H. C., M.A. (Sept. 1, 1914). Capt., Acting Maj., R.A.S.C. (M.T.). Palestine. *D.* Palestine, 1918, 1919.

1904 Doyne,* P. G., B.A. (Feb. 16, 1916). Capt. R.A.M.C. (T.F.).

1900 Duckworth, F. R. G., M.A. (Dec. 19, 1914). Lt. R.F.A. Capt. Special Lists (specially empld.). Salonika. *M.B.E.* (Mil.). *D.* Salonika, 1916, 1918.

1906 Dugdale, C. J. G., B.A. (Oct. 1914). Lt. 8th London Regt. (Post Office Rifles), attd. F.O. at Washington.

1893 Duguid McCombie, W. McC., B.A. (Serving Aug. 4, 1914). Maj., Bt.-Lt.-Col., 2nd Dragoons. France, Belgium. *D.S.O.*, Jan. 1, 1919. Order of St. Stanislas (2nd Class) (with Swords). *D.* France, 1914, 1918, 1919.

1881 Dun, F., M.A. (Nov. 9, 1914). Capt. 10th King's (Liverpool Regt.) (T.F. Res.).

1912 **Dun,* L. F.** (Aug. 6, 1914). ‡2nd 10th King's (Liverpool Regt.) (Capt.). France, Belgium. Killed in action near Ypres on Sept. 28, 1915.

1914 Duncan, P. C. (Feb. 18, 1915). Capt. and Adjt. 4th Queen's (R. W. Surrey Regt.). France. *M.C.*, Jan. 1, 1919.

1905 Dunell, O. H. C. (Sept. 1916). Lt., Acting Capt., R.G.A. France, Belgium, Italy. Croce di Guerra. *D.* Italy, 1918.

1911 Dunn, A. J., M.A. (Apr. 1917). 2nd Lt. R.G.A. France.

1919 Dymond, F. R. (Sept. 1914). Lt. R.A.F. France, 1915; Macedonia, 1915–16; France, 1916–17.

1919 Dyson, F. N. (Sept. 20, 1914). ‡Lt. 15th Light Armoured Motor Batt. France, 1915–16; Mesopotamia, 1917–18; Persia, 1918–19.

1873 Earle, Sir H., Bt., *D.S.O.* (Nov. 21, 1914). G.S.O. 3. Medijieh, 5th Class.

1899 Eastwood, H., B.A. (July 7, 1915). Lt. R.F.A.

1900 Eberle, G. S. J. F., M.A. (Aug. 5, 1914). Lt.-Col. 5th R. Sussex Regt. France, 1915–17; Italy, 1917–18. *D.S.O.*, June 3, 1918. *D.* France, 1915; Italy, 1918 twice.

1905 Eberle, V. F., M.A. (Aug. 8, 1914). ‡Maj. 474th (S. Midland) Field Coy. R.E. France, 1915–17; Italy, 1917–19. *M.C.*, June 3, 1918. *D.* France, 1917; Italy, 1919.

1895 Eccles, J. H. (Sept. 7, 1916). Capt. 1st Dock Bn. King's (Liverpool Regt.).

1919 Eckstein, B. (Aug. 15, 1914). Capt. 2nd E. Surrey Regt., attd. R.A.F. (1918). France.

1905 Edlmann, F. J. F., M.A. (Aug. 5, 1914). ‡Maj., Acting Lt.-Col., Northumberland Fusiliers. France and Belgium. *D.S.O.*, Jan. 1, 1917. *D.* France, 1916 twice.

1900 Edwards, G. J., B.A. (Serving Aug. 4, 1914). Capt., Acting Lt.-Col., 4th Coldstream Guards. France, 1914–19. *D.S.O.*, June 3, 1919. *M.C.*, Jan. 1, 1917. *D.* France, twice.

Edwards, H. E. (Oct. 10, 1914). Lt. 3rd, attd. 2nd, R. Warwickshire Regt. France. Killed in action on Sept. 8, 1915.

1907 Edwards, J. B. (Apr. 29, 1915). Lt. 3rd Monmouthshire Regt., attd. S. Wales Borderers.

1897 Egerton Warburton, C. W., M.A. (Sept. 24, 1914). Capt. 7th London Bde. R.F.A. (Lt.-Col.). Asst. Controller of Salvage, I.E.F. France, 1915–16, 1917; Italy, 1917–18. *D.* Italy, 1919. (Invalided.)

1913 Ehrenborg,* R. K. (Dec. 16, 1914). Lt., Acting Capt., Border Regt. France, Italy.

1919 Eissler, C. W. (Aug. 24, 1915). Lt. R.G.A. France, 1915–17; India, 1918–19.

1903 **Elcho, Lord** (Mobilized Aug. 4, 1914). Capt. R. Gloucestershire Hussars. Egypt. *D.* Egypt, 1917. Killed in action at Katia, Sinai, on Apr. 23, 1916.

1902 Eliot, V. A. G. Lt. Canadian Inf.
1896 Elliot, F. B., M.A. (Sept. 1914). Capt. 5th R. Berkshire Regt., attd. Ministry of Food. Belgium and France. *C.B.E.* (Civil). Officer of the Order of the Crown of Italy. Officer of the Order of Leopold II. Croix de Chevalier de la Légion d'Honneur.
1912 Ellis,* C. M. J., B.A. (Oct. 21, 1914). Lt., Acting Capt., 2/5th Hampshire Regt., attd. Intelligence Corps. India, 1914–17; Egypt and Palestine, 1917–18; Syria, 1918. *D.* Palestine, 1918.
1919 Ellison, G. W. (Apr. 15, 1917). Lt. R.G.A. France, 1917–19.
1903 Emden, C. S., M.A. (Aug. 4, 1914). ‡Capt. R. W. Kent Regt., attd. R.A.F. (1917–19). France, 1915–16, 1918. *D.F.C.*, June 3, 1919.
1906 Entwisle, T., B.A. (Serving Aug. 4, 1914). Capt. 5th Loyal N. Lancashire Regt. France. *M.C.*, Oct. 20, 1916. *D.* France, 1916.
1919 Errington, E. (Sept. 20, 1918). 2nd Lt. Gordon Highlanders (on demobilization).
1904 **Estridge, E. W.** (1915). ‡2nd Lt. 3rd E. Yorkshire Regt. France. Killed in action on Nov. 13, 1916.
1882 Ewing, G. B., M.A. (Oct. 1914). Capt. General List; District Officer No. 1. C.C. and D.H.R. France, 1917–19.
1911 Eyres, L. E., B.A. (Sept. 16, 1914). Pte. 1/4th Somerset L.I. India, Mesopotamia, 1915. (Prisoner of war in Turkey, 1916–18.)
1906 Farebrother, Rev. F. S., M.A. (Apr. 10, 1916). Chaplain to the Forces (4th Class), attd. 1/15th London Regt. (Civil Service Rifles). *D.* § Mar. 1918.
1884 Ferguson, V. (Mobilized Aug. 4, 1914). Maj. Res. of Officers (empld. War Office). Russia, 1914–15; France, 1918. Order of S. Stanislas (2nd Class). Order of St. Anne (2nd Class). *D.* § Feb. 1917.
1915 **Fernald,* V. D.** (1916). Lt. 3rd Queen's (R. W. Surrey Regt.). Lt. Observer, R.A.F. France, Italy. Order of St. Stanislas (2nd Class). Order of St. Anne (2nd Class) (with Swords). Died as prisoner, 1918.
1903 Field, M. G., B.A. (Serving Aug. 4, 1914). Capt. D. Batt. 242nd Bde. R.F.A. France, 1915–16; Belgium, 1917. (Discharged on account of wounds, Oct. 1918.)
1891 **Field, O.**, B.A. (1915). Lt. 9th Durham L.I. France. Killed in action on July 18, 1915.
1900 Field, S. R., B.A. (Mobilized Aug. 4, 1914). Maj. R.F.A. (T.F.).
1912 Field,* W. O., B.A. (Aug. 15, 1914). ‡Capt. 4th, attd. 16th, R. Warwickshire Regt. Belgium, 1914–15; France, Belgium, and Italy, 1916–18. *M.C.*, June 3, 1918; *Bar*, Dec. 2, 1918.
1899 Fisher, Rev. T. L. T., M.A. (Serving Aug. 4, 1914). ‡Chaplain (4th Class), attd. 1st R. Fusiliers. France, 1916–17; Italy, 1917–19. *M.C.*, June 3, 1918.
1901 Flanagan, J. H. W. (Nov. 25, 1914). Lt. R.N.V.R., R.N.A.S.
1905 Flemmer, W. K. S. African Inf.
1902 **Flemming, D. S.**, M.A. (Jan. 28, 1915). 2nd Lt. 8th King's Own (R. Lancaster Regt.). France. Died on June 1, 1917, of wounds received in action.
1919 Flemming, G. N. (June 5, 1916). Lt. 7th Rifle Brigade. France.
1913 Fletcher,* J. H., B.A. (Sept. 29, 1914). Lt., Acting Capt., 11th S. Lancashire Regt. France.

1893 Flint, R. B. (Serving Aug. 4, 1914). Maj. 2nd Loyal N. Lancashire Regt. Maj. empld. Record Office.

1901 Flowers, J., B.A. ‡Lt. R.A.S.C. *D.* § Mar. 1919.

1913 Forbes,* J. B. M. M. (Sept. 1914). Capt. 3rd Seaforth Highlanders. France.

1899 **Forster, A. P.,** B.A. (Sept. 25, 1914). Capt. K.R.R.C., attd. M.G.C. France. *D.* France, 1916, 1917. Died on Sept. 25, 1918, of illness contracted on active service.

1912 **Forster,* W. J.,** B.A. (Aug. 15, 1914). Capt. 3rd attd. 8th E. Lancashire Regt. France. Killed in action on May 31, 1917.

1911 Foster,* L. L., B.A. (Nov. 20, 1914). Maj. R.M.A. France. *M.C.*, July 26, 1918. *D.* France, 1916.

1906 **Fowler, C. J.,** M.A. (Mar. 25, 1915). 2nd Lt. 22nd R. Fusiliers. France. Died on June 1, 1916, of wounds received in action.

1919 Franklin, A. D. (May 22, 1917). Lt. 1st (Garr.) Bn. Highland L.I. India, 1918–19.

1912 Franklin,* A. P., M.A. (Aug. 26, 1914). Lt. R.F.A. (T.F.). Egypt, 1916; Salonika, 1916–18.

1895 Fraser, Rev. A. G., M.A. (Sept. 11, 1917). Chaplain to the Forces (4th Class).

1907 Freeman,* A. F. (Mobilized Aug. 4, 1914). Capt. Montgomeryshire Yeomanry, attd. 25th R. Welch Fusiliers. Palestine. *M.C.*, Jan. 18, 1918.

1912 **French,* B. St. G.** (Oct. 20, 1914). Lt., temp. Capt., 15th King's (Liverpool Regt.), attd. R. Inniskilling Fusiliers. Gallipoli, Salonika. Killed in action on July 1, 1916.

1900 **Fulton, E. A.,** M.A. (July 1, 1916). 2nd Lt. 25th Middlesex Regt. France. Missing, presumed killed in action on Oct. 4, 1916.

1900 Furlong, A. W., M.A. (May 24, 1915). ‡Lt. R.G.A. Dardanelles (in H.M.S. *Monica*), 1915; France, 1916–19.

1905 Furse, H. R., B.A. (Sept. 9, 1914). Lt. 9th Lancers. Belgium, France, Germany, 1914–19.

1895 Gaine, H. H., B.A. (June 22, 1915). Lt. 4th Devonshire Regt.

1893 Gainsford, E. A., B.A. (Sept. 20, 1914). Maj. 352nd Siege Batt., R.G.A. Egypt, Salonika, France. Croix de Guerre. *D.* France, 1917, 1918.

1914 Gahan, F., B.A. (Jan. 13, 1916). Pte. 32nd Res. Bn. Canadian E.F. S.Q.M.S. (W.O., Class 2), Estates Branch, Overseas Mil. Forces of Canada. *D.* § Feb. 1917.

1913 **Gale,* W. N.** (Oct. 1914). Capt. 2/4th York and Lancaster Regt. Belgium, France. Believed killed in action at Bullecourt on May 3, 1917.

1903 Gardner, C. J., B.A. (1917). Lt., Acting Capt. and Adjt., R.F.A. France, 1917; Italy, 1917–19. *M.C.*, June 3, 1919. *D.* Italy, 1919.

1894 Garnier, Rev. T. V., M.A. (Dec. 22, 1915). Chaplain to the Forces (4th Class). Salonika. *O.B.E.* (Mil.). *D.* Salonika, 1917, 1918.

1913 Gaskell,* F. R. (Aug. 1914). Lt. 10th Hussars. France, Belgium.

1919 Gent, G. E. J. (Aug. 14, 1914). Capt., Acting Maj., 3rd D.C.L.I. France, 1914–16, 1917; Italy, 1918. *D.S.O.*, Jan. 1, 1919. *M.C.*, Jan. 1, 1917. *D.* France, 1916, 1918.

1909 Gent, R. M., B.A. (Jan. 1, 1916). Lt. R.A.S.C. Egypt. *M.C.*, Apr. 11, 1918. *D.* Egypt, 1917.

1913 **Gent,* T. S.** (Aug. 22, 1914). 2nd Lt. 7th Rifle Brigade. France and Belgium. Killed in action in Belgium on July 24, 1915.

1899 Gibbon, W. D., M.A. (Sept. 21, 1914). Maj. 9th Worcestershire Regt. (Lt.-Col.). Gallipoli, Mesopotamia, Persia, Russia. *D.S.O.*, Mar. 17, 1917. *M.C.*, Feb. 2, 1916. Medal of La Solidaridad (3rd Class). *D.* Mesopotamia, 1916, 1917, 1918, 1919.

1905 Gibson,* P. L., B.M., M.A. (Serving Aug. 4, 1914). Surgeon Lt.-Commdr. R.N. H.M.S. *Yarmouth*, H.M.H.S. *Soudan*, H.M.S. *Queen Elizabeth*, 1914–20.

1919 Gielgud, V. H. (Sept. 23, 1918). 2nd Lt. Grenadier Guards.

1911 **Gilbanks,* R. P.,** B.A. (Aug. 26, 1914). Lt. 6th Border Regt. Gallipoli. Killed in action in Gallipoli, Aug. 7–11, 1915.

1919 Gildard, J. G. A. (July 14, 1917). Lt. 6th Bde., R.F.A. N. Russia.

1903 **Gilkison, J. D.** (Serving Aug. 4, 1914). Lt. 1st Arg. & Suth'd. Highlanders. France. Killed in action at Le Cateau on Aug. 26, 1914.

1912 Gilligan, J. V. (Aug. 11, 1914). Capt. R. Munster Fusiliers. France, 1914–15.

1908 **Gilmour,* A.,** B.A. (Mobilized Aug. 4, 1914). Capt. 2nd Lovat's Scouts, attd. Q.O. Cameron Highlanders. Egypt and Palestine. Died on Dec. 16, 1917, of wounds received in action.

1920 Glen, A. (Apr. 10, 1915). Maj. 8th The Black Watch. France, Belgium. *M.C.*, Oct. 15, 1918.

1867 Gloucester, Bishop of, D.D. (Serving Aug. 4, 1914). Chaplain (1st Class) (T.F.), attd. R. Gloucestershire Hussars.

1901 Glover, H., M.A. (Sept. 1, 1916). Lt. R.G.A. (S.R.).

1912 Goad,* F. L., B.A. (1914). ‡2nd Lt. 23rd Manchester Regt. France,

1897 Goad, H. E., M.A. (May 2, 1916). Capt. Special Lists. Staff-Captain. Salonika. *O.B.E.* (Mil.). Cavalier, Order of the Crown of Italy. Croce di Guerra. *D.* Salonika, 1917, 1918.

1898 Godefroi, J. W. H., B.A. (Mar. 11, 1916). ‡Lt. R.A.O.C. France, 1918.

1909 Godfrey, A. H. (Oct. 17, 1914). Lt. R.A.

1911 Godson, C. L., B.A. (Nov. 25, 1914). Lt. 100th Field Coy., R.E. Salonika.

1907 Godson,* E. A., B.A. (Mobilized Aug. 4, 1914). Capt. 10th Res. Regt. of Cavalry. G.S.O. 3. France. *M.C.*, Sept. 25, 1916 ; *Bar*, Mar. 8, 1919. Belgian Croix de Guerre. *D.* France, 1917.

1903 Godson, G. E., B.A. (Aug. 4, 1914). Capt. 7th Worcestershire Regt.

1888 Goff, Sir P., M.A. King's Messenger.

1895 Goodacre, R. F., M.A. (May 2, 1915). 2nd Lt., Unattached List, T.F., Glenalmond O.T.C.

1895 Goodden, J. B. H., B.A. (Mobilized Aug. 1914). Maj. Dorset Yeomanry (Lt.-Col.). Egypt, Gallipoli.

1864 Goodden, J. R. P., M.A. (Mobilized Aug. 4, 1914). Hon. Col. Dorset Yeomanry. T.D.

1897 Goodford, J. W., B.A. (Mobilized Aug. 4, 1914). Maj. W. Somerset Yeomanry.

1912 **Gordon, C. C. B.** (Nov. 1914). 2nd Lt. 3rd, attd. 8th, Somerset L.I. France. Killed in action on Apr. 28, 1917.

1919 Gordon, P. L. (July 31, 1915). Lt. 3rd York and Lancaster Regt. France, 1916, 1917.

1887 Gordon, W. A. (Aug. 1914). Col. 9th R. Warwickshire Regt. Gallipoli, 1915; Mesopotamia, 1916–19. *C.M.G. C.I.E. D.S.O.*, Feb. 2, 1916. *D.* Gallipoli, 1915; Mesopotamia, 1917, 1918; § Feb. 1917.

1913 Gordon-Hall,* W. A. (Nov. 27, 1914). Capt. 8th R. Scots Fusiliers. France, Salonika, Egypt.

1900 Gore, C. H. (Jan. 28, 1915). Capt. R.A.S.C., attd Egyptian Army. Egypt. *O.B.E.* (Mil.).

1903 Gore, J. F. (Aug. 4, 1914). Capt. Bedfordshire Yeomanry. Staff-Captain. France and Belgium, 1915–18. *D.* France, 1917.

1900 **Gorell, Lord,** M.A. (Mobilized Aug. 4, 1914). Capt., temp. Maj., 7th London Bde., R.F.A. (T.F.). France. *D.S.O.*, Nov. 2, 1916. *D.* France, 1916. Died on Jan. 16, 1917, of wounds received in action.

Goslett, J. S. (Oct. 27, 1914). Lt. Norfolk Yeomanry. Gallipoli. Killed in action on Nov. 11, 1915.

1900 Gossell, K. O. T., B.A. (Mobilized Aug. 4, 1914). Capt. 1st County of London Yeomanry. Gallipoli, Salonika, Egypt, Palestine, Syria. *M.C.*, Mar. 26, 1918.

1919 Graham, A. C. (Aug. 14, 1915). Lt. 3rd Q.O. Cameron Highlanders (Capt.). France, 1916–17; N. Russia, 1918–19. Order of St. Anne (3rd Class) (with crossed swords and bow).

1901 Graham, A. J., B.A. (Apr. 8, 1915). ‡Lt. King's (Liverpool Regt.) (Liverpool Scottish), attd. Foreign Office. *O.B.E.* (Civil).

1907 Graham, C. R., M.A. (Oct. 10, 1914). Capt. General List. G.S.O. 3. France, 1914–19. *O.B.E.* (Mil.). *D.* France, 1916, 1917.

1909 Graham,* H. F., M.A. (Sept. 1, 1914). Lt. 108th Bde., R.F.A. (Maj.). Egypt, Serbia, France. *D.* France, 1919.

1910 Graham,* O. B. (Serving Aug. 4, 1914). Capt. 1st Rifle Brigade. Lt.-Col. Special Lists. France. *D.S.O.*, June 4, 1917. *D.* France, 1918.

Gray, P. W. (Jan. 1916). 2nd Lt. R.F.A. France, 1917. Died on May 9, 1917, of wounds received in action at Agnez-lez-Duisans.

1919 Green, C. A. H. (1918). Inns of Court O.T.C., and No. 16 O.C.B.

1904 Greenly, J. H. M., B.A. (Mobilized Aug. 4, 1914). Maj. 1st Herefordshire Regt. Staff Captain, Ministry of Munitions. *O.B.E.* (Mil.). *D.* § Mar. 1918.

1914 Gregory, A. S. (Nov. 3, 1917). 2nd Lt. R.F.A.

1919 Gregory, J. S. (Nov. 7, 1916). ‡2nd Lt. R.F.A. (T.F.). France and Belgium.

1911 Grey,* N. F. E. (Oct. 7, 1914). Lt. 78th Bde., R.F.A. France and Belgium, 1915–19.

1919 Griffin, A. K. (Dec. 1915). Lt. 220th Bn. C.E.F. Lt. R.G.A. France, N. Russia.

1894 Griffith, Rev. H. A., B.A. (Feb. 19, 1917). Chaplain to the Forces (4th Class).

1909 Griffiths, I. H. (July 2, 1917). 2nd Lt. R.A.S.C.

1885 Grindley, Rev. R. D., M.A. (Feb. 16, 1916). Chaplain to the Forces (4th Class).

1902 **Gunner, J. H.** (Mobilized Aug. 4, 1914). Capt. Hampshire Yeomanry, attd. 15th Hampshire Regt. France. Died on Aug. 9, 1918, of wounds received in action.

1904 Gurney, S. (Oct. 25, 1916). Lt. 6th Norfolk Regt.

1895 Gurney Salter, F., M.A. (Sept. 2, 1914). ‡Lt. 5th Rifle Brigade. France, 1915–16.

1919 Hagen, J. L. (Dec. 3, 1917). Pte. 23rd Engineers, U.S. Army. France, 1918–19.

1885 Haig, A. E. (Serving Aug. 4, 1914). Maj. K.O. Scottish Borderers. France. *D.* France, 1914. (Prisoner of war, 1914.) *D.* May 5, 1919.

1910 Hale, R., B.A. (Nov. 1917). ‡2nd Lt. Board of Contracts and Adjustments, afterwards 163rd Inf., U.S. Army. France, 1917–18.

1913 Hall, D. L., B.A. (Oct. 17, 1914). Lt. and Adjt. 60th Bde., R.F.A. Egypt, Serbia, 1915; Salonika, 1915–17.

1909 Hall, E. W., M.A. (Sept. 1914). ‡Capt. R.A.F. (Maj.). France. (Wounded and prisoner of war, July 1916 to Sept. 1917.)

1897 **Hall, J. E. K.,** B.A. (Feb. 17, 1915). 2nd Lt. 3rd S. Wales Borderers. Gallipoli. Died on Sept. 22, 1915, of wounds received in action in Gallipoli.

1912 Hamilton,* A. F., B.A. (Oct. 2, 1914). Lt. 1/4th Hampshire Regt. (Capt.). India, 1914–16; Mesopotamia, 1916–17; Persia, 1918; Turkestan, 1918–19.

1905 **Hamilton Grierson, J. G.,** B.A. (Oct. 24, 1914). 2nd Lt. 1/5th R. Scots Fusiliers. Gallipoli. Killed in action in Gallipoli on July 12, 1915.

1901 Hamilton Grierson, P. F., B.A. (Aug. 7, 1914). ‡Capt. 1/5th R. Scots Fusiliers. (Staff-Captain). Gallipoli, Egypt, Sinai, Palestine, Syria. *D.* Egypt, 1916; Palestine, 1919.

1908 Hamlyn,* G. A., B.A. (Oct. 13, 1916). Lt. R.E.

1919 Hammond, S. A. (Oct. 20, 1916). ‡2nd Lt. R.E. France, 1917–18.

1903 Hannain, C. D., B.A. (Sept. 1914). Capt. 2/7th W. Yorkshire Regt. France. *M.C.*, July 26, 1917.

1899 Hannay, A. K., M.A. (Sept. 2, 1914). Capt. King's (Liverpool Regt.).

1899 **Harley, J.,** M.A. (Feb. 8, 1915). Lt. 13th Worcestershire Regt., attd. K.O. Scottish Borderers. Gallipoli. Killed in action in Gallipoli on June 4, 1915.

1884 Harris, A. Butler, B.M., M.A. (Aug. 5, 1914). Maj., Bt. Lt.-Col., R.A.M.C. T.D.

1919 Harris, E. L. (Jan. 3, 1917). Lt. 4th K.O. Scottish Borderers. France and Belgium, 1917–18.

1897 **Harrison, B. C.,** B.A. (Dec. 21, 1914). Capt. 11th Border Regt. France. *D.* France, 1917. Killed in action on Aug. 12, 1918.

1893 Harrison, C. N. M., B.A. Nairobi Defence Force.

1888 Harrison, J. K. M., M.A. (Oct. 1914). Capt. R.F.A. Staff-Captain.

1907 **Harvey,* B. S.,** M.A. (Sept. 28, 1914). Lt., temp. Capt., 5th London Regt. (London Rifle Brigade). France. Killed in action in the Battle of the Somme on July 1, 1916.

1902 Hasluck, N. R. (Apr. 10, 1915). 2nd Lt. E. Surrey Regt.

1907 **Hastings, L.,** B.A. (Serving Aug. 4, 1914). Capt. Indian Army, attd. 102nd King Edward's Own Grenadiers. Persia. Killed in action in the Persian Gulf on Jan. 21, 1916.

1905 **Hatton, B.** (Mar. 1, 1915). 2nd Lt. Worcestershire Yeomanry. Egypt. Killed in action at Katia, Sinai, on Apr. 23, 1916.

1892 Havers, H. L. (Mobilized Aug. 4, 1914). Maj. 1/1st Sussex Batt., R.F.A. (T.F.). India. Mesopotamia. (Invalided Apr. 1918.)

1919 Haworth, P. K. (Sept. 24, 1914). ‡Capt. 7th K.R.R.C. France, 1915–17. *M.C.* Oct. 18, 1917.

1910 Hayes Sadler,* C. W., B.A. (Aug. 6, 1914). ‡Lt. R.E. France, 1914–15. 1916–19; Germany, 1919. Croix de Guerre.

1914 **Hayward, H. W.** (Dec. 22, 1914). 2nd Lt. K.O.Y.L.I., attd. 8th Northamptonshire Regt. France. Killed in action on the Somme in July, 1916.

1905 **Heberden, A. C.,** B.Mus., M.A. (June 22, 1915). 2nd Lt. 6th K.R.R.C. France. Killed in action on July 10, 1917.

1913 **Hemingway,* J.** (Aug. 15, 1914). 2nd Lt. 3rd, attd. 1st, Seaforth Highlanders. France and Belgium. Killed in action on May 9, 1915.

1907 Henderson,* G. L. P., B.A. (Sept. 30, 1914). ‡Lt.-Col. R.A.F. (Wing Commander). France. *M.C.* Jan. 22, 1916. *A.F.C.* June 3, 1919. *D.* § Feb. 1917; June 1918; Jan. 1919.

1899 Henderson, W. E B., M.A. (Mar. 1916). Lt. R.G.A.

1901 **Henderson Hamilton, C. C.,** B.A. (1915). Capt. 12th Cameronians, attd. 1st K.O. Scottish Borderers. Gallipoli. Killed in action in Gallipoli on Aug. 21, 1915.

1917 Hervey, F. A. R. (Jan. 4, 1918). 2nd Lt. 3rd York and Lancaster Regt., attd. 11th E. Yorkshire Regt. Belgium, France.

1912 Hervey, G. A. K., B.A. (Oct. 1, 1914). ‡Lt. Special Lists. (Staff-Captain R.T.O.) France, Belgium.

1906 Hervey, G. S., B.A. (Aug. 30, 1914). ‡Lt. Seaforth Highlanders. France. Italy. *M.C.* Sept. 24, 1918.

1913 Heseltine, C. L., B.A. (Dec. 14,1914). Lt. 13th Arg. & Suth'd. Highlanders, afterwards Lt. M.G.C., attd. Ministry of Munitions. France.

1883 Hewett, H. T., B.A. (May 7, 1915). Capt. Special Lists. A.P.M.

1899 Heyland, Rev. A. K., M.A. (Oct. 31, 1916). Chaplain to the Forces (4th Class). France and Belgium, 1916–18.

1911 **Hickman, A. K.** (Mar. 6, 1915). Lt. 3rd R. Welch Fusiliers. France. Killed in action, Apr. 4–5, 1916.

1909 Higham, T. F., M.A. (Dec. 22, 1914). Capt. General List. Staff-Captain (Intelligence Corps.) Salonika, 1916–18; Constantinople, 1918. Greek medal for Military Merit (4th Class). *D.* Salonika, 1918.

1899 Hill, W. F., B.A. (Aug. 1914). Capt. 3rd Highland L.I. France. (Retired on account of wounds, Apr. 1918.)

1909 Hills,* A. L. F. (Aug. 12, 1914). Capt. 3rd Cheshire Regt. France and Belgium.

1914 Hoare, A. J. L. (Sept. 1915). 2nd Lt. Suffolk Regt., attd. M.G.C. France, Palestine, 1916.

1898 Hoare, E. G. (1915). Capt. K.O.Y.L.I. Acting Lt.-Col. 5th King's Own (R. Lancaster Regt.). France. *D.S.O.* June 3, 1919. *D.* France, 1918.

1904 **Hodges, H. A.,** M.A. (Aug. 27, 1914). Capt. 3rd Monmouthshire Regt., attd. 11th S. Lancashire Regt. France. *D.* France, 1917 twice. Killed in action near Ham on Mar. 24, 1918.

1908 Hodges, R. J., B.A. (Sept. 18, 1914). Capt. Denbighshire Yeomanry. Egypt, 1916–17; Palestine, 1917–18; France, 1918–19.

1906 Hodgson, D. K. (Feb. 20, 1915). Hon. Lt. R.N.V.R.

1903 Hodgson, P. K., M.A. (Mobilized Aug. 4, 1914). Maj. Suffolk Yeomanry (Asst. Mil. Sec. to G.O.C. 3rd Army). Egypt, 1916; France, 1916–19. *O.B.E.* (Mil.) *D.* France, 1918.

1895 **Holland, E.** (Mobilized Aug. 4, 1914). Lt. Worcestershire Yeomanry. 2nd Lt. Scots Guards (from Apr. 1916). Egypt, Gallipoli, France. *M.C.* June 3, 1916. *D.* Gallipoli, 1916. Killed in action on Sept. 13, 1916.

1908 **Holland, T. E.,** M.A. (Sept. 19, 1914). Capt. 11th Rifle Brigade. Capt. General List, empld. War Office. France. *M.C.* Sept. 16, 1918. Croix de Chevalier de la Légion d'Honneur. Died on Jan. 11, 1919.

1919 Hollis, A. M. (Jan. 4, 1918). 2nd Lt. Guards M.G. Regt.

1913 **Holt,* L. G.** (1914). ‡Capt. 3rd Loyal N. Lancashire Regt. France. *M.C.* Aug. 19, 1916. Killed in action on Sept. 28, 1916.

1920 Hopkins, G. M. (Aug. 1916). Lt. R.A.F. France, Germany.

1910 Hordern, C. W. (June 15, 1915). Lt. R. Fusiliers.

1908 Hornby,* R. F., B.A. (Serving Aug. 4, 1914). Lt., Acting Capt., 8th Hussars.

1912 Howard,* H. Ll. (Sept. 2, 1914). ‡Capt., Acting Maj., 36th Divl. Signal Coy., R.E. France, Belgium. *M.C.* June 4, 1917. *D.* France, 1916, 1919.

1912 Howard, W. J., B.A. (Feb. 12, 1915). Capt., Acting Maj., R.G.A. *M.C.* Aug. 25, 1916. *D.* France, 1917.

1902 Howard Vyse, R. G. H. (Serving Aug. 4, 1914). Maj., Bt.-Lt.-Col., R. Horse Guards (Brig.-General). France, Palestine. *C.M.G. D.S.O.*, June 23, 1915. *D.* France, 1917, 1918.

1899 Howarth, E. G., M.A. (May 11, 1915). Lt. Q.O. Oxfordshire Hussars. France and Belgium. *D.* France, 1918.

1896 Howell, C. M. H., D.M. (Sept. 5, 1914). Capt. R.A.M.C., attd. 1st London General Hospital.

1892 Howkins, J. D., M.A. (Feb. 8, 1915). Lt. R.N.V.R.

1898 Hull, J. H., B.A. (Jan. 2, 1916). Lt. 5th, attd. 10th, Essex Regt.

1904 Humbert, O. J., B.A. (July 10, 1916). Lt. R.A.S.C.

1897 **Hume, E. A.,** B.A. (Dec. 11, 1914). Capt. 7th S. Staffordshire Regt. Gallipoli. Died at sea on Aug. 27, 1915, of wounds received in action on July 25, 1915.

1904 Hunt, H. V. (Aug. 21, 1914). Capt. R.A.S.C. *D.* § Feb. 1917.

1899 Hunter, Rev. E. T. G., M.A. (June 25, 1915). Chaplain to the Forces (4th Class), attd. No. 1 Dispersal Station, Ripon (S.C.F.). France, 1916.

1911 Hurst,* H., M.A. (Sept. 1914). ‡Capt. 4th Leicestershire Regt. Salonika, Black Sea. *D.* Salonika, 1918.

1919 Hutchings, R. H. (May 18, 1915). Capt. 16th Welsh Regt. France.

1919 Hutton, A. P. (Feb. 21, 1917). Lt. R.A.F. (Capt.). France, 1917–18.

1894 Ingram, B. S., B.A. (Dec. 22, 1915). Lt. R.G.A. Capt. Special Lists, whilst Staff-Captain. France. *M.C.* June 3, 1918. *D.* France, 1917.

1913 Ivens, C. H., B.A. (Aug. 28, 1914). Lt. 9th R. Warwickshire Regt., attd. 51st Devonshire Regt. Gallipoli, Mesopotamia.

1913 Jack,* F. C. (Aug. 25, 1914). Lt. 255th Bde., R.F.A. (Maj.). France and Belgium, 1915–18; Egypt and Palestine, 1919. *D.S.O.*, Sept. 16, 1918. *M.C.*, Sept. 26, 1917; *Bar*, Jan. 18, 1918. *D.* France, 1918.

1895 James, A. G. (Aug. 3, 1915). Capt. R.A.S.C. (Staff-Captain, D.A.A.G., War Office.) Egypt, 1916. *C.B.E.* (Civil). *O.B.E.* (Mil.).
1897 Jamison, R., B.M., M.A. (May 14, 1917). Maj. R.A.M.C. N. Russia.
1919 Jaques, L. H. (Sept. 21, 1917). 2nd Lt. 179th Bde., R.F.A. France. *M.C.* June 3, 1919.
1919 Jeppé, H. P. (June 6, 1917). Lt. R.G.A. Lt. R.A.F. France.
1904 Johnston, S. F. S., B.A. (Aug. 1914). Capt. R.A.S.C. France, 1914–18. *D.* France, 1917.
1916 Jones, A. G. K. S. (Feb. 15, 1917). 2nd Lt. 35th T.M. Batt., R.F.A. Belgium and France, 1917–19.
1893 **Jones, E. Ll. H.,** M.A. (1914). 2nd Lt. 12th R. Welch Fusiliers. Gallipoli and Egypt. Killed in action on Mar. 26, 1917.
1890 Jones, J. R., B.A. (Sept. 23, 1914). Capt. R.A.
1915 **Joscelyne, L. A.** (1917). 2nd Lt. Somerset L.I. France. *M.C.*, Oct. 18, 1917. Died on Oct. 1, 1917, of wounds received in action.
1910 **Joy,* G. B.,** B.A. (Aug. 15, 1914). Lt. 3rd Welsh Regt. France. Died on May 21, 1915, of wounds received in action.
1919 Juta, H. C (Aug. 5, 1918). 2nd Lt. Coldstream Guards.
1919 Kamm, G. E. (June 29, 1917). Lt. 382nd Batt., R.F.A. France.
1886 Karslake, J. B. P., M.A. (Mobilized Aug. 4, 1914). Lt.-Col. Berkshire Yeomanry. France. *D.* § Feb. 1917.
1911 Keble White,* A. F., M.A. (Nov. 4, 1914). Lt. 6th Suffolk Regt. Acting Capt. Technical Officer R.A.F.
1900 **Keenlyside, C. A. H.,** B.A. (Mobilized Aug. 4, 1914). Capt. 1st Cambridgeshire Regt. Belgium, France. Killed in action at Armentières on July 20, 1915.
1906 Kempson, C. J., B.A. (July 9, 1915). Lt. I.A.R.O.
1911 Kern, E. E., B.A. (1917). Lt. Field Artillery, U.S. Army. France.
1898 Kershaw, F., M.A. (1916). A.B., R.N.V.R. ‡Capt. R.A.F. Grand Fleet.
1919 Kinchin Smith, F. J. (Sept. 6, 1914). ‡Lt. 4th Shropshire L.I. Far East, 1914–17; France, 1917–18. (Prisoner of war in Germany, 1918.)
1912 **King, A. N.** (Dec. 23, 1914). Lt. R.F.A. France. Killed in action on May 10, 1916.
1919 King, D. P. (Apr. 14, 1918). Pte. Inns of Court O.T.C.
1907 Kirk, P. (Mar. 20, 1917). 2nd Lt. 6th W. Riding Regt.
1904 Knapp Fisher, Rev. G. E., M.A. (Serving Aug. 4, 1914). Chaplain R.N., H.M.S. *Donegal*. Africa, 1914–15; Dardanelles, 1915–16; Atlantic, 1917–18.
1913 **Knapp Fisher,* S. B.** (Oct. 3, 1914). 2nd Lt. 3rd N. Staffordshire Regt. Died 1915.
1913 Knight, D. J., B.A. (Sept. 15, 1914). ‡Lt. Grenadier Guards (S.R.) Belgium, France.
1904 Knyvett, Rev. C. F., M.A. (June 6, 1916). Chaplain to the Forces (4th Class). France and Belgium, 1916–19. *O.B.E.* (Mil.). *D.* France, 1919.
1905 Krabbé, C. B. (Mobilized Aug. 1914). Maj. Berkshire Yeomanry and R.A.F. Egypt, Gallipoli, France. *O.B.E.* (Mil.). *D.* France, 1918; § Mar. 1918.
1900 Krabbé, C. F., B.A. (Nov. 13, 1914). Capt. General List (T.F. Res.). *O.B.E.* (Mil.). *D.* § Feb. 1917.

1912 Laithwaite, J. G., B.A. (Jan. 1915). ‡Lt. 4th Lancashire Fusiliers (Adjt.), attd. War Office. France, 1917–18.

1905 Lascelles, A. F., M.A. (Mobilized Aug. 4, 1914). Capt. Bedfordshire Yeomanry. France. *M.C.*, Jan. 1, 1919. *D.* France, 1916.

1889 Latter, A., M.A. Capt. Unattached List T.F., King's School, Canterbury, O.T.C. *D.* § Mar. 1919.

1914 Latter, J. C. (Dec. 23, 1914). Capt. 5th Lancashire Fusiliers (Staff Captain). France, Italy. *M.C.*, Nov. 26, 1917.

1900 Lattey, R. T., B.Sc., M.A. (Dec. 1915). Lt. R.A.F. (Capt.).

1912 **Lawrence, G. F.** (Dec. 23, 1914). Lt. Grenadier Guards (S.R.), attd. 2nd Bn. Palestine. *D.* Palestine, 1917. Killed in action on Aug. 27, 1918.

1912 Leck, D. H., M.A. (Aug. 27, 1914). Capt. 3rd Border Regt. (Maj. M.G.C.). France, 1915, 1916–18. *M.C.*, Jan. 1, 1918.

1906 Lee, A. K. (Dec. 12, 1914). Lt. 1/4th Somerset L.I. (Capt. A.P.M.). India, Mesopotamia, Andaman Islands.

1918 Legate, J. M., B.A. (Jan. 8, 1915). Lt. 3rd S. African Inf. Bde. German S.W. Africa, German E. Africa.

1889 Legge, Rev. H., M.A. (Feb. 1915). Acting Chaplain, Ambulance Unit, afterwards Gunner R.G.A. Serbia.

1893 Legge, W. T., B.A. (Sept. 2, 1914). Capt. Coldstream Guards. France and Belgium. *D.* France, 1916.

1913 Lemberger, J., M.A. (July 30, 1915). Pte. 91st Field Ambulance, R.A.M.C. France and Belgium, 1915–19.

1891 Leslie, A. S., B.A. (Mobilized Aug. 4, 1914). Lt.-Col. Scottish Horse, attd. Directorate of Forestry, G.H.Q. Gallipoli, France. *C.M.G.*, Jan. 1, 1918. Ordre du Mérite Agricole. *D.* France, 1917.

1907 Leslie, J. (Serving Aug. 4, 1914). Lt. 12th Lancers. Maj. 6th Bn. Tank Corps. France, 1914, 1917–18; Egypt and Senussi, 1915, 1916; *D.S.O.*, Jan. 1, 1919. *M.C.*, June 3, 1916. *D.* Egypt, 1915, 1916; France, 1918.

1920 Lett, S. (Apr. 1915). Capt. and Adjt. 46th Bn. C.E.F. France, Belgium, 1915, 1917–19. *M.C.*, Dec. 2, 1918.

1913 Levy, M. P. (Dec. 4, 1915). Lt. Hampshire Regt. *D.* Order of Aviz.

1919 Lewis, H. G. (Apr. 15, 1918). 2nd Lt. R.A.F. France.

1897 Lewisohn, F., M.A. (May 23, 1917). Gnr. Canadian Field Artillery. ‡Lt. General List, attd. 63rd (Royal Naval) D.A.C. France and Belgium, 1918.

1911 Lister-Kaye, K. A. (Aug. 1914). Lt. (Hon. Capt.) W. Yorkshire Regt. France.

Littledale, W. J. (Dec. 16, 1914). Lt. 2nd Oxf. & Bucks. Lt. Infty. Italy. Killed in action on Mar. 23, 1918.

1910 Lloyd,* C. E. H., M.A. (Mobilized Aug. 4, 1914). Lt., Acting Capt., R.F.A. (T.F.).

1919 Lloyd, E. J. B. (Apr. 5, 1915). ‡Sub-Lt. Hawke Bn. R.N.D. (Lt.). Gallipoli, 1915; France.

1919 Lockhart, D. D. A. (Apr. 15, 1915). Lt. 1st Gordon Highlanders, attd. 52nd Gordon Highlanders. France.

1910 Lockhart,* J. G., B.A. (Aug. 21, 1914). Capt. 1/4th Wiltshire Regt. India, Egypt, Palestine.

1890 Lofthouse, Rev. W. F., M.A. (Jan. 7, 1916). Chaplain to the Forces (4th Class). Salonika, 1916–17.

1920 Lole, E. F. (Apr. 20, 1917). Lt. 1st (Garr.) Bn. Worcestershire Regt. India.

1904 Lorimer, W. L., M.A. (Sept. 28, 1914). 2nd Lt. 11th Gordon Highlanders.

1913 **Lott, J. C.** (Aug. 1914). ‡2nd Lt. 3rd E. Lancashire Regt. France, 1915–16, 1916–18. *M.C.*, Sept. 17, 1917. Killed in action between Merris and Vieux Berquin on Apr. 13, 1918.

1911 Lott,*R. C., M.A. (Aug. 1914). Lt. 12th Lancashire Fusiliers, attd. General Staff, War Office. Salonika, 1916. *D.* Salonika, 1916; §Mar. 1919.

1905 Lowe, R. D. T., M.A. (June 2, 1915). Lt. R. Monmouthshire Engineers.

1911 Lowinsky, T. E. (Aug. 1914). Lt. Scots Guards (S.R.). France, Germany.

1892 Lubbock, G. (Mobilized Aug. 1914). Maj. N. Somerset Yeomanry. France. *D.* France, 1915 twice, 1916.

1903 Luke, H. C., B.Litt., M.A. (Dec. 31, 1914). Lt.-Commdr. R.N.V.R. Syria, Dardanelles, Salonika. Italian Bronze Medal for Valour.

1903 Lupton, A. M. (Serving Aug. 4, 1914). Capt. R.F.A. (Maj.). France and Belgium. *M.C.*, June 4, 1917. Croix de Guerre.

1910 Luttman Johnson,* F. M. (Aug. 15, 1914). Lt. 19th Hussars (S.R.). A.D.C. Chevalier, Order of the Star of Rumania (with swords).

1899 Luxmoore, A. A., M.A. (Aug. 4, 1916). Capt. Northumberland Fusiliers. Capt. General List.

1902 Lyle, A. M. P., M.A. (Mobilized Aug. 4, 1914). Lt. Scottish Horse. Maj. 13th The Black Watch. Gallipoli, Egypt, Macedonia, France. *M.C.* Jan. 18, 1918. *D.* Gallipoli, 1916.

1911 Lyman, E., B.A. (1917). Lt. 7th M.G. Bn., U.S. Army. France, 1918–19.

1912 McBean,* D. R., B.A. (Sept. 23, 1914). Lt. Rifle Brigade. Capt. General List. A.D.C. France. *M.C.* June 3, 1919. *D.* France, 1918.

1911 Macbeth,* J. N., B.A. (Sept. 1, 1914). 2nd Lt. 14th London Regt. (London Scottish).

1901 McBride, W., B.A. (Nov. 18, 1914). Capt. 9th London Regt. (Queen Victoria's Rifles) attd. Tank Corps.

1910 McCleland,* K. C. (May 5, 1915). Cpl. 4th Australian M.G. Squadron. Egypt, Palestine, Syria. *D.C.M.*, Mar. 1918. *D.* Palestine, 1918.

1901 MacClellan, J. P., M.A. (Aug. 5, 1914). Sergt. 14th London Regt. (London Scottish). Belgium and France, 1914–15. (Discharged as result of wounds Feb. 28, 1918.)

1911 **McClelland, T.,** B.A. (Sept. 5, 1914). 2nd Lt. 7th King's (Liverpool Regt.), (T.F.). France. Killed in action on May 16, 1915.

1906 McClure, G. B., B.A. (Sept. 1, 1914). Capt. 9th London Regt. (Queen Victoria's Rifles), empld. 33rd London Regt. France. *D.* France, 1915.

1910 McClure, W. F. C. (Sept. 26, 1914). Maj. 1/8th Arg. & Suth'd. Highlanders (Lt.-Col.). France, 1915–16, 1917–19. *M.C.*, Nov. 14, 1916; *Bar*, Sept. 26, 1917.

1913 **Macculloch,* S. H.** (Jan. 10, 1915). 2nd Lt. 2nd Seaforth Highlanders. France. *D.* France, 1915. Died in Jan. 1916, of wounds received in action.

1909 Macgregor, D. C., M.A. (Aug. 1914). Lt. 8th Q.O. Cameron Highlanders. Lt. General List (Intelligence Corps). France. *D.* France, 1919.

1899 **MacGregor, J. A.,** M.A. (Apr. 10, 1915). 2nd Lt. Coldstream Guards. France, 1916. Killed in action on Sept. 26, 1916.

1919 Macgregor, J. C. S. (July 13, 1915). ‡Lt. R.G.A. (S.R.), attd. Intelligence Corps, G.H.Q., France. France and Belgium, 1915, 1916, 1917, 1918, 1919.

1919 Macgregor, N. E. (Sept. 19, 1914). Capt. 1st Lovat's Scouts. Gallipoli, Egypt, Salonika, France.

1910 Mackenzie, K. A. I., B.M. (Dec. 18, 1916). Surgeon Lt. R.N.

1910 **Mackenzie,* K. FitzP.** (Sept. 29, 1914). Lt. 5th Q.O. Cameron Highlanders. Belgium, France. Killed in action at the Hohenzollern Redoubt on Sept. 25, 1915.

1899 McKenzie, K. W. (Oct. 10, 1914). Maj., Acting Lt.-Col., R.A.M.C. France. *D.S.O.*, 1919. *M.C.*, Oct. 20, 1916; *Bar*, Feb. 6, 1917. *D.* France, 1917, 1918.

1912 Mackenzie, R. M. B., M.A. (July 31, 1916). Sub-Lt. R.N.V.R. Capt. R.A.F.

1893 McLaren, A. E., B.A. (Apr. 28, 1915). Lt. 6th N. Staffordshire Regt.

1914 McLellan, H. (Dec. 20, 1914). Lt. R.E. (Signal Service). France, 1915–16; Palestine, 1917–19.

1919 McNeill, J. (May 28, 1918). 2nd Lt. 1st The Black Watch. France.

1914 Macpherson, I. G. (Nov. 2, 1914). Lt. 1st Q.O. Cameron Highlanders. France, Belgium, Germany, 1916–19.

1895 Mahon, H. M., B.A. (May 1916). ‡Lt. R.G.A. France, 1917–19.

1893 Malcolm, G. H., M.A. (Nov. 4, 1914). Maj. 8th Arg. & Suth'd. Highlanders. Governor of Sinai, 1918. Egypt and Palestine, 1917–19.

1905 **Mappin, F. T.,** B.A. Canadian Air Force. France. Killed in an accident during training.

1911 Marshall,* E. N., B.A. (Sept. 2, 1914). Capt. 1/4th W. Riding Regt. France and Belgium, 1915–16, 1916–19. *M.C.*, Jan. 1, 1918. *D.* France, 1916.

1910 Marshall, G. L., B.A. (Jan. 1915). Capt. 4th Canadian Inf. France, 1916–18. *D.* France, 1919.

1909 Marshall,* H. R., B.A. (Mobilized Aug. 4, 1914). Capt. Lanarkshire Yeomanry. G.S.O. 2. Gallipoli, 1915; Sinai, Egypt, 1916–17; Palestine, 1917–19.

1905 Marshall, J. R., B.A. (Mobilized Aug. 5, 1914). Capt. 1/1st Lothians and Border Horse. France, 1915; Salonika, 1915–18.

1901 Marston, J. A., M.A. (June 6, 1916). ‡2nd Lt. R. Welch Fusiliers. France, 1918.

1884 Mason, A. E. W., B.A. (Dec. 19, 1914). Capt. Manchester Regt. Maj. R. Marines. Staff-Captain.

1893 Mason, C. R. (Dec. 1, 1915). Pte. S. African Medical Corps, afterwards Pte. S.A. Overseas Inf. German E. Africa, France.

1910 Mathers, E. P., B.A. Pte. Middlesex Regt.

1895 Mathias, W. D., M.A. (Feb. 25, 1915). A.B., R.N. Anti-Aircraft Corps, afterwards 2nd Lt. R.G.A. (Capt.; G.S.O. 3). (Retired on account of ill health, Jan. 1918.)

1890 Matthew, G. W. (Sept. 18, 1914). Capt. 4th R. Irish Rifles. *D.* § Aug. 1919.

1882 Maude, E. A. (Mobilized Aug. 4, 1914). Lt.-Col. N. Irish Horse.

1908 Maufe, C. G., M.A. (Sept. 1914). ‡Lt. 1/6th W. Yorkshire Regt. France. *D.* France, 1918, 1919.

1885 Mavrojani, S., B.C.L., M.A. (Oct. 29, 1914). Capt. 5th R. Fusiliers.

1902 Mead, G. G. (Oct. 13, 1914). Capt. R.A.S.C.

1889 Meade, G. H., B.A. (Dec. 24, 1914). Capt. N. Somerset Yeomanry.

1910 Melly,* E. E., B.A. (Sept. 10, 1914). Capt. and Adjt. 1/5th York and Lancaster Regt. France, 1915–19. *M.C.*, June 3, 1918; *Bar*, Sept. 16, 1918.

1911 Meyer, E. A., B.A. Pte. R. Warwickshire Regt.

1899 Milburn, L. E., B.A. (Mobilized Aug. 2, 1914). Capt., temp. Maj., 4th Suffolk Regt. A.P.M. France. *M.C.*, Jan. 14, 1916. *D.* France, 1916.

1908 **Miles, A. O.,** B.A. (1914). ‡2nd Lt. Gloucestershire Regt. Belgium, France. Killed in action near Richebourg l'Avoué on June 30, 1916.

1919 Miller, C. T. (Aug. 1917). Lt. R.A.F. Dunkirk, 1918.

1919 Miller, F. P. (Oct. 4, 1917). ‡1st Lt. 58th Coast Art. Corps, U.S. Army.

1908 **Milligan,* J. R.** (1915). Lt. I.A.R.O., attd. 59th Rifles. Mesopotamia. Missing, believed killed in action in Mesopotamia on Mar. 8, 1916.

1900 Mills, E. E., B.A. (Sept. 22, 1914). Capt. 7th S. Wales Borderers. Salonika. *M.C.*, Jan. 1, 1918. *D.* Salonika, 1917.

1894 Milsted, G. H., M.A. (Jan. 10, 1916). ‡2nd Lt. R.G.A.

1909 Mitchell, P. E. Lt. King's African Rifles. Nairobi Defence Force. E. Africa.

1907 **Mitchell,* P. M.,** B.A. (Mar. 9, 1915). Lt. 1st Herefordshire Regt. Egypt and Palestine. Killed in action on Nov. 6, 1917.

1895 **Mitchell, R. W.** (Oct. 18, 1914). Lt., Acting Capt., R. E. Kent Yeomanry, attd. 10th The Buffs (E. Kent Regt.). Egypt and Palestine. Died on Nov. 19, 1917, of wounds received in action.

1907 Monk,* J. M., M.A. (Serving Aug. 4, 1914). Capt., Bt.-Maj., Worcestershire Regt. G.S.O. 2. France. *M.C.*, Jan. 14, 1916; *Bar*, Nov. 26, 1917. *D.* France, 1915, 1917, 1918.

1913 Monro, C. C. A., B.A. (Sept. 1, 1914). Lt., Acting Capt., M.G.C.

1906 Monteath, D. T., B.A. (Jan. 1918). Lt. R.N.V.R.

1890 Montgomerie, H. S., B.A. (Mobilized Aug. 4, 1914). Maj. 9th Middlesex Regt.

Moore, R. (Aug. 31, 1915). 2nd Lt. W. Yorkshire Regt. France. Killed in action in France on July 15, 1916.

1894 **Morgan, J. C.,** M.A. (Oct. 4, 1914). Capt. 6th Yorkshire Regt. Gallipoli. Killed in action in Gallipoli on Aug. 7, 1915.

1894 Morgan, J. H., M.A. (1917). Superintendent, French Hospital, Nevirs. France, 1917. Médaille de la Reconnaissance française de 2e classe en argent.

1919 Morris, C. R. (Sept. 5, 1916). Lt. R.G.A. (S.R.). France.

1914 Morris, H. M., B.A. (Mar. 16, 1915). ‡Lt. 4th Shropshire L.I.

1906 **Moseley,* H. G. J.,** M.A. (Oct. 17, 1914). 2nd Lt. R.E. (Signal Officer 38th Bde.). Gallipoli. Killed in action in Gallipoli on Aug. 10, 1915.

1894 Moss, W. E., M.A. (Mobilized Mar. 1915). Lt.-Col. 4th W. Lancs. (Howr.) Bde., R.F.A., 1915–1916, afterwards Hon. Lt.-Col. R.H. and R.F.A. (T.F.).

1903 **Mowat, C. J. C.,** M.A. (Aug. 14, 1914). Capt. 8th Cameronians. France. Killed in action on June 28, 1915.

1890 Muir, W. E. (Mar. 1917). Conducteur, Section Sanitaire Anglaise, No. 10, Croix rouge française. France, Verdun.

1908 Mundey, H. R., M.A. (Sept. 15, 1914). Capt. 11th R. Fusiliers (attd. XIX Corps School). France. *D.* France.

1893 **Murdoch, L. F. C.** (Feb. 1916). 2nd Lt. 2nd Scots Guards. France. Died on Sept. 19, 1916, of wounds received at Ginchy on Sept. 15, 1916.

Murray, G. L. (Aug. 30, 1917). 2nd Lt. R.A.F. France. Killed in action in May, 1918.

1913 Murray, L. D., M.A. (1914). Cpl. 1st King Edward's Horse. France. (Prisoner of war, 1918.) *D.C.M.*, Mar. 31, 1918.

1909 **Napier,* L. R. M.**, B.A. (Serving Aug. 4, 1914). Capt. 1st Q.O. Cameron Highlanders. France. Killed in action in Aug. 1916.

1911 **Narey,* V. G.**, B.A. (Aug. 23, 1915). Lt. 11th W. Riding Regt. France. Killed in action on Oct. 15, 1916.

1901 Nash, L. C. F., B.A. (Sept. 2, 1914). Capt. Rifle Brigade.

1911 Naumann, F. C. G. (Aug. 5, 1914). ‡Lt. 76th Bde., R.F.A. (Maj.). Egypt, France, Italy. *M.C.*, June 4, 1917. *D.* France, 1916; Italy, 1918.

1915 Need, W. F. (Feb. 8, 1916). Lt. 8th Loyal N. Lancashire Regt. France, 1916–18; Egypt, 1918–19.

1910 Nelson,* J. H. (Aug. 4, 1914). ‡Lt. R.F.A. France. (Invalided on account of wounds, Jan. 1918.)

1906 Newman, W. P. M. (Nov. 10, 1912). ‡2nd Lt. R.F.A. Capt. R.A.F. Staff Captain, Air Ministry. France.

1908 Nicholas, D. L. (1918). 2nd Lt. R.A.F.

1913 Nichols, R. M. B. (Oct. 13, 1914). 2nd Lt. 104th Bde., R.F.A. France. (Invalided on account of wounds.)

1914 Nicolson, G. W. H. (Dec. 2, 1914). Capt. 8th R. Berkshire Regt. France. *M.C.*, Feb. 1, 1919; *Bar*, Feb. 1, 1919.

1890 Noble, P. E. (Sept. 1, 1914). Lt. Northumberland Yeomanry (T.F. Res.). *D.* §.

Norbury, P. G. (Dec. 1914). Lt. 7th The Buffs (E. Kent Regt.). France. Killed in action in Battle of the Somme on July 1, 1916.

1908 Norman,* C. L., M.A. (Mobilized Aug. 4, 1914). Capt. 1/4th R. W. Kent Regt. India.

1909 Nuttall, E., M.A. (Mobilized Aug. 1914). Capt. 1st E. Lancashire Bde., R.F.A. Egypt, Gallipoli, Sinai, France.

1919 Nuttall-Smith, R. N. (June 23, 1917). ‡2nd Lt. R.A.F.

1909 **O'Callaghan, D. M. M.** (Aug. 15, 1914). 2nd Lt. 3rd, attd. 2nd, D.C.L.I. France. Killed in action at Neuve Chapelle on Mar. 15, 1915.

1880 Ogle, C., M.A. (Aug. 1914). Capt. R.A.M.C., attd. 4th London General Hospital.

1877 Ogle, Rev. W. R., M.A. (Mobilized Aug. 4, 1914). Chaplain (4th Class) (T.F.), attd. 7th Middlesex Regt.

1905 Okell, Rev. F. J., M.A. (Dec. 22, 1915). Chaplain to the Forces (4th Class). France and Belgium, 1915–19. *D.* France, 1917.

1903 Oliphant, K., M.A. (Sept. 9, 1914). ‡Maj. Hertfordshire Regt. (D.A.D.L. London District). France. *M.C.*, Jan. 14, 1916. *D.* France, 1915.

1903 Ormerod, Rev. J. C., M.A. (Nov. 18, 1915). Chaplain to the Forces (4th Class). France.

1886 Ormiston, T. L., M.A. (Serving Aug. 4, 1914). Lt.-Col. Indian Army.
1895 Otter, F. R. (Aug. 19, 1914). Lt. 5th Dragoon Guards, Res. of Officers.
1919 Owen, H. D. (Jan. 15, 1912). Lt. R.N., H.M.A.S. *Australia*. North Sea.
1903 Parker, Rev. G. W., M.A. (July 4, 1917). Chaplain R.N.
1896 Parker, R. F., B.A. (1914). Capt. 21st Manchester Regt. Capt. General List. Staff-Captain. France, Italy. *O.B.E.* (Mil.). *M.C.*, June 4, 1917. *D.* France, 1916; Italy, 1918.
1895 Parkin, A. J., B.A. (Sept. 2, 1914). Capt. 3rd R. Sussex Regt.
1909 Parkin, G. M., B.A. (Aug. 4, 1914). Maj. R.F.A., attd. G.H.Q., Ireland. France. *M.C.*, Oct. 18, 1917.
1875 Parry, L. E. S., *D.S.O.*, T.D. (Mobilized Aug. 1914). Lt.-Col. Denbighshire Yeomanry (T.F. Res.), attd. Staff. *C.B.E.* (Mil.). *D.* § Feb. 1917.
1907 Paterson, G. M., M.A. (Feb. 15, 1914). Lt. Unattached List, T.F., Cheltenham College O.T.C.
1882 Paterson, Rev. G. W., M.A. (1914). Chaplain to Lowland Mtd. Bde.
1913 Paterson,* H. D. L., B.A. (Oct. 11, 1914). Lt. Field Coys., R.E. France.
1919 Paton, R. R. D. (Aug. 1917). Lt. 1st Welsh Guards. France, Belgium, Germany. *M.C.*, Feb. 1, 1919.
1911 Peach, E. W. A., B.A. (Dec. 22, 1914). Capt. Bedfordshire Regt., empld. War Office.
1899 Pearson, Rev. T. N., M.A. (Aug. 20, 1916). Chaplain to the Forces (4th Class).
1910 Peat,* C. U., B.A. (Sept. 1914). ‡Capt. City of London Yeomanry. Egypt, Salonika, Palestine. *M.C.*, Jan. 1, 1918.
1905 Peat, R. M., M.A. (Sept. 1914). Capt. City of London Yeomanry. Egypt, Gallipoli.
1911 Pedder, G. R. (Feb. 25, 1915). Lt. 13th Hussars.
1911 Pedley, J. E., B.A. (Aug. 1914). Tpr. King Edward's Horse. ‡Capt. 57th Rifles, I.A.R.O., attd. as G.S.O., Headquarters, N.W.F.F., Peshawar. France, India, N.W. Frontier. *M.C.*, Jan. 1, 1917.
1914 Peebles-Chaplin, C. J. (Nov. 4, 1914). Capt. 3rd The Black Watch (attd. Staff). France.
1913 **Peel, G.** (Jan. 25, 1915). Lt. 6th Bedfordshire Regt. France. Killed in action on July 18, 1917.
1889 Peel, Hon. S. C., M.A. (Mobilized Aug. 4, 1914). Lt.-Col. Bedfordshire Yeomanry, attd. F.O. (1918), attd. British Delegation, Peace Conference (1919). France. *D.S.O.*, June 4, 1917. T.D. *D.* France, 1916, 1917.
1907 Pemberton,* R. B. (Sept. 1914). Capt. 7th Oxf. & Bucks. Lt. Infty. G.S.O. 3, 28th Div. France, 1915; Salonika, 1915–18.
1919 Penniman, T. K. (Sept. 4, 1918). Pte. 5th Dev. Bn., Camp Upton, New York.
1900 **Pennington, H. E.,** B.A. (Dec. 30, 1914). 2nd Lt. 9th R. Sussex Regt. France. Killed in action at Loos on Sept. 25, 1915.
1919 Pennington, K. M. (Apr. 1916). ‡Lt., Flying Officer, R.A.F. (Capt.). German E. Africa, Mesopotamia, Persia, Russia. *A.F.C.*, Dec. 2, 1918. *D.* Mesopotamia, 1919.
1898 Pereira, H. A. de C., B.A. (Mar. 4, 1915). ‡Capt R.A.O.C. France.
1906 Peterson,* W. G., M.A. (July 26, 1914). Maj. 73rd R. Canadian Regt. Bermuda, France, Belgium, Germany. *D.S.O.*, June 3, 1918. *D.* France, 1917.

1906 Petrie, F. E., M.A. (Sept. 15, 1914). ‡Capt. 6th R. Fusiliers. France, 1917, 1918; Italy, 1917–18.

1888 Phillips, Rev. E. S., M.A. (Serving Aug. 4, 1914). Chaplain R.N.

1905 **Phillips, J. A.,** B.A. (Nov. 4, 1914). Lt. 13th King's (Liverpool Regt.). France. Killed in action on May 3, 1917.

1912 **Phillpotts,* F. C.** (Aug. 22, 1914). Lt. 7th Gloucestershire Regt. Gallipoli. Died on Aug. 9, 1915, of wounds received in action in Gallipoli.

1913 **Pinsent, L. A.** (Aug. 29, 1914). Lt. 7th N. Staffordshire Regt. Gallipoli. *D.* Gallipoli, 1915. Died on Aug. 15, 1915, of wounds received in action in Gallipoli.

1910 **Plummer, A. H.** (Oct. 19, 1914). 2nd Lt. 5th King's (Liverpool Regt.). France. Killed in action near La Bassée on May 17, 1915.

1909 **Plummer,* Rev. C. B.,** M.A. (Nov. 24, 1914). Chaplain to the Forces (4th Class). France. Killed in action on Mar. 12, 1917.

1919 Plummer, J. E. B. (Sept. 1914). Capt. 12th King's (Liverpool Regt.). France and Belgium, 1916–18. *M.C.*, Jan. 1, 1918. *D.* France, 1917.

1906 **Podmore,* H.,** B.A. (Sept. 22, 1914). Maj. 6th Northamptonshire Regt. (Lt.-Col.). France. *D.S.O.*, May 31, 1916. *D.* France, 1916 twice. Accidentally killed on Dec. 31, 1917.

1913 Pogson-Smith, J. E. (Jan. 7, 1915). Lt. 8th Oxf. & Bucks. Lt. Infty. Salonika.

1919 Pollock, J. (July 28, 1915). Lt. N. Irish Horse. France, 1916–17.

1885 Pollok-Morris, W. P. M., *D.S.O.* (Aug. 21, 1914). Lt.-Col. 18th Hussars, attd. 5th Res. Regt. of Cavalry. *C.M.G.*, Mar. 8, 1918. *D.* § Feb. 1917; § Aug. 1919.

1899 Ponsonby, Rev. M. G. J., M.A. (Dec. 4, 1914). Chaplain to the Forces (4th Class), attd. Guards Bde. (S.C.F., 19th Div.) France. *M.C.*, Jan. 26, 1917. *D.* France, 1915, 1916.

1909 Poole,* J. C., B.A. (Sept. 27, 1915). Lt., Acting Maj., R.F.A. (S.R.). France. *M.C.*, July 26, 1917; *Bar*, Feb. 15, 1919. *D.* France, 1917.

1904 Poole, R. H., M.A. (Mar. 30, 1915). Lt., Acting Maj., R.E., attd. R.A.O.C. (Assistant to C.I.O.O.D., Ordnance G.H.Q.) France, 1915, 1918–19. *D.* France.

1894 Porch, R. B., M.A. (Dec. 1915). ‡Lt. Unattached List, T.F., Malvern College O.T.C.

1910 Poston, G. (Serving Aug. 4, 1914). ‡Capt. 1/5th E. Surrey Regt. India, Mesopotamia, 1914–19.

1919 Potts, C. V. (Mobilized Aug. 5, 1914). Capt. 3rd Northumberland Fusiliers. France, 1917.

1915 Prickett, W., B.A. (Sept. 13, 1917). 2nd Lt. Field Artillery, U.S. Army. Lt. Flying Force. France.

1896 Prideaux, H. H., M.A. (Aug. 28, 1914). ‡Capt., temp. Maj., 3rd Northumberland Fusiliers. D.A.A.G. France and Belgium. *D.S.O.*, June 3, 1918. *M.C.*, June 3, 1916. Belgian Croix de Guerre. *D.* France, 1916, 1917, 1918.

1899 Prideaux, Rev. S. P. T., D.D. (Nov. 18, 1916). Chaplain to the Forces (4th Class).

1902 Proby, G., M.A. (Mobilized Aug. 1914). Capt. Bedfordshire Yeomanry. France.

1910 **Pumphrey,* J. L.** (1914). Northumberland Yeomanry. France. Killed in action on Oct. 25, 1914.
1912 **Purvis,* J. R.** (Sept. 1, 1914). Capt. 9th Rifle Brigade. France and Belgium. Killed in action at Bellewaarde Ridge, near Hooge, on Sept. 25, 1915.
1882 Quiller-Couch, Sir A. T., M.A. Capt. D.C.L.I.
1910 **Quiller-Couch,* B. B.** (Aug. 5, 1914). Capt. R.F.A. (S.R.), attd. 9th Batt. France, Germany. *D.S.O.*, June 3, 1919. *M.C.*, Jan. 14, 1916. *D.* France, 1915, 1918, 1919. Died at Düren on Feb. 6, 1919, of illness contracted while on active service.
1919 Raleigh, F. V. (Jan. 28, 1918). 2nd Lt. R.A.F.
1908 Rainy, G. R., B.A. (Serving Aug. 4, 1914). Capt., Bt.-Maj., commanding 100th Batt., R.F.A., 28th Div. France, Aug. 1914–16; Macedonia, 1916–18. *M.C.*, Jan. 1, 1915. Greek Military Cross (2nd Class). *D.* France, 1914.
1891 Ratcliffe-Ellis, A. (Aug. 8, 1914). Maj. 2/5th Manchester Regt. France, 1915, 1916, 1917. *D.* § Feb. 1917.
1906 Raven, M. O., M.A. (Aug. 6, 1914). Surgeon Lt. R.N., attd. No. 1 Ambulance, R.N.D. France.
1906 Rawle, W., B.A. (Oct. 1914). Capt. Grenadier Guards. China, Turkey, France.
1907 Rees,* R. D., M.A. ‡2nd Lt. R.F.A. (since Nov. 1918). France, 1918.
1912 Reid, H. T. (Dec. 17, 1914). Lt. R.A. (Capt.).
1897 Richards, Rev. G. S., M.A. (Mar. 5, 1918). Chaplain to the Forces (4th Class).
1901 Rider, Rev. J. S. D., M.A. (Aug. 31, 1915). Chaplain to the Forces (3rd Class). France, *M.C.*, Jan. 1, 1919.
1902 Ridley, E. D. (Serving Aug. 4, 1914). Capt. 3rd Grenadier Guards (Staff-Captain). France. *M.C.*, June 23, 1915. *D.* France, 1915.
1912 **Rigby,* A. G.** (Aug. 29, 1914). Capt. 8th W. Yorkshire Regt. G.S.O. 3. France and Belgium. *M.C.*, Jan. 1, 1918. *D.* France, 1915. Killed in action on Oct. 12, 1917.
1912 **Rissik, B.** (Nov. 4, 1914). 2nd Lt. 9th Rifle Brigade. E. Africa. *D.* E. Africa, 1916. Killed in action on June 23, 1915.
1914 Rissik, H., B.C.L., M.A. (Jan. 14, 1915). 2nd Lt. 15th Rifle Brigade. Capt., Acting Staff-Captain, S. African Defence Force (Bde.-Maj.). German S.W. Africa, 1915; E. Africa, 1915–18. *M.C.*, Jan. 1, 1918. *D.* E. Africa, 1916.
1919 Rissik, P. U., B.A. (Oct. 1914). ‡2nd Lt. S. African Forces (Staff-Captain) A.D.C. to G.O.C., 1918. S.W. Africa, E. Africa. *D.* E. Africa, 1919.
1911 Ritchie, D. M., M.A. (Sept. 1, 1914). Capt., Acting Staff-Captain, 55th Div. Artillery, R.A. France and Belgium, 1915–19. *M.C.*, Oct. 20, 1916.
1913 Ritchie, J. R. (Aug. 29, 1914). Lt., Acting Capt., R.F.A. France. *M.C.*, Oct. 28, 1917.
1919 Ritchie, Hon. P. C. T. (Jan. 7, 1918). 2nd Lt. Suffolk Regt. Salonika.
1910 **Ritchie,* R. A.** (Dec. 9, 1914). Lt. 2nd Norfolk Regt. Persia. Killed in action in the Persian Gulf on Nov. 29, 1915.
1898 Ritchie, W. T. D., B.A. (Aug. 5, 1914). Capt. Leicestershire Yeomanry (T.F. Res.).

1896 Rivington, W. G., M.A. (Aug. 26, 1916). Lt. Coldstream Guards. France.

1909 Roberts,* E. H. G., B.A. (Oct. 28, 1914). Capt. 5th R. Welch Fusiliers, attd. G.H.Q., E.E.F. Egypt and Palestine, 1917–19. *M.C.*, June 4, 1917. *D.* Palestine, 1919.

1904 **Robertson, G. H. M.,** B.A. (Sept. 8, 1915). Lt. Special Lists. Lt. Nigeria Regt. W. Africa. Died on Mar. 10, 1919, at Sandhead, Wigtownshire, of illness.

1906 **Robertson,* H. J. G.,** B.A. (Oct. 1, 1914). Lt. 3rd, attd. 1st, The Black Watch. France. Killed in action in the Battle of Loos on Sept. 25, 1915.

1894 **Robertson, M. A.** (Sept. 15, 1914). Capt. 10th R. Inniskilling Fusiliers. France. Killed in action in the Battle of Somme on July 1, 1916.

1887 Robins, Rev. W. A., M.A. (Feb. 20, 1917). Chaplain to the Forces (4th Class).

1919 Robinson, A. E. (Nov. 24, 1916). Lt. 17th, afterwards 29th, Batt. R.F.A. France and Belgium, 1917–19. *M.C.*, Dec. 17, 1917 ; *Bar*, Dec. 2, 1918.

1911 Robinson, C. R. (1914). Lt. 9th R. Sussex Regt., and M.G.C.

1913 Robinson, G. G., B.A. (Nov. 1914). Capt. and Adjt. Guards Divl. Train, R.A.S.C. France.

1910 Robinson, W. M., B.A. (Dec. 1914). Capt. Sherwood Foresters. France, 1915, 1916, 1917, 1918. Belgian Croix de Guerre.

1891 Robson, J., B.A. (June 1915). Maj. Arg. & Suth'd Highlanders. D.A.D.L. and Asst. Labour Commdt., III Corps. *O.B.E.* (Mil.). *D.* §

1912 Rodocanachi, J. E., B.A. (Oct. 5, 1914). Lt. R.F.A. France, 1917–18 ; Salonika, 1918–19.

1919 Rogers, J. E. M. (Aug. 19, 1918). 2nd Lt. R.A.F.

1897 Rogers, W. L. Y., M.A. (Serving Aug. 4, 1914). Maj., Acting Lt.-Col., R.F.A. France. *D.S.O.*, Jan. 1, 1918. *D.* France, 1917, 1918.

1900 Ronaldson, T. M., M.A. (Sept. 23, 1915). Capt. and Adjt. No. 2 (Devon and Cornwall) Fire Command, R.G.A.

1911 **Roper,* W. E.,** B.A. (Nov. 10, 1914). Capt. 5th King's Own (R. Lancaster Regt.). France and Belgium. Killed in action on July 31, 1917.

1908 Rose,* A. R., B.C.L., M.A. (Sept. 6, 1914). ‡Lt. 5th K.O.Y.L.I. Belgium, France, Germany. *M.C.*, Jan. 11, 1919.

1919 Ross, A. H. H. (Oct. 11, 1915). Lt. R.E. (T.F.), attd. Tyne E.E.R.E.

1919 Routh, R. J. (May 11, 1916). Lt. General List, attd. S. Persia Rifles (Capt.). Persia.

1913 Rudd, B. G. D'U., B.A. (Dec. 15, 1914). 2nd Lt. Arg. & Suth'd. Highlanders. Lt. M.G.C. Lt., Acting Maj., Tank Corps. France. *M.C.*, Feb. 18, 1918.

1909 Rugg, R. F., M.A. (Sept. 1, 1914). ‡Capt. 3rd R. Welch Fusiliers. France and Belgium, from 1915.

1919 Runge, C. H. S. (Sept. 2, 1914). Maj. 12th Middlesex Regt. D.A.Q.M.G. 58th (London) Div. France and Belgium, 1915–18. *D.S.O.*, June 3, 1918. *M.C.*, Jan. 1, 1917 ; *Bar*, Nov. 6, 1918. *D.* France, 1917, 1918.

1916 **Rushton, W.** Stores Dept. American Red Cross, U.S. Army. Died on board ship on the way home.

1903 Russell, J. G., B.A. (Feb. 8, 1915). Capt. R.A.S.C.

1919 Rutherford, E. V. (Mar. 1916). Lt. 21st Lancers. India.

1914 Ryves, T. E., B.A. (Dec. 21st, 1915). 2nd Lt. A/106th Bde., R.F.A. France, 14 months.

1919 St. Hill, H. (June 11, 1915). Lt. 3rd, attd. 51st, Devonshire Regt. France, 1916, 1919; Germany, 1919.

1910 Sampson, H. F., B.A. (Aug. 6, 1914). ‡Lt. Border Regt. Lt., Kite Balloon Officer, R.A.F. France, Gallipoli.

1896 Samuel, A. H., M.A. (June 17, 1916). Pte. R.A.F. Salonika, 1916–18.

1907 Samuelson, B. G. (Dec. 22, 1915). Lt. Grenadier Guards (S.R.), empld. 39th R. Fusiliers.

1912 Sanderson,* B., B.A. (Sept. 5, 1914). Capt. Duke of Lancaster's Own Yeomanry. Maj. G.S.O. 2. France. *M.C.*, Nov. 14, 1915; *Bar*, Sept. 16, 1918. Belgian Croix de Guerre. *D.* France, 1917, 1919.

1902 Sandover, W. L., M.A. (Mobilized Aug. 4, 1914). Maj. 1/6th E. Surrey Regt. India, 1914–17; Aden Field Force, 1917–18. *D.* Aden.

1912 Sargeaunt,* W. T., B.A. (Aug. 1914). Capt. Wiltshire Regt., attd. Tank Corps. France, Belgium, Germany. *D.* France, 1915.

1911 **Sartoris,* C. F.** (Sept. 12, 1914). Lt. 7th Leicestershire Regt., attd. R. Inniskilling Fusiliers. Gallipoli. Killed in action in Gallipoli on June 24, 1915.

1897 Sedgwick, J. R., M.A. 2nd Lt. London Regt.

1912 Shand,* J. L., B.A. (Oct. 1, 1914). Lt. 2nd Life Guards.

1902 Shaw, Hon. A. M. P., M.A., *M.P.* (Aug. 30, 1915). Lt. R.M.A. France, 1916.

1909 **Shears,* E. H.,** B.A. (May 1915). Lt. 1st Irish Guards. France, Belgium, 1917. Killed in action at Boesinghe on July 4, 1917.

1913 Sheepshanks, T. H. (Oct. 21, 1914). Capt. 4th Norfolk Regt., attd. 11th Suffolk Regt. France.

1912 Shennan, K. G. W. (Mar. 1915). Lt. R. Horse Guards. France.

1908 Shepherd, W. S., M.A. (May 28, 1915). Lt. I.A.R.O.

1898 Sheppard, S. T. Lt. 15th Bombay Bn. I.D.F. Capt. Special Lists, whilst Staff-Captain.

1892 Shipman, Rev. R., M.A. (Jan. 1, 1916). Chaplain to the Forces (4th Class). France.

1909 Sidebottom,* R. (Mobilized Aug. 4, 1914). Capt. 1/1st Staffordshire Yeomanry. Egypt, 1915–16; Palestine and Syria, 1916–19. *D.* Egypt.

1908 Simeon, C. B., B.A. (Oct. 14, 1914). Capt. R. Monmouthshire R.E. (S.R.).

1897 **Simonds, C. F.** (Sept. 24, 1914). Maj. 13th K.R.R.C. France, 1915–16. Killed in action on June 29, 1916.

1896 Simpson, L., *M.V.O.* (Serving Aug. 1914). Maj. 2nd K.O.Y.L.I. Belgium, France, Aug. 1914. (Wounded and prisoner of war, Aug. 26, 1914, till Nov. 1918.) *M.C.*, May 5, 1919.

1911 Skaife, W. F., B.A. (Dec. 7, 1914). Lt. R.F.A. France. *D.* France, 1917.

1903 Skinner, E. L., M.A. (June 8, 1915). Capt. Special Lists, whilst specially empld.

1886 Slaughter, E. M. (Mobilized Aug. 5, 1914). Maj. Berkshire Yeomanry. Egypt and Palestine.

1904 Slingsby, J., M.A. (June 6, 1917). Gunner R.G.A.

Smith, G. A. C. (Mar. 31, 1915). Capt. 14th Arg. & Suth'd. Highlanders. France. *M.C.*, Nov. 25, 1916. Killed in action on Sept. 28, 1918.

1907 Smith, H. A. N., B.A. (Aug. 1915). Lt. 1/4th D.C.L.I. India, Aden, Egypt, Palestine.

1913 Smith, Rev. N. C., M.A. (July 12, 1916). Chaplain to the Forces (4th Class).
1886 Smith Bosanquet, G. R. (1914). Maj. 3rd Res. Regt. of Cavalry.
1906 **Snowden, H. J.,** M.A. (Sept. 26, 1915). Lt. 1st Hertfordshire Regt. France and Belgium. Killed in action on Jan. 11, 1915.
1869 Southam, F. A., B.M., M.A. (Mobilized Aug. 4, 1914). Lt.-Col. R.A.M.C. (T.F.).
1896 Stanford, G. D., B.A. (Aug. 1, 1917). 2nd Lt. King's Own (R. Lancaster Regt.).
1898 Stansfeld, J. A. H., B.A. (1915). Capt. and Adjt. Cameronians.
1911 Staveley, T., B.A. (Sept. 19, 1914). Lt. E. Lancashire Regt.
1906 Steell,* J. W. G., M.A. (Mobilized Aug. 4, 1914). Capt. R.A.M.C. (S.R.).
1895 Stephenson, F. L., B.C.L., M.A. (Dec. 1916). Lt. R.G.A. (Capt.).
1919 Steward, N. O. W. (May 20, 1918). ‡2nd Lt. R.G.A.
1898 Stewart, H. S., B.A. (Mobilized Aug. 4, 1914). Capt. Lothians and Border Horse.
1914 **Stilwell, M. J.** (Mar. 1, 1915). Lt. R.W. Kent Regt. France. Presumed killed in action near Aveluy on June 30, 1918.
1906 Stirling, A. C., B.A. (Aug. 19, 1917). 2nd Lt. R.G.A. (S.R.).
Stoer, F. C. (Oct. 17, 1914). 2nd Lt. 6th D.C.L.I. France. Killed in action on Mar. 17, 1916.
1890 Stohr, F. O., D.M. (Aug. 16, 1915). Capt. R.A.M.C.
1903 Strange, C., M.A. (Nov. 22, 1916). Lt. 1st Loyal N. Lancashire Regt.
1909 Stride, Rev. W. F. A., B.A. (July 20, 1918). Chaplain to the Forces (4th Class).
1904 **Strutt, R. N.** (Jan. 5, 1915). 2nd Lt. 12th, attd. 2nd, R. Scots. France. Killed in action near Loos on Sept. 26, 1915.
1905 Sutcliffe, N., B.A. (Apr. 5, 1915). Lt. 5th York and Lancaster Regt. (Capt.).
1893 Swanston, J. C. (1914). Lt. R. Defence Corps. Capt. Labour Corps.
1897 Swanston, J. F. A. (Oct. 19, 1914). Lt. Queen's (R. W. Surrey Regt.) Acting Maj. M.G.C.
1908 Swayne,* J. G. des R., B.A. (Serving Aug. 4, 1914). Capt. Somerset L.I., attd. R.E. Signal Service.
Sweet-Escott, W. A. (1917). Lt. R.G.A. (S.R.). France. Died on Oct. 14, 1918, of wounds received in action.
1890 Sykes, Rev. S. F., M.A. (Aug. 15, 1917). Chaplain to the Forces (4th Class).
1905 Symes, H., M.A. (Dec. 28, 1914). 2nd Lt. Unattached List, T.F., King's School, Bruton O.T.C.
1912 Synge,* R. M., B.A. (Aug. 15, 1914). Capt. Coldstream Guards (S.R.), attd. 1st Bn. France.
1919 Taberer, T. C. M. (Mar. 31, 1916). Lt. 3rd Hampshire Regt. (Capt.). France, Belgium. *D.S.O.*, Sept. 26, 1917. *D.* France, 1918.
1910 Tait, R. H., B.A. (Aug. 20, 1914). Maj. R. Newfoundland Regt. Gallipoli, Egypt, France, Belgium. *M.C.*, Nov. 26, 1917.
1911 Tate,* C. T., M.A. (Nov. 12, 1914). Capt. 13th London Regt., empld. Ministry of Food. France, 1916.
1909 Tate, G. V. (Aug. 14, 1914). Capt. 6th, attd. 1st, Middlesex Regt. France. *M.C.*, Mar. 8, 1919.

1902 Tate, H. B. (Mobilized Aug. 4, 1914). Lt. Warwickshire Yeomanry. Capt. M.G.C.

1901 Taylor, A. E., B.M., M.A. (Dec. 28, 1914). Capt. R.A.M.C.

1913 **Taylor, G. B.** (1914). Lt. 48th Canadian Highlanders, C.E.F. France and Belgium. Killed in action near Ypres on Apr. 24, 1915.

1897 Taylor Morgan, G. W., B.A. (Mobilized Aug. 1914). ‡Lt. 74th Bde., R.F.A. Egypt and Aden, 1915–16; France, 1917–18; Germany, 1918–19. *M.C.*, Feb. 15, 1919.

1895 Teichmann Derville, M., M.A. (Feb. 22, 1915). Maj. R.A.S.C. *O.B.E.* (Mil.). *D.* § Mar. 1918.

1897 Tennyson, A. B. S. (Apr. 23, 1915). Lt. R. Wiltshire Yeomanry. Lt. Leicestershire Yeomanry.

1908 Thelwall, J. W. F. (Feb. 15, 1915). Lt., temp. Capt., Special Lists. G.S.O. 3. France. *M.C.*, June 4, 1917.

1918 Thomas, B. (Mar. 14, 1917). Lt. R.A.F. France, 1917–18.

1895 Thomas, J. H., B.M. (Oct. 24, 1914). Capt. R.A.M.C. (Lt.-Col.). France and Belgium. *D.S.O.*, Jan. 1, 1918. *D.* France, 1916, 1917.

1902 Thompson, G., M.A. (Jan. 28, 1915). British Red Cross Society, 1915–18. Capt. Special Lists (Intelligence Corps). Belgium, 1915; Italy, 1915–19; Jugo-Slavia, 1919–20. Italian Bronze Medal for Military Valour. *D.* Italy, 1919.

1914 Thomson, J. E. (Jan. 1, 1916). Lt. 7–8th K.O. Scottish Borderers. France. *D.* France, 1917, 1918.

1901 **Thornton, G. M.,** B.A. (1914). Capt. Seaforth Highlanders, attd. 8th Bn. France. Killed in action on Aug. 22, 1917.

1900 Thornton, H. R. H., M.A. (Sept. 29, 1914). 2nd Lt. Labour Corps, S. African Forces.

1887 Thornton, Rev. H. S. R., M.A. (Sept. 14, 1914). French Red Cross (until Sept. 1916), afterwards Chaplain to the Forces (4th Class). France, 1914–16; E. Africa, 1917–19.

1904 Thornton, W. H., B.A. Pte. R. Sussex Regt.

1919 Thorold, G. P. (Apr. 27, 1915). Capt. R. Marines. Gallipoli, 1915; Salonika, 1916; France, 1916.

1906 Thorpe, J. H., B.A., *M.P.* (Mobilized Aug. 4, 1914). Capt. 7th Manchester Regt. France, Egypt. *O.B.E.* (Mil.). *D.*

1879 Thurburn, A. H., M.A. (Sept. 21, 1914). Maj. 8th R. Scots Fusiliers. Temp. Maj. Scottish Command Depot.

1888 Thursfield, J. H., D.M. (Sept. 1914). Maj. R.A.M.C., attd. 14th Gen. Hospital, B.E.F. France, 1917–19.

1897 Thynne, R. G. (Oct. 1, 1914). Lt. Scots Guards (S.R.).

1898 **Tiddy, R. J. E.,** M.A. (Feb. 16, 1915). Lt. 2/4th Oxf. & Bucks. Lt. Infty. France. Killed in action on Aug. 11, 1916.

1902 **Tompson, R. F. C.** (Oct. 2, 1915). 2nd Lt. Grenadier Guards. France. Killed in action on Sept. 11, 1916.

1914 Trewhella, E. C., B.A. (Jan. 8, 1916). Lt., Acting Capt., R.G.A., attd. H.Q. 65th Bde. France. *D.* France, 1919.

1912 Tribe, F. N., B.A. (Mar. 23, 1915). Capt. A.S.C. Capt. Gen. List. Staff-Captain. France. *O.B.E.* (Mil.). *D.* France, 1918.

1901 Tribe, W. H., M.A. (1914). Capt. 4th R. Sussex Regt. (Resigned.)

1913 Trier,* M. B. (1914). ‡Lt. E. Yorkshire Regt.

1909 **Trinder, J. R.,** B.A. (Mobilized Aug. 4, 1914). Capt., temp. Maj., 18th London Regt. (London Irish Rifles). France. *M.C.*, Jan. 14, 1916. *D.* France, 1915. Killed in action on the Somme on Sept. 15, 1916.

1887 Tuckett, P. D., M.A. Inns of Court O.T.C. Res.

1883 Tuckey, Rev. J. G. W., M.A. (Serving Aug. 4, 1914). Asst. Chaplain Gen. France and Belgium, Aug. 1914–15. *C.B.E.* (Mil.). *D.* France, 1915 twice; § Mar. 1918.

1907 **Turner, F. H.,** B.A. (Serving Aug. 4, 1914). Lt. 10th King's (Liverpool Regt.). France and Belgium. Killed in action on Jan. 11, 1915.

1880 Turney, H. G., D.M. (Aug. 1914). Capt. R.A.M.C.

1919 Tuttle, N. (May 15, 1917). 1st Lt. Chem. Warfare Serv., U.S. Army (Capt.). France.

1918 Twidell, J. T. (May 1918). Cadet O.C.B.

1893 **Tyser, H. E.** (Feb. 15, 1915). 2nd Lt. 8th The Black Watch. France. Killed in action on Apr. 9, 1917.

1912 Van der Noot, G. E. F. (Oct. 1, 1914). Lt. Irish Guards (Capt.). Egypt, 1914; India, 1915–16; S. Africa, 1917; France and Germany, 1917–19.

1919 Van der Riet, E. F. (Feb. 1917). Lt. R.A.F. (Capt.). France, 1917. *D.F.C.*, Aug. 3, 1918.

1911 Vansittart,* G. N., B.A. (Serving Aug. 4, 1914). Capt. 39th King George's Own Central India Horse.

1919 Vassall, L. S. (Jan. 10, 1918). ‡2nd Lt. K.O.Y.L.I. France.

1896 **Vaughan, H.,** B.A. (Oct. 29, 1915). Lt. R.F.A. (S.R.). France and Belgium. Killed in action on July 31, 1917.

1902 **Vaughan Thompson, R. H.** (Sept. 12, 1914). Capt. 11th R. Fusiliers. France. *D.* France, 1916. Killed in action on Sept. 26, 1916.

1909 Vawdrey, D. Ll., B.A. (Sept. 20, 1914). ‡Lt. 5th Worcestershire Regt., attd. No. 4 O.C.B. (Capt. 2nd Worcestershire Regt.). France, 1915–17.

1893 Veitch, G. D., B.A. (May 11, 1915). 2nd Lt. W. Riding Regt. (Resigned.)

1899 **Vickers, N. M.,** M.A. (Sept. 10, 1915). Lt. 13th W. Yorkshire Regt. France. Killed in action on Aug. 4, 1916.

1906 Voules, H. St. G. (1915). ‡2nd Lt. R.A.O.C. *D.* § Aug. 1919.

1902 **Wace, P. B.,** M.A. (1914). Capt. 5th R. Berkshire Regt. France. *D.* France, 1916. Killed in action in the Battle of the Somme on July 3, 1916.

1898 Wadmore, J. M., M.A. (Sept. 21, 1914). Maj., Bt.-Lt.-Col. 9th R. Fusiliers. France. *D.* § Mar. 1918.

1912 Wadsworth,* W. W., B.A. (Aug. 29, 1914). Capt. R.F.A. France and Belgium, 1915–18. (Invalided Aug. 1918.) *M.C.*, June 4, 1917. *D.* France, 1917.

1903 Waggett, J. L., M.A. (Sept. 16, 1914). Lt. 1st Dragoon Guards. France, India. *M.C.*, Nov. 29, 1919.

1883 Wait, H. W. K., M.A. (Mobilized Aug. 1914). Maj. R.G.A. France.

1913 **Wakeford, G. T.** (July 4, 1915). 2nd Lt. 4th R. Berkshire Regt. France. Killed in action on July 23, 1916.

1905 Wansbrough, R. W., B.A. (Dec. 2, 1916). Lt., Acting Capt., Tank Corps. France. *D.* France, 1918 twice.

1906 Ward, Rev. D'A. W., M.A. (May 3, 1918). Chaplain to the Forces (4th Class).

1909 Warner, K. C. H., B.A. (Mobilized Aug. 1914). Maj. Kent Cyclist Bn. (Lt.-Col. 7th York and Lancaster Regt.). France. *D.S.O.*, June 3, 1919. *D.* France, 1919.

1908 **Warren,* J. C.,** M.A. (Mobilized Aug. 4, 1914). Capt. 7th Sherwood Foresters. France. *M.C.*, Nov. 12, 1915. *D.* France, 1915. Killed in action at Bullecourt on Mar. 21, 1918.

1912 Waterlow,* A., B.A. (Aug. 8, 1914). Capt. 19th London Regt. France, 1915. *D.* § Aug. 1919.

1912 Watson,* H. B., M.A. (Aug. 29, 1914). 2nd Lt. 7th W. Yorkshire Regt. Capt. 3rd Skinner's Horse, Indian Army. France, 1915–16; India, 1917–19. *M.C.*, Jan. 1, 1919.

1899 Whitaker, G. C. (Aug. 7, 1914). Capt., Acting Maj., Guards M.G. Regt. France, 1914–19.

1910 **Whitaker, H. J. I.** (1914). Sub-Lt. R.N.V.R., Nelson Bn., R.N.D. Gallipoli. Killed in action in Gallipoli on May 3, 1915.

Whitehead, G. W. E. (1914). Lt. R.F.A., attd. R.A.F. France and Belgium. Killed in action at Lauwe, near Courtrai, on Oct. 17, 1918.

1909 **Whitehead, J. H. E.** (Sept. 1914). 2nd Lt. R. W. Kent Regt. Died on Mar. 13, 1919, of illness contracted on active service.

1892 Whitehead, W. J., M.A. (Mobilized Aug. 4, 1914). Maj. 6th London Regt. France. *D.S.O.*, Jan. 1, 1917. *D.* France, 1916; § 1919.

1896 Whitworth, A. W., M.A. (Dec. 19, 1915). Lt. Unattached List, T.F., Eton College O.T.C.

1913 Wilkes, J. F. R., B.A. (Aug. 4, 1914). ‡2nd Lt. R.A., afterwards Capt. H.Q. Staff, C.E.F., Siberia. Siberia.

1919 Wilkinson, A. L. (Sept. 28, 1917). 2nd Lt. R.F.A. France, 1918–19.

1912 Wilkinson, H. M., B.A. (May 24, 1915). Lt., Acting Capt., 3rd Cheshire Regt. France. *M.C.*, July 26, 1918. *D.* France, 1918.

1908 Williams, T. R. (1914). Rhodesian Defence Force. Africa.

1912 Williams, W. K., B.A. (Aug. 1917). Paymaster R.N.V.R. Bermuda, 1917, 1919.

1906 Williamson, R. H. (1914). Enslin's Horse, S. African Force. S. Africa.

1901 Wilson, A. B. H., B.A. (Sept. 9, 1914). Lt., 220th Field Coy., R.E. (Capt.). Salonika, 1915–17; France, 1917–19. *D.* France, 1919.

1914 Wilson, J. H., B.A. (Aug. 20, 1917). 1st Lt. Field Artillery, U.S. Army (Capt.). France.

1905 Wilson, R. W., B.A. (Mobilized Aug. 4, 1914). Lt. R. Horse Guards. France.

1906 Witts, F. H., M.A. (Aug. 12, 1914). Capt. Irish Guards, Bde.-Maj. France and Belgium. *D.S.O.*, June 3, 1919. *M.C.*, Jan. 1, 1917. *D.* France, 1917, 1918, 1919.

1919 Wood, G. F. (Mobilized July 28, 1914). ‡Maj. R.E. France. *M.C.*, Jan. 1, 1919.

1901 Woods, M. H., B.A. (Nov. 26, 1914). Capt. R. W. Kent Regt.

1894 Wortham, O. O. (Oct. 22, 1914). Maj. R.A.O.C. *D.* § Mar. 1918.

1913 Wright,* C. S., M.A. (Dec. 6, 1914). Capt. 23rd R. Welch Fusiliers. France and Belgium, 1917.

1898 Wynne Willson, L. F. (Aug. 8, 1914). Lt. 5th Norfolk Regt. (T.F.). (Lt.-Col. 13th Gloucestershire Regt., Nov. 1916–Mar. 1917), afterwards Maj. No. 7 Training Squadron, R.A.F. France and Belgium. *D.* France, 1917.

1895 Young, H. G. M. (Oct. 29, 1914). Capt. 4th Queen's (R. W. Surrey Regt.). Asst. Inspector of Q.M.G. Services. Staff-Captain. *D.* § Aug. 1918.

1898 Young, R. F., M.A. (Mar. 30, 1917). Lt. R.N.V.R.

1912 Young,* V. C. H., B.A. (Dec. 21, 1915). ‡Lt. 4th Essex Regt. France. (Wounded and taken prisoner, Mar. 7, 1917.)

1890 Zanzibar, Rt. Rev. Bishop of, D.D. Hon. Maj. Zanzibar Carrier Corps. German E. Africa. *O.B.E.* (Mil.). *D.* E. Africa, 1916.

1912 Zorn, P. W., M.A. (May 29, 1915). 2nd Lt. Unattached List, T.F., Malvern College O.T.C.

ST. JOHN'S COLLEGE

1916 Ackerson, L. (1918). Pte. Ordnance Dept., U.S. Army.

1908 **Adams,* C. J. N.,** B.A. (Serving Aug. 4, 1914). 2nd Lt. 2nd Grenadier Guards. France. Died on Nov. 14, 1918, of wounds received in action at Wargnies-le-Petit.

1911 **Adamson, G.** (Nov. 27, 1914). 2nd Lt. 12th Highland L.I. France, 1915. Killed in action at Loos on Sept. 25, 1915.

1898 Adamson, J. D., M.A. R.G.A.

1910 Ainsworth, T. W., M.A. (July 24, 1917). 2nd Lt. Labour Corps.

1919 Alderson, C. W. (Apr. 10, 1918). Cadet No. 8 O.C.B.

1895 Alexander, W. A., B.A. (Mobilized Aug. 1914). Maj. Dorset Yeomanry. Maj. attd. General Staff, War Office. Egypt, 1915, 1916.

1903 Allan, Rev. A. P., M.A. (Oct. 29, 1915). Chaplain to the Forces (4th Class).

1893 Allan, B., B.A. (Serving Aug. 4, 1914). Maj., Acting Lt.-Col., VI Div. Amm. Col., R.G.A. Gallipoli, 1915; France. *O.B.E.* (Mil.). Croix de Guerre. *D.* France, 1918.

1909 **Allen, D. G. A.** (Aug. 13, 1915). Lt. Durham L.I. Capt., Flight Commdr., R.A.F. India, France. Killed in action on Oct. 8, 1918.

1887 Allen, Rev. R., M.A. (Aug. 11, 1914). Acting Naval Chaplain on H.M. Hospital Ship *Rohilla.* (Resigned owing to illness subsequent on his ship being wrecked.)

1913 **Almack, A. C. T.** (Feb. 27, 1915). 2nd Lt. 3rd Northamptonshire Regt. M.G.C. France. Killed in action in the Battle of the Somme on Sept. 27, 1916.

1912 Alston, G. R. G. (Aug. 8, 1914). ‡Capt. R.F.A. (Maj.). France, 1914–15, 1916–18. *M.C.*, Feb. 15, 1919. *D.* France, 1918.

1915 Anderson, K. T. A. (Dec. 28, 1915). Lt. 5th Middlesex Regt. France and Belgium, 1916–17.

1900 Anderson-Morshead, R. Y., B.A. (Mobilized Aug. 1914). Capt. and Adjt. 1/4th Devonshire Regt. India, 1914–16, 1919; Mesopotamia, 1916–17.

1914 Anthony, R. M. (July 29, 1915). Lt. 3rd King's Own (R. Lancaster Regt.). France.

1911 **Armitage, G. D.** (Nov. 1914). 2nd Lt. 11th E. Surrey Regt., attd. 2nd Hampshire Regt. Gallipoli. Killed in action at Achi Baba on Aug. 6, 1915.

1911 Armstrong, C. W. W., B.M. (Jan. 1918). Surgeon Lt. R.N. Adriatic, 1918; White Sea, 1919.

1912 Armstrong, G. R., B.A. (Oct. 21, 1914). 2nd Lt. W. Riding Regt.

1912 Armstrong, J. R. (1914). ‡Lt. R.F.A. (S.R.). Salonika. *D.* Salonika, 1917.

1903 Arrowsmith, Rev. W. L., M.A. (Dec. 5, 1916). Chaplain to the Forces (4th Class). France. *M.C.*, Jan. 1, 1919.

1899 Aston, Rev. B., M.A. (July 1915). Chaplain to the Forces (4th Class), attd. 36th Inf. Bde. 12th Div. France, 1915–19. *D.S.O.*, Aug. 25, 1916. *D.* France, 1916, 1918.

1907 Atkin, A. L., M.A. (Sept. 1, 1915). Instructor Lt. R.N. Grand Fleet, 1916–19.

1904 Atkinson, A. W., B.A. (Mar. 25, 1915). Lt. R.F.A. (S.R.) (Capt.).

1891 Atkinson, E. C., M.A. (Sept. 9, 1914). Lt. T.F. Res., Bde. Musketry Officer, School of Musketry. (Visiting Officer, D.I.G.A. (T.), Inspection Dept., Woolwich Arsenal.)

1896 Austen, Rev. A. S. C., M.A. (July 5, 1917). Chaplain to the Forces (4th Class).

1908 Aylward, J. A. S., B.A. (Mar. 1916). Lt. R. E. Kent Yeomanry. Egypt, Palestine, France. *M.C.*, Feb. 4, 1918.

1915 Bacon, S. (Jan. 11, 1916). ‡Lt. 2/4th York and Lancaster Regt. France, 1916–18.

1919 Bagley, C. R. (Mar. 2, 1917). Capt. 321st Inf., U.S. Army (Maj.). France.

1919 Bagnall, A. G. (July 23, 1917). Telegraphist R.N.V.R. H.M.S. *Victory.*

1877 Bagnall, Rev. R. H. (Aug. 15, 1916). Chaplain to the Forces (4th Class).

1899 Bailey, Rev. R. C. S., M.A. (July 17, 1917). Chaplain to the Forces (4th Class). France. *M.C.*, July 26, 1918.

1907 Bailey, W. A., M.A. (Oct. 6, 1916). Lt. I.A.R.O. India.

1919 Baines, E. R. (May 9, 1918). ‡2nd Lt. Rifle Brigade (on demobilization).

1907 Baines, J. E., M.A. (1914). 28th London Regt. (Artists Rifles).

1908 Baker, A. S., M.A. (Oct. 25, 1916). Lt. 3rd Suffolk Regt.

1919 Baker, C. E., B.A. (Dec. 24, 1915). Lt. 140th Canadian Inf. France, 1917.

1905 Bald, Rev. E. M., M.A. (May 16, 1918). Chaplain to the Forces (4th Class).

1908 Baldwin, A. C. J., M.A. (May 14, 1915). Lt. I.A.R.O. India.

1914 Barbour, D. N. (Dec. 23, 1914). Lt. 9th King's Own (R. Lancaster Regt.). Instructor, Inns of Court O.T.C. Mesopotamia, 1916; Egypt, India.

1898 Barnby, F. H., M.A. (Serving Aug. 4, 1914). Lt. Unattached List, T.F., St. Peter's School O.T.C.

1900 Barnes, C. A., B.A. (1914). Pte. Loyal N. Lancashire Regt.

1913 Barnes, D. T. (Dec. 22, 1914). Capt. 2nd Oxf. & Bucks. Lt. Infty. France. *D.S.O.*, June 4, 1917. *D.* France, 1917. (Wounded and prisoner, Mar. 1918.)

1899 **Barrett, J. A.** (1914). 2nd Lt. 16th Rifle Brigade. France and Belgium. Killed in action on July 31, 1917.

1910 **Barrow, G. S.** (Oct. 10, 1914). 2nd Lt. Cyclists' Corps, 8th Div. (Interpreter). Lt. R.F.A. (Capt. G.H.Q., France). France, 1914–18. *O.B.E.* (Mil.). *D.* France, 1918, 1919. Died on Dec. 26, 1918, of illness contracted while on active service.

1904 Barry, A. H., B.A. (Feb. 9, 1915). Lt. R.E. (Postal Section) (Lt.-Col.). France, Salonika. *D.* France, 1915.

1912 Barton, F. T., B.A., B.Litt. (Mar. 24, 1916). 2nd Lt. R.A.S.C.

1912 **Bashforth, J. F. C.** (July 1915). 2nd Lt. 9th Norfolk Regt. Belgium and France. Killed in action at Ginchy on Sept. 15, 1916.

1884 Bastard, W. E. P., B.A. (Mobilized Aug. 1914). Lt.-Col. R.E. (Devon Fortress). *O.B.E.* (Mil.). *D.* § Feb. 1917.

1914 Batchelor, H. V. (Feb. 23, 1915). Lt. 9th R. Berkshire Regt. Capt., Acting Maj., 60th Bn. M.G.C. France, 1915–16 ; Egypt and Palestine, 1917–19. *M.C.*, June 3, 1919.

1901 Bate, Rev. E. Y., M.A. (Serving Aug. 4, 1914). Chaplain to the Forces (4th Class). France, Mesopotamia. *M.C.*, Jan. 1, 1917. *D.* France, 1916 ; Mesopotamia, 1918.

1900 Bates, M., B.M. (Oct. 10, 1914). Capt. R.A.M.C. (Maj.). Egypt, Sinai, Palestine. *O.B.E.* (Mil.). *D.* Palestine, 1917, 1918, 1919.

1916 Bates, M. S., M.A. (Oct. 1918). Candidate, F.A. Officer's Training School, U.S. Army. Mesopotamia, 1917–18 (with Y.M.C.A.).

1897 Bax, R. E. V., M.A. (Oct. 24, 1914). Lt. 9th Middlesex Regt. Capt. Intelligence Staff. Gallipoli, 1915.

1912 Bebb, H. I. M. (Dec. 30, 1914). Lt. 9th S. Wales Borderers.

1901 Beedle, Rev. C. H., M.A. (Sept. 1, 1917). Chaplain to the Forces (4th Class).

1907 Beeson, C. F. C., M.A. (May 1916). Capt. R.A.M.C. Mesopotamia.

1900 **Belas, G. H.,** M.A. (Sept. 29, 1914). Capt. R.F.A. France. Killed in action on June 3, 1917.

1912 **Bell, P. L.** (Aug. 26, 1914). Lt. 10th Hampshire Regt. Gallipoli. Killed in action at Suvla Bay on Aug. 10, 1915.

1908 Bell,* V. G. (Mar. 28, 1915). ‡2nd Lt. General List. Belgium, Egypt, Palestine.

1894 Benson, A. C. (Sept. 30, 1914). Capt. 8th K.O.Y.L.I.

1896 Benson, G. R. (Jan. 25, 1917). Lt. Shropshire Yeomanry.

1919 Berry, E. W. (Sept. 29, 1918). Lt. R.A.F.

1919 Berthoud, F. G. (Dec. 28, 1917). 2nd Lt. R.F.A. France, 1918.

1913 Bertie, L. W. H., M.A. (June 1915). Staff-Lt. (2nd Class) Intelligence Corps. Lt. R.A.F., H.Q. (S.E. area).

1893 Bevers, E. C., B.M., M.A. (Mobilized Aug. 4, 1914). Maj. R.A.M.C. (T.F.), 3rd Southern General Hospital. *D.* § Aug. 1919.

1910 Bickersteth, C. W., B.A. (Sept. 7, 1914). ‡Capt. W. Yorkshire Regt. France.

1876 Bickersteth, Rev. S., D.D. (Aug. 1914). Chaplain (2nd Class) 7th W. Yorkshire Regt. T.D.

1918 Bilson, C. F. (Nov. 1915). Lt. R.E. France. *M.C.*, Sept. 26, 1917.

1919 Bingen, E. A. (Feb. 1917). Lt. 5th R. Sussex Regt. Lt. 2nd Balloon Wing, R.A.F. France, 1917–18.

Black, N. (Aug. 6, 1916). Flight Lt. R.N.A.S. France and Belgium. Died on Oct. 12, 1917, of wounds received in action near Wynendaele.

1913 Blackledge, G. G., B.A. (Sept. 19, 1914). Capt., Acting Maj., 1/6th King's (Liverpool Regt.). France, 1915–16, 1917–19. *M.C.*, Jan. 14, 1916 ; *Bar*, Sept. 16, 1918. *D.* France, 1915.

1906 Bonnor, A. D. D., M.A. (May 11, 1915). Lt. 5th Middlesex Regt. Lt. M.G.C.

1912 Booker, H. G., B.A. (Aug. 21, 1914). Capt. 5th Shropshire L.I. Capt. General List, attd. H.Q. 2nd Corps. Belgium, France, Germany.

1912 **Booker,* S. C.** (Aug. 1914). ‡Lt. 2/7th Worcestershire Regt. France. *M.C.*, Sept. 22, 1916. Killed in action near Neuve Chapelle on Oct. 10, 1916.

1909 Bosman, H. F. (Sept. 15, 1914). Lt. Special Lists, R.T.O. France. *D.* France, 1916.

1919 Boucher, N. (July 28, 1915). Lt. 76th Squadron, R.A.F. (Capt.). France and Belgium.

1902 Bourdillon, B. H., B.A. (1914). ‡Lt. I.A.R.O., attd. 7th United Provinces Horse. India.

1900 **Bourns, C.,** M.A. (Oct. 7, 1914). Lt. 6th, attd. 4th, Rifle Brigade. France. Killed in action on May 28, 1915.

1919 Bowey, T. B. (Feb. 11, 1916). A.B. H.M.S. *Vivid,* R.N. N. Russia.

1906 **Boys-Stones, G. L.,** B.A. (Serving Aug. 4, 1914). Capt. 7th Hariana Lancers, Indian Army. Staff-Captain 6th Cavalry Bde. (Bde.-Maj.). Mesopotamia. *M.C.*, June 4, 1917. *D.* Mesopotamia, 1915, 1917 twice. Died on Mar. 30, 1917, of wounds received in action near Baguba.

1914 Boys-Stones, H. (Mar. 30, 1915). Lt. 1st King's Own (R. Lancaster Regt.) (Capt.). France. *D.* France, 1919.

1912 Boys-Stones,* R., B.A. (Aug. 15, 1914). Capt. 9th Durham L.I. Bde.-Maj. 25th Inf. Bde. France and Belgium, 1915–19. *M.C.*, Jan. 1, 1916; *Bar*, Sept. 16, 1918. *D.* France, 1918, 1919.

1913 Bradley,* L. R. (July 14, 1915). 2nd Lt. 6th Middlesex Regt.

1911 Braund, H. B. L., B.A. (Aug. 1914). Capt. Wiltshire Regt. Staff-Captain 10th Inf. Bde., Quetta. Gallipoli, Egypt, Mesopotamia.

1919 Brebner, J. B. (Mar. 25, 1915). ‡2nd Lt. R.G.A. Salonika, 1915–17.

1909 **Bridson,* C. E. R.** (Serving Aug. 4, 1914). Capt. 3rd King's Own (R. Lancaster Regt.). France, Belgium, 1914, 1915, 916. *D.* France, 1914. Died on Apr. 4, 1916, of wounds received in action at St. Edouard.

1904 Briscoe, R. B. C., B.A. (Mobilized Aug. 4, 1914). Surgeon R.N.V.R. (until Apr. 1916). Capt. R.A.M.C. France.

1911 Brown,* F. D., B.A. (Aug. 29, 1914). Lt. 5th Durham L.I.

Brown, G. H. J. (Sept. 1914). Pte. 16th Middlesex Regt. Belgium, France. Killed in action on Jan. 12, 1916.

1911 **Brown,* J. W.** (Aug. 1914). Capt. 11th R. Scots. France. *M.C.*, Sept. 2, 1916. Killed in action at Arras on Mar. 21, 1917.

1885 Brown, L. J., M.A. (Mobilized Aug. 4, 1914). Capt. R. Defence Corps.

1895 Brown, S. R. S., M.A. (Dec. 19, 1916). Lt. 2nd Hampshire Regt.

1913 Brown,* W. E. (Oct. 1, 1914). ‡Lt. R.F.A. (Capt.). France and Belgium, 1916–18. *M.C.*, July 26, 1918. *D.* France.

1885 Browne, D. S. (Aug. 4, 1914). Capt. 8th R. Scots Fusiliers. Staff-Captain Embarkation Staff.

1919 Buck, A. H. (Sept. 10, 1918). 2nd Lt. R.W. Kent Regt. (on demobilization).

Buckley, H. P. S. (Dec. 1914). Capt. 7th E. Yorkshire Regt. Belgium and France. *D.* France, 1916. Killed in action near Rœux on July 29, 1917.

1903 **Bullock, H. A. L.,** B.A. (May 21, 1915). Lt. 7th R. Warwickshire Regt. France. Killed in action near Pozières on July 14, 1916.

1902 Bumpus, T. H., M.A. (Apr. 20, 1915). Lt. Unattached List, T.F., King's School, Warwick, O.T.C.

1914 **Bunce, H. P.** (Mar. 17, 1916). 2nd Lt. 8th N. Staffordshire Regt. France and Belgium, 1915–16. Accidentally killed on Oct. 5, 1916.

1916 Burbank, J. H., B.A. (Jan. 24, 1917). Pte. H.A.C. France, 1917. (Wounded and invalided, May, 1917.)

1910 **Burges,* E. L. A. H.,** B.A. (Aug. 1914). 2nd Lt. 2nd Wiltshire Regt. Belgium. Killed in action at Reutel, near Ypres, on Oct. 23, 1914.

1919 Burgoyne-Johnson, R. P. (Jan. 4, 1915). Lt. R.F.A. France and Belgium, 1915, 1916, 1917; Salonika, 1916; Italy, 1918–19. *M.C.*, Dec. 17, 1917. *D.* Italy, 1919.

1888 Burnett, Rev. W. R., M.A. (Sept. 23, 1916). Chaplain to the Forces (4th Class). *D.* § Mar. 1918.

1911 **Burnie,* J. G.** (Sept. 1914). Pte. 23rd R. Fusiliers. France. Killed in action at Delville Wood on July 27, 1916.

1884 Burr, Rev. E. G., D.D. (Aug. 1914). Chaplain (4th Class), 5th R. W. Kent Regt. (T.F.).

1902 Burrough, Rev. C. J., M.A. (June 1, 1917). Chaplain to the Forces (4th Class).

1904 Burrough, Rev. E. G., M.A. (Mar. 13, 1917). Chaplain R.N.

1919 Burrows, R. H. (Oct. 1917). Lt. R.A.F. Submarine Patrol, Orkney and Shetland, 1918-19. *A.F.C.*, Nov. 2, 1918.

1909 Butcher, W. H., M.A. (Aug. 8, 1914). Surgeon Lt. R.N. H.M.S. *Druid*, 1st Destroyer Flotilla, 1914; H.M.S. *Iphigenia*, White Sea Mine Sweeping Flotilla, 1915; H.M.S. *Constance*, Grand Fleet, 1916. H.M.S. *Osmaniah*, E. Mediterranean Squadron, 1917; H.M.S. *Paris*, 2nd Minelaying Squadron, 1918.

1907 **Butler, L. G.,** M.A. (Nov. 1914). Lt. 3rd Rifle Brigade (Capt.). France. Killed in action near Guillemont on Aug. 21, 1916.

1901 **Cairns, G. M.,** B.A. (June 12, 1915). ‡2nd Lt. 6th The Black Watch. France. Killed in action at Beaumont Hamel on Nov. 13, 1916.

1912 Caldecott, C. D'A., B.A. (Sept. 28, 1914). Lt. 10th E. Yorkshire Regt. Lt. R.E. Egypt, 1915–16; France, 1916–18; Palestine, 1918–19.

1910 Campbell, C. J. H., B.A. (Dec. 8, 1914). Maj. R.A.S.C. Maj. Gen. List. Legal Advisor, Egyptian Forces. Egypt and Palestine, 1917–19. *D.* Egypt, 1917, 1918 twice.

1898 Campbell, F. A. B., B.A. (May 12, 1915). 2nd Lt. 3rd Wiltshire Regt.

1910 Cannon,* G. H. F. (Aug. 19, 1916). Lt., temp. Capt., Special Lists (R.T.O.). Italy. *D.* Italy, 1919.

1913 Capes,* R. S. H. (Sept. 23, 1914). Lt. 21st London Regt.

1919 Caple, G. R. (Feb. 2, 1917). Lt. 129th Heavy Batt. R.G.A. France, Belgium, Germany.

1908 Capon, R. S., B.A. (Nov. 8, 1915). 2nd Lt. 7th King's (Liverpool Regt.). Lt. Flying Officer R.A.F. France. *D.* Air Ministry, Dec. 1919. (Prisoner of war.)

1909 Carlton,* C. H., B.M. (Aug. 5, 1914). Capt. R.A.M.C. France, 1914, 1916–19; W. Africa, 1915. *M.C.*, Sept. 16, 1918.

1896 Carlyon, T., B.A. (Serving Aug. 4, 1914). Maj. R.A. Bde.-Maj. France. *D.S.O.*, Jan. 14, 1916. *D.* France, 1915.

1903 Carrington, R. C., B.A. (Mar. 1, 1915). Capt. 7th S. Wales Borderers.

Carter, G. F. (Apr. 6, 1915). 2nd Lt. 7th K.R.R.C. France and Belgium. Died on July 30, 1915, of wounds received in action.

1919 Carter, W. H. (1918). Cadet 3rd O.C. School, Parkhurst, I. of W.

1908 [Casson, S., M.A.] (Aug. 15, 1914). Capt. 3rd E. Lancashire Regt. G.S.O. 3, G.H.Q., British Salonika Force. Belgium, 1915; Salonika, 1916–18; Turkey, 1918-19. Greek Order of the Redeemer. *D.* Salonika, 1918.

1911 Castledine, H. W. G. Ceylon Planters Rifle Corps.
1899 Chadwick, B. N., B.A. (Nov. 7, 1914). Lt. 5th Sussex Regt. Staff-Lt.
1908 Chalmers, J. A. G. (July 2, 1915). Lt. 3rd Suffolk Regt., attd. R.E. (Signal Service). France. *M.C.*, Oct. 20, 1916. Belgian Croix de Guerre.
1914 **Chambers, E. C. E.** (June 15, 1915). 2nd Lt. 19th Lancashire Fusiliers. France, 1915–16. Killed in action at Authuille Wood on July 1, 1916.
1919 Champneys, F. C. (Mar. 17, 1918). 2nd Lt. Seaplane Officer, R.A.F.
Chase, P. H. (Oct. 1914). 2nd Lt. Middlesex Regt. (Capt.). France, 1915–16. *D.* France, 1916. Died on July 1, 1916, of wounds received in action on the Somme.
1919 Chatfield, T. R. (Jan. 4, 1918). 2nd Lt. 19th Bn. Tank Corps.
1910 **Chester, G. A. B.,** B.A. (Serving Aug. 4, 1914). 2nd Lt. 1st N. Staffordshire Regt. France and Belgium, 1914. Killed in action near Hazebrouck on Oct. 13, 1914.
1909 Childs,* C. B. M., B.A. (Feb. 25, 1917). Lt. Special Lists, empld. Land Branch.
1899 Chorlton, A. F. T. (June 15, 1915). Pte. R.A.S.C. (M.T.). Egypt, Palestine, Syria.
1909 Christopherson, *Rev. N. C., M.A. (Aug. 11, 1916). Chaplain to the Forces (4th Class). France. *D.* France, 1918.
1913 **Clarke,* A. A.** (July 1914). Capt. 7th Leicestershire Regt. France and Belgium. *M.C.*, Sept 26, 1916. Killed in action at Polygon Wood on Oct. 1, 1917.
1919 Clarke, A. F. (Mar. 14, 1917). ‡Lt. 100th Squadron R.A.F. Ochey, Independent Air Force, 1917–18. (Prisoner of war, Feb.–Nov. 1918.)
1912 Claypole,* G. H., B.A. (Serving Aug. 4, 1914). Lt. Unattached List, T.F. Lt. 5th K.R.R.C.
1919 Collander-Brown, W. H. (Apr. 23, 1917). ‡Lt. R.A.F. France, 1918.
1909 Collins, O. H., B.A. (Oct. 27, 1914). Lt. 4th R. Berkshire Regt.
1911 **Collins, P. G. F.** (Oct. 1914). ‡Lt. 6th D.C.L.I. France, 1915–16. Killed in action in Delville Wood on Aug. 18, 1916.
1919 Constant, H. (Dec. 10, 1916). Lt. R.A.F., attd. Seaplane Section.
1905 Constant, M., B.A. Driver R.A.S.C. (M.T.).
1919 Cooke, E. A. (Mar. 1917). Lt. R.A.F. France. (Prisoner of war in Germany for 15 months.)
1908 Cooper, G. M. (1914). ‡2nd Lt. I.A.R.O., attd. Chota Nagpur Light Horse. India.
1907 Copleston, R. T. (Oct. 27, 1915). 2nd Lt. King's Own (R. Lancaster Regt.). Lt. I.A.R.O., attd. 1/26th Punjabis. India.
1897 Corbett, A. F., B.A. S. African Expeditionary Force.
1912 Costin,* W. C., B.A. (Sept. 2, 1914). Capt. 6th Gloucestershire Regt. France, 1915–18. *M.C.*, Sept. 26, 1916. *D.* § Aug. 1919.
1919 Cotton, J. H. (Aug. 1, 1917). Signaller 18th Welsh Regt. France.
1911 Cotton, W. F., M.A. (Mar. 24, 1915). Lt. Northamptonshire Regt. (Capt.), attd. Hampshire Regt. Gallipoli, 1915–16 ; Palestine, 1916–19.
1887 Covernton, J. G., M.A., *C.I.E.* Rangoon Volunteer Rifles.
1915 Cowley, J. D. (Apr. 14, 1916). Lt. M.G.C. France, 1916–17, 1918.
1903 Cox, R. F. de L. (June 5, 1915). Lt. R.F.A. (T.F.) (specially empld).
1901 Cragg, Rev. R. H., M.A. (Jan. 9, 1918). Chaplain to the Forces (4th Class).

1910 Crawford, S. J. (Jan. 1915). Gunner, Madras Artillery. India.
1899 Crawfurd, H. E., B.A. (1915). Capt. R.A.F. (Acting Maj.).
1887 Cree, H. E., M.A. Anti-Aircraft Corps, R.N.V.R.
Creese, A. R. (Apr. 1917). Flight Lt. R.A.F. France, 1917; Italy, 1918. Died on Nov. 19, 1918.
1906 Creswick, H. F., B.A. (Mobilized Aug. 4, 1914). Capt. King Edward's Horse (S.R.) (Maj.). France and Italy.
1918 Cross, D. G. T. K. (Aug. 4, 1914). ‡2nd Lt. 10th Bedfordshire Regt. Lt. Gold Coast Regt., W. African Frontier Force. Cameroons, Sierra Leone, 1915–18.
1901 Cryer, Rev. C., M.A. (May 28, 1915). Chaplain to the Forces (4th Class). France.
1919 Cuckow, M. W. (Feb. 26, 1915). Capt. 7th R. Berkshire Regt. Salonika, Balkans, 1916–19. *M.C.*, Dec. 17, 1917.
1909 **Cuthbert,* O. R.** (1914). ‡Capt. York & Lancaster Regt. France. Killed in action in the Battle of the Somme on July 1, 1916.
1918 Cutler, L. S., B.A. (Dec. 25, 1915). Sergt. 8th Canadian Inf. France and Belgium.
1906 Daniell,* Rev. M. A., M.A. (Aug. 1, 1916). Chaplain to the Forces (4th Class). France.
1913 Darragh, C. Q. (Dec. 2, 1914). Lt. R. Irish Fusiliers. Lt. General List. Staff-Lt. (2nd Class).
1914 Dashwood, M. A. R.A.M.C.
1897 Dauglish, Rev. J., M.A. (Serving Aug. 4, 1914). Chaplain R.N., H.M.S. *Queen Elizabeth*. Grand Fleet.
1897 Daukes, H. C. (1914). Lt. R.G.A. (S.R.).
1907 David, A. N. (May 1916). Lt. R.A.F. Macedonia, 1916–17.
1903 Davies, T. G., M.A. R.A.S.C.
1919 Davis, G. (1915). ‡Lt. R.A.F. (Capt.). German E. Africa, 1916; Egypt, Italy, 1917–18; France, 1918. *D.F.C.*, Jan, 1, 1919.
1911 Davis, H., M.A. (July 14, 1916). ‡Lt. R.G.A. France. *D.* France, 1918.
1919 Dechert, R. (May 11, 1917). ‡Capt. 7th Inf., U.S. Army. France, 1918; Germany, 1918–19.
1899 de la Hey, Rev. T. C., M.A. (Mar. 12, 1917). Chaplain to the Forces (4th Class).
1906 De Morgan, R. C., B.A. (Oct. 5, 1916). Lt. R.G.A. (Staff-Capt.). Italy. *D.* Italy, 1918.
1896 Dene, A. P. (Serving Aug. 4, 1914). Maj., Bt.-Lt.-Col. D.C.L.I. Temp. Lt.-Col. attd. 7th R. Berkshire Regt. France, Belgium, Salonika, Trans-Caucasia. *C.M.G.*, Dec. 12, 1919. *D.S.O.*, July 26, 1917. Croix d'Officier de la Légion d'Honneur. *D.* France, 1915; Salonika, 1916, 1917.
1911 Dickins, A. R. A. (Oct. 9, 1914). Capt. 6th S. Staffordshire Regt. France, 1915 onwards.
1900 **Dickins, G.,** M.A. (Nov. 1914). Capt. 13th K.R.R.C. France, 1915–16. Died on July 17, 1916, of wounds received in action.
1919 Dixey, R. N. (Aug. 29, 1914). Maj. 1/1st N. Midland Bde. R.F.A. (T.F.). France, Belgium, Germany, 1915–19.
1913 Dixon,* G. G., B.A. (Aug. 1914). Lt. 9th Essex Regt. France, Belgium.

1900 Douglas, C. G., B.Sc., D.M. (Oct. 10, 1914). Lt.-Col. R.A.M.C. France. *C.M.G.*, June 3, 1919. *M.C.*, Jan. 1, 1916. *D.* France, 1916, 1917, 1918, 1919.
1909 Douglas, L. D. (Dec. 28, 1914). Capt. R.G.A., attd. R.E. France, 1915–19. *M.C.*, 1919.
1899 Dover, H. B., B.A. (1915). Lt. Special Lists, R.T.O., Uganda Railway.
1919 Dowdell, E. H. (Mar. 14, 1917). Lt. R.G.A. France.
1919 Dowling, W. (Mar. 1917). Lt. R.A.F. France, 1918 ; Germany, 1918–19.
1909 Drew, D. L. McC., M.A. (Dec. 28, 1914). Lt. R.G.A. France. *M.C.*, June 3, 1919.
1919 Dunkin, J. C. (Aug. 29, 1914). Capt. 1/4th Dorsetshire Regt., attd. Staff. India, 1914–16 ; Mesopotamia, 1916–19.
1919 Dyer, W. E. (Jan. 1918). Hon. 2nd Lt. R.A.F.
1913 Dyson, W. G. (Aug. 1914). Maj. R.F.A. France. *M.C.*, Oct. 20, 1916 ; *Bar*, Feb. 13, 1917 ; *2nd Bar*, Dec. 2, 1918. *D.* France, 1915.
1908 East, A. G., B.M. (June 1916). Capt. R.A.M.C. France, 1916–17.
1916 Easum, C. V., M.A. (Nov. 27, 1917). Lt. 6th Inf., U.S. Army. Instructor in Army Schools. France, 1918 ; Germany, 1919.
1910 Eccles,* H. B. (Serving Aug. 4, 1914). Capt. R.F.A. (Maj.). France. *D.* France, 1918, 1919.
1914 Eden-Eadon, S. W. D., B.A. (Sept. 1, 1916). Paymaster Lt. R.N.V.R.
1919 Edmunds, H., B.A. (Nov. 1915). Lt. R.G.A. (S.R.). France.
1919 Egerton, A. H. (Sept. 22, 1914). Pte. 48th Field Ambulance, R.A.M.C. France, 1915–19.
1911 Ellingham, C. J., M.A. (July 1, 1916). Signalman R.N.V.R. H.M.S. *King Alfred*, 9th Cruiser Squadron, and N. Atlantic Convoy.
1915 **Elliott, V. A. E.** (Jan. 4, 1916). Capt. and Adjt. R.F.A. France and Belgium, 1916–18. Killed in action on Mar. 25, 1918.
1908 Ellis, R. P., B.A. (May 6, 1915). Lt. 7th Durham L.I. (Maj.), attd. M.G.C. France, 1916–17 ; Egypt and Palestine, 1918–19.
1913 Elton,* L. S. (Aug. 21, 1914). Capt. 9th King's (Liverpool Regt.). France and Belgium, 1915–17 ; Palestine, 1918–19. *M.C.*, Nov. 26, 1917.
1904 Elwell, Rev. W., M.A. (June 18, 1915). Chaplain to the Forces (4th Class).
1890 Elwes, Rev. A. C., M.A. Chaplain to the Forces (4th Class).
1907 Enoch, H. A., M.A. (Nov. 24, 1916). Lt. Tank Corps.
1904 Evans, C. W. (Sept. 1914). Lt. Bedfordshire Regt. France, 1915–16.
1915 Evans, J. V. (Jan. 7, 1916). Lt. Monmouthshire Regt., attd. R. Welsh Fusiliers. Egypt, 1917 ; Palestine, 1917–18 ; France, 1918.
1909 Evans, N. D. (Dec. 1914). Lt. 5th Rifle Brigade (Capt.). France, 1916, 1917–18.
1912 Ewert, A., M.A. (1914). ‡Lt. 1st Bn. Canadian Inf. France, 1914 ; Gallipoli, France, 1915–16 ; Salonika, Egypt, 1916 ; France 1918.
1912 Farnell,* R. L., B.A. (Sept. 2, 1914). ‡Lt. 3rd R. W. Kent Regt. (Capt.). Salonika, 1915–17 ; Palestine, 1917–18 ; France, 1918.
1916 Faucett, L. W., B.A. (Apr. 1, 1918). Lt. R.A.F.
1912 **Featherstone, G. H.** (July 3, 1915). 2nd Lt. 9th K.O.Y.L.I. France, 1915–16. Killed in action at Fricourt on July 1, 1916.
1913 **Fedden, R. H.** (Aug. 1914). ‡2nd Lt. 2nd H.A.C. France. Killed in action at Bullecourt on May 3, 1917.
1919 Ferguson, H. C. (July 19, 1915). Lt. R.F.A. France, 1916–18.

1886 Ffoulkes, C. J., B.Litt. (Oct. 9, 1914). Lt. R.N.V.R. Maj. R. Marines. France, 1917, 1918.

1912 Fiddes,* E. S., B.A. (Aug. 29, 1914). Capt. 9th R. Scots. Instructor No. 10 O.C.B. France, 1915–18.

1919 Finberg, H. P. (Sept. 20, 1918). Cadet No. 2 O.C.B.

1913 Findlay,* L. F., M.A. (Aug. 4, 1914). Lt. 9th Middlesex Regt. Lt. M.G.C. (Capt.), attd. Indian Army. India, Afghanistan Frontier.

1916 Finger, W. L. (Aug. 25, 1917). Capt. 136th U.S. Field Artillery. France.

1919 Finn, R. A. (Oct. 21, 1918). Gunner R.G.A.

1898 Firth, R. W., B.A. R.A.S.C.

1899 Fisher, C. D., B.A. (Nov. 9, 1914). Captain R.A.S.C. France, 1915, Macedonia, 1915–18; Egypt, 1917.

1911 Flex,* Rev. W. R., M.A. (Dec. 8, 1914). Chaplain to the Forces (4th Class). Lemnos, Gallipoli, Egypt.

1903 **Foreshew, H. J. H.** (Aug. 1914). ‡2nd Lt. 6th, attd. 3rd, Rifle Brigade. France. Killed in action at Loos on April 15, 1917.

1901 Foreshew, T. W. C. (Mar. 31, 1915). Lt. 3rd Oxf. & Bucks. Lt. Infty. France.

1904 Foster, Rev. H. C., B.A. (Sept. 15, 1914). Chaplain R.N. Gallipoli. *D.* Gallipoli, 1916.

1913 **Foulkes, G. B.** (Sept. 8, 1914). Capt. R. Scots Fusiliers. France. Killed in action near Martinpuich on Aug. 12, 1916.

1919 Frampton, H. J. (Oct. 5, 1916). Lt. 9th W. Riding Regt. (Capt.). France, 1917–19. *M.C.*, Mar. 8, 1919.

1914 Freeman, F. L. (Nov. 28, 1914). Capt. 7th S. Staffordshire Regt. G.S.O. 3, VIII Corps H.Q. Lemnos and Imbros, 1915–16; Suez Canal, 1916; France and Belgium, 1916–19. *D.* France, 1917, 1919.

1910 **Freeman,* T.,** B.A. (Sept. 1914). Lt. 3rd Worcestershire Regt. Belgium. Killed in action at Wytschaete on Mar. 12, 1915.

1904 Frewer, F. (Dec. 30, 1914). ‡Lt. 7th R. Sussex Regt. France, Belgium, 1915–17.

1902 **Fry, H.** (Sept. 1914). ‡Sub-Lt. Howe Bn. R.N.D. (Capt.). Gallipoli, 1915; France, 1916. Killed in action at Beaumont Hamel on Nov. 16, 1916.

1873 Gaisford, R. B., B.A., *C.B.*, *C.M.G.* (Mobilized Aug. 4, 1914). Lt.-Col. Special Lists. Brig.-Gen. Inspector of infantry.

1910 Galpin,* C. J., B.A. (Mar. 30, 1915). Capt. R.A.F. (Staff-Maj., Air Ministry). Gallipoli, France, North Sea Air Patrol. *D.S.O.*, June 22, 1917 (for destruction of Zeppelin L 22). *D.* § Jan. 1919.

1914 Gandell, H. L. (Apr. 29, 1915). Lt. 2/7th King's (Liverpool Regt.). Lt. R.F.A. France.

1912 **Gaussen,* D. N.** (Sept. 1914). Lt. 1st Bedfordshire Regt. France. Killed in action on July 31, 1916.

1911 George, R. E. G., B.Litt., M.A. (Oct. 1916). Lt. Central India Horse. India, Egypt.

1907 George, Rev. T. P., M.A. (Sept. 18, 1914). Chaplain to the Forces (4th Class).

1919 Gibbons, J. M. B. (Aug. 23, 1915). Lt. 1st R. Irish Regt. Salonika, 1916–17; Palestine, 1917–19.

1912 Gibbons, P. A., B.A. (June 22, 1915). Lt. Bedfordshire Regt. Lt. Army Cyclist Corps. France, 1916.

1907 Gibbs, A. H. (Dec. 31, 1914). Capt. R.F.A. (Maj.), attd. Staff. France. *M.C.*, Sept. 26, 1917.

1895 Gidley, C. de B. (Serving Aug. 4, 1914). Maj. 20th Batt., R.F.A. (Lt.-Col.). India, Mesopotamia. *D.S.O.*, Feb. 7, 1918. *D.* Mesopotamia, 1917, 1919.

1885 Gidley, J., M.A. (Dec. 7, 1914). Capt. 1st (Garr.) Bn. Oxf. & Bucks Lt. Infty. (Maj.). India.

1912 Gifford, F. R., M.A. (Mobilized Aug. 4, 1914). Capt. 1/10th Middlesex Regt. Capt. 2/10th Gurkha Rifles, Indian Army. India, 1914–19; Egypt, 1914; Afghanistan, 1919.

1913 Giles,* M. F., B.A. (1914). ‡2nd Lt. 6th London Regt.

1913 **Gill, J. W.** (Sept. 1914). ‡2nd Lt. 6th K.O.Y.L.I. France, Belgium. Killed in action at Ypres on Nov. 19, 1915.

1910 Gimlette,* G. T., B.M. (Dec. 29, 1915). Capt. R.A.M.C. France, 1916; Mesopotamia, 1916; Egypt, Palestine, 1917–19. *D.* Mesopotamia, 1918.

1895 Giveen, C. M. (Jan. 1916). Lt. R.F.A. (S.R.). France. *D.* France, 1917.

1919 Godet, H. M. (Feb. 22, 1918). Pte. 28th London Regt. (Artists' Rifles). Gnr. R.F.A.

Godet, L. de G. (Dec. 26, 1916). Lt. R.A.F. France. Killed in action near Metz on June 1, 1918.

1907 Goldberg, G. H. A. Lt., Acting Capt., I.A.R.O., attd. 91st Punjabis. Egypt and Palestine. *D.* Palestine, 1918, 1919.

Goldsmith, L. W. (Aug. 1914). Capt. 7th Yorkshire Regt. France. Killed in action on Nov. 5, 1916.

1896 Goodall, A. H. (June 12, 1915). Lt. 3rd The Buffs (E. Kent Regt.).

1917 Goodliffe, J. B., B.A. (Dec. 7, 1914). Capt. 8th Leicestershire Regt.

1890 Goodwyn, W. M. (Serving Aug. 4, 1914). Lt.-Col. Devonshire Regt.

1913 Gordon,* F. W. (Oct. 22, 1914). 2nd Lt. 10th Gordon Highlanders. Lt. 32nd Bn. M.G.C. (Maj.). Belgium and France. *M.C.*, Jan. 1, 1919; *Bar*, Apr. 2, 1919. *D.* France.

1919 Gordon, K. (Aug. 14, 1915). Capt. 3rd E. Surrey Regt., attd. M.G.C. France, 1916, 1917–19; Germany, 1919. *M.C.*, Feb. 4, 1918.

1882 Gough, Rev. A. W., M.A. (Serving Aug. 4, 1914). Chaplain to the Forces (4th Class), attd. R.A.

1910 Gracey,* H. M. K., B.A. (Serving Aug. 4, 1914). Capt. 1/101st Grenadiers, Indian Army, attd. 2/101st Grenadiers. India.

1919 Graves, C. P. R. (Nov. 2, 1917). 2nd Lt. 3rd R. Irish Fusiliers.

1919 Graves, R. von R. (Aug. 12, 1914). Capt. 3rd R. Welch Fusiliers, attd. O.C.B. France, 1915–16 (attd. 1st and 2nd R. Welch Fusiliers). (Invalided on account of wounds.)

1919 Gray-Jones, A. J. (July 1915). Lt. 15th R. Welch Fusiliers. France, 1916, 1917, 1918.

1903 Grazebrook,* H. B. D., M.A. (Sept. 7, 1916). 2nd Lt. R.A.F.

1919 Green, C. S. (Sept. 22, 1914). Capt. 6th E. Yorkshire Regt. Gallipoli, 1915; Egypt, 1916; France, 1916–19. *D.* France, 1917.

1895 Green, H. F., M.A. (June 1916). ‡Capt. R. Fusiliers, attd. 26th Bn., afterwards Capt. R.A.F. (transferred on account of wounds). France, Belgium, Italy.

1904 Green, L. H., M.A. (Mobilized Aug. 4, 1914). Capt. 8th R. Warwickshire Regt. (T.F. Res.), empld. Recruiting Duties.

1908 Green,* R. B., B.A. (Sept. 15, 1914). ‡2nd Lt. Army Cyclist Corps. Capt. General List; D.A.P.M. France and Belgium, 1915–17, 1918. *M.C.*, Oct. 18, 1917.

1907 Greenhill, E. H. Interpreter, Special Lists.

1912 Greenhow,* E. L. (Sept. 1914). Capt. 2nd Essex Regt. Capt. 32nd Lancers, Indian Army. India, 1918; Afghanistan Frontier, 1918.

1900 Greig, A. D. (Serving Aug. 4, 1914). Maj. R.G.A. France. *O.B.E.* (Mil.). *M.C.*, June 4, 1917. Croix de Guerre. *D.* France, 1919.

1909 **Grey-Smith,* M.,** B.A. Capt. 2/3rd Gurkha Rifles, Indian Army. Egypt, Mesopotamia, Palestine. Killed in action at Beersheba on Nov. 20, 1917.

1898 [Griffith, I. O., M.A.] (Sept. 5, 1915). Maj. Technical Officer R.A.F. *A.F.C.* Nov. 2, 1918.

1913 Griffiths, B. P., B.A. (Jan. 1915). Lt. 4th Welsh Regt. Staff-Lt., Gen. Staff Intelligence. Egypt and Palestine.

1908 Gurner,* S. R. K., M.A. (Dec. 17, 1914). Lt. Army Cyclist Corps, attd. War Office. France. *M.C.*, June 18, 1917. *D.* France, 1917.

1905 Gutch, Rev. A. L., M.A. (Jan. 4, 1916). Chaplain to the Forces (4th Class).

1902 Gwynne, C. W., B.A. (Apr. 1, 1917). ‡Lt., temp. Maj., I.A.R.O. India. *D.* India, 1919.

1910 Haines, Rev. I. M., M.A. (June 21, 1916). Chaplain to the Forces (4th Class).

1910 **Hall, A. J. M.,** B.A. (May 1915). 2nd Lt. 20th London Regt. France. Killed in action at High Wood on Sept. 15, 1916.

1891 Hall, H. R. H., M.A., D.Litt. (Mar. 15, 1916). Capt. Special Lists. Staff-Lt. (2nd Class), Intelligence H.Q. France, 1916; Mesopotamia, 1918–19. *M.B.E.* (Mil.). *D.* § Mar. 1918.

1919 Hall, J. G. (Sept. 11, 1914). ‡Lt. 4th Leicestershire Regt. France and Belgium. (Prisoner of war in Germany for 12 months.)

1919 Hamilton, F. W. G. (Sept. 1914). Capt. 6th King's Own (R. Lancaster Regt.). Maj. General List. France, 1915–16. *D.* France, 1916.

1906 Hammond, G. H., B.A. (Nov. 23, 1914). Capt. 7th W. Yorkshire Regt. (T.F.). France and Belgium, 1916–19.

1891 Hammond, J. L. Le B., B.A. (Sept. 1915). 2nd Lt. Lowland Bde., R.F.A. (T.F.), afterwards 2nd Lt. T.F. Res.

1895 Hance, J. E., M.A. (Sept. 22, 1915). Hon. Lt. Riding Master R.F.A. *D.* § Feb. 1917.

1903 **Handyside, J.,** M.A. (July 8, 1915). 2nd Lt. 16th King's (Liverpool Regt.). France. Died on Oct. 18, 1916, of wounds received in action on the Somme.

1913 Harris,* G. G. (Aug. 4, 1914). Capt. Norfolk Regt. (Adjt.). Lt. 1/155th Pioneers, Indian Army. France, 1915; India, 1915–19.

1914 Harris, H. J. M. (Oct. 1914). Capt. 9th R. W. Kent Regt. France. *M.C.*, Aug. 25, 1916; *Bar*, Nov. 6, 1917; *2nd Bar*, Feb. 1, 1919.

1902 Harrison-Jones, C., B.A. (Jan. 29, 1915). Lt. 5th London Regt. (London Rifle Brigade) (Capt.). (Bde. Intelligence Officer.) France, 1917–18.

1908 Harter, G. J. (Apr. 15, 1916). Capt. R.A.F.

1898 Hartley, G. W. C. (Mobilized Aug. 4, 1914). Capt. 5th Cheshire Regt. France. *D.* France, 1916.

1904 **Harvey, E. A.,** B.A. (Nov. 1, 1917). 2nd Lt. I.A.R.O., attd. 29th Lancers (Deccan Horse). Mesopotamia. Died on Nov. 13, 1917, of illness contracted on active service.

1905 **Harvey, J.** (Mobilized Aug. 4, 1914). Capt. 7th King's (Liverpool Regt.) (T.F.). France. Killed in action on May 16, 1915.

1910 Hatfeild, A. C., B.A. (1914). ‡Capt. R.A.F. (Flight Commdr.). France. (Prisoner of war.)

1895 Hay, J. S., B.A. (Sept. 9, 1914). Capt. Intelligence Corps. Staff-Lt. (1st Class). *D.* § Feb. 1917.

1897 Heath, E. L., M.A. (Dec. 1, 1914). Capt. Special Lists, empld. War Office. *D.* § Mar. 1919.

1897 Heathcote, D. K. P., B.A. (Feb. 10, 1915). Lt. R.G.A.

1896 Hebb, J. H., B.M. (Apr. 27, 1915). Capt. R.A.M.C. (Maj.). Egypt, 1915; Mediterranean, 1916; India, 1916; France, 1916–19. *O.B.E.* (Mil.). *D.* France, 1917, 1918.

1894 Hedges, F. R., B.A. (Mobilized Aug. 1914). Maj. 4th R. Berkshire Regt. Belgium and France.

1917 Hemsted, E. C. E. (Jan. 1917). Capt. S. Nottinghamshire Hussars, attd. 52nd Inf. Bde. H.Q. France.

1907 Hesketh, P. L. Sub-Lt. R.N.V.R. (Motor-boat service.) (Invalided.)

1895 Hibbert, Rev. E. H., B.A. (July 26, 1918). Chaplain to the Forces (4th Class).

1919 Hicks, E. C. (Apr. 27, 1917). 2nd Lt. R.E. (Signals). France.

1911 Higgs-Walker, J. A., B.A. (Aug. 25, 1914). Capt. 5th Worcestershire Regt. Egypt, Salonika, Mesopotamia, Italy.

1919 Hill, A. C. (Aug. 10, 1917). 2nd Lt. 3rd, attd. 2nd, Shropshire L.I. Salonika, 1918; Batum, 1918–19.

1908 **Hill, G. G.** Pte. Singapore Volunteers. India. Killed in Singapore Rebellion on July 16, 1915.

1895 Hill, G. L. W., B.A. (June, 1916). Capt. R.G.A. (Commission Internationale de Ravitaillement, 1918–19.) *M.B.E.* (Civil).

1919 Hill, P. H. (Apr. 9, 1915). ‡Lt. R. Sussex Regt. (Capt.). France and Belgium.

1906 Hill,* R. H., B.A. R.F.A.

1902 Hilliard, S. C. (Aug. 30, 1914). ‡Lt. 8th R. Scots Fusiliers (Capt.). France, Salonika. (Relinquished Commission on grounds of ill health contracted on active service.)

1894 Hillman, R. F. C., M.A. (Oct. 31, 1914). Capt. Somerset L.I. Staff-Capt.

1896 Hills, R. P., B.A. (Feb. 1, 1915). Capt. 7th K.O. Scottish Borderers. Maj. General List, D.A.A.G. France. *M.C.*, June 4, 1917. *O.B.E.* (Mil.). *D.* France, 1915, 1916.

1912 Hirst, T. W. (Aug. 18, 1914). Lt. Q.O. Yorkshire Dragoons (Capt. and Adjt.).

1907 Hobday, W. E. (Sept. 3, 1914). Capt. I.A.R.O., attd. 33rd Punjabis and 93rd Burma Inf. Egypt, 1914–15; France, 1915; Mesopotamia, 1916; India, 1916–19.

1904 **Hodges, A. G.,** B.A. (Dec. 23, 1914). 2nd Lt. 8th Bedfordshire Regt. (Capt.). France, 1915–16. Killed in action near Ginchy on Sept. 15, 1916.

1900 Hodges, Rev. C. H. N., B.A. (Mar. 13, 1917). Chaplain to the Forces (4th Class).

1911 **Hodgkinson, A.** (Aug. 1914). Lt. 2nd R. Warwickshire Regt. (Capt.). France. *D.* France, 1915. Killed in action in the Battle of the Somme on July 1, 1916.

1913 Hodson,* E. M., B.A. (Aug. 28, 1914). Capt. 5th, attd. 3rd, D.C.L.I. France and Belgium, 1916–18. *D.* France, 1917.

1898 Hodson, S. S., B.A. (Mobilized Sept. 18, 1914). Capt. 93rd Burma Inf., Indian Army. Egypt, 1914–15; France, 1915; Mesopotamia, 1916–18; Palestine, 1918–19. *D.* Palestine, 1918.

1913 Hogg, G. R. D. (Feb. 21, 1916). ‡2nd Lt. R.E. 2nd Lt. R.A.F. (Lt.). Salonika, Egypt, Palestine.

Hoggard, E. J. (1915). 2nd Lt. 3rd Queen's (R. W. Surrey Regt.), attd. M.G.C. France, 1916. Killed in action on Oct. 6, 1916.

1908 Holcroft, H. R., M.A. (Sept. 5, 1914). Capt. 2/8th Worcestershire Regt. G.S.O. 3, XI Corps. France, 1916–19. *M.C.*, June 3, 1919.

1914 **Holdsworth, J. A.** (June 15, 1915). 2nd Lt. 11th Gordon Highlanders. Lt. 2/8th Lancashire Fusiliers (Capt.). France. *M.C.*, Nov. 26, 1917. Died as prisoner in Saxony on June 17, 1918, of wounds received in action at Hargicourt on Mar. 21, 1918.

1909 Holland,* J. W. T., M.A. (Oct. 4, 1914). Capt. 7th King's (Liverpool Regt.) (T.F.). France, 1915–16.

1914 Holman, E. F. (1918). U.S. Medical Corps.

1906 Hope, Rev. V., M.A. (Oct. 14, 1915). 2nd Lt. Unattached List, T.F. Lt. R.G.A. France.

1908 Hopwood, J. S. N. (June 13, 1915). 2nd Lt. 9th R. W. Kent Regt.

1913 Hore-Belisha, L., B.A. (Aug. 1914). ‡Maj. R.A.S.C. France, 1914–17; Salonika, Egypt, 1917–18. *D.* Salonika, 1918.

1906 Horsfield,* H. E., B.A. (Oct. 6, 1916). Lt., temp. Capt., I.A.R.O. (Cavalry). Staff-Capt. E. Indies. India, E. Indies.

1913 Horsley,* S. M. (Aug. 5, 1914). ‡2nd Lt. Gordon Highlanders. France, 1914–15. (Relinquished Commission on account of ill health, Nov. 1915.)

1905 Houlder, H. F., M.A. (Jan. 25, 1915). Sergt. 56th Field Ambulance, R.A.M.C. France, 1915–18. (Prisoner of war, 1918.) *M.M.*, Mar. 1917.

1914 Howell, A. R. (May 15, 1915). 2nd Lt. 16th K.R.R.C.

1905 Hoyle,* A. L., B.A. (July 22, 1916). Lt., temp. Capt., I.A.R.O. (Cavalry). India.

1899 Hudson, H. H., M.A. (Nov. 9, 1914). Lt.-Col. W. Yorkshire Regt. France, Belgium, Italy. *D.S.O.*, Oct. 28, 1917. *M.C.*, June 3, 1916. Italian silver medal for valour. *D.* France, 1917; Italy, 1918, 1919.

1918 Humphreys, C. R. L. (Oct. 5, 1914). ‡2nd Lt. 8th E. Lancashire Regt. France, 1915–16. (Invalided on account of wounds, Sept. 1917.)

1911 Humphreys,* R. M., B.M. (Aug. 11, 1914). Capt. 7th R. Welch Fusiliers (relinquished Commission). Capt. R.A.M.C. Gallipoli, 1915; India, 1918; E. Persia, 1918–19.

1914 **Hunt, F. F.** (Oct. 1914). Lt. 4th London Regt. (R. Fusiliers). France, 1915. Killed in action at Richebourg St. Vaast on June 27, 1915.

1915 Hunt, G. G. (Dec. 3, 1915). Lt. 4th London Regt. (R. Fusiliers). France, 1917.

1919 Huntley, M. J. (Aug. 16, 1916). Lt. R.F.A. France, 1917; Italy, 1918–19.

1919 Huntsman, C. 28th London Regt. (Artists' Rifles), and 3rd County of London Yeomanry.

1906 **Hurstbourne, W. H.** (June, 1915). 2nd Lt. R.F.A. France, 1916–17. Killed in action on June 23, 1917.

1919 Hutchins, R. (Aug. 1918). 2nd Lt. Tank Corps.

1917 Idjidovitch, S. (Sept. 1, 1914). Pte. Telegraphic Section, Serbian Army. Serbia, Durazzo.

1909 Iliffe,* A. P., M.A. (Jan. 23, 1916). Lt. 2/1st Warwickshire Yeomanry. *D.* § Aug. 1919.

1903 Imbert-Terry, D. P. (Apr. 6, 1915). Lt. 7th The Buffs (E. Kent Regt.).

1919 Impey, L. A. (June 4, 1917). ‡Lt. Coldstream Guards. France. Croix de Guerre.

1911 Inch, P. G., M.A. (Dec. 28, 1914). Capt. 15th Middlesex Regt. Maj. M.G.C.

1908 Inder, R. W., B.A. (Aug. 28, 1916). Lt. I.A.R.O. (Inf.). India.

1897 Inman, H. M., B.A. (Serving Aug. 4, 1914). Maj. Indian Medical Service (Lt.-Col.). France, 1914–16; E. Africa, 1917–19. *D.* E. Africa, 1918.

1918 Jacot, B. L., B.A. (Nov. 17, 1915). Capt. R.F.A. (T.F.).

1905 Jamieson, J. P., B.A. (July 1916). ‡Capt. 4th Middlesex Regt. France. *D.S.O.*, Dec. 2, 1918. *D.* France, 1918.

1901 Japp, D. N. (1915). Maj. R.F.A. Salonika. *M.C.*, June 4, 1917. Order of the White Eagle (4th Class) (with swords). Greek Military Cross (2nd Class).

1911 Jardine, A. C., M.A. (Sept. 5, 1914). ‡Capt. 9th Yorkshire Regt. France, 1915–16, 1916–17; Italy, 1917–18; France, 1918–19. *M.C.*, Nov. 19, 1917. *D.* Italy, 1918.

1909 **Jeayes, H. L.,** B.A. Sergt. Essex Regt. France. Killed in action on Mar. 26, 1917.

1907 Jeffries, C. S. (Sept. 1, 1914). Coy. Sergt.-Maj. 1/28th London Regt. (Artists' Rifles). France and Belgium, 1914–18.

1910 Jennings, M. R. N. (Feb. 23, 1916). Flight Lt. R.A.F. (Maj. Flight Commdr.). France. *M.C.*, Sept. 16, 1918. *A.F.C.*, June 3, 1919.

1912 Jerman,* R. H., B.A. (Aug. 4, 1914). ‡Maj. R. Welch Fusiliers, attd. R.A.F. G.S.O. 2. France, 1914–18. *M.C.*, Jan. 1, 1918. *D.* France, 1917.

1895 Johnson, B. C., B.A. (Aug. 29, 1914). Lt. Warwickshire Yeomanry (Capt.), attd. 2/5th E. Lancashire Regt. Transport Officer. Egypt, Gallipoli, France, Belgium.

1912 Johnson, C. B. (Jan. 22, 1915). Lt. 10th Suffolk Regt. (invalided 1917). Rejoined as Lt. R.E. Gallipoli, 1915.

1911 **Johnson,* G. R.** (Aug. 26, 1914). 2nd Lt. 7th Gloucestershire Regt. Gallipoli. Died on Aug. 7, 1915, of wounds received in action at Suvla Bay.

1908 **Johnson,* J. F.,** B.A. (Sept. 1914). Lt. 1/4th Leicestershire Regt. France, 1915. Died on Oct. 30, 1915, of wounds received in action at the Hohenzollern Redoubt on Oct. 13, 1915.

1920 Johnson, K. H. (Sept. 8, 1915). Lt. R.A.S.C. Capt. I.A.R.O., attd. 1/123rd Outram's Rifles. Salonika, 1917–18; India, 1918–19.

1913 **Johnson,* R. H. J.** (Aug. 1914). 2nd Lt. 2nd Essex Regt. France and Belgium. Killed in action at Ploegsteert on Mar. 13, 1915.

1913 Johnstone,* J. C. (Aug. 29, 1914). Capt. 1/7th Devonshire Regt., attd. Intelligence Corps. France, Germany. *M.C.*, June 3, 1919. *D.* France, 1919.

1918 Johnstone, R. F. (Nov. 29, 1915). Sergt. 2nd S. African Field Ambulance. German E. Africa. (Invalided.)

1913 Jones, A. E., B.A. (Oct. 12, 1914). Capt. 4th R. W. Kent Regt. (Lt.-Col.). France.

1899 Jones, W. A. F. (Serving Aug. 4, 1914). Maj., Bt. Lt.-Col. 290th Bde., R.F.A. France and Belgium, 1914–18. *D.S.O.*, June 3, 1916. *D.* France, 1915, 1916 twice, 1917, 1919.

1909 **Jones-Savin,* J. S.** (Aug. 22, 1914). Lt. 8th R. Welch Fusiliers. France, Egypt, Salonika. Killed in action in Macedonia on Mar. 27, 1917.

1905 Jordan, J. P. (Nov. 4, 1914). Lt. R.A. France. *M.C.*, Nov. 14, 1916.

1919 Keeble, H. M. (Sept. 2, 1917). ‡2nd Lt. R.E. Signals. France and Germany.

1884 Kent, H. E. H., B.A. (June 1915). Lt. 22nd Rifle Brigade. Egypt, Cyprus, Mudros, 1916; Salonika, 1916–17. (Invalided Jan. 1918, on account of ill health contracted on active service.)

Kerr, G. A. L'E. (May 1, 1917). 2nd Lt. Bedfordshire Regt. France, 1918. Killed in action near Albert on June 30, 1918.

1908 Kerry,* A. H. G., M.A. (Aug. 7, 1914). ‡Capt. R.E. France, 1914–15; Egypt, 1916–19.

1909 Kettelwell, J., B.A. (May 1, 1915). Paymaster Sub-Lt., R.N.R.

1888 Kilburn, Rev. E. E., M.A. (Aug. 13, 1914). Chaplain R.N. H.M. Hospital Ship *Rewa No.* 5, 1914–15.

1919 King, S. E. (Mar. 1, 1917). Lt. 48th Bn. M.G.C. France, 1917; Italy, 1917–19. *D.* Italy, 1918.

1904 [Kirk,* Rev. K. E., M.A.] (Sept. 28, 1914). Chaplain to the Forces (3rd Class). France and Belgium.

1908 **Kirk,* L. C.,** B.A. (Sept. 1914). Capt. 9th W. Yorkshire Regt. France and Belgium, 1916–17. Killed in action near Poelcappelle on Oct. 9, 1917.

1918 Kirkwood, W. C. (Oct. 29, 1914). Maj. R.G.A. France and Belgium. *M.C.*, Jan. 1, 1918. (Discharged on account of wounds, June 1919.)

1906 Kitchin, A. E., M.A. (Serving Aug. 4, 1914). Capt. Unattached List, T.F., Shrewsbury School O.T.C.

1912 Lakin, C. H. A., B.A. (Dec. 28, 1914). Lt. 8th S. Wales Borderers.

1881 Lancaster, E. Le C., B.A. (Mobilized Aug. 4, 1914). Lt.-Col. R.A.M.C.

1896 Landon, C. W. (Sept. 1, 1914). Maj. R.A.S.C.

1913 Lascelles, L., M.A. (Nov. 3, 1914). Lt. 3rd Divl. Train R.A.S.C. France.

1898 Latimer, H. (Jan. 1915). ‡Lt. I.A.R.O., attd. 37th Lancers. N.W. Frontier, 1917–18; Palestine and Egypt, 1918–19.

1905 Lawrence, A. S., B.A. (Oct. 7, 1915). Lt. 6th K.R.R.C. Lt. M.G.C.

1904 Lawrence,* M. R., B.M., M.A. (Dec. 27, 1916). Capt. R.A.M.C.

1909 **Lawrence,* W. G.,** B.A. (Apr. 1915). Lt. 3rd Oxf. & Bucks. Lt. Infty., attd. R.F.C. France. Killed in aerial action near St. Quentin on Oct. 23, 1915.

1912 **Laycock, L. J. P.,** B.A. (July 16, 1915). Lt. 7th Northamptonshire Regt. France and Belgium, 1916–17. Killed in action near Zillebeke on July 31, 1917.

1913 Leach,* A. C., B.A. (Jan. 18, 1915). Lt. R.A.S.C.

1919 Leach, C. H. (July 19, 1917). 2nd Lt. 2nd Cavalry Res. Regt.
1913 **Leake, R. M.** (Sept. 1914). ‡Capt. 1st Loyal N. Lancashire Regt. France. *M.C.*, May 11, 1917; *Bar*, Jan. 18, 1918. Killed in action on Sept. 18, 1918.
1913 Leclerq, F. D. K. U.S. Navy.
1909 Lester Garland,* A. G., B.A. (Aug. 5, 1914). 2nd Lt. 1/4th Hampshire Regt. Capt. 1/153rd Punjabis, Indian Army (Lt.-Col.). India, Mesopotamia, Palestine. *M.C.*, Mar. 8, 1919.
1913 Lester Garland, G. H., B.A. (Sept. 1914). ‡Lt. Dorsetshire Regt., attd. M.G.C. India and Mesopotamia. *D.* Mesopotamia, 1919.
1912 Lever, W. G. T. (Nov. 30, 1915). Lt. 5th Cheshire Regt.
1910 Levy,* F. D., M.A. (Aug. 14, 1914). Lt. 2/21st London Regt. Lt. R.A.F. France, Salonika, Egypt, Palestine.
1914 **Lewis, C. S.** (Feb. 1915). Lt. 2/6th Gloucestershire Regt. France. Died on Sept. 19, 1916, of wounds received in action at Armentières.
1912 **Lewis,* C. W. V.** (Aug. 15, 1914). Lt. 6th Middlesex Regt. France. Accidentally killed on Oct. 3, 1917.
1911 **Lewis, J. N.** (Aug. 14, 1914). Lt. 8th Welsh Regt. (Pioneers) (Capt.). Gallipoli. Killed in action on Chocolate Hill on Aug. 8, 1915.
1912 Lewis,* L. C. St. A. (1914). 2nd Lt. 3rd, attd. 2nd, Welsh Regt.
1915 **Lightbourn, R.** (Jan. 8, 1916). 2nd Lt. 8th Gloucestershire Regt. (Capt.). France and Belgium. Killed in action near Ypres on July 26, 1917.
1907 Lissant, S. P., B.A. (Mar. 17, 1915). Lt. A/106th Batt., R.F.A. (Maj.). France and Belgium, 1915–18.
1914 Liveing, E. G. D., B.A. (June 4, 1915). Lt. 12th London Regt. (The Rangers). Staff-Lt.
1897 Lloyd, C. M., M.A. (Feb. 1915). Capt. 22nd Manchester Regt. Capt. General List, Staff-Capt., attd. 115th Inf. Bde. Egypt, France. *M.C.*, June 3, 1919.
1920 Lockett, M. V. (July 18, 1918). Pte. 1/28th London Regt. (Artists' Rifles).
1904 Lockyer, Rev. E. R., M.A. (Oct. 17, 1914). Chaplain to the Forces (4th Class). Mediterranean, 1915; Egypt, 1915 onwards. *D.* Egypt, 1918.
1908 Logan, H. T., M.A. (Apr. 22, 1916). ‡Maj. 4th Canadian M.G.C. France and Belgium. *M.C.*, Feb. 1, 1919. *D.* France, 1918.
1905 Logan, W., M.A. (Mobilized Aug. 4, 1914). Capt. 1/4th Devonshire Regt. (Staff-Captain and D.A.Q.M.G.) Mesopotamia, 1916–19.
1914 **Loveitt, A. P. C.** (Aug. 21, 1915). 2nd Lt. 3/7th R. Warwickshire Regt. France. Killed in action near Pozières on July 27, 1916.
1918 Lowndes, G. A. N. (Dec. 31, 1915). Capt. 16th London Regt. (Queen's Westminster Rifles). France, 1916, 1918. *M.C.*, June 22, 1918.
1887 McDonald, A., B.A. (Mobilized Aug. 4, 1914). Capt. 14th London Regt. (London Scottish).
1886 MacDonald, K. L., M.A., *D.S.O.* (Mobilized Aug. 4, 1914). Maj. Lovat's Scouts. Hon. Lt.-Col. Gallipoli. *D.* Gallipoli, 1916.
1908 McDougall,* J. H. G., B.A. Uganda Volunteer Reserve.
1908 Mackarness,* C. G. M. (1914). ‡Lt. I.A.R.O. (Capt.). India.
1919 McKenzie, A. C. Cadet O.C.B.

1891 Mackenzie, W. K. S., B.A. (Serving Aug. 4, 1914). Lt.-Col. A.I.F. France. *D.S.O.*, Jan. 1, 1917. Order of St. Stanislas (2nd Class). *D.* France, 1916, 1917.

1906 **Maclear, G. D'O.,** B.A. (Feb. 1915). Lt. I.A.R.O., attd. 39th Garhwal Rifles (Capt.). Mesopotamia, 1916–18; Salonika, 1918. *M.C.*, Jan. 11, 1919. Died on Jan. 29, 1919, of illness contracted on active service.

1919 McMillan, E. D. (June 26, 1918). Cadet R.G.A.

1903 **McMinn, H. B.,** B.A. (Oct. 1914). Maj. Special Lists, D.A.D. Rly. Transport. Belgium and France. Died on July 29, 1918, of illness contracted on active service.

1916 Macnamara, Rev. A. (Mar. 21, 1917). Chaplain to the Forces (4th Class). Belgium and France.

1897 McNeile, A. M., M.A. (Serving Aug. 4, 1914). Capt. Unattached List, T.F., Eton College O.T.C.

1919 Maitland, A. G. C. (Feb. 28, 1918). 2nd Lt. R.G.A.

1909 Maitland, J. E., M.A. (Aug. 8, 1914). ‡Lt. R.F.A. (T.F.), attd. War Office Intelligence Dept. (Capt.). France and Belgium, 1917–18.

1918 Mann, R. L., B.A. (Aug. 3, 1915). Lt. R.G.A. France, 1917.

1907 Marsden,* P., B.A. (July 4, 1918). 2nd Lt. 9th Hodson's Horse, Indian Army. East Persia, 1918–19.

1910 **Marsden,* W. A. J.** (Aug. 4, 1914). 2nd Lt. R.F.A. France. Died on July 20, 1917, of wounds received in action on the Somme.

1904 Marsh-Roberts, C. F., M.A. (Jan. 4, 1915). 2nd Lt. R.F.A.

1908 Matthews,* Rev. H. J., M.A. (Feb. 26, 1917). Chaplain R.N.

1910 Matthews,* T. H., B.A. (Feb. 21, 1916). Instructor Lt. R.N., H.M.S. *New Zealand.*

1904 Maufe, E. B., M.A. (Sept. 22, 1914). A.B., R.N.V.R. ‡Lt. R.A. Staff-Lt., A.D.C. to G.O.C. R.A. XII Corps. Macedonia and Turkey.

1910 **Maurice, F. T.,** B.A. (Sept. 1914). ‡Lt. 3rd, attd. 1st, Grenadier Guards. France, Italy. Died on Oct. 29, 1918, of illness contracted while on active service.

1919 Maurice, L. S. P. (Nov. 9, 1917). 2nd Lt. 18th Middlesex Regt. France.

1909 May,* J. I. C., B.A. (Jan. 11, 1915). Lt. King's African Rifles. E. Africa.

1914 Mayo, T. F. (1916). American Amb. 1916, afterwards Lt. U.S. Naval Reserve Force, Aviation Service. France, 1916, 1918–19.

1911 **Meek, H. K.,** B.A. (Feb. 2, 1915). Lt. 14th K.R.R.C. Gallipoli, 1915; France, 1916. Died on Sept. 15, 1916, of wounds received in action on the Somme.

1907 Menzies-Jones,* Ll. F., B.A. (Mar. 1915). 2nd Lt. 13th E. Surrey Regt. Lt. 95th T.M.B. (Capt.). France.

1913 Merriman,* Rev. T. F., M.A. (June 22, 1918). Pte. R.A.M.C. (Sergt.). Army Education Lecturer. France, 1917–18 (with Church Army).

1913 **Messer,* A. E.** (Aug. 1914). Capt. 5th, attd. 1st, K.R.R.C. France and Belgium, 1915, 1916. Died at Calais on Feb. 17, 1916, of wounds received in action at Festubert on Jan. 22.

1898 Meyrick, Rev. C. H., M.A. (Jan. 1, 1916). Chaplain to the Forces (4th Class). France, 1916–17. *D.* France, 1917.

1914 Michell, J. K., B.A. (Jan. 1915). 2nd Lt. R. Warwickshire Regt. Lt. 42nd Bn. M.G.C. (Capt.). France. *M.C.*, Aug. 25, 1916; *Bar*, Mar. 8, 1919.

1907 Middleton, Rev. R. D., M.A. (Dec. 30, 1915). Chaplain to the Forces (4th Class). *D.* § Mar. 1918.

1919 Millett, H. J. C. (May 30, 1915). Capt. R.A.S.C., M.T., attd. R.G.A. France, 1916–18.

1894 Milligan, J. W., B.A. (Aug. 5, 1914). Maj. E. African Mounted Rifles. Asst. Director Requisitioning Services. British E. Africa, German and Portuguese E. Africa. *D.S.O.*, Jan. 1, 1918. *D.* E. Africa, 1917, 1918.

1908 **Mitchell, J. B.,** B.A. (Dec. 1914). ‡Capt. 8th London Regt. (Post Office Rifles). France and Belgium. *M.C.*, June 24, 1916. Killed in action on the Somme on Sept. 15, 1916.

1912 **Moody,* A.** (Sept. 8, 1914). Capt. 5th Dorsetshire Regt. Gallipoli. Presumed killed in action near Suvla Bay on Aug. 21, 1915.

Moore, R. C. D. (Apr. 26, 1917). 2nd Lt. H.A.C. France and Belgium. Killed in action on Oct. 9, 1917.

1900 Moore, W. A. (Feb. 15, 1915). Capt. 5th Rifle Brigade. Salonika. *M.B.E.* (Mil.). Serbian Order of the White Eagle. *D.* Salonika, 1917.

1919 Morgan, L. R. (Jan. 3, 1916). Pte. 2nd Rhodesian Inf. Flight Cadet R.A.F. E. Africa.

1890 Morrah, H. A. (Sept. 29, 1917). Lt. R.N.V.R.

1914 Mortimer, L. P. W. A. (Mar. 15, 1915). 2nd Lt. 7th Northamptonshire Regt., afterwards Pte. 6th Tank Corps. France and Belgium. (Relinquished Commission, 1916, on account of ill health. Re-enlisted in ranks, 1917.)

1914 Neal, L. E. (Jan. 1915). ‡Lt. 3rd Wiltshire Regt. France.

1902 Negus, R. E., M.A. (Mobilized Aug. 1914). Lt.-Col. 7th Shropshire L.I. Belgium and France. *D.S.O.*, Oct. 20, 1916. *D.* France, 1916 twice.

1879 Nelson, A., B.A. (Serving Aug. 4, 1914). Maj. General List. *O.B.E.* (Mil.).

1919 Nesbit, T. (May 15, 1917). ‡Lt. 303rd F.A., U.S. Army (Capt.). France.

1901 Newcomb, C., D.M. (Mobilized Sept. 17, 1914). Capt. Indian Medical Service, 9th Indian General Hospital. Mesopotamia, 1914–16. (Prisoner of war, 1916–18, captured at Kut-el-Amara.)

1911 Newsam, F. A. (Oct. 7, 1915). Lt. 4th R. Irish Regt. Lt. 1/30th Punjabis, Indian Army (Capt.). Belgium, France, Punjab, 1916–18 ; Afghanistan, 1919. *M.C.*, Sept. 16, 1918. *D.* France, 1916.

1908 **Newsome,* R. H. A.,** B.A. (Apr. 1914). Capt. R.E. France, 1914, 1918 ; Egypt and Mediterranean, 1915–16. *M.C.*, June 3, 1916. *D.* France, 1915 ; Egypt, 1916. Died on Aug. 29, 1918, of wounds received on Aug. 26, 1918, at the Hindenburg Line.

1908 Nicholls, B. C. H., B.A. (Aug. 29, 1914). ‡Lt. 1/7th W. Yorkshire Regt. France and Belgium, 1918.

1900 Nicholls, Rev. R. M., M.A. (Sept. 29, 1915). Chaplain R.N. H.M.S. *Bellerophon*, *Powerful*, and *Hecla*, 1915–19.

1903 Nicholson, K. (Mobilized Aug. 4, 1914). Capt. 6th W. Riding Regt., attd. R.A.F.

1907 Nixon, C. F. (Apr. 12, 1916). 2nd Lt. Household Cavalry.

1909 North, E. H., B.A. (Feb. 12, 1915). Lt. 4th Q. O. Oxfordshire Hussars. France, 1916–17, 1918–19.

1903 Northcote, H. B. S., M.A. (Dec. 20, 1915). ‡Capt. R.A.S.C. Mesopotamia and Persia.

1894 Norwood, C., M.A. (Serving Aug. 4, 1914). Capt. Unattached List, T.F., Bristol Grammar School O.T.C.

1908 Nottidge, W. R., B.A. (Aug. 28, 1914). Capt. 4th Bedfordshire Regt. Belgium and France. *D.* France, 1916 ; § Mar. 1919.

1910 Ockenden, J. R., B.A. (Apr. 20, 1915). Lt. 21st London Regt., attd. M.G.C.

1909 O'Donoghue, G. H., B.A. R.G.A.

1918 Olivier, A. E. (Jan. 23, 1916). Lt. R.F.A. France. (Invalided 1918.)

1910 Osborne,* D. G. H., B.A. (Oct. 2nd, 1914). Capt. 1/4th Hampshire Regt. Baluchistan, Mesopotamia, N. Persia.

1903 Oswell, Rev. B. H., M.A. (Feb. 19, 1914). Chaplain R.N. H.M.S. *Monarch*, Grand Fleet, 1914–15 ; H.M.S. *Cumberland*, N. Atlantic Squadron, 1915–16 ; H.M.S. *Devonshire*, N. Atlantic Squadron, 1916–17 ; H.M.S. *Ajax*, Grand Fleet, 1917–19.

1912 Owen, Sir J. A., Bt. (Sept. 9, 1915). Lt. 9th Somerset L.I.

1905 Owen, Rev. L., M.A. (Nov. 29, 1916). Chaplain to the Forces (4th Class).

1898 Page, Rev. R. St. C., M.A. (Feb. 12, 1918). Chaplain to the Forces (4th Class).

1906 [Parker, Rev. C. L., M.A.] (Jan. 1, 1915). Chaplain to the Forces (4th Class). (Resigned on account of ill health.)

1919 Parker, F. G. Pte. H.A.C.

1910 Parker,* F. V., B.A. (Aug. 15, 1914). Capt. 2nd Bedfordshire Regt. France.

1920 Parker, R. H. (Apr. 1, 1917). ‡Lt. 2nd Coldstream Guards. France and Belgium, 1918–19 ; Poland, Austria, Hungary, Bohemia, 1919.

1909 Parsons,* H. (Nov. 13, 1914). Lt. I.A.R.O., attd. 119th Inf. Mesopotamia, 1915.

1909 **Pascall, P. M.,** M.A. (Jan. 1915). ‡Capt. Middlesex Regt., attd. King's African Rifles. France and Belgium, Cameroons, German E. Africa. *M.C.*, June 4, 1917. *D.* E. Africa, 1917. Died on Jan. 13, 1918, of wounds received in action.

1919 Patterson, R. M. (May 18, 1917). 2nd Lt. R.F.A. France, 1918. (Prisoner of war, Mar.–Dec. 1918.)

1900 Payne, Rev. G. S., M.A. (Apr. 9, 1918). Chaplain to the Forces (4th Class), attd. 11th R. Sussex Regt. N. Russia.

1917 Payne, S. R. Cadet Tank Corps.

1914 Pearson, D. A. G. (Feb. 24, 1915). 2nd Lt. 8th R. Scots (T.F.). France, 1915–16. (Relinquished Commission on account of ill health, May 1916.)

1910 Pearson,* L. J., B.A. (Apr. 21, 1915). 2nd Lt. R.E. Lt. Flying Officer R.A.F. France. (Prisoner of war.) *D.* Air Ministry, Dec. 1919.

1907 Pearson,* N. G., M.A. (Sept. 19, 1914). Capt. 1st Gordon Highlanders (Maj.). France, 1915, 1916–17, 1918. *M.C.*, Jan. 11, 1919. *D.* France, 1918.

1903 Pentycross, G. H., B.A. R. Fusiliers.

1919 Peregrine, R. L. T. (Sept. 20, 1918). Cadet No. 2 O.C.B.

1919 Peters, W. (Dec. 4, 1916). Wireless Telegraphist R.N.V.R. Canadian and U.S.A. Atlantic Coasts.

1912 Philips,* R. O., B.A. (Sept. 14, 1914). Lt. 16th Manchester Regt. (Capt.). France.

1888 Phillips, G. I., B.Litt., M.A. (Aug. 31, 1914). Maj. R. Warwickshire Regt. Bt.-Lt.-Col. General Staff, War Office. France, 1914, 1917. *C.B.E.* (Mil.). *D.* France, 1917.

1909 Pocock,* L. G. (Dec. 2, 1915). Lt. D/102nd Bde., R.F.A. Italy. *M.C.*, June 3, 1919. *D.* Italy, 1918.

1891 Pollok, A. G., B.A. (Serving Aug. 4, 1914). Lt.-Col. Ayrshire Yeomanry (T.F. Res.). T.D.

1888 Pollok-McCall, J. B. (Serving Aug. 4, 1914). Col. R. Scots Fusiliers (Brig.-Gen.). Egypt and Palestine. *C.M.G. D.S.O.*, Apr. 6, 1918. *D.* Egypt, 1916, 1917.

1908 Poole,* A. L., M.A. (Dec. 10, 1914). Lt. 8th Gloucestershire Regt., attd. O.C.B. France and Belgium, 1915–16, 1917.

1912 Popert, A. H., B.A. (Dec. 22, 1914). Lt. 12th Worcestershire Regt. Capt. T.M.B.

1911 Porri,* C., M.A. (Sept. 9, 1914). Lt. 10th Lincolnshire Regt. Capt. R.A.F. France, Belgium, Germany.

1910 Porter,* J. D., B.A. (Aug. 9, 1914). Capt. 6th R. Welch Fusiliers. Temp. Maj. D.A.A.G., 21st Corps, Egyptian E.F. Gallipoli, 1915; Egypt, Palestine, Syria, 1916–19. *O.B.E.* (Mil.). Order of the Nile (4th Class). *D.* Egypt, 1917; Palestine, 1918, 1919.

1905 **Pound,* J. R.,** M.A. (Serving Aug. 4, 1914). Capt. 3rd, attd. 2nd, Shropshire L.I. France. Killed in action on Apr. 28, 1915.

1914 Powe, A. B. (Feb. 1, 1916). Lt. R.G.A. France and Belgium, 1916–18.

1913 **Powell,* R. K.** (Nov. 30, 1914). Capt. 10th N. Staffordshire Regt., attd. S. Lancashire Regt. France, 1915–16. Killed in action on Oct. 4, 1916.

1903 Poyser, A. H. R. W., B.A. (Sept. 1, 1914). ‡Capt. Inns of Court O.T.C. Maj. M.G.C. Mesopotamia, N. Persia. *D.* Mesopotamia, 1919.

1896 Poyser, C. L. (1915). Lt. R.G.A. (S.R.). Italy. *D.* Italy, 1918.

1910 Pritchard,* E. W. (Aug. 1915). Lt. Durham L.I. Lt. R.A.F. (Capt.). France.

1913 **Proud,* J. R. S.** (Oct. 16, 1914). 2nd Lt. 7th R. W. Kent Regt. 2nd Lt. R.F.C. France. Killed in action at Ath on Apr. 6, 1917.

1908 Pugh,* C. H. W., B.C.L., M.A. (Sept. 9, 1914). ‡Lt. 3rd, attd. 6th, Shropshire L.I. (Capt.). France, 1915–19. *M.C.*, Feb. 18, 1918.

1903 Pullman, G. C., M.A. (Mobilized Aug. 1914). Capt. 1/6th E. Surrey Regt. (Maj.). D.A.A.G. Aden Field Force. India, 1914–17; Aden, 1917–19. *O.B.E.* (Mil.). *D.* Aden, 1919.

1913 Rands, R. S. J., B.A. (Oct. 16, 1915). Lt. 4th Suffolk Regt. France, 1917.

1919 Raphael, C. M. (June 7, 1918). 2nd Lt. The Buffs (E. Kent Regt.).

1901 **Raphael, J. E.,** B.A. (Sept. 1914). Lt. 18th K.R.R.C. A.D.C. France and Belgium. Died on June 11, 1917, of wounds received in action at Messines Ridge.

1909 Rawson, G. F. (May, 1915). Lt. R.A.S.C.

1903 Raymer, Rev. W. H., M.A. (Sept. 28, 1918). Paymaster Sub-Lt. R.N.V.R.

1919 Rayner, F. (Nov. 6, 1918). Pte. K.O.Y.L.I. Cadet R.E., O.C.B.

1903 Raynor, K., B.A. (May 1916). Lt. 4th The Black Watch (Capt.). Lt. Intelligence Dept. (2nd Class Agent). France, 1916; Palestine, 1918.

1911 Reckitt,* G. L., B.A. (Aug. 22, 1914). Capt. 7th R. Sussex Regt. France, 1915–16, 1916–19. *M.C.*, May 13, 1918; *Bar*, Jan. 11, 1919.

1912 Reed, L. N. (Sept. 1914). ‡Capt. I.A.R.O. (Inf.). India, Mesopotamia. *M.C.*, Feb. 7, 1918. *D.* Mesopotamia, 1917.

1910 **Reed, M. J. B.** (Feb. 1916). Pte. 3/20th London Regt. Died on Apr. 5, 1916, of illness contracted on active service.

1905 Reynish, J. B., M.A. (Mar. 1915). ‡Capt. R.E. (Anti-Gas Service). *M.B.E.* (Mil.). *D.* § Mar. 1918.

1911 Reynolds, F. G. B. (Aug. 5, 1914). Capt. 1st Bucks. Bn. Oxf & Bucks. Lt. Infty., attd. R.A.F. France.

1889 Reynolds, T. W., M.A. (Serving Aug. 4, 1914). Capt. Suffolk Regt.

1905 Roberts, G. D., B.A. (Aug. 4, 1914). Maj. 8th Devonshire Regt. Maj. General List, D.A.A.G. France and Belgium, 1915–19. *O.B.E.* (Mil.). *D.* France, 1916, 1917, 1918; § Mar. 1918.

1909 Robertson,* N. W., M.A. (Aug. 26, 1914). Capt. 10th, attd. 3rd, Cameronians. France. *M.C.*, Oct. 15, 1918; *Bar*, Dec. 2, 1918.

1875 **Robertson-Macdonald, D. M.,** M.A. (Aug. 4, 1914). C.P.O., R.N.V.R. Anti-Aircraft Div. Died on July 13, 1919.

1910 Robinson,* E. L. D., B.A. (Nov. 24, 1914). Lt. Oxf. & Bucks. Lt. Infty. France, 1916; Salonika, 1917–18.

1911 Robinson,* J. D., M.A. (Jan. 18, 1915). Capt. 13th Essex Regt. France. (Prisoner of War, Dec. 1917–18.) *D.* France, 1918.

1914 Robinson, V. P. (July 10, 1916). ‡Lt. Durham L.I. Belgium and France, Germany, 1917–19.

1910 **Roe,* A. J. H.** (Aug. 22, 1914). 2nd Lt. 7th K.R.R.C. France. Killed in action in France on Aug. 9, 1915.

1911 Rogers, W. McM., B.A. (1917). Capt. U.S. Field Artillery. France. *O.B.E.*

1907 Romanes, F. J. (Aug. 15, 1914). Capt. 1st King Edward's Horse. France. (Invalided Apr. 1919.)

1905 Rose, E. D. (Aug. 1914). Capt. R.F.A. (Maj.). India, Afghanistan.

1908 Rose, G. T. (Serving Aug. 4, 1914). Capt. Hampshire Regt.

1911 Rosling,* A., B.A. (Nov. 7, 1914). Capt. and Adjt. Suffolk Yeomanry, attd. 15th Suffolk Regt. Egypt, 1916–17; Palestine, 1917–18; France, 1918. *D.* France, 1919.

1896 Rowlands, P., M.A. (Dec. 10, 1914). Lt. 4th Somerset L.I.

1913 Russell, E. F. L. (Oct. 31, 1914). Lt. 1st King's (Liverpool Regt.) (Capt.). France. *M.C.*, Jan. 1, 1917; *Bar*, Sept. 16, 1918; *2nd Bar*, Feb. 1, 1919.

1892 Ryman-Hall, B., B.A. (July 6, 1916). Lt. R.A.S.C.

1907 St. Quintin, R. G., M.A. (Dec. 24, 1914). ‡Lt. Welsh Regt. (Capt.). France.

1908 Sale, R., B.A. (Jan. 28, 1915). Capt. 8th Shropshire L.I.

1897 Sandford, Rev. J. H., B.A. (June 26, 1917). Chaplain to the Forces (4th Class).

1899 Savory, D. L., M.A. (Sept. 1, 1917). Lt. R.N.V.R., Naval Staff (Intelligence Div.).

1914 Saxby, C. O. (May 6, 1915). 2nd Lt. 4th R. Berkshire Regt. Capt. 11th Bn. M.G.C. France, 1916–19.

1911 Saxton,* A. E. (Sept. 1, 1914). 2nd Lt. 6th D.C.L.I.. Lt. Special Lists, (Intelligence Corps). France. Croix de Guerre. *D.* France, 1919.

1913 **Saye,* L. H.** (Feb. 24, 1915). 2nd Lt. 6th R. Berkshire Regt. France, 1915–16. Died on July 11, 1916, of wounds received in action on the Somme.

1871 Scarth, L. E., M.A. (Oct. 1914). Capt. Wiltshire Regt. Maj. Special Lists, empld. Recruiting Duties.

1913 Scattergood, T. A. (Sept. 16, 1914). ‡Lt. R.A.S.C. France, 1915; Salonika, 1916–18. Chevalier, Order of the Redeemer.

1904 Scothern, A. E., M.A. (Dec. 31, 1914). Lt.-Col. 9th Sherwood Foresters. Gallipoli, France. *C.M.G. D.S.O.*, Jan. 1, 1918. *D.* Gallipoli, 1915; France, 1916, 1917.

1905 Scott,* E., B.M. (Aug. 7, 1914). Capt. R.A.M.C. (Maj.). France. *D.S.O.*, Jan. 1, 1917. *D.* France, 1916, 1917.

1901 Scott, W., M.A. (Dec. 1914). Capt. 13th Yorkshire Regt. France, 1916–18. *D.* France, 1918.

1900 Seal, F. J., M.A. (Oct. 19, 1914). ‡Sub-Lt. R.N.V.R.

1900 Sedgwick, L. G. T. (Nov. 15, 1915). Lt. A.O.D. Capt. Technical Officer, R.A.F. *D.* § Mar. 1918.

1908 Seed, C. J. (Dec. 10, 1915). Capt. E. Yorkshire Regt. Staff-Capt. Station Staff Officer, Lucknow Bde. India.

1912 Sellar,* H. H., M.A. (Aug. 1, 1916). Instructor Lt., R.N., H.M.S. *Resolution*. Grand Fleet.

1912 Sever, J., M.A. (July 3, 1915). Lt. 9th Shropshire L.I.

1893 Sewell, Rev. A. H., M.A. (May 1915). Chaplain to the Forces (3rd Class). Serbia, 1915; Switzerland, 1917–18. Order of St. Sava (4th Class).

1913 Sharkey, L. I. J., M.A. (June 24, 1915). Capt. R.F.A.

1895 **Shaw, A. J. M.** (Feb. 2, 1915). Capt. 1st K. O. Scottish Borderers. France. Killed in action in the Battle of the Somme on July 1, 1916.

1911 Sharp, E. G., M.A. (Aug. 8, 1914). ‡Lt. H.A.C. (Capt.). France, 1914–15, 1916–19.

1887 Shea, R. P., M.A. (Serving Aug. 4, 1914). Maj. 5th Leicestershire Regt. France. *D.* France, 1917; § Aug. 1918.

1912 Shephard, H. H., M.A. (Feb. 23, 1915). Lt. 6th E. Lancashire Regt. Gallipoli, Egypt, Mesopotamia.

1868 Sheppard, Rev. E., D.D. (Serving Aug. 4, 1914). Chaplain to the Forces (4th Class), attd. 4th London Regt.

1911 Shipley, J. le R., M.A. (Apr. 18, 1917). Assist. Surgeon U.S. Naval Res. (Lt.). Atlantic Fleet, 1917–19.

1901 Shirreff, A. G., B.A. (July 15, 1918). 2nd Lt. I.A.R.O., attd. 39th Central India Horse. India.

1914 Shuffrey, F. A., B.A. (Mar. 1915). 2nd Lt. W. Riding Regt. Lt. M.G.C. (Capt.). France, Belgium, Italy, Austria. *M.C.*, Nov. 26, 1917.

1901 Shuttleworth, L. H. C., B.A. (Feb. 16, 1915). Capt. 3rd E. Surrey Regt., empld. Ministry of Labour.

1912 Simes,* C. E. W., M.A. (Aug. 25, 1914). Lt. 1/7th Worcestershire Regt. Lt. General List. France, 1915.

1911 Simmons, C. E. (Oct. 10, 1915). Lt. Supply and Transport Corps, Indian Army, attd. 3rd Lahore Div. Train (Capt. and Adjt.). Mesopotamia, 1916–18; Palestine, 1918 onwards. *D.* Mesopotamia, 1917.

1912 **Simpson, C. F. B.** (Aug. 21, 1914). Capt. 9th, attd. 14th, Durham L.I. Egypt, France, 1917. Died on Dec. 3, 1917, of wounds received in action at Marcoing.

1882 Simpson, S., M.A., T.D. (Mobilized Aug. 1914). Lt.-Col. R.F.A. (T.F.). France, 1916, 1917.

1919 Sims, H. V., B.A. (Sept. 1, 1914). ‡Lt. M.G.C. France. *M.C.*, Nov. 10, 1917.

1912 **Sinnett Jones, G. L.** (Sept. 1914). Capt. 8th R. Welch Fusiliers. Gallipoli, Mesopotamia. Killed in action in Mesopotamia on Apr. 9, 1916.

1906 Sitzler, E. A., B.A. (July 9, 1915). Lt. I.A.R.O. India.

1886 Sladen, D. R., *D.S.O.* (Serving Aug. 4, 1914). Lt.-Col. 1st K.O. Scottish Borderers. Temp. Brig.-Gen. Southern Brigade, India. India, Gallipoli, France. *C.M.G.* *D.* France, 1917.

1912 Smith,* A. C., B.A. (Aug. 4, 1914). ‡Lt. R.F.A. (Capt.). France and Italy. *M.C.*, Jan. 1, 1919. *D.* France, 1916, 1917; Italy, 1918.

1914 Smith, D. C. (Aug. 16, 1915). Lt. R.F.A.

1904 [Smith, H. A., M.A.] (Dec. 12, 1914). 2nd Lt. 8th Oxf. & Bucks. Lt. Infty. Capt. M.G.C., attd. Ministry of Information. France, 1915–16.

1919 Smith, J. R. A. (June 22, 1917). Lt. 366 Batt., R.F.A. Palestine, France

1919 Smith, P. A. (Sept. 9, 1917). 2nd Lt. R.G.A.

1914 Smith, V. E. A. (Dec. 22, 1914). Lt. 8th Lincolnshire Regt.

1912 Smith-Pearse, T. L. H., B.A. (Sept. 4, 1914). ‡Capt. and Adjt. R.F.A., attd. R.E. (Signal Service). Egypt, Arabia, Palestine, Syria. *D.* Palestine, 1918.

1911 **Solomon, K. M. H.** (Aug. 6, 1914). ‡2nd Lt. 11th Gloucestershire Regt., attd. 4th Worcestershire Regt. Gallipoli. Died on Sept. 18, 1915, of wounds received in action at Suvla Bay on Aug. 22.

1919 Sollis, C. J. (Aug. 4, 1915). Victualling Asst. R.N.

1906 Sothers, D. B., B.A. (Jan. 15, 1915). Lt. I.A.R.O. Inf. India.

1894 South, Rev. H. G., M.A. (July 3, 1917). Chaplain to the Forces (4th Class).

1913 Southee, E. A., M.A. (Oct. 1914). ‡Capt. 23rd Div. Train, R.A.S.C. (Maj.). France and Belgium, 1915–17; Italy, 1917–19. *O.B.E.* (Mil.). *D.* Italy, 1918, 1919.

1913 Spaulding, G. F., M.A. (Aug. 8, 1917). Lt. R.A.F. (Capt.). France, 1915–16 (with American Field Ambulance); Egypt, 1917–18.

Speight, J. L. (Jan. 11, 1916). Capt. 6th W. Yorkshire Regt. France and Belgium. Killed in action in Oct. 1917.

1910 Spencer, C. E., B.A. (Dec. 20, 1914). Lt. R.G.A.

1903 Spencer-Smith, R. O., B.A. (Serving Aug. 4, 1914). Capt. 2nd Hampshire Regt. (Maj.). India, Gallipoli, Egypt, France, Russia. *D.* Gallipoli, 1915, 1916.

1913 Spurway,* F. E., B.A. (Oct. 3, 1914). Lt. 2/5th Somerset L.I. (Capt.). India.

1881 Squire, W. Harold, M.A. (Sept. 14, 1915). Maj. 1st Cadet Bn. R. Fusiliers.

1905 Stanbridge, Rev. G. C., M.A. (Nov. 1, 1917). Chaplain to the Forces (4th Class). France, Belgium, 1918, 1919.

1919 Standen, A. O. (Feb. 20, 1917). 2nd Lt. R.F.A. (Lt.). France. (Prisoner of war, May–Dec. 1918.)

1884 Standen, Rev. J. E., M.A. (Mobilized Aug. 1914). Chaplain to the Forces (4th Class), attd. 5th Lincolnshire Regt. *D.* § Sept. 1918.

1911 Stanford,* J. K., M.A. (Nov. 14, 1914). ‡Capt. Suffolk Regt. Capt. 14th Bn. Tank Corps. (Bde.-Maj.). France, 1915. *M.C.*, June 3 1919. *D.* France, 1918.

1897 Stapleton, H. E., B.Sc., M.A. (Apr. 29, 1915). Lt. I.A.R.O., attd. 123rd Outram's Rifles (Capt. attd. 24th Punjabis.). Mesopotamia, 1915. (Prisoner of war, captured at Kut-el-Amara, 1916–18.)

1908 Stark, R. G. W., B.A. (Aug. 1914). 2nd Lt. 5th Shropshire L.I. Capt. Tank Corps. France, 1915–16; Palestine, 1917–18.
1884 Staveley-Hill, H. S. (Sept. 1914). Lt.-Col. 2/1st Staffordshire Yeomanry. T.D. *D.* § Feb. 1917.
1919 Steel, J. L. Cadet O.C.B. R.E.
1913 Stephens, F. D. (Apr. 1917). Capt. 5th F.A., U.S. Army, attd. Artillery Headquarters, 3rd Army Corps. France, 1917–18. Chevalier de l'Ordre de la Couronne. Order of the White Eagle.
1913 Stephens,* H. C. (Oct. 6, 1914). ‡2nd Lt. R.E. Lt. R.A.F. France.
Stevenson, P. W. J. (Aug. 29, 1914). 2nd Lt. 23rd London Regt. France. Killed in action on May 24, 1915.
1919 Stiff, F. E. (Nov. 10, 1915). Cpl. 5th Worcestershire Regt. (Sergt. Instructor). France.
1901 Stocks,* J. L., M.A. (Nov. 21, 1914). Lt. 13th K.R.R.C. Capt. General List, attd. No. 19 O.C.B. France, 1915–16. *D.S.O.*, Mar. 3, 1917. *D.* France, 1917; § Aug. 1918.
1903 Stoker, K., M.A. (Mar. 1916). ‡Capt. 12th King's (Liverpool Regt.). France, 1916–18.
1896 Stooke-Vaughan, J. S., B.A. (Feb. 22, 1918). Lt. R.G.A. Lt. R.A.F. (Staff-Officer).
1898 **Stratford, L.,** B.A. (Oct. 1915). Lt. 1st Rifle Brigade. France. Killed in action at Fampoux on Mar. 28, 1918.
1906 Street, W. G., B.A. (Sept. 2, 1914). ‡Lt. 8th Middlesex Regt. (T.F.) attd. R.F.A. (Capt.).
1897 Streeten, R. C. (Mar. 1917). Lt. Cape Coloured Regt. (Adjt.). German E. Africa.
1917 Subotitch, D. (Sept. 19, 1914). Military Censor. Serbian Army.
1914 Sullivan, W. M. (1917). 1st Lt. Inf., U.S. Army. France.
1914 Sumner, F. D. C. (Feb. 8, 1915). Orderly, Serbian Relief Ambulance. Lt. 380th Siege Batt., R.G.A. Serbia, 1915; France, 1916; Palestine, Egypt, 1917–19.
1905 Sutton, E. W., M.A. (Jan. 5, 1916). Lt. Special Lists. Staff-Lt.
1915 Swash, S. V. (Oct. 1915). Capt. B/88th Bde., R.F.A. France and Belgium, 1916–18. *M.C.*, Oct. 18, 1917; *Bar*, Sept. 16, 1918.
1919 Switzer, C. W. (Sept. 25, 1915). Lt. 2nd The Buffs (E. Kent Regt.). France, 1916; Salonika, 1917.
1905 Tacon, D. G. T. (Aug. 14, 1914). ‡Lt. 7th Lincolnshire Regt. Capt. 25th Div. Artillery, R.F.A. France, 1915–19. *D.* France, 1919.
1908 Tate, E. D. Cadet 28th London Regt. (Artists' Rifles).
1889 Taylor, Rev. F. H. W., M.A. (June 19, 1917). Chaplain to the Forces (4th Class).
1902 Taylor, J. F. G., M.A. (Aug. 31, 1914). ‡2nd Lt. 3rd King's (Liverpool Regt.). France and Belgium, 1915.
1914 Taylor, P. J. (Apr. 10, 1915). Lt. 9th Lincolnshire Regt. France and Belgium.
1913 **Terry,* S. F.** (Sept. 1914). ‡Capt. and Adjt. 1st Wiltshire Regt. France, 1915–18. *M.C.*, June 3, 1918. Killed in action near Bapaume on Mar. 24, 1918.
1891 Thelwall, F. W., B.A. S. African Heavy Artillery.
1913 Theodosius,* A. W. H., B.A. (Mar. 25, 1915). Lt. Kent Cyclist Bn.

1906 **Thomas, A. L.,** B.A. (Aug. 1, 1917). 2nd Lt. 3rd Northamptonshire Regt. France. Killed in action on Apr. 24, 1918.

1919 Thomas, L. H. (Dec. 29, 1916). Lt. T.M.B., R.F.A. France, 1917–18; Mesopotamia, 1918–19.

1913 Thompson, * C. D. (Aug. 1914). ‡Lt. Flight Officer R.A.F. (Capt.). Egypt, Sinai, Aden, 1915–16; France, 1917. (Prisoner of war, 1917–18.) *D.* Air Ministry, Dec. 1919.

1907 [**Thompson,* H.,** M.A.] (Aug. 15, 1914). Lt. 3rd, attd. 1st, Northamptonshire Regt. France. Killed in action at Festubert on May 9, 1915.

1911 **Thompson, M. B.,** B.A. (Sept. 19, 1914). Lt. 8th R. Berkshire Regt. Lt. M.G.C. France, 1916–17. Killed in action at Monchy-le-Preux on May 3, 1917.

1906 Thompson,* T. O., D.M. (Jan. 20, 1914). Capt. R.A.M.C., attd. 48th Div. (Maj.). Belgium, 1914–15; France, 1915–17; Italy, 1917–18. Croce di Guerra. *D.* Italy, 1919.

1897 [Tod, M. N., M.A.] (Dec. 15, 1915). Capt., 1st Class Agent, Intelligence Corps. Salonika, 1915–19. *O.B.E.* (Mil.). Croix de Guerre. *D.* Salonika, 1916, 1917, 1918, 1919.

1898 Tordoff, B., B.M. (Serving Aug. 4, 1914). Capt. Unattached List, T.F., O.T.C.

1909 Tower, G. de B., M.A. (Jan. 5, 1915). Pte. 14th London Regt. (London Scottish), attd. R.A.M.C. Egypt, 1916–19.

1904 Townroe, B. S., B.A. (Mobilized Aug. 4, 1914). Capt. 4th S. Lancashire Regt. Staff-Lt. France. *D.* France.

1911 Tribe, M. O., B.A. (Sept. 2, 1914). ‡Lt. 10th W. Riding Regt. France, 1915–16. *M.C.*, Nov. 14, 1916.

1909 Trotter, H. (Dec. 1, 1914). ‡Capt. 2nd Gurkha Rifles. Egypt, 1915–16; Indian Frontier, 1916; Mesopotamia, 1916–17.

Truman, A. H. (May 4, 1915). 2nd Lt. 3rd, attd. 1st, Oxf. & Bucks. Lt. Infty. Mesopotamia. Killed in action on Apr. 6, 1916.

1911 Turner,* C. W., B.A. (Sept. 1, 1914). Capt. 8th D.C.L.I. (Maj.). France, 1915; Macedonia, 1915–19. *M.C.*, Oct. 28, 1917.

1911 Turner, J. H. (Nov. 16, 1914). 2nd Lt. 13th Middlesex Regt.

1899 Turner, R. Ll., B.A. (Jan. 26, 1915). Lt. R.E. France, 1915–19. *D.* France, 1919.

1914 **Turner, W. G. D.** (Nov. 16, 1914). 2nd Lt. 13th Middlesex Regt. Lt. R.F.C. France. Killed in action on May 24, 1917.

1919 Turney, G. L. (Sept. 1, 1916). Lt. 274th Siege Batt., R.G.A. France, 1917–19.

1895 Tweedy, Rev. H. H., M.A. (Apr. 5, 1918). Chaplain to the Forces (4th Class).

1907 Tylden, J. R. (Mobilized Aug. 4, 1914). Capt. 1/1st R. E. Kent Yeomanry. Camp Commandant H.Q., 6th Div. Gallipoli, Egypt, France, Belgium, Germany.

Upham, H. E. R. (Nov. 1915). Lt. R.M.L.I. France. Killed in action on Nov. 13, 1916.

1910 **Upstone,* C. D.** (Aug. 1914). 2nd Lt. 1/4th Devonshire Regt. India, 1914; Mesopotamia, 1916. Died on July 11, 1916, of illness contracted on active service.

1896 Vale, Rev. J. T., M.A. (Feb. 6, 1917). Chaplain to the Forces (4th Class).

Van Fleet, E. H. (Oct. 10, 1917). Cpl. Co. C. 308th U.S. Field Signal Bn. Died on Jan. 17, 1918, of illness on Transport *Mercury* while on active service.

1902 Varley, G. H., B.M. (Aug. 13, 1914). Capt. R.A.M.C.

1906 Varley, J. E. R. Berkshire Regt.

1899 Vasey, G. H., B.A. (Dec. 29, 1914). Capt. 2nd Dorsetshire Regt. Capt. No. 1 Combined British Inf. Depot (Maj.). India.

1902 Vasey, P. W. (Mobilized Aug. 1914). Capt. 3rd Dorsetshire Regt., empld. Ministry of National Service.

1894 **Vernède, R. E.,** B.A. (1914). ‡2nd Lt. Rifle Brigade. France, 1915–17. Died on Apr. 9, 1917, of wounds received in action.

1916 Vidacovitch, A., B.A. (Sept. 1915). Pte. Serbian Militia. Serbia.

1889 Viener, Rev. H. D. L., M.A. (Serving Aug. 4, 1916). Chaplain R.N. Chaplain-in-Chief, attd. R.A.F. Channel, Mediterranean, Dardanelles, 1915. *C.B.E.* (Mil.).

1908 Vince,* W. B., B.A. (Aug. 19, 1914). Maj. 8th London Regt. (Post Office Rifles). France. *D.S.O.*, Feb. 18, 1918. *M.C.*, Jan. 1, 1917. *D.* France, 1916, 1918.

1912 Vincent,* J. D., M.A. (Oct. 17, 1914). Lt. 11th Devonshire Regt. Lt. General List. France, 1916–18. *M.C.*, Nov. 25, 1916 ; *Bar*, Oct. 18, 1917.

1909 Vipan,* G., B.A. (Nov. 27, 1914). 2nd Lt. 6th Queen's (R. W. Surrey Regt.). Lt. R.E. France. *M.C.*, June 3, 1918.

1919 Vise, E. C. (July 24, 1915). Capt. 3/4th R. W. Kent Regt. France, 1917–19.

1919 Vivian, P. (Feb. 19, 1917). Gnr. Australian F.A. France, 1918.

1907 Vowles, G. R., M.A. Home Guard, Fargo. N. Dakota.

1910 Wagner,* A. W. S., B.A. (Aug. 22, 1914). Lt. 8th Shropshire L.I. (Capt.). Lt. R.A.F. Egypt, Aegean Sea, Macedonia. (Invalided out of Army, June 1918. Re-commissioned R.A.F., Oct. 1918.)

1910 Wakefield,* H. E. K., M.A. (Sept. 13, 1914). ‡Capt. R.E., attd. Signal Coy. G.H.Q. France, 1915 ; Salonika and Black Sea, 1915–19. *M.C.*, June 3, 1918. *D.* Salonika, 1918 twice.

1908 **Wakeman, E. O. R.,** B.A. (Jan. 4, 1915). 2nd Lt. Grenadier Guards (S.R.), attd. 1st Bn. France. *D.* France, 1915. Killed in action on May 16, 1915.

1919 Waker, W. J. (Mar. 3, 1916). Rfln. 18th London Regt. (London Irish). France, 1917–19.

Walker, A. J. (Oct. 8, 1914). Capt. 11th W. Yorkshire Regt., attd. 6th Manchester Regt. Gallipoli. Killed in action on Aug. 7, 1915.

1919 Walker, R. H. (May 2, 1918). 2nd Lt. 18th Sqdn. R.A.F. France and Germany.

1881 Walker, W. G., M.A., **V.C.** (Serving Aug. 4, 1914). Maj-Gen. Indian Army, (Maj.-Gen. 2nd Div. B.E.F.). France, 1914–17. *C.B.* *D.* France, 1915, 1916.

1910 **Wallis,* A. B.,** B.A. (Oct. 6, 1914). Lt. 6th Sherwood Foresters. France. Killed in action on Mar. 21, 1918.

1901 **Walter, C.** (Mar. 1915). Lt. 9th Devonshire Regt. (Capt.). France and Belgium. Killed in action near Polygon Wood on Oct. 8, 1917.

1919 Warr, J. C. (Apr. 5, 1917). 2nd Lt. R.F.A. France, 1918–19.

1899 **Watson, G. L.** (Oct. 13, 1914). Capt. 3rd, attd. 1st, E. Surrey Regt. France and Belgium. Killed in action near Ypres on Apr. 21, 1915.

1919 Watson, H. St. J. B. (Feb. 28, 1917). 2nd Lt. 5th N. Staffordshire Regt. France, 1917–18. *M.C.*, May 13, 1918. (Prisoner of war, Mar. to Dec. 1918.)

1912 Watt, W. E., B.A. (July 28, 1915). 2nd Lt. King Edward's Horse. Lt. Flight Officer R.A.F. France and Belgium. *A.F.C.*, June 3, 1919.

1911 **Wayman,* W. A.** (Sept. 1914). Capt. 1/4th Oxf. & Bucks. Lt. Infty. France, 1914–16. Missing, believed killed in action at Pozières on Aug. 14, 1916.

1919 Webb, F. A. (Sept. 1914). ‡2nd Lt. Essex Regt. (Invalided, Jan. 1917.) Rejoined in 1918 as 2nd Lt. Gloucestershire Regt. Belgium and France.

1919 Wells, A. Q. (Nov. 1915). Surgeon Sub-Lt. R.N.V.R. H.M.S. *Plassy*, H.M.S. *Ulysses*, North Sea.

1919 Wells, C. J. L. (Mar. 3, 1915). Capt. 231st Field Ambulance, R.A.M.C. Egypt, Palestine.

1905 Wemyss, A. B. (Oct. 3, 1914). Capt. 2/4th Dorsetshire Regt. Capt. I.A.R.O., attd. No. 2 Combined British Inf. Depot. India.

1901 **West, F. C. B.**, B.A. (Mobilized Aug. 4, 1914). Lt.-Col. 243rd Bde., R.F.A. (T.F.). (Group Commdr. 48th Div. Artillery.) France, 1915–16. *D.* France, 1915, 1916. Killed in action near Pozières on Sept. 28, 1916.

1917 Whitlock,* T. G. (Mar. 2, 1918). 2nd Lt. R.M.A.

1902 Whytehead, Rev. R. L., M.A. (Sept. 25, 1915). Chaplain to the Forces (4th Class), attd. 3/5th Sherwood Foresters. France, 1916–19.

1897 Wigan, W. C., B.A. (Feb. 1917). Capt. Nyasaland Field Force. Nyasaland, E. Africa. *D.* E. Africa.

1917 Wilcox, H. N. (May, 1918). Cpl. Signal Corps, U.S. Army.

1896 Wilder, G. (Sept. 15, 1915). Lt. R.N.V.R.

1914 Wilkes, S. H. (Oct. 8, 1915). Lt. 1/8th Worcestershire Regt. (Capt.). Belgium and France, 1916–17; Italy, 1918. *M.C.*, June. 4, 1917; *Bar*, Sept. 26, 1917; *2nd Bar*, Dec. 2, 1918.

1907 **Williams, J. W.**, B.A. (Jan. 1915). Lt. Canadian Grenadier Guards. Belgium and France. Killed in action in the Battle of the Somme on Nov. 18, 1916.

1919 Williams, L. C. (July 29, 1918). Pte. R.A.F.

1912 **Williams, O. M.** (Aug. 1914). ‡2nd Lt. 16th Welsh Regt. (Capt.). France. Missing, presumed killed in action at La Bassée on Apr. 9, 1916.

1912 Willmore,* E. G., M.A. (Apr. 10, 1915). Lt. 90th Siege Batt., R.G.A. France. *M.C.*, June 4, 1917. (Placed on retired list owing to wounds, Apr. 1918.)

1919 Wilson, A. M. P. (Jan. 6, 1916). Lt. 31st Batt., R.F.A. France and Belgium, 1916–17; Italy, 1917–18.

1903 Wilson, E. A. R. (Mar. 25, 1915). 2nd Lt. 13th London Regt.

1903 Wilson, E. W., B.A. (Mar. 6, 1915). Lt. 16th London Regt. (Queen's Westminster Rifles).

1919 Woodcock, T. A. (Oct. 4, 1916). Lt. 3rd W. Riding Regt. France.

1911 Wooddy, C. H., B.A. (1918). Pte. and Sergt., Psychological Div. Medical Dept., U.S. Army.

1909 Woodford,* C. E. M. (Feb. 11, 1915). Lt. 14th Sherwood Foresters.

1914 **Woods, E. J.** (Apr. 10, 1915). Lt. 17th W. Yorkshire Regt. France and Belgium, 1916, 1917. Killed in action near Passchendaele on Oct. 9, 1917.

1908 [Woodward, E. Ll., M.A.] (Oct. 1914). Lt. R.F.A. Lt. Special Lists, Staff Lt. (2nd Class), empld. Foreign Office. France, 1915–16; Salonika, 1916–18.

1886 Worrall, A. H., M.A. (Mobilized July 13, 1915). Capt. 5th Lincolnshire Regt. (T.F.). France. T.D.

1907 **Worster,* F. C.,** B.A. (Oct. 21, 1915). Lt. 1st Worcestershire Regt. (Capt.). Belgium and France. *M.C.*, Sept. 24, 1918. Died on May 30, 1918, of wounds received in action near Soissons.

1919 Wright, R. F. (Dec. 8, 1916). Cadet R.A.F. Russia.

1913 **Wright,* V. A. B.** (Oct. 1914). ‡2nd Lt. 12th Essex Regt. Gallipoli. Killed in action in Gallipoli on Dec. 3, 1915.

1910 Yates, A. Gnr. Canadian F.A.

1900 Young, Rev. R. E., B.A. (Aug. 18, 1915). Chaplain to the Forces (4th Class). Chaplain (3rd Class) (attd. 4th Cavalry Div.) Gallipoli, 1915; Mesopotamia, Egypt, and Macedonia, 1916; Palestine and Syria, 1917–19. *D.* Mesopotamia, 1916.

JESUS COLLEGE

1912 Acheson,* G. J., M.A. (Sept. 1, 1914). ‡Capt. 21st W. Yorkshire Regt. Gallipoli, Egypt, France. (Wounded and prisoner of war, Sept. 1, 1918.)

1899 **Alderson, Rev. A. G. J.,** M.A. (Sept. 1915). Lt. 2/5th D.C.L.I. (Capt.). Lt. M.G.C. Accidentally killed on Oct. 19, 1916.

Allan, F. C. (Sept. 1915). 2nd Lt. 13th Durham L.I. France. Died on Sept 29, 1916, of wounds received in action at Martinpuich.

1906 **Andrew, M.,** M.A. (1914). 2nd Lt. 20th Lancashire Fusiliers. France. Killed in action on Nov. 4, 1918.

1920 Arch, T. W. (May 8, 1916). ‡Lt. M.G.C. France, 1917–18.

1903 Armstrong, C. W., B.A. (Feb. 1, 1917). Capt. R.A.M.C. Mesopotamia. *D.* Mesopotamia, 1918.

1911 **Armstrong,* H. W. T.** (Aug. 22, 1914). 2nd Lt. 7th E. Surrey Regt. France. Killed in action in France on July 14, 1915.

1911 Arnold,* H., M.A. (Aug. 15, 1914). Capt. 5th Worcestershire Regt., attd. Gold Coast Regt. Gallipoli, 1915; E. Africa, 1915–18; W. Africa, 1919. *D.* E. Africa, 1918.

1906 Atkin, R., M.A. (Dec. 3, 1915). Lt. 5th Gordon Highlanders. Lt. R.E. France and Italy. *D.* France, 1917.

1908 Attenborough, C. R., M.A. (Mar. 1917). Paymaster Sub-Lt. R.N.V.R. (Decoding Officer). H.M.S. *Hilary*, H.M.S. *Virginian*, H.M.S. *Victorian*, H.M.S. *City of London*.

1914 Attwater, H. F. (Dec. 22, 1914). Lt. 15th Northumberland Fusiliers, attd. 153rd Squadron R.A.F. Gallipoli, 1915; Egypt, 1916; France, 1916–17.

1907 Ault, W. O., M.A .(Mar. 1918). ‡2nd Lt. F.A. Reserve Corps, U.S. Army.

1908 Backhouse,* Rev. A. G., B.A. (Oct. 27, 1916). Chaplain to the Forces (4th Class).

1907 Bacon,* G. H., B.A. (Jan. 25, 1915). Lt. 3rd W. Yorkshire Regt. France, 1915, 1916. (Invalided on account of wounds.)

1913 Baker, J. N. L. (Dec. 22, 1914). 2nd Lt. 16th King's (Liverpool Regt.). Lt. 119th Infantry, Indian Army.

1899 **Baker, S. H.,** M.A. (Jan. 27, 1915). Maj. 14th Gloucestershire Regt. Belgium, France, Macedonia. Killed in action at Failouiel, near La Fère, on Mar. 23, 1918.

Bamkin, H. C. (Aug. 12, 1914). 2nd Lt. 7th Suffolk Regt. France, Belgium. Killed in action at Ploegsteert on July 19, 1915.

1912 Bangham,* D. H., M.A. (Oct. 10, 1914). Capt. 3rd King's (Liverpool Regt.). France. *M.C.*, Aug. 16, 1917.

1913 Barratt, A. J. (June 1917). ‡2nd Lt. 32nd Middlesex Regt.

1888 Barron, A. H., M.A. (Sept. 1914). Maj. R.A.S.C. France. *D.* France, 1917.

1901 Beards, C., B.M., M.A. (July 2, 1917). Lt. R.A.M.C.

1910 **Beddow,* J. F. H.,** B.Litt. (Mobilized Aug. 4, 1914). Capt. 3rd, attd. 4th, Essex Regt. France. Killed in action on Nov. 3, 1917.

Beddy, K. C. (1915). 2nd Lt. 3rd Hampshire Regt. Lt. R.A.F. Egypt, Palestine. Killed in flying accident at Amesbury on Feb. 6, 1918.

1913 Bell, H. C., M.A. (Dec. 2, 1914). Lt. 7th R. Dublin Fusiliers. Gallipoli, 1915; Serbia, 1915; Salonika, 1915–17.

1917 Benjamin, H. D., B.A. (Oct. 2, 1917). ‡2nd Lt. 5th Loyal N. Lancashire Regt. France.

1884 Benoy, Rev. J., B.D. (Serving Aug. 4, 1914). Chaplain to the Forces (1st Class). Asst. Chaplain General. *D.* § Feb. 1917.

1919 Benson, K. L. (June 28, 1918). Cadet R.A.F.

1919 Beynon, A. C. (Sept. 17, 1915). 2nd Lt. 14th Cheshire Regt. Lt. 3/153rd Rifles, Indian Army. Waziristan, Palestine, Egypt.

1919 Beynon, I. Ll. (Jan. 29, 1917). Pte. 11th W. Yorkshire Regt. France, 1917; Italy, 1917–19.

1913 Bolt, C. A. (Sept. 28, 1914). Signaller 18th Squadron M.G.C. (Cavalry). Egypt, Palestine, Syria.

1910 Bosustow, G. W., M.A. (Jan. 11, 1915). Capt. 7th Durham L.I. France.

1920 Bowen, H. R. (Aug. 31, 1914). ‡Lt. 6th York and Lancaster Regt. France and Belgium, 1915–18.

1919 Bowen, T. B. (Feb. 11, 1916). A.B., H.M.S. *Vivid* (attd. N. Russian E.F.). N. Russia.

1911 **Bradfield,* W. L.,** B.A. (Sept. 3, 1914). Pte. 15th W. Yorkshire Regt. France. Killed in action near Couin on Dec. 5, 1916.

1919 Brain, H. A. (Nov. 29, 1917). Pte. 3rd E. Surrey Regt.

1908 Brett, E. N. J., M.A. Pte. R.A.M.C. Died, 1919.

1913 Brierley, A. H. M., M.A. (Apr. 1918). Pte. R. Fusiliers, attd. Intelligence Dept. Italy.

1887 Briscoe, T. F. H., M.A., T.D. (Mobilized Aug. 4, 1914). Maj. and Q.M. 2nd Eastern General Hospital, R.A.M.C.

1890 Brown, Rev. H. H., M.A. (Jan. 24, 1918). Chaplain to the Forces (4th Class).

1913 Bryant, F. S., B.A. (Aug. 1917). Lt. 347th F.A., U.S. Army. France, 1918.

1913 Buchanan,* A. (Nov. 27, 1914). Capt. 4th S. Wales Borderers. Gallipoli, 1915; Mesopotamia, 1916. *M.C.*, June 3, 1916. Order of St. Vladimir, (4th Class) (with Swords.) *D.* Gallipoli, 1916; Mesopotamia, 1916. **V.C.** won at Falaniyah Lines, Mesopotamia, on Apr. 5, 1916.

For most conspicuous bravery. During an attack an officer was lying out in the open severely wounded about 150 yards from cover. Two men went to his assistance and one of them was hit at once. Captain Buchanan, on seeing this, immediately went out and, with the help of the other man, carried the wounded officer to cover under heavy machine gun fire. He then returned and brought in the wounded man, again under heavy fire.

1907 **Bull, B. A.,** B.A. (Aug. 1914). Capt. R.A.M.C., attd. London Regt. France and Belgium. Killed in action at Boesinghe on Sept. 16, 1917.

1900 **Butler, C. H.,** M.A. (Oct. 21, 1914). ‡Lt. 5th, attd. 6th, The Black Watch. France. Killed in action at Arras on Apr. 23, 1917.

1913 Butler,* T. W. (Dec. 1915). ‡2nd Lt. M.G.C. France, 1916–17; 1918–19.

1913 **Champion, R. J.** (Oct. 1914). ‡Lt. Scots Guards (attd. T.M.B.) France and Belgium, 1915, 1916, 1917. Killed in action at Ypres on July 18, 1917.

1910 Clark,* F. L., B.A. (Apr. 1915). ‡Lt. 8th Border Regt. France and Belgium.
1904 Clarke, H. E., M.A. (Jan. 7, 1915). Lt. R.A.M.C.
1914 Clearihue,* J. B., B.C.L., M.A. (Sept. 11, 1916). Lt. Canadian Field Artillery. France. *M.C.*, Apr. 2, 1919.
1919 Cleverley, H. N. (Aug. 8, 1914). ‡Lt. 3rd Gloucestershire Regt. (Capt.). S.W. Africa, 1914–16; France, 1916–17, 1918; Egypt and Palestine, 1917–18.
1910 Cochrane, Rev. R. A. (Oct. 14, 1918). Chaplain to the Forces (4th Class).
1901 Cole, F. J., D.Sc. (Oct. 1916). Lt. 4th Essex Regt.
1917 Colegrove, R. (Sept. 27, 1917). 2nd Lt. 11th Tank Corps. France, 1918–19.
1911 Collier,* L. J., B.A. (Sept. 1914). Lt. R.A.F. Salonika, Egypt. *D.F.C.*, Jan. 1, 1918. *D.* Salonika, 1918.
1920 Constable, F. J. (Mar. 20, 1917). Pioneer, 'P' Special Coy., Special Bde. R.E. France.
1919 Cooke, A. M. (Nov. 18, 1917). Flight Cadet, 70th Squadron, R.A.F.
1919 Cooper, J. F. (Jan. 30, 1917). ‡2nd Lt. 10th London Regt. France, 1918.
1899 Cooper, J. H., B.A. (Jan. 1916). Capt. 23rd Middlesex Regt. France and Belgium. *D.* France, 1917.
1911 **Cooper,* L. G.** (Aug. 1914). 2nd Lt. 4th S. Wales Borderers. Gallipoli. Killed in action in Gallipoli on Aug. 9, 1915.
1919 Cooper, S. (Sept. 15, 1916). Wireless Operator, R.N.V.R. H.M. Minesweeper, *Darvel Stroud*; France.
1907 Corbin, J. E. B., M.A. (Aug. 6, 1914). ‡2nd Lt. R.G.A. (Invalided on account of ill health, Sept. 1918.)
1893 Costley-White, E., B.A. (Sept. 1916). Capt. Special Lists, empld. Nyasaland Field Force. Africa. *O.B.E.*
1908 Craig, J. D., B.A. (Aug. 9, 1915). Capt. R.F.A., attd. H.Q. 320th Inf. Bde. France.
1913 Crease, L. G., M.A. (Nov. 1915). Pte. 1st (Garr.) Bn. Worcestershire Regt.
1905 Crockett,* H. L., M.A. (Feb. 1915). Lt., Acting Capt., R. Welch Fusiliers, attd. O.C.B. France, 1915–16; Egypt, 1918–19. *D.* Egypt, 1919.
1911 **Crofts,* G. R. M.** (Sept. 1914). Lt. 2nd Welsh Regt. France, 1915. Killed in action south of Rue du Bois on May 9, 1915.
1919 Cross, E. G. (Aug. 7, 1917). Pioneer R.E. France and Belgium, 1918–19.
1908 Cruce, Rev. F. G. L., M.A. (Aug. 8, 1914). Chaplain R.N. W. Indies and Mediterranean.
1904 Cunningham, C. E., B.A. (July 1915). Capt. Cheshire Regt. France, 1916–18.
1905 Dainton, A. H., M.A. (Oct. 31, 1914). Lt. Unattached List, T.F., Durham University O.T.C.
1905 Dale, J. A., B.A. (Mobilized Aug. 4, 1914). Capt. 8th London Regt. (Post Office Rifles). Asst. Principal Surveyor-General of Supply Dept.
1912 David, T. N. T., B.A. (Sept. 10, 1914). ‡Lt. 1st Welsh Regt. (Capt.). Egypt, Salonika.
1919 Davies, A. M. (Apr. 1, 1918). ‡Midshipman, R.N.V.R. 2nd Lt. R.A.F. (Meteorological Branch).
1902 Davies, A. W., M.A. (May 5, 1915). Lt. 438th (Cheshire) Field Coy., R.E. France and Belgium.

1905 Davies,* D., B.A. (Serving Aug. 4, 1914). Capt. Unattached List, T.F., Merchant Taylors' School O.T.C., afterwards Lt. 1/13th London Regt. (Capt.). France. *M.C.*, June 3, 1918.

1908 **Davies,* D. C. P.** (Oct. 29, 1914). Capt. 9th S. Wales Borderers. Gallipoli, Egypt, France. Killed in action in France, May 1916.

1920 Davies, E. (Mar. 12, 1915). Capt. 14th Welsh Regt. France, from 1915. *M.C.*, Jan. 1, 1917.

1898 Davies, Rev. E. T., M.A. Chaplain, Welsh Regt. (Resigned.) Died.

1912 Davies, G. C., M.A. (Oct. 5, 1914). ‡2nd Lt. 6th R. Welch Fusiliers. Capt. I.A.R.O., attd. 16th Rajputs. Gallipoli, 1915; Egypt and Palestine, 1918; India, 1918–19. *M.C.*, Feb. 18, 1918.

1905 Davies, Rev. J. Alban (Sept. 4, 1915). Chaplain to the Forces (4th Class), attd. R.F.A.

1909 Davies, J. Allan, M.A. (Dec. 29, 1915). Lt. 7th R. Welch Fusiliers.

1915 Davies, J. T. D., B.A. (Nov. 15, 1916). Pte. 2/2nd Monmouthshire Regt.

1910 Davies,* Rev. J. Rhys, M.A. (Mar. 15, 1917). Chaplain to the Forces (4th Class), attd. R.G.A. Mesopotamia, Palestine.

1919 Davies, L. J. (Feb. 1917). Pte. R. Dublin Fusiliers. France.

1906 Davies,* P. V., M.A. (Aug. 28, 1914). Capt. 6th Lancashire Fusiliers (Staff-Captain, Gen. Staff). Egypt, 1914–15; Gallipoli, 1915; France, 1916–17, 1918–19.

1912 Davies, W. V., B.A. (Dec. 1915). Cpl. R.E. (Meteorological Section). France, 1916–18; Germany, 1918–19.

1912 Davis, D., B.A. (Sept. 18, 1914). Lt. 1/7th Hampshire Regt. India, 1914–18; Aden, 1918–19.

1914 Davis, J. L., B.A. (Feb. 1916). ‡Lt. R.G.A. France and Belgium.

1913 **Davis,* W. A. J.** (Aug. 15, 1914). 2nd Lt. 1st E. Surrey Regt. Belgium. Killed in action near Ypres on Apr. 21, 1915.

1915 **Dawes, S. F.** (Mar. 1, 1916). 2nd Lt. 236th Siege Batt., R.G.A. Belgium and France. Killed in action near Bohain on Oct. 8, 1918.

1906 Dawson, Rev. T. S., M.A. (Oct. 1, 1918). Chaplain to the Forces (4th Class).

1914 **Deakin, R. H.** (Nov. 1914). 2nd Lt. 10th Jats, Indian Army, attd. R.A.F. (Adjt.). India, 1915–16; France, 1916–17. Killed in action on July 22, 1917.

1906 **de la Bere,* Rev. C. E.,** M.A. (Sept. 1914). ‡Capt. and Adjt. R.G.A. France. Killed in action on Sept. 10, 1918.

1915 Denis, A. G. (Aug. 5, 1914). Pte., Belgian Army (Génie Prospecteur). Belgium and France.

1902 Denny, E. M. C., B.A. (Aug. 6, 1914). ‡Capt. 7th D.C.L.I. France, 1916, 1917, 1918. *M.C.*, Nov. 15, 1916; *Bar*, Jan. 9, 1918. *D.* France, 1917.

1911 Denny, M. C. M., B.A. (Sept. 1914). ‡Capt. 11th King's (Liverpool Regt.). France, Belgium. *D.* France, 1917. (Invalided, May, 1919.)

1907 Dodd, P. W., M.A. (Aug. 21, 1914). Capt. 2/6th W. Yorkshire Regt. France.

1894 Donaldson, C. L. (Oct. 1917). Sergt. R.G.A., attd. as Sergt. Instructor to 51st (Grad.) Bn. Manchester Regt.

1912 Dugdale, J. A. (Aug. 1914). ‡2nd Lt. Norfolk Regt. Capt. R.E. Mesopotamia, 1915–16, 1916–17, 1918–19; India, 1916, 1918. *D.* Mesopotamia, 1917. Died on Oct. 22, 1919.

1914 **Ebery, W.** (Mar. 1915). 2nd Lt. 10th Sherwood Foresters. France and Belgium. Killed in action at St. Eloi on Feb. 14, 1916.
1901 Edwards, A. C. W., B.A. (Nov. 9, 1914). Capt. 9th Welsh Regt. France. *D.* Mar. 1919.
1919 Edwards, D. V. (Oct. 1, 1917). Pte. 7th R. W. Kent Regt. France.
1913 Edwards, E. A., M.A. (Aug. 1914). Lt. 1st Monmouthshire Regt. France, 1915.
1909 Edwards, J. G., M.A. (Nov. 1914). ‡Capt. and Adjt. 1/4th R. Welch Fusiliers. France, 1918–19.
1911 **Edwards,* J. T.** (Sept. 1914). ‡2nd Lt. 3rd King's (Liverpool Regt.). France. Killed in action at Neuve Chapelle on Sept. 13, 1915.
1914 Edwards, W. G. T. (Nov. 23, 1914). Capt. 5th S. Wales Borderers, attd. Labour Corps (11th H.Q.). France. *M.C.*, July 27, 1916.
1908 **Ellerton, C. F.,** M.A. (Dec. 16, 1914). Capt. 10th Cheshire Regt. France. Killed in action at Vimy Ridge on May 19, 1916.
1910 Elliot, W. G. H. H.A.C.
1901 Elliott, V. A., M.A. (Serving Aug. 4, 1914). 2nd Lt. Unattached List, T.F., Mill Hill School O.T.C.
1917 Ellis, C. D. B. (Jan. 19, 1915). Lt. Leicestershire R.H.A. France. *M.C.*, July 27, 1917. *D.* France, 1917.
1908 **Ellis, H. L. M.,** M.A. (Oct. 1914). ‡2nd Lt. 1st R. Welch Fusiliers. (Capt. 10th Manchester Regt.) France. Died on May 5, 1917, of wounds received in action at Bullecourt.
1919 Evans, D. C. R. J. (Jan. 25, 1918). 2nd Lt. R.G.A.
1920 Evans, D. L. (July 26, 1915). Lt., 11th, afterwards 3rd, W. Riding Regt. France. *D.* France, 1917.
1912 Evans, D. M., M.A. (Oct. 1915). ‡Lt. 4–5th Welsh Regt. Egypt, Palestine, Syria.
1908 Evans, Rev. E. G. M., M.A. (Aug. 23, 1916). Chaplain to the Forces (4th Class).
1900 Evans, E. O., M.A. (June 21, 1915). Pte. R.A.M.C., 2/2nd S.M.F. Ambulance, attd. H.Q. 61st Div. France.
1894 Evans, F. Taynton, B.A. (Jan. 1915). ‡Lt. 1st Monmouthshire Regt. (T.F.) (Capt.). France, 1915, 1917–19.
1896 Evans, Gomer. ‡Lt. Welsh Regt. France.
1910 Evans, H. Ll., M.A. (1917). Lt. R.G.A.
1916 Evans, H. R. (Oct. 1916). Lt. 3rd Welsh Regt. (Capt.). France and Belgium. *M.C.*, Dec. 2, 1918.
1893 Evans,* H. T., D.M. (Sept. 1916). Lt. R.A.M.C. France.
1914 Evans, I. G., B.A. (July 15, 1915). ‡Lt. 9th Yorkshire Regt. France, 1915–16, 1917.
1919 Evans, J. R. (July 9, 1918). Pte. 4th R. Welch Fusiliers (Lce.-Cpl.).
1899 Fenn, R. P., B.A. (Sept. 1, 1916). ‡Lt., Acting Capt. and Adjt., 9th, attd. 2/4th, Hampshire Regt. Palestine, 1917–18; France and Germany, 1918–19. *M.C.*, Nov. 4, 1918.
1909 Ferguson,* J. G. W., M.A. (Aug. 4, 1916). ‡Lt. Tank Corps. E. Africa, 1915; France, 1917–18.
1912 Field, F. W., B.A. (Aug. 14, 1915). 2nd Lt. 14th W. Yorkshire Regt. Lt. R.A.F. France, 1916–17.
1903 Fielden, T. P. (Nov. 20, 1915). Lt. R.F.A. (S.R.).

1897 Fisher, Rev. B. H., M.A. (Nov. 3, 1914). Lt. Unattached List, T.F., Dover College O.T.C.

1908 Fox,* G. A. (Aug. 20, 1915). Paymaster Sub-Lt. R.N.R. H.M.S. *Liverpool*, 1915; H.M.S. *Gibraltar*, 1915–17.

1919 Francis, D. G. (Dec. 5, 1915). Staff-Sergt. Instructor 17th R. Welch Fusiliers. France.

1920 Franks, A. W. (July 11, 1918). Pte. 1st Dorsetshire Regt.

1919 Fraser, K. (Feb. 12, 1917). ‡Lt. 144th Sqdn. R.A.F. Palestine, 1918; Salonika, 1918; Egypt, 1918.

1893 Gane, P. C., M.A. (May 8, 1917). 2nd Lt. R.F.A. India.

1884 Garstang, W., M.A., D.Sc. (Nov. 23, 1916). ‡2nd Lt. 5th Vol. Bn. W. Yorkshire Regt.

1910 George, F. J., M.A. (Jan. 19, 1916). 1st Class Aircraftsman R.A.F. France, Italy, Belgium. *D.*

1911 George, H. J., M.A. (Sept. 1914). ‡Lt. 8th R. Welch Fusiliers (Maj.) (attd. Ministry of Munitions Explos. Dept.). Gallipoli, 1915; Egypt, 1916; Mesopotamia, 1916; India, 1916–17.

1910 **Gibbs, I. R.,** B.A. (Sept. 19, 1914). Capt. 10th Gloucestershire Regt. France. Killed in action in the Battle of Loos on Sept. 25, 1915.

1919 Gibson, F. A. (Aug. 29, 1916). Lt. 1st R. Guernsey L.I. France.

1910 Gilleland,* G., M.A. (Apr. 4, 1916). Gnr. R.G.A. (Sergt.-Maj.). Salonika.

1919 Goddard, G. R. (May 1, 1918). 2nd Lt. R.F.A. Died on Oct. 26, 1919.

1919 Goehring, R. R. (1917). U.S. Army.

1915 Gordon-Smith, A. G. C. (Jan. 5, 1916). ‡Lt. 4th S. Staffordshire Regt. Lt. M.G.C. France.

1912 Gough, T. J., B.A. (May 1915). Capt. and Adjt. 5th K.O. Scottish Borderers (Maj.) (Staff-Captain). France and Belgium, Germany. *M.C.*, Sept. 16, 1918.

1907 Gowan,* C. H. (Nov. 7, 1914). Lt. 13th Hussars (Capt. and Adjt.). Mesopotamia. *D.* Mesopotamia, 1918.

1915 Gracie, A. L. (1914). Lt. 5th K.R.R.C. France. *M.C.*, Sept. 17, 1917.

1910 Grant, A. E., M.A. (Dec. 1, 1914). ‡Capt. Welsh Regt. France.

1910 Gregory, E. K., M.A. (Sept. 26, 1916). Sergt. R.A.V.C. France.

1914 **Griffin, S. J.** (Apr. 23, 1915). Capt. 3rd, attd. 1st, Oxf. & Bucks. Lt. Infty. Mesopotamia. Died on Mar. 26, 1918, of wounds received in action at Khan Baghdadi.

1903 Griffiths, Rev. J. A. S., M.A. (Feb. 1, 1916). Chaplain to the Forces (4th Class). France, 1916–17.

1900 Griffiths, O. D., M.A. (May 3, 1915). Lt., Acting Capt., 290th Siege Batt., R.G.A. (Maj.). Egypt, France.

1899 Gruffydd, W. J., M.A. (Nov. 21, 1915). Lt. R.N.V.R. North Sea, 1915; Suez Canal, 1916–17.

1909 [Guillaume, A., M.A.] (Sept. 21, 1914). ‡Lt. Lancashire Fusiliers. Capt. Special Lists, Arab Bureau, Cairo. France and Egypt. *D.* Egypt, 1919.

1915 Gwilliam, C. E. (June 18, 1916). Lt. Seaplane Pilot, R.A.F. Dunkirk.

1907 Hall,* Rev. E. F., M.A. (Serving Aug. 4, 1914). Lt. Unattached List, T.F., Exeter School O.T.C.

1919 Hall, S. (June 29, 1918). 3rd Air Mechanic, Wireless School, R.A.F.

1919 Hallam, H. J. B. (Dec. 9, 1915). ‡Lt. 4th Welsh Regt. France, 1917–18.

1912 Hambly, W. D., B.Sc. (Nov. 5, 1914). ‡Lt. R.N.V.R. Gallipoli, France.

1906 **Hanby, F. J.,** B.A. (Dec. 23, 1915). 2nd Lt. R. Sussex Regt. France. Killed in action near Richebourg on June 30, 1916.

1919 Handley, G. (June 5, 1917). ‡Lt. 29th Bn. M.G.C. Belgium, France, Germany.

1913 Hankinson, W. C. (Sept. 14, 1914). ‡Capt. 14th York and Lancaster Regt. Egypt, 1915–16; France, 1916, 1917, 1918. *M.C.*, Nov. 28, 1918.

1919 Harcombe, S. (Nov. 3, 1915). ‡Lt. R.E.

1909 Hardie,* H. R., B.A. (Jan. 19, 1912). 2nd Lt. 1st R. Welch Fusiliers.

1896 Harding, H. H., B.A. (Mar. 1916). ‡Lt. 5th Gordon Highlanders. Capt. Special Lists. Maj. D.A.A.G. France and Germany.

1919 Harris, C. G. (July 29, 1916). Cadet No. 5 Wing R.A.F. (Cadet BE). France.

1919 Harris, S. (May 10, 1918). Pte. 39th R. Fusiliers. Egypt and Palestine.

1919 Hart, W. J. (Mar. 11, 1918). Telegraphist R.N.V.R. Baltic Sea, 1918–19.

1919 Harvey, A. (Nov. 9, 1917). ‡2nd Lt. N. Staffordshire Regt. Belgium and France.

1919 Harwin, S. (Aug. 10, 1917). Pte. 28th London Regt. (Artists' Rifles). France. Accidentally killed on June 6, 1920.

1919 Havard, Rev. W. T. (Aug. 1915). Chaplain to the Forces (3rd Class), attd. Guards Brigade. France and Belgium. *M.C.*, Jan. 1, 1918. *D.* France, 1916.

1919 Hayward, S. P. (July 15, 1915). Lt. 7th W. Riding Regt. (Capt.). France. *M.C.*, Feb. 4, 1918.

1907 **Hazard,* C. P.,** B.A. (Mar. 13, 1915). 2nd Lt. 3rd Shropshire L.I. France, 1915; Belgium, 1916. Killed in action on Ypres–Langemarck Road, Apr. 21–22, 1916.

1916 Heaton, W. R. (May 23, 1917). ‡Lt. R.A.F. (Pilot). France, 1918.

1906 **Hemming,* F. W.,** B.A. (Aug. 1914). Capt. 1/8th Worcestershire Regt. Belgium and France. Killed in action at Guillemont Farm, near Péronne, on Apr. 24, 1917.

1883 Hemsley, W. J., M.A. (Apr. 14, 1915). ‡Maj. R.A.S.C. Salonika, 1917–18.

1919 Heppenstall, L. D. (Mar. 30, 1917). 2nd Lt. 3rd Devonshire Regt. France, 1918–19.

Herbert, R. S. (July 1915). Lt. 2/11th London Regt. (Finsbury Rifles). France, 1917. Killed in action at Bullecourt on May 21, 1917.

1911 Herbertson, J. J. W. (Sept. 25, 1915). Capt. Special Lists. G.S.O. 3. France. *O.B.E.* (Mil.). *D.* France, 1916, 1917, 1918.

1919 Herring, H. H. (Jan. 22, 1918). Cadet (Gnr.) R.G.A. 2nd Lt. (on demobilization).

1905 Hide, Rev. S., M.A. (Jan. 28, 1917). Chaplain to the Forces (4th Class).

1906 Higgs, H. V., B.A. (Sept. 4, 1914). Pte. 18th R. Fusiliers. (Discharged medically unfit through an accident, Mar. 3, 1915.)

1911 Hill, Rev. A. F. J., M.A. (Jan. 1, 1918). Chaplain to the Forces (4th Class). Salonika, 1918; Black Sea, 1919.

1908 Hill,* J. J. S. (Sept. 18, 1916). Capt. Special Lists (Dental Surgeon).

1911 **Hiscock,* E. H.** (Aug. 20, 1914). Capt. 9th Worcestershire Regt. Gallipoli, Egypt, Mesopotamia. Killed in action in Mesopotamia on Jan. 25, 1917.

1902 Hocart, A. M., M.A. (Sept. 6, 1914). Capt. General List. Staff Lt. France. *D.* France, 1917.

1904 (Hodgkinson, J., M.A.) (Mobilized Aug. 4, 1914). Capt. 5th N. Staffordshire Regt. Temp. Maj. Tank Corps. France, 1917, 1918–19.

1911 Hoey,* J. T. S., B.A. (Aug. 1914). ‡Lt. 7th Oxf. & Bucks. Lt. Infty. France, 1915; Salonika, 1915–16. Croix de Guerre. *D.* French Dispatches, 1916.

1911 Hoffert, W. H., M.A. (Aug. 25, 1914). Lt. 11th Manchester Regt., afterwards Capt. R.A.F. Gallipoli, 1915; Paris, 1918.

1919 Hollis, A. W. (May 10, 1916). Gnr. 6th Motor Batt. M.G.C. Egypt, Palestine, Mesopotamia.

1919 Hopkins, T. (Dec. 1915). Pte. 14th R. Welch Fusiliers. France and Belgium.

Horn, J. B. (Apr. 1917). 2nd Lt. 2/4th Loyal N. Lancashire Regt. France and Belgium. Killed in action at Poelcappelle on Oct. 26, 1917.

1919 Hubbell, P. E., M.A. (May 26, 1918). Pte. H.Q. Coy., 323rd Inf., U.S. Army. France.

Huby, H. (Mar. 6, 1916). Pte. 2/6th W. Riding Regt. France. Killed in action at Cambrai on Nov. 20, 1917.

1919 Hudson, D. E. (Dec. 12, 1917). Sergt. U.S. Army Student Detachment. Italy, France.

1919 Hughes, A. R. (Sept. 14, 1916). Lt. 4th, attd. 2nd, Dorsetshire Regt. Egypt and Palestine, 1917–19.

1908 Hughes, A. S., B.A. (Oct. 1, 1917). Pte. Canadian Forestry Corps.

1919 Hughes, A. W. (Apr. 7, 1915). ‡Lt. M.G.C. France, 1915–18.

1919 Hughes, B. E. (Oct. 1, 1915). 2nd Lt. 13th Lancashire Fusiliers. Lt. 23rd Bn. M.G.C. France, Italy.

1913 Hughes,* F. Ll. (Oct. 26, 1914). 2nd Lt. 4th King's (Liverpool Regt.). Capt. General Staff. France and Belgium, 1915–18. *M.C.*, Jan. 1, 1917. *D.* France, 1916; § Mar. 1919.

1904 Hughes, J. Augustine (Sept. 1914). Pte. 7th R. Berkshire Regt. France, 1915; Salonika, 1916–18.

1919 Hughman, R. N. H. (Mar. 28, 1917). Lt. 9th Sqdn. R.A.F. Belgium, 1917–18.

1906 Humphreys,* W. W., M.A. (Aug. 5, 1914). Capt. 8th D.C.L.I. Maj. 7th S. Wales Borderers (Lt.-Col.). France, 1915; Salonika, 1919. *D.* Salonika, 1917, 1918, 1919.

1903 Imison, J. A., B.A. (Oct. 8, 1915). Lt., Acting Capt., 1st E. Surrey Regt. Belgium and France. *M.C.*, Aug. 16, 1917; *Bar*, Mar. 8, 1919.

1919 Ingleson, H. (Aug. 20, 1917). 2nd Lt. R.E. (Signal Service). France, Germany.

1911 Inglis,* W. F., B.A. (Sept. 14, 1914). ‡2nd Lt. King's (Liverpool Regt.). France, Belgium, 1915–18.

1906 James, H. B., M.A. ‡Lt. Essex Regt. W. Africa.

1911 James, H. C., M.A. (Sept. 2, 1914). ‡Capt. 14th Welsh Regt. Capt. Indian Army. France and India. *D.* France, 1917.

1910 James, J. Elwyn, M.A. (Apr. 20, 1916). Paymaster Sub-Lt. R.N.V.R. North Atlantic Patrol.

1920 James, W. T. (Dec. 1915). ‡Lt. 1st London Regt. France. *M.C.*, Aug. 25, 1917.

1908 Jenkins, D. W. (Jan. 25, 1917). Lt. 13th Welsh Regt. France. *M.C.*, Dec. 2, 1918.

1919 Jenkins, G. (Aug. 9, 1915). Lt. M.G.C. France, 1916–18. *M.C.*, Jan. 9, 1918.

1919 Jenkins, J. L. (May 1916). ‡2nd Lt. R. Fusiliers (Lt.). France, 1916–17.

1913 Jenkins, O., B.A. (Sept. 1914). ‡Lt. R. Welch Fusiliers. Capt. R.E. France, 1915–18; Palestine, 1918–19.

1907 Johnson,* C. B., B.A. (Oct. 14, 1914). Lt. 4th Lancashire Fusiliers. Belgium.

1900 **Jones, A. S. B.,** B.A. (May, 1915). ‡Lt. 1st Canadian Pioneers. France, 1916–18. Died on Feb. 9, 1919, of illness contracted while on active service.

1912 **Jones, C.,** B.A. (Jan. 1916). ‡2nd Lt. R. Welch Fusiliers. France and Belgium. Killed in action at Ypres on Aug. 1, 1917.

1907 Jones, D. Hedog, M.A. Capt. Grenada Defence Force.

1907 Jones,* Rev. G. D., B.A. (Sept. 16, 1916). Chaplain to the Forces (4th Class), attd. R.A.F.

1912 **Jones, G. M.,** B.A. (Sept. 1914). Lt. Westmorland and Cumberland Yeomanry. Died of illness at Matlock on Dec. 13, 1918.

1904 Jones, H., M.A. (Aug. 5, 1914). ‡Capt. 3rd R. Welch Fusiliers. Nigeria, 1914–15; France, 1916–17.

1919 Jones, H. H. (Feb. 6, 1918). 2nd Lt. R.G.A.

Jones, H. H. S. (Aug. 1916). 2nd Lt. Queen's (R. W. Surrey Regt.). France. Killed in action at Clery-sur-Somme on Mar. 4, 1917.

1903 Jones, Rev. J. D., M.A. (July 17, 1915). Chaplain to the Forces (4th Class). Gallipoli, Egypt, Sinai, Palestine, German E. Africa.

1888 Jones, Rev. J. G., B.A. (July 17, 1915). Chaplain to the Forces (4th Class).

1906 **Jones,* J. H. R.** (Aug. 1914). ‡Lt. 7th S. Lancashire Regt. France, 1915–16. Killed in action on the Somme on July 4, 1916.

1919 Jones, Ll. R. (Dec. 1914). ‡Lt. 17th R. Welch Fusiliers, attd. King's African Rifles. Staff Officer. France, B. E. Africa, Portuguese, and Central Africa.

1903 Jones, Ll. W. (July 1916). Capt. R.A.F.

1908 Jones,* O. P., B.A. (Mobilized Aug. 4, 1914). Capt. 5th R. Scots Fusiliers (T.F. Res.), empld. Min. of Munitions.

1919 Jones, R. (May 21, 1918). Flight Cadet 191st Squadron R.A.F.

1899 Jones, S. Harrison, B.A. (Sept. 4, 1914). Cpl. (226th Divl. Employment Coy.), 16th Middlesex Regt. France.

1897 Jones,* Rev. T. W. A., M.A. (July 4, 1915). Chaplain to the Forces (4th Class), attd. 26th Gen. Hospital, France. France and Belgium, 1915–19. *M.C.*, July 18, 1917.

1906 Jones,* Rev. W. Alcuin, M.A. (Jan. 1, 1916). Chaplain to the Forces (4th Class), attd. 24th R. Welch Fusiliers. Egypt and Palestine, 1916–18; France, 1918–19. *M.C.*, Jan. 18, 1918; *Bar*, Apr. 22, 1918.

1903 **Jones, W. H.** Pte. R. Welch Fusiliers. Killed in action.

1919 Jones, W. P. (May 9, 1916). Driver R.A.S.C. (M.T.). France, 1917–19.

1909 Jordan,* A. B., B.A. (May 1916). ‡Lt. Malay States Volunteer Rifle Corps. Malay.

1904 Kemp, F. J., M.A. (Serving Aug. 4, 1914). Capt. Unattached List, T.F.

1909 Ker, N.B., B.A. Lt. Unattached List, T.F., Stafford School O.T.C.

1919 King, C. G. (July 26, 1915). ‡Lt. 11th London Regt. (Finsbury Rifles). France. *M.C.*, Oct. 27, 1917.
1897 Kingsford, H. S., M.A. (June 1917). Paymaster Sub-Lt., R.N.V.R.
1916 Kozomaritch, G., B.A. (Sept. 5, 1914). Volunteer Pte. Serbian Army. Serbia.
1902 Langman, T. W., B.A. (Sept. 1, 1914). Capt. 5th Welsh Regt. (Staff-Captain). France. *O.B.E.* (Mil.). *D.* France, 1918.
1913 **Lawrence,* F. H.** (Aug. 31, 1914). Lt. 3rd, attd. 1st, Gloucestershire Regt. France. Killed in action at Richebourg L'Avoué on May 9, 1915.
1907 [Lawrence,* T. E., B.A.] (Oct. 1914). Col. Special Lists. Egypt, Arabia and Syria. *C.B.* *D.S.O.*, May 13, 1918. Croix de Chevalier de la Légion d'Honneur. Italian Silver Medal for Military Valour. Croix de Guerre. *D.* Egypt, 1915; Hedjaz, 1918.
1907 Lawson, Rev. A. C., M.A. (Jan. 16, 1917). Chaplain to the Forces (4th Class). France and Belgium.
1914 Lawson, F. A. (Apr. 16, 1915). Lt. 10th R. Welch Fusiliers, attd. R.A.F. France.
1918 Lay, F. C. (July 26, 1915). Lt. 1/4th Oxf. & Bucks. Lt. Infty., attd. 86th Training Res. Bn. France, 1916–17.
1919 Leake, S. A. (Jan. 1, 1915). Pte. 19th R. Fusiliers. France, 1915–16.
1915 Lee, F. R. M. (Dec. 11, 1915). ‡2nd Lt. 1/6th Rifle Brigade. France, 1916–19.
1911 Lee, L. G., M.A. (Nov. 28, 1914). Lt. 9th Yorkshire Regt. France, 1915–16. *M.C.*, Jan. 1, 1917.
1913 Leeming,* A. (Aug. 28, 1914). ‡Lt. 106th Hazara Pioneers, Indian Army. Egypt, 1916–17; France, 1917; Mesopotamia, Persia, 1918–19.
1912 Levy, R., B.A. (Feb. 1916). ‡Capt. General Staff, attd. Intelligence Corps H.Q. Mesopotamia.
1920 Lewis, C. G. (Apr. 14, 1915). ‡Capt. Welsh Regt. France. *M.C.* Mar. 8, 1919.
1896 Lewis, D. J. (June 10, 1915). Capt. R.A.M.C.
1910 Lewis, Rev. H. C. Colvin, M.A. (Nov. 29, 1916). Chaplain to the Forces (4th Class). France and Belgium.
1913 Lewis, H. T., M.A. (May 21, 1917). Lt. 12th Bedfordshire Regt.
1908 **Lewis,* Rev. I. M.,** B.A. (Sept. 4, 1914). Chaplain R.N., H.M.S. *Goliath.* Dardanelles. Drowned at sea on May 13, 1915.
1902 Lewis, Rev. J. F. O., M.A. (Dec. 3, 1915). Chaplain to the Forces (4th Class). France.
1919 Lisle, F. B. (Aug. 1916). Gnr. 1/B Batt. H.A.C. Palestine.
1906 Littler, Rev. H. D., M.A. (Apr. 1915). Lt. Unattached List, T.F., attd. Liverpool College O.T.C.
1902 Llewellyn, J. T. (June 10, 1915). Lt. Northumberland Fusiliers (Capt. and Adjt.).
1898 Lloyd, Rev. A. E., B.A. Pte. R.A.M.C. Chaplain to the Forces (4th Class).
1919 Lloyd, T. M. (Feb. 15, 1918). 2nd Lt. R.G.A.
1910 Lloyd-Jones, Rev. T., B.A. (Aug. 22, 1917). Chaplain to the Forces (4th Class). France and Belgium.
1918 Locke, H. O. (June 7, 1915). Lt. 3rd R. Irish Fusiliers. France and Belgium, 1916.

1901 Lockyer, S. H., M.A. Pte. R. Fusiliers.
1898 Longdon, Rev. J. S., M.A. (Dec. 21, 1914). Chaplain to the Forces (4th Class), attd. Fortress Engineers, R.E. (T.F.).
1892 Love, Rev. R. D. D. (Serving Aug. 4, 1914). Chaplain to the Channel Islands Militia.
1901 **Loud, Rev. G. E.,** B.A. (Feb. 1917). Pte. London Regt. France. Died in hospital as a prisoner of war on June 27, 1918.
1902 Lumb, Rev. T. W., M.A. (Serving Aug. 4, 1914). Lt. Unattached List, T.F., Merchant Taylors' School O.T.C.
1919 McConaghie, J. R. (1917). U.S. Army.
1904 Mackie, J. D., M.A. (Serving Aug. 4, 1914). Capt. 14th Arg. & Suth'd. Highlanders (Maj.). France. *M.C.*, Jan. 1, 1917.
1908 MacMahon, P. S., B.Sc. (Aug. 13, 1916). Lt. Irish Guards. Staff-Lt.
1895 Maine, J. P., B.A. (Mar. 25, 1915). Lt. 6th Sherwood Foresters, attd. Staff.
1911 **Manderson, H. L.** (Mar. 10, 1915). 2nd Lt. 11th Loyal N. Lancashire Regt. Mesopotamia. Killed in action on Apr. 9, 1916.
1914 Manley, N. W. (Sept. 1915). Gnr. 174th Bde., R.F.A. France, 1916–18. *M.M.*, July 1917.
1919 Mansell, E. D. (Feb. 1917). Lt. 20th Cameronians.
1896 Martindell, E. W., M.A. (Sept. 1914). 2nd Lt. 11th Sherwood Foresters. Capt. General List, attd. War Office. France.
1910 Martyr, W. A. J., M.A. (July 29, 1915). Lt. 10th E. Lancashire Regt. Lt. 52nd Rifle Brigade. France, 1916–17; Germany, 1919.
1908 Matthews, G. M., M.A. Gnr. R.F.A.
1913 Mayers, W. H., M.A. (June 1916). ‡Lt., Acting Capt., 1/5th Bedfordshire Regt. Palestine. *M.C.*, Nov. 7, 1918.
1919 Megicks, W. (Jan. 22, 1916). Pte. 1/5th Norfolk Regt. France, Palestine. *M.M.*, July 31, 1917.
1919 Miles, R. B. (Mar. 11, 1918). 2nd Lt. R. Welch Fusiliers.
1911 Miles, W. H., B.A. (Sept. 18, 1917). Pte. R. Welch Fusiliers.
1911 Molyneux, P. L. (Dec. 1914). ‡2nd Lt. 7th Oxf. & Bucks. Lt. Infty. Capt. Garhwal Rifles, Indian Army. France, 1915; Salonika, 1915–17; India, 1917–19.
1915 Moodey, H. S. (Aug. 16, 1916). Leading Aircraftsman R.A.F. France.
1908 Morgan,* J., M.A. (Sept. 1915). ‡Lt. 1/10th London Regt. Egypt and Palestine.
1904 Morgan, W., B.A. Nigerian Land Contingent.
1919 Morgan, W. L. (May 21, 1917). Lt. 26th R. Welch Fusiliers. France and Belgium.
1909 Morgan-Richards, Rev. W., M.A. (Jan. 15, 1916). Chaplain to the Forces (4th Class). France, Germany.
1920 Morris, E. (Nov. 9, 1915). ‡Lt. 51st Welsh Regt. France.
1913 **Morris,* N. D.** (Sept. 1914). Lt. 8th S. Lancashire Regt. (Capt.). France. *D.* France, 1916. Died on May 12, 1916, of wounds received in action on Vimy Ridge.
1903 Musgrave, J. K. D., M.A. (July 3, 1916). Lt. R.G.A., attd. 56th Siege Batt. France. *M.C.*, June 3, 1919. *D.* France, 1918.
1919 Newell, E. Ll. (Apr. 11, 1917). Lt. R.F.A. India, 1917–19.
1900 Newell, G. G. (Sept. 8, 1914). Capt. Labour Corps. Capt. Special Lists (Interpreter).

1910 Newsam, W. O., B.A. (Nov. 1, 1917). Lt. I.A.R.O., attd. 15th Lancers. India, 1917–19.

1868 Nicholas, Rev. W. L., M.A. (Serving Aug. 4, 1914). Chaplain to the Forces (1st Class), attd. 5th R. Welch Fusiliers.

1908 Nicholls,* G. B. T., B.A. (Aug. 21, 1915). Lt. R.A.O.C. Egypt and Palestine. *O.B.E.* (Mil.). *D.* Palestine, 1918, 1919.

1910 Nicholson,* W. E., B.A. (1914). ‡Lt. Special Lists, attd. W. African Field Force. W. Africa.

1909 Norman,* D. R., B.A. (July 22, 1916). Lt. I.A.R.O., attd. 81st Pioneers. Capt. Recruiting Officer, Byjapur District, India.

Norris, F. G. (Nov. 1916). 2nd Lt. 4th Cheshire Regt., attd. 7th R. W. Kent Regt. France and Belgium. Killed in action on Apr. 2, 1918.

1912 **Norwood,* R. C.** (Sept. 2, 1914). 2nd Lt. Bucks. Bn. Oxf. & Bucks. Lt. Infty. France. Missing, believed killed in action in Sept. 1917.

1919 O'Connor, B. V. (Sept. 4, 1916). 2nd Lt. R.F.A. (S.R.). France.

1903 Odgers, A. G., B.A. (Oct. 1914). ‡Pte. A.I.F. Lt. R.E. (Gas Coy.). Gallipoli, 1915; Egypt, France.

1900 Ogier, L. L'H., M.A. Capt. 3rd R. Jersey Militia. *O.B.E.* (Mil.). *D.* § Feb. 1917.

1886 Overend, F. L., B.A. (Mobilized Aug. 4, 1914). Maj. 5th S. Staffordshire Regt. France. T.D.

1907 Owen, Ll. G., M.A. (Feb. 1915). Maj. I.A.R.O., attd. 116th Mahrattas. N.W. Frontier, India, 1916; Mesopotamia, 1917–19.

1914 **Owen, M.** (Mar. 1916). ‡2nd Lt. 9th Welsh Regt. France and Belgium. Killed in action on July 31, 1917.

1900 Owens, Rev. W. J., B.A. (Dec. 7, 1914). Chaplain (4th Class) A.I.F.

1919 Page, J. H. (June 18, 1918). 2nd Lt. R.H. and R.F.A.

1903 Pallister, J. (Mar. 6, 1915). Lt. R.G.A. (S.R.).

1908 Parker,* F. L. (1914). ‡Lt. 6th Worcestershire Regt.

1903 Partridge, H. C., B.A. (Aug. 31, 1914). Capt. 2/20th London Regt. France, 1915–16; Macedonia, 1916–17; Palestine, 1917; Egypt, 1917–18.

1894 Patterson, R. F., B.A. (Oct. 17, 1914). Lt. Unattached List, T.F., Christ's Hospital O.T.C.

1907 Pearson,* Rev. C. G. G., M.A. (Dec. 8, 1914). Chaplain R.N. H.M.S. *Jupiter*, 1914–15; H.M.S. *Roxburgh*, 1915–18; H.M.S. *Albion*, 1918. Order of St. Anne (3rd Class).

1914 Pemberton, R. E. K. (Mar. 1917). ‡Lt. 5th Bedfordshire Regt. France, 1918–19.

1898 Pereira, Rev. H. A. da C., M.A. (1914). ‡Lt. R.A.O.C.

1919 Peters, J. F. J. (Dec. 10, 1915). ‡2nd Lt. 211th Squadron, R.A.F. France, 1918. (Prisoner of war in Holland Aug.–Nov. 1918.)

1914 Philip, A. (Dec. 22, 1914). Lt. 11th Durham L.I. (Capt.). France. *D.* France, 1917.

1917 Phillips, A. H. (Aug. 31, 1917). 2nd Lt. 69th Siege Batt., R.G.A. France, 1918–19; Germany, 1919.

1915 Phillips, J. (Jan. 10, 1916). Gnr. R. Marine Artillery. H.M.S. *Attentive II*. Belgium.

1904 Phillips, M. H., B.A. (Aug. 7, 1914). Pte. Inns of Court O.T.C. and 21st

R. Fusiliers (Invalided Dec. 1914). Lt. R.A.S.C. (from Oct. 1915). Italy.

1919 Phillips, R. V. (Jan. 8, 1918). Aircraftsman, R.A.F.

1910 Phillips,* T. S., B.A. (Sept. 28, 1914). Lt. W. African Frontier Force. German E. Africa; Portuguese E. Africa.

1920 Phillips, W. G. (Aug. 30, 1915). 2nd Lt. Welsh Regt. Lt. attd. 1/7th R. Welch Fusiliers. France, Belgium, Egypt, Palestine, Syria. *D.*

1906 Phoenix,* A. D., M.A. (Nov. 11, 1914). ‡Capt. R.E. Belgium, France, Germany, 1916–19.

1895 Pike, D. R., B.M., M.A. (Nov. 1, 1915). Capt. R.A.M.C.

1919 Porter, C. W. (Oct. 21, 1914). Capt. and Adjt. 41st Bn. M.G.C. Belgium, France, and Italy.

1912 Powel, T. R., M.A. (Jan. 17, 1916). Sapper R.E. (Inland Waterways and Docks, Salonika). Salonika, 1917–18; Caucasus, 1918–19.

1902 Powell, T. G., M.A. (Aug. 11, 1910). Capt. Unattached List, T.F., Glenalmond College O.T.C. *D.* § Mar. 1919.

1919 Price, A. J. (Oct. 5, 1917). Lt. R.A.F. (Seaplane Officer). France.

1912 **Price, D. E.** (1914). ‡2nd Lt. Welsh Regt. France. Missing, believed killed in action in Sept. 1916.

1910 Price,* S. L., M.A. (Oct. 16, 1914). ‡Lt. Special Lists, empld. W. African Field Force. Nigeria.

1908 Prys-Jones,* A. G., M.A. (Oct. 14, 1914). Lt. Unattached List, T.F., Dulwich College O.T.C.

1911 Pugh,* T. E. (Sept. 6, 1914). Lt., Acting Capt., 104th Wellesley Rifles, Indian Army. Aden, 1914–15; India, 1915–18; Mesopotamia, 1918–19.

1909 Purchas, F. S., M.A. (Aug. 20, 1917). Lt. Nigeria Regt. E. Africa, 1917–18.

1901 Reed, J. S. B., B.A. (Apr. 1916). ‡Lt. R.N.V.R., attd. Naval War Staff. H.M.S. *Cyclops*, H.M.S. *President*. *O.B.E.* (Mil.).

1919 Rees, B. P. (Jan. 6, 1916). ‡2nd Lt. R.F.A. France. *M.M.*, Aug. 1917.

1912 Rees, W., M.A. (Oct. 1915). Lt. 3rd W. Riding Regt. France, 1917–19.

1913 **Reeves,* G. F. J.** (Aug. 15, 1914). 2nd Lt. 2nd Hampshire Regt. Gallipoli. Killed in action near Krithia on June 6, 1915.

1875 Reichel, Sir H. R., M.A. (Serving Aug. 4, 1914). Capt. Unattached List, T.F., Bangor University O.T.C.

1910 Rhys, B., B.A. (Jan. 30, 1916). Paymaster Sub-Lt. R.N.V.R., attd. Signal Div., Admiralty. 10th Cruiser Squadron, 1916–17.

1919 Richards, J. G. M. (Nov. 12, 1918). Cadet No. 2 B Artillery Reception Brigade.

1893 Richards, Rev. T. H., M.A. (Jan. 5, 1915). Chaplain to the Forces (3rd Class), attd. 68th Welsh Div. *D.* § Feb. 1917.

1914 Richardson, D. D. (June 23, 1915). Lt. 4th E. Surrey Regt. (Capt.), attd. R.A.F. (Flying Officer, Observer). Salonika, 1905; France, 1916–18. (Wounded and prisoner of war, Mar. 1918.)

1919 Roberts, C. E. (June 4, 1918). Cadet 6th Cadet Bn. Northamptonshire Regt. 2nd Lt. Reserve of Officers (on demobilization).

1912 **Roberts,* F. J.** (Aug. 14, 1914). Capt. 3rd, attd. 1st, King's (Liverpool Regt.). France. *D.* France, 1915. Killed in action at Cuinchy on Sept. 27, 1915.

1919 Roberts, G. G. (Sept. 10, 1914). ‡Lt. 3rd R. Welch Fusiliers. France.

1919 Roberts, H. (Dec. 20, 1915). Lt. R.G.A. France.

1914 Robertson, D. (Dec. 23, 1914). Capt. 16th, attd. 1st and 2nd, Lancashire Fusiliers. France, 1915–17. *M.C.*, June 4, 1917.

1908 Rosser, D. C., B.A. (Oct. 1914). Paymaster Lt. R.N.V.R.

1907 Rowbotham,* R. N., B.A. (Aug. 14, 1914). ‡Capt. R.F.A. Gallipoli, Egypt, France.

1915 Rowlands, A. (Jan. 20, 1916). Capt. Army Cyclist Corps, attd. Special Service Office, G.H.Q., Mesopotamia. Mesopotamia, 1916–19. *M.B.E.* (Mil.). *D.* Mesopotamia, 1919.

1895 Rowlands, Rev. D. E., M.A. (Jan. 18, 1916). Chaplain to the Forces (4th Class). France and Belgium.

1903 Ruddy, Rev. H. E., M.A. (Nov. 21, 1918). Chaplain to the Forces (4th Class), attd. R.A.F.

1919 Rugginz, K. H. (July 4, 1917). 2nd Lt. R.G.A. (S.R.). France, 1918.

1904 **Salmon, S.,** B.A. (Sept. 9, 1914). ‡2nd Lt. 9th Welsh Regt. France. Killed in action in N.W. France on July 19, 1917.

1919 Sanborn, F. W. (1917). U.S. Army.

1919 Sands, S. E. (May 16, 1917). ‡Lt. 247th Siege Batt., R.G.A., Belgium, Italy. Croce di Guerra.

1919 Sansome, G. H. (May 16, 1917). Bombardier R.G.A., attd. Labour Corps. France, 1917–18.

Scott, K. W. L. (July 26, 1915). 2nd Lt. 11th Cheshire Regt. France, 1916. Killed in action in attack on Schwaben Redoubt on Oct. 21, 1916.

1913 **Scott, R. M.** (Sept. 1, 1914). 2nd Lt. R.E. (Signalling Service). Mesopotamia, 1917; Palestine, 1918. Died on Dec. 25, 1918, of illness contracted on active service.

1914 **Seel, H. A.** (Mar. 3, 1915). 2nd Lt. 2/7th Cheshire Regt. Gallipoli. Killed in action at Suvla Bay on Dec. 7, 1915.

1866 Sharkey, Sir S. J., D.M. (Mobilized Aug. 4, 1914). Lt.-Col. R.A.M.C. (T.F. Res.).

1912 Shillito,* J. E., B.A. (Nov. 13, 1914). Lt. 9th E. Yorkshire Regt. Macedonia.

1920 Shilton, D. W. F. (Apr. 1917). ‡2nd Lt. Tank Corps.

1908 **Silvester,* A. L.,** B.A. (Aug. 6, 1914). Lt. 2nd R. Sussex Regt. France and Belgium. Killed in action near Cuinchy on Dec. 31, 1914.

1913 **Simmance,* A. J. S.** (Aug. 10, 1914). Capt. 4th King's (Liverpool Regt.). France, 1915–16. Killed in action at Delville Wood on Aug. 18, 1916.

1913 Sladden, A. F. S., D.M. (Serving Aug. 4, 1914). Capt. R.A.M.C., attd. Asst. Ad. in Pathology, 1st Army. France, 1914–19. Médaille des Epidémies (en argent). *D.* France, 1919.

1887 Smart, Rev. J. R., M.A. (Dec. 18, 1917). Chaplain to the Forces (4th Class).

1905 Smith, A., M.A. (Dec. 2, 1914). Capt. 16th, attd. 2nd Lancashire Fusiliers. France.

1919 Smith, R. B. (Jan. 30, 1918). Aircraftsman (2nd Class), R.A.F.

1919 Smith, S. H. (Aug. 29, 1917). ‡2nd Lt. Observer R.A.F. France.

1919 Sneyd, A. W. (Aug. 14, 1918). Pte. 53rd Welsh Regt.

1912 **Sprunt,* E. L.** (Aug. 1914). Pte. H.A.C. France and Belgium. *D.* France, 1915. Killed in action at Château Hooge on June 16, 1915.

1886 [Stenning, J. F., M.A.] (Mobilized Aug. 1914). Lt.-Col. O.U.O.T.C., attd. No. 4 O.C.B. Liaison Officer between the University and War Office. *C.B.*, 1916. *C.B.E.* (Mil.). *D.* § Aug. 1917; § Mar. 1918.

1909 Stephens, C. R., M.A. (Jan. 15, 1915). ‡Lt. Manchester Regt. (Capt.). France, 1915–16. *D.* France, 1917.

1906 Stone, Rev. C. E., M.A. (Apr. 5, 1918). Chaplain to the Forces (4th Class).

1919 Sutton, W. G. L. (Apr. 4, 1918). Cadet, Inns of Court O.T.C.

1911 Tedd, H. G., M.A. (Nov. 28, 1914). Capt. King's (Liverpool Regt.). Capt. R.E. (Gas Service). France and Belgium.

1904 Thomas, C. E. H., M.A. (Apr. 1915). Lt. 5th Bn. M.G.C. (C.E.F.). France. (Invalided on account of wounds, Oct. 1917.)

1914 Thomas, D. E. (Feb. 9, 1916). Pte. 23rd Welsh Regt. Macedonia.

1911 Thomas,* E. H., B.A. (Sept. 15, 1914). ‡Lt. 3rd R. Fusiliers (Capt.). Malta, 1914; Khartoum, 1915; Gallipoli, 1915; France, 1917–18. (Discharged May 2, 1919, on account of wounds received in action.)

1897 Thomas, G. J., M.A. (June 16, 1915). 2nd Lt. 4th Welsh Regt.

1903 Thomas, Rev. H. A., M.A. (1914). Pte. R.A.M.C. ‡Chaplain R.N., attd. R.A.F. Gallipoli.

1919 Thomas, I. S. (Jan. 7, 1915). Lt. 12th R. Welch Fusiliers. Lt. R.A.F. France, 1916–17, 1917–18.

1905 **Thomas, L. M.** (Apr. 1916). ‡Sub-Lt. R.N. Div. France. Died on Feb. 15, 1917, of illness contracted on active service.

1892 Thomas, Rev. R. O. R., M.A. Pte. 13th Northumberland Fusiliers.

1909 Thomas, S., M.A. (Feb. 17, 1917). ‡Lt. Labour Corps. Education Officer. Salonika and Germany.

1919 Thomas, T. J. (Nov. 30, 1914). ‡Lt. 3rd R. Welch Fusiliers. France and Belgium, 1915–18. *M.C.*, Mar. 8, 1919. *D.* France, 1918.

1911 Thomas, W. D., M.A. (May 1916). Lt. 3rd Bn. C.E.F. France.

1909 Thomas-Jones, Rev. D., M.A. (Sept. 22, 1916). Chaplain to the Forces (4th Class), attd. Res. Bns. of Monmouthshire and Herefordshire Regts. Egypt, Palestine, France.

Thomson, G. F. M. (Jan. 25, 1915). 2nd Lt. 16th King's (Liverpool Regt.). France. Died on May 19, 1917, of wounds received in action.

1904 Thomson, J. C., B.Sc., M.A. (Dec. 12, 1915). Maj. 20th Siege Batt., R.G.A. France and Belgium, 1916–19. *M.C.*, July 26, 1918. *D.* France 1917, 1918 twice.

1910 Threlkeld, T. P., B.A. (1914). Capt. R.G.A.

1919 Todd, A. (May 21, 1918). Flight Cadet, R.A.F.

1911 Toms, H. W., B.M. (Aug. 1915). Lt. R.A.F. (Medical Service). H.M. Hospital Ship *Ghoorkha*, 1915.

1912 Townsend,* T. S. (Nov. 16, 1916). 2nd Lt. R.E.

1908 Tracey, A. G. (Dec. 29, 1915). Lt. R.G.A. Lt. R.A.O.C.

1905 Venner, I. P., M.A. (Sept. 3, 1914). ‡2nd Lt. R.E. Capt. R.A.F. France.

1912 **Vyvyan,* B. H.** (Aug. 31, 1914). ‡Capt. 121st Bde., R.F.A. Belgium and France. *D.* France, 1915, 1916, 1917. Died on Aug. 18, 1917, of wounds received in action at Pilkem Ridge.

1914 Vyvyan, M. (Oct. 22, 1914). Capt. R.G.A., attd. R.A.F. France and Belgium. *M.C.*, Aug. 18, 1917. *D.* France, 1916, 1917.

1919 Waddington, H. (Jan. 18, 1915). Capt. R.G.A. France.
1889 Wales, Archbishop of, D.D., Hon. D.C.L. (Serving Aug. 4, 1914). Chaplain to the Forces (2nd Class), attd. Welsh Border Mounted Bde. *D.* § Feb. 1917.
1904 Walmsley, A. M., M.A. (July 1915). Lt. 128th Heavy Batt., R.G.A. (Capt.). France, Belgium, Germany, 1916–19. *D.* France, 1918.
Walton, F. (May 1916). Gnr. Tank Corps. Palestine. Died on Oct. 27, 1917, of illness contracted as a prisoner of war at Nigdi, Asia Minor.
1912 Warr,* S. W., B.A. (Sept. 1914). Lt., temp. Maj., 7th Middlesex Regt., attd. 8th R. Berkshire Regt. France. *M.C.*, Feb. 1, 1919. *D.* France, 1917, 1919.
1911 Waugh, H. R., B.A. (Dec. 1914). Capt. K.O. Scottish Borderers, attd. 5th Lancashire Fusiliers. Gallipoli, 1915; Arabia, 1917; Belgium, 1917–19. *M.C.*, July 26, 1918. *D.* France, 1918.
1912 **Webb,* J. P.** (Sept. 29, 1914). Capt. 12th Gloucestershire Regt. France. Died on Aug. 22, 1918, of wounds received in action near Achiet-le-Petit.
1904 **Webber, Rev. W. F.,** B.A. (Serving Aug. 4, 1914). Chaplain R.N. H.M.S. *Black Prince*. Grand Fleet, Cruiser Squadron. Killed in action at the Battle of Jutland on May 31, 1916.
1910 Wells,* T. C., B.A. (Aug. 7, 1914). Maj. 6th Welsh Regt., attd. General Staff. France, 1914, 1916; Egypt and Salonika, 1915–16. *M.C.*, Jan. 1, 1917.
1899 Weston, L. N., B.A. (Aug. 1, 1916). Gnr. 182nd Siege Batt., R.G.A. France, 1917–18.
1919 Wheeler, E. I. (Mar. 24, 1915). Lce.-Cpl. Labour Corps, attd. I. W. & D. (R.E.). Salonika, 1916–19.
1919 Whelan, J. C. D. (Sept. 25, 1915). Lt. 5th Leinster Regt., afterwards Lt. R.A.F. (Capt.). Belgium and France.
1911 Whiston,* J. R. H., M.A. (Oct. 4, 1914). 2nd Lt. 8th Sherwood Foresters, afterwards Capt. R.A.F. France. *D.* § Aug. 1919.
1900 White, O. C., B.A. (Sept. 18, 1914). ‡Lt. 4th S. Staffordshire Regt. France, 1916–19.
1910 Whiteley,* G. C., B.A. Nigerian Land Contingent.
1907 Whitelock,* A. T. (Sept. 21, 1914). ‡Maj. R.A.F. France and Belgium. *D.* France, 1915.
1910 **Whyatt,* P.,** B.A. (Oct. 1914). Capt. 11th Sherwood Foresters. France and Belgium. *M.C.*, Jan. 1, 1918. *D.* France, 1917. Killed in action near Ypres on Oct. 18, 1917.
1915 Willan, H. C. (Jan. 3, 1916). Lt. R.G.A. France, India. *M.C.*, Aug. 16, 1917.
1919 Williams, C. A. (May 1, 1917). Pte. 5th R. Fusiliers. Belgium.
1898 Williams, Rev. David, M.A. (Oct. 18, 1916). Chaplain to the Forces (4th Class). Palestine.
1913 Williams, D. O., B.A. (Aug. 1915). ‡Lt. 4th Siege Coy., R. Monmouthshire R.E. France till 1919.
1914 Williams, E. Ll. (Feb. 22, 1916). ‡2nd Lt. M.G.C. France 1916, 1918.
1919 Williams, H. Ll. (Aug. 27, 1917). Pioneer R.E. (Signals).
1908 Williams, I., M.A. (Apr. 1917). Gnr. R.G.A. Mesopotamia.
1902 Williams, I. E., M.A. Pte. R. Welch Fusiliers.

1913 Williams, J. Penry, M.A. (June 12, 1915). Lt. 1st Leicestershire Regt. (Capt.). France, 1916–18.
1919 Williams, J. R. (1917). U.S. Army.
1913 Williams, L. E. H. (Sept. 11, 1914). ‡Lt. 17th R. Welch Fusiliers. France, Belgium, Salonika.
1912 Williams, L. St. C. G., B.A. (Sept. 27, 1914). ‡Lt. 10th S. Wales Borderers. France and Belgium. *M.C.*, Sept. 27, 1917.
1901 Williams, R., M.A. (Aug. 19, 1915). Lt. 119th Heavy Batt., R.G.A. France, Belgium, Germany. *M.C.*, Jan. 1, 1918.
1895 Williams, Rev. S. B., M.A. (May 1, 1918). Chaplain to the Forces (4th Class).
Williams, S. M. (Scholar elect) (Aug. 1916). Lt. 2/50th Kamaon Rifles. Indian Army. India.
1904 Williams, T. P., M.A. (Oct. 19, 1914). ‡Capt. 3rd, attd. 1st, Oxf. & Bucks. Lt. Infty. Mesopotamia, 1916–19.
1897 Williams, Rev. W. J., M.A. (Feb. 28, 1916). Chaplain to the Forces, attd. R. Sussex Regt. France. *M.C.*, Jan. 1, 1918.
1913 **Wilson,* K. F.** (Feb. 9, 1915). Lt., Acting Capt., 7th Essex Regt. Egypt and Palestine. Killed in action near Jerusalem on Nov. 2, 1917.
1906 Winckworth, R., M.A. (Aug. 11, 1914). ‡Paymaster Lt. R.N.R. Dunkirk, Oct. 1914; Auxiliary Patrol, 1915–17; "Q" Boat off Morocco, 1918.
1915 Wood, A. C. (Feb. 15, 1916). ‡2nd Lt. 16th Cheshire Regt. France and Belgium. (Discharged on account of wounds.)
1904 Wood, Rev. A. R. C., M.A. Chaplain R.N.
1910 Wood, F., M.A. (Dec. 13, 1916). 2nd Lt. R.E. France, 1917–19.
1897 Woodward, Rev. C. S., M.A. (May 16, 1916). Chaplain to the Forces (4th Class), attd. 142nd Inf. Bde. *M.C.*, Nov. 14, 1916.
1882 Wykes, J. T., B.A. (Oct. 1, 1914). Capt. 5th Sherwood Foresters.
1914 Wynne-Jones, E. I. (Feb. 8, 1915). Capt. 8th Welsh Regt.
1914 Young, W. A., B.A. (July 3, 1916). Pioneer R.E. (Special Companies). France and Belgium, 1916–18.

WADHAM COLLEGE

1902 **Abbott, G.,** B.A. (Sept. 17, 1915). Lt. 1st Hertfordshire Regt., attd. 7th Bedfordshire Regt. France. Killed in action on Aug. 23, 1918.

1914 Abell, E. T., B.A. (July 3, 1917). 2nd Lt. Labour Corps.

1908 Abraham,* J. C. (Dec. 10, 1914). Capt. Special Lists, whilst with Nyasaland Field Force. E. Africa. *M.B.E.* (Mil.). *D.* E. Africa, 1915, 1917.

1903 [Allen, Rev. G. B., B.D.] (Mar. 23, 1917). Chaplain to the Forces (4th Class), 1917; Chaplain, R.A.F., 1918.

1896 Allison, F. W., B.A. Bombay Volunteers, I.D.F. India.

1903 Anderson Robertson, J. H., B.A. R.A.F., Mechanical Dept.

1903 Andrew, Rev. W. S., M.A. (Jan. 22, 1918). Chaplain to the Forces (4th Class). France. *M.C.*, Mar. 8, 1919.

1919 Andrews, H. B. (Apr. 17, 1918). Gnr. R.F.A., attd. 434th Agric. Coy.

1899 Annesley, P. de V., B.A. (Feb. 24, 1918). 2nd Lt. Special Lists. Lt. Labour Corps.

1896 Annesley, Rev. W. M. (Apr. 10, 1917). Chaplain to the Forces (4th Class).

1893 Archer, R. L., M.A. (Sept. 1915). Lt. Unattached List, T.F., University College of N. Wales O.T.C.

1914 Ardagh, L. V., B.A. (Apr. 2, 1915). Lt. 351st Bde., R.F.A. France and Belgium. *M.C.*, Feb. 4, 1918.

1911 Armitage, A. H. (Nov. 4, 1915). Driver R.E. Mesopotamia and India.

1907 Arrowsmith, Rev. H. S., M.A. (Sept. 28, 1917). Chaplain to the Forces (4th Class). Mesopotamia.

1919 Ashby, P. T. H. (Mar. 8, 1915). Sergt. Canadian M.G.C. France, Belgium.

1881 Baines, Rev. C. F., M.A. (Serving Aug. 4, 1914). Chaplain to the Forces (1st Class) (Asst. Chaplain-General). France, 1915–18. *D.S.O.*, Jan. 1, 1918. *D.* France, 1915, 1917, 1918.

1919 Baker, L. K. (July 4, 1917). ‡Flight Lt., 80th Squadron, R.A.F. France, 1918. *D.F.C.*, Nov. 2, 1918.

1908 Balk,* T. O., B.A. (June 29, 1915). Capt. 7th R. Warwickshire Regt., attd. R.E. (Army Signals). France. *M.C.*, June 3, 1919.

1914 **Bambridge, B. S.** (Apr. 1915). 2nd Lt. 7th The Buffs (E. Kent Regt.). France, 1916. Killed in action at Grandcourt on Nov. 18, 1916.

1911 Bardsley, F. S. E., B.A. (May 26, 1915). Lt. 6th King's (Liverpool Regt.). France. (Invalided on account of wounds.)

1919 Barfield, A. O. (Apr. 10, 1917). ‡2nd Lt. Signal Service, R.E. France, 1918.

1884 Barnett, R. Wheildon, B.C.L., M.A., *M.P.* (Sept. 15, 1914). Capt. Special Lists.

1897 **Barnsley, A.** (Apr. 18, 1915). Capt. 6th Gloucestershire Regt. France and Belgium. Killed in action near Ypres on Oct. 25, 1914.

1919 Bateman, L. R. (Dec. 7, 1917). 2nd Lt. 5th Somerset L.I., attd. M.G.C.

1919 Bayley, T. D. S. (Apr. 30, 1917). Lt. R.E. Belgium, France.
1904 [Bazett, H. C., D.M.] (Aug. 4, 1914). Capt. R.A.M.C. Capt., Medical Officer, R.A.F., attd. No. 14 General Hospital. France. *O.B.E.* (Mil.). *M.C.*, Jan. 14, 1916. *D.* France, 1915 twice.
1911 Beard, H. K. (1918). Pte. 69th Artillery, U.S. Army. France.
1905 Bearder, H. L., M.A. (Mar. 4, 1918). 2nd Lt. R.G.A. (S.R.). France.
1919 Beasley, F. R. (May 10, 1915). ‡Lt. 11th Inf. Bn., A.I.F. Gallipoli, 1915; Egypt, France, 1916–18, 1918–19.
1919 Beckett, W. E. S. (Dec. 21, 1914). Lt., Acting Capt., 3rd Cheshire Regt. G.S.O. 3. France, 1915; Macedonia, 1916–18; Caucasus, 1919. *D.* Salonika, 1917.
1885 [Bennett, E. N., M.A.] (Serving Aug. 1914). Capt. 4th Oxf. & Bucks. Lt. Infty (T.F. Res.). R.C.S. Commissioner in Belgium, France, and Serbia. Order of the White Eagle (3rd Class).
1893 Bentley, H. C., M.A. (Feb. 1916). ‡Lt. R.G.A. (Capt.). France.
1905 Berry, A., B.A. (Aug. 6, 1914). ‡Lt. 9th King's (Liverpool Regt.). France, 1917–19. *D.* France, 1919.
1919 Bewsher, R. (Aug. 7, 1914). ‡2nd Lt. R.G.A. France, Belgium, Egypt, Macedonia.
1913 Bingley, H. J. (Serving Aug. 4, 1914). Lt., Acting Capt., R.G.A. Lt. R.H.A. Palestine, 1917–18.
1891 [Birkenhead, Lord, B.C.L., M.A.] (Mobilized Aug. 1914). Hon. Capt. Q.O. Oxfordshire Hussars. Lt.-Col. Headquarters Staff, Indian Army Corps. Belgium and France. *D.* France, 1915.
1903 Bissett, A. M. S. African Defence Force.
1905 Blackman, Rev. G. D'A., M.A. (Nov. 21, 1916). Chaplain to the Forces (4th Class). France.
1901 Blackwell, C. P., B.A. (Aug. 4, 1916). Lt. General List, empld. Ministry of National Service. *M.B.E.* (Mil.).
1906 Blake, J. H., M.A. (Mobilized Aug. 1914). Capt. 1/5th Somerset L.I. India, 1914–17; Egypt and Palestine, 1917–19.
1915 Bland, A. A. (Apr. 28, 1916). Lt. 2nd H.A.C. France, Belgium, Italy, Austria.
1910 Blank,* A. L., M.A. (Aug. 14, 1916). 2nd Lt. 13th Rajputs, Indian Army. India.
1899 Blencowe, A. J. W. (Dec. 26, 1914). Maj. 1st Lancashire Fusiliers. France. *M.C.*, June 23, 1915. *D.* France, 1915 twice, 1916.
1907 Bolter,* A. E., B.A. (Jan. 26, 1917). Lt. M.G.C. France.
1913 Boodle, J. F., M.A. (Sept. 3, 1914). ‡Lt. 6th E. Surrey Regt., attd. 52nd Sherwood Foresters.
1919 Boodle, W. A. C., B.A. (Mar. 27, 1918). 2nd Lt. 5th R. Fusiliers. Belgium, 1918–19.
1896 Booth, C. R. (Oct. 1918). Lt. R.A.F. S. Russia.
1902 Bostock,* J. K., M.A. (July 26, 1918). 3rd Air Mechanic, R.A.F.
1890 Bowell, E. W., M.A. (May 29, 1917). Capt. R.A.M.C. Mesopotamia, India.
1914 Bowron, E. L. D. (Oct. 1916). ‡Lt. 21st Lancers.
1907 Boyd,* Rev. N. R., B.A. (May 20, 1918). Chaplain, R. Marine Depot, Deal.
1881 Bradshaw, Rev. F. T., B.A. (Sept. 1, 1917). Chaplain to the Forces (4th Class).

1914 Branscomb, B. H., B.A. (June 1918). 5th Infantry, U.S. Army.
1907 Bren, R., M.A. (May 1918). Pte. Inns of Court O.T.C.
1912 Bridges,* F. J., B.A. (Nov. 16, 1914). Lt. 15th Hussars, attd. M.G.C. France. *M.C.*, Jan. 18, 1918. (Prisoner of war.)
1909 **Bridges, G. E.** (Feb. 10, 1917). Lt. R.F.A. France. Died of illness on Nov. 11, 1918.
1920 Bromet, W. G. H. (Mar. 1917). 2nd Lt. 24th Squadron, R.F.A. France and Belgium.
1906 Brown, C. C., B.A. R.G.A., Sierra Leone.
1919 Brown, R. E. (July 1916). ‡Lt. 5th Norfolk Regt. India, 1917–18; Mesopotamia, 1918–19.
1899 Browne, F. W., B.M., M.A. (Apr. 2, 1917). Capt. R.A.M.C. Salonika.
1919 Brundrit, D. F. (Jan. 31, 1917). 2nd Lt. Tank Corps. France. (Prisoner of war, Nov. 1917.)
1919 Bryant, C. G. S. (Jan. 8, 1918). Wireless Operator, Merchant Service Transport.
1912 **Buckman, J. L.** (Nov. 11, 1914). Capt. 12th E. Surrey Regt. France. Killed in action at Flers on Sept. 15, 1916.
1904 Burgess, M. G., B.A., B.Mus. (June 1, 1915). Pte. R.A.M.C. Mesopotamia, 1916–19.
1893 **Burrow, G. D'A.,** B.A. (1914). Pte. British Columbia Regt. France. Killed in action on Apr. 24, 1915.
1919 Burton, C. W. M. (Feb. 4, 1918). 2nd Lt. 18th K.R.R.C. Belgium.
1912 **Burton,* H. P. C.** (Aug. 15, 1914). Lt. 4th, attd. 1st, Bedfordshire Regt. France, 1915–16. Killed in action on July 27, 1916.
1909 Burton, R. W., B.A. (July 28, 1916). Lt. M.G.C. France. *M.C.*, Jan. 1, 1918. *D.* France, 1916.
1915 Butler, L. (Dec. 31, 1915). Lt., Flying Officer, R.A.F. France. (Prisoner of war in Germany, Mar. 1917.)
1914 Butlin, J. H. (Nov. 21, 1914). Lt. 3rd Dorsetshire Regt. France, 1915–16, 1917.
1893 Butt, A. G. Eddy, B.A. 128th Batt., R.G.A. (Invalided.)
1902 Butterfield, H. G., D.M. (Nov. 4, 1914). Capt. R.A.M.C. (T.F. Res.).
1911 Campion, C. A. G., M.A. (Aug. 4, 1914). ‡Capt. R.F.A. France, 1915–17. *D.* France, 1916, 1917.
1919 Canney, E. E. (Aug. 4, 1914). ‡Capt. Durham L.I. France, Belgium, 1915–17. *M.C.*, Oct. 20, 1916. *D.* France, 1916.
1920 Canney, J. R. (Aug. 4, 1914). ‡Lt. R.G.A. France, 1914–15, 1916, 1918–19; Germany, 1919.
1913 Carmichael, O. C., B.Sc. (1917). Lt. Inf., U.S. Army. France.
1909 Cartwright, K. T. St. G., M.A. (Sept. 1914). ‡2nd Lt. Rifle Brigade (Resigned). 2nd Lt. R.F.A. and General List. France and Belgium, 1915–16, 1916–18.
1894 Caspersz, Rev. T. W. L., M.A. (Serving Aug. 4, 1914). Chaplain, R.N. Hospital, Haslar.
1913 Cave, C. G. (Jan. 21, 1915). 2nd Lt. R. Sussex Regt. Lt. R.A.S.C. France and Belgium.
1889 Chadwick, H. F., B.A. (Oct. 23, 1914). Capt. 9th K.O.Y.L.I. Capt. Labour Corps.
1896 Chisolm, R. A. (Nov. 1916). Hon. Capt., Physician in charge of Red

Cross Hospital. France, 1916–19. Bronze Medal Della Salute Publica (Italy).
1905 Clark-Turner, R., B.A. (Dec. 7, 1915). Lt., Acting Capt., R.F.A. France.
1905 **Clarke, W. J.** Pte. Middlesex Regt. France. Killed in action in Nov. 1916.
1909 Cockey,* C. E. E., B.A. (Apr. 24, 1915). Lt. 3rd Devonshire Regt., attd. Gloucestershire Regt. France and Salonika. *D.* Salonika, 1919.
1914 Cohen, R. (Dec. 11, 1915). Signaller R.F.A. France.
1910 **Coldwells,* F. B.,** B.A. (July 12, 1915). 2nd Lt. 3rd Devonshire Regt. France. Killed in action in the Battle of the Somme on July 1, 1916.
1912 Collier, L. W., M.A. (Apr. 5, 1915). Lt. Somerset L.I. 2nd Lt. (Hon. Lt.), Technical Officer, R.A.F. France.
1898 Cooke, H. E., B.A. (Sept. 3, 1914). ‡Lt. Pembrokeshire Yeomanry. Capt. D.A.P.M. France.
1906 Cooper, W. L., M.A. (June 26, 1915). Lt. R.F.A. (S.R.). Capt. Education Officer. France, 1916–18. *M.C.*, Jan. 6, 1917. Cruz del Guerra (3rd Class).
1910 **Corbett,* H.,** B.A. (Aug. 15, 1914). Lt. 3rd Devonshire Regt., attd. 6th Gloucestershire Regt. France and Belgium, 1915, 1916. Killed in action in the Battle of the Somme on July 22, 1916.
1902 Corney, Rev. A. F., M.A. (Sept. 1915). Chaplain to the Forces and Interpreter. Salonika. Greek Cross of the Holy Saviour.
1902 Cosser, Rev. J. W., B.A. (June 30, 1915). Chaplain to the Forces, attd. M.G. Bn., 60th Div. Gallipoli, 1915–16 ; E. Africa, 1916–18 ; Egypt, 1918–19.
1898 Cotton, J. C., M.A. Lt. Nigerian Land Contingent. W. Africa.
1893 Cotton, W. B. (Mar. 19, 1915). Capt. I.A.R.O., attd. Wazaristan Rifles. India, 1916–18.
1906 Coulon, J. P. E. (1914). French Army. France.
1913 **Crombie,* I. O.** (Aug. 1914). Capt. 11th Middlesex Regt. France, 1915, 1916. Killed in action near Pozières on July 28, 1916.
1911 Crowe, L. A. (June 24, 1916). Lt. Special Lists (Interpreter).
1893 Curwen, Rev. R. M., M.A. (July 19, 1915). Chaplain to the Forces (4th Class). Belgium, France.
1902 [Cushing, R. W. J. A., B.M., M.A.] (Aug. 1915). Capt. R.A.M.C. (T.F. Res.). France, 1917–18.
1907 Cuthbert, Rev. M. W., B.A. (Dec. 15, 1916). Chaplain to the Forces (4th Class). France, 1917–19.
1912 Dakyns, F. H. (Oct. 7, 1914). Capt. Northern Cyclist Bn. (T.F.).
1919 Dale, A. P. (Feb. 1916). Lt. 111th Heavy Batt., R.G.A. France and Belgium. *M.C.*, June 3, 1918.
1901 Daniel, J. F. R., M.A. (Serving Aug. 1914). Lt. O.T.C.
1908 **Davies,* B. J.** (Aug. 4, 1914). Capt. 2nd S. Wales Borderers. Gallipoli, Egypt, and France. Killed in action at Monchy on May 19, 1917.
1919 Davies, D. B. (Sept. 1917). ‡2nd Lt. Welsh Guards. France. *M.C.*, Feb. 1, 1919.
1909 Davies, Rev. E. E., B.A. (Sept. 2, 1918). Chaplain to the Forces (4th Class).
1913 Davies, R. S. (Apr. 1, 1918). Lt., Observer Officer, R.A.F.
1919 Davis, B. E. C. (Sept. 1917). ‡Sub-Lt. R.N.V.R. Lt. R.A.F. Italy.

1905 Dearden, V. C. H. (Apr. 2, 1917). Lt. R.A.M.C. France, Salonika.
1908 De Hart,* J., B.A. R.G.A., Sierra Leone (4th Res. Bn.).
1898 De Labillière, Rev. P. F. D., M.A. (Mar. 21, 1916). Chaplain to the Forces (4th Class). Egypt. *D.* § Mar. 1918.
1910 **Derrick, A. J.,** B.A. (July 18, 1916). 2nd Lt. 6th Northumberland Fusiliers. France. Missing, presumed killed in action in Nov. 1916.
1893 De Visme, R. S. J. (Serving Aug. 1914). Maj. Channel Islands Militia.
1919 Dewey, G. H. (Feb. 23, 1918). 2nd Lt. R.G.A.
1900 Dickson, H. R. P. (Serving Aug. 1914). Capt. Indian Cavalry. India, Mesopotamia. *C.I.E.* *D.* Mesopotamia, 1917.
1907 Dobie,* M. R., B.A. (Aug. 4, 1914). ‡Lt. Special Lists. Staff-Lt. (2nd Class) Intelligence Corps. France, Belgium, Germany.
1910 Dodds, J. L., B.A. (Oct. 1914). Lt., Acting Capt., R.G.A. France, Belgium.
1894 Dowson, L. S. (Dec. 20, 1916). Lt. 2nd Oxf. & Bucks. Lt. Infty. France.
1897 Drinkwater, G. C., M.A. (Aug. 7, 1914). ‡Lt., temp. Capt., R.F.A. Bde. Maj. R.A. France, 1915–16; Egypt, 1916–17, 1918–19; Palestine, 1917–18. *M.C.*, Mar. 26, 1918. *D.* Palestine, 1918.
1895 Dudley, O. H. T. (1914). Pte. M.G. Section, 35th Poona Bn., I.D.F. India.
1909 Dutton, E. R., B.A. (Oct. 18, 1918). Pte. H.A.C. (Infantry).
1898 Earle, Rev. H. Chaplain Canadian E.F. France and Belgium.
1910 Edwards,* E. J. R., B.A. (Dec. 11, 1916). Lt. R.G.A. France.
1913 Edwards, R. D., B.A. (Dec. 1915). Lt. R.F.A. Egypt and Palestine.
1886 Ellaby, Rev. G. A., B.A. (Jan. 22, 1914). Chaplain, Rangoon Cantonments. India.
1898 Ellis, A. (Mar. 2, 1915). ‡2nd Lt. R. Warwickshire Regt. France.
Ellis, B. H. (Sept. 22, 1914). Lt. 5th Shropshire L.I. France and Belgium. Killed in action in Belgium on June 18, 1915.
1906 Ellis,* W. A., B.A. (Apr. 20, 1915). Lt. R. Irish Rifles. France.
1884 Elrington, N., B.A. (Oct. 1, 1916). Capt. R.A.M.C.
1919 Evans, J. H. F. (Nov. 29, 1915). Lt. R.G.A. (Capt.). France. *M.C.*, Nov. 1, 1918.
1897 Evans, S. E., M.A. (Oct. 15, 1914). Capt. General List (T.F. Res.). France, 1918. *M.B.E.* (Mil.). *D.* § Feb. 1917.
1903 Evelyn White, H. G., M.A. (Sept. 18, 1914). ‡2nd Lt. 6th Lancashire Fusiliers. Egypt. (Invalided.)
1906 Falle, T. de C., B.A. (Oct. 1, 1915). Lt., Acting Maj., 4th R. Irish Fusiliers. France and Belgium. *M.C.*, Dec. 2, 1918. *D.* France, 1917.
1912 Farquhar, F. W., B.A. (Sept. 13, 1915). Lt. 12th Highland L.I., empld. Command Depot. France, 1916.
1908 Farrar,* H., M.A. (Dec. 10, 1915). ‡Lt., Acting Capt., W. Yorkshire Regt., empld. 1/6th W. Riding Regt. France, 1916–19. *M.C.*, Apr. 2, 1919.
1903 **Farrell, H. P.,** M.A. Capt. Karachi Artillery Volunteers. India. Died in Nov. 1916.
1919 Feather, G. A. (July 6, 1917). Pte. U.S. Marine Corps.
1919 Fellows, L. E. H. (Apr. 17, 1918). Cadet No. 2 Cavalry Officers' Cadet School.
1902 Felton, A. L., M.A. (Sept. 26, 1917). 2nd Lt., Acting Capt. and Adjt., 17th R. Fusiliers. France. *M.C.*, June 3, 1919. *D.* France, 1918.

1919 Fenwick, F. C. A. (May 10, 1918). 2nd Lt. S. Staffordshire Regt.
1896 Ferguson, K. B., B.A. (Serving Aug. 4, 1914). Interpreter, General Staff. Maj. R.G.A. France, Aug. 1914–17 ; Germany, 1919.
1906 Ferris, Rev. W. A., M.A. (May 26, 1916). Chaplain to the Forces (4th Class).
1919 Field, D. R. (Feb. 1918). 2nd Lt. R.A.F.
1900 Firmstone, F. S. J. B., M.A. (Nov. 7, 1914). A.B. (H.G.) R.N.V.R., U.P.S. Bn., R.N.D. Cadet R.N.V.R. Gallipoli, 1915 ; France, 1916.
1903 Fish, B. W., M.A. (Sept. 1914). Capt. 8th Loyal N. Lancashire Regt. France. *M.C.*, Sept. 22, 1916.
1910 Fish, R. C. (Feb. 2, 1915). 2nd Lt. 3rd W. Yorkshire Regt. France. (Resigned on account of ill health caused by wounds.)
1911 Fitz, E. W., B.A. (July 23, 1917). Pte. 149th Batt., F.A., U.S. Army. France, 1918 ; Germany, 1918–19.
1897 Floud, Rev. H. A., M.A. (Aug. 15, 1915). Chaplain to the Forces (4th Class). Egypt and Palestine, Mediterranean.
1912 Forbes, Rev. H. N. (Nov. 30, 1915). Chaplain to the Forces (4th Class). France. *D.* France, 1916.
1902 **Fox, V. W. D.,** B.A. (Dec. 23, 1914). Lt. Irish Guards. France and Belgium. Killed in action in Belgium on May 18, 1915.
1897 Frankland, Rev. H., M.A. (June 27, 1916). Chaplain to the Forces (4th Class). Egypt, Salonika, Mediterranean.
1881 Franks, W. Temple, B.C.L., M.A., *C.B.* (Oct. 1914). Sub-Lt. R.N.V.R. Anti-Aircraft Defences.
1919 Frisby, A. W. (Oct. 22, 1916). A.B., R.N.V.R., Naval Intelligence Office. Jamaica, 1917–19.
1905 Frost, R. T., M.A. (Aug. 12, 1915). Capt. Cheshire Regt. France.
1891 Fry, C. B., M.A. (Aug. 27, 1914). Hon. Commdr. R.N.R.
1908 Fullbrook-Leggatt,* L. E. W. O. (Nov. 29, 1915). Lt. 3rd Oxf. & Bucks. Lt. Infty. (Capt.). France, Germany, 1917–19. *M.C.*, Feb. 18, 1918 ; *Bar*, July 26, 1918.
1902 Gardner, O. J., M.A. Pte. 28th London Regt. (Artists' Rifles). Cadet O.C.B.
1914 Gentry, C. S., B.A. (1917). Engineer, Forestry Corps, U.S. Army. France.
1919 Gibbon, A. M. (Dec. 10, 1915). ‡Lt. King's Own (R. Lancaster Regt.). France, 1916 ; Macedonia, 1917–18.
1901 Gibbon, D. S., B.A. (Mar. 31, 1915). Lt. 3rd R. Welch Fusiliers. Salonika. *M.C.*, June 4, 1917.
1906 Gibson, G. C., M.A. (Aug. 15, 1914). Capt. 3rd Essex Regt. Staff-Capt. Gallipoli and France.
1895 Gillett, A. B. (Dec. 9, 1915). Lt. 1st (Garr.) Bn. R. Warwickshire Regt., attd. 4th Somerset L.I.
1884 Goddard, H. L., M.A. (Sept. 15, 1914). Maj. 4th Leicestershire Regt.
1908 Goddard, T. N., B.A. Capt. Vol. Bn., Falkland Islands.
1902 Goddard-Jones, E. A., B.A. (Apr. 6, 1916). Pte. 9th R. Sussex Regt. France, 1916–18.
1910 Goldingham,* P. R., B.A. (Aug. 25, 1914). Capt. R.A.S.C., attd. 27th Bde., R.G.A. France, 1914–19. *D.* France, 1916 twice.
1910 **Gordon, A. C. M.** (Nov. 24, 1914). 2nd Lt. 6th R. Scots Fusiliers. France. Died on Mar. 1, 1917, of wounds received in May, 1916.

1914 Gordon Stewart, S. A. 2nd Lt. Seaforth Highlanders. France.
1914 Gorman, J. P. (Dec. 1915). Lt. 1/1st Warwick Heavy Batt., R.G.A. France, Italy. *D.* Italy, 1918.
1903 Gough, Rev. P. C., B.A. (Serving Aug. 4, 1914). Chaplain, R.N., H.M.S. *Kent.* Dardanelles, 1914; North Sea, 1915–17; Africa (Cape Station), 1917–18; N. Russia, 1919.
1913 **Green,* A. P.** (Aug. 1914). Lt. 7th Norfolk Regt. France. Killed in action near Albert on July 6, 1916.
1901 Green, H. M. C., B.M., M.A. (June 10, 1915). Capt. R.A.M.C. France, 1915; Salonika, 1915–19.
Greenup, J. B. (Aug. 1916). 2nd Lt. 5th, attd. 1st, Rifle Brigade. France and Belgium. Killed in action near Poelcappelle on Oct. 13, 1917.
1907 Griffith, C. R. W., M.A. (Oct. 1915). 2nd Lt. 12th Bengal Cavalry. Lt., Army H.Q., Delhi. Mesopotamia, 1916–17; India, 1917–18.
1911 Grove, G. F., B.A. (Oct. 1914). Lt. 1st Gloucestershire Regt. France, 1916; Egypt and Palestine, 1918–19.
1892 Grundy, Rev. E. P. R. B., M.A. (Dec. 27, 1916). Chaplain to the Forces (4th Class). France.
1909 Guillaume, A., M.A. (Sept. 21, 1914). Lt. Lancashire Fusiliers. ‡Capt. Special Lists, Arab Bureau, Cairo. France and Egypt. *D.* Egypt, 1919.
1906 Gurney,* S. D. (July 8, 1917). Lt. S. Nottinghamshire Hussars, attd. M.G.C. Salonika, Egypt, and Palestine.
1904 Haines, Rev. T. T., B.A. (June 14, 1915). Chaplain to the Forces (4th Class). France.
1898 Hamilton, N. C. (Serving Aug. 4, 1914). Maj. R.A.S.C. (Lt.-Col.). D.A.D. of Transport. Gallipoli, France. *O.B.E.* (Mil.). *D.S.O.*, May 2, 1916. *D.* Gallipoli, 1915, 1916; France, 1916 twice, 1917, 1919.
1907 Hare, A. K., B.A. (Sept. 25, 1914). Lt. 25th (Cyclist) Bn. London Regt. (T.F. Res.). Belgium.
1905 Harper, C. H. L., B.M. (July 6, 1916). Hon. Capt. R.A.M.C. (Red Cross Hospital, Netley).
Harrington, P. W. (Dec. 22, 1915). 2nd Lt. Worcestershire Regt. France, 1916; Mesopotamia, 1917. Killed in action on the Tigris on Jan. 13, 1917.
1920 Hart, F. J. A. (Oct. 28, 1914). Lt. 'F' Batt., R.H.A. (Capt. 1917–19). Gallipoli, 1915–16; Egypt, 1916; France and Belgium, 1916–19. *D.* France, 1918 twice.
1913 **Hartert,* J. C.,** B.A. (Sept. 1914). ‡Lt. 8th E. Yorkshire Regt. (Capt.). France. Killed in action at Serre on Oct. 28, 1916.
1901 Harvey, Rev. G. L. H., B.A. (Dec. 9, 1915). Chaplain to the Forces (4th Class). 2nd Lt. Yorkshire Regt. (1919).
1904 Hatton, G. C., B.A. (Nov. 20, 1915). Lt. R.G.A. (Adjt.). Egypt and Palestine.
1894 Hawkes, Rev. S. F., M.A. (July 3, 1917). Chaplain to the Forces (4th Class). France, Belgium, Germany.
1919 Hazell, E. (Oct. 2, 1915). ‡Lt. 143rd Squadron R.A.F. France, Belgium.
1911 Heawood,* G. L., M.A. (Aug. 26, 1914). Lt. 4th Wiltshire Regt. Acting Capt. No. 19 O.C.B. India, 1914–15; Mesopotamia, 1915–16. (Prisoner of war, May–Oct. 1916.)

1908 Helm, C.von P. (1914). ‡†2nd Lt. 5th London Regt. (London Rifle Brigade). France, 1914–17.
1919 Henson, E. F. L., B.A. (Aug. 8, 1914). ‡Lt. 2nd D.C.L.I. Salonika, 1917–18.
1897 Hepple, Rev. J. D., M.A. (Aug. 29, 1915). Chaplain to the Forces (4th Class). Egypt, France, and Mesopotamia.
1912 Herbert,* C. G. (Oct. 16, 1914). Lt. 16th Middlesex Regt., attd. 6th Queen's (R. W. Surrey Regt.) (Capt.). France. *D.* France, 1918.
1901 Hett, W. S., M.A. (Serving Aug. 1914). Capt. Unattached List, T.F., Brighton College O.T.C.
1907 Hickes, A. G. R., B.A. Inns of Court O.T.C. (Invalided.)
1920 Hicklin, R. P. (Nov. 13, 1917). 2nd Lt. 8th Sqdn. R.A.F. France, Belgium.
1907 Hocking, A. V., B.A. Inns of Court O.T.C. (Invalided.)
1904 Hodson, C. B., M.A. (Oct. 4, 1918). Chaplain to the Forces (4th Class). N. Russia.
1919 Hodson, F. L. C. (Aug. 1914). Capt. 7th Gloucestershire Regt. Gallipoli, Mesopotamia. *M.C.*, Mar. 17, 1917. Cavalier, Order of the Crown of Italy.
1906 Hodson, Rev. R. V., M.A. (Feb. 17, 1916). Chaplain R.N., H.M.S. *New Zealand.*
1901 Hodson, T. A., M.A. (Aug. 1, 1917). 2nd Lt. R.A.S.C. France and Belgium.
1919 Holden, J. M. (Jan. 5, 1916). Lt. R.G.A. (S.R.). France.
1904 Hollway, H. S., B.A. S. African Expeditionary Force. Africa.
1894 Hooper, J. McK., M.A. (May 1916). ‡2nd Lt. Suffolk Regt. Lt., Administrative Officer, R.A.F. France.
1894 Hooper, W. W., B.A. (Sept. 22, 1914). Pte. Imp. Camel Corps. Egypt and Palestine.
1901 **Hornsey, J. F.,** B.M. (July 1917). Lt. R.A.M.C., attd. Shropshire L. I. France. Killed in action near St. Quentin on Mar. 24, 1918.
1907 **Horridge,* R.,** B.A. (Mobilized Aug. 4, 1914). Lt. 4th, attd. 2nd, Manchester Regt. (Capt.). France and Belgium. Killed in action at Wulverghem on Nov. 17, 1914.
1914 Horwill, L. C. (June 28, 1916). Capt. 21st Cavalry Regt., I.A.R.O. Mesopotamia, 1918–19.
1898 Houghton, A. T., B.A. (Aug. 7, 1914). Capt. 4th Loyal N. Lancashire Regt. France and Belgium. *M.C.*, Nov. 26, 1917.
1915 House, C. A. V., B.A. (Aug. 1, 1917). 2nd Lt. 13th London Regt. France. (Invalided.)
1913 **Howard,* W. L.** (Nov. 20, 1914). 2nd Lt. 7th Somerset L.I. Lt. M.G.C. France and Belgium. Died on Aug. 16, 1917, of wounds received in action at Langemarck.
1919 Howe, C. W. (May 3, 1915). Lt. 9th Devonshire Regt. France.
1913 Howes, *B. E. (Sept. 2, 1914). Capt. 9th R. Warwickshire Regt. Gallipoli, 1915; India, Mesopotamia, 1916–18. *M.C.*, Mar. 8, 1919.
1911 **Huckett,* A. W.** (Aug. 29, 1914). Lt. 5th Wiltshire Regt. Gallipoli, 1915. Killed in action in Gallipoli on Aug. 10, 1915.
1919 Hudson, A. K. (May 1, 1918). Gunner R.F.A. Cadet O.C.B.
1911 Hudson,* Æ. H., B.A. (Mobilized Aug. 4, 1914). Capt. 1st London Regt. France and Belgium, 1917.
1904 Hughes, Rev. W. B., M.A. (May 5, 1916). Chaplain to the Forces (4th Class). France.

1909 **Hughes-Jones, H. L.**, B.A. (Jan. 28, 1915). Lt. 11th Middlesex Regt. France. Killed in action on Mar. 3, 1916.

1895 Hunt, A. E., M.A. (Sept. 1914). ‡Capt. R.F.A. India, 1917–18.

1907 Hunt,* Rev. E. S., B.A. (Aug. 1917). Chaplain to the Forces (4th Class). Lce.-Cpl. 28th London Regt. (Artists' Rifles) (since Jan. 1918). France.

1919 Hunter, S. K., B.A. (July, 1917). Conducteur, Section Sanitaire Anglaise, No. 20, Croix rouge française. France.

1919 Hurst, H. N. (Oct. 5, 1917). 2nd Lt. 14th Worcestershire Regt. France.

1914 Hurst, J. H. D., B.A. (Jan. 28, 1915). Lt. 6th, attd. 10th, Arg. & Suth'd. Highlanders. France.

1913 Hussey-Jones, B. A. R.A.M.C. Salonika.

1912 **Ibbotson, R.** (Sept. 7, 1914). ‡Lt. 3rd, attd. 2nd, R. Irish Fusiliers. France and Salonika, 1915–17. Killed in action on Salonika Front on May 2, 1917.

1906 Inman, A. C., B.M., M.A. (Mar. 1915). Hon. Capt. R.A.M.C. France.

1899 Irwin, C. J., B.A. (Jan. 8, 1917). Lt. Nagpur Volunteer Rifles. Palestine. *D.* Palestine, 1919.

1915 Isaac, B. J. (Mar. 1916). ‡Lt. 19th Welsh Regt. France, 1917–19.

1918 Ivamy, E., B.A. (Sept. 1, 1914). Pte. 1/15th London Regt. (Civil Service Rifles). France, 1915.

1912 Jacks, M. L., M.A. (Nov. 24, 1914). Lt. K.R.R.C. Acting Capt. No. 4 O.C.B. France, 1915–16.

1892 Jackson, Rev. C. J., M.A. (Feb. 23, 1915). Pte. 24th R. Fusiliers. Chaplain to the Forces (4th Class). France. *D.* France, 1918.

1913 Jardine, L. W. (Mobilized Aug. 4, 1914). Capt. 1/5th Queen's (R. W. Surrey Regt.). India, 1914–15; Mesopotamia, 1915–19. *D.* Mesopotamia, 1918.

1902 **Jeffries, H. J. F.**, B.A. (Mobilized Aug. 1914). Maj. 5th Leicestershire Regt. (T.F.). France and Belgium, 1915. Killed in action near Hooge on Sept. 26, 1915.

1893 [Jenkins, Rev. N. Ll., M.A.] (Sept. 1915). Chaplain to the Forces (4th Class). 2nd Lt. S. Wales Borderers. France, 1915–16.

1900 Jones, Rev. C. Mortimer. Chaplain to the Forces (4th Class), N.Z.E.F. France.

1919 Jones, E. G. A. (June 28, 1915). 2nd Lt. 4th York and Lancaster Regt. Lt. R.A.F. France, 1916–18. *M.C.*, Mar. 3, 1917. *D.* France, 1917.

1908 **Joy,* T. C. B.**, B.A. (Aug. 1914). Capt. 1st Devonshire Regt., attd. 2nd Dorsetshire Regt. France and Mesopotamia. Killed in action in Mesopotamia on Dec. 11, 1915.

1914 **Joyce, G. E.** (Jan. 11, 1915). Lt. 10th Leicestershire Regt. France. Killed in action on Sept. 19, 1916.

1904 Kay, A. S., B.A. (Mar. 26, 1915). Lt. R.G.A. (S.R.).

1912 **Keep, D. S. H.** (Aug. 4, 1914). ‡Capt. 7th Bedfordshire Regt. France and Belgium, 1915–17. *M.C.*, Nov. 25, 1916. Killed in action at Ypres on July 14, 1917.

1919 Keep, N. H. (June 1917). Cadet R.F.A. France.

1908 **Keith, D. H.**, B.A. (Feb. 1915). 2nd Lt. 17th Highland L.I., attd. 18th Durham L.I. (Capt.). France and Belgium. Killed in action near Arras on Aug. 31, 1917.

1893 Kirkaldy, A. W. (Nov. 7, 1916). 2nd Lt., temp. Lt. O.T.C. (T.F.).
1893 Lake, F. J. C. (Sept. 29, 1918). Pte. 2/28th London Regt. (Artists' Rifles).
1908 Lane-Davies, Rev. J. G., M.A. (Mar. 20, 1917). Chaplain to the Forces (4th Class). France. (Prisoner of war in Germany.) *M.C.*, June 3, 1918.
1910 Lazarus, K. M., M.A. (Sept. 10, 1914). ‡Lt. 6th Worcestershire Regt. Maj. M.G.C. France, 1915, 1917, 1918. *D.* France, 1919.
1910 **Leadbitter,* G. G.,** B.A. (Oct. 18, 1914). 2nd Lt. 1/4th Northamptonshire Regt. Gallipoli, Egypt and Palestine, 1915–17. Killed in action at the Second Battle of Gaza on Apr. 19, 1917.
1908 **Learoyd,* D. G.,** B.A. (Jan. 1916). Lt. Inland Water Transport R.E. Mesopotamia. Died of fever at Basra on Dec. 13, 1917.
1911 **Ledger,* R. K.** (Aug. 1914). Lt. 6th Rifle Brigade, attd. 1st R. Welch Fusiliers. France. *D.* France, 1915. Killed in action near Neuve Chapelle on Apr. 13, 1915.
1910 Lee,* D. J. N., B.A. (Apr. 29, 1915). Capt. R.G.A., attd. Indian Army. India, Burma, Aden, 1916 ; Palestine, 1918–19.
1894 Legard, G. S., B.A. (Aug. 11, 1914). Capt. 3rd Durham L.I. France and Belgium.
1913 **Leigh,* J. C. T.** (Aug. 26, 1914). Capt. 6th The Buffs (E. Kent Regt.). France. Killed in action in the Battle of the Somme on July 3, 1916.
1904 Lennard, R. V., M.A. (Aug. 1917). ‡Paymaster Sub-Lt., R.N.V.R.
1891 Leslie, D. (Apr. 1, 1917). Capt. Volunteer Bn., Nagpur–Bengal Rly.
1911 Lewis, N. P., B.A. (Nov. 27, 1914). Lt. R. Fusiliers. France.
1909 Lingard,* A. L., B.A. (June 15, 1915). Capt., Technical Officer, R.A.F.
1911 Lithiby, J. S., B.A. (Dec. 31, 1914). Capt. 11th Manchester Regt. Staff-Capt. General List, empld. O.C.B. Gallipoli, Egypt, and Palestine. *D.* Gallipoli, 1916 ; § Aug. 1918.
1888 Llewellyn, J. C. T. (Oct. 30, 1914). Capt. 3rd Devonshire Regt., attd. Labour Corps.
1913 Lowdermilk, W. C., B.A. (1917). Engineer, Forestry Corps, U.S. Army. France.
1884 Luckley, Rev. H. O., M.A. (Nov. 28, 1916). Chaplain to the Forces (4th Class).
1904 Ludlow Hewitt, A. A. T., B.A. (Mar. 23, 1915). Capt. R.A.S.C. France. *D.* France, 1919.
1897 McClure, A., B.A. Maj. R.E. E. Africa.
1897 Macfadyen, Hon. E., B.A. (Dec. 2, 1917). 2nd Lt. R.G.A. France.
1907 Macfarlane,* W. A., B.A. (May 23, 1915). Lt. R.A.S.C. France and Salonika. *D.* Salonika, 1919.
1919 Machin, M. I. (Apr. 7, 1915). Lt. 4th Dorsetshire Regt. and M.G.C. Mesopotamia, Egypt, and Palestine.
1908 Mackain, C. A., M.A. (Feb. 3, 1916). Sub-Lt. R.N.V.R. H.M.S. *Pembroke*, H.M.S. *Almanzora*, H.M.S. *Orvieto*, N. Atlantic Squadron.
1899 Mackay, Rev. H. W., M.A. (Nov. 1915). Chaplain to the Forces (4th Class). France.
1912 Mackay,* R. J., B.A. (Sept. 14, 1914). ‡Lt., temp. Maj., 9th London Regt. (Queen Victoria's Rifles). Instructor whilst empld. with Military Mission, U.S.A. France.
1904 Mackenzie, J. L., B.A. 70th Bn. Signallers R.E. (T.F.). Egypt, Palestine, France.

1907 Mackintosh,* C., B.A. (Sept. 22, 1914). Capt. 1/4th R. Scots. Staff-Capt. 229th Inf. Bde. H.Q. Gallipoli, Egypt, Palestine, and France. *M.C.*, June 3, 1919. *D.* Palestine, 1918.

Maclagan, P. W. (Sept. 5, 1914). 2nd Lt. 5th Border Regt. France. *D.* France, 1915. Killed in action on Apr. 16, 1916.

1910 **Macleod,* G. C.,** B.A. (Sept. 8, 1914). ‡Lt. K.O. Scottish Borderers. Gallipoli, Egypt, and Palestine. Killed in action at the Second Battle of Gaza on Apr. 19, 1917.

1911 MacLeod, N., B.A. (Sept. 22, 1914). Lt. 1st K.O. Scottish Borderers, attd. 2nd Bn. Slavo-British Legion (Capt.). Gallipoli, Egypt, France, N. Russia. (Prisoner of war in Germany.) *D.* May 5, 1919.

1903 Macmahon, N. C. M., B.A. (Mobilized Aug. 4, 1914). Maj. 5th London Bde, R.F.A. Staff-Captain, Dept. of Adjt.-Gen., War Office. France, 1915. *D.* § Aug. 1917.

1919 McNeill, W. M. (Nov. 5, 1918). Pte. R.A.F.

1909 Macqueen,* W. (Sept. 21, 1914). 2nd Lt. R.F.A. France. (Invalided on account of wounds.)

1891 Macvey, T. (July 19, 1915). Maj. General List. G.S.O. 3, Censor Staff. France. *O.B.E.* (Mil.). *D.* France, 1917, 1918, 1919.

1896 Madden, C. H. (May 30, 1917.) Lt. 3rd, attd. 8th, Somerset L.I. France. *M.C.*, Dec. 2, 1918; *Bar*, Feb. 15, 1919.

1901 Maddison, Rev. W., M.A. (Oct. 11, 1915). Chaplain to the Forces (4th Class), attd. 75th Inf. Bde. H.Q. Belgium, France.

1904 Mann, A. J., M.A. (Sept. 4, 1914). 2nd Lt. 7th E. Lancashire Regt. Staff-Captain (H.Q. Staff), Air Ministry, R.A.F. Salonika.

1909 Manson, A. G. B. (Dec. 14, 1914). Lt. Lancashire Fusiliers. France.

1903 Marrs, R., M.A. (Oct. 1914). Capt. Bombay Volunteer Artillery. Maj. Political Dept., M.E.F. Mesopotamia, 1915–19. *C.I.E.* *D.* Mesopotamia, 1919.

1914 Marsden, H. W., B.A. (July 8, 1915). Lt. S. Lancashire Regt. France. *D.* France, 1917.

1899 Marsh, C. H., B.A. (Oct. 21, 1916). 2nd Lt. I.A.R.O.

1910 **Marsh,* C. W. B.,** B.A. (Aug. 26, 1914). Lt. 6th The Buffs (E. Kent Regt.). France. Killed in action in France on Oct. 13, 1915.

1903 Marshall, C. J., B.A. (Mar. 30, 1915). Lce.-Cpl. R.A.S.C. (M.T.). France, 1915–19.

1911 Marshall, R., B.A. (Sept. 1, 1914). ‡Lt. R.N.V.R., Flag Lt., H.M.S. *Rameses*. German S.W. Africa, 1915; German E. Africa, 1915–17; Egypt, 1917; Minelaying Squadron, 1918. *D.* E. Africa, 1916.

1891 Marshall, R. (Jan. 10, 1917). Capt. R.E. (Inland Water Transport). Egypt.

1907 **Martin,* W. H.,** B.A. (Oct. 1914). ‡2nd Lt. 24th London Regt. (The Queen's). France, 1915, 1916. Killed in action at High Wood on Sept. 14, 1916.

1895 **Martyn, Rev. C. R.** (Sept. 7, 1917). Chaplain to the Forces (4th Class). France. *D.* France, 1916, 1918. Died on Mar. 3, 1919, at Rouen, of illness contracted while on active service.

1919 Marwood, B. V. (Aug. 20, 1917). Lt. R.E. (Signals). France and Belgium, 1918–19.

1909 Mathewson,* W. G., B.A. (Oct. 19, 1914). Capt. 7th The Black Watch. France. (Invalided.)

1894 Matthew, Rev. H. H., M.A. (Jan. 1, 1916). Chaplain to the Forces (4th Class). France.

1912 **Maxwell,* J. H.** (Sept. 1914). Pte. 9th R. Scots. France and Belgium. Killed in action near Ypres on May 22, 1915.

1919 Meade, R. F. (Jan. 8, 1918). Cadet O.C.B., R.A.S.C. France (attd. British Consulate, Dieppe and Havre).

1903 Measham, R. J. R. (Oct. 12, 1914). Capt., Acting Lt.-Col., Asst. Director Postal Services, R.E. France and Belgium. *O.B.E.* (Mil.). *D.* France, 1918, 1919.

1898 **Medley, E. F.** Pte. Canadian E.F. France and Belgium. Died on May 28, 1918, of wounds received in 1917.

1906 Merrick, H., M.A. (Sept. 4, 1914). ‡Capt. 1st Gloucestershire Regt. France. *M.C.*, June 19, 1917.

1898 Michell, Rev. G. L., M.A. (May 1917). Chaplain to the Forces (4th Class). France and Belgium, 1917–19.

1919 Millard, F. A. C. (Dec. 8, 1916). Lt. R.F.A., attd. H.Q. 49th Divl. Artillery, R.F.A. (Capt. and Adjt.). France and Belgium, 1917–19.

1908 Milne, Rev. J. L., B.A. (Feb. 16, 1917). Chaplain to the Forces (4th Class), attd. 11th Welsh Regt. Salonika. *O.B.E.* (Mil.). *D.* Salonika, 1919.

Mockridge, G. E. 2nd Lt. M.G.C. France. Killed in action on July 21, 1916.

1913 Monck, H. G. H. (Dec. 30, 1914). Lt. 3rd, attd. 7th, Shropshire L.I. France.

1896 Monro, F. R. D'O., B.A. (May 1916). Lt. R.G.A. France, 1917–18.

1907 Moorwood, J., B.A. (Aug. 29, 1917). Lt. R.A.S.C.

1895 Moran, C. G., B.A. (Oct. 14, 1919). Capt. 14th Middlesex Regt. Capt. General List, specially empld. Gallipoli, 1915; France, 1915–18.

1912 Morris, A. E., M.A. (Nov. 28, 1917). 2nd Lt., Acting Capt., 2nd R. Fusiliers. France.

1919 Morris, F. G. (Sept. 25, 1918). Pte. 58th Wing, R.A.F.

Morris, F. St. V. (Aug. 7, 1915). 2nd Lt. 3rd Sherwood Foresters, attd. R.F.C. France. Died on Apr. 29, 1917, of wounds received in action.

1900 Morris, H. H., M.A. (Mobilized Aug. 1914). Capt. 6th Gloucestershire Regt. Salonika. (Invalided.)

1902 Morrison, J. H. (Oct. 16, 1914). ‡Lt. R.N.V.R. H.M.S. *Benbow*, H.M.S. *Plover*.

1888 Mumford, Rev. J. T., M.A. (Nov. 30, 1914). Chaplain to the Forces (4th Class). France. *D.* § Mar. 1919.

1898 Murray, Rev. A. C. R., B.A. Chaplain to the Forces (4th Class).

1920 Napier, J. L. (Aug. 1914). ‡Lt. 2/4th York & Lancaster Regt. (Capt.). France, 1916–19.

1898 Nash, E. C., M.A. (Feb. 25, 1915). Capt. 38th Divl. Train, R.A.S.C. France. *D.* France, 1917 twice.

1910 Nethersole, M. H. B., B.A. (Sept. 27, 1914). ‡Maj., Flying Officer, R.A.F. France, 1914–18; Germany, 1919. *D.S.O.*, Feb. 8, 1919. Croix de Guerre.

1919 Newall, G. A. (Aug. 9, 1918). 2nd Lt. Middlesex Regt.

1919 Newton, R. E. (1918). 2nd Lt. R.F.A. (after demobilization).

1911 Nicholson, J. W., B.A. (Aug. 4, 1914). Tpr. King Edward's Horse. Lt. I.A.R.O., attd. 12th Cavalry. India, 1916–17; Mesopotamia, 1917–19.

1902 Nicholson, R. H., B.A. (Apr. 1, 1918). Capt., Acting Maj., Technical Officer, R.A.F.

1909 Norton,* Rev. H. R., B.A. (Dec. 27, 1916). Chaplain to the Forces (4th Class). Egypt, Palestine, India.

1904 **Orde Ward, A. P.,** B.A. (Apr. 1, 1916). ‡Lt. 4th (Res.) Lincolnshire Regt., attd. M.G.C. (Capt.). France, 1916, 1917, 1918. Accidentally killed at Grantham on Nov. 11, 1918.

1911 Osborn, A. S. J. (Jan. 3, 1916). Lt. 4th, attd. 5th, Norfolk Regt. France.

1905 Osborne, R. B., B.A. (Apr. 1, 1917). Lt. 5th Grenadier Guards. France. *M.C.*, June 3, 1919.

1914 Osborne Jones, D. G., B.A. (Mar. 25, 1915). Lt. M.G.C. (Lt. and Adjt.). France, 1916, 1917; Italy, 1917–18.

1913 Osmaston,* B. H. (Feb. 17, 1915). Lt. 3rd Dragoon Guards. France.

1906 [Owen, Rev. R. H., M.A.] (Aug. 1914). Lt. Unattached List, T.F., Uppingham School O.T.C.

1907 Owen Williams, I., B.A. (July 1, 1918). Cpl. 23rd R. Welch Fusiliers.

1897 Page, L. M. S. (Serving Aug. 4, 1914). Maj., Bt.-Lt.-Col., R.A.S.C., Asst. Director of Transport. France, 1914–18. *D.S.O.*, Jan. 1, 1917. *D.* France, 1915, 1916 twice, 1917, 1918, 1919.

1912 Paine, G. I., B.A. (Nov. 27, 1914). Capt. R.E. France, Belgium. *D.* France, 1918.

1919 Palmer, C. D. (May 3, 1918). 2nd Lt. R. Sussex Regt.

1919 Palmer, C. H. (Mar. 16, 1918). 3rd Air Mechanic, R.A.F.

1919 Palmer, F. N. (Sept. 9, 1915). ‡Lt. 5th Essex Regt., attd. Ministry of Labour. France, 1916–17.

1914 Palmer, G. H. (Nov. 28, 1915). 2nd Lt. 12th Rifle Brigade. France. (Invalided.) Died in Oxford on Oct. 27, 1918.

1913 Parker, E. H. T., B.A. (Feb. 27, 1915). Lt. R.F.A., empld. Ministry of Munitions. France.

1919 Paton, S. H. (Aug. 10, 1918). 2nd Lt. 140th Heavy Batt., R.G.A. France, Belgium.

1913 Pawsey,* C. R., B.A. (Sept. 2, 1914). Capt. 1/8th Worcestershire Regt. France, 1915–17; Italy, 1917–18. *M.C.*, Jan. 14, 1916; *Bar*, June 18, 1917. *D.* France, 1915.

1903 Peck, L. J., M.A. (July 13, 1915). Lt. Indian Cavalry, I.A.R.O., attd. 2nd Lancers. France, India, Mesopotamia. *M.C.*, Jan. 18, 1918.

1887 Peckett, R. G., B.A. Chief Mechanical Engineer (with rank of Lt.-Col.), Egyptian Railway Transport. Egypt. *C.B.E.* (Civil).

1909 Peel, G. A., B.A. (Sept. 16, 1914). ‡Lt. Cheshire Regt., attd. R.G.A.

1919 Peeler, E. F. (Feb. 1917). Lt. 1st (Garr.) Bn. Suffolk Regt. Egypt, 1918–19.

1907 Peers,* J., M.A. (July 1, 1915). Lt., Acting Capt., R.G.A. France.

1896 Percival, Rev. S. T., M.A. (June 19, 1917). Chaplain to the Forces (4th Class). France, Italy, Belgium.

1899 Pittman, W., B.A. Enslin's Horse, Southern Force, S. Africa.

1903 Porcher, Rev. G. L., M.A. (July 13, 1916). Chaplain to the Forces (4th Class). France and Belgium, 1916–18.

1893 Potter, J. R., M.A. (Aug. 3, 1915). Lt. R.N.V.R. Maj., Technical Officer, R.A.F.

1911 Pounsford, C. (Oct. 8, 1914). Major R.A.S.C. Dep. Asst. Director General of Transport. France.

1912 **Powers,* H. G.** (Sept. 2, 1914). Capt. 5th Hampshire Regt. Acting Capt. and Adjt. I.A.R.O., attd. 1st Gurkha Rifles. India, 1914; Mesopotamia, 1916–18; Palestine, 1918. *M.C.*, Aug. 25, 1917. *D.* Mesopotamia, 1917; Palestine, 1918. Killed in action in Palestine on Sept. 19, 1918.

1904 Price, B. M., B.C.L. (May, 1917). Capt. U.S. Inf.

1919 Price, S. J. W. (Sept. 1918). Ord. Seaman R.N.V.R. H.M.S. *Victory VI.*

1920 Price, W. A. B. (Oct. 8, 1914). ‡2nd Lt. 1/6th Welsh Regt. France.

1914 Pritchard, L. A. T., B.A. (June 26, 1915). Capt. R.A.F. France, Belgian Coast.

Puckridge, C. V. N. (Feb. 21, 1915). 2nd Lt. 5th Gloucestershire Regt. France. Missing, presumed killed in action in Aug. 1916.

1905 Pullein Thompson,* H. J., B.A. (Jan. 10, 1917). Capt. 1st Queen's (R. W. Surrey Regt.) (Bde. Maj.). France. *M.C.*, Jan. 1, 1919.

1914 **Pulling, O. L.** (Mar. 26, 1915). 2nd Lt. R.G.A. France. Missing, believed killed in action in Sept. 1915.

1912 Ramage, W. E., M.A. (Aug. 23, 1915). Lt. 6th The Black Watch.

1919 Rau, A. (July 31, 1917). Pte. Middlesex Regt. (Cpl.). France.

1919 Read, J. H. (Sept. 5, 1918). 2nd Lt. D.C.L.I. (on demobilization).

1919 Redhouse, H. E., B.A. (July, 1915). Lt. 8th Middlesex Regt. France.

1900 Redman, Rev. C. W. C., M.A. Chaplain to the Forces (4th Class). India.

1920 Rees, B. (July 3, 1917). Bomdr. 57th Batt., 15th Bde., R.G.A. (Cpl.). France, 1918–19; Germany, 1919.

1919 Rees, G. S. (Mar. 8, 1917). ‡2nd Lt. Cheshire Regt. Belgium, France, 1917–18.

1912 Rees, R. N. K., B.A. (Dec. 22, 1914). Lt. Sherwood Foresters. Lt. R.E. attd. for Army Signals. France.

1912 Rhodes,* R. F. E., B.A. (Nov. 12, 1914). Lt. 15th Hussars. France. *M.C.*, July 26, 1918.

1899 Richards, F. C. M., M.A. (Sept. 14, 1914). ‡Lt. 1st (Garr.) Bn. Essex Regt. Egypt, 1916; Sudan, 1917; Arabia, 1917; Palestine, 1918; Macedonia, 1918; Montenegro, 1919; Albania, 1919.

1904 **Richards, J. D. E.,** B.A. (Aug. 1914). ‡Lt. 2nd R. Sussex Regt. France, Belgium. Killed in action at Loos on Sept. 25, 1915.

1888 Ritson, F. W., M.A. (Serving Aug. 4, 1914). Capt. and Q.M. Durham University O.T.C.

1909 Roberton, W. P., B.A. (Sept. 4, 1914). ‡Capt. 12th Hampshire Regt. France, 1915; Salonika, 1916–18; Danube, 1919.

1899 Roberts, P., B.A. (1917). Ambulance Corps, U.S. Army.

1908 Roberts,* P., M.A. (July 7, 1916). Lt. R.F.A. France. Croix de Guerre.

1909 Rochford,* C. E., M.A. (June 1, 1916). Capt. 3rd London Regt., attd. M.G.C. France.

1920 Russell, A. J. A. (Jan. 25, 1915). Pte. R.A.M.C., attd. No. 2, General Hospital, B.E.F. (Cpl.). France.

1887 Rutherford, C. R., M.A. (Jan. 1917). 2nd Lt. R.A.S.C.

1867 Ryan, Rev. V. J., M.A., V.D. (Mobilized Aug. 4, 1914). Chaplain to the Forces (1st Class). (Retired Oct. 1916.) *D.* § Feb. 1917.
1886 Sadler, F. J., D.M. (May 25, 1915). Capt. R.A.M.C.
1919 Samuel, A. (Dec. 15, 1915). Lt. R.G.A. (S.R.). France.
1919 Sarif, N. (Aug. 18, 1915). Pte. S. Rhodesia Column. German E. Africa, NE. Rhodesia.
1919 Savage, J. de la M. (Feb. 22, 1916). Tpr. Q.O. Oxfordshire Hussars. France and Belgium.
1919 Scott, G. C. (Feb. 4, 1917). 2nd Lt. R.F.A. (S.R.). France.
1910 **Selbie,* R. J.,** B.A. Lt. Highland L.I., Canadian E.F. France. Killed in action on June 13, 1916.
1912 **Seymour,* L. T.** (Aug. 4, 1914). ‡Lt. 2nd York & Lancaster Regt. France and Belgium. Killed in action at Beaumont Hamel on Aug. 13, 1916.
1912 Shannon, R. W. (Mobilized Aug. 1914). Lt. Somerset L.I. (S.R.). France and India.
1920 Shedden, H. R. G. (Nov. 1917). R.F.C., afterwards 2nd Lt. Irish Guards (S.R.).
1909 Sheldon, A. F. B., B.A. Middlesex Regt. (Invalided.)
1910 **Sherriff, J. G.** (Mobilized July, 1914). Lt. 7th Arg. & Suth'd. Highlanders (T.F.). France and Belgium. Killed in action near St. Julien on Apr. 25, 1915.
1892 Simon, Rt. Hon. Sir John, M.A., *K.C.V.O.* (Sept. 1917). Maj. R.A.F. France. *O.B.E.* (Mil.). *D.* France, 1918.
1919 Single, J. (May 1, 1918). Gnr. 46th Res. Bde., R.F.A.
1907 Sinkinson, A. P. le M., B.A. (Aug. 15, 1914). Capt. 5th R. Fusiliers. Staff-Captain, G.H.Q., France. France and Belgium, 1914–15, 1916–19; Mediterranean E.F., 1915. *O.B.E.* (Mil.). *D.* France, 1919.
1897 Smallhorn, C. A., B.M., M.A. (Jan. 12, 1915). Lt. R.A.M.C. France. *D.* France, 1915.
1919 Smart, J. E. (Oct. 1914). Lt., Acting Capt., attd. 1/5th Manchester Regt. France, Belgium, 1916–18. *M.C.*, Jan. 1, 1918. Belgian Croix de Guerre.
1919 Smith, P. F. (Aug. 1914). ‡Lt., Acting Capt., K.R.R.C., attd. 34th London Regt. France, 1915–16, 1917, 1918–19; Italy, 1917–18. *M.C.*, Nov. 19, 1917.
1913 Smith, R. W., M.A. 2nd Lt. Unattached List, T.F., King William's College O.T.C.
1913 **Snell, C.** (Aug. 1914). ‡2nd Lt. 10th W. Riding Regt. France, 1915–16. Died on July 14, 1916, of wounds received in action on the Somme.
1897 Snow, C. A., M.A. (Apr. 23, 1915). Lt. Indian Army, attd. 1st Gurkha Rifles. India, 1915–16; Mesopotamia, 1916; Persia, 1919. *D.* Mesopotamia, 1918.
1919 Spear, E. N. (Jan. 5, 1917). Lt. R.F.A. (S.R.). France.
1911 Squire,* E. A., M.A. (Dec. 22, 1914). Lt. 8th Gloucestershire Regt. France. (Prisoner of war in Germany, 1917–18.)
1919 Stafford, G. W. (Apr. 26, 1917). Lt. 4th Northumberland Fusiliers.
1900 Stanford, W. (Sept. 25, 1914). Maj. R.F.A., attd. R.E. France, 1914–19. *O.B.E.* (Mil.). *D.* France, 1918.
1886 Stenning, J. F., M.A. (Mobilized Aug. 4, 1914). Lt.-Col. O.U.O.T.C.,

attd. No. 4 O.C.B. Liaison Officer between the University and War Office. *C.B.*, 1916. *C.B.E.* (Mil.). *D.* § Aug. 1917; § Mar. 1918.

1905 Stewart, Rev. P. A., M.A. (Sept. 3, 1914). Pte. R.A.M.C. ‡Chaplain to the Forces (3rd Class). France, 1915–17; Mesopotamia, Egypt, 1918–19. *M.C.*, Dec. 11, 1916. *D.* France, 1916.

1889 Stocks, E. V., M.A. (Oct. 1914). 2nd Lt. Unattached List, T.F., Durham University O.T.C.

1908 Stockton, W. T., B.A. (1917). Capt. 320th Batt., F.A., U.S. Army.

1898 Storr, F. H., B.A. (Oct. 25, 1914). ‡Capt. General List, attd. Staff. France. *O.B.E.* (Mil.). *D.* France.

1911 Stott,* T. M. (Sept. 30, 1914). Capt. 5th Manchester Regt. Gallipoli, Salonika, France.

1893 Strachan-Davidson, K. D. B., M.A. (Jan. 13, 1915). Pte. 23rd R. Fusiliers. ‡2nd Lt. R. Defence Corps. France, Egypt. (Invalided.)

1894 Struben, R. H. (Nov. 15, 1916). Maj. Army Remount Service. France, 1917; Belgium and Germany, 1919. *O.B.E.* (Mil.). *D.* § Mar. 1919.

1913 Sukuna, J. L. V., B.A. French Foreign Legion. France.

1900 Summers, Rev. G. E., M.A. (Sept. 5, 1916). Chaplain to the Forces (4th Class).

1915 **Sutcliffe, O.** (Dec. 31, 1915). 2nd Lt. 4th K.O.Y.L.I. France. Killed in action on Nov. 3, 1916.

1913 Swain, F. G., B.A. Lt. U.S. Army Res.

1919 Tapley, R. A. B. (May 1917). 2nd Lt. R.F.A. France, Germany.

1896 Taylor, J., M.A. Driver R.A.S.C.

1897 Tennent, H. M. (Apr. 20, 1915). Capt., Acting Maj., R.A.S.C. *O.B.E.* (Mil.). *D.* § Feb. 1917.

1914 Thatcher, J. S. (Dec. 22, 1914). Lt. Somerset L.I. France.

1898 Thirkell White, E. H. (Dec. 19, 1916). Capt. 28th S. Andaman Coy., I.A.R.O.

1911 **Thomas,* D. C.** (Feb. 1915). Rfln. 1st Rifle Brigade. France. Killed in action on Oct. 18, 1916.

1899 **Thorp, H.,** B.A. Pte. Friends Ambulance, R.A.M.C. France. *M.M.* Died on Sept. 22, 1917, of wounds received in action.

1906 Thorp,* M., B.A. (May 7, 1915). Capt. I.A.R.O. Staff-Captain Persian Lines of Communication. Mesopotamia and Persia. *D.* Mesopotamia, 1919.

1898 Townley, R. (Dec. 1915). Gnr. R.F.A. (Bomdr.). France and Belgium.

1892 Trewby, C. M. A. K.R.R.C. France.

1897 Turnbull, T. M. (Oct. 10, 1914). Capt. R.A.S.C. (M.T.). Capt. Q.-M.G. 3, War Office. France, 1914–16. *M.B.E.* (Mil.). *D.* § Mar. 1918, Mar. 1919.

1898 **Turner, J. P.,** M.A. (Sept. 25, 1915). 2nd Lt. 3rd, attd. 14th, R. Warwickshire Regt. France and Belgium. Killed in action on Oct. 26, 1917.

1919 Unmack, E. W. (July 30, 1916). Lt. R.A.F. Aegean Sea and Eastern Mediterranean. *D.F.C.*, June 3, 1919.

1898 **Ussher, B.** (Serving Aug. 4, 1914). Capt. Leinster Regt. Bde. Maj. 29th Div. Gallipoli. Killed in action in Gallipoli on June 22, 1915.

1919 Vigne, J. C. L. (Nov. 11, 1914). ‡Lt. R.A.F. German S.W. Africa, German E. Africa.

1912 **Von Winckler, M. W.** (June 16, 1915). Lt. Middlesex Regt. France. Killed in action on Aug. 1, 1917.

1907 Wade-Gery, H. T., M.A. (Sept. 1914). Maj. 19th Lancashire Fusiliers. France, 1915–18. *M.C.*, June 3, 1918.

1908 Wainwright, C. D. Pte. R.A.M.C.

1904 Walker,* G. W. H., B.A. (Nov. 17, 1915). Lt. R.E. France.

1894 **Walsh, L. P.** (Oct. 2, 1915). Capt. Dublin Fusiliers. France. Died on July 4, 1916, of wounds received in action on the Somme.

1914 Walsh, W. C. de C. (Dec. 5, 1914). Lt., Acting Capt., R.A. France. *D.* France, 1918.

1906 Walsham How, Rev. W. H., B.A. (Feb. 4, 1918). Chaplain R.N., H.M.S. *Chester*. Grand Fleet.

1901 Wanstall, F. E. B. 2/1st Cambridgeshire Regt.

1920 Ward, F. E. (Apr. 30, 1917). Lce.-Cpl. 1/8th Essex Regt.

1910 Wardroper,* P. R. 2nd Lt. N. Rhodesian Police. German E. Africa. *D.* E. Africa, 1918.

1906 **Wathes,* T. S.,** B.A. (Sept. 1914). Capt. 6th R. Warwickshire Regt. France. Missing, believed killed in action on July 29, 1916.

1912 **Watts, R. C.,** B.A. (Mar. 1917). Pte. A.S.C. Drowned in sinking of H.M.T. *Transylvania* on May 4, 1917.

1898 **Webster, E. W.,** M.A. (Mar. 1915). Capt. 13th K.R.R.C. France. *D.* France, 1917. Killed in action at Monchy le Preux on Apr. 9, 1917.

1912 Weir,* P. M. A. (Sept. 3, 1914). Maj., Acting Lt.-Col., R.A.S.C. France, Mesopotamia, Kurdistan. *O.B.E.* (Mil.). *D.* Mesopotamia, 1919; Kurdistan, 1919.

1919 Wells, S. C. (Sept. 5, 1914). ‡Capt. 9th Northumberland Fusiliers. France and Belgium.

1919 Wernham, J. W. K. (May 6, 1915). Capt., Acting Maj., 18th Bn. M.G.C. France, Belgium. *M.C.*, Jan. 14, 1918.

1919 West, S. G. (Jan. 27, 1915). Lt. Hampshire Regt. (Capt.). Egypt, Senussi Campaign, 1916; Salonika, 1916; France, 1917.

1913 **Westmore,* L. A.** (Nov. 1915). 2nd Lt. 1st Hampshire Regt. France. Killed in action in the Battle of the Somme on July 1, 1916.

1919 Whitney, E. P. (May 10, 1918). Cadet No. 20 O.C.B. 2nd Lt. (after demobilization).

1883 Whittington, Rev. F. B. B., M.A. (Serving Aug. 1914). Chaplain (3rd Class), attd. Cambridgeshire Regt.

1901 Whittington, R. P., M.A. (May 1, 1916). Lce.-Cpl. 25th Canadian Inf. France, 1916–18. *M.M.*, Sept. 5, 1917.

1898 **Whitworth, J. H.,** M.A. (Oct. 1914). Maj. 2/6th Manchester Regt. France, 1917–18. *D.S.O.*, June 22, 1918. *M.C.*, Sept. 28, 1917. *D.* France, 1918. Died on Mar. 31, 1918, of wounds received in action near Dompierre.

1911 Willett,* L. H. (Oct. 18, 1915). Capt. 3rd The Black Watch, attd. War Office. France and Mesopotamia.

1911 Williams, C. D., B.A. (Nov. 10, 1914). Lt. 2/7th Northumberland Fusiliers (Capt.). France and Belgium, 1915; Egypt, 1917; Sudan, 1918.

1892 Williams, Rev. F. E. A., M.A. (July 1916). Chaplain to the Forces (4th Class). France, Belgium, Italy, 1916–18. *M.C.*, Feb. 1, 1919. *D.* Italy, 1918.

1914 Williams, G. B. (Mar. 12, 1915). Capt. 4th, Lt. 5th, Leicestershire Regt. France. *M.C.*, June 3, 1916; *Bar*, Sept. 16, 1918. (Prisoner of war in Germany, 1918.)
1919 Williams, J. E. (Feb. 1917). Cadet No. 16 O.C.B.
1911 Williams,* L. F. M., B.A. (Aug. 5, 1914). Capt. and Adjt. 1/6th R. Sussex Regt.
1900 Williams, R. F., B.A. (Apr. 8, 1915). Maj. 1st Dock Bn. King's (Liverpool Regt.).
1919 Willison, W. L. P. (Sept. 2, 1914). Capt. 1/6th Hampshire Regt. India.
1895 Wilson, A. R., D.M. (Serving Aug. 1914). Lt. R.A.M.C.
1907 Wing, S. T., M.A. (Oct. 26, 1918). 2nd Lt. U.S. Infantry, Liaison Service. France (État-Maj., 8th Region, Bourges, Cher.). Médaille d'Honneur des Affaires Étrangères.
1913 Wire, L. T. (Sept. 29, 1914). Lt. 11th Hampshire Regt. France.
1906 Wood, F. P., M.A. (Nov. 28, 1914). ‡Lt. 1/6th Suffolk Regt. France, Belgium.
1919 Wood, K. S. (Feb. 24, 1916). ‡Lt. R.A.F. (Capt.). France, 1917; Italy, 1918.
1897 Woodward, Rev. Canon C. S., M.A. (Dec. 27, 1916). Chaplain to the Forces (4th Class). France. *M.C.*, Sept. 25, 1918.
1919 Woolley, A. R. (Dec. 10, 1917). 2nd Lt. R. Warwickshire Regt. (on demobilization).
1906 Woolley,* H. W. (Jan. 27, 1915). Lt., Acting Capt., R.F.A. France. *M.C.*, Jan. 1. 1917.
1908 **Wright,* A. A.,** B.A. (Apr. 3, 1915). Lt. 3rd, temp. Capt. 12th, E. Surrey Regt. France. Killed in action on Sept. 4, 1918.
1902 Wright, Rev. C. H. T. (June 27, 1918). Chaplain to the Forces (4th Class). 2nd Lt. R.A.S.C. (M.T.). France.
1909 **Wright,* E. T.,** B.A. (Oct. 27, 1914). Capt. 20th R. Fusiliers. France. Killed in action on Mar. 13, 1916.
1909 Wylie, C. E. F. (Aug. 1, 1917). 2nd Lt. Oxf. & Bucks. Lt. Infty. Salonika.
1904 Young, R. B., B.A. (Serving Aug. 4, 1914). Capt., Bt.-Maj., Sherwood Foresters, Bde. Maj. India, 1914; France, 1914–15.
1910 Ziegler, W. A., B.A. (1917). Capt. Artillery, U.S. Army.

PEMBROKE COLLEGE

1891 Adams, J. W. B., M.A. (Aug. 20, 1914). ‡2nd Lt. R.A.S.C. France, Belgium.

1914 Ainscough, J. P. (Apr. 16, 1915). 2nd Lt. 10th S. Lancashire Regt. Lt. 21st Bn. M.G.C. France, 1916–18. (Prisoner of war, Mar.–Dec. 1918.)

1907 Aldworth,* A. A., M.A. (Sept. 12, 1914). Maj. Leicestershire Regt. (Lt.-Col.). France. *M.C.*, Nov. 25, 1916.

1903 Allen, Rev. G. B., B.D. (Mar. 23, 1917). Chaplain to the Forces (4th Class), (1917); Chaplain, R.A.F. (1918).

1898 Amcoats, Rev. W. (Apr. 9, 1918). Chaplain to the Forces (4th Class). France. *D.* France, 1917, 1918. (Prisoner of war.)

1878 Andrewes, Sir F. W., D.M. (Mobilized Aug. 1914). Maj. R.A.M.C., attd. 1st London General Hospital. *O.B.E.* (Mil.).

1919 Angus, W. S. (Sept. 5, 1917). 2nd Lt. 5th N. Staffordshire Regt. France.

1906 Archibald, M. T. (Jan. 31, 1917). Lt., Acting Capt., Tank Corps. France. *M.C.*, Feb. 8, 1918.

1919 Ashton, F. (Oct. 3, 1914). ‡Lt. R.F.A. (S.R.) (Capt.). France, Belgium. *M.C.*, Jan. 1, 1919. *D.* France, 1917.

1919 Bailey, A. G. (Nov. 30, 1914). ‡Lt. 277th Siege Batt., R.G.A. Gallipoli, 1915; France, 1917–19.

1910 Baldwyn,* C. F., B.A. (Oct. 3, 1914). Capt. and Adjt. 2nd Worcestershire Regt. France.

1898 Balleine, Rev. R. W., M.A. (Sept. 12, 1914). Chaplain to the Forces (4th Class). France. *M.C.*, Jan. 1, 1918.

1912 **Ballinger,* F. A.** (Aug. 1914). 2nd Lt. 4th King's (Liverpool Regt.). France, Belgium. Killed in action at Richebourg l'Avoué on May 22, 1915.

1903 Bancroft, W., M.A. (Apr. 9, 1917). Lt. 5th R. Welch Fusiliers.

1893 Barker, S. L. P. (1914). Capt. 6th The Buffs (E. Kent Regt.) (Res. of Officers).

1909 Barnes, H. A., B.A. (Jan. 30, 1915). ‡Lt. 13th W. Yorkshire Regt. Gallipoli, Egypt, Salonika.

1919 Barnes, H. C. (June 21, 1918). Lce.-Cpl. 2/28th London Regt. (Artists' Rifles) (Cpl.).

1911 Barnes, T. B., M.A. (Dec. 5, 1914). Lt. 11th Essex Regt. France, 1915–16.

1916 **Barrows, M. D.** (Aug. 23, 1917). 2nd Lt. 1/5th Sherwood Foresters (Capt. and Adjt.). France. *M.C.*, Sept. 24, 1918. Killed in action near Bellenglise on Oct. 3, 1918.

1913 **Bass, P. B.** (Nov. 13, 1914). Lt. 5th Cheshire Regt. France. Killed in action in the Battle of the Somme on July 1, 1916.

1911 Bates, S. F. (Oct. 11, 1914). ‡Lt. 1st S. Lancashire Regt. Mesopotamia, 1915–17; India, 1918–19.

1900 Battersby, C. H. (Nov. 10, 1914). Capt. W. Somerset Yeomanry, attd. 7th D.C.L.I.

1913 **Beaumont, E. P.** (May 1915). Lt. 17th King's (Liverpool Regt.) (Capt.). France, 1916–18. *M.C.*, July 31, 1917. Died on Apr. 2, 1918, of wounds received in action near St. Quentin on Mar. 22.

1907 Beckett, R. C., B.C.L. (May 11, 1917). Capt. 1st Bn. Trench Artillery, U.S. Army. France, 1918.

1900 Bell, S. L. (Sept. 8, 1914). ‡Capt. 9th W. Yorkshire Regt. France. *M.C.*, Jan. 1, 1917.

1910 **Benson, C. S.** (Dec. 22, 1914). Lt. 6th Oxf. & Bucks. Lt. Infty. (Capt.). France, Belgium. Killed in action at Trescoult on Apr. 24, 1917.

1920 Bertram, C. A. G. (Dec. 29, 1915). Lt. 3rd York & Lancaster Regt. Instructor, No. 10 O.C.B. France.

1914 Betts, R. N., B.A. (May 26, 1915). Lt. 1/7th King's (Liverpool Regt.). France, Belgium. *M.C.*, June 3, 1919.

1919 Bezzant, J. (June 19, 1917). Artificer (Engine room) H.M.S. *Victory*. H.M.S. *Robina*, Western Channel Patrol, 1917–18.

1918 Bharucha, J. S. (Sept. 17, 1917). Cpl. Bombay University Inf., I.D.F. India.

1919 Birks, S. (Sept. 12, 1914). Sergt. 1/5th N. Staffordshire Regt., attd. Gas Services. France, 1915, 1916–18; Egypt, 1915–16.

1915 Bisson, L. A. (May 9, 1917). Pte. R.A.M.C., afterwards Spr. R.E. France, Belgium.

1908 Blair-Fish, W. W. (Jan. 25, 1916). Pte. 3/14th London Regt. (London Scottish).

1908 **Blount-Dinwiddie,* J. T.,** B.A. (Aug. 1914). Capt. 1st Border Regt. German S.W. Africa, Gallipoli. *D.* German S.W. Africa, 1915; Gallipoli, 1915. Died on Sept. 13, 1915, of wounds received on Aug. 21 at Anafarta Ridge.

1903 Boughton, Rev. J. N., M.A. (Mar. 10, 1918). Chaplain to the Forces (4th Class). France, Belgium.

1907 **Brandreth,* A. K. B.,** M.A. (1914). Pte. Public Schools Bde., R. Fusiliers. France. Killed in action on Nov. 1, 1916.

1919 Bray, F. (Jan. 26, 1915). ‡2nd Lt. N. Staffordshire Regt. Gallipoli, Egypt, German E. Africa. *M.S.M.* *D.* E. Africa.

1919 Bridges, A. E. (Sept. 14, 1918). 2nd Lt. R.M.A.

1898 Brooks, J. H. (Dec. 16, 1914). Capt. R.G.A. S. Africa, 1915–16; Malta, 1918–19.

1913 Brooks-King,* M. (Oct. 14, 1914). Lt. 2/5th Somerset L.I. Burma, India.

1919 Broome, L. G. B. (Apr. 26, 1917). Pte. R. Berkshire Regt. (Lce.-Cpl.). France. (Invalided on account of wounds, Nov. 1918.)

1914 Brown, F. (Mar. 1917). Spr. R.E. France.

1905 **Brown, J. R.,** M.A. (Mobilized Aug. 4, 1914). Capt. 7th Highland L.I. Gallipoli, 1915; Egypt, Palestine, 1916–17. Died on Apr. 23, 1917, of wounds received in action at Gaza.

1912 Bryars, W. D. (Aug. 4, 1914). Sergt. R.A.M.C. France, Belgium, 1914–19.

1920 Bubb, C. H. L. (Feb. 1917). ‡Lt. 6th London Regt. (Capt.). France.

1897 Buchanan, G. A., M.A. (Nov. 16, 1916). Lt. Grenadier Guards. France.

1915 Buchler, M., B.A. (Feb. 8, 1916). Pte. 2/19th London Regt. (C.S.M.). Egypt, Palestine.

1906 Burnand,* R. F., M.A. (Mobilized Aug. 1914). Capt. 6th Northumberland Fusiliers. Maj., Chief Instructor, M.G. Training Centre. France. *O.B.E.* (Mil.). *D.* France, 1918.

1914 Butler, E. D. (July 26, 1915). Lt. 116th Heavy Batt., R.G.A., afterwards empld. in Research Dept., Ministry of Munitions. France, 1915–16.

1903 **Cadle, L. M.** (1916). Capt. 18th Bn. A.I.F. France. Killed in action on May 14, 1918.

1899 Campbell, D. (Serving Aug. 4, 1914). Maj. 8th Arg. & Suth'd. Highlanders (Lt.-Col.). France. T.D. *D.* § Aug. 1917.

1912 **Card, S. H.** (Feb. 1915). ‡2nd Lt. 1st Somerset L.I. France. Killed in action at Fampoux, near Arras, on Apr. 10, 1917.

1891 Carden, Sir F. H. W., Bt. (Serving Aug. 4, 1914). Maj. 1st Life Guards. France, 1914–15.

1904 Carothers, N. (Dec. 6, 1917). Capt. General Staff, U.S. Army.

1919 Carr, H. R. C. (Aug. 18, 1915). Sub-Lt. R.N.V.R. France.

1905 Casswell,* J. D., B.A. (Dec. 28, 1914). Maj. R.A.S.C. France, 1915–17. *D.* France, 1917.

1882 **Chaplin, C. S.** (Serving Aug. 4, 1914). Lt.-Col. 9th K.R.R.C. France, Belgium, 1915. Killed in action at Messines on July 30, 1915.

1911 **Chapman, R. S.,** B.A. (Dec. 1915). Rfln. 2/5th London Regt. (London Rifle Brigade). France, Belgium. Died on Sept. 22, 1917, of wounds received in action on Sept. 20.

1907 Chappell,* R. G. (Oct. 18, 1915). Sub-Lt. R.N.V.R.

1919 Charles, H. C. (Jan. 13, 1915). Lt. 4th R. Irish Rifles (Capt.). France, Macedonia.

1891 Chichester, C. H. (Serving Aug. 4, 1914). Maj. 2nd Devonshire Regt. Maj. Labour Corps. *D.* § Feb. 1917.

1919 Churchill, H. C. (Serving Aug. 4, 1914). ‡Lt. Gold Coast Regt. 1914–15. Lt. 1st Bedfordshire & Hertfordshire Regt. Togoland, 1914; Cameroons, 1915–16; India, 1917–19.

1908 Clark, J. F., M.A. (Sept. 1914). Capt. 8th Border Regt. (Invalided.)

1909 Clark,* W. S., B.A. (Oct. 4, 1915). Lt. 7th Arg. & Suth'd. Highlanders, attd. 4th S. Wales Borderers.

1920 Clarke, E. A. (Mobilized Aug. 1914). Capt. R.F.A. (T.F.). France, 1917 (attd. R.F.C.).

1911 Coady, J. M. C., B.A. Canadian Engineers.

1908 Collings,* Rev. H. C., M.A. (July 3, 1917). Chaplain to the Forces (4th Class), attd. R. Guernsey L.I. France, 1917–19.

1916 Collins, T., B.A. (Apr. 1917). Pte. R.A.M.C. France.

1880 Congreve, Sir W. N., **V.C.**, *M.V.O.* (Serving Aug. 4, 1914). Lt.-Gen. Commanding VII Army Corps. France, 1914–18. *K.C.B.* Croix de Commandeur de la Légion d'Honneur. Order of St. Anne (1st Class). *D.* France, 1915, 1916, 1917, 1918 twice.

1904 Conway, H. P. (Sept. 25, 1914). 2nd Lt. 16th Lancers (S.R.).

1912 **Cook, C. E.** (Jan. 30, 1915). 2nd Lt. 3rd, attd. 2nd, R. Sussex Regt. France. Died on July 8, 1916, of wounds received in action on the Somme.

1910 Corballis, J. C. J. (Aug. 15, 1914). Capt. 5th Leinster Regt. (Adjt.). France.

1904 Corfield, E. T. (Apr. 25, 1915). Capt. R.M.A.

1907 Cranmer,* J. E. A., B.A. (Sept. 2, 1914). Lt. 1/4th Oxf. & Bucks. Lt. Infty. Belgium. (Invalided, July 14, 1916.)

1898 **Crawford, G. S.,** M.A. (1914). Maj. 6th S. Wales Borderers. France. Died on Aug. 10, 1917, of wounds received in action.

1917 Creed, T. P. (June 6, 1915). ‡Lt. 5th Leicestershire Regt. France, 1916–17. *M.C.*, Mar. 3, 1917.

1908 **Croft,* R. W. S.** (Sept. 1914). Capt. 7th Yorkshire Regt. France. *D.* France, 1915, 1916. Killed in action near Arras on May 12, 1917.

1903 Cross, S. T., M.A. (Mobilized Aug. 4, 1914). Capt. 3rd Gloucestershire Regt. G.S.O. 3. France. *D.* France, 1917.

1919 Croydon, F. E. (Aug. 5, 1914). ‡Lt. Labour Corps. France, Belgium.

1907 Cryer, J. B., M.A. (Dec. 10, 1915). Lt. 3rd R. W. Kent Regt., attd. 15th Hampshire Regt. France, Belgium, 1917–18. *M.C.*, Sept. 16, 1918.

1912 Cullen, A. A., B.A. (Mobilized Aug. 4, 1914). 2nd Lt. 6th R. Dublin Fusiliers. Lt. R.A.F. Gallipoli, 1915; Serbia, 1915; Salonika, 1916, 1917; Egypt, 1917–18; Mesopotamia, 1918; Persia, 1918. *D.* Salonika, 1917. (Prisoner in Turkey, Aug.–Nov. 1918.)

1913 Cullen, W. J. (Sept. 26, 1914). Lt. 7th Leinster Regt. (Capt.). France, 1915–16. *M.B.E.* (Mil.).

1877 **Dauber, J. H.,** B.M., M.A. (Dec. 1914). Lt.-Col. R.A.M.C., E. Anglian C.C.S. Lost in H.M. Transport *Royal Edward* on Aug. 13, 1915.

1919 Davies, C. B. (Aug. 6, 1914). ‡Staff-Captain Intelligence Corps, G.H.Q., Great Britain. E. Africa, 1914–16. *M.B.E.* (Mil.). *D.* § Mar. 1919.

1919 Davies, R. W. H. (Jan. 6, 1916). Lt., Acting Capt., Y/4th T.M.B., R.F.A. France, 1916–19.

1897 De la Motte, R. B. (Serving Aug. 4, 1914). Maj. Supply & Transport Corps, Indian Army. Mesopotamia. *D.S.O.*, June 3, 1916. Order of the White Eagle (5th Class) (with swords). *D.* Mesopotamia, 1916.

1897 Demuth, W. E., M.A. (Aug. 4, 1914). Pte. Nyasaland Vol. Res. ‡Capt. 3rd Tank Bde., Tank Corps. Nyasaland, 1914–15; France, Belgium, 1917–19. *M.C.*, Jan. 1, 1919. *D.* France, 1918.

1913 Derbyshire, H. A., M.A. (Oct. 1914). 2nd Lt. 15th Sherwood Foresters. France, 1916.

1908 **Derrick,* J. L.,** B.A. (Sept. 4, 1914). ‡Capt. 6th Yorkshire Regt. Egypt, France, Belgium. Killed in action at Langemarck on Aug. 27, 1917.

1913 Dickinson, J., M.A. (May 26, 1915). Lt. 2/7th King's (Liverpool Regt.), attd. 2/4th K.O.Y.L.I. (Capt.). France.

1910 **Dodgson,* K. V.,** B.A. (Aug. 22, 1914). Lt. 8th Devonshire Regt. France. Killed in action at Loos on Sept. 25, 1915.

1902 Done, W. E. P., M.A. (Sept. 26, 1914). Capt. 5th R. Sussex Regt. Staff-Captain. Salonika, Egypt, Italy. *M.C.*, Jan. 1, 1918. Croce di Guerra. *D.* Italy, 1918.

1914 Donkin, H. A. L. (Nov. 24, 1914). Capt. 7th R. Berkshire Regt. France, 1915; Salonika, 1915–16, 1917–19. *M.C.*, Jan. 1, 1919.

1906 Doré, R. H., B.A. (Aug. 1914). 2nd Lt. 9th Welsh Regt. (Relinquished Commission on account of ill health, Jan. 1915.)

1920 Doty, J. D. (Aug. 28, 1917). Capt. 19th Inf., 18th Div., U.S. Army.

1911 **Downes, O.** (Aug. 25, 1915). 2nd Lt. 2/8th Durham L.I. Died on June 7, 1916, of illness contracted while on active service.

1910 Drew, A., M.A. Pte. M.T. Coy., R.A.S.C. France.
1902 **Drew, R.** (Sept. 1914). Sergt. 22nd R. Fusiliers. France, Belgium. Killed in action at Vimy Ridge on May 23, 1916.
1913 Duncan, G. W., M.A. (Jan. 11, 1915). Lt. 9th Durham L.I.
1913 Dymoke,* L. M. (May 30, 1915). Lt. 8th Middlesex Regt.
1905 Eady, R. B. (Dec. 21, 1916). Lt. R.A.S.C.
1896 Eastwood, F. N. (Oct. 1914). Lt.-Col. 2/22nd London Regt. (The Queen's). France, 1916; Salonika, 1916–17; Egypt and Palestine, 1917–19. *M.C.*, Jan. 8, 1918. *O.B.E.* (Mil.). *D.* Salonika, 1917; Palestine, 1917; Syria, 1919.
1912 Eck,* C. R. (May 1, 1916). ‡Lt. R.A.F. (Observer). France.
1912 Edwards,* C. V. (Sept. 1, 1914). 2nd Lt. 3rd Suffolk Regt., afterwards Cpl. Q. O. Cameron Highlanders. France. (Invalided, Mar. 31, 1916; afterwards re-enlisted.)
1898 Eldridge, J. M., M.A. (Sept. 17, 1914). ‡Maj. 14th King's (Liverpool Regt.). France, 1915; Macedonia, 1915–18; France, 1918.
1886 Ellison, Rev. H. B., M.A. (May 1, 1915). Chaplain to the Forces (4th Class), attd. 33rd Div. France, 1915–17.
1908 Ellwood, V. T., D.M. (Nov. 16, 1915). Capt. R.A.M.C. (T.F.).
1911 English, H. B., B.A. (Sept. 1917). ‡Capt. Sanitary Corps., U.S. Army.
1920 Evans, A. G. (Sept. 4, 1914). Cpl. 108th Bde., R.F.A. France, 1915–17.
1919 Evans, E. V. (Sept. 19, 1914). ‡Lt. Welsh Regt. France.
1910 Evill, C. G. (Sept. 1914). ‡Capt. 12th R. Sussex Regt., afterwards Lt. M.T. Coy., R.A.S.C. France.
1893 Fanshawe, L. A., B.A. (Serving Aug. 4, 1914). Maj., Acting Lt.-Col., R.A.O.C. India, 1914–18; Mesopotamia, 1918–19. *D.S.O.*, June 3, 1916. *O.B.E.* (Mil.). *D.* India, 1916; Mesopotamia, 1919.
1919 Farrell, J. (July 5, 1917). 2nd Lt. Rifle Brigade. France. (Prisoner of war, May–Dec. 1918.)
1919 Farrimond, W. (Feb. 1, 1916). ‡Lt. 14th R. Warwickshire Regt. (Capt.). Belgium, France, Italy. *M.C.*, Aug. 15, 1918. *D.* Italy, 1918.
1914 Faulkner, R. (Dec. 5, 1915). Capt. 3rd Queen's (R. W. Surrey Regt.). France. *M.C.*, Aug. 25, 1916.
1912 **Fergusson,* E. K. O.** (Sept. 10, 1914). Capt. 8th Seaforth Highlanders. France. *D.* France, 1915. Killed in action at Loos on Jan. 26, 1916.
1919 Field, H. F. (Jan. 6, 1917). Bandsman 6th Oxf. & Bucks. Lt. Infty. France, Belgium.
1908 Filleul,* D. S. A. (Aug. 16, 1914). 2nd Lt. R. Jersey Artillery. (Relinquished Commission on account of ill health, Nov. 12, 1917.)
1891 Fleming, Rev. H. J., M.A. (Serving Aug. 4, 1914). Chaplain to the Forces (2nd Class). France. *C.M.G.* *D.* France, 1915, 1916.
1919 Floyd, T. H. (Jan. 25, 1916). ‡Lt. 2/5th Lancashire Fusiliers. France, Belgium, Germany. *D.* France, 1919.
1899 Fox, C. V. (Serving Aug 4, 1914.) Maj. Scots Guards. France, Belgium. *D.S.O.*, Oct. 1914. Medjidieh (3rd Class). *D.* France, 1914, 1915; May 5, 1920. (Wounded and taken prisoner at Kruiseik, Oct. 1914, escaped July 1917.)
1902 Fox, G. D., B.A. (Nov. 26, 1914). Lt. 4th Lincolnshire Regt. (Capt.). France. *M.C.*, Sept. 26, 1918.

1898 Franklin, H. E. H., B.A. (Sept. 1, 1917). 2nd Lt. R.G.A.
1908 French, A. K. (1914). 2nd Lt. R.F.A.
1886 Gainsford, Rev. G. B., M.A., T.D. (Serving Aug. 4, 1914). Chaplain (3rd Class) (T.F.), attd. Hertfordshire Regt.
1919 Gainsford, G. J. (Aug. 27, 1917). 2nd Lt. Suffolk Regt. Lt. Labour Corps. France.
1907 Gedge,* A. L. C., B.A. S. African Mounted Rifles. German S.W. Africa, 1915.
1906 Gibbs, G. B. (Sept. 14, 1914). Pte. 2/1st Warwickshire Yeomanry.
1903 Giles, P. B. (Aug. 10, 1914). Cpl. Hauraki Coy., Auckland Regt., N.Z.E.F. (Sergt.). Egypt, 1914, 1915; Gallipoli, 1915. (Invalided, Sept. 1915.)
1907 Gill, W. R. de H. (1914). Pte. 17th R. Fusiliers.
1920 Ginever, A. H. (Sept. 5, 1914). ‡Lt. R.A.S.C., attd. 215th Siege Batt., R.G.A. Egypt, 1916; Salonika, 1916–17; France, 1917–19.
1900 Gist, F. (Nov. 27, 1914). Capt. 2/1st Northamptonshire Yeomanry. France, 1916–17.
1908 Gladstone,* F. C., D.M. (July 26, 1915). Surgeon R.N. H.M.S. *Centurion*, Grand Fleet, 1915–17.
1911 Godfrey, C. H. W. (1914). ‡Flight Lt. R.N.A.S. *D.*
1919 Goldsmith, E. E. (July 29, 1916). Signalman R.N.V.R.
1899 Goodchild, C. O., B.A. (Mobilized Aug. 4, 1914). Capt., Acting Maj., R.H.A. (T.F.). France. *M.C.*, June 3, 1918.
1909 **Goody,* G. R.** (Sept. 1914). ‡Lt. K.R.R.C. France. Accidentally killed in France on July 13, 1918.
1896 Goudge, Rev. W. H., M.A. (Serving Aug. 4, 1914). Chaplain and Instructor Commdr. R.N., H.M.S. *King George V*. Grand Fleet, 1914–17.
1901 Graham, R. S. (Oct. 6, 1914). Lt. R.A.O.C.
1894 **Gray, L.,** M.A. (Oct. 15, 1914). Lt. 5th Essex Regt. (Capt.). Gallipoli, Egypt, Palestine. Died at Alexandria on July 31, 1917, of illness contracted while on active service.
1911 Greig, P. H. (Nov. 1, 1915). Lt. 7th The Buffs (E. Kent Regt.). Egypt, Palestine. *M.C.*, Aug. 3, 1919.
1919 Gruchy, E. Ll. (May 5, 1917). Gnr. R.G.A. France, Belgium, 1917–18.
1908 **Guest-Williams, W. A.,** M.A. (Serving Aug. 4, 1914). Capt. 2nd R. Berkshire Regt. India, France, Belgium. Killed in action near Bois Grenier on Sept. 25, 1915.
1911 Gunderson, H. A., B.A. (Aug. 27, 1917). Capt. 57th M.G. Bn., U.S. Army (Maj.).
1883 Gwynne, R. J. (Serving Aug. 4, 1914). Brig.-Gen. Headquarters Staff, Ottawa. Director-General of Mobilization, Canada. *C.M.G.* *D.* 3 times.
1904 Hadley, P. E., M.A. (Dec. 1, 1916). Lt. Special Lists.
1909 Haines, Rev. R. E. M., B.A. (Jan. 1916). Chaplain to the Forces (4th Class). E. Africa, 1916–17; France, 1917–19. *D.*
1894 Halford-Thompson, R. (Mobilized Aug. 1914). Capt., Hon. Maj., R.F.A. (S.R.). Salonika, Egypt.
1892 Hall, W. (Mobilized Aug. 4, 1914). Lt. Col. Arg. & Suth'd. Highlanders. France.
1919 Hamblen, H. J. (Oct. 1915). ‡Capt. 3rd R. Inniskilling Fusiliers. Egypt, Palestine, 1917; France, 1918.

1902 Hancock, F. W. (Oct. 12, 1915). Capt. Special Lists, whilst Adjt. Prisoners of War camp.

1908 Hardman, T. P., M.A. (Aug. 1917). Capt. American Red Cross. France, 1918–19.

1878 Hawkins, H. P., D.M. (Mobilized Aug. 6, 1914). Lt.-Col., Bt.-Col., R.A.M.C. *C.B.E.* (Mil.). *D.* § Feb. 1917, § Mar. 1919.

1919 Hayman, P. B. (July 9, 1915). ‡Lt. 30th Bn., A.I.F. France, 1916–18.

1919 Heath, H. C. (May 16, 1916). ‡2nd Lt. Cheshire Regt. France, Belgium, Germany.

1913 Hedges, W. P. (Nov. 9, 1914). Lt. 130th Bde., R.F.A. Belgium, Egypt, Salonika.

1905 **Henson, S. B.** (Serving Aug. 4, 1914). 2nd Lt. Somerset L.I. France. Killed in action on Dec. 27, 1914.

1914 Henson, S. B., B.A. (Dec. 30, 1915). Lt. 3/5th The Buffs (E. Kent Regt.), afterwards Lt., Technical Officer, R.A.F. France, 1917 ; Mesopotamia, 1918–19.

1919 Henwood, W. E. (Jan. 30, 1918). Cadet R.A.F. Lce.-Cpl. Inns of Court O.T.C.

1914 Hewitt, R. M. (Oct. 19, 1915). Lt. E. Lancashire Regt., attd. War Office.

1909 Heyworth,* T. F., B.A. (Jan. 4, 1916). Lt., Acting Capt., Arg. & Suth'd. Highlanders, attd. 9th O.C.B. France.

1913 **Hichens, W. T.** (Aug. 1914). 2nd Lt. 1st D.C.L.I. France. Killed in action at Guillemont on Sept. 3, 1916.

1913 Hickley, T. N. (Aug. 1914). H.A.C. France. (Invalided.)

1912 **Hill,* R. B. T.** (Aug. 1914). Capt. 11th Essex Regt. France. Killed in action near Lens on June 3, 1917.

1898 Hingston, A. (Aug. 1916). Maj. R.A.F. France, 1918. *M.B.E.* (Mil.).

1919 Hoare, C. F. C. (Mar. 25, 1915). Lt. 1st D.C.L.I. (Capt.). France, 1915–17 ; Salonika, 1918.

1911 Hoby, J. C. J., D.Mus. (Serving Aug. 4, 1914). Lt. R. Marines. France, 1917.

1913 Hodgkins, S. K. (Dec. 1914). Capt. 4th Leicestershire Regt. France, 1915, 1918.

1912 Holford, W. F., M.A. (Apr. 30, 1915). Lt. 3rd Queen's (R. W. Surrey Regt.), attd. 6th Cavalry Bde. India, Mesopotamia.

1913 **Holme, G. W.** (Apr. 1915). 2nd Lt. R.F.A. France. Killed in action at Longueval on Dec. 22, 1916.

1902 Hopkyns, D. K., M.A. (Nov. 24, 1914). Maj. R.E., Postal Section. Salonika, 1915–16 ; France, 1916–18 ; Italy, 1918–19. *D.* France, 1917 ; Italy, 1918 ; Salonika, 1919.

1903 Hughes, Rev. H., B.A. (Serving Aug. 4, 1914). Capt. Unattached List, T.F., King's School, Worcester O.T.C.

1899 Humphreys-Davies, G. A. (1914). Lt. Res. of Officers, late Imperial Yeomanry.

1913 **Hutcheson, A. G.** (Aug. 1914). Capt. and Adjt. 9th Cameronians. France. *M.C.*, Jan. 14, 1916. *D.* France, 1915. Killed in action at Montauban on July 14, 1916.

1911 Hutcheson, J. H., B.A. (Sept. 28, 1914). Capt. 11th Arg. & Suth'd. Highlanders. France. *D.* § Mar. 1919.

1911 Iliffe, Rev. E. E. C., M.A. (Sept. 8, 1918). Chaplain to the Forces (4th Class). Died on Jan. 1, 1920.

1905 Illingworth, C. H. (Feb. 17, 1916). Lt. R.N.V.R.

1890 Incledon-Webber, W. B., M.A. (Sept. 9, 1914). ‡Capt. 3rd County of London Yeomanry. France, 1917. (Relinquished Commission on account of ill health, May, 1919.)

1919 Ingrams, L. S. (Nov. 20, 1917). 2nd Lt. Coldstream Guards (S.R.).

1919 Jack, R. H. (Mar. 11, 1915). ‡Lt. Essex Regt., attd. 1st Manchester Regt. France, India, Mesopotamia, Egypt, Palestine.

1905 **Jalland,* H. H.,** M.A. (Dec. 4, 1915). Lt. 3rd, attd. 10th, The Black Watch. Palestine. *D.* Palestine, 1918. Killed in action on Oct. 18, 1918.

1894 Jesse, J. L. (Serving Aug. 4, 1914). Lt.-Col. R.A.S.C. (Col.). France, 1914–18; Italy, 1918–19. *C.M.G.*, Jan. 1919. *D.S.O.*, Jan. 1, 1916. *D.* France, 1914, 1915; Italy, 1918.

1910 **Jones, J. L.** (Sept. 1914). ‡2nd Lt. 3rd Welsh Regt. France. Died on Aug. 13, 1917, of illness contracted while on active service.

1900 Jones, Rev. J. W. P., M.A. (Sept. 21, 1917). Chaplain to the Forces (4th Class).

1908 Jukes, M. N., B.A. (Nov. 24, 1914). 2nd Lt. 8th Cheshire Regt. Gallipoli, 1915. (Invalided on account of wounds, July 6, 1916.)

1906 Kane,* J. L. K., B.A. (Serving Aug. 4, 1914). Capt. 1/109th Infantry, Indian Army. Persia. *O.B.E.* (Mil.).

1902 Keely, T. C. S. (May 21, 1915). Lt. 3rd King's (Liverpool Regt.) (Capt.). France, 1916; Mesopotamia, 1917; Egypt, Palestine, Syria, 1918–19.

1905 Kerr, W. B. (Aug. 14, 1915). Lt. 11th Gordon Highlanders.

1913 **Kewley, G. R.** (June 1915). 2nd Lt. 11th Loyal N. Lancashire Regt. France. Killed in action at Vimy Ridge on May 20, 1916.

1911 Kidd, W. R., B.A. (June 25, 1915). Lt. 4th R. Dublin Fusiliers, attd. R.A.F. France, 1916, 1917–19. *M.C.*, Sept. 22, 1916.

1913 **King, C.** (Oct. 8, 1914). Capt. 9th Queen's (R. W. Surrey Regt.). Maj. 44th Coy., M.G.C. France, 1916–17. *D.* France, 1916. Killed in action at Monchy on Apr. 11, 1917.

1919 King, F. J. (June 15, 1916). Pte. 32nd Bn. M.G.C. France, Belgium, Germany.

1906 **Knight,* R. E.,** M.A. (Aug. 1914). ‡2nd Lt. 1/5th Gloucestershire Regt. France. *D.C.M.* Died on July 22, 1916, of wounds received in action at La Bassée.

1913 Knott, E. H. (Sept. 1, 1914). Lt. 9th R. Fusiliers.

1919 Knowles, J. (Oct. 8, 1916). Lt., Acting Capt., 4th Lancashire Fusiliers. France, 1917–19.

1907 **Kurten, G. P.** (Feb. 7, 1916). Maj. 291st Siege Batt., R.G.A. France, Belgium. *D.* France, 1917, 1918. Killed in action at Villers Bretonneux on Apr. 24, 1918.

1910 Labey,* C. C., M.A. (Sept. 2, 1914). Capt. R.A.S.C. (Maj.). France, 1914–19.

1916 Lane, C. R. (Dec. 1917). 2nd Lt. R.F.A. Italy.

1897 Largie, Rev. W. G., M.A. (1916). Chaplain to the Forces (4th Class). France, Belgium, 1916–17, 1918–19. *D.* France, 1917.

1915 Leatherdale, R., B.A. (Jan. 6, 1916). Sergt. R.A.M.C.

1902 Lee, A. L., B.A. (Mobilized Aug. 1914). Pte. Ceylon Planters Rifle Corps.
1910 Lee, J. H. (Nov. 4, 1915). Lt., Acting Capt., K.R.R.C. France. *D.S.O.*, Nov. 2, 1916. *D.* France, 1916.
1901 Lenton, Rev. C. H., M.A. (Serving Aug. 4, 1914). Chaplain (4th Class) (T.F.), attd. 5th Lincolnshire Regt.
1919 Levy, I. (Aug. 16, 1915). Pte. 1/19th London Regt. (Sergt.). France.
1909 **Liddell,* J. H. T.,** B.A. (Aug. 8, 1914). Lt. 1st K.R.R.C. France. Died on Nov. 17, 1916, of wounds received in action at Beaumont Hamel on Nov. 13.
1905 Lindop, K. (Mar. 28, 1915). Lt. 7th Devonshire Regt.
1881 Longe, H. D. (Feb. 20, 1915). Capt. R. Defence Corps.
1904 Longuet Higgins, Rev. H. H. L., M.A. (Aug. 15, 1915). Chaplain to the Forces (4th Class), attd. 1st Northamptonshire Regt. and 2nd R. Sussex Regt. S. Africa, 1915–17; France, 1917–18; Germany, 1918–19. *M.C.*, June 3, 1919. *D.* France, 1919.
1914 Loughton, H. E. (July 12, 1915). Lt. 5th Norfolk Regt. (Capt.), attd. R.A.F. (1917–18). France.
1911 MacGill, H. C. (Nov. 18, 1914). 2nd Lt. 6th S. Staffordshire Regt.
1919 McKenzie, A. D. F. (Feb. 1917). Cpl. Army Pay Corps.
1909 Mainwaring,* A. J., B.A. (Sept. 21, 1914). Lt. I.A.R.O. Mesopotamia.
1899 Mallam, P. P., M.A. (Feb. 8, 1916). ‡Lt. Coldstream Guards. France, 1916, 1918. *M.C.*, Oct. 16, 1918.
1903 Mansel, E. P. B. (Aug. 1914). ‡Lt. R.N.V.R., Anti-Submarine Div. Gallipoli, Mediterranean, S. Italy.
1914 Marburg, T. (Oct. 1914). Lt., Acting Capt., R.A.F. (Flight Commdr.). France, 1915–16. *A.F.C.*, Jan. 1, 1919.
1919 Margerison, L. C. (Apr. 6, 1917). Pte. 3rd S. Wales Borderers. (Invalided, Feb. 1, 1918.)
1912 Marsh, R. J., M.A. (Mar. 19, 1915). Lt. 1/7th Essex Regt. Egypt, Palestine.
1887 Martyn-Linnington, Rev. R. L., M.A. (Sept. 1, 1918). Chaplain to the Forces (4th Class).
1914 **Mason, V. K.** (Oct. 23, 1914). Pte. C.C.S. Canadian E.F. ‡2nd Lt. 10th Suffolk Regt. France, 1914–16. Killed in action on Aug. 4, 1916.
1903 Meade-King, R. E. B. (Oct. 4, 1915). Lt. 42nd Divl. M.T. Coy., R.A.S.C. France. *D.* France, 1918.
1919 Menzies, Rev. K. (June 6, 1916). Gnr. R.G.A. (1916). ‡Chaplain to the Forces (4th Class), attd. M.G.C.
1919 Millard, N. F. (Jan. 25, 1916). Cpl. R.A.F. (Sergt.). France, Belgium.
1896 Miller, H. N., M.A. (July 1917). Lt. R.N.V.R. Died on Feb. 15, 1919.
1899 Milner, Rev. G., M.A. (Nov. 15, 1917). Chaplain to the Forces (4th Class).
1892 Moffat, W. K. (Oct. 15, 1915). Lt. 13th R. Scots Fusiliers.
1900 Montgomery, J. E., M.A. (Aug. 1914). Capt. Unattached List, T.F., Felsted O.T.C.
1907 Moore,* J. L. M. (Nov. 8, 1914). ‡Maj. R.E. France, Belgium. *M.C.*, July 26, 1918. *D.* France, 1916, 1918.
1887 Moseley, O. G. (Jan. 30, 1915). 2nd Lt., Acting Adjt., 2/1st Cheshire Yeomanry, attd. Manchester Regt.
1901 Moseley, R. (June 12, 1915). Lt. R.N.V.R. Egypt, Salonika.
1910 **Moxly,* J. H. S.** (Aug. 15, 1914). 2nd Lt. 1st Bedfordshire Regt. France, Belgium. Killed in action at Ypres on Mar. 13, 1915.

1919 Mulholland, W. J., B.Litt. (May 6, 1915). ‡Capt. Special Lists, Asst. Director of Education, A.I.F. Gallipoli, 1915–16; Egypt, 1916; France, 1916–19.

1891 Muntz, R. A., B.A. (Oct. 14, 1914). Maj. 2/1st Northamptonshire Yeomanry.

1900 Murley, Rev. J. R. de C. O'G., M.A. (Dec. 29, 1916). Chaplain to the Forces (3rd Class). Salonika. *O.B.E.* (Mil.). Order of the White Eagle (4th Class). *D.* Salonika, 1918, 1919.

1903 Mustard, D. (Oct. 13, 1914). Maj. R.A.S.C.

1903 Nelson, W. H. (Oct. 24, 1914). Lt. R.F.A.

1908 **Nicholl-Carne, O. W.** (1915). 2nd Lt. Welsh Regt. France, Belgium. Killed in action on Aug. 1, 1917.

1910 **Nicoll, F. J.** (Nov. 13, 1914). Lt. 12th Highland L.I. France. Killed in action at Loos on Sept. 25, 1915.

1919 Nicoll, J. F. (Apr. 1917). ‡2nd Lt. 2nd S. Lancashire Regt. France.

1909 Nixon,* E., B.A. (Oct. 19, 1914). Lt., Acting Capt., 7th Northumberland Fusiliers. France. *D.* France, 1919.

1905 Nortjé, P. le F. (1914). Capt. S. African Medical Corps. German S.W. Africa.

1919 Nye, C. W. (Oct. 1, 1914). Cpl. R.A.M.C. France, Belgium, 1917–19.

1902 Oberlé, L. J., M.A. (1914). S. African Mounted Rifles. S. Africa.

1919 O'Brien, J. E. N. (Jan. 23, 1918). 2nd Lt. 2nd Cavalry Res. Regt., Hussars.

1919 Okell, J. D. (May 21, 1915). Lt. 528th Siege Batt., R.G.A. (Capt.). France, Belgium, 1916–17, 1918. *D.* France, 1918.

1904 **Oliphant, M. F.,** B.A. (Jan. 1915). ‡2nd Lt. 5th Norfolk Regt. Gallipoli. Died on Aug. 12, 1915, of wounds received in action at Suvla Bay.

1919 Onslow, F. H. (June 12, 1917). ‡Lt. R. Marines. N. Russia.

1912 Outhwaite, F. O. (June 2, 1915). Lt. 7th Northumberland Fusiliers (Capt.). France, 1916, 1916–17, 1918–19. *M.C.*, July 19, 1917.

1919 Oxtoby, F. E. (Aug. 14, 1916). Pte. Army Pay Corps. France.

1910 Packard, E. W. S., B.A. (Aug. 26, 1916). ‡2nd Lt. 3rd Oxf. & Bucks. Lt. Infty., attd. M.G.C. France, 1917.

Parkes, T. D. (Aug. 1914). ‡Capt. 1st S. Staffordshire Regt. France, Belgium, 1914–17. Killed in action at Polygon Wood on Oct. 5, 1917.

1910 Parry, G. W. R. M., M.A. (Jan. 13, 1915). Pte. 3/5th London Regt., afterwards Pioneer, Special Coy., Special Bde., R.E. Belgium, 1916–19.

1919 Parsons, A. V. (Sept. 7, 1914). ‡Capt. 9th R. Welch Fusiliers. France.

1911 Parsons, F. J. (Sept. 15, 1914). Pte. Herefordshire R.A.M.C. (T.F.), afterwards Sergt. Meteorological Section, R.E. France, Belgium, 1915–19. *D.* France, 1916.

1919 Parsons, K. F. (Aug. 4, 1915). Lt. 3rd Queen's (R. W. Surrey Regt.). France, 1917.

1919 Pattisson, J. R. (Mar. 11, 1917). Lt. 241st Squadron, R.A.F. France. (Interned in Holland.)

1913 Patton, F. L., M.A. (June 14, 1918). 2nd Lt. 41st Coast Artillery Corps, U.S. Army (Capt.).

1910 Pearce, H. K. (Dec. 18, 1914). Capt. 10th London Regt. and R.A.F. France, 1917.

Pearson, A. J. W. (Sept. 3, 1914). ‡2nd Lt. 14th R. Fusiliers, attd. 1st R. Dublin Fusiliers. Gallipoli, 1915–16; Egypt, 1916; France, 1916. Killed in action before Beaumont Hamel on July 1, 1916.

1892 **Pease, J. R.** (1914). Maj. R.G.A. France. Killed in action, Oct. 1915.

1911 Pedley, J. W. D. (1915). H.A.C.

1919 Peterson, H. W. C. (Aug. 28, 1915). Pte. 24th R. Fusiliers. ‡2nd Lt. R.A.F. (after demobilization). France, 1915–17.

1912 Philipson, H. (Mar. 25, 1915). Lt. Scots Guards, empld. Guards M.G. Regt.

1919 Philpott, F. H. (Feb. 5, 1916). Cpl. R.A.F.

1911 Pim,* A. S. (Aug. 15, 1914). Capt. 2nd R. Irish Regt. (Maj.). France, 1914–15, 1917–18. *M.C.*, Feb. 8, 1918. (Prisoner of war, Mar. 21–Dec. 20, 1918.)

1914 Plumptre, R. H. (Dec. 28, 1914). Capt. R.A.S.C. Salonika.

1903 Plunkett, O. (Dec. 18, 1915). Capt. R.A.S.C.

1913 Powell, T. B., M.A. (Oct. 8, 1915). Pte. R.A.M.C. (Lce.-Cpl.). Belgium, France.

1913 Pritchard, E. C. (Oct. 13, 1914). Lt. R.F.A. France. *M.C.*, July 26, 1918.

1892 Prowse, W. B., B.M., M.A. (Mobilized Aug. 4, 1914). Capt. R.A.M.C. (T.F.), 3rd Southern General Hospital.

1913 Ramage,* C. B. (Sept. 22, 1914). Capt. 1/4th R. Scots (Staff-Captain 233rd Inf. Bde.) (Bde. Maj.). Gallipoli, 1915; Egypt, Palestine, 1916–19. *M.C.*, June 3, 1919. Order of the Nile (4th Class). *D.* Palestine, 1918.

1905 Raymond,* H., M.A. (Aug. 14, 1914). Maj. General List. D.A.A.G. 19th Div. France, 1915–19. *O.B.E.* (Mil.). *M.C.*, Jan. 1, 1918. *D.* France, 1916, 1917, 1918, 1919.

1919 Regan, L. W. A. (May 1917). Pte. 1st H.A.C. France.

1919 Rendall, L. A. (Nov. 1, 1915). ‡Lt. 6th London Regt. France, Belgium, 1916–17; France, 1918–19.

1894 Richardson, P. N., M.A. (Dec. 12, 1915). Lt. Special Lists (Graves Registration). France, Belgium.

1919 Richmond, A. S. (Nov. 1914). ‡Capt. 10th R. W. Kent Regt. France, Belgium, 1915–17.

1893 Ricketts, S. T., M.A. (Mar. 4, 1915). Capt. and Adjt. 5th Vol. Bn. Devonshire Regt.

1919 Rickword, J. E. (Sept. 1916). ‡Lt. 5th R. Berkshire Regt. France. *M.C.*, Mar. 8, 1919.

1906 Riley,* L. A. M., B.A. (Oct. 19, 1914). 2nd Lt. R. Jersey Militia.

1908 Riley, R. C. B. (Apr. 19, 1915). Lt. Warwickshire Yeomanry. Lt. R.A.F. France. (Relinquished Commission, Oct. 15, 1918, on account of ill health caused by wounds.)

1902 Roberts, A. N., M.A. (Aug. 6, 1914). ‡Lt. 5th Middlesex Regt. France.

1904 Roberts, Rev. W. K., M.A. (Oct. 8, 1917). Chaplain to the Forces (4th Class). France, 1918–19.

1913 Robinson,* R. W. E. (Aug. 21, 1914). 2nd Lt. 7th Gloucestershire Regt. (Invalided, Nov. 1915.) Afterwards Sergt. 3rd Gordon Highlanders. Gallipoli, 1915.

1908 Rogers, G. L., M.A. (Sept. 1, 1914). Capt. 10th Durham L.I. France, Belgium. *M.C.*, June 3, 1919.
1911 Rogers,* R. B., B.A. (Aug. 28, 1914). Lt. 6th Oxf. & Bucks. Lt. Infty. Lt. M.G.C. (Capt. and Adjt.). France, 1915–16.
1907 Rowland-Thomas, A. R. W., B.A. (Jan. 12, 1915). Capt. 11th S. Wales Borderers. Russia, 1918–19.
1920 Russell, J. F. (Sept. 9, 1916). ‡Lt. 3rd, attd. 51st, Sherwood Foresters. France, 1917; Italy, 1917–18; Germany, 1919.
1904 Ryland, Ll. M. (Sept. 2, 1914). Capt. Special Lists, empld. Ministry of National Service.
1903 Sale, A. B., M.A. (Dec. 27, 1914). Maj. 9th R. Warwickshire Regt. Mesopotamia, India, Salonika, Caucasus. *M.C.*, Aug. 25, 1917.
1898 Salmon, T. G. (Serving Aug. 4, 1914). Capt. 3rd W. Yorkshire Regt.
1919 Sanders, J. N. (Oct. 8, 1917). 2nd Lt. 1st London Regt.
1894 Sandys, G. J., M.A. (1914). Lt. Household Cavalry.
1905 Schofield, Rev. R., B.A. (July 15, 1915). Chaplain to the Forces (4th Class). France, 1917–18.
1898 **Scott, J. C.,** M.A. (Oct. 1914). ‡Lt. Worcestershire Regt. (Adjt.). France. Killed in action on Oct. 18, 1916.
1910 Selbie, W. P., M.A. (Jan. 14, 1915). Capt. 8th E. Surrey Regt. France, 1916–17; Italy, 1917–18; France, Belgium, 1918. *M.C.*, Feb. 1, 1919.
1903 Shepherd, D. A., M.A. (Nov. 27, 1915). Pte. Labour Corps. France, Belgium.
1909 Shepherd, G. H. G., M.A. (Nov. 5, 1914). Lt. 2/4th Oxf. & Bucks. Lt. Infty., attd. R.A.F. France, 1916–17.
1902 Shepherd, Rev. H. F., M.A. (Mar. 5, 1918). Chaplain to the Forces (4th Class), attd. 151st Inf. Bde. France.
1919 Sheppard, E. B. M. (May 12, 1915). Lt. 4th K.R.R.C. (A.D.C.). Egypt, 1916; Salonika, 1916–18.
1920 Simpson, G. F. (Dec. 1916). Capt. 533rd Siege Batt., R.G.A. France, Belgium, 1917–18.
1890 Slator, Rev. T., B.A. (Serving Aug. 4, 1914). Instructor-Commdr. R.N., attd. R.N.A.S. and R.A.F. France, 1916–17.
1900 Smart, R. R. (Sept. 10, 1914). ‡Capt. N. Irish Horse. Staff-Captain 51st (H.) Div. (Maj.). France. *M.C.*, June 3, 1918. *D.* France, 1918.
1916 Smith, A. G. (Sept. 1, 1916). Lt. 17th Batt., R.F.A. France, Belgium, Germany. *M.C.*, Dec. 2, 1918. *D.* France, 1919.
1910 Smith, C. B., M.A. (June 1917). Lt. W. African Service Brigade. W. Africa.
1919 Smith, C. E. (Nov. 22, 1915). Pte. 2/23rd London Regt. France, 1915; Salonika, 1916–17; Egypt and Palestine, 1917–18; Belgium, 1918–19.
1899 Smith, E. A. W. 2nd Lt. A.I.F.
1910 Smith,* H. R. W., M.A. (Jan. 29, 1916). Lt. 16th Manchester Regt. France, 1916–17; Salonika, 1918.
1919 Smith, L. H. (Sept. 1916). ‡Lt. 32nd Bn. M.G.C. (Capt. and Adjt.). France, Belgium, Germany, 1917–19. *M.C.*, Mar. 8, 1919.
1912 Smith, R. S., B.A. (Oct. 1914). Lt. 10th Middlesex Regt., attd. 1st Leinster Regt. Lt. 2/1st Brahmans, Indian Army. Egypt, 1916; Salonika, 1916–17; Palestine, 1917–18; India and Arabia, 1919. *M.C.*, Mar. 26, 1918.

1912 **Smith-Howard, K. O. H.** (Aug. 1915). 2nd Lt. 12th R. Sussex Regt. France. Killed in action on Oct. 18, 1916.

1896 Snowden, R. C. (Aug. 25, 1915). Lt. 5th Bedfordshire Regt.

1919 Spurway, B. J. C. (May 10, 1918). 2nd Lt. 3rd Dorsetshire Regt.

1908 Stead, J., B.A. (1914). Lt. 3rd Norfolk Regt.

1907 Stent, J. P. H., B.A. (Sept. 1, 1916). Lt. I.A.R.O., attd. 103rd Mahratta L.I. (Staff-Capt. Bushire Force). India, Persia. *D.* Persia, 1919.

1912 **Sterling,* R. W.** (Aug. 1914). Lt. 3rd, attd. 1st, R. Scots Fusiliers. France, Belgium, 1915. Killed in action near Ypres on Apr. 23, 1915.

1914 Stokoe, H. N. (Nov. 28, 1914). Lt. 1/4th Loyal N. Lancashire Regt. (Capt.). France, 1915–16, 1918–19. *M.C.*, June 24, 1916.

1912 Stone,* H. J., M.A. (Nov. 2, 1915). ‡Lt. 10th Queen's (R. W. Surrey Regt.). France, 1916; Belgium, 1917, 1918–19; Italy, 1917–18. *M.C.*, Oct. 14, 1918. *D.* France, 1918.

1911 **Sutton,* C. J.** (Sept. 23, 1915). 2nd Lt. R.F.A., attd. Special Bde., R.E. France. Killed in action at Thiepval on July 1, 1916.

1913 Sutton, N. P. (Oct. 1914). Lt. 1st (Garr.) Bn. R. Warwickshire Regt. (Capt.). Gallipoli, Egypt, Palestine.

1906 **Symons, Rev. C. F. J.,** B.A. (Sept. 11, 1914). ‡Lt. 9th R. Welch Fusiliers. France. Killed in action at Loos on Sept. 25, 1915.

1908 Symons, N. J., M.A. (1916). Lt. 2nd Central Ontario Regt., Canadian E.F.

1892 Tetley, J. G. W. (1914). Maj. General List (T.F. Res.).

1919 Tetley, J. N. (Dec. 28, 1917). 2nd Lt. 5th W. Yorkshire Regt., attd. 18th Yorkshire Regt.

1910 Thomas,* E. S. de V. (Sept. 1914). ‡Lt. Shropshire L.I. (Capt.). France, Belgium, 1916–17, 1918–19.

1902 Thomas, W. J., B.A. (Oct. 29, 1914). Lt. 4th The Buffs (E. Kent Regt.), empld. Board of Agriculture and Fisheries (Maj.).

1919 Thompson, H. D. (Jan. 28, 1918). Lce.-Cpl. Inns of Court O.T.C. (Flight-Cadet R.A.F.).

1902 **Thornton, G. R. H.,** B.A. (Apr. 1916). ‡2nd Lt. 16th Batt., R.G.A. France. Killed in action near Laventie on Apr. 9, 1918.

1888 Tod, Rev. W. McL., M.A. (Serving Aug. 4, 1914). Chaplain to the Forces (4th Class). France, 1918–19.

1909 Toogood, E. S., M.A. (1914). ‡Lt. R.A.S.C. France.

1909 Trewhella, F. J. (Aug. 23, 1915). Lt. No. 5 G.H.Q. Res. M.T. Coy., R.A.S.C. Belgium, France, 1915–18.

1902 Trist, F. W. (May 9, 1917). Pte. (1st Class) R.A.F. (Cpl.).

1916 Tue, G. A. (Oct. 1915). Lt. 8th York & Lancaster Regt. (Capt.). France, Belgium.

1905 Tunstall-Behrens, B., M.A. (Mar. 24, 1915). Capt. R.E. France, 1916–17; Italy, 1917–19. Italian Silver Medal for Valour.

1897 Turnbull, Rev. W. H., M.A. (Nov. 9, 1914). Chaplain to the Forces (3rd Class), attd. 27th Div. France, 1915; Salonika, 1915–17.

1919 Turner, J. T. (May 29, 1915). ‡2nd Lt. 9th R. Warwickshire Regt. Lt. R.A.F. Lemnos, Egypt, India.

1897 Twisleton-Wykeham-Fiennes, N. I. E. (Serving Aug. 4, 1914). Maj. 66th Batt., 4th Bde., R.F.A. (Lt.-Col.). Mesopotamia, 1917; Palestine, 1918. *D.S.O.*, Jan. 11, 1919. *D.* Mesopotamia, 1917, 1918.

1919 Tyler, W. J. (Jan. 22, 1918). 2nd Lt. R.F.A. France, Germany.
1909 Tyndall, Rev. E. D., B.A. (Nov. 20, 1915). Chaplain to the Forces (4th Class). France. *M.C.*, Jan. 1, 1918; *Bar*, Oct. 16, 1918.
1895 Tyrrell, F. G. (Jan. 15, 1915). Capt. and Adjt. 13th Yorkshire Regt. (Bde. Maj. 32nd Inf. Bde.). Gallipoli, Egypt, France, Russia. *D.* Gallipoli, 1916.
1919 Usill, H. V. (Apr. 6, 1915). Pte. R.A.M.C. Sergt. 1/10th London Regt. Cadet O.C.B., Egypt. Mudros, Egypt, Palestine.
1916 van Raalte, G. F. (Mar. 1917). Aircraftsman (1st Class) R.A.F., attd. R.G.A. as Wireless Operator. France, Belgium, Germany, 1917–19.
1903 Vowles, C. E., M.A. (Aug. 1915). Lt. 10th D.C.L.I. France, Belgium, Germany.
1917 Walker, J. W. (Nov. 30, 1917). Cadet, O.C.B. Pte. Labour Corps. (Invalided, May 1918.)
1911 **Walsh,* G. P.** (Aug. 1914). Lt. 2nd Sherwood Foresters. France, Belgium. *D.* France, 1915. Killed in action near Hooge on Aug. 9, 1915.
1908 Walton, B. S., B.A. (July 1917). 2nd Lt. R.G.A. France, Belgium.
1907 **Ward,* R. L.,** B.A. (Sept. 10, 1914). ‡Lt. 3rd, attd. 2nd, York & Lancaster Regt. Belgium. Killed in action near Boesinghe on Apr. 21, 1916.
1885 **Wardell, W. H.** (Serving Aug. 4, 1914). Maj. 1/39th Garhwal Rifles, Indian Army (Lt-Col.). France, Belgium, 1914. Killed in action at Festubert on Nov. 24, 1914.
1905 Wardle, C. E. (Aug. 6, 1914). ‡Capt. R.A.F. (Lt.-Col., G.S.O. 1). France, Egypt.
1904 Warne, H. F. M., B.A. (Mobilized Aug. 1914). Maj. 15th London Regt. (Civil Service Rifles). France, Belgium, 1916–17. (Prisoner of war, 1917–18.)
1910 Watson, G. H. A., M.A. (Sept. 1914). Lt. 11th K.E.O. Lancers, Indian Army (transferred from 1st Nigerian Regt.). Cameroons, French W. Sudan, E. Africa.
1911 **Watt, N. L.** (1914). ‡Lt. King Edward's Horse and R.F.C. France, 1915, 1916–17. Killed in action on July 27, 1917.
1912 Watts, R. P., B.A. (Aug. 26, 1914). Capt. Hampshire Regt. France.
1896 Way, L. J. U. (Jan. 22, 1916). Lt. 4th N. Staffordshire Regt., attd. 9th K.O.Y.L.I. France, Belgium. (Invalided, Apr. 1918.)
1905 Weaving, H. W., M.A. (Oct. 20, 1914). 2nd Lt. 4th R. Irish Rifles. France. (Invalided.)
1919 Weaving, L. A. (Sept. 9, 1915). Lt. 8th R. Berkshire Regt. France.
1908 Weaving, R. J. (Aug. 4, 1915). Lt. R.G.A.
1911 Webb, B., B.A. (Aug. 7, 1915). Lt. 3rd N. Staffordshire Regt., attd. M.G.C. (Capt.). France, 1916–18. *D.* France, 1918.
1867 **Webber, H.,** B.A. (1916). Lt. S. Lancashire Regt. France. *D.* France, 1916. Died on July 21, 1916, of wounds received in action.
1912 Weir, R. (July 13, 1917). Pte. 463rd Agricultural Coy. Spr. R.E.
1907 **Weld-Blundell, R. S.** (1914). 2nd Lt. 7th King's (Liverpool Regt.). Died on Jan. 1, 1916, while on active service.
1914 Wells, H. D., B.A. (May 1, 1917). Lt. 1st Middlesex Regt. France, 1917.
1897 Welman, C. W., M.A. (Mobilized Aug. 1914). Lt. Gold Coast Volunteers.

1919 Westlake, J. V. (Sept. 25, 1915). Sergt. 5th Worcestershire Regt. France, 1916–17.
1911 Wethey, E. N. J., B.A. (Sept. 9, 1914). Capt. 6th W. Yorkshire Regt. France.
1919 Wiblin, M. (July 1918). Cadet R.A.F.
1900 Wicks, A. T., M.A. (Jan. 3, 1916). Lt. R.G.A. (S.R.).
1900 Wicksteed, F. (Dec. 19, 1912). Capt. 1/1st W. Somerset Yeomanry. Adjt. Light Armoured Motor Bde. Gallipoli, Egypt, Palestine. *D.* Gallipoli, 1916.
1901 Wicksteed, H., M.A. (Mobilized Aug. 4, 1914). Capt. 1/6th Devonshire Regt. India, Mesopotamia.
1904 Wilberforce-Bell, H. (Serving Aug. 4, 1914). Maj. Indian Army; G.S.O. 3. Asst. Military Secretary to C.-in-C., India (1918). France, 1915; Waziristan, 1917; India.
1908 Wilkins, P. V. (Jan. 1916). 2nd Lt. 68th Batt., R.G.A. France, Belgium, 1916–17.
1919 Wilkinson, J. H. (Mar. 21, 1916). Lt. R.A.F. France.
1919 Williams, C. F. V. (Jan. 20, 1916). Lce.-Cpl. 1st Seaforth Highlanders, attd. Staff (Cpl.). Mesopotamia, 1916; India, 1917; Egypt, 1918–19.
1911 **Williams, L. V.** (Aug. 1914). Capt. 7th S. Wales Borderers. France, Salonika. Killed in action at Salonika on May 26, 1917.
1902 Williams, R. H., M.A. (June 1916). Lt. R.A.S.C. Mesopotamia. *D.* Mesopotamia, 1918.
1913 **Williams, W. C.** (Dec. 2, 1914). Lt., Acting Adjt., 12th Hampshire Regt. France, Salonika. Killed in action at Salonika on Sept. 24, 1916.
1913 Willis, N. S., M.A. (Sept. 8, 1914). Lt. 6th Loyal N. Lancashire Regt. (Staff-Captain). Gallipoli, 1915; Mesopotamia, 1916–17; India, 1917–19.
1905 **Wilson, C. R.** (Jan. 5, 1916). 2nd Lt. M.G.C. France, 1916–17. *M.C.*. June 18, 1917. Killed in action on May 24, 1917.
1898 Winnifrith, Rev. D. P., M.A. (Serving Aug. 4, 1914). Chaplain to the Forces (3rd Class). France, 1914–15, 1917–18. *O.B.E.* (Mil.). *D.* France, 1915; May 5, 1919.
1908 **Wood, G.** (1916). Lt. 58th Bn., A.I.F. France. Died on Dec. 11, 1917, of wounds received in action.
1919 Wood, W. R. (Apr. 4, 1917). Lt. R.A.F. Egypt.
1899 Woodd, G. N., M.A. (July 28, 1916). 2nd Lt. Unattached List, T.F., Bury Grammar School O.T.C.
1905 Wright, F. A. P., M.A. Malay States Vol. Rifles.
1917 Wright, F. M. (Feb. 18, 1918). 2nd Lt. R.A.F.
1904 Wright, W. W., M.A. (May 12, 1916). ‡2nd Lt. Worcestershire Regt. France, 1916–18.
1913 Yandell, B., M.A. (Oct. 5, 1914). ‡Lt. 14th Manchester Regt., afterwards Lt. R.A.F. Gallipoli, 1915; Belgium, France, 1917.
1912 Yeates,* S., M.A. (1914). 2nd Lt. 11th Essex Regt. (Invalided.)
1917 Young-Evans, J. B. (Sept. 10, 1918). 2nd Lt. S. Wales Borderers (on demobilization).

WORCESTER COLLEGE

1903 Abbott, E. J. W. (Mobilized Aug. 1914). Lt. 4th R. Inniskilling Fusiliers.
1919 Adams, R. F. G. (Nov. 15, 1915). Lt. 19th Punjabis, Indian Army (Capt.). Persia and Transcaspia. *D.* Persia, 1919.
1912 Adye,* L. C., M.A. (Aug. 15, 1914). Capt. 3rd W. Riding Regt. Belgium, France, till 1916.
1895 **Aldridge, R. J. P. D.,** B.A. (Serving Aug. 4, 1914). Capt. 2nd R. Sussex Regt. (Q.M. and Adjt.). France, 1914. Killed in action at Troyon on Oct. 7, 1914.
1904 Allen, C. B., B.A. (Sept. 12, 1914). Lt. Unattached List, T.F., Loretto School O.T.C. Lt. Grenadier Guards.
1916 Alleyn, R. R. (Oct. 1917). Lt. 10th Canadian Res. Bn., C.E.F.
1904 Allum, G. G., B.A. (Jan. 22, 1916). ‡Lt. 1st Canadian Res. Regt. France and Belgium, 1916–17.
1909 Alsop,* G. P. R. (Aug. 4, 1914). Capt. 3rd Dragoon Guards. France, Belgium, 1915–19. *M.C.*, July 26, 1918.
1895 **Amphlett, E. B.,** M.A. (Aug. 4, 1914). Capt. 12th Worcestershire Regt., attd. 2nd R. Fusiliers (Adjt.). Gallipoli. Killed in action in Gallipoli on June 4, 1915.
1907 Annetts, H. H., B.A. (Aug. 10, 1914). Asst. Transport Officer, Nigerian Land Contingent. Africa.
1911 **Aplin, K. S.** (Serving Aug. 4, 1914). 2nd Lt. 2nd R. Inniskilling Fusiliers. France and Belgium. Killed in action near Messines on Nov. 1, 1914.
1919 Bach, V. C. S. (Sept. 2, 1917). Lt. R.A.F. France.
1912 **Badcock,* E. D.** (Aug. 1914). Lt. 1st Northamptonshire Regt. (Bde. Pioneer). France. Killed in action near Contalmaison on July 22, 1916.
1888 Baghot de la Bere, Rev. J., M.A. (Nov. 1915). Chaplain to the Forces (4th Class), attd. G.H.Q., Palestine. Mediterranean, Egypt, Palestine, 1915–19.
1913 Bamber, M. C. K. (Mobilized Aug. 1914). Capt. 13th London Regt., attd. O.C.B. France.
1912 Banks,* E. G. le B., B.A. (Oct. 1914). 2nd Lt. 5th Welsh Regt. Gallipoli. *D.* Gallipoli, 1916. (Invalided.)
1893 Barnes, Rev. S. R. (Mobilized Aug. 4, 1914). Chaplain to the Forces (3rd Class), attd. 49th Division. France, 1915–19. *O.B.E.* (Mil.). T.D. *D.* France, 1918.
1912 **Barrington,* N. S.** (Serving Aug. 4, 1914). 2nd Lt. R. Irish Rifles. France. Killed in action at Neuve Chapelle on Mar. 10, 1915.
1878 Bartram, Rev. H., M.A. Chaplain to the Forces (4th Class).
1905 Baskerville, H. D., B.A. (Mar. 1917). Gnr. I.D.F. India.
1893 Batchellor, F. H., M.A. (Serving Aug. 4, 1914). Instructor Commdr., R.N., H.M.S. *Marlborough*. Black Sea and Mediterranean, 1919.
1919 Bateman, S. M. (Aug. 20, 1917). 2nd Lt. 'L' Corps, Sig. Coy., R.E. France, 1918; Belgium, 1918–19; Germany, 1919.

1919 Baxter, F. W. (Apr. 30, 1917). 2nd Lt. N.Z. Engineers (Signals) (Capt.). France.

1910 **Beach,* L. H. F.,** B.A. (Oct. 1914). Capt. 2/4th Queen's (R.W. Surrey Regt.) (Maj.). Gallipoli, 1915; Egypt and Palestine, 1916, 1917–18. *D.S.O.*, Aug. 16, 1917. *D.* Palestine, 1917. Died on Nov. 28, 1918, of illness subsequent to wounds.

1909 Beaudry, L. J., M.A. (1917). Lt. 236th Bn. Canadian Inf.

1914 **Bedells, C. A.** (Jan. 25, 1915). 2nd Lt. 11th Essex Regt. France. Died on Sept. 26, 1915, of wounds received in action at the Battle of Loos.

1912 Belcher,* W. H., M.A. (Dec. 22, 1914). Lt., Acting Capt., Signal Service, R.E. France, 1915–18. *M.C.*, July 26, 1918. *D.* France, 1917.

1919 Bell, S. (May 23, 1917). ‡Lt. 1st Res. (Garr.) Bn. Worcestershire Regt., attd. 16th (Garr.) Bn. K.O.Y.L.I. France, 1917–19; Germany, 1919.

1899 Beyts, C. F. (May 1915). Lt. 9th Suffolk Regt. Capt. M.G.C. France. *M.C.*, Jan. 22, 1916. *D.* France, 1915.

1891 Billups, H. B., B.M., M.A. (Jan. 1, 1916). Capt. R.A.M.C. Malta, Alexandria, Black Sea, Mediterranean, France.

1912 **Birch, L.** (Nov. 1914). Capt. 7th Border Regt. France. Killed in action at Monchy-le-Preux on Apr. 23, 1917.

1906 Bircham, H. T., B.A. (Aug. 20, 1914). Lt. 6th Durham L.I. France, 1915–19. *M.C.*, Jan. 1, 1917.

1906 Bishop, A. G., M.A. (Dec. 1914). Lt. 10th, attd. 3rd, Worcestershire Regt. France, Belgium. *M.B.E.* (Mil.). *D.* France, 1917.

1919 Blackley, T. R. (Sept. 28, 1917). 2nd Lt. R.F.A. France.

1914 Booth, J. C. (May 6, 1915). Lt. 9th Sherwood Foresters. France, 1917–19.

1903 Boulton, C. E., B.A. (Serving Aug. 4, 1914). Capt. 1/5th, attd. 1/6th, L.I., Indian Army. India.

1891 Bourne, W. K., B.A. (Serving Aug. 4, 1914). Lt.-Col. 20th Deccan Horse, commanding 2/35th Sikhs, Indian Army. India, France. *D.* France, 1916 twice.

1920 Boustead, H. (Aug. 4, 1914). Sub-Lt. R.N., H.M.S. *Hyacinth*. ‡Capt. S. African Scottish Regt., attd. Indian Army. E. Africa, W. Africa, 1914–15; Egypt, 1916; France, 1916–17, 1918–19; India, 1917–18; S. Russia, 1919–20. *M.C.*, July 26, 1917; *Bar*, Aug. 25, 1919. Order of Vladimir.

1902 Bowman, J. H. (Aug. 1914). Capt. 7th Durham L.I. N. Russia, 1918–19. Order of S. Anne (3rd Class) (with crossed swords).

1906 **Bradshaw, A. E.,** M.A. (Serving Aug. 4, 1914). Capt. 14th Lancers, Indian Army, attd. 15th Hussars. India, France. Killed in action at Bout-del-Ville, near Estaires, on Oct. 13, 1914.

1897 Bradshaw, Sir A. F., M.A., *K.C.B.* (Serving Aug. 4, 1914). Surg.-Maj.-Gen. Hon. Consulting Physician to the Military Hospitals in Oxford and neighbourhood.

1912 Braund,* A. E., M.A. (Aug. 31, 1915). 2nd Lt. 7th Northumberland Fusiliers (T.F.). France.

1913 Brewin,* J. V. (Aug. 22, 1914). Lt. Northamptonshire Regt. (Capt.). France, Belgium, 1915–19. *M.C.*, Feb. 18, 1918. *D.* France, 1917.

1919 Bridge, M. F. (Sept. 12, 1914). Capt. 19th Divl. Train, A.S.C. Capt. R.A.F. France, Italy.

1890 Broad, Rev. A. S. L., M.A. (June, 1916). Chaplain to the Forces (4th Class), afterwards Capt. R.G.A.
1920 Brockman, J. D. (Sept. 1, 1918). 2nd Lt. R. Marines.
1913 Brodie, P. H., B.A. (Aug. 27, 1917). 1st Lt. 3rd Infantry, U.S. Army (Bn.-Comdr.).
1907 Brown,* J. H., B.A. (Sept. 1914). 2nd Lt. M.G.C. Gallipoli, 1915; Egypt, 1915–17; France, 1917–18.
1905 Brown, L. N., M.A. (Apr. 23, 1915). Lt. I.A.R.O., attd. 8th Rajputs. India, Mesopotamia.
1914 Browning, C. R. (Oct. 3, 1915). Lt. 5th Queen's (R.W. Surrey Regt.). France.
1907 Browning, W. H., M.A. (Sept. 21, 1917). 2nd Lt. R.F.A.
1890 Bruce, Rev. F. R. C., D.D. (Serving Aug. 4, 1914). Chaplain to the Forces (4th Class). France, 1915.
1913 Bruce, H. L., M.A. (1917). Capt. Coast Artillery Corps, U.S. Army. France.
1919 Burnaby, H. E. (Aug. 2, 1914). Lt. R.N., H.M.S. *Dragon.* Atlantic, Mediterranean, North Sea, Indian Ocean.
1897 Burnet, W. C., M.A. (May, 1916). Lt. R.G.A.
1911 Butler, V. K., M.A. (May, 1917). Lt. 62nd Heavy Artillery, U.S. Army, Capt. 9th Aero Squadron, U.S. Air Force. France, 1918; Germany, 1918–19.
1914 Bygott, J. F. (July 24, 1915). Lt. 4th S. Staffordshire Regt. (Staff Capt.). France, Belgium, 1916–17; Italy, from 1917. *M.C.*, June 3, 1919.
1920 Cameron, S. S. (Aug. 14, 1915). ‡Lt. Q.O. Cameron Highlanders. France, 1916–17, 1918–19; Germany, 1919.
1907 Campbell, C. M. Lt. Natal Mounted Rifles. Africa.
1910 Cemlyn-Jones, J. (Mobilized Aug. 1914). Maj. 6th R. Welch Fusiliers, attd. R.A.F., 1915–19. France. *D.* France, 1915.
1901 Chadwick, P. S., B.A. 3rd Sanitary Section, R.A.M.C.
1907 Challenor, Rev. B. M., M.A. (Nov. 28, 1915). Chaplain to the Forces (4th Class). France, Belgium. *D.* France, 1918.
1907 Chaning-Pearce, M. S., B.A. (Aug. 29, 1914). Capt. 1/4th Dorsetshire Regt. (Adjt.), attd. Political Dept. M.E.F. India, 1914–16; Mesopotamia, 1916–19.
1906 **Channer, E. W.,** B.A. Pte. Leicestershire Regt. France. Killed in action near Vermelles on July 7, 1917.
1909 **Chaytor, A. K.** (Dec. 30, 1914). 2nd Lt. 3rd Worcestershire Regt. France. Died on May 26, 1915, of wounds received in action near La Clytte.
1913 Chegwidden, T. S. (Feb. 28, 1917). Lt. R.E. France.
1912 Chevallier,* C. T., M.A. (Aug. 15, 1914). Lt., Acting Capt., 3rd Oxf. & Bucks. Lt. Infty. France, 2½ years. *D.* France, 1916.
1919 Christopherson, I. (Dec. 7, 1917). 2nd Lt. 277th Siege Batt., R.G.A. France.
1897 **Clapham, B. A.,** M.A. (Aug. 1914). Lt. 1/4th Essex Regt. (Capt.). Egypt, Palestine, 1916. Died on Mar. 27, 1917, of wounds received in action at the first Battle of Gaza on Mar. 26, 1917.
1899 **Clayton, G. E. C.,** M.A. (Aug. 4, 1914). 2nd Lt. R. Marines. Antwerp, Belgium. Died on Sept. 2, 1915, of illness contracted on active service.
1889 Clayton, J. (Oct. 12, 1914). ‡2nd Lt. Labour Corps. Burma, 1916–17; France, 1917–18.

1906 Cobb, F., B.A. (Mar. 21, 1915). Lt. 1st London Regt. (R. Fusiliers).
1905 **Colborne, Rev. R. A. P.,** M.A. (Mar. 1917). Chaplain to the Forces (1st Class). France. Killed in action near Arras on May 28, 1918.
1919 Colchester, B. M. (Mar. 23, 1918). Midshipman, R.N.V.R.
1896 Coldstream, J., B.A. (Apr. 1, 1915). Capt. Special Lists; Staff Lt. (1st Class).
1896 Cole-Hamilton, Rev. R. M., M.A. (Aug. 18, 1915). Chaplain to the Forces (4th Class). Gallipoli, 1915; Suez Canal, 1916; N.W. Frontier, India, 1916.
1919 Coles, A. J. (Aug. 24, 1917). ‡2nd Lt. 8th R. Berkshire Regt. France.
1899 Colles, H. C., B.Mus., M.A. (Aug. 1916). Lt. R.G.A. (Capt.). Macedonia, 1917. Greek Military Medal.
1894 Collis, H. G., B.A. (Apr. 1916). ‡Lt. R.G.A. France.
1908 Coningham, W. F. M. (Aug. 28, 1916). ‡2nd Lt. R.A.S.C. (M.T.). France, 1916–17; Italy, 1918. (Invalided Jan. 29, 1917.)
1913 Cooke, B. K. (Aug. 22, 1914). Maj. 5th Oxf. & Bucks. Lt. Infty., afterwards 18th Gloucestershire Regt. (Lt.-Col.). France, 1915–19. *M.C.*, Jan., 1918; *Bar*, Sept. 16, 1918.
1912 **Cottrell,* P. B.** (Sept. 1914). ‡2nd Lt. 19th R. Fusiliers. Lt. General List; Staff-Lt. (3rd Class) (Intelligence Corps). France, 1915; Salonika, 1916–18. *M.C.*, Feb. 1, 1919; Greek Order of the Redeemer. Greek Military Cross. *D.* Salonika, 1918. Died on Sept. 27, 1918, of wounds received in action at Snevce.
1893 Couchman, Rev. R. H., M.A. (Serving Aug. 4, 1914). Chaplain to the Forces (4th Class), attd. 4th Devonshire Regt.
1906 Cresswell,* J. A., B.A. (Sept. 12, 1916). Lt. 30th Bn. Canadian E.F.
1874 Crofton, Rev. W. d'A., M.A. (Mobilized, 1914). Chaplain to the Forces (1st Class), attd. 1st Hertfordshire Regt. Gallipoli, 1915. T.D.
1892 Crombie, C. H., M.A. (1914). Pte. 15th London Regt. (Civil Service Rifles). (Invalided Apr. 15, 1915.)
1904 **Crossman, G. D. M.,** M.A. (Aug. 23, 1915). 2nd Lt. 13th Welsh Regt. France. Killed in action at Mametz Wood on July 10, 1916.
1905 Crouch, Rev. G. H., M.A. (Oct. 7, 1914). Chaplain R.N. H.M.S. *Canada*.
1915 Crowther, C. C. (Jan. 27, 1916). ‡Lt. 2nd W. Riding Regt. Lt. General List (Intelligence Corps). France.
1914 Cruise, W. Lce.-Cpl. S. Lancashire Regt.
1909 Cumberlege, G. F. J., M.A. (Aug. 1914). Capt. Oxf. & Bucks. Lt. Infty. (Bde. Maj.). France, 1915–18; Italy, 1918. *D.S.O.*, Apr. 17, 1917. *M.C.*, Jan. 1, 1919. Croce di Guerra. *D.* France, 1917 twice; Italy, 1918.
1911 **Curran,* N. W.** (Aug. 1914). Lt. 2nd R. Irish Regt. France, 1914–16. *M.C.*, Apr. 15, 1915. Croix de Guerre. *D.* France, 1915. Killed in action on Oct. 4, 1916.
1902 David-Devis,* W. E., M.A. (Aug. 1914). Capt., Acting Maj., 13th London Regt., attd. R.A.O.C. France.
1919 Davies, H. D. K. (Sept. 26, 1914). Capt. 4th Northumberland Fusiliers. France. *M.C.* Jan. 1, 1918. *D.* France, 1916 twice.
1920 Davies, H. S. (June 1, 1917). ‡Lt. 51st Hampshire Regt. France, 1918; Germany, 1919–20.

1905 de la Cour, J. C., B.A. (Sept. 1915). ‡2nd Lt. R.A.S.C. Lt. 16th London Regt. (Queen's Westminster Rifles) (Capt.). France, 1916–17, 1918–19.

1920 Denney, L. E. (May 22, 1917). Lt. 1st (Garr.) Bn. Norfolk Regt. India, 1918–19.

1907 Dennis,* A. H. W., M.A. (Serving Aug. 4, 1914). 2nd Lt. Rossall School O.T.C. Capt. 5th S. Lancashire Regt. France, 1915–16; Burmah and India, 1918–19.

1909 **Dent, P. M.** (Aug. 1914). Pte. 4th Seaforth Highlanders. France. Killed in action at Neuve Chapelle on Apr. 28, 1915.

1907 **de Rougemont,* G.**, B.A. (Dec. 6, 1915). Cpl. R.A.S.C. Macedonia. Died on Aug. 10, 1919, of illness contracted while on active service.

1913 Dickinson,* A. S. H., B.A. (June 24, 1915). Lt. R. N. Devon Yeomanry, attd. 16th Devonshire Regt. Egypt, Palestine, France.

1919 Dilworth, A. (Jan. 3, 1918). Lce.-Cpl. 7th W. Yorkshire Regt.

1912 Dixon, C. E. T., M.A. (Aug. 1914). Capt. Bt.-Maj., 7th, afterwards 51st Leicestershire Regt. France, 1915–19; Germany, 1919. *M.C.*, Dec. 17, 1917. *D.* France, 1916, 1918.

1888 Donald, Rev. J. R., M.A. (June 14, 1915). Pte. R.A.S.C. (M.T.). France.

1905 Draper, H. C., B.A. (Aug. 1, 1915). ‡2nd Lt. 28th R. Fusiliers. France.

1882 Ducat, C. T., B.A. (Serving Aug. 4, 1914). Lt.-Col. Indian Army (Supernumerary List). India.

1903 **Duncan,* A. B.** 2nd Lt. I.A.R.O., attd. Indian Cavalry. India, Persia. *D.* India. Died on Aug. 5, 1916, of wounds received on Persian border of Baluchistan.

1919 Dyson, G. (July, 1915). Lt. 5th W. Riding Regt. (Capt.). France, 1917–18.

1904 **Eastwood, L.**, M.A. (Sept. 1, 1914). 2nd Lt. 6th King's Own (R. Lancaster Regt.). Gallipoli. Died at Alexandria on Sept. 19, 1915, of illness contracted on active service.

1909 Eccles, L. W. G. (Dec. 12, 1914). ‡Lt. Coldstream Guards (Capt.). Rhodesia, East Africa, France, 1914–17; Russia, 1919. *M.C.*, Dec. 17, 1917. *D.* France, 1917. (Prisoner of war in Russia, 1919–20.)

1912 **Edgar, G. G.** (Nov. 24, 1914). 2nd Lt. 14th K.R.R.C. France. Died on Aug. 28, 1916, of wounds received in action at Delville Wood.

1912 **Ellis,* Y. L.** (Oct. 1914). Lt. 13th Hampshire Regt. France. Killed in action near Bethune on May 29, 1916.

1911 **Elmhirst,* W.**, B.A. (Dec. 1914). Capt. 8th E. Yorkshire Regt. France. Killed in action at Serres on Nov. 13, 1916.

1896 Elwell, C. S., B.A. (Aug. 11, 1916). Capt. General List, T.F. Res., empld. Ministry of National Service.

1894 **Everitt, R. E.**, M.A. (Dec. 11, 1916). 2nd Lt. R.G.A. France and Belgium. Killed in action near Poperinghe on June 24, 1917.

1912 Ewing, I. L. Orr (Dec. 2, 1914). 2nd Lt. 3rd, attd. 1st, Scots Fusiliers. Lt. Scots Guards (Capt.). France and Belgium.

1912 **Farquharson, F. L.** (1914). Lt. 6th Gordon Highlanders. France. Killed in action near Givenchy on June 3, 1915.

1920 Farthing, F. B. (Aug. 1916). ‡Lt. 24th D.M.T. Coy., R.A.S.C. France, Belgium. *D.* France, 1919.

1882 Fawcus, L. E., B.A. (Jan. 15, 1915). Lt.-Col. 19th Northumberland Fusiliers.

1911 **Feild, J. F.** (Oct. 1914). 2nd Lt. D.C.L.I. France. Killed in action near Gueudecourt on Sept. 16, 1916.

1912 Firminger, J. E. (Sept. 1914). Capt. Bucks. Bn. Oxf. & Bucks. Lt. Infty. Belgium, France, Italy. *M.C.*, Dec. 2, 1918. Italian Silver Medal for Valour. *D.* Italy, 1918.

Fisher, J. H. (Aug. 1, 1917). 2nd Lt. 6th W. Yorkshire Regt., attd. 2/4th K.O.Y.L.I. France. *M.C.*, Jan. 11, 1919. Croix de Guerre. Died on Sept. 7, 1918, of wounds received in action.

1912 Fletcher,* C. A., B.A. (Aug. 15, 1914). Lt. 3rd Devonshire Rgt. Capt. and Adjt. 84th Bn. Labour Corps. France and Belgium, 1915.

1919 Fletcher, R. M. (Apr. 21, 1915). Lt. 2/9th London Regt. (Queen Victoria's Rifles). Lt. No. 22 T.D.S., R.A.F. France, Belgium.

1897 Flower, C. T., M.A. (Nov. 4, 1915). Lt. 143rd Siege Batt., R.G.A., attd. War Office. France. Croix de Guerre.

1901 Foley, R. E., B.A. (May 26, 1915). 2nd Lt. 5th (Res.) Middlesex Regt., attd. R.A.O.C.

1912 Forty,* J. E. H., M.A. (Aug. 22, 1914). Lt.-Col. 6th E. Yorkshire Regt., attd. 14th Worcestershire Regt. Gallipoli, 1915–16; Egypt, 1916; France and Belgium, 1916–19. *D.* France, 1919.

1904 Foster, G. N. (Oct. 10, 1914). Lt. E. Riding of Yorkshire Yeomanry, attd. M.G.C. (Capt. and Adjt.). Egypt, Palestine, France.

1920 Fox-Pitt-Rivers, G. H. L. (Serving Aug. 4, 1914). Capt. 1st R. Dragoons. France, Belgium.

1914 Freeman,* C. T. (Sept. 1914). ‡Maj., Seaplane Officer, R.A.F. North Sea. *D.S.C.* (for attack on Zeppelin), Oct. 25, 1916. *A.F.C.*, Nov. 2, 1918. *D.* 1917.

1913 Frost,* E. G., B.A. (Oct. 29, 1914). Capt. 1/4th Queen's (R. W. Surrey Regt.). Gallipoli, Egypt, Palestine, India.

1896 Furley, G. M., B.A. (July 9, 1915). Lt. 5th R. Welch Fusiliers.

1908 Gallwey, H. W. D. (Mobilized Aug. 1914). Lt. 3rd, attd. 1st, Somerset L.I. France.

1905 Garle, H. A. (Sept. 11, 1914). Capt., Acting Maj., R.F.A. (T.F.). Mesopotamia. *D.* Mesopotamia, 1919.

1910 Garle, J. A. B. (Sept. 21, 1914). Capt. I.A.R.O., attd. Cavalry. India, Palestine.

1912 Garrard,* J. D. (Sept. 1916). Lt. 7th Lincolnshire Regt. France.

1898 Garratt, E. V., M.A. (Oct. 19, 1914). Pte. 23rd R. Fusiliers (1st Sportsman's). France, 1915–16. *M.M.*, Oct. 21, 1916.

1905 Gattie, V. R. M., M.A. (Feb. 13, 1916). Capt. Special Lists. D.A.A.G. Headquarters Staff (attd. British Mil. Delegation, Peace Conference, 1919). *C.B.E.* (Mil.). *D.* § Feb. 1917.

1919 Gaunt, W. (July 16, 1918). Lce.-Cpl. 51st (Grad.) Bn. Durham L.I.

1888 Gibbons, Rev. W. J. B. E., B.A. (Apr. 29, 1918). Chaplain to the Forces (4th Class).

1913 Gilligan, F. W., B.A. (Oct. 18, 1914). Capt. 3rd Essex Regt. Belgium, France. *D.* § Aug. 1919.

1904 Gilshenan, T. S., B.A. (Sept. 26, 1916). ‡Capt. 37th Bn. M.G.C. France. *D.* France, 1918.

1895 Girling, Rev. E. M., M.A. (July 24, 1917). Chaplain to the Forces (4th Class). France, 1917–18.

1911 **Golightly, F. W.,** B.A. (Aug. 23, 1915). Gnr. 72nd Batt. S. African Heavy Artillery. France, 1916. Killed in action near Thiepval on July 21, 1916.

1919 Gompertz, R. H. L. (Feb. 15, 1918). Pte. 28th London Regt. (2nd Artists' Rifles O.T.C.). Cadet R.A.F.

1903 Gore-Browne, E., B.A. (Mobilized Aug. 1914). Capt., Bt.-Maj., 8th London Regt. (Post Office Rifles). D.A.Q.M.G. France, Belgium, 1915–19. *D.S.O.*, Jan. 1, 1918. Croix de Guerre. *D.* France, 1917, 1919.

1905 Gottwaltz, L. H. (Mar. 11, 1915). Capt. R.F.A. France. *M.C.*, Mar. 26, 1918.

1919 Grange, G. G. (Mar. 1915). ‡Lt. 9th London Regt. (Queen Victoria's Rifles). France, 1917–18.

Green, C. A. (Feb. 1, 1916). 2nd Lt. R.G.A. France, 1917. *M.C.*, Apr. 23, 1917. Killed in action at Arras on July 13, 1917.

Green, W. E. (Aug. 1914). Capt. 1st Dorsetshire Regt. France. Died on July 6, 1916, of wounds received July 1, 1916, in Battle of the Somme.

1889 Griffiths, Rev. T., M.A. (Jan. 8, 1916). Chaplain to the Forces (4th Class). France, 1916–18; Switzerland, 1918. *O.B.E.* (Mil.).

1908 Grisman,* J. R., B.A. (July 1915). Instructor Lieut. R.N. H.M.S. *Neptune*, 1916–18.

1907 Grundy,* Rev. K. E., M.A. (Mar. 9, 1916). Chaplain, R.N., attd. 4th Light Cruiser Squadron. Atlantic, North Sea.

1888 Gurney, Rev. A. G. H., M.A. (Serving Aug. 4, 1914). Chaplain to the Forces (4th Class), attd. Hampshire Regt.

1889 Gwynne, H. V., B.A. (Nov. 8, 1915). Capt. 56th Divl. Train, R.A.S.C. France and Belgium, 3½ years.

1914 Haarhoff, T. J., B.Litt. (Apr. 1915). S. African Defence Force. German S.W. Africa.

1919 Hadwen, E. H. L. (June 15, 1918). Cadet, R.A.F.

1919 Hall, C. B. (May 4, 1917). Lt. Grenadier Guards. France, 1918.

1911 Hall,* R. A., M.A. (Aug. 9, 1915). Lt. 8th Manchester Regt. France, 1916–17. (Invalided June 29, 1918.)

1903 **Hall, T. S. I.** (Nov. 24, 1914). 2nd Lt. 4th King's Own (R. Lancaster Regt.). Mesopotamia. Killed in action at Sanna-i-yat on Apr. 9, 1916.

1893 Hall, W. G. C., B.C.L., M.A. (Mobilized Aug. 1914). Maj. 19th London Regt.

1912 Halloran, G. B., B.A. (Mar. 28, 1917). Lt. 3rd R. Berkshire Regt., attd. 2/94th Russell's Infantry, Indian Army. India.

1910 Hampson, H. B. (Dec. 1914). ‡Lt. 5th R. Dublin Fusiliers, attd. 48th Bn. M.G.C. France, Italy.

1919 Hands, A. S. (Mar. 23, 1915). Lt. A.S.C. Lt. 1st Dorsetshire Regt. (Maj.). Mesopotamia, France. *M.C.*, Jan. 1, 1918.

1908 **Hardy, A. H.,** B.A. (Sept. 19, 1914). 2nd Lt. R. E. Kent Yeomanry, attd. R.F.C. Accidentally killed near Forfar on Oct. 14, 1915.

1913 Harrison, F. H. (Dec. 13, 1915). Lt. The Cameronians. Salonika, 1917–18.

1910 Harrower, A. B. (Sept. 3, 1914). ‡Capt. R.A.S.C., attd. 10th S. Wales Borderers. France and Belgium, 1915, 1916, 1917–18.

1901 Harry, G. D., M.A. (Mar. 28, 1916). Lce.-Cpl. 305th Works Coy., Labour Corps.

Hartley, N. C. (Feb. 1917). 2nd Lt. R.F.A. France, 1917–18. Killed in action near Marcoing on Jan. 20, 1918.

1919 Hayes, E. A. (Sept. 28, 1917). 2nd Lt. 14th Bn. Tank Corps. France.

1919 Henriques, E. F. Q. (Sept. 28, 1917). ‡2nd Lt. 'D' Batt., Anti-Aircraft R.F.A. France, Belgium.

1904 Henry, R. L., B.C.L. (May 1, 1917). Maj., General Staff, Washington, U.S. Army.

1910 Hetherington, E. B. (Nov. 6, 1916). Sergt. 2nd R. Welch Fusiliers.

1895 **Hewetson, Rev. G. H.,** B.A. (Aug. 1914). Chaplain, R.N., H.M.S. *Bulwark*. Killed on Nov. 26, 1914, in explosion in H.M.S. *Bulwark*.

1909 **Higgs, J. P.** (June 1, 1915). Lt. Q. O. Oxfordshire Hussars, attd. 4th Bn. M.G.C. France. Died on Apr. 14, 1918, of wounds received in action on Apr. 1 at Rifleman Wood near Domat.

Hirsch, D. P. (Apr. 1915). Capt. 4th Yorkshire Regt. France, Belgium. *D.* France, 1916. Killed in action at Arras on Apr. 23, 1917. **V.C.** won near Wancourt, France, on Apr 23, 1917.

For most conspicuous bravery and devotion to duty in attack.

Having arrived at the first objective, Captain Hirsch, although already twice wounded, returned over fire-swept slopes to satisfy himself that the defensive flank was being established.

Machine-gun fire was so intense that it was necessary for him to be continually up and down the line encouraging his men to dig and hold the position.

He continued to encourage his men by standing on the parapet and steadying them in the face of machine-gun fire and counter-attack until he was killed.

His conduct throughout was a magnificent example of the greatest devotion to duty.

1889 Hirst, W. A., B.A. (Aug. 31, 1914). Lt. R. Defence Corps. France, 1916.

1914 **Hodgkinson, H. G.** (Sept. 1914). 2nd Lt. 10th W. Riding Regt. Lt. King's African Rifles. France, 1915–16; E. Africa, 1916–17. Killed in action at Mtua, near Lindi, on Oct. 17, 1917.

1898 Hodgson, E., M.A. (May 19, 1916). 2nd Lt. Unattached List, T.F., Sherborne School O.T.C.

1909 Hodgson-Smith, W. B., M.A. (Aug. 21, 1914). Capt. 6th R. W. Kent Regt. (Maj.). France, 1915–17. (Prisoner of war, Nov. 1917–Dec. 1918.)

1892 Holden, Rev. H. H., B.A. (May 15, 1918). Chaplain to the Forces (4th Class). France and Germany.

1911 Homan,* C. W. F. B., M.A. (Aug. 26, 1914). Capt. and Adjt. 1/4th Wiltshire Regt. India, 1914–17; Palestine and Egypt, 1917–19. *M.C.*, Jan. 1, 1919.

1911 Hooper, K. A. (July 16, 1916). Lt. R.G.A. France, 1915–16 (with B.R.C.S.); Singapore, 1917–18; Hong Kong, 1918–19.

1896 **Hooper, R. M.,** M.A. (Dec. 21, 1915). Lt. R.G.A., attd. R.E. France. Killed in action on March 21, 1918.

1906 Hopkinson, C. E., M.A. (Sept. 2, 1915). Lt. Intelligence Corps. France, 1916, 1917–19. *M.C.*, Jan. 1, 1919.

1899 **Horley, E. L. R.,** B.A. (May 22, 1915). 2nd Lt. 2nd Manchester Regt. France and Belgium. Killed in action at Coxyde on Sept. 4, 1917.

1910 Howard, F. C., B.A. (Aug. 30, 1914). ‡Lt. 9th London Regt. (Queen Victoria's Rifles) (Capt.). France and Belgium.

1919 Howland, A. H. (Jan. 3, 1918). 2nd Lt. Queen's (R.W. Surrey Regt.), attd. R.A.F.

1919 Hughes-Games, C. M. (Feb. 11, 1915). Lt., Acting Capt., 2/5th Gloucestershire Regt. France and Belgium, 1916–19. *M.C.*, June 18, 1917; *Bar*, Feb. 4, 1918.

1911 Humble, G. M. A., B.A. (Sept. 22, 1914). Lt. 13th Sherwood Foresters, attd. Lancashire Fusiliers. France.

1910 Hyslop,* R. M. (Oct. 19, 1914). Capt. 5th King's (Liverpool Regt.), attd. 20th Rifle Brigade. Egypt and Palestine.

1911 Iliffe,* C. W., M.A. (Aug. 27, 1914). Capt. 7th R. Warwickshire Regt. (T.F.)

1910 Irwin,* H. S. (Serving Aug. 4, 1914). Lt. Scots Guards (A.D.C.). France, 1916–17.

1919 Ivory, L. J. (Dec. 14, 1914). ‡Capt. N.Z.F.A., attd. as Secretary, Dept. of Education, N.Z.E.F., London. Gallipoli, 1915; France, 1916–18. *D.* § Aug. 1919.

1897 Jack, A., M.A. (July 27, 1918). 2nd Lt. R.A.S.C. Italy.

1919 Jackson, J. B. (Mar. 30, 1917). 2nd Lt. R.F.A. France.

1913 Jenner, C. H. (Oct. 20, 1914). Lt. 5th Hampshire Regt., attd. 23rd Pioneers, Indian Army. India.

1919 Jennings, A. C. (Mar. 10, 1918). 2nd Lt. 76th Field Coy., R.E. Germany, 1919.

1896 Johnson, N. H., B.A. (Sept. 2, 1914). ‡Capt. R.A.O.C. France. *D.* France, 1917.

1882 Jones, Rev. J. H. W., M.A. (Serving Aug. 4, 1914). Chaplain (4th Class), attd. 6th Welsh Regt.

1911 Jones,* O. J., B.A. (Serving Aug. 4, 1914). Capt. R.F.A., D.T.M.O. 38th Division. France, 1914–19. *M.C.*, Jan. 1, 1917. *D.* France, 1917.

1902 Kenion, T. D., M.A. (Aug. 8, 1915). Lt. 23rd Cheshire Regt. (Capt.). France, 1918.

1908 **Kidner, F. E.,** B.A. (Sept. 7, 1914). Rfln. 16th London Regt. (Queen's Westminster Rifles) (Lce.-Cpl.). Belgium, France. Died on Feb. 20, 1915, of wounds received in action near Armentières.

1911 Kitson, A. B., B.A. (Jan. 15, 1915). Capt. 11th Devonshire Regt. France.

1919 Knight, S. W. (Sept. 4, 1914). Sergt. 28th London Regt. (Artists' Rifles) (Signal Sergt.). France.

1901 Knollys, W. E. (Aug. 4, 1914). ‡Capt. Special Lists, attd. Mil. Audit Dept., E. Africa. E. Africa, 1916–17.

1893 Knowles, Rev. K. D., M.A. (Serving Aug. 4, 1914). Chaplain to the Forces (4th Class), attd. 33rd Bde. France, 1916.

1907 Lacy, B. R., B.A. (1917). Chaplain, Field Artillery, U.S. Army. France.

1912 Lamb, W., M.A. (Nov. 15, 1915). Lt. 5th Lincolnshire Regt. (T.F.). *D.* § Aug. 1919.

1908 Landon,* A. H. W. (Mar. 11, 1915). Capt., Acting Maj., R. (Nova Scotia) Canadian Regt., C.E.F. France and Belgium, Russia. *O.B.E.* (Mil.). *M.C.*, Jan. 1, 1918. Croix de Guerre. *D.* France, 1916, 1919; Russia, 1919.

1914 Lang, R. S., B.A. (Mar. 27, 1918). 2nd Lt. Cheshire Regt.

1898 Lawrence, Lord A. G. (Aug. 28, 1914). Maj. 2/11th London Regt. (Finsbury Rifles). France.

1908 Legge-Wilkinson, L. C. (Feb. 22, 1915). Lt. 6th S. Lancashire Regt. Lt. Flying Officer, R.A.F. Mesopotamia.

1902 Lejeune, H. (Apr. 15, 1915). Capt. Technical Officer, R.A.F. France. *M.C.*, Jan. 1, 1917.

1891 Lemprière, L. R., B.A. (May 1915). Capt. R.A.M.C., M.O., 1st A.H.Q. France. *O.B.E.* (Mil.). Médaille des Epidémies (en argent). *D.* France, 1918, 1919.

1901 Lewis, Rev. P., M.A. (Dec. 20, 1915). Chaplain to the Forces (4th Class). Egypt, 1915–17; Mesopotamia, 1917–18; India, 1918–19. *O.B.E.* (Mil.). *D.* Mesopotamia, 1918.

1910 Liebermann, Rev. B., M.A. (Jan. 16, 1917). Chaplain to the Forces (4th Class). France.

1911 Liesching, W. M., B.A. (Sept. 3, 1914). ‡Lt. 4th E. Surrey Regt. France, 1916–17, 1917–19.

1914 Lindsay, R. (Dec. 7, 1914). Capt. 11th Northumberland Fusiliers.

1910 Lindsay-Smith, L. (Mobilized Aug. 1914). Lt. City of London Yeomanry. Capt. R.A.O.C. Egypt, Gallipoli. *M.B.E.* (Mil.).

1906 Lob, R., M.A. (June 1915). Cpl. R.E. (Research Physicist). France, 1915–17.

1908 Long,* B., B.A. (Mobilized Aug. 1914). Capt. 4th Oxf. & Bucks. Lt. Infty., attd. M.G.C. (Maj.). France, Belgium, Italy. *M.C.*, Jan. 14, 1916; *Bar*, Apr. 2, 1919. *D.* France, 1915, 1916; Italy, 1918.

1907 Loveridge, S. G. (Mobilized Aug. 1914). Capt. Staffordshire Yeomanry. Egypt, France, Germany.

1901 Low, Rev. P. W., M.A. (Apr. 16, 1915). Chaplain to the Forces (4th Class). Belgium, France.

1911 Lowry,* G. L. B. (Sept. 12, 1914). Lt. 8th N. Staffordshire Regt. Lt. General List, attd. T.M.B. France and Belgium. *M.C.*, Aug. 25, 1916.

1913 Lund,* R. J. S. (Sept. 2, 1914). Capt. 4th R. Berkshire Regt. Capt. 60th Squadron, R.A.F. France, 1915–16, 1917, 1918–19.

1892 **Lydall, Rev. C. Wykeham,** M.A. (Serving Aug. 4, 1914). Chaplain, R.N., H.M.S. *Lion*. Grand Fleet. Killed in action in the Battle of Jutland on May 31, 1916.

1891 Lyne, R. F., M.A. (Sept. 14, 1914). Lt., Acting Capt. and Adjt., R.F.A. (T.F.). Egypt and Palestine. *D.* Palestine, 1918.

1919 McCallum, R. B. (Apr. 23, 1917). Lt. No. 4 Coy. Labour Corps. France.

1907 McClymont, C. J. (Nov. 3, 1914). 2nd Lt. Unattached List, T.F., King's School, Warwick, O.T.C.

1919 McCracken, C. J. N. (Nov. 14, 1916). Lt. D/130th Bde., R.F.A. Salonika.

1907 Macfarlane,* A. G., B.A. (1914). ‡Lt. 8th London Regt. (Post Office Rifles). France.

1902 **Machebeuf, L. M. L. J.** (1914). Lt. de Reserve au 166e d'Infanterie. France. Killed in action on Nov. 12, 1914.

1881 **Mack, A. P.** (Sept. 1914). Lt.-Col. 9th Suffolk Regt. France. *D.* France, 1916. Killed in action near Ginchy on Sept. 15, 1916.

1904 MacLean, J., M.A. (Apr. 1917). Cpl. 78th Canadian Inf. France, 1918.

1898 McLellan, F. R. H., M.A. (Serving Aug. 4, 1914). Lt. Unattached List, T.F. Maj. 16th R. Welch Fusiliers.

1902 McNaught, W., B.A. (Jan. 29, 1915). Lce.-Cpl. 2nd London Field Ambulance, R.A.M.C. France, 1916–19.

1913 **Macrae, C. M.** (Mobilized Aug. 1914). Lt. 4th Hampshire Regt. Persian Gulf. Killed in action at Gurma Sapha on July 5, 1915.

1912 **Malet, F. L.** (Nov. 7, 1914). Lt. 12th R. Warwickshire Regt., attd. 2nd Hampshire Regt. Gallipoli. Killed in action in Gallipoli on June 4, 1915.

1919 Mallett, J. L. (Sept. 1914). Capt. 6th S. Staffordshire Regt. Maj. M.G.C. Gallipoli, Egypt, Mesopotamia, Persia.

1909 **Maltby, C. C.** (1914). ‡Lt. (and Adjt.) 12th Rifle Brigade. France and Belgium. Died on Aug. 26, 1916, of wounds received near Guillemont.

1911 Marsden, R., B.A. (Aug. 26, 1914). Capt. 6th King's Own (R. Lancaster Regt.). Gallipoli, Egypt.

1896 **Martin, C.** (Feb. 4, 1916). 2nd Lt. Coldstream Guards. France. Killed in action at St. Quentin Ridge on Dec. 1, 1917.

1909 **Mathias,* C. A. S.,** B.A. (Sept. 1914). ‡2nd Lt. 7th The Buffs (E. Kent Regt.). France. *M.C.*, Apr. 17, 1917. Killed in action near Chérisy on May 3, 1917.

1903 **Maufe, E. G.,** B.A. (May 30, 1916). Pte. R. W. Kent Regt. France. Killed in action at Le Sars on Oct. 6, 1916.

Mead, R. E. C. (Feb. 1, 1917). 2nd Lt. The Buffs (E. Kent Regt.), attd. 7th Bn. France and Belgium. Killed in action in Belgium on Sept. 29, 1917.

1911 **Mears,* E. de Q.** (Sept. 1914). 2nd Lt. 10th Essex Regt. France. Killed in action in Trônes Wood on July 14, 1916.

1919 Meek, H. G. (Aug. 4, 1914). ‡Lt. 23rd Inf. A.I.F. Lt. 12th K.O.Y.L.I., attd. 2nd West Inf. Bde. (Staff-Captain). France, Belgium, Germany. *D.* France, 1918.

1914 Meredith, P. R. (Apr. 13, 1915). Lt., Acting Capt., 7th R. Scots. Gallipoli, 1915; Egypt and Palestine, 1916–17; France, 1918–19. *M.C.*, Apr. 2, 1919.

1919 Millard, E. N. (May 1918). ‡2nd Lt. The Buffs (E. Kent Regt.).

1903 **Milligan, H. W.,** B.A. (Aug. 1914). ‡Lt. Lancashire Fusiliers. Egypt, 1915; Gallipoli, 1915; France, 1916–17. Killed in action at Noyelles on Nov. 21, 1917.

1904 **Mills, F.,** B.A. (Mar. 1916). Interpreter, attd. R.E. (Signallers' Wireless Section). France. Killed in action at Sailly-Sallisel on Mar. 14, 1917.

1919 Milnes, W. H. G. (Aug. 16, 1916). 2nd Lt. R. Warwickshire Regt., attd. R.F.C. Lt. 37th T.D.S., R.A.F. (Flight-Commdr.). France. *M.C.*, June 22, 1918.

1889 Moberly, G. K. (Nov. 1, 1916). Maj. S. African Medical Corps.

1904 Mockett, V. B., M.A. (Aug. 22, 1914). Lt. 1/4th The Buffs (E. Kent Regt.). Mesopotamia. *M.B.E.* (Mil.). *D.* Mesopotamia, 1919.

1901 **Moilliet, J. L.,** B.A. (1915). Lce.-Cpl. 72nd Canadian Seaforth Highlanders (Sergt.). France. Killed in action near Vimy Ridge on June 28, 1917.

1907 Morgan,* H. de R., B.A. (Serving Aug. 4, 1914). Capt. 2nd The Buffs (E. Kent Regt.) (Lt.-Col.). Maj. Tank Corps. France. *D.S.O.*, Sept. 16, 1918. *D.* France, 1915, 1918.

1902 **Morgan-Owen, J. G.,** B.A. (Feb. 1915). 2nd Lt. 4th S. Wales Borderers. Egypt, Mesopotamia. *D.* Mesopotamia. Killed in action at the Battle of Sanna-i-yat on Apr. 9, 1916.

1907 Morrow, McK. F., B.A. (1918). Pte. 3rd Training Bn., U.S. Signal Corps.
1909 Morton,* E. S., B.A. (Oct. 19, 1914). Pte R.A.M.C. Pte. No. 2 Cadet Reception Bn. (Cpl.). France, 1915, 1916–18; Egypt, 1915–16.
1876 Moseley, Rev. R., B.A. (Serving Aug. 4, 1914). Chaplain to the Forces (1st Class).
1919 Munton, E. (Aug. 10, 1917). Sapper, 5th Field Survey Bn., R.E. France.
1907 Murray, J. M., B.A. General Botha's Staff, German S.W. Africa. German S.W. Africa.
1904 Murray, R. M., M.A. (June 1, 1917). Lt. British W. Indies Regt. Belgium, France. *M.B.E.* (Mil.).
1914 Narborough, F. D. V., B.A. (Sept. 4, 1918). Pte. 2/6th Suffolk Regt. (Lce.-Cpl.).
1913 Naylor, W. R. N., B.A. (Oct. 16, 1916). Guardsman, Coldstream Guards (Cpl.). 2nd Lt. Worcestershire Regt. (on demobilization). France.
1902 **Nicholas, O. R.,** B.C.L., M.A. (Aug. 15, 1914). Lt. 3rd R.W. Kent Regt., attd. Connaught Rangers. Mesopotamia. Killed in action in Apr. 1916.
1907 Nicholson,* A. R., B.A. (May 28, 1915). Capt. I.A.R.O., attd. 1/102nd Grenadiers. A.D.C. to G.O.C. Poona Division. India, Mesopotamia. *D.* Mesopotamia, 1917.
1903 Nicol, Rev. W. H., M.A. (May 3, 1916). Chaplain to the Forces (4th Class). France, 1916–17; Italy, 1917; Egypt, 1917; Hospital Ship in Mediterranean, 1917.
1913 Noble, G. B., B.A. (1917). 1st Lt. 168th Inf., U.S. Army. France. *American D.S.C.*
1897 Odling, W. A. (Serving Aug. 4, 1914). Maj. Middlesex Regt. Temp. Lt.-Col. N. Staffordshire Regt.
O'Farrell, A. H. (Jan. 3, 1918). 2nd Lt. Irish Guards. France. Killed in action at Flesquières on Sept. 27, 1918.
Olivier, J. G. (Jan. 16, 1915). 2nd Lt. D.C.L.I. France, 1916. Killed in action near Albert on Sept. 19, 1916.
1919 Oswell, H. T. W. (Feb. 26, 1915). Lt. 13th Cheshire Regt. Lt. Flying Officer, 188th N.T. Squadron, R.A.F. France, 1915–16.
1914 Owen, A. T. (Sept. 26, 1916). Lt. R.E. (T.F.).
1906 Owen, Rev. R. H., M.A. (Aug. 1914). Lt. Unattached List, T.F., Uppingham School O.T.C.
1911 **Oxland N.** (Sept. 1914). Lt. 6th Border Regt. Gallipoli. Killed in action at Suvla Bay on Aug. 9, 1915.
Page, J. K. S. (Aug. 1914). Capt. 9th R. Warwickshire Regt., attd. 1/5th Lancashire Fusiliers. Gallipoli, Egypt, France. *M.C.*, Sept. 16, 1918. Died on Aug. 22, 1918, of wounds received in action.
1906 Palmer, C. A., B.A. (Nov. 7, 1914). Capt. 12th Lancashire Fusiliers, attd. O.C.B. Salonika. *D.* § Mar. 1919.
1919 Parks, W. R. (Dec. 1915). Pte. 88th Perth Infantry (Aust.). ‡2nd Lt. 3rd Gordon Highlanders.
1919 Parry, J. I. (Aug. 5, 1914). ‡2nd Lt. 3rd Cheshire Regt. France and Belgium, 1915–16, 1918. *M.C.*, Sept. 24, 1918.
1915 Peaker, A. P. (Oct. 1915). Capt. K.R.R.C., attd. No. 17 O.C.B. France, Belgium, 1916–17. *M.C.*, Oct. 28, 1917.

1909 Pearce,* J. J. (Mobilized Aug. 1914). Capt. Q.O. Oxfordshire Hussars. France.

1911 **Pearce,* M. L.** (Nov. 18, 1914). Lt. R. Sussex Regt. Adjt. attd. 12th Hampshire Regt. France, 1915; Salonika, 1915–16. Presumed killed in action at Salonika on Sept. 24, 1916.

1910 **Pearson,* G. T.,** B.A. (Aug. 31, 1914). Lt. 9th Worcestershire Regt. (Capt.). Gallipoli. Killed in action at Kabbak Kuyu on Aug. 12, 1915.

1914 Peel, G. W. E. (Oct. 13, 1914). Lt., Acting Capt., Army Cyclist Corps. France. *D.* France, 1918.

1907 Peel, H. W. (Feb. 7, 1917). Lt. R.F.A.

1909 Peirson,* N. J., B.A. (Nov. 4, 1914). Capt. 7th Oxf. & Bucks. Lt. Infty. Salonika. *D.* Salonika, 1918.

1915 Phillips, W. P. (June 1916). ‡Lt. York & Lancaster Regt., attd. No. 21 O.C.B. France.

Pilcher, G. A. (Jan. 26, 1915). Lt. D. Batt. 159th Bde., R.F.A. France and Belgium. Died on Oct. 26, 1917, of wounds received in action at Langemarck.

1914 Pitts, H. C. M. (Mar. 6, 1915). 2nd Lt. 13th Worcestershire Regt. Lt. M.G.C. Salonika, 1916; Egypt and Palestine, 1918–19; Constantinople, 1919.

1887 Pode, C. A., M.A. (July 24, 1915). Capt. (War Dept. Land Agent) Special Lists. (Resigned on account of ill health, Feb. 1918.)

1886 Powles, Rev. E., M.A. (Mobilized Aug. 5, 1914). Chaplain to the Forces (2nd Class). Egypt, 1916–17. T.D.

1885 Price, Rev. C., M.A. (Serving Aug. 4, 1914). Chaplain to the Forces (3rd Class). India.

1919 Priestley, L. S. (Jan. 10, 1916). ‡Lt. 95th Siege Batt., R.G.A. Belgium, France.

1920 Pritt, W. A. (Sept. 1916). Lt. 141st Squadron, R.A.F. (Capt.). France. *M.C.*, Sept. 26, 1917.

1911 **Rae, J. E. P.** (Sept. 15, 1914). Maj. 7th D.C.L.I. (Col.). France, 1915–17. Killed in action at Les Rues Vertes on Nov. 30, 1917.

1914 Rammell, J. C. (May 31, 1917). ‡2nd Lt. R.G.A.

1892 Randall-MacIver, D., B.Sc., M.A. (Sept. 8, 1914). 2nd Lt., Interpreter, Special Lists. Capt., D.A.D. of Labour. France, 1914–15; Salonika, 1916–18. *D.* Salonika, 1918.

1899 Rankin, T. W., B.A. Pte. R. Fusiliers.

1913 **Raynes, A. H.** (Oct. 1914). Lt. 11th Essex Regt. France, 1915. Missing, believed killed in action at Loos, on Sept. 26, 1915.

1919 Read, G. N. (Mar. 16, 1917). Lt. No. 2 Res. Bde., R.F.A. France.

1902 Relton, F. E. (Sept. 28, 1916). 2nd Lt. R.G.A.

1909 Revely, Rev. O. P., M.A. (1917). Chaplain R.N., H.M.S. *Highflyer*.

1899 Reynell, D., B.C.L., M.A. (Mobilized 1914). Sergt. 5th Punjab Light Horse I.D.F. (Squadron Sergt.-Maj.). India.

1909 Riddle, A. E. S. (Sept. 15, 1914). ‡Lt. 2nd Oxf. & Bucks. Lt. Infty. France, 1915; Mesopotamia, 1916–18.

1908 Ridgeway, Rev. N. V., B.A. (Sept. 1914). Lt. Unattached List, T.F., Tonbridge School O.T.C. Chaplain to the Forces (4th Class). France, 1917.

1895 Robinson, R. M., M.A. (Aug. 20, 1914). Lt. 6th W. Riding Regt. (T.F.). Asst.-Instructor M.G.C. France. *D.* France, 1917.

1901 **Rogers, R.,** M.A. (June 13, 1915). 2nd Lt. 7th Rifle Brigade. France. Killed in action at Flers on Sept. 15, 1916.

1896 Rolfe, Rev. G. C., M.A. (Mar. 1, 1917). Chaplain to the Forces (4th Class), attd. 153rd Inf. Bde. France.

1903 Rose, Rev. A. C. W., M.A. (Aug. 19, 1914). Chaplain R.N., H.M.S. *Marlborough*, 1st Battle Squadron. Gallipoli, Italy.

Round, H. C. (Dec. 4, 1915). Lt., Acting Capt., 9th Rifle Brigade. France and Belgium. *D.S.O.*, Aug. 16, 1917. *M.C.*, Nov. 14, 1916. *D.* France, 1917. Killed in action near Passchendaele on Aug. 24, 1917.

1919 Rowney, L. C. (Jan. 1915). ‡Lt. Middlesex Regt. Lt. 'M' Flight, R.A.F. Salonika, Egypt, France, Germany.

1919 Ruck, S. K. (Jan. 17, 1918). 1st Aircraft Mechanic, R.A.F.

1919 Russell, P. G. (May 12, 1917). 2nd Lt. 2/4th K.O.Y.L.I. France and Germany.

1913 **Saunders,* C. F.** (Sept. 1, 1914). 2nd Lt. 7th Northamptonshire Regt. France. Killed in action at Guillemont on Aug. 18, 1916.

1913 Seymour,* A. H. (Aug. 29, 1914). Lt. 4th D.C.L.I. Capt. 2/4th Gurkha Rifles, Indian Army. India, Mesopotamia, Afghanistan.

1913 Seyrig, H. A. (Dec. 16, 1914). Lt. 2ᵉ Artillerie de Montagne, French Army. France. Croix de Guerre.

1901 Shapland, Rev. C. B. (Mar. 15, 1917). Chaplain to the Forces (4th Class).

1909 Sheehan-Dare,* Rev. C. A., B.A. (Jan. 8, 1917). Chaplain to the Forces (4th Class). H.M. Hospital Ship *Wendilla.*

1902 **Sheppey-Greene, Rev. N. G.,** M.A. (Sept. 15, 1915). 2nd Lt. R. W. Kent Regt. France. Died on June 14, 1918, of wounds received in action.

1913 **Simpson,* B.** (Aug. 14, 1914). Lt. 2nd Cameronians. France. Killed in action near Fromelles on May 9, 1915.

1906 **Smith, E.,** B.A. (Aug. 1914). ‡2nd Lt. R. W. Kent Regt. France. Died in France on Oct. 16, 1916, of illness contracted while on active service.

1907 Smith, F. Eardley, B.A. (Serving Aug. 4, 1914). Capt. Militia Artillery, Bermuda. Bermuda, 1914–18.

1883 Smith, H. W. T., B.A. (Serving Aug. 4, 1914). Maj., Bt. Lt.-Col., R.G.A. France. *D.S.O.*, Feb. 2, 1916. *D.* France, 1915, 1916, 1917 twice, 1918.

1898 Spooner, R. W. W., B.A. (June 15, 1916). Lt. R.A.S.C. France.

1900 Stockdale, A. (Oct. 20, 1916). Lt. 5th Cheshire Regt. (T.F.).

1919 Stevens, J. T. (Dec. 23, 1914). Staff Sergt-.Maj. 14th Div. H.Q., R.A.S.C. France. *M.S.M.*, June 1917. Belgian Croix de Guerre. *D.* France, 1916.

1889 Street, Rev. G., M.A. (Apr. 8, 1916). Chaplain to the Forces (4th Class). Egypt, Salonika.

1902 Sullivan, C. E. E., B.A. Capt. Intelligence Dept., B. E. African Force. E. Africa.

1919 Sutton, C. (Aug. 21, 1914). ‡2nd Lt. S. African Horse. 2nd Lt. R.F.A. German S.W. Africa, German E. Africa, France.

1913 **Sweet-Escott,* L. W.** (Aug. 1914). Lt. 5th Oxf. & Bucks. Lt. Infty. France and Belgium. Killed in action at Bellewaerde Farm, near Ypres, on Sept. 25, 1915.

1910 Sykes,* J., M.A. (May 5, 1915). Lt., Acting Capt., M.G.C. France, 1916–17, 1917–19. *D.* France, 1919.

1898 Symons, C. T., B.A. (Sept. 1914). ‡Lt. Ceylon Motor Cyclist Corps (O.C.). Ceylon.

1911 Talbot, J. W., B.A. (May 2, 1915). Lt. 10th Gloucestershire Regt. Lt. 1st Field Survey Bn., R.E. (Capt.). France, 1915–18. *D.* France, 1917.

1908 **Tasker,* R. G.,** B.A. (Aug. 1914). Capt. 10th Worcestershire Regt. France, 1915–16. Killed in action at La Boisselle on July 3, 1916.

1919 Tatton, E. (May 30, 1917). ‡2nd Lt. 2nd Welsh Regt. France.

1907 Thatcher, R. S., B.A. (Sept. 1914). ‡Capt. 3rd Somerset L.I. (Maj.). D.A.Q.M.G. Belgium, France, Italy, Germany. *O.B.E.* (Mil.). *M.C.*, Jan. 1, 1918. Croix de Guerre. Chevalier of the Order of the Crown of Italy. *D.* France, 1918.

1919 Thomas, C. C., B.A. (June 21, 1917). 2nd Lt. R.G.A. France, 1917.

1909 **Thomas, *F. S.,** B.A. (Nov. 9, 1914). Capt. 4th Welsh Regt. Gallipoli, Egypt, and Palestine. Died on Apr. 20, 1917, of wounds received in action at Gaza on Apr. 19.

1883 Thomas, Rev. P. C., M.A. (Mobilized Aug. 4, 1914). Chaplain to the Forces (2nd Class), attd. 1/7th Worcestershire Regt. Belgium, 1915; France, 1916. T.D.

1908 Thompson,* C. W., B.A. (Aug. 14, 1914). ‡ Lt. K.O.Y.L.I., empld. No. 2 O.C.B. France and Belgium, from 1915.

1882 Thompson, Rev. R. B., M.A. (Aug. 1915). Chaplain to the Forces (4th Class), attd. 1/3rd N. Mid. Division.

1911 Thompson, Rev. W. (Aug. 30, 1916). Chaplain to the Forces (4th Class).

1900 Tidswell, E. S. W., M.A. (Serving Aug. 4, 1914). Capt. and Bt.-Maj. Temp. Lt.-Col. 1st Leicestershire Regt. (attd. Gen. Staff). France, Belgium, Salonika. *D.S.O.*, Feb. 18, 1915. *O.B.E.* (Mil.). Star of Roumania. Order of the White Eagle (4th Class) (with swords). *D.* France, 1915 twice; Salonika, 1916, 1917, 1918, 1919.

1910 Timpson,* G. F., M.A. (Oct. 25, 1916). Lt. 4th Northamptonshire Regt.

1919 Todd, R. M. (Feb. 8, 1915). Sub-Conductor (1st Class W. O.) R.A.O.C. France, 1915–18.

1896 **Townshend, D. R.,** B.A. (Serving Aug. 4, 1914). Capt. Unattached List, T.F. Capt. 11th Loyal N. Lancashire Regt. Gallipoli, 1915. Killed in action at Suvla Bay on Aug. 21, 1915.

1919 Tranter, A. R. McIntyre (May 5, 1917). Lt. 7th Border Regt. France, 1917–18.

1911 Tristram, A. M., B.A. (Sept. 1914). Lt. 4th Manchester Regt. France.

1898 Truslove, R., M.A. (Mobilized Aug. 1914). Maj. 4th Seaforth Highlanders. Staff-Captain in the 51st Div. France, 1914–15, 1916–18.

1883 Trustram, E. J., M.A. (Sept. 10, 1916). Capt. 2nd Vol. Bn. London Regt. (R. Fusiliers) (Capt. and Adjt.).

1895 Turner, R. B., B.A., *D.S.O.* (June 25, 1917). Maj. S. African Def. Force. Lt.-Col. Special Lists, A.Q.M.G. E. Africa. *C.M.G.* *D.* E. Africa, 1918 twice.

1904 Tyndale, A. C., M.A. (Nov. 1914). Maj. Dy. Field Accountant General, Military Accounts Dept. Mesopotamia, 1914–16, 1919–20; India, 1916–19.

1898 Tyrwhitt, T. (Feb. 6, 1915). A.B., R.N.V.R., Anti-Aircraft Corps. ‡2nd Lt. R.G.A.

1913 **Vacher,* G. H.** (Aug. 1914). 2nd Lt. 2nd R. Warwickshire Regt. Belgium. Killed in action at Zandvoorde on Oct. 30, 1914.

1919 Valentine, A. B. B. (Sept. 20, 1918). Cadet No. 2 O.C.B.

1886 Vallings, Rev. Canon G. R., M.A. (Apr. 25, 1915). Chaplain to the Forces (2nd Class), D.A.C.G., V Corps. France. *D.S.O.*, Jan. 1, 1918. *D.* France, 1916, 1917.

1919 Vezey, P. H. (Oct. 16, 1916). Lt. 195th Siege Batt., R.G.A. France, 1918. Germany, 1918–19.

1906 Vidal, H. S. G. (Apr. 1, 1915). Capt. R.A.S.C. Lt. R.F.A. *D.* § Mar. 1919.

1919 Vigne, C. (Feb. 17, 1918). 2nd Lt. R.A.F.

1912 Vigo,* D. S. (Aug. 15, 1914). Lt. R.F.A. (T.F.).

1906 Wace, W. M., B.A. (Aug. 21, 1914). Capt. 3rd Bedfordshire Regt. France, Belgium (with 6th Bn.). *M.C.*, Sept. 26, 1916.

1906 **Waddell-Dudley, R. R.,** B.A. (Serving Aug. 4, 1914). Lt. 3rd R. Fusiliers. France. Killed in action on Apr. 15, 1915.

1912 Waddy,* B. H., B.A. (Serving Aug. 4, 1914). Lt. Gloucestershire Regt. France, 1914–15, 1915–16, 1918; Italy, 1917–18. *M.C.*, June 3, 1915. *D.* France, 1915 twice.

1919 Waight, G. (Aug. 18, 1914). ‡Lt. General List. Lt. R.A.F. France, 1915–17, 1918.

1899 Waithman, Rev. F. W. T., M.A. (Feb. 1918). Chaplain to the Forces (4th Class). France, 1918–19.

1914 Walter, J. H. (Nov. 3, 1914). Lt. R.A.S.C.

1901 Warman, W. H., B.A. (Sept. 17, 1914). Lt. 12th R. Irish Rifles. Capt. Army Cyclist Corps. Capt. Tank Corps. France.

1904 Wathen, A. R., M.A. (Nov. 1914). Capt. Unattached List, T.F., Bradfield College O.T.C.

1919 Watts, P. S. (Feb. 2, 1916). Lt. R.M.L.I. France, 1917–18.

1903 Weir, A. G., B.A. (Nov. 22, 1914). Capt. R.A.F. France. (Prisoner of war, July 1915.)

1903 Weller, A. J., M.A. (Serving Aug. 4, 1914). Lt. Unattached List, T.F. Shrewsbury School O.T.C.

1911 Wells, R. C. O., M.A. (Apr. 3, 1916). Capt. R.A.S.C.. *M.B.E.* (Mil.).

1914 Wetenhall, J. P., B.A. (Sept. 1916). ‡Lt. Tank Corps. France. (Wounded and prisoner of war, Nov. 1917–Dec. 1918.)

1900 Whaley, J. B. (Dec. 1915). ‡Lt. 50th Divl. Train, R.A.S.C. France.

1900 Whatley, C., M.A. (Sept. 15, 1914). Maj. R.A.S.C. France, 1916; Russia, 1918–19. Order of S. Anne. *D.* N. Russia, 1919.

1911 Whinney, C. T., M.A. (Aug. 22, 1914). Lt. Middlesex Regt., attd. 52nd Devonshire Regt. France; N. Russia, 1919. *M.C.*, Oct. 3, 1919. *D.* § Aug. 1919.

1919 White, A. G. F. (Aug. 10, 1917). 2nd Lt. R.F.A. France, from 1918.

1916 **Whitelock, C. R.** (Aug. 1917). Lt. Independent Air Force. France. Killed in action near Charmes on July 16, 1918.

1919 Whitrow, R. H. (Sept. 1, 1916). Lt. 148th Bde., R.F.A. (Capt. and Adjt.). France.

1907 Whittall, F. J. G., B.A. (Sept. 1, 1914). Capt. 17th Manchester Regt. France. *M.C.*, Sept. 26, 1916. *D.* France, 1916.

1906 Wilkinson, C. H., M.A. (Dec. 23, 1914). Capt. Coldstream Guards (Maj.). G.S.O. 2. Belgium and France, 1915–17; Italy, 1917–19. *M.C.*, June 3, 1918. Croix de Guerre. Croce di Guerra. *D.* France, 1917.

1908 **Wilkinson, H. U.,** B.A. (1914). Rfln. King's African Rifles. Africa. Died in March 1916.

1907 **Wilkinson,* J. R. M.,** B.A. (Serving Aug. 4, 1914). Lt. 4th Middlesex Regt. Belgium. Killed in action at Obourg, near Mons, on Aug. 23, 1914.

1907 Williams, A. D. (Dec. 3, 1914). Lt. 12th R. Welch Fusiliers.

1893 Williams, G. R. K. (Serving Aug. 4, 1914). Maj. Indian Army, Supernumerary List, attd. Burma Police. India.

1914 Williamson, G. A., B.A. (Mar. 25, 1915). Capt. 7th Northamptonshire Regt. France, 1916–17, 1917–19. *M.C.*, Sept. 16, 1918.

1919 Wilmott, B. A. (Aug. 15, 1918). 2nd Lt. R.G.A. (on demobilization).

1904 Wilson, Rev. C. C. C., M.A. (Oct. 21, 1915). Chaplain to the Forces (4th Class) (Asst. A.C.G.). France. *D.* France 1919.

1909 **Wilson, R. E.** (Jan. 25, 1917). 2nd Lt. 7th Queen's (R. W. Surrey Regt.). France, Belgium. Missing, presumed killed in action at Inverness Copse on Aug. 10, 1917.

1910 Winterbottom, L. (Nov. 2, 1914). Lt. Q.O. Oxfordshire Hussars. France.

1919 Witts, W. (July 24, 1917). Lt. 11th N. Staffordshire Regt. Lt. No. 4 Traffic Control Coy. France. *D.* France, 1918.

1906 **Wood, H.,** M.A. (July 1915). Lt., Acting Capt., 1/20th London Regt. France. Killed in action at St. Pierre Vaast on Sept. 1, 1918.

1891 Woollcombe, Rev. C. R., M.A. (May 1, 1918). Chaplain to the Forces (4th Class), attd. 4th Queen's (R. W. Surrey Regt.).

1908 Woolley, H. C. W., B.A. (June 4, 1915). Capt. Labour Corps.

1902 Wright, Rev. C. J. C., M.A. (July 1917). Chaplain to the Forces (4th Class), attd. 21st W. Yorkshire Regt. France, 1917–18.

1919 Wright, J. S. (June 18, 1916). Capt. R.A.F. France. *D.S.C.*, Nov. 2, 1917.

1913 Young,* R. E. M. (Sept. 2, 1914). Capt. 1st Bucks. Bn., Oxf. & Bucks. Lt. Infty. France, 1915–19.

HERTFORD COLLEGE

1910 Abbot, C. H., B.A. (Apr. 27, 1915). Lt., Acting Capt., 4th D.C.L.I. Mesopotamia, India.

1919 Adams, C. F. (Aug. 17, 1917). 2nd Lt. Unattached List, T.F., attd. Dean Close School O.T.C.

1919 Adams, D. T. (Sept. 4, 1914). Pte. 103rd Field Ambulance. Egypt, 1914–16; Palestine, 1917–18; France, 1918.

1902 **Allan, Rev. H. S.,** M.A. (Mobilized Aug. 1914). ‡2nd Lt. 6th London Regt. (Rifles). India, 1914–16; France, 1916. Died on Oct. 2, 1916, of wounds received in action between High Wood and Flers.

1895 Allchin, B. C., M.A. (Dec. 10, 1915). Capt. Unattached List, T.F., serving with O.U.O.T.C. (Capt. and Adjt.).

1897 **Almond, G. H.-H.,** B.M., M.A. (Nov. 1915). Capt. R.A.M.C., attd. 3rd Cavalry Field Ambulance. Sicily, France. Killed in action at Caix on Aug. 9, 1918.

1907 Anderson, D. S. (Aug. 26, 1914). Capt. 8th The Black Watch. Temp. Capt. General List. Acting Maj. while comdg. Reception Camp. France.

1898 Armitstead, W. K., M.A. (Dec. 3, 1914). Lt. 5th, attd. 13th, Cheshire Regt. (Capt.). France, Belgium, 1916, 1917.

1904 Ascroft, G. B., M.A. (Sept. 12, 1914). Capt. 1st Herefordshire Regt. (T.F.), empld. under N. & A.C.B.

1913 Ashmole,* B., B.A. (Oct. 6, 1914). Capt. 5th R. Fusiliers. France. *M.C.*, Feb. 2, 1917.

1914 **Atkins,* B. E.** (Mar. 17, 1915). Capt. 7th N. Staffordshire Regt. Mesopotamia. *D.* Mesopotamia, 1917. Killed in action in Mesopotamia on Feb. 25, 1917.

1909 **Atkinson,* L. E. M.,** B.A. (Aug. 15, 1914). Lt. 3rd, attd. 2nd, R. Berkshire Regt. France. Killed in action on May 9, 1915.

1919 Atkinson, R. d'E. (Mar. 1, 1917). 2nd Lt. 12th Batt., 35th Bde., R.F.A. France, 1917; Italy, 1917–19.

1912 Bagshawe, F. E. G. (Sept. 17, 1914). ‡2nd Lt. Lanarkshire Yeomanry, empld. Imp. Camel Corps, afterwards Capt. Tank Corps. Egypt, 1915, 1916–17; France, 1917–19; Germany, from May 1919.

Baring, C. C. (Mar. 1916). ‡2nd Lt. 8th R. W. Kent Regt. (Staff-Lt.). France. Died on Mar. 21, 1918, of wounds received in action.

1910 Baring, H. (Oct. 14, 1914). Capt. 4th R. W. Kent Regt., attd. R.A.F. France.

1912 Barnard,* A. S. C., M.A. (Aug. 22, 1914). Lt. 6th York & Lancaster Regt. Gallipoli, France. (Prisoner of war in Germany.)

1905 Barringer, K. A. (Aug. 20, 1916). Lt. R.A.S.C. (M.T.) (previously serving as Ambulance Driver under St. John's Amb. Association). France, 1914–18; Germany, 1918–19.

1900 Batterbee, H. H., M.A. (Serving Aug. 4, 1914). Capt. Unattached List, T.F., Blundell's School O.T.C. Lt., Acting Capt., 60th Siege Batt., R.G.A. (Maj.). France, 1916–18.

1908 Batterbury, T. K. E., M.A. (Sept. 1914). Lt. Unattached List, T.F., Bedford Grammar School O.T.C.

1898 Bean, C. E. W. (Sept. 28, 1914). Commonwealth Correspondent with the Australian Contingent (graded as Capt.). Gallipoli, 1915; France, 1916–19. *D.* Gallipoli, 1916.

1912 **Beatty,* D. H.** (Aug. 1914). 2nd Lt. 4th, attd. 2nd, E. Surrey Regt. Belgium. Died on Feb. 21, 1915, of wounds received in action at Ypres.

1898 Bell-Cox, L. C. (Sept. 16, 1915). 2nd Lt. 5th Loyal N. Lancashire Regt.

1885 Bennett, E. N., M.A. (Mobilized Aug. 1914). Capt. 4th Oxf. & Bucks. Lt. Infty. (T.F. Res.). (Attd. H.Q. IX Div., B.E.F., 1917). Instructor, 2nd Army College, Cologne. France, Belgium, 1914, 1915, 1917; Serbia, 1914–15; Germany, 1919. Order of the White Eagle (3rd Class).

1905 Bentley, W. C., M.A. (Aug. 26, 1915). Lt. R.E. (T.F.). Salonika.

Betley, E. (Jan. 1916). Lt. R.G.A., attd. R.F.C. France. Missing, believed killed while flying near Villers-Brettoneux on Mar. 28, 1918.

1881 Bevan, E. L., Bishop of Swansea, D.D. (Mobilized Aug. 1914). Chaplain (1st Class), Breconshire Bn., S. Wales Borderers. Aden, India.

1915 Bevir, A. (July 8, 1915). Capt. 2/7th King's (Liverpool Regt.), attd. 171st Inf. Bde. France, 1917–18. *D.* France, 1917, 1918, 1919.

1907 **Bevir,* R.,** B.A. (Aug. 1914). ‡2nd Lt. 10th R. Fusiliers. France. Killed in action at Pozières on July 15, 1916.

1912 Blacker,* C. H. B., B.A. (Aug. 1914). Lt. 5th Dragoon Guards (until Aug. 1918) (Capt. and Adjt.). Lt. R.A.F. France.

1907 Blackett, Rev. H. M. (July 27, 1918). 2nd Pte. R.A.F. Armament School, Uxbridge.

1902 Blake, W. J. Pte. R.A.S.C. (M.T.).

1912 **Bland,* C. E.** (Aug. 1914). Capt. 11th Hampshire Regt. France, 1915–16. Killed in action near Cuinchy on Sept. 9, 1916.

1910 Bleckly,* H., B.A. (Dec. 16, 1914). Lt. 2/1st Cheshire Yeomanry, attd. 6th Cyclist Bde., Signal Section, R.E.

1913 **Bourne,* J. C.** (Aug. 22, 1914). 2nd Lt. 9th Worcestershire Regt. Gallipoli. Killed in action in Gallipoli in July 1915.

1912 Boyce,* H. F., B.A. (Oct. 29, 1915). Lt. Devonshire Regt., attd. 6th Somerset L.I. France. (Prisoner of war in Germany.)

1911 Boyd,* A. K., B.A. (Aug. 15, 1914). Lt., temp. Capt., 4th Lancashire Fusiliers, attd. M.G.C. France, 1915–16.

1919 Boyd, R. McD. (Apr. 30, 1918). Cadet Pilot (C. Q.-M.) 10th Squadron, Miami, U.S. Naval Res. Flying Corps.

1899 **Bradburn, T. S.,** M.A. (Sept. 21, 1914). Temp. Surgeon R.N., attd. British Armoured Car Squadron. White Sea, North Sea. Russian Order of St. Anne (3rd Class) (with swords). Died on Mar. 8, 1918, of illness contracted while on active service.

1906 Brailsford, H. E. L. Rhodesian Regt. Africa.

1907 Brandon,* R. C. L., B.A. (1914). ‡Lt. 5th, attd. 3rd, Middlesex Regt. Salonika.

1908 Brett,* W. B. Behar Light Horse. India.

1906 **Brinsley-Richards, R. H. W.,** M.A. (June 1915). 2nd Lt. W. Riding Regt. France. Killed in action near Pozières on July 29, 1916.

1884 Broadbent, Sir J. F. H., Bt., M.A. (Mobilized Aug. 1914). Capt. R.A.M.C. (T.F.), 3rd London General Hospital.

1902 Broadley, R. A. L., B.A. (Sept. 27, 1915). Lt. R.A.S.C. (Capt.).

1908 Brodrick, A. L., B.A. (Mobilized Aug. 1914). Capt. 1st County of London Yeomanry.

1890 **Bromfield, H. H.,** *D.S.O.* (Mobilized Aug. 1914). Maj. 1st Welsh Guards. France. Killed in action in the Battle of the Somme on Sept. 10, 1916.

1918 Brown, A. S. (Aug. 5, 1914). Q.S., R.N.D. (A.B.). Antwerp, Oct. 1914. (Interned in Holland, 1914–18.)

1913 Brown,* J. B., B.A. (Mar. 21, 1915). Lt., Acting Capt., 12th R. Scots. France.

1919 Brown, J. H. H. (Aug. 31, 1914). Capt. 6th Bedfordshire Regt. France, Belgium.

1914 Brown,* R. H., M.A. (Dec. 1916). ‡Lt. 19th Middlesex Regt. (Adjt.). France, 1918; Germany, 1919.

1919 Browning, R. G. (Aug. 10, 1915). Lt. 8th Northumberland Fusiliers (Capt. and Adjt.). France.

1913 Bruchholz, H. V. (Aug. 27, 1917). 1st Lt. 346th Field Artillery, U.S. Army. France, 1918–19.

1910 Bryan, H. M., M.A. (1918). 2nd Lt. F.A. Reserve Corps, U.S. Army.

1897 Buchanan-Riddell, W. R., M.A. (Aug. 24, 1914). ‡Capt. 9th Hampshire Regt. India, Siberia.

1904 Buckingham, F. R., B.A. (Sept. 9, 1914). Capt. 1/4th Devonshire Regt. Mesopotamia, Palestine.

1913 **Burkett,* H. W. B.** (Jan. 12, 1915). Lt. 1st Wiltshire Regt. (Capt. and Adjt.). France, Belgium. Killed in action at Crucifix Corner, near Bailleul, on Apr. 14, 1918.

1900 **Burnett, C. G. A.** (Aug. 1914). ‡Lt. 7th Northumberland Fusiliers. Belgium and France. Killed in action at Wytschaete on June 30, 1916.

1913 **Cambie, E. M. B.** (Sept. 1914). ‡Lt. 9th K.O.Y.L.I. (Adjt.). France, 1916. Killed in action near Thiepval on July 1, 1916.

1912 Cameron A. C., M.A. (Aug. 1914). ‡Capt. and Adjt. 8th Devonshire Regt. France, Belgium, 1915–17; Italy, 1917–19. *M.C.*, Jan. 1, 1918. *D.* France, 1916; Italy, 1918, 1919.

1905 [**Campbell, A. U.**] (Oct. 1915). Lt., Acting Lt.-Commdr., R.N.V.R., R.N.D., attd. T.M.Batt. France. *M.C.*, Jan. 1, 1917; *Bar*, Mar. 13, 1917. Croix de Guerre with Palm. *D.* France. Killed in action on Dec. 30, 1917.

1910 Campbell,* I. P. F., B.A. (Mobilized Aug. 1914). Capt. 9th Hampshire Regt. (T.F.). India, Mesopotamia, Russia. *O.B.E.* (Mil.). *D.* Siberia, 1919.

1903 Campbell, Rev. J. McL., M.A. (Aug. 12, 1914). Chaplain to the Forces (3rd Class), attd. 51st and 4th Divs. France, 1915–19. *M.C.*, Jan. 1, 1919. *D.* France, 1917.

1913 **Campbell,* W. P.** (Aug. 1914). 2nd Lt. 3rd, attd. 2nd, Wiltshire Regt. Belgium, France. Killed in action near Ypres on Oct. 24, 1914.

1901 Campion, G. F. M., M.A. (July 31, 1914). Capt. R.A.S.C. France, 1914–16. (Commission relinquished on account of illness contracted on active service, June 1917.)

1914 Campion,* J. T., B.A. (Dec. 22, 1914). Lt. R.G.A. Belgium, France.

1896 Canny, J. C. M., *D.S.O.* (Serving Aug. 4, 1914). Maj., Bt.-Lt.-Col., R.A.S.C., Asst. Director of Transport. France, Mesopotamia. *C.B.E.* (Mil.). *D.* France, 1915; Mesopotamia, 1919.

1906 **Cardew, G. E.,** B.A. (Nov. 1914). Capt. 6th Durham L.I. Belgium, France. *M.C.*, Sept. 16, 1918. Killed in action at La Gorgue, near Estaires, on Apr. 9, 1918.

1910 Cardwell, N. (Oct. 20, 1914). Lt. 3rd K.O.Y.L.I. France, 1915.

1918 Carew, E. H. (Aug. 6, 1914). A.B., R.N.D. (L.S.). Antwerp, 1914. (Interned in Holland, 1914–18.)

1894 Carey, Rev. W. J., M.A. (Aug. 11, 1914). Chaplain R.N. H.M.S. *Mars*, 1914; H.M.S. *Warspite*, 1915–17.

1906 Carlisle,* C. V., B.A. (Aug. 15, 1914). Lt. 16th Lancers (S.R.). France, 1915–17, 1918.

1911 Carnegy, P. C. A., M.A. (Feb. 7, 1916). Sergt. Army Cyclist Corps.

1919 Cassidy, J. G. (Dec. 13, 1917). Sergt. Ordnance Dept., U.S. Army. France.

1903 Catterall, C., B.A. (June 14, 1915). Capt. and Adjt. R.A.S.C. France. *D.* France, 1917, 1919.

1887 Cecil, Lord Hugh, The Rt. Hon., M.A., *M.P.* (Apr. 1915). Capt. R.A.F.

1896 Champain, F. H. B., B.A. (Oct. 1914). Lt. 9th Rifle Brigade. Acting Capt. R.A.O.C. France. *D.* France, 1917.

1912 Chance,* K. M. (Aug. 22, 1914). Maj. Border Regt., attd. 1/4th K.O. Scottish Borderers. Gallipoli, 1915; Egypt, 1916; France, 1916–17, 1918. *D.S.O.*, June 4, 1917. *D.* France, 1917.

1913 Chapman,* W. H. G. (June 1915). Lt. 11th Queen's (R. W. Surrey Regt.), attd. No. 10 O.C.B. France.

1906 Chappell, Rev. C. R., M.A. (Dec. 1914). Chaplain to the Forces (4th Class), attd. 15th W. Yorkshire Regt. Egypt, 1915–16; France, 1916–18.

1914 Charles,* W. E., B.A. (Dec. 22, 1914). Lt. Bedfordshire Regt. Belgium, France.

1904 **Chavasse, A. R.,** B.M., M.A. (Oct. 1914). Capt. R.A.M.C., attd. No. 2 General Hospital, B.E.F. France, 1914–16. Died on Mar. 12, 1916, of illness contracted while on active service.

1913 Chavasse,* C. C. H., B.A. (Aug. 14, 1914). Lt. 4th, attd. 2nd, R. Warwickshire Regt. (Invalided, Nov. 1915). Surgeon Sub-Lt. R.N.V.R. (from July 1918). France, 1915; Mudros, Constantinople, Black Sea, 1918–19. *D.* France, 1915.

1913 **Church, A. G. W.** (Aug. 1914). Capt. 1/6th Devonshire Regt. India, Egypt, Palestine, France. Killed in action at Marfaux on July 20, 1918.

1912 **Clarke,* H. J.** (Aug. 1914). Lt. 3rd, attd. 1st, R. Berkshire Regt. France. Killed in action at Richebourg L'Avoué on May 16, 1915.

1919 Clarke, O. F. (Dec. 28, 1916). Lt. H.Q. 13th (T.) Group, R.A.F.

1908 Clarke,* R. D., M.A. (Oct. 1914). Capt. R.A.S.C. France, Salonika.

1911 **Clayton, F. H.,** B.A. (Sept. 15, 1914). Pte. 11th R. Fusiliers. France. Believed killed in action on Sept. 26, 1916.

1914 Clease,* W. E. G. (Nov. 5, 1915). Lt. 1st Shropshire L.I. (Capt. and Adjt.). France.

1907 Clerke, A. H. Sergt. Australian Medical Corps. ‡Lt. Education Service, A.I.F. France.

1914 Cluver, E. H., B.A. (Aug. 22, 1918). Capt. S. African Medical Corps. Belgium.

1911 Coates,* P. A., B.A. (1915). Lt. 4th Essex Regt. France.

1905 **Coffin, S. E.** (June 11, 1915). 2nd Lt. 3rd, attd. 1st, R. Scots. France. Died on Dec. 20, 1915, of wounds received in France.

1902 Cook, Rev. A. M., M.A. (Oct. 5, 1915). Chaplain to the Forces (4th Class), attd. 69th Div. Belgium, France, 1915–16.

1914 Cook, W. C., B.A. (Feb.–Mar. 1918). Pte. Ordnance Dept., U.S. Army. France.

1903 Cooke, Rev. G. C. R., M.A. (Mar. 20, 1915). Chaplain to the Forces (4th Class). France, 1915–16, 1916–18; Germany, 1919. *M.C.*, Dec. 17, 1917. (Prisoner of war, Mar.–Dec. 1918.)

1919 Cooper, A. E. (1917). 2nd Lt. 323rd Field Artillery, U.S. Army. France.

1910 Coote, C. M. J. (Aug. 3, 1914). ‡Lt. Huntingdonshire Cyclist Bn., attd. 4th Gloucestershire Regt. France. (Prisoner of war in Germany.)

1895 Cousens, H. S., M.A. (Dec. 7, 1914). Capt. 7th R. Sussex Regt. France, Belgium. *D.* France, 1918 twice.

1908 Crailsham, E. H. (Sept. 12, 1914). Lt. 10th Cameronians, empld. Recruiting Duties.

1910 Crooks, T. T., B.A. (1917). 2nd Lt. Sanitary Corps, U.S. Army. France.

1911 Crow, G. H., B.A. (Autumn 1915). Lt. 7th R. Warwickshire Regt. (T.F.). France. (Invalided.)

1903 Crowder, E. N. (Dec. 13, 1914). 2nd Lt. Res. of Cavalry.

1906 Cruttwell, C. R. M. F., M.A. (Aug. 19, 1914). Capt. 1/4th R. Berkshire Regt., attd. General Staff, War Office (Mil. Intelligence). France, Belgium, 1915.

1900 Cullen, J. G. C. (June 28, 1915). Capt. R.F.A. Capt. Special Lists.

1900 Currie, T. C., M.A. (Serving Aug. 4, 1914). Capt. Unattached List, T.F., Cheltenham College O.T.C.

1884 Curry, Rev. R. H. A., M.A. (Mar. 31, 1915). Chaplain R.N., H.M.S. *Actaeon*. North Sea.

1902 Dain, J. R., B.A. Behar Light Horse. India.

1897 Dalton, F. W. (Nov. 13, 1916). Lt. 6th Bn. Canadian Railway Troops.

1919 Dalton, W. E. (June 16, 1918). Cadet Household Bde. O.T.C.

1910 Darnley-Smith,* H. W., B.A. (Aug. 31, 1914). ‡Lt. 2/6th Devonshire Regt. (Capt.). India, Mesopotamia, Persia, 1914–19.

1908 David, C. W., B.A. (1917). Capt. University of Washington O.T.C.

1889 Davies, C. R., B.A., V.D. (1914). Lt.-Col. General List, A.I.F. Gallipoli, France. *O.B.E.* (Mil.).

1919 Davies, C. R. (Mar. 15, 1915). Capt. 51st Manchester Regt. Belgium, France, Germany.

1905 Davies, W. F. de R., B.A. (Apr. 17, 1915). Lt., Acting Capt., 4th Welsh Regt. Gallipoli, Egypt, Palestine. *D.* Palestine, 1918, 1919.

1911 Davis,* F. C. (Aug. 21, 1914). Capt. 3rd London Regt. (R. Fusiliers). Malta, 1914; France, 1915–18. *D.* France, 1917.

1919 Davis, M. H. (June 9, 1917). 1st Lt. 345th Infantry, U.S. Army. France. Croix de Guerre.

1912 Dawson,* C. A., B.A. (Aug. 14, 1916). ‡2nd Lt. 688th M.T. Coy., R.A.S.C. Salonika, 1917–19.

1911 Dawson, W. N., B.A. (Nov. 14, 1914). ‡2nd Lt. 10th W. Riding Regt. France.

1904 Day, G. D., M.A. (Dec. 1915). Lt. R.A.S.C., attd. Egyptian Camel Transport Corps, afterwards Maj. Special Lists, Political Officer,

Intelligence Branch, E.E.F. Egypt, Senussi Campaign, Palestine, Syria. *D.* Palestine, 1918.

1910 de Blaby,* G. T., B.A. (Aug. 21, 1914). Capt. 1st Leinster Regt. Gallipoli, 1915; Salonika, 1916–17; Palestine, 1917–18.

1919 de Caux, L. H. (Apr. 17, 1918). 2nd Lt. R.F.A.

1907 De Ganay, H. O. E. French Army. France.

1906 Denniston, J. D., M.A. (Sept. 1914). Capt. 7th K.O. Scottish Borderers, afterwards Maj. General List. G.S.O. 2, War Office. France, 1915. 1916. *O.B.E.* (Mil.). Croix de Guerre.

1910 **Digby,* J. K.,** B.A. (Aug. 1914). ‡2nd Lt. 7th Norfolk Regt. (Lt.). France. Killed in action near Armentières on Aug. 4, 1915.

1912 Dixey,* H. G., B.A. (Jan. 1915). Lt. 298th Bde., R.F.A. (Adjt.). France, 1917–18.

1908 Dore, F. R., B.A. (Aug. 1914). Capt. 12th–13th Northumberland Fusiliers. France, Belgium. *D.* France, 1918.

1910 Duckworth-King, Sir G. H. J., Bt. (Serving Aug. 4, 1914). Capt. 5th (Res.) Grenadier Guards (A.D.C.). France.

1906 Dugdale, W. G. (Oct. 29, 1914). Lt. Shropshire Yeomanry (Capt.). France. *M.C.*, Jan. 1, 1918.

1919 Dunlop, M. T. (Mar. 12, 1917). ‡2nd Lt. R.F.A.

1903 **Dunn, E. C.** (Aug. 5, 1914). Sergt. 7th Bn. Canadian E.F. Belgium, France. Killed in action near Zillebeke on June 3, 1916.

1919 Dunt, R. C. (Sept. 9, 1918). 2nd Lt. R.G.A. (after demobilization).

1908 Durnford,* H. W. (Oct. 1914). Lt. 9th Lancers (S.R.). France, 1915–18. *D.* France, 1918.

1899 **Dyson, C.** (Oct. 1914). Capt. 2/8th W. Yorkshire Regt. France. Killed in action at Écourt on Apr. 6, 1917.

1903 Edwards, A. T., M.A. (Nov. 1, 1915). A.B., R.N., H.M.S. *Apollo*. Grand Fleet and 4th Destroyer Flotilla.

1912 Edwards,* E. J. O., M.A. (Aug. 31, 1917). Sergt. R.G.A.

1919 Edwards, H. (May 20, 1915). ‡Lt. 9th London Regt. (Queen Victoria's Rifles). France, Belgium.

1913 Edwards,* H. C. R., B.A. (Feb. 1917). ‡2nd Lt. 64th P. of W. Coy., Labour Coy. France, 1918.

1908 Elliott, V. J. H. (Oct. 24, 1916). ‡2nd Lt. 5th, attd. 27th, King's (Liverpool Regt.).

1876 Errington, F. H. L., M.A. (Aug. 1914). Lt.-Col. Inns of Court O.T.C. (attd. Staff, XI Corps). G.S.O. 2, 8th Bde., R.A.F. *C.B.*, Jan. 1, 1916. *D.* § Feb. 1917; § Air Ministry, June 1919.

1907 **Evan-Jones,* H. G.,** B.A. (Serving Aug. 4, 1914). Lt. 1st Welsh Regt. France and Belgium. *D.* France, 1915. Killed in action near Ypres on Feb. 16, 1915.

1906 Evans, C. S. (Dec. 20, 1914). Capt. and Adjt. 20th Divl. Train. R.A.S.C. France, 1915–19. *D.* France, 1919.

1919 Evans, D. M. (Sept. 1918). Cadet No. 18 O.C.B.

1911 **Evans, R. S.** (Sept. 1, 1914). 2nd Lt. 1/5th Welsh Regt. (Capt.). Gallipoli. Missing, presumed killed in action at Suvla Bay on Aug. 10, 1915.

1919 Everiss, E. W. (Aug. 31, 1914). ‡Lt., Flying Officer, R.A.F. Egypt, Salonika, France.

1919 Farquhar, G. N. (Feb. 6, 1916). Capt. 150th Bde., R.F.A. France, 1916–19. *M.C.*, June 3, 1918.

1907 **Farrer,* L. H. St. G.,** B.A. (Nov. 13, 1914). 2nd Lt. 6th Oxf. & Bucks. Lt. Infty. France, 1915. Died in France on Oct. 28, 1915, of illness contracted while on active service.

1901 Fergusson, R. D. (June 3, 1916). ‡Lt. Highland L.I.

1908 **Fife, G. S.** (May 1, 1915). Lt., Acting Capt., Princess Patricia's Canadian L.I. France, Belgium. Killed in action at Sanctuary Wood on June 2, 1916.

1912 Fighiera,* C. G. C. Pte. London Regt.

1919 Fisher, H. (Dec. 13, 1916). Pte. 1/28th London Regt. (Artists' Rifles). France, Belgium, 1917.

1895 Fitzpatrick, Rev. F., M.A. (Dec. 1915). Chaplain to the Forces (4th Class). Salonika, 1915–18.

1910 **FitzPatrick, P. N. G.** (Sept. 1914). ‡Maj. 1st Siege Batt., S. African Heavy Artillery. S. Africa (Rebellion), 1914; German S.W. Africa, 1914–15; France, Belgium, 1916, 1917. Killed in action on Dec. 14, 1917.

1914 **Fletcher,* W. G.** (Oct. 19, 1914). 2nd Lt. 11th S. Lancashire Regt. France. Died on Oct. 14, 1916, of illness resulting from wounds.

1919 Flood, J. W. (Mar. 29, 1918). Spr. Coy. A, 305th Engineers, U.S. Army. France.

1903 **Flowers, H.** (Sept. 1914). ‡Lt. R. W. Kent Regt. France. Killed in action at Delville Wood on Aug. 31, 1916.

1919 Ford, J. N. C. (July 1917). 2nd Lt. R.G.A. France, 1918–19.

1907 Forder,* C. J. (Aug. 23, 1915). Maj. S. African Heavy Artillery. France.

1903 **Forsyth, S. S.,** B.C.L., M.A. (Aug. 5, 1914). ‡Lt. 23rd Bde., R.F.A. (A.D.C.). France, Belgium. *D.* France, 1915. Killed in action at Hooge on Sept. 25, 1915.

1903 Foster, J. B. (Aug. 4, 1914). Maj. Yorkshire Dragoons. France, 1915–18.

1904 Foster, P. B. (Mobilized Aug. 1914). Lt., Hon. Maj., R.H.A. (T.F. Res.).

Fox, F. N. W. (Sept. 1914). Lt. 14th Welsh Regt. France, Belgium. Killed in action at Passchendaele on July 31, 1917.

1913 Fox,* L. W. (Dec. 19, 1914). Capt. 9th W. Riding Regt. D.T.M.O., 36th Div. France, Belgium. *M.C.*, Aug. 25, 1916. Belgian Croix de Guerre. *D.* France, 1917.

1894 Fox, R. W., B.A. (Serving Aug. 4, 1914). Maj. 2nd R. Warwickshire Regt. France. Croce di Guerra. *D.* France, 1916.

1901 Foxell, J. T. (Dec. 16, 1915). Lt. R.E. (Postal Section) (Maj.). France, 1915–17; Italy, 1917–19. *D.* France, 1916; Italy, 1918.

1919 Franklin, K. J. (Sept. 1916). Lt. C/152nd Bde., R.F.A. France, Belgium.

1894 Fraser, C. E. W., M.A. (Mobilized Aug. 1914). Capt., Hon. Maj., R.F.A. (T.F. Res.).

1911 Freeman,* D., B.A. (Aug. 22, 1914). Capt. 9th Essex Regt., attd. No. 4 O.C.B. France, 1915.

1904 Freeman, Rev. F., M.A. (Nov. 1917). Chaplain R.N. Atlantic, Murman Coast.

1895 Fremantle, J. M., M.A. (Serving Aug. 4, 1914). Maj. 3rd County of London Yeomanry. Intelligence Officer to Nigeria Regt. E. Africa, *M.B.E.* (Civil).

1905 Friend, A. L. I., B.A. (Serving Aug. 4, 1914). Capt. 7th Dragoon Guards, France. *M.C.*, Jan. 1, 1919. *D.* France, 1918.

1911 **Fry, A. C.**, B.A. (Sept. 19, 1914). ‡2nd Lt. 2/4th Oxf. & Bucks. Lt. Infty. France. Died on Feb. 28, 1917, of wounds received in action at Ablaincourt.

1912 Fry,* E. B. (Apr. 1915). Pte. 2nd Welsh Field Ambulance, R.A.M.C. Palestine.

1906 Fulcher, E. A. (Oct. 6, 1914). Lt. 11th Hussars (S.R.).

1919 Fulcher, P. M. (July 23, 1917). Pte. American Field Service. France. Croix de Guerre.

1914 **Gale,* J. H.** (Mar. 19, 1916). 2nd Lt. 70th Squadron, R.F.C. France. Killed in action in France on Sept. 14, 1916.

1893 Gallup, H. C. (Aug. 22, 1914). Lt. 1/5th Hampshire Batt., R.F.A. (T.F.). India, 1914–15; Mesopotamia, 1915–16. (Prisoner of war (Kut), Apr. 1916–Dec. 1918.)

1907 Garnett,* A. R. V. (Jan. 18, 1917). Lt. R.A.S.C.

1907 Garratt,* G. T., B.A. (Apr. 30, 1915). Lt. I.A.R.O., attd. 21st Indian Cavalry. India.

1901 Garrett, R. J. C., M.A. (Serving Aug. 4, 1914). Lt., Acting Capt., Unattached List, T.F., Bedford Grammar School O.T.C.

1903 Gaskell, W. R. (Sept. 11, 1914). Capt. K.O. Scottish Borderers. France, 1915, 1916, 1918–19; Egypt, 1915–16.

1905 Gatey, K., B.A. (Sept. 1, 1914). ‡Lt. 2nd Devonshire Regt. (Capt.). France, 1916, 1917, 1917–18. *M.C.*, Oct. 20, 1916.

1906 Gent, P., M.A. (Jan. 19, 1916). Lce.-Sergt. 75th Training Res. Bn.

1919 Gibson, L. A. (Sept. 3, 1914). ‡Capt. 7th Oxf. & Bucks. Lt. Infty. Egypt, Salonika.

1918 Gilbert, F. J. (Aug. 11, 1914). A.B., London Div., R.N.V.R. Antwerp, 1914. (Interned in Holland, Oct. 1914–1918.)

1904 Gillam, T. H. J., B.A. (Serving Aug. 4, 1914). Capt. W. Riding Regt., Bde. Maj. 35th Inf. Bde. France. *D.* France, 1917.

1919 Girdlestone, G. O'D. (Sept. 1, 1916). Lt. R. Marines. H.M.S. *Donegal*, Atlantic, 1917–18; H.M.S. *Furious*, Grand Fleet, 1918–19.

1902 Gotelee, G. L., B.A. (Aug. 30, 1914). ‡2nd Lt. Army Cyclist Corps.

Gourlay, W. N. (Aug. 10, 1914). ‡Capt. 5th Q.O. Cameron Highlanders. France. Died on June 6, 1917, of wounds received in action on May 1, in France.

1878 Gowring, G. H. (Apr. 1916). Capt. 28th Manchester Regt.

1914 Gowring, J. S. (Jan. 11, 1915). Lt. 8th Wiltshire Regt., afterwards Lt., Acting Maj., 17th Bn. M.G.C. France. *M.C.*, Feb. 1, 1919. *D.* France.

1909 Gravell,* Rev. G. T., B.A. (July 7, 1916). Chaplain to the Forces (4th Class). France, Belgium, 1916–17.

1910 **Gregory,* R. H.** (Sept. 1914). Capt. 9th Sherwood Foresters. Belgium, Egypt, France. *M.C.*, Sept. 26, 1916. Killed in action at Wytschaete Ridge on June 8, 1917.

1899 Grellet, R. C. (Sept. 4, 1914). Lt.-Col. 8th Yorkshire Regt. Belgium, France, Italy. *D.S.O.*, Oct. 27, 1917. *D.* France, 1916, 1917; Italy, 1919.

1910 Greswell, E. A., B.A. (Nov. 1, 1916). Capt. I.A.R.O. Punjab (India).

1908 Grundy,* J., B.A. (Serving Aug. 4, 1914). Lt. Repton School O.T.C. (until Jan. 1, 1916), afterwards Lt. R.F.A. France, Italy.

1887 Gundry, J. (Mobilized Aug. 1914). Maj. Dorset Yeomanry. Egypt, Palestine.

1919 Guy, H. W. (Oct. 27, 1914). 2nd Lt. 14th R. Fusiliers. Capt. 11th Wing H.Q., R.A.F. France, 1915–18. *D.* France, 1918.

1905 Hacker, K. (Apr. 28, 1917). Lt. R.A.S.C.

1914 Hadcock,* N. (Oct. 3, 1914). Lt. R.F.A. France, 1915; Salonika, 1915–17. *D.* Salonika, 1917.

1906 Hall, F. V. (Sept. 9, 1917). 2nd Lt. Unattached List, T.F., Leeds University O.T.C. *D.* § Mar. 1919.

1899 Hamer, J. L. P., M.A. (Sept. 29, 1914). Capt. Cheshire Regt., attd. 2nd British W. Indies Regt. Egypt (Western Desert) and Aegean Sea, 1916; Palestine, 1917, 1918.

1910 Hamilton, K. T. (Aug. 24, 1914). ‡Lt. 3rd Australian Light Horse Regt. Gallipoli, Egypt, Palestine.

1911 Hardie,* A. N., M.A. (Oct. 5, 1914). Lt., Acting Capt., R.G.A. France. *D.* France, 1916.

1899 Harding, E. J., M.A. (Nov. 1915). 2nd Lt. R.G.A. *C.M.G.*

1909 Hardy,* R. L. (1914). ‡Lt. Bedfordshire & Hertfordshire Regt. Africa, France. *M.C.*, May 5, 1919. (Prisoner of war in Germany.)

1895 Harré, R. W., M.A. (Nov. 21, 1915). Lt. 4th R. Sussex Regt. (Capt.).

1881 Harris, Rev. R. W., M.A. (Dec. 4, 1915). Chaplain to the Forces (4th Class), attd. 10th Cyclist Bde.

1896 Hart, J. R. B., B.A. (Mar. 13, 1917). Lt., Recruiting Officer, Special Lists.

1913 Hartley,* S. (Sept. 9, 1914). Lt. 10th Worcestershire Regt. France, 1915–18. *M.C.*, Jan. 1, 1918.

1913 **Harvey, E. J.** (Jan. 2, 1917). Pte. 28th London Regt. (Artists' Rifles). France. Killed in action at La Barque on Aug. 22, 1918.

1906 Havard-Jones, D. C. (Feb. 6, 1915). Capt. 5th Somerset L.I. (Capt. and Adjt.). France.

1889 Hawes, I. H. S. (May 15, 1915). Capt. R.A.M.C. France and Belgium.

1910 **Hawkins, H. G.** (Aug. 1914). 2nd Lt. 11th Middlesex Regt. France. Died at Armentières on July 24, 1915, of wounds received in action at Houplines.

1919 Haynes, E. J. W. E. (Dec. 8, 1917). 2nd Lt. 7th Bde., R.H.A. France.

1895 **Hazel, A. W.,** B.A. Lt.-Col. General List, Inspector of Recruiting (Egypt). Egypt. *O.B.E.* Order of the Medjidieh and Order of the Nile (3rd Class) (pre-war). *D.* Egypt, twice. Killed on Mar. 24, 1919, by a sniper while on duty in Upper Egypt.

1895 Hebard, S. C., M.A. (Nov. 16, 1915). Lt. 7th K.R.R.C. France.

1919 Hemingway, G. Y. (Jan. 12, 1918). 2nd Lt. R.E.

1895 Henderson, Hon. A. P. (Aug. 26, 1914). Lt., Hon. Maj., Berkshire Yeomanry (T.F. Res.).

1904 Herbert, S. M. (1914). ‡Capt. Northumberland Fusiliers. France, Belgium.

1910 **Heywood, G. G.** (Aug. 8, 1914). Pte. 1st H.A.C. France, Belgium, 1914–15. Died on Mar. 12, 1915, of wounds received in action near Ypres on Feb. 15.

1890 Hichens, B. S. (Sept. 5, 1914). ‡Lt. 60th Div. Ammunition Column, R.F.A. (Capt.). France, Salonika, Palestine. *D.* Palestine, 1919.

1920 Hicks, H. A. H. G. (Apr. 30, 1917). Lt. Seaforth Highlanders. France.

1919 Hill, H. A. (May 15, 1917). ‡Capt. M.T.C., U.S. Army. France.

1913 Hinshelwood,* A. S. (Sept. 12, 1914). Lt. 9th Devonshire Regt., afterwards Lt. M.G.C. (Maj.). France, 1915, 1916, 1917, 1918; Italy, 1917–18.

1908 Hobbs,* F. W. (May 1915). Lt. 255th Siege Batt., R.G.A. France. *D.* France, 1917.

1912 **Hodges,* H. W.** (Sept. 1914). 2nd Lt. 6th, attd. 2nd, K.R.R.C. (Capt.). France, Belgium. Killed in action in an attack on Aubers Ridge on May 9, 1915.

1897 Hodgson, F. H. B., M.A. (Dec. 22, 1915). Lt. 4th Loyal N. Lancashire Regt.

1896 Hodgson, J. W. B., M.A. (Oct. 1916). Lt. R.A.S.C. (M.T.), attd. R.G.A., 1917–18. France, 1917–19.

1908 [Hodgson,* Rev. L., M.A.] (Jan. 4, 1918). 2nd Lt. Unattached List, T.F., O.U.O.T.C.

1896 [Hollins, A. M.] (May 1915). Capt. 11th Loyal N. Lancashire Regt. *D.* § Feb. 1917.

1919 Holmes, A. J. (Jan. 19, 1918). 2nd Lt. R.F.A. France.

1881 Hooper, H. R., M.A. (Apr. 21, 1915). Capt. R.E. (Staff-Captain). *O.B.E.* (Mil.). *D.* § Feb. 1917, Mar. 1918.

1906 Howell-Jones, H. G. (Mar. 5, 1916). 2nd Lt. 3rd, attd. 1/5th, R. Welsh Fusiliers.

1919 Hoyt, J. D. H. (July 9, 1917). ‡2nd Lt. Ordnance Res. Corps, U.S. Army. France.

1909 Hughes, Rev. J. D., M.A. (Mar. 22, 1916). Chaplain to the Forces (4th Class), attd. 62nd Div.

1903 **Hughes-Hughes, W. M.**, M.A. (Aug. 1914). Capt. 9th Welsh Regt. France. Killed in action at Givenchy on Sept. 25, 1915.

1919 Humphries, C. M. (Aug. 7, 1916). Lt. 3rd Seaforth Highlanders. France, 1917, 1918–19.

1899 Hutchison, R O., B.A. (1914). Capt. Hong-Kong Volunteers. A.D.C. to Governor of Hong-Kong.

1910 Inglis,* T. G., M.A. (Oct. 23, 1916). ‡Lt. R.G.A. (S.R.).

1907 **Inman, L. Y.** (1914). ‡2nd Lt. 3rd R. Scots, attd. 5th Wiltshire Regt. Mesopotamia. Died on Apr. 6–7, 1916, of wounds received in action near Kut.

1903 Irby, L. M. A., B.A. (May 1, 1916). ‡Lt. R.A.O.C. France, 1916.

1919 Jeffreys, Rev. J. A. (Mar. 6, 1917). Gnr. Australian F.A., afterwards Chaplain (4th Class), 6th Inf. Bde., A.I.F. Egypt, France.

1914 Jepson, W. C., B.A. (July, 1916). American Ambulance, attd. French Army, afterwards 1st Lt. U.S. Air Service. France. Croix de Guerre.

1911 Jeune, R. D., B.A. (Sept. 8, 1914). Lt. General List, Intelligence Corps (Capt.). France. *D.* France, 1917.

1900 Johns, W. H., M.A. (Sept. 22, 1914). Capt. 2nd County of London Yeomanry, empld. War Office. France.

1912 Jolley,* G. C. K., B.A. (Nov. 13, 1914). Capt. 8th W. Riding Regt., afterwards Lt. R.G.A. Gallipoli, 1915.

1907 Jollye,* H. C. B., B.A. (Sept. 8, 1916). Lt. I.A.R.O., attd. Indian Munitions Board (Capt.). N.W. Frontier, India.

1903 Jones, O. K., M.A. (1916). ‡Lt. R.F.A. France. *D.* France, 1917.

1904 **Jones, W. D. P.,** B.A. (Apr. 22, 1915). Pte. 23rd R. Fusiliers. France. Died on Nov. 18, 1916, of wounds received in action in the Battle of the Ancre.

1908 Joyce,* H. C., M.A. (Sept. 5, 1914). ‡Lt. 9th, attd. 1st, Oxf. & Bucks. Lt. Infty. France, 1915; Mesopotamia, 1917–19.

1897 Joyce, T. A., M.A. Capt. Special Lists, attd. General Staff, War Office. *O.B.E.* (Mil.). *D.* § Feb. 1917.

1900 Kay-Mouat, J. R., M.A. (Aug. 29, 1914). Surgeon Lt., Acting Staff Surgeon, R.N.V.R. Belgium, 1914; Gallipoli, Egypt, France, W. Africa. *D.* Admiralty, 1919.

1912 Kealy,* J. H., B.A. (Aug. 3, 1914). ‡Lt. General List (Staff-Lt.). Gallipoli, Egypt, Palestine.

1899 Kennedy-Cox, R. (Aug. 17, 1914). ‡Lt. 3rd Hampshire Regt., attd. 3rd K.R.R.C. (Capt.). France, 1914–15; Egypt, 1916; Salonika, 1916–18; Caucasus and Turkey, 1919. *D.* 1919.

1919 Kerr, W. B. (Mar. 31, 1916). Gnr. Canadian F.A. France.

1920 Kilburn, D. (Sept. 15, 1918). Lt. 1st Grenadier Guards.

1919 Kingdon, F. D. (Oct. 1916). ‡2nd Lt. No. 2 Res. Bde., R.F.A. France, 1917–18. *M.C.*, Dec. 2, 1918.

1909 **Kingdon,* R. C. H.,** B.A. (Feb. 1916). 2nd Lt. 123rd Batt., R.F.A. France, 1916–17. Killed in action at Vimy Ridge on Apr. 9, 1917.

1906 Kirby, Rev. J. A., M.A. (Sept. 1917). Chaplain to the Forces (4th Class), attd. 3rd R. Dublin Fusiliers.

1917 Knapp, K. C. (Nov. 11, 1917). ‡Probationary Flight Officer, R.N.A.S. France.

1914 Knight, W. F. J. (Nov. 1, 1915). ‡Lt. Signal Service, R.E. France, 2 years.

1907 **Kriegler, S. G.,** B.Sc. (1914). Capt. 2nd Mounted Bde., S. African Medical Corps. German S.W. Africa. Died in hospital at Johannesburg on Aug. 2, 1916.

1893 Labouchere, C. E. E., B.A. (Sept. 27, 1916). Capt. Special Lists, empld. I.W.T. France. *D.* France, 1919.

1912 Lacey-Smith, L., M.A. (July 16, 1915). Lt. 5th Devonshire Regt., attd. Casualty Branch, 3rd Echelon, G.H.Q., France (Capt.). France.

1914 **Lamb, T.** (Dec. 1915). 2nd Lt. 4th K.O.Y.L.I. Accidentally killed at bombing practice at Clipston Camp on June 30, 1916.

1914 Lambert, P. H. (Apr. 13, 1915). Capt. R.A.S.C. Aegean Islands, 1915–16; Egypt, 1916–19.

1906 Langley, C. K., B.A. (1914). ‡2nd Lt. R. Warwickshire Regt. France. (Invalided on account of wounds.)

1909 Lardelli, M. S. (May 26, 1917). 2nd Lt. R.F.A. (S.R.), empld. Ministry of Munitions.

1919 Larwill, G. J. (June 16, 1917). Gnr. 119th Siege Batt., R.G.A. Belgium, France, 1917–19.

1914 Law, A. N. (Apr. 26, 1915). Capt. 1/4th Northamptonshire Regt. Staff-Captain, Mil. Government Staff, Jerusalem. Gallipoli, 1915; Egypt, 1916; Sinai and Palestine, 1917–18. *M.C.*, June 3, 1918.

1902 Lean, J. V. (Sept. 22, 1914). Lt. 6th Res. Regt. of Cavalry, empld. Army Horse Lines.

1888 [Leathes, C. de M.] (Mobilized Aug. 1914). Maj. 5th (Extra Res.) R. Irish Rifles. *D.* § Feb. 1917.

1914 **Leicester,* D. N.** (Dec. 1914). 2nd Lt. 12th Gloucestershire Regt. France, Belgium. Killed in action at Fresnoy on May 8, 1917.

1911 Levy, S. L., B.A. (1917). Master Yeoman, U.S. Navy. France.

1898 Lewis, Rev. H. A., M.A. (May 19, 1915). Acting Chaplain R.N. H.M.S. *Sutlej*.

1903 Lidbury, D. J., B.A. (Aug. 4, 1914). Maj., Acting Col., R.E. (Postal Section). France, 1914–19; Germany, 1919. *D.S.O.*, June 3, 1916. Military Order of Aviz. *D.* France, 1915, 1916.

1888 Liversidge, H. W., B.C.L., M.A. (1918). Lt. R.A.F.

1903 Lloyd-Jones, G. (Sept. 15, 1914). Capt. Berkshire Yeomanry. G.S.O. 3. Egypt, Palestine.

1914 Lomax,* G., B.A. (Oct. 1915). Lt. 5th Lancers. France, 1917, 1918–19.

1901 Luby, T., M.A. (Serving Aug. 4, 1914). Lt., Acting Capt., Chota Nagpur Regt., I.D.F. India.

1913 **Lucas,* F. G. B.** (Aug. 28, 1914). Capt. 6th Bedfordshire Regt. France, Belgium. *M.C.*, Sept. 22, 1916. Died on Aug. 10, 1917, of wounds received in action near Bailleul on Aug. 9.

1903 Lucy, A. W., M.A. (Serving Aug. 4, 1914). Capt. Unattached List, T.F., Bedford Grammar School O.T.C. (Resigned owing to ill health, Aug. 1916.)

1903 Lupton, R. H., B.A. (Mar. 31, 1915). Capt. 17th R. Sussex Regt. France. *M.C.*, Mar. 8, 1919. *D.* France, 1916.

1912 Lurcott,* R. G. (Sept. 20, 1914). ‡Capt. 12th Sherwood Foresters. Capt. I.A.R.O. France, 1916–17; Palestine, 1918–19.

1889 Lury, Rev. H. E., M.A. (Apr. 23, 1916). Chaplain to the Forces (4th Class).

1890 Lynam, R. G., M.A. (Mar. 1915). Capt. R.A.M.C., 3rd Southern General Hospital.

1919 Lysons, E. (June 8, 1915). ‡2nd Lt. 14th Worcestershire Regt. France, 1915–16, 1917, 1918–19.

1902 Macassey, Rev. E. L., M.A. (Mobilized Aug. 1914). Chaplain to the Forces (4th Class), attd. 8th Middlesex Regt. France, Belgium.

1904 McEacharn, N. B. W. (Aug. 1914). Capt. 5th K.O. Scottish Borderers. Salonika. *M.B.E.* (Mil.). *D.* Salonika, 1918.

1919 McElligott, G. L. M. (Aug. 15, 1914). Capt. 3rd R. Munster Fusiliers. Acting Maj. attd. Gold Coast Regt. France, Belgium, 1915–16; E. Africa, W. Africa, 1917–18.

1901 McIver, C. D. (Sept. 1914). ‡Capt. 2/4th Queen's (R. W. Surrey Regt.), attd. R.A.F. Gallipoli, Egypt.

1902 McKaig, J. B., M.A. (Mobilized Aug. 1914). Maj., Acting Lt.-Col., 6th King's (Liverpool Regt.) (T.F.). France. *D.S.O.*, June 4, 1917; *Bar*, Feb. 18, 1918. *D.* France, 1916, 1917, 1919.

1910 **Mackenzie,* F. T.** ‡2nd Lt. R.F.A. (T.F.) (from July 1, 1917). France. Missing, now presumed killed in action near St. Quentin on Mar. 23, 1918.

1910 **Mackie,* N. L.,** B.A. (Sept. 1, 1914). Capt. 14th London Regt. (London Scottish). France, Belgium. *D.* France, 1915. Killed in action near Loos on Sept. 25, 1915.

1913 Macmahon, P. A. M. (Dec. 1914). 2nd Lt. 10th King's Own (R. Lancaster Regt.). Gallipoli, 1915. (Invalided.)

1912 **McNeill,* N.** (July 8, 1914). 2nd Lt. 3rd, attd. 1st, The Black Watch. France, Belgium. Killed in action near Ypres on Nov. 11, 1914.

1903 Madeley, C. F. (May 26, 1915). Lt. R.N.V.R.

1919 Mailer, M. L. (Nov. 1915). Pte. Malay States Volunteer Rifles. Malay States.

1911 **Mallinson, C. H.,** B.A. (Oct. 1914). ‡Capt. E. Lancashire Regt. France. Died as prisoner of war at Ingolstadt on June 26, 1918, of wounds received in action at Oppy on Dec. 4, 1917.

1913 Mann,* P. D. (Sept. 1914). ‡Lt. 6th Durham L.I., afterwards Acting Capt. General List, attd. No. 22 (G.) O.C.B., Cambridge. France, Belgium, 1915–16.

Marsh, J. T. T. (Aug. 9, 1917). 2nd Lt. 15th Bde., R.F.A. France, 1918. Died on June 28, 1918, of wounds received in action near Aire.

1919 Marshall, H. J. O. (Nov. 5, 1918). 2nd Lt. R.M.A.

1919 Martin, W. M. E. ‡2nd Lt. New Zealand A.S.C. (from Oct. 30, 1917). France.

1910 Marwood,* S. L., B.A. (Sept. 14, 1914). Capt. I.A.R.O. (Signals) (Maj.). India, 1914–17; Mesopotamia, 1917–19.

Masterman, R. C. (Aug. 1914). ‡Lt. Lancashire Fusiliers (Capt.). Gallipoli, France. Killed in action at Thiepval on July 1, 1916.

1909 Mather,* N. F. H., B.A. (Dec. 4, 1915). Lt. 8th Rifle Brigade (Asst. Adjt.). France.

1909 **Maxwell,* I. B.,** B.A. (Mobilized Aug. 1914). Capt. 3rd, attd. 1st, S. Wales Borderers. Belgium, Oct. 1914. Killed in action at Gheluvelt on Oct. 31, 1914.

1900 Micklem, C., M.A. (Sept. 2, 1914). Maj. Howitzer Bde., R.M.A. Gallipoli, Egypt, Belgium, France. *D.S.O.*, Jan. 1, 1919. *D.* France, 1916, 1917, 1918.

1895 Micklem, Rev. P. A., M.A. (Apr. 1916). Chaplain, A.I.F.

1898 Monro, Rev. R. E., M.A. (Aug. 1916). Chaplain to the Forces (4th Class). France.

1919 Mooney, H. F. (Oct. 25, 1916). ‡Lt. 12th (Bengal) Cavalry, Indian Army. India, 1917–19.

1919 Moor, R. (Sept. 5, 1916). Pte. 15th Bn. M.G.C. France.

1898 Moore-Gwyn, J. G. (Mobilized Aug. 4, 1914). Maj. 1/1st Glamorganshire Yeomanry (Lt.-Col.). Egypt, Palestine, France, 1916–17, 1918. T.D.

1910 Moore, J. S. H., B.A. (Aug. 26, 1914). 2nd Lt. 6th R. Dublin Fusiliers. Capt. M.G.C. Capt. General List. Staff-Captain. Gallipoli. *O.B.E.* (Mil.). *D.* § Aug. 1918.

1899 **Moore, S. C. L.** (Sept. 1914). Pte. 29th Bn. Canadian Infantry. France, Belgium. Died on May 31, 1916, of wounds received in action at St. Eloi on Apr. 6.

1908 **Morgan,* C. E.** (Mobilized Aug. 1914). Capt. 3rd, attd. 1st, Hampshire Regt. Belgium, France, 1914. Accidentally drowned off Gibraltar on July 3, 1915, while en route for Gallipoli.

1906 Morgan, Rev. J., M.A. (Jan. 10, 1916). Chaplain to the Forces (4th Class). Egypt.

1903 Morton, L. S., M.A. (Oct. 3, 1914). Lt., Acting Capt., Unattached List, T.F., Maidstone Grammar School O.T.C. *D.* § Mar. 1919.

1900 Mosenthal, H. R. (1916). Maj. R.A.F.

1919 Mulliner, H. G. (Apr. 25, 1917). ‡2nd Lt. 1st King's (Liverpool Regt.). France.

1919 Munn, L. S. (Aug. 3, 1915). Lt. 6th Shropshire L.I. France. (Prisoner of war in Germany.)

1909 Murphy, N. R., M.A. (Oct. 2, 1914). ‡Capt. 3rd R. Irish Fusiliers, attd. Tank Corps. France, Salonika.

1920 Murray, A. J. R. (Feb. 24, 1918). Lt. R.A.F. (Scout Squadron, Home Defence).

1919 Murray, M. (May 29, 1917). 2nd Lt. 7th London Regt.

1912 **Nash,* J.** (Jan. 1915). 2nd Lt. 4th, attd. 1st, E. Surrey Regt. France, Belgium. Killed in action near Ypres on Apr. 2, 1915.

1912 Nicholas,* F. W. H. (Aug. 6, 1914). Capt. 1st Bedfordshire Regt., attd. Staff (Bde. Maj.). Gallipoli, Egypt, Palestine, France. *M.C.*, June 3, 1919. *D.* Palestine, 1918.

1909 Nicolls, G. (Jan. 21, 1916). Lt. 14th W. Yorkshire Regt.

1913 **Nicolls,* R. J.** (Sept. 1, 1914). Capt. 11th Sherwood Foresters. Gallipoli, France. Killed in action near Le Sars on Oct. 1, 1916.

1919 Nicolson, J. F. W. (Sept. 26, 1916). Lt. R.A.F. France and Italy.

1913 Niles, E. H., B.A. (May 14, 1917). Capt. 313th Field Artillery, U.S. Army. France.

1907 Norie-Miller,* S., M.A. (Aug. 8, 1914). Capt. 9th, attd. 4/5th The Black Watch, and Staff. France, Belgium, 1915–18. *M.C.*, Jan. 1, 1918. *D.* France, 1916.

1919 Norwood, D. (Aug. 19, 1918). Cadet R.A.F.

1909 **Oldham,* J. H.,** B.A. (Aug. 4, 1914). 2nd Lt. 3rd D.C.L.I., attd. K.O.Y.L.I. France, Belgium. Killed in action at Hill 60 on Apr. 18, 1915.

1905 Oldrey, H. C., B.A. (Aug. 25, 1915). Lt. R.E. (T.F.), attd. M.G.C.

1897 Ord, E. M. (Nov. 23, 1916). ‡Lt. R.A.S.C.

1906 Orr, G. B. (Sept. 23, 1914). Capt. R.G.A. Salonika. *M.C.*, June 4, 1917. *D.* Salonika, 1917.

1897 **O'Sullivan, A. M.,** M.A. (Serving Aug. 4, 1914). Capt. 1st R. Irish Rifles. France, 1914–15. *D.* France, 1915. Killed in action at Fromelles on May 9, 1915.

1906 Overell, E. V., B.A. (Jan. 1915). Lt. M.G.C. France.

1917 Owen, A. V. P. (Oct. 1917). 2nd Lt. 1st R. Berkshire Regt. France, Germany, 1918–19.

1908 Owen, G. E., B.A. Behar Light Horse. India.

1912 Ozanne,* H. ff., M.A. (Aug. 14, 1914). Capt. R.F.A. Staff-Captain R.A., 9th Div. France, Belgium. *M.C.*, Jan. 1, 1919. Belgian Croix de Guerre. *D.* France, 1917 twice.

1905 Ozanne,* R. C., B.M., M.A. (Sept. 25, 1914). Capt., Bt.-Maj., No. 2 C.C.S., R.A.M.C. France. *D.* France, 1915.

1909 **Paget, F. A. E.** (Apr. 1915). Pte. 24th R. Fusiliers. France. Killed in action in Delville Wood on July 31, 1916.

1911 Parish, C. D. W. (Mobilized Aug. 1914). 2nd Lt. 3rd County of London Yeomanry. Capt. Coldstream Guards (S.R.). A.D.C. France.

1919 Park, D. C. (1917). 1st Lt. 115th Infantry, U.S. Army. France.
1913 Parker,* H. M. D. (Apr. 29, 1915). Lt. 7th (Res.) King's (Liverpool Regt.).
1902 Parker, R. I., M.A. (Nov. 19, 1914). ‡Lt. Dorset Yeomanry, attd. 7th Hussars. Egypt, Palestine.
1919 Parkes, J. W. (Jan. 3, 1916). ‡Lt. 10th Queen's (R. W. Surrey Regt.) (Capt. and Adjt.). France, 1916, 1917.
1903 Parkin, A. D. (Jan. 1915). Lt., Acting Capt., 11th Sherwood Foresters. France, Belgium, 1916–18. *M.C.*, Nov. 26, 1917.
1895 Patch, Rev. B. H., M.A. (Jan. 4, 1918). Chaplain to the Forces (4th Class).
1900 **Patey, E.,** B.A. (Sept. 2, 1914). ‡Capt. 8th Rifle Brigade. France, Belgium. Killed in action near Ypres, July 31–Aug. 2, 1917.
1908 Payton,* Rev. C. H., B.A. (Feb. 3, 1915). Chaplain R.N., H.M.S. *Juno*. E. Indies, Persian Gulf, African Coast, Red Sea, 1915–19.
1919 Peeke, C. K. (Feb. 22, 1917). Signaller 1st Devonshire Regt. Italy, 1918; France, 1918.
1900 Peel, B. L., M.A. (July 5, 1915). Lt. 8th Q.O. Cameron Highlanders, attd. No. 1 O.C.B. France, 1915.
1911 Peel,* R. T., B.A. (Oct. 10, 1914). Capt. 6th Seaforth Highlanders, attd. No. 5 O.C.B. (Capt. and Adjt.). France, 1915–17. *M.C.*, Jan. 1, 1918. *D.* France, 1916.
1905 Peggs, J. H., B.A. (Mobilized Aug. 4, 1914). Lt. 4th R. Dublin Fusiliers. (Resigned.)
1912 **Pelham-Burn,* M. E.** (Aug. 26, 1914). Lt. 8th The Black Watch. France, Belgium, 1915, 1917. Killed in action at Vimy Ridge on Apr. 9, 1917.
1919 Pendock, H. V. M. (May 10, 1918). 2nd Lt. 5th Rifle Brigade (on demobilization).
1919 Pendock, P. E. C. (Nov. 24, 1914). Lt. 7th, afterwards 3rd, N. Staffordshire Regt. (Capt.). Gallipoli, Mesopotamia.
1910 Penn, J. R. P., M.A. (Aug. 14, 1914). 2nd Lt. 4th Welsh Regt., afterwards Lt. R.E. (Signal Service). France, 1915, 1916–17.
1910 Perkins,* G., B.M. (July 1916). Capt. R.A.M.C. E. Africa, 1916–19. *M.C.*, Sept. 16, 1918.
1908 Pigot, A. P. V., B.A. (Aug. 15, 1914). Capt., Acting Maj., 3rd, attd. 2nd, S. Lancashire Regt. E. Africa, 1914–16; France, 1918–19.
1887 Plum, H. V., M.A. (June 11, 1915). Lt. Unattached List, T.F., Kelly College O.T.C.
1912 Plummer,* A. E. B., B.A. (Aug. 26, 1914). Capt. 8th Northumberland Fusiliers. Gallipoli, 1915; Egypt, 1916; France, 1916, 1917, 1918–19. *M.C.*, Apr. 2, 1919.
Plummer, F. R. (June 23, 1915). Lt. Anti-Aircraft Section, R.G.A. France, 1916–17, 1917–18. Died on Nov. 2, 1918, at Cambrai of illness contracted on active service.
1889 **Poore, R. A.** *D.S.O.* (Mobilized Aug. 1914). Maj. R. Wiltshire Yeomanry (Lt.-Col.), attd. as Maj. R. Welch Fusiliers. France, Belgium. *D.* France. Killed in action at Zonnebeke Wood on Sept. 26, 1917.
1912 Popham, R. F. (Oct. 10, 1914). ‡Capt. 9th Norfolk Regt. France.
1919 Poultney, L. F. (Aug. 2, 1914). Signaller R.N.D. Antwerp, 1914. (Interned in Holland, Oct. 1914–Feb. 1918.)
1911 Preece, W. H. A. (Aug. 7, 1915). Lt. R.F.A. (S.R.).

1902 Pretty, A. H. F., B.C.L., M.A. (June 18, 1915). Capt. 22nd London Regt. (The Queen's), empld. Ministry of National Service.
1911 Price,* O. W., B.A. (Aug. 3, 1914). Lt. 2nd W. Riding Regt. Belgium, France. (Prisoner of war in Germany.)
1910 **Price,* W. E.** B.A. (Aug. 1914). 2nd Lt. 5th R. Sussex Regt. France. Killed in action near Neuve Chapelle on May 2, 1915.
1909 Pridham,* R. P., B.A. (Sept. 1, 1914). Capt. 9th Devonshire Regt. (Maj.). France, Belgium, Italy. *M.C.*, Jan. 18, 1918; *Bar*, Apr. 2, 1919. *D.* France, 1917.
1919 Priest, C. V. (Oct. 25, 1918). Cadet R.G.A.
1919 Prouty, E. S. (May 12, 1917). 1st Lt. 8th Infantry, U.S. Army. France.
1899 Pullman, H. J., B.A. (Nov. 3, 1914). ‡Capt. Bucks. Bn. Oxf. & Bucks. Lt. Infty. France, Belgium, 1915–17; Italy, 1917–18. *M.C.*, Oct. 18, 1917.
1901 Purnell, A. L. (Oct. 17, 1914). Capt. W. Somerset Yeomanry, afterwards Lt. R.A.S.C. German E. Africa, 1917–19.
Raynor, H. A. L. (Sept. 7, 1917). 2nd Lt. 3rd Rifle Brigade. France. Died on June 7, 1918, of wounds received in action at Cambrai l'Abbaye.
1893 Raynor, W. D., B.A. (Feb. 20, 1916). Lt. I.A.R.O., attd. 123rd Outram's Rifles (Capt.). Egypt, Palestine, Syria.
1891 Read, Rev. F. P., M.A. (Serving Aug. 4, 1914). Chaplain to the Forces (2nd Class). Gibraltar. *D.* § Mar. 1918.
1894 Reeve, T. H., M.A. (July 11, 1918). Capt. Special Lists.
1904 Reid, J. L., B.A. (Oct. 1914). Capt., Acting Maj., 2nd County of London Yeomanry, attd. Imperial Camel Corps. Gallipoli, Egypt, Palestine, 1915–19. *D.* Palestine, 1919.
1905 Reid, R. A. (Oct. 1, 1914). Lt. R. Marines, afterwards Staff-Maj. R.A.F. France, 1914–15; Gallipoli, 1915. *O.B.E.* (Mil.).
1919 Reynolds, P. K. B. (Mar. 16, 1915). Lt. 310th (W. Riding) Bde., R.F.A. France.
1919 Richardson, R. D. (Jan. 3, 1916). 2nd Writer R.N. Dover Patrol, Dunkirk.
1912 Riddell,* P. C. O., M.A. (Aug. 15, 1914). Capt. 3rd Wiltshire Regt., attd. R.A.F. France, 1914, 1917–19.
1907 Rifai, E. H. Staff-Lt. Intelligence Corps, Egyptian E.F. Egypt.
1900 Riley, Rev. S. P., M.A. (Dec. 12, 1916). Chaplain to the Forces (4th Class).
1903 Ripley, G. A. (Oct. 23, 1914). Lt. R. Dragoons (S.R.), attd. R.A.F., 1917–18. France, 1915, 1918.
1906 Rivington, G. S., B.A. (Sept. 4, 1914). ‡Lt. 1/6th Sherwood Foresters (Capt.). Belgium, France.
1907 **Robinson, E. W.** (Serving Aug. 4, 1914). Lt. 5th R. Irish Lancers. France, Belgium. Killed in action at Hollebeke on Oct. 27, 1914.
1907 Rodd, E. F. S. (Mobilized Aug. 1914). Capt. W. Somerset Yeomanry (Maj.). Gallipoli, Egypt, Palestine, France. *D.* Egypt, 1917.
1902 Rogers, W. H. M., M.A. (Aug. 24, 1914). ‡Capt. Shropshire L.I. (S.R.). Gallipoli, Egypt, Mesopotamia, France. *M.C.*, June 3, 1919. *D.* France, 1918.
1919 Rose, H. J. (Dec. 2, 1915). Capt. 2nd R. Sussex Regt. Belgium, Germany.
1904 Ross, H. J. (Oct. 3, 1914). Lt. 2/7th The Black Watch, afterwards Lt. 43rd Aux. (Petrol) Coy., R.A.S.C. (M.T.). France.

1908 Rowlands, J. W., B.A. (Feb. 1915). ‡Lt. 2/7th Lancashire Fusiliers. (Resigned on account of ill health, 1917.)

1892 **Russell, C.,** M.A. (1914). ‡Lt. 9th E. Yorkshire Regt., afterwards Capt. I.A.R.O., attd. Gurkha Rifles. Egypt, Gallipoli, Mesopotamia, Burmah, Palestine. Killed in action in Palestine on Nov. 22, 1917.

1909 **Russell,* D. L.,** B.A. (Mobilized Aug. 1914). Capt. 8th London Regt. (Post Office Rifles). France. Died on May 24, 1915, of wounds received in action at Festubert.

1909 Russell,* L. A., B.A. (June 17, 1915). Capt. Northern Rhodesian Police. German S.W. Africa, German E. Africa, 1915–18. *D.* E. Africa.

1914 Rypins, S. I. (1918). Sergt. Intelligence Corps, U.S. Army.

1906 Salter, M. G., B.A. (Dec. 6, 1916). Lt. I.A.R.O. (Capt. 1918–19), attd. 30th Lancers, and Combined Depot, Kut. India, 1916–17; Mesopotamia, 1917–19.

1890 Salwey, R. (Mar. 31, 1916). Lt. Labour Corps (Capt.).

1899 Sampson, L. H. W., B.A. (Oct. 1, 1917). 2nd Lt. 925th Coy., 75th Divl. Train, R.A.S.C. Egypt, Palestine, 1917–18.

1899 **Samson, O. M.,** M.A. (Oct. 1916). 2nd Lt. 143rd Siege Batt., R.G.A. (Lt.). France. Died on Sept. 17, 1918, of wounds received in action.

1920 Sanford, C. (May 30, 1918). Pte. 1st Devonshire Regt. (Sergt.).

1911 Sanger, C. W., B.A. (Sept. 1, 1914). ‡Lt. 41st Bn. M.G.C. France, Belgium, Germany.

1901 Schomberg, Rev. E. St. G., M.A. (July 4, 1916). Chaplain to the Forces (4th Class), attd. 17th Div. France. Serbian Order of St. Sava (5th Class). *D.* France, 1917.

1910 Scott, Rev. B. J., M.A. (Feb. 27, 1917). Chaplain R.N., H.M.S. *Neptune*, Grand Fleet, 1917–19; H.M.S. *Lord Nelson*, Mediterranean and Constantinople, 1919.

1895 Scrivenor, J. B., M.A. (Feb. 1915). ‡Temp. 2nd Lt. R.E. (57th Div. Coy.). Malay, 1915–16; France, 1918.

1907 Seaman, C. K., M.A. (Mobilized Aug. 1914). ‡2nd Lt. I.A.R.O., attd. 2/91st Punjabis. India.

1903 **Seers, G. O.** (Aug. 1914). Pte. 23rd London Regt. France. Killed in action at Givenchy on May 25, 1915.

1910 Selke,* E. A., M.A. Cpl. 6th S. African Infantry. E. Africa. (Invalided.)

1914 **Shaw,* M. M.** (June 26, 1915). Lt. 2nd Sherwood Foresters (Capt.). France, 1916–18. *M.C.*, Sept. 17, 1917. Killed in action at Lagnicourt on Mar. 21, 1918.

1909 Shearme, J. H. E. Assam Valley Light Horse. India.

1909 Sheppard,* E. W., B.A. (Oct. 3, 1914). Capt. R. W. Kent Regt., attd. Lancashire Fusiliers. Capt. General List. G.S.O. 3, War Office. France. *O.B.E.* (Mil.). *M.C.*, Sept. 26, 1916.

1910 **Sidebotham,* J. F.,** B.A. (1914). ‡Lt. 6th Shropshire L.I. France. Killed in action on Feb. 12, 1916.

1914 Sillar,* F. C. (May 15, 1915). Sub-Lt. R.N.V.R., Nelson Bn., R.N.D. Gallipoli. (Invalided, Aug. 1916.)

1900 Simonds, J., M.A. (Sept. 22, 1914). Maj., Acting Lt.-Col., Hertfordshire Regt.

1908 Smith, F. M., B.A. (Sept. 9, 1916). Pte. R.A.S.C. (M.T.). France.

1906 Smith,* J. N., B.A. (Serving Aug. 4, 1914). Capt. 3rd Oxf. & Bucks. Lt. Infty, empld. N. Nigeria. Cameroons, 1915–16.

1911 Smith, M. G., B.A. (1917). Maj. U.S. Coast Artillery Corps. France.

1888 Smith, Rt. Rev. M. L., D.D. (Apr. 9, 1915). Chaplain to the Forces (3rd Class), attd. 30th Div. France, Belgium, 1915–17. *D.S.O.*, Jan. 1, 1917. *D.* France, 1916.

1911 Snell,* J. B., M.A. (Aug. 17, 1914). Lt. R.E. (Wireless Observation Group). Gallipoli, 1915; Egypt, Sudan, 1916–18; Palestine and Syria, 1918–19. *D.* Darfour, 1916.

1904 Snell, W. A. F., M.A. (May 23, 1916). Lt. Scots Guards. France, Belgium, Germany, from 1916.

1905 Somerset, E. J., M.A. (Nov. 19, 1915). 2nd Lt. 101st Training Res. Bn.

1901 Spafford, A. O., M.A. (Nov. 6, 1914). Lt. R.E. (Postal Service) (Maj.). France, 1919. *O.B.E.* (Mil.). *D.* § Feb. 1917.

1902 Stephenson, P. K., B.A. (Jan. 5, 1915). Lt., Acting Capt., Grenadier Guards, attd. Guards M.G. Regt. France, 1915–17. Croix de Guerre.

1903 Steward, F. L., M.A. (Aug. 1914). ‡Lt. 6th S. Staffordshire Regt. (T.F.), empld. Ministry of National Service. Belgium.

1920 Stock, E. E. (Jan. 1917). Lt. R.A.F. France, 1917–18. *M.C.*, Mar. 28, 1918.

1914 **Stockley,* P. L.** (Dec. 1914). 2nd Lt. 10th S. Staffordshire Regt., afterwards Capt. M.G.C. Belgium, France. Killed in action at Verbranden Molen, near Ypres, on Apr. 26, 1918.

1919 Stoughton-Harris, G. (Mar. 1915). Lt. 5th W. Yorkshire Regt., attd. 1st W. Yorkshire Regt. and R.E. (Signals). France, 1916–17.

1919 Surridge, C. E. N. (Mar. 25, 1918). 2nd Lt. R.M.A. Land Defences, Scapa Flow.

1919 Swatland, D. C. (1917). 1st Lt. 2nd Pioneer Infantry, U.S. Army. France.

1912 Sykes,* F. A. (Sept. 4, 1914). Lt. 4th Hussars (Capt.). France and Belgium, 1915–19. Croix de Guerre.

1911 Symes,* J. D., B.A. (Aug. 11, 1914). Capt. 4th Dorsetshire Regt. Mesopotamia, Egypt, Palestine, Indian Frontier.

1910 **Tanner,* T. L.**, M.A. (Sept. 2, 1914). Capt. 4th R. W. Kent Regt. France. Killed in action on Sept. 18, 1918.

1911 Tetley,* E. W. (Aug. 22, 1914). Capt. K.R.R.C., now Capt. S. Lancashire Regt., General Res. of Officers. France, Belgium, 1915–18. *M.C.*, June 4, 1917; *Bar*, July 26, 1918.

1919 Thomas, J. G. S. (Jan. 2, 1915). Lt. 10th Worcestershire Regt., afterwards Lt., Acting Capt., M.G.C. France, 1916–17, 1918–19. *M.C.*, Oct. 18, 1917.

1913 Thomas,* M. D. (Sept. 1914). Lt. Grenadier Guards. France. *M.C.*, May 5, 1919. (Prisoner of war in Germany, Apr. 1918.)

1916 Thorburn, J. W. A. (Oct. 1917). 2nd Lt. 319th Works Coy., Labour Corps. France, 1918.

1909 Thornhill,* Rev. J. F., M.A. (Apr. 16, 1917). Chaplain to the Forces (4th Class). *D.* § Aug. 1919.

1909 Thornhill,* Rev. R. W., M.A. (July 4, 1916). Chaplain to the Forces (4th Class). France. *M.C.*, Feb. 1, 1919.

1898 Thornton, C. E. C., M.A. (Feb. 25, 1916). Lt. Special Lists, empld. Recruiting Duties.

1900 Tilleard, M. F. (Nov. 25, 1914). Capt. R.A.S.C. France.
1919 Tindal-Atkinson, C. P. (Aug. 31, 1914). Capt. 10th Loyal N. Lancashire Regt. 2nd Lt., Hon. Capt., 31st Training Depot Station, R.A.F. France, 1915–16; France, Belgium, 1916–17.
1919 Tisdall, O. R. (Nov. 17, 1917). 2nd Lt. C/251st Bde., R.F.A. France.
1919 Todd, Rev. J., B.A. (June 28, 1916). Chaplain to the Forces (4th Class). Egypt, 1916; Salonika, 1916–17; Italy, 1917; France, 1917–18; Germany, 1919.
1920 Tong, J. A. (Aug. 8, 1917). ‡2nd Lt. Pilot, 1st Prov. Wing, Air Service, U.S. Army.
1888 Tongue-Croxall, E. R. (Oct. 27, 1914). Capt. R.F.A., afterwards Capt. R.A.F. France, Belgium, 1915, 1916–18.
1899 Townshend, D. L. (Mar. 1916). ‡Lt. 2/1st Duke of Lancaster's Own Yeomanry, attd. 21st Manchester Regt. France, 1918–19.
1901 Toyne, S. M., M.A. (May 23, 1914). Lt. Unattached List, T.F., St. Peter's School, York O.T.C. (Maj. 11th York & Lancaster Regt.).
Tracy, L. T. (Sept. 8, 1914). 2nd Lt. 5th Yorkshire Regt. (T.F.), attd. 4th Seaforth Highlanders. France, Belgium. Killed in action at St. Eloi on June 4, 1916.
1920 Tredgold, R. C. (May 20, 1918). Pte. 2/28th London Regt. (Artists' Rifles). 2nd Lt. General List (after demobilization).
1912 **Tuck,* D. J.** (June 1914). Capt. 5th Oxf. & Bucks. Lt. Infty. Belgium, France, 1915–16. Died on July 3, 1916, of wounds received in action at Arras on June 17.
1905 Tupper, F. G., B.A. (Nov. 13, 1915). Lt. 55th Divl. Train, R.A.S.C. France and Belgium.
1893 Underwood, W. W. (Apr. 16, 1915). Capt. 9th Cheshire Regt. France.
1907 Van Neck, C. (Oct. 1914). 2nd Lt. 23rd London Regt. France, 1915. (Invalided on account of wounds, 1915.)
1913 Waddington,* C. (Aug. 15, 1914). Capt. 3rd E. Lancashire Regt. France, 1915, 1916. (Prisoner of war in Germany, Oct. 1916–Dec. 1918.)
1919 Waldock, F. A. (Apr. 3, 1917). Lt. B/108th Bde., R.F.A. France. *D.* France, 1919.
1919 Waldock, H. F. (Oct. 23, 1917). 2nd Lt. R.M.L.I. Lt. R.A.F.
1907 Walker, Rev. E. F., M.A. (Aug. 1, 1916). Chaplain to the Forces (4th Class), attd. 66th Div. France, Belgium, 1917–18.
1919 Walker, R. L. (May 11, 1915). Lt. 1/4th Northamptonshire Regt., attd. M.G.C. (Maj.). Egypt, Palestine, 1915–18.
1900 Walker, Rev. T. R., M.A. (Oct. 16, 1914). Chaplain R.N., H.M.S. *Iron Duke*. Grand Fleet.
1905 **Wallis, H.,** M.A. (1916). Naval Instructor, R.N., H.M.S. *Indefatigable*. Grand Fleet. Killed in action in the Battle of Jutland on May 31, 1916.
1905 Ward, C. E., B.A. (Sept. 19, 1914). Capt. 3rd, attd. 6th, Shropshire L.I. Political Officer, German E. Africa. France, E. Africa.
Ward, E. A. H. (Oct. 1915). Lt. 3/6th W. Yorkshire Regt. Lt., Flight Commdr., attd. R.F.C. Belgium. Killed in action in flight over German lines on Aug. 11, 1917.
1910 Ward,* W. W., B.A. (Sept. 20, 1914). Maj. 2nd Siege Batt., R.M.A. France, 1915–19. *D.* France, 1917.

1919 Wareham, H. A. (Feb. 28, 1916). ‡Lt. 5th N. Staffordshire Regt., attd. Labour Corps. France.

1910 **Wareing,* W. R. A.,** M.A. (Aug. 29, 1914). Lt., Acting Capt., 11th King's (Liverpool Regt.). France, Belgium. *M.C.*, July 26, 1918. Killed in action at Flavy le Martel, near St. Quentin, on Mar. 23, 1918.

1900 Warren, G. K., M.A. R.A.M.C.

1898 **Warren, R. D.** (Oct. 1914). Maj. 11th Leicestershire Regt. (Lt.-Col.). France, Belgium, 1915–16, 1917–18; Salonika, 1916–17. Killed in action at Ypres on Apr. 7, 1918.

1898 Warwick, P. H., M.A. (Mobilized Aug. 4, 1914). Maj. S. Nottinghamshire Hussars (Lt.-Col.). Egypt, Gallipoli, 1915; Salonika, 1916–17; Palestine, 1917–18; France, 1918. *D.S.O.*, Jan. 1, 1918. *D.* Palestine, 1918.

1914 Watkins,* E. H. (Dec. 31, 1915). Lt. 100th F.A. Bde., R.F.A. Salonika, Dedeagatch.

1910 **Watkins,* H. H.** (Aug. 14, 1914). 2nd Lt. 3rd, attd. 1st, S. Wales Borderers. France, Belgium. Killed in action at Langemarck, near Ypres, on Oct. 21, 1914.

1893 Watson, F. B., M.A. (Dec. 1914). Capt. 1st London Regt. (R. Fusiliers), afterwards Lt. R.A.S.C. Malta, Gallipoli, Egypt, France.

Welch, V. E. O. (Dec. 31, 1914). Capt. 5th London Regt. (London Rifle Brigade). France. Killed in action N.W. of Bullecourt on Aug. 30, 1918.

1913 **West,* H. M. P.** (Nov. 13, 1914). Capt. 11th Northumberland Fusiliers. France, Belgium, 1915, 1916, 1917. Killed in action in Belgium on Sept. 20, 1917.

1903 Whatley, N., M.A. (Mobilized Aug. 1914). Capt. Unattached List, T.F., O.U.O.T.C., afterwards Capt. Intelligence Corps. France, 1916, 1918. Bt.-Maj., 1919. *D.* § Feb. 1917.

1913 Whelpton,* G. E., B.A. (Aug. 26, 1914). Capt. 4th R. Berkshire Regt. (Invalided.)

1885 White, T. A., B.A. (Jan. 14, 1915). Capt. 13th Gloucestershire Regt. Courts Martial Officer, 23rd Training Res. Bde.

Whitehead, H. M. (Aug. 6, 1914). ‡Lt. 8th R. Sussex Regt. France, Belgium. *D.* France, 1918. Killed in action near Rémigny on Mar. 21, 1918.

1908 Whitehead, P., B.A. Bomdr. 349th Siege Batt., R.G.A. France.

1914 Whittaker,* G. W. (May 15, 1915). Lt.-Commdr. R.N.V.R., Drake Bn., 63rd (R.N.) Div. E. Mediterranean, France, Belgium. *D.S.O.*, Feb. 13, 1917. *D.* France, 1917.

1911 Willans,* P. W., B.A. (Jan. 18, 1915). Lt. 118th A.A. Section, R.G.A. (Capt.). Mesopotamia.

1919 Williams, H. D. (Sept. 1914). Lt. 49th Batt., R.F.A. (Capt.). Belgium, France. *D.* France, 1917, 1918.

1910 **Williams-Vaughan, J. C. A.** (Apr. 21, 1915). 2nd Lt. S. Wales Borderers, attd. M.G.C. France. Killed in action in the Battle of the Somme on July 15, 1916.

1893 Willimott, Rev. J. S. (Feb. 19, 1918). Chaplain to the Forces (3rd Class).

1913 Wilmot,* E. (Sept. 2, 1914). Capt. 1st Herefordshire Regt. Gallipoli, 1915; Egypt, Palestine, 1916–18; France, 1918.

1919 Wood, E. C. (Aug. 4, 1916). Pte. 3/5th Loyal N. Lancashire Regt., afterwards Pte. 15th Bn. M.G.C. France, Belgium.

1908 Wood, E. S., M.A. (Mobilized Aug. 4, 1914). Capt. 6th Sherwood Foresters, afterwards Lt., Flying Officer, R.A.F. France, Belgium.

1886 Woodard, A. M. W. (Sept 15, 1915). Lt. Sherwood Foresters (T.F. Res.), empld. Ministry of Munitions. 2nd Lt. Labour Corps.

1907 **Woodd,* Rev. A. B. P.,** M.A. (Nov. 1916). ‡2nd Lt. 10th W. Yorkshire Regt. (Lt.). France. Died on Aug. 25, 1918, of wounds received in action at Thiepval.

1908 Woodhead,* F. C. T., B.A. (May 22, 1915). Lt. 5th Worcestershire Regt. (S.R.), attd. M.G.C. (Capt.). Egypt, 1915–16; France, 1916, 1917, 1918–19; Mesopotamia, 1917–18.

1907 **Woodward, E. H. H.,** B.A. (Sept. 1914). ‡2nd Lt. 10th Queen's (R. W. Surrey Regt.) (Capt.). France, Belgium, 1915–16. Killed in action near Wytschaete on Dec. 24, 1916.

1898 Woodyatt, G. E. S. (Sept. 14, 1914). Capt. 4th Lancashire Fusiliers. Bimbashi, attd. Egyptian Army. Cameroons, 1915–16; Egypt, 1917–19.

1907 Woollcombe,* Rev. E. P., M.A. (June 2, 1915). Chaplain to the Forces (3rd Class), attd. 1st Army H.Q. France, Belgium. *O.B.E.* (Mil.). *D.* France, 1917 twice.

1911 Worsley, R. S. L. (Mobilized Aug. 1914). 2nd Lt. 4th R. Sussex Regt. France. (Wounded and prisoner of war in Germany.)

1915 Worthington, H. B. (Sept. 29, 1916). Gnr. R.G.A., afterwards Pioneer, London Air Defence Area, Signal Coy., R.E.

1896 Wrey, R. C. (Serving Aug. 4, 1914). Maj. Devonshire Regt.

1909 **Wright,* C. J. S.,** B.A. (Mobilized Aug. 3, 1914). Capt. 7th Leicestershire Regt. France. Killed in action at Bazentin-le-Petit on July 14, 1916.

1919 Wright, E. M. (Apr. 11, 1918). Pte. 14th Photo Section, U.S. Army. France.

1905 **Wynter, F. C. W.,** B.A. (Serving Aug. 4, 1914). Capt. 1st Oxf. & Bucks. Lt. Infty. India, Mesopotamia. Killed in action at Ctesiphon on Nov. 22, 1915.

1908 **Yates,* J. S.,** B.A. (Serving Aug. 4, 1914). 2nd Lt. 3rd, attd. 6th, R. W. Kent Regt. France, 1915. Killed in action near Hulluch on Oct. 8, 1915.

ST. EDMUND HALL

1918 Ager, W. E. (Oct. 17, 1914). ‡Lt. 2nd Wiltshire Regt. (Capt.). France and Belgium.

1912 Ainscow,* H. M., M.A. (Mar. 23, 1915). Lt. 5th Lancashire Fusiliers (Capt.). France. (Prisoner of war, 1916–18.)

1901 Allen, Rev. M. Y., M.A. (Sept. 12, 1918). Chaplain to the Forces (4th Class).

1910 Andrews,* W. E., M.A. (1914). ‡2nd Lt. 5th Bn. I.D.F. India.

1912 Ashenden,* N. E., M.A. (July 1, 1915). Lt. F/4th Res. Bde., R.F.A. France.

1911 Atkins,* W. V. (May 29, 1915). Lt. 3rd Manchester Regt., attd. 2/35th Sikhs, Indian Army. Mesopotamia, 1916–18; Persia, 1918–19.

1912 Baker,* L. D., B.A. (Aug. 1914). ‡Lt., Acting Capt., 5th R. Dublin Fusiliers, attd. R.A.F. France, 1916–19.

1919 Barnes-Lawrence, H. A. (Apr. 18, 1917). Cadet R.A.F.

1919 Barrett, H. B. (Nov. 20, 1915). Lt. 25th Batt., R.F.A. Salonika, France.

Barrow, L. A. H. (Aug. 1914). ‡2nd Lt. 10th, attd. 11th, R. Sussex Regt. France. Killed in action in the Battle of the Somme on Sept. 1, 1916.

1908 Bateman,* Rev. G. H., B.A. (July 3, 1917). Chaplain to the Forces (4th Class). France.

1911 Beatty,* T. R. (Aug. 4, 1914). Lt. R.N., H.M.S. *Onslaught.* White Sea, 1914; North Sea, 1914–18; Atlantic, 1918.

1919 Beddow, F. M. (Nov. 30, 1915). C.M.S. 1/28th London Regt. (Artists' Rifles). France. *D.C.M.*

1904 Berlyn, Rev. B. H. A. F. (Oct. 2, 1915). 2nd Lt. 4th R. Irish Rifles. (Invalided.)

1907 **Bevan, P. J.,** B.A. (Dec. 30, 1914). Lt. 6th, attd. 1st, K.R.R.C. France. Killed in action in Mar. 1915.

1903 Bickerdike, Rev. K. C., M.A. (1916). ‡2nd Lt. R. Berkshire Regt., attd. 7th Wiltshire Regt. France. *M.C.*, Feb. 15, 1919.

1918 Bird, D. H. (Dec. 1914). ‡Lt. R. Fusiliers.

1911 Blaxland,* A. B., B.A. (Serving Aug. 4, 1914). Capt. and Adjt. 16th Rajputs, Indian Army. France, 1915; S. Persia, 1917–19.

1876 Blucke, Rev. R. S. K., M.A. (Feb. 19, 1916). Chaplain to the Forces (4th Class). *D.* § Aug. 1919.

1914 Bluett, A. F. (Dec. 17, 1915). Lt. 2nd D.C.L.I. (Capt.). Egypt, 1916; Salonika, 1916–18; Caucasus, 1918–19.

1919 Bluett, R. J. (Jan. 1, 1918). Cadet, R.G.A., No. 2 O.C.B. 2nd Lt. (on demobilization).

1907 **Bott, G.,** B.A. (Sept. 2, 1914). ‡2nd Lt. 6th, attd. 3rd, Rifle Brigade. France, 1915, 1916, 1917. Killed in action near Loos on Feb. 9, 1917.

1915 Boultbee, J., B.A. (July 1917). ‡2nd Lt. 2nd R. Berkshire Regt. France.

1910 Brear, G. W. W. (July 1, 1915). Capt. R.A.S.C. France. *D.* France, 1917.

1908 Browne-Wilkinson, Rev. A. R., M.A. (Jan. 1, 1918). Chaplain to the Forces (4th Class). France. *D.* France, 1918.

1919 Browne-Wilkinson, C. V. (Sept. 9, 1916). Pte., Acting Lce.-Cpl., 11th Sherwood Foresters (Cpl.). Italy, 1917–18; France, 1918.

1919 Buckle, F. J. (July 16, 1916). Leading Aircraftsman R.A.F.

1894 Burkitt, Rev. C. E., M.A. (Jan. 30, 1917). Chaplain to the Forces (4th Class).

1919 Burnett, F. (Dec. 2, 1914). ‡Capt. R.E. (Signals). France and Germany. *M.C.*, Oct. 19, 1917; *Bar*, Sept. 16, 1918.

1892 Calver, Rev. S. C., M.A. (July 14, 1915). Chaplain to the Forces (4th Class). *D.* § Aug. 1917.

1919 Carlson, P. A. (1917). Sergt. Medical Dept., 328th M.G. Bn., U.S. Army. France.

1919 Cavalier, F. B. (Mar. 1915). Lt. Bedfordshire Yeomanry. France, 1916–19.

1919 Chapman, A. E. (Sept. 10, 1914). Pte. 2/4th Oxf. & Bucks. Lt. Infty.

1891 Chappell, Rev. W. H., M.A. (Serving Aug. 4, 1914). Chaplain R.N. H.M.S. *Argyll*, H.M.S. *Defiance*.

1905 Chevallier, J. F. E., B.A. (July 28, 1916). Lt. Interpreter, Special Lists.

1915 Christie, A. F. G., B.A. (Jan. 1916). Lt. 3rd Queen's (R. W. Surrey Regt.).

1919 Clark, J. D. (Sept. 20, 1917). Sergt. and Cadet U.S. Infantry. France, 1918–19.

1904 Coad, Rev. W. S., M.A. (Feb. 11, 1916). Chaplain to the Forces (4th Class).

1918 Cole, C. (Aug. 14, 1916). Lce.-Cpl. 36th Training Res. Bn. (Discharged disabled, Mar. 12, 1918.)

1916 Cole, H. (Jan. 16, 1916). Pte. 1st (Garr.) Bn. Worcestershire Regt.

1911 Cole,* W., M.A. (Jan. 27, 1916). 2nd Lt. Unattached List, T.F., Oundle School O.T.C.

1908 Coles, Rev. L. H., M.A. (Serving Aug. 4, 1914). Maj. Res. of Officers. Chaplain R.N., H.M.S. *Isis*. North Sea.

1915 Connell, R. F. (Jan. 4, 1916). 2nd Lt. 5th K.R.R.C., attd. R.A.F. (Lt.). France, 1917, 1918.

1910 **Cook,* H. M.** (Sept. 1914). ‡Lt. 5th R. Berkshire Regt. Lt. 12th Bn. M.G.C. France. *D.* France. Killed in action at Dernancourt, near Albert, on Aug. 9, 1918.

1919 Cooper, G. P. (Sept. 14, 1914). Lt., Acting Capt., 12th E. Surrey Regt. Belgium, Italy, France, Germany.

1904 Crabbe, Rev. H. M., M.A. (Aug. 8, 1916). Chaplain to the Forces (4th Class), attd. 17th and 18th Lancashire Fusiliers. France and Belgium.

1904 **Dallas, Rev. W. L. S.,** M.A. (Aug. 1915). Chaplain to the Forces (4th Class), attd. 5th King's (Liverpool Regt.). France and Belgium. Killed in action at Pommern Castle, near Ypres, on Sept. 20, 1917.

1899 Davies, D. G. W., B.A. (Oct. 26, 1914). ‡Lt., Acting Capt. and Adjt., 8th Divl. Ammn. Col., R.F.A. France, 1916–19.

1912 Day,* H. J. T., M.A. (Sept. 14, 1914). Capt. 10th Welsh Regt. Capt. General List. Staff-Captain G.H.Q., France. France and Belgium. *D.* France, 1918.

1919 Denduyts, N. E. (Dec. 1915). ‡Lt. R.A.S.C. (M.T.). France, Belgium, Cape Colony, E. Africa, Egypt.
1919 Dewar, W. G. F. (May 2, 1917). ‡2nd Lt. 8th Rifle Brigade. France, 1917–18.
1919 Downes, R. M. (Aug. 13, 1914). ‡Capt. 1st Lancashire Fusiliers. Egypt, 1915; France, 1916–17. *M.C.*, June 18, 1917; *Bar*, Nov. 26, 1917.
1919 Duer, E. L. (1917). ‡2nd Lt. F.A., U.S. Army.
1908 Edwards,* Rev. R., M.A. (Apr. 1917). Chaplain to the Forces (4th Class), attd. 2/15th London Regt. (Civil Service Rifles). Belgium and France.
1907 [Emden, A. B., M.A.] (Nov. 29, 1915). A.B. R.N.V.R., H.M.S. *Parker* (P.O.). Grand Fleet, 1916–19.
1919 Espley, T. H., B.A. (Aug. 4, 1914). ‡Lt. 1/4th Shropshire L.I. France and Belgium.
1914 **Evans, A. J.** (Dec. 22, 1914). Capt. 10th S. Wales Borderers. France. Killed in action at Léalvilliers on July 2, 1918.
1902 Field, Rev. C. T. F., B.A. (Aug. 1914). Chaplain R.N.
1912 Foster,* R. S., B.A. (Sept. 2, 1914). ‡Lt. 3rd Shropshire L.I., attd. (as Q.-M.) King's African Rifles. France, 1915, 1916; E. Africa, 1917–18. *D.* E. Africa, 1919.
1919 Freeman, P. T. (Nov. 24, 1915). Capt. R.E. (T.F.). *M.B.E.* (Mil.).
1898 Fyffe, Rev. J. E., M.A. (July 5, 1918). Chaplain to the Forces (4th Class).
1919 Gabriel, H. S. (1917). 1st Lt. 316th Infantry, U.S. Army.
1919 Gallop, M. W. (Sept. 2, 1914). ‡Lt. R.F.A., attd. 35th Squadron, R.A.F. France and Belgium.
1912 Gardner, G. C., M.A. (Dec. 30, 1915). Lt. 4th The Buffs (E. Kent Regt.), attd. No. 1 Eastern Command Travelling Musketry School.
1909 **Gare, J. H.,** B.A. (Sept. 21, 1916). Sergt. 1/28th London Regt. (Artists' Rifles). France. Killed in action at Cambrai on Dec. 30, 1917.
1919 Garland, H. G. (Aug. 27, 1917). 1st Lt. 61st Infantry, U.S. Army. France.
1919 Garrett, C. E. (Aug. 5, 1915). Paymaster Sub-Lt. R.N.R.
1891 Goddard, Rev. G. H. G., B.A. (July 21, 1916). Chaplain to the Forces (4th Class), attd. 4th Wiltshire Regt.
1919 Godwin, E. T. H. (Sept. 22, 1914). Lt. 9th R. Sussex Regt. Maj. M.G.C. France, 1915–16. *M.C.*, Nov. 4, 1915. *D.* France, 1915; § Mar. 1919.
1919 Goldberg, L. W. (Sept. 1917). R.O.T.C., Yale University, U.S.A., until June, 1918. Pte. 3rd R. W. Kent Regt.
1910 **Goodbarne-Chatterton, A. H.,** B.A. (Aug. 14, 1915). Lt. R.F.A. (T.F.), attd. H.Q. 215th Bde., R.F.A. Mesopotamia. Died at Baghdad on July 21, 1917, of illness contracted on active service.
1893 Gough, Rev. W. R., M.A. (May 24, 1916). Chaplain to the Forces (4th Class).
1911 Gould, Rev. T. C. P., M.A. (Jan. 1, 1918). Chaplain to the Forces (4th Class), attd. 1/5th Loyal N. Lancashire Regt. France and Belgium.
1902 Gower, H. D. Pte. 21st Sherwood Foresters.
1894 Gray, R., M.A. (Oct. 29, 1914). Capt. 1/5th E. Surrey Regt., attd. Gen. Knox's Mission (Lt.-Col. while attd. 6th Loyal N. Lancashire Regt., 1917–18). India, 1914; Mesopotamia, 1916; Persia and Caucasia, 1918; Siberia, 1919. *M.C.*, Jan. 11, 1919. Order of St. Anne. *D.* Mesopotamia, 1917.

1918 Green, F. L. (1914). Lt. Worcestershire Regt.
1903 Green, Rev. G., M.A. (Serving Aug. 4, 1914). Chaplain (2nd Class) A.I.F.
1917 Greenidge, J. T. W. (Dec. 27, 1917). 2nd Lt. R.G.A.
1919 Grieve, M. D. (Feb. 7, 1917). 2nd Lt. 3rd Lincolnshire Regt. France. (Prisoner of war at Stralsund, May–Dec. 1918.)
1910 Griffiths, D. P. S. (Mar. 3, 1915). Lt. 2nd Brecknockshire Bn., S. Wales Borderers. (Invalided, Oct. 29, 1918.)
1907 Griffiths, Rev. J. M. T., M.A. (July 5, 1918). Chaplain to the Forces (4th Class).
1910 **Griggs,* H. E.** (Aug. 25, 1914). Capt. 9th Essex Regt. France. Killed in action on Oct. 5, 1915.
1917 Grinter, J. H. D. (June 6, 1918). 2nd Lt. Grenadier Guards (S.R.).
1897 Gull, C. B., M.A. (Mar. 1915). Capt. and Adjt. R.G.A. Capt. Tank Corps. Belgium and France.
1891 **Gunson, Rev. H. E.,** M.A. (Mar. 15, 1915). Chaplain to the Forces (4th Class). Died in Ireland on Aug. 23, 1918.
1909 Hadenfeldt,* R. A., M.A. (Mar. 1916). Sergt. 7th (I.L. Coy.) Middlesex Regt. France and Belgium.
1914 Hall,* R. J. (1914). R. Fusiliers.
1905 [Handover, Rev. S. J., M.A.] (Oct. 1915). Chaplain to the Forces (4th Class), attd. Hospital Ship *Goorkha*.
1913 Hart, L. W. (Sept. 9, 1914). ‡Lt. 2/12th London Regt. (The Rangers), attd. Indian Army (Capt.). France, Belgium, N.W. Frontier, India.
1911 Harvey,* E. L., B.A. (May 6, 1916). ‡Lt. 3rd The Buffs (E. Kent Regt.). France, 1916–17; N.W. Frontier, India, 1918.
1910 Hawkins,* R. H., M.A. (Oct. 3, 1914). Capt. 3rd S. Staffordshire Regt. Lt., Hon. Capt., S.E. Area Flying Instructors' School, R.A.F. France, 1915; Salonika, 1915–17; Egypt, 1917.
1888 Hawtrey, G. H. C., M.A. (Oct. 6, 1914). ‡Sub-Lt. R.N.D., R.N.V.R. Lt. 7th Worcestershire Regt. and Labour Corps (Staff-Lt. G.H.Q. Staff). France.
1902 Heath, Rev. R. A. D., M.A. (Mar. 9, 1915). Pte. R.A.M.C. (Cpl.). France and Belgium.
1915 Hedges, D. H. (Jan. 9, 1917). ‡Lt. R.A.S.C. (M.T.). Mesopotamia, Persia, S. Russia.
1919 Herbert, T. D. C. (Apr. 17, 1915). Lce.-Sergt. 10th Welsh Guards (C.Q.M.S.). Belgium, France.
1905 Hodson, Rev. R. L., M.A. (Sept. 6, 1918). Chaplain to the Forces (4th Class).
1919 Horwood, H. J. (Feb. 15, 1917). ‡2nd Lt. 6th Leicestershire Regt. France.
1910 **Houlston, E. C.,** B.A. (July 27, 1915). Chaplain to the Forces (4th Class). Drowned on May 4, 1917.
1919 Howard, S. A., B.A. (Serving Aug. 4, 1914). Capt. R.E. (S.R.). France, Aug. 1914–15.
1897 Hubble, Rev. H. O. (June 1, 1918). Chaplain to the Forces (4th Class).
1919 Hustwayte, H. L. (Jan. 31, 1915). Pte. 66th Field Ambulance, R.A.M.C. France, 1915; Balkans, 1915–19.
1909 Irving,* H. C., B.A. (Mar. 3, 1917). Lt. R.F.A. France.
1914 **James, B. L.** (Aug. 1915). 2nd Lt. 4th The Buffs (E. Kent Regt.), attd. Loyal N. Lancashire Regt. France. Died on Nov. 25, 1916, of wounds received in action near Dernancourt.

1919 Janes, A. R. (Nov. 20, 1914). Pte. 55th Field Ambulance, R.A.M.C. France, 1916; Salonika, 1917; Palestine, 1917; France, 1918.
1919 Jefferson, P. T. (May 5, 1915). ‡Lt. R.A.S.C. Gallipoli, Egypt, Palestine. *D.* Palestine, 1918.
1915 Jenkins, J. L. (Jan. 26, 1916). A.B. R.N., H.M.S. *Royal Sovereign.*
1919 Johnson, B. C. W. (Aug. 23, 1915). ‡Lt. M.G.C. France, Belgium, Germany.
1919 Johnson, J. (June 20, 1918). Pte. 4th D.C.L.I.
1910 Johnston, Rev. G. F., B.A. (Oct. 14, 1915). Chaplain to the Forces (4th Class).
1909 Karn,* J. C. (Serving Aug. 4, 1914). Capt. 3rd R. Welch Fusiliers. *D.* § Mar. 1919.
1903 Knight-Adkin, Rev. W. K., B.A. (Serving Aug. 4, 1914). Chaplain R.N., H.M.S. *Revenge.* Mediterranean Fleet, Atlantic Fleet. *O.B.E.* (Mil.).
1906 Lace, R. D., B.A. (Aug. 6, 1915). Lt. 3rd The Black Watch. Capt. Labour Corps. France. *D.* France, 1917.
1914 Lambeth,* W. E. (Nov. 24, 1914). Lt. 3rd Queen's (R. W. Surrey Regt.) France, 1918.
1905 Lancaster, Rev. C. H., M.A. (Apr. 8, 1918). Chaplain to the Forces (4th Class).
1913 Lane, H. G. (Aug. 1914). ‡Capt. 62nd Bn. M.G.C. France, Germany. *M.C.*, Feb. 15, 1919.
1919 Law, H. R. McK. (Mar. 29, 1915). Lt. 1st (Garr.) Bn. Gordon Highlanders. France, Belgium, 1915–16; India, 1917–19.
1918 Laxon, F. (Sept. 12, 1914). ‡Lt. 9th R. Scots. France, Belgium.
1912 **Leslie,* L. F. E.** (Serving Aug. 4, 1914). ‡Lt. King's African Rifles. German E. Africa, 1916–17. Killed in action at Luwuka on Aug. 20, 1917.
1919 Lickes, H. G. (Jan. 14, 1915). ‡Lt. 11th Oxf. & Bucks. Lt. Infty. Salonika, France, Germany.
1919 Livesey, H. (Nov. 1915). Lt. 4th S. Lancashire Regt. France. (Discharged on account of ill health caused by wounds, Feb. 1919.)
1918 Lowe, D., B.A. (Jan. 10, 1915). Pte. 17th King's (Liverpool Regt.). France, 1915–16. (Discharged on account of wounds, Aug. 1916.)
1918 Lowe, G. (Aug. 1914). ‡Lt. R.F.A. France.
1918 McGowan, F., B.A. (July 22, 1915). Lt. W. Riding Regt. Lt. M.G.C. France, 1916–17.
1913 Mackintosh, A. C. (July 7, 1915). Lt. 6th Devonshire Regt.
1913 Maiden,* S. J. F. (Oct. 4, 1915). Lt. The Buffs (E. Kent Regt.), attd. O.C.B.
1919 Markley, G. H. (Sept. 17, 1917). Sergt. 311th Infantry, U.S. Army. France.
1920 Martin, W. R. (May 26, 1916). Lt. 5th R. Irish Rifles (S.R.). France.
1904 Mathias, Rev. H. S., M.A. (Oct. 4, 1918). Chaplain to the Forces (4th Class).
1904 Mathias, L. S. (Oct. 5, 1915). Capt. 3rd Leinster Regt.
1914 Maund, A. E., B.A. (Apr. 1917). Lt. Labour Corps, i/c No. 318 (H.S.) Works Coy.
1912 Meredith,* W. M., M.A. (Dec. 24, 1915). Lt. 10th E. Yorkshire Regt. Capt. General List. Staff-Captain.
1920 Millen, Rev. E. L. (Oct. 31, 1916). Chaplain to the Forces (4th Class), attd. R.A.F. Palestine and Egypt, 1917–19.

1861 Milner, Rev. W. H. (Serving Aug. 4, 1914). Chaplain (1st Class), attd. 1st Life Guards (Retired). Distinguished Service Reward.

1920 Mohan, T. G. (Dec. 1916). Cpl. 1st Wiltshire Regt. Belgium and France.

1903 Molyneux, Rev. E. G., M.A. (May 2, 1917). Chaplain to the Forces (4th Class). Acting Asst. Chaplain-General, No. 4 Area. France and Belgium, 1917–19.

1886 Monckton, Rev. R. G., M.A. (Mar. 28, 1916). Chaplain to the Forces (4th Class).

1919 Moore, G. T. (May 29, 1916). ‡2nd Lt. R.G.A. France and Belgium, 1917.

1907 Mortimer, Rev. E. C., M.A. (Sept. 29, 1916). Chaplain to the Forces (4th Class), attd. 19th Bde., R.M.A. (S.C.F.). Egypt, Palestine, Syria.

1903 Noble, P. W. H. Tpr. King Edward's Horse.

1903 North, G. R. (Nov. 26, 1914). Lt. 9th Queen's (R. W. Surrey Regt.). Capt. Labour Corps.

1919 O'Connor, G. J. (Aug. 14, 1914). ‡Lt. Gloucestershire Regt. Belgium, 1915–16; France, 1918.

1887 O'Donovan, Rev. R. H., B.A. (Serving Aug. 4, 1914). Chaplain R.N.

1919 Palmer, H. (Sept. 4, 1914). ‡Lt. 2/7th Lancashire Fusiliers. France, Belgium. *M.M.* (Prisoner of war in Germany.)

1919 Parsons, D. J. (Aug. 16, 1915). ‡2nd Lt. 3rd S. Wales Borderers. France, 1915–17, 1918–19.

1912 **Partridge,* A. J.,** B.A. (July 8, 1915). 2nd Lt. 9th, attd. 5th, R. Berkshire Regt. France. Killed in action at Ovillers on July 3, 1916.

1890 Peacock, Rev. C. A., M.A. (July 1, 1916). Chaplain to the Forces (1st Class). Asst. Chaplain-General. *C.B.E.* (Mil.).

1919 Porter, J. F. A. (Apr. 1918). 2nd Lt. 5th Devonshire Regt. France, 1918–19.

1909 Priestley, E. C., M.A. (Aug. 26, 1914). Lt. 8th Essex Regt. Capt. and Adjt. Indian Army, attd. 67th Punjabis. India.

1913 Proctor, A. H. (Dec. 1915). ‡2nd Lt. 1/5th King's (Liverpool Regt.). Egypt, 1915–18; France and Belgium, 1918–19. *M.C.*, Feb. 1, 1919.

1887 Proctor, Rev. F. O., M.A. (Apr. 23, 1917). Chaplain to the Forces (3rd Class).

1904 Ramsay, Rev. R. E., M.A. (May 23, 1916). Chaplain to the Forces (4th Class).

1918 **Ransom, H. B.** (Dec. 1914). Lt. 3rd Wiltshire Regt. France. (Invalided.) Died on Oct. 30, 1918.

1918 Raven, J. W. (Jan. 1915). 2nd Lt. 10th Border Regt. France.

1919 Ray, F. E. (June 15, 1918). Pte. R. W. Kent Regt. (Cpl.).

1918 Reardon, W. J. R. (Mobilized Aug. 1914). Capt. 4th R. Irish Regt. (Invalided.)

1920 Reddick, P. G. (July 21, 1915). Rfln. 16th K.R.R.C. France, 1916.

1912 Rees,* A. P. C. (Aug. 21, 1914). Capt. R. Welch Fusiliers. Gallipoli, 1915–16; Mesopotamia, 1916.

1897 Reid, Rev. E., M.A. (June 1915). Chaplain to the Forces (4th Class). France and Belgium, 1916–17.

1914 Robathan, F. N., B.A. (Dec. 22, 1914). Lt. Army Cyclist Corps, attd. 1/6th Norfolk Regt. (Capt.). France, 1916.

1919 Robertson, H. C. (Nov. 18, 1914). ‡Lt. 3rd Seaforth Highlanders (Capt.). France, 1915–19. *M.C.*, Mar. 8, 1919.

1910 **Robinson,* L. H. F.** (Aug. 22, 1914). Lt. 7th E. Surrey Regt. France. Killed in action at the Hohenzollern Redoubt on Mar. 15, 1916.
1906 Rossborough, Rev. V. W. A., M.A. (Oct. 2, 1917). Chaplain to the Forces (4th Class).
1897 Rowley, J. C., B.A. (Mar. 12, 1917). Lt. R.F.A. (S.R.).
1913 Salmon,* G. H. (July 27, 1915). Lt. 6th Devonshire Regt.
1919 Sampson, C. (July 6, 1915). Pte. H.A.C. France and Belgium, 1916–17. (Discharged on account of wounds, Aug. 2, 1918.)
1897 Sampson, M. F. W. (Dec. 14, 1916). Capt. R.A.F.
1902 Sargeant, F. N., B.A. (Aug. 2, 1915). Volontaire (Sous-Chef) Section Sanitaire Anglaise, Croix rouge française, attd. 15th Div. French Army. France, 1915, 1916, 1917. *D.* French Dispatches, 1917.
1913 Sayle, R., B.A. (June 28, 1915). ‡Lt. Yorkshire Regt. (Staff-Captain, Admin. Staff, H.Q. Northern Command).
1919 Schlueter, W. H. (Sept. 19, 1917). Color-Sergt. 314th Engineers, U.S. Army. France, 1918; Germany, 1918–19.
1901 Scott, Rev. F. K. (Sept. 5, 1914). Chaplain to the Forces (4th Class) (Senior Divl. Chaplain).
1909 Seaver,* G. F., M.A. (Feb. 1915). Lt. Connaught Rangers. France, for 18 months.
1914 Selwyn, A. B., B.A. (July 25, 1916). Cpl. 1/7th Devonshire Regt. (Lce.-Sergt.).
1915 Sharpe, G. H. (Jan. 21, 1916). ‡2nd Lt. 2nd Worcestershire Regt. France, 1916–17, 1918, 1919.
1919 Shaw, F. C. L. (Feb. 21, 1917). Pte. 978th M.T. Coy., R.A.S.C.
1919 Shaw, J. (May 27, 1918). Sergt. 138th Infantry, 35th Div., U.S. Army. France.
1913 **Shaw,* W. B.** (Nov. 13, 1914). Lt. 9th R. Sussex Regt. France. Killed in action at Vimy Ridge on Apr. 12, 1917.
1919 Shearman, H. C. (Dec. 4, 1915). ‡2nd Lt. R.A.F. Mesopotamia, 1916–17; India, 1917; Egypt, 1917–19.
1909 Shirley,* F. J. J., M.A. (Dec. 1915). 2nd Lt. R.M.L.I. Sub-Lt. R.N.V.R. (Intelligence).
1918 Simpson, I. L. (Serving Aug. 4, 1914). Lt. 4th E. Lancashire Regt., attd. 4th S. Lancashire Regt. (Capt.). Egypt, 1914; Gallipoli, 1915; France and Belgium, 1915–17.
1919 Smalley, F. A. (Serving Aug. 4, 1914). Cpl. 1st Rifle Brigade. France, 1914. (Prisoner of war in Germany, Aug. 1914–Dec. 1918.)
1919 Soulsby, M. J. (May 29, 1916). Bomdr. R.G.A. France, Belgium.
1913 **Spencer,* G. W. S.** (Sept. 1914). 2nd Lt. 8th Norfolk Regt. France. Died on Feb. 24, 1916, of wounds received at Albert on Sept. 12, 1915.
1914 Spriggs, P. B. (Dec. 10, 1915). ‡Lt. R.A.O.C. France, 1917–18.
Standring, W. S. ‡2nd Lt. 17th King's (Liverpool Regt.) (Lt.). France. Killed in action near Guillemont on July 30, 1916.
1914 Stephens, G. W. (Aug. 11, 1914). Lt. 14th Gloucestershire Regt. France and Belgium, 1916–19.
1918 Swannell, F. C. (Nov. 27, 1914). ‡Lt. R.G.A., attd. R.E. France, N. Russia.
1910 Taylor,* E. F. L., B.A. (Aug. 15, 1914). Lt. 3rd Devonshire Regt. Lt. Technical Officer, R.A.F. Belgium and France, 1915; Egypt, 1917–19.

1909 Tennant,* J. S., B.A. (Dec. 1, 1914). 2nd Lt. 2/5th W. Yorkshire Regt. (Invalided.) Capt. and Adjt. 7th Vol. Bn. W. Yorkshire Regt.

1909 Thomas, Rev. M. W., B.A. (Nov. 20, 1917). Senior Chaplain to the Forces. France.

1899 Thorne, Rev. H. W., M.A. (May 4, 1917). Chaplain to the Forces (4th Class).

1911 Todd, C. F., B.A. (Nov. 1, 1916). Pte. 28th London Regt. (Artists' Rifles). (Invalided.)

1912 Trevor, C. H. J., M.A. (Feb. 10, 1916). Lt. R.G.A. (S.R.).

1919 Vickers, H. H. (Sept. 17, 1915). ‡Lt. 11th Leicestershire Regt. Belgium and France.

1908 Walker, C. D., B.A. (Dec. 23, 1914). Capt. 13th, afterwards 51st Manchester Regt. France, 1915, 1918–19; Salonika, 1915–18; Germany, 1919. *D.* Salonika, 1918.

1919 Walkington, J. J. G. (Aug. 5, 1914). ‡Lt. 6th Lincolnshire Regt. (Capt. and Adjt.). France.

1919 Wallace, D. J. (Dec. 13, 1917). 2nd Lt. 100th Aero Squadron, U.S. Army. France.

1904 Wand, Rev. J. W. C., M.A. (July 27, 1915). Chaplain to the Forces (4th Class). Instructor, 2nd Army College, Cologne. Egypt and Gallipoli, 1915; France, 1915–18; Germany, 1919.

1912 Warner, L. C., B.A. (Sept. 16, 1915). Gnr. 'K' A.A. Batt., R.G.A. France, 1918–19.

1910 Warner, W. R., M.A. (Jan. 8, 1916). 2nd Lt. Army Cyclist Corps, attd. 1/23rd London Regt.

1914 Waters, H. B. (Nov. 27, 1914). Lt. R.E. (Signals).

1914 **Watson, K. C. F.** (July 24, 1915). Lt. 3rd S. Lancashire Regt., attd. 2/7th R. Warwickshire Regt. France and Belgium. *M.C.*, Jan. 1, 1918. Killed in action near Robecq on Apr. 12, 1918.

1919 Welford, P. G. (Nov. 1915). Pte. R. Fusiliers.

1918 West, H. (Aug. 4, 1914). ‡2nd Lt. R.F.A. Lt. 1st Bn. Tank Corps (Capt.). France and Belgium, 1914–17. (Invalided on account of wounds, 1918.)

1919 White, R. B. (Jan. 8, 1915). Lce.-Cpl. Q.O. Oxfordshire Hussars. France, Belgium.

1913 Williams, C., M.A. (Aug. 25, 1915). Lt., Acting Capt., 4th (Res.) The Buffs (E. Kent Regt.), attd. R.A.F.

1919 Williams, E. S. (Nov. 1, 1915). Lt. 4th The Buffs (E. Kent Regt.). France.

1920 Williams, T. E. (June 1, 1915). Driver 'B' Batt., H.A.C. Egypt, Palestine, Syria, 1916–19.

1917 **Willoughby, J. F.** (1918). Cadet No. 6 O.C.B. Died on Oct. 29, 1918, of illness contracted on active service.

1919 Winston, C. K. (Aug. 1, 1917). Cpl. 111th Engineers, U.S. Army. France.

1919 Wood, F. J. (May 21, 1918). Flight Cadet R.A.F.

1914 Wood, J. B., B.A. (July 1, 1918). Lce.-Cpl. 1st (Garr.) Bn. Worcestershire Regt.

1910 Worster,* Rev. P. W., M.A. (Nov. 1917). Chaplain to the Forces (4th Class). Malta, 1918–19; Russia, 1919.

1914 Yelverton, Rev. E. E., B.D. (June 7, 1918). Chaplain to the Forces (4th Class), attd. Dragoon Bde., Cavalry Div., Rhine Army. France and Belgium, 1918–19; Germany, from 1919. *O.B.E.* (Mil.).

KEBLE COLLEGE

1886 Abbott, Rev. W. H., M.A. (Sept. 9, 1914). Chaplain to the Forces (4th Class). France. *M.C.*, June 23, 1915. *D.* France, 1915.

1903 Abraham, C. W. R., B.A. Bowker's Horse, British E. Africa.

1916 Acheson, A. B. (Aug. 14, 1914). ‡Lt. 7th Rifle Brigade. Capt. 9th Bn. M.G.C. France and Belgium, for 2½ years. Croix de Guerre. *D.* France, 1918.

1899 Adam, T. W., M.A. (Feb. 12, 1918). Chaplain to the Forces (4th Class). France, 1918–19.

1910 Adams, F. K. Pte. 11th Bn. A.I.F.

1911 Adams,* L. F., B.A. (Serving Aug. 4, 1914). Capt. 10th Devonshire Regt. Capt. General List. Staff-Lt. Salonika, 1915; France, 1918.

1897 Adkin, J. H. K., B.A. (Mobilized Aug. 4, 1914). Lt. 4th Gloucestershire Regt (Capt.). Lt. O.T.C., T.F., Unattached List. France, Belgium.

1907 Adolphus,* E. M., M.A. (1914). ‡Lt. R. Defence Corps.

1913 **Aldana,* J. M.** (Nov. 14, 1914). Lt. 4th Worcestershire Regt. (Capt.). France. Killed in action at Monchy, near Arras, on Apr. 20, 1917.

1900 Aldred, Rev. C. C., M.A. (Oct. 4, 1915). Chaplain to the Forces (4th Class). (Resigned.)

1914 Aldred-Brown,* G. R. P., B.A. (Dec. 30, 1915). Capt. R.A., attd. IX Heavy T.M.B., R.G.A. France.

1906 Aldridge,* Rev. H. E. G., B.A. (Aug. 2, 1918). Chaplain to the Forces (4th Class).

1919 Alexander, R. G. (June 7, 1918). Cadet No. 17 O.C.B.

1887 Allen, F. J., M.A. (Sept. 12, 1914). Capt. R.A.S.C. France, Belgium, Germany, 1915–19. *O.B.E.* (Mil.). *D.* France, 1916, 1919.

1897 Allen, R. S. (Serving Aug. 4, 1914). Maj., Bt. Lt.-Col., temp. Lt.-Col., Hampshire Regt. G.S.O. 1, D.A.A.Q.M.G. France. *D.S.O.*, Jan. 1, 1919. *D.* France, 1915, 1917 twice, 1918.

1895 Allsop, B., M.A. (Feb. 2, 1916). 2nd Lt. Unattached List, T.F., Aldenham School O.T.C.

1906 Appleton, Rev. J. A., M.A. (Apr. 4, 1916). Chaplain to the Forces (4th Class) (S.C.F.) Egypt, 1916; Imbros, 1916; Salonika, 1916–18.

1919 Archer, C. H. (Dec. 30, 1915). Lt. R.F.A. Lt. Kite Balloon Officer, R.A.F. France, 1916–19.

1903 Archibald, G. K. (Serving Aug. 4, 1914). Capt., Bt.-Maj., Acting Lt.-Col. R.A.S.C. France, Mesopotamia. *D.S.O.*, Sept. 17, 1917. *D.* France, 1915; Mesopotamia, 1917, 1918, 1919.

1912 Ardagh, F. D., M.A. (Mobilized Aug. 4, 1914). Capt. 1/5th Queen's (R. W. Surrey Regt.), attd. M.G.C. (Maj.). India, 1914–15; Mesopotamia, 1915–19. *D.* Mesopotamia, 1919.

1919 Arden-Davis, G. H. (Oct. 22, 1914). 2nd Lt. 6th Somerset L.I. (Resigned.) France, 1917.

1895 Arkwright, A. J., B.A. (Feb. 22, 1915). Lt. 10th E. Surrey Regt. Lt. Labour Corps.

1909 Armstrong, F. H. C., B.A. (Serving Aug. 4, 1914). Capt. 67th Punjabis, Indian Army. (Mil. Attaché to British Embassy at Constantinople.) Mesopotamia. (Prisoner of war in Turkey after the fall of Kut.) *O.B.E.* (Mil.).

1916 Armstrong, T. H. W. (May 15, 1917). ‡2nd Lt. R.G.A. (S.R.). France, 1917–19.

1914 Ashworth, N. B. (July 23, 1915). ‡Lt. R.A.S.C. (M.T.). France.

1914 Askin, A. T. C. (Jan. 21, 1915). Lt. Wiltshire Regt., attd. 1/8th Hampshire Regt. Gallipoli, 1915; Egypt, 1916; Palestine, 1917. (Wounded and taken prisoner at Gaza, Apr. 19, 1917.)

1919 Austen, A. C. (May 3, 1915). Lce.-Cpl. 18th Divl. Sig. Coy., R.E. France and Belgium, 1915–19. *M.M.*, Aug. 1917; *Bar*, Oct. 1918.

1907 Austen, H. C. H. P. (Jan. 5, 1915). 2nd Lt. 14th Middlesex Regt. A.P.M. General List.

1901 Aylen, Rev. C. A. W., M.A. (July 11, 1916). Chaplain R.N., H.M.S. *St. Vincent.* North Sea.

1912 Baddeley,* W. H., M.A. (Dec. 2, 1914). Maj. 8th E. Surrey Regt. (Lt.-Col.). France and Belgium. *D.S.O.*, June 3, 1919. *M.C.*, Aug. 16, 1917; *Bar*, Sept. 16, 1918. *D.* France, 1917 twice, 1918, 1919.

1915 Bagott, H. W. H. (Mar. 1, 1916). ‡Lt. 113th Heavy Batt., R.G.A. France, 1917–18.

1905 Bailey, Rev. E. F., M.A. (Aug. 26, 1918). Chaplain to the Forces (4th Class).

1911 Baily,* R. G. (Dec. 21, 1914). Capt. 7th Dorsetshire Regt. Lt. General List. (Invalided.)

1905 Baker, A. C., B.A. (June 11, 1916). Lt. 10th Loyal N. Lancashire Regt. Capt. 3rd Class Agent, Intelligence Corps. France and Belgium, 1917, 1918. *M.C.*, Nov. 26, 1917.

1919 Baker, A. J. K. (Apr. 17, 1916). ‡Lt. 10th Bn. A.I.F. France and Belgium.

1910 Baker,* G. A. A. (Mar. 9, 1915). Lt. Denbighshire Yeomanry. Lt. M.G.C. (Cavalry).

1917 Baldry, A. F. H. (Jan. 19, 1917). 2nd Lt. R.E. Lt. Special Lists, R.T.O. France.

1901 Bankes-Jones, Rev. R. M., M.A. (Oct. 27, 1914). Chaplain to the Forces (4th class). Lt. Flying Officer R.A.F. France, Palestine.

1908 Banks,* L. J. (Jan. 7, 1915). 2nd Lt. 7th R. Berkshire Regt. Lt. R.E. France.

1901 Barber, C. A., M.A. (Serving Aug. 4, 1914). Capt. 15th Hampshire Regt. (Staff-Captain). Belgium and France, 1916–19. *M.C.*, Mar. 8, 1918.

1909 Barber,* E. K., M.A. (May 26, 1915). Lt., Acting Capt. 298th Siege Batt., R.G.A. (Maj.). France.

1900 Barber, Rev. H. S., M.A. (Jan. 25, 1918). Lt. R.N.V.R. H.M. Naval Wireless Station, Aden.

1900 Barlow-Poole, Rev. G. D., M.A. (Mar. 15, 1915). Chaplain to the Forces (3rd Class), attd. 63rd (R.N.) Div. France and Belgium. *M.C.*, Sept. 16, 1918.

1897 Barlow-Poole, Rev. R. E., M.A. (May 2, 1916). Chaplain to the Forces (4th Class). (Resigned.)

1893 Barnard, B. H. F. (Mobilized Feb. 1915). Pte. Malay States Volunteer Rifles (Sergt.).

1896 Barnes, A. C., B.A. (Sept. 28, 1914). Lt. 4th Yorkshire Regt. Acting Capt. Special Lists (whilst Bde. Bombing Officer).

1898 Barnes, A. F., B.A., B.Mus. (Mar. 5, 1915). Capt. 5th Gloucestershire Regt., attd. Irish Guards. France. (Prisoner of war in Germany.) *M.C.*, Jan. 1, 1917.

1919 Barrett, R. T. (Aug. 22, 1914). Sub-Lt. R.N.D. Antwerp. (Prisoner of war, interned in Holland.)

1894 Barter, E. B., B.A. (Mar. 27, 1915). 2nd Lt. 4th Somerset L.I. (Resigned.)

1913 **Bartlett,* R. N. O.** (Sept. 17, 1914). ‡Capt. 6th E. Lancashire Regt. Gallipoli, 1915; Mesopotamia, 1916. Died on Apr. 6, 1916, of wounds received in action at Felahiyeh.

1915 Barton, R. M. (Dec. 15, 1915). Sergt. 1/3rd S.M. Field Ambulance, R.A.M.C. Italy.

1914 Barugh, W. H. (Jan. 6, 1916). ‡Lt. 4th Northumberland Fusiliers. France, 1916–17. *D.* § Aug. 1919.

1906 Basset,* Rev. G. H., M.A. (Jan. 3, 1916). Chaplain to the Forces (4th Class). France.

1911 **Batson,* L. H.** (Nov. 26, 1914). 2nd Lt. 6th The Buffs (E. Kent Regt.). France. Killed in action at Albert on July 3, 1916.

1896 Baylay, Rev. M., M.A. (July 3, 1917). Chaplain to the Forces (4th Class). France, 1917–19.

1914 Bazeley, O. E. S. (Dec. 22, 1914). 2nd Lt. 11th Gloucestershire Regt. Lt. 273rd Coy., M.G.C. (Capt.). Gallipoli, 1915; Egypt, 1915; Mesopotamia, 1915–19. *D.* Mesopotamia, 1919.

1904 Bazell, C., B.A. (Oct. 29, 1914). Capt. Singapore Volunteer Rifles.

1897 Beavan, A. Trooper Worcestershire Yeomanry. Egypt and Palestine. (Wounded and prisoner in Turkey, Apr. 1917.)

1919 Beckingham, D. V. (May 14, 1915). Signalman R.N.V.R., afterwards 2nd Lt. R.A.F. At sea, 1915–19.

1896 Beckwith, Rev. C., M.A. (July 3, 1917). Chaplain to the Forces (4th Class), attd. 47th Gen. Hospital, B.E.F. France and Belgium. (Retired July 3, 1918.)

1910 Belcher,* W. B., M.A. (Sept. 1914). ‡Lt., temp. Capt. 3rd R. Berkshire Regt. Staff-Captain Eastern Div. (Bde.-Maj.). France, Belgium, Germany, 1916–19. *M.C.*, Jan. 1, 1919.

1913 Bennett, A. H. (Sept. 2, 1914). ‡Capt. 2/5th Devonshire Regt. Egypt, 1915–16; Mesopotamia, 1916–19.

1914 Bennett, S. G. (Aug. 28, 1915). Capt. R.E. France. *M.C.*, June 3, 1918. *D.* France, 1917.

1904 Beresford-Peirse, Rev. J. W. de la P., M.A. (Oct. 14, 1918). Chaplain to the Forces (4th Class).

Berkeley, C. (Oct. 1915). Lt. Coldstream Guards (S.R.). 2nd Lt. R.A.F. Died on Jan. 30, 1919, as a result of a flying accident at Northolt.

1889 Berkeley, G. Fitz H., B.A. (Dec. 2, 1914). Capt. T.F. Res., attd. Claims and Requisitions Directorate. France, Italy.

1909 Besant,* T. L. (Nov. 21, 1914). Lt. 3rd R. Warwickshire Regt., empld. O.C.B. (Capt.). France. *M.C.*, Jan. 14, 1916. *D.* France, 1915.

1900 **Beswetherick, W. J.,** B.A. (Nov. 26, 1915). Pte. 5th S. African Inf.

German E. Africa, 1916. Died on July 15, 1916, at Nairobi, of illness contracted on active service.

1913 **Biggerton-Evans,*** A. B. G. (Dec. 1914). Capt. 7th S. Wales Borderers. Gallipoli, 1915; France, 1916; Macedonia, Bulgaria, 1918–19. Greek Order of the Redeemer. Chevalier, Order of King George I (Greece). Died at Philippopolis in Dec. 1919 of illness contracted on active service.

Bird, H. T. (Sept. 1, 1916). 2nd Lt. R.F.A. France. Killed in action at Bullecourt on Mar. 21, 1918.

1904 **Birrell, S. E.,** B.A. (Aug. 29, 1914). Capt. 6th Somerset L.I. Belgium and France. Killed in action at Arras on July 11, 1916.

1919 Bivar, H. G. S. (Sept. 29, 1916). Lt. R.F.A. France and Belgium, 1917–18.

1911 **Black,* E. O.** (Serving Aug. 4, 1914). Lt. 2nd Lincolnshire Regt. Belgium. Killed in action at Aubers Ridge on May 9, 1915.

1895 Blencowe, E. P., B.A. (Serving Aug. 4, 1914). Maj., Bt. Lt.-Col. R.A.S.C., attd. 56th Divl. Train. France, 1914–19. *D.S.O.*, Jan. 1, 1916. *D.* France, 1915, 1916, 1917, 1919.

1908 Blogg,* W. G. V., B.A. 2nd Lt. Bahamas Volunteer Corps.

1919 Boggon, J. H. (Mar. 16, 1915). ‡Lt. 1st Hertfordshire Regt. France, 1915–16, 1918.

1914 Bolton, H. O. (Apr. 8, 1915). Lt. and Adjt. 4th Inniskilling Fusiliers (Capt.). Palestine, Macedonia, France. *D.* Palestine, 1918.

1889 Bond, A. G., B.A. (May 25, 1915). Capt. Special Lists, Staff-Captain, R.T.O. France.

1906 Bonser, C. A., B.A. (Oct. 1916). Bombardier R.G.A., H.Q. IV Corps, R.A. Gibraltar, Belgium, France.

1914 Boobbyer, P. W., B.A. (Feb. 1916). ‡Lt. R.F.A. France, 1916–17.

1903 **Booth, A.,** B.M. Capt. S. African Medical Corps. Lt. R.A.M.C. France. Killed in action on Apr. 29, 1916.

1905 Boswell, Rev. P. E., B.A. (Feb. 9, 1915). Chaplain R.N., H.M.S. *Crescent.* North Sea, 1916.

1909 Boulter,* J. S., B.A. (Oct. 20, 1914). Lt. Unattached List, T.F., St. Bees O.T.C.

1894 Bouquet, Rev. J. A., M.A. (Feb. 5, 1918). Chaplain to the Forces (4th Class), attd. M.G.C. France.

1911 **Bourn,* J.,** B.A. (Jan. 29, 1915). Lt. N. Staffordshire Regt. France and Belgium. Killed in action at Klein Zillibeke on July 31, 1917.

1887 Bowden-Smith, Rev. H., M.A. (Feb. 1918). Chaplain to the Forces (4th Class), attd. No. 47 Gen. Hospital, Le Treport. France, 1918.

1919 Bowen, T. (Sept. 21, 1916). Gunner R.F.A. (Bombardier). Belgium and France.

1907 Bower,* A. J., M.A. (Sept. 1914). ‡2nd Lt. 11th York and Lancaster Regt., afterwards Lt. Haileybury College O.T.C.

1919 Bowman, E. S. S. (Aug. 28, 1917). Gent. Cadet R.M.A., Woolwich.

1910 Bowman,* Rev. H., M.A. (July 3, 1916). Chaplain to the Forces (4th Class). France, Belgium, Germany.

1897 Boyd, Rev. F. W., M.A. (Sept. 25, 1917). Chaplain to the Forces (4th Class) (S.C.F.). France and Germany, 1917–19.

1914 **Box, H. F.** (Feb. 17, 1915). Capt. 5th Essex Regt., attd. R.E. (Signals). France. Killed in action on Oct. 29, 1918.

1888 Brackenbury, E. A., B.A. (Oct. 1914). Capt. The Buffs (E. Kent Regt.), Res. of Officers, attd. Nigeria Regt. Staff-Officer. Cameroons, 1914–16. *D.* Cameroons, 1916.
1919 Bradshaw, A. R. (Oct. 19, 1918). Gnr. 211th Batt., R.F.A.
1910 **Bramley,* C. R.** (Aug. 1914). ‡Capt. 2/5th K.O.Y.L.I. France. Killed in action at Beaumont Hamel on Feb. 20, 1917.
1919 Brightman, A. L. (May 21, 1915). ‡Lt. Bucks. Bn. Oxf. & Bucks. Lt. Infty. France, Belgium, Italy.
1920 Brisley, C. W. (Oct. 16, 1916). Lt. Irish Guards. France, 1917–19.
1894 Brooke, Rev. J. C. H., M.A. (Nov. 1914). Chaplain 3rd Mounted Bde., S. African Contingent. German S.W. Africa.
1913 Brooke,* T. B., B.A. (Aug. 1918). Gnr. R.G.A., afterwards attd. Intelligence Corps. France, 1918–19.
1898 Brookes, C. B., M.A. (Oct. 10, 1914). Pte. 23rd R. Fusiliers. France, 1915–17. (Prisoner of war, Apr. 1917–Dec. 1918.)
1915 Brookes, J. A. (Apr. 11, 1916). ‡2nd Lt. 1st Queen's (R. W. Surrey Regt.). France, 1916–17, 1918.
1880 Broughton, Rev. R. E., M.A. (Serving Aug. 4, 1914). Chaplain 7th Cheshire Regt.
1919 Brown, C. L. B. (Aug. 1915). 2nd Lt. 17th Durham L.I., afterwards Capt. and Adjt. Labour Corps, attd. H.Q. XVII Corps. France, for 2 years 8 months.
1887 Brown, R. C. (May 6, 1915). Capt. 7th Rifle Brigade. France, 1915–17. *M.C.*, Nov. 14, 1916.
1891 Browne, Rev. L. (Serving Aug. 4, 1914). Chaplain (4th Class), 5th D.C.L.I.
Bruce, R. L. (Sept. 22, 1914). Lt. 11th Cameronians. France. Killed in action on Nov. 19, 1916.
1910 Bruce-James, L. W. Pte. R. Fusiliers. (Discharged.)
1914 **Brutton,* E. W.** (Apr. 8, 1915). Lt. 3rd Devonshire Regt. and M.G.C. France, Belgium. *M.C.*, Sept. 26, 1916. Killed in action at Ravelsburg Ridge, near Neuve Eglise, on Apr. 14, 1918.
1912 Buckley,* C. H. S., B.A. (Sept. 30, 1914). ‡Capt. 1st Devonshire Regt. France, 3 years; Italy, 4 months.
1919 Buckley, J. D. (Mar. 15, 1917). Pte. 275th Area Employment Coy., XVII Corps H.Q., Labour Corps. France, 1917–19.
Buckmaster, R. N. L. (Sept. 1, 1915). Capt. 4th Loyal N. Lancashire Regt. (Adjt.). France, Belgium, 1916–17. *D.* France, 1917. Killed in action near Vauxcalette Farm, Epéhy, on Nov. 30, 1917.
1907 Bull,* W. R., B.A. (Dec. 11, 1914). Capt. R.A.S.C. France.
1919 Burgess, D. S. (Dec. 13, 1916). Gnr. 111th Howitzer Batt., A.I.F. France.
1909 Burn,* E. F. (Nov. 9, 1914). Lt. 9th Somerset L.I. Capt. General List. Staff-Lt. France. *O.B.E.* (Mil.). *D.* France, 1918.
1901 Burne, Rev. R. V. H., M.A. (Aug. 14, 1917). Chaplain to the Forces (4th Class). France, 1917–19.
1894 Burnett, K., M.A. (1914). ‡Lt. R.A.S.C.
1907 **Burr,* F. B.,** M.A. (Aug. 5, 1914). 2nd Lt. 3rd Worcestershire Regt. (Capt.). France, Belgium, 1914–15. Killed in action at Kemmel on Mar. 12, 1915.
1912 Burrell, B. R. (formerly Isaacs, B. R. B.) (Mar. 28, 1915). Lt. 8th Middlesex Regt. (Invalided.)

1909 Burton,* R. C. (July 26, 1915). Capt. R.A.S.C. France, 1915–16, 1918.
1900 **Bury, W. E.,** B.A. (Dec. 1914). Pte. 1st Canadian Mounted Rifles. France, Belgium, 1915–17. Died on Nov. 15, 1917, of wounds received in action at Passchendaele on Nov. 13.
1911 Bye, T. F. (1915). Pte. R. Fusiliers.
1913 **Caesar,* C. P.** (Aug. 1914). Lt. 7th Shropshire L.I. France, Belgium. Killed in action in the Battle of the Somme on July 14, 1916.
1911 **Cameron, R. D.** (Aug. 29, 1914). Lt. 6th Q.O. Cameron Highlanders. France. Killed in action at the Battle of Loos on Sept. 26, 1915.
1894 Camm, C. B., B.A. (Dec. 12, 1914). Capt. 4th Hampshire Regt. Staff-Capt. to Adjt.-General.
1883 Camm, Rev. Dom Bede, B.A. (Aug. 27, 1915). Chaplain to the Forces (4th Class) (R.C.), attd. Command Depot, Mustapha, Alexandria. Egypt, 1915–19.
1904 Campbell, Rev. E. C., M.A. (Jan. 20, 1917). Chaplain to the Forces (4th Class). France, Belgium, 1917, 1918.
1919 Candy, R. (June 1, 1916). ‡2nd Lt. M.G.C. France.
1919 Card, H. (Apr. 23, 1917). 1st Class Aircraftsman, R.A.F.
1914 **Carey, M. E.,** B.A. (Apr. 4, 1917). 2nd Lt. 6th The Buffs (E. Kent Regt.) (Capt.). France. *M.C.*, Apr. 22, 1918. Missing, believed killed in action on Nov. 30, 1917.
1898 Carleton, Rev. E. B., B.A. (Sept. 6, 1918). Chaplain to the Forces (4th Class).
1899 Carleton, H. H., D.M. (May 6, 1915). Capt. R.A.M.C. France.
1907 **Carrington,* E. W.,** B.M., B.Ch., M.A. (Aug. 1914). Capt. R.A.M.C. M.O. 2nd Worcestershire Regt. France. *M.C.*, Feb. 18, 1915. *D.* France, 1915 twice. Killed in action at the Battle of Loos on Sept. 27, 1915.
1919 Cartridge, L. E. (Jan. 1918). ‡2nd Lt. E. Yorkshire Regt. attd. R.A.F.
1903 Caswell, Rev. H. C., M.A. (Aug. 1918). Chaplain to the Forces (4th Class). France, Belgium, Germany.
1903 [Caton-Thompson, A. P.] (1914). 2nd Lt. Border Regt. (Resigned.)
1912 Cattley,* L. A., M.A. (Oct. 2, 1914). Maj. 11th E. Yorkshire Regt. Egypt, 1915–16; France, 1916–18. (Wounded prisoner of war in Germany, Apr.–Dec. 1918.) *M.C.*, Jan. 1, 1918.
1901 Caudwell, L. V., M.A. (June, 1916). Lt. 4th E. Surrey Regt. (Maj.). France.
1888 **Cawood, W. B. C.,** M.A. (Mobilized Aug. 4, 1914). Capt. R.F.A. India. Died in India on May 24, 1915.
1887 [Cecil, Rt. Hon. Lord Hugh, M.A., *M.P.*] (Apr. 1915). Capt., Administrative Officer, R.A.F.
1891 Champernowne, Rev. J. E., M.A. (July 3, 1918). Pte. R.A.M.C.
1914 Chandler, G. E., B.A. (Oct. 17, 1915). Lt. 11th Essex Regt. France.
1914 Chatfield, A. W. F., B.A. Pte. Inns of Court O.T.C.
Chepmell, W. D. (Sept. 22, 1914). Lt. 9th R. Sussex Regt., attd. T.M.B. France. Killed in action at Souchez on Apr. 12, 1917.
1885 Child, Rev. A. G., M.A. (Sept. 1914). Chaplain 1/7th Cheshire Regt. (Chaplain, 3rd Class). Gallipoli, Egypt, Palestine. *D.* Egypt, 1916.
1908 Churchill,* Rev. R. R., M.A. (Sept. 1, 1915). Chaplain R.N., H.M.S. *Monarch*. Grand Fleet.

1912 Churchyard,* J. H., B.A. (Aug. 30, 1914). Capt. R.A.S.C. (Maj.). France, Belgium. *D.* § Mar. 1918.

1913 Clark,* A. N. L. (Aug. 5, 1914). Capt., Acting Maj., 10th W. Yorkshire Regt. France, Belgium.

1919 Clarke, E. A. C. (Oct. 7, 1917). Pte. Army Pay Corps.

1893 Clarke, L. E., B.A. (Nov. 1914). Maj. R.A.S.C. Salonika.

1917 Clarke, W. K., B.A. (Sept. 3, 1914). ‡Lt. 3rd Bedfordshire Regt., attd. No. 4 O.C.B. France, 1915–16.

1919 Clarkson, T. C. (June 6, 1917). 2nd Lt. 11th Rifle Brigade. France.

1888 Clauss, P. R., M.A. (Sept. 1914). Lt. Unattached List, T.F., Cheltenham College O.T.C.

1902 Clayton, Rev. J. F., M.A. (June 6, 1916). Chaplain to the Forces (4th Class). France. *M.C.*, July 26, 1918.

1919 Clift, A. H. (Apr. 5, 1917). Signaller R.G.A. Italy.

1903 Close,* Rev. R. B. M., M.A. (Sept. 18, 1914). Chaplain R.N. Gallipoli, 1915; Grand Fleet, 1916–17; France, 1917–18. *O.B.E.* (Mil.). *D.* Gallipoli, 1916.

1914 Clutsom, C. A. (Dec. 22, 1914). Lt. 5th Oxf. & Bucks. Lt. Infty. (Capt.). France, 1915–16, 1917–18.

1919 Cobby, A. H. (Aug. 14, 1914). ‡Lt. 430th Batt., 53rd Bde., R.F.A. (Capt.). Egypt, 1915; Salonika, 1915–17; Palestine, 1917–19.

1919 Cocker, C. S. (July 31, 1915). Lt. 2/5th Loyal N. Lancashire Regt. France.

1911 Cocker, N. A., M.A. (July 30, 1915). Lt. 10th Manchester Regt. Egypt.

1915 **Coles, A. E.** (Mar. 28, 1916). ‡2nd Lt. 1st Somerset L.I., attd. T.M.B. France, Belgium. Killed in action on Oct. 4, 1917.

Collen, N. O. (July 1915). 2nd Lt. 1st E. Yorkshire Regt. France, 1916. Killed in action near Flers on Sept. 25, 1916.

1919 Collignon, P. L. (Feb. 27, 1918). Pte. 15th Queen's (R. W. Surrey Regt.), afterwards Sergt. H.Q. XVII Corps R.L.C. France, 1918–19. *M.S.M.*, June 3, 1919.

1897 Collins, L. P. (Jan. 5, 1901). Maj., temp. Lt.-Col., 4th Gurkha Rifles, Indian Army. India, France, Gallipoli. *D.S.O.*, May 8, 1915. *D.* Gallipoli, 1915, 1916.

1900 Collinson, Rev. H., B.A. (Jan. 2, 1918). Chaplain to the Forces (4th Class), attd. 52nd R. Sussex Regt. France, Belgium, Germany.

1919 Colthurst, R. T. (July 27, 1917). 2nd Lt. C/235th Bde., R.F.A. France, 1918–19.

1892 Compton, Rev. J., M.A. (July 3, 1917). Chaplain to the Forces (4th Class).

1908 **Comyn,* R. M.** Pte. 9th Cameronians. France. Died at Avesnes on Jan. 6, 1917, of illness contracted on active service.

1918 Coney, H. R. H., B.A. (Aug. 4, 1914). Cpl. 15th London Regt. (Civil Service Rifles). France, Belgium, 1915–17. *M.S.M.*, Oct. 18, 1916. *D.* France, 1916.

1911 Constable,* O. C., B.A. (July 12, 1915). Lt. 6th Worcestershire Regt., attd. No. 4 O.C.B. France, 1916–17.

1910 **Cooke,* D.**, B.A. (Mar. 22, 1914). Capt. 3rd, attd. 1st, The Black Watch. France, Belgium, 1914–15, 1916–18. Killed in action at Givenchy on Apr. 18, 1918.

1911 Cooke,* L. D. (Sept. 19, 1914). Capt. 5th Dorsetshire Regt. Gallipoli, 1915; France, 1916–19.

1912 Cooke-Yarborough,* G. M., B.A. (Aug. 22, 1914). Lt. R. Monmouth Engineers (S.R.). Italy. Croce di Guerra. *D.* Italy, 1918.

1894 Cooper, H. E. S., M.A. (Nov. 25, 1915). Lt. 5th Essex Regt. (Capt.).

1909 Cooper,* H. G. (Oct. 28, 1915). ‡Capt. I.A.R.O., attd. King George's Own Baluchis (Staff-Capt.). E. Africa, 1914–17; India, 1917–18; Persia, 1918–19. *M.C.*, Jan. 1, 1918. *D.C.M.*, July 14, 1917. *D.* E. Africa, 1916.

1901 Cooper, Rev. W., M.A. (Dec. 20, 1915). Chaplain to the Forces (4th Class).

1919 Corbishley, J. W. (Dec. 25, 1915). Lt. R.H.A. (T.F.), attd. Ministry of Munitions. France, 1916.

1908 Cory,* Rev. A., M.A. (Apr. 2, 1917). Chaplain to the Forces (4th Class). France, 1918.

1908 **Cotterill,* J. H.,** B.A. (June 8, 1915). 2nd Lt. 3rd, attd. 2nd, The Black Watch. Mesopotamia. Died on Mar. 15, 1917, of wounds received in action at Mashadie.

1919 Coulson, C. S. L. (Oct. 12, 1916). ‡Lt. R.A.F. (Capt.). France, 1918. *D.F.C.*, Aug. 9, 1918. *D.* France, 1918.

1909 Court,* Rev. N. H., M.A. (Aug. 7, 1918). Chaplain to the Forces (4th Class). France.

1912 Courtney,* L. G., B.A. (May 18, 1916). Lt. 18th Bn. Army Cyclist Corps (T.F.) (Capt.). France, 1917–18, 1918–19.

1904 **Coutts, N. V.,** M.A. (Dec. 22, 1914). 2nd Lt. 9th E. Surrey Regt. France. Killed in action on Oct. 11, 1915.

1902 Cowland-Cooper, Rev. C. P. (Sept. 19, 1916). Chaplain to the Forces (4th Class). Palestine.

1882 Craddock, Sir R. H., *K.C.S.I.* Hon. Comdt. 18th Rangoon Bn., I.D.F.

1908 **Crane,* R. H.,** B.A., B.Sc. (Jan. 27, 1916). ‡2nd Lt. E. Yorkshire Regt. France, Belgium. Killed in action at Polygon Wood on Oct. 4, 1917.

1905 Crawford, O. G. S., B.A. (Sept. 1, 1914). ‡2nd Lt. R. Berkshire Regt., afterwards Lt. R.A.F. (Staff-Lt.). France, 1914–18. *D.* France, 1918. (Prisoner of war, Feb.–Dec. 1918.)

1907 Creasy,* Rev. L. S., M.A. (Feb. 1917). Chaplain R.N., H.M.S. *Thunderer*. Grand Fleet.

1901 **Creighton, Rev. O.,** M.A. (Nov. 16, 1914). Chaplain to the Forces (4th Class). France. *D.* France, 1915. Killed in action on Apr. 15, 1918.

1877 Crofts, E. S. (Serving Aug. 4, 1914). Lt.-Col. 13th Hampshire Regt. (Resigned.) Re-employed by Ministry of National Service.

1910 **Crowley,* C. H.,** B.A. (Aug. 5, 1914). 2nd Lt. 4th, attd. 2nd, R. Warwickshire Regt. France. Killed in action on Apr. 25, 1915.

1896 **Crowley, J. C.,** M.A. (Mobilized Aug. 4, 1914). Lt., temp. Capt., 4th Queen's (R. W. Surrey Regt.). India, 1914–16; Mesopotamia, 1916. Killed in action at Nasiriyeh on Sept. 11, 1916.

1913 Crowley,* R. (Aug. 15, 1914). Lt. 3rd R. Sussex Regt. France, 1914. (Invalided.)

1903 Cruickshank, Rev. G. C., M.A. (Oct. 29, 1915). Chaplain to the Forces (4th Class), attd. N.Z.E.F. France.

1905 Curtis, Sir R. C. M., Bt., B.A. (Dec. 13, 1915). Capt. R.A.S.C. France. *D.* France, 1917.

1919 Dakin, G. F. (July 8, 1915). Capt. 8th York and Lancaster Regt. France, Belgium, 1917; Italy, 1917–18; Fiume, Austria, 1918–19. *M.C.*, Jan. 1, 1919. Croce di Guerra.

1905 Dalton, J. C. (Mar. 1, 1915). Capt. Northamptonshire Yeomanry. France, 1916–17.

1913 Dancaster, A. C., B.A. (Nov. 18, 1916). ‡2nd Lt. R.G.A. France, 1917, 1918–19.

1893 Dansey, G. R. (May 23, 1916). Pte. 50th Bn., C.E.F. France.

1913 **Darby,* W. E. C. A.** (Mar. 12, 1915). Lt. 1st Monmouthshire Regt. France. Killed in action on Oct. 13, 1915.

1893 Darvell, S., M.A. (Oct. 19, 1914). Capt. Denbighshire Hussars, attd. 5th S. Wales Borderers. France, Belgium.

1893 Dashwood, C. W. L., B.A. (Mar. 12, 1917). Pte. 3rd (Garr.) R. Welch Fusiliers.

1878 Daubeny, C. W. (Nov. 2, 1914). Capt. 7th Shropshire L.I.

1910 David,* A. C. R., B.A. (Nov. 30, 1914). Lt., Acting Maj., 112th Bde., R.F.A. France, 1915–17, 1918–19. *M.C.*, Sept. 26, 1917.

1914 David, T. L. (July 8, 1915). Capt. York and Lancaster Regt., attd. 75th T.M.B. Gallipoli, 1915; Egypt, 1916; France, 1916–18. *D.* France, 1918.

1910 **David,* T. W.,** B.A. (Dec. 1, 1914). Capt. 15th Welsh Regt. France, Belgium, 1917. Killed in action at Ypres on July 27, 1917.

1913 Davies, B. K., B.A. (July 27, 1918). Asst. Paymaster R.N.V.R.

1911 **Davies, Rev. E. G. E.,** B.A. A.B., Hawke Bn., R.N. Div. France. Killed in action on Jan. 27, 1916.

1911 **Davies, H. B.** (June 26, 1915). 2nd Lt. 3rd, attd. 1st, W. Yorkshire Regt. France. Killed in action on Apr. 23, 1916.

1919 Davies, H. R. (Sept. 16, 1914). ‡Lt., Acting Capt., 14th R. Welch Fusiliers, attd. H.Q. Staff, 38th Div. France, 1915–19. *M.C.*, Dec. 2, 1918.

1919 Davies, J. E. E. (Dec. 6, 1917). Pte. 4th E. Surrey Regt. Acting Cpl. 2nd Reception Bn., Salisbury. France.

1915 Davies,* J. L. J., B.A. (Dec. 11, 1915). Pte. S. Wales Borderers. (Discharged.)

1911 [Davies, J. L. T., B.A.] (Dec. 22, 1914). Lt. 10th R. Welch Fusiliers, afterwards Lt. and Adjt. R.A.F. Belgium, France, 1915–16.

1908 Davies, Rev. J. T., M.A. (Oct. 4, 1915). Chaplain to the Forces (4th Class).

1913 Davies, J. T. (Sept. 30, 1914). Capt. 6th Welsh Regt., attd. Labour Corps.

1907 Davies,* Rev. R. H., B.A. S. African Field Ambulance.

Davies, T. D. Pte. R. Fusiliers. France. Missing, believed killed in action on July 23, 1916.

1919 Day, G. E. (June 19, 1918). 2nd Lt. R.E. (on demobilization).

1902 Deane, Rev. E. N., B.A. (June 25, 1916). Chaplain to the Forces (4th Class).

1898 De Fontaine, B. L., B.A. Hartigan's Horse, S. Africa.

1906 Dennis,* A. W., B.M., M.A. (Aug. 20, 1914). Capt. R.A.M.C. France. *D.* France, 1916, 1917, 1919.

1915 Dennis, C. P. L. (May 29, 1916). ‡2nd Lt. R.A.S.C. Italy, Salonika, Trans-Caucasia.

1919 Derry, R. L. (Aug. 9, 1917). Lt. 3rd R. Inniskilling Fusiliers. France, Belgium.
1919 de Saram, R. S. (Jan. 1918). Pte. Ceylon Medical Corps. Ceylon.
1919 de Smidt, H. E. (Sept. 29, 1918). 2nd Lt. R.A.F.
1919 Dewar, Rev. L. (Aug. 10, 1916). Chaplain to the Forces (4th Class). France, 1916–17.
1913 Dickinson,* C. J., B.A. (Feb. 10, 1915). 2nd Lt. 8th R. W. Kent Regt. Capt. Administrative Officer, R.A.F.
1914 Dickinson, E. D. (Mar. 4, 1917). ‡2nd Lt. 10th King's (Liverpool Regt.). France, Salonika.
1911 Dickinson, F. G. C. (Feb. 10, 1915). Lt. 3rd Gloucestershire Regt. Lt. Administrative Officer, R.A.F.
1894 Dickson, E. A. (Jan. 26, 1918). Lt. R.A.S.C. Egypt, Palestine.
1910 **Dingle,* A. J.,** B.A. (Sept. 1914). Lt. 6th E. Yorkshire Regt. (Capt.). Gallipoli. Killed in action at Suvla Bay on Aug. 22, 1915.
1919 Doak, J. S. B. (Feb. 25, 1918). Gnr. 1st Bde. Australian F.A.
1899 Dolben, A. C. F., B.A. (Nov. 1914). ‡Lt. M.G.C. (Capt.). India.
1919 Donne, E. F. (Aug. 21, 1917). Lce.-Cpl. 3/5th London Regt. (London Rifle Brigade). France, for 9 months.
1919 Donovan, C. P. M. (May 1, 1918). Cadet R.F.A., No. 3 Cadet School.
1890 Douglas, Rev. A. W., M.A. (Apr. 23, 1917). Chaplain R.N., H.M.S. *Lucia.*
1919 Douglas, D. C. (Aug. 9, 1918). Pte. Inns of Court O.T.C.
1902 Douglas, J. A., B.Sc., M.A. (Sept. 9, 1914). Capt. 3rd Gordon Highlanders (attd. R.E.). France, Belgium.
1915 Douthwaite, P. H. (July 12, 1916). Pte. 18th Durham L.I. France, 1917, 1918; Italy, 1917–1918.
1919 Dowden, H. J. (Jan. 1, 1917). Lt. 'B' Batt., 312th Bde., R.F.A. France, Belgium, Germany. *M.C.*, Jan. 11, 1919.
1900 Downing, H. C., M.A. (Oct. 6, 1914). Capt. 5th Welsh Regt. Gallipoli, Egypt, Palestine. *D.* Palestine, 1917.
1910 **Doyne,* P. D.,** B.A. (Sept. 1914). Lt. 1/4th Oxf. & Bucks. Lt. Infty. (Capt.). France, 1915. Killed in action at Hébuterne on Dec. 28, 1915.
1910 Drake, B. J. L., B.A. (Feb. 23, 1915). 2nd Lt. D.C.L.I. Lt. M.G.C.
1914 Draper, J. G. B. (Mar. 13, 1915). Lt. 3rd, attd. 2nd, K.O.Y.L.I. France.
1919 Drewe, E. M. (May 17, 1917). Pte. 1st Res. Bn. H.A.C.
1913 **Drummond, H. M.** (Aug. 22, 1914). 2nd Lt. 8th, attd. 9th The Black Watch. France. Died on May 26, 1916, of wounds received in action.
1919 Drummond-Hay, J. C. (Sept. 20, 1916). Cpl. 29th Bn. A.I.F. France, Belgium, 1917.
1908 Dudley, Ed., M.A. (May 30, 1918). Pte. Inns of Court O.T.C.
1903 Dudley, Eus., B.A. (Apr. 28, 1916). Lt. Saskatchewan Regt., C.E.F.
1919 Duncan, D. A. (June 15, 1916). Lt. 4th King's Own (R. Lancaster Regt.). France, Belgium, 1917–18. *M.C.*, Feb. 15, 1919.
1900 Duppuy, Rev. C. R., M.A. (Mar. 5, 1918). Chaplain to the Forces (4th Class). France.
1887 Durell, T. C. D., B.A. (Apr. 23, 1916). Lt. Special Lists. Staff-Lt. (1st Class). R.T.O. Chevalier, Ordre du Mérite Agricole.
1899 Durst, W. H., B.A. (Sept. 4, 1914). Maj. 9th King's Own (R. Lancaster Regt.). Temp. Lt.-Col. 9th Border Regt. France, 1915; Salonika, 1915–19; Constantinople, 1919. *M.C.*, Nov. 25, 1916.

1913 Dutton, E. A. T. (Aug. 21, 1914). Maj. 9th W. Yorkshire Regt. Gallipoli. *D.* Gallipoli, 1915. (Invalided.)

Eagar, D. G. (July 1917). 2nd Lt. R.F.A. France, Belgium. Killed in action at Wytschaete Wood on Sept. 28, 1918.

1898 Eardley-Wilmot, Rev. H. V., M.A. (June 10, 1918). Chaplain to the Forces (4th Class).

1899 Eaves, J. M. (Oct. 3, 1914). Capt. R.A.S.C. (D.A.Q.M.G., 19th Div.). France, Belgium, 1915–19; Germany, 1919. *D.* France, 1918.

1906 Edington, Rev. A. F. H., B.A. (Oct. 5, 1915). Rifleman 5th London Regt. (London Rifle Brigade), afterwards Chaplain to the Forces (4th Class). France, 1915–19. *M.M.*, July 1, 1916.

1908 Edkins,* F. J., M.A. (Aug. 10, 1915). Lt. 3rd City of London Regt. (R. Fusiliers), attd. Min. of Mun. (Capt.). France, Belgium, 1915–16.

1899 Edwards, Rev. H. T. A., M.A. (Oct. 9, 1914). Chaplain to the Forces (4th Class).

1919 Edwards, W. L. (May 5, 1915). Lt. Lancashire Fusiliers, attd. 1/5th Bn. (Capt.). Sinai, 1916–17; France, 1917–18; Germany, 1919.

1896 Elgood, Rev. H. F., M.A. (Jan. 13, 1915). Chaplain to the Forces (3rd Class). France. *M.C.*, Aug. 25, 1917. *D.* France, 1916, 1919.

1905 Elias, T. (Mar. 11, 1915). Capt. 15th R. Welch Fusiliers.

1910 Ellis,* J. C., B.A. (Apr. 6, 1915). Capt. 16th R. Welch Fusiliers, empld. War Office.

1912 Ellis,* W. E., B.A., B.Sc. (Sept. 1, 1914). Cpl. Wessex Div. Sig. Coy., R.E. France, 1914. (Invalided.)

1908 Ellwood,* Rev. C. J., M.A. (June 25, 1917). Chaplain to the Forces (4th Class).

1903 Elstob, N. C., M.A. (Jan. 1, 1915). Capt. 2nd Monmouthshire Regt. France.

1894 Elwell, J. H., M.A. (May 11, 1915). Lt., temp. Capt., General List. Staff-Lt. (2nd Class). France. *D.* France.

1899 **Elwell, R. W. D.,** M.A. (1915). Pte. 56th Canadian Inf. Died at Calgary on Oct. 31, 1915.

1909 **Emmet,* F. H.,** B.A. (Aug. 1914). Capt. 9th Leicestershire Regt. France, 1915–16. Killed in action at Bazentin Wood on July 14, 1916.

1900 Eteson, Rev. F. B., B.A. (Mar. 18, 1918). Chaplain to the Forces (4th Class).

1911 Evans, Rev. C. N. M., M.A. (Apr. 5, 1918). Chaplain to the Forces (4th Class).

1907 Evans, Rev. D. G., M.A. (Oct. 4, 1915). Chaplain to the Forces (4th Class), attd. 1st Lancashire Fusiliers. Gallipoli, Mediterranean, France.

1913 Evans,* G. M. O. (Mar. 21, 1915). Lt. Brecknock Bn., S. Wales Borderers.

1908 Evans,* J. F., M.A. (Aug. 1914). ‡Lt., Acting Capt., 12th Norfolk Regt., attd. No. 1 O.C.B. France, 1915–16.

1912 Evans-Jones,* P. J. D., B.A. (Jan. 1915). 2nd Lt. 6th R. Welch Fusiliers. Lt. 3rd King's (Liverpool Regt.). Acting Staff-Captain Embarkation Dept., Indian Army. Gallipoli, Egypt, India, 1915–19. *D.* India.

1889 Everington, E. A., B.A. Anti-Aircraft Corps.

1919 Fair, H. I. (Apr. 15, 1917). 1st Lt. 101st Inf., U.S. Army (Capt.). France. *D.* American Divl. Orders, twice.

1881 Fairbrother, W. H., M.A. (Oct. 12, 1914). Capt. 4th R. Warwickshire Regt., attd. O.C.B. *D.* § Feb. 1917.

1900 Falkner, E. B., M.A. (May 17, 1916). Lt. R.N.V.R., afterwards Capt. R.A.F.

1913 Farmar, F. W., M.A. (Sept. 2, 1914). Pte. 13th R. Fusiliers. France, 1915–18.

1911 Farrar,* A. D. M., M.A. (Sept. 1914). Maj. 17th R. Welch Fusiliers, attd. No. 16 O.C.B. Gallipoli, 1915; Mesopotamia, 1916–17. *D.S.O.*, Mar. 17, 1917. *D.* Mesopotamia, 1917.

1880 Farrar, R. A., D.M. (Mobilized Aug. 4, 1914). Maj. R.A.M.C. (Sanitary Section). France. Chevalier de l'Ordre de la Couronne.

1892 Faunthorpe, B. P., B.A. (Dec. 9, 1917). 2nd Lt. Labour Corps (Capt.).

1899 Fawcett, E., B.A. (July 1915). Capt. 2nd Durham L.I. France. *M.C.*, Feb. 4, 1918. (Prisoner of war.)

1902 Felton, R. H., M.A. (Apr. 17, 1915). Lt. 8th Wiltshire Regt. Capt. M.G.C. Education Officer, attd. General Staff (Maj.). Mesopotamia, 1916–19. *D.* Mesopotamia, 1917.

1894 Fenn, B. S., B.A. (Feb. 23, 1917). 2nd Lt. R.A.S.C.

1904 **Fenton, B. L.,** M.A. (1914). Maj. 1st Dorsetshire Regt. France. Killed in action in the Battle of the Somme on July 15, 1916.

Field, C. C. (Sept. 1914). 2nd Lt. R.W. Kent Regt., attd. Suffolk Regt. France, Belgium. Killed in action at St. Eloi on Mar. 30, 1916.

1919 Fieldhouse, S. W. (May 14, 1918). Rfln. 7th W. Yorkshire Regt. (Leeds Rifles).

1890 Fielding-Ould, R., D.M. (Serving Aug. 4, 1914). Capt. R.A.M.C. (resigned).

1896 Field Richards, J. C. (Serving Aug. 4, 1914). Maj. Hampshire Regt.; Dep. Asst. Mil. Sec., War Office. *O.B.E.* (Mil.). Croix de Guerre with palm. *D.* § Mar. and Aug. 1918.

1889 Finch, H. E. Capt. N.Z. Medical Corps.

1902 Firth, D. (Serving Aug. 4, 1914). Maj. 2nd W. Riding Regt., attd. No. 13 O.C.B. France. *D.* § Mar. 1919.

1910 Firth,* F. J. W., M.A. (Serving Aug. 4, 1914). Capt. 6th King Edward's Own Cavalry, Indian Army (Maj.). India; France, 1916–18; Palestine, 1918; Syria; Asia Minor, 1919.

1894 Fisher, H. J., B.A. (1914). Lt. Inns of Court O.T.C. (spec. empld.).

1905 Fisher, Rev. W. F. O'N., M.A. (June 1917). Pte. Canadian A.M.C. ‡ Chaplain Canadian E.F. (Hon. Capt.). France, Belgium, Germany.

1902 FitzGerald, S. G. V., M.A. (June 20, 1918). 2nd Lt. I.A.R.O., attd. 3/153rd Rifles. India.

1913 **FitzGibbon, B. N. R.** (Oct. 1914). Lt. 6th R. Irish Regt. France, Belgium, 1915–16. *D.* France, 1916. Killed in action in Belgium on Aug. 21, 1916.

1901 [Flack, M. W., B.M., M.A.] (Oct. 21, 1915). Hon. Maj. R.A.M.C. Hon. Wing-Commdr. (Lt.-Col.) Director of Medical Research, R.A.F. *C.B.E.* (Mil.). *D.* § Aug. 1917.

1891 Floyd, Rev. T. O., M.A. (Aug. 1917). Chaplain to the Forces (4th Class).

1904 Foord, Rev. N. F. E., M.A. (Mar. 12, 1917). Chaplain to the Forces (4th Class).

1920 Formby, E. L. (Aug. 10, 1915). Capt., Staff Capt., X Corps H.Q., R.A. France, 1915–17; France, Germany, 1918–19.

1912 **Forrest,* A. L.** (Sept. 1914). 2nd Lt. 11th K.R.R.C. France, 1916. Killed in action on Sept. 3, 1916.

1915 Forrest, J. D. D. (May 5, 1917). Lt. 2/90th Punjabis, Indian Army (Capt.). India.

1902 Forsdyke, E. J., M.A. (Apr. 20, 1915). Capt. R.H.A. (T.F.). France.

1902 Foster-Palmer, Rev. C., M.A. (Nov. 1, 1918). Chaplain to the Forces (4th Class). France, Holland.

1919 Fothergill, E. L. (Aug. 8, 1918). Cadet, R.E., O.C.B.

Fox, A. (Mar. 26, 1915). 2nd Lt. 3rd, attd. 1st, Shropshire L.I. (Capt.). France. *M.C.*, May 31, 1916. Killed in action on May 8, 1917.

1912 Fox,* D. G. A., B.A. (Jan. 26, 1916). Lt. 4th Gloucestershire Regt. France, 1916–17. (Invalided.)

1912 **Fox,* W. A.** (Aug. 4, 1914). 2nd Lt. 1/4th Lincolnshire Regt. France, Belgium. Killed in action at Hill 60 on July 29, 1915.

1902 Francis, A. J. H., B.A. (June 29, 1917). 2nd Lt. 82nd Siege Batt., R.G.A. France, 1918; Germany, 1919.

1897 Francis, Rev. G. H., M.A. (May 24, 1917). Chaplain to the Forces (4th Class), attd. 3rd Tank Bde. France, 1917–19.

1913 Fraser, Rev. A. E. (Aug. 7, 1914). Chaplain R.N. North Sea.

1901 **Freestone, Rev. W. H.,** M.A. (June 6, 1916). Chaplain to the Forces (4th Class). Mesopotamia. Killed in action on Dec. 14, 1916.

1902 French, Rev. A., B.A. Pte. Inf. Bn. Canadian E.F.

1912 Frere, J. G., B.A. (Dec. 17, 1914). Lt., temp. Capt., Suffolk Regt., attd. M.G.C. (Maj. C.M.G.O.), attd. Headquarters, V Corps. France, Belgium, 1914–16, 1917–19. *D.S.O.*, June 3, 1919. *M.C.*, Jan. 1, 1918. *D.* France, 1915, 1916 twice, 1919.

1899 Fulford, G. L., B.A. (Aug. 1914). ‡Lt. 2/6th, attd. 1/4th, Devonshire Regt. (Capt.). India, 1914–16; Mesopotamia, 1917.

1902 **Furley, R. B.,** B.A. Pte. 28th R. Fusiliers. France. Killed in action on Oct. 7, 1916.

1895 Gallop, Rev. E. H., M.A. (June 7, 1916). Chaplain to the Forces (4th Class).

1891 Gantz, Rev. W. L., M.A. (May 1, 1918). Chaplain to the Forces (4th Class).

1899 Gardner, Rev. E. A., M.A. (Serving Aug. 1914). Chaplain to the Forces (3rd Class), attd. 6th Essex Regt. Gallipoli, Egypt. *M.C.*, June 3, 1916. Order of the Nile (3rd Class). *D.* Gallipoli, 1916.

1919 Gargery, E. J. (July 16, 1917). Pte. R.A.O.C. Mesopotamia.

1911 **Garland,* W.** (Dec. 1914). 2nd Lt. 7th Oxf. & Bucks. Lt. Infty. (Capt.). France, Salonika, Balkans. *D.* Salonika, 1917. Killed in action on Salonika Front on May 9, 1917.

1899 Gaul, Rev. A. C., M.A. (Oct. 20, 1914). Pte. 12th (Pretoria) Regt., S.A.F., afterwards Chaplain S.A. Overseas Bde. German S.W. Africa, 1915; France, 1916–18; India, 1918–19; Aden, 1919.

1919 Gay, P. (Feb. 27, 1915). Lt. 3rd Devonshire Regt. (Capt. and Adjt.). France.

1910 Geary,* B. H. (Aug. 14, 1914). Capt. 4th E. Surrey Regt. France, Belgium, 1914–15, 1916–18. **V.C.**

For most conspicuous bravery and determination on Hill 60, near Ypres, on Apr. 20 and 21, 1915, when he held the left crater with his platoon, some men of the Bedfordshire Regiment, and a few reinforcements who came up during the evening and night. The crater was first exposed to very heavy artillery fire which broke down the defences, and afterwards throughout the night to repeated bomb attacks which filled it with dead and wounded. Each attack was, however, repulsed, mainly owing to the splendid personal gallantry and example of 2nd Lt. Geary. At one time he used a rifle with great effect, at another threw hand grenades, and exposed himself with entire disregard to danger in order to see by the light of flares where the enemy were coming on. In the intervals between the attacks he spent his whole time arranging for the ammunition supply and for reinforcements. He was severely wounded just before daylight on Apr. 21.

1919 Geer, A. M. (Oct. 9, 1917). Pte., Acting-Cpl., 'A' Bn., 302nd F.A., U.S. Army. France, 1918.

1913 Gethen,* R., B.A. (Aug. 10, 1914). Maj. 7th Norfolk Regt. (Lt.-Col.). France, 1915–19. *M.C.*, July 18, 1917. *D.* France, 1919.

1898 Gibbins, Rev. W. H., M.A. (Oct. 3, 1914). Chaplain R.N. (resigned).

1900 Gibbon, Rev. R. H., B.A. (Oct. 22, 1915). Chaplain to the Forces (4th Class).

1915 Gibbon, W. M. (Jan. 22, 1916). 2nd Lt. R.A.S.C. France, 1916–17.

1913 Gibbons,* A. G., B.A. (Dec. 22, 1914). 2nd Lt. 9th Oxf. & Bucks. Lt. Infty. Lt. R.E. France. *M.C.*, Apr. 22, 1918.

1904 **Gibbs, Rev. E. R.,** M.A. (Sept. 18, 1917). Chaplain to the Forces (4th Class). France, 1917–18. Killed in action on April 5, 1918.

1898 Gibbs, Rev. J. S., M.A. (Jan. 1915). Chaplain to the Forces (4th Class), attd. 3rd Cav. Div. (D.A.C.G.). France, 1915–19. *M.C.*, Jan. 1, 1919. *D.* France, 1917.

1893 Gibson, B. T., M.A. Tpr. 5th Punjab Light Horse.

1908 Gibson,* C. F. L., B.A. (Nov. 2, 1914). Capt. 5th R. Warwickshire Regt. France. *M.C.*, July 26, 1918. *D.* France, 1918.

1909 Gilbert, E. W., B.A. (July 3, 1918). Inns of Court O.T.C.

1902 Gilbertson, Rev. A. D., M.A. (Serving Aug. 4, 1914). Chaplain R.N. H.M.S. *Powerful*, 1914–16; H.M.S. *Tiger*, 1916–18; H.M.S. *Ganges*, 1918–19.

1919 Giles, Rev. R. A. (Apr. 15, 1918). Chaplain to the Forces, 13th Inf. Bde., 4th Div., A.I.F. France, Belgium.

1908 Gillett,* G. H., B.A. (Sept. 18, 1914). Lt. Unattached List, T.F., Honiton O.T.C.

1901 Gittins, Rev. O. E., M.A. (May 15, 1915). Chaplain to the Forces (4th Class) (Chaplain, 3rd Class). France, Egypt, Palestine, 1915–19. *D.* Palestine, 1918.

1912 Glaisyer, H., M.A. (Apr. 1, 1918). Lt. Technical Officer, R.A.F.

1906 Gleave, E. T., M.A. (Jan. 27, 1915). Capt. R.A.S.C., attd. Guards Div. France, Belgium, Germany.

1911 **Glenday,* F. G.** (Sept. 1914). Capt. 12th Northumberland Fusiliers, attd. R.F.C. France, 1915–16. Killed in aerial action on Sept. 15, 1916.

1917 Goch, W. S. (Oct. 1914). Pte. 1st Infantry Bn., A.I.F. Egypt, France.

1919 Gofton-Salmond, R. C. S. (Nov. 3, 1916). 2nd Lt. 2nd R. Sussex Regt., attd. Base Censor's Office, Alexandria. Egypt, 1917–19.

1888 Goodwin, A. C., B.M., M.A., M.Ch. (Oct. 5, 1914). Maj., Acting Lt.-Col., R.A.M.C. Palestine. *D.* Palestine, 1918.

1910 Goodwin,* J. C. (Mobilized Aug. 1914). Capt. 3rd King's Own (R. Lancaster Regt.).

1900 Goody, C. E. (Nov. 22, 1916). Lt. 6th, attd. 2nd, Rifle Brigade. France.
1912 Goody,* G. R., B.A. (Aug. 6, 1915). Lt. 2/4th Dorsetshire Regt., attd. 2/154th Indian Infantry (Capt.). India, 1916–17; Egypt, 1917–19. Died, July, 1919.
1898 Gordon, Rev. G., M.A. (Nov. 24, 1914). Lt. R.N.V.R., i/c M.L. 143. Mediterranean, Malta, Italy, 1918.
1894 Gordon, M. H., B.Sc., D.M. Hon. Lt.-Col. R.A.M.C. Officer i/c of Cerebrospinal Fever Lab. *C.M.G.*, Jan. 1, 1919. *C.B.E.* (Mil.). *D.* § July, 1917.
1910 Gore,* E. S. (Apr. 9, 1915). Lt. 4th N. Staffordshire Regt. France, 1916–17.
1903 [Goss, L. S., B.A.] (Mobilized Aug. 4, 1914). Pte. 28th London Regt. (Artists' Rifles), afterwards Surgeon Lt., R.N. France, 1914–15; Egypt, Red Sea, 1915–19. *O.B.E.* (Mil.). *D.* Egypt, 1917.
1914 Gosselin, G. (July 1, 1915). Lt. 4th R.W. Kent Regt. France, 1917.
1919 Gowing, L. E. (Nov. 27, 1917). 2nd Lt. Worcestershire Regt.
1919 Grabner, F. C. (July 3, 1917). Ordnance Sergt. 2nd Coy., 5th P.O.D., U.S. Army. France.
1912 Graves, Rev. L. A. W., M.A. (Apr. 5th, 1918). Chaplain to the Forces (4th Class). France, 1918–19.
Gray, C. S. (Aug. 1914). ‡2nd Lt. 3rd, attd. 1st, Wiltshire Regt. France, 1915–17. Died on Apr. 21, 1917, of wounds received in action.
1891 Greaves, Rev. A. I., M.A. (Aug. 6, 1917). Chaplain to the Forces (4th Class) (S.C.F.). France, 1917–18.
1897 Greaves, D. S. W., M.A. R.E.
1894 Greaves, H. M., B.A. (Serving Aug. 4, 1914). Maj. R.A. G.S.O. 2.
1919 Greene, G. S. (Sept. 4, 1914). ‡Capt. 5th Oxf. & Bucks. Lt. Infty. France, 1916–17.
1914 Gregory*, E. D., B.A. (June 22, 1915). Capt. 8th Devonshire Regt. France, 1916–17; Italy, 1917–19.
1882 Griffith, A. E., B.A. (Feb. 1915). Lt. R. Defence Corps.
1919 Griffith, P. (July 1917). Gentleman Cadet, R.M.C., Sandhurst.
1908 Griffiths,* A. W. M. (1914). ‡Lt. Rhodesia Regt. France. *D.C.M.*
1919 Grinham, R. (Aug. 4, 1914). ‡Lt. 8th Bn. Tank Corps. India, 1914–16; France, 1917–19.
1919 Groves, E. (Dec. 18, 1917). ‡2nd Lt. R.A.F.
Groves, R. F. (Oct. 19, 1916). Sapper, R.E. (A.D.D.). Died on Jan. 21, 1917, of illness contracted on active service.
1911 **Gruby,* T. W.,** B.A. (Aug. 26, 1915). 2nd Lt. 8th Border Regt. France. Died on July 19, 1916, of wounds received in action on the Somme.
1919 Gurley, R. H. (May 6, 1917). Sergt. 123rd M.G. Bn., U.S. Army (Sergt. (1st Class) Med. Dept.). France, 1918, 1919.
1910 **Hale,* D. P.,** B.A. Pte. A.S.C. Sept. 25, 1918.
1888 Hales, H. M. A. (Serving Aug. 4, 1914). Lt.-Col. 11th Gloucestershire Regt. France.
1892 Hales, Rev. J. R., M.A. (Aug. 5, 1914). Chaplain to the Forces (4th Class).
1909 Halet, Rev. J. P. H., M.A. (Mar. 16, 1916). Chaplain to the Forces (4th Class), attd. 1st Somerset L.I. France, 1916–19.
1908 **Hall, W. H.,** B.A. (Nov. 1915). ‡2nd Lt. R.F.A. France, Belgium. Killed in action on Sept. 28, 1917, at Zonnebeke.

1905 Hallows, N. F., D.M., M.A. (Aug. 13, 1914). Capt. R.A.M.C. France, Aug. 1914–15, 1917.

1897 Hammond, Rev. T. G., M.A. (Apr. 2, 1918). Chaplain to the Forces (4th Class).

1886 Hampson, J. N., B.A. (Sept. 24, 1914). Lt., 59th Protection Coy., R. Defence Corps.

1905 Hanbury, J. H. F., M.A. (Aug. 8, 1915). Pte. 16th Middlesex Regt., afterwards Cpl. R.A.F. France, Belgium, 1916–17. *D.C.M.* *M.M.* Belgian Croix de Guerre.

1913 **Hanforth,* C. H.** Pte. 12th York & Lancaster Regt. Died on Feb. 9, 1915.

1913 Harding,* J. A., M.A. (Nov. 24, 1914). Lt. Kent Cyclist Bn. India, 1916–19.

1904 Harding, J. B., B.A. (Jan. 20, 1915). Lt. 4th, attd. 6th, Shropshire L.I.

1916 **Harper, O. T.** (May 1916). 2nd Lt. Leicestershire Regt. France, 1918. Killed in action near Lagnicourt on Mar. 22, 1918.

1912 Harris,* R. C. (Serving Aug. 4, 1914). Lt. 1st Lancashire Fusiliers, attd. O.C.B. France, 1914–16.

1907 Harrison, W. A., M.A. (Mobilized Aug. 4, 1914). Capt. 4th, attd. 1/5th, The Buffs (E. Kent Regt.). India, Aden, 1914–16; Mesopotamia, 1916–19. *D.* Mesopotamia, 1917.

1912 Hartland-Rowe, R. C. (Nov. 1914). Lt. 1st Leinster Regt., attd. R.A.F. (1917). France, 1915; Salonika, 1916; Egypt, 1917.

1919 Harwood, F. (Oct. 5, 1917). 2nd Lt. 5th Sherwood Foresters. France, 1918.

1899 Hawkes, Rev. E. A., M.A. (Nov. 1917). Chaplain to the Forces (4th Class). France, 1918–19.

1900 Hawley-Edwards, S. F. (Apr. 25, 1916). Lt. Army Pay Dept. France. *D.* France, 1917.

1919 Haworth, R. A. L. (May 1, 1917). W/T Officer, Mercantile Marine, Naval Transport, and Fleet Auxiliary. Far East, S. America, Mediterranean.

1919 Haysom, R. A. (Sept. 6, 1914). ‡Capt. I.A.R.O. (31st Punjabis), attd. Mesopotamian Political Dept. India (Baluchistan Frontier), 1914–15; Mesopotamia, 1915–19.

1919 Haythornthwaite, R. A. (May 10, 1917). ‡Lt. R.F.A. France.

1913 Hayton,* J. S., M.A. (Oct. 6, 1914). Lt. R.H.A. France. *M.C.*, Aug. 16, 1917.

1901 Hayward, A. G. (May 5, 1915). Maj. 13th Essex Regt. Temp. Lt.-Col., 51st Devonshire Regt. France. *M.C.*, Sept. 26, 1916. *D.* France, 1917.

1913 **Hayward,* G. H.** (Nov. 25, 1914). Pte. 1st R. Fusiliers. France. Killed in action on April 5, 1917.

1901 Heald, Rev. B., M.A. (Serving Aug. 4, 1914). Capt. Unattached List, T.F., Epsom College O.T.C.

1919 Heath, N. (Mar. 16, 1917). ‡2nd Lt. Wiltshire Regt. France.

1919 Heaton, C. S., B.A. (Oct. 5, 1915). 2nd Lt. 4th Northumberland Fusiliers, afterwards Lt. R.A.F. (Capt.). France.

1908 Hedley,* Rev. P. F., M.A. (May 3, 1918). Chaplain to the Forces (4th Class).

1899 Helms, P. V., B.A. R.A.M.C.

1899 **Henderson, Rev. R. M.,** M.A. (March 29, 1914). Chaplain to the Forces (4th Class). Died on Feb. 3, 1919, of illness contracted while on active service.

1887 Henley, L. M., B.A. (March 24, 1915). Capt. R.A.S.C. *D.* § Mar. 1918.
1879 Henley, Rev. O. P. (Sept. 28, 1917). Chaplain to the Forces (4th Class). *D.* § Aug. 1919.
1901 Herklots, C. L., M.A. (Sept. 9, 1914). Capt. R.A.M.C. France, Salonika.
1873 Herringham, Sir W. P., D.M. (Serving Aug. 4, 1914). Maj.-Gen. Army Medical Service, Consulting Physician to Expeditionary Force. France, Belgium. *K.C.M.G.*, June 3, 1919. *C.B.* *D.* France, 1916, 1917, 1918, 1919.
1902 Hewitt, Rev. G. H., M.A. (Aug. 5, 1914). Chaplain, R.N., H.M.S. *Glory*.
1898 **Heywood, C. C.** (Nov. 10, 1915). Lt. B. Batt., 88th Bde., R.F.A. France, Belgium, 1917–18. Killed in action at Kemmel Hill on April 25, 1918.
1912 Higgins,* B., M.A. (Sept. 8, 1914). ‡Lt. 8th R. W. Kent Regt. France.
1910 Higgs,* Rev. H. R., M.A. (April 5, 1918). Chaplain to the Forces (4th Class). France, 1917–18.
1907 Higham, Rev. E. R. W., M.A. (Nov. 16, 1917). Chaplain R.N., H.M.S. *Astraea*.
1908 Hill,* E. E. St. L., B.A. (May, 1915). 2nd Lt. 19th Lancashire Fusiliers. Lt. R.N.V.R., H.M.S. *President*. Italy.
1908 Hill, Rev. J. Ll. G., M.A. (Apr. 29, 1916). Chaplain to the Forces (4th Class). France, 1916–19. *M.C.*, Oct. 16, 1918.
1904 Hill, W. S. (May 27, 1916). ‡Capt. K.O.Y.L.I., attd. No. 3 O.C.B. France. *M.C.*, Oct. 18, 1917.
1919 Hills, J. F. T. (Sept. 13, 1916). Gnr. 2/B Batt., H.A.C. France, Belgium, 1917–19.
1907 Hillyard,* Rev. G., B.A. (June 7, 1918). Chaplain to the Forces (4th Class).
1912 Hinchliffe, A. H. S. (Sept. 1914). ‡Lt. 1/5th N. Staffordshire Regt. (Capt.). France, 1915; India, 1916–19. *D.* India. (Invalided on account of wounds, Apr. 1918.)
1898 Hind, D. A. D.C.L.I.
1898 Hind, N. S. (Nov. 26, 1915). Lt. R.N.V.R.
1900 [Hingston,* J. H. N., B.A.] (Jan. 3, 1916). Sapper 99th Field Coy., R.E. Salonika.
1911 **Hirst,* C. P.** (June 20, 1915). 2nd Lt. 9th Devonshire Regt. France, 1915–16. Killed in action at Fricourt on July 1, 1916.
1884 **Hirst, H. D.,** M.A. (Serving Aug. 4, 1914). Lt.-Col. The Buffs (E. Kent Regt.). *D.* § Feb. 1917. Died on May 16, 1918.
1919 Hoar, F. P. (July 28, 1916). Signaller, 33rd Siege Batt., R.G.A. France, 1917–19.
1913 **Hobbs,* H. E.** (Aug. 1914). 2nd Lt. 2nd Northumberland Fusiliers. France, Belgium. Killed in action at Hooge, near Ypres, on May 25, 1915.
1919 Hodges, C. (Feb. 20, 1918). 2nd Lt. 277th Siege Batt., R.G.A. France, Germany.
1909 Hodgkin,* A. E., B.A. (Mobilized Aug. 4, 1914). Capt. 5th Cheshire Regt. Acting Maj. commanding 'A' Special Coy., R.E. France, 1915–19. *M.C.*, Jan. 1, 1919.
1902 Hoggarth, A. H. G., M.A. (Aug. 16, 1918). 2nd Lt. Border Regt.
1915 Hole, H. E. M. (March 11, 1915). Lt. R.F.A. (Capt.). France, India, N.W. Frontier.

1904 Holland, C. F., B.A. (Sept. 2, 1915). Lt. 4th Gloucestershire Regt. France. *M.C.*, Sept. 22, 1916; *Bar*, May 26, 1917.

1919 Holman, R. (Sept. 1917). Sergt. U.S. Army Ambulance Service, attd. French Army. France. Croix de Guerre.

1895 Holmes, Rev. C. F. J., M.A. (Oct. 16, 1914). Chaplain to the Forces (3rd Class). Egypt, Palestine, Syria. *D.S.O.*, July 3, 1918. Croix de Chevalier de la Légion d'Honneur. *D.* Egypt, 1915; Palestine, 1918.

1887 Hook, W. A. (Aug. 3, 1915). Capt. 7th W. Yorkshire Regt.

1920 Hope, R. S. G. (Nov. 25, 1915). Pte. R.A.M.C., attd. 40th Gen. Hospital, Mesopotamia. Mesopotamia, 1916–19.

1895 Hopkins, T. H. C., M.A. (Jan. 1916). Capt. Yorkshire Regt., afterwards Maj. Unattached List, T.F. France. T.D.

1904 Hopkyns, H. C., M.A. (June 29, 1915). 2nd Lt. 15th R. Fusiliers. Lt. Training Reserve.

1919 Hopwood, D. (Feb. 28, 1917). Mechanic R.N.A.S., afterwards 2nd Lt. R.G.A. France.

1896 Houghton, C. E. J., M.A. (Serving Aug. 4, 1914). Capt. Unattached List, T.F., Woodbridge School O.T.C.

1889 How, F. A. W., B.A. (Aug. 5, 1914). Maj. 8th Worcestershire Regt. France. *D.* France, 1915.

1911 Howell,* W. A. G. (Oct. 4, 1915). Lt. 3rd D.C.L.I. *D.* § Aug. 1919.

1915 **Howells, G. D.** (Jan. 17, 1916). ‡2nd Lt. 1st Monmouthshire Regt., attd. 15th Cheshire Regt. France, Belgium, 1917–18. Killed in action near Langemarck on Feb. 28, 1918.

1912 **Hudson,* A. H.** (Aug. 31, 1914). Capt. 9th Berkshire Regt. France, Belgium. *D.* France, 1917. Killed in action on July 31, 1917.

1906 Hudson,* Rev. H. H., B.A. (Feb. 23, 1916). Chaplain to the Forces (4th Class).

1902 **Hughes, E. T.,** B.A. (Nov. 1917). Rfln. 16th London Regt. (Queen's Westminster Rifles). France, Belgium. Killed in action at Croisilles on Aug. 28, 1918.

1903 **Hughes, L. R.** (Aug. 15, 1914). 2nd Lt. 4th N. Staffordshire Regt. France. Died on May 19, 1915, of wounds received in action.

1911 Hughes,* V. G., B.A. (Aug. 22, 1914). Lt. 8th Rifle Brigade. Belgium, 1915–16.

1905 Hughes-Davies, Rev. E. H., M.A. (Feb. 15, 1916). Chaplain to the Forces (4th Class). (Resigned).

1918 Hulburd, G. S. (Mar. 1914). ‡Lt. 10th W. Riding Regt. France, Belgium, 1915, 1916, 1917.

1902 **Humble-Crofts, A. M.,** B.A. (1914). ‡Capt. Technical Officer, R.A.F. Died on Nov. 19, 1919, of illness contracted while on active service.

1915 Hunter, J. (Aug. 15, 1917). 2nd Lt. 7th Middlesex Regt. France, 1918.

1919 Hurley, A. V. (June 21, 1915). ‡Flying Officer, R.A.F. (Flight Commander). France, Belgium, 1917; N. Russia, 1919.

1913 Hurt,* C. N. B., B.A. (Oct. 17, 1914). Capt. 6th E. Lancashire Regt., afterwards Capt. General List, empld. Min. of Nat. Service. Gallipoli, 1915.

1883 Hussey, G., M.A. (Aug. 26, 1916). Driver, S. African M.T., A.S.C. ‡2nd Lt. Labour Corps. German E. Africa, 1916–17; France, 1918.

1914 Hutchins, W. T. (May 25, 1915). Lt. 7th Gloucestershire Regt. Mesopotamia, N. Persia, Caucasus, 1916–19.

1906 Huxley, Rev. T. S., B.A. (July 31, 1918). Chaplain to the Forces (4th Class). France.

1904 Huyshe, O. F., B.A. (June 1916). Capt. R.A.S.C. France. *M.C.*, June 3, 1918.

1915 Hyder, M. G. G., B.A. (Jan. 24, 1916). ‡2nd Lt. R.E. (Special Bde.). France, 1916–18.

1904 Insley, F. P., B.A. (Feb. 1, 1915). Capt., R.G.A. (Maj.). France.

1919 Ireland, S. J. (Apr. 30, 1917). Cpl. R. Sussex Regt. France. (Prisoner of war, Mar.–Nov. 1918.)

1901 Irvin, Rev. H. M., B.A. (May 5, 1917). Chaplain to the Forces (4th Class). France. *M.C.*, Jan. 1, 1918.

1899 Irwin, Rev. R. J. B., M.A. (Serving Aug. 4, 1914). Senior Chaplain, Indian Ecc. Establishment (promoted for valuable service). Asst. Chaplain-Gen., 4th Army Headquarters. Mesopotamia, France. *D.S.O.*, Dec. 22, 1916. *M.C.*, Jan. 14, 1916; *Bar*, Dec. 25, 1916. Croix de Guerre. *D.* France, 1915, 1918; Mesopotamia, 1916.

1910 Jackson,* Rev. G., M.A. (Jan. 1, 1918). Chaplain to the Forces (4th Class), attd. 6th Division. France, Belgium.

1903 Jackson, Rev. K. C., M.A. (Aug. 4, 1914). Chaplain to the Forces (4th Class). France. *M.C.*, Oct. 20, 1916.

1889 Jacob, Rev. C. W., M.A. (Aug. 25, 1916). Chaplain to the Forces (4th Class) (S.C.F.). *D.* § Mar. 1918.

1885 Jacob, Ven. J. A. (July 20, 1916). Chaplain (3rd Class), N.Z.E.F.

1919 James, B. V. (May 26, 1916). Sergt. R.E. (Signals). France, Belgium, Germany, 1919; Italy, 1917–18.

1890 Jeffcock, C. A. C., M.A. (1914). ‡Lt. R.G.A.

1901 Jenkins, E. D. T., M.A. (Jan. 15, 1916). 2nd Lt. 9th K.O.Y.L.I. (until July 1916), afterwards Lt. 25th (Works) Bn., Durham L.I. France, 1916.

1910 **Jenkins, E. S.** (Feb. 12, 1916). ‡2nd Lt. 18th Welsh Regt. France. Killed in action at Bourlon Wood on Nov. 24, 1917.

1909 Jenner,* R. F. (Nov. 9, 1914). Capt. 1st Worcestershire Yeomanry.

1892 Jephson, Rev. W. V. (Serving Aug. 4, 1914). Chaplain to the Forces (3rd Class), attd. 9th Hampshire Regt. *D.* § Mar. 1919.

1906 Jermyn, L. A. S., B.A. (Dec. 4, 1915). 2nd Lt. 13th Hampshire Regt. (Invalided Feb. 24, 1916.)

1912 Johns,* H. S. (Jan. 25, 1915). 2nd Lt. 9th Welsh Regt. (Resigned.)

1919 Johnston, R. T. (May 23, 1917). 2nd Lt. Lancashire Fusiliers. France, Belgium, Germany, 1918–19.

1888 Johnstone, O. R. B. (Mobilized Aug. 4, 1914). Maj. 2/1st London Field Coy., R.E. (T.F. Res.) (C.R.E. 58th Division). France, 1916. T.D.

1910 Jolliffe,* J. E. A., M.A. (Jan. 3, 1916). 2nd Lt. Unattached List, T.F., St. Bees O.T.C.

1901 Jones, Rev. A. Ll., M.A. (May 1915). Chaplain to the Forces (3rd Class), attd. 66th Div. France. *M.C.*, Nov. 14, 1916.

1919 Jones, A. M. (July 5, 1917). Pte., Acting Lce.-Cpl., 6th R. Fusiliers. France, 1918.

1919 Jones, A. W. B. (Aug. 14, 1915). Lt. R. Welch Fusiliers, attd. King's African Rifles. E. Africa, 1917–19.

1901 Jones, Rev. B. D., M.A. (Nov. 4, 1914). Chaplain to the Forces (4th Class)

(Staff-Capt., Intelligence Dept.). Gallipoli, 1915; E. Africa, 1915–18; Palestine, 1918. *O.B.E.* (Mil.). *D.* E. Africa, 1918.

1913 Jones,* J. E. O., B.A. R.A.S.C. (M.T.). German E. Africa, 1917–18.

1905 **Jones, S. D. S.,** B.A. (Oct. 1914). ‡Lt. 117th Batt., R.F.A. German S.W. Africa, France, 1916. Killed in action in the Battle of the Somme on Sept. 2, 1916.

1908 **Jones, W. B. L.,** B.A. (Sept. 26, 1914). Flight Observer, R.N.A.S. France, Dardanelles, Italy. Lost at sea on Jan. 7, 1918, while on Patrol Flight near Italy. *D.* twice.

1913 Joyce,* W., B.A. (Aug. 24, 1914). Lt. 6th Bedfordshire Regt., attd. R.A.F. France. (Prisoner of war, March 1916–Nov. 1918.)

1902 Jullyan, Rev. E. A., M.A. (May 3, 1918). Chaplain to the Forces (4th Class).

1911 **Keatinge,* E. G. L.,** B.A. (Oct. 3, 1914). Lt. 3rd Northumberland Fusiliers, attd. 2nd Durham L.I. (Capt.). France, Belgium. Killed in action in France on April 13, 1918.

1912 Keble,* J. H. C., B.A. (Oct. 17, 1914). Lt. 7th Oxf. & Bucks. Lt. Infty., attd. No. 4 O.C.B. France, 1915; Salonika, 1915–16; France, 1918–19.

1907 **Keller, F. F.** (Sept. 1914). ‡Lt. 2/6th London Regt. (Rifles) (Capt.). France. Died on May 22, 1917, of wounds received in action at Bullecourt.

1910 Kelly, E. R. (Feb. 1, 1915). Lt. 2nd Essex Regt. (Capt.). France, 1915–16, 1917–18, 1918–19.

1904 Kenyon, Rev. H. J., B.A. (Feb. 2, 1917). Chaplain to the Forces (4th Class). Salonika, 1917–19.

1919 Ker, R. A. (Sept. 22, 1914). Capt. 3rd Lincolnshire Regt. France, 1915–17.

1908 Kerby,* A. M., B.A. (Aug. 27, 1915). Lt. R.F.A. (S.R.), attd. C/241st S. Mid. Bde., R.F.A. (T.F.). *D.S.O.*, Sept. 24, 1918. *M.C.*, Mar. 3, 1917. France; Italy, 1917–18. *D.* France, 1917; Italy, 1918.

Kestell-Cornish, R. V. (June 7, 1915). Capt. 3rd, attd. 1st, Dorsetshire Regt. France. *M.C.*, June 29, 1915; *Bar*, Feb. 13, 1917. *D.* France, 1918. Died on June 17, 1918, of wounds received in action.

1906 Ketchley, C. P. G., M.A. (Nov. 13, 1916). Lt. R.G.A. (S.R.).

1908 Ketchley, Rev. L. G., M.A. (Nov. 21, 1916). Chaplain to the Forces (4th Class).

1881 Kettle, W. H. H. A., B.A. (Jan. 25, 1915). Lt. Border Regt.

1909 King,* A. A., B.A. Inns of Court O.T.C.

1917 King, H. C. (Jan. 3, 1918). ‡2nd Lt. R.F.A.

1909 King,* Rev. N., B.A. (Aug. 11, 1916). Chaplain to the Forces (4th Class).

1913 King,* W. L., B.A. (Sept. 16, 1914). Lt., Acting Capt., 13th Middlesex Regt., attd. No. 4 O.C.B. France. *M.C.*, Oct. 20, 1916.

1887 Kingdon, Rev. R. A., M.A. (Oct. 6, 1914). Chaplain to the Forces (4th Class).

1919 Kirby, A. G. (Feb. 28, 1916). Lt. 7th Northamptonshire Regt. France, Belgium, 1917–19.

1904 [Kirk, Rev. K. E., M.A.] (Sept. 1914). Chaplain to the Forces (3rd Class). France, 1915–17.

1907 Kirkley,* Rev. S. E., M.A. (April 12, 1917). Chaplain R.N., H.M.S. *Lowestoft*. Adriatic.

1886 Kirwan, Rev. E. C., M.A. (Serving Aug. 4, 1914). Chaplain to the Forces (2nd Class), attd. 5th Queen's (R. W. Surrey Regt.).
1882 **Kirwan, Rev. R. M.,** M.A. Chaplain, Indian Army. India. Died on May 23, 1916.
1901 Kitching, A. F., M.A. (Serving Aug. 4, 1914). Capt., Unattached List, T.F., Monkton Combe O.T.C.
1913 **Kite,* R. B.** (Nov. 11, 1914). Capt. 2nd Oxf. & Bucks. Lt. Infty. France, 1914–16. *M.C.*, Oct. 20, 1916. *D.* France, 1916. Died on Dec. 10, 1916, of wounds received in action at Beaumont Hamel on Nov. 13, 1916.
1892 Kitson, Rev. J. A., B.A. (Jan. 1917). Chaplain to the Forces (4th Class), attd. 2nd Rifle Brigade. France, Belgium.
1900 **Knight, R. B.** (July 5, 1916). Capt. Bedfordshire Regt. France. Killed in action on Sept. 5, 1918.
1882 Kyffin, J. (Mobilized Aug. 4, 1914). Lt.-Col. R.A.M.C. (T.F.). Officer of the Military Order of Savoy.
1905 Lacon, C. C. R., B.A. (Jan. 23, 1915). Capt. 16th R. Warwickshire Regt.
1907 Laidler,* W. (1914). ‡Lt. Flying Officer, R.A.F.
1896 Lambert, J. A. P., M.A. Nigerian Land Contingent. W. Africa.
1902 Lancaster, H. de Z. 2nd Lt. Malay States Rifles. Malay.
1919 Lancelot, R. (June 26, 1918). Cadet Guards O.C.B.
1912 Lane,* G. L. H. D., M.A. (Apr. 17, 1916). Capt. R.A.F.
1905 Larr, Rev. O. G. O., M.A. (Aug. 2, 1917). Chaplain to the Forces (4th Class).
1912 Latter,* A. H., B.A. (Oct. 27, 1914). Lt. 5th R. Sussex Regt. France. (Invalided Nov. 1917.)
1908 **Lauria,* J. V.** (July 15, 1915). 2nd Lt. 14th Sherwood Foresters, attd. R.E. France. Died on June 18, 1916, of wounds received in action.
1908 Law, Rev. J. T. S., M.A. Chaplain R.N. Chaplain R.A.F.
1891 Lea, Rev. J. W. (Jan. 1, 1918). Chaplain to the Forces (4th Class).
1918 Lee, C. I. R.A.F. (Invalided.)
1890 Lee, Rev. C. P., M.A. (July 24, 1917). Chaplain to the Forces (4th Class).
1892 Lee, Rev. H., M.A. (June 17, 1916). Chaplain to the Forces (4th Class).
1912 Lee-Jones, J. L., B.A. (Oct. 22, 1914). Capt. 9th King's (Liverpool Regt.). France, 1916–19.
1915 le Liévre, P. D. (Oct. 25, 1916). Lt. M.G.C. France, 1917–18. *M.C.*, Sept. 16, 1918.
1883 Le Maistre, W. de V., M.A. (June 27, 1916). Lt. Special Lists. Staff-Lt. (Interpreter).
1903 Lester, R., M.A. (Dec. 24, 1914). Capt. I.A.R.O., attd. Supply and Transport Corps. India, 1915; Aden, 1916–19; Baluchistan, 1919.
1896 Lewis, E. N., B.A. (May 15, 1916). 2nd Lt. R.A.S.C.
1919 Lewis, J. A. L. M. (July 20, 1918). Midshipman R.N.V.R., H.M.S. *Sylph*. North Sea, 1919.
1912 Lewis,* P. S. (Nov. 23, 1914). Lt. R.F.A. Mesopotamia, 1915–16; France, 1917. (Prisoner of war.)
1913 Lewis, R. H. M. (Dec. 7, 1914). Lt. 13th K.R.R.C., empld. Min. of Munitions. France, 1915–16.
1894 **Limpus, B. H.** R. Fusiliers. France. Killed in action on Mar. 12, 1917.
1909 Lloyd,* E. G. R., M.A. (Aug. 20, 1914). Capt. 1st Shropshire L.I. (Maj.). France, Belgium, 3 years. *D.S.O.*, Sept. 26, 1917. *D.* France, 1917.

1917 Lloyd, H. W. B. (Jan. 2, 1918). ‡2nd Lt. R.G.A. France.
1910 Lloyd,* J. P., M.A. (Nov. 23, 1915). Lt. Welsh Regt. (Capt. spec. empld.). France, 1917.
1907 **Lloyd, R.,** M.A. (1917). R.A.S.C. Died, 1918.
1901 Lock, J. B. (July 22, 1918). Rfln. 6th London Regt. (Rifles).
Loft, P. T. (Aug. 1, 1917). 2nd Lt. 6th K.R.R.C. France, 1917, 1918; Italy, 1917–18. Killed in action at Frémicourt on Mar. 24, 1918.
1891 Lomax, Rev. C., B.A. (July 18, 1916). Chaplain to the Forces (2nd Class).
1877 London, Right Rev. A. F., Lord Bishop of, D.D. (Mobilized Aug. 1914). Chaplain to the Forces (1st Class), attd. London Rifle Brigade. France, Salonika. *K.C.V.O.* Grand Cross, Order of the Redeemer. *D.* France, 1915.
1878 Longden, Rev. H. J., M.A. (May 20, 1916). Chaplain to the Forces (4th Class).
1912 Lord, C. T., M.A. (Sept. 29, 1917). Sergt. R.A.M.C. Instr. Army Education Dept. France.
1909 Lord, W. F., M.A. (Oct. 28, 1914). A.B., R.N.V.R. Anti-Aircraft Corps (C.P.O.).
1919 Lott, D. B. (May 8, 1918). 2nd Lt. R. W. Kent Regt. (on demobilization).
1913 Lowe, E. G. T. (Oct. 13, 1914). Lt. 10th Somerset L.I. France, 1915.
1913 Lowe, W. F., B.A. (Sept. 2, 1914). ‡Lt. 1/1st Derbyshire Yeomanry (Staff-Captain). Egypt, 1915; Macedonia, 1916–19; S. Russia, 1919. *M.C.*, Nov. 19, 1917. *D.* Salonika, 1917.
1896 Loynes, Rev. O. J., B.A. (Dec. 3, 1914). Inns of Court O.T.C. (formerly Chaplain to the Forces).
1919 Lucette, E. H. (Apr. 2, 1915). Capt. 8th Northumberland Fusiliers. France, 1915–18, 1918–19. *M.C.*, Sept. 17, 1917.
1908 Lumb,* Rev. J. R. B. B., M.A. (Aug. 6, 1918). Chaplain to the Forces (4th Class). France, 1918–19.
1911 Lush,* A. J. (Aug. 15, 1914). Capt. 6th Rifle Brigade, attd. Intelligence Dept., War Office. France, 1915.
1914 **Lutener, R. A. M.** (Dec. 1914). 2nd Lt. 6th Shropshire L.I. France and Belgium. Killed in action at Ypres on April 6, 1916.
1891 Luxmoore, Rev. W. C., M.A. (Serving Aug. 4, 1914). Chaplain 5th Leicestershire Regt.
1919 McCarthy, W. (May 10, 1915). Eng.-Lt.-Commdr., R.N., Instructor at R.N. College, Osborne.
1890 Macdonald, A. H., M.A. (Oct. 1914). A.B., R.N.A.S.
1892 Mace, A. C., M.A. (Sept. 1, 1915). ‡Lt. R.A.S.C. Italy, 1917–19.
1908 **Macfarlane-Grieve,* A. R.,** M.A. (Nov. 3, 1914). Lt. 8th Arg. & Suth'd Highlanders. France, 1916–17. Killed in action at Rodincourt, Arras, on Mar. 17, 1917.
1911 Mackenzie.* D. B., B.A. (Serving Aug. 4, 1914). Capt. and Adjt. 58th Vaughan's Rifles, Indian Army (Maj.). France, India, Egypt, Palestine, 1915–19. *D.* Palestine, 1919.
1919 McKenzie, T. H. F. (Oct. 5, 1914). Capt. 79th Bde., R.G.A. (Maj.). France, 1915, 1917, 1918, 1919. *D.* France, 1916.
1919 Maclagan, W. D. (Feb. 12, 1918). Lce.-Cpl. Army Pay Corps.
1919 McLaughlin, M. C. (June 26, 1918). 3/Air Mechanic R.A.F.

1910 **Macrae, K. M.,** B.A. (Nov. 17, 1914). Maj. R.F.A. France and Belgium. *M.C.*, June 3, 1918. *D.* France, 1917. Killed in action at Ingoyghem, near Courtrai, on Nov. 1, 1918.

1903 Malden, J. W. S., B.A. (June 20, 1915). Lt. 1st Northamptonshire Yeomanry. France and Italy, 1916–18.

1903 Malet, G. C. W. (Nov. 19, 1914). Capt. 1st Somerset L.I. France.

1909 **Mallam,* C. A.,** B.A. (Sept. 1914). ‡Capt. and Adjt. 3rd, attd. 5th, R. Berkshire Regt. France and Belgium, 1916–18. *M.C.*, Jan. 1, 1918; *Bar*, Jan. 11, 1919. *D.* France, 1917.

Manley, D. H. G. (Sept. 1914). ‡Capt. 6th R. Welch Fusiliers. Suvla Bay, Gallipoli, Egypt, Palestine. Killed in action at Tel Khuweilfeh on Nov. 6, 1917.

1919 Manson, T. L. (July 15, 1915). Capt. 2nd Queen's (R. W. Surrey Regt.). France, Belgium, Italy, 1916–19. *M.C.*, June 3, 1918.

Margerison, G. J. Pte. King's (Liverpool Regt.). France. Killed in action on Nov. 8, 1918.

1919 Marsden, A. W. (Dec. 29, 1917). Lt. R.A.F.

1905 **Marsh, Rev. H. A.,** M.A. (July 23, 1918). Chaplain U. S. Army. France. Died of pneumonia on Oct. 7, 1918, after being gassed at Vittel, Vosges.

1901 Marshall, E. R., M.A. (July 1916). Lt. Coldstream Guards (S.R.), attd. 4th Bn. France.

1914 Marshall, H. G., B.A. (Nov. 7, 1916). Lce.-Cpl. 36th Bn. M.G.C. France and Belgium.

1913 Marshall, K. R., B.A. (Sept. 1914). ‡Lt. 5th Dorsetshire Regt. Capt. and Adjt. 1st Yemen Infantry, Aden Field Force. France, 1915; India, 1916–17; Egypt, 1917–18; Aden, 1918–19.

1916 Martindale,* Rev. H., M.A. (June 24, 1916). Chaplain to the Forces (4th Class). Mesopotamia. *D.* Mesopotamia, 1917.

1909 Martyn,* Rev. C. W. (July 1918). Chaplain to the Forces (4th Class). France, Belgium, Germany.

1911 Mashiter,* E., M.A. (Aug. 29, 1914). Maj. 4th Border Regt., attd. 74th Bn. M.G.C. Burmah, India, 1914–18; Egypt, 1918; France, 1918–19.

1912 Mason, A. S. (Aug. 4, 1914). ‡Lt. R.F.A. France. (Invalided on account of wounds, Oct. 1, 1918.)

1904 Mason, Rev. J. H., B.A. Pte. R.A.S.C. France.

1910 **Matheson,* C. B.,** B.A. (Mar. 9, 1917). ‡2nd Lt. 5th, attd. 2nd, Rifle Brigade. France and Belgium, 1917. Killed in action near Warneton on Sept. 24, 1917.

1902 Matheson, F. W., M.A. (Mobilized Aug. 1914). Lt.-Col. O.U.O.T.C., attd. No. 4 O.C.B. *M.B.E.* (Mil.). T.D. *D.* § Feb. 1917.

1916 Matheson, K. I. G. (Mar., 1916). ‡Lt. 4th Arg. & Suth'd. Highlanders. France, 1917–18.

1899 Matthews, Rev. C. Ll., M.A. (July 10, 1915). Chaplain to the Forces (4th Class).

1914 **Matthews, St. J. B.** (Dec. 2, 1914). 2nd Lt. 6th R. Berkshire Regt. France. Died on Nov. 25, 1915, of wounds received in action.

1886 Maud, A. R. (Oct. 24, 1914). Sergt. Brandt's Horse. German S.W. Africa.

1911 Maude,* J. D. (1915). Maj. Seaplane Officer, R.A.F. Sea Patrol. *D.*

1875 Maurice, W. J., B.M., M.A. (Oct. 19, 1914). Lt.-Col. Bt.-Col. R.A.M.C., 3rd S. Gen. Hospital. *D.* § Feb. 1917.

1899 **Maxwell, J. W.,** B.A. (Sept. 9, 1914). Maj. 7th Rifle Brigade, attd. 8th K.R.R.C. (Lt.-Col.). France and Belgium. *D.S.O.*, Jan. 1, 1918. *M.C.*, June 3, 1916. *D.* France. Died on Dec. 4, 1917, of wounds received in action.

1905 **Medd, A. W.,** B.A. Pte. Queen's (R. W. Surrey Regt.). France. Killed in action on Sept. 5, 1918.

1906 Medd,* E. N., B.A. Pte. Durham L.I.

1912 Meredith, J. H. M., B.A. (1914). ‡Lt. 4th E. Surrey Regt.

1899 Mertens, Rev. R. H. C., M.A. (Serving Aug. 4, 1914). Capt., Unattached List, T.F. Cranleigh School O.T.C.

1915 Micklethwaite, D. M. (July 11, 1916). 2nd Lt. E. Yorkshire Regt., afterwards Lt. Labour Corps. France, 1917–19.

1911 Millar, J. G., B.A. (Oct. 6, 1916). Lt. I.A.R.O., attd. 19th Punjabis. India.

1919 Miller, G. C. (Sept. 22, 1914). Capt. 7th Oxf. & Bucks. Lt. Infty. France, Salonika, 1915–19. *M.C.*, Nov. 14, 1916.

1905 **Miller-Stirling, H. J. G.,** B.A. (Apr. 1915). Lt. 1st Nigeria Regt. French Soudan and German E. Africa. Killed in action in German E. Africa on Oct. 16, 1917.

1908 Millington, Rev. C., B.A. (July 1915). Chaplain to the Forces (4th Class), attd. 1st Life Guards. France.

1889 Mills, H. P., B.A. (Nov. 1, 1914). Maj. S. African Infantry. France. *O.B.E.* (Mil.). *D.* § Nov. 1918.

1914 Milman, H. R. (Dec. 22, 1914). Lt. 7th S. Lancashire Regt., afterwards Lt. 203rd Bde. Signal School.

1901 Milner, Rev. C., M.A. (Feb. 4, 1916). Chaplain to the Forces (4th Class). France, 1916–19.

1912 Minifie-Hawkins,* S. M. (Aug. 15, 1914). Capt. 3rd, attd. 2nd, Oxf. & Bucks. Lt. Infty. France.

1919 Minshull, M. J. M. (Mar. 25, 1918). Pte. Labour Corps.

1897 Mitford, B. L. (July 21, 1915). 2nd Lt. Montgomeryshire Yeomanry.

1910 Mocatta,* W. E., B.A. (July 18, 1914). Lt. 1st W. Yorkshire Regt. (Interpreter). France. *D.* France, 1918.

1911 **Moll,* J. A.** (Mobilized Aug. 1914). ‡Lt. R.F.A. France, 1915–16. Died on Sept. 21, 1919, of wounds received in action on June 21, 1916.

1904 Molyneux, Rev. F. M., M.A. (Nov. 11, 1916). Chaplain to the Forces (4th Class), attd. G.H.Q. Mesopotamia. *M.B.E.* (Mil.). *D.* Mesopotamia, 1917.

Monro, K. E. (Nov. 7, 1914). 2nd Lt. 3rd, attd. 1st, Northamptonshire Regt. France. Died on May 14, 1915, of wounds received in action.

1914 Morgan, C. G. N., B.A. (Oct. 4, 1915). Lt. 3rd R. Welch Fusiliers (Capt.). France, 1916–18. *M.C.*, July 18, 1917; *Bar*, Sept. 5, 1917.

1903 Morgan, Rev. D. J., M.A. (July 3, 1915). Chaplain to the Forces (4th Class).

1906 Morgan,* Rev. S. M., B.A. (June 14, 1915). Chaplain to the Forces (4th Class). France, 1915–16.

1910 Morgan,* T. G. (Dec. 7, 1914). Capt. 1st Welsh Regt. France, Salonika. *M.C.*, Apr. 17, 1917.

1908 Morgan-Brown,* W. N. Lt. (Dental Surgeon) S. African Pioneers.

1895 Morres, H. F. M., M.A. (1914). 2nd Lt. 1st (Garr.) Bn. Worcestershire Regt.

1913 **Morris,* C. G. N.** (Nov. 24, 1914). Lt. 9th, attd. 6th, Oxf. & Bucks. Lt. Infty. France, 1916. Killed in action near Guedecourt on Oct. 7, 1916.

1918 Morson, P. A., B.A. (Jan. 4, 1915). ‡2nd Lt. 11th R. Warwickshire Regt. France, 1915–16.

1908 Morson, Rev. R. F., M.A. (Nov. 1, 1917). Chaplain to the Forces (4th Class). Salonika.

1919 Mortimer, T. (Aug. 22, 1914). 2nd Lt. Somerset L.I., afterwards attd. 85th Provisional Bn. (Invalided, Oct. 12, 1917.)

1918 Morton, P. (Nov. 10, 1916). ‡2nd Lt. 3rd Shropshire L.I. France and Belgium, 1917.

1898 Mott, Rev. L. O. (Oct. 17, 1914). Capt. 11th Sherwood Foresters. (Resigned.)

1890 Moxon, S. C. (Sept. 3, 1914). Lce.-Cpl. 3rd Suffolk Regt. France, 1915–18.

1919 Moyle, F. W. (Aug. 12, 1915). 2nd Lt. 12th R. Sussex Regt. France. (Wounded and prisoner of war, June 1916–Nov. 1918.)

1906 Mullins,* A. G., B.A. (1915). Maj. S. African Heavy Artillery. Acting Maj. R.G.A. France. *D.S.O.*, June 4, 1917. *D.* France, 1916, 1917.

1887 Mullins, G. J. H. (Serving Aug. 4, 1914). Temp. Brig.-Gen. R.N. Division. Gallipoli. Croix de Guerre. *D.* Gallipoli, 1916.

1900 Mullins, H. R. (Aug. 1914). Surgeon-Capt., Acting Maj., S. African Medical Corps, attd. 1st S.A. General Hospital. German S. W. Africa 1914–15; France, 1916–19. *O.B.E.* (Mil.). *D.* German S.W. Africa, twice; France, 1918.

1891 Mullins, R. C., D.M. (Feb. 22, 1917). Capt. S. African Medical Corps. S. Africa, France.

1913 Munn,* R. B. S. (Dec. 15, 1914). Capt. 1st Shropshire L.I., attd. M.G.C. France. *M.C.*, Sept. 16, 1918.

1904 Mylne,* Rev. A. M., B.A. (June 12, 1917). Chaplain to the Forces (4th Class). France, 1917–18. *D.* France, 1918 twice.

1895 Mylne, Rev. C. H., M.A. (June 12, 1917). Chaplain to the Forces (4th Class). France.

1902 **Mylne, E. G.** (Oct. 12, 1914). Capt. 1st Irish Guards. France. *D.* France, 1916. Died at Rouen on June 12, 1915, of wounds received in action.

1908 Mylne, K. M., B.A. (Sept. 2, 1914). Capt. 1/8th Worcestershire Regt. (Capt. and Adjt.). France, 1915–17.

1906 Nankivell,* Rev. J. C., M.A. (Oct. 1914). Chaplain to the Forces (4th Class).

1916 Nash, G. C. (Oct. 25, 1915). Lt. 4th Arg. & Suth'd. Highlanders. France, 1917.

1911 **Neilson,* D. F.** (Aug. 15, 1914). Lt., Acting Capt., 3rd Lincolnshire Regt. France. *D.S.O.*, July 26, 1918. *M.C.*, Jan. 1, 1917. *D.* France, 1918. Killed in action on April 15, 1918.

1909 Nethersole, J. M. Pte. 15th London Regt. (Civil Service Rifles).

1911 Nevill,* R. H. R. (Sept. 5, 1914). Capt. Norfolk Regt. (Staff-Captain). France and Belgium, 1915–16, 1917.

1911 Newill, H. S., M.A. (Jan. 15, 1915). Lt. 8th Shropshire L.I. France, 1915; Salonika, 1915–16. (Invalided Mar. 1918.)

1912 Newman,* B. R., M.A. (Aug. 8, 1914). Capt. 6th Middlesex Regt., attd. M.G.C. (Maj.). France, 1915, 1917–19. *D.* France, 1918.

1906 Newman,* Rev. G. F., B.A. (Oct. 5, 1915). Lt., Unattached List, T.F., Radley College O.T.C.

1908 Newman, Rev. G. G., M.A. (June 12, 1917). Chaplain to the Forces (4th Class). France, Russia.

1909 Newman,* H. G., B.A. (Mobilized Aug. 1914). Capt. 1/8th Worcestershire Regt. Education Officer, Cambrai Sub-Area H.Q. France, from 1915.

1908 Newman,* Rev. R. E. G., M.A. (Feb. 15, 1916). Chaplain to the Forces (3rd Class). France. *M.C.*, Sept. 26, 1917 ; *Bar*, Sept. 16, 1918.

1919 Nicholls, C. W. (Jan. 31, 1916). ‡Lt. 55th Bn. A.I.F. Egypt, 1916 ; France, 1917–19.

1896 Nicolls, O. C. C., B.A. (Serving Aug. 4, 1914). Maj. R.G.A. France, 1915–16.

1910 Nield, Rev. O., M.A. (Sept. 13, 1918). Chaplain to the Forces (4th Class).

1914 **Nightingale, E.** (Dec. 1914). Lt. 7th The Buffs (E. Kent Regt.), afterwards Lt. R.A.F. France. Killed in action near Proyart on June 25, 1918.

1886 Ninis, Rev. R. D., M.A. (Oct. 14, 1914). Senior Chaplain, Ecclesiastical Establishment, Bengal. France, 1915–16 ; India, 1916–19. *D.* France, 1916.

1892 Nixon, Rev. L. H., M.A. Acting Chaplain, R.M.A.

1895 Nockolds, S., B.M., M.A. (Dec. 14, 1915). Capt. R.A.M.C.

1919 Noel-Cox, E. L. (Mar. 8, 1918). Pte. 3rd Gloucestershire Regt. Cadet Garr. O.C.B.

1919 Norfor, R. C. (Jan. 12, 1917). Sergt. 469th Emp. Coy., Labour Corps. *D.* § Mar. 1919.

1906 **Norris, G. H.,** B.A. (Aug. 1, 1916). Capt. 13th K.R.R.C. France. Died on Mar. 9, 1918, of wounds received in action.

1914 Nosworthy, H., B.A. Pte. K.R.R.C. (Discharged.)

1911 Notley, J. B. S. (Oct. 7, 1914). ‡Lt. 8th Devonshire Regt. France. (Invalided Feb. 5, 1918.)

1891 Nussey, C. A., B.A. (Serving Aug. 4, 1914). Capt. (V.) attd. 1st Cadet Bn. London Regt. (The Queen's). V.D.

1920 Nuttall-Smith, H. R. (Mar. 19, 1918). Gnr., 1/1st Essex Heavy Batt., R.G.A. France, Belgium, Germany, 1918–19.

1905 Olive, G. F., M.A. Sergt. London Regt.

1906 **Onslow, A. D.,** B.A. (Aug. 1914). 2nd Lt. 4th, attd. 11th, R. Warwickshire Regt. France. *M.C.*, Sept. 22, 1916. Killed in action at Bazentin on Aug. 13, 1916.

1903 Orr, Rev. G. F., M.A. M.G.C., A.I.F. (Discharged.)

1907 Orr,* Rev. H. C., M.A. (Nov. 30, 1915). Chaplain to the Forces (4th Class). Malta.

1907 Osborn,* Rev. A. H., M.A. (May 21, 1918). Chaplain to the Forces (4th Class).

1901 Osborn, Rev. J. E. N., M.A. (Aug. 29, 1916). Chaplain (3rd Class), A.I.F. France, Belgium. *M.C.*, Jan. 1, 1918.

1919 Osborne, J. (Mar. 19, 1916). 2nd Lt. 3rd D.C.L.I., afterwards Lt. M.G.C. France and Belgium.

1910 Otto,* F. A., M.A. (Mobilized Aug. 4, 1914). 2nd Lt. 3rd N. Staffordshire Regt.

1899 Ovans, H. L. (Serving Aug. 4, 1914). Maj. Northumberland Fusiliers empld. Ministry of National Service. *D.* § Feb. 1917.

1883 Overend, W., B.M. (Feb. 18, 1915). Lt. R.A.M.C.
1905 Owen, Rev. A., M.A. (Feb. 7, 1916). Chaplain to the Forces (4th Class).
1914 Owen, A. G. J. (Jan. 11, 1916). Capt. 15th, attd. 52nd, Welsh Regt. Belgium and France. *M.C.*, Jan. 1, 1918.
1905 Owen, Rev. B. E., B.A. (Dec. 20, 1915). Chaplain to the Forces (4th Class).
1897 Owen, J. H. H. (Aug. 27, 1915). Lt. R.E. (Signal Service).
1907 Owen, L. V. D., M.A. (Aug. 26, 1915). Lt., Acting Capt., 3rd, attd. 5th, Oxf. & Bucks. Lt. Infty. France and Belgium (till 1918). (Prisoner of war at Mainz from Apr. 1918–Nov. 1918.)
1907 Owen,* R. C. D., B.A. (Aug. 1914). Capt. 3rd R. Welch Fusiliers. France, 1915; Mesopotamia, 1918.
1906 Page,* E., B.A. (Aug. 1914). ‡Capt. 7th K.R.R.C., afterwards Capt. General List, Staff-Captain (Maj.) France. *M.C.*, June 4, 1917. *D.* France, 1916, 1917, 1918.
1912 Page,* J. C. (Aug. 21, 1914). Capt. and Adjt., 6th The Buffs (E. Kent Regt.). France. *M.C.*, Jan. 10, 1917. *D.* France, 1916, 1917.
1910 Palethorpe,* R. F. (Dec. 1915). Pte. E. Africa Defence Force. British E. Africa.
1920 Palmer, R. W. V. (Sept. 16, 1914). ‡Lt. 1st Suffolk Regt. (Capt.). France, 1915; Egypt, 1915; Salonika, 1915–18; Constantinople, 1918–19. *D.* Salonika, 1919.
1900 Pardoe, F. S., B.A. (Nov. 1, 1915). Lt. 16th R. Irish Rifles. Lt. General List (Capt.). *D.* § Aug. 1919.
1907 **Park,* J. W. H.,** B.A. (Serving Aug. 4, 1914). Capt. 22nd Cavalry, Indian Army. Mesopotamia. *D.* Mesopotamia, 1917. Killed in action on Jan. 14, 1917.
1913 Parkes,* D. W., B.A. (Dec. 2, 1914). Lt., Acting Captain, 18th Middlesex Regt. France, 1916–19. *M.C.*, Mar. 12, 1917.
1910 Parry, J. G. M. (Dec. 9, 1916). 2nd Lt. 6th K.R.R.C., attd. Labour Corps.
1908 Parry-Okeden,* Rev. C. E. G., M.A. (July 3, 1917). Chaplain to the Forces (4th Class). France. *M.C.*, Sept. 16, 1918.
1919 Parsley, E. W. (Aug. 15, 1918). Cadet R.F.A. 2nd Lt. (on demobilization).
1900 **Parsons, A. H.** (Serving Aug. 4, 1914). Capt. 9th Gurkha Rifles, Indian Army. India, France, Mesopotamia, 1914–16. Killed in action in Mesopotamia on Mar. 8, 1916.
1907 Parsons,* Rev. O. B., M.A. (July 6, 1915). Chaplain to the Forces (4th Class). France, 1915–17; Salonika, 1918–19. *D.* France, 1917 twice.
1906 Parsons, W. A., B.A. (Dec. 1915). ‡Lt. R.G.A. (S.R.) (Maj.). France.
1910 **Pastfield, J. T. R.,** B.A. (Aug. 15, 1914). 2nd Lt. Middlesex Regt. France. Killed in action on Dec. 22, 1914.
1905 **Patterson,* C. B.,** B.A. 2nd Lt. I.A.R.O., attd. 1/1st Gurkha Rifles. Mesopotamia. Killed in action on Dec. 30, 1916.
1910 **Payne,* E. G.,** B.A. (Oct. 26, 1914). Capt. 9th R. Welch Fusiliers. France. Killed in action at the Battle of Loos on Sept. 25, 1915.
1915 Peacock, A. C. (Feb. 15, 1916). ‡2nd Lt. R.E. (Anti-Gas Establishment, Chemical Warfare Dept., Min. of Mun.). France, 1916–18.
1903 Pearson, Rev. H. W., M.A. (May 1918). ‡2nd Lt. 2nd Cavalry Div. M.T. Coy., R.A.S.C. France.

1899 Peile, Rev. H. G., M.A. (Mar. 9, 1916). Chaplain to the Forces (4th Class). *D.* § Mar. 1918.

1911 Pendlebury, W. J. von M., B.A. (Mobilized Aug. 4, 1914). Maj. R.F.A. (T.F.). Egypt and Palestine.

1909 Pennefather,* J. B., B.A. (Sept. 17, 1914). Capt. 6th Loyal N. Lancashire Regt. Capt. General List. Military Forwarding Officer. Mesopotamia. *O.B.E.* (Mil.). *D.* Mesopotamia, 1918.

1873 Perry, Rev. Preb. G. H., M.A. (Serving Aug. 4, 1914). Chaplain to the Forces (3rd Class), attd. R.E.

1913 Perry-Gore,* H. W., B.A. (Jan. 6, 1915). Lt. 2nd S. Lancashire Regt. Gallipoli, 1915; Mesopotamia, 1916–17; Italy, 1918; France, 1918–19.

1919 Pettitt, D. S. T. (Apr. 18, 1917). ‡Lt. R.A.F.

1911 **Peyton,* J. A. W.,** B.A. (Mar. 19, 1915). Lt. 3rd, attd. 7th, Norfolk Regt. France. Killed in action on Aug. 22, 1918.

1894 Phillips, Rev. B. S., M.A. (Feb. 1916). Chaplain to the Forces (4th Class).

1919 Phillips, E. R. S. (Apr. 15, 1915). 2nd Lt. R.A.F.

1918 Phillips, F. E. (Mobilized Aug. 4, 1914). Capt. 7th W. Riding Regt. (T.F.).

1899 Phillips, Rev. J. L., B.D. (July 5, 1915). Lt. R.A.O.C. *D.* § Aug. 1918.

1910 **Phillips,* O. S.** (Aug. 26, 1914). 2nd Lt. 4th S. Wales Borderers. Gallipoli. Killed in action in Gallipoli on Aug. 21, 1915.

1910 Phillips, Rev. S. T., M.A. (May 1918). Chaplain to the Forces (4th Class). France, 1918–19.

1913 Phipps,* H. R. (Aug. 14, 1914). Lt. 1st Northamptonshire Regt., attd. No. 13 O.C.B. (Capt.) France. *M.C.*, May 31, 1916.

1905 Phipps, P. C., B.A. (1914). ‡Lt. 18th London Regt. (London Irish Rifles). France, N. Russia.

1915 **Pickard, L. D.** (1916). 2nd Lt. 5th Queen's (R. W. Surrey Regt.). France and Belgium. Killed in action at Inverness Copse on Aug. 10, 1917.

1900 **Pilling, E.,** M.A. (Nov. 22, 1915). 2nd Lt. R.F.A. (S.R.). France. Killed in action on April 23, 1917.

1919 Pinchbeck, H. W. (Oct. 16, 1914). Pte. 1/1st N. Midland Field Amb., R.A.M.C. France, 1915–19.

1896 Platt, A. H., B.A. (Serving Aug. 4, 1914). Instr. Commdr., R.N., Keyham College. H.M.S. *Tamal*, Hong-Kong, 1914–15; H.M.S. *Erin*, 5th Battle Squadron, 1916.

1908 **Playford,* A. B.,** M.A. (Oct. 6, 1914). Capt. 1st S. Wales Borderers. France. Killed in action near Loos on Sept. 25, 1915.

1919 Plummer, A. J. (Apr. 6, 1915). ‡Lt. 21st Manchester Regt., attd. King's African Rifles (Capt.). France, 1915–17; E. Africa (Jubaland), 1918–19.

1919 Poignand, G. C. I. (Aug. 4, 1914). Capt. R.A.S.C. France, 1915–16.

1886 Pollock-Hill, Rev. W., M.A. (Mar. 26, 1918). Chaplain to the Forces (4th Class). France, 1918–19; Germany, 1919–20.

1901 Poole, Rev. G. C., M.A. (Aug. 15, 1918). Chaplain to the Forces (4th Class).

1909 Poole,* J. C., M.A. (Aug. 15, 1914). Lt., Acting Capt., 3rd R. Sussex Regt., attd. No. 4 O.C.B. France, 1914–15.

1899 Pope, R. M., M.A. (Mobilized Aug. 4, 1914). Capt. 5th R. Sussex Regt. R.T.O.

1919 Porter, C. H. (Apr. 19, 1918). ‡2nd Lt. 3rd (Garr.) Bn. R. Welch Fusiliers.

1920 Potts, G. C. (July 21, 1917). Pte. Border Regt. Cpl. R.E. (Searchlights). France, 1918.

1916 Powell, G. B. (June 11, 1917). Lt. R.A.F. (Flight Commdr.). *A.F.C.*, Jan. 1, 1919.

1902 Powell, J. Ll., M.A. (May 8, 1911). 2nd Lt. R. Warwickshire Regt. (T.F. Res.). Capt. R. Defence Corps.

1914 Powell, V. (Dec. 18, 1914). Gnr. 215th Bde., R.F.A. (Bombardier). India, 1916; Mesopotamia, 1916–19.

1905 **Powell,* V. H. de B.,** B.A. (Mar. 1915). Maj. Canadian F.A. France and Belgium. *M.C.*, Nov. 14, 1916. Died on Jan. 2, 1918.

1905 Power, C. J. (Apr. 26, 1915). Capt. 26th R. Welch Fusiliers. France, 1916–19.

1887 Preedy, Rev. W. W., M.A. (May 15, 1917). Chaplain to the Forces (4th Class), attd. 5th Div. Art. France, Belgium, Italy.

1906 Price,* T. L., B.A. (Oct. 1914). ‡Capt. R.A.M.C. Belgium and France.

1909 [Priestley,* E. C., M.A.] (Aug. 26, 1914). Lt. 8th Essex Regt. Lt. Indian Army, attd. 1/67th Punjabis. India.

1913 Procter,* N. P., B.A. (Sept. 18, 1914). Lt. 1st Middlesex Regt. (Capt.), attd. 21st Punjabis, 1918–19. Gallipoli, Egypt, Palestine. *M.C.*, Feb. 18, 1918.

1911 Prosser-Evans,* L., B.A. (Mar. 30, 1915). Lt. R.A.

1904 Protheroe, Rev. W. L. M., M.A. (Jan. 12, 1916). Chaplain to the Forces (4th Class). France. *M.C.*, Jan. 1, 1919.

1919 Pryce-Jones, J. (Aug. 10, 1917). ‡Lt. R.A.F. Coastal Patrol, S. Coast.

1913 Pugh, R. W. B., B.A. (Jan. 1916). Sergt. Intelligence Corps, afterwards Educational Staff Training (G.S.), G.H.Q., France. France.

1905 Pugh, Rev. W., M.A. (May 3, 1917). Chaplain to the Forces (4th Class), attd. 8th Oxf. & Bucks. Lt. Infty. Salonika, Danube, Black Sea, 1917–19.

1908 Punton-Smith,* Rev. S. P., M.A. (Aug. 21, 1917). Chaplain to the Forces (4th Class).

1905 **Radford, O. C.,** B.A. (Serving Aug. 4, 1914). Capt. 12th K.R.R.C. France. Died on Feb. 26, 1916, of wounds received in action.

1908 Raikes,* K. C., B.A. (Sept. 15, 1914). ‡Capt. Monmouthshire Regt. Maj. D.A.Q.M.G., G.H.Q., France. France, 1915–16; Egypt, 1916; France, 1916–19. *O.B.E.* (Mil.). *D.* France, 1917, 1918.

1904 Railton, Rev. D., M.A. (Jan. 10, 1916). Chaplain to the Forces (3rd Class). France. *M.C.*, Nov. 25, 1916. *D.* France, 1917.

1907 Railton,* Rev. N. G., M.A. (Sept. 7, 1915). Chaplain to the Forces (4th Class). France, 1915, 1917–19; Salonika, 1916.

1911 Rawlinson, A. C., M.A. (Sept. 29, 1914). ‡Capt. and Adjt. 1st Q.O. Oxfordshire Hussars. France and Belgium, 1916–17, 1918–19.

1903 Reed, Rev. J. B., B.A. (Jan. 1, 1916). Chaplain to the Forces (4th Class).

1912 Rees,* A. J. L. (June 1, 1915). Capt. 17th Welsh Regt. (Invalided.)

1919 Reeves, Rev. A. W. (Nov. 6, 1916). Cpl., Canadian A.M.C. Belgium and France.

1896 Reeves, T. S. (July 17, 1915). Capt. R.A.M.C.

1894 Reinold, Rev. C., M.A. (Aug. 11, 1914). Chaplain, R.N., H.M.S. *Argonaut.* Atlantic Ocean and English Channel.

1909 Renfree,* Rev. R. S., M.A. (Dec. 4, 1917). Chaplain to the Forces (4th Class). Mesopotamia. *D.* Mesopotamia, 1919.

1908 Reynolds,* H. R., B.A. (Jan. 13, 1915). Lt. R.A.S.C., attd. 15th Hampshire Regt. (Capt.). France, Belgium, Germany. *M.C.*, Mar. 8, 1919.

1911 Reynolds, J. W., M.A. (Aug. 1915). 2nd Lt. 9th S. Wales Borderers, afterwards Lt. I.A.R.O., attd. 2/151st Infantry. France, N.W. Frontier, India, Palestine.

1913 Rice-Oxley, F. B., B.A. (Jan. 5, 1916). Lt. 21st Durham L.I.

1911 Rice-Oxley, L., M.A. (Jan. 22, 1916). Capt. 18th London Regt. (London Irish Rifles), attd. No. 4 O.C.B., afterwards attd. School of Education, Oxford and Newmarket.

1882 Rich, Rev. L. J., M.A. (Serving Aug. 4, 1914). Chaplain to the Forces (4th Class), attd. R.E.

1912 Richards, E. G. C., B.A. (Aug. 22, 1914). Lt. 5th Coldstream Guards. France, 1915–16, 1917–18.

1907 Richardson,* R. J. (Aug. 22, 1914). Capt. 16th R. Sussex Regt. France.

1906 **Ridley, H. L.** (June 1915). 2nd Lt. 5th Essex Regt. France. Killed in action on July 29, 1916.

1876 Rimington, M. F., B.A. (Serving Aug. 4, 1914). Col. 6th Dragoons. Maj.-Gen. Indian Contingent (Lt.-Gen.). France. *C.B.* *C.V.O.*, Croix de Commandeur de la Légion d'Honneur. *D.* France, 1916, 1919; § Feb. 1917.

Roberts, C. L. N. (May 16, 1915). 2nd Lt., Acting Captain, 3rd R. Warwickshire Regt. France and Belgium. *D.* France, 1917. Killed in action at Ypres on Oct. 9, 1917.

1909 Roberts,* H. O., M.A. (Serving Aug. 4, 1914). Capt. Unattached List, T.F., St. Bees O.T.C.

1919 Roberts, M. E. (Sept. 1917). ‡2nd Lt. 60th Engineers, U.S. Army (Capt.). France.

1898 Robertson, F. A. de V., M.A. (Serving Aug. 1914). Lt. I.A.R.O. 2nd Lt. (Hon. Lt.) Technical Officer, R.A.F. France and Belgium. *D.* § Aug. 1919.

1920 Robinson, V. L. (Apr. 22, 1917). ‡2nd Lt. 7th London Regt. (Rifles) France, 1918–19.

1919 Rock, P. E. (Dec. 1915). ‡Lt. R.G.A. (S.R.). France, 1917.

1919 Rogers, G. T. (May 10, 1918). 2nd Lt. E. Surrey Regt. (on demobilization).

1909 Rogers,* M. H., M.A. (Nov. 9, 1914). Lt. 4th, attd. 18th, R. Welch Fusiliers (Capt.).

1904 Rogers, Rev. V. R., B.A. (Mar. 13, 1916). Chaplain to the Forces (4th Class), afterwards 2nd Lt. R.G.A. France, 1916–17.

1920 Rolfe, J. J. (Feb. 15, 1917). Pte. 262nd Siege Batt., R.G.A. Pte. 406th M.T. Coy., R.A.S.C. France and Belgium, 1917–18; Germany, 1918–19.

1919 Rolleston, J. M. (Sept. 20, 1914). Lt. 2/4th Oxf. & Bucks. Lt. Infty. France, 1916–19.

1898 Rorison, Rev. H. G. G., M.A. (Serving Aug. 4, 1914). Chaplain, R.N., H.M.S. *Hercules*. Grand Fleet, Mediterranean, Naval Armistice Commission in German ports.

1915 Ross, J. K. (April 3, 1916). ‡Capt. 11th Oxf. & Bucks. Lt. Infty. France, Germany.

1900 **Ross, Rev. T. E.,** B.A. (Sept. 7, 1915). Chaplain R.N., 1915–16. Died on Aug. 13, 1918.
1918 Roundhill, J. H. (Sept. 5, 1914). Lt. 3rd W. Yorkshire Regt. France and Belgium, 1915–18.
1899 Rowband, Rev. C. P. N., M.A. (Nov. 1, 1917). Chaplain to the Forces (4th Class). France, 1918.
1905 Rowbotham, C. J. (Aug. 23, 1916). 2nd Lt. I.A.R.O., attd. 93rd Burmese Infantry.
1911 **Rowley,* W. A.** (Sept. 1914). ‡2nd Lt. 3rd, attd. 8th, Leicestershire Regt. France and Belgium. Killed in action on July 17, 1917.
1908 **Ruck-Keene, Rev. B. C.,** B.A. (Jan. 10, 1917). Chaplain to the Forces (4th Class), attd. 8th E. Yorkshire Regt. France and Belgium. Killed in action at Passchendaele on Sept. 26, 1917.
1901 Russell, H. L. (July 6, 1916). 2nd Lt. 5th Sherwood Foresters (T.F. Res.).
1908 Russell, S. F. (Dec. 15, 1914). Capt. 14th London Regt. (London Scottish).
1903 Salmon, Rev. D. M., M.A. (Aug. 29, 1916). Chaplain to the Forces (4th Class).
1898 Salmon, Rev. G. E., M.A. (Nov. 1, 1918). Chaplain to the Forces (4th Class). France.
1913 Samler, W. H. G., B.A. (Oct. 10, 1914). Capt. 1/4th Somerset L.I. India, Mesopotamia, Salonika.
1907 Sampson, E. Pte. 28th London Regt. (Artists' Rifles). (Invalided.)
1906 Sanders, Rev. F. H., M.A. (Nov. 27, 1917). Chaplain to the Forces (4th Class).
1897 Sandford, Rev. E. J., M.A. (Oct. 31, 1916). Chaplain to the Forces (4th Class), attd. 1st E. Surrey Regt. France, Belgium, Italy. *M.C.*, Dec. 2, 1918.
1896 Sandford, T. C. G., B.A. (Serving Aug. 4, 1914). Capt., Unattached List, T.F., Marlborough College O.T.C.
1919 Sanger, G. F. (Jan. 13, 1917). Lt. R.M.A. France and Belgium, 1917–19.
1914 **Sauer,* P. F.** (Apr. 1918). Rfln. 2/7th London Regt. (Rifles). France and Belgium. Killed in action at Messines Ridge on Sept. 28, 1918.
1910 **Saunderson,* R. de B.,** B.A. Lt. Gold Coast Regt. Africa. Killed in action on Oct. 18, 1917.
1907 Savage, R., B.A. (Nov. 9, 1914). Capt. 6th (Garr.) Bn. R. Welch Fusiliers (Deputy-Asst. Mil. Sec. to Gen. Allenby). Egypt and Palestine. *D.* Palestine, 1918.
1894 Scatliff, H. H. E., M.A. (Serving Aug. 4, 1914). Capt. R.G.A., afterwards Capt. R.A.M.C. T.D.
1904 Scott, A. M. C., B.A. (Sept. 23, 1914). Lt. 21st London Regt. Capt. Technical Officer, R.A.F.
1904 Seccombe, Rev. C. E., M.A. (June 5, 1917). Chaplain to the Forces (4th Class). France and Belgium. *D.* France, 1918.
1912 Sellors,* Rev. J., M.A. (Nov. 29, 1917). Chaplain to the Forces (4th Class). Salonika.
1913 **Sewell,* W. A.** (Nov. 10, 1914). Lt. 4th Border Regt. and R.F.C. France. Killed in action on Nov. 12, 1917.
1919 Sexton, Rev. H. E. (Apr. 11, 1916). Chaplain to the Forces (4th Class), A.I.F. Belgium, 1917; France, 1918–19. *D.* France, twice.
1912 Sharp,* P. B. (Sept. 1, 1914). 2nd Lt. 6th Lincolnshire Regt. (Commission

relinquished, Jan. 1915). Pte. R.A.S.C. (M.T.) (Cpl.) from Feb. 1917. E. Africa.

1911 Sharpe,* A. J. M., M.A. (Oct. 1917). Pte. R.A.S.C. France, 1918.

Shaw, A. G. (Dec. 12, 1914). Lt. 4th Sherwood Foresters. France. Killed in action on Dec. 24, 1915.

1910 **Shaw,* R. E. F.,** B.A. (Oct. 14, 1914). Lt.-Col. 13th London Regt. France. *M.C.*, Jan. 1, 1918. *D.* France. Killed in action on Aug. 23, 1918.

1914 Shaw, W. (July 12, 1915). 2nd Lt. 11th N. Staffordshire Regt. Lt., temp. Capt., General List. Adjt. N. Riding Vol. Regt.

1895 Shelley, A., B.M., M.A. (Mar. 1917). Capt. R.A.M.C. France and Italy, 1917–19. *D.* Italy, 1919.

1912 **Shields,* W. F. W.,** B.A. (Oct. 8, 1914). Lt. 9th, attd. 5th, Shropshire L.I. France and Belgium. Killed in action in Belgium on Sept. 25, 1915.

1919 Siepmann, C. A. (Sept. 8, 1917). 2nd Lt. R.F.A. Italy. *M.C.*, Sept. 24, 1918.

1915 Simmonds, B. C. (Feb. 1, 1916). Lt. 15th Coy., M.G.C. France and Belgium, 1917–19.

1903 Simons, Rev. A. F., M.A. (Dec. 1, 1914). Pte. 2/3rd E. Anglian Field Ambulance, R.A.M.C. ‡Chaplain to the Forces (4th Class). France and Belgium.

1894 Simpson, Rev. H. W., M.A. (Sept. 1918). Pte. Canadian Engineers.

1904 Sisson, J. J. L. (Nov. 27, 1916). Lt. R.G.A. (S.R.).

1907 **Slater, G. J. L.** (Aug. 9, 1914). Lt. and Adjt. 8th Worcestershire Regt. (Capt.). France. Killed in action at Fonque Villers, near Hèbuterne, on April 30, 1916.

1919 Sleight, R. S. (Aug. 7, 1918). Pte. 28th London Regt. (Artists' Rifles).

1908 Smith, Rev. E., B.A. (May 1, 1917). Chaplain to the Forces (4th Class).

1919 Smith, H. (June 23, 1917). Pte. 87th Training Res. Bn.

1903 Smith, L. E. (Serving Aug. 4, 1914). Lt., Acting Capt. Unattached List, T.F., Bloxham O.T.C.

1908 Smith,* M. de B., M.A. (Aug. 22, 1914). Lt. 8th K.R.R C. Capt. General List, empld. Min. of Nat. Serv. France, 1915.

1911 Smith,* R. E. C., B.A. (Jan. 30, 1918). 2nd Lt. 8th Manchester Regt., attd. 11th Durham L.I. France, 1917–19.

1914 Smith, W. A. (Jan. 11, 1915). Lt. 16th Durham L.I., afterwards Lt. General List. France and Belgium, 1915–16.

1914 **Smith-Masters,* G. A.** (Aug. 21, 1914). 2nd Lt. 2/6th Bedfordshire Regt. France and Belgium. Killed in action on Aug. 20, 1915.

1909 Smith-Masters,*Rev. H. A., M.A. (June 21, 1917). Chaplain to the Forces (4th Class). France. (Prisoner of war.)

1910 Spafford,* D. N., M.A. (Nov. 15, 1915). Lt. R.H.A. Mesopotamia, 1916–18. *D.* Mesopotamia, 1918.

1896 **Speke, Rev. H.,** M.A. (Oct. 1914). Maj. 10th Lancashire Fusiliers. France and Belgium, 1915. Killed in action on Aug. 2, 1915.

1888 Spencer, C. G. Madras Guards, I.D.F.

1885 Spencer, E. V., B.A. (Mar. 19, 1915). Capt. 3rd London Field Coy., R.E. (T.F. Res.).

1913 **Spink, E. M.** (Sept. 7, 1914). ‡Lt. 7th N. Staffordshire Regt. (Capt.). Mesopotamia, 1916–18; S. Russia, 1918. Killed in action at Baku on Sept. 14, 1918.

1891 Stallard, Rev. L. B., M.A. (April 25, 1916). Chaplain to the Forces (4th Class). France, 1916–19.

1907 **Stantial, F. E.** (Nov. 1914). 2nd Lt. 3rd, attd. 2nd, Suffolk Regt. France and Belgium. Killed in action at Ypres on May 4, 1915.

1902 Steeds, P. E. L., B.A. (Oct. 27, 1917). Q.M. Sergt., R.N.A.S.

1887 Steel, Rev. C. H., M.A. (Oct. 10, 1916). Chaplain, R.N.

1908 Stephenson, A., B.Mus. (Sept. 5, 1916). Lt. 5th E. Lancashire Regt.

1911 **Stevens, H. F. B.,** B.A. (Aug. 1914). Lt. 6th R. W. Kent Regt. France. Killed in action at Armentières on Sept. 17, 1915.

1919 Stickland, H. A. N. (May 4, 1918). ‡2nd Lt. 1/6th Cheshire Regt. France, Germany.

1906 **Stock, J. L. W.,** B.A. (Dec. 1915). ‡2nd Lt. 3rd Dorsetshire Regt., attd. 6th Somerset L.I. France, 1916–17. Died on May 3, 1917, of wounds received in action at Wancourt.

1909 **Stock,* J. M. T.,** B.A. (Sept. 1914). Capt. 8th E. Lancashire Regt. France. Killed in action at Beaumont Hamel on Nov. 16, 1916.

1906 Strahan,* G. C., B.A. (Serving Aug. 4, 1914). Capt. 2/6th Gurkha Rifles, Indian Army, attd. 7th Gurkha Rifles (Maj.). India, Mesopotamia, Salonika, Trans-Caucasia, Asia Minor, N.W. Frontier, India, 1915–19. *O.B.E.* (Mil.).

1912 **Street,* T. A.** (Sept. 1914). ‡Lt. 10th Gloucestershire Regt. France and Belgium. Killed in action at Het Sas, Belgium, on Jan. 27, 1918.

1910 **Strickland,* A. R.,** B.A. Pte. 2nd London Regt. France. Killed in action at Passchendaele on Oct. 26, 1917.

1905 Strickland,* Rev. O. F., B.A. (Jan. 4, 1917). Chaplain to the Forces (4th Class). *D.* § Aug. 1919.

1919 Strouts, C. R. N. (May 8, 1918). 2nd Lt. The Buffs (E. Kent Regt.), attd. 7th Queen's (R. W. Surrey Regt.). France.

Stuart, K. B. (Oct. 5, 1914). 2nd Lt. 6th Durham L.I. France. Killed in action on Nov. 5, 1916.

1916 Stuart-Shepherd, G. S. (Aug. 14, 1917). ‡2nd Lt. Indian Army, attd. 1/95th Russell's Infantry. India.

1880 Stubbs, J. H. (Serving Aug. 4, 1914). Maj. R.E. (retired). France. *D.* France, 1917.

1912 **Stubbs, R. A.** (Aug. 1914). ‡2nd Lt. 4th R. Munster Fusiliers, and R.F.C. France, 1916. Killed in action near Arras on June 8, 1916.

1907 Sumner,* W. C. (Nov. 1915). Sergt. 21st Signal Coy., R.E. France, for 3 years. *M.M.*

1893 Sutcliffe, Rev. F. E., B.A. (Serving Aug. 4, 1914). Chaplain R.N. Malta.

1911 Sutcliffe, P. R.A.F. (late R.N.A.S.).

1909 Sweet,* Rev. G. C. W., M.A. (Aug. 6, 1918). Chaplain to the Forces (4th Class), attd. 3rd Lowland Bde. H.Q., Army of the Rhine. Germany. Accidentally drowned on Aug. 7, 1919.

1904 Swift, E. M., B.A. Inns of Court O.T.C.

1883 Swift, R. M. P. (Mobilized Aug. 4, 1914). Maj. R. Dublin Fusiliers (Res. of Officers).

1912 **Swift,* W. H.** (Sept. 2, 1914). Lt. 6th Hampshire Regt. Mesopotamia. *D.* Mesopotamia, 1917. Died on April 22, 1917, of wounds received in action.

1913 **Swindells,* C. G. R.** (Oct. 1914). 2nd Lt. 7th Leicestershire Regt. France, Mesopotamia. Killed in action at Sanna-i-Yat on Jan. 19, 1917.

1919 Sykes, P. H. (Sept. 7, 1915). Lt. 4th Yorkshire Regt. France and Belgium, 1916.
1912 Talbot,* E. P., B.A. (Sept. 19, 1914). Capt. 9th Welsh Regt. France.
1919 Tandy, G. (Apr. 22, 1918). ‡2nd Lt. R.A.
1912 Tanner,* B. W., M.A. (Sept. 15, 1914). ‡Lt., Acting Capt., 3rd R. Fusiliers. France, 1915; Salonika, 1915–18; France, 1918–19. *M.C.*, Apr. 2, 1919.
1911 **Tanner,* C. P.** (Oct. 1914). ‡Capt. S. Wales Borderers. Capt. M.G.C. France. Killed in action on Nov. 30, 1917.
Tanner, J. C. (Feb. 14, 1916). Capt. R.A.F. France. Accidentally killed on Aug. 1, 1918.
1911 **Tanner,* J. H.,** B.A. (Aug. 1914). Lt. 10th Hampshire Regt. Gallipoli, 1915; France, 1916. Killed in action in the Battle of the Somme on Sept. 15, 1916.
1904 Taylor, A. T., B.A. (Aug. 1914). Capt. 1/2nd London Regt. (R. Fusiliers). Malta, 1914–15; France and Belgium, 1915–19. *M.C.*, Jan. 1, 1919. *D.* France, 1916.
1916 Tenison, E. H. R. (Mar. 21, 1917). Capt. 17th S. Lancashire Regt.
1919 Tetley, S. (Dec. 2, 1915). 2nd Lt. 2/7th W. Yorkshire Regt. France, 1917–18.
1906 Thicknesse, Rev. C. C., M.A. (June 15, 1915). Chaplain to the Forces (4th Class). France and Belgium. (Invalided May, 1917.)
1914 Thirlway, M. H. (July 8, 1915). Lt. 9th Lancashire Regt. Egypt.
1909 Thomas,* Rev. H. C., M.A. (Mar. 21, 1917). Chaplain to the Forces (4th Class), attd. 19th Bde., R.H.A. Egypt, Sinai Desert, Palestine.
1887 Thomas, L. G., B.A. (Serving Aug. 4, 1914). Capt. Unattached List, T.F., Edinburgh Academy O.T.C. *D.* § Mar. 1919.
1919 Thomas, M. W. (Oct. 2, 1918). 2nd Aircraftsman R.A.F.
1891 Thomas, Rev. R. R., M.A. (Jan. 12, 1916). Chaplain to the Forces (4th Class). France, 1916–17.
1919 Thomas, T. W. B. (Jan. 26, 1918). Midshipman R.N.V.R.
1904 Thomas, Rev. W. G. K., B.A. (Aug. 1, 1918). Chaplain to the Forces (4th Class).
1919 Thompson, B. B. (Apr. 30, 1917). Lt. 219th Field Coy., R.E. France, Germany, 1918–19.
1919 Thompson, E. F. L. (Apr. 23, 1915). ‡Lt. R.A.S.C., attd. 1/8th R. Warwickshire Regt. France, 1915–17; Italy, 1918.
1903 Thompson, R. L. (May 29, 1918). 2nd Lt. London Regt. France, 1918.
1896 Thompson, W. E., B.A. (Jan. 1916). Cpl. 1/28th London Regt. (Artists' Rifles) (Sergt.). France, 1916–19.
1912 Thorpe, E., M.A. (Jan. 21, 1916). Pte. 5th Norfolk Regt. Macedonia, Palestine.
1901 Tinley, Rev. S. G., M.A. (Apr. 15, 1915). Chaplain to the Forces (4th Class). Egypt, Palestine, 1915–17.
1898 Tireman, C. L., M.A. (Serving Aug. 4, 1914). Capt. R.F.A. (Resigned.)
1910 Tobutt, R. L. W., B.A. (Jan. 1916). ‡2nd Lt. R.F.A. (S.R.). France.
1908 **Todd,* A. C.,** B.A. Chota Nagpur Light Horse. India. Died on Nov. 2, 1917.
1897 **Todd, N. H.,** M.A. (Apr. 1916). Rfln. 16th London Regt. (Queen's Westminster Rifles). France, 1916. Killed in action on Oct. 7, 1916.

1898 **Todd, O. E.** (Serving Aug. 4, 1914). Major, 5th Gurkha Rifles, Indian Army. India. Accidentally killed on July 10, 1916.

1899 **Tollemache, L. de O.** (Serving Aug. 4, 1914). Capt. 1st Lincolnshire Regt. France and Belgium. *D.* France, 1914. Killed in action at Wytschaete on Nov. 1, 1914.

1910 **Tombs,* J. D.,** B.A. (Dec. 28, 1914). Lt. 7th Border Regt. France. Died on active service on Feb. 17, 1916.

1900 Torrance, Rev. W. J., M.A. (Nov. 1914). Chaplain to the Forces (4th Class), attd. 19th Div. France. *D.* France.

1912 Treadgold, G. W. R., M.A. (Aug. 2, 1916). Lt. 6th Middlesex Regt. Mesopotamia, 1917; India, 1917–18.

1913 **Tree,* P. B.** (Sept. 1914). ‡2nd Lt. M.G.C. France, 1915–16, 1917–18. Killed in action at Peronne on March 24, 1918.

1901 Tulk, J. A., B.A. (Jan. 17, 1917). Lt. R.G.A. France and Belgium.

1919 Tunnadine, H. C. (May 29, 1915). 2nd Lt. 3rd Loyal N. Lancashire Regt. Lt. 104th M.G. Bn. German E. Africa, 1916–18; France, 1918.

1914 Turk, F. W. (Jan. 25, 1915). Lt. 3rd The Buffs (E. Kent Regt.). Egypt, 1915–16; Mesopotamia, 1916.

1912 **Turner,* A.** Pte. 12th Gloucestershire Regt. Died on May 7, 1915.

1897 **Turner, N. P. J.** (Sept. 4, 1914). Lt. 3rd, attd. 1st, S. Wales Borderers. France. *D.* France, 1915. Died on May 14, 1915, of wounds received in action.

1898 Tyson, R. W., M.A. (May 17, 1918). 2nd Lt. Unattached List, T.F., Imperial College O.T.C.

1904 Vassall, Rev. W., M.A. (Aug. 2, 1918). Chaplain to the Forces (4th Class). Russia, Persia, 1918–20.

1895 Vaughan, C. G., B.A. (Dec. 1915). Pte. Cheshire Regt. Salonika.

1914 Veazie, H. P., B.A. (1918). Cadet, Guards M.G. Regt.

1919 Veitch, S. N. (Oct. 13, 1915). 2nd Lt. Durham L.I. Maj. R.A.F. France and Belgium, 1916–17.

Vinter, R. B. W. (Feb. 3, 1915). Lt. 6th Worcestershire Regt. France, 1915, 1916. *M.C.*, July 28, 1916. Killed in action near Les Boeufs on Oct. 31, 1916.

1907 **Wade,* H. W.** (Serving Aug. 4, 1914). Lt. 3rd Brahmans, Indian Army. France, 1914. Killed in action on Oct. 28, 1914.

1911 **Walker, E. W.,** B.A. (Aug. 8, 1914). Capt. 7th R. Welch Fusiliers. Palestine. *D.S.O.*, Aug. 16, 1917. *D.* Palestine, 1917. Killed in action on Nov. 6, 1917.

1903 Walker, R. C., M.A. Middlesex Regt. (Discharged.)

1909 **Walters,* E. C.,** B.A. (Aug. 15, 1914). 2nd Lt. 3rd Gloucestershire Regt. France. Killed in action on Dec. 21, 1914.

1895 **Walton, Rev. C. A.,** M.A. (1915). Chaplain, R.N., H.M.S. *Chester*. Grand Fleet. Killed in action in the Battle of Jutland on May 31, 1916.

1908 Wanstall, H. J. B., M.A. (Dec. 23, 1914). Lt. Unattached List, T.F., Wellington College O.T.C.

1902 Ward, H. A., B.A. (Nov. 22, 1915). Lt. 14th Gloucestershire Regt.

1919 Ward, H. B. (Sept. 15, 1915). Lt. 7th Cheshire Regt. (Capt.). France, 1917–19.

1908 Warde,* Rev. G. H., M.A. (June 21, 1916). Chaplain to the Forces (4th Class). Salonika.

1909 Warne,* G. L. M. (Feb. 1915). Hon. Capt. Uganda Volunteer Reserve, attd. Political Dept. German E. Africa.

1910 Warne,* O. H., B.A. (Serving Aug. 4, 1914). Capt. 1st Manchester Regt., attd. as Maj., Egyptian Army. Togoland, Palestine, Egypt. *M.C.*, June 3, 1919. *D.* Palestine, 1918.

1919 Waterhouse, R. D. (June 1, 1917). 2nd Lt. R.F.A. France, 1918.

1907 Waters, E. G. R., M.A. (Aug. 30, 1915). ‡Lt. Queen's (R. W. Surrey Regt.) Staff-Lt. Intelligence Corps. France, Italy.

1911 Waters, K. F. D., B.M. (Sept. 6, 1915). Surgeon Probationer, R.N.V.R. Lt. Medical Officer, R.A.F.

1899 Watkins, H. B., M.A. (Aug. 5, 1916). ‡Lt. 1st D.C.L.I. France, 1917.

1903 Watmough, C. W., B.A. (July 4, 1918). 2nd Lt. R.A.S.C.

1897 Watmough, F. C., B.A. R.F.A.

1895 Watson, H. T., B.A. (June 17, 1917). 2nd Lt. 3rd R. Welch Fusiliers.

1900 **Watts, H. V. I.,** M.A. (Oct. 1914). Capt. 7th, attd. 2nd, Devonshire Regt. Belgium. Died on Aug. 11, 1917, of wounds received in action at Third Battle of Ypres.

1898 Waudby, C. (Serving Aug. 4, 1914). Capt. 18th Hussars. Maj. M.G.C. France.

1890 Waugh, Rev. W. L., M.A. (Serving Aug. 4, 1914). Chaplain (3rd Class) R. Wiltshire Yeomanry.

1894 **Weatherhead, G. E.,** B.A. (Serving Aug. 4, 1914). Capt. King's Own (R. Lancaster Regt.). Killed in action, May 8–9, 1915.

1877 Weigall, Rev. G., M.A. (Oct. 1, 1914). Chaplain to the Forces (4th Class). India.

1913 Weir,* N. A. C. (Aug. 26, 1914). Capt. Arg. & Suth'd. Highlanders, attd. No. 21 O.C.B. (Staff-Captain). France, 1915–16. *D.* France, 1916.

1903 Westby, Rev. J. T., B.A. (Jan. 15, 1917). Capt. R.A.M.C.

1897 Wetherall, C. R., M.A. (Jan. 1, 1915). Capt. 2/5th Devonshire Regt. Egypt, 1915–16; Mesopotamia, 1916–19.

1911 Wheeler,* C., M.A. (Sept. 21, 1914). Maj. 7th Oxf. & Bucks. Lt. Infty. (Lt.-Col. Worcestershire Regt.). France, 1915; Salonika, 1915–19. *D.S.O.*, July 26, 1917. Greek Military Cross. *D.* Salonika, 1917.

1917 Wheeler, R. E. (Aug. 9, 1918). Cadet, No. 11 O.C.B.

1896 Whitaker, Rev. C. G., B.A. (June 4, 1915). Pte. 44th Field Ambulance, R.A.M.C. France.

1899 Whitaker, R. McF. A., M.A. (July 14, 1915). 2nd Lt. 6th Dorsetshire Regt.

1906 White,* A. P., M.A. (Aug. 15, 1914). Lt. 3rd, attd. 1st, Northamptonshire Regt. France.

1905 White, S. B., B.M. (June, 1917). Capt. R.A.M.C.

1910 Whitehead,* Rev. H., B.A. (Jan. 4, 1918). Chaplain to the Forces (4th Class).

1912 **Whitehouse,* A. G. R.** (Sept. 1, 1914). Maj. 1st Herefordshire Regt. Gallipoli, Egypt, Palestine, France, 1915–18. *M.C.*, Jan. 1, 1918. *D.* Gallipoli, 1916; Palestine, 1917. Killed in action at Soissons on Aug. 1, 1918.

1909 **Whiteside,* C. H. M.,** B.A. (Nov. 13, 1914). Capt. and Adjt. 7th Border Regt. France. Died on Nov. 1, 1916, of wounds received in action at the Battle of the Somme.

1913 Whitrow,* P. B. (Sept. 13, 1914). Lt. 5th R. W. Kent Regt. France. (Prisoner of war in Germany, Mar.–Dec. 1918.)

1904 Wilken, Rev. A. G., M.A. (Feb. 5, 1915). Tpr. Canadian Mounted Rifles. ‡Chaplain to the Forces, attd. 4th Canadian Division. France, 1915–16, 1919. (Prisoner of war in Germany, 1916–18.) *D.* May 5, 1919.

1893 Wilkinson, F. H. (Oct. 1915). ‡Flag Lt. R.N.V.R. (Commdr.). Mine-Sweeper Flotilla.

1912 Wilkinson, F. R. (1914). Lt. Indian Army, attd. 12th Pioneers. India. Died, Feb. 1920.

1919 Wilkinson, G. L. B. (May 6, 1918). Cadet R.A.F.

1888 Wilkinson, W. E., M.A. (1914). ‡Lt. Special Lists (whilst with Nyasaland Field Force). France, E. Africa.

Willans, G. R. (Sept. 26, 1917). 2nd Lt. 3rd, attd. 2nd, Lancashire Fusiliers. France. Died on Mar. 29, 1918, of wounds received in action near Arras.

1909 Williams, C. à B., M.A. (Sept. 11, 1914). Capt. 6th Devonshire Regt., attd. War Office. (Invalided, July, 1916.)

Williams, F. C. D. (May 9, 1915). 2nd Lt. 3rd E. Surrey Regt., attd. R. Berkshire Regt. France. Killed in action on July 19, 1916.

1909 Williams, H. M. (Jan. 19, 1916). Lt. Indian Army, attd. 74th Punjabis (Capt.). India.

1914 Williams, W. H. H. (Aug. 16, 1915). 2nd Lt. 11th York & Lancaster Regt. Lt. M.G.C. France, 1916.

1904 Willis, Rev. E. M. (Sept. 18, 1917). Chaplain to the Forces (4th Class).

1898 Willson, T. O., M.A. (Nov. 9, 1914). ‡2nd Lt. General List (T.F. Res.) (lent to Foreign Office for special duty). *C.B.E.* (Civil). Chevalier de l'Ordre de la Couronne.

Wilmshurst, E. R. (Sept. 1914). ‡Lt. 20th R. Fusiliers (Capt.). France and Belgium. Died on Dec. 1, 1916, of wounds received in action at Le Transloy.

1911 **Wilson,* A. A.,** B.A. (June 2, 1916). 2nd Lt. 3rd, attd. 2nd, Arg. & Suth'd. Highlanders. France, 1916–17. Killed in action on Apr. 23, 1917.

1912 **Wilson,* B. W.** (Sept. 3, 1914). ‡2nd Lt. 19th London Regt., attd. R.A.F. France. Killed in action near St. Quentin on Sept. 23, 1918.

1916 Wilson, R. M. (Jan. 12, 1916). ‡Lt. M.G.C. France, 1917–18; Italy, 1918.

1904 Wilson, Rev. W. S., B.A. (Jan. 6, 1915). Chaplain to the Forces (4th Class). Gallipoli, Sinai, Palestine, France, 1915–19.

1886 Winter, E. S. (Mobilized Aug. 4, 1914). Maj. R.A.M.C. (4th Northern General Hospital).

1884 Wood, Rev. G. R., M.A. (May, 1917). Chaplain to the Forces (2nd Class). T.D.

1910 Wood, J. H., B.A. (Apr. 20, 1915). Capt. 4th Highland L.I. Mesopotamia, 1916, 1917–18; India, 1916–17.

1910 **Woodhams,* G.** (Aug. 1914). Capt. 7th R. Sussex Regt. France, Belgium. *D.* France, 1915, 1916. Killed in action near the Hohenzollern Redoubt on Mar. 19, 1916.

1913 **Woodruff,* A. H. W.** (Feb. 18, 1915). 2nd Lt. 4th Dorsetshire Regt. Mesopotamia. Killed in action on Sept. 26, 1917.

1913 **Woods,* G.** (Jan. 8, 1915). Capt. 9th London Regt. (Queen Victoria's Rifles). France. Killed in action on Sept. 9, 1916.

1904 Wood-Smith, Rev. T. J. M., M.A. (Feb. 12, 1918). Chaplain to the Forces (4th Class), attd. R.A.F.

1889 Woollcombe, Rev. H. St. J. S., M.A. (Serving Aug. 4, 1914). Chaplain W. Yorkshire Regt.

1903 Worlock, H. T., B.A. (Sept. 3, 1914). ‡Capt. R.F.A. (Maj.). France and Belgium.

1899 Worrall, P. R. (Serving Aug. 4, 1914). Maj., Bt. Lt.-Col. Devonshire Regt. France, 1914, 1917, 1918; Gallipoli, 1915; Italy, 1917–18. *D.S.O.*, Jan. 1, 1918. *M.C.*, Feb. 18, 1915. *D.* France, 1917, 1918; § Feb. 1917.

1915 Wrenford, C. R. B. (July 16, 1916). Lt. 5th R. Berkshire Regt. France, 1917, 1918, 1919.

1897 Wright, E. E. V., M.A. (Nov. 30, 1914). Petty Officer (1st Class), Recruiting Staff, R.N.V.R.

1907 Wright, H. L., B.A. (Apr. 1, 1917). Lt. 2/32nd Madras and S. Mahratta Railway Rifles, I.D.F. India.

1919 Wyers, G. H. (Mar. 14, 1917). ‡2nd Lt. 6th Siege Batt., R.G.A. France, Belgium, Germany, 1918–19.

1880 Yates, Rev. A. G., M.A. (Serving Aug. 4, 1914). Chaplain R.N.

1912 Young,* W. R. B., M.A. (Jan. 1, 1915). Lt. 9th Welsh Regt., attd. 52nd Cheshire Regt. *D.* § Aug. 1919.

NON-COLLEGIATE

1905 **Abrams, R. A.,** M.A. (July 4, 1915). Lt. 8th Sherwood Foresters. France. Killed in action on Mar. 5, 1917.
1907 Ainslie, J. R. (Apr. 19, 1915). Lt. 4th R. Dublin Fusiliers.
1909 Aldridge, M., M.A. (Mar. 1915). Capt. R.A.O.C. Belgium, France.
1906 [Amery, G. D., M.A.] (Dec. 11, 1914). Maj. 15th Hampshire Regt. France. *M.C.*, Jan. 1, 1917.
1920 Anderson, J. S. S. (Aug. 19, 1914). Maj. 4th Bn. A.I.F. Bde.-Maj. 3rd Australian Bde. Egypt, 1914; Gallipoli, 1915; Egypt and Sinai, 1916; France and Belgium, 1916–19. *D.S.O.*, Jan. 1, 1919. *M.C.*, Jan. 14, 1916. *D.* Gallipoli, 1915; Egypt, 1916; France, 1918.
1905 Annis, W. F., M.A. (July 1917). Pte. Dispatch Rider, R.A.S.C. France, Belgium, Germany.
1908 Arnett, M. G., M.A. (Mar. 1, 1915). Capt. 7th Oxf. & Bucks. Lt. Infty. Maj. M.G.C., attd. O.C.B. Salonika.
1912 Attale, W. M. E., B.A. (Dec. 23, 1914). Lt. M.G.C. France.
1914 Ault, F. T., B.A. (Sept. 1917). Gnr. R.G.A.
1889 Aylmer-Stark, Rev. W. (Apr. 20, 1916). Chaplain to the Forces (4th Class).
1898 **Baker, T.,** B.A. (Sept. 9, 1914). Capt. 10th Lincolnshire Regt. France. Killed in action in the Battle of the Somme on July 1, 1916.
1897 Barber, C. H., D.M. (Serving Aug. 4, 1914). Maj. Indian Medical Service. Mesopotamia, 1914–16; at sea, H.M. Hospital Ship (for 13 months). *D.S.O.*, June 3, 1919. *D.* Mesopotamia, 1915, 1916 twice.
1909 Barker, W. G. (Apr. 9, 1917). 2nd Lt. R.G.A.
1919 Barry, E. (Oct. 2, 1917). Lce.-Cpl. 1/6th Manchester Regt., attd. 127th T.M.B. France, 1918–19.
1912 Barry, Rev. V. A. A., B.Litt. (Mar. 1915). Chaplain, R.N., 1st Battle Squadron. East Mediterranean, North Sea.
1892 Barton, H. H., B.A. (Serving Aug. 4, 1914). Instructor Commander, R.N.
1900 Bavin, J. T. (Serving Aug. 4, 1914). Maj. Queen's (R. W. Surrey Regt.). *D.* § Feb. 1917.
1913 Beechey,* O. P. (July 22, 1915). Lt. 5th Somerset L.I.
1905 Bell, Rev. H. C., M.A., V.D. (Mobilized Sept. 1914). Chaplain to the Forces (1st Class), attd. 17th London Regt. (Senior Chaplain 47th Div.). France.
1919 Biggers, W. N. (Mar. 6, 1916). Pioneer, Special Bde., R.E. France.
1913 Billings, Rev. A. J., M.A. (Sept. 28, 1917). Chaplain to the Forces (4th Class). France and Belgium.
1919 Blunt, H. S. (Jan. 1915). Capt. 3rd Gordon Highlanders. France, 1915–17.
1903 Bode, F. T., B.A. (Sept. 23, 1916). Rfln. 33rd London Regt. (Rifle Brigade). France.
1909 **Bonsey, E. K.,** B.A. (Feb. 20, 1917). 2nd Lt. R.G.A. France. Died from effects of gas poisoning on July 2, 1918.

1919 Boyd, J. (May 2, 1916). Pte. 10th Durham L.I. France. (Discharged, June 2, 1917.)

1917 Boyes, J. N. T. (Aug. 4, 1914). Q.M.S. 3rd City of London Field Amb., R.A.M.C. (Sergt.-Maj.). France, Belgium. *D.* France, 1915.

1908 Brittain, E. R., B.A. (July 16, 1915). Capt. Manchester Regt.

1905 Brooker, Rev. A. B., M.A. (Dec. 5, 1915). Chaplain to the Forces (4th Class). Belgium, France. *D.* France, 1917.

1912 **Brooks, E. W.,** B.A. (Dec. 22, 1914). Capt. 6th Oxf. & Bucks. Lt. Infty. France and Belgium. Killed in action on Sept. 20, 1917.

1911 Brown,* A. C., B.A. (Aug. 9, 1914). Pte. 4th M.G.C. (Cavalry). France.

1920 Brown, J. A. (Nov. 24, 1914). ‡Lt. 2nd Northumberland Fusiliers. Gallipoli, 1915; France, 1916, 1917, 1918–19.

1899 Buck, H. C., M.A. (Nov. 29, 1915). Sergt. R.A.M.C. France and Belgium.

1914 Burborough, A. W. (July 19, 1915). ‡Lt. M.G.C. France.

1914 **Burrows, A. C.** (Dec. 22, 1914). 2nd Lt. 14th, attd. 8th, Cheshire Regt. Mesopotamia. Died at Karachi on June 5, 1916, of wounds received in action in Mesopotamia.

1908 Burton, A. A. C., M.A. (Sept. 13, 1916). ‡Lt. R.G.A. (S.R.). France, 1917.

1914 Bye, W. R. G., M.A. (Aug. 1914). Capt. 8th Queen's (R. W. Surrey Regt.). Staff-Captain General List. France, 1915–18. *D.S.O.*, Jan. 1, 1918. *M.C.*, May 31, 1916. *D.* France, twice.

1901 Calway, Rev. L. J. (Oct. 26, 1915). Chaplain to the Forces (4th Class).

1918 Campbell, D. (Aug. 4, 1914). ‡Lt. I.A.R.O. Capt. R.A.M.C. India, Burma, Egypt, Mediterranean, France. *D.* Mediterranean, 1915.

1913 **Cann, T.** (1914). Sergt. 7th Gloucestershire Regt. Died at Tidworth Military Hospital on Apr. 1, 1915.

1912 **Carpenter,* B. M.,** B.A. (Apr. 1916). 2nd Lt. 6th Middlesex Regt. France, 1916–17; Italy, 1917–18; France, 1918. Died on Apr. 3, 1918, of wounds received in action on Mar. 25.

1900 Carpenter, G. D. H., D.M. (Aug. 26, 1914). Capt. Uganda Medical Service. German and Portuguese E. Africa. *M.B.E.* (Mil.).

1919 Carter, H. S. (1917). 2nd Lt. U.S. Army.

1900 Casey, E. C., M.A. (July 12, 1915). Lt. General List. Staff. Lt. Intelligence Corps. France and Belgium.

1895 Chatterton, E. K., B.A. (Sept. 11, 1914). Lt. R.N.V.R.

1919 Chenoweth, Rev. C. W. (1917). Chaplain U.S. Army.

1920 Clark, A. M. (Oct. 26, 1916). Cpl. 5th Res. Bde., R.F.A. Salonika.

1910 **Clarke, H. F.,** B.A. (Aug. 22, 1914). Lt. 5th Oxf. & Bucks. Lt. Infty. Belgium, France. Missing, believed killed in action at the Battle of Loos on Sept. 25, 1915.

1916 Clarke,* L. F. (Dec. 1, 1916). Lt. 5th R. Welch Fusiliers. France.

1909 Clarkson, R. M., B.A. (Jan. 13, 1915). Capt. 4th Highland L.I.

1919 Clavel, M. A. F. Y. M. (Sept. 5, 1914). ‡Capt. 81st Regt. of Infantry, French Army (Bn.-Commdr.). France. Croix de Guerre. *D.* French Orders.

1904 Clifford, Rev. E. O., B.A. (June 4, 1915). Chaplain to the Forces (4th Class). *D.* § Mar. 1918.

1909 Coldicott, H. R. S., B.Litt. (Sept. 23, 1914). Capt. 21st London Regt. France. *M.C.*, Feb. 18, 1918. *D.* France, 1916.

1915 **Cole, H. T. S.** (Sept. 3, 1915). 2nd Lt. 19th London Regt., attd. K.O.Y.L.I. France, 1917. Died on Feb. 12, 1917, of wounds received in action.
1901 Coleman, R. H. F., M.A. (Mar. 27, 1915). Capt. 9th N. Staffordshire Regt. Education Officer, 4th Corps. France, Belgium, 1916–18. *D.* France, 1919.
1918 Coles, Rev. H. H. (Aug. 24, 1916). Chaplain to the Forces (4th Class), attd. 1st Bn. A.I.F. France, Belgium, 1918–19.
1919 Collins, Rev. D. J. (Feb. 16, 1916). Pte. 11th Depot Bn., A.I.F. ‡Chaplain (Maj.) 4th Australian Div. H.Q. France.
1914 Compton, S. A. (Oct. 17, 1915). 2nd Lt. Somerset L.I.
1898 Connor, Rev. H. L., M.A. (May 15, 1915). Chaplain to the Forces (4th Class).
1908 Constable, A. B., M.A. Pte. 28th London Regt. (Artists' Rifles).
1917 Cook, S. C. (Sept. 14, 1914). Pte. 1/4th Oxf. & Bucks. Lt. Infty. Belgium, France.
1914 Cox, J. A., B.A. (Aug. 8, 1918). Sergt. R.A.F. Cadet Bde.
1919 Cressy, R. (Sept. 1, 1914). ‡Lt. 17th Lancashire Fusiliers (Capt.). France, Belgium, 1916–19.
1913 **Crichton, H. C.** (July 24, 1915). 2nd Lt. 18th Manchester Regt. France. Killed in action on Oct. 7, 1916.
1903 Crowe, G. L. (Jan. 20, 1915). Lt. and Adjt. 6th Worcestershire Regt.
1908 Danbury, Rev. C. G., M.A. (Apr. 27, 1915). Chaplain to the Forces (4th Class). France, 1915; Salonika, 1915–16; H.M.H.S. *Kalyan*, 1918.
1919 Daniell, E. H. (Feb. 24, 1915). ‡2nd Lt. R.F.A. (on demobilization). France, 1917–18.
1906 Dann, C. H., M.A. (July 7, 1916). Lt. 6th R. W. Kent Regt., attd. O.C.B.
1907 **Dann, E.,** M.A. (Aug. 26, 1914). Lt. 6th Bedfordshire Regt. France. Died on Nov. 22, 1915, of wounds received in action.
1898 Dann, E. W., M.A. (Mobilized Aug. 1914). Capt. 8th Essex Regt. Maj. M.G.C. France, Belgium, 1917.
1911 Darby, G. (Oct. 8, 1915). Lt., temp. Capt., R.F.A. Staff-Captain. France, N. Russia. *M.C.*, June 3, 1918. *D.* France, 1918, 1919; N. Russia, 1919.
1917 Darby, P. R., B.A. (1918). Cadet O.C.B.
1883 Davenport, Rev. F., M.A. (Sept. 14, 1915). Chaplain to the Forces (4th Class).
1919 Davies, T. J. (Feb. 3, 1915). ‡Lt. 14th Welsh Regt. France.
1902 Davis, Rev. R. K., M.A. (Dec. 1, 1915). Chaplain to the Forces (4th Class). Malta, 1916–17; H.M.H.S. *Llandovery Castle*, 1917; Salonika, 1917; France, 1918–19.
1900 Dawson, W. H., M.A. (Nov. 5, 1914). Capt. 4th Loyal N. Lancashire Regt. Staff-Captain, G.S.O. 3. France, Belgium, 1917–19. *D.* France, 1917, 1918.
1909 De la Bere, Rev. C. E. (July 3, 1917). Chaplain to the Forces (4th Class).
1906 Dell, A. M., M.A. (May 10, 1916). ‡2nd Lt. R.A.S.C. Egypt and Palestine.
1906 **Dell, R.,** B.A. (Apr. 1915). Lt. 10th Bedfordshire Regt. Lt. M.G.C. France. Died as a prisoner of war on May 8, 1918, from effects of wounds.
1908 Denham, S. T. (Jan. 21, 1916). Lt. 10th London Regt.

1914 De Wolodkowicz, J. J. Praporshik, 5th Obozny Bn. 21st Transport, Russian Army. Russia.
1894 **Dibb, W. R.** (May 11, 1916). Capt. R.F.A., attd. T.M.B. France. *M.C.*, Feb. 6, 1917. Died at Tourastre on May 27, 1918, of wounds received in action.
1915 Dickenson, E. C. Lce.-Cpl. R.E.
1897 **Dickinson, G. R. W.,** M.A. Pte., Canadian E. F. France, Belgium. Killed in action in Nov. 1917.
1919 Dickson, H. E. B., B.A. (Mar. 25, 1915). ‡Lt. 3rd Devonshire Regt. France. (Prisoner of war, 1917–18.)
1919 Dixon, S. (Jan. 2, 1915). ‡Lt. M.G.C. France, 1915–16, 1917, 1918.
1900 Dodson, C. W., M.A. (Mobilized Aug. 1914). Capt. 5th Queen's (R. W. Surrey Regt.).
1916 Dolley, S. P. B. Pte. Oxf. & Bucks. Lt. Infty.
1901 Dougan, J. L., M.A. (May, 1915). Director, Missing and Wounded Dept. Mediterranean Area, B.R.C.S. France, Malta, Egypt, Gallipoli.
1914 Downes, G. R. (July 26, 1915). Rfln. 5th London Regt. (London Rifle Brigade). France, Belgium, Germany
1909 Druce, C. J., M.A. (Mar. 1, 1916). ‡Lt. 12th Gloucestershire Regt. France.
1914 **Dunn, H. J.** (Jan. 20, 1916). Lt. 4th R. W. Kent Regt. France. Killed in action on Nov. 26, 1917.
1914 **Dunstan, Rev. S.** (May 2, 1918). Chaplain to the Forces (4th Class), attd. 84th Training Res. Bn. Died on July 16, 1918, of illness contracted on active service.
1913 Dwyer, Rev. J. (Jan. 10, 1916). Chaplain to the Forces (4th Class).
1919 Dyer, T. R. (1917). 2nd Lt. U.S. Army.
1907 **Dyott,* K. M.,** B.A. (July 24, 1915). Surgeon, R.N. Grand Fleet. Drowned on Dec. 13, 1917, in sinking of H.M.S. *Stephen Furness*.
1903 Elwell, J. A. W., B.A. Gnr. R.A.
1891 Evans, J. H., D.M. Motor Ambulance Convoy, B.E.F. France.
1909 Evans, Rev. J. H. (Jan. 1, 1918). Chaplain to the Forces (4th Class).
1899 Farquharson, Rev. E. E., M.A. (May 1, 1917). Chaplain to the Forces (4th Class).
1888 Fernsby, Rev. A. R., M.A. (July 27, 1915). Chaplain to the Forces (4th Class).
1913 Ferrall, K. J. S. (Sept. 2, 1914). ‡2nd Lt., Acting Capt., General List. Gas Officer, H.Q. 46th Division. Gallipoli.
1919 Firth, F. (Aug. 1914). ‡Capt. 9th York & Lancaster Regt. Capt. Tank Corps. France, 1915–16, 1917–18. Croix de Guerre avec palme.
1910 Fischer, G. (Oct. 22, 1915). Lt. R.A.O.C.
1900 Fitzgerald, T. P., B.A. (Nov. 18, 1916). Lt. 1st Central Ontario Regt., Canadian E.F. France.
1906 Fletcher, Rev. A. F. G. (Mar. 13, 1915). Chaplain to the Forces.
1919 Foreman, H. J. C. (May 9, 1917). Chaplain, Maj. A.I.F. France.
1898 Franscombe, L. J., M.A. Pte. Queen's (R.W. Surrey Regt.).
1904 Gale, E. E. H. R.A.S.C. (M.T.).
1900 **Garth, H.,** B.A. Lce.-Cpl. R. Fusiliers. France. Killed in action on Sept. 27, 1916.
1915 Gaskin, A. D., Pte. H.A.C.
1903 Gee.* F. S., M.A. (May 1, 1917). 2nd Lt. R.A.S.C. E. Africa, 1918–19.

1895 Gibson, S., M.A. (May 25, 1916). Cpl. 22nd K.R.R.C. Cpl. R.A.F., Intelligence Section, Air Ministry (Sergt.).

1914 Gilbert, U. B. (Aug. 21, 1915. Lt. R.G.A. 2nd Lt. Administrative Officer, R.A.F.

1888 Gillmor, Rev. F. J. C., M.A. (Aug. 1914). Chaplain to the Forces (3rd Class). *D.* § Aug. 1919.

1907 Graham, Rev. P. G. (July 18, 1916). Chaplain to the Forces (4th Class).

1910 Grant, Rev. A. R. H., B.D. (Jan. 1916). Chaplain to the Forces (4th Class), attd. 3rd Cavalry Division. France, 1916, 1918.

1905 Grant, Rev. E. E. B., B.A. (Oct. 4, 1918). Chaplain to the Forces (4th Class).

1911 Grant,* R. G., B.A. (Feb. 19, 1915). Capt. Tank Corps, attd. 20th London Regt.

1905 **Green, Rev. H. J. B.** (Sept. 6, 1918). Chaplain to the Forces (4th Class). Died on Dec. 8, 1918.

1918 Green, S. W. (Aug. 26, 1914). Capt. 12th London Regt. (The Rangers).

1913 Greenhalgh, J. A. G. (Oct. 6, 1915). ‡2nd Lt. 12th Worcestershire Regt.

1892 Gregory, E. D. W., B.A. (Serving Aug. 1914). Lt.-Col. Middlesex Regt., (T.F. Res.) *D.* § Feb. 1917.

1910 Gurney,* F. J. W. (July 24, 1915). Lt. 5th Bedfordshire Regt.

1900 Hadfield, J. A., M.A. (Apr. 1917). Surgeon, R.N. Capt. R.A.M.C. H.M.S. *Thunderer*, Grand Fleet, 1917–18.

1907 Hadland, F. W., B.A. (Mar. 25, 1915). 2nd Lt. 11th W. Riding Regt. (Resigned.)

1908 Hadland, R. C., B.A. (April 1915). 2nd Lt. K.R.R.C. France. (Invalided, 1917.)

1889 Hainsselin, Rev. M. T., B.A. (Serving Aug. 4, 1914). Chaplain, R.N.

1906 Hale, H. E., M.A. (May 1, 1918). 2nd Lt. 1st and 2nd Oxf. & Bucks. Lt. Infty.

1900 Hanbury, C. E. C., B.A. (Dec. 1, 1914). ‡Lt. Special Lists (Intelligence Corps). France, 1915–18; Germany, 1919.

1913 Hardy, C. T. (Jan. 29, 1915). Lt. Q.O. Oxfordshire Hussars. France, 1916–19.

1875 Harford, W. A. (Nov. 16, 1914). Maj. Remount Service.

1911 Harlow, C. M. (Sept. 8, 1916). 2nd Lt. I.A.R.O.

1911 Harman, W., M.A. (Oct. 1916). ‡2nd Lt. 2/7th R. Warwickshire Regt. France.

1910 Harris, Rev. W. G., M.A. (July 6, 1916). Chaplain to the Forces (4th Class).

1901 Hartley, A. F. (June 21, 1916). Pte. King's Own (R. Lancaster Regt.). France, Germany. (Prisoner of war, Mar. 1918.)

1912 Hathaway, T. W., M.A. (Nov. 28, 1914). 2nd Lt. 9th Oxf. & Bucks. Lt. Infty. (Invalided Dec. 8, 1915.)

1912 Haydock, G. H. (Sept. 13, 1915). 2nd Lt. 10th Highland L.I. 2nd Lt. General List.

1896 Headlam, G. E. (Oct. 20, 1914). Lt. Unattached List, T.F.

1914 Heaton, G. H. (Jan. 25, 1915). Lt. 1/1st Kent Cyclist Bn. Lt. R.A.F. India, Egypt, France.

1913 Heaton,* R. R. (Oct. 16, 1914). Lt. Kent Cyclist Bn. Lt. Flying Officer, R.A.F.

1919 Hemming, C. D. (Aug. 11, 1916). 1st Aircraftsman, Wireless Section, R.A.F. France, Belgium.
1898 Heslop, Rev. G. L. A., M.A. (Aug. 7, 1915). Chaplain to the Forces (4th Class).
1920 Hewer, R. K. (Aug. 14, 1914). ‡Maj. A/187th Bde., R.F.A. (London Div.). France, 1915–19; Germany, 1919. *M.C.*, Apr. 23, 1918. *D.* France, 1917.
1895 Hickey, V. C. F., B.A. (Nov. 13, 1916). Lt. R.G.A. (S.R.).
1904 Hill, Rev. H., M.A. (Sept. 19, 1918). Chaplain to the Forces (4th Class).
1911 Hill, R. H., M.A. (Dec. 7, 1915). Sergt. 15th G.H.Q. Res. M.T. Coy., R.A.S.C. France, Belgium.
1916 Hind, H. C. (July 14, 1917). Sergt. Leicestershire Regt.
1907 Hipkins, B. R., M.A. (1915). ‡Lt. 5th N. Staffordshire Regt.
1876 Hobbes, Rev. W. E., M.A. (Aug. 8, 1918). Chaplain to the Forces (4th Class).
1909 Hodges, P. J., B.A. (Aug. 26, 1914). Lt., Acting Capt., 5th Northamptonshire Regt.
1919 Hoffmann, Rev. M. M. (1917). Chaplain, U.S. Army.
1919 Howells, J. T. (Sept. 21, 1914). ‡Lt. 18th Welsh Regt. France, 1915–17.
1896 Howson, F., M.A. (1915). Capt. A.M.C., A.I.F. France.
1919 Huckle, F. A. (July 17, 1915). Pte. 1/7th Essex Regt. Palestine, 1917–19.
1904 Hudgell, E. W. G., M.A. 28th London Regt. (Artists' Rifles).
1897 Hughes, Rev. P. E., M.A., B.Mus. (May 12, 1916). Chaplain to the Forces (4th Class).
1909 Hurn, A. S., B.Litt., M.A. (Feb. 1, 1915). ‡Capt. and Adjt., 9th Bedfordshire Regt. Gallipoli, 1915; Egypt, 1915; India, 1917–19.
1903 Irby, L. M. A., B.A. Pte. R. Sussex Regt.
1919 Ives, N. (1917). 2nd Lt. U.S. Army.
1910 James,* F. H., M.A. (Oct. 1, 1914). Capt. 13th R. Scots. France, 1915. (Invalided, June 1917, on account of shell-shock.)
1906 James, Rev. M. G., M.A. (Aug. 5, 1914). Maj. (Retired, Indian Army) Labour Corps.
1903 Jefferson, E. W., M.A. (Nov. 13, 1916). Lt. R.G.A. (S.R.).
1911 Johnson, F. H., B.A. (Aug. 14, 1914). ‡Capt. 7th Oxf. & Bucks. Lt. Infty., empld. Ministry of National Service. *D.* § Aug. 1917.
1913 Jones, D. J. C., B.A. (Aug. 1914). ‡Lt. General List, attd. King's African Rifles. France, 1915; E. Africa, 1917.
1906 Jones, O., B.A. Ceylon Planters Rifle Corps.
1914 Jones, W. P. B., B.A. (July 1916). Pte. M.G.C. Salonika, 1917–19.
1876 Jowett, Rev. G. T. (June 1914). Chaplain to the Forces (4th Class).
1901 Kendrew, W. G., M.A. (Aug. 19, 1917). 2nd Lt. R. Irish Rifles. 2nd Lt. General List, attd. Censor's Dept., Boulogne. France.
1911 Kimbell, R. R., M.A. R.N.V.R.
1904 **King, N. G. B.** (Jan. 9, 1915). Lt. Wiltshire Regt. France. Killed in action on June 7, 1917.
1919 Kirkpatrick, Rev. G. D. (1917). Chaplain U.S. Army.
1888 Knapp, H. H. G., D.M. (Serving Aug. 4, 1914). Maj. Indian Medical Service. I.G. of Prisons, Burma. India.
1913 Kusik, H. M. (1914). Russian Air Service. Russia.

1910 **Lakin, C.,** B.A. (May 6, 1915). Lt. 4th Oxf. & Bucks. Lt. Infty. France. Died on Aug. 21, 1916, of wounds received in action.
1909 Lanctôt, G. Lt. Canadian E.F. France.
1915 Lander, Rev. W. B. (Oct. 12, 1917). Chaplain to the Forces (4th Class).
1915 Langford, R. A. (May 25, 1916). ‡2nd Lt. 3rd Oxf. & Bucks. Lt. Infty. France, 1917, 1918.
1906 Leach, T. H. de B. (Sept. 1915). ‡Lt. Tank Corps. Belgium, France.
1884 Lee, W. L. Melville, M.A. Maj. late Queen's (R. W. Surrey Regt.). Secretary, Oxfordshire T.F. Association. *D.* § Aug. 1917.
1911 Leeds, G. N. (Dec. 30, 1915). Lt. Tank Corps.
1910 **Lewis, C.,** B.A. Lt. Devonshire Regt. France. Killed in action on Mar. 21, 1918.
1913 Lewis, H. D. (Mar. 10, 1915). 2nd Lt. R.G.A. 2nd Lt. Observer Officer, R.A.F.
1907 Lewis, P. E. (1914). ‡Lt., Acting Capt., 13th R. Fusiliers. France. *M.C.*, Jan. 11, 1919. *D.* France, 1917.
1912 Lloyd, J. E., B.A. (July 24, 1915). 2nd Lt., Acting Lt., S. Wales Borderers (T.F.)
Lloyd-Williams, D. G. 2nd Lt. 6th King's Own (R. Lancaster Regt.). Gallipoli. Missing, presumed killed in action on Aug. 10, 1915.
1912 Lord, V. S. (Apr. 2, 1917). ‡Lt. Technical Officer, R.A.F.
1914 Loughton, H. E. (July 12, 1915). Lt. 1st Norfolk Regt. (Capt.). France.
1912 Lucas, G. C. Pte. Northumberland Fusiliers. France.
1909 Luce, H. W. (Feb. 19, 1915). Lt. R.A. (T.F.).
1880 Luffman, Rev. S. (June 19, 1916). Chaplain to the Forces (4th Class).
1916 **Macdonald, D. J.** (Mar. 1917). Lce.-Cpl. 7th Seaforth Highlanders. France, Belgium, 1918. Killed in action at Meteren on June 28, 1918.
1911 McGee, N., B.A. (Dec. 22, 1914). Lt. 9th King's Own (R. Lancaster Regt.). France, Salonika.
1918 McHaffie, W. H. (Jan. 1915). ‡Lt. 17th R. Fusiliers (Capt.). France, Germany.
1888 Manvell, Rev. A. E. W., M.A. Chaplain to the Forces (4th Class).
1919 Marshall, A. D. (June 30, 1915). ‡2nd Lt. Middlesex Regt. France, 1916–18.
1898 Marshall, R. L., M.A. Pte. R. Defence Corps.
1917 Martyn-Roberts, Rev. C. J. Chaplain to the Forces.
1892 Matthews, Rev. W. N., M.A. (July 11, 1916). Chaplain to the Forces (4th Class).
1915 Mercolino, E. (1915). Italian Army. Italy.
1894 **Merrikin, Rev. G. H.,** M.A. (Dec. 18, 1917). 2nd Lt. 2nd London Regt. France. Killed in action on Aug. 27, 1918.
1919 Miles, H. (July 2, 1917). Bombardier R.G.A. France.
1913 Miller,* H., B.A. (Mar. 17, 1915). Lt. 4th S. Wales Borderers. Mesopotamia. *D.* Mesopotamia, 1918, 1919.
1891 Mills, C. M. de V. (Oct. 13, 1914). Capt. R.A.S.C.
1908 **Milne, W. C.** Lt. I.A.R.O. Killed in action on Oct. 29, 1917.
1911 Moore, F. W., B.A. (Aug. 24, 1914). ‡Lt. 10th Essex Regt. France, 1915–16; Salonika, 1916–18.
1913 **Moore, J. A.** (Aug. 1914). Lt. 7th S. Staffordshire Regt. Gallipoli. Killed in action at Anafarta Hill on Aug. 9, 1915.

1910 Moore, Rev. R. C., M.A. (Nov. 18, 1915). Pte. R.A.M.C. ‡2nd Lt. 5th Wiltshire Regt. Mesopotamia, 1916–18; India, 1918–19.

1887 Moreton, Rev. A. C., M.A. (Serving Aug. 4, 1914). Chaplain, R.N. H.M.S. *Invincible*, Heligoland and Falkland Islands, 1914–15; H.M.S. *Impregnable*, 1915–17; Malta, 1917–19.

1886 Moreton, Rev. T. P., M.A. (May 11, 1915). Chaplain to the Forces (2nd Class). France. *D.* France, 1917.

1889 Morley, Rev. R. A., M.A. (Aug. 9, 1917). Chaplain to the Forces (4th Class).

1911 Morley, R. S., M.A. (Mar. 11, 1915). ‡Lt. 5th Lancashire Fusiliers. France, Belgium, 1917–18. (Prisoner of war, 1918.)

1910 Morris, C. G. M., B.A. (Jan. 25, 1915). Capt. R. Berkshire Regt. *D.*

1912 **Morris, J. H. C.** (Aug. 29, 1914). Pte. 1/4th Oxf. & Bucks. Lt. Infty. Died on Feb. 11, 1915, of illness contracted on active service.

1890 Morris, W., M.A. (July 15, 1915). Lt. Sherwood Foresters. Capt. whilst specially empld.

1919 Mulligan, H. (1917). U.S. Army.

1892 Muschamp, Rev. E. G., M.A. (Dec. 1, 1915). Chaplain to the Australian Forces (3rd Class). Egypt, 1916; France, Belgium, 1916–19.

1911 [**Neale, A. C.**] (July 11, 1916). 2nd Lt. 10th Cameronians. France, Belgium. Killed in action near Ypres on Aug. 1, 1917.

1919 Northey, W. E. (Oct. 3, 1916). Gnr. R. Australian Artillery. France, Belgium.

1905 Northrop, G. N. (1917). 1st Lt., Adjt. Gen.'s Dept., N.A. 88th Div., U.S. Army.

1913 Oatway,* S. H. (1914). ‡Lt. I.A.R.O., attd. 93rd Burma Inf. India, Burma.

1911 O'Donnell, P. S. G., B.Mus. (Serving Aug. 4, 1914). Bandmaster, R.M.A.

1882 Oldfield, J., M.A., D.C.L. (Mobilized Aug. 5, 1914). Lt.-Col. R.A.M.C. (T.F.). T.D. *D.* § Feb. 1917.

1905 Oliphant, F. M. (Sept. 12, 1914). Maj. 7th Seaforth Highlanders. Maj. General List. France. Croix de Chevalier de la Légion d'Honneur.

1913 Osmond, W. P. (Sept. 3, 1914). 2nd Lt. 3rd Hampshire Regt. France, 1915, 1916, 1918.

1919 Oswell, F. A. (Jan. 14, 1918). G. L. Operator, R.N.V.R. France.

1903 Ovenell, W. H., M.A. R.A.M.C.

1907 Owden, J. S. (Nov. 12, 1915). Lt. I.A.R.O., attd. R.A.F. India, Aden. *D.* Aden, 1919.

1917 [Owen, A. V. P.] (Oct. 1917). 2nd Lt. 1st R. Berkshire Regt. France, Germany, 1918–19.

1907 Owen, R. W. (May, 1918). Capt. American Red Cross. France, 1918–19.

1907 Owens, H. R. (July 22, 1917). Lt. R.G.A. France. *D.* France, 1917.

1911 Patterson, T., B.M., M.A. Lt. R.A.M.C.

1908 Patton, Rev. J. V., B.Litt., M.A. (Jan. 27, 1916). Chaplain to the Forces (4th Class). France, 1916; Salonika, 1916–17; Egypt and Palestine, 1917–19.

1919 Pearse, A. E. E. (Apr. 16, 1917). Pte. 25th Bn. A.I.F. France.

1902 Penson, J. F., B.M., M.A. (May 18, 1916). Capt. 1/4th London Field Amb., R.A.M.C. India, Egypt, Palestine, France.

1914 Phelps, A. E. (Nov. 14, 1914). Lt. 6th Lincolnshire Regt. Lt. General List, attd. Indian Army.
1902 Phillips, C. T. E. (Dec. 19, 1916). 2nd Lt. 8th Seaforth Highlanders.
1897 Philpott, Rev. R. G. K. F., M.A. (May 24, 1918). Chaplain to the Forces (4th Class).
1912 **Phipps, P. L. S.** (1915). Lce.-Cpl. 9th Oxf. & Bucks. Lt. Infty. Died in Hospital at Weymouth on Mar. 1, 1916.
1913 Pigott, Rev. L. F. (May 5, 1916). Chaplain to the Forces (4th Class). France. *M.C.*, Nov. 6, 1918.
1885 Ping, Rev. A., M.A. (June 12, 1917). Chaplain to the Forces (4th Class), attd. 1st N. General Hospital.
1909 Ping, A. W., B.A. (Aug. 19, 1914). Capt. 3rd York & Lancaster Regt. France, Belgium, 1914–15. (Invalided from France on account of wounds.)
1901 **Pitcairn, H. F.,** M.A. (May 1, 1916). 2nd Lt. A.S.C. France. Killed in action on June 3, 1917.
1896 **Pollard, G. H.** (Nov. 18, 1915). 2nd Lt. Arg. & Suth'd. Highlanders, attd. R.F.C. France. Died on June 7, 1917, of wounds as a prisoner in Germany.
1905 Powles, F. B., B.A. (1915). Italian Army. Italy.
1911 Price, W. H., M.A. (Sept. 15, 1914). ‡Lt. 8th Queen's (R. W. Surrey Regt.). Capt. General List, attd. 89th Inf. Bde. H.Q. France, 1915–18.
1887 Prince, Rev. J. H., M.A. (Serving Aug. 4, 1914). Chaplain (4th Class) (T.F).
1905 Pugh, Rev. H. S., M.A. (June 18, 1917). Chaplain to the Forces (4th Class), attd. R.G.A. France. *M.C.*, Jan. 1, 1919. *D.* France, 1918.
1918 Puleston, F. J. Warrant Officer (Class 2) Regular Forces.
1880 Pulling, Rev. E. H. (Serving Aug. 4, 1914). Chaplain to the Forces (1st Class). *D.* § Feb. 1917 ; § Mar. 1919.
1911 Rau, S. R., B.A. 9th Lancers.
1916 Rees, Rev. S. (Feb. 6, 1918). Chaplain to the Forces (4th Class), attd. 9th Border Regt. Macedonia, 1918–19 ; Turkey in Europe, 1919.
1907 Rees, W. E., B.A. A.B., R.N.
1912 Richards, Rev. D. M., B.A. (Sept. 6, 1917). Chaplain to the Forces (4th Class).
1915 Richards,* J. D. M. (June 19, 1915). Lt. R. Welch Fusiliers. France.
1919 Richards, J. E. (June 26, 1917). Pte. 2nd R. Scots. N. Russia.
1912 Richards, J. M., M.A. (July 15, 1915). Lt., Acting Capt., 1/7th R. Welch Fusiliers. Egypt, Palestine. *M.C.*, Aug. 16, 1917.
1919 Rigby, E. A. (June 20, 1916). ‡2nd Lt. Border Regt. France, 1917–18.
1919 Robertson, H. G. Canadian E.F. France.
1910 Robertson, Rev. T. G. Chaplain A.I.F.
1912 Robinson, L. T., B.A. (Mobilized Aug. 1914). ‡2nd Lt. 1/4th Oxf. & Bucks. Lt. Infty. France, 1915–16 ; Italy, 1918–19.
1892 Rowley, C. E. (1918). Pte. R.A.M.C. Italy.
1880 Sammons, H. (Jan. 2, 1916). Lt. R.A.S.C. *D.* § Mar. 1919.
1906 Samson, Rev. A. M. Chaplain to the Forces (4th Class).
1911 Sanders, F. C., B.A. (1914). ‡Lt. 11th Lancashire Fusiliers.
1907 Sansom,* F. G., B.A. (Jan. 28, 1915). Capt. Wessex Divl. Train, A.S.C. Lt. 4th Res. Regt. Cavalry.

1908 Seccombe, Rev. R. B., M.A. (Apr. 19, 1917). Chaplain to the Forces (4th Class).
1910 Sellar, F. C., B.A. (June 28, 1918). Pte. 28th London Regt. (2nd Artists' Rifles O.T.C.).
1912 Sharpe, F. (Oct. 1, 1914). ‡2nd Lt. 2/5th Lincolnshire Regt. France, 1916, 1917–18.
1891 Shepherd, Rev. W. M., M.A. (May 1, 1917). Chaplain to the Forces (4th Class).
1893 Shepherd-Smith, Rev. P. W., M.A. (Apr. 8, 1918). Chaplain to the Forces (4th Class).
1917 Sholl, H. P. G. (Oct. 27, 1917). 2nd Lt. R.E. Signal Service.
1911 **Shrewsbury, C. B.** (Mar. 5, 1915). 2nd Lt. 5th Lincolnshire Regt. France. Killed in action in France, Oct. 11–13, 1915.
1913 Sirry, M. A. H. Naval Ex. Services, Egypt. Egypt.
1917 Slater, O. R. (Jan. 13, 1918). ‡2nd Lt. 11th Field Coy., R.E. France.
1909 Smth, A. E. B. (July 12, 1916). 2nd Lt. Unattached List, T.F., Lancing School O.T.C.
1919 Smith, F. H. C. (Feb. 2, 1916). Pte. R. Welch Fusiliers.
1896 Smith, P. L. J., M.A. (July 22, 1916). 2nd Lt. Unattached List, T.F., Loretto School O.T.C.
1907 Snowden,* H. P., M.A. (Aug. 4, 1914). Capt. 5th Gloucestershire Regt., attd. Educational Staff, Oxford Hospitals. Belgium, 1915; France, 1915–17. *M.C.*, Sept. 26, 1916.
1915 Sopote, S. C. R.E. Signals.
1874 Spencer, Rev. R. F. A., M.A. Chaplain, R.N.
1914 **Spencer, S.**, B.A. (July 12, 1915). Lt. 2/5th, attd. 7th, Norfolk Regt. France. *M.C.*, Feb. 15, 1919. Killed in action near Epéhy on Sept. 24, 1918.
1905 Stace, J. A., M.A. (June 25, 1917). Capt. 5th Oxf. & Bucks. Lt. Infty., attd. 18th Gloucestershire Regt. France. *D.* France.
1905 Stansfield, E. M., M.A. (Dec. 1914). Lt. Lancashire Fusiliers (Capt.). Lt. General List, attd. King's African Rifles. Education Officer. France, 1916; E. Africa, 1918–19.
1872 Stevenson, G. J. H. Maj. Recruiting Officer.
1902 Stewart, Rev. G. W., M.A. (June 26, 1917). Chaplain to the Forces (4th Class).
1917 Stewart, K. B. Sergt.-Observer R.A.F.
1907 Streat, Rev. C., B.A. (June 19, 1916). Chaplain to the Forces (4th Class).
1899 Summers, Rev. H. H., M.A. (Mar. 12, 1916). Chaplain to the Forces (4th Class).
1913 Sutcliffe,* R., M.A. (Sept. 18, 1914). ‡Lt. 28th Durham L.I. (Capt.). France.
1894 Sweatman, S. E., M.A. (Mar. 2, 1916). Lt. Unattached List, T.F., Oakham School O.T.C.
1899 Tapply, Rev. F. M., M.A. Chaplain to the Forces (4th Class).
1911 Taunton, E. (Mar. 11, 1915). Capt. R.A.M.C.
1906 Taylor,* F. W., M.A. (Serving Aug. 4, 1914). Lt. 4th Oxf. & Bucks. Lt. Infty. (Capt.), empld. Nigeria. Nigeria.
1895 Thomas, A. R., B.C.L., M.A. (May 29, 1916). C.S.M., Instructor, Corps School of Musketry.
1903 Thomas, J. J. (Nov. 10, 1915). 2nd Lt. R.F.A.

1901 **Thomas, T. G.,** B.A. (Feb. 21, 1915). Lt. W. Ontario Regt. C.E.F. (Capt.). France. *D.* France, 1918. Died on Aug. 12, 1918, of wounds received in action at Foucquescourt.

1911 Thompson, J. F. (1917). Capt. Coast Artillery Corps, U.S. Army.

1911 Thompson, Rev. W. (Dec. 8, 1916). Chaplain to the Forces (4th Class).

1912 Thomson, D. H. W. (Aug. 26, 1914). Lt. 8th W. Riding Regt.

1916 Thorburn, J. W. A. (Dec. 16, 1917). 2nd Lt. Labour Bn., Labour Corps.

1919 Tooth, Rev. R. (Nov. 20, 1914). Pte. 22nd Mounted Bde. Field Amb. ‡Chaplain to the Forces (4th Class). Egypt and Palestine, 1915–19.

1900 Towler, F., M.A. (Mar. 23, 1916). Sapper, 106th Field Coy., R.E. France.

1910 **Troman, T. J. B.** (Mar. 1, 1915). ‡2nd Lt. N. Staffordshire Regt., attd. M.G.C. France, 1915–16. Killed in action in the Battle of the Somme on July 14, 1916.

1915 Trotman, R. R., B.A. (May 1, 1918). Sapper, 3rd Bridging Bn., R.E.

1919 Turner, A. M. (Feb. 17, 1915). Pte. 18th R. Fusiliers (1st Public Schools Bn.) France. (Prisoner of war in Germany for 22 months.)

1919 Turner-Smith, N. A. (Apr. 14, 1915). Capt. 4th Highland L.I., attd. R.E. France, Belgium.

1909 Twisaday, J. H. C. (Oct. 15, 1915). 2nd Lt. A.S.C. (Invalided Apr. 1916.)

1919 Twycross, J. (Jan. 7, 1916). ‡2nd Lt. General List. E. Africa, 1916–17.

1914 **Unwin, G. S.** (Dec. 22, 1914). 2nd Lt. 11th Sherwood Foresters. France. Killed in action on July 30, 1916.

1914 Van Sertima, S. J. (Nov. 23, 1915). Cpl. 9th Manchester Regt. France, Belgium. (Prisoner of war, Mar.–Dec. 1918.)

1908 Vernon, H. R., M.A. (Aug. 3, 1915). ‡Lt. R.G.A. (Capt.). France, Belgium. *D.* France, 1917, 1918.

1907 Wakefield, J. A. (Mar. 1917). Sergt. 22nd Northumberland Fusiliers (C.S.M.). Belgium, France.

1902 Walkden, Rev. A. T., M.A. (Mar. 7, 1916). Chaplain to the Forces (4th Class).

1913 **Walton, O. T.** (Apr. 22, 1915). 2nd Lt. 3rd S. Lancashire Regt., attd. R.F.C. France. Killed in action on Apr. 12, 1917.

1909 Ward, Rev. J. E., M.A. (June, 1915). Chaplain to the Forces (4th Class) (District Senior Chaplain). France, Belgium.

Ward, T. H. H. 2nd Lt. 1st Dorsetshire Regt. Killed in action in Apr. 1915.

Warland, F. L. (Jan. 25, 1917). 2nd Lt. 3rd, attd. 12th, E. Surrey Regt. France. Missing, presumed killed in action on Mar. 25, 1918.

1916 Warner, W. E. (Sept. 26, 1917). 2nd Lt. W. Yorkshire Regt. France. (Prisoner of war.)

1909 Watts, A. L., B.M., M.A. (Dec. 21, 1916). Surgeon Lt., R.N.

1901 Weston, Rev. G. A., M.A. (June 16, 1915). Chaplain to the Forces (4th Class).

1896 Weston, H. E., M.A. (1915). Cpl. 4/3rd Home Counties Field Amb., R.A.M.C. (T.F.); afterwards Lt. R.A.S.C.

1903 Wheatley, A., M.A. (Mobilized Aug. 1914). Maj. 17th London Regt., attd. Rifle Brigade. Egypt and Palestine. *D.* Palestine, 1919.

1915 Wheeller, E. T. S., B.A. (Mar. 15, 1917). Driver R.A.S.C. (M.T.), attd. 2nd Tank Group. Belgium, France, 1917–19.

1901 White, Rev. A. C., M.A. (June 29, 1915). Chaplain, R.N., H.M.S. *Ramillies*. Gallipoli, Balkan Peninsula, 1915–17; Grand Fleet, 1917–19.

1897 White, R. M., M.A. (July 12, 1918). Pte. R.M.L.I.

1911 **Whitlock, F. W.,** B.A. (Dec. 2, 1914). 2nd Lt. 6th Oxf. & Bucks. Lt. Infty. France, Belgium. Killed in action at the Battle of Loos on Sept. 25. 1915.

1913 Whymont, N. J. (Sept. 5, 1917). 2nd Lt. Labour Corps.

1914 **Wicks, E. E.** (Nov. 16, 1915). Sub-Lt. R.N.D. France, 1917–18. Killed in action on Sept. 3, 1918.

1906 Wilcock, C. A. (Nov. 15, 1915). Lt. R.A.S.C.

1901 **Wilkes, S. A.,** M.A. (May 30, 1917). 2nd Lt. 4th, attd. 7th, The Black Watch. France. Killed in action on Aug. 24, 1918.

1908 Wilkins, P. V. (Nov. 1915). ‡2nd Lt. 17th Bde., R.G.A. France, Belgium, 1916–17.

1914 Williams, E. O., B.A. Welsh Regt.

1908 Williams, G. O., M.A. Cadet, O.C.B.

1914 [**Williams, H. M.**] (Mar. 1916). 2nd Lt. 10th Welsh Regt. France, Belgium. Killed in action at Ypres on June 24, 1917.

1911 Wilsdon,* H. A., M.A. (Sept. 1, 1914). Lt. 4th Oxf. & Bucks. Lt. Infty. Lt. (Hon. Capt.), Technical Officer, R.A.F. Belgium, France. *D.* § Jan. 1919.

1911 Wilsher,* R. V., B.A. (Nov. 27, 1914). 2nd Lt. 7th S. Lancashire Regt. Lt. General List (Capt.). France and Italy, 1915–19.

1904 Wilson, Rev. J. A. S., B.A. (Jan. 3, 1917). Chaplain to the Forces (4th Class). Egypt.

1907 **Wilson, T. P. C.** (Aug. 1914). ‡Capt. 10th Sherwood Foresters (Staff-Captain). France. *D.* France, 1917. Killed in action on Mar. 23, 1918.

1902 Wimbush, N. N., B.A. (Serving Aug. 4, 1914). ‡Lt. 2nd King's Own (R. Lancaster Regt). France, 1914–15. (Invalided on account of wounds, Nov. 1916.)

1911 Winship, E. R. (Sept. 17, 1914). ‡Lt. 8th Middlesex Regt. Lt. Musical Director, 1st Army. France. *M.C.*, Dec. 2, 1918.

1882 Witt, Rev. A. R., M.A. (May 28, 1915). Chaplain to the Forces (1st Class). *D.* § Mar. 1918.

1914 Wolff, F. van S., B.A. (May 21, 1917). Pte. 18th Cyclist Bn., Army Cyclist Corps. France, Belgium.

1882 Wolverton, Lord. Hon. Col. Middlesex Regt.

1910 **Wood, T. H. H.,** B.A. (Nov. 28, 1914). 2nd Lt. 3rd Dorsetshire Regt. France. Killed in action on Apr. 13, 1915.

1892 Woodard, E. H. J. (Sept. 22, 1914). Lt. 9th R. Warwickshire Regt. Lt. General List, R.T.O.

1913 **Wooldridge, A. J.** Sapper, Forest Group, R.E. France. Killed in action on Aug. 21, 1917.

1914 Woolford, F. H. (Nov. 15, 1915). Pte. 9th R. Warwickshire Regt. France, 1916; Mesopotamia, 1916; India, 1917–19.

1912 Wright, D. S. S. (1914). ‡Lt. R.A.S.C. France, Salonika. Serbian Gold Medal for Zealous Service.

1869 Wright, G. A., B.M. (May, 1915). Lt.-Col. R.A.M.C. Consulting Surgeon to Military Hospital. *D.* § Sept. 1917.

1899 Yarnold, D. E., M.A. (Dec. 21, 1915). Lt. 5th Norfolk Regt.

1904 Youens, Rev. F. A. C., M.A. (Jan. 1, 1917). Chaplain to the Forces (4th Class).

PRIVATE HALLS

ST. ALBAN HALL

1880 **Sharpe, W. S.** Maj. A.P.M. *C.M.G.* Accidentally killed on Apr. 20, 1917.

MARCON'S HALL

1893 Bell, W. E. D. (Sept. 1914). Maj. Middlesex Regt. *D.* § Mar. 1918.
1906 Bircham, H. T., B.A. (Aug. 20, 1914). Lt. 6th Durham L.I. France, 1915–19. *M.C.*, Jan. 1, 1917.
1904 Bostock, N. F., B.A. (Sept. 1914). Capt. 173rd Siege Batt., R.G.A. France.
1901 Browne, Rev. L. W., M.A. (June 8, 1916). Chaplain to the Forces (4th Class). *D.* § Aug. 1919.
1907 Bull, Rev. A. A., M.A. (June 12, 1916). Chaplain to the Forces (4th Class).
1905 **Campbell, A. U.** (Oct. 1915). Lt., Acting Lt.-Commdr. R.N.V.R., R.N.D., attd. T.M.B. France. *M.C.*, Jan. 1, 1917; *Bar*, Mar. 13, 1917. Croix de Guerre with palm. *D.* France. Killed in action on Dec. 30, 1917.
1895 Carr, R. (Oct. 12, 1914). Lt. Interpreter. Maj. King's African Rifles. Africa.
1908 Carter, H. T. (Mobilized Aug. 4, 1914). Capt. R.A.S.C. (T.F.), Adjt. 3rd Advanced Supply Depot. France and Belgium.
1903 Caton Thompson, A. P. (1914). 2nd Lt. Border Regt. (Resigned.)
1907 Cocker, N. (1917). ‡2nd Lt. Lincolnshire Regt.
1901 Cope, L. F. (Serving Aug. 4, 1914). Surgeon Lt.-Commdr. R.N.
1905 **Cozens-Hardy, R.** (Sept. 1914). Lt. 1st Norfolk Regt. (Capt.). France and Belgium. Killed in action at Polderhoek on Oct. 9, 1917.
1902 Cushing, R. W. J. A., B.M., M.A. (Aug. 20, 1915). Capt. R.A.M.C. (T.F.).
1911 Davies, J. L. T., M.A. (Dec. 22, 1914). Lt. R. Welch Fusiliers. Lt. and Adjt. R.A.F. France and Belgium, 1915–16.
1885 Disraeli, C. R. (Mobilized Aug. 1914). Maj. R. Bucks. Hussars, attd. R.A.F.
1896 Ellis, H. C. (Oct. 28, 1916). 2nd Lt. R.G.A. (S.R.).
1900 Evans, J. S. P. (Oct. 1914). Capt. 3rd Q.O. Cameron Highlanders.
1911 Fielding, M. G., M.A. (1914). ‡Lt. 2nd Oxf. & Bucks. Lt. Infty. (Capt.). France. *M.C.*, Feb. 13, 1917.
1908 French, A. K. (1914). ‡2nd Lt. R.F.A. (Resigned.)

1903 Goss, L. S., B.A. (Mobilized Aug. 4, 1914). Pte. 28th London Regt. (Artists' Rifles), afterwards Surgeon Lt. R.N. France, 1914–15; Egypt, Red Sea, 1915–19. *O.B.E.* (Mil.). *D.* Egypt, 1917.

1911 [Grove, G. F., B.A.] (Oct. 1914). Lt. 1st Gloucestershire Regt. France, 1916; Egypt and Palestine, 1918–19.

1904 Hadley, P. E., M.A. (Dec. 1, 1916). Lt. Special Lists, empld. Recruiting Duties.

1906 **Hatfeild, C. E.** (Mobilized Aug. 4, 1914). Capt. R. E. Kent Yeomanry, attd. 10th The Buffs (E. Kent Regt.). Gallipoli, Egypt, Palestine, France. *M.C.*, Feb. 15, 1919. *D.* Palestine, 1917. Killed in action near Cambrai on Sept. 21, 1918.

1908 [Hemelryk, C. J., M.A.] (Aug. 5, 1914). Pte. A. Coy., H.T., A.S.C. (Lce.-Cpl.). France, 1915–17. (Discharged on account of injuries received on active service.)

1906 Herbert, Hon. G. S. (Mobilized Aug. 1914). Maj. 1/4th Wiltshire Regt. India.

1914 Hewitt, R. M. (Oct. 9, 1915). Lt. E. Lancashire Regt., empld. War Office.

1910 Hingston, J. H. N., B.A. (Jan. 3, 1916). Sapper 99th Field Coy., R.E. Salonika.

1895 Holland, Hon. S. L. (Aug. 5, 1914). Capt. 6th Dragoons, Res. of Officers, A.P.M. France. *D.* France, 1919.

1910 [Holley, E. J. H., B.A.] (Mobilized Aug. 1914). Capt. Royal 1st Devon Yeomanry, attd. 16th Devonshire Regt. (Lt.-Col.). Gallipoli, Egypt, Palestine, France. *M.C.*, Jan. 1, 1918. *D.* France, 1919.

1896 [Hollins, A. M.] (May 1915). Capt. 11th Loyal N. Lancashire Regt. *D.* § Feb. 1917.

1893 Jenkins, Rev. N. Ll., M.A. (Sept. 1915). Chaplain to the Forces (4th Class), afterwards 2nd Lt. S. Wales Borderers. France, 1915–16.

1915 Leatherdale, R. (Jan. 6, 1916). Sergt. R.A.M.C.

1888 Leathes, C. de M. (Mobilized Aug. 1914). Maj. 5th (Extra Res.) R. Irish Rifles. *D.* § Feb. 1917.

1908 Lewis, G., M.A. (1914). R.A.S.C. (M.T.).

1904 Manbey, P. H., B.A. (Oct. 1914). Capt. 4th Essex Regt.

1888 [**Manning, P.,** M.A.]. Protection Coy., R. Defence Corps. Died on service on Feb. 28, 1917.

1893 [Masters, G.] (Serving Aug. 4, 1914). Maj., Acting Lt.-Col., R.F.A. France. *D.S.O.*, Sept. 16, 1918. Croix de Chevalier de la Légion d'Honneur. Croix de Guerre. *D.* France, 1914, 1918 twice.

1905 Mathews, P. D., B.A. (Oct. 10, 1914). Lt. 5th Connaught Rangers, attd. 12th Irish Rifles.

1896 Meadows, E. B. King's Own (R. Lancaster Regt.).

1909 Moon, C. H. (Nov. 21, 1914). Lt. 10th London Regt. (Invalided.)

1912 Nicholas, F. W. H. (Aug. 6, 1914). Capt. 1st Bedfordshire Regt. Bde. Maj., attd. Staff. Gallipoli, Egypt and Palestine, France. *M.C.*, June 3, 1919. *D.* Palestine, 1918.

1911 Paramore, J. R. P. (Jan. 27, 1915). Lt. 3rd D.C.L.I. (Capt.), attd. R.A.F. (1917–19). France, 1915, 1916–17.

1904 [Peel, R., M.A.] (Dec. 18, 1914). 2nd Lt. 9th Oxf. & Bucks. Lt. Infty. Lt. R.A.F.

1895 **Perry-Ayscough, H. G. C.,** M.A. (Oct. 1914). Capt. 4th Connaught Rangers. Belgium, France. Chinese Order of the Excellent Crop (6th Class). Wounded and missing, believed killed in action at Hooge on Sept. 25, 1915.
1899 Philips, H. V. (Oct. 1914). Capt. Northumberland Fusiliers.
1897 [Rowley, J. C., B.A.] (Mar. 12, 1917). 2nd Lt. R.F.A. (S.R.).
1907 Scott, Rev. W. F. (Serving Aug. 4, 1914). Chaplain R.N., H.M.S. *Renown*. Grand Fleet.
1893 Shuttleworth, P. P. (Dec. 23, 1914). Lt. Nottinghamshire Yeomanry.
1893 Skeeles, C. S. (1914). Lt. Special Lists, empld. Recruiting Duties.
1908 Stead, J., M.A. (Apr. 1, 1915). Lt. Norfolk Regt.
1915 Sutcliffe, A. L. ‡Lt. 6th S. Staffordshire Regt.
1907 **Thompson, H.,** M.A. (Aug. 15, 1914). Lt. 3rd, attd. 1st, Northamptonshire Regt. France. Killed in action at Festubert on May 9, 1915.
1905 Vaux, F. G., B.A. (Aug. 5, 1914). ‡Lt. 5th Durham L.I. (Capt.). France, 1916–19.
1906 [Vickers, J. H., B.A.] (Oct. 1, 1915). Capt., Acting Maj., Airship Officer, R.A.F. *D.* § Jan. 1919.
1889 Watson, W. F. (Feb. 20, 1915). Capt. 74th Divl. Train, R.A.S.C. Egypt and Palestine. *O.B.E.* (Mil.). *D.* Palestine, 1918.
1910 Wilkinson, W. A. C., B.A. (Nov. 3, 1914). Lt. Coldstream Guards. France. *M.C.*, Sept. 26, 1917; *Bar*, Feb. 18, 1918.
1902 Winterton, E., Earl (Mobilized Aug. 1914). Maj. Sussex Yeomanry, empld. Imperial Camel Corps. Egypt, Palestine. Order of the Nile (4th Class). *D.* Egypt, 1917; Palestine, 1919.

CAMPION HALL

1906 Bellanti, Rev. L. E. (Mar. 17, 1917). Chaplain to the Forces (4th Class), attd. R.F.A. France, Italy, Germany. *M.C.*, Dec. 17, 1917.
1901 Butler, Rev. W. E., M.A. (Mar. 27, 1917). Chaplain to the Forces (4th Class). France, Belgium.
1903 Campbell, Rev. N. J., M.A. (Mar. 27, 1917). Chaplain to the Forces (4th Class). France, 1917–19.
1901 Gallagher, Rev. G. F., M.A. (Mar. 27, 1917). Chaplain to the Forces (4th Class), attd. 17th Divl. Art. France and Belgium.
1902 Garrold, Rev. R. P., M.A. (Oct. 29, 1915). Chaplain to the Forces (4th Class), 7th Cavalry Bde., attd. 119th C.C.F.A. France, 1915–16; E. Africa, 1916–18. Mesopotamia, 1918–19. *D.* E. Africa, 1918.
1896 Irwin, Rev. F. (Apr. 26, 1917). Chaplain to the Forces (4th Class). France.
1900 **Monteith, Rev. R. J.,** M.A. (Mar. 1917). Chaplain to the Forces (4th Class), attd. 15th Divl. Ammunition Column. France. Killed in action at Ribécourt on Nov. 27, 1917.
1897 Steuart, Rev. R. H. J. (Oct. 13, 1916). Chaplain to the Forces (4th Class), attd. 12th Highland L.I., and afterwards VI Corps Troops. France and Belgium, 1916–19; Germany, 1919. *D.* France, 1919.
1904 Woodlock, Rev. J., M.A. (Mar. 21, 1917). Chaplain to the Forces (4th Class), attd. 2nd Rifle Brigade. France and Belgium.

ST. BENET'S HALL

1897 Byrne, Rev. W. A., M.A. Chaplain to the Forces (4th Class). France and Belgium, 1916–19; Germany, 1919.

1915 Lightbound, Rev. A. A. (Apr. 11, 1917). Chaplain to the Forces (4th Class). Mesopotamia, 1917–19.

TURRELL'S HALL

1884 **Turrell, A. G.,** B.A. (Oct. 1914). Pte. 2nd Sportsmen's Bn. R. Fusiliers. France, 1915–18. Died at Ventnor on Sept. 19, 1919, of illness contracted while on active service.

INDEX

www.ingramcontent.com/pod-product-compliance
Ingram Content Group UK Ltd.
Pitfield, Milton Keynes, MK11 3LW, UK
UKHW042133270426
12128UKWH00002B/21

9 789354 045943